Auditing &
Assurance Services

Auditing & Assurance Services

Timothy J. Louwers, PhD, CPA, CISA, CFF
Director of the School of Accounting and
KPMG Eminent Professor in Accounting

Allen D. Blay, PhD, CPA
Associate Professor of Accounting
Florida State University

David H. Sinason, PhD, CPA, CIA, CFE, CFSA, CRMA
PwC Professor of Accountancy
Northern Illinois University

Jerry R. Strawser, PhD, CPA
KPMG Chair of Accounting
Texas A&M University

Jay C. Thibodeau, PhD, CPA
Rae D. Anderson Professor of Accounting
Bentley University

Mc
Graw
Hill
Education

AUDITING & ASSURANCE SERVICES, SEVENTH EDITION

Published by McGraw-Hill Education, 2 Penn Plaza, New York, NY 10121. Copyright © 2018 by McGraw-Hill Education. All rights reserved. Printed in the United States of America. Previous editions © 2015, 2013, and 2011. No part of this publication may be reproduced or distributed in any form or by any means, or stored in a database or retrieval system, without the prior written consent of McGraw-Hill Education, including, but not limited to, in any network or other electronic storage or transmission, or broadcast for distance learning.

Some ancillaries, including electronic and print components, may not be available to customers outside the United States.

This book is printed on acid-free paper.

1 2 3 4 5 6 7 8 9 LWI 21 20 19 18 17

ISBN 978-1-259-57328-6
MHID 1-259-57328-1

Chief Product Officer, SVP Products & Markets: *G. Scott Virkler*
Vice President Portfolio & Learning Content: *Michael Ryan*
Managing Director: *Tim Vertovec*
Marketing Director: *Natalie King*
Brand Manager: *Patricia Plumb*
Director, Product Development: *Rose Koos*
Associate Director of Digital Content: *Kevin Moran*
Lead Product Developers: *Michele Janicek / Kristine Tibbetts*
Senior Product Developer: *Rebecca Mann*
Product Developer: *Randall Edwards*
Marketing Manager: *Cheryl Osgood*
Digital Product Analyst: *Xin Lin*
Director, Content Design & Delivery: *Linda Avenarius*
Program Manager: *Daryl Horrocks*
Senior Content Project Managers: *Dana M. Pauley / Angela Norris*
Buyer: *Laura M. Fuller*
Design: *Matt Diamond*
Content Licensing Specialists: *Shawntel Schmitt / Lori Slattery*
Cover Image: *The-Lightwrighter/Getty Images*
Compositor: *SPi Global*
Printer: *LSC Communications*

All credits appearing on page or at the end of the book are considered to be an extension of the copyright page.

Library of Congress Cataloging-in-Publication Data

Names: Louwers, Timothy J., author.
Title: Auditing & assurance services / Timothy J. Louwers, James Madison
  University, David H. Sinason, Northern Illinois University, Jerry R.
  Strawser, Texas A&M University, Jay C. Thibodeau, Bentley College, Allen
  D. Blay.
Other titles: Auditing and assurance services
Description: Seventh edition. | New York, NY: McGraw-Hill Education, [2018]
Identifiers: LCCN 2016042220 | ISBN 9781259573286 (alk. paper)
Subjects: LCSH: Auditing.
Classification: LCC HF5667 .A815 2018 | DDC 657/.45—dc23
LC record available at https://lccn.loc.gov/2016042220

The Internet addresses listed in the text were accurate at the time of publication. The inclusion of a website does not indicate an endorsement by the authors or McGraw-Hill Education, and McGraw-Hill Education does not guarantee the accuracy of the information presented at these sites.

mheducation.com/highered

Some people come into our lives and quickly go. Some stay awhile and leave footprints on our hearts and we are never quite the same.

Anonymous

We dedicate this book to the following educators whose footprints we try to follow:

Professor Homer Bates
(University of North Florida)

Professor Stanley Biggs
(University of Connecticut)

Professor Lewis C. Buller
(Indiana State University)

Professor Patrick Delaney
(Northern Illinois University)

Professor William Hillison
(Florida State University)

Professor John Ivancevich
(University of Houston)

Professor Richard Kochanek
(University of Connecticut)

Professor John L. "Jack" Kramer
(University of Florida)

Professor Jack Robertson
(University of Texas at Austin)

Professor Robert Strawser
(Texas A&M University)

Professor Sally Webber
(Northern Illinois University)

Professor "IBM Jim" Whitney
(The Citadel)

Meet the Authors

Courtesy James
Madison University

Timothy J. Louwers *is the Director of the School of Accounting and KPMG Eminent Professor in Accounting at James Madison University.*

Professor Louwers received his undergraduate and master's degrees from The Citadel and his PhD from Florida State University. Prior to beginning his academic career, he worked in public accounting with KPMG, specializing in financial, governmental, and information systems auditing. He is a certified public accountant (South Carolina and Virginia) and a certified information systems auditor. He is also certified in financial forensics.

Professor Louwers's research interests include auditors' reporting decisions and ethical issues in the accounting profession. He has authored or coauthored more than 60 publications on a wide range of accounting, auditing, and technology-related topics, including articles in the *Journal of Accounting Research, Accounting Horizons,* the *Journal of Business Ethics, Behavioral Research in Accounting, Decision Sciences,* the *Journal of Forensic Accounting, Issues in Accounting Education,* the *Journal of Accountancy,* the *CPA Journal,* and *Today's CPA.* Some of his published work has been reprinted in Russian and Chinese. He is a respected lecturer on auditing and technology-related issues and has received teaching excellence awards from the University of Houston and Louisiana State University. He has appeared on both local and national television news broadcasts, including MSNBC and CNN news programs.

Courtesy Kallen M. Lunt

Allen D. Blay *is an Associate Professor of Accounting at Florida State University.*

Professor Blay completed his PhD at the University of Florida in 2000. He teaches auditing at all levels and teaches a seminar in auditing research in the doctoral program. His research interests relate to auditor judgment and decision making. Professor Blay has authored or coauthored publications on a wide range of accounting and auditing topics in journals such as *Contemporary Accounting Research, Auditing: A Journal of Practice and Theory, Organizational Behavior and Human Decision Processes,* the *Journal of Business Ethics, Behavioral Research in Accounting, Issues in Accounting Education,* the *International Journal of Auditing,* and the *Journal of Accounting, Auditing, and Finance.* He is currently Associate Editor for *Issues in Accounting Education* and serves on several editorial boards.

Professor Blay has been active in the American Accounting Association, serving on the auditing education committee and the annual meeting committee as Accounting, Behavior, and Organizations section chair, among other committees. He is also active in the American Institute of CPAs, serving in various volunteer roles relating to the Uniform CPA Exam. Prior to entering academics, Professor Blay worked in public accounting auditing financial institutions. He currently directs the accounting doctoral program at Florida State University.

Courtesy Northern Illinois
University

David H. Sinason *is the PwC Professor of Accountancy at Northern Illinois University (NIU) and director of the NIU Internal Audit program.*

Professor Sinason received a BS in engineering from the University of Illinois, a BS in History from Northern Illinois University, a BBA and MAcc in accounting from the University of North Florida, and a PhD in accounting from Florida State University. He has certifications as a certified public accountant, a certified internal auditor, a certified financial services auditor, and a certified fraud examiner. He also has certification in risk management assurance. Professor Sinason has written more than 50 articles, mostly in the areas of assurance services, fraud prevention and detection, and auditor liability.

Professor Sinason has taught in the areas of accounting information systems, auditing and assurance services, and financial accounting. He has received teaching awards at each of the universities where he has taught including the 2002–2003 Department of Accountancy and Northern Illinois University Awards for Excellence in Undergraduate Teaching.

Courtesy Jerry R. Strawser

Jerry R. Strawser *is Executive Vice President and Chief Financial Officer at Texas A&M University and holds the KPMG Chair in Accounting.*

Prior to his current appointment, Professor Strawser served as dean of Mays Business School at Texas A&M University, interim executive vice president and provost at Texas A&M University, interim dean of the C. T. Bauer College of Business at the University of Houston, and Arthur Andersen & Co. Alumni Professor of Accounting.

Professor Strawser has coauthored three textbooks and more than 60 journal articles. In addition to his academic experience, he had prior public accounting experience at two Big Five accounting firms. He has also developed and delivered numerous executive development programs to organizations such as AT&T, Centerpoint Energy, Continental Airlines, ConocoPhillips, Halliburton, KBR, KPMG, Minute Maid, PricewaterhouseCoopers, McDermott International, Shell, Southwest Bank of Texas, and the Texas Society of Certified Public Accountants. Professor Strawser is a certified public accountant in the state of Texas and earned his BBA and PhD in Accounting from Texas A&M University.

Courtesy Bentley University

Jay C. Thibodeau *is the Rae D. Anderson Professor of Accounting at Bentley University.*

Professor Thibodeau is a certified public accountant and a former auditor. He received his bachelor's degree from the University of Connecticut in 1987 and his PhD from the University of Connecticut in 1996. He joined the faculty at Bentley in 1996 and has remained there. At Bentley, he serves as the coordinator for all audit and assurance curriculum matters. His off-campus commitments include consulting with the Audit Learning and Development group at KPMG.

Professor Thibodeau's scholarship focuses on audit judgment and decision making and audit education. He is a coauthor of two textbooks and has written more than 40 book chapters and articles for academics and practitioners in journals such as *Auditing: A Journal of Practice & Theory, Accounting Horizons,* and *Issues in Accounting Education.*

Professor Thibodeau served as the President of the Auditing Section of the American Accounting Association for the 2014/2015 academic year. He served on the Executive Committee for the Auditing Section from 2008 to 2010. He has received national recognition for his work five times. First, for his thesis, winning the 1996 Outstanding Doctoral Dissertation Award presented by the ABO section of the AAA. Three other times, for curriculum innovation, winning the 2001 Joint AICPA/AAA Collaboration Award, the 2003 Innovation in Assurance Education Award, and the 2016 Forensic Accounting Teaching Innovation Award. Finally, for outstanding service, receiving a Special Service Award from the Auditing Section for his work in helping to create the "Access to Auditors" program sponsored by the Center for Audit Quality.

Look Beneath the Surface . . .

As auditors, we are trained to investigate beyond appearances to determine the underlying facts—in other words, to *look beneath the surface.* From the Enron and WorldCom scandals of the early 2000s to the financial crisis of 2007–2008 to present-day issues and challenges related to significant estimation uncertainty, understanding the auditor's responsibility related to fraud, maintaining a clear perspective, probing for details, and understanding the big picture are indispensable to effective auditing. With the availability of greater levels of qualitative and quantitative information ("big data"), the need for technical skills and challenges facing today's auditor is greater than ever. The author team of Louwers, Blay, Sinason, Strawser, and Thibodeau has dedicated years of experience in the auditing field to this new edition of *Auditing & Assurance Services,* supplying the necessary investigative tools for future auditors.

Cutting-Edge Coverage

The seventh edition of *Auditing & Assurance Services* continues its tradition as the most up-to-date auditing text on the market. All chapters and modules have been revised to incorporate the latest professional standards, recodifications, and proposals from the International Auditing and Assurance Standards Board, Auditing Standards Board, and Public Company Accounting Oversight Board. To acquaint students with the professional standards, each chapter or module begins with a list of the relevant professional standards that are covered in that chapter. Importantly, this text incorporates the reorganized PCAOB standards effective December 31, 2016.

As a team, we use a variety of contacts and resources to stay informed of ongoing developments that affect learning objectives in the financial statement auditing course(s). In fact, changes to key learning goals and objectives are usually prompted by interactions with colleagues from practice.

In that spirit, since the publication of our sixth edition, we have been working hard to stay in touch with developments in practice so we can always respond to your needs in the financial statement auditing classroom. Among our many observations, one trend has emerged as a potential sea change in the financial statement auditing process, the "big data" challenge.

Indeed, based on our collective observations, we believe that students should be prepared to make the best use possible of relevant data using state-of-the art analytical tools. In fact, the terms *big data* and *data analytics* are frequently being used to describe a growing movement among audit professionals. Our collective view is that students must be prepared to meet the "big data" challenge.

To help students be prepared, the seventh edition of *Auditing & Assurance Services* has been revised deliberately to help students critically think about the use of increased data and analytical tools in the financial statement audit. In addition, we would like to help students learn how to effectively document their conclusions in the current "big data" environment.

In a recent white paper, PwC (2015)[1] lists five "new" skills that will be required of auditors moving forward. Although many of these skills require special statistical or programming knowledge, the first listed skill is one that is applicable to all auditors: "Research and identify anomalies and risk factors in underlying data." Although

[1]"Data Driven: What Students Need to Succeed in a Rapidly Changing Business World." Available at: http://www.pwc.com/us/en/faculty-resource/assets/PwC-Data-driven-paper-Feb2015.pdf.

extraction and analysis from client accounting data are critical skills for newly minted auditors, we are unaware of sufficient materials to assist professors in integrating data analytics into the auditing classroom. Thus, an important goal of the seventh edition is to provide a clear and implementable method to fully integrate a leading data analysis tool, the IDEA data analysis software, into the auditing class.

To start, McGraw-Hill Education is excited to announce a partnership with the developers of the IDEA software. We believe that IDEA provides an outstanding platform to illustrate the steps that auditors need to take related to data and data analysis while completing the financial statement audit. Leading auditing professionals have confirmed that using IDEA is an outstanding way for an entry-level auditing professional to begin the journey into the world of "big data" and "data analytics." Simply stated, big data is manifested in the financial statement auditing process through the use of tools like IDEA.

Overall, our revisions related to the big data challenge were designed to provide instructors a set of tools and mechanisms to bring data and analytics into the classroom in a meaningful way. Through the use of these tools, students can be sure they are prepared to enter practice with an appreciation for and knowledge of the increasing importance of data and analytics in the auditing profession. We hope that everyone enjoys our attempts to help students get ready for the big data challenge.

Of course, and perhaps most importantly, the seventh edition of *Auditing & Assurance Services* also continues to be the most up-to-date auditing text on the market. The book has fully integrated the reorganized PCAOB Auditing Standards. In addition, all chapters and modules in the seventh edition have been revised to incorporate the two new standards (AS 2701 and AS 2410) adopted by the PCAOB that relate to the auditor's work on supplementary information provided in the financial statements and related parties. In addition, all chapters and modules have been revised to incorporate the latest updates from the international standards of auditing (ISAs) and the Auditing Standards Board (ASB). With *Auditing & Assurance Services,* seventh edition, students are prepared to take on auditing's latest challenges.

The Louwers author team uses a conversational, yet professional tone—hailed by reviewers as a key strength of the book.

Flexible Organization

Auditing & Assurance Services teaches students auditing concepts by emphasizing real-life contexts when describing the auditing process. The authors use chapters and modules to

> *"The format allows you to integrate the modules into the chapter material in any way you would find useful."*
> —Frank J. Beil, *University of Minnesota*

Chapters	Modules
The 12 chapters cover the auditing process extensively with a multitude of cases designed to give students a better understanding of how a best-practice concept developed from real-world situations.	Modules A–H provide instructors additional material that can be used throughout the course. Topics such as fraud, ethics, sampling, and technology are covered in the modules, which are designed to be taught whenever instructors want to introduce the topic in their course.

achieve this goal. Although the chapters follow a logical sequence that we recommend professors consider for their classes, **the modules have been written to be used on a stand-alone basis.** In essence, the modules have been deliberately prepared for entirely flexible implementation of these topics without excessive reliance on chapter sequencing. We encourage you to integrate these modules into your syllabi in a manner that best suits your approach to the auditing course.

Engage Your Students with Real Examples

"The tone of the textbook is in a conversational manner that allows for more student-friendly reading material."
—Aretha Hill, *Florida A&M University*

An effective accounting textbook integrates real-world scenarios with theoretical discussion. *Auditing & Assurance Services* places the student in the role of a decision maker, by illustrating the application of auditing concepts using actual situations experienced by accounting firms and companies such as:

Each chapter or module opens with a "real-world" example that draws upon concepts discussed within that chapter or module. Finally, a series of mini-cases have been developed for use by instructors to further bring text material to life. These mini-cases feature real situations experienced by the following companies, individuals, or accounting firms [new cases to the seventh edition are noted with an asterisk (*)].

- Arthur Andersen (failure of auditors to detect fraud at Enron)
- Bernie Madoff Investment Securities (failure of auditors and regulators to detect fraud)*
- Crazy Eddie's (failure of auditors to detect fraud)*
- Daily Journal Corporation (auditor changes and reporting on internal control)*
- General Electric (audit fees and services provided by auditors)
- General Motors (going-concern report by auditors)
- HealthSouth Corporation (failure of auditors to detect fraud)
- KPMG (competition in the audit marketplace)
- Lehman Brothers (estimation uncertainties in the audit and disclosure concerns)*
- Parmalat (failure of auditors to detect fraud)
- Satyam Computer Services Ltd. (failure of auditors to detect fraud)
- Scott London, KPMG partner (failure of auditor to follow the AICPA Code of Conduct)*

Fraud Awareness

The fraud coverage in *Auditing & Assurance Services* is the most extensive available and is complemented by real-world examples chosen to engage students through the following tools:

- Auditing Insights integrated throughout the text.
- Mini-cases that may be assigned to supplement text chapters and modules that expose students to

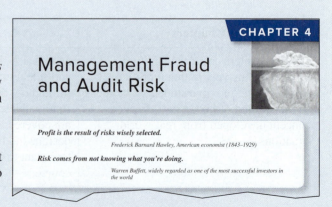

CHAPTER 4

Management Fraud and Audit Risk

Profit is the result of risks wisely selected.
Frederick Barnard Hawley, American economist (1843–1929)

Risk comes from not knowing what you're doing.
Warren Buffett, widely regarded as one of the most successful investors in the world

landmark fraud cases at Bernie Madoff Investment Securities, Enron, HealthSouth, Parmalat, PTL Club, and Satyam Computer Services.

- Specific discussion of management fraud (Chapter 4), employee fraud (Chapter 6), and the Certified Fraud Examiner Exam (Module D).
- **Apollo Shoes Case,** the only stand-alone fraud audit case on the market (available online).

Create a State-of-the-Art Learning Environment: Instructor Resources

The author team and McGraw-Hill are dedicated to providing instructors with the best teaching resources available. In addition to the solutions manual, test bank, and PowerPoint Presentations, and the Apollo Shoe Case, the following resources are also available.

The Updated Auditor

The author team scrutinizes leading business and academic publications for relevant issues and research that sheds light on auditing and the audit process. Recent findings from academic research and discussions from professional literature are drawn from the following publications:

- *Accounting Horizons*
- *Accounting Today*
- *Auditing: A Journal of Practice & Theory*
- *Behavioral Research in Accounting*
- *Bloomberg Businessweek*
- *CFO.com*
- *CPA Journal*
- *Journal of Accountancy*
- *Journal of Accounting and Economics*
- *The Accounting Review*
- *The Wall Street Journal*

These excerpts are highlighted throughout the text as Auditing Insights to allow for easy identification and review by instructors and students.

In addition to the use of Auditing Insights, on a monthly basis, the author team provides an *Updated Auditor* briefing, which summarizes the content of relevant business and academic publications on a chapter-by-chapter basis, to allow students to apply current developments in the profession with material discussed in class. The *Updated Auditor* briefing is available in Connect. With the *Updated Auditor,* instructors will always be at the cutting edge of auditing practice!

IDEA Software and Workbook

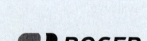

With the availability of unprecedented amounts of quantitative and qualitative information and tools available to access and process that information, it is imperative that students learn and utilize the latest technologies used by auditing professionals. As previously stated, McGraw-Hill Education has forged a partnership with Caseware Analytics for the use of the IDEA data analysis tool. Chapters 3 (audit planning), 4 (risk assessment), 5 (internal control), 7–9 (operating cycle chapters), Module F (attributes sampling), and Module G (variables sampling) have been revised to reference the use of IDEA within the chapter or module.

In addition, the seventh edition includes end-of-chapter exercises utilizing **author-developed databases** exclusively for use with *Auditing & Assurance Services* as well as supplemental materials available in Connect to complement the IDEA workbook and provide hands-on instructions on using the IDEA software. The authors also provide implementation guidance to instructors and detailed solutions and explanations on this new content. Overall, the author team has provided significant resources to prepare students for the auditing environment in 2017 and beyond.

Roger CPA Review

McGraw-Hill Education has partnered with Roger CPA Review, a global leader in CPA Exam preparation, to provide students a smooth transition from the accounting classroom to successful completion of the CPA Exam. While many aspiring accountants wait until they have completed their academic studies to begin preparing for the CPA Exam, research shows that those who become familiar with exam content earlier in the process have a stronger chance of successfully passing the CPA Exam. Accordingly, students using these McGraw-Hill materials will have access to sample CPA Exam Multiple-Choice questions and Task-based Simulations from Roger CPA Review, with expert-written explanations and solutions. All questions are either directly from the AICPA or are modeled on AICPA questions that appear in the exam. Task-based Simulations are delivered via the Roger CPA Review platform, which mirrors the look, feel and functionality of the actual exam. McGraw-Hill Education and Roger CPA Review are dedicated to supporting every accounting student along their journey, ultimately helping them achieve career success in the accounting profession. For more information about the full Roger CPA Review program, exam requirements and exam content, visit www.rogercpareview.com.

TestGen

TestGen is a complete, state-of-the-art test generator and editing application software that allows instructors to quickly and easily select test items from McGraw Hill's TestGen testbank content and to organize, edit and customize the questions and answers to rapidly generate paper tests. Questions can include stylized text, symbols, graphics, and equations that are inserted directly into questions using built-in mathematical templates. With both quick-and-simple test creation and flexible and robust editing tools, TestGen is a test generator system for today's educators.

Association to Advance Collegiate Schools of Business (AACSB) Statement

McGraw-Hill Education is a proud corporate member of AACSB International. Understanding the importance and value of AACSB accreditation, *Auditing & Assurance Services*, 7e, recognizes the curricula guidelines detailed in the AACSB standards for business accreditation by connecting selected questions in the text and test bank to the eight general knowledge and skill guidelines in the AACSB standards. The statements contained in *Auditing & Assurance Services*, 7e, are provided only as a guide for the users of this textbook. The AACSB leaves content coverage and assessment within the purview of individual schools, their mission, and their faculty. Although *Auditing & Assurance Services*, 7e, and the teaching package make no claim of any specific AACSB qualification or evaluation, we have within *Auditing & Assurance Services*, 7e, labeled selected questions according to the eight general knowledge and skills areas.

MCGRAW-HILL CUSTOMER EXPERIENCE GROUP CONTACT INFORMATION

At McGraw-Hill Education, we understand that getting the most from new technology can be challenging. That's why our services don't stop after you purchase our products. You can contact our Product Specialists 24 hours a day to get product training online. Or you can search the knowledge bank of Frequently Asked Questions on our support website. For Customer Support, call 800-331-5094 or visit www.mhhe.com/support. One of our Technical Support Analysts will be able to assist you in a timely fashion.

New to the Seventh Edition of

In response to feedback and guidance from numerous auditing accounting faculty, the authors have made many important changes to the seventh edition of *Auditing & Assurance Services*, including the following:

Highlights of *Auditing & Assurance Services*, 7e

- The seventh edition of *Auditing & Assurance Services* features Connect and SmartBook.

- All chapter and modules have been revised to incorporate professional standards adopted through May 2016. In addition, the reorganized PCAOB framework (which becomes effective December 31, 2016) has been utilized throughout the text.

- **Auditing Insight boxes** have been added and updated throughout the textbook to place issues discussed within the text into a real-world context. These boxes incorporate numerous examples from business and academic publications as well as actual company annual reports and audit reports.

- Examples using the Caseware IDEA software have been added in Chapters 3, 4, 5, 7, 8, 9, Module F, and Module G. In addition, end-of-chapter exercises using **author-developed databases** exclusively for use with *Auditing &*

Assurance Services as well as supplemental materials to complement the IDEA workbook are provided.

- Coverage in the cycle chapters has been standardized to focus on the risk assessment process for each relevant assertion. In addition, the chapters provide a consistent focus on how auditors respond to assessed risk of material misstatement, through the incorporation of easy-to-read tables throughout Chapters 6 through 10 to highlight the key issues and risks faced by auditors in the examination of different accounts. These tables take the students through the risk assessment process for each cycle on a step-by-step basis to mirror the methodology used in current audit practice.

- Five new Mini-cases have been added that feature Bernie Madoff Investment Securities (failure of auditors and regulators to detect fraud); Crazy Eddie's (failure of auditors to detect fraud); Daily Journal Corporation (auditor changes and internal control reporting); Lehman Brothers (estimation uncertainties in the audit and failure to make informative disclosures); and Scott London, KPMG Partner (failure of auditor to follow the AICPA Code of Conduct).

Part I: The Contemporary Auditing Environment

CHAPTER 1: Auditing and Assurance Services

- Our discussion about the CPA exam has been revised to fully reflect the substantial changes being made to the exam as of April 1, 2017. Due primarily to the outsourcing of routine tasks and significant advances in information technology, the job of a newly licensed CPA has changed. The AICPA responded with a revised exam that has an increased emphasis on higher-order skills like problem solving, critical thinking, and analytical ability. The changes are fully described in the text.

- Increased our emphasis about the importance of audit quality in the current environment and added an Auditing Insight that describes the audit quality indicators project recently completed by the PCAOB in 2015.

- Added a new exhibit that provides an example of the 2014/2015 Sustainability Report for the Coca-Cola Company. We also added a new exhibit that features Mickey Mantle's baseball card from 1961.

- Increased our emphasis on the emergence of big data in the auditing environment and added an Auditing Insight that describes what students need to succeed in a world characterized by big data.

CHAPTER 2: Professional Standards

- Summarized recent academic research related to the impact of PCAOB inspections and results of inspections on audit quality, client attraction and retention, and audit fee growth rates (including research specifically related to the Deloitte vignette in the introduction of this chapter).

- Summarized recent independence issues encountered by EY and KPMG.

- McDonald's 2016 audit report, which demonstrates the contents of an actual audit report and how this report reflects the guidance in the reporting principle.

- Included an Auditing Insight regarding controversy over PCAOB inspection of audits of Alibaba Group Holding Limited, which have been impacted by China's ban of PCAOB inspections.

- Summarized PCAOB inspections of 2012, 2013, and 2014 audits conducted by Big Four firms and expanded analysis to summarize the number of audits in which the client's report on internal control was revised as a result of the inspection.

Part II: The Financial Statement Audit

CHAPTER 3: Engagement Planning

- Added a discussion to emphasize the importance of identifying all of the significant accounts and each of the relevant financial statement assertions during the engagement planning process.
- Included a new table to help facilitate the understanding of significant accounts and relevant financial statement assertions and to show how this might be documented in the audit work papers.
- Added an Auditing Insight to describe the importance of audit quality and why planning is such an important aspect in helping to ensure that the engagement plan has been developed to achieve quality outcomes on the audit.
- Added a discussion about the availability of big data on the audit and included a demonstration problem of how to access a client's data using IDEA.

CHAPTER 4: Management Fraud and Audit Risk

- Increased focus on the importance of assessing the risk of material misstatement for each relevant financial statement assertion for each significant account and disclosure. This focus is entirely consistent with the audit approaches of each of the largest audit firms in the world. This focus will be very helpful in preparing students to enter the auditing environment in 2017 and beyond.
- Added a new easy-to-read table to highlight the importance of identifying "what can go wrong" for each relevant assertion identified in the planning process. This process is instrumental for assessing the risk of material misstatement for each relevant assertion.
- Moved our discussion of an audit client's risk management system to Chapter 5, where it is incorporated into our discussion of the risk assessment component of an effective internal control system as defined by COSO. By moving this section, students are able to better focus on inherent risk assessment in this chapter.
- Added an Auditing Insight to illustrate the potential dangers of analyst expectations at Bankrate and an Auditing Insight to illustrate the difficulty involved in auditing percentage of completion estimates at Toshiba. These examples are used to emphasize the importance of considering a client's business and operating environment during the risk assessment process.
- Incorporated newly released PCAOB Auditing Standard 2410 about Related Parties into the chapter.

CHAPTER 5: Risk Assessment: Internal Control Evaluation

- Fully integrated the specifics of the COSO 2013 update to its internal control framework. The update adds 17 explicit principles that are associated with the five components of internal control (i.e., control environment, risk assessment, control activities, information and communication, and monitoring). The chapter now includes five new exhibits to help clarify and make these principles salient to students.
- Added a new easy-to-read table to reinforce the importance of identifying "what can go wrong" to help assess the risk of material misstatement for each relevant assertion that provides a foundation to help identify control activities that might mitigate that risk. This is an important aspect of the audit process employed by each of the large audit firms, and the table is designed to help students better understand that process.
- Added a section on internal control testing alternatives with a focus on how auditors can use a tool such as IDEA to test the entire population of control instances in today's environment. We also added two new problems where students can complete exception tests using IDEA.

CHAPTER 6: Employee Fraud and the Audit of Cash

- Added two easy-to-read tables to allow for a focus on the risk assessment process for each relevant assertion related to cash. For each relevant assertion, students can see how the risk of material misstatement was assessed and how the auditors might respond to the assessed risks with tests of control and substantive tests. The step-by-step process mirrors the methodology used in current audit practice.
- Improved the flow and organization of the chapter by integrating the section on controls designed to mitigate the risk of employee fraud into the section on internal control testing for the cash account. In addition, the section on proof of cash has been moved to the extended fraud procedures section to better align the chapter with current audit practice.
- Added an Auditing Insight describing the fraud perpetrated by a controller at a Pepsi-Cola Bottler and how he escaped to the Appalachian trail for an extended period of time.

CHAPTER 7: Revenue and Collection Cycle

- Revised format tracking the audit process beginning with identification of significant accounts and relevant assertions.
- Added four new tables outlining risks and tracking them through the audit process, including tests of controls and substantive procedures.
- Updated discussion of revenue recognition restatements.
- Increased discussion of risks related to data breaches, including an Auditing Insight on the Target Corp. data breach.
- Added a discussion of the new revenue recognition standards, including examples from financial statements of Apple Inc.

- Updated PCAOB inspection findings through the latest inspection reports.
- Includes a focus on data and analytics that integrates several IDEA exercises, including new author-created content and end-of-chapter materials.

CHAPTER 8: Acquisition and Expenditure Cycle

- Revised format tracking the audit process beginning with identification of significant accounts and relevant assertions.
- Added five new tables outlining risks and tracking them through the audit process, including tests of controls and substantive procedures.
- Increased discussion of risks related to accounts payable.
- Updated PCAOB inspection findings through the latest inspection reports.
- Includes a focus on data and analytics that integrates several IDEA exercises, including new author-created content and end-of-chapter materials.

CHAPTER 9: Production Cycle

- Revised format tracking the audit process beginning with identification of significant accounts and relevant assertions.
- Added six new tables outlining risks and tracking them through the audit process, including tests of controls and substantive procedures.
- Extensive discussion of the production process and key reports of interest to the auditors.
- Updated PCAOB inspection findings through the latest inspection reports.
- Includes a focus on data and analytics that integrates several IDEA exercises, including new author-created content and end-of-chapter materials.

CHAPTER 10: Finance and Investment Cycle

- Revised format tracking the audit process beginning with identification of significant accounts and relevant assertions.
- Added five new tables outlining risks and tracking them through the audit process, including tests of controls and substantive procedures.

Part III: Stand-Alone Modules

MODULE A: Other Public Accounting Services

- New section added on PCAOB broker–dealer standards, including an Auditing Insight describing compliance issues that led to the new standards.

- Added a new Auditing Insight regarding Verizon's purchases, including the recent proposed purchase of Yahoo!
- Added a new Auditing Insight describing off-balance-sheet risk for Citigroup.
- Expanded discussion of auditing accounting estimates and fair values, with discussion of extreme estimation uncertainty and an Auditing Insight on the Lehman Brothers collapse.
- Added a discussion of blockchain technology and Bitcoin transactions.
- Updated PCAOB inspection findings through the latest inspection reports.

CHAPTER 11: Completing the Audit

- New introductory vignette discusses Valeant's year-end financial troubles and the effect on the auditors trying to complete the company's audit. Added discussion of AS 16's increased responsibilities to communicate with those charged with governance.

CHAPTER 12: Reports on Audited Financial Statements

- New introductory vignette discusses KPMG's report on the audit of Rolls-Royce and the identification of critical audit matters in this report.
- Discuss recently approved and proposed standards of audit report disclosures and practices related to critical audit matters, naming of the engagement partner, and audits of group financial statements.
- Summarize recent academic research related to the disclosure of critical audit matters, disclosure of engagement partner identity, receipt and issuance of going concern reports, and inclusion of explanatory paragraphs in otherwise unmodified audit opinions.
- Included examples from recent auditors' reports of Abbott Laboratories, Alaska Air, Best Buy Co. Inc., Caesars Entertainment Corporation, The Coca-Cola Company, General Electric, Harris Teeter Supermarkets Inc., The Kroger Co., Penske Automotive Group, and Softbank Corp. to illustrate how auditors modify their reports for situations encountered in practice.
- Include results of an Audit Analytics research report summarizing 15 years of data regarding going-concern reports.

- Updated for the revised standards on accounting and review services, including a section on preparation engagements.
- A new table clarifies the differences between preparation engagements and services that are not preparation engagements.

MODULE B: Professional Ethics

- Opened the module with the story of disgraced former KPMG partner Scott London who sacrificed his career to share confidential client information with a friend.
- Added a discussion of Aristotelian virtue ethics to already existing discussions of Kantian categorical imperatives and utilitarianism.
- Added a discussion of the role of the PCAOB's Division of Enforcement and Investigations.

MODULE C: Legal Liability

- Updated the introductory vignette on litigation involving BDO Seidman for its audits of E.S. Bankest to include the ultimate resolution of this litigation.
- Updated the summary of major settlements involving Big Four accounting firms to include settlements occurring since 2008.
- Expanded the discussion of academic research examining auditor litigation to include recent studies that investigated the factors affecting the litigation risk faced by audit firms.

MODULE D: Internal Audits, Governmental Audits, and Fraud Examinations

- Updated the coverage of the reliance of Congress on the GAO.
- Discussed the variety of services provided by internal auditors.
- Added Benford's law to the fraud investigation discussion.

MODULE E: Overview of Sampling

- New introductory vignette involve the recent U.S. Supreme Court ruling on use of sampling methods to determine monetary damages against Tyson Foods in an employment dispute.
- Revised walk-through example of the use of sampling to address a nonauditing issue.
- Auditing Insight address how sampling risk affected predictions in the 2015 United Kingdom general elections for David Cameron and the Conservative Party.
- Included a brief example of sampling in the evaluation of internal control to illustrate the major steps and decisions made in the sampling process.

MODULE F: Attributes Sampling

- Introductory section provide an overview of the audit engagement, the use of the audit risk model, and the role of attributes sampling in the audit engagement to place the attributes sampling process in context.
- IDEA is used in the determination of sample size, selection of sample items, and evaluation of sample results to supplement the use of AICPA sampling tables.
- Additional end-of-chapter items provide students with the opportunity to use IDEA in various stages of the attributes sampling process.
- Summarized a recent academic study that surveyed the sampling practices of six international accounting firms with respect to establishing parameters and selecting sample items.

MODULE G: Variables Sampling

- Introductory section provides an overview of the audit engagement, the use of the audit risk model, and the role of variables sampling in the audit engagement to place the variables sampling process in context.
- IDEA is used in the determination of sample size, selection of sample items, and evaluation of sample results to supplement the use of formulae in MUS.
- Additional end-of-chapter items to provide students with the opportunity to use IDEA in various stages of MUS applications.
- Auditing Insight summarize the results of a recent academic study that surveyed the sampling practices of six international accounting firms.
- Previous content on classical variables sampling and nonstatistical sampling has been expanded and relocated into appendixes to provide instructors with flexibility in addressing these topics.

MODULE H: Auditing and Information Technology

- Significantly revised (and simplified) the module throughout to reinforce how the client's use of automated transaction processing systems affects the major stages of the audit team's study and evaluation of internal control.
- Provided an example of how students encounter IT general and app controls when using a smartphone.
- Added additional end-of-chapter material that requires students to identify tests of controls that would be used to evaluate the operating effectiveness of general and automated application controls.

McGraw-Hill Connect®
Learn Without Limits

Connect is a teaching and learning platform that is proven to deliver better results for students and instructors.

Connect empowers students by continually adapting to deliver precisely what they need, when they need it, and how they need it, so your class time is more engaging and effective.

73% of instructors who use Connect require it; instructor satisfaction increases by 28% when Connect is required.

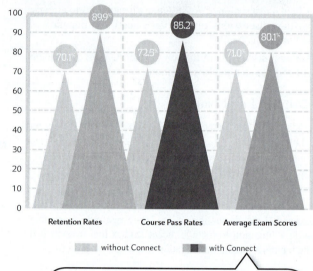

Connect's Impact on Retention Rates, Pass Rates, and Average Exam Scores

- Retention Rates: 70.1% (without Connect), 89.9% (with Connect)
- Course Pass Rates: 72.5% (without Connect), 85.2% (with Connect)
- Average Exam Scores: 71.0% (without Connect), 80.1% (with Connect)

without Connect | with Connect

Using **Connect** improves retention rates by **19.8%**, passing rates by **12.7%**, and exam scores by **9.1%**.

Analytics

Connect Insight®

Connect Insight is Connect's new one-of-a-kind visual analytics dashboard that provides at-a-glance information regarding student performance, which is immediately actionable. By presenting assignment, assessment, and topical performance results together with a time metric that is easily visible for aggregate or individual results, Connect Insight gives the user the ability to take a just-in-time approach to teaching and learning, which was never before available. Connect Insight presents data that help instructors improve class performance in a way that is efficient and effective.

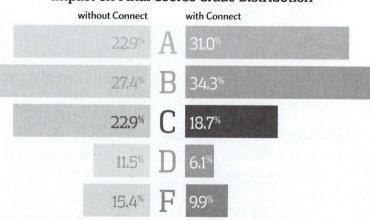

Impact on Final Course Grade Distribution

	without Connect	with Connect
A	22.9%	31.0%
B	27.4%	34.3%
C	22.9%	18.7%
D	11.5%	6.1%
F	15.4%	9.9%

Adaptive

THE **ADAPTIVE** **READING EXPERIENCE** DESIGNED TO TRANSFORM THE WAY STUDENTS READ

More students earn **A's** and **B's** when they use McGraw-Hill Education **Adaptive** products.

SmartBook®

Proven to help students improve grades and study more efficiently, SmartBook contains the same content within the print book, but actively tailors that content to the needs of the individual. SmartBook's adaptive technology provides precise, personalized instruction on what the student should do next, guiding the student to master and remember key concepts, targeting gaps in knowledge and offering customized feedback, and driving the student toward comprehension and retention of the subject matter. Available on tablets, SmartBook puts learning at the student's fingertips—anywhere, anytime.

Over **8 billion questions** have been answered, making McGraw-Hill Education products more intelligent, reliable, and precise.

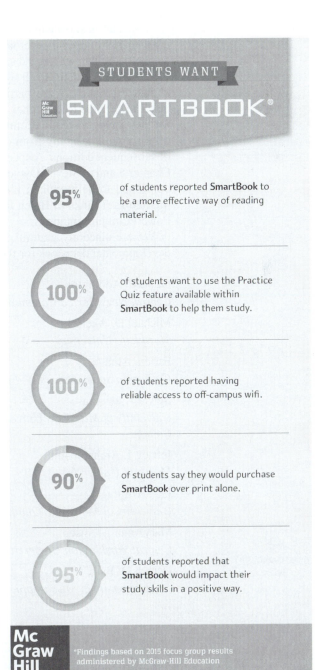

STUDENTS WANT

Mc Graw Hill Education **SMARTBOOK**®

95% of students reported **SmartBook** to be a more effective way of reading material.

100% of students want to use the Practice Quiz feature available within **SmartBook** to help them study.

100% of students reported having reliable access to off-campus wifi.

90% of students say they would purchase **SmartBook** over print alone.

95% of students reported that **SmartBook** would impact their study skills in a positive way.

Mc Graw Hill Education

*Findings based on 2015 focus group results administered by McGraw-Hill Education

www.mheducation.com

Acknowledgments

OUR SINCEREST THANKS . . .

The American Institute of Certified Public Accountants (AICPA) has generously given permission for liberal quotations from official pronouncements and other AICPA publications, all of which lend authoritative sources to the text. In addition, several publishing houses, professional associations, and accounting firms have granted permission to quote and extract from their copyrighted material. Their cooperation is much appreciated because a great amount of significant auditing thought exists in this wide variety of sources.

A special acknowledgment is due to the Association for Certified Fraud Examiners (ACFE). It has been a generous contributor to the fraud auditing material in this text. The authors also acknowledge the valuable inclusion of the educational version of IDEA software in the seventh edition, which significantly enhances the practical application of the book.

Also, the authors are particularly grateful to Meghann Cefaratti (Northern Illinois University), Brad Roof (James Madison University), and Yigal Rechtman (Pace University) for their many insightful comments over the past several years. The feedback they contributed while teaching from our text has contributed greatly to the clarity and accuracy of subsequent editions. A special thanks to Michael K. Shaub for his valuable critique of Chapter 5 and to Steven Dwyer, Suzanne McLaughlin, and Frank Wimer for the example developed to help explain the difference between general and application controls in Module H. Thanks to Helen Roybark for her help with the preparation of the instructor PowerPoint presentations.

We are sincerely grateful for the valuable input of all those who helped guide our developmental decisions for the past seven editions of *Auditing & Assurance Services:*

Dawn P. Addington,
Central New Mexico Community College

Michael D. Akers,
Marquette University

Fatima Alali,
California State University–Fullerton

Sylvia Anderson,
University of Maryland University College

Jeffrey J. Archambault,
Marshall University

Jack Armitage,
University of Nebraska–Omaha

MaryAnne Atkinson,
Central Washington University

Dereck D. Barr,
The University of Mississippi

LuAnn Bean,
Florida Institute of Technology

Frank J. Beil,
University of Minnesota

Marie Blouin,
Penn State University–Harrisburg

David Blum,
Moraine Park Technical College

Russell F. Briner,
University of Texas at San Antonio

Alexander K. Buchholz,
Brooklyn College of the City University of New York

Suzanne M. Busch,
California State University–East Bay

Eric Carlsen,
Kean University

Meghann Cefaratti,
Northern Illinois University

John Critchett
Madonna University

Karl Dahlberg,
Rutgers University

John E. Delaney,
Southwestern Texas University

Marcus Mason Doxey,
University of Kentucky

Raymond Elson,
Valdosta State University

Tom English,
Boise State University

Patricia Feller,
Nashville State Community College

Marilyn Fisher,
Corinthian Colleges

Diana R. Franz,
University of Toledo

John Gabelman,
Columbus State Community College

Clyde Galbraith,
West Chester University

Andy Garcia,
Bowling Green State University

David Gelb,
Seton Hall University

Earl Godfrey,
Gardner-Webb University

Judith G. Grant,
*Northern Virginia Community
College at Annandale*

Emily Elaine Griffith,
The University of Georgia

Richard Hale,
Midway College

James Hansen,
University of Illinois at Chicago

Aretha Hill,
Florida A&M University

Steven C. Hunt,
Western Illinois University

Venkataraman Iyer,
*The University of
North Carolina at Greensboro*

Keith Jones,
George Mason University

Bonita K. Peterson Kramer,
Montana State University–Bozeman

Joseph M. Larkin,
St. Joseph's University

Rose Layton,
University of Southern California

Pamela Legner,
College of DuPage

Philip Levine,
Berkeley College

R. D. Licastro,
Penn State University–University Park

Maureen Mascha,
Marquette University

Dorothy McMullen,
Rider University

Heidi H. Meier,
Cleveland State University

Bharat Merchant,
Baruch College

Eddie Metrejean,
Georgia Southern University

Charles Miller,
California Polytech University

Perry Moore,
Lipscomb University

Fowler A. Murrell,
Lehman College

Ramesh Narasimhan,
Montclair State University

Vincent Owhoso,
Northern Kentucky University

Dwight M. Owsen
Long Island University Brooklyn

Gary Peters,
University of Arkansas

Byron Pike,
Minnesota State University–Mankato

Marshall Pitman,
University of Texas–San Antonio

Sharon Polansky,
Texas A&M University–Corpus Christi

Kathy Pollock,
Indiana University–Purdue University Fort Wayne

Duane Ponko,
Indiana University of Pennsylvania

Dwayne Powell,
Arkansas State University

Abdul Qastin,
North Carolina A&T State

Linda Quick,
University of South Carolina

Hema Rao,
SUNY–Oswego

Jason T. Rasso,
University of South Florida

Yigal Rechtman,
Pace University

Barbara Reider,
University of Montana

Raymond Reisig,
Pace University

John Rigsby,
Mississippi State University

Pamela Roush,
University of Central Florida

Maria Sanchez,
Rider University

Kristen Kelli Saunders,
University of South Carolina

Tammi Schaefer,
University of South Carolina

Bunney L. Schmidt,
Utah Valley State College

Timothy Andrew Seidel,
University of Arkansas

Carol Shaver,
Louisiana Tech University

Jaysinha Shinde,
Eastern Illinois University

Adrianne Slaymaker,
Metropolitan State University

Duane Smith,
Brescia University

Beverly Strachan,
Troy University at Montgomery

Iris Stuart,
California State University

Christine N. Todd,
Colorado State University–Pueblo

John Trussel,
Penn State University–Harrisburg

Jerry L. Turner,
University of Memphis

Frank Venezia,
State University at Albany

Barbara Vinciguerra,
Moravian College

Bobby Waldrup,
University of North Florida

Rick Warne,
University of Cincinnati

J. Donald Warren Jr.,
Rutgers University

Christian Wurst,
Temple University

Tu Xu,
Georgia State University

Xu Zhaohui,
University of Houston–Clear Lake

Lin Zheng,
Northeastern Illinois University

Douglas Ziegenfuss,
Old Dominion University

In addition, we would like to recognize our outstanding staff at McGraw-Hill: Managing Director, Tim Vertovec; Brand Manager, Pat Plumb; Marketing Manager, Cheryl Osgood; Product Developers, Rebecca Mann and Randall Edwards; Senior Content Project Managers, Dana Pauley and Angela Norris; Buyer, Laura Fuller; and Designer, Matt Diamond. For their encouragement, assistance, and guidance in the production of this book, we are grateful.

Few understand the enormous commitment of time and energy that it takes to put together a textbook. As authors, we are constantly scanning *The Wall Street Journal* and other news outlets for real-world examples to illustrate theoretical discussions, rereading and rewriting each other's work to make sure that key concepts are understandable, and double-checking our solutions to end-of-chapter problems. Among the few who do understand the time and energy commitment are our family members (Barbara Louwers; Kristin, Jackson, Elijah, Jonah, Ansley, and Laney Grace Blay; Karen, Matthew, Joshua, and Adam Sinason; Susan and Meghan Strawser; and Ellen, Jenny, Eric, and Jessica Thibodeau) who uncomplainingly endured endless refrains of, "I just need a couple more minutes to finish this section." Words cannot express our gratitude to each of them for their patience and unending support.

Tim Louwers

Allen Blay

Dave Sinason

Jerry Strawser

Jay Thibodeau

Brief Contents

Contents

xxviii *Contents*

Custody 348
Periodic Reconciliation 348
Testing of Operating Effectiveness of Internal Control 349
Tests of Controls 349
Substantive Analytical Procedures and Tests of Details 351
Open Purchase Orders 351
Audit Risk Model Applied 359
Fraud Cases: Extended Audit Procedures (ISA/AS 2301) 361
Audit Issues in the Expense and Acquisition Cycle 364
Summary 365
Key Terms 365
Multiple-Choice Questions for Practice and Review 366
Exercises and Problems 369
Appendix 8A
Internal Control Questionnaires 377

Appendix 8B
Audit Plans 380

Appendix 8C
The Payroll Cycle 382

Multiple-Choice Questions for Practice and Review 390
Exercises and Problems 392

Chapter 9

Production Cycle 394

Phar-Mor Inc. 395
Production Cycle: Typical Activities 396
Significant Accounts and Relevant Assertions 400
Risk of Material Misstatement 402
Internal Control Activities and Design Evaluation 404
Testing of Operating Effectiveness of Internal Control 408
Substantive Analytical Procedures and Tests of Details 411
Inventory Circumstances 416
Audit Risk Model Applied 421
Fraud Case: Extended Audit Procedures (AS 2301) 421
Summary 423
Key Terms 425
Multiple-Choice Questions for Practice and Review 426
Exercises and Problems 429
Appendix 9A
Internal Control Questionnaires 439

Appendix 9B
Audit Plans 441

Chapter 10
Finance and Investment Cycle 443

Introduction 444
Finance and Investment Cycle: Typical Activities 445
Financing the Entity through Debt and Stockholder Equity 446
Financial Planning (1) 447
Raising Capital (2) 447
Investing Transactions: Investments and Intangibles (3) 449
Significant Accounts and Relevant Assertions 452
Risk of Material Misstatement 453
Fair Market Value 454
Related-Party Transactions 455
Lease Accounting 455
Loan Covenants 456
Impairments 457
Presentation and Disclosure 457
Internal Control Activities and Design Evaluation 458
Control Considerations 460
Tests of Operating Effectiveness of Internal Control 460
Control over Accounting Estimates 463
Authorization 464
Record Keeping 464
Custody 465
Summary: Control Risk Assessment 465
Substantive Analytical Procedures and Tests of Details 466
Auditing Fair Value Measurements (AS 2502) 472
Derivative Instruments, Hedging Activities, and Investments in Securities (AS 2503) 473
Long-Term Liabilities and Related Accounts 474
Stockholders' Equity: Substantive Procedures 476
Auditing Stock-Based Compensation Plans 476
Fraud Cases: Extended Audit Procedures (AS 2301) 477
Summary 482
Key Terms 484
Multiple-Choice Questions for Practice and Review 484
Exercises and Problems 488
Appendix 10A
Internal Control Questionnaires 496

Appendix 10B
Substantive Audit Plans 497

Chapter 11

Completing the Audit 500

Introduction 501
Audit Timeline 502
Procedures Performed During Fieldwork 504

Cases

Index   I1

CHAPTER 1

Auditing and Assurance Services

Our system of capital formation relies upon the confidence of millions of savers to invest in companies. The auditor's opinion is critical to that trust.

> James R. Doty, Chairman, Public Company Accounting Oversight Board (PCAOB)

Professional Standards References

Topic	AU-C/ISA Section	AS Section
Overall Objectives of the Independent Auditor	200	1001, 1005, 1010, 1015
Consideration of Fraud in a Financial Statement Audit	240	2401
Audit Evidence	500	1105
Attestation Standards	AT 101	AT 101
Compliance Auditing Considerations in Audits of Recipients of Governmental Financial Assistance	935	6110

LEARNING OBJECTIVES

You are about to embark on a journey of understanding how auditors work to keep the capital markets safe and secure for the investing public. You should know that students demonstrate success in the auditing course quite differently than they do in other accounting courses. For example, when taking financial accounting, students typically demonstrate success by correctly identifying the proper journal entry for a given set of facts and circumstances. In auditing, success is typically demonstrated by completing multiple-choice, short-answer, and simulation-type questions based on the professional standards that regulate the auditing process. Overall, this book provides you with a comprehensive set of materials that will allow you to master these professional auditing standards. Chapter 1 provides an introduction to the auditing and assurance profession.

Your objectives are to be able to:

LO 1-1 Define *information risk* and explain how the financial statement auditing process helps to reduce this risk, thereby reducing the cost of capital for a company.

LO 1-2 Define and contrast *financial statement auditing, attestation,* and *assurance services.*

LO 1-3 Describe and define the assertions that management makes about the recognition, measurement, presentation, and disclosure of the financial statements and explain why auditors use them as the focal point of the audit.

LO 1-4 Define *professional skepticism* and explain its key characteristics.

LO 1-5 Describe the organization of public accounting firms and identify the various services that they offer.

LO 1-6 Describe the audits and auditors in governmental, internal, and operational auditing.

LO 1-7 List and explain the requirements for becoming a certified public accountant (CPA) and other certifications available to an accounting professional.

USER DEMAND FOR RELIABLE INFORMATION

LO 1-1

Define *information risk* and explain how the financial statement auditing process helps to reduce this risk, thereby reducing the cost of capital for a company.

In 2002, the Sarbanes–Oxley Act was passed as a direct response to a wave of major financial statement frauds that had just occurred at companies like **Enron, WorldCom, and Tyco.** While the law was passed many years ago, the effect of this landmark legislation on financial statement auditing has been far reaching. Perhaps the most important change ushered in by the law is that financial statement auditing of public companies is regulated. Specifically, the Public Company Accounting Oversight Board (PCAOB) is now responsible for setting all audit standards to be followed on audits of public companies. In addition, the PCAOB is required to perform inspections of the audit work completed and the quality control processes employed by audit firms. As a direct result, accounting students should know that if they plan to work as financial statement auditors, they will be entering a world that is focused on audit quality. Consider the following Auditing Insight.

 AUDITING INSIGHT   Audit Quality

In July 2015, the PCAOB released a concept statement that detailed 28 different indicators of audit quality. The indicators were categorized within three broad categories. The first category, audit professionals, focused on measures such as partner workload and industry expertise of professionals. The second category, audit process, focused on measures such as compliance with independence requirements and PCOAB inspection results. The third category, audit results, focused on measures such as number of client restatements and client frauds. The list is a clear indication to students that quality matters more than anything else in their future work as auditing professionals.

Source: PCAOB Concept Release on Audit Quality Indicators: Release No.2015-005, July 1, 2015. Available at http://pcaobus.org/Rules/Rulemaking/Docket%20041/Release_2015_005.pdf.

Why is audit quality so important? Well, both investors and creditors depend on reliable financial statement information to make their investment and lending decisions about a company. As a result, the confidence of investors and creditors is shaken each and every time that audit quality is compromised. In fact, before we think about audit quality any further, we must first explain the vital role that financial statement auditors play in supplying key decision makers with useful, understandable, and timely information. When you have a better understanding of why auditing is so critical to help ensure the liquidity of the world's capital markets, we will then explore in detail the process auditors take to help ensure that audit quality is achieved. Because many of you are likely planning to enter the public accounting profession and work as an auditor, we hope that you will work hard to acquire this knowledge so that you may do your part in playing a key role in maintaining the public's confidence in both the auditing profession and the capital markets.

Information Risk in a Big Data World

All businesses make a countless number of decisions each and every day. Decisions to purchase or sell goods or services, lend money, enter into employment agreements, or buy or sell investments depend in large part on the quality of useful information. These decisions affect business risk, which is *the risk that an entity will fail to meet its objectives.* For example, **business risk** includes the chance a company takes that customers will buy from competitors, that product lines will become obsolete, that taxes will increase, that government contracts will be lost, or that employees will go on strike. If the company fails to meet its objectives enough times, the company may ultimately fail. To minimize these risks and take advantage of other opportunities presented in today's competitive business environment, decision makers such as chief executive officers (CEOs) demand *timely, relevant,* and *reliable* information. Similarly, investors and creditors demand high-quality information to make educated financial decisions. Information professionals such as accountants and auditors help satisfy this demand.

In recent years, as a result of ever-increasing computing power, the decision-making environment is rapidly being transformed into one that is characterized by the availability of significant amounts of data and information. Let's face it, the amount of information that organizations are seeking to manage is larger than anyone could have possibly imagined just 10 years ago. You are entering a world where upper management teams are placing more emphasis than ever on how to make sense of this seemingly ever-increasing availability of data and information. To help you prepare for this "big data" challenge, we will be drawing upon this theme in multiple chapters throughout this book.

There are at least four environmental conditions in this "big data" world that increase user demand for relevant and reliable information:

1. *Complexity.* Events and transactions in today's global business environment are numerous and often very complicated. You may have studied derivative securities and hedging activities in other accounting courses, but investors and other decision makers may not have your level of expertise when dealing with these complex transactions. Furthermore, these decision makers are not trained to collect, compile, and summarize the key operating information themselves. They need the services provided by information professionals to help make the information more understandable for their decision processes.

2. *Remoteness.* Decision makers are usually separated from current and potential business partners not only by a lack of expertise but also by distance and time. Investors may not be able to visit distant locations to check up on their investments. They need to employ full-time information professionals to do the work they cannot do for themselves.

3. *Time sensitivity.* Today's economic environment requires businesses, investors, and other financial information users to make decisions more rapidly than ever before. The ability to promptly obtain high-quality information is essential to businesses that want to remain competitive in our global business environment.

4. *Consequences.* Decisions can involve a significant investment of resources. The consequences are so important that reliable information, obtained and verified by information professionals, is an absolute necessity. Enron's aftermath provides a graphic example of how decisions affect individuals' (as well as companies') financial security and well-being. Enron's stock dropped from $90 to $0.90 in little more than a year, leaving employees who had invested their life savings in the company virtually penniless. To put this drop in perspective, an investor's $5 million investment in Enron stock in 2000 (enough for an enjoyable retirement) was worth only $50,000 a year later.

A further complication in effective decision making is the presence of information risk. **Information risk** is *the probability that the information circulated by a company will be false or misleading.* Decision makers usually obtain their information from companies or organizations with which they want to conduct business, to provide

AUDITING INSIGHT — The Consequences of Fraudulent Financial Information

Bernard Madoff, a former chairman of the NASDAQ stock market and a respected Wall Street adviser and broker for 50 years, was arrested after his sons turned him in for running "a giant Ponzi scheme," bilking investors out of billions of dollars. Many investors, including actors, investment bankers, politicians, and sports personalities, lost their life savings. Some who had already retired, now in their 70s and 80s, were forced to go back to work. Others lost their retirement homes. Charities and pensions that had invested heavily were wiped out.

Although some of the world's most knowledgeable investors fell prey to the scam, numerous red flags were present for all who were wise enough to see them. First, Madoff's fund returned 13–16 percent per year, every year, no matter how the markets performed. Second,

his stated strategy of buying stocks and related options to hedge downside risk could not have occurred because the number of options necessary for such a strategy did not exist. Third, although his firm claimed to manage billions of dollars, its auditing firm had only three employees, including a secretary and a 78-year-old accountant who lived in Florida.

Sources: "Fund Fraud Hits Big Names," *The Wall Street Journal,* December 13, 2008, pp. A1, A7; "Fees, Even Returns and Auditor All Raised Flags," *The Wall Street Journal,* December 13, 2008, p. A7; "Top Broker Accused of $50 Billion Fraud," *The Wall Street Journal,* December 12, 2008, pp. A1, A14; "Probe Eyes Audit Files, Role of Aide to Madoff," *The Wall Street Journal,* December 23, 2008, pp. A1, A14.

loans, or to buy or sell stock. Because the primary source of information is the target company itself, an incentive exists for that company's management to make its business or service appear to be better than it actually is, to put its best foot forward. As a result, preparers and issuers of financial information (directors, managers, accountants, and other people employed in a business) might benefit by giving false, misleading, or overly optimistic information. This potential *conflict of interest* between information providers and users, along with financial statement frauds such as those of Enron and WorldCom, leads to a natural skepticism on the part of users. Thus, they depend on information professionals to serve as independent and objective intermediaries who will lend credibility to the information. This *lending of credibility* to information is known as providing **assurance**. When the assurance is provided for specific assertions made by management, we refer to the assurance provided as **attestation**. When the assertions are embodied in a company's financial statements, we refer to the attestation as **auditing**. More specifically, when their work is completed, the auditors supply an opinion as to whether the financial statements and related footnotes are presented fairly in all material respects. The actual compilation and creation of the financial statements is completed by the company's accountants.

✔ REVIEW CHECKPOINTS

1.1 What is a business risk?

1.2 What conditions increase the demand for reliable information?

1.3 What risk creates a demand for independent and objective outsiders to provide assurance to decision makers?

AUDITING, ATTESTATION, AND ASSURANCE SERVICES

LO 1-2
Define and contrast *financial statement auditing, attestation,* and *assurance services.*

Now that you understand why decision makers need independent information professionals to provide assurance on key information, we further define auditing and expand the discussion of attestation and assurance services in this section, and explain their roles in today's information economy.

Definition of Financial Statement Auditing

The focus of this book is on the financial statement auditing process, by far and away the most common type of auditing and assurance service provided in today's market. Many years ago, the American Accounting Association (AAA) Committee on Basic Auditing Concepts provided a very useful general definition of *auditing* as follows:

> *Auditing* is a systematic process of objectively obtaining and evaluating evidence regarding assertions about economic actions and events to ascertain the degree of correspondence between the assertions and established criteria and communicating the results to interested users.[1]

A closer look at the definition reveals several ideas that are important to any type of auditing engagement. Auditing is a *systematic process*. It is a purposeful and logical process and is based on the discipline of a structured approach to reaching final decisions. It has a logical starting point, proceeds along established guidelines, and has a logical conclusion. It is not haphazard, unplanned, or unstructured.

The process involves obtaining and evaluating *evidence*. Evidence consists of all types of information that ultimately guide auditors' decisions and relate to *assertions made by management about economic actions and events*. When beginning a financial statement audit engagement, an independent auditor is provided with financial statements and other disclosures by management. In doing so, management essentially makes assertions about the financial statement balances (that the inventory on the balance sheet really does exist, that revenue transactions recorded on the income statement really did occur, that the list of liabilities on the balance sheet is complete, etc.) as well as assertions that the financial statement disclosures are fairly presented.

 AUDITING INSIGHT

Although most of the largest public accounting firms (collectively referred to as the "Big Four") trace their roots to the turn of the 19th century, auditing in the United States has a rich history. When the Pilgrims had a financial dispute with the English investors who financed their trip, an "auditor" was sent to resolve the difference. George Washington sent his financial records to the Comptroller of the Treasury to be audited before he could be reimbursed for expenditures he made during the Revolutionary War. One of the first Congress's actions in 1789 was to set up an auditor to review and certify public accounts. Even the "modern" concept of an audit committee is not so modern; the bylaws of the Potomac Company, formed in 1784 to construct locks on the Potomac River to increase commerce, required that three shareholders annually examine the company's records.

Source: D. Flesher, G. Previts, and W. Samson, "Auditing in the United States: A Historical Perspective," *Abacus* 41 (2005), pp. 21–39.

External auditors generally begin their work with a focus on these assertions (explicit representations) made by management about the financial statement amounts and information disclosed in footnotes, and then they set out to obtain and evaluate evidence to prove or disprove these assertions or representations. Other types of auditors, however, often are not provided with explicit representations. For example, an internal auditor may be assigned to evaluate the cost effectiveness of the company's policy to lease, rather than to purchase, heavy equipment. A governmental auditor may be assigned to determine whether goals of providing equal educational opportunities to all have been achieved with federal grant funds. Oftentimes, the latter two types of auditors must develop the explicit performance criteria or benchmarks for themselves.

The purpose of obtaining and evaluating evidence is to ascertain the degree of correspondence between the assertions made by the information provider and the established criteria. Auditors will ultimately communicate their findings to interested users.

[1] American Accounting Association Committee on Basic Auditing Concepts, *A Statement of Basic Auditing Concepts* (Sarasota, FL: American Accounting Association, 1973).

To communicate in an efficient and understandable manner, auditors and users must have a common basis for measuring and describing financial information. This basis is the established criteria essential for effective communication.

Established criteria may be found in a variety of sources. For independent auditors, the criterion is whatever the applicable financial reporting framework is, whether it is Generally Accepted Accounting Principles (GAAP) in the United States or International Financial Reporting Standards (IFRS) in other jurisdictions. Internal Revenue Service (IRS) auditors rely heavily on criteria specified in the Internal Revenue Code. Governmental auditors may rely on criteria established in legislation or regulatory agency rules. Bank examiners and state insurance board auditors look to definitions, regulations, and rules of law. Internal and governmental auditors rely a great deal on financial and managerial models of efficiency and effectiveness. Of course, all auditors rely to some extent on the sometimes elusive criteria of general truth and fairness. Exhibit 1.1 depicts an overview of financial statement auditing.

The AAA definition already presented is broad and general enough to encompass external, internal, and governmental auditing. The more specific viewpoint of external auditors in public accounting practice is reflected in the following statement about the financial statement audit made by the American Institute of Certified Public Accountants (AICPA), the public accounting community's professional association:

> The purpose of an audit is to enhance the degree of confidence that intended users can place in the financial statements. This is achieved by the expression of an opinion by the auditor on whether the financial statements are prepared, in all material respects, in accordance with an applicable financial reporting framework. In the case of most general purpose frameworks, that opinion is on whether the financial statements are presented fairly, in all material respects, in accordance with the framework. An audit conducted in accordance with generally accepted auditing standards and relevant ethical requirements enables the auditor to form that opinion. (AU-C 200.11)

Auditing in a Big Data Environment

The auditing environment is rapidly being transformed into an environment characterized by the availability of significant amounts of data and cutting-edge analytical tools. As a direct result, entry-level professionals are being asked to join public accounting firms

EXHIBIT 1.1
Overview of Financial Statement Auditing

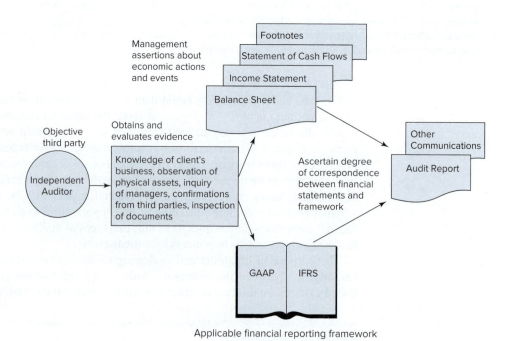

Applicable financial reporting framework

having completed coursework related to the use of data and analytical tools. The accompanying Auditing Insight provides some examples.

AUDITING INSIGHT

What Students Need to Succeed in a "Big Data" World

A recent report published by PwC, "Data Driven: What Students Need to Succeed in a Rapidly Changing Business World," clearly indicates that the skills needed by entry-level auditing professionals must include proficiency in data analytics and technology.

For example, insights from a CEO survey discussed in the PwC report reveal that "businesses are preparing for a future that's different from today. And they expect their talent to adapt. One implication of this rapidly changing business environment is clear—today's accounting curriculum should be updated to equip students with new skills, especially in technology and data analytics" (p. 4).

Overall, it seems clear that the world has changed and the set of skills acquired by students must also change to adapt to the new world. Most importantly, while the PwC report is published by only one firm, our conversations with professionals and observations indicate that the other Big Four firms (e.g., KPMG, Deloitte, and EY) are largely in agreement with this approach.

Source: "Data Driven—What Students Need to Succeed in a Rapidly Changing Business World," PwC, February 2015.

Among the critical issues for students is how to identify the right data to analyze given a set of facts and circumstances, and then how to present data analyses in a compelling format while documenting the results of their work. Frankly, these steps are important to learn even before completing analyses of data using the latest analytical tools. In addition, while analytical tools can rely on data sources that are both internal and external to the client, our current understanding is that staff audit professionals in today's environment need to first learn how to make the best use of data that is internal to the client in order to provide useful insights to the audit team. Throughout this book, we will be providing examples of how to make the best use of such internal client data.

In fact, as your study of external auditing continues, you will find that auditors perform many tasks designed to reduce the risk of giving an inappropriate opinion on financial statements. Auditors are careful to work for trustworthy clients, to gather and analyze evidence about the assertions in financial statements, and to take steps to ensure that audit personnel report properly on the financial statements when adverse information is known.

Attestation Engagements

Many people appreciate the value of auditors' attestations on historical financial statements, and as a result, they have found other types of information to which certified public accountants (CPAs) can attest. The all-inclusive definition of an **attestation engagement** is

> An engagement in which a practitioner is engaged to issue a report on subject matter, or an assertion about subject matter that is the responsibility of another party. (AT 101.01)

By comparing the AAA's earlier definition of auditing with the definition of attestation, you can see that the auditing definition is a specific type of attestation engagement. According to the earlier definition, in an audit engagement, an auditor (more specific than a *practitioner*) issues a report on assertions (financial statements) that are the responsibility of management. For example, as more and more companies and organizations seek to demonstrate their efforts related to corporate social responsibility, demand is growing for attestation services related to sustainability reporting. The following Auditing Insight indicates the significance of this emerging market for public accounting firms.

In today's global business environment, activist shareholders are increasingly pressuring board of director members and upper management teams regarding issues of social responsibility, the environment, and other matters related to sustainability. As a direct result, more companies than ever are directly integrating their sustainability initiatives

AUDITING INSIGHT ▷ Sustainability Reporting—An Emerging Market for CPAs

The Global Reporting Initiative (GRI) is a nonprofit organization that was established to promote environmental sustainability to organizations throughout the world. Perhaps most importantly, the GRI has established a reporting framework that leading companies use to report key information about their efforts to promote sustainability in their business practices. The GRI last issued its Sustainability Reporting Guidelines in May 2013 and the current Guidelines are in transition to a set of GRI Sustainability Reporting Standards. The new

GRI Standards will likely be finalized at some point in 2017. KPMG LLP reported that as of the end of 2015, 92 percent of the 250 largest global companies issue some type of corporate responsibility report.

Sources: https://www.globalreporting.org/standards/transition-to-standards/Pages/default.aspx; http://www.kpmg.com/CN/en/IssuesAndInsights/ArticlesPublications/Documents/kpmg-survey-of-corporate-responsibility-reporting-2015-O-201511.pdf.

into their overall business strategy and then seeking to quantify their sustainability and social responsibility efforts with measurable outputs. These measurements might help to quantify the company's performance in areas such as the environment, labor, and human rights. For example, Coca-Cola reports in the 2014–2015 Sustainability Report about their goals and progress on improving energy efficiency. Exhibit 1.2 shows Coca-Cola's change in energy use and energy use ratio. Although sustainability is a prominent example of an attestation engagement, other examples of attestation engagements completed by CPAs (discussed more in Module A) appear in the following box.

EXHIBIT 1.2

The Coca-Cola System Energy Use from 2007 to 2014

Systemwide total based on estimated total use (billion megajoules)

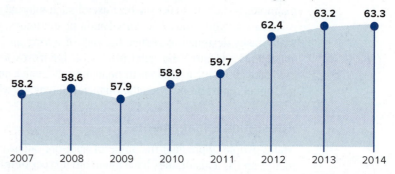

The Coca-Cola System Energy Use Ratio from 2007 to 2014

Average plant ratios based on collected data (megajoules/liter of product)

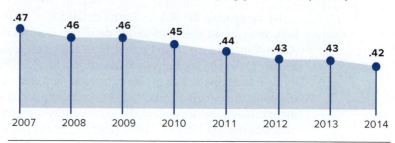

Examples of Attestation Engagements

- **Agreed Upon Procedures Engagements** (AT 201), such as verifying inventory quantities and locations.
- **Financial Forecasts and Projections** (AT 301), such as analysis of prospective or hypothetical "what-if" financial statements for some time period *in the future*.
- **Reporting on Pro Forma Financial Information** (AT 401), such as retroactively analyzing the effect of a proposed or consummated transaction on the *historical* financial statements "as if" that transaction had already occurred.

- **Compliance Attestation** (AT 601), such as ascertaining a client's compliance with debt covenants.
- **Examination of Management's Discussion and Analysis** (AT 701), prepared pursuant to the rules and regulations of the Securities and Exchange Commission (SEC).
- **Reporting on Controls at a Service Organization** (AT 801), such as organizations that provide outsourced processes that are likely to be relevant to the user entities' internal control over financial reporting.

Assurance Services

Although *auditing* refers specifically to expressing an opinion on financial statements and *attestation* refers more generally to expressing an opinion on any type of information or subject matter that is the responsibility of another party (such as sustainability measures), *assurance services* includes an even broader set of information, including nonfinancial information. The following Auditing Insight indicates how the quality of information can assist both buyers and sellers in today's market.

AUDITING INSIGHT

Exhibit 1.3 shows two 1961 **Topps** Mickey Mantle baseball cards. The card on the right was offered on eBay with the seller's representation that the card was in Near Mint/Mint condition. This representation is a standard description and is the equivalent of a grade 8 on a standard 10-point scale used in grading the quality of a trading card. The card was purchased on **eBay** for $205.50.

Within a week, a second 1961 Topps Mickey Mantle baseball card was sold on eBay. Again, this card was offered with the seller's representation that the card was in Near Mint/Mint condition (card on the left). The only difference was that this card had been sent to **Professional Sports Authenticator** (PSA), a company that verifies the authenticity and quality of sports items. Note that PSA does not buy or sell sports merchandise; it acts only as an independent third party expressing a professional opinion regarding the merchandise in question. This card sold for $585.

The only difference between the two transactions was that the buyers of the card on the left had more information concerning the risk inherent in the transaction. Why was the first transaction riskier? What were the buyers' concerns? Were the concerns only from intentional misstatements? How did the grading of the card by PSA reduce these

EXHIBIT 1.3 Professional Sports Authenticator as Third-Party Assuror

© Allen Blay

concerns? What are the incentives for PSA to grade the card accurately? How does the business of PSA relate to the profession of auditing?

Although the primary focus of our earlier discussion of information risk was in the context of economic decisions, information risk is present whenever someone must make a decision without having complete knowledge. The AICPA expanded the profession's traditional focus on accounting information to include all types of information, both financial and nonfinancial. The expanded services are collectively referred to as **assurance services**, which the AICPA defines as independent professional services that improve the quality of information, or its context, for decision makers. The major elements, and boundaries, of the definition are

- *Independence.* CPAs want to preserve their attestation and audit reputations and competitive advantages by preserving integrity and objectivity when performing assurance services.[2]

- *Professional services.* Virtually all work performed by CPAs (accounting, auditing, data management, taxation, management, marketing, finance) is defined as a professional service as long as it involves some element of judgment based on education and experience.

- *Improving the quality of information or its context.* The emphasis is on information, CPAs' traditional stock in trade. CPAs can enhance quality by assuring users about the reliability and relevance of information, and these two features are closely related to the familiar credibility-lending products of attestation and auditing services. *Context* is relevance in a different light. For assurance services, improving the context of information refers not to the information itself but to how the information is used in a decision-making context. An example would be providing key information in a database that management could use to make important decisions.

- *For decision makers.* The decision makers are the consumers of assurance services, and they personify the consumer focus of different types of professional work. The decision makers are the beneficiaries of the assurance services. Depending upon the assignment, decision makers may be a very small, targeted group (e.g., managers of a database) or a large targeted group (e.g., potential investors interested in a mutual fund manager's performance).

Examples of Assurance Services

Although they are subsets of assurance services, attestation and auditing services are highly structured and intended to be useful for large groups of decision makers (e.g., investors, lenders). On the other hand, assurance services other than audit and attestation services tend to be more customized for use by smaller, targeted groups of decision makers. For example, many companies and organizations have used public accounting firms to conduct a comprehensive assessment of risks the enterprise faces. This type of enterprise risk assessment can then be used to show stakeholders that the management team understands and is properly managing risks the enterprise faces. We also present a few more examples of assurance services to illustrate the variety of services that fall under the assurance service umbrella. Some will look familiar and others may defy imagination. Be aware, however, that public accounting firms must pick and choose the services that they wish to provide to the market based on the expertise that resides within the firm. Nobody believes or maintains that all public accounting firms will want or be able to provide all types of assurance services.

- XBRL (eXtensible Business Reporting Language) reporting.
- Information risk assessment and assurance.
- Regulatory compliance.
- Third-party reimbursement maximization.
- Customer satisfaction surveys.
- Evaluation of investment management policies.
- Fraud and illegal acts prevention and deterrence.
- Cyber risk assessment and assurance.
- Internal audit outsourcing.

Attestation and financial statement auditing services are special types of assurance services, but consulting services are not. In providing consulting services, CPAs use their

---

[2]A survey commissioned by the AICPA found that CPAs are viewed more positively than any other business professional by both business decision makers and investors. Sixty-nine percent of investors and 74 percent of business decision makers feel that "CPAs have a unique perspective that is valuable when making business and financial decisions, even when those decisions are not directly related to accounting." In terms of attributes ascribed to CPAs, they are most associated with integrity, competence, and objectivity ("Brand Research Shows CPAs Viewed Positively in Marketplace," *AICPA News Update,* October 20, 2008).

EXHIBIT 1.4

The Relationships among Audit, Attestation, and Assurance Engagements

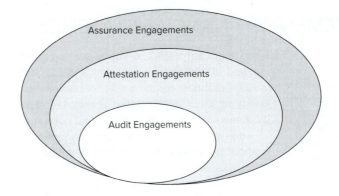

professional skills and experiences to provide recommendations to a client for outcomes such as information system design and operation; in assurance services, the focus is entirely on the information that decision makers use. However, like consulting services, assurance services do have a "customer focus," and CPAs develop assurance services that add value for customers (i.e., decision makers). Exhibit 1.4 depicts the relationships among assurance, attestation, and auditing services.

Although audits are specific types of assurance engagements and auditors can be described more generally as information assurors, hereafter we will use the term *auditor* instead of *information assuror* because of the specific responsibilities that auditors have under generally accepted accounting standards (GAAS) as well as under regulatory bodies such as the Securities and Exchange Commission (SEC) and the Public Company Accounting Oversight Board (PCAOB). However, many of the procedures that auditors perform as part of an audit engagement are similar to those performed as part of other information assurance engagements. Throughout this book, we will point out these shared procedures when appropriate.

AUDITING INSIGHT | XBRL Reporting

Advances in information technology have allowed for more efficient reporting platforms that better meet the needs of decision makers. In that spirit, the AICPA is currently focused on a number of initiatives to help auditors meet the needs of their clients. Among the initiatives, the need to help companies with XBRL implementations for SEC reporting has taken center stage. XBRL (also referred to by the SEC as interactive data) is an information format designed specifically for business reporting. Through the "tagging" of specific data items (cash, inventory, sales transactions, etc.), XBRL facilitates the collection, summarization, and reporting of financial information in a medium that users can easily transform for their own decision-making purposes.

The SEC now requires all U.S. public companies and foreign private issuers listed with the SEC to use XBRL for SEC filings. Recently, the AICPA helped to launch the XBRL U.S. Center for Data Quality in an attempt to improve the utility of XBRL financial data filed with the SEC even more.

Sources: *AICPA SOP 13-02,* "Performing Agreed-Upon Procedures Engagements That Address the Completeness, Mapping Consistency, or Structure of XBRL-Formatted Information"; *SEC 2009 Release No. 33-9002,* "Interactive Data to Improve Financial Reporting"; "XBRL US Center for Data Quality." All three are available through the AICPA's website (www.aicpa.org).

☑ REVIEW CHECKPOINTS

1.4 Define and explain auditing. What would you answer if asked by a communications major, "What do *auditors* do?"

1.5 What is an *attestation engagement*?

1.6 What is an *assurance service engagement*?

1.7 In what ways are assurance services similar to attestation services (including audits of financial statements)?

1.8 What are the four major elements of the broad definition of assurance services?

MANAGEMENT'S FINANCIAL STATEMENT ASSERTIONS

LO 1-3

Describe and define the assertions that management make about the recognition, measurement, presentation, and disclosure of the financial statements and explain why auditors use them as the focal point of the audit.

From your earlier studies, you know that accounting is the process of recording, classifying, and summarizing a company's transactions into financial statements that will create assets, liabilities, equities, revenues, expenses, and related disclosures. It is the means of satisfying users' demands for financial information that arise from the forces of complexity, remoteness, time sensitivity, and consequences.

Auditing does not include the function of producing financial reports. The function of **financial reporting** is to provide statements of financial position (balance sheets), results of operations (income statements, statements of shareholders' equity, and statements of comprehensive income), changes in cash flows (statements of cash flows), and accompanying disclosures to outside decision makers who do not have access to management's internal sources of information. A company's accountants, under the direction of its management team, perform this function. In fact, auditing standards emphasize that the financial statements are the responsibility of a company's management. Thus, the financial statements contain management's assertions about the *transactions and events* that occurred during the period being audited (primarily the income statement, statement of shareholders' equity, statement of comprehensive income, and statement of cash flows), assertions about the *account balances* at the end of the period (primarily the balance sheet), and assertions about the financial statement *presentation and disclosure* (primarily the footnote disclosures).

AUDITING INSIGHT — Sarbanes–Oxley and Management's Responsibility for Financial Reporting

Congress passed the Sarbanes–Oxley Act in 2002 in an attempt to address a number of weaknesses found in corporate financial reporting as a result of the frauds at companies such as WorldCom and Enron. Although the preparation of the financial statements has always been the responsibility of management, Sarbanes–Oxley has enhanced the disclosure provisions to create a heightened sense of accountability. One of its most important provisions (Section 302) states that key company officials must certify the financial statements. Certification means that the company's chief executive officer and chief financial officer must sign a statement indicating

1. They have read the financial statements.

2. They are not aware of any false or misleading statements (or any key omitted disclosures).

3. They believe that the financial statements present an accurate picture of the company's financial condition.

Management must also make assertions regarding the effectiveness of the company's internal controls over financial reporting. In addition, the auditors are required to issue an attestation report (Section 404) on the system of internal controls to provide assurance that the system of internal controls over financial reporting has been designed and is operating effectively.

Source: U.S. Congress, *Sarbanes–Oxley Act of 2002,* Pub. L. No. 107-204, 116 Stat. 745 (2002).

As the Auditing Insight about Sarbanes–Oxley makes clear, the upper management team at public companies must certify the correctness of the financial statements and the effectiveness of the internal control system for financial reporting. Given the current focus on internal controls, first-year audit professionals are expected to understand the relationship between a company's internal control activities and the relevant financial statement assertions about the financial statement account balances. We suggest that as a new auditing professional, a detailed understanding of this relationship will provide you with the opportunity to immediately contribute to the audit team. As a result, we are hopeful that this book can provide a foundation of knowledge to help simplify the relationship, which is paramount in the post-Sarbanes–Oxley auditing environment.

When planning the audit engagement, auditors use management's assertions to assess external financial reporting risks by determining the different types of misstatements that could occur for each of the relevant management assertions identified and then develop auditing procedures that are appropriate in the circumstances. The auditing procedures are completed to provide the evidence necessary to persuade the auditor that there is no material misstatement related to each of the relevant assertions. Once the auditor is satisfied that the evidence has supported each of the relevant assertions, the auditor issues a report to provide assurance to financial statement users that the financial statements are free of material misstatement in accordance with generally accepted accounting principles. As an auditor, you must keep in mind the importance of understanding management's financial statement assertions and always remember that you are serving the entire public interest, including stakeholders such as bankers, investors, and employees when ultimately reporting that the financial statements are free of material misstatement.

When studying and learning about the assertions, a student of auditing must always remember that each assertion gives rise to a question that can be answered with audit evidence. In that spirit, Exhibit 1.5 provides a list of all of management's financial statement assertions and some of the key questions that the audit team must address, with evidence, about each assertion. Note that column 1 in Exhibit 1.5 denotes the assertions currently identified by the PCAOB for public company audits.[3] The PCAOB auditing standards do allow auditors to use different management assertions at their discretion, provided that the assertions cover the pertinent risks in each significant account. In that spirit, the Auditing Standards Board (ASB)[4] provides an additional set of management assertions (columns 2, 3, and 4 in Exhibit 1.5). You will note that the ASB set of assertions, while in direct alignment with the PCAOB assertions, does provide greater detail and clarity for students of auditing to conceptualize. As a result, largely all of the firms auditing public companies with international operations feature the ASB assertions as a starting point to guide their auditing processes. The key questions (column 5) indicate how each of these assertions must be thought about when evaluating specific aspects of management's financial statements and disclosures. Each of the assertions is defined and described in detail in the following sections, organized along the lines of the PCAOB assertions identified in column 1, with the aligned ASB assertion(s) following in parentheses.

Existence or Occurrence (Existence, Occurrence)

The numbers listed on the financial statements have no meaning to financial statement users unless the numbers *faithfully represent* the actual transactions, assets, and liabilities of the company. *Existence* asserts that each of the balance sheet and income statement balances actually exist. *Occurrence* asserts that each of the income statement events and transactions actually did occur. As a general rule, the *occurrence* assertion relates to events, transactions, presentations, and footnote disclosures (as indicated in columns 2 and 4 of Exhibit 1.5), and the *existence* assertion relates to account balances (as indicated in column 3). Therefore, auditors must test whether the balance sheet amounts reported as assets, liabilities, and equities actually *exist*. To test the existence assertion, auditors typically verify cash with banks and count the physical inventory, verify accounts receivables and insurance policies with customers, and perform other procedures to obtain evidence whether management's assertion is in fact supported. Similarly, management asserts that each of the revenue and expense transactions summarized on the income statement or disclosed in the financial statement footnotes really did occur during the period being audited. To test the occurrence assertion, auditors complete procedures to ensure that the reported sales transactions really did occur and were not created to fraudulently inflate the company's profits.

[3]The Public Company Accounting Oversight Board (PCAOB) is a nonprofit corporation established by Congress to oversee the audits of public companies. The PCAOB is discussed in more detail in Chapter 2.

[4]The ASB was established by the profession to issue auditing standards. Standards issued by the ASB apply to audits of private companies. The ASB is discussed in more detail in Chapter 2.

EXHIBIT 1.5 **Management Assertions**

| (1) PCAOB Assertions | ASB Assertions | | | (5) Key Questions |
	(2) Assertions about Events and Transactions	(3) Assertions about Account Balances	(4) Assertions about Presentation and Footnote Disclosures	
Existence or occurrence	Occurrence	Existence	Occurrence	Do the assets listed really exist?
				Did the recorded sales transactions really occur?
Rights and obligations		Rights and obligations	Rights and obligations	Does the company really own the assets?
				Are all legal responsibilities to pay the liabilities identified?
Completeness	Completeness	Completeness	Completeness	Are the financial statements (including footnotes) complete?
				Were all transactions recorded?
	Cutoff			Are transactions included in the proper period?
Valuation or allocation	Accuracy	Valuation and allocation	Accuracy	Are the accounts valued correctly?
			Valuation and allocation	Are expenses allocated to the period(s) that were benefited?
Presentation and disclosure	Classification		Classification	Were all transactions recorded in the correct accounts?
			Understandability	Are the disclosures understandable to users?

AUDITING INSIGHT | Q: When Is a Sale of Computer Disk Drives Not a Sale? A: When They Are Bricks.

Miniscribe was a manufacturer of computer disk drives. When sales did not occur at a sufficient level to support the company's efforts to obtain outside financing, management generated fictitious sales to fraudulently boost the company's net income. After first sending obsolete inventory to customers who never ordered the goods, the company packaged bricks (about the same size and shape as the company's disk drives of that time) in disk drive boxes and shipped them to "customers" that were, in fact, company-owned warehouses.

Source: "A $128.1 Million Settlement Reached in Miniscribe Case," *The New York Times,* June 4, 1992, available at: http://www.nytimes.com/1992/06/04/business/company-news-a-128.1-million-settlement-reached-in-miniscribe-case.html.

Rights and Obligations (Rights and Obligations)

In the financial statements, management asserts that they have ownership rights for all amounts reported as assets on the company's balance sheet and that the amounts reported as liabilities represent the company's own obligations. In simpler terms, the objective for an auditor is to obtain evidence that the assets are really owned and that the liabilities are really owed by the company being audited. You should be careful about *ownership,* however, because the assertion extends to include assets for which a company may not actually hold title. For example, an auditor will have a specific objective of obtaining evidence about the amounts capitalized for leased property. Likewise, *owing* includes accounting liabilities a company may not yet be legally obligated to pay. For example, specific objectives would include obtaining evidence about the estimated liability for product warranties. The auditor also has an obligation to ensure that the details of the company's obligations are properly disclosed in the footnotes to the financial statements.

Completeness (Completeness, Cutoff)

In the financial statements, management asserts that all transactions, events, assets, liabilities, and equities that should have been recorded have been recorded. In addition, management asserts that all disclosures that should have been included in the footnotes have been presented. Thus, auditors' specific objectives include obtaining evidence to determine whether, for example, all inventory is included, all accounts payable are included, all notes payable are included, all expenses are recorded, and so forth. A verbal or written management representation saying that all transactions are included in the accounts is not considered a sufficient basis for deciding whether the completeness assertion is true. Auditors need to obtain persuasive evidence about completeness.

Cutoff is a more detailed expression of the completeness assertion. **Cutoff** refers to accounting for revenue, expense, and other transactions in the *proper period* (neither postponing some recordings to the next period nor accelerating next-period transactions into the current-year accounts). Simple cutoff errors can occur when (1) a company records late December sales invoices for goods not actually shipped until early January; (2) a company records cash receipts through the end of the week (e.g., Friday, January 4) when the last batch of receipts for the year should have been processed on December 31; (3) a company fails to record accruals for expenses incurred but not yet paid, thus understating both expenses and liabilities; (4) a company fails to record purchases of materials shipped free on board (FOB) shipping point but not yet received and, therefore, not included in the ending inventory, thus understating both inventory and accounts payable; and (5) a company fails to accrue unbilled revenue through the fiscal year-end for customers on a cycle billing system, thus understating both revenue and accounts receivable. In auditor's jargon, the *cutoff date* generally refers to the client's year-end balance sheet date.

Valuation and Allocation (Accuracy or Valuation)

In the financial statements, management asserts that the transactions and events have been recorded accurately and that the assets, liabilities, and equities listed on the balance sheet have been valued in accordance with GAAP (or IFRS). The audit objective related to valuation and allocation is to determine whether proper values have been assigned to assets, liabilities, and equities. *Allocation* refers to the appropriate percentage of an asset or liability balance being recorded on the income statement in accordance with GAAP (or IFRS). For example, has the proper depreciation expense been calculated for each fixed asset amount? *Accuracy* refers to the appropriate recording of the transactions involving these items. Auditors obtain evidence about specific valuations and mathematical accuracy by comparing vendors' invoices to inventory prices, obtaining lower-of-cost-or-market data, evaluating collectability of receivables, recalculating depreciation schedules, and so forth. Many valuation, accuracy, and allocation decisions amount to reaching conclusions about the proper application of GAAP (or IFRS). For example, due to the complexity in the accounting standards related to fair value (i.e., *ASC Topic 820*), there has been an increased focus on the valuation assertion.

Presentation and Disclosure (Classification, Understandability)

In the financial statements, management asserts that all transactions and events have been presented correctly in accordance with GAAP (or IFRS) and that all relevant information has been disclosed to financial statement users, usually in the footnotes to the financial statements. This assertion embodies several different components. First, disclosures must be relevant, reliable, and understandable or transparent to financial statement users. In addition, auditors will test to make sure that all have the proper disclosures made in accordance with GAAP (or IFRS). To complete this step, auditors will often use a disclosure checklist that highlights all the disclosures that should be made for a particular entity.

Second, transactions must be classified in the correct accounts (e.g., proper classification of transactions as assets or expenses). To test this assertion, auditors perform audit procedures such as analyzing repair and maintenance expenses to ensure that that they should in fact have been expensed rather than capitalized. Similarly, auditors will test from the opposite direction, examining additions to buildings and equipment to ensure that transactions that should have been expensed were not in fact capitalized in error (or fraud). The Auditing Insight about the WorldCom fraud provides an example of the importance of this financial statement assertion.

AUDITING INSIGHT — Is Your Telephone Bill an Asset?

WorldCom routinely leased telephone lines from local telephone companies (to carry its voice transmissions). However, rather than record the cost of these telephone lines as an expense on the income statement, the company capitalized them as assets on the balance sheet, resulting in an estimated $11 *billion* fraudulent overstatement of net income. WorldCom management argued that because the leased telephone lines were not fully used to capacity, the expense should be deferred until the lines started to produce revenue (i.e., the matching concept). Moreover, because they controlled the telephone lines as a result of the long-term lease agreements, no one else could use the telephone lines and, therefore, the exclusivity rights should be treated as an asset. (This explanation is analogous to your saying that your monthly phone bill expense is really an asset because no one else can use your phone number while you use it.) An internal auditor uncovered the fraud and reported her findings to the company's board of directors.

Source: WorldCom Board of Directors' Special Investigative Committee Report, June 9, 2003.

Third, to be useful to decision makers, information must be understandable. *Statement of Financial Accounting Concepts (SFAC) No. 2,* "Qualitative Characteristics of Accounting Information," defines *understandability* as "the quality of information that enables users to perceive its significance." The responsibility levied on auditors is to make sure that the financial statements are "transparent." In other words, investors should be able to understand how the company is doing by reading its financial statements and footnotes and should not have to rely on financial experts or lawyers to help them figure out what the fine print is saying. Another way to regard this assertion is to ask whether the disclosures have been written in *plain English.* Consider the following Auditing Insight highlighting the financial disclosures at Enron.

AUDITING INSIGHT — Say What?

Financial analysts generally regarded Enron's financial disclosures in its annual report as incomprehensible. In fact, Enron's management took pride in the fact that no one could figure out what they were doing to generate incredibly high revenues. A 2003 Congressional Joint Committee on Taxation concluded that Enron's tax avoidance schemes (including 692 partnerships in the Cayman Islands) were "so complex that the IRS has been unable to understand them" (*The New York Times,* February 13, 2003). Following is an excerpt from *Enron's 2001 Annual Report* describing some of its business activities:

Trading Activities. Enron offers price risk management services to wholesale, commercial and industrial customers through a variety of financial and other instruments including forward contracts involving physical delivery, swap agreements, which require payments to (or receipt of payments from) counterparties based on the differential between a fixed and variable price for the commodity, options and other contractual arrangements. Interest rate risks and foreign currency risks associated with the fair value of the commodity portfolio are managed using a variety of financial instruments, including financial futures.

Unfortunately, due in large part to the incomprehensibility of its financial disclosures, no one realized the extreme risks that Enron was taking until it was too late. The company, which reported the fifth-highest revenues in the United States in 2000, filed for bankruptcy in 2001.

Source: Enron 2001 Annual Report.

Importance of Assertions

The financial statement assertions are important and at times can be difficult to comprehend. A student of auditing must remember that the key questions that must be answered about each assertion become the *focal points* for the audit procedures to be performed. In other words, audit procedures are the means to answer the key questions posed by management's financial statement assertions. When evidence-gathering audit procedures are specified, you need to be able to relate the evidence produced by each procedure to one or more specific assertions. In essence, the secret to writing and reviewing a list of audit procedures is to ask, "Which assertion(s) does this procedure produce evidence about?" Then ask, "Does the list of procedures (the *audit plan*) cover all the assertions?" Exhibit 1.6 illustrates how the assertions relate to the financial statements.

EXHIBIT 1.6 **Management Assertions and Their Relationship to the Financial Statements**

STATEMENT OF FINANCIAL CONDITION
APOLLO SHOES INC.
in thousands

As of December 31	2017	2016
Assets		
Cash	$3,245	$3,509
Accounts Receivable (Net of Allowances of $1,263 and 210, respectively) (Note 3)	15,148	2,738
Inventory (Note 4)	15,813	13,823
Prepaid Expenses	951	352
Current Assets	$35,157	$20,422
Property, Plant, and Equipment (Note 5)	1,174	300
Less Accumulated Depreciation	(164)	(31)
	$1,010	$269
Investments (Note 6)	613	613
Other Assets	14	0
Total Assets	$36,794	$21,304
Liabilities and Shareholders' Equity		
Accounts Payable and Accrued Expenses	$4,675	$3,556
Short-Term Liabilities (Note 7)	10,000	0
Current Liabilities	$14,675	3,556
Long-Term Debt (Note 7)	0	0
Total Liabilities	$14,675	3,556
Common Stock	8,105	8,105
Additional Paid-in Capital	7,743	7,743
Retained Earnings	6,271	1,900
Total Shareholders' Equity	$22,119	$17,748
Total Liabilities and Shareholders' Equity	$36,794	$21,304

The accompanying notes are an integral part of the consolidated financial statements.

Existence—Does this cash really exist?

Rights and Obligations—Does the company really own this inventory?

Valuation or Allocation—Are these investments properly valued?

Occurrence—Did these sales transactions really take place?

Completeness—Are all the expenses included? Are they recorded in the correct period?

STATEMENTS OF INCOME
APOLLO SHOES INC.
in thousands (except per share data)

For year ended December 31,	2017	2016
Net Sales (Note 2)	$240,575	$236,299
Cost of Sales	$141,569	$120,880
Gross Profit	$99,006	$115,419
Selling, General and Administrative Expenses	$71,998	$61,949
Interest Expense (Note 7)	$875	0
Other Expense (Income)	($204)	($1,210)
Earnings from Continuing Operations Before Taxes	$26,337	$54,680
Income Tax Expense (Note 10)	$10,271	$21,634
Earnings from Continuing Operations	$16,066	$33,046
Discontinued Operations, Net of tax benefit		($31,301)
Extraordinary Item, Net of tax benefit (Note 11)	($11,695)	
Net Income	$4,371	$1,745
Earnings Per Common Share		
From Continuing Operations	$1.98	$4.08
Other	($1.44)	($3.86)
Net Income	$0.54	$0.22
Weighted shares of common stock outstanding	8,105	8,105

The accompanying notes are an integral part of the consolidated financial statements.

NOTES TO CONSOLIDATED FINANCIAL STATEMENTS
APOLLO SHOES, INC.

1. Summary of Significant Accounting Policies

Business activity The Company develops and markets technologically superior podiatric athletic products under various trademarks, including *SIREN, SPOTLIGHT*, and *SPEAKERSHOE*.

Marketable Securities Investments are valued using the market value method for investments of less than 20%, and by the equity method for investments greater than 20% but less than 50%.

Cash equivalents Cash equivalents are defined as highly liquid investments with original maturities of three months or less at date of purchase.

Inventory valuation Inventories are stated at the lower of First-in, First-out (FIFO) or market.

Property and equipment and depreciation Property and equipment are stated at cost. The Company uses the straight-line method of depreciation for all additions to property, plant, and equipment.

Intangibles Intangibles are amortized on the straight-line method over periods benefited.

Net Sales Sales for 2017 and 2016 are presented net of sales returns and allowances of $4.5 million, and $0.9 million, respectively, and net of warranty expenses of $ 1.1 million, and $0.9 million, respectively.

Income taxes Deferred income taxes are provided for the tax effects of timing differences in reporting the results of operations for financial statements and income tax purposes, and relate principally to valuation reserves for accounts receivable and inventory, accelerated depreciation and unearned compensation.

Net income per common share Net income per common share is computed based on the weighted average number of common and common equivalent shares outstanding for the period.

Reclassification Certain amounts have been reclassified to conform to the 2016 presentation.

2. Significant Customers

Approximately 15%, and 11% of sales are to one customer for years ended December 31, 2017 and 2016, respectively.

Presentation and Disclosure—Are these disclosures understandable? Has everything been disclosed that should be?

Although standards-setting bodies such as the PCAOB and ASB try to neatly categorize transactions, balances, and disclosures according to the different assertions, the *real world* is seldom as orderly. For example, although cutoff procedures provide evidence about completeness, they also provide evidence about valuation and existence. Prematurely recording sales transactions inflates revenue and/or asset values because the transaction did not *occur* by the income statement date. Similarly, if a cutoff test shows a delay in recording a liability, the liability is not only incomplete but *undervalued* as well. Thus, errors in financial statements may affect multiple management assertions.

✅ REVIEW CHECKPOINTS

1.9   What is the difference between financial statement auditing and financial accounting?

1.10 List and briefly explain each of the Auditing Standards Board's management assertions. List at least one key question that auditors must answer with evidence related to each management assertion.

1.11 Why is the Auditing Standards Board's set of management assertions important to auditors? Do these assertions differ from those included in PCAOB standards? If so, how are they different?

PROFESSIONAL SKEPTICISM

LO 1-4
Define *professional skepticism* and explain its key characteristics.

> ### *"Doveryai, no Proveryai" (Trust, but Verify)*
> President Ronald Reagan to Soviet Prime Minister Mikhail Gorbachev during Cold War missile reduction talks

Professional skepticism is defined in the professional auditing standards as having an attitude that "includes a questioning mind and a critical assessment of evidence." Essentially, it is an auditor's responsibility to *not* accept management assertions without corroboration. Stated differently, an auditor must ask management to "prove" each of the relevant assertions with documentary evidence. The occurrence of errors and fraud in financial reports highlights the following basic premise, which underlies the importance of professional skepticism: *A potential conflict of interest always exists between the auditors and the management of the company being audited.* This potential conflict arises because management wants to present the company in the best possible light whereas auditors must ensure that the information about the company's financial condition is "presented fairly."

 AUDITING INSIGHT   Why Be Skeptical?

When **Lehman Brothers** filed for bankruptcy in September 2008, it was reportedly the largest bankruptcy in U.S. history. How could such a large firm seem to collapse so suddenly? Some observers blamed the auditors. In fact, back in 2010, auditors at **Ernst & Young** (EY) were identified, along with other investment bankers and senior Lehman executives, for having played a role in the bank's demise in a civil fraud lawsuit filed by the attorney general of New York. The lawsuit described a "cozy" relationship between Lehman and EY because "two of Lehman's chief financial officers were former EY employees"

and "Ernst & Young charged Lehman $150 million in audit fees over a seven-year period of time." EY settled the lawsuit in April 2015 for $10 million without the admission of any wrongdoing by its professionals. However, the lawsuit serves as a reminder for auditors to always exhibit professional skepticism.

Sources: "Ernst Accused of Lehman Whitewash," *The Wall Street Journal,* December 22, 2010, p. C1; "Ernst & Young Reaches Settlement with N.Y. Attorney General," *The Wall Street Journal,* April 16, 2015, p. C1.

With full awareness of this potential conflict of interest, auditors must always remain professionally skeptical in their relationships with management, but not adversarial or confrontational. Nevertheless, knowing that a potential conflict of interest always exists causes auditors to perform procedures to search for errors and frauds that could have a material effect on the financial statements. And, even though the vast majority of audits do not contain fraud, auditors have no choice but to exercise professional skepticism at all times and on all audits because of misdeeds perpetrated by just a few people in a few companies. The professional standards emphasize the importance of maintaining and then applying an attitude of professional skepticism throughout the entire audit process.

Auditing firms have long recognized the importance of exercising professional skepticism when making professional judgments. In fact, as illustrated in the following Auditing Insight, firms have increasingly stressed the importance of being skeptical when evaluating documentary evidence. As an auditing student, you can definitely expect to encounter difficult economic transactions as an auditor. When auditors encounter a difficult transaction, they must take the time to fully understand the economic substance of that transaction and then critically evaluate, with skepticism, the evidence provided by the client to justify its accounting treatment. No shortcuts are allowed. Rather, auditors are required to be unbiased and objective when making their professional judgments.

AUDITING INSIGHT — Overcoming Judgment Biases: The Importance of Professional Judgment

Judgment and decision-making researchers in auditing have long known about common biases that can interfere with or obstruct auditors from making excellent professional judgments. One example is the *anchoring bias,* which recognizes the possibility that an auditor might "anchor" on a number provided by a client manager (e.g., an estimate for the allowance for doubtful accounts) and then have difficulty adjusting to the economically correct amount. In its monograph, entitled "Elevating Professional Judgment in Accounting and Auditing," KPMG (2011) outlines a professional judgment framework designed to help auditors to mitigate professional judgment biases like the anchoring bias. In order to do so, auditors must first be aware of the possibility that these biases might interfere with their professional judgment. Beyond awareness, the monograph argues that auditors must follow a disciplined process that includes (1) clarifying the issues and objectives, (2) considering the possible alternatives, (3) gathering and evaluating the relevant evidence, (4) reaching an audit conclusion, and (5) carefully documenting their rationale for the professional judgment reached. And, perhaps most importantly, the monograph emphasizes the importance of an auditor exercising professional skepticism throughout the entire process.

Source: "Elevating Professional Judgment in Accounting and Auditing: The KPMG Professional Judgment Framework" (Montvale, NJ: KMPG, 2011).

Persuading a skeptical auditor is not impossible, just somewhat more difficult than persuading a normal person in an everyday context. Skepticism is a manifestation of objectivity, holding no special concern for preconceived conclusions on any side of an issue. In fact, the auditor should not care about the impact that an economic transaction has on the "bottom line" of a company, only that the accounting rules were followed and were properly applied and that the financial statements are appropriate for the user's needs. Skepticism is not being cynical, hypercritical, or scornful. The properly skeptical auditor asks questions such as the following: (1) What do I need to know? (2) How well do I know it? (3) Does it make sense? and (4) What can go wrong?

Auditors understand that receiving explanations from an entity's management is merely the first step in the professional judgment process, not the last. Auditors must listen to the explanation, and then always test it by examining sufficient competent audit evidence. The familiar phrase "healthy skepticism" should be viewed as a show-me attitude, not a predisposition to accepting unsubstantiated explanations. Auditors must gather the evidence needed, uncover all the implications from the evidence, and then arrive at the most appropriate and supportable conclusion. Time pressure to complete a financial statement audit engagement is no excuse for failing to exercise professional skepticism. Too many auditors have gotten themselves into trouble by accepting a manager's glib explanation and stopping too early in an investigation without seeking corroborating evidence.

AUDITING INSIGHT | Professional Skepticism

In its Staff Audit Practice Alert about professional skepticism, the PCAOB expressed serious concern about "whether auditors consistently and diligently apply professional skepticism." The alert recognizes that there are a number of factors that could "impede" the application of professional skepticism but stresses the importance of taking whatever actions are necessary to make sure that professional skepticism is applied in an appropriate manner throughout the audit process.

THE HURTT SKEPTICISM SCALE

How skeptical are you? Answer the following 30 questions to find out. As a benchmark, business students typically fall between 90 to 150 points; auditors score much higher.

Questions	Strongly Disagree					Strongly Agree
1. I often accept other people's explanations without further thought.	1	2	3	4	5	6
2. I feel good about myself.	1	2	3	4	5	6
3. I wait to decide on issues until I can get more information.	1	2	3	4	5	6
4. The prospect of learning excites me.	1	2	3	4	5	6
5. I am interested in what causes people to behave the way that they do.	1	2	3	4	5	6
6. I am confident of my abilities.	1	2	3	4	5	6
7. I often reject statements unless I have proof that they are true.	1	2	3	4	5	6
8. Discovering new information is fun.	1	2	3	4	5	6
9. I take my time when making decisions.	1	2	3	4	5	6
10. I tend to immediately accept what other people tell me.	1	2	3	4	5	6
11. Other people's behavior does not interest me.	1	2	3	4	5	6
12. I am self-assured.	1	2	3	4	5	6
13. My friends tell me that I usually question things that I see or hear.	1	2	3	4	5	6
14. I like to understand the reason for other people's behavior.	1	2	3	4	5	6
15. I think that learning is exciting.	1	2	3	4	5	6
16. I usually accept things I see, read, or hear at face value.	1	2	3	4	5	6
17. I do not feel sure of myself.	1	2	3	4	5	6
18. I usually notice inconsistencies in explanations.	1	2	3	4	5	6
19. Most often I agree with what the others in my group think.	1	2	3	4	5	6
20. I dislike having to make decisions quickly.	1	2	3	4	5	6
21. I have confidence in myself.	1	2	3	4	5	6
22. I do not like to decide until I've looked at all of the readily available information.	1	2	3	4	5	6
23. I like searching for knowledge.	1	2	3	4	5	6
24. I frequently question things that I see or hear.	1	2	3	4	5	6
25. It is easy for other people to convince me.	1	2	3	4	5	6
26. I seldom consider why people behave in a certain way.	1	2	3	4	5	6
27. I like to ensure that I've considered most available information before making a decision.	1	2	3	4	5	6
28. I enjoy trying to determine if what I read or hear is true.	1	2	3	4	5	6
29. I relish learning.	1	2	3	4	5	6
30. The actions people take and the reasons for those actions are fascinating.	1	2	3	4	5	6

Sources: Kathy Hurtt, "Development of a Scale to Measure Professional Skepticism," *Auditing: A Journal of Practice & Theory 29*, no. 1 (May 2010), pp. 149–171; Public Company Accounting Oversight Board, *Staff Audit Practice Alert No. 10: Maintaining and Applying Professional Skepticism in Audits* (Washington, DC: PCAOB, 2012).

Although the SEC places constraints on the common practice of auditors' joining public clients that they have previously audited, close relationships often exist between former colleagues now employed by the client and members of the audit team. In these cases, the audit team must guard against being too trusting in accepting representations about the client's financial statements. Of more concern is the fact that former colleagues have inside knowledge of the firm's practices and procedures, knowing where the audit team will probably look (and where they might not look).

To summarize, due care requires an auditor to be professionally skeptical and question all material representations made by management (whether written or oral) during the professional judgment process. Although this attitude must be balanced by maintaining healthy client relationships, auditors should never assume management to be perfectly honest. The key lies in auditors' skeptical attitude toward gathering and evaluating the evidence necessary to reach supportable conclusions.

☑ REVIEW CHECKPOINT

1.12 Why should auditors act as though there is always a potential conflict of interest between the auditor and the management of the enterprise under audit?

PUBLIC ACCOUNTING

LO 1-5
Describe the organization of public accounting firms and identify the various services that they offer.

The practice of public accounting is conducted in thousands of practice units ranging in size from sole proprietorships (individuals who "hang out a shingle" in front of their homes) to the largest international firms with thousands of professionals. Furthermore, many public accounting firms no longer designate themselves as *CPA firms*. Many of them describe their businesses and their organizations as *professional services firms* or some variation on this term. Exhibit 1.7 shows an organization for a typical public accounting firm. However, some firms differ in their organization. For example, some have other departments such as small business advisory and forensic accounting. Other firms may be organized by industry (e.g., entertainment, oil and gas, health care, financial institutions) to take advantage of firmwide expertise. And still some other firms have different names for their staff and management positions.

Assurance Services

Generally speaking, assurance services involve lending credibility to information, whether that information is financial or nonfinancial. While financial statement auditing services remain the dominant service area, CPAs have also provided assurance to vote counts (Academy Awards), dollar amounts of prizes that sweepstakes have claimed to award, accuracy of advertisements, investment performance statistics, and characteristics claimed for computer software programs. Although assurance services (separate and distinct from auditing) currently represent a fairly small part of a normal firm's operating revenues, the AICPA continues to make an effort to market these additional services to the public and businesses.

EXHIBIT 1.7
Public Accounting Firm Organization

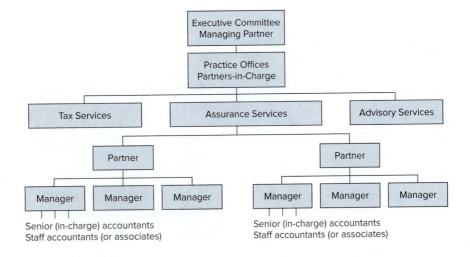

AUDITING INSIGHT Pushing the Envelopes

On Oscar night, Hollywood's Best Kept Secret Award surely goes to the hard-working team of accountants from PwC. For 79 years running, PwC has maintained its role of overseeing the validity of the entire voting process and making sure that integrity is upheld. The system employed by PwC includes the exact tallying of each and every ballot case by voters and making sure that the results are kept confidential from the press. In fact, the two partners assigned to lead the team even commit the winners to memory in case one of the starry-eyed presenters loses the envelope. And, as you may have guessed, these two partners are positioned backstage during the entire event, handing the official ballot to the award presenters as they approach the podium.

Source: www.pwc.com.

At the present time, assurance services primarily include financial statement audit engagements and other nonaudit and attestation engagements. We discuss these services as key examples of assurance services that public accounting firms offer.

Financial Statement Auditing Services

Most of the large, international accounting (Big Four) firms were founded around the turn of the 20th century (late 1800s/early 1900s) during the Industrial Revolution as European financiers sent representatives (individuals whom we now refer to as *auditors*) to check up on their investments (mostly railroads) in the United States. As such, the primary focus of many large international accounting firms' practice has been traditional accounting and auditing services. Audits of traditional financial statements remain the most frequent type of assurance engagement that public companies (and most large and medium nonpublic companies) demand. Exhibit 1.8 shows the auditing (and other assurance services) revenues of the Big Four accounting firms based on their 2015 annual reports. This level of auditing activity usually drops as the size of the public accounting firm decreases. In other words, smaller firms usually provide more nonaudit and attestation services for their clients.

Nonaudit and Attestation Engagements

Basic accounting and review services are "nonaudit" services, performed frequently for medium and small businesses and not-for-profit organizations. Small public accounting firms perform a great deal of this type of nonaudit work. For example, CPAs can perform a *compilation,* which consists of preparing financial statements from a client's books and records, without performing any evidence-gathering work. They can also perform a *review,* in which limited evidence-gathering work is performed but which is narrower in scope than an audit. Although these are the most common attestation engagements, CPAs

EXHIBIT 1.8 **Revenues for the Big Four CPA Firms**

	Deloitte	EY	KPMG	PwC
Total revenues (in billions)	$35.2	$28.7	$24.4	$35.4
Auditing and assurance services revenues (in billions and as a percent of revenue)	$13.3 38%	$11.3 40%	$10.0 41%	$15.2 43%
Tax revenues (in billions and as a percent of revenue)	$6.7 19%	$7.5 26%	$5.3 22%	$8.9 25%
Consulting and advisory services revenues (in billions and as a percent of revenue)	$15.2 43%	$9.9 34%	$9.1 37%	$11.3 32%

Sources: Deloitte, Global Report 2015; EY, Global Review 2015; KPMG International Review 2015; PwC, Global Annual Review 2015.

also can attest to the accuracy of management's discussion and analysis (MD&A) that accompanies the financial statements in an annual report, an entity's internal controls, and hypothetical "what-if" projections relating to mergers or acquisitions.

Tax Services

Local, state, national, and international tax laws are often called "accountant and attorney full-employment acts." The laws are complex, and CPAs perform tax planning services and tax return preparation in the areas of income, gift, estate, property, and other taxation. A large proportion of the practice in small public accounting firms is tax related. Tax laws change frequently, and tax practitioners must spend considerable time in continuing education and self-study to keep current. Exhibit 1.8 shows the tax revenues of the Big Four accounting firms based on their 2015 annual reports. Smaller public accounting firms tend to conduct more tax consulting engagements and fewer audit engagements.

The role of tax consulting in a professional services firm has at times faced scrutiny. The *Statements on Responsibilities in Tax Practice* specifically state that "A CPA has both the right and responsibility to be an advocate for the client" in arguing tax positions with the IRS [TX 112.04]. Can the CPA be an advocate for the client with respect to tax matters and maintain objectivity with regard to other audit matters? Recent guidance from the Public Company Accounting Oversight Board (PCAOB) prohibits an accounting firm from providing auditing services to a public company if the accounting firm provides tax consulting on aggressive interpretations of tax laws or "listed" transactions (those included on the U.S. Treasury Department's list of questionable tax strategies), if contingent fees (i.e., fees depending on a certain outcome) are involved, or if the public accounting firm provides tax services for key company executives. In all three cases, the PCAOB argues that auditor independence would be impaired. Providing normal corporate tax return preparation and advice is permissible as long as the audit committee discusses with the accounting firm the implications of the tax consulting fees on auditor independence and preapproves the relationship in writing. As a result, this remains a common service area for firms to provide to their audit clients, but the firm must always maintain its independence and objectivity.

Consulting and Advisory Services

Prior to the turn of this century (the 1990s), the largest public accounting firms handled a great deal of consulting business. Consulting and management advisory services seemed to present a great new revenue opportunity, and the field appeared to be virtually unlimited. Public accounting firms tried to become "one-stop shopping centers" for clients' auditing, taxation, and business advice needs.

The Securities and Exchange Commission (SEC), the governmental agency charged with investor protection, expressed reservations as to whether the performance of nonaudit services (such as consulting) impaired a public accounting firm's ability to conduct an independent audit. The SEC's concern was that the large amount of revenues generated from consulting services might sway the auditor's opinion on the company's financial statements. The public accounting firms, on the other hand, argued that the provision of consulting services allowed them a closer look at the client's operations, providing a synergistic, positive effect on the audit.

In response to the spate of corporate frauds, Congress resolved this difference of opinion, in part, by passing the Sarbanes–Oxley Act of 2002 (hereafter referred to as *Sarbanes–Oxley*), a broad accounting and corporate governance reform measure. Sarbanes–Oxley prohibits public accounting firms from providing any of the following services to a public audit client: (1) bookkeeping and related services; (2) design or implementation of financial information systems; (3) appraisal or valuation services; (4) actuarial services; (5) internal audit outsourcing; (6) management or human resources services; (7) investment or broker/dealer services; and (8) legal and expert services (unrelated to the audit). As already stated, public accounting firms may provide general corporate tax return preparation and advice and other nonprohibited services to public audit clients if the company's audit committee has approved them in advance.

To briefly summarize these restrictions, Sarbanes–Oxley prohibits public accounting firms from performing any consulting or advisory services in which the auditors may find themselves making managerial decisions or that would result in the firm auditing its own work (e.g., completing a financial information system implementation for its audit client). As a result of Sarbanes–Oxley, most of the large firms now provide consulting only for companies that they do not audit. However, the Big Four firms have still been able to dramatically increase the size of their consulting and advisory services in recent years. As shown in Exhibit 1.8, firm consulting revenues ranged between 32 and 43 percent of the Big Four firms' total revenues in 2015. Of course, public accounting firms are not required to follow Sarbanes–Oxley guidelines for their non-SEC clients, and in those situations, firms can provide an array of consulting and advisory services provided they maintain their independence and objectivity when completing the financial statement audit.

⊘ REVIEW CHECKPOINTS

1.13 What are some examples of assurance services performed on nonfinancial information?

1.14 What are some of the major areas of public accounting services?

OTHER KINDS OF ENGAGEMENTS AND INFORMATION PROFESSIONALS

LO 1-6
Describe the audits and auditors in governmental, internal, and operational auditing.

The AAA and the AICPA definitions of auditing clearly apply to the independent financial statement auditors who work in public accounting firms. The word *audit,* however, is also used in other contexts to describe broader types of work. The variety of engagements performed by different kinds of information assurors causes some problems with terminology. In this textbook, *independent auditor, external auditor,* and *CPA* will refer to people doing financial statement audit work with public accounting firms. In the internal and governmental contexts discussed here, auditors are identified as *operational auditors, internal auditors,* and *governmental auditors.* Although all of these professionals are information assurors (and many are certified public accountants), the term *CPA* in this book will refer to financial statement auditors engaged in public practice.

Internal Auditing

The Board of Directors of the Institute of Internal Auditors (IIA) defines **internal auditing** and states its objective as follows:

> Internal auditing is an independent, objective assurance and consulting activity designed to add value and improve an organization's operations. It helps an organization accomplish its objectives by bringing a systematic, disciplined approach to evaluate and improve the effectiveness of risk management, control, and governance processes.[5]

Internal auditors are employed by organizations such as banks, hospitals, city governments, and industrial companies or work for CPA firms that provide internal auditing services. Internal auditors often perform *operational audits.* **Operational auditing** refers to the study of business operations for the purpose of making recommendations about the efficient and effective use of resources, effective achievement of business objectives, and

---

[5]This definition and other information about internal auditing may be found on the Institute of Internal Auditors' website (www.theiia.org).

compliance with company policies. The goal of operational auditing is to help managers discharge their management responsibilities and improve profitability.

Internal auditors also perform audits of financial reports for internal use or limited external distribution (e.g., reports to regulatory agencies) much like external auditors audit financial statements distributed to outside users. Thus, some internal auditing work is similar to the auditing described elsewhere in this textbook. In addition, the services provided by internal auditors include (1) reviews of internal control systems to ensure compliance with company policies, plans, and procedures; (2) compliance with laws and regulations; (3) appraisals of the *economy* and *efficiency* of operations; and (4) reviews of effectiveness in achieving program results in comparison to established objectives and goals.

It should be noted that the AICPA defines operational auditing performed by independent CPA firms as a distinct type of management consulting service whose goal is to help a client improve the use of its capabilities and resources to achieve its objectives. So, internal auditors consider operational auditing integral to internal auditing and external auditors define it as a type of assurance service offered by public accounting firms. In fact, providing these types of internal auditing services continues to be a growing business for many large CPA firms. However, both the SEC and the PCAOB prohibit CPA firms from providing these services to their own public audit clients.

Governmental Auditing

The U.S. Government Accountability Office (GAO) is an accounting, auditing, and investigating agency of the U.S. Congress, headed by the U.S. Comptroller General. In one sense, GAO auditors are the highest level of internal auditors for the federal government. Many states have audit agencies similar to the GAO. These agencies answer to state legislatures and perform the same types of work described in this section for GAO auditors. In another sense, GAO and similar state agencies are really external auditors with respect to government agencies they audit because they are organizationally independent.

Many government agencies have their own internal auditors and inspectors general. Well-managed local governments also have internal audit departments. For example, most federal agencies (Department of Defense, Department of Human Resources, Department of the Interior), state agencies (education, welfare, controller), and local governments (cities, counties, tax districts) have internal audit staffs. Governmental and internal auditors have much in common.

The GAO shares with internal auditors the same elements of *expanded-scope* services. The GAO, however, emphasizes the accountability of public officials for the efficient, economical, and effective use of public funds and other resources. The generally accepted government auditing standards (GAGAS) define and describe three broad types of audits that may be performed. They are financial audits, attestation engagements, and performance audits.

Financial-related audits include determining whether financial information is presented in accordance with the established and applicable financial reporting framework. There are many types of attestation engagements, including whether the governmental entity's internal control system is suitably designed and implemented to achieve the applicable control objectives.

Attestation engagements would also include a compliance audit function applied with respect to applicable laws and regulations. All government organizations, programs, activities, and functions are created by law, and most are surrounded by regulations that govern the things they can and cannot do. For example, a program established to provide school meals to low-income students must comply with regulations about the eligibility of recipients. A compliance audit of such a program involves a study of schools' policies, procedures, and actual performance in determining eligibility and handing out meal tickets.

Performance audits refer to a wide range of governmental audits that include (1) economy and efficiency audits and (2) program audits. Governments are concerned about accountability for the appropriate use of taxpayers' resources; performance audits are a means of seeking to improve accountability for the efficient and economical use of resources and the achievement of program goals. In addition, the program audit helps determine whether the financial resources being spent are truly helping the government achieve its stated objectives for a particular program. Performance audits, like internal auditors' operational audits, involve studies of the management of government organizations, programs, activities, and functions.

GAO Engagement Examples

- *Federal Information Security: Agencies Need to Correct Weaknesses and Fully Implement Security Programs* (GAO-15-714, September 29, 2015).
- *Federal Student Loans: Education Could Do More to Help Ensure Borrowers Are Aware of Repayment and Forgiveness Options* (GAO-15-663, September 17, 2015).
- *Management Report: Improvements Needed in Controls over the Processes Used to Prepare the U.S. Consolidated Financial Statements* (GAO-15-630, July 30, 2015).

- *Food Safety: Additional Actions Needed to Help FDA's Foreign Offices Ensure Safety of Imported Food* (GAO-15-183, February 27, 2015).
- *Central America: Information on Migration of Unaccompanied Children from El Salvador, Guatemala, and Honduras* (GAO-15-362, February 27, 2015).

Regulatory Auditors

For the sake of clarity, other kinds of auditors deserve separate mention. The U.S. Internal Revenue Service employs auditors. They take the "economic assertions" of taxable income made by taxpayers in tax returns and determine their correspondence with the standards found in the Internal Revenue Code. They also audit for fraud and tax evasion. Their reports can either clear a taxpayer's return or claim that additional taxes are due.

State and federal bank examiners audit banks, savings and loan associations, and other financial institutions for evidence of solvency and compliance with banking and other related laws and regulations. As a result of the financial crisis of 2008/2009 and the resulting Dodd-Frank Act of 2010, these examiners have been in the news frequently as they work to help ensure the safety and security of the U.S. banking system.

> ### ✓ REVIEW CHECKPOINTS
>
> 1.15 What is *operational* auditing? How does the AICPA view operational auditing?
> 1.16 What are the three broad types of governmental audits described by the GAGAS issued by the GAO?
> 1.17 Define what is meant by *compliance* auditing.
> 1.18 Name some other types of auditors in addition to external, internal, and governmental auditors.

BECOME A PROFESSIONAL AND GET CERTIFIED!

LO 1-7
List and explain the requirements for becoming a certified public accountant (CPA) and other certifications available to an accounting professional.

If you plan to begin your career in accounting (which we hope you do since you are reading this book!), you are on your way to being known as an accounting professional. Congratulations! Being part of a profession implies a higher level of societal responsibility. In order to meet this responsibility, it is absolutely essential that you acquire the knowledge required to do your job; and certification indicates that you have acquired that knowledge. In that spirit, being certified as a CPA is generally regarded as the highest mark of distinction and is required to practice as a financial statement auditor in the United States. In Australia, Canada, and the United Kingdom, the chartered accountant (CA) designation is required to practice as a financial statement auditor. For an information technology (IT) audit professional, a certified information systems auditor (CISA) is the key mark of distinction. In fact, depending on your area of professional service within public accounting, a certified fraud examiner (CFE), certified forensic accountant (CFA), certified information systems security professional (CISSP), or even a certified internal auditor (CIA) certification may be just as important. Outside of public accounting, certification as a certified management accountant (CMA) or as a certified information technology professional (CITP) may be the most appropriate. Regardless of your career choice, a certification adds credibility that will assist you throughout your entire career.

Education

While education requirements vary across the different certifying organizations, we focus on the CPA certification in this book because of its importance to financial statement auditors. For the CPA, the specific education requirements vary by state for both having permission to take the CPA examination and for receiving a CPA certificate. As a result, students must visit the website of their own state's board of accountancy and search for the exact regulations that apply in their home state. As we approach 2020, most states are requiring you to take 150 semester hours of college education before you receive a CPA certificate, but many states now allow you to take the CPA examination after only 120 semester hours of college education. Still other certifications (such as the CIA) allow you to take the exam before you have graduated.

In addition to entry-level education requirements, all certifying organizations have regulations about *continuing professional education* (CPE). At present, the AICPA and most state boards of accountancy require 120 hours of CPE over three years (with no less than 20 hours in any one year). Once certified, accounting professionals obtain CPE hours in a variety of ways: continuing education courses, in-house training, and even college courses. These types of courses range in length from one hour to two weeks, depending on the subject. Many CPE providers offer courses online. If in-house training is not an option, many CPAs obtain their CPE by taking part in training sessions offered by their home state's professional accounting organization or other industry conferences.

Examination

When working as a financial statement auditor, CPAs have a critically important role in protecting the public interest when they attest to the reliability of a company's financial statements. As a result, the profession needs to make sure that only qualified individuals can become certified and then licensed as CPAs. To do so, the AICPA creates and then administers the Uniform CPA Examination. When creating the exam, the AICPA works hard to ensure that the knowledge and skills covered on the exam are aligned with those that are needed to protect the public interest in current practice. In fact, the AICPA just recently conducted a thorough practice analysis to "ensure that the exam measures the right knowledge and skills to protect the public interest and meet the needs of the boards of accountancy as they license CPAs."[6] The practice analysis led the AICPA to make substantial changes to the CPA exam as of April 1, 2017. Due primarily to the outsourcing of routine tasks and significant advances in information technology, the job of a newly licensed CPA has changed, and the AICPA responded with a revised exam, which is now described.

The new CPA exam has an increased emphasis on higher-order skills like problem solving, critical thinking, and analytical ability. The exam still covers Auditing and Attestation (AUD), Financial Accounting and Reporting (FAR), Regulation (REG), and Business Environment and Concepts (BEC). However, the exam is now 16 hours, instead of 14, and the emphasis has shifted toward the completion of more task-based

[6]http://www.journalofaccountancy.com/news/2016/apr/new-cpa-exam-201614166.html

simulations, which allows higher-order skills to be more accurately tested and measured. In the required AUD section, candidates will have four hours to complete 72 multiple-choice questions and eight to nine task-based simulations. The exam score is equally weighted between the multiple-choice questions and task-based simulations. To help candidates prepare for the exam, the AICPA has published detailed blueprints for each of the four sections. Each blueprint is designed to provide clarity about the knowledge content, skills, and types of tasks that might be tested for each exam. The summary blueprint for the AUD section is provided in the accompanying table (with rough approximations of weights given to each content area and skill allocation):

Content Area Allocation	Weight
Ethics, Professional Responsibilities, and General Principles	15–25%
Assessing Risk and Developing a Planned Response	20–30%
Performing Further Procedures and Obtaining Evidence	30–40%
Forming Conclusions and Reporting	15–25%
Skill Allocation	**Weight**
Evaluation	5–15%
Analysis	15–25%
Application	30–40%
Remembering and Understanding	30–40%

Source: http://www.aicpa.org/BECOMEACPA/CPAEXAM/NEXTEXAM/Pages/next-cpa-exam.aspx. Summary blueprints for REG, FAR, and BEC can also be found at this site.

Generally speaking, each section of the new CPA exam consists of multiple-choice question and task-based simulations (except for BEC, which also includes graded written communication). The task-based simulations are short case studies in which you will be asked to apply your auditing and accounting knowledge. A simulation may involve identifying a potential problem, electronically researching the topic using a database of authoritative standards, and reporting your findings. Each section's exam blueprint is designed specifically for candidates to help prepare for the exam. Throughout this book, you will have many opportunities to acquire the knowledge necessary to pass the AUD section of the exam.

General information about the new CPA exam can be obtained from a special site set up by the AICPA (available at www.aicpa.org). Because qualifications for taking the CPA examination vary from state to state, you will need to contact your state board of accountancy for an application or more information. You can find your state board of accountancy website through the National Association of State Boards of Accountancy (NASBA) website (www.nasba.org). Exhibit 1.9 lists the requirements for the most commonly recognized professional certifications.

Experience

Although not required to *sit* for a professional exam, experience is required to *become certified.* Most states and territories require a person who has attained the education level and passed the CPA examination to have a period of experience working under a practicing CPA before awarding a CPA certificate. Experience requirements vary across states, but most jurisdictions require two to three years of experience. A few states require that the experience be obtained in a public accounting firm, but most of them accept experience in other organizations (GAO, internal audit, management accounting, Internal Revenue Service, and the like) as long as the applicant performs work requiring accounting judgment and is supervised by a competent accountant, preferably a CPA. Other certifying organizations also have experience requirements.

EXHIBIT 1.9   **Certification Requirements**

	Certified Public Accountant (CPA)	Certified Information Systems Auditor (CISA)	Certified Internal Auditor (CIA)	Certified Fraud Examiner (CFE)	Certified Management Accountant (CMA)
Education Level	Varies by state; Check with your state board of accountancy	No specific degree requirement	Bachelor's degree or its educational equivalent	Bachelor's degree or its educational equivalent	Bachelor's degree, or pass the CPA examination, or score in the 50th percentile on the GMAT
Experience	Varies by state; Check with your state board of accountancy	5 years of professional information system (IS) auditing, control, or security work experience for certification	2 years of internal auditing experience or its equivalent for certification	2 years of professional experience for certification	2 continuous years of professional experience in management accounting and/ or financial management
Exam Coverage	1. Auditing and attestation (AUD) 2. Financial accounting and reporting (FAR) 3. Regulation (REG) 4. Business environment and concepts (BEC)	1. The process of auditing information systems 2. Governance and management of IT 3. Information systems acquisition, development, and implementation 4. Information systems operations, maintenance, and service management 5. Protection of information assets	1. Internal audit basics 2. Internal audit practice 3. Internal audit knowledge elements	1. Fraud prevention and deterrence 2. Financial transactions and fraud schemes 3. Investigation 4. Law	1. Financial reporting, planning, performance, and control 2. Financial decision making
Test Length	4 parts, 16 hours (as of April 1, 2017)	1 part, 4 hours (150 mc questions)	3 parts, 6.5 hours (325 mc questions)	4 parts (125 mc questions each), 10 hours	2 parts (100 mc questions and two 30-minute essays, each) 8 hours
Passing Score	75%	450 (on an 800-point scale)	600 (on a 750-point scale)	75%	360 per part (on a 500-point scale)
Test Dates	On demand in 1st two months of each calendar quarter	June, Sep, Dec	On demand	Self-administered	On demand during the months of Jan, Feb, May, Jun, Sep, and Oct
Administering Body	American Institute of Certified Public Accountants	Information Systems Audit and Control Association	Institute of Internal Auditors	Association of Certified Fraud Examiners	Institute of Management Accountants
Website	www.aicpa.org	www.isaca.org	www.theiia.org	www.acfe.com	www.imanet.org

State Certificate and License

The AICPA does not issue CPA certificates or licenses to practice. Rather, all states and territories have state accountancy laws and state licensing boards to administer them. After satisfying state requirements for education and experience, successful candidates receive their CPA *certificate* from their state board of accountancy. At the same time, new CPAs must pay a fee to obtain a state *license* to practice or work for a CPA firm that is licensed to practice in their state. Thereafter, state boards of accountancy regulate the behavior of CPAs under their jurisdiction (enforcing state codes of ethics) and supervise the continuing education requirements.

After becoming a CPA licensed in one state, a person can obtain a CPA certificate and license in another state by filing the proper application with the second state board of accountancy, meeting that state's requirements, and obtaining another CPA certificate. Many CPAs hold certificates and licenses in several states. From a global perspective, individuals must be licensed in each country. Similar to CPAs in the United States, *chartered accountants (CAs)* practice in Australia, Canada, Great Britain, and India.

AUDITING INSIGHT   Auditors Make a Run for the Border

Efforts are currently under way through the AICPA and the National Association of State Boards of Accountancy (NASBA) to streamline the licensing process so that CPAs can practice across state lines without having to have 50 different licenses. Under the concept of **substantial equivalency**, as long as the licensing (home) state requires (1) 150 hours of education, (2) successful completion of the CPA exam, and (3) one year of experience, a CPA can practice (either in person or electronically) in another substantial equivalency state without having

to obtain a license in that state. The super majority of states and the District of Columbia have enacted provisions to allow CPAs licensed in other states to practice without notification (but agreeing to be under the state's automatic jurisdiction). This *uniform mobility* arrangement is temporary though, because a CPA who relocates to another state must ultimately seek licensing in that state.

Source: AICPA State Regulation and Legislation Team at www.aicpa.org.

Skill Sets and Your Education

The requirements to become certified are rather strenuous, but they may not be enough! Let us take you on a brief tour of the core competencies listed by the AICPA, the Association of Certified Fraud Examiners (ACFE), the Institute of Internal Auditors (IIA), the Institute of Management Accountants (IMA), the Information Systems Audit and Control Association (ISACA), and other guidance-providing groups: mathematics, international culture, psychology, economics, statistics, political science, inductive and deductive reasoning, ethics, group dynamic processes, finance, capital markets, managing change, history of accounting, regulation, information systems, taxation, and (oh, yes) accounting and auditing. Add administrative capability, analytical skills, business knowledge, communication skills (writing and speaking), efficiency, intellectual capability, marketing and selling, model building, people development, capacity for putting client needs first, and more.

We hope you are suitably impressed by this recitation of virtually all of the world's knowledge. You will be very old when you accomplish a fraction of the skill development and education suggested. Now the good news: (1) not everyone needs to be completely knowledgeable in all of these areas upon graduation from college, (2) learning and skill development evolve over a lifetime, and (3) no one expects you to know everything and operate as a "Lone Ranger." Audit teams composed of members specializing in some areas with other members specializing in other areas seem to work best in practice. We do, however, stress the need to continue your education even after you leave school. Learning should be a lifelong pursuit, not something that ends when you receive your diploma.

✔ REVIEW CHECKPOINTS

1.19 Why is continuing education required to maintain certification?

1.20 Why do you think experience is required to become certified?

1.21 What are some of the functions of a state board of public accountancy?

1.22 What are some of the limitations to practicing public accounting across state and national boundaries?

Summary

Decision makers need more than just information; they need reliable and credible information that they can rely upon. Internet buyers rely on website information when purchasing online. Financial analysts and investors use financial reports to help make stock investment decisions. Suppliers and creditors use financial reports to decide whether to grant credit and bank loans. Labor organizations use financial reports to help determine a company's ability to pay wages. Government agencies and Congress use financial information in preparing analyses of the economy and in making laws concerning taxes, subsidies, and the like. These various users rely on independent information assurors such as CPAs to reduce information risk. Auditors (and other information assurance providers) assume the role of certifying (or attesting to) published financial information, thereby offering users the valuable service of providing assurance that information risk is low.

This chapter began by defining information risk and explained how auditing and assurance services play a role in minimizing this risk. The financial statements were explained in terms of the primary assertions that management makes in them, and these assertions were identified as the focal points of the auditors' evidence-gathering work. Auditing is practiced in numerous forms by various practice units, including public accounting firms, the Internal Revenue Service, the U.S. Government Accountability Office, internal audit departments in companies, and several other types of regulatory auditors. Fraud examiners, many of whom are internal auditors and inspectors, have also found a niche in auditing-related activities.

The public accounting profession recognizes that, in today's information economy, information risk exists in areas outside of financial transactions. Assurance services is a broad category of information-enhancement services that build on CPAs' auditing, attestation, accounting, and consulting skills to create products useful to a wide range of decision makers (customers). While reliable information helps make capital markets efficient and helps people know the consequences of a wide variety of economic decisions, CPAs practicing the assurance function are not the only information professionals at work in the economy. Bank examiners, IRS auditors, state regulatory agency auditors (e.g., auditors in a state's insurance department), internal auditors employed by a company, and federal government agency auditors all practice information assurance in one form or another.

Most financial statement auditors aspire to become certified public accountants, which involves successfully completing a rigorous examination, obtaining practical experience, and maintaining competence through continuing professional education. Auditors also obtain credentials as certified internal auditors, certified management accountants, certified information systems auditors, and certified fraud examiners. Each of these fields has large professional organizations that govern the professional standards and quality of practice of its members.

Key Terms

assurance: The lending of credibility to information.

assurance services: The independent professional functions that improve the quality of information, or its context, for decision makers.

attestation: An accounting service resulting in a report on subject matter or an assertion about subject matter that is the responsibility of another party.

attestation engagement: The provision of an opinion on subject matter or an assertion about the subject matter that is the responsibility of another party.

auditing: The systematic process of objectively obtaining and evaluating evidence regarding assertions about economic actions and events to ascertain the degree of correspondence between the assertions and established criteria and communicating the results to interested users.

business risks: Those factors, events, and conditions that could prevent the organization from achieving its business objectives.

completeness: Management assertion that all of the transactions, events, assets, liabilities, equity interests, and other disclosures that should have been recorded in the financial statements have been recorded.

cutoff: Management assertion that refers to accounting for revenue, expense, and other transactions in the proper period. The cutoff date generally refers to the audit client's year-end balance sheet date.

existence: Management assertion that all assets, liabilities, and equity interests do actually exist.

financial reporting: Process of providing statements of financial position (balance sheets), results of operations (income statements, statements of shareholders' equity, and statements of comprehensive income), changes in cash flows (statements of cash flows), and accompanying disclosure to outside decision makers who do not have access to management's internal sources of information; a company's accountants, under the direction of its management, perform this function.

information risk: The probability that the information circulated by an entity will be false or misleading.

internal auditing: An examination service provided to a company to assist the company to meet its corporate goals and objectives by evaluating and recommending risk management, control, and governance processes.

occurrence: Management assertion that all of the transactions and events that have been recorded are valid, pertain to the entity, and have actually taken place.

operational auditing: An examination designed to evaluate the processes and procedures of an organization or an area within an organization to ensure the process or area is operating efficiently and effectively.

presentation and disclosure: Management assertion that all transactions and events have been presented correctly and that all relevant information has been disclosed to financial statement users, usually in the footnotes to the financial statements.

professional skepticism: A state of mind that is characterized by appropriate questioning and a critical assessment of audit evidence.

rights and obligations: The entity is entitled to all rights of the assets, the liabilities are the legal responsibility of the entity, and all of the disclosed events and transactions pertain to the entity.

substantial equivalency: The process through which CPAs licensed in one state can practice in another state.

valuation or allocation: Management assertion that all assets, liabilities, and equity interests of the entity have been valued in accordance with the relevant financial reporting standards (e.g., GAAP) and are listed in the financial statements at the proper amount and any resulting valuation adjustments have been appropriately recorded in the financial statements.

Multiple-Choice Questions for Practice and Review

connect All applicable questions are available with *Connect.*

LO 1-2

1.23 Which of the following would be considered an assurance engagement?

 a. Giving an opinion on a prize promoter's claims about the amount of sweepstakes prizes awarded in the past.

 b. Giving an opinion on the conformity of the financial statements of a university with generally accepted accounting principles.

 c. Giving an opinion on the fair presentation of a newspaper's circulation data.

 d. Giving assurance about the average drive length achieved by golfers with a client's golf balls.

 e. All of the above.

LO 1-4

1.24 It is always a good idea for auditors to begin an audit with the professional skepticism characterized by the assumption that

 a. A potential conflict of interest always exists between the auditor and the management of the enterprise under audit.

 b. In audits of financial statements, the auditor acts exclusively in the capacity of an auditor.

 c. The professional status of the independent auditor imposes commensurate professional obligations.

 d. Financial statements and financial data are verifiable.

LO 1-2

1.25 In an attestation engagement, a CPA practitioner is engaged to

 a. Compile a company's financial forecast based on management's assumptions without expressing any form of assurance.

 b. Prepare a written report containing a conclusion about the reliability of a management assertion.

 c. Prepare a tax return using information the CPA has not audited or reviewed.

 d. Give expert testimony in court on particular facts in a corporate income tax controversy.

LO 1-6   1.26 A determination of cost savings obtained by outsourcing cafeteria services is most likely to be an objective of
a. Environmental auditing.
b. Financial auditing.
c. Compliance auditing.
d. Operational auditing.

LO 1-6   1.27 The primary difference between operational auditing and financial auditing is that in operational auditing
a. The operational auditor is not concerned with whether the audited activity is generating information in compliance with financial accounting standards.
b. The operational auditor is seeking to help management use resources in the most effective manner possible.
c. The operational auditor starts with the financial statements of an activity being audited and works backward to the basic processes involved in producing them.
d. The operational auditor can use analytical skills and tools that are not necessary in financial auditing.

LO 1-2   1.28 According to the AICPA, the purpose of an audit of financial statements is to
a. Enhance the degree of confidence that intended users can place in the financial statements.
b. Express an opinion on the fairness with which they present financial position, results of operations, and cash flows in conformity with accounting standards promulgated by the Financial Accounting Standards Board.
c. Express an opinion on the fairness with which they present financial position, results of operations, and cash flows in conformity with accounting standards promulgated by the U.S. Securities and Exchange Commission.
d. Obtain systematic and objective evidence about financial assertions and report the results to interested users.

LO 1-1   1.29 Bankers who are processing loan applications from companies seeking large loans will probably ask for financial statements audited by an independent CPA because
a. Financial statements are too complex for the bankers to analyze themselves.
b. They are too far away from company headquarters to perform accounting and auditing themselves.
c. The consequences of making a bad loan are very undesirable.
d. They generally see a potential conflict of interest between company managers who want to get loans and the bank's needs for reliable financial statements.

LO 1-5   1.30 The Sarbanes–Oxley Act of 2002 prohibits public accounting firms from providing which of the following services to an audit client?
a. Bookkeeping services.
b. Internal auditing services.
c. Valuation services.
d. All of the above.

LO 1-1   1.31 Independent auditors of financial statements perform audits that reduce
a. Business risks faced by investors.
b. Information risk faced by investors.
c. Complexity of financial statements.
d. Timeliness of financial statements.

LO 1-6   1.32 The primary objective of compliance auditing is to
a. Give an opinion on financial statements.
b. Develop a basis for a report on internal control.
c. Perform a study of effective and efficient use of resources.
d. Determine whether client personnel are following laws, rules, regulations, and policies.

LO 1-7   1.33 What requirements are *usually* necessary to become licensed as a certified public accountant?
a. Successful completion of the Uniform CPA Examination.
b. Experience in the accounting field.
c. Education.
d. All of the above.

LO 1-6

1.34 The organization primarily responsible for ensuring that public officials are using public funds efficiently, economically, and effectively is the
    a. Governmental Internal Audit Agency (GIAA).
    b. Central Internal Auditors (CIA).
    c. Securities and Exchange Commission (SEC).
    d. Government Accountability Office (GAO).

LO 1-6

1.35 Performance audits usually include [two answers]
    a. Financial audits.
    b. Economy and efficiency audits.
    c. Compliance audits.
    d. Program audits.

LO 1-3

1.36 The objective in an auditor's review of credit ratings of a client's customers is to obtain evidence related to management's assertion about
    a. Completeness.
    b. Existence.
    c. Valuation and allocation.
    d. Rights and obligations.
    e. Occurrence.

LO 1-4

1.37 Jones, CPA, is planning the audit of Rhonda's Company. Rhonda verbally asserts to Jones that all expenses for the year have been recorded in the accounts. Rhonda's representation in this regard
    a. Is sufficient evidence for Jones to conclude that the completeness assertion is supported for expenses.
    b. Can enable Jones to minimize the work on the gathering of evidence to support Rhonda's completeness assertion.
    c. Should be disregarded because it is not in writing.
    d. Is not considered a sufficient basis for Jones to conclude that all expenses have been recorded.

LO 1-1

1.38 The risk to investors that a company's financial statements may be materially misleading is called
    a. Client acceptance risk.
    b. Information risk.
    c. Moral hazard.
    d. Business risk.

LO 1-3

1.39 When auditing merchandise inventory at year-end, the auditor performs audit procedures to ensure that all goods purchased before year-end are received before the physical inventory count. This audit procedure provides assurance about which management assertion?
    a. Cutoff.
    b. Existence.
    c. Valuation and allocation.
    d. Rights and obligations.
    e. Occurrence.

LO 1-3

1.40 When auditing merchandise inventory at year-end, the auditor performs audit procedures to obtain evidence that no goods held on consignment are included in the client's ending inventory balance. This audit procedure provides assurance about which management assertion?
    a. Completeness.
    b. Existence.
    c. Valuation and allocation.
    d. Rights and obligations.
    e. Occurrence.

LO 1-3

1.41 When an auditor reviews additions to the equipment (fixed asset) account to make sure that fixed assets are not overstated, she wants to obtain evidence as to management's assertion regarding

a. Completeness.

b. Existence.

c. Valuation and allocation.

d. Rights and obligations.

e. Occurrence.

LO 1-5

1.42 The Sarbanes–Oxley Act of 2002 generally prohibits public accounting firms from

a. Acting in a managerial decision-making role for an audit client.

b. Auditing the firm's own work on an audit client.

c. Providing tax consulting to an audit client without audit committee approval.

d. All of the above.

LO 1-7

1.43 Substantial equivalency refers to

a. An auditor's tendency not to believe management's assertions without sufficient corroboration.

b. Providing consulting work for another firm's audit client in exchange for the other firm's providing consulting services to one of your clients.

c. The waiving of certification exam parts for an individual holding an equivalent certification from another professional organization.

d. Permitting a CPA to practice in another state without having to obtain a license in that state.

LO 1-2

1.44 Which of the following best describes the relationship between auditing and attestation engagements?

a. Auditing is a subset of attestation engagements that focuses on the certification of financial statements.

b. Attestation is a subset of auditing that provides lower assurance than that provided by an audit engagement.

c. Auditing is a subset of attestation engagements that focuses on providing clients with advice and decision support.

d. Attestation is a subset of auditing that improves the quality of information or its context for decision makers.

LO 1-3

1.45 During an audit of a company's cash balance on a company with operations in only one country, the auditor is most concerned with which management assertion?

a. Existence.

b. Rights and obligations.

c. Valuation or allocation.

d. Occurrence.

LO 1-3

1.46 When auditing an investment in another company, an auditor most likely would seek to conduct which audit procedure to help satisfy the valuation assertion?

a. Inspect the stock certificates evidencing the investment.

b. Examine the audited financial statements of the investee company.

c. Review the broker's advice or canceled check for the investment's acquisition.

d. Obtain market quotations from *The Wall Street Journal* or another independent source.

LO 1-3

1.47 Cutoff tests designed to detect valid sales that occurred before the end of the year but have been recorded in the subsequent year would provide assurance about management's assertion of

a. Presentation and disclosure.

b. Completeness.

c. Rights and obligations.

d. Existence.

LO 1-3

1.48 Which of the following audit procedures probably would provide the most reliable evidence related to the entity's assertion of rights and obligations for the inventory account?

    a. Trace test counts noted during physical count to the summarization of quantities.

    b. Inspect agreements for evidence of inventory held on consignment.

    c. Select the last few shipping advices used before the physical count and determine whether the shipments were recorded as sales.

    d. Inspect the open purchase order file for significant commitments to consider for disclosure.

LO 1-3

1.49 In auditing the accrued liabilities account on the Balance Sheet, an auditor's procedures most likely would focus primarily on management's assertion of

    a. Existence or occurrence.

    b. Completeness.

    c. Presentation and disclosure.

    d. Valuation or allocation.

LO 1-2

1.50 Which of the following *best* describes the focus of the following engagements?

Auditing Engagement	Attestation Engagement	Assurance Engagement	Consulting Services Engagement
a. Any information	Financial statements	Advice and decision support	Financial information
b. Financial information	Advice and decision support	Financial statements	Any information
c. Advice and decision support	Any information	Financial information	Financial statements
d. Financial statements	Financial information	Any information	Advice and decision support

LO 1-7

1.51 Which of the following is a reason to obtain professional certification?

    a. Certification provides credibility that an individual is technically competent.

    b. Certification often is a necessary condition for advancement and promotion within a professional services firm.

    c. Obtaining certification is often monetarily rewarded by an individual's employer.

    d. All of the above.

LO 1-3

1.52 During an audit of an entity's stockholders' equity accounts, the auditor determines whether there are restrictions on retained earnings resulting from loans, agreements, or state law. This audit procedure most likely is intended to verify management's assertion of

    a. Existence or occurrence.

    b. Completeness.

    c. Valuation or allocation.

    d. Presentation and disclosure.

LO 1-3

1.53 When auditing the accounts receivable account on the balance sheet, an auditor's procedures most likely would focus primarily on management's assertion of

    a. Existence.

    b. Completeness.

    c. Presentation and disclosure.

    d. Rights and obligations.

LO 1-3

1.54 An auditor selected items for test counts from the client's warehouse during the physical inventory observation. The auditor then traced these test counts into the detailed inventory listing that agreed to the financial statements. This procedure most likely provided evidence concerning management's assertion of

    a. Rights and obligations.

    b. Completeness.

    c. Existence.

    d. Valuation.

LO 1-3

1.55 An auditor's purpose in auditing the information contained in the pension footnote most likely is to obtain evidence concerning management's assertion about

    a. Rights and obligations.

    b. Existence.

    c. Presentation and disclosure.

    d. Valuation.

Exercises and Problems

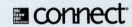 All applicable Exercises and Problems are available with *Connect.*

LO 1-2

1.56 **Audit, Attestation, and Assurance Services.** Following is a list of various professional services. Identify each by its apparent characteristics as audit engagement, attestation engagement, or assurance engagement. Because audits are a subset of attestation engagements, which are a subset of assurance engagements, choose the most specific description. In other words, if you believe the engagement is an audit engagement, select only audit engagement rather than checking all three. Similarly, the choice of assurance engagement for an audit, while technically correct, would not be the best choice.

	Audit Engagement	Attestation Engagement	Assurance Engagement
Real estate demand studies			
Ballot for awards show			
Utility rates applications			
Newspaper circulation audits			
Third-party reimbursement maximization			
Annual financial report to stockholders			
Rental property operation review			
Examinations of financial forecasts and projections			
Customer satisfaction surveys			
Compliance with contractual requirements			
Benchmarking/best practices			
Evaluation of investment management policies			
Information systems security reviews			
Productivity statistics			
Internal audit strategic review			
Financial statements submitted to a bank loan officer			

LO 1-4

1.57 **Controller as Auditor.** The chairman of the board of Hughes Corporation proposed that the board hire as controller a CPA who had been the manager of the team that conducted Hughes Corporation's audit engagement. The chairman thought that hiring this person would make the annual audit unnecessary and would consequently result in saving the professional fee paid to the auditors. The chairman proposed to give this new controller a full staff to conduct such investigations of accounting and operating data as necessary. Evaluate this proposal.

LO 1-3

1.58 **Management Assertions.** Complete the following chart indicating the corresponding Auditing Standards Board assertions and whether the assertion relates to transactions, balances, or disclosures.

PCAOB Assertion	Corresponding ASB Assertion	Nature of Assertion
Existence or Occurrence		
Rights and Obligations		
Completeness		
Valuation and Allocation		
Presentation and Disclosure		

LO 1-3

1.59 **Management Assertions.** Your audit manager has asked you to explain the PCAOB assertions by using an account on the balance sheet at your audit client. For the accounts receivable account, please define each of the PCAOB assertions, using the accounts receivable account as a way to illustrate each assertion. You are encouraged to reference Exhibit 1.5 to help you answer this question.

LO 1-5, 1-6

1.60 **Operational Auditing.** Bigdeal Corporation manufactures paper and paper products and is trying to decide whether to purchase Smalltek Company. Smalltek has developed a process for manufacturing boxes that can replace containers that use fluorocarbons for expelling a liquid product. The price may be as high as $45 million. Bigdeal prefers to buy Smalltek and integrate its products while leaving the Smalltek management in charge of day-to-day operations. A major consideration is the efficiency and effectiveness of Smalltek's operations. Bigdeal wants to obtain a report on the operational efficiency and effectiveness of the Smalltek sales, production, and research and development departments.

Required:

Who can Bigdeal engage to produce the report resulting from this operational audit? Several possibilities exist. Are there any particular advantages or disadvantages in choosing from among them?

LO 1-1, 1-2

1.61 **Auditor as Guarantor.** Your neighbor, Loot Starkin, invited you to lunch yesterday. Sure enough, it was no "free lunch" because Loot wanted to discuss the annual report of Dodge Corporation. He owns Dodge stock and just received the annual report. Loot says, "Our auditors prepared the audited financial statements and gave an unqualified opinion, so my investment must be safe."

Required:

What misconceptions does Loot Starkin seem to have about the auditor's role with respect to Dodge Corporation?

LO 1-6

1.62 **Identification of Audits and Auditors.** Audits may be characterized as (a) financial statement audits, (b) compliance audits, (c) economy and efficiency audits, and (d) program results audits. The work can be done by independent (external) auditors, internal auditors, or governmental auditors (including IRS auditors and federal bank examiners). Following is a list of the purposes or products of various audit engagements:

	Type of Audit	Type of Auditor
1. Analyze proprietary schools' spending to train students for low-demand occupations.		
2. Determine whether an advertising agency's financial statements are fairly presented in conformity with GAAP.		
3. Study the effectiveness of the Department of Defense's expendable launch vehicle program.		
4. Compare costs of municipal garbage pickup services to comparable services subcontracted to a private business.		
5. Investigate financing terms of tax shelter partnerships.		
6. Study a private aircraft manufacturer's test pilot performance in reporting on the results of test flights.		
7. Conduct periodic examinations by the U.S. Comptroller of Currency of a national bank for solvency.		
8. Evaluate the promptness of materials inspection in a manufacturer's receiving department.		
9. Report on the need for the states to consider reporting requirements for chemical use data.		
10. Render a public report on the assumptions and compilation of a revenue forecast by a sports stadium/racetrack complex.		

Required:

For each of the engagements listed, indicate (1) the type of audit (financial statement, compliance, economy and efficiency, or program results) and (2) the type of auditors you would expect to be involved.

LO 1-3

1.63 **Financial Assertions and Audit Objectives.** You are engaged to examine the financial statements of Spillane Company for the year ended December 31. Assume that on November 1, Spillane borrowed $500,000 from Second National Bank to finance plant expansion. The long-term note agreement provided for the annual payment of principal and interest over five years. The existing plant was pledged as security for the loan. Due to the unexpected difficulties in acquiring the building site, the plant expansion did not begin on time. To use the borrowed funds, management decided to invest in stocks and bonds and on November 16, invested the $500,000 in publicly traded securities.

Required:

Develop specific assertions (audit objectives) related to securities (assets) based on management's five (PCAOB) general assertions.

LO 1-7

1.64 **Internet Exercise: Professional Certification.** Each state has unique rules for certification concerning education, work experience, and residency. Visit the website for your state board of accountancy and download a list of the requirements for becoming a CPA in your state. Although not all of the state boards of accountancy have websites, you can find those of most states by accessing the National Association of State Boards of Accountancy at its website (www.nasba.org).

LO 1-7

1.65 **Internet Exercise: Professional Certification.** Visit the website of the Institute of Internal Auditors (www.theiia.org), the Institute of Management Accountants (www.imanet.org), the Association of Certified Fraud Examiners (www.acfe.com), or the Information Systems Audit and Control Association (www.isaca.org). Review the information regarding the certifications available. Does the organization explain the benefits of having its certification? What topics are covered on the certification exam? What are the minimum requirements to take the exam? What additional experience is required to receive the certification?

CHAPTER 2

Professional Standards

In today's regulatory environment, it's virtually impossible to violate rules.

> Bernard Madoff, money manager, approximately one year prior to being arrested for embezzling $50 billion from investors in a Ponzi scheme

Professional Standards References

Topic	AU-C/ISA Section	AS Section
Overall Objectives of the Independent Auditor	200	1001, 1005, 1010, 1015
Quality Control for an Audit Engagement	220	1220
Audit Planning	300	2101
Supervision of the Audit Engagement	300	1201
Identifying and Assessing the Risks of Material Misstatement	315	2110
Materiality	320	2105
Audit Evidence	500	1105
Reporting on Financial Statements	700	3101
Modifications to Reports on Financial Statements	705	3101
Quality Control	QC 10	1110, QC 10

LEARNING OBJECTIVES

Chapter 2 discusses the standards that govern the conduct of audit examinations (generally accepted auditing standards) and how these standards offer the explicit guidance that must be followed during audits. In addition, Chapter 2 identifies important policies and procedures implemented by auditing firms (through a system of quality control) to ensure that the firms' audits comply with appropriate professional standards and can withstand scrutiny by regulatory bodies. Finally, the chapter discusses external monitoring efforts that evaluate the quality of audit firms' work.

Your objectives are to be able to:

LO 2-1 Understand the development and source of generally accepted auditing standards.

LO 2-2 Describe the fundamental principle of *responsibilities* and how this principle relates to the characteristics and qualifications of auditors.

40

LO 2-3   Describe the fundamental principle of *performance* and identify the major activities performed in an audit.

LO 2-4   Understand the fundamental principle of *reporting* and identify the basic contents of the auditors' report.

LO 2-5   Understand the role of a system of quality control and monitoring efforts in enabling public accounting firms to meet appropriate levels of professional quality.

INTRODUCTION

The introductory quote from Bernie Madoff suggests that a strong regulatory environment results in compliance with established rules (despite the fact that Madoff himself did not do so!). Who sets the rules and standards for audits? Until 2002, the accounting profession was *self-regulated;* that is, the standards governing audits were established by members of the profession themselves through the **American Institute of Certified Public Accountants (AICPA)**. Although critics indicated that self-regulation was akin to having university students establish the systems used to determine their grades, this practice continued for more than 60 years and, although some concerns were raised during this time, remained largely unchanged.

Motivated to a great extent by the audit failures related to **Enron** and **WorldCom,** Congress passed the Sarbanes–Oxley Act of 2002 (Sarbanes–Oxley). Among other reforms, this act created the **Public Company Accounting Oversight Board (PCAOB)** to provide external and independent oversight over the audits of public entities. (A **public entity** is one that offers registered securities, such as stocks and bonds, for sale to the general public.) Among other matters, the PCAOB is responsible for registering public accounting firms, establishing and enforcing standards for audit engagements, and inspecting the quality of audits conducted by registered public accounting firms.

The PCAOB's inspection process and public reporting of results have received a great deal of media attention. As one of the "Big Four" accounting firms along with **EY, KPMG,** and **PwC, Deloitte** is a premier provider of accounting and auditing services. With worldwide revenues of more than $35 billion in 2015 and more than 225,000 employees operating in more than 150 countries, Deloitte's professionals provide services to leading organizations throughout the world.[1] Clearly, it is important for firms such as Deloitte to implement policies, procedures, and standards to ensure the quality of their work to their clients as well as others who rely on their work in making economic decisions.

In 2011, the PCAOB publicly released portions of an inspection report that criticized Deloitte's internal policies and procedures. (This was the first public disclosure of this nature involving a Big Four firm.) This report concluded that "important issues may exist" regarding procedures established by Deloitte related to

- The comprehensiveness of its audits.
- The professional skepticism of its personnel.
- The quality of its training programs for its professional staff.
- Systems for assessing and monitoring the work of its member firms in other countries.[2]

A recent academic study[3] concluded that the release of this information resulted in a reduction in Deloitte's ability to retain existing clients and attract new clients. In addition, Deloitte's audit fee growth rates declined following the release of this information. These

---

[1] Data are drawn from Deloitte's 2015 *Global Report.*

[2] "Audit Watchdog Criticized Deloitte Quality Controls in '08," *The Wall Street Journal,* October 18, 2011, p. C3. Each of the remaining Big Four firms have been the subject of similar PCAOB reports.

[3] J. P. Boone, I. K. Khurana, and K. K. Raman, "Did the 2007 PCAOB Disciplinary Order against Deloitte Impose Actual Costs on the Firm or Improve Its Audit Quality?" *The Accounting Review,* March 2015, pp. 405–441.

findings suggest that the PCAOB's actions imposed actual costs on Deloitte through less favorable perceptions of the firm and its work. In all, since 2007, the PCAOB has levied four monetary sanctions against Big Four firms totaling $6.5 million.[4]

This vignette illustrates the public scrutiny placed on policies and procedures implemented by firms to conduct quality audits. Although situations like these, as well as the Madoff fraud referenced in the opening quote to this chapter, are exceptions rather than the rule, accounting firms clearly are being held to a higher standard for the quality of their work, and failures are receiving intense attention in the media. The development of professional auditing standards, actions taken by audit firms to ensure that their audits comply with these standards, and monitoring efforts by external bodies (such as the PCAOB) to evaluate the quality of audit firms' work are the focal points of this chapter.

GENERALLY ACCEPTED AUDITING STANDARDS (GAAS)

LO 2-1
Understand the development and source of generally accepted auditing standards.

At least two historical milestones had a significant impact on the development of auditing standards. In 1938, a scandal of epic proportions broke at **McKesson & Robbins,** a large pharmaceutical company. Price Waterhouse & Co. (now PwC), the company's auditor for more than 10 years, failed to discover that the company had inflated inventory and receivables through the falsification of supporting documents (including one phony shipment from the United States to Australia by truck!). Auditors merely accepted management's assertions about inventory and receivables balances without verifying their existence. The accounting profession reacted quite strongly to the scandal by tasking the AICPA to develop standards that served as the basis for audits of both public and nonpublic (private) entities. From 1939 through 2002, the AICPA's Auditing Standards Board issued *Statements on Auditing Procedure* (1939–1972) and *Statements on Auditing Standards (SASs)* (1972–present) to provide guidance for the conduct of audits.[5]

A second defining moment in the development of auditing standards was the massive frauds at Enron and WorldCom (and the inability of those entities' auditors to identify the frauds). In response to these failures, Sarbanes–Oxley (which was passed by a vote of 99-0 in the U.S. Senate!) created the PCAOB and delegated the responsibility for developing standards for the audits of public entities to this body. The PCAOB issues *Auditing Standards,* which are subject to the formal approval of the Securities and Exchange Commission (SEC). The authorization for developing standards for the audits of nonpublic entities continues to remain with the Auditing Standards Board of the AICPA.

Until recently, PCAOB standards consisted of a combination of *Auditing Standards* issued by the PCAOB and standards issued by the AICPA that had not been superseded by the PCAOB (referred to as *Interim Auditing Standards*). Effective December 31, 2016, the PCAOB has reorganized and combined these standards into a single body of pronouncements. Appendix 2A illustrates how auditors utilize the PCAOB and ASB standards in providing appropriate professional guidance.

The relevant pronouncements of the AICPA and PCAOB are collectively referred to as **generally accepted auditing standards (GAAS)**.[6] GAAS are auditing standards that identify necessary qualifications and characteristics of auditors and guide the conduct of the audit examination. The purpose of GAAS is to meet the objectives of an audit examination, which are (AU-C 200.12):

---

[4]See pcaobus.org/Enforcement/Decisions/Pages/default.aspx for a complete listing of settled disciplinary orders.

[5] *Statements on Auditing Standards (SAS)* are authoritative AICPA pronouncements on auditing theory and practice. *Statements on Auditing Procedure (SAP) Nos. 1–54* were codified into *SAS 1* in 1972.

[6]The auditing standards for public entities are sometimes referred to as *PCAOB Standards* to distinguish them from the standards for nonpublic entities.

- To obtain reasonable assurance about whether the financial statements as a whole are free of material misstatement, whether due to fraud or error.
- To issue a report on the financial statements.

Generally, auditors who do not follow the guidance provided in GAAS are presumed to have performed deficient audits. The auditing standards also includes *interpretive publications* (which includes *Interpretations,* exhibits, *AICPA Audit and Accounting Guides,* and *AICPA Auditing Statements of Position*). Although officially considered less authoritative and less binding than the guidance in the *SASs* and *Auditing Standards,* auditors still must justify any departures from these publications, which provide guidance on the application of GAAS in specific circumstances, including engagements for entities in certain industries. The relationship among these various pronouncements is summarized in the following graphic.

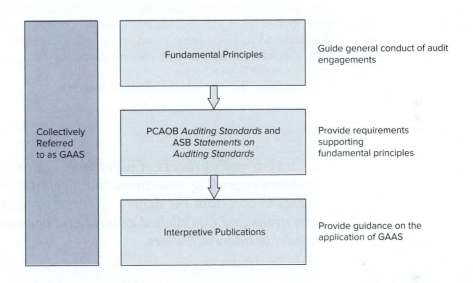

Auditing standards are quite different from *audit procedures.* **Audit procedures** are the particular and specialized actions that auditors take to obtain evidence in a specific audit engagement. **Auditing standards**, on the other hand, are quality guides to the audit that apply to all audits. For example, auditing standards indicate that auditors must determine that recorded accounts receivable are based on actual sales to customers. An audit procedure used to satisfy that standard is to confirm accounts receivable with the company's customers. This difference is the reason auditors' reports refer to an audit "conducted in accordance with *standards* of the Public Company Accounting Oversight Board" [emphasis added] rather than in accordance with audit procedures.

In addition to the standards for U.S. public and nonpublic entities, it is important to note that separate auditing standards have been developed for governmental and foreign entities. A summary of the body charged with establishing standards as well as the standards themselves for various types of audits follows.

	Public Entities	Nonpublic Entities	Governmental Entities	Foreign Entities
Rule-making body	Public Company Accounting Oversight Board (PCAOB)	AICPA Auditing Standards Board (ASB)	U.S. Government Accountability Office (GAO)	International Auditing and Assurance Standards Board (IAASB)
Standards	*Auditing Standards (ASs)*	*Statements on Auditing Standards (SASs)*	*Government Auditing Standards* (The Yellow Book)	*International Standards on Auditing (ISAs)*
Website	www.pcaobus.org	www.aicpa.org	www.gao.gov	www.ifac.org

If an accounting firm audits public and private entities throughout the world, that firm may be subject to multiple (sometimes conflicting) standards issued by the ASB, PCAOB, and IAASB, among others. For this reason, auditors and regulators have a great interest in *convergence*—that is, making the standards coordinated, if not uniform, throughout the world. The *ISAs* are a first step in the development of one consistent set of guidelines that auditors worldwide can follow. Although the focus in this text will be on audits of U.S. public, and nonpublic entities (and therefore pronouncements of the PCAOB and ASB), it is important that students be aware that additional standards exist related to the audits of governmental and foreign entities.

Organization of GAAS

The body of GAAS is based on three fundamental principles identified by the ASB that underlie all audits. These fundamental principles (related to responsibilities of the audit team, performance of the audit, and reporting the results of the engagement) are established to meet the objectives of an audit and are supported by objectives and requirements of specific *SASs*. While these principles have been issued by the ASB and are not formally applicable to the audits of public entities, they are consistent with and reflect the requirements of GAAS for audits of public entities.

Recall from Chapter 1 the definition of *auditing* as

> *. . . a systematic process of objectively obtaining and evaluating evidence regarding assertions about economic actions and events to ascertain the degree of correspondence between the assertions and established criteria and communicating the results to interested users.*

Closer examination of the fundamental principles reveals that they closely parallel that definition. For example, the *responsibilities* principle defines objectivity and identifies the important role that objectivity plays in the audit. The *performance* principle requires, among other things, auditors to plan the work (i.e., conduct the audit using a "systematic process") and to "obtain and evaluate evidence" through assessing the risk of material misstatement and gathering sufficient appropriate evidence. Finally, the *reporting* principle provides guidance for "communicating the results" of the audit about whether the financial statements are prepared using "established criteria" (an applicable financial reporting framework, or GAAP).

☑ REVIEW CHECKPOINTS

2.1 Define *generally accepted auditing standards (GAAS)*. What is the purpose of GAAS?

2.2 Who is responsible for developing standards for the audits of public entities? Who is responsible for developing standards for the audits of nonpublic entities?

2.3 Identify the role of the following bodies in the auditing standards-setting process: (1) the AICPA; (2) the PCAOB; (3) the SEC.

2.4 Identify the three fundamental principles underlying GAAS.

FUNDAMENTAL PRINCIPLE: RESPONSIBILITIES

LO 2-2
Describe the fundamental principle of *responsibilities* and how this principle relates to the characteristics and qualifications of auditors.

The fundamental principle of *responsibilities* relates to the personal integrity and professional qualifications of auditors. This principle addresses the following responsibilities of auditors:

> *Auditors are responsible for:*
> - *Having appropriate competence and capabilities to perform the audit.*
> - *Complying with relevant ethical requirements.*
> - *Maintaining professional skepticism and exercising professional judgment throughout the planning and performance of the audit.*

As shown in the following figure, most of the issues related to responsibilities are addressed before a firm accepts a prospective client. However, professional skepticism and professional judgment must be considered and exercised by the auditor throughout the entire engagement.

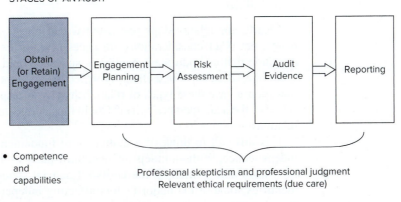

STAGES OF AN AUDIT

Competence and Capabilities

Competence and *capabilities* begin with education in accounting because auditors hold themselves out as experts in accounting standards, financial reporting, and auditing. In addition to university-level education prior to beginning their careers, auditors are required to participate in continuing professional education throughout their careers to ensure that their knowledge keeps pace with changes in the accounting and auditing profession. In fact, one of the important requirements for maintaining a CPA license is sufficient continuing professional education.

Education is only one element of competence and capabilities. Another important dimension is *experience,* which is gained with hands-on practice and on-the-job training. An important component of this experience is the ability to develop and apply professional judgment in real-world audit situations. These situations include various judgments related to gathering evidence as to the fairness of an entity's financial statements and evaluating whether that evidence indicates that the financial statements are prepared according to generally accepted accounting principles. (Professional judgment is also an important component of the performance principle, which will be discussed later.)

Independence and Due Care

The responsibilities principle requires auditors to comply with appropriate ethical requirements; two important requirements relate to *independence* and *due care*. Auditors must maintain independence in mental attitude; that is, auditors are expected to be unbiased and impartial with respect to the financial statements and other information they audit. This "state of mind" is often referred to as the auditor possessing **independence in fact**. This independence allows auditors to form an opinion on the entity's financial statements without being affected by influences that might compromise that opinion.

It is not only important for auditors to be unbiased; they must also *appear* to be unbiased. **Independence in appearance** relates to others' (particularly financial statement users') perceptions of auditors' independence. For example, imagine that the son or daughter of your professor was enrolled in your class. While your professor may truly be unbiased and evaluate their child fairly, it is unlikely that you and your classmates would believe your professor to be independent.

Although independence is a complex concept and many different threats to independence exist, two general types of relationships that are believed to jeopardize (or compromise) independence are

1. *Financial relationships,* such as owning shares of stock in a client or having a loan outstanding to or from a client.
2. *Managerial relationships,* such as the ability to act in a decision-making capacity on behalf of a client or to provide advice on systems or information that will subsequently be audited.

Clearly, the relationships just listed would impair perceptions of auditors' independence, but other considerations are necessary. For example, although it seems safe to conclude that an audit team member's spouse should be restricted from the preceding types of relationships for a client for which the team member is providing services, could that spouse have these types of relationships with respect to a client served by a distant office of the team member's firm? Could the audit team member's third cousin have such relationships?

It is difficult to think of a matter more fundamental to the value of an audit than independence. Without independence, third-party users are not able to rely on the auditor's work and opinion on the entity's financial statements. The preceding discussion identifies some of the major factors affecting independence, but the possible relationships involving auditors, entities, and their personnel are endless; the complexities of these relationships have resulted in a number of interpretations and ethics rulings regarding auditor independence. Many individuals fundamentally question whether auditors can be independent given the fee arrangement they have with their clients. (Imagine the situation if you directly paid your professor instead of the university for your tuition!) In addition, the often long-standing relationships between auditors and their clients have resulted in some attempts to require periodic rotation of audit firms to lessen the impact of financial relationships between these two parties and enhance independence.

Issues related to auditor independence may provide some significant challenges in practice. For example, an investigation in 2000 of independence violations at PwC revealed that ". . . approximately 86.5 percent of PwC partners and 10.5 percent of all other PwC professionals had independence violations."[7] Some more recent examples of independence issues facing major accounting firms are summarized in the accompanying Auditing Insight.

This section introduces the concept of auditor independence and provides a limited overview of issues that impact auditor independence. A detailed discussion of AICPA and SEC rules related to independence (and various interpretations of those rules) is provided in Module B.

---

[7]"Independent Consultant Finds Widespread Independence Violations at PricewaterhouseCoopers," *SEC Press Release 2000–4*, January 6, 2000.

AUDITING INSIGHT   Independent Auditors?

The following recent incidents illustrate the wide range of issues that can affect auditor independence:

- In 2014, EY withdrew its 2012 and 2013 opinions on the financial statements of **Ventas Inc.** (a Chicago-based real estate investment trust) because of an "inappropriate personal relationship" involving one of its partners (who participated in the audit engagement) and Ventas's chief accounting officer. EY subsequently paid $9.3 million to settle charges related to this matter.

- In July 2014, the SEC charged EY with violating independence rules by inappropriately lobbying congressional staff on behalf of two audit clients, indicating that ". . . [these activities] put the firm

in the position of being an advocate for those audit clients." (Both incidents occurred prior to 2009, and EY no longer engages in lobbying activities on behalf of its audit clients.)

- In January 2014, KPMG agreed to an $8.2 million settlement with the SEC for providing prohibited nonaudit services (including corporate finance, bookkeeping, and payroll services) to three unnamed audit clients.

Sources: "Ventas Audit Reports Pulled Due to Inappropriate Relationship," *The Wall Street Journal Online*, July 9, 2014; "Ernst & Young to Pay $9.3 Million to Settle Charges," *The Wall Street Journal Online*, September 19, 2016. "EY Runs Afoul of Auditor-Independence Rules Again," *CFO.com*, July 15, 2014; "KPMG Settles Auditor Independence Charges," *CFO.com*, January 14, 2014.

A second ethical requirement identified by the responsibilities principle is that of due care. **Due care** reflects a level of performance that would be exercised by reasonable auditors in similar circumstances. This standard is often referred to as that of a prudent auditor; auditors are expected to possess the skills and knowledge of others in their profession but are not expected to be infallible. This aspect relates to the competence and capabilities of the auditor to perform the engagement and issue appropriate reports. One specific element of due care noted by the standards is the need for auditors to plan and perform the audit with an appropriate level of professional skepticism as discussed in the following section.

Professional Skepticism and Professional Judgment

Professional skepticism and professional judgment are necessary responsibilities of auditors throughout the entire audit process. **Professional skepticism** (which was introduced in Chapter 1) is a state of mind that is characterized by appropriate questioning and a critical assessment of audit evidence. When exhibiting professional skepticism, auditors do not assume that management is dishonest, nor do they assume that management is unquestionably honest. Rather, auditors evaluate and consider

- Contradictory audit evidence obtained through different procedures.
- The reliability of documentary evidence.
- The reliability of information obtained from management and those charged with governance of the entity (e.g., the audit committee).

Although the preceding discussion suggests that professional skepticism is a relatively straightforward concept, situations occur during the audit that could impede auditors' ability to apply appropriate levels of professional skepticism. A PCAOB *Staff Practice Alert*[8] identified the following conditions that present challenges for auditors maintaining appropriate levels of professional skepticism; these conditions may result in auditors failing to appropriately question, assess, and evaluate evidence, and, ultimately, reach the correct conclusion during their engagement:

- Financial incentives and pressures (such as building or maintaining a long-term audit engagement, facing pressures to keep audit fees low, achieving high levels of client satisfaction, and providing other fee-related services to clients).
- Time pressures (such as completing the audit and report prior to deadlines and scheduling and workload demands on partners and other audit team members).
- Personal relationships developed with clients that provide auditors with an inappropriate level of trust or confidence in management.

[8] *Staff Audit Practice Alert No. 10,* "Maintaining and Applying Professional Skepticism in Audits," PCAOB, December 4, 2012.

Professional judgment is the application of relevant training, knowledge, and experience in making informed decisions about appropriate courses of action during the audit engagement. These judgments relate to the evidence obtained during the audit and the conclusions reached based on this evidence. Auditors are required to demonstrate this characteristic throughout the entire audit process as they do professional skepticism. Professional judgment is required as auditors gather evidence, evaluate evidence, and draw conclusions based on evidence. Professional judgment is particularly important in evaluating the reasonableness of various management estimates required in preparing the entity's financial statements.

In addition to demonstrating appropriate levels of professional judgment, auditors are required to carefully document their professional judgment in such a manner that experienced auditors with no previous relationship with the audit can understand the judgments made in reaching conclusions on significant issues.

AUDITING INSIGHT　　Madoff and the Responsibilities Principle

A preliminary investigation of the actions of David Friehling (the individual responsible for the audits of **Bernard L. Madoff Investment Securities LLC**) illustrated the following potential violations of elements of the responsibilities principle:

- Friehling did not verify the existence of assets or securities trades made by Madoff's company, suggesting a lack of professional skepticism and a lack of due care.

- Friehling was the sole auditor at Friehling and Horowitz, raising the question as to whether a "one-man" firm has the capability to effectively audit a company as large as Madoff's.

- Friehling and his family had investment accounts at Madoff's company worth more than $14 million, a conflict of interest that raises questions about his independence.

Source: "Accountant Arrested for Sham Audits," *The Wall Street Journal*, March 19, 2009, p. C1.

✓ REVIEW CHECKPOINTS

2.5 Distinguish between independence in fact and independence in appearance. Can auditors be independent in fact yet not be perceived to be independent in appearance?

2.6 What is *due care*? To what standards are auditors held with respect to due care?

2.7 Define *professional skepticism* and *professional judgment*. During what stages of the audit are auditors required to demonstrate these characteristics?

FUNDAMENTAL PRINCIPLE: PERFORMANCE

LO 2-3
Describe the fundamental principle of *performance* and identify the major activities performed in an audit.

The fundamental principle of *performance* sets forth general quality criteria for conducting an audit. As noted in the preceding section, in addition to the elements of this principle, the performance of the audit is influenced by the need for auditors to exercise *professional skepticism* and *professional judgment* throughout the audit process. The performance principle states that:

> *To express an opinion, the auditor obtains reasonable assurance about whether the financial statements as a whole are free from material misstatement, whether due to fraud or error. To obtain reasonable assurance, which is a high but not absolute level of assurance, the auditor:*
>
> · *Plans the work and properly supervises any assistants.*
>
> · *Determines and applies appropriate materiality level or levels throughout the audit.*

> · *Identifies and assesses risks of material misstatement, whether due to fraud or error, based on an understanding of the entity and its environment, including the entity's internal control.*
> · *Obtains sufficient appropriate audit evidence about whether material misstatements exist, through designing and implementing appropriate responses to the assessed risks.*

As the preceding reflects, the performance principle contains five elements: (1) reasonable assurance, (2) planning and supervision, (3) materiality, (4) risk assessment, and (5) audit evidence. These are discussed in the remainder of this section.

Reasonable Assurance

The concept of **reasonable assurance** recognizes that a GAAS audit may not detect all material misstatements and auditors are not "insurers" or "guarantors" regarding the fairness of the entity's financial statements. However, auditors should provide a high level of assurance (or confidence) regarding their work. Auditors provide reasonable assurance through considering various risks relating to the likelihood of material misstatement in the financial statements and performing audit procedures to limit the overall risk to an acceptably low level. This is done through the risk assessment process, an additional element of the performance principle.

Planning and Supervision

After obtaining or retaining the engagement, the next major stage of the audit is planning, as in the following figure. The professional standards contain several considerations for planning and supervising an audit. They are concerned with (1) preparing an audit plan and supervising the audit work, (2) obtaining knowledge of the client's business, and (3) dealing with differences of opinion among the accounting firm's own personnel.

GAAS require the preparation of a written audit plan. An **audit plan** is a list of the audit procedures that auditors need to perform to gather sufficient appropriate evidence on which to base their opinion on the financial statements. The procedures in an audit plan should be stated in enough detail to instruct the assistants about the work to be done. (You will see detailed audit plans later in this textbook.)

STAGES OF AN AUDIT

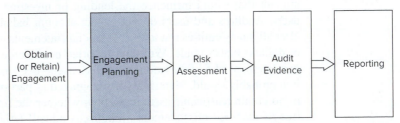

Auditors are also required to obtain an understanding of the client's business and industry. This knowledge helps auditors identify areas for special attention (the accounts or classes of transactions where frauds or errors might exist), evaluate the reasonableness of accounting estimates made by management, evaluate management's responses to inquiries, and make judgments about the appropriateness of management's choices among accounting principles. Auditors gain this understanding of a business through discussions with management and other client personnel; through experience with other entities in the same industry; and by reviewing AICPA accounting and audit guides, industry publications, other entities' financial statements, business periodicals, and textbooks.

Just as having advance notice of assignments and examinations makes it easier for you (as a student) to perform better on those assignments, timing is important for audit planning. To have time to plan an audit, auditors should be engaged before the client's fiscal year-end. The more advance notice auditors have, the better they are able to provide enough time for planning. The audit team may be able to perform part of the audit at an interim date—a date some weeks or months before year-end—and thereby make the rest of the audit work more efficient. For example, in examining property, plant, and equipment, auditors may evaluate activity in the account balance up to some date during the year (say, September 30) prior to year-end (December 31) and then evaluate activity occurring between that date and December 31 following year-end (the roll-forward period), as shown in the following graphic. Essentially, at December 31, auditors have evaluated the account balance through the interim date (in this case, September 30) and will evaluate the remainder of the activity following year-end. Doing so permits audit work to be "shifted" from after year-end to prior to year-end and allows the audit to be completed on a more timely basis.

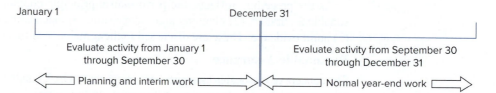

Engagement planning is discussed in greater detail in Chapter 3. In addition, planning activities related to the audit of various accounts and cycles are discussed in Chapters 6, 7 8, 9, and 10.

 AUDITING INSIGHT   Too Late

In its *Form 12b-25* filing with the SEC, **U.S. Premium Beef LLC** disclosed that it dismissed KPMG as its auditor and engaged PwC on February 28, 2012. Because of the late appointment of PwC and its inability to plan and perform the audit on a timely basis (U.S. Premium

Beef had a December 31 year-end), the company was unable to meet the deadline for filing its financial statements with the SEC.

Sources: *U.S. Premium Beef LLC Form 12b-25* (dated March 29, 2012); *U.S. Premium Beef LLC Form 8-K* (dated February 28, 2012).

Materiality

The concept of **materiality** recognizes that auditors should focus on matters that are important to financial statement users. One common way of viewing materiality is the dollar amount that would influence the lending or investing decisions of financial statement users. Auditors and users do not expect account balances to be accurate to the penny; after all, many entities round their financial statements to the thousands, or even millions, of dollars! For example, **Walmart** reported net income of $15 billion in 2016; clearly, a misstatement of $1,000 would not affect users' decisions, but a misstatement of $1 billion probably would. Materiality is recognized as part of the objective of an audit, which is "to obtain reasonable assurance about whether the financial statements as a whole are free of *material* misstatement" [emphasis added] (AU-C 200.12). Materiality is commonly established based on percentages of key financial statement subtotals, such as net income, sales or revenues, and total assets.

The audit team considers materiality in planning the audit, performing the audit, and evaluating the effect of misstatements on the entity's financial statements. Auditors are responsible only for providing reasonable assurance that misstatements *material* to the entity's financial statements are identified. Stated another way, auditors are not responsible for detecting misstatements that are not material to the financial statements.

Although the concept of materiality appears to be relatively straightforward, implementation of materiality during the audit requires high levels of professional judgment. For example, suppose a small dollar misstatement (in absolute terms) resulted in an entity meeting its earnings expectations or resulted in an entity reporting higher earnings than in the previous year. Certainly, these impacts would likely influence investment decisions, even if the dollar amount is relatively small. Circumstances such as these are referred to as qualitative materiality factors and should also be considered by auditors. The role of materiality in the planning stages of the audit is discussed in more detail in Chapter 3.

Risk Assessment

An important part of the performance principle is for auditors to identify important concerns (or risks) they face in the audit. This process is referred to as *risk assessment:*

STAGES OF AN AUDIT

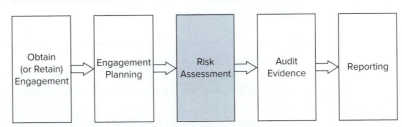

The risk assessment process requires an understanding of the client, its operating environment, and its industry. This includes internal controls operating within the client's accounting information systems that ultimately produce the client's financial statements. **Internal control** may be defined as the policies and procedures implemented by an entity to prevent or detect material accounting frauds or errors and provide for their correction on a timely basis. Satisfactory internal control reduces the probability of frauds or errors in the accounts. This understanding provides the foundation for the work auditors do in assessing the **risk of material misstatement**, a combination of **inherent risk** (the probability that a material misstatement, either an error or fraud, will occur) and **control risk** (the probability that a material misstatement, either an error or fraud, will not be prevented or detected on a timely basis by the entity's internal controls). One way to think of the risk of material misstatement is the likelihood that an error or fraud will exist in the financial statements prior to considering the auditors' work.

The primary purpose of assessing the risk of material misstatement is to help auditors determine the *nature, timing, and extent of further audit procedures* necessary for gathering evidence about the fairness of the entity's financial statements. The process of risk assessment presumes two necessary relationships:

1. Effective internal control reduces the control risk, and auditors thus have a reasonable basis for reducing the necessary effectiveness of further audit procedures.
2. Ineffective internal control increases control risk, and auditors must increase the necessary effectiveness of further audit procedures.

Because these audit procedures are used to obtain evidence with respect to the fairness of the account balance (i.e., to "substantiate" the account balance), they are referred to as **substantive procedures**. The auditors' substantive procedures are reflected in the determination of detection risk, which is discussed in the next section. A depiction of this relationship follows:

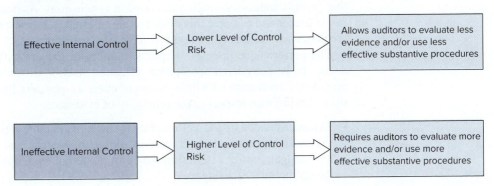

The importance of internal control in the audit examination is evidenced by an increase in auditors' responsibility for internal control in the audit of public entities that auditors evaluate (through testing the operating effectiveness of specific controls) and report on the effectiveness of a public entity's internal control over financial reporting. This is one example of auditors' responsibility in the audit of a public entity exceeding that for the audit of a nonpublic entity. Internal control (and the related reports on internal control) is discussed in more detail in Chapter 5; in addition, important elements of internal control related to the audit of various accounts and cycles are discussed in Chapters 6, 7, 8, 9, and 10.

☑ REVIEW CHECKPOINTS

2.8 Define *reasonable assurance*. How does the audit team provide reasonable assurance in the engagement?

2.9 What is an *audit plan*? During which stage of the audit is an audit plan prepared?

2.10 Why is the timing of the auditors' appointment an important matter in the conduct of a financial statement audit?

2.11 What is *materiality*? During what stages of the audit do auditors consider materiality?

2.12 For what reasons do auditors obtain an understanding of a client's internal control?

2.13 What is the basic relationship between the effectiveness of the client's internal control and the necessary effectiveness of substantive procedures?

Audit Evidence

The final element of the performance principle requires that the audit team collects and evaluates sufficient appropriate evidence to provide a reasonable basis for their opinion.

STAGES OF AN AUDIT

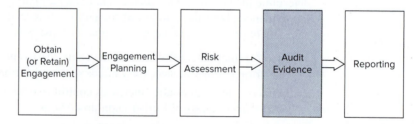

Evidence is the information that auditors use in arriving at the conclusions on which to base the audit opinion and includes the underlying accounting data and all available corroborating information. Examples of evidence include minutes of meetings, confirmations with independent third parties, invoices, analyst reports, and all other information that permits auditors to reach valid, logical conclusions. As noted, the methods auditors use to gather and evaluate this evidence are referred to as *substantive procedures,* which are performed following the auditors' risk assessment process.

The performance principle requires auditors to gather "sufficient appropriate" evidence. To be considered **appropriate**, evidence must be trustworthy (*reliable*) and must provide the audit team with information of interest (*relevant*). Professional standards note the following with respect to the reliability of evidence:

- Evidence created by sources external to the entity is more reliable than that created by the entity. From most to least reliable, sources of evidence are auditors (direct personal knowledge), parties external to the entity (external evidence), and parties internal to the entity (internal evidence).

- Evidence created by sources outside the entity is more reliable when received directly from the external source (direct external evidence) than when received from sources internal to the entity (external-internal evidence).
- Evidence obtained from entities with more effective internal controls is more reliable than that obtained from entities with less effective internal controls.
- Evidence obtained from original source documents is more reliable than that obtained from photocopies, facsimiles, or electronic documents.

AUDITING INSIGHT   Whom Can You Trust?

"The level of fraud and financial deception that took place at Health-South is a blatant violation of investor trust, and Ernst & Young is as outraged as the investing public." In a public statement, the accounting firm asserted that HealthSouth, one of its largest clients, tried to deceive the firm's audit team by creating false documents to support fraudulent journal entries. To support the firm's claim, the statement cited a court hearing in which a former HealthSouth employee testified that "he knew of at least three occasions where company executives prepared false documents specifically to conceal fraud from Ernst."

Source: "Did HealthSouth Auditor Ernst Miss Key Clues to Fraud Risks?" *The Wall Street Journal*, April 10, 2003, pp. C1, C3.

Relevance refers to the nature of information provided by the audit evidence; for example, when auditors confirm accounts receivable with customers, this audit procedure provides evidence that the account is legitimate (i.e., the sale actually took place) but does not provide evidence that the account will ultimately be collectible. The nature of information provided by evidence is operationalized through the management assertions identified and discussed in Chapter 1.

Appropriateness relates to evidence *quality,* and **sufficiency** relates to evidence *quantity.* For large entities, auditors do not audit all of the transactions and components but examine a sample of these items in drawing their conclusions. Sufficiency relates to the number of transactions or components evaluated.

The sufficiency and appropriateness of evidence are reflected in the necessary level of detection risk. **Detection risk** represents the risk that the audit team's substantive procedures will fail to detect a material misstatement. As auditors require a higher quality of evidence (lower detection risk), they must gather more relevant and reliable evidence (appropriateness) and evaluate more transactions or components (sufficiency). Evidence-gathering procedures are discussed in more detail in Chapter 3. In addition, specific approaches to gathering evidence in the examination of various accounts and cycles are discussed in Chapters 6, 7, 8, 9, and 10.

Exhibit 2.1 summarizes the key characteristics of evidence just discussed. Note that both the sufficiency and the appropriateness of audit evidence affect detection risk. Also note that the appropriateness is affected by both the relevance of the evidence and its reliability.

EXHIBIT 2.1
Key Characteristics of Audit Evidence

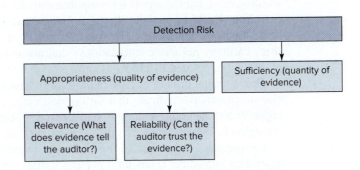

FUNDAMENTAL PRINCIPLE: REPORTING

LO 2-4

Understand the fundamental principle of *reporting* and identify the basic contents of the auditors' report.

The ultimate objective of the audit—the report on the audit—is guided by the fundamental principle of reporting, which states

> *Based on evaluation of the evidence obtained, the auditor expresses in the form of a written report, an opinion in accordance with the auditor's findings, or states that an opinion cannot be expressed. The opinion states whether the financial statements are presented fairly, in all material respects, in accordance with the applicable financial reporting framework.*

As the following graphic shows, reporting is the final stage of an audit and occurs following the gathering of audit evidence.

STAGES OF AN AUDIT

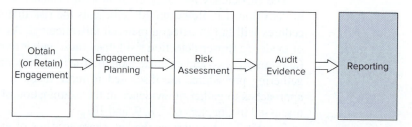

An example of an auditors' report is shown in Exhibit 2.2, and you should review it in relation to the following discussion.

The report in Exhibit 2.2 is the report form used for public entities; differences in wording exist, but the report for nonpublic entities conveys essentially the same information. You should understand the term *financial statements* to include not only the traditional financial statements, but also all footnote disclosures and additional information (e.g., earnings per share calculations) that are integral elements of the basic financial presentation required by GAAP.

The reporting principle requires the auditor to express an opinion on the entity's financial statements (or indicate that an opinion cannot be expressed). With respect to this requirement, the opinion paragraph of Ernst & Young's report begins with the phrase "In our opinion," which represents the expression of an opinion.

In expressing this opinion, the auditor is required to assess the financial statements against an applicable financial reporting framework. A **financial reporting framework** is a

EXHIBIT 2.2 Example Auditors' Report for Public Company (McDonald's Corporation)

Report Title	Report of Independent Registered Public Accounting Firm
Addressee	The Board of Directors and Shareholders of McDonald's Corporation
Introductory Paragraph	We have audited the accompanying consolidated balance sheets of McDonald's Corporation as of December 31, 2015 and 2014, and the related consolidated statements of income, shareholders' equity, and cash flows for each of the three years in the period ended December 31, 2015. These financial statements are the responsibility of the Company's management. Our responsibility is to express an opinion on these financial statements based on our audits.
Scope Paragraph	We conducted our audits in accordance with the standards of the Public Company Accounting Oversight Board (United States). Those standards require that we plan and perform the audit to obtain reasonable assurance about whether the financial statements are free of material misstatement. An audit includes examining, on a test basis, evidence supporting the amounts and disclosures in the financial statements. An audit also includes assessing the accounting principles used and significant estimates made by management, as well as evaluating the overall financial statement presentation. We believe that our audits provide a reasonable basis for our opinion.
Opinion Paragraph	In our opinion, the financial statements referred to above present fairly, in all material respects, the consolidated financial position of McDonald's Corporation at December 31, 2015 and 2014, and the consolidated results of its operations and its cash flows for each of the three years in the period ended December 31, 2015, in conformity with U.S. generally accepted accounting principles.
Internal Control Paragraph	We also have audited, in accordance with the standards of the Public Company Accounting Oversight Board (United States), McDonald's Corporation's internal control over financial reporting as of December 31, 2015, based on criteria established in *Internal Control–Integrated Framework* issued by the Committee of Sponsoring Organizations of the Treadway Commission (2013 framework) and our report dated February 25, 2016 expressed an unqualified opinion thereon.

Ernst & Young LLP (signed)
Chicago, Illinois
February 25, 2016

set of criteria used to determine the measurement, recognition, presentation, and disclosure of material items in the financial statements; three examples of financial reporting frameworks are GAAP, *International Financial Reporting Standards (IFRS)*, or a special purpose framework (such as cash or tax bases). Again, referring to Ernst & Young's report in Exhibit 2.2, the opinion paragraph concludes that **McDonald's** financial statements present its financial condition, results of operations, and cash flows ". . . in conformity with U.S. generally accepted accounting principles" (GAAP). In this case, GAAP are the applicable financial accounting framework.

The report in Exhibit 2.2 is an example of an unmodified (or unqualified) opinion, which concludes that the entity's (in this case, McDonald's) financial statements present its financial condition, results of operations, and cash flows in conformity with GAAP. Other types of opinions that can be expressed include the following:

- An adverse opinion concludes that the entity's financial statements are not presented in conformity with GAAP (or other financial reporting framework such as IFRS).
- A qualified opinion concludes that *except for* a relatively isolated (usually limited) departure, the entity's financial statements are presented in conformity with GAAP (or other financial reporting framework, such as IFRS).
- In some cases (e.g., if the auditors lack independence), auditors may choose not to express an opinion on the entity's financial statements. This type of report is referred to as a disclaimer of opinion. (A disclaimer of opinion is an indication that an opinion cannot be expressed.)

When these situations are encountered, auditors add an explanatory paragraph to their report and would then modify some of the paragraphs of the report shown in Exhibit 2.2. These and other report modifications are discussed further in Chapter 12.

One important phrase in the opinion paragraph is "in all material respects. . . ." The concept of materiality has been discussed previously as part of the *performance* principle; used in a reporting context, it communicates that the audit team is unaware of any material misstatements in the financial statements. The choice of report (unqualified, qualified, or adverse) depends on the nature and materiality (significance) of the effect of the GAAP departure.

The report shown in Exhibit 2.2 expresses the auditors' conclusion on the fairness of McDonald's financial statements. The last paragraph of this report references a report on McDonald's internal control over financial reporting. This report is also presented along with McDonald's financial statements and expresses the auditors' conclusion regarding the effectiveness of McDonald's internal control over financial reporting. This report and the process through which auditors evaluate the effectiveness of internal control are discussed in Chapter 5. Audit reporting is discussed in greater detail in Chapter 12.

☑ REVIEW CHECKPOINTS

2.19 What is a *financial reporting framework?* How is it related to the auditors' reporting responsibilities?

2.20 What are the four types of audit opinions? What is the conclusion of each one?

EVALUATING THE QUALITY OF PUBLIC ACCOUNTING FIRMS' PRACTICES

LO 2-5
Understand the role of a system of quality control and monitoring efforts in enabling public accounting firms to meet appropriate levels of professional quality.

To this point in the chapter, we have discussed the professional standards related to audit engagements. Many organizations are interested in ensuring that public accounting firms meet these engagement standards and maintain high levels of quality in their practices. For example, the SEC provides general oversight of the accounting and auditing professions, investigates audit failures (situations in which auditors fail to detect material financial statement misstatements), and levies fines against firms that have been found negligent in conducting audits. In addition, the PCAOB inspects the work of audit firms to ensure that their audits comply with professional standards.[9]

However, one important issue that has not been addressed is the nature of actions that firms themselves routinely take to ensure that their work is of high quality and meets the professional standards discussed in this chapter. For example, how do firms ensure that the personnel assigned to engagements are independent with respect to the client and have the appropriate level of competence to handle the assignment? What process do firms use when deciding either to accept or continue an audit engagement? The answers to these and other questions are reflected in policies and procedures that firms implement as part of a system of quality control, which is the focus of this section.

System of Quality Control

Statement on Quality Control Standards No. 8 (SQCS 8), "A Firm's System of Quality Control," notes that the purpose of a **system of quality control** is to provide the firm reasonable assurance that the firm and its personnel:

- Comply with professional standards and applicable regulatory and legal requirements.
- Issue reports that are appropriate in the circumstances.

[9]Firms auditing only nonpublic entities undergo a peer review process conducted by the AICPA's National Peer Review Committee.

Simply stated, a system of quality control is implemented by firms to ensure that their work is of high quality and meets the expectations of professional standards. Section 103 of Sarbanes–Oxley established broad areas of quality control standards that were required of registered public accounting firms. These areas serve as the basis for the following six elements of a system of quality control identified by *SQCS 8:*

1. **Leadership responsibilities for quality within the firm ("tone at the top").** Undoubtedly, you have heard the phrase "leadership by example." In order for quality control standards to be effective, it is important that the firm's management take a lead role in clearly and consistently demonstrating its own commitment to quality control and high-quality work. Doing so will make it clear to all personnel that high-quality work is valued and will be rewarded. Some examples of how this can be done include

   - Assigning management responsibilities in such a manner that financial considerations do not override the quality of work performed.
   - Basing performance evaluation, compensation, and promotion opportunities for personnel on the quality of work performed.
   - Devoting sufficient resources for developing, communicating, and supporting the firm's quality control policies and procedures.

   It may seem unusual to specify that personnel decisions should be based on the quality of work performed. After all, what other basis should be used? Both the Enron and WorldCom cases provided anecdotal evidence that suggested the fear of losing a key client (and the impact of that loss on individual auditors' performance evaluations and opportunities within the firm) contributed to the audit failures in those cases.

2. **Relevant ethical requirements.** Earlier in this chapter, we discussed independence and the importance of independence to the auditing profession. Firms should take various actions to ensure that personnel assigned to engagements are both independent in fact and independent in appearance with respect to the firm's clients, such as

   - Communicating independence requirements to personnel.
   - Identifying circumstances and relationships that create threats to independence and taking appropriate action to eliminate those threats or reduce them to an acceptable level.
   - Obtaining written confirmation from all firm personnel with respect to their compliance with appropriate independence requirements.

3. **Acceptance and continuance of client relationships and specific engagements.** As discussed in Chapter 3, one of the most important decisions facing an audit firm is that of accepting an engagement (for a new client) or continuing to perform an engagement (for an existing client). When making this decision, firms should focus on three important issues:

   1. The integrity and business reputation of the client.
   2. The firm's ability to adequately perform the engagement with an appropriate level of professional competence.
   3. The firm's ability to comply with legal and ethical requirements related to the engagement.

   The purpose of this process is to avoid association with a client whose management lacks integrity and to ensure that the firm can perform the engagement at an appropriate level.

   If firms decide to withdraw from an engagement after considering the preceding matters, *SQCS 8* notes that the firm should document significant issues, consultations, conclusions, and the basis for any conclusions related to its decision to withdraw.

4. **Human resources.** The quality of any professional services organization (such as an audit firm) is based on the quality of its people. Effective quality control policies and procedures should be implemented to ensure that firms hire quality personnel, assign these personnel to engagements for which they have the appropriate capabilities, provide

professional development opportunities to those individuals, and effectively evaluate, compensate, and promote them. These practices will increase the likelihood that a high-quality audit is conducted by ensuring that the firm has high-quality personnel and that these individuals have the ability to assume the responsibilities assigned to them.

5. **Engagement performance.** The performance principle (discussed earlier in this chapter) addressed a number of significant issues related to the conduct of an audit engagement. Firms frequently use manuals and other standardized forms of documentation to meet the preceding objectives.

   An important element of quality control is the practice of conducting **engagement quality control reviews** for engagements meeting specified criteria identified by the firm (for example, engagements in a highly volatile industry or engagements that meet certain risk criteria). An engagement quality control review includes an internal evaluation of the significant judgments made by the audit team and the conclusions reached in formulating its report.

6. **Monitoring.** The purpose of monitoring is to provide the firm with reasonable assurance that policies and procedures composing the system of quality control are operating effectively and complied with in practice. Examples of procedures used to monitor quality control include

   - Reviews of selected administrative and personnel records.
   - Reviews of engagement documentation, reports, and the client's financial statements.
   - Discussions with firm personnel.
   - Assessments of the (1) appropriateness of the firm's guidance materials and professional aids, (2) compliance with policies and procedures on independence, (3) effectiveness of continuing professional education, and (4) decisions regarding the acceptance and continuance of client relationships and specific engagements.

Firms may accomplish these monitoring activities through either an ongoing post-issuance review of engagement documentation or targeted inspection procedures for a sample of engagements conducted by the firm.

PCAOB Inspection of Firms

Earlier in this chapter, we addressed the role of the PCAOB in establishing auditing standards. In addition to this role, the PCAOB is charged with *monitoring* the quality of work performed by firms auditing public entities and bringing appropriate action against those firms if substandard work is identified. This monitoring is referred to as an **inspection** and is conducted as follows:

- For firms performing audits of more than 100 public entities, inspections are conducted on an annual basis.
- For firms performing audits of 100 or fewer public entities, inspections are conducted at least every three years.

Based on information from the PCAOB's website, more than 2,000 accounting firms are registered with the PCAOB. As of January 1, 2016, 569 of these firms issue audit reports but only 10 were required to have annual inspections because they conducted audits for more than 100 companies.

PCAOB inspections are conducted by individuals chosen by the PCAOB who are full-time employees of the PCAOB. These inspections consist of a review of a sample of audit engagements conducted by the firm as well as an overall evaluation of the firm's system of quality control (policies related to audit performance, training, compliance with independence requirements, and client management). Copies of the PCAOB's inspection reports can be found (on a firm-by-firm basis) on the PCAOB's website. These reports detail the deficiencies identified by the PCAOB on the sample of audit engagements (the name of the client is not identified); information regarding deficiencies in the firm's quality control are not publicly disclosed and will be disclosed only if the firm fails to address those deficiencies within a year following the inspection. One challenge facing the PCAOB is

AUDITING INSIGHT · No Inspections for Alibaba

Alibaba Group Holding Limited is a Chinese e-commerce company that provides sales, electronic payment, search, and cloud computing services.

While Alibaba trades on the New York Stock Exchange, it is based in China and audited by a Hong Kong affiliate of PwC. Because China bars PCAOB inspections, Alibaba's shareholders are not provided with the potential benefits and improvements in audit quality resulting from these inspections. In fact, one of the risk factors identified by Alibaba in its most recent annual report is that the lack of PCAOB inspections

may result in lower confidence of shareholders in their reported financial information and quality of their financial statements. However, recent developments suggest that the PCAOB may be granted access to review audits of Alibaba and **Baidu** (a Chinese web services company).

Source: "Alibaba's SEC Probe: The Red Flags Are Flying Higher," *The Wall Street Journal*, May 26, 2016, p. C8; "Overheard," *The Wall Street Journal*, May 27, 2016, p. C8.; "U.S. May Finally Get a Peek at the Books of Alibaba, Baidu," *The Wall Street Journal Online*, August 5, 2016.

a limitation imposed on the ability to investigate audits conducted by foreign affiliates of U.S. firms, as noted in the Auditing Insight "No Inspections for Alibaba".

A study by Church and Shefchik[10] on the inspection reports of large accounting firms (those auditing more than 100 issuers) from 2005 to 2009 concluded that:

- The most frequent deficiencies cited by the PCAOB were related to the failure to gather or document sufficient audit support (53.3 percent of deficiencies) followed by the failure of the firm to adequately evaluate an accounting issue (28.0 percent of deficiencies).
- 11.4 percent of all identified deficiencies resulted in accounting misstatements.
- The number of deficiencies has significantly declined over the period investigated.[11]

The Auditing Insight "Grading the Firms" provides a summary of reported deficiencies for audits conducted by Big Four firms. Although that information summarizes audits conducted by large accounting firms, evidence suggests that a significant number of deficiencies has also been observed in audits conducted by smaller firms.[12]

AUDITING INSIGHT · Grading the Firms

Year	Number of Audits Inspected	Audits in Which Deficiencies Were Identified	Number of Deficiencies Identified	Audits in Which Departure from GAAP Not Identified by Firms	Audits in Which Report on Internal Control was Revised
2015 reports (2014 audits)	217	76	158	1	7
2014 reports (2013 audits)	215	86	176	4	5
2013 reports (2012 audits)	205	76	179	5	2

These results illustrate a general decrease in the number of audits in which a deficiency was identified as well as the number of deficiencies identified. In addition, the number of audits in which the deficiency resulted in a failure to identify a departure from GAAP is still relatively small. Both of these findings suggest that audit quality is

improving as a result of PCAOB inspections. However, it appears that inspections have resulted in an increasing number of revisions to auditors' reports and opinions on internal control over financial reporting.

Source: PCAOB website (http://pcaobus.org/Inspections/Reports/Pages/default.aspx).

---

[10]B. Church and L. Shefchik, "PCAOB Inspections and Large Accounting Firms," *Accounting Horizons*, March 2012, pp. 43–63.

[11]For a summary of inspection reports issued to smaller accounting firms (those with 100 or fewer issuer clients), see D. R. Hermanson, R. W. Houston, and J. C. Rice, "PCAOB Inspections of Smaller CPA Firms: Initial Evidence from Inspection Reports," *Accounting Horizons*, June 2007, pp. 137–152. In addition, B. Daugherty and W. Tervo, "PCAOB Inspections of Smaller CPA Firms: The Perspective of Inspected Firms," *Accounting Horizons*, June 2010, pp. 189–219 provide an interesting summary of the perceptions of smaller CPA firms to the PCAOB's inspection process.

[12]"Smaller Auditors Get So-So Grades," *The Wall Street Journal*, February 26, 2013, p. C2.

The very public nature of the PCAOB inspection process and controversies surrounding that process raise the question as to whether inspection reports measure audit quality and are useful to various parties in their decision processes. The following Auditing Insight summarizes academic research that examined how the inspection process and results influence the behavior of both audit firms and their clients. The PCAOB recently indicated that it is considering shifting the focus of its investigations from evaluating audit deficiencies to assessing the firms' systems of quality control.[13]

AUDITING INSIGHT | Academic Research on PCAOB Inspections

- Abbott et al. concluded that clients were more likely to dismiss smaller (triennially inspected) audit firms when those firms received PCAOB inspection reports indicating that they failed to detect a departure from GAAP.

- Gramling et al. found that audit firms receiving a PCAOB inspection report that identified deficiencies were more likely to issue more severe audit opinions for clients experiencing financial difficulties following the inspection report compared to prior to the inspection report.

- Nagy concluded that audit firms receiving public disclosure of quality control criticisms suffered a significant loss in market share, consistent with perceptions that these reports are credible signals of audit quality.

- Abbott et al. found that auditors having favorable inspection reports received more favorable selection recommendations than those having unfavorable inspection reports.

- Lamoreaux found that audit firms subject to PCAOB inspections in a nonmandatory inspection regime conducted higher qual-

ity audits (as measured by a greater incidence of issuing going-concern opinions and reporting material weaknesses in internal control and lower client earnings management activities).

Sources: L. J. Abbott, K. A. Gunny, and T. C. Zhang, "When the PCAOB Talks, Who Listens? Evidence from Stakeholder Reaction to GAAP-Deficient PCAOB Inspection Reports of Small Auditors," *Auditing: A Journal of Practice & Theory,* May 2013, pp. 1–31; A. A. Gramling, J. Krishnan, and Y. Zhang, "Are PCAOB-Identified Audit Deficiencies Associated with a Change in Reporting Decisions of Triennially Inspected Audit Firms?" *Auditing: A Journal of Practice & Theory,* August 2011, pp. 59–79; A. L. Nagy, "PCAOB Quality Control Inspection Reports and Auditor Reputation," *Auditing: A Journal of Practice & Theory,* August 2014, pp. 87–104; L. J. Abbott, V. L. Brown, and J. L. Higgs, "The Effects of Prior Manager-Auditor Affiliation and PCAOB Inspection Reports on Audit Committee Members' Auditor Recommendations," *Behavioral Research in Accounting,* Spring 2016, pp. 1–14; P. T. Lamoreaux, "Does PCAOB Inspection Access Improve Audit Quality? An Examination of Foreign Firms Listed in the United States," *Journal of Accounting and Economics,* April–May 2016, pp. 313–337.

☑ REVIEW CHECKPOINTS

2.21 What is a *system of quality control*? Identify the six elements of a system of quality control.

2.22 What factors should auditors consider in deciding whether to accept or continue the engagement with a particular client? What should firms do if they decide to withdraw from an engagement?

2.23 Provide examples of procedures that firms have used to monitor their quality control policies and procedures.

2.24 What role does the PCAOB play in connection with monitoring and regulating public accounting firms?

2.25 How frequently are firms required to have PCAOB inspections?

Summary

This chapter discussed the professional standards that apply to audit engagements and identified important mechanisms that enable public accounting firms to provide professional services to meet those standards. From an auditing standpoint, generally accepted auditing standards form the basis for professional engagements and the necessary

---

[13]"Auditing the Auditors: U.S. Rethinks Approach," *The Wall Street Journal Online,* May 6, 2016.

qualifications and characteristics of auditors. These standards are based on three basic principles, which reflect the overall conduct of the audit examination:

1. Responsibilities, which require auditors to possess competence and capabilities, comply with relevant ethical requirements, maintain professional skepticism, and exercise professional judgment.
2. Performance, which involves planning the work and supervising assistants, determining and applying appropriate materiality levels, identifying and assessing the risk of material misstatement, and obtaining sufficient appropriate audit evidence.
3. Reporting, which requires that auditors express an opinion about the fairness of the entity's financial statements.

To provide reasonable assurance of compliance with these standards, firms develop systems of quality control that prescribe policies and procedures related to (1) the responsibilities of firm leadership for quality, (2) ethical requirements, (3) acceptance and continuance of client relationships and specific engagements, (4) human resources, (5) engagement performance, and (6) monitoring of the effectiveness of the system of quality control. Under Sarbanes–Oxley, firms conducting audits of public entities are required to have inspections of selected engagements and their systems of quality control by the PCAOB. The purpose of these inspections is to identify deficiencies in engagements conducted by the firms and provide suggestions for improvements in their systems of quality control.

Following is a summary of the professional standards and monitoring activities for audits of public and nonpublic entities.

	Professional Standards	Monitoring Requirements
Public entity	*Auditing Standards* issued by the PCAOB	Annual or triennial inspections conducted by the PCAOB (frequency depends upon number of audits performed by the firm)
Nonpublic entity	*Statements on Auditing Standards* issued by the ASB of the AICPA	Triennial peer reviews conducted through the AICPA National Peer Review Committee

Key Terms

American Institute of Certified Public Accountants (AICPA): As related to professional auditing standards, the body charged with establishing auditing standards for the audits of nonpublic entities through *Statements on Auditing Standards (SASs)* issued by the Auditing Standards Board.

appropriate (audit evidence): Characteristics related to the quality (relevance and reliability) of audit evidence.

audit plan: A comprehensive list of the specific audit procedures that the audit team needs to perform to gather sufficient appropriate evidence on which to base their opinion on the financial statements.

audit procedures: The specialized actions auditors take to obtain evidence in an engagement.

auditing standards: The audit quality guides that apply to all audits.

control risk: The likelihood that the client's internal control policies and procedures fail to prevent or detect a material misstatement.

detection risk: The likelihood that the auditors' substantive procedures will fail to detect a material misstatement that exists within an account balance or class of transactions.

due care: A level of performance that would be exercised by reasonable auditors in similar circumstances; auditors are expected to possess the skills and knowledge of others in their profession and are not expected to be infallible.

engagement quality control review: An internal evaluation of the significant judgments made by the audit team and the conclusions reached in formulating its report on an engagement conducted by that firm.

evidence: The information used by auditors in arriving at the conclusion on which the audit opinion is based, which includes the underlying accounting data and all available corroborating information.

financial reporting framework: The financial reporting standards (i.e., GAAP, IFRS, etc.) adopted by management and, when appropriate, those charged with governance (audit committee or board of directors) in the preparation of the financial statements.

generally accepted auditing standards (GAAS): Standards that identify necessary qualifications and characteristics of auditors and guide the conduct of the audit examination.

independence in appearance: The extent to which others (particularly financial statement users) perceive auditors to be independent.

independence in fact: Auditors' mental attitude and impartiality with respect to the client.

inherent risk: The probability that in the absence of internal controls, material errors or frauds could enter the accounting system used to develop financial statements.

inspection: An evaluation of an accounting firm's audit engagements and system of quality control conducted by the PCAOB and required for any firms providing auditing services to public entities.

internal control: A process, effected by an entity's board of directors, management, and other personnel, designed to provide reasonable assurance regarding the achievement of objectives in the reliability of financial reporting, the effectiveness and efficiency of operations, and compliance with applicable laws and regulations.

materiality: An amount or event that is likely to influence financial statement users' decisions.

professional judgment: The application of relevant training, knowledge, and experience in making informed decisions about appropriate courses of action during the audit engagement.

professional skepticism: A state of mind that is characterized by appropriate questioning and a critical assessment of audit evidence.

Public Company Accounting Oversight Board (PCAOB): As related to professional auditing standards, the body charged with establishing auditing standards for the audits of public entities through the issuance of *Auditing Standards*. The PCAOB is also responsible for inspecting firms that perform audits of public entities.

public entity: An entity that offers registered securities, such as stock and bonds, for sale to the general public.

reasonable assurance: The concept that recognizes that the costs of control activities should not exceed the benefits that are expected from the control activities.

risk of material misstatement: The combined probability that a material misstatement (error or fraud) will occur and not be prevented or detected on a timely basis by the entity's internal controls. The risk of material misstatement is a combination of inherent and control risk.

substantive procedures: The detailed audit and analytical procedures designed to detect material misstatements in account balances and footnote disclosures.

sufficiency (audit evidence): The measure of the quantity of audit evidence (the number of transactions or components evaluated).

system of quality control: The policies and procedures implemented by a firm to provide with reasonable assurance that the firm and its personnel (1) comply with professional standards and applicable regulatory and legal requirements and (2) issue reports that are appropriate in the circumstances.

Multiple-Choice Questions for Practice and Review

All applicable questions are available with *Connect*.

LO 2-3

2.26 Which of the following categories of principles is most closely related to gathering audit evidence?
   a. Performance.
   b. Reasonable assurance.
   c. Reporting.
   d. Responsibilities.

LO 2-2

2.27 Which of the following is *not* related to ethical requirements of auditors?
   a. Due care.
   b. Independence in appearance.
   c. Independence in fact.
   d. Professional judgment.

LO 2-5

2.28 One of an accounting firm's basic objectives is to provide professional services that conform to professional standards. Reasonable assurance of achieving this objective can be obtained by following
   a. Generally accepted auditing standards.
   b. Standards within a system of quality control.
   c. Generally accepted accounting principles.
   d. International auditing standards.

LO 2-2

2.29 Which of the following best demonstrates the concept of professional skepticism?
   a. Relying more extensively on external evidence rather than internal evidence.
   b. Focusing on items that have a more significant quantitative effect on the entity's financial statements.
   c. Critically assessing verbal evidence received from the entity's management.
   d. Evaluating potential financial interests held by auditors in the client.

LO 2-3

2.30 The primary purpose for obtaining an understanding of the entity's environment (including its internal control) in a financial statement audit is
   a. To determine the nature, timing, and extent of substantive procedures to be performed.
   b. To make consulting suggestions to the entity's management.
   c. To obtain direct sufficient appropriate audit evidence to afford a reasonable basis for an opinion on the financial statements.
   d. To determine whether the entity has changed any accounting principles.

LO 2-3

2.31 Ordinarily, what source of evidence should least affect audit conclusions?
   a. External documentary evidence.
   b. Inquiry of management.
   c. Documentation prepared by the audit team.
   d. Inquiry of entity legal counsel.

LO 2-3

2.32 The most reliable evidence regarding the existence of newly acquired computer equipment is
   a. Inquiry of management.
   b. Documentation prepared externally.
   c. Evaluation of the client's procedures.
   d. Physical observation.

LO 2-3

2.33 Which of the following procedures would provide the most reliable audit evidence?
   a. Inquiries of the client's internal audit staff.
   b. Inspection of prenumbered client purchase orders filed in the vouchers payable department.
   c. Inspection of vendor sales invoices received from client personnel.
   d. Inspection of bank statements obtained directly from the client's financial institution.

LO 2-3

2.34   Breaux & Co. CPAs require that all audit documentation indicate the identity of the preparer and the reviewer. This procedure provides evidence relating to which of the following?

a. Independence.

b. Adequate competence and capabilities.

c. Adequate planning and supervision.

d. Gathering sufficient appropriate evidence.

LO 2-2

2.35   Which of the following concepts is *least* related to the standard of due care?

a. Independence in fact.

b. Professional skepticism.

c. Prudent auditor.

d. Reasonable assurance.

LO 2-3

2.36   The evidence considered most appropriate by auditors is best described as

a. Internal documents such as sales invoice copies produced under conditions of strong internal control.

b. Written representations made by the president of the entity.

c. Documentary evidence obtained directly from independent external sources.

d. Direct personal knowledge obtained through physical observation and mathematical recalculation.

LO 2-3

2.37   Auditors' understanding of the internal control in an entity provides information for

a. Determining whether members of the audit team have the required competence and capabilities to perform the audit.

b. Ascertaining the independence in mental attitude of members of the audit team.

c. Planning the professional development courses the audit staff needs to keep up to date with new auditing standards.

d. Planning the nature, timing, and extent of substantive procedures on an audit.

LO 2-5

2.38   Which of the following elements of a system of quality control is related to firms receiving independence confirmations from its professionals with respect to clients?

a. Acceptance and continuance of client relationships and specific engagements.

b. Engagement performance.

c. Monitoring.

d. Relevant ethical requirements.

LO 2-2

2.39   Which of the following is most closely related to the responsibilities principle?

a. The auditors' responsibility to issue a report as a result of their examination.

b. The requirement that auditors gather sufficient, appropriate evidence upon which to base an opinion on the financial statements.

c. The auditors' compliance with relevant ethical requirements of independence and due care.

d. The auditors' responsibility to plan the audit and properly supervise assistants.

LO 2-2

2.40   Kramer, CPA, consulted an independent appraiser regarding the valuation of fine art for a not-for-profit museum. Consultation with the appraiser in this case would

a. Be considered as exercising proper due care.

b. Be considered a failure to follow generally accepted auditing standards because Kramer should have known how to value fine art before accepting the engagement.

c. Not be considered a violation of generally accepted auditing standards because generally accepted auditing standards does not apply to not-for-profit entities.

d. None of the above.

LO 2-4

2.41   Which of the following topics is *not* addressed in the auditors' report for a public entity?

a. Responsibilities of the auditor and management in the financial reporting process.

b. Absolute assurance regarding the fairness of the entity's financial statements in accordance with GAAP.

c. A description of an audit engagement.

d. A summary of the auditors' opinion on the effectiveness of the entity's internal control over financial reporting.

LO 2-3

2.42 Which of the following recognizes that an audit conducted under generally accepted auditing standards may not detect all material misstatements?

a. Absolute assurance.

b. Professional judgment.

c. Reliability of audit evidence.

d. Reasonable assurance.

LO 2-3

2.43 Which of the following combinations would provide the auditor the most reliable evidence?

Source of Evidence	Effectiveness of Internal Control
a. Internal	More effective
b. Internal	Less effective
c. External	More effective
d. External	Less effective

LO 2-3

2.44 Which of the following is most closely related to the relevance of audit evidence?

a. Auditors decide to physically inspect investment securities held by a custodian instead of obtaining confirmations from the custodian.

b. In addition to confirmations of accounts receivable, auditors perform an analysis of the aging of accounts receivable to evaluate the collectability of accounts receivable.

c. In response to less effective internal control, auditors increase the number of customer accounts receivable confirmations mailed compared to that in the prior year.

d. Because of a large number of transactions occurring near year-end, auditors decide to confirm a larger number of receivables following year-end instead of during the interim period.

LO 2-3

2.45 Which of the following statements is *not* true with respect to the performance principle?

a. Auditors are required to prepare a written audit plan during the planning stages of initial audits but are not required to do so in continuing audits.

b. Audit teams consider materiality in planning the audit, performing the audit, and evaluating the effect of misstatements on the entity's financial statements.

c. In assessing the risk of material misstatements, the audit team considers the effectiveness of the entity's internal controls in preventing and detecting misstatements.

d. Auditors are required to consider both the relevance and the reliability of evidence in evaluating whether the evidence they have gathered is appropriate.

LO 2-5

2.46 Which of the following is true with respect to PCAOB inspections of accounting firms?

a. All firms performing audits of public companies are required to have annual inspections conducted by the PCAOB.

b. PCAOB inspections review a sample of audits conducted by firms as well as the firm's systems of quality control.

c. All results of PCAOB inspections are made available to the public following the inspection.

d. Firms performing audits of 100 or fewer public entities may elect to have a peer review conducted through the AICPA in lieu of a PCAOB inspection.

LO 2-1

2.47 The particular and specialized actions that auditors take to obtain evidence during a specific engagement are known as

a. Audit procedures.

b. Audit standards.

c. Interpretive publications.

d. *Statements on Auditing Standards.*

LO 2-1

2.48 Which of the following combinations of standards and types of audits are most closely related to the activities of the Public Company Accounting Oversight Board?

a. Develop *Auditing Standards* for the audits of nonpublic entities.

b. Develop *Auditing Standards* for the audits of public entities.

c. Develop *Statements on Auditing Standards* for the audits of nonpublic entities.

d. Develop *Statements on Auditing Standards* for the audits of public entities.

LO 2-4

2.49 Which of the following best describes the general contents of the introductory paragraph of the auditors' report?

a. A description of an audit examination, including the fact that the audit was conducted under standards established by the PCAOB.

b. The auditors' conclusion with respect to the fairness of the entity's financial statements.

c. Statements identifying the responsibility of auditors and management in the financial reporting process.

d. The auditors' conclusion with respect to the effectiveness of the entity's internal control over financial reporting.

LO 2-4

2.50 Which of the following opinions would be issued if auditors believed that the entity's financial statements were *not* presented in conformity with GAAP?

a. Adverse opinion.

b. Disclaimer of opinion.

c. Qualified opinion.

d. Unmodified opinion.

LO 2-4

2.51 Which of the following principles is most closely associated with the auditors' conclusion as to the fair presentation of the entity's financial statements?

a. Communication principle.

b. Performance principle.

c. Reporting principle.

d. Responsibilities principle.

Exercises and Problems

 All applicable questions are available with *Connect*.

LO 2-1, 2-5

2.52 **AICPA and PCAOB Responsibilities.** The creation of the PCAOB by the Sarbanes–Oxley Act has affected both the standards-setting process and the periodic review of the quality of an audit firm's work.

Required:

a. Identify the responsibilities of the AICPA, PCAOB, and SEC in the auditing standards-setting process.

b. Which standard(s) provide guidance for the audits of public entities? Which standard(s) provide guidance for the audits of nonpublic entities?

c. What role do the AICPA and PCAOB play in the periodic review of the quality of audit firms' work?

LO 2-1

2.53 **Professional Guidance.** A challenge facing auditors is the wide array of professional guidance available to them in the audits of different types of entities.

Required:

Describe *Statements on Auditing Standards* and *Auditing Standards*. In your description, identify which professional body(ies) is(are) responsible for issuing the standards and the types of audits in which the standards are applicable.

LO 2-2

2.54 **Independence.** You are meeting with executives of Cooper Cosmetics Corporation to arrange your firm's engagement to audit the corporation's financial statements for the year ending December 31. One executive suggests the audit work be divided among three staff members. One person would examine asset accounts, a second would examine liability accounts, and the third would examine income and expense accounts to minimize audit time, avoid duplication of staff effort, and curtail interference with entity operations.

Advertising is the corporation's largest expense, and the advertising manager suggests that a staff member of your firm whose uncle owns the advertising agency that handles the corporation's advertising be assigned to examine the Advertising Expense account because the staff member has a thorough knowledge of the complex contact between Cooper Cosmetics and the advertising agency.

Required:

   a. To what extent should auditors follow the client's suggestions for the conduct of an audit? Discuss.

   b. List and discuss the reasons that audit work should not be assigned solely according to asset, liability, and income and expense categories.

   c. Should the staff member of your accounting firm whose uncle owns the advertising agency be assigned to examine advertising costs? Discuss.

LO 2-2

2.55 **Independence.** Generally accepted auditing standards require auditors to be independent. Included within this standard are the concepts of independence in fact and independence in appearance.

Required:

   a. Define *independence in fact* and *independence in appearance.*

   b. What two general types of relationships would normally compromise auditors' independence?

   c. For each of the following separate situations, discuss whether you believe the auditors' independence has been compromised.

     1. The auditors' firm provides extensive consulting services to the client; these services provide revenues to the firm that exceed revenues received from the audit engagement.

     2. The spouse of the partner in charge of the audit engagement occupies an executive-level position within the client.

     3. A distant relative of a partner within the firm occupies an entry-level position within a client of the firm. (The audit is conducted by another office of the firm with which the partner has infrequent contact.)

     4. A staff member within the firm owns shares of stock of one of that firm's clients. (She is not a member of the engagement team serving that client.)

LO 2-2

2.56 **Professional Skepticism.** An important principle for auditors is the need to maintain an appropriate level of professional skepticism.

Required:

   a. Define *professional skepticism.*

   b. During which stages of the audit are auditors required to exhibit professional skepticism?

   c. How does each of the following independent issues potentially relate to the principle of professional skepticism?

     1. The auditor's firm has served the client for a long period of time, and strong friendships have developed between the firm personnel and client's officers.

     2. Auditors are anxious to complete the audit shortly because of other workload demands and deadlines related to other engagements.

     3. The client has mentioned on a number of occasions its desire to reduce (or limit) the audit fee.

LO 2-2

2.57 **Responsibilities Principle.** Martin is considering submitting a proposal to conduct the audit examination of Phillip Inc., a manufacturer and distributor of automotive parts to the large automobile manufacturers. Martin learned of this client opportunity through one of its staff accountants, who is a cousin of Phillip's chief financial officer. In evaluating this opportunity, Martin first inquired with Phillip as to the reason for a change in auditors and was assured that the former auditors decided not to continue auditing Phillip Inc. because it no longer possessed the necessary expertise to audit clients in the automotive parts industry. A conversation with Phillip's former auditors confirmed this explanation, so Martin is currently evaluating this opportunity.

Phillip is a particularly attractive engagement for Martin because it would allow the firm to enter into the manufacturing market. Most of Martin's clients are in the services industry and are much smaller than Phillip. Martin is concerned about the numerous locations of Phillip's warehouses and the ability to conduct an appropriate observation of Phillip's year-end inventory balances; however, Martin's staff accountant noted that the firm could engage component auditors to assist with this aspect of the audit engagement. As a manufacturing entity, inventory (and the related cost of goods sold) is highly material to Phillip's financial statements. Alternatively, Phillip indicated that its previous auditors would observe physical inventory at the different warehouses on different days, reducing the need for them to rely on the work of others. To ensure that inventory was not transferred from one location to another and "double counted," the auditors obtained a written statement from Phillip indicating that no such transfers occurred.

After considering these factors, Martin has decided to submit a proposal for the audit of Phillip. If accepted, Martin will take appropriate actions to ensure that the appropriate firm personnel are independent in fact and in appearance with respect to Phillip.

Required:

Identify issues related to the responsibilities principle that Martin should consider in its decision to submit a proposal to conduct the audit of Phillip.

LO 2-3

2.58 **Performance Principle: Planning.** Your public accounting practice is located in a city of 15,000 people. The majority of your work, conducted by you and two assistants, consists of compiling clients' monthly statements and preparing income tax returns for individuals from cash data and partnership returns from books and records. You have a small number of audit clients; given the current size of your practice, you generally consider it a challenge to accept new audit clients.

One of your corporate clients is a retail hardware store. Your work for this client has been limited to preparing the corporate income tax return from a trial balance submitted by the bookkeeper.

On December 26, you receive from the president of the corporation a letter containing the following request:

We have made arrangements with First National Bank to borrow $500,000 to finance the purchase of a complete line of appliances. The bank has asked us to furnish our auditors' certified statement as of December 31, which is the closing date of our accounting year. The trial balance of the general ledger should be ready by January 10, which should allow ample time to prepare your report for submission to the bank by January 20. In view of the importance of this certified report to our financing program, we trust you will arrange to comply with the preceding schedule.

Required:

From a theoretical viewpoint, discuss the difficulties that are caused by such a short notice audit request.

(AICPA adapted)

LO 2-3

2.59 **Performance Principle: Evidence.** Generally accepted auditing standards (the performance principle) require auditors to gather *sufficient appropriate* evidence on which to base an opinion.

Required:

a. Briefly define the characteristics "sufficient" and "appropriate" as they relate to audit evidence.
b. What are *relevance* and *reliability* (as they relate to audit evidence)? How do these concepts relate to the auditors' requirement to gather sufficient appropriate evidence?
c. How does the source of evidence affect its reliability?
d. How does the effectiveness of the entity's internal control affect the sufficiency and appropriateness of evidence gathered by auditors?

LO 2-3

2.60 **Performance Principle.** You have accepted the engagement of auditing the financial statements of the C. Reis Company, a small manufacturing firm that has been your client for several years. Because you were busy writing the report for another engagement, you sent a staff accountant to begin the audit with the suggestion that she start with accounts receivable. Using the prior year's audit documentation as a guide, she prepared a trial balance of the accounts, aged them, prepared and mailed positive confirmation requests, examined underlying support for charges and credits, and performed other work she considered necessary to obtain evidence about the validity and collectability of the receivables. At the conclusion of her work, you reviewed the audit documentation she prepared and found she had carefully followed the prior year's audit documentation.

Required:

The opinion rendered by auditors states that the audit was made in accordance with generally accepted auditing standards. Identify the important components of the performance principle and relate them to the audit of C. Reis Company by indicating how they were fulfilled or, if appropriate, how they were not fulfilled.

(AICPA adapted)

LO 2-3

2.61 **Performance Principle.** Identify how each of the following statements relates to the performance principle by considering which element(s) of the principle are related to that statement. (A statement may be related to more than one element.) Use the following elements in providing your response:

- Reasonable assurance
- Planning and supervision
- Materiality
- Risk assessment
- Audit evidence
  a. Evaluating the effectiveness of the client's internal control in preventing or detecting misstatements.
  b. Obtaining an understanding of the client's business and industry.
  c. Acknowledging that the risk of failing to detect a material misstatement cannot be reduced to zero.
  d. Obtaining confirmations from the client's customers as to the ending balances in accounts receivable.
  e. Preparing a written audit plan.
  f. Designing audit procedures to identify misstatements that would have a significant effect on financial statement users' decisions.
  g. Considering the likelihood that the account balance contains a material misstatement.
  h. Failing to detect material misstatements because of audit team mistakes and misinterpretations in evaluating evidence.

LO 2-2, 2-3

2.62 **Responsibilities and Performance Principles.** Respond to each of the following comments that you heard related to the audit of Swan Company, a public entity.
  a. "We don't need to consider the risk of material misstatement in our work because we really can't do anything to reduce that risk."
  b. "Because the client has not implemented effective internal controls, we need to gather more reliable evidence. This means we need to test a greater number of transactions and obtain more reliable forms of evidence."
  c. "We will really need to spend a lot of time and effort on this audit. Because this client has just filed for a bond offering, we can't allow for any misstatements in the financial statements. We need to guarantee the accuracy of the client's financial statements."
  d. "Because this company has $140 million in revenues, we really shouldn't be concerned about smaller accounts because they are not likely to have a major impact on the financial statements."
  e. "I know it will be more time consuming and expensive, but we are required to physically inspect the stock certificates held by the client rather than obtain confirmation from the custodian. After all, our own direct observation is more reliable than receiving a confirmation."

LO 2-4

2.63 **Reporting Principle.** The reporting principle requires auditors to express their opinion through the issuance of a written report.

Required:
  a. What is the purpose of the auditors' opinion and report?
  b. What are the major paragraph(s) in the auditors' report on the examination of a public entity? What are the major contents of each of these paragraphs?
  c. What are the four types of opinions that auditors can issue?
  d. How does the concept of materiality influence the auditors' report?

LO 2-2, 2-3, 2-4

2.64 **Comprehensive Principles Case Study.** Ray, the owner of a small entity, asked Holmes, CPA, to conduct an audit of the entity's records. Ray told Holmes that the audit was to be completed in time to submit audited financial statements to a bank as part of a loan application. Holmes immediately accepted the engagement and agreed to provide an auditors' report within three weeks. Ray agreed to pay Holmes a fixed fee plus a bonus if the loan was granted.

Holmes hired two accounting students to conduct the audit and spent several hours telling them exactly what to do. Holmes told the students not to spend time reviewing the controls but instead to concentrate on proving the mathematical accuracy of the ledger accounts and on summarizing the data in the accounting records that support Ray's financial statements. The students followed Holmes' instructions and, after two weeks, gave Holmes the financial statements, which did not include footnotes. Holmes studied the statements and prepared an unmodified auditors' report. The report, however, did not refer to generally accepted accounting principles or to the fact that Ray had changed to the accounting standard for capitalizing interest.

Required:
Briefly describe each of the principles and indicate how the action(s) of Holmes resulted in a failure to comply with these principles.

(AICPA adapted)

LO 2-2, 2-3, 2-4

2.65 **Fundamental Principles (Comprehensive).** In each of the following, identify which of the elements of the fundamental principles is most applicable. In addition, discuss what action(s) (if any) you believe auditors should take with respect to these issues.

a. An entity has contacted you about performing its audit engagement. You have not previously served a client in the entity's industry, which has many industry-specific accounting issues that are both technical and complex.

b. An entity has entered into a number of lease agreements. Based on the requirements of GAAP, you believe that these obligations meet the criteria for being classified as capital leases; however, the entity has elected to treat these leases as operating leases, providing full and complete disclosure of this treatment in the footnotes to the financial statements.

c. Because of a disagreement with its current auditors, an entity has contacted you about conducting its current-year audit. However, because the previous auditors have just recently resigned from the engagement, you have some questions as to whether an audit can be completed in time to meet the entity's deadlines for providing audited financial statements to a lender.

d. Based on the effectiveness of the entity's internal control, you have assessed control risk at low levels and decided that a smaller number of customer accounts need to be confirmed.

e. An entity has contacted you about performing its audit engagement. This entity became aware of your firm because the husband of one of your partners is currently serving as the entity's chief financial officer.

f. One of your clients is currently a potential defendant in several cases because of the damage caused by one of its products. Because this entity does not believe that it is likely to receive an unfavorable outcome from this litigation, it did not disclose the potential litigation in the footnotes accompanying their financial statements.

g. You are performing tests of the client's controls over the processing of revenue transactions to determine whether these controls are operating effectively and can be relied upon to prevent or detect misstatements.

h. One of your supervisors has requested a number of clarifications based on her review of your work on an audit engagement. A subsequent meeting with her has resolved these clarifications, and you both have concluded that your work supports the opinion on the client's financial statements.

LO 2-2, 2-3, 2-4

2.66 **Fundamental Principles (Comprehensive).** Identify which of the major fundamental principles (responsibilities, performance, or reporting) is most closely related to each of the following:

a. The need for auditors to consider their financial relationships with prospective clients.

b. An auditor has raised some questions with respect to management's response to various inquiries concerning pending litigation facing the client.

c. The auditors' consideration of the effectiveness of the entity's internal control on the nature, timing, and extent of substantive procedures.

d. The auditors' evaluation of the magnitude of a misstatement that would impact perceptions of the entity's profitability.

e. The auditors' issuance of a disclaimer of opinion because of a significant scope limitation.

f. Relevant education and experience requirements for CPA licensure.

g. The inability of an audit examination to provide absolute assurance with respect to detecting all material misstatements.

h. The requirement that auditors possess the skills and knowledge of others in their profession.

i. The preparation of a written audit plan that guides the conduct of the audit engagement.

j. The auditors' issuance of a qualified opinion because of a departure from GAAP.

LO 2-2, 2-3, 2-4   2.67 **Fundamental Principles (Comprehensive).** Comment upon each of the following statements you heard in a conversation between two newly hired staff auditors.

a. "Of course, I'm qualified to be assigned to this engagement. I have an accounting degree from a top university and was an honors graduate. I know some of the accounting rules have changed since I graduated, but I'll be able to figure that out as we go through the audit."

b. "It doesn't really matter what others think. . . . I'm completely independent of Acme Industries and should be a member of the audit team. While I own some stock, it's a small amount and I'm holding it for the long term, anyway."

c. "You really have to question everything the client tells you. That's what professional skepticism is all about. It's a shame you can't believe a word they say."

d. "The evidence is lower in quality, but we typically use internal evidence when we audit property, plant, and equipment. It just takes too much time and costs too much to get more reliable evidence."

e. "On that last job, we really planned the audit well. We were able to finish everything by November 1 and didn't need to do any work after year-end."

f. "We're not too worried about internal control. We always do the same substantive procedures anyway, so why take the time to look at the client's controls?"

g. "Because the client isn't accounting for its leases properly, we need to issue either a qualified opinion or a disclaimer of opinion. Just how large a dollar impact does this have on the financial statements?"

h. "When we evaluate items for materiality, the only thing we need to worry about is the absolute dollar amount. There really isn't anything else we need to consider."

LO 2-5   2.68 **System of Quality Control.** Each of the following quality control policies and procedures is typical of ones that can be found in public accounting firms' systems of quality control. Identify each of them with one of the six elements of quality control identified by *SQCS 8*.

a. Assign management responsibilities in such a manner that commercial considerations do not override the quality of work performed.

b. Establish policies and procedures for resolving differences of opinion among firm personnel that arise during professional engagements.

c. Develop policies and procedures to ensure that professionals are provided appropriate professional development opportunities.

d. Review engagement documentation, reports, and the client's financial statements.

e. Develop effective performance evaluation, compensation, and advancement procedures.

f. Identify circumstances and relationships that create threats to independence and take appropriate action to eliminate those threats or reduce them to an acceptable level.

g. Identify whether the firm possesses the competency, capability, and resources to appropriately serve a specific client.

h. Devote sufficient resources to develop, communicate, and support the firm's quality control procedures.

i. Retain engagement documentation for a sufficient period of time to satisfy the needs of the firm, professional standards, laws, and regulations.

LO 2-5   2.69 **Evaluating Quality Control.** Firms auditing public entities are required to have periodic inspections conducted by the PCAOB.

Required:

a. What are the major characteristics of PCAOB inspections?

b. What types of firms typically have PCAOB inspections? How frequently are these evaluations conducted?

LO 2-5

2.70 **Internet Exercise: Public Company Accounting Oversight Board Inspection Reports.**
Refer to the website of the Public Company Accounting Oversight Board (PCAOB) (www.
pcaobus.org), review the information under "Inspections," and select the most current
inspection report for one of the Big Four firms (Deloitte, EY, KPMG, and PwC).

Required:

a. What information is contained in the "public" version of the PCAOB's inspection
reports? Is there any additional information that you would like to see?

b. What categories of practices, policies, and procedures are evaluated in the PCAOB's
inspection of the firm's quality control system?

c. For the firm you selected, how many practice offices had audits inspected by the PCAOB?

d. For the firm you selected, for how many audits (issuers) did the PCAOB find deficiencies?

e. Identify five deficiencies that were cited in the PCAOB's inspection report. For each
deficiency, to which of the elements of the principles does it most closely relate? (If the
firm had fewer than five deficiencies, evaluate all of the deficiencies identified in the
report.)

f. Briefly summarize the firm's response (if any) to the PCAOB's inspection report.

Appendix 2A

Referencing Professional Standards

Shown here is a comparison of the categories of standards issued by the PCAOB and Auditing Standards Board (ASB). (Section numbers are shown in parentheses for each category.) These general categories parallel the majors stages of an audit engagement and serve as an appropriate starting point when researching the professional auditing literature with respect to an issue that may be encountered during the audit examination.

ASB	PCAOB
General Principles and Responsibilities (200–299)	General Auditing Standards (1000–1300)
Risk Assessment and Response to Assessed Risks (300–499)	Audit Procedures (2100–2900)
Audit Evidence (500–599)	Audit Procedures (2100–2900)
Using the Work of Others (600–699)	Incorporated in General Auditing Standards and Audit Procedures
Audit Conclusions and Reporting (700–799)	Auditor Reporting (3100–3300)
Special Considerations (800–899)	Other Matters Associated with Audits (6101–6115)
Special Considerations in the United States (900–999)	Other Matters Associated with Audits (6101–6115) Matters Related to Filings Under Federal Securities Laws (4101–4105)

EXAMPLE: AUDITING REPORTING

Assume that you were seeking guidance on the appropriate wording for the auditors' report. For public entities, "Auditor Reporting" is covered under AS sections 3100–3300. Reviewing AS 3101 ("Reports on Audited Financial Statements"), paragraph 8 contains the wording for the auditors' report. In documenting your reference to the professional standards, you would cite AS 3101.08 as the appropriate source of professional guidance.

For nonpublic entities, "Audit Conclusions and Reporting" are covered under AU-C sections 700–799. AU-C section 700 ("Forming an Opinion and Reporting on Financial Statements") specifically relates to the content of the auditors' report. When you access AU-C section 700, you will see the source identified as *SAS No. 122* and *SAS No. 131*. If future pronouncements issued by the ASB affect audit reporting, AU-C section 700 will be updated to include those pronouncements. In this way, auditors can find all of the appropriate professional guidance for an area under one AU-C section rather than needing to reference several individual pronouncements.

Each AU-C section includes a number of paragraphs that address various matters related to that topic. AU-C section 700 has 59 paragraphs outlining the professional guidance for reporting and 63 other paragraphs (referred to as Application and Other Explanatory Material) to provide more specific guidance for applications of the standard. Paragraph A63 (the "A" refers to the application paragraph) provides sample auditors' reports. In documenting your reference to the professional standards, you could refer to either *SAS No. 122/SAS No. 131* or AU-C 700.A63.

EXAMPLE: AUDIT CONFIRMATIONS

You are seeking guidance for the use of confirmations in the audit of a public entity; specifically, you want to know what alternative procedures should be performed for nonresponses to confirmations. Reviewing the categories of standards, "Audit Procedures" (AS sections 2100–2900) appears to be most applicable; a review of standards within this category allows you to identify AS 2310, "The Confirmation Process." Reviewing this standard, paragraphs 31 and 32 describe the auditors' responsibility for performing alternative procedures if replies to confirmations are not received. In documenting your reference to the professional standards, you would cite AS 2310.31-32.

For the audits of nonpublic entities, audit evidence is covered under AU-C sections 500–599. AU-C section 505 ("External Confirmations") specifically relates to the use of external confirmations. When you access section 505, you will see the source identified as *SAS No. 122*. Paragraphs A24–A26 provide guidance for auditors' responsibility for nonresponses to confirmations. In documenting your response, you could cite either *SAS No. 122* or AU-C 505.A24–A26.

The preceding examples illustrate that individual pronouncements of the ASB (*Statements on Auditing Standards*) may contain guidance on a variety of topics. For example, *SAS No. 122* addresses both auditor reporting and confirmations (along with other topics). As a result, when referring to professional guidance in the audit of nonpublic entities, it is more appropriate to use the AU-C referencing to allow the specific source of guidance to be easily identified.

Engagement Planning

Professional Standards References

Topic	AU-C/ISA Section	AS Section
Overall Objectives of the Independent Auditor	200	1001, 1005, 1010, 1015
Terms of Engagement	210	1301
Communication Between Predecessor and Successor Auditors	510	2610
Quality Control for an Audit Engagement	220	1220
Communications with Audit Committees	260	1301
Supervision of the Audit Engagement	220, 300	1201
Audit Documentation	230	1215
Consideration of Fraud in a Financial Statement Audit	240	2401
Consideration of Laws and Regulations	250	2405
Audit Planning	300	2101
Consideration of Internal Control in an Integrated Audit	265	2201
Identifying and Assessing the Risks of Material Misstatement	315	2110
Materiality	320	2105
Auditors' Responses to Risks of Material Misstatement	330	2301
Audit Considerations Relating to an Entity Using a Service Organization	402	2601
Audit Evidence	500	1105
External Confirmations	505	2310
Substantive Analytical Procedures	520	2305
Related Parties	550	2410
Consideration of the Internal Audit Function in a Financial Statement Audit	610	2605
Using the Work of an Audit Specialist	620	1210

LEARNING OBJECTIVES

During the planning phase of an engagement, the professional standards emphasize that risk assessment underlies the entire audit process. Motivated by the importance of risk assessment, standards setters at both the PCAOB and ASB have each recently adopted a suite of standards related to the auditor's assessment of, and response to, risk in a financial statement audit. Collectively, the standards also include guidance related to audit planning, supervision, materiality, and other related topics. In this chapter, we cover engagement planning, beginning with pre-engagement activities, supervision, and materiality. Next, we cover the types of audit procedures that can be completed, including computer-assisted audit techniques (CAATs). In Chapter 4, we provide a comprehensive explanation of an auditor's assessment of risk.

Your objectives are to be able to:

LO 3-1 List and describe the required pre-engagement activities that auditors undertake before beginning an audit engagement.

LO 3-2 Understand the importance of planning the audit engagement so that it is conducted in accordance with professional standards.

LO 3-3 Define *materiality* and explain its importance in the audit planning process.

LO 3-4 List and describe the eight general types of audit procedures for gathering evidence.

LO 3-5 List and discuss matters of planning that auditors should consider related to the client's computer environment and describe how CAATs can be used to improve the efficiency of the audit process.

LO 3-6 Define what is meant by the proper form and content of audit documentation.

INTRODUCTION

The post-Sarbanes–Oxley auditing environment demands that the information needs of investors be met with reliable financial statement information. Although this has always been the expectation for audit professionals, the emergence of the PCAOB as a strong regulatory agency has forced audit firms to have a never-ending focus on audit quality. In order to achieve high-quality outcomes on each engagement, audit professionals must take the time to develop an outstanding plan. The following Auditing Insight provides a powerful reminder of what can go wrong when audit planing falls short.

 AUDITING INSIGHT   A Failure to Plan at Enron

In a planning memo dated February 6, 2001, the **Arthur Andersen** audit team assigned to the **Enron** engagement discussed whether Andersen should remain as Enron's auditor. Specifically, the engagement planning team had identified some questionable investment practices and expressed concern that Enron was engaging in "intelligent gambling." Despite these reservations, the Andersen engagement planning team concluded that the firm had the "appropriate people and processes in place to serve Enron and manage our engagement risks." Less than a year later, Enron was in bankruptcy and Andersen was in the midst of a federal investigation that would lead to its ultimate dissolution. Please refer to the case "Andersen: An Obstruction of Justice?" about Andersen's audit of Enron in 2001.

Source: William C. Powers, Jr., Raymond S. Troubh, Herbert S. Winokur, Jr., *Report of Investigation by the Special Investigative Committee of the Board of Directors of Enron Corp.,* February 1, 2002.

What went wrong in Arthur Andersen's planning process? Well to start, the audit team did not adequately assess and/or plan the procedures necessary to manage the engagement risks on the Enron audit. This chapter is devoted to the audit planning process with close attention to auditors' early identification of the risks that exist that the financial statements may be materially misstated. In fact, the primary reason for engagement planning is for the auditor to be exhaustive in identifying the risks of material misstatement for each of the relevant financial statement assertions. Next, the auditor must design testing procedures (both substantive and tests of control) that, when completed, will reduce these risks. Finally, once these risks have been reduced to an acceptable level, the auditor can issue an opinion (most often unmodified) on the fairness of the financial statements. However, before beginning to work on the audit plan, the auditor must complete a number of pre-engagement activities, required by the professional standards, that will help to determine whether to accept a new client or agree to work with an existing client for another year.

PRE-ENGAGEMENT ACTIVITIES (AU-C 300, AS 2101)

LO 3-1
List and describe the required pre-engagement activities that auditors undertake before beginning an audit engagement.

Public accounting firms try to reduce their own business risks by carefully managing their audit engagements. To do so, public accounting firms undertake several activities before beginning any audit engagement. In general, these activities can be called *risk management activities*. Risk in an audit engagement generally refers to the probability that the firm could issue a clean, unmodified audit opinion when in fact a material misstatement *does* exist in the financial statements and the opinion should have been modified. Because of the importance of these activities, the most recent professional standards state that the auditor should perform the following activities: (1) perform procedures regarding the acceptance or continuance of the audit client relationship, (2) determine compliance with independence and ethics requirements, and (3) reach a contractual understanding with the client for the terms and conditions of the audit engagement. Each of these areas is now discussed.

Client Acceptance or Continuance

An important element of a public accounting firm's quality control policies and procedures is a system for deciding whether to accept a new client and, on a continuing basis, whether to continue providing services to existing clients. Public accounting firms are not obligated to accept undesirable clients, nor are they obligated to continue to serve clients when relationships deteriorate or when the management comes under a cloud of suspicion. The process activities are clearly focused on understanding and managing risk to the audit firm. In fact, to mitigate their business risk, public accounting firms devote substantial time to make sure that the audit clients that they serve do not become the next Enron, **WorldCom, Waste Management,** or even **Bernard L. Madoff Securities.**

STAGES OF AN AUDIT

Obtain (or Retain) Engagement	Engagement Planning	Risk Assessment	Substantive Procedures	Reporting

AUDITING INSIGHT   Accounting Firms Will Walk Away from Risky Clients

After Sarbanes–Oxley was passed in 2002, the most prestigious public accounting firms became far more vigilant about walking away from clients that they believed posed a high risk to the firm. When deciding whether to accept a new engagement or continue with an existing client, firms undertake a process to carefully investigate the management team's reputation and integrity. Audit firms typically perform criminal background checks on the important members of the management team and the audit committee. This process is completed to reduce the possible risk of working with a client that would be willing to engage in illegal or unethical financial reporting practices.

Performing audits of public companies involves significant reputation and litigation risks to public accounting firms because they are lending their credibility to the client's financial statements filed with the SEC. As a result, each of the large firms takes dramatic steps to protect its reputation and avoid working with risky clients.

Source: "In-Depth Guide to Public Company Auditing: The Financial Statement Audit," *Center for Audit Quality,* May, 2011 (available at www.thecaq.org).

Auditing a client that has integrity generally results in a problem-free engagement. Conversely, despite conducting an audit in accordance with generally accepted auditing standards, it is difficult for a public accounting firm to avoid appearing "guilty by association" with a client that lacks integrity. The public accounting firm that has been terminated or has voluntarily withdrawn from the engagement (whether the audit has been completed or not) is known as the **predecessor auditor**. To reduce the risk of accepting a problem client, auditing standards require a prospective auditor to initiate contact with and *attempt* to obtain basic information directly from the predecessor regarding issues that reflect directly on the *integrity of management*. The audit client must grant its approval before the communication can occur between the prospective auditor and the predecessor auditor. In addition, client acceptance and continuance policies and procedures generally include

- Obtaining and reviewing financial information about the prospective client: annual reports, interim statements, registration statements, Form 10-Ks, and reports to regulatory agencies.
- Acquiring detailed criminal background checks of all senior managers.
- Inquiring of the prospective client's bankers, legal counsel, underwriters, analysts, or other persons who do business with the entity for information about it and its management.
- Considering whether the engagement would require special attention or involve unusual risks to the public accounting firm.
- Evaluating the public accounting firm's independence with regard to the prospective client.
- Considering the need for individuals possessing special skills or knowledge to complete the audit (e.g., IT auditor, valuation specialist, industry specialist).

The firms also search for news articles, lawsuits, and bankruptcy court outcomes naming the entity, the chairman of the board, the CEO, the CFO, and other high-ranking officers. In fact, the firms often engage private investigators to conduct additional searches for information when the prospective clients are financial institutions, companies accused of fraud, companies under SEC or other regulatory investigation, companies that have changed auditors frequently, and companies showing recent losses. These characteristics are red flags of potential problems, and public accounting firms want to know as much as they can about the companies and their officers before entering into a relationship with them. Without a doubt, management integrity (or lack thereof) is the primary reason for accepting (or not accepting) an audit engagement.

Client continuance decisions are similar to acceptance decisions except that the firm will have more firsthand experience with the entity. These types of client retention reviews are typically done annually and also with the occurrence of major events such as changes in management, directors, ownership, legal counsel, financial condition, litigation status, nature of the client's business, or scope of the audit engagement. In general, conditions that would have caused a public accounting firm to reject a prospective client can develop and lead to a decision to discontinue the engagement. For example, a client company could expand and diversify on an international scale so that a small public accounting firm might not have the resources to continue the audit. In addition, it would not be unusual to see newspaper stories about public accounting firms dropping clients after directors or officers admit to falsification of financial statements or to theft and misuse of corporate assets.

As stated previously, for a new audit engagement, public accounting firms are required to attempt to communicate with the predecessor auditor, if any, for information on management's integrity; on disagreements with management about accounting principles, audit procedures, or similar matters; and the reasons for a change of auditors. Companies are free to, and often do, change auditors periodically, sometimes as a result of corporate policy to rotate auditors, sometimes because of fee considerations, and sometimes

To reduce the possible damage to its reputation, **Deloitte** decided to withdraw as auditor for **WPT Enterprises Inc.,** the creator of the World Poker Tour, just as the company was starting its new online poker enterprise. When announcing the decision, the Big Four firm cited additional "audit risks" associated with the new gaming venture that would consume too many resources to adequately audit this client. Not noted in its resignation letter were concerns about the legality of online gaming. It is illegal in the United States, and part of the audit team's responsibilities would have included investigating whether any online gambling customers were residing in the United States. Additionally, online gambling requires complex software that involves a general lack of transparency.

Source: "For Audit Firms, All Bets Are Off," *The Wall Street Journal*, July 21, 2005, p. C3.

because of arguments about the scope of the audit or the acceptability of accounting principles. It is possible that a change in auditors occurred for the purpose of procuring new auditors who will agree with management's treatment of questionable accounting practices. Not surprisingly, these types of disagreements between auditors and management would be of interest to investors and future auditors.

As a result, when a public company changes auditors, the company must file a *Form 8-K* report with the SEC and disclose that the board of directors approved the change. **Form 8-K**, the "special events report," is required whenever certain significant events such as changes in control and legal proceedings occur. Public companies also must report any disagreements with the former auditors concerning matters of accounting principles, financial statement disclosures, or auditing procedures. At the same time, the former auditor must submit a letter stating whether the auditors agree with the explanation and, if not, provide particulars. These documents are available to the public through the SEC's Electronic Data Gathering, Analysis, and Retrieval (EDGAR) system, available on the SEC's website (www.sec.gov). The purpose of these public disclosures is to make information available about client–auditor conflicts that have occurred.

If you read closely, professional standards require only that the auditors *attempt* to communicate with the predecessor auditors. The AICPA Code of Professional Conduct does not permit the predecessor to provide information obtained during any audit engagements without the explicit consent of the client. Confidentiality remains even when the auditor–client relationship ends. Therefore, auditing standards require the prospective public accounting firm to ask that the consent be given to permit the predecessor auditor to speak. If this consent is refused, the refusal should be regarded as a *red flag,* and the prospective auditor should be cautious about accepting the engagement.

Compliance with Independence and Ethical Requirements

If you recall from Chapter 2, the *responsibilities principle* requires auditors to comply with appropriate ethical requirements for each audit engagement; two important requirements relate to *independence* and *due care*. Auditors must maintain independence *in mental attitude;* that is, auditors are expected to be unbiased and impartial with respect to the financial statements and other information they audit. This "state of mind" is often referred to as the auditor possessing **independence in fact**. This independence allows auditors to form an opinion on the entity's financial statements without being affected by influences that might compromise that opinion. Not only is it important for auditors to *be* unbiased, but they must *appear* to be unbiased. **Independence in appearance** relates to others' (particularly financial statement users') perceptions of auditors' independence.

In fact, if the auditor is not independent, the financial statements are considered unaudited for all practical purposes. A lack of independence can result in disciplinary action by regulators and/or professional organizations and litigation by those who relied on the financial statements (e.g., clients and investors). The profession as a whole depends on the value of independence in that the auditor's opinion on the financial statements loses its value if the auditor is not considered to be independent from the management of the firm. As a result of the importance placed on independence, public accounting firms must have a process in place to ensure that they are independent of the company being audited.

Because public accounting firms are subject to strict independence rules, they actively monitor the key relationships and the investment portfolios of their individual partners. These processes are in place to help ensure that the firm is independent of any relationship that might impact the firm's professionals from maintaining objectivity when making professional judgments on each audit. In fact, even after an audit client has passed the client acceptance process, independence rules must continue to be rigorously maintained. The importance of this process is exemplified by the way that **KPMG** handled a recent situation involving a rogue partner, described in the following Auditing Insight.

AUDITING INSIGHT　　Auditor Resignation

KPMG LLP was forced to resign from two large audit clients, **Herbalife Ltd.** and **Skechers USA Inc.,** because Scott London, the partner assigned to each client, admitted to providing stock tips about the two audit clients to a friend in exchange for cash and gifts. The friend is believed to have made more than $1 million from trading on the insider information. By providing confidential insider information, London directly violated the AICPA Code of Professional Conduct regarding confidential client information. As a result, the firm immediately fired him and resigned as the external auditor for the two clients. The resignation was necessary because London "violated the firm's rigorous policies and protections, betrayed the trust of clients as well as colleagues, and acted with deliberate disregard for KPMG's longstanding culture of professionalism and integrity." There was a fear that the firm's independence and objectivity toward the clients would potentially be compromised as a result of this partner's actions. In addition to resigning from the two audits, KPMG decided to withdraw its audit report on the financial statements of Herbalife for the three previous years and for Skechers for the previous two years. In doing so, KPMG stated that it did not believe there were any errors in the financial statements. However, because of London's actions, the firm believed doing so was appropriate. London pleaded guilty to a federal insider-trading charge on July 1, 2013, publicly admitting that he did reveal confidential information about his clients to a friend. The friend used the information to make over $1 million. London was sentenced to serve 14 months in a federal prison in April 2014.

Sources: J. Eaglesham, J. Chung, and H. Karp, "Trading Case Embroils KPMG," *The Wall Street Journal,* April 10, 2013, p. A1; M. Geller and E. Flitter, "FBI Probes Trading as KPMG Quits Herbalife, Skechers Audits." Reuters.com, April 9, 2013, available at www.reuters.com/article/2013/04/09/us-herbalife-auditor-idUSBRE9380N920130409; S. Pfeifer, "Former KPMG Partner Scott London Pleads Guilty to Insider Trading." *Los Angeles Times,* July 1, 2013, available at http://articles.latimes.com/2013/jul/01/business/la-fi-mo-kpmg-scott-london-insider-trading-20130627; S. Pfeifer, "Former KPMG Partner Sentenced for Insider." *Los Angeles Times,* April 24, 2014, available at http://www.latimes.com/business/la-fi-kpmg-london-20140425-story.html.

Engagement Letters

Professional standards require auditors to reach a mutual understanding with clients concerning engagement requirements and expectations and to document this understanding, usually in the form of a written letter. When a new client is accepted or when an audit engagement continues from year to year, an **engagement letter** should be prepared. This letter sets forth the understanding with the client, including in particular (1) the objectives of the engagement, (2) management's responsibilities, (3) the auditors' responsibilities, and (4) any limitations of the engagement. Other matters of understanding, such as the ones shown in Exhibit 3.1, also may be included in the letter. For example, the additional internal control considerations required by the Public Company Accounting Oversight Board are specifically mentioned in the example engagement letter. In fact, a close review of this exhibit reveals the importance of an auditor being quite detailed when completing the engagement letter.

In effect, the engagement letter acts as a contract. Thus, it serves as a means for reducing the risk of misunderstandings with the client and as a means of avoiding legal liability for claims that the auditors did not perform the work promised.

Many public accounting firms also have policies about sending a **termination letter** to former clients. Such a letter is a good idea because it provides an opportunity to deal

EXHIBIT 3.1 **Engagement Letter**

September 15, 2017

Dear Mr. Lancaster:

This letter will confirm our understanding of the arrangement for our audit of the financial statements of Dunder-Mifflin Inc. for the year ending December 31, 2017.

We will audit the Company's balance sheet at December 31, 2017, and the related statements of income, comprehensive income, stockholders' equity, and cash flows for the year then ended, for the purpose of expressing an opinion on them. We will also audit whether Dunder-Mifflin Inc. maintained effective internal control over financial reporting as of December 31, 2017, based on criteria established in Internal Control—Integrated Framework issued by the Committee of Sponsoring Organizations of the Treadway Commission (COSO criteria). Dunder-Mifflin Inc.'s management is responsible for these financial statements and for maintaining effective internal control over financial reporting. Management is also responsible for making financial records and related information available for audit and for identifying and ensuring that the company complies with the laws and regulations that apply to its activities. Our responsibility is to express an opinion on these financial statements and an opinion on the effectiveness of the company's internal control over financial reporting based on our audits. If, for any reason, we are unable to complete the audit or are unable to form or have not formed an opinion, we may decline to express an opinion or decline to issue a report as a result of the engagement.

We will conduct our audits in accordance with the standards of the Public Company Accounting Oversight Board (United States). Those standards require that we plan and perform the audit to obtain reasonable assurance about whether the financial statements are free of material misstatement and whether effective internal control over financial reporting was maintained in all material respects. Our audit of the financial statements includes examining, on a test basis, evidence supporting the amounts and disclosures in the financial statements, assessing the accounting principles used and significant estimates made by management, and evaluating the overall financial statement presentation. Our audit of internal control over financial reporting includes obtaining an understanding of internal control over financial reporting, testing and evaluating the design and operating effectiveness of internal control, and performing such other procedures as we considered necessary in the circumstances. We believe that our audits provide a reasonable basis for our opinions.

Our fee for these services will be at our regular hourly rates, plus travel and other out-of-pocket costs. Invoices will be rendered on a monthly basis and are payable on presentation. If this letter correctly expresses your understanding, please sign the enclosed copy where indicated and return it to us.

Very truly yours,

Smith & Smith, CPAs

DUNDER-MIFFLIN Inc.

By _____

Date _____

with the subject of future services, in particular, (1) access to audit documentation by successor auditors, (2) reissuance of the auditors' report when required for SEC reporting or comparative financial reporting, and (3) fee arrangements for such future services. The termination letter also may include a report of the auditors' understanding of the circumstances of termination (e.g., disagreements about accounting principles and audit procedures, fees, or other conflicts). These matters can be of great interest to prospective auditors who should always remember to ask for a copy of the termination letter.

✅ REVIEW CHECKPOINTS

3.1 What sources of information can auditors use in connection with deciding whether to accept a new client?

3.2 Why do predecessor auditors need to obtain the client's consent to give information to prospective auditors? What information should prospective auditors try to obtain from predecessor auditors?

3.3 What benefits are obtained by having an *engagement letter?* What is a *termination letter?*

AUDIT PLAN (AU-C 300, AS 2101)

LO 3-2

Understand the importance of planning the audit engagement so that it is conducted in accordance with professional standards.

An **audit plan** is a comprehensive list of the specific audit procedures that the audit team needs to perform to gather sufficient appropriate evidence on which to base their opinion on the financial statements. The professional standards require that the auditor plan each audit engagement, including the establishment of an overall strategy for each audit engagement. Specifically, when planning the engagement, the auditor needs to develop and document a plan that describes the nature, timing, and extent of further audit procedures to be performed to assess the risk of material misstatement at the financial statement and the assertion level. Next, the auditor must carefully plan the nature, timing, and extent of control tests and substantive tests that are designed to mitigate these risks to an acceptable level. This planning process is required to be led by the assigned engagement partner.

STAGES OF AN AUDIT

The professional standards are absolutely clear that the nature and extent of work completed during engagement planning will depend on the company's size, complexity, and industry. In addition, the auditor's prior experience with the company, including any major changes from prior years, will have an impact on the nature and extent of planning activity. As a result, audit firms spend a considerable amount of time on risk assessment at both the financial statement level and the management assertion level for the client being audited.

Importantly, this process begins with a detailed understanding of the client's business, industry, and strategy to achieve a competitive advantage in its marketplace. During this process, the auditor should obtain an understanding of important events that have affected the client, its operations, the financial statements, and ultimately the management assertions. This understanding provides the base of knowledge necessary to assess audit risk, providing the underlying basis to construct the audit plan.

For example, the evaluation of the risk of material misstatement is likely to vary for different financial statement accounts and may even vary for different classes of significant transactions related to the same financial statement account. Ultimately, the audit plan will need to identify each of the relevant financial statement assertions (i.e., *existence, occurrence, completeness, cutoff, rights and obligations, valuation and allocation, accuracy, classification,* and *understandability*) for each of the significant financial statement accounts and disclosures identified at an audit client. Because of the importance of risk assessment to the financial statement audit process, we devote exclusive attention to this subject in Chapter 4.

The risk assessment process provides the basis to determine the nature, timing, and extent of internal control tests and substantive tests of account balances and disclosures at an audit client. That is, for each relevant assertion, the auditor must determine the combination of control and substantive tests that will be necessary to gather enough evidence to persuade the auditor that no material misstatement exists for the relevant assertion being audited. When the tests have been completed, audit team members will often indicate the date that the procedure was performed and where the evidence is documented in the audit plan. Thus, audit plans are used not only for quality control and supervision but also as documentation to show that the audit engagement was planned and supervised in accordance with professional standards.

Although risk assessment is absolutely critical in the audit planning process, there are many other aspects of audit planning. The remainder of this chapter will focus on all other aspects of engagement planning. So, one must remember that the professional standards require that when planning, the auditor should establish the overall audit strategy for the company being audited, which includes the risk assessment procedures that will be performed and ultimately the auditor's plan to respond to each of the assessed risks of material misstatement with specific auditing procedures. The ultimate goal of engagement planning is to establish an acceptable level of detection risk so that the auditors find potential misstatements and have them corrected by the client. Essentially, the audit plan should contain the following three goals of audit planning:

- To make sure that the firm has the requisite staff to conduct the audit in accordance with professional standards in a timely and profitable manner;
- To determine materiality; and
- To outline the specific audit procedures, including tests of control and substantive tests that need to be executed properly in order to mitigate assessed risks of material misstatment and be in compliance with professional standards.

Staffing the Audit Engagement

When a new client is obtained, most public accounting firms assign a full-service team to the engagement. For a typical audit engagement, this team usually consists of the **audit engagement partner** (the person with final responsibility for the audit and usually an industry specialist), an audit manager, an information technology (IT) audit specialist, a tax specialist, a **quality assurance partner** (the second audit partner who reviews the audit team's work in critical audit areas), and audit staff. The assignment of staff depends on the riskiness of the engagement. For new clients, companies with complex significant transactions and public companies, more experienced staff members are typically assigned. No matter the type of engagement, planning meetings should include all team members and focus on the financial statement accounts that represent the highest risk of material misstatement.

AUDITING INSIGHT   Plan for Quality

The Center for Audit Quality (CAQ) is a nonprofit organization that is dedicated to promoting "high quality performance by public company auditors," which helps to ensure the highest level of "investor confidence" in the capital markets. In providing the financial support for the CAQ, the public company auditing firms recognize the importance of working together to achieve audit quality.

The importance of planning was recently elevated by the CAQ when it released its own set of Audit Quality Indicators. In fact, one of the four key themes of audit quality outlined by the CAQ was the "engagement team knowledge, experience, and workload." Among other issues, the report stressed that "The knowledge, experience, and workload of the audit engagement partner and certain other members of the engagement team are important elements in the execution of an audit. It is the responsibility of the engagement partner to determine that, collectively, the engagement team has the appropriate experience and competencies, and that specialists are engaged, as needed. The level of detail that may be provided on changes in the composition of the engagement team is dependent on the audit committee's needs and expectations, size of the engagement team, and other considerations."

Sources: *CAQ Approach to Audit Quality Indicators,* April 24, 2014, available at http://www.thecaq.org/reports-and-publications/caq-approach-to-audit-quality-indicators/caq-approach-to-audit-quality-indicators; *Audit Quality Indicators: Journey and Path Ahead,* January 12, 2016, available at http://www.thecaq.org/reports-and-publications/audit-quality-indicators-journey-and-path-ahead/audit-quality-indicators-journey-and-path-ahead.

These planning meetings help to ensure that the engagement is properly planned and that the audit team (especially new) members are properly supervised. The meetings also are intended to be brainstorming sessions to (1) ensure that all audit team members are informed about potential risks in the engagement and (2) increase team members' awareness for potential fraud. This required brainstorming session is discussed in more detail in Chapter 4.

Considering the Work of Internal Auditors (AU-C 610, AS 2605)

External auditors must obtain an understanding of a client's internal audit department and its work as part of the understanding of the client's internal control system. Internal auditors were discussed briefly in Chapter 1 and will be discussed in more detail in Module D, but here we talk about the working relationship between internal and external auditors. Audit efficiency can be realized when the two groups work together. However, prior to relying on the work of internal auditors, external auditors should consider internal auditors' *objectivity* and *competence:*

- *Objectivity.* Internal auditors can never be considered *independent* in the same sense that external auditors are because internal auditors are either directly employed or paid as contractors by the client; however, they can (and should) be *objective.*[1] Internal auditors' objectivity is investigated by learning about their organizational status and lines of communication in the company. The theory is that objectivity is enhanced when the internal auditors report directly to the audit committee of the board of directors. Objectivity is questioned when the internal auditors report to divisional management, line managers, or other persons with a stake in the outcome of their findings. Objectivity is especially questioned when managers have some power over the pay or job tenure of the internal auditors. Similarly, objectivity is questioned when individual internal auditors have relatives in audit-sensitive areas or are scheduled to be promoted to positions in the activities under internal audit review.

- *Competence.* Internal auditors' competence is investigated by obtaining evidence about their educational and experience qualifications, their certifications (CPA, CIA, CISA, etc.) and continuing education status, the department's policies and procedures for work quality and for making personnel assignments, the supervision and review activities, and the quality of reports and audit documentation. This evidence enables the external auditors to evaluate internal auditors' performance.

Favorable conclusions about competence and objectivity enable external auditors to rely on the work completed by the internal audit department related to gaining an understanding of and testing of a company's internal control system. Internal auditors also can assist (under the supervision of the independent audit team) with performing some substantive testing of balances on the audit, reducing the external auditors' work, and avoiding duplication of effort. As an example, internal auditors can conduct observations and make test counts during physical inventory counts. By relying in part on the work of the internal audit department, external auditors may be able to reduce the nature, timing, or extent of their own procedures for these accounts. Be careful to note, however, that this utilization of internal auditors' work cannot be a complete substitute for the external auditors' own procedures. Indeed, the work completed by external auditors must always provide the basis for the auditors' opinion. Consider, for example, substantive procedures related to difficult accounting judgments and material financial statement balances. These types of procedures must be performed by the external auditors.

The external auditors can never delegate responsibility for audit decisions to the internal auditors. Rather, they must supervise, review, evaluate, and perform independent testing of the work performed by internal auditors. This requirement applies to both the work of obtaining an understanding of the internal control system and the work of using internal auditors' substantive test work completed on account balances. In other words, internal auditors should never be delegated tasks that require the external auditors' *professional judgment.* Thus, although internal auditors may investigate accounts receivable confirmation exceptions, they normally would not be involved in assessing the reasonableness of the company's allowance for doubtful accounts. Following is an illustration of how one Big Four firm addresses the use of internal auditors on its engagements. Note that internal auditors' work can be utilized more extensively without reperforming a

---

[1]Internal auditors refer to their level of objectivity as *independence.* This concept is discussed further in Module D.

percentage of the work when the account balance involves low professional judgment and risk, and internal auditors are considered to be more competent and objective.

Reliance on Internal Auditors

	Objectivity and Competence	
	Low	High
High judgment/risk	Auditor should not rely on internal auditors' work	Auditor should not rely on internal auditors' work
Low judgment/risk	Auditor can rely on internal auditors' work but should reperform some of the work	Auditor can rely on internal auditors' work and may want to reperform some of the work

Using the Work of an Audit Specialist (AU-C 620, AS 1210)

Gaining an understanding of the business can often lead to acquiring information that reveals the need to employ *audit specialists* on the audit. **Audit specialists** are persons skilled in fields other than accounting and auditing—actuaries, appraisers, attorneys, environmental engineers, and geologists—who are not members of the audit team. Auditors are not expected to be experts in all fields of knowledge that can contribute information to the financial statements. When an audit specialist is engaged, auditors must know about his or her professional qualifications, experience, and reputation. An audit specialist should be unrelated to the company under audit if possible. It is imperative that the audit professional gain a detailed understanding of the methods and assumptions of an audit specialist, including detailed tests on the data that were provided by the client to the specialist. Provided that some additional auditing work is done on the data that the audit specialist uses in reaching his or her conclusions, auditors may rely on the work of an audit specialist in connection with audit decisions. Normally, audit specialists are not referred to in the auditor's report unless the audit specialist's findings (e.g., a difference in an estimate from that of management) cause the auditors' report to be modified (e.g., because of a GAAP departure). In these cases, references to the findings of the audit specialists may facilitate a better understanding of the nature of the GAAP departure.

Use of IT Auditors

When planning the engagement, the partner or manager will likely determine that the technological environment is complex for a number of different reasons. Whenever a complex computing environment exists, specialized information technology skills are needed to evaluate the effect of computerized processing on the audit process. These IT auditors are members of the audit team and are called on when the need for their specialized skills arises, just as statistical sampling specialists or SEC specialists are available when their expertise is needed. For example, the audit team could need specialized skills relating to various methods of data processing, programming languages, software packages, or computer-assisted audit techniques. For largely all audits of large companies in today's environment, IT auditors will be required and included on the engagement team.

Time Budget

The timing of the work and the number of hours that each segment of the engagement is expected to take are detailed in a preliminary time budget. *Time budgets* are used to maintain control of the audit by identifying problem areas early in the engagement, thereby ensuring that the engagement is completed on a timely basis. Time budgets are usually based on the prior-year's performance for continuing clients while considering changes in the client's business. In a first-time audit, the budget may be based on a predecessor auditor's experience or on general experience with similar companies. Extra time also may be assigned to those accounts containing the highest amount of audit risk. A simple time budget for an audit engagement follows.

	Audit Time Budget (Hours)	
	Interim	Year-End (Final)
Gain an understanding of business	15	
Evaluate internal audit function	10	
Understand internal control system	30	10
Prepare audit plan	25	
Investigate related party transactions	5	15
Meet with client personnel	10	18
Complete cash substantive testing	10	15
Complete accounts receivable substantive testing	15	5
Complete inventory substantive testing	35	20
Complete accounts payable substantive testing	5	35
Evaluate legal letters		20
Review financial statement		25
Prepare audit report		12

This time budget is illustrative—actual time budgets are much more detailed and complex. Most budgets specify the expected time according to the level of staff people on the team (partner, manager, in-charge accountant, staff assistant, IT specialist, tax specialist). The illustration shows time at *interim* and at *year-end.* **Interim audit work** refers to procedures performed several weeks or months before the date of the financial statements. (Account balances audited during interim are later *rolled forward* at year-end.) **Year-end audit work** refers to procedures performed shortly before and after the date of the financial statements. Public accounting firms typically spread the workload during the year by scheduling interim audit work so they will have enough time and people available when several audits have year-ends on the same date. (December 31 is quite common.) For many public accounting firms, the auditing "busy season" runs from September through March of the following year. The interim work typically consists of risk assessment work, internal control testing, and substantive testing of balances as they exist at the interim date.

Everyone who works on the audit engagement is typically required to report the time taken to perform procedures for each phase of the audit. These time reports are recorded by budget categories for the purposes of (1) evaluating the efficiency of the audit team members, (2) compiling a record for billing the client, and (3) compiling a record for planning the next audit. Although the purposes of a time budget are straightforward, these budgets create job pressures. Staff members are under pressure to meet the budget, and beginning auditors often experience frustration over learning how to complete their audit work in an efficient manner.

✓ REVIEW CHECKPOINTS

3.4 What is the purpose of a planning memorandum?

3.5 List some items normally documented in a planning memorandum.

3.6 What must external auditors do to use the work of internal auditors in the audit of an entity's financial statements?

3.7 What must external auditors do to use the work of audit specialists in the audit of an entity's financial statements?

3.8 For a typical audit engagement, describe the people and skills that are normally assigned to a full-service audit team.

MATERIALITY (AU-C 320, AS 2105)

LO 3-3

Define *materiality* and explain its importance in the audit planning process.

As you already know, financial statement measurements and information in some footnote disclosures are not flawlessly accurate. As recognized in the scope paragraph of the auditor's standard report for public companies, the financial statements are a function of the "accounting principles used and significant estimates made by management." The choices of depreciation method (straight line versus accelerated), inventory valuation method (e.g., FIFO, LIFO, weighted average cost), or classification of marketable securities (available for sale, trading, or held to maturity) all affect final financial statement numbers. Furthermore, many financial measurements are based on estimates such as the estimated depreciable lives of fixed assets or the estimated amount of uncollectible accounts receivable. Thus, you must think of net income not as the one "true" figure but as one possible measure in a range of potential net income figures allowable under the relevant reporting framework (e.g., GAAP or International Financial Reporting Standards [IFRS]).

Because of the range permitted, some amount of inaccuracy is allowed in financial statements because (1) unimportant inaccuracies do not affect users' decisions and hence are not material, (2) the cost of finding and correcting small misstatements is too high, and (3) the time taken to find them would delay issuance of the financial statements. Although accounting numbers are not absolutely accurate, accountants and auditors want to maintain that financial reports are materially accurate and do not contain material misstatements.

As a result, to plan the nature, timing, and extent of further audit procedures to be performed, an auditor "should establish a **materiality** level for the financial statements as a whole that is appropriate in light of the particular circumstances. This includes consideration of the company's earnings and other relevant factors." The professional standards also now require that the "materiality level for the financial statements as a whole needs to be expressed as a specified amount."[2]

Auditors cannot really think usefully about how to mitigate the risk of material misstatement at the financial statement and assertion levels without also thinking about the size of the misstatement that would be considered material in the marketplace for the audit client. Information is material if it is likely to influence financial statement users' decisions. Thus, *material information* is a synonym for *important information*. The emphasis is on the financial statement users' point of view, not on the auditors' or managers' point of view. Although financial statement users are expected to have a basic knowledge of business and financial statements as well as an understanding of the limitations of the audit process, auditors remain conservative when setting the materiality level.

As referenced in PCAOB AS No. 2105: In interpreting the federal securities laws, the Supreme Court of the United States has held that a fact is material if there is "a substantial likelihood that the . . . fact would have been viewed by the reasonable investor as having significantly altered the 'total mix' of information made available." As the Supreme Court has noted, determinations of materiality require "delicate assessments of the inferences a 'reasonable shareholder' would draw from a given set of facts and the significance of those inferences to him."[3]

As a result, the engagement partner needs to think carefully about the appropriate level of materiality during the planning process. By doing so, the auditor helps to avoid unnecessary surprises on the audit engagement. Suppose that near the end of an audit, the partner decided that all misstatements of more than $50,000 should be considered material but then realized that the nature, timing, and extent of substantive procedures had been completed assuming a materiality level of $250,000! As a result, the nature, timing, and

[2]PCAOB *Auditing Standard No. 2105*, "Consideration of Materiality in Planning and Performing an Audit," August 2010.

[3]Ibid.

extent of further audit procedures would have to be modified significantly, which would likely be an unpleasant surprise for the engagement team.

The professional standards also require the auditor to evaluate the facts and circumstances of each engagement carefully to determine whether particular accounts or disclosures for which amounts are lower than the established overall financial statement materiality level might influence the professional judgment of a reasonable user of the financial statements. If that is determined to be the case, the auditor must determine an amount that would be considered a tolerable misstatement when completing risk assessment procedures and then planning and performing audit procedures considered necessary given the audit engagement's exacting facts and circumstances. One way to consider the difficulty auditors face when determining materiality is to think about driving down a mountain road, as shown in the following picture. How close does the auditor want to come "to the edge" of determining the amount of a misstatement that would be considered material by a reasonable investor?[4]

Therefore, auditors use *performance materiality* (an amount less than materiality for the financial statements as a whole) to make sure that the aggregate of uncorrected and undetected immaterial misstatements does not exceed materiality for the financial statements as a whole. For example, auditors may use different amounts (smaller than overall financial statement materiality) when auditing particular classes of significant transactions, account balances, or disclosures. The audit team cannot look at every significant transaction, so the concept of performance materiality takes this risk into account. When auditors use sampling, performance materiality is referred to as *tolerable misstatement*.

The extent to which performance materiality is based on the overall materiality is a matter of professional judgment and, as a result, the amount may vary from auditor to auditor, so you should not be surprised that auditors use different methods for assigning performance materiality to accounts. The auditing standards do not even require that the overall materiality amount be assigned to individual accounts in dollar amounts. You will find many different thought processes and methods used in practice. However, most start with a top-down approach: judging an overall material amount for the financial statements (e.g., $200,000 would materially misstate an entity's balance sheet) and then determining performance materiality to particular accounts (e.g., receivables, inventory) to help determine the amount of work to be done in each area. Such a top-down approach is considered theoretically preferable because this method requires the audit team to think first about the financial statements taken as a whole.

How close "to the edge" does the auditor want to come
when determining overall materiality?

[4]Ibid.

Materiality Calculation

Although some accountants wish that standard setters could issue definitive, quantitative materiality guidelines, many fear the rigidity that such guidelines would impose. Therefore, in the end, materiality is a matter of professional judgment that the engagement partner must decide on each audit engagement. However, on each audit engagement, the planning process begins with a calculation of a preliminary materiality amount that is based on a relevant benchmark and a rule of thumb percentage applied to that benchmark.

The choice of appropriate benchmark relates directly back to the financial statement users. When making an initial determination of materiality, the auditor should consider what is most important to users. For example, for an asset management company or a hedge fund, it is likely that total net assets would be the most appropriate benchmark. However, for a company in the manufacturing industry, profit before tax (PBT) is likely to be most appropriate. If PBT fluctuates widely, a normalized, or average, PBT over recent years may be substituted for the current-year PBT, or the relation may be to the trend change of PBT. For a high-technology start-up, perhaps total revenue would be best. The benchmark for nonprofit entities may be gross revenue, total contributions, or a figure important in the statement of cash flows. Although many different benchmarks may be used, auditors most commonly use PBT, total net assets, or total revenues as the benchmark for their initial determination of materiality. Of course, in the end, it is a matter of professional judgment.

The best rule of thumb depends upon the relevant benchmark selected for the client within a particular industry. For example, 3–5 percent of PBT or 1/2–1 percent of revenue or total assets are often used as starting points for the determination of materiality. Once again, the rule of thumb varies depending on the facts and circumstances of the audit engagement. The SEC, however, cautions auditors about overreliance on certain quantitative benchmarks to assess materiality, noting that "misstatements are not immaterial simply because they fall beneath a numerical threshold."[5] Thus, auditors must examine both quantitative and qualitative factors when assessing materiality. Some of the more common qualitative factors that auditors use in making materiality judgments are the nature of the item or issue, engagement circumstances, and possible cumulative effects—all discussed in the following paragraphs.

Nature of the Item or Issue

An important qualitative factor is the descriptive nature of the item or issue. An illegal payment is important primarily because of its nature as well as because of its absolute or relative amount. In addition, the auditor would consider any type of fraud committed by a member of management material regardless of the amount. Finally, generally speaking, potential errors in the more liquid assets (cash, receivables, and inventory) are considered more important than potential errors in other accounts (such as fixed assets and deferred charges).

Engagement Circumstances

An auditor's legal liability is always a relevant consideration when determining materiality. That is, auditors generally place extra emphasis on the detection of misstatements in financial statements that will be widely used (such as those of public companies) or used by important outsiders (such as bank loan officers). The likelihood of an engagement being selected for inspection by the PCAOB is also a relevant consideration. In addition, troublesome political events in foreign countries can cause auditors to try to be more accurate with measurements and disclosures. Other circumstances that affect quantitative materiality involve amounts that could turn a net loss into a profit or allow a company to meet earnings expectations. In these circumstances, when management can exercise discretion over an accounting treatment, auditors tend to exercise more care and use a more stringent quantitative materiality criterion. Finally, matters surrounded by uncertainty about the outcome of future events usually come under more stringent quantitative materiality considerations.

---

[5]SEC *Staff Accounting Bulletin No. 99,* "Materiality," August 12, 1999.

Possible Cumulative Effects

At the end of each audit engagement, auditors must also evaluate the aggregate sum of known or potential misstatements. For example, consider an audit for which overall materiality is set at $50,000. If the audit test work revealed five individual $15,000 misstatements, they would each, on their own, be considered immaterial. However, what if all five misstatements each had the effect of increasing net income? In that situation, the auditor must factor in the probability that the aggregate of uncorrected and undetected misstatements could exceed overall materiality for the financial statements.

 AUDITING INSIGHT | Things Add Up at HealthSouth

Regardless of the materiality level established, auditors should always be on the lookout for indicators of fraud. Consider that **HealthSouth** was able to conceal its $1.4 billion accounting fraud from its auditors, EY, in part because it broke it up into smaller pieces. Knowing that the auditors were examining all expenses over $5,000, HealthSouth capitalized approximately $1 billion in expenses with transaction amounts ranging between $500 and $4,999. By capitalizing a significant number of smaller transactions (and then depreciating them over a long period of time) rather than expensing them in the current year, HealthSouth was able to report significantly higher net income for the current year.

Source: "Ex-Employee Took His Case to Auditors, Then Internet—but Convinced No One," *The Wall Street Journal,* May 20, 2003, pp. A1, A13.

Although we have presented a number of different factors affecting overall materiality, decisions about materiality ultimately remain a function of auditors' professional judgment. Many experienced auditors will state that these judgments are among the most difficult they make. And materiality is one of the most important audit concepts you will learn about because of its pervasive effect on the audit engagement. To summarize, on an audit engagement, the audit team uses materiality three ways:

- As a guide to *planning substantive testing procedures*—directing attention and audit work to those items or accounts that are important, uncertain, or susceptible to material misstatements.

- As a guide for determining *performance materiality* to help make sure that the aggregate of uncorrected and undetected immaterial misstatements does not exceed the materiality level for the financial statements as a whole. For example, auditors may use an amount smaller than overall financial statement materiality when auditing particular classes of significant transactions, account balances, or disclosures.

- As a guide for making *decisions about the audit report.* An account such as inventory can be material in an audit context because of its size or its place in the financial statements.

 REVIEW CHECKPOINTS

3.9   What is meant by material information in accounting and auditing?

3.10 How does an audit team use materiality on an audit engagement?

AUDIT PROCEDURES FOR OBTAINING AUDIT EVIDENCE (AU-C 500, AS 1105)

LO 3-4
List and describe the eight general types of audit procedures for gathering evidence.

Auditors use audit procedures for three purposes. First, they use audit procedures to gain an understanding of the client and the risks associated with the client (*risk assessment procedures*). These procedures are covered in detail in Chapter 4. Second, auditors use audit procedures to test the operating effectiveness of client internal control activities (*tests of controls*) discussed in Chapter 5. Finally, auditors use audit procedures to produce evidence about management's assertions (i.e., relating to *existence, occurrence, completeness, cutoff, rights and obligations, valuation and allocation, accuracy, classification,* and *understandability*) related to the amounts and disclosures in a client's financial statements. Exhibit 3.2 shows the relationship among the assertions, the types of evidence available to the auditor, and the procedures most closely related to each.

Once the risk assessment procedures have been completed and the relevant financial statement assertions have been identified, an auditor then considers whether specific control activities are in place to prevent or detect a misstatement related to each of the relevant financial statement assertions. Ultimately, the audit plan needs to specify a list of procedures that must be completed to gather sufficient and appropriate evidence directed toward achieving particular audit objectives. For example, an **internal control audit plan** would contain the specific procedures needed to obtain an understanding of the client's internal control system and test that understanding for those controls that relate to the relevant financial statement assertions. If the auditor decides to rely on specific internal control activities, the plan would also identify the specific types of tests of controls that would need to be completed to validate the operating effectiveness of the internal control activities.

A **substantive audit plan** would contain a list of audit procedures for gathering evidence related to the relevant assertions identified for an audit client's significant financial statement accounts and disclosures. The substantive audit plan (i.e., the *nature, timing, and extent* of futher procedures) depends almost exclusively upon the assessment of risk at an audit client. As an example, consider the nature of procedures. There are two ways to conduct substantive tests: (1) substantive analytical procedures and (2) tests of details.

EXHIBIT 3.2 **Assertions, Evidence, and Audit Procedures**

PCAOB Assertions	ASB Assertions	What Can Go Wrong?	Examples of Evidence Available	Representative Audit Procedures
Existence or occurrence	Existence	Do the assets recorded really exist?	The physical presence of the assets	Inspection of tangible assets
	Occurrence	Did the recorded sales transactions really occur?	Client shipping documents	Inspection of records or documents (vouching)
Rights and obligations	Rights and obligations	Does the entity really own the assets? Are related legal responsibilities identified?	Statements by independent parties	Confirmation
Completeness	Completeness	Are the financial statements (including footnotes) complete?	Documents prepared by the client	Inspection of records or documents (tracing)
	Cutoff	Were all transactions recorded in the proper period?	Client receiving, shipping reports	Inspection of records or documents (tracing or vouching)
Valuation and allocation	Valuation or allocation	Are the accounts valued correctly?	Client-prepared accounts receivable aging schedule	Reperformance
	Accuracy	Were transactions recorded accurately?	Vendor invoices	Inspection of records or documents (tracing or vouching)
Presentation and disclosure	Classification	Were all transactions recorded in the proper accounts?	Comparisons of current-year amounts with those from the prior year	Analytical procedures
	Understandability	Are the presentations and disclosures understandable to users?	Management-prepared financial statements and footnotes	Inquiry

EXHIBIT 3.3A

Dunder-Mifflin Trial Balance, December 31, 2017

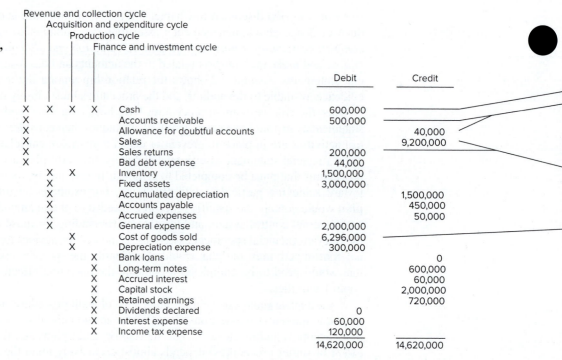

					Debit	Credit
Revenue and collection cycle						
	Acquisition and expenditure cycle					
		Production cycle				
			Finance and investment cycle			
X	X	X	X	Cash	600,000	
X				Accounts receivable	500,000	
X				Allowance for doubtful accounts		40,000
X				Sales		9,200,000
X				Sales returns	200,000	
X				Bad debt expense	44,000	
	X	X		Inventory	1,500,000	
	X			Fixed assets	3,000,000	
	X			Accumulated depreciation		1,500,000
	X			Accounts payable		450,000
	X			Accrued expenses		50,000
	X			General expense	2,000,000	
		X		Cost of goods sold	6,296,000	
		X		Depreciation expense	300,000	
			X	Bank loans		0
			X	Long-term notes		600,000
			X	Accrued interest		60,000
			X	Capital stock		2,000,000
			X	Retained earnings		720,000
			X	Dividends declared	0	
			X	Interest expense	60,000	
			X	Income tax expense	120,000	
					14,620,000	14,620,000

When completing analytical procedures to gather evidence, the auditor must develop an independent expectation of what he or she thinks the account balance should be. Once this is developed, the expectation is compared to the recorded amount. Any significant differences must be investigated and then corroborated with evidence. When applying substantive test of details, the auditor must seek to understand the account balance and/or economic transaction to ensure, based on valid and reliable evidence, that the amount was recorded in accordance with the applicable financial reporting framework. In general, analytical procedures are considered more efficient while a test of details is considered more effective. Thus, an auditor must take great care in determining the nature of the testing procedure (i.e., substantive analytical procedure or test of detail) to specify in the audit plan.

To simplify the audit plan, auditors typically group the accounts into *cycles* (see Exhibit 3.3A). A *cycle* is a set of accounts that are logically grouped in the internal control system, which has been designed to produce the financial statements and notes (see Exhibit 3.3B). Most audit firms recognize four cycles, and each of these cycles is featured in a chapter of this book: (1) the revenue and collection cycle (Chapter 7), (2) the acquisition and expenditure cycle (Chapter 8), (3) the production cycle (Chapter 9), and (4) the finance and investment cycle (Chapter 10). Using the revenue and collection cycle as an example, the idea of the cycle organization is to group accounts (sales, accounts receivable, cash) related to one another by the transactions that normally affect them all. This cycle starts with a sale to a customer along with recording an account receivable, which is later collected in cash or provided for in the allowance for doubtful accounts.

☑ REVIEW CHECKPOINTS

3.11 What are the two primary ways to conduct substantive tests? Explain how the tests are different.

3.12 Identify the four cycles featured in Dunder-Mifflin's accounting system featured in Exhibit 3.3A. Next, list the financial statement accounts that can be identified within each of the cycles identified as featured in Exhibit 3.3B.

EXHIBIT 3.3B   Dunder-Mifflin Unaudited Financial Statements

FINANCIAL POSITION

Cash	$ 600,000	Accounts payable	$ 450,000
Accounts receivable	460,000	Accrued expenses	110,000
Inventory	1,500,000	Current debt	200,000
Current Assets	$2,560,000	Current Liabilities	$ 760,000
Fixed assets (net)	$3,000,000	Long-term debt	$ 400,000
Accum. depreciation	(1,500,000)	Capital stock	2,000,000
Fixed Assets (net)	$1,500,000	Retained earnings	900,000
		Total Liabilities	
Total Assets	$4,060,000	and Stockholder Equity	$4,060,000

RESULTS OF OPERATIONS

Sales (net)	$9,000,000
Cost of goods sold	6,296,000
Gross Profit	$2,704,000
General expenses	$2,044,000
Depreciation expense	300,000
Interest expense	60,000
Operating income before taxes	$ 300,000
Income tax expense	120,000
Net Income	$ 180,000

CASH FLOWS

Operations:	
Net income	$ 180,000
Depreciation	300,000
Increase in accounts receivable	(141,500)
Decrease in inventory	50,000
Decrease in accounts payable	(25,000)
Decrease in accrued expenses	(15,000)
Decrease in accrued interest	(20,500)
Cash Flow from Operations	$ 328,500
Investing Activities:	
Purchase Fixed Assets	$ 0
Financing Activities:	
Repay bank loan	$(275,000)
Repay notes payable	(200,000)
Financing Activities	$(475,000)
Increase (decrease) in cash	$(146,500)
Beginning balance	746,500
Ending Balance	$ 600,000

NOTES TO FINANCIAL STATEMENTS
1. Accounting Policies
2. Inventories
3. Plant and Equipment
4. Long-Term Debt
5. Stock Options
6. Income Taxes
7. Contingencies
Etc.

In general, auditors use eight general audit procedures to gather evidence: (1) inspection of records and documents (*vouching, tracing, scanning*), (2) inspection of tangible assets, (3) observation, (4) inquiry, (5) confirmation, (6) recalculation, (7) reperformance, and (8) analytical procedures. For each relevant assertion, auditors need to gather enough evidence to conclude that the risk of material misstatement for that assertion has been reduced to an acceptably low level. In the following sections, we discuss each of these audit procedures in more detail.

1. Inspection of Records and Documents

Much auditing work involves gathering evidence by examining authoritative documents prepared by independent parties and by the client. Auditors frequently inspect such documents to ensure they contain the correct information and/or authorization. Such documents can provide "evidence of varying degrees of reliability, depending on their nature and source," regarding many of management's financial statement assertions.

Documents Prepared by Independent Outside Parties

The most reliable form of documentary evidence is external, which means that the document was received directly from an independent outside third party (e.g., a bank). The signatures, seals, engraving, or other distinctive artistic attributes of formal authoritative documents make such sources more reliable (less susceptible to alteration) than ordinary documents prepared by outsiders. Remember, when either type of document is received directly from an independent outside party, the evidence is considered reliable. Some examples of both types of documents are:

Formal Authoritative Documents	Ordinary Documents
1. Bank statements received directly from the bank by the auditor	1. Vendors' invoices
2. Title papers (e.g., automobiles)	2. Customers' purchase orders
3. Insurance policies	3. Loan applications
4. Notes receivable (on unique forms)	4. Notes receivable (on standard bank forms)
5. Securities certificates	5. Insurance policy applications
6. Indenture agreements	6. Simple contracts
7. Complex sales contracts	7. Written correspondence

In addition, a great deal of documentary evidence is considered external-internal, which means that the documents were initially prepared by an external third party but they were received by the client first and then given to the auditor. Since the client had possession of the documents, there is always a possibility that the client altered the documents. As a result, external-internal documents are not as reliable as external documents.

Documents Prepared and Processed by the Client

Documentation of this type is referred to as internal evidence. Some of these documents may be quite informal and not very authoritative or reliable. When such documents are prepared by the client but are mailed to third parties, they become slightly more reliable. However, as a general proposition, the reliability of these documents depends on the quality of internal control under which they were produced and processed. Because the client produces the evidence, an auditor must perform additional testing on this type of information before placing any reliance at all on the internal evidence. Some of the most common of these documents are:

Internal Documents	
1. Sales invoice copies	7. Shipping documents
2. Sales summary reports	8. Receiving reports
3. Cost distribution reports	9. Requisition slips
4. Loan approval memos	10. Purchase orders
5. Budgets and performance reports	11. Credit memos
6. Documentation of significant transactions with subsidiaries	12. Transaction logs

Vouching—Examination of Documents

When testing the existence or the occurrence assertion, the auditor will take the vouching direction when examining documents. The important point about *vouching* is that the auditor begins the search for evidence by focusing on transactions that have already been recorded in the financial statements. In **vouching,** an auditor selects an item in the financial records, usually from a journal or ledger, and follows its path back through the processing steps to its origin (i.e., the *source documentation* that supports the item selected from the ledger). Consider a revenue entry made in the financial statements. For that entry, the auditor will find the journal entry, the sales summary, the sales invoice copy, the shipping documents, and, finally, the sales order from the customer. Vouching of documents can help auditors decide whether all recorded significant transactions are adequately supported (the *existence* and *occurrence* assertions), but vouching does not provide evidence to show whether all significant transactions were actually recorded (the *completeness* assertion). However, if the auditors verify amounts during their testing, evidence regarding *valuation and allocation* also may be obtained while vouching documents.

Tracing—Examination of Documents

When testing the completeness assertion, the auditor will take the tracing direction when examining documents. When taking the **tracing** direction, the auditor selects a basic source document and follows its processing path *forward* to find its final recording in a summary journal or ledger and ultimately the financial statements. For example, samples of shipping documents can be obtained from the warehouse and then traced to sales invoices, the sales journal, and ultimately their recording in the financial statements as revenue earned.

Using tracing, an auditor can decide whether all significant transactions and events that should have been recorded actually were recorded (the *completeness* assertion). In doing so, the auditor complements the evidence obtained by vouching. This implies that an auditor must always be alert to events that were not entered into the accounting system. For example, the search for unrecorded liabilities for raw materials purchases must include examination of invoices received in the period following the fiscal year-end and examination of receiving reports dated near the year-end. In practice, it is important to remember that the direction of the examination of documents is critical in relation to the assertion being tested.

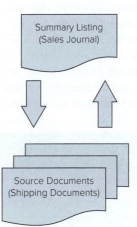

Vouching
(Would be used to test the existence or occurrence assertion. The audit test would be designed to answer the following question: Did all recorded sales occur?)

Summary Listing (Sales Journal)

Tracing
(Would be used to test the completeness assertion. The audit test would be designed to answer the following question: Were all shipments made to customers actually recorded as sales?)

Source Documents (Shipping Documents)

Scanning—Examination of Documents

Scanning is the way auditors exercise their general alertness to unusual items and events in clients' documentation. A typical scanning directive in an audit plan is: "Scan the expense accounts for credit entries; vouch any to source documents."

In general, scanning is an "eyes-open" approach of looking for anything unusual. The scanning procedure usually does not produce direct evidence itself, but it can raise questions related to other evidence that must be obtained. Scanning can be accomplished on digital records using computerized audit software to select records to be printed out for further audit investigation. Typical items discovered by the scanning effort include debits in revenue accounts, credits in expense accounts, unusually large accounts receivable write-offs, unusually large paychecks, unusually small sales volume in the month following the year-end, and large cash deposits just prior to year-end. Scanning can contribute some evidence related to the existence of assets and the completeness of accounting records, including the proper cutoff of significant transactions.

2. Inspection of Tangible Assets

Inspection of tangible assets includes examining property, plant, and equipment; inventory; and securities certificates. Physical inspection of tangible assets provides compelling evidence of *existence* and may provide tentative evidence of *valuation*. For example, audit team members can verify the existence of specific pieces of equipment listed on the client's fixed asset register by locating them and noting their condition (*valuation*). However, inspection does not necessarily provide evidence that the entity owns the assets (*rights*). For example, fixed assets on the client's premises may be leased under operating lease agreements, and inventory inspected by auditors may be held on consignment.

3. Observation

Although inventory observation often refers to the physical inspection of inventory (i.e., tangible assets), auditors use *observation* when they view the client's physical facilities and personnel on an inspection tour, when they watch personnel carry out accounting and control activities (such as observing client inventory counts), and when they participate in a surprise payroll distribution. Observation also can produce a general awareness of events in the client's offices. In this sense, observation is commonly used as a test of controls.

4. Inquiry

Inquiry is a procedure that generally involves the collection of verbal evidence from independent parties and management (commonly referred to as *management representations*). Important inquiries and responses should be documented by the auditor in the workpapers. Auditors typically use inquiry procedures during the early planning stages of the engagement. Evidence gathered by formal and informal inquiry generally cannot stand alone as convincing, and auditors must corroborate responses with independent findings based on other procedures. In fact, the professional standards state that "inquiry alone" is never enough to reach an audit conclusion. An exception to this general rule might be a negative statement in which someone volunteers adverse information such as an admission of theft, fraud, or use of an accounting policy that is misleading. However, even in such a situation, an auditor would most likely follow up to obtain documentary evidence to support the negative statement.

 AUDITING INSIGHT | Verbal Inquiry = Interview

Auditors conduct interviews almost every day. Sometimes these seem more like casual conversations than "interviews." Nevertheless, the following guidelines for the inquiry/interview procedure can help you obtain good information and maintain good relations with client personnel.

1. *Prepare.* Think about the information you want to obtain, the questions to ask, and the best person to interview.

2. *Make an appointment.* Call in advance for a time or at least ask permission to interrupt: "Do you have time to talk with me about [subject]?" Introduce yourself and make enough conversation to warm up the person without wasting time.

3. *Be conversational.* Try to get the person to describe the accounting, the controls, or whatever the subject in his or her own words. You will get more information. Just firing off questions makes the meeting an interrogation. Most auditors find it difficult to think of all of the right questions ahead of time anyway. Don't exhibit

a questionnaire or checklist; doing so makes the interview too mechanical. You can take informal notes to remember the substance of the interview.

4. *Ask questions.* Fill in the gaps in the person's description or explanation by asking prompting questions to elicit additional descriptions and explanations. Start with broad, open-ended questions and use specific questions to obtain more detail.

5. *Listen carefully.* Repeat items you don't completely understand.

6. *Be noncommittal.* Refrain from expressing your own value judgments or criticisms while you talk with the client personnel. Don't reveal any audit-sensitive information.

7. *Close gracefully.* Thank the person for the time and information. Ask permission to return later for "anything I forgot."

8. *Document the interview.* Write a memorandum for the audit documentation. Now you can get out the questionnaire or checklist, complete it, and see whether you overlooked anything important.

5. Confirmation

Confirmation by direct correspondence with independent parties is a procedure widely used in auditing. It can produce evidence of *existence* and *rights and obligations* and sometimes of *valuation* and *cutoff.* Auditors typically limit their use of confirmation to significant transactions and balances about which outside parties could be expected to provide information. A selection of confirmation applications includes the following:

- Banks—cash and loan balances.
- Customers—receivables balances.
- Borrowers—note terms and balances.
- Agents—inventory on consignment or in warehouses.
- Lenders—note terms and balances.
- Policyholders—life insurance contracts.
- Vendors—accounts payable balances.
- Registrar—number of shares of stock outstanding.
- Attorneys—litigation in progress.
- Trustees—securities held, terms of agreements.
- Lessors—lease terms.

Several points about confirmations are important to remember. First, confirmation letters are typically printed on the client's letterhead and signed by a client officer; third parties usually do not release information without client permission. Second, confirmation requests should seek information the recipient can supply, such as the amount of a balance or the amounts of specified invoices or notes. Third, the audit firm should control confirmations rather than giving them to client personnel for mailing. The audit team should be very careful that the recipient's address is reliable and not subject to alteration by the client in such a way as to misdirect the confirmation. Fourth, responses should be returned directly to the audit firm, not to the client. And lastly, auditors are increasingly executing their confirmation procedures electronically. The increased use of electronic confirmations is covered in detail in Chapter 6.

6. Recalculation

Auditor recalculation of computations previously performed by client personnel produces compelling evidence. A client calculation must always be mathematically accurate. Client calculations performed by computer programs can be recalculated using computer-assisted audit techniques (CAATs) with differences printed out for further audit investigation. Mathematical evidence can serve the objectives of *existence* and *valuation* for financial statement amounts that exist principally as calculations, for example, depreciation, interest expense, pension liabilities, actuarial reserves, bad debt reserves, and product guarantee liabilities. Recalculation, in combination with other procedures, is also used to provide evidence of *valuation* for all other financial data.

7. Reperformance

Although similar to recalculation, reperformance is much broader in approach. As discussed in Chapter 4, reperformance is commonly used by auditors while completing walkthroughs when gaining an understanding of a client's internal control system. In fact, reperformance can generally be completed for any client control procedure such as matching vendor invoices with supporting purchase orders and receiving reports. Reperformance may be done either manually or with the assistance of CAATs. An auditor, for example, can verify that an accounts receivable aging schedule was prepared properly by sorting accounts receivable by due date.

8. Analytical Procedures

Auditors can evaluate financial statement accounts by developing expectations about what an account balance should be based on an analysis of relevant financial and nonfinancial data. When an auditor compares the expectation to a recorded balance, **analytical procedures** are being performed. Auditors are required to use them when planning the audit and when performing the review of the financial statements near the end of the audit before the audit report is issued. In addition, auditors use analytical procedures to provide evidence about management's financial statement assertions during the testing phase of the audit.

Analytical procedures take the following five general forms. Auditors need to be careful to use independent, reliable information for analyses. The sources of information shown for the analytical procedures are very important, and auditors must gain comfort over the information that is used to develop expectations during analytical procedures.

Analytical Procedures	Sources of Information
1. Comparison of current-year account balances to balances of one or more comparable periods	Financial account information for comparable period(s) *Example: Current-year cost of goods sold compared to last year's balance*
2. Comparison of current-year account balances to anticipated results found in the company's budgets and forecasts	Company budgets and forecasts *Example: Current-year cost of goods sold compared to the company's budgeted amount*
3. Evaluation of the relationships of current-year account balances to other current-year balances for conformity with predictable patterns based on the company's experience	Financial relationships among accounts in the current period *Example: Relationship between inventory and cost of goods sold*
4. Comparison of current-year account balances and financial relationships (e.g., ratios) with similar information for the industry in which the company operates	Industry statistics *Example: Comparing inventory and cost of goods sold levels to comparable companies in the industry*
5. Study of the relationships of current-year account balances with relevant nonfinancial information (e.g., physical production statistics)	Nonfinancial information such as physical production statistics *Example: Comparing the number of unfilled orders to inventory and cost of goods sold levels*

Because analytical procedures completed during planning are required and used only to direct attention to unusual relationships, some auditors are reluctant to use analytical procedures during the substantive testing of balances. Instead, many auditors feel more comfortable with tests of details such as recalculation, observation, confirmation, and the inspection of documents. However, you should resist this temptation. In fact, the professional standards clearly indicate that a well-planned analytical procedure conducted during the substantive testing phase can be quite effective if executed properly. Most importantly, when applying substantive analytical reviews to gather evidence in this manner, any significant differences must be investigated and corroborated with evidence.

Because of their effectiveness in directing attention to high-risk areas, professional standards require that analytic procedures be used during *planning* and during *final evaluation* phases of the audit. Although not required to be used during the *substantive testing* phase of the engagement, auditors must consider the value of analytical procedures, especially because they are usually less costly than more detailed, document-oriented procedures. Consequently, analytical procedures often take a prominent place in the *audit plan*.

AUDITING INSIGHT | Potholes in the Audit Procedures Road

Performing specified audit procedures might not be enough. The following true stories highlight the need for caution in the conduct of audit procedures.

RECALCULATION

An auditor calculated inventory valuations (quantities × price) thinking the measuring unit was the actual number of items counted when the client had actually recorded counts in dozens (12 units for each item listed), thus causing the inventory valuation to be 12 times the actual measure.

INSPECTION OF TANGIBLE ASSETS

Despite observing the fertilizer tank assets in ranch country, the auditor was fooled when the manager was able to move them to other locations and place new identification numbers on them. The auditor "observed" the same tanks many times.

OBSERVATION

A team visited a building restoration client's job site to verify that the company was actually performing the restoration services. Unbeknownst to the team, the client (**ZZZ Best**) had rented the vacant building for the day, put up its "building restoration" signs, and had its employees in hard hats milling around for the audit team's benefit.

CONFIRMATION

Executives at an Italian grocery company (**Parmalat**) faxed a forged bank confirmation to auditors in order to conceal a $5 billion fraud. The auditors never questioned why they received a fax from the bank rather than a mailed confirmation.

INQUIRY

Seeking evidence of the collectability of accounts receivable, the auditors "audited by conversation" and took the credit manager's word about the collection probabilities on the over-90-day past due accounts. They sought no other evidence.

INSPECTION OF RECORDS AND DOCUMENTS (VOUCHING)

In the HealthSouth audit, auditors requested supporting documentation for an asset purchased for one of the company's Kansas locations. The problem was that it was a fraudulent transaction recorded as an asset to avoid treating the transaction properly as an expense. To conceal the fraud from the auditors, a vice president in the accounting department found a similar purchase invoice for an asset purchased for another location, scanned it into her computer, and then electronically changed the shipping information to match the invoice requested by the auditors.

INSPECTION OF RECORDS AND DOCUMENTS (SCANNING)

The auditors extracted a list of all of the bank's loans for more than $1,000. They neglected to perform a similar scan for loans with negative balances, a condition that should not occur. The bank had information processing problems that caused many loan balances to be negative, although the trial balance balanced!

 REVIEW CHECKPOINTS

3.13 What is meant by (a) vouching, (b) tracing, and (c) scanning? What is the difference between vouching and tracing?

3.14 Identify and then briefly explain the eight general audit procedures used to gather evidence. Next, please provide an example for each of the eight procedures.

3.15 What are the five types of general analytical procedures? List five sources of information for analytical procedures.

3.16 When are analytical procedures required during an audit engagement?

PLANNING IN A COMPUTERIZED ENVIRONMENT

LO 3-5
List and discuss matters of planning that auditors should consider related to the client's computer environment and describe how CAATs can be used to improve the efficiency of the audit process.

The technology application (e.g., SAP, Sage 50) used to process accounting transactions will affect an entity's financial reporting process and influence the procedures and techniques used to accomplish the organization's financial reporting goals and objectives. The following are characteristics that an auditor needs to consider when evaluating a client's computerized environment:

- *Possibility of temporary transaction trails.* An **audit trail** is a chain of evidence provided through coding, cross-references, and documentation connecting account balances and other summary results with the original transaction source documents. Some computerized systems are designed so that a complete transaction trail, useful for audit purposes, could exist only for a short time or only in computer-readable form. Often the loss of hard copy documents and reports and the temporary nature of the audit trail require external auditors to alter both the timing and the nature of audit procedures.

- *Uniform processing of transactions.* Computerized processing subjects similar transactions to the same processing instructions. Consequently, computerized processing virtually eliminates the occurrence of random errors. As a result, programming errors (or other similar systematic errors in either the computer hardware or software) will result in all similar transactions being processed incorrectly when those transactions are processed under the same conditions.

- *Potential for errors and frauds.* The potential for individuals to gain unauthorized access to or alter data without visible evidence as well as to gain access (direct or indirect) to assets is significant in computerized information systems. Employees have more access to information through numerous terminals hooked together in a common computer network. Less human involvement in handling transactions processed by computers can reduce the potential for observing errors and frauds. Errors or fraud made in designing or changing application programs can remain undetected for long periods of time.

- *Potential for increased management supervision.* Computerized information systems offer management a wide variety of analytical tools to review and supervise the company's operations. The availability of these additional controls can enhance the entire system of internal control and, therefore, reduce control risk. For example, traditional comparisons of actual operating ratios with those budgeted as well as reconciliation of accounts frequently are available for review on a timelier basis when such information is computerized.

- *Initiation or subsequent execution of transactions by computer.* With automatic transaction initiation, certain transactions can be initiated or executed automatically by a computerized system without human review. Computer-initiated transactions include the generation of invoices, checks, shipping orders, and purchase orders. Without a human-readable document indicating the transaction event, the correctness of automatic transactions can be difficult to judge. In addition, management's authorization of transactions can be implicit in its acceptance of the design of the accounting system. For example, authorization of transactions occurs when certain flags are installed in programs or records (e.g., inventory quantity falling below reorder point). Therefore, authorization can be difficult to trace to the proper person. Control procedures must be designed into the system to ensure the genuineness and reasonableness of automatic transactions and to prevent or detect erroneous transactions.

- *Use of cloud computing applications.* With cloud computing, an audit client may be accessing certain software applications and data contained in the "cloud" via the Internet with its laptop, tablet, smartphone, or other computing device. By accessing software applications and data in this manner, a client may save substantial computing costs because it need not purchase its own software site licenses and/or data storage hardware. However, this decision is not without risk because data security, service interruptions, and data migration issues can occur. Control procedures must be designed to ensure the completeness and accuracy of the informational flows to and from the cloud and that data security within the cloud is ensured.

Effect of Client's Computerized Processing on Audit Planning

Largely, all organizations use computers to process their data. Although client automation raises some difficulties (e.g., temporary transaction trails, potential for fraud), auditors can use the speed and accuracy of their own laptops to increase audit efficiency and effectiveness. Accordingly, when evaluating the effect of a client's computerized processing on an audit of financial statements, auditors should consider matters such as the following:

- The complexity of the computer operations used by the entity (e.g., batch processing, online processing, outside service centers).
- The organizational structure of the computerized processing activities.

- The availability of data required by the auditor.
- The computer-assisted audit techniques (CAATs) available to increase the efficiency of audit procedures.
- The need for specialized skills.

Complexity of Computerized Operations

When assessing the complexity of computerized information processing, the audit team members should consider his or her training and experience relative to the methods of information processing. A review of the client's computer hardware could show the extent of complexity involved. If the client *outsources* significant accounting applications (e.g., payroll), the audit team might need to coordinate audit procedures with service auditors at the processing center. This topic is covered in more detail in Module A.

Organizational Structure of Computerized Processing

Clients can exhibit great differences in the way that their computerized processing activities are organized. The degree of centralization inherent in the organizational structure can vary. A highly centralized organizational structure generally has all significant computerized processing controlled and supervised at a central location. The control environment, the computer hardware, and the computerized systems can be uniform throughout the company. Auditors can obtain most of the necessary computerized processing information by visiting the central location. At the other extreme, a highly decentralized organizational structure generally allows various departments, divisions, subsidiaries, or geographical locations to develop, control, and supervise computerized processing in an autonomous fashion. In this situation, the computer hardware and the computer systems are usually not uniform throughout the company. Thus, auditors might need to visit many locations to obtain the necessary audit information.

Availability of Data

Computerized systems provide an ability to store, retrieve, and analyze large amounts of data. Input data, certain computer files, and other data that the audit team needs might exist for only short periods or only in computer-readable form. In some computerized information systems, hard copy input documents may not exist at all because information is entered directly. For example, electronic signatures have replaced manual signatures on electronic purchase orders sent directly to vendors via electronic data interchange with the consequence that the auditors are not able to examine a hard copy signature. The client's data retention policies may require auditors to arrange for some information to be retained for review. Alternatively, auditors might need to plan to perform audit procedures when the information is still available.

In addition, certain information generated by the computerized system for management's internal purposes can be useful in performing analytical procedures. For example, because storage is easy, the client can save large amounts of operating information (*data warehousing*) such as sales information by month, by product, and by salesperson. Such information can be accessed (*data mining*) for use in analytical procedures to determine whether the revenue amounts are reasonable. Auditors also can drill down to examine individual transactions that compose a general ledger account balance.

The Need for Specialized Skills

CPA firms generally have auditors who are specially trained to evaluate computerized controls and processes. Often they may be called on to write specialized computer programs to retrieve and analyze data. See Module H for more discussion of how to audit computerized controls and processes.

Computer-Assisted Audit Techniques (CAATs)

One major trend in current auditing practice is the use of data analysis tools like CAATs to take full advantage of the growing amounts of data available in the financial statement audit process. In fact, we collectively believe that auditing students of today have an opportunity to capitalize on opportunities that have emerged as a result of the increased focus on data and analytical tools that have helped to characterize the current public accounting environment. Indeed, because the largest auditing firms are focused on this issue, a key goal of this book is to help you learn the tools that will help you succeed in today's environment. Simply stated, the auditing world has changed, and we desire to help you adapt to the new world that you are about to enter.

In general, CAATs allow auditors to complete a number of important tasks through the use of the cutting-edge devices (e.g., tablets, laptops) that are available to auditors. CAATs allow the auditor to directly access a client's dataset for the year under audit. In addition, in today's environment, auditors use their own laptops and/or tablets regularly to perform steps such as preparing the working trial balance, posting adjusting entries, computing comparative financial statements and common ratios for analytical procedures, preparing supporting audit documentation schedules, and producing draft financial statements. Many auditors also use technology tools to help assess control risk, perform sophisticated analytical functions on individual accounts, access public and firm databases for analysis of unusual accounting and auditing problems, and utilize decision support software to make complex evaluations.

Most CAAT software packages consist of a set of preprogrammed editing, operating, and output subroutines so that original programming is not required and the same software can be used on different clients' computerized systems. For the most part, the widely used CAAT packages (e.g., IDEA, ACL) are very similar. In addition, most have been developed from standard spreadsheet and database applications, so if you understand spreadsheet software, you can use most of the audit-specific functions. The applications, however, have been modified so that auditors can perform common audit tasks at the touch of a button by accessing predeveloped "macros" to analyze data. In this book, we have integrated a leading CAAT used by many audit professionals—the IDEA software package—to help students understand how to make the best use of firm data during the audit.

Based on conversations with audit professionals, we believe that learning how to use a CAAT like IDEA is one of the best ways for entry-level auditing professionals to begin their journey into the world of big data. Simply stated, in today's auditing environment, big data is leveraged in the financial statement auditing process through the use of a tool like IDEA. As a result, we believe that this will be an efficient and effective way for students to begin their journey. There are, of course, other options for incorporating big data and analytics into the introduction to auditing classroom, including competing products (ACL) and visualization tools (Tableau), among many others. However, we chose IDEA as a first step primarily because of its common usage in practice and the relative ease of implementing it into the classroom. The following "Using IDEA in the Audit" excerpt is designed to help you begin this journey.

Computerized accounting applications capture and generate voluminous amounts of data that usually are available only on machine-readable records. As illustrated earlier, CAATs can be used to access the data and organize it into a format useful to the

USING IDEA IN THE AUDIT   Accessing Client Data

The first step in using a CAAT like IDEA is to gain access to the client's data. The data may be available in multiple forms, depending on the audit client's unique computing environment. However, IDEA is designed to be flexible enough to handle multiple computing environments. Your instructor will provide you with access to the IDEA software and the electronic version of the IDEA Data Analysis Workbook: IDEA Version Ten (the IDEA Workbook). Your instructor will also provide you with access to the data files for the audit procedures to be completed for Accounts Receivable, Accounts Payable, and Inventory.

For each set of files, your first step is to import the client's data into the IDEA software. We suggest that you complete this step for each of the areas that have been assigned by your instructor.

To proceed, please refer to the following pages in the Workbook provided by your instructor:

- *Accounts Receivable:* Please follow the steps that begin on page 25 and end on page 44 of the IDEA Workbook to properly import the sample data files for accounts receivable into IDEA.

- *Accounts Payable:* Please follow the steps that begin on page 95 and end on page 119 of the IDEA Workbook to properly import the sample data files for accounts payable into IDEA.

- *Inventory:* Please follow the steps that begin on page 187 and end on page 200 of the IDEA Workbook to properly import the sample data files for inventory into IDEA.

audit team. The software can be used to accomplish many different audit procedures such as the following:

- *Recalculation.* The audit software can be used to test the accuracy of client computations and to perform analytical procedures to evaluate the reasonableness of account balances. Examples of this use are to (1) recalculate depreciation expense; (2) recalculate extensions on inventory items; (3) compute file totals; and (4) compare budgeted, standard, and prior-year data with current-year data.

- *Confirmation.* Auditors can program statistical or judgmental criteria for selecting customers' accounts receivable, loans, and other receivables for confirmation. In addition, although not a CAAT, the use of electronic confirmations by auditors (e.g., confirmation.com) has led to improvements in both the effectiveness and the efficiency of the confirmation process.

- *Scanning.* Auditors can use CAATs to examine records to determine quality, completeness, consistency, and correctness. This is the computerized version of scanning the records for exceptions to the auditors' criteria. For example, scan (1) accounts receivable balances for amounts over the credit limit, (2) inventory quantities for negative balances or unreasonably large balances, (3) payroll files for terminated employees, or (4) loan files for loans with negative balances.

- *Analytical procedures.* CAATs functions can match data in separate files to help extract the data necessary to make comparisons between financial and nonfinancial information. In addition, CAATs can be used to extract the data necessary to make comparisons to other companies in the same industry.

- *Fraud investigation.* CAATs can be used in a variety of ways to search for fraudulent activities. For example, lists of vendor addresses can be compared to employee address files to see whether employees are paying invoices to companies that they own or operate. Duplicate payments can be found by sorting payments by invoice number and amount paid. Telephone records can be quickly sorted and scanned to ensure that employees are not misusing company telephones.

Notwithstanding the powers of the computer, several general audit procedures are outside its reach. The computer cannot observe and count physical things (e.g., inventory), but it can compare auditor-made counts to the computer records. The computer cannot examine external and internal documentation; thus, it cannot vouch accounting output to sources of basic evidence. (An exception would exist in a computerized system that stores the basic source documents on magnetic media.) However, when manual vouching is involved, computer-assisted selection of sample items is quick and easy. Finally, CAATs can never take the place of the auditor's professional judgment (e.g., determining the reasonableness of the allowance for doubtful accounts).

REVIEW CHECKPOINTS

3.20 What are CAATs?

3.21 What are some audit procedures that can be performed using CAATs?

3.22 What advantages are derived from using CAATs in the financial statement audit? When answering this question please specifically consider performing when an auditor has to perform recalculations and selecting a sample of accounts receivable balances to be confirmed.

AUDIT DOCUMENTATION (AU-C 230, AS 1215)

LO 3-6
Define what is meant by the proper form and content of audit documentation.

An engagement is not complete without preparation of proper documentation. PCAOB AS 1215 defines **audit documentation** as

> The written record of the basis for the auditor's conclusions that provides the support for the auditor's representations, whether those representations are contained in the auditor's report or otherwise.

In other words, audit documentation provides the auditors' record of compliance with generally accepted auditing standards. The documentation (usually in the form of either electronic files or hard copy *workpapers*) should contain support for the decisions regarding planning and performing the audit, procedures performed, evidence obtained, and overall conclusions reached near the end of the audit. Even though the auditors legally own the audit documentation, professional ethics require that the files not be transferred without the client's consent because of the confidential information recorded in them.

Auditors often use the term *workpapers,* but it is becoming a misnomer. Public accounting firms rarely use *paper* to document their findings anymore; more commonly, firms are using electronic documents. Today, automated audit software allows auditors to create, share, edit, review, correct, approve, and finalize audit documentation without the "paper," thereby reducing the storage space requirements of hard copy workpapers. In addition to reduced storage costs, auditors' use of electronic documentation can result in improved efficiency because the electronic documents can be easily updated and modified from year to year. Finally, automated audit software reduces the time spent on numbering, referencing, initialing, dating, and reviewing ("ticking and tying") by automating these tasks through the use of macro programs. In the past, these largely clerical tasks consumed large quantities of audit effort that is now directed more productively to more critical aspects of the audit. Most automated audit engagement management programs utilize commonly used word processor and spreadsheet applications to prepare audit documentation, audit plans, and audit memos.

Audit documentation can be classified in two categories: (1) *permanent files* (which contain information that is relevant to ongoing client relationships) and (2) *current files* (which relate to just one year of the client relationship). The following sections describe the information contained in each file in more detail.

Permanent Files

The **permanent files (or continuing audit files)** contain information of *continuing audit significance* over many years' audits of the same client. The audit team may use this file year after year, but each year's current audit documentation is stored after the files have served their purpose. Documents of permanent interest and applicability include

1. Copies or excerpts of the corporate or association charter, bylaws, or partnership agreement.
2. Copies or excerpts of continuing contracts such as leases, bond indentures, and royalty agreements.
3. A history of the company, its products, markets, and background.

4. Copies or excerpts of minutes of meetings of stockholders and/or directors on matters of lasting interest.

5. Continuing schedules of accounts with balances that are carried forward for several years, such as owners' equity, retained earnings, partnership capital, and the like.

6. Copies of prior-years' financial statements and audit reports.

7. Client organization chart.

Copies of financial statements and auditors' reports from prior years also may be included. Public accounting firms collect articles and other information regarding a client and key personnel throughout the year. This information is often placed in the permanent file to facilitate a review of the client prior to continuing the relationship. Because of the importance of the documents contained and summarized in this one place, the permanent file is a ready source of information for familiarization with the client by new personnel on the engagement.

Current Files

The current files include all client acceptance or continuance documentation along with planning documentation for the year under audit. They usually include the engagement letter, staff assignment notes, conclusions related to understanding the client's business, results of preliminary analytical procedures, assessments of audit risks, and determination of audit materiality. Many public accounting firms follow the practice of summarizing these data in a **planning memorandum** with specific directions about the impact on the audit.

Basically, the planning memo summarizes all important overall planning information and documents that the audit team is following generally accepted auditing standards. All planning becomes a basis for preparing the audit plan, which is a list of the audit procedures to be performed by the audit team to gather sufficient appropriate evidence on which to base the opinion on the financial statements. Auditing standards require a *written* audit plan for each relevant assertion on the audit.

As illustrated in Exhibit 3.4, the planning documentation must include a listing of each significant account and disclosure in the client's financial statement. According to the professional standards, if there is a chance the account could contain a misstatement that is material, it should be identified as significant. The documentation also must include a listing of each relevant financial statement assertion related to the significant accounts and disclosures. According to the professional standards, if the assertion has "a reasonable possibility of containing a misstatement that would cause the financial statements to be materially misstated," it must be categorized as relevant. Documentation of the significant accounts and disclosures, along with the relevant assertions, forms the basis of the current file documentation.

Audit documentation should be prepared in sufficient detail to provide a clear understanding of its purpose, its source, and the overall conclusions reached near the end of the audit. The audit documentation communicates the quality of the audit, so it must be clear, concise, complete, neat, well indexed, and informative. Each workpaper must be complete in the sense that it can be removed from the audit documentation file and considered on its own with proper cross-references available to show how the document coordinates

EXHIBIT 3.4
Significant Accounts and Relevant Assertions

Significant Accounts	Relevant Assertions
Cash	Existence
	Valuation
	Presentation and Disclosure
Accounts Receivable	Existence
	Completeness
	Valuation

with other audit documentation. In other words, the documentation must be sufficient to enable an experienced auditor, having no previous connection with the engagement, to understand (1) the nature, timing, extent, and results of procedures; (2) the overall conclusions reached with respect to the area covered by the audit documentation; and (3) the audit team member performing the work, the date of work, the audit team member reviewing the work, and the date of review. The audit documentation should also be sufficient to allow another auditor to reperform the work if necessary.

The most important facet of the current audit evidence documentation files is the requirement that they show the auditors' conclusions. The documentation must record the management assertions that were audited, the evidence gathered about them, and final conclusions. Professional audit standards require the audit documentation show that (1) the client's accounting records agree or reconcile with the financial statements, (2) the work was adequately planned and supervised, (3) a sufficient understanding of the client's internal control was obtained, and (4) sufficient appropriate audit evidence was obtained as a reasonable basis for an audit opinion. Common sense also dictates that the audit documentation be sufficient to show that the financial statements conform to the relevant accounting framework and that the disclosures are adequate. The audit documentation also should explain how exceptions, unusual accounting questions, and findings contradictory to the audit team's final conclusions were resolved or treated. In addition, the resolution of any differences among audit team members must be documented. Taken altogether, these features should demonstrate that all auditing standards were observed and executed.

Audit Documentation Arrangement and Indexing

Each public accounting firm has a different method of arranging and indexing audit documentation files. In general, however, the documentation is grouped (or electronically hyperlinked) in order behind the trial balance according to balance-sheet and income-statement captions. Usually, the current assets appear first, followed by fixed assets, other assets, liabilities, equities, income, and expense accounts. A **lead schedule** is a summary of the accounts or components in an account group. For cash, the lead schedule includes all of the company's cash accounts. For inventory, the lead schedule may include inventory amounts by product line, cost of goods sold, and reserves for obsolescence. The amounts on the lead schedule should agree with prior-year numbers, the current-year general ledger amounts, and, after any adjustments, the audited financial statements. Although this is normally accomplished in the electronic workpaper files, the typical arrangement is shown in writing in Exhibit 3.5.

Several audit documentation preparation techniques are quite important for the quality of the finished product. The points explained here are illustrated in Exhibit 3.6.

- *Indexing.* Each document (whether electronic or paper) is given an index number, like a book page number, so it can be found, removed, and replaced without loss.
- *Cross-referencing.* Numbers or memoranda related to other documents carry the index of the other documents so the connections can be followed.
- *Heading.* Each document is titled with the name of the company, the balance-sheet date, and a descriptive title of the document's contents.
- *Signatures and initials.* The auditor who performs the work and the supervisor who reviews it must sign the audit documentation so personnel can be identified.
- *Dates of audit work.* The dates of performance and review are recorded on the documents so reviewers of the documentation can tell when the work was performed.
- *Audit marks and explanations.* Audit marks (or "tick marks") are the auditor's shorthand for abbreviating comments about work performed. Audit marks always must be accompanied by a full explanation of the auditing work. (Notice in Exhibit 3.6 the auditor's confirmation of the disputed account payable liability.) On electronic documents, comments can be hyperlinked so that reviewers can find additional explanations of audit procedures performed.

EXHIBIT 3.5
Current Audit
Documentation File

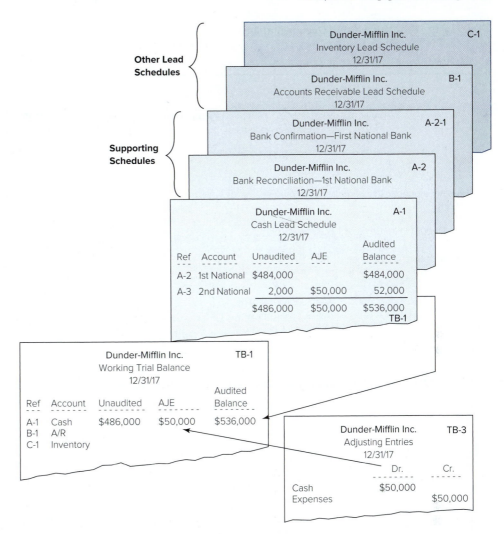

AS 1215 requires that audit documentation, including workpapers and other documents that form the basis of the engagement, be retained for seven years following the conclusion of the engagement (usually the audit report release date). AS 1215 also stresses that audit documentation to be retained include those workpapers that document any discussions and subsequent resolution of differences in professional judgment among the audit team members. PCAOB regulations also require that all documentation be finalized within 45 days of the audit report's release date. With sufficient (documented) justification, auditors may subsequently add, but may not remove, documentation after the 45-day period. Although the AS 1215 requirements are only for public companies, most public accounting firms use the same requirements for their nonpublic clients.

✓ REVIEW CHECKPOINTS

3.23   What information would you expect to find in a permanent audit file?

3.24   What information would you expect to find in a current audit file?

3.25   What is considered the most important content of the auditor's current audit documentation files?

3.26   What are the documentation retention requirements of AS 1215?

EXHIBIT 3.6 **Illustrative Audit Documentation**

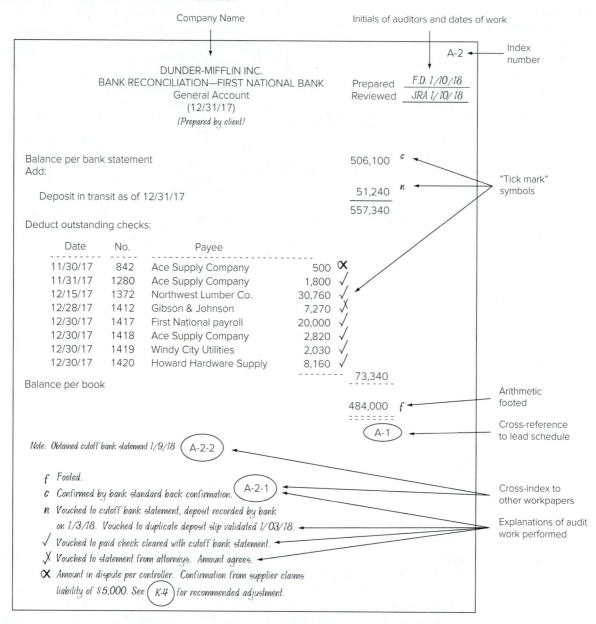

Company Name

Initials of auditors and dates of work

A-2 — Index number

DUNDER-MIFFLIN INC.
BANK RECONCILIATION—FIRST NATIONAL BANK
General Account
(12/31/17)
(Prepared by client)

Prepared — F.D. 1/10/18
Reviewed — JRA 1/10/18

Balance per bank statement   506,100 *c*   "Tick mark" symbols
Add:

  Deposit in transit as of 12/31/17   51,240 *n*
                                         557,340

Deduct outstanding checks:

Date	No.	Payee		
11/30/17	842	Ace Supply Company	500	⊗
11/31/17	1280	Ace Supply Company	1,800	✓
12/15/17	1372	Northwest Lumber Co.	30,760	✓
12/28/17	1412	Gibson & Johnson	7,270	✗
12/30/17	1417	First National payroll	20,000	✓
12/30/17	1418	Ace Supply Company	2,820	✓
12/30/17	1419	Windy City Utilities	2,030	✓
12/30/17	1420	Howard Hardware Supply	8,160	✓
			73,340	

Balance per book

                                         484,000 *f* — Arithmetic footed

                                         A-1 — Cross-reference to lead schedule

Note: Obtained cutoff bank statement 1/9/18   A-2-2

f Footed.
c Confirmed by bank standard back confirmation.   A-2-1   — Cross-index to other workpapers
n Vouched to cutoff bank statement, deposit recorded by bank
     on 1/3/18. Vouched to duplicate deposit slip validated 1/03/18.   — Explanations of audit work performed
✓ Vouched to paid check cleared with cutoff bank statement.
✗ Vouched to statement from attorneys. Amount agrees.
⊗ Amount in dispute per controller. Confirmation from supplier claims
   liability of $5,000. See K-4 for recommended adjustment.

Summary

This chapter contains a description of the specific set of planning activities that auditors undertake when completing an engagement. *Pre-engagement activities* start with the work of deciding whether to accept a new client and, on an annual basis, whether to continue the engagement for existing clients. Public accounting firms are not obligated to provide audit services to every company or organization that requests them, and they regularly exercise discretion when deciding which they choose to undertake. For audit engagements, the investigation may involve the cooperative task of communicating with the organization's former (predecessor) auditors. In addition, firms need to make sure that they are in compliance with both independence and ethical requirements before deciding whether to accept a new client or continue with an existing client.

The *audit plan* is a comprehensive list of the specific audit procedures that the audit team needs to perform to gather sufficient appropriate evidence on which to base its opinion on the financial statements. Although risk assessment (discussed in Chapter 4) provides the basis to determine the nature, timing, and extent of procedures to be performed at an audit client, many other aspects of audit planning are also discussed in this chapter. Other planning issues include properly staffing the audit, using IT auditors, considering the work of audit specialists and using the work of internal auditors, and creating the time budget.

Because financial statement measurements and footnote disclosure information are not flawlessly accurate, auditors need to ultimately ensure that the financial statements are materially accurate and do not contain material misstatements. Information is material if it is likely to influence financial statement users' decisions. As a result, the engagement team needs to think carefully about the appropriate level of materiality during the planning process. The auditor will then use this materiality as a guide to (1) plan and execute substantive testing procedures, (2) evaluate audit evidence, and (3) make final decisions about the auditor's report.

Auditors then use a variety of procedures to gather evidence about management's assertions related to the amounts and disclosures in a client's financial statements. In general, auditors use eight different types of audit procedures to gather evidence: (1) inspection of records and documents (*vouching, tracing, scanning*), (2) inspection of tangible assets, (3) observation, (4) inquiry, (5) confirmation, (6) recalculation, (7) reperformance, and (8) analytical procedures. One or more of these procedures may be used no matter what account balance, control procedure, class of transactions, or other information is under audit. Auditors must consider a number of factors when planning based on the audit client's computing environment. And of course, the selection of procedures to be completed must always be tailored to the exacting nuances of the client's computing environment. Finally, CAATs can improve both engagement effectiveness and efficiency and are used by auditors on most engagements.

The closing topic in this chapter is a brief overview of audit documentation with some basic pointers about their form, content, and overall purpose. At this stage in the audit process, we have accepted (or retained) the client, considered the types of audit procedures that might be performed to gather evidence, and thought about the impact of a client's technological environment. The next step in the audit process is the assessment of inherent risk in both the financial statement account balances and footnote disclosures, which serves as the focus of the next chapter.

Key Terms

analytical procedures: Procedures that allow auditors to evaluate financial information by studying relationships among both financial and nonfinancial data. When used near the end of the audit, analytical procedures allow auditors to assess the conclusions reached during the audit and evaluate the overall financial statement presentation.

audit documentation: The written basis for the auditor's conclusions that provides the necessary support for the auditor's assertions and representations made in the auditor's report.

audit engagement partner: The person with the final responsibility for the audit, and usually an industry specialist.

audit plan: A comprehensive list of the specific audit procedures that the audit team members need to perform to gather sufficient appropriate evidence on which to base their opinion on the financial statements. The professional standards require that the auditor plan each audit engagement, including the establishment of an overall strategy for each audit engagement.

audit trail: The chain of evidence provided through coding, cross-references, and documentation connecting account balances and other summary results with the original transaction source documents.

continuing audit files (or permanent files): The audit documentation containing information of *continuing audit significance* for current and past audits of the same client.

engagement letter: This letter sets forth the understanding with the client, including in particular (1) the objectives of the engagement, (2) management's responsibilities, (3) the auditors' responsibilities, and (4) any limitations of the engagement.

Form 8-K: The "current events" report filed periodically at the occurrence of major events, such as earnings releases, major asset sales, acquisitions, and auditor changes.

independence in appearance: The extent to which others (particularly financial statement users) perceive auditors to be independent.

independence in fact: Auditors' mental attitude and impartiality with respect to the client.

interim audit work: The procedures performed several weeks or months before the balance-sheet date.

lead schedule: A summary of the accounts in or components of an account group.

materiality: An amount or event that is likely to influence financial statement users' decisions. Thus, *material information* is a synonym for *important information.* The emphasis is on the financial statement users' point of view, not on the auditors' or managers' points of view.

permanent files (or continuing audit files): The audit documentation containing information of *continuing audit significance* for current and past audits of the same client.

planning memorandum: The document summarizing the preliminary analytical procedures and the materiality assessment with specific directions about the effect on the audit.

predecessor auditor: The public accounting firm that has been terminated or has voluntarily withdrawn from an audit engagement (whether the audit has been completed or not).

quality assurance partner: The second audit partner on the audit team as required for audits of financial statements filed with the SEC who reviews the audit team's work in critical audit areas (those areas with the highest potential audit risk).

specialists: The persons skilled in fields other than accounting and auditing—actuaries, appraisers, attorneys, engineers, and geologists—who are not members of the public accounting firm.

substantive audit plan: Document that contains a list of audit procedures for gathering evidence related to the relevant assertions identified for the significant financial statement accounts and disclosures on an audit client.

termination letter: The documentation provided to former clients dealing with the subject of future services, in particular (1) access to audit documentation by new auditors, (2) reissuance of the auditors' report when required for SEC reporting or comparative financial reporting, and (3) fee arrangements for such future services. The termination letter also can contain a report of the auditor's understanding of the circumstances of termination (e.g., disagreements about accounting principles and audit procedures, fees, or other conflicts).

tracing: An audit procedure in which the auditor selects a basic source document and follows its processing path *forward* to find its final recording in a summary journal or ledger. In practice, however, the term *tracing* may be used to describe following the path in either direction.

vouching: An audit procedure in which an auditor selects an item of financial information, usually from a journal or ledger, and follows its path back through the processing steps to its origin (i.e., the *source documentation* that supports the item selected).

year-end audit work: The procedures performed shortly before and after the balance-sheet date.

Multiple-Choice Questions for Practice and Review

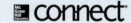 All applicable questions are available with *Connect.*

LO 3-1

3.27 When initiating communications with predecessor auditors, prospective auditors should expect

   a. To take responsibility for obtaining the client's consent for the predecessor to give information about prior audits.

   b. To conduct interviews with the partner and manager in charge of the predecessor public accounting firm's engagement.

   c. To obtain copies of some or all of the predecessor auditors' audit documentation.

   d. All of the above.

LO 3-2

3.28 Generally accepted auditing standards require that auditors always prepare and use

   a. A written planning memorandum explaining the auditors' understanding of the client's business.

   b. A written client consent to discuss audit matters with prospective auditors.

c. A written audit plan.

d. The written time budgets and schedules for performing each audit.

LO 3-2   3.29 When planning an audit, which of the following is *not* a factor that affects auditors' decisions about the quantity, type, and content of audit documentation?

a. The auditors' need to document compliance with generally accepted auditing standards.

b. The auditors' need to verify the existence of new sales contracts important for the client's business.

c. The auditors' judgment about their independence with regard to the client.

d. The auditors' judgments about materiality.

LO 3-6   3.30 Audit documentation that shows the detailed evidence and procedures regarding the balance in the accumulated depreciation account for the year under audit will be found in the

a. Current file audit documentation.

b. Permanent file audit documentation.

c. Administrative audit documentation in the current file.

d. Planning memorandum in the current file.

LO 3-6   3.31 An auditor's permanent file audit documentation most likely will contain

a. Internal control analysis for the current year.

b. The most recent engagement letter.

c. Memoranda of conference with management.

d. Excerpts of the corporate charter and bylaws.

LO 3-3   3.32 Which of the following is *not* a benefit claimed for the practice of determining materiality in the initial planning stage of an audit?

a. Being able to fine-tune the audit work for effectiveness and efficiency.

b. Avoiding the problem of doing more work than necessary (overauditing).

c. Being able to decide early what type of audit opinion to issue.

d. Avoiding the problem of doing too little work (underauditing).

LO 3-5   3.33 Spreadsheet software would be most useful for which of the following audit activities?

a. Testing internal controls over computerized accounting applications.

b. Preparing an audit plan.

c. Preparing a comparison of current-year expenses with those from the previous year.

d. Drafting a planning memorandum.

LO 3-5   3.34 Which of the following is an advantage of computer-assisted audit techniques (CAATs)?

a. All the CAATs programs are written in one computer language.

b. The software can be used for audits of clients that use differing computer equipment and file formats.

c. The use of CAATs has reduced the need for the auditor to study input controls for computer-related procedures.

d. The use of CAATs can be substituted for a relatively large part of the required testing.

LO 3-5   3.35 A primary advantage of using CAATs in the audit of an advanced computerized system is that it enables the auditor to

a. Substantiate the accuracy of data through self-checking digits and hash totals.

b. Utilize the speed and accuracy of the computer.

c. Verify the performance of machine operations that leave visible evidence of occurrence.

d. Gather and store large amounts of supportive audit evidence in machine-readable form.

LO 3-2   3.36 An audit engagement letter should normally include which of the following matters of agreement between the auditor and the client?

a. Schedules and analyses to be prepared by the client's employees.

b. Methods of statistical sampling the auditor will use.

c. Specification of litigation in progress against the client.

d. Client representations about availability of all minutes of meetings of the board of directors.

LO 3-2

3.37 When auditing Vandalay Jewelry, Costanza, CPA, was not familiar with the quality and cut of the company's precious jewel inventory. To address this shortcoming, Costanza hired Benes, an expert in jewel valuation, to assist as an audit specialist for the inventory valuation. Should Costanza refer to Benes's work in the audit report?

a. Yes, the auditors' report should mention the fact that an audit specialist was used.

b. The auditors' report should mention the use of the audit specialist only when the audit specialist's findings affect the auditors' conclusions.

c. The use of an audit specialist need not be mentioned if the auditors decide not to take responsibility for the audit specialist's findings.

d. The auditors' report should mention the audit specialist only if Vandalay agrees with the audit specialist's findings.

LO 3-2

3.38 Which of the following engagement planning procedures would most likely assist the auditor in identifying related-party transactions before the balance-sheet date?

a. Interviewing internal auditors about their reporting responsibilities.

b. Reviewing accounting records for recurring transactions occurring near year-end.

c. Inspecting communications with the client's legal counsel regarding recorded contingent liabilities.

d. Scanning the minutes for significant transactions with members of the board of directors.

LO 3-2

3.39 Which of the following communications is most likely to be written before the balance-sheet date?

a. A report to the audit committee on the results of testing of internal control over cash receipts.

b. Confirmation letters to vendors confirming the amounts they owe to the client.

c. An attorney's letter regarding contingent liabilities.

d. An engagement letter.

LO 3-2

3.40 Which of the following procedures would most likely be performed during planning?

a. Surprise counting of the client's petty cash fund.

b. Reporting internal control deficiencies to the audit committee.

c. Performing a search for unrecorded liabilities.

d. Identifying related parties.

LO 3-1

3.41 Prior to accepting a new audit engagement, a public accounting firm should

a. Attempt to contact the predecessor auditors.

b. Evaluate the integrity of management.

c. Assess the firm's resources to ensure that they are sufficient to permit the firm to accept the engagement.

d. All of the above.

LO 3-2

3.42 An audit plan contains

a. Specifications of audit standards relevant to the financial statements being audited.

b. Specifications of procedures the auditors believe appropriate for the financial statements under audit.

c. Documentation of the assertions under audit, the evidence obtained, and the conclusions reached.

d. Reconciliation of the account balances in the financial statements with the account balances in the client's general ledger.

LO 3-4

3.43 The revenue cycle of a company generally includes which accounts?

a. Inventory, accounts payable, and general expenses.

b. Inventory, general expenses, and payroll.

c. Cash, accounts receivable, and sales.

d. Cash, notes payable, and capital stock.

LO 3-4

3.44 When auditing the existence assertion for an asset, auditors proceed from the
   a. Financial statement amounts back to the potentially unrecorded items.
   b. Potentially unrecorded items forward to the financial statement amounts.
   c. General ledger back to the supporting original transaction documents.
   d. Supporting original transaction documents to the general ledger.

LO 3-4

3.45 Confirmations of accounts receivable provide evidence primarily about which two assertions?
   a. Completeness and valuation.
   b. Valuation and rights and obligations.
   c. Existence and rights and obligations.
   d. Existence and completeness.

LO 3-3

3.46 With respect to the concept of materiality, which of the following statements is correct?
   a. Materiality depends only on the dollar amount of an item relative to other items in the financial statements.
   b. Materiality depends on the nature of a transaction rather than the dollar amount of the transaction.
   c. Materiality is determined by reference to AICPA guidelines.
   d. Materiality is a matter of professional judgment.

LO 3-4

3.47 When evaluating whether accounting estimates made by management are reasonable, the audit team would be most interested in which of the following?
   a. Key factors that are consistent with prior periods.
   b. Assumptions that are similar to industry guidelines.
   c. Measurements that are objective and not susceptible to bias.
   d. Evidence of a conservative systematic bias.

LO 3-4

3.48 Which of the following would be considered an analytical procedure?
   a. Testing purchasing, shipping, and receiving cutoff activities.
   b. Comparing inventory balances to recent sales activities.
   c. Projecting the deviation rate of a statistical sample to the population.
   d. Reconciling physical counts to perpetual records and general ledger balances.
   (AICPA adapted)

LO 3-2

3.49 Which of the following procedures would a CPA most likely perform in planning a financial statement audit?
   a. Make inquiries of the client's lawyer concerning pending litigation.
   b. Perform cutoff tests of cash receipts and disbursements.
   c. Compare financial information with nonfinancial operating data.
   d. Recalculate the prior-years' accruals and deferrals.
   (AICPA adapted)

LO 3-4

3.50 Which of the following statements is correct concerning analytical procedures used in planning an audit engagement?
   a. They often replace the tests of controls that are performed to assess control risk.
   b. They typically use financial and nonfinancial data aggregated at a high level.
   c. They usually involve the comparison of assertions developed by management to ratios calculated by an auditor.
   d. They are often used to develop an auditor's preliminary judgment about materiality.
   (AICPA adapted)

LO 3-2

3.51 The company being audited has an internal auditor who is both competent and objective. The independent auditor wants to assign tasks for the internal auditor to perform. Under these circumstances, the independent auditor may
   a. Allow the internal auditor to perform certain tests of internal controls.
   b. Allow the internal auditor to audit a major subsidiary of the company.

    c. Not assign any task to the internal auditor because of the internal auditor's lack of independence.

    d. Allow the internal auditor to perform analytical procedures but not be involved with any tests of details.

(AICPA adapted)

LO 3-1

3.52 Which of the following conditions most likely would pose the greatest risk in accepting a new audit engagement?

    a. Staff will need to be rescheduled to cover this new client.

    b. There will be a client-imposed scope limitation.

    c. The firm will have to hire a specialist in one audit area.

    d. The client's financial reporting system has been in place for 10 years.

(AICPA adapted)

Exercises and Problems

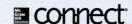 All applicable Exercises and Problems are available with *Connect*.

LO 3-4

3.53 **General Audit Procedures and Financial Statement Assertions.** The eight general audit procedures produce evidence about the principal management assertions in financial statements. However, some procedures are useful for producing evidence about certain assertions, and other procedures are useful for producing evidence about other assertions. The assertion being audited can influence the auditors' choice of procedures.

Required:

Opposite each general audit procedure, write the management assertions most usefully audited by using each procedure.

Audit Procedures	PCAOB Assertions	ASB Assertions
a. Inspection of records or documents (vouching)		
b. Inspection of records or documents (tracing)		
c. Inspection of records or documents (scanning)		
d. Inspection of tangible assets		
e. Observation		
f. Confirmation		
g. Inquiry		
h. Recalculation		
i. Reperformance		
j. Analytical procedures		

LO 3-4

3.54 **Audit Procedures.** Auditors use different types of audit procedures to gather the evidence necessary to conclude that the risk of material misstatement for each relevant assertion has been reduced to an acceptably low level. List eight different types of procedures auditors can use during an audit of financial statements, and give an example of each.

LO 3-4

3.55 **Confirmation Procedure.** A CPA accumulates various types of evidence on which to base the opinion on financial statements. Among this evidence are confirmations from third parties.

Required:

    a. What is an audit confirmation?

    b. What characteristics of the confirmation process and the recipient are important if a CPA is to consider the confirmation evidence appropriate?

LO 3-4

3.56 **Potential Audit Procedure Failures.** For each of the general audit procedures of (1) recalculation, (b) observation, (c) confirmation (accounts receivable, securities, or other assets), (d) inquiry, (e) inspection of internal documents, (f) recalculation, (g) reperformance, and (h) analytical procedures, discuss one way the procedure could be misapplied or the auditors could be misled in such a way as to render the work (audit evidence) misleading or irrelevant. Give examples that are different from the examples in this chapter.

LO 3-6

3.57 **Audit Documentation.** The preparation of audit documentation is an integral part of an auditor's examination of financial statements. On a recurring engagement, auditors review the audit plans and audit documentation from the prior audit while planning the current audit to determine their usefulness for the current-year work.

Required:

a. (1) What are the purposes or functions of audit documentation?
   (2) What records may be included in audit documentation?

b. What factors affect the auditors' judgment of the type and content of the audit documentation for a particular engagement?

c. What should be included in audit documentation to support auditors' compliance with generally accepted auditing standards?

d. How can auditors make the most effective use of the prior-year audit plans in a recurring audit?

(AICPA adapted)

LO 3-1

3.58 **Communications between Predecessor and Successor Auditors.** Assume that Smith & Smith, CPAs, audited Apollo Shoes Inc., last year. Now CEO Larry Lancaster wishes to engage Anderson, Olds, and Watershed, CPAs (AOW) to audit its annual financial statements. Lancaster is generally pleased with the services provided by Smith & Smith, but he thinks the audit work was too detailed and interfered excessively with normal office routines. AOW has asked Lancaster to inform Smith & Smith of the decision to change auditors, but he does not wish to do so.

Required:

List and discuss the steps AOW should follow with regard to dealing with a predecessor auditor and a new client before accepting the engagement.

LO 3-1

3.59 **Predecessor and Successor Auditors.** The president of Allpurpose Loan Company had a genuine dislike for external auditors. Almost any conflict generated a towering rage. Consequently, the company changed auditors often.

The firm of Wells & Ratley (W&R), CPAs, was recently hired to audit the 2017 financial statements. W&R succeeded the firm of Canby & Company (C&C), which had obtained the audit after Albrecht & Hubbard (A&H) had been fired. A&H audited the 2016 financial statements and rendered a report that contained an additional paragraph explaining an uncertainty about Allpurpose Loan Company's loan loss reserve. Goodbye A&H! The president then hired C&C to audit the 2017 financial statements, and Chris Canby started the work, but before the audit could be completed, Canby was fired and W&R was hired to complete the audit. C&C did not issue an audit report because the audit was not finished.

Required:

Does the Wells & Ratley firm need to initiate communications with Canby & Company? With Albrecht & Hubbard? With both? Explain your response in terms of the purposes of communications between predecessor and successor auditors.

LO 3-1

3.60 **Client Selection.** You are a CPA in a regional public accounting firm that has 10 offices in three states. Mr. Shine has approached you with a request for an audit. He is president of Hitech Software and Games Inc., a five-year-old company that has recently grown to $500 million in sales and $200 million in total assets. Shine is thinking about going public with a $25 million issue of common stock, of which $10 million would be a secondary issue of shares he holds. You are very happy about this opportunity because you know Shine is the new president of the Symphony Society board and has made quite a civic impression since he came to your medium-size city seven years ago. Hitech is one of the growing employers in the city.

Required:

a. Discuss the sources of information and the types of inquiries that you and the firm's partners may make in connection with accepting Hitech as a new client.

b. Do professional audit standards require any investigation of prospective clients?

c. Suppose Shine also told you that 10 years ago his closely held hamburger franchise business went bankrupt, and on investigation, you learn from its former auditors (your own firm in another city) that Shine was fraudulent in its application of franchise-fee income recognition rules and presented such difficulties that your firm resigned from the audit (before the bankruptcy). Do you think the partner in charge of the audit practice should accept Hitech as a new client?

LO 3-2

3.61 **Using the Work of Internal Auditors.** North, CPA, is planning an independent audit of the financial statements of General Company. In determining the nature, timing, and extent of the audit procedures, North is considering General's internal audit function, which is staffed by Tyler.

Required:

a. In what ways can the internal auditor's work be relevant to North, the independent auditor?

b. What factors should North consider, and what inquiries should North make in deciding whether to use Tyler's internal audit work?

(AICPA adapted)

LO 3-5

3.62 **Using the Computer to Discover Intentional Financial Misstatements in Transactions and Account Balances.** AMI International is a large office products company. Headquarters management imposed pressure on operating division managers to meet profit forecasts. The division managers met these profit goals using several accounting manipulations involving the record-keeping system that maintained all transactions and account balances on computer files. Employees who operated the computer accounting system were aware of the modifications of policy the managers ordered to accomplish the financial statement manipulations. The management and employees carried out these activities:

1. Deferred inventory write-downs for obsolete and damaged goods.
2. Kept open the sales entry system after the quarterly and annual cutoff dates, recording sales of goods shipped after the cutoff dates.
3. Recorded as sales transactions that had been coded as leases of office equipment.
4. Recorded shipments to branch offices as sales.
5. Postponed recording vendors' invoices for parts and services until later, but the actual invoice date was faithfully entered according to accounting policy.

Required:

Describe one or more procedures that could be performed with CAATs to detect signs of each of these transaction manipulations. Limit your answer to the actual work accomplished by the computer software.

CHAPTER 4

Management Fraud and Audit Risk

Profit is the result of risks wisely selected.

> Frederick Barnard Hawley, American economist (1843–1929)

Risk comes from not knowing what you're doing.

> Warren Buffett, widely regarded as one of the most successful investors in the world

Professional Standards References

Topic	AU-C/ISA Section	AS Section
Overall Objectives of the Independent Auditor	200	1001, 1005, 1010, 1015
Consideration of Fraud in a Financial Statement Audit	240	2401
Consideration of Laws and Regulations	250	2405
Communications with Audit Committees	260	1301
Consideration of Internal Control in an Integrated Audit	265	2201
Audit Planning	300	2101
Identifying and Assessing the Risks of Material Misstatement	315	2110
Materiality	320	2105
Auditors' Responses to Risks of Material Misstatement	330	2301
Audit Evidence	500	1105
Substantive Analytical Procedures	520	2305
Auditing Accounting Estimates	540	2501
Auditing Fair Value Measurements and Disclosures	540	2502
Related Parties	550	2410

LEARNING OBJECTIVES

The professional standards emphasize the importance of an auditor's identification and assessment of the risks of material misstatement that exist related to an audit client. Once each of the risks is identified and assessed, the auditor then needs to plan an appropriate response. Given the importance of risk assessment, it is not surprising that the professional standards state that the risk assessment process underlies the entire audit process. In Chapter 3, we covered the engagement planning process, beginning with pre-engagement activities, supervision, materiality, and the emerging importance of computer-assisted audit techniques (CAATs). In this chapter, we provide comprehensive coverage of an auditor's risk assessment and its impact on the audit process.

Your objectives are to be able to:

LO 4-1 Define *audit risk* and describe how it can be broken down into the three separate components of the audit risk model to help assess and respond to such risks during the audit planning process.

LO 4-2 Explain auditors' responsibility for fraud risk assessment and define and explain the differences among several types of fraud and errors that might occur in an organization.

LO 4-3 Explain an auditor's responsibility to assess inherent risk, including a description of the type of risk assessment procedures

that should be performed when assessing inherent risk on an audit engagement.

LO 4-4 Understand the different sources of information and the audit procedures used by auditors when assessing risks, including analytical procedures, brainstorming, and inquiries.

LO 4-5 Explain how auditors complete and document the overall assessment of inherent risk.

LO 4-6 Explain auditors' responsibilities with respect to a client's failure to comply with laws or regulations.

LO 4-7 Describe the content and purpose of an audit strategy memorandum.

INTRODUCTION

Take a step back in time to March 2001. **Enron,** one of the world's largest energy companies, reported revenues that ranked it among the top 10 companies in the United States. The company had doubled its revenues from 1999 to 2000, and company management predicted that it would do so again for the 2001 fiscal year. **Andersen,** then one of the world's five largest public accounting firms, provided auditing and consulting services to Enron, earning Andersen a million dollars a week in fees. While the auditors expressed concerns with respect to some of Enron's aggressive accounting practices, the future appeared strong for both companies. Andersen's planning team projected both increased growth for Enron and increased fees for Andersen.

Fast-forward nine months. By December 2001, Enron was a shell of its former self. The company had terminated almost its entire workforce, leaving its Houston skyline-dominating complex of buildings dark and empty. Enron's share price had plummeted from $90 in August 2000 to less than a dollar by December 2001, leaving many of its employees, who had invested their life savings in the high-flying energy company, out of work and virtually penniless. Enron's failure struck an irreparable blow to Andersen's reputation; one by one, Andersen's other clients decided to find new audit firms rather than be associated with a firm that was now labeled by the business press as "low quality." Beset with shareholder lawsuits and government-led investigations of its audit practices, the firm struggled to maintain its very existence. After providing auditing services for almost a century to some of America's largest companies, Andersen decided to leave the practice of auditing public companies by August 31, 2002. Most of the firm's personnel also left the failing firm, attempting to find positions with other firms that had picked up Andersen's former clients. The firm's partnership equity, depleted by litigation and shareholder settlements, had been reduced to almost nothing, leaving new partners with nothing to show for the hundreds of thousands of dollars they paid to buy into the firm's partnership. Accounting students with prestigious (and lucrative) offers from Enron and Andersen found themselves scrambling for jobs when their offers were rescinded late in the recruiting season.

How could one of the oldest and most venerable auditing firms (Andersen) miss the financial statement fraud going on at one of its largest audit clients, resulting in the firm's ultimate dissolution? To start, the audit team assigned to the Enron engagement failed to identify and then assess the risks of material misstatement. In addition, for those risks that were identified and assessed properly, the auditors failed to adequately respond to those risks of material misstatement. In this chapter, we will describe how auditors identify, assess, and then properly respond to the risks of material misstatement that exist at their audit clients.

AUDIT RISK (AU-C 320, AS 1101)

LO 4-1
Define *audit risk* and describe how it can be broken down into the three separate components of the audit risk model to help assess and respond to such risks during the audit planning process.

Audit Risk

Audit risk is the probability that an audit team will express an inappropriate audit opinion when the financial statements are materially misstated (i.e., give an unmodified opinion on financial statements that are misleading because of material misstatements that the auditors failed to discover). Such a risk always exists, even when audits are well planned and carefully performed. Of course, the risk is much higher in poorly planned and carelessly performed audits. The auditing profession has no official standard for an acceptable level of overall audit risk except that it should be "appropriately" low. In practice, audit risk is evaluated at both the overall financial statement level (as a whole) and for each *significant account and disclosure* through a focus on the *relevant assertions* identified. A **significant account or disclosure** is an account or disclosure that has a reasonable possibility of containing a material misstatement regardless of the effect of internal controls. A **relevant assertion** is a management assertion that has a reasonable possibility of containing a material misstatement without regard to the effect of internal controls. The concern an auditor has regarding any particular assertion depends on the significant account that the auditor is testing (or to which the assertion relates). For example, an auditor may deem the occurrence assertion to present more risk when testing revenue than the completeness assertion presents. Most companies want to report a healthy stream of revenue, so it is unlikely that they will omit sales that would violate the completeness assertion. It is more likely that a company reports sales that did not occur to present more revenue, which would violate the occurrence assertion.

To help better understand and ultimately mitigate audit risk, the professional standards break down overall audit risk (see Exhibit 4.1) into the risks (1) that a material misstatement will even occur (*inherent risk*), (2) that it would not be prevented or detected by client internal controls (*control risk*), and (3) that is not detected by the auditor's own procedures (*detection risk*). Because inherent risk and control risk are related to the company and its overall environment, these two components are combined into the **risk of material misstatement (RMM)**, which is the risk a material misstatement exists in the financial statements before auditors apply their own procedures. Each of these components is now discussed in detail.

EXHIBIT 4.1 Inherent, Control, and Detection Risk

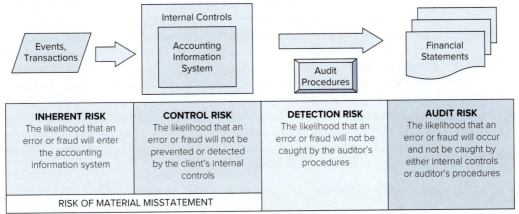

Inherent Risk

Inherent risk is the probability that, in the absence of internal controls, material errors or frauds could enter the accounting system used to develop financial statements. You can think of inherent risk as the *susceptibility* of the account to misstatement. Inherent risk is a function of the nature of the client's business and strategy to achieve competitive advantage, the major types of transactions, and the effectiveness and integrity of its managers and accountants. It is important to understand that for different accounts, various *assertions* are riskier than others. For cash, *existence* is riskier than *completeness* because it is more likely that a client would try to include more cash than it really had on its balance sheet rather than less; and for accounts payable, *completeness* is riskier than *existence* because it is more likely that a client would try to understate what it really owed rather than overstate the amount. As a result, auditors focus their attention on *relevant assertions*. Finally, it is important for students to remember that auditors do not create or control inherent risk. They can only try to assess its magnitude in an appropriate manner. This will be discussed in more detail later in the chapter.

Control Risk

Control risk is the probability that the client's internal control activities will *fail* to prevent or detect material misstatements provided that such misstatements enter or would have entered the accounting system in the first place. So, for misstatements that could occur, what is the audit client doing about such occurrences? Does it have the proper systems, processes, and controls in place to either prevent or detect misstatements? Recall from our discussion of auditing standards in Chapter 2 that one of the major purposes of an internal control system is to ensure appropriate processing and recording of transactions for the production of reliable financial statements. Similar to inherent risk, auditors do not create or manage control risk. They can only evaluate an entity's internal control system and assess its magnitude in an appropriate manner.

External auditors' task of control risk assessment begins with learning about an entity's internal controls that are designed to prevent and detect material misstatements related to each relevant assertion for each significant account and disclosure. The auditors then perform tests of controls if appropriate to determine whether they are operating effectively. This process is discussed in detail in Chapter 5.

Detection Risk

Detection risk is the probability that the auditor's own procedures will *fail* to detect material misstatements provided that any have entered the accounting system in the first place and have not been prevented or detected and corrected by the client's internal controls. In contrast to inherent risk and control risk, auditors *are* responsible for performing the evidence-gathering procedures that manage and establish detection risk. These audit procedures represent the auditors' opportunity to detect material misstatements that may exist in the financial statements. In other words, unlike inherent risk and control risk, auditors can and do influence the level of detection risk.

In Chapter 3, you learned about substantive procedures, the procedures used to detect material misstatements that may exist in the significant account balances and disclosures presented in the financial statements and footnotes. The two categories of *substantive procedures* are (1) tests of details of transactions and balances, which provide specific evidence directly supporting assertions; and (2) substantive analytical procedures, which study plausible relationships among financial and nonfinancial data. Auditors are able to reduce detection risk by completing more and stronger substantive tests. Generally speaking, in response to a higher assessed risk of material misstatement for a relevant assertion being audited, auditors must reduce detection risk to an appropriate level by planning appropriate substantive procedures. This relationship is now further illustrated with a discussion of the audit risk model.

Audit Risk Model

The three components of audit risk can be expressed in a conceptual model that is designed to help auditors understand how the assessment of each component affects the overall audit risk being faced on the engagement. It is important to stress that the following discussion is conceptual in nature. It is also important to point out that the audit risk model assumes that each of the elements is *independent*. Thus, the risks can be expressed in a model form as follows:

$$\text{Audit risk (AR)} = \text{Inherent risk (IR)} \times \text{Control risk (CR)} \times \text{Detection risk (DR)}$$

Assume that auditors want to perform an audit of a particular assertion or disclosure well enough to hold the AR to a relatively low level (e.g., 0.05, which means that, on average, 5 percent of audit opinions would be wrong). For example, suppose that an audit team thought *valuation* of a particular inventory balance was subject to great inherent risk (say, IR = 0.90) and that the client's internal control was not very effective (say, CR = 0.50). Thus, RMM would be 0.45 (0.90 × 0.50). If auditors wanted to keep audit risk at a low level (say, AR = 0.05), according to the model, this example would produce the following results:

$$\text{AR} = \text{IR} \times \text{CR} \times \text{DR}$$

$$0.05 = 0.90 \times 0.50 \times \text{DR}$$

Solving for DR: DR = 0.111 (rounded to 0.11)

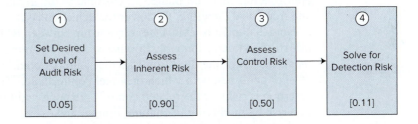

①	②	③	④
Set Desired Level of Audit Risk	Assess Inherent Risk	Assess Control Risk	Solve for Detection Risk
[0.05]	[0.90]	[0.50]	[0.11]

You should notice that the assessment of inherent risk (IR) and control risk (CR) led to a determination of detection risk (DR). As a result, detection risk depends on and is planned for based on the assessment of the other risk factors. DR is calculated and derived from the others by solving the risk model equation. It is not an independent judgment. Hence,

$$\text{DR} = \text{AR}/(\text{IR} \times \text{CR})$$

$$\text{DR} = 0.11 = 0.05/(0.90 \times 0.50)$$

While *detection risk* is defined as the risk that the auditors' procedures *fail* to detect material misstatements, it is important that you understand that the *application* of DR is different. The 11 percent represents *the amount of risk the auditors can allow* and still maintain overall audit risk at 0.05. Conceptually then, auditors must design procedures so that DR will not exceed 0.11 (approximately). Exhibit 4.2 provides a visual display of the steps in the audit risk process.

EXHIBIT 4.2

Audit Risk Model

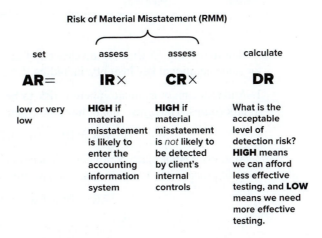

Risk of Material Misstatement (RMM)

set	assess	assess	calculate
AR=	**IR**×	**CR**×	**DR**
low or very low	**HIGH** if material misstatement is likely to enter the accounting information system	**HIGH** if material misstatement is *not* likely to be detected by client's internal controls	What is the acceptable level of detection risk? **HIGH** means we can afford less effective testing, and **LOW** means we need more effective testing.

Based on the allowable or planned level of detection risk (which is always based on the assessment of IR and CR), auditors modify the *nature*, the *timing*, and the *extent* of further audit procedures. The *nature* of an audit procedure refers to the type of procedure (e.g., observation, recalculation, inquiry) and the purpose of the procedure (e.g., test of controls, substantive procedure). When determining the nature of the audit procedure, the auditor is considering *what* to do. When doing so, the auditor considers the overall effectiveness of different types of audit procedures in detecting misstatements. While inquiry of management about whether accounts receivable listed on the balance sheet really exist is an audit procedure, it would not be an *effective* one. A much more effective procedure would be to confirm accounts receivable directly with the client's customers. *Timing* refers to *when* the audit procedures will be completed. To do so, the auditor typically considers whether to complete the procedures at an interim date or at the balance sheet date. While confirmation of accounts receivable may be performed at an interim date, auditors are expressing an opinion on year-end balances. The closer the procedures are performed to year-end (the balance sheet date), the more effective they are because there is less chance of a material misstatement occurring between the interim confirmation date and year-end. Finally, *extent* refers to the number of tests performed. Clearly, the larger the number of accounts receivable confirmations that are mailed to customers, the greater the chance of finding errors and fraud, and therefore, the lower the detection risk.

Note that there is an inverse relationship between RMM (i.e., inherent risk and control risk) and detection risk. In other words, the greater the risk of material misstatement, the lower the detection risk that auditors could allow in order to maintain the level of audit risk with which they feel comfortable. This makes sense. If the relevant assertion is risky or the related controls are poor, auditors would want to reduce detection risk by modifying the nature, timing, and extent of further procedures to increase their effectiveness. On the other hand, if the account is not risky and controls are strong, the auditor could employ less effective (and presumably less costly) substantive audit procedures.

The practical problem here is knowing whether the audit has been planned and performed well enough to limit the detection risk to as low as 0.11. Remember that the audit risk model is only a conceptual tool. Auditors cannot calculate the *exact* level of DR (or, for that matter, IR or CR), so the model represents more of a way to think about audit risks than a way to calculate them. However, the AICPA *Audit Sampling* Guide does use this model to calculate risks and the related sample sizes.

The Impact of Detection Risk Allowed on the Nature, Timing, and Extent of Further Audit Procedures

	Lower Detection Risk Allowed	Higher Detection Risk Allowed
Nature	More effective tests	Less effective tests
Timing	Testing performed at year-end	Testing can be performed at interim
Extent	More tests	Fewer tests

Before moving on with our discussion of audit risk, the conceptual model does allow for some additional key insights, including these:

1. Auditors cannot estimate inherent risk to be zero and omit other evidence-gathering procedures. Thus, you *cannot* have the condition

$$AR = IR\ (= 0) \times CR \times DR = 0$$

2. Auditors cannot place complete reliance on internal controls to the exclusion of other audit procedures. Thus, you cannot have the condition

$$AR = IR \times CR\ (= 0) \times DR = 0$$

3. Auditors would not seem to exhibit due professional care if the level of audit risk was too high, for example:

$$AR = IR\ (= 0.80) \times CR\ (= 0.80) \times DR\ (= 0.50) = 0.32$$

4. Although permissible, audit teams rarely choose to rely exclusively on evidence produced by substantive procedures. Even if they think that control risk is high, auditors often perform some tests of controls to make sure the controls are in place. The concern is that if the controls are so weak (or nonexistent) as to fail to detect material misstatements, an audit team would probably not feel comfortable relying solely on substantive procedures. For example, this combination would generally not be considered wise:

$$AR = IR\ (= 1.00) \times CR\ (= 1.00) \times DR\ (= 0.05) = 0.05$$

Up to this point, the components of the audit risk model have been expressed *quantitatively* (as numbers). In practice, largely all firms use *qualitative* measures of audit risk such as "low," "moderate," and "high." In fact, it is not likely that you will ever "solve" for AR on your audit engagement. Yet whether expressed quantitatively or qualitatively, audit theory places both inherent risk and control risk on a probability continuum. Consider the following illustration for control risk (Exhibit 4.3) where qualitative control risk categories are expressed in terms of representative control risk probabilities.

EXHIBIT 4.3

Qualitative and Quantitative Control Risk

Control Risk Categories (Qualitative)	Representative Control Risk Probabilities (Quantitative)
Low control risk	0.10–0.45
Moderate control risk	0.40–0.70
Control risk slightly below the maximum	0.60–0.95
Maximum control risk	1.00

When risk is measured qualitatively, how do firms solve an equation to determine the appropriate level of detection risk? The simple answer is they do not. Rather, firms typically use a matrix approach similar to the one shown in Exhibit 4.4. Auditors find the appropriate detection risk by reading the cell at the intersection of the assessed levels of inherent risk and control risk.

EXHIBIT 4.4

Matrix Approach to Detection Risk (DR) Determination

		Control Risk (CR)		
		Low	Moderate	High
Inherent Risk (IR)	Low	DR—High	DR—Moderate to High	DR—Moderate
	Moderate	DR—Moderate to High	DR—Moderate	DR—Low to Moderate
	High	DR—Moderate	DR—Low to Moderate	DR—Low

FRAUD RISK (AU-C 240, AS 2401)

LO 4-2

Explain auditors' responsibility for fraud risk assessment and define and explain the differences among several types of fraud and errors that might occur in an organization.

In our previous discussion about the audit risk model, you likely noticed that there was no specific mention of fraud risk. This does not mean that auditors can ever ignore fraud risk. On the contrary, auditors are required to consider fraud risk on each audit engagement for each relevant assertion related to each significant account and disclosure identified for an audit client. In effect, fraud risk is a special case of the risk of material misstatement related to those situations where management intended to mislead the marketplace by issuing fraudulent financial statements.

Thus, when applying the audit risk model and assessing the risk of material misstatement, the auditor must always remember that a misstatement in the financial statements may be caused by an error or a fraud. The key difference is *intent*. Specifically, did a manager at the client intend to commit a fraud? Or, was the misstatement due to an error made by an employee? Most importantly, according to the professional standards, an auditor is responsible for assessing the risk of material misstatement due to an error or fraud on every engagement. However, because of the damage to the capital markets caused by fraudsters who have intentionally misstated their financial statements, auditors must carefully assess fraud risk on every audit engagement. The following Auditing Insight identifies a number of CEO fraudsters from the recent past.

AUDITING INSIGHT | When CEOs Go Bad*

Perpetrator (age at trial)	Company	Verdict	Punishment
Conrad Black (62)	Hollinger International Inc.	Found guilty of three counts of mail fraud and one count of obstruction of justice related to the looting of his company of millions of dollars.	Successfully appealed two of the fraud convictions. Served a total of 3 years in federal prison.
Bernie Ebbers (63)	WorldCom	Found guilty on fraud and conspiracy charges related to an $11 billion accounting scandal.	Sentenced to 25 years in federal prison.
Walter Forbes (64)	Cendant	Found guilty of conspiracy to commit securities fraud and two counts of making false statements.	Sentenced to more than 12 years in prison; ordered to pay $3.3 billion in restitution.
Dennis Kozlowski (59)	Tyco International	Found guilty of stealing $600 million from the company.	Served a total of 6.5 years in a New York state prison.
Sanjay Kumar (44)	Computer Associates 28 International Inc. (CA)	Pleaded guilty to obstruction of justice and securities fraud charges related to CA's $3.3 billion accounting scandal.	Fined $8 million, sentenced to 12 years in prison, and ordered to pay $798.6 million in restitution.

Perpetrator (age at trial)	Company	Verdict	Punishment
Ken Lay (64)	**Enron**	Found guilty of securities fraud and related charges.	Suffered a massive coronary and passed away while awaiting sentencing.
Bernie Madoff (71)	**Madoff Investment Securities**	Pleaded guilty to securities fraud, money laundering, filing false statements with the SEC, wire fraud, mail fraud, and several other charges.	Sentenced to 150 years in prison.
Angelo R. Mozilo (72)	**Countrywide Financial**	Settled with the SEC over securities fraud and insider trading charges.	Agreed to pay $67.5 million in fines and accepted a lifetime ban from serving as an officer or director of any public company.
John Rigas (80)	**Adelphia Communications Inc.**	Found guilty on 18 felony counts of fraud and conspiracy.	Sentenced to 12 years in federal prison. Federal judge ordered his release due to diagnosis of terminal bladder cancer.
Richard Scrushy (52)	**HealthSouth**	Was acquitted of 36 criminal conspiracy charges related to the fraud but was later found guilty of other bribery, conspiracy, and mail fraud charges.	Settled civil charges with the SEC for $81 million; also in 2009, judge ruled that Scrushy was responsible for HealthSouth's fraud and ordered him to pay $2.87 billion. Served almost 5 years in federal prison.
Jeffrey Skilling (52)	**Enron**	Found guilty of securities fraud and related charges.	Originally sentenced to 24 years in prison; after many challenges to the punishment, in 2013 the sentence was reduced to 14 years.
Calisto Tanzi (70)	**Parmalat**	Found guilty of securities laws violations related to his company's 2003 collapse amid a giant financial fraud.	Currently serving a 17-year prison sentence.
Henry Yuen (53)	**Gemstar-TV Guide International**	Lost a civil trial for his role in fraudulently inflating revenues between 2000 and 2002.	Ordered to pay civil fines of $22.3 million, Yuen is currently "at large" and remains a fugitive as of 2016.

Sources: "Ebbers Is Sentenced to 25 Years for $11 Billion WorldCom Fraud," *The Wall Street Journal,* July 14, 2005, p. A1; "Daewoo Founder Gets Prison Term," *The Wall Street Journal,* May 31, 2006, p. B9; "Scrushy Is Convicted in Bribery Case," *The Wall Street Journal,* June 30, 2006, p. A3; "Ahold's Ex-CEO, Finance Chief Are Found Guilty in Fraud Case," *The Wall Street Journal,* May 23, 2006, p. B9; "Ex-CEO of Cendant Is Found Guilty in Third Trial," *The Wall Street Journal,* November 1, 2006, p. C3; "Skilling Gets 24 Years in Prison," *The Wall Street Journal,* October 24, 2006, p. C1; "Gemstar's Yuen Said He Destroyed Evidence; Judge: 'A No-Brainer,'" *The Wall Street Journal,* April 25, 2006, p. A1; "Yao Guilty in Fraud Case," *The Wall Street Journal,* March 15, 2007, p. C5; "Press Baron Black Guilty in Fraud Case," *The Wall Street Journal,* July 14, 2007, p. A3; "Former Sentinel Executives Agree to Settle Fraud Suit," *The Wall Street Journal,* May 20, 2008, p. C7; "Ex-CEO Agrees to Give Back $620 Million," *The Wall Street Journal,* December 7, 2007, p. A1; "Authorities Rule Out Samuel Israel Suicide," *The Wall Street Journal,* June 17, 2008, p. C7; "Trial Ends for Samsung Ex-Chairman," *The Wall Street Journal,* July 11, 2008, p. B5; "Former Samsung Chairman Found Guilty," *The Wall Street Journal,* July 17, 2008, p. B6; "Scandal-Plagued Samsung Chairman Quits," *BusinessWeek,* April 22, 2008, www.businessweek.com/globalbiz/content/apr2008/gb20080422_646584.htm (referenced August 10, 2010); "Parmalat Founder Gets Prison Term," *The Wall Street Journal,* December 19, 2008, p. B2: "Ex-General Re CEO Gets 2 Years," *The Wall Street Journal,* December 16, 2008; p. C7, Laurence Viele Davidson, "HealthSouth's Scrushy Liable in $2.88 Billion Fraud (Update 3)," *Bloomberg,* June 18, 2009; www.bloomberg.com/apps/news?pid=newsarchive&sid=a89tFKR4OevM (referenced August 10, 2011); Adam Liptak "Justices Limit Law Used for Corruption Cases," *The New York Times,* June 25, 2010, p1; Gretchen Morgenson, "Angelo Mozilo of Countrywide Settles Fraud Case for $67.5 Million," *The New York Times,* October 16, 2010, p.1; A. Smith, "Ex-Enron CEO Skilling Has 10 Years Lopped Off Sentence," CNN.com, June 21, 2013, http://money.cnn.com/2013/06/21/news/companies/skilling-enron-resentencing/index.html.

Given the damage that can occur to the capital markets as a result of fraud, the professional standards require auditors to hold a brainstorming session to consider the risk of fraud on every audit engagement. While the required brainstorming session will be discussed later in this chapter, it is important for students to recognize that the nature, timing, and extent of audit work should change as a result of the auditor's ultimate fraud risk assessment. In general, the lower the risk of material misstatement due to fraud, the less persuasive the audit evidence needs to be. It therefore follows that when fraud risk factors are identified, the auditor generally must obtain more persuasive audit evidence. Most importantly, once fraud risk factors are identified, the auditor should clearly identify the fraud risks and then design and perform procedures that respond directly to fraud risks. However, before continuing our discussion of fraud risk assessment and an auditor's response to fraud risk, it is important to provide some basic definitions about fraud and fraud risk factors.

Fraud

Fraud is the act of knowingly making material misrepresentations of fact with the intent of inducing someone to believe the falsehood and act on it and, thus, suffer a loss or damage. Through both fraud and aggressive financial reporting, some companies have caused financial statements to be misstated, usually by (1) overstating revenues and assets, (2) understating expenses and liabilities, and (3) giving disclosures that are misstated or that omit important information.[1] Fraud that affects financial (or other) information and causes financial statements to be materially misstated often arises from the perceived need to get through a difficult period. The difficult period may be characterized by cash shortage, increased competition, cost overruns, and similar events that cause financial difficulty. Managers usually view these conditions as temporary, believing that getting a new loan, selling stock, or otherwise buying time to recover can overcome them. In the meantime, falsified financial statements are used to benefit the company. Generally, fraudulent financial statements show financial performance and ratios that are more favorable than current industry experience or than the company's own history. Exhibit 4.5 illustrates three categories of factors that might indicate increased risk of fraudulent financial reporting.

EXHIBIT 4.5 **Fraud Risk Factors**

Management's Characteristics and Influence	Industry Conditions	Operating Characteristics and Financial Stability
• Management has a motivation (bonus compensation, stock options, etc.) to engage in fraudulent reporting.	• Company profits lag those of its industry.	• A weak internal control environment prevails.
• Management decisions are dominated by an individual or a small group.	• New requirements are passed that could impair stability or profitability.	• The company is not able to generate sufficient cash flows to ensure that it is a going concern.
• Management fails to display an appropriate attitude about internal control and financial reporting.	• The company's market is saturated due to fierce competition.	• There is pressure to obtain capital.
• Managers' attitudes are very aggressive toward financial reporting.	• The company's industry is declining.	• The company operates in a tax haven jurisdiction.
• Managers place too much emphasis on earnings projections.	• The company's industry is changing rapidly.	• The company has many difficult accounting measurement and presentation issues.
• Management participates excessively in the selection of accounting principles or the determination of estimates.		• The company has significant transactions or balances that contain estimates that are difficult to audit.
• The company has a high turnover of senior management.		• The company has significant and unusual related-party transactions.
• The company has a known history of violations.		• Company accounting personnel are lax or inexperienced in their duties.
• Managers and employees tend to be evasive when responding to auditors' inquiries.		
• Managers engage in frequent disputes with auditors.		

[1]An academic study (see M. Nelson, J. Elliott, and R. Tarpley, "How Are Earnings Managed? Examples from Auditors," *Accounting Horizons,* November 2002) examined more than 500 attempts to manage earnings that were detected by auditors. The majority (more than 50 percent) of the attempts involved improper expense reductions, approximately 20 percent involved improper revenue increases, and the remainder involved business combinations and other accounting artifices.

A very common reason cited for falsifying financial statements is so a company can meet its earnings projections either provided by management or set by financial analysts. Simply stated, when a company fails to meet earnings projections, its stock price usually falls and the managers of the company face great scrutiny. As a result, managers work very hard to meet expectations set by analysts. In fact, sometimes a company's performance will exactly meet the earnings targets announced by management months earlier. To avoid the negative outcomes that typically accompany a failure to meet expectations, managers sometimes commit fraud. The accompanying Auditing Insight illustrates an example that recently occurred at Bankrate.

AUDITING INSIGHT | Meeting Analyst Expectations at Bankrate

While reviewing the preliminary financial results for the second quarter of 2012, the Chief Financial Officer, VP of Finance, and Director of Accounting at **Bankrate Inc.** concluded that their quarterly performance was going to fall dramatically short of analyst expectations. In order to avoid possible repercussions from Wall Street, the managers directed two different divisions to record additional revenue totaling $800,000, without supporting documentation or analysis. Eventually, the company's auditors, Grant Thornton, discovered and flagged the unsupported revenue. In July 2015, Bankrate restated its financial statements for the second quarter of 2012. In addition, in September 2015, Bankrate was fined $15 million to settle the accounting fraud charges.

Sources: Accounting and Auditing Enforcement Release No. 3683, September 8, 2015 (available at: https://www.sec.gov/litigation/admin/2015/33-9901.pdf); Michael Cohn, "Bankrate to Pay $15 Million to Settle Accounting Fraud Charges," *Accounting Today*, September 8, 2015 (available at: www.accountingtoday.com/news/audit-accounting/bdo-settle-sec-charges-false-misleading-audit-opinions-75733-1.html).

On the other hand, there are times when management may find it beneficial to commit fraud by understating assets and revenues and overstating expenses and liabilities. Such behavior is likely to occur during times when profits are high and management wants to put reserves in a "cookie jar"[2] that can be used to increase profits in future years and "smooth earnings" at the discretion of the management team. Understating profits also can be desirable if the company is under scrutiny by governmental bodies, taxing authorities, labor unions, or competitors. Therefore, auditors must be aware of the potential for fraudulent activity in both directions, depending on the relevant facts and circumstances.

When assessing the risk of fraud, auditors need to know about the *red flags*, those telltale signs and indications that have accompanied many frauds that have occurred in the past. Because of the double-entry bookkeeping system, fraudulent accounting entries always affect at least two accounts and two places in financial statements. Because many frauds involve improper recognition of assets, there is a theory of the "dangling debit," which is an asset amount that can be investigated and found to be false or questionable. Frauds may involve the omission of liabilities, but the matter of finding and investigating the dangling credit is normally very difficult. It "dangles" off the books. In other words, the "dangling credit" is a credit that was never recorded to a liability account, resulting in an omission of a liability that should have been recorded. (Consider the implications for the completeness assertion in this scenario.) Misstated disclosures also present difficulty, mainly because they involve words and messages instead of numbers. Omissions may be difficult to notice, and misleading inferences may be very subtle. Exhibit 4.5 presents some of the other risk factors that have characterized situations in which frauds have occurred. Among the fraud risk factors identified, when a company has difficult

---

[2]*Cookie jar* reserves are overaccruals created by a company (credit accrual, debit expense). In times when the company struggles, it reverses the overaccrual (debit accrual, credit expense) to pump up profits. Once the "cookie jar" reserve has been established, auditors are in a fix because it may be difficult to object to the company correcting the overaccrual.

accounting issues or has balances that contain difficult estimates to audit, these issues can be very challenging for auditors.

Types of Fraud

Remember, financial statements may be materially misstated as a result of *errors* or *fraud*. While accounting errors are usually unintentional, fraud consists of knowingly making material misrepresentations of fact with the *intent* of inducing someone to believe the falsehood and act on it and, thus, suffer a loss or damage. This definition encompasses all means by which people can lie, cheat, steal, and dupe other people. **Management fraud** is deliberate fraud committed by management that injures investors and creditors through materially misstated information. Because management fraud usually takes the form of deceptive financial statements, management fraud is sometimes referred to as **fraudulent financial reporting**. AU-C 240.A2 defines fraudulent financial reporting as "intentional misstatements, including omissions of amounts or disclosures in financial statements to deceive financial statement users. It can be caused by the efforts of management to manage earnings in order to deceive financial statement users by influencing their perceptions about the entity's performance and profitability."

 AUDITING INSIGHT | Wayward CFOs Often Coerced by CEOs, Study Says

When CFOs are caught fudging the numbers, it's more likely they were pressured by upper management than looking for some immediate financial benefit. At least that's the way **The Conference Board** sees it after analyzing more than 20 years of accounting and auditing enforcement actions by the Securities and Exchange Commission. The study found that CFOs have an inherently higher risk of litigation in accounting manipulation cases, yet they often do not get the personal financial benefits of cooking the books. However, when CEOs apply enough pressure, CFOs may acquiesce and set aside their role as watchdog of financial reporting quality.

Source: T. Whitehouse, *Compliance Week*, May 20, 2011.

Exhibit 4.6 shows some acts and devices that are often involved in financial frauds. Notice that these actions may be perpetrated *by* the organization or may be perpetrated *upon* the organization. Collectively, these are known as **white-collar crimes**—the misdeeds of people who wear ties to work and steal with a pencil or a computer terminal. White-collar crime produces ink stains instead of bloodstains.

It is important to note that audit teams are concerned with fraud *only as it affects the financial statements.* That is, audit teams are not responsible to detect all fraud but are responsible to detect cases where fraudulent activity results in *materially* misstated financial statements. For example, if a warehouse employee is misappropriating inventory but that embezzlement does not result in materially misstated financial statements, auditors do not necessarily have a responsibility for detecting this type of fraud. However, if management is materially misstating revenues in order to meet earnings expectations, auditors *are* responsible for detecting this misstatement. That is not to say that auditors would ignore immaterial fraud (indeed, any instance of fraud would cause auditors to re-evaluate their assessment of management's integrity), but only that auditors' primary responsibility is to design procedures to provide *reasonable assurance* that *material* frauds that might misstate the financial statements are detected.

Other Definitions Related to Fraud

Employee fraud is the use of fraudulent means to misappropriate funds or other property from an employer. It usually involves falsifications of some kind: using false documents, lying, exceeding authority, or violating an employer's policies. It consists of

EXHIBIT 4.6
Overview of Types of Frauds

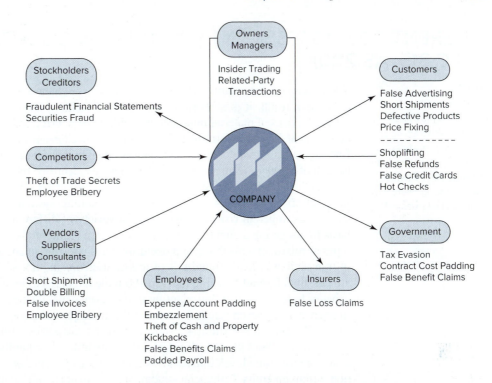

three phases: (1) the fraudulent act, (2) the conversion of the funds or property to the fraudster's use, and (3) the cover-up. Employee fraud can be classified as either embezzlement or larceny. This type of fraud is discussed in detail in Chapter 6.

Embezzlement is a type of fraud involving employees or nonemployees wrongfully misappropriating funds or property entrusted to their care, custody, and control, often accompanied by false accounting entries and other forms of deception and cover-up.

Larceny is simple theft; for example, an employee misappropriates an employer's funds or property that has not been entrusted to the custody of the employee.

Defalcation is another name for employee fraud, embezzlement, and larceny. Auditing standards also call it *misappropriation of assets*.

Errors are unintentional misstatements or omissions of amounts or disclosures in financial statements. Errors are not considered fraud because they occur unintentionally.

Auditing standards require that auditors specifically assess the risk of material misstatement due to fraud for each engagement. Fraud risk factors relate to both misstatements arising from *fraudulent financial reporting* and misstatements arising from *misappropriations of assets* (usually as a result of employee theft and the related attempt to conceal this theft through erroneous journal entries). Furthermore, auditors should consider these risk factors when determining what audit procedures to perform. With regard to the audit risk model, fraud risk is always considered as a key factor when an auditor assesses inherent risk. A complete discussion of inherent risk assessment now follows.

✓ REVIEW CHECKPOINTS

4.5 What is the primary difference between a material misstatement due to fraud or error?

4.6 What is the auditor's responsibility regarding fraud risk?

4.7 What are the defining characteristics of (a) white-collar crime, (b) employee fraud, (c) embezzlement, (d) larceny, (e) defalcation, (f) management fraud, and (g) errors?

4.8 Identify three different categories of fraud risk factors. Next, for each category, what are some of the conditions that can help contribute to a higher likelihood of financial statement fraud?

INHERENT RISK ASSESSMENT—"WHAT CAN GO WRONG?" (AU-C 315, AS 2110)

LO 4-3
Explain an auditor's responsibility to assess inherent risk, including a description of the type of risk assessment procedures that should be performed when assessing inherent risk on an audit engagement.

The professional standards make clear that risk assessment underlies the entire audit process. As a result, it is absolutely essential that auditors take great care to appropriately assess the risks of material misstatement, either due to error or fraud that exists on an audit engagement. When performing risk assessment procedures to accomplish this objective, the first step taken by auditors is often to assess inherent risk for each relevant assertion related to each of the significant accounts and disclosures identified on an audit engagement.

Recall that inherent risk is the probability that, in the absence of internal controls, material errors or frauds could enter the accounting system used to develop financial statements. Inherent risks can arise from a variety of different sources, and an auditor's basis for assessing a client's inherent risk is often found in his or her familiarity with the types of misstatements that could occur for each assertion in any account balance or class of transactions. Clearly, hundreds of innocent errors and not-so-innocent fraud schemes are possible. Instead of trying to learn about the hundreds of possible errors and frauds, it is better to begin with an introduction to the seven general categories of errors and fraud. In a sense, these seven categories answer the audit question: "What can go wrong?" in the financial statements. Exhibit 4.7 shows the seven categories with some examples.

In effect, at both the overall financial statement level and at the management financial statement assertion level, inherent risk refers to the exposure or susceptibility of an assertion within an entity's financial statements to a material misstatement without regard to the system of internal controls. A detailed understanding of an audit client's business model, including its products and services, is an essential part of an auditor's inherent risk assessment process at both the financial statement and the financial statement assertion

EXHIBIT 4.7 General Categories of Misstatements

What Can Go Wrong?	Error Examples	Fraud Examples	Assertion Violated
1. Invalid transactions are recorded.	A computer malfunction causes a sales transaction to be recorded twice.	Fictitious sales are recorded and charged to nonexistent customers.	Occurrence
2. Valid transactions or disclosures are omitted from the financial statements.	Shipments to customers are never recorded because of problems in the company's information processing system.	Shipments are made to an employee's friend and intentionally never recorded.	Completeness
3. Transaction or disclosure amounts are inaccurate.	An employee calculates depreciation incorrectly.	A company "short ships" a shipment to a customer and bills the customer for the full amount ordered.	Accuracy
4. Transactions are classified in the wrong accounts.	Sales to a subsidiary company are recorded as sales to external parties instead of intercompany sales, or the amount is charged to the wrong customer account receivable record.	A loan to the company's CEO (not permitted under Sarbanes–Oxley) is classified as an account receivable to conceal the transaction.	Classification
5. Transaction accounting and posting are incorrect.	Sales are posted in total to the accounts receivable control account, but some are not posted to individual customer account records.	Repairs and maintenance expenses are recorded as additions to property, plant and equipment accounts to keep expenses off the income statement.	Accuracy
6. Transactions are recorded in the wrong period.	The company fails to record a shipment that was sent by a supplier FOB shipping point in December, but the shipment was not received (or recorded) until January.	Shipments made in January (of the next fiscal year) are backdated and recorded as sales in December.	Cutoff
7. Disclosures are incomplete or misleading.	The company did not include the effective tax rate reconciliation in the footnotes.	Management fails to disclose litigation against the company.	Presentation and Disclosure

levels. Inherent risk assessment helps to guide the auditor in allocating more and stronger resources to test specific accounts and disclosures that present a higher likelihood of material misstatement and therefore present a higher level of inherent risk. In effect, inherent risk assessment provides the basis for executing an appropriate response to the risks identified. Remember that the assessment of inherent risk can be based on a variety of types of information. The risk assessment process is summarized in Exhibit 4.8.

At a preliminary level, the best indicator of the risk of a material misstatement in the year under audit is a material misstatement that was discovered during the previous audit. Also, changes in transaction types, technology, personnel, or accounting principles may increase the risk of material misstatement. The nature of the client's business can produce complicated transactions and calculations that are subject to information processing and accounting treatment error. For example, real estate, franchising, and oil and gas transactions are frequently complicated and subject to accounting error. Some types of inventories are more difficult than others to count, value, and keep accurately in perpetual records. The following factors have been suggested as being related to the susceptibility of accounts to misstatement or fraud:

- *Dollar size of the account.* The higher the account balance, the greater the chance of having errors or fraud in the account.
- *Liquidity.* The greater the account's liquidity (ability to be easily converted to cash), the more susceptible the account is to fraud. For example, cash is more susceptible to theft than, say, a building.
- *Volume of transactions.* The higher the volume of transactions, the higher the chance of error or fraud occurring in the transactions.
- *Complexity of the transactions.* Very complex transactions (e.g., those involving derivative securities or hedging transactions) tend to have a higher percentage of errors than simple transactions.

EXHIBIT 4.8　　**The Risk Assessment Process**

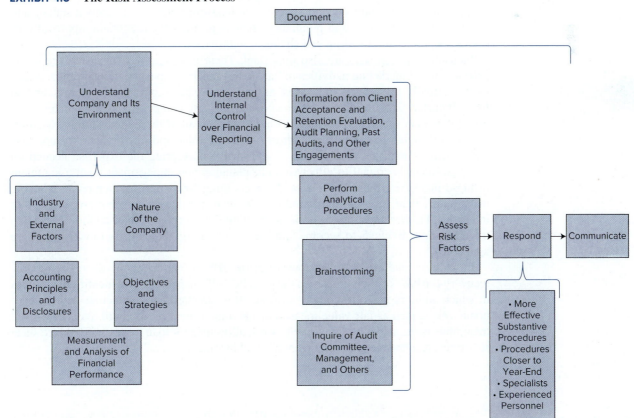

- *Subjective estimates.* Subjective measurements (e.g., estimating the allowance for doubtful accounts) tend to have more errors and fraud than objective measurements (e.g., counting petty cash). Simply stated, the more subjective the measurement, the easier it is to manipulate.

Understanding the Client's Business and Its Environment

Gaining a detailed understanding and knowledge of the client's business and its environment within the context of its industry is essential in an audit. Auditing standards require auditors to obtain a thorough understanding of the business to plan and perform the audit work. Obtaining an understanding of the client's business includes understanding:

- Relevant industry, regulatory, and other external factors.
- The nature of the company and related parties.
- The effect of client computerized processing (discussed in Chapter 3).
- The company's selection and application of accounting principles, including related disclosures.
- The company's objectives and strategies and those related business risks that might reasonably be expected to result in risks of material misstatement.
- The company's measurement and analysis of its financial performance.

Industry, Regulatory, and Other External Factors

Auditors must obtain an understanding of relevant industry, regulatory, and other external factors that encompasses the client's competitive environment. This includes a detailed understanding of: the regulatory environment, including the applicable financial reporting framework (e.g., U.S. GAAP or IFRS). Auditors must also understand the broad economic environment in which the client operates, including such things as the effects of national economic policies (e.g., price regulations and import/export restrictions), the geographic location and its economy (e.g., northeastern states versus sunbelt states), and developments in taxation and regulatory areas (e.g., industry regulation, approval processes for products in the drug and chemical industries).

Industry characteristics are also important. There is a great deal of difference in the production and marketing activities of banks, insurance companies, mutual funds, supermarkets, hotels, oil and gas industries, agriculture organizations, manufacturers, and so forth. Industry expertise also involves knowledge of the competition and an understanding of the client's market. Few auditors are experts in all of these areas. Public accounting firms must have experts in all industries they examine and rely on them to supervise audits in their industry of expertise. This is why considering the expertise needed on an engagement is crucial to effective audit planning and engagement team assignment in those industries. Indeed, some public accounting firms have reputations for having many audit clients in a particular industry while others have a larger presence in other industries. Further, most large public accounting firms organize their auditors by industry, allowing individuals to become familiar with issues in the industry to which they are assigned.

In addition, auditors should be aware of the effects that economic distress and slow recovery can have on their clients. In the past, PCAOB inspectors have identified instances in which auditors failed to comply with auditing standards in connection with an economic crisis, such as fair value measurements, impairment of goodwill, indefinite-lived intangible assets, and other long-lived assets, allowance for loan losses, off-balance sheet structures, revenue recognition, inventory, and income taxes.[3]

---

[3]Report on Observations of PCAOB Inspectors Related to Audit Risk Areas Affected by the Economic Crisis, September 29, 2010.

The Nature of the Company

Obtaining an understanding of the nature of the company includes understanding:

- *The company's organizational structure and management personnel.* Is the client centralized or decentralized? Who makes the decisions? Are senior managers familiar with accounting and reporting requirements? Do they value the importance of good controls? Are any officers, employees, or shareholders involved in related-party transactions?

- *The sources of funding of the company's operations and investment activities.* Is the company funded by debt or equity? Are there restrictions placed by lenders that management must meet (e.g., debt covenants)? Does it have the financing in place to meet future cash requirements? Are any lenders or shareholders involved in related-party transactions?

- *The company's significant investments.* Is the company invested in other companies for strategic purposes? Do investments provide a significant source of income? What is the company's investment policy? Do overseas investments present a risk of nationalization? Are any subsidiaries involved in related-party transactions? Is the company planning to acquire another company? As the following Auditing Insight reveals, there are additional risks for auditors if their client is either about to be acquired by or planning to acquire another company.

- *The company's operating characteristics, including its size and complexity.* Does the company operate internationally? Do subsidiaries operate in diverse industries?

- *The sources of the company's earnings, including the relative profitability of key products and services, and key supplier and customer relationships.* Are there any threats to loss of revenue from losing suppliers or customers? Could key products be overtaken by competitors' products? Could advances in technology make the client's products obsolete? Are any customers or suppliers *related parties?*

AUDITING INSIGHT Did Hewlett-Packard Overpay for Autonomy?

When **Hewlett-Packard** (HP) admitted that it overpaid when it acquired **Autonomy** for $11.1 billion in October 2011, the management team did not accept responsibility for the blunder. Rather, an investigation completed by HP concluded that there were serious "accounting improprieties" and "outright misrepresentations" found on Autonomy's financial statements. According to HP CEO Meg Whitman, "There appears to have been a willful sustained effort" to inflate Autonomy's revenue and profitability. "This was designed to be hidden." For its part, **Deloitte UK** defends its audit work completed at the company. In fact, a spokesman for Deloitte UK "categorically denies that it had any knowledge of any accounting improprieties or any misrepresentations in Autonomy's financial statements, or that it was complicit in any accounting improprieties or misrepresentations."

Source: "HP Says It Was Duped, Takes $8.8 Billion Charge," *The Wall Street Journal,* November 21, 2012, p. A1.

Related Parties

Related parties include those individuals or organizations that can influence or be influenced by decisions of the company, possibly through family ties or investment relationships. According to the professional standards, an auditor's primary objective in regard to related parties is to obtain the evidence needed to determine whether "related parties and relationships and transactions with related parties have been properly identified, accounted for, and disclosed in the financial statements."[4] Because one of the basic assumptions of historical cost accounting is that transactions are valued at prices agreed on by two *independent* parties (i.e., "arm's-length transactions"), *valuation* of

[4]AS 2410.02

related-party transactions is particularly troublesome. For example, auditors must remember that the economic substance of a particular transaction (and its effect on the financial condition of the entity) could be significantly different from its legal form (e.g., capitalized leases versus operating leases).

Auditors strive to identify related-party relationships and transactions during the planning stage to be able to obtain evidence that the financial accounting and disclosure for them are proper. Some methods include reviewing the board of directors' meeting minutes, making inquiries of key executives, and reviewing stock ownership records (5 percent ownership in the company is usually used as a good cutoff). Auditors also should question the persuasiveness of the evidence obtained from related parties because the source of the evidence may be biased. Hence, auditors should obtain evidence of the purpose, nature, and extent of related-party transactions and their effect on financial statements, and the evidence should extend beyond inquiry of management.

AUDITING INSIGHT   The Perils of Related-Party Transactions

ENRON

Although related-party transactions are approved by some company boards, various critics charge that such transactions do not pass the "smell test" and should be avoided, especially given the spate of recent accounting scandals. A recent study noted that 40 percent of the S&P 500 companies had business relationships with other companies that are somehow related.

Enron CFO Andrew Fastow made millions by managing investment partnerships that had significant dealings with Enron. By "selling" appreciated assets to Fastow's **LJM** partnerships, Enron was able to record profits before the company would normally earn them. The financing vehicles were also instrumental in keeping significant debt off Enron's balance sheet. The problem was that Fastow's millions came at Enron's expense. Although there were safeguards in place to prevent such conflicts of interest, Enron's board of directors waived the rules preventing such transactions. Board members later stated that they had not realized how much Fastow was making from the deals (approximately $45 million). Arthur Andersen expressed concern about the related-party transactions but withdrew its reservations when the board signed off on the relationship. The risky partnerships, based on overvalued assets and collateralized with

Enron stock, represented one of the primary reasons for Enron's ultimate collapse.

XINHUA FINANCE LTD.

Loretta Fredy Bush, who became well known in Asia as the U.S. chief executive of **Xinhua Finance Ltd.,** was indicted on U.S. fraud charges along with two associates. The charges filed in U.S. District Court by the District of Columbia, set forth in a grand-jury indictment, allege "conspiracy to defraud the U.S. Securities and Exchange Commission, investors and others and to enrich themselves through a series of undisclosed and disguised related-party transactions and insider trading." In one series of transactions over a number of years, prosecutors allege Bush and Dennis Pelino sold Xinhua Finance stock valued at more than $25 million and concealed the fact from investors with the help of Shelly Singhal, who made it appear the shares were pledged as loan collateral. Finance shares dropped to ¥1,390 each in Tokyo, down from more than ¥75,000 in March 2007.

Sources: "'Related-Party' Deals Abound at Companies," *The Wall Street Journal,* December 3, 2004, p. C3; "Visionary's Dream Led to Risky Business; Opaque Deals, Accounting Sleight of Hand Built an Energy Giant and Ensured Its Demise," *The Washington Post,* July 28, 2002, p. A1; "Global Finance: Xinhua Finance Founders Charged," *The Wall Street Journal,* May 12, 2011, p. C.3.

Selection and Application of Accounting Principles, Including Related Disclosures

Auditors should evaluate whether the company's selection and application of accounting principles are appropriate for its business and consistent with the applicable financial reporting framework and accounting principles used in the relevant industry. Auditors should pay attention to significant changes in the company's accounting principles, financial reporting policies, or disclosures and the reasons for such changes; significant accounting principles in controversial or emerging areas; and the methods the company uses to account for significant and unusual transactions.

Accounting estimates are a concern because numerous fraud cases have involved the deliberate manipulation of estimates to increase net income. **Accounting estimates** are approximations of financial statement numbers and are often included in financial statements. Examples include valuation of investment securities, net realizable value of accounts receivable, depreciation expense, insurance loss reserves, percentage-of-completion contract revenues, impairment of goodwill, pension expense, warranty liabilities, fair value of financial instruments, and many more. Management is responsible for making accounting estimates. Auditors are responsible for determining that all appropriate estimates have been made, that they are reasonable, and that they are presented in conformity with GAAP and adequately disclosed. The following Auditing Insight provides a brief description of "what went wrong" at Toshiba related to an important accounting estimate.

AUDITING INSIGHT   Percentage of Completion Estimates at Toshiba

In early September 2015, the Japanese conglomerate Toshiba announced a $1.9 billion earnings writedown that involved the past seven fiscal years. The accounting irregularities were primarily related to "percentage of completion" estimates that were used to account for both revenue and costs for various infrastructure projects that included railway system, hydroelectric, and nuclear projects. The accounting rules specify that the estimates are supposed to represent reasonable estimates of the extent of contract progress. However, due to the subjectivity involved in the estimates, there is always an opportunity for management bias to occur during the estimation process and for a fraud to occur. As a result, auditors must always be aware of this possibility whenever they are auditing an accounting estimate.

Sources: Eric Pfanner and Megumi Fugukawa, "Toshiba Slashes Earnings for Past Seven Years," *The Wall Street Journal,* September 7, 2015 (available at http://www.wsj.com/articles/toshiba-slashes-earnings-for-past-7-years-1441589473); David Katz, "Accounting Rife with Estimates Haunted Toshiba," CFO.com, September 9, 2015 (available at http://ww2.cfo.com/financial-reporting-2/2015/09/accounting-rife-estimates-haunted-toshiba/).

With respect to auditing accounting estimates, auditors are supposed to monitor the differences between management's estimates and the closest reasonable estimates supported by the audit evidence and evaluate the differences taken altogether for indications of a systematic bias. For example, management may estimate an allowance for doubtful accounts to be $50,000, and the auditors may estimate that the allowance could be $40,000 to $55,000. In this case, management's estimate is within the auditors' range of reasonableness. However, the auditors should note that the management estimate leans toward the conservative side (more than the auditors' $40,000 lower estimate but not much less than the auditors' higher $55,000 estimate). If other estimates exhibit the same conservatism and the effect is material, the auditors will need to evaluate the overall reasonableness of the effect of all estimates taken together.

Company Objectives, Strategies, and Related Business Risks

An auditor needs to gain a detailed understanding of the audit client's strategy to achieve a competitive advantage within its industry. The purpose of obtaining an understanding of the company's objectives and strategies is to identify business risks that could reasonably be expected to result in material misstatement of the financial statements. The best starting point is with management, whose job it is to be knowledgeable about the company's business risks. Any risks that could adversely affect a company's ability to achieve its objectives and execute its strategies are called **business risks**. Although not all business risks are relevant to auditors, the following are examples of situations in which business risks might result in material misstatement of the financial statements:

- *Industry developments,* for example, a potential related business risk might be that the company does not have the personnel or expertise to deal with the changes in the industry.
- *New products and services,* for example, a potential related business risk might be that the new product or service will not be successful.
- *Expansion of the business,* for example, a potential related business risk might be that the demand for the company's products or services has not been accurately estimated.

- *The effects of implementing a strategy,* particularly any effects that will lead to new accounting requirements.
- *Financing requirements,* for example, a potential related business risk might be the loss of financing due to the company's inability to meet financing requirements.

If you think about the financial statements as a window into the operations and results of a business, you can imagine peering through them to see activities of thousands of employees, suppliers, and customers working to achieve their goals. You should also be able to see the effects of the industry environment, including economic and political events, weather occurrences, technological advances, and social and demographic patterns. Given this view of financial statements, it's easier to understand why auditors need to take the time to carefully acquire knowledge about a client's business, industry, and strategy to achieve competitive advantage. This foundation of company- and industry-specific knowledge allows the auditor to better understand the client's business risk, which is a precursor to assessing inherent risk and audit risk.

Indeed, the professional standards recognize that most business risks are eventually reflected in the financial statements. So auditors devote a significant amount of time to gain an understanding of their clients' business risks. Firms believe they must learn more about their clients' business strategies and processes to understand whether the financial statements are fairly presented. As you can see in the Auditing Insight about Enron, a change in strategy can have a major impact on the accounting used for the financial statements.

AUDITING INSIGHT   Change in Strategy, Change in Accounting

At Enron, the industry environment changed dramatically in the mid-1980s due to the government's decision to deregulate the once highly regulated energy industry. Previously, the government had dictated the prices that pipeline companies (such as Enron) could pay for gas and the prices they could charge customers for it. However, deregulation meant that the market forces of supply and demand then could dictate prices and the volumes sold. As a result, Enron changed its strategy by becoming involved in natural gas trading and financing. Specifically, Enron served as an intermediary among producers who contracted to sell their gas to Enron and customers who contracted to purchase it from Enron. The company then collected as profits the difference between the prices at which it sold the gas less the prices at which it purchased it.

In response to the problem of getting producers to sign long-term contracts to supply gas, Enron started giving such producers cash up front instead of paying over the life of the contract. Enron then allowed

for the natural gas contracts it devised—which were quite complex and variable, depending on different pricing, capacity, and transportation parameters—to be traded in the marketplace. This new strategy of trading energy contracts led Enron to formally ask the SEC if it could use mark-to-market accounting for its trading business. Often, these mark-to-market calculations involved complex models that determined the present value of projected cash inflows and cash outflows under the contract. Because the inputs to these models were often highly subjective, the use of mark-to-market accounting for contract revenues and expenses was open to interpretation and became far more difficult to audit.

Sources: J. C. Thibodeau and D. Freier, *Auditing and Accounting Cases: Investigating Issues of Fraud and Professional Ethics,* 4th ed. (New York: McGraw-Hill Irwin, 2014), p. 85; B. McLean and P. Elkind, *The Smartest Guys in the Room: The Amazing Rise and Scandalous Fall of Enron* (New York: Penguin Group, 2003), p. 39.

Gaining an understanding of strategies and processes involves gathering evidence in areas not historically addressed by auditors. Auditors might ask production personnel about labor problems or marketing personnel about product quality or competition. The process has been criticized by some as being more consulting than auditing, but it is essential in order to assess the risk of material misstatements. It addresses factors that audit team members could miss by getting lost in the details of an approach that simply started with the financial statements. Business risk assessment also makes auditors much more knowledgeable about their client's business and its environment. We should note that, even when taking a top-down approach that starts with an understanding of the risks faced by the client in executing its strategy within the industry, the audit team ultimately still has to focus its procedures on the significant accounts and relevant management assertions.

Company Performance Measures

The purpose of obtaining an understanding of the company's performance measures is to determine what information management and others deem to be key indicators of company performance that may affect the risk of material misstatement. A key step for auditors to consider is to try to understand those measures to which management or financial statement users might be sensitive. For example, measures used to determine management compensation or analysts' ratings might place pressure on management to manipulate financial results. Also, auditors might gain a better understanding of their clients by reviewing measures management uses to monitor operations, such as budget variances or trend analysis. Finally, those measures might be indicators of qualitative factors that should be considered when determining materiality, as discussed in Chapter 3.

✓ REVIEW CHECKPOINTS

4.9   Why is it important for an auditor to carefully assess inherent risk on each audit engagement?

4.10 What is meant by the nature of the company, and why is it important to inherent risk assessment?

4.11 Why should auditors understand their clients' performance measures when assessing inherent risk?

4.12 What is the major concern for auditors related to evidence obtained from related parties?

GATHERING INFORMATION AND PRELIMINARY ANALYTICAL PROCEDURES

LO 4-4
Understand the different sources of information and the audit procedures used by auditors when assessing risks, including analytical procedures, brainstorming, and inquiries.

Auditors have a responsibility to keep up with developments within their clients' businesses, industries, and the overall economy. Remember from our discussion in Chapter 1 that the auditing environment is rapidly being transformed into an environment characterized by the availability of "Big Data." Only a few of the many different sources of information available are described briefly in this section. The AICPA industry accounting and auditing guides are often a very good place to start. These guides explain the typical transactions and accounts used by various types of businesses and not-for-profit organizations. Many databases and information sources are available on the Internet, such as the Library of Congress E-resources Online Catalog (http://eresources.loc.gov/). Auditors should make sure to read public information about the company, such as company-issued press releases, company-prepared presentation materials for analysts or investor groups, and analyst reports, as well as observe or read transcripts of earnings calls and, to the extent publicly available, of other meetings with investors or rating agencies. Auditors also need to obtain an understanding of compensation arrangements with senior management, including incentive compensation arrangements, changes or adjustments to those arrangements, and special bonuses by reviewing the documents and discussing the arrangements with management. Board of directors compensation committee minutes often contain useful information about the intent of such arrangements.

General Business Sources

Most industries have specialized trade magazines and journals. You may not choose to read *Grocer's Spotlight* for pleasure, but magazines of this special type are very valuable for learning and maintaining an industry expertise. In addition, specific information about public companies can be found in registration statements and 10-K reports filed with the SEC. General business magazines and newspapers often contribute insights about an industry, an entity, and individual corporate officers. Many are available, including such leaders as *Bloomberg Businessweek, Forbes, Fortune, Harvard Business Review, Barron's,* and *The Wall Street Journal.* Auditors typically read several of these regularly.

Additionally, many companies present "company story" information on their websites. A visit to company websites can provide a wealth of information about products, markets, and strategies. For public companies, auditors should also monitor the client's daily stock price for any unusual trading activity that might indicate new information that affects the company's business risk.

Company Sources

Other early information-gathering activities include (1) reviewing the corporate charter and bylaws or partnership agreement; (2) reviewing contracts, agreements, and legal proceedings; and (3) reading the minutes of the meetings of directors and committees of the board of directors. The minutes provide a history of the company, critical events and significant transactions, and future company intentions. A company's failure to provide minutes is a significant scope limitation that could result in the public accounting firm's disclaiming an opinion on the company's financial statements.

Information from Client Acceptance or Continuance Evaluation, Audit Planning, Past Audits, and Other Engagements

A great deal of information about the client is gathered in the pre-engagement planning process discussed in Chapter 3. Auditors evaluate the competence and integrity of management and the riskiness of the business before taking or continuing a client. As noted, the best indicator of the risk of a material misstatement is the presence of misstatements in previous audits that required adjusting entries. For example, for nonpublic clients, public accounting firms often develop client income tax provisions once the audit is complete; thus, the income tax adjusting entry would show up as an adjustment every year. Finally, auditors who have industry expertise often have more than one client in that industry, so they can transfer general knowledge of risks encountered in other clients while maintaining confidentiality standards required by the profession.

What's in the Minutes of Meetings?

Boards of directors are responsible for monitoring their companies' businesses. The minutes of their meetings and the meetings of their committees (e.g., executive committee, finance committee, compensation committee, and audit committee) frequently contain information of vital interest to the independent auditors. Some information examples follow:

- Amount of dividends declared.
- Elections of officers and authorization of officers' salaries.
- Authorization of stock options and other incentive compensation arrangements.
- Acceptance of contracts, agreements, and lawsuit settlements.
- Approval of major purchases of property and investments.
- Discussions of possible mergers and divestitures.

- Authorization of financing by stock issuance, long-term debt issuance, and leases.
- Approval to pledge assets as security for debts.
- Discussion of negotiations on bank loans and payment waivers.
- Approval of accounting policies and accounting for significant and unusual transactions.
- Authorizations of individuals to sign bank checks.

Auditors take notes or make copies of important parts of these minutes and compare them to information in the accounts and disclosures (e.g., compare the amount of dividends declared to the amount paid, compare officers' authorized salaries to amounts paid, compare agreements to pledge assets to proper disclosure in the notes to financial statements).

Preliminary Analytical Procedures (AU 520-C, AS 2110)

Auditors are required to complete preliminary analytical procedures on each engagement. When completing analytical procedures, auditors are required to develop an expectation about what an account balance should be and then compare that expectation to the recorded balance. When doing so, auditors typically use the prior-year balances as the starting point for their expectation for each account balance. At this stage, **analytical procedures** are *reasonableness tests;* auditors compare their expectation for each of the account balances with those recorded by management. According to auditing standards, *analytical procedures* must be applied in the preliminary stages of each audit. During this critical point of the engagement, auditors use analytical procedures to identify potential problem areas so that subsequent audit work can be designed to reduce the risk of missing something important. Analytical procedures during the preliminary stages also provide an organized approach—a standard starting place—for becoming familiar with the client's business. Auditors need to remember that preliminary analytical procedures are based on unaudited data, so they should consider the effectiveness of controls over their reliability when deciding how much weight to place on the results.

Auditors should perform five steps when completing analytical procedures:

1. *Develop an expectation.* A variety of sources can provide evidence for auditors' expectations of the balance in a particular account:

   - Balances for one or more comparable periods (e.g., vertical and horizontal analyses).
   - Anticipated results found in the company's budgets and forecasts.
   - Leveraging predictable patterns among account balances based on the company's experience.
   - Relevant information from third party sources for the industry in which the company operates.
   - Relevant nonfinancial information (e.g., physical production statistics, sales orders).

2. *Define a significant difference.* Basically, the question is, "What percentage (or dollar) difference from your expectation can still be considered reasonable?" It is important that this decision be made *before* making the comparison to prevent auditors from rationalizing differences and failing to follow up.

3. *Compare expectation with the recorded amount.* Many auditors start with comparative financial statements and calculate year-to-year changes in balance-sheet and income-statement accounts (**horizontal analysis**). They next calculate common-size statements (**vertical analysis**) in which financial statement amounts are expressed as percentages of a base, such as sales for the income-statement accounts or total assets for the balance-sheet accounts. These initial calculations (see Exhibit 4.9) provide a basis for describing the financial activities for the current year under audit. Although vertical and horizontal analyses are fairly basic, other analytical procedures—including mathematical time series and regression calculations, comparisons of multiyear data, and trend analyses—can be more complex.

4. *Investigate significant differences.* Auditors typically look for relationships that do not make sense as indicators of problems in the accounts, and they use such indicators to plan additional audit work. In the planning stage, analytical procedures are used to identify potential problem areas so that subsequent audit work can be designed to reduce the risk of missing something important. The application demonstrated here can be described as *attention directing:* pointing out accounts that could contain errors and frauds. The insights derived from *preliminary* analytical procedures do not provide direct evidence about the numbers in the financial statements. Although the insights derived from preliminary analytical procedures provide only limited evidence about the numbers in the financial statements, they do help auditors identify risks as an aid in preparing the audit plan.

5. *Document each of the preceding steps.* For companies that have not undergone any significant changes in operations, current-year recorded amounts should be fairly similar to those of the prior year (step 1). Because changes are not expected, auditors can identify any changes that are more than 10 percent and $100,000 as deserving additional attention (step 2). Note that the threshold is *both* 10 percent *and* $100,000 instead of just one trigger or the other. A change in an account balance from $100 to $200 is a 100 percent change, but the change is clearly immaterial. Similarly, an increase

EXHIBIT 4.9 Dunder-Mifflin Inc.—Preliminary Analytical Procedures Data

	Prior Year		Current Year		Change	
	Balance	Common Size	Balance	Common Size	Amount	Percent Change
Income						
Sales (net)	$9,000,000	100.00%	$9,900,000	100.00%	$ 900,000	10.00%
Cost of goods sold	6,750,000	75.00	7,200,000	72.73	450,000	6.67
Gross margin	2,250,000	25.00	2,700,000	27.27	450,000	20.00
General expense	1,590,000	17.67	1,734,000	17.52	144,000	9.06
Depreciation	300,000	3.33	300,000	3.03	0	0.00
Operating income	360,000	4.00	666,000	6.46	306,000	85.00
Interest expense	60,000	0.67	40,000	0.40	(20,000)	−33.33
Income taxes (40%)	120,000	1.33	256,000	2.59	136,000	113.33
Net income	$ 180,000	2.00%	$ 370,000	3.74%	$ 190,000	105.56%
Assets						
Cash	$ 600,000	14.78%	$ 200,000	4.12%	($400,000)	−66.67%
Accounts receivable	500,000	12.32	900,000	18.56	400,000	80.00
Allowance for doubtful accounts	(40,000)	−0.99	(50,000)	−1.03	(10,000)	25.00
Inventory	1,500,000	36.95	1,600,000	32.99	100,000	6.67
Total current assets	2,560,000	63.05	2,650,000	54.63	90,000	3.52
Equipment	3,000,000	73.89	4,000,000	82.47	1,000,000	33.33
Accumulated depreciation	(1,500,000)	−36.95	(1,800,000)	−37.11	(300,000)	20.00
Total assets	$4,060,000	100.00%	$4,850,000	100.00%	$ 790,000	19.46%
Liabilities and Equity						
Accounts payable	$ 500,000	12.32%	$ 400,000	8.25%	($100,000)	−20.00%
Bank loans, 11%	0	0.00	750,000	15.46	750,000	
Accrued interest	60,000	1.48	40,000	0.82	(20,000)	−33.33
Total current liabilities	560,000	13.79	1,190,000	24.53	630,000	112.50
Long-term debt, 10%	600,000	14.78	400,000	8.25	(200,000)	−33.33
Total liabilities	1,160,000	28.57	1,590,000	32.78	430,000	37.07
Capital stock	2,000,000	49.26	2,000,000	41.24	0	0.00
Retained earnings	900,000	22.17	1,260,000	25.98	360,000	40.00
Total liabilities and equity	$4,060,000	100.00%	$4,850,000	100.00%	$ 790,000	19.46%

in sales from $9.9 million to $10 million meets the $100,000 threshold but does not appear unreasonable in percentage terms. In step 3, auditors compare expectations with the recorded balances. Exhibit 4.9 contains financial balances for the prior year (consider them audited) and the current year (consider them unaudited at this stage). Common-size statements (vertical analysis) are shown in parallel columns, and the dollar amount and percentage change (horizontal analysis) are shown in the last two columns.

The investigation of significant differences (step 4) is probably the most critical step in the analytical procedures process. After generating basic financial data and relationships, the next step is to determine whether the financial changes and relationships actually describe what is going on within the company. According to the current-year unaudited financial statements in Exhibit 4.9, the company increased net income by increasing sales 10 percent, reducing cost of goods sold as a proportion of sales, and controlling other expenses. At least some of the sales growth appears to have been prompted by easier access to credit (accounts receivable increased by 80 percent) and more service (more equipment in use). The company also appears to have used most of its cash and borrowed more to purchase equipment, make payments on long-term debt, and pay dividends. Inventory and cost of goods sold, on the other hand, remained fairly consistent compared to the previous year, with both accounts increasing by only 6.7 percent.

The next step is to ask, "What could be wrong?" and "What errors and frauds, as well as legitimate explanations, could account for these financial results?" As an example of how analytical procedures are used, we limit our attention to the Accounts Receivable and Inventory accounts. At this point, some other ratios can help support the analysis. Exhibit 4.10 contains several familiar ratios. (Appendix 4A at the end of this chapter contains these ratios and their formulas.)

- *Question:* Are the accounts receivable collectible? (*Alternative:* Is the allowance for doubtful accounts large enough?) Easier credit can lead to more bad debts. The company has a much larger amount of receivables, the days' sales in receivables has increased significantly, the receivables turnover has decreased, and the allowance for doubtful accounts is smaller in proportion to the receivables. If the prior-year allowance for bad debts at 8 percent of receivables was appropriate and conditions have not become worse, it could be that the allowance should be closer to $72,000 than $50,000. The auditors should work carefully on the evidence related to accounts receivable valuation.

- *Question:* Could the inventory be overstated? (*Alternative:* Could the cost of the goods sold be understated?) Overstatement of the ending inventory would cause the cost of goods sold to be understated. The percentage of cost of goods sold to sales shows a decrease. If 75 percent of the prior year represents a more accurate cost of goods sold amount, then the income before taxes could be overstated by $225,000 (75 percent of $9.9 million minus $7.2 million unaudited cost of goods sold). The days' sales in inventory and the inventory turnover remained the same, but you could expect them to change in light of the larger volume of sales. Careful work on the physical count and valuation of inventory appears to be needed.

EXHIBIT 4.10
Dunder-Mifflin Inc.—
Selected Financial
Ratios

	Prior Year	Current Year	Percent Change
Balance-Sheet Ratios			
Current ratio	4.57	2.23	− 51.29%
Days' sales in receivables	18.40	30.91	67.98
Doubtful accounts ratio	0.0800	0.0556	− 30.56
Days' sales in inventory	80.00	80.00	0.00
Debt/equity ratio	0.40	0.49	21.93
Operations Ratios			
Receivables turnover	19.57	11.65	− 40.47
Inventory turnover	4.50	4.50	0.00
Cost of goods sold/Sales	75.00%	72.73%	− 3.03
Gross margin percentage	25.00%	27.27%	9.09
Return on beginning equity	6.62%	12.76%	92.80
Financial Distress Ratios (Altman)			
Working capital/Total assets	0.49	0.30	− 38.89
Retained earnings/Total assets	0.22	0.26	17.20
EBIT/Total assets	0.09	0.14	54.87
Market value of equity/Total debt	2.59	1.89	− 27.04
Net sales/Total assets	2.22	2.04	− 7.92
Discriminant Z-score	4.96	4.35	− 12.32

Other questions can be asked and other relationships derived when industry statistics are available. Industry statistics can be obtained from such services as Yahoo! Finance, Google Finance, Dun & Bradstreet, and Standard & Poor's. These statistics include industry averages for important financial benchmarks such as gross profit margin, return on sales, current ratio, debt/net worth, and various others. A comparison with client data can reveal out-of-line statistics, indicating a relatively strong feature of the company, a weak financial position, or possibly an error or misstatement in the client's financial statements. However, care must be taken with industry statistics. A particular company could or could not be well represented by industry averages.

Comparing reported financial results with internal budgets and forecasts also can be useful. If the budget or forecast represents management's estimate of probable future outcomes, planning questions can arise for items that fall short of or exceed the budget. If a company that expected to sell 10,000 units of a product sold only 5,000 units, the auditors would want to plan a careful analysis of the inventory of unsold units for obsolescence (*valuation*). If 15,000 were sold, an auditor would want to audit for sales validity (*occurrence*). Budget comparisons can be tricky, however. Some companies use budgets and forecasts as goals rather than as expressions of probable outcomes. Also, meeting the budget with little or no shortfall or excess can result from managers' manipulating the numbers to "meet the budget." Auditors must be careful to know something about an entity's business conditions from sources other than the internal records when analyzing comparisons with budgets and forecasts to determine inherent risk.

Cash flow analysis enables the auditors to see the crucial information of cash flow from operating, investing, and financing activities. A cash flow deficit from operations can signal financial difficulty. Companies fail when they run out of cash (no surprise) and are unable to pay their debts when they become due. Professional auditing standards state that auditors are responsible for letting financial statement users know whether they have substantial doubts as to whether the client will be able to survive into subsequent periods (i.e., whether the company can remain a *going concern*), and cash flow analysis is a good starting place.

AUDITING INSIGHT   Some Examples of Analytical Procedures

- Auditors noticed large quantities of rolled steel in the company's inventory. Several 60,000-pound rolls were entered in the inventory list. The false entries were detected because the auditor knew the company's forklift trucks had a 20,000-pound lifting capacity.

- Auditors could have compared the total quantity of vegetable oils the company claimed to have inventoried in its tanks to the storage capacity reported in national export statistics. The company's "quantity on hand" amounted to 90 percent of the national supply and greatly exceeded its own tank capacity.

- A comparison of the current year's balance in accrued wages payable to the prior year's balance revealed a dramatic decrease in the current year. Based on the analytical procedure, it was learned that the company failed to accrue for a significant percentage of its wages payable at the end of the current year.

- Auditors developed a complex regression model to estimate the electric utility company's total revenue. They used empirical relations of fuel consumption, meteorological reports of weather conditions, and population census data in the area. The regression model estimated revenue within close range of the reported revenue.

- Auditors for a small regional airline calculated an estimate of airline revenue by multiplying the number of company planes times an estimate of the number of flights made by each plane in a year times the number of seats on each plane times an estimate of the average ticket price. The revenue reported by the airline was significantly higher than the auditors' estimate, meaning that either more than one person was sitting in the same seat at the same time or that the auditors needed to more closely examine recorded revenue transactions. Additional investigation discovered that the airline was in fact fraudulently overstating its revenues.

As previously stated, professional standards require auditors to perform analytical procedures during the planning stages of the audit "with the objective of identifying unusual or unexpected relationships" involving significant financial accounts "that might indicate a material misstatement, including material misstatement due to fraud." When doing so, the auditor should consider all types of relevant data to help improve their understanding of risk on the audit. Importantly, professional standards allow the use of "data that is preliminary or data that is aggregated at a high level" when completing analytical procedures at the planning stages. As a result, the increased use of big data and analytical tools has the potential to improve the effectiveness of this type of risk assessment procedure.[5]

Indeed, auditors now have the opportunity to use new types of analyses that utilize third-party data to supplement their "traditional" analytical procedures. The additional data can help auditors refine their expectations and improve the results of preliminary analytical procedures, which form initial beliefs about the nature, timing, and extent of audit evidence to be gathered from an audit client. While this type of access to increased volumes of data on the client has the potential to improve audit effectiveness, it also can have an initial negative impact on audit efficiency if audit professionals are unable to efficiently execute such additional procedures.

For example, consider the visualization featured in Exhibit 4.11, which is a text analysis that examines the words most commonly used in social media to describe a high-technology client's new product during the year under audit. As you may already know, words that appear more often in social media are larger, and words often used together in social media are closer to each other. This type of data might be helpful to auditors when determining the reasonableness of recorded sales for its newest products. In this situation, if the client's new product was a portable gaming system, the analysis might provide evidence that would confirm sales of the new product. However, if the client's new product was a wearable fitness watch, the analysis might provide evidence that would serve to question whether any sales actually occurred for the new product. Most importantly, when using this type of evidence, auditors must make sure of the data's reliability, completeness, and accuracy before relying on it as evidence.

While the availability of even more third-party data offers considerable promise for auditors when completing preliminary analytical procedures, audit professionals in today's environment also need to learn how to make the best use of internal client data when completing such procedures. For example, when completing preliminary analytical procedures, the availability of largely all of the client's internal data can allow for a more robust trend analysis (i.e., year over year) on a multitude of financial and nonfinancial data. Auditors are encouraged to consider the facts and circumstances of each audit engagement and utilize computer-assisted audited techniques to facilitate the most useful trend analyses for the financial statement audit. The following box provides guidance on how IDEA can be used to improve the efficiency of analytical procedures.

EXHIBIT 4.11
Social Media Text Analysis

[5]See PCAOB Auditing Standard No. 2110, Identifying and Assessing Risks of Material Misstatement, paragraphs 46–48.

USING IDEA IN THE AUDIT — Analytical Procedures

The IDEA software package may also be helpful when summarizing internal client data for purposes of analytical procedures used during the planning process. For example, on page 16 of the IDEA Data Analysis Workbook: IDEA Version Ten (the IDEA Workbook), it is stated that "IDEA can help with the preparation of figures for an analytical review. In particular, IDEA can generate analyses that would not otherwise be available. The **Stratification** task (from the **Analysis** tab on the IDEA Ribbon) generates a profile of the population in value bands, groups of codes, or dates. This is particularly useful when auditing assets such

as accounts receivable, inventories, or loans or for a breakdown of transactions. Additionally, the information can be summarized by particular codes or subcodes. Figures can also be compared against previous years to determine trends. A chart can be produced if required."

At the end of this chapter, problems 4.67, 4.68, and 4.69 can be completed to illustrate the use of IDEA during preliminary analytical procedures. To be most useful, each of these analyses would have to be completed for multiple years so comparisons could be made and meaningful expectations could be developed.

Before moving forward, here are a few more thoughts about analytical procedures. Professional standards mandate that analytical procedures are performed at the beginning of an audit—the preliminary stage application of analytical procedures discussed in this chapter and at the end of an audit when the partners in charge review the overall quality of the work and look for apparent problems. Analytical procedures can also be used as a substantive testing procedure to gather evidence about the relevant assertion being tested. When using substantive analytical procedures, the auditor must take great care to develop an independent expectation that is based on reliable information. When this has been developed, the expectation is compared to the recorded amount, and any significant differences must be investigated and corroborated with documentary evidence. The procedure to provide evidence about an assertion must be conducted with exacting precision and a high degree of rigor. Regardless of when analytical procedures are performed, auditors conclude their analytical procedures test work by documenting the team's findings (step 5).

AUDITING INSIGHT — Analytical Procedures in Practice

Interviews with 36 practicing auditors found that the corporate scandals that occurred in the late 1990s/early 2000s and the ensuing Sarbanes–Oxley Act, along with the advent of improved technology, have led to the following changes in how firms perform analytical procedures:

- Increased use of analytical procedures.
- Development of more precise, quantitative expectations.
- Gathering broader industry and company information, including nonfinancial information.

- Reliance on analytical procedures more to decrease substantive tests of detail.
- Less experienced staff to conduct (but not to design) a larger portion of analytical procedures.
- Increased consideration of underlying controls.

Source: G. Trompeter and A. Wright, "The World Has Changed—Have Analytical Procedure Practices?" *Contemporary Accounting Research* 27, no. 2 (2010), pp. 669–700.

Audit Team Brainstorming Discussions

On every audit engagement, the risk assessment process includes *required* audit team brainstorming sessions in which critical audit areas are discussed. These sessions update audit team members on important aspects of the audit and heighten team members' awareness of the potential for fraud and errors in the engagement. Items typically discussed include previous experiences with the client, how a fraud might be perpetrated and concealed by the client, and procedures that might detect fraud. When studying a business operation, auditors' ability to think like a criminal and devise ways to steal can help in creating procedures to determine whether fraud has happened. Often, imaginative extended procedures can be employed to unearth evidence of fraudulent activity.

A secondary objective of the discussions is to set a proper tone for the engagement. These sessions address not only fraud risk, but also other client business and audit-related risk assessments. While these brainstorming sessions typically begin during the planning stage of engagements, they should be held on a continual basis through the conclusion of the engagement.

Many firms have fraud specialists that assist audit teams throughout the risk assessment process. If an auditor's specialists are assigned to the audit, his/her involvement during brainstorming sessions is particularly important because, as a result of his/her experience, he/she is particularly adept at identifying critical audit areas and how these areas influence the risk of misstatement due to fraud.

AUDITING INSIGHT   Some Best Practices in Brainstorming

- An engagement partner or an auditor's forensic specialist is the best choice to lead the brainstorming session, but the use of group decision software (which protects individuals' identities) allows each engagement team member to participate freely without fear of intimidation or repercussion. Managers and partners should be active participants.

- Audit team members should be reminded of the purpose of the brainstorming session and stress the importance of professional skepticism.

- A good strategy is to discuss material misstatements found in previous audits and/or frauds found on similar engagements.

- When checklists are used, fully discuss each item on the list and don't limit discussions solely to items on the checklist. In other words, consider what might have been left off the checklist.

- The idea-generation phase should be separated from the idea-evaluation phase. Considering each threat as it is brought up may cause individuals to feel slighted and may inhibit further idea generation. Engagement team members should be encouraged to discuss why they feel an identified risk is important.

- An information technology audit specialist should attend.

- The session should be held during preplanning or early in the planning stage.

- It should include discussion of how management might perpetrate fraud and audit responses to fraud risk.

- Time should be set aside at the end of the session to indicate how the audit plan should be modified as a result of the discussions.

Sources: M. Landis, S. Jerris, and M. Braswell, "Better Brainstorming," *Journal of Accountancy,* October 2008, pp. 70–73; J. F. Brazel, T. D. Carpenter, and J. G. Jenkins, "Auditors' Use of Brainstorming in the Consideration of Fraud: Reports from the Field," *The Accounting Review* 85, no. 4 (2010), pp. 1273–1301.

Inquiry of Audit Committee, Management, and Others within the Company

Interviewing the entity's management, internal auditors, directors, the audit committee, and other employees is a required audit process that can bring auditors up to date on changes in the business and the industry. Such inquiries of client personnel have the multiple purposes of building personal working relationships, observing the competence and integrity of client personnel, obtaining a general understanding of the client or company, and probing for problem areas that could harbor financial misstatements. Issues to discuss include selection of accounting principles; susceptibility to errors and fraud, including known or suspected fraud; and how management controls and monitors fraud risks. Other company employees to question might include operations or marketing managers or those involved in significant and unusual transactions.

Another source of information is company discussion boards where anonymous whistleblowers can post information that management may not wish to disclose to auditors.

AUDITING INSIGHT | Auditors Fail to Respond to Warning Signs at HealthSouth

After failing to get the auditors' attention through direct e-mail, former **HealthSouth** bookkeeper Michael Vines tried to expose HealthSouth's accounting fraud on Yahoo's bulletin board forum devoted to the company. He wrote, "What I know about the accounting at [HealthSouth] will bring [the company] to its knees . . . what is going on at [HealthSouth], if discovered by the right people will bring change to the accounting department if not the entire company." Although it was prophetic, the auditors did not heed his warnings. They were,

however, noticed by HealthSouth security personnel who were able to identify Vines through his Yahoo ID (which contained some digits from his social security number). What HealthSouth officials intended to do with the information never came to light. One month later, the SEC filed a civil lawsuit alleging "massive accounting fraud" followed quickly by criminal indictments of key executives.

Source: "Ex-Employee Took His Case to Auditors, Then Internet—But Convinced No One," *The Wall Street Journal,* May 20, 2003, pp. A1, A13.

OVERALL ASSESSMENT AND DOCUMENTATION OF INHERENT RISK ASSESSMENT (AU-C 500, AS 1105; AU-C 265, AS 2201)

LO 4-5

Explain how auditors complete and document the overall assessment of inherent risk.

The overall goal of the risk assessment process that has been described in this chapter is to identify and then properly assess the risks of material misstatement that exist at an audit client. Once the risk assessment process is complete, auditors have a basis to plan and then implement an appropriate testing response for each of the assessed risks. This process must be completed in a very detailed manner for each relevant assertion related to each significant financial statement account and disclosure. In a sense, auditors need to think about how all of the risks identified at the company and the financial statement level could affect risks of material misstatement at the relevant assertion level. If you recall from our discussion of the audit risk model, the overall risk of material misstatement includes both inherent risk and control risk. We will discuss the assessment of control risk and the effect of tests of control in Chapter 5. For now, we will focus on the assessment of inherent risk, which needs to be evaluated without regard to the system of internal controls.

The assessment of inherent risk needs to occur for each significant financial statement account and disclosure. An account or disclosure is significant if there is a chance that it could contain a material misstatement. When making this determination, the auditor should evaluate both the quantitative and the qualitative risk factors associated with the financial statement account or disclosure. When doing so, clearly the overall materiality level is a critically important factor. However, it is possible that an account or disclosure could be significant even though its balance is below materiality. For example, an account balance may be understated or a disclosure could be omitted, among a host of other factors. Once each of the significant accounts and disclosures have been identified, the auditor then needs to identify the relevant financial statement assertions.

Relevant Assertions

According to the professional standards (AS 2201.28), a financial statement assertion is relevant if it has a "reasonable possibility of containing a misstatement that would cause the financial statements to be materially misstated." Therefore, based on all of the risk assessment procedures performed, auditors must identify those assertions that have a meaningful bearing on whether the account is fairly stated. For example, the valuation assertion would only be relevant to the cash account if the audit client had cash accounts that were denominated in a foreign currency. However, due to the nature of cash, it is likely that the existence assertion would always be relevant.

Once each relevant assertion is identified for each significant account and disclosure, the auditor must then identify the likely sources of misstatements that could cause the financial statements to be materially misstated. It is important that this step is completed at a detailed and almost granular level. To do so, the professional standards suggest that

EXHIBIT 4.12   What Can Go Wrong?

Significant Accounts	Relevant Assertions	What Can Go Wrong?
Cash	Existence	The cash balance may not exist in the company's bank accounts.
	Valuation	The cash balance that is held in foreign countries may not have been translated properly.
	Presentation and disclosure	There may be restrictions on the cash balance that were not properly disclosed.
Accounts Receivable	Existence	Accounts receivable balances are inflated and don't really exist.
	Completeness	Not all accounts receivable have been recorded.
	Valuation	Receivables are not included in financial statements at the appropriate amount, and valuation adjustments are not recorded properly.

an auditor should consider "what can go wrong" when thinking about each of the relevant financial statement assertions. The comprehensive identification of "what can go wrong" for each relevant financial statement assertion is the foundation for the risk assessment process and ultimately the audit plan. Exhibit 4.12 provides a summary of this process.

Once the likely sources of misstatements that could cause the financial statements to be materially misstated have been identified, the auditors' next task is to assess the types of risk present, the likelihood that material misstatement has occurred, the magnitude of the risk, and the pervasiveness of the potential for misstatement. This lays the groundwork for the identification of internal controls that the client should have in place to mitigate the various risks of material misstatement, which will be explored in detail in Chapter 5.

Document Risk Assessment

Auditors must carefully document the risk assessment process in the workpapers to provide a record of the procedures performed. Items that must be documented include the following:

- Discussions with engagement personnel.
- Procedures to identify and assess risk.
- Significant decisions during discussion.
- Specific risks identified and audit team responses.
- Explanation of why improper revenue recognition is *not* a risk.
- Results of audit procedures, particularly procedures regarding management override.
- Other conditions causing auditors to believe that additional procedures are required.
- Communications to management and those charged with governance, such as the audit committee.

Fraud and Other Significant Risks (AU-C 330, AS 2301)

In addition to the risk assessment based on factors previously identified, auditing standards require several other fraud risk assessments to be made. First, auditors must presume that improper revenue recognition is a fraud risk. Another risk is that, despite the existence of controls, management might override the controls through force of authority. Because several major frauds were committed through year-end adjusting entries (such as **WorldCom**'s capitalization of telephone line expenses), auditors must examine journal entries and other adjustments (especially those made close to year-end). If any significant and unusual accounting entries are identified, auditors must evaluate the business rationale behind the significant transactions. Team members gather information necessary to identify key fraud risk factors (red flags) indicating an increased potential for fraud to occur.

In addition, while completing risk assessment procedures, auditors may determine that an identified risk represents a significant risk. **Significant risks** are those risks that require special audit consideration because of the nature of the risk or the likelihood and potential magnitude of misstatement related to the risk. By definition, fraud risks are significant risks. Auditors should specifically examine controls and design tests to address significant risks. Auditors should evaluate quantitative and qualitative risk factors based on the likelihood and potential magnitude of misstatements. They should consider whether the risk is related to recent significant economic, accounting, or other developments; the complexity of transactions; whether the risk involves related parties; the degree of complexity or judgment required and uncertainty involved; and whether the risk involves significant transactions that are unusual or outside the company's normal course of business.

Auditors must next respond to the results of the risk assessments. Using the audit risk model, the auditor adjusts detection risk for *significant accounts* and *relevant disclosures*. Additional considerations must be made for risks identified as *significant risks*. For example, if the potential for fraud is high, auditors should include more experienced team members. Other responses include examining more transactions, performing **extended procedures**, including targeting tests toward higher risk areas, performing more tests of transactions at year-end rather than at interim points, and gathering higher quality evidence. Finally, the auditors should use less predictable audit procedures such as "surprise" inventory observations in which management is not told at which company warehouse locations auditors will show up to watch the client counting inventory or extended procedures such as using larger sample sizes.

Finally, when collecting evidence to support the financial statements throughout the audit, auditors must remain vigilant against the potential for fraud. Discrepancies in the accounting records, conflicting evidence, and missing documentation are all symptomatic of financial statement fraud. When such instances are identified, auditors must follow up with management to identify the source of the problems. Management's response is a key source of evidence; vague, implausible, or inconsistent responses to inquiries can be a key indicator of the pervasiveness of the fraud. Similarly, problematic or unusual reactions such as refusal to cooperate, hostility, or management delays in responding to the auditors are often present in financial statement frauds. The evaluation for potential fraud continues throughout the audit. Audit team members must be on the lookout for unusual findings or events and, upon discovery, not simply write them off as isolated occurrences.

Communication of Fraud Risks

Auditors must always exercise significant care because accusations of fraud are taken very seriously by audit clients. For this reason, if preliminary findings indicate fraud possibilities, auditors should enlist the cooperation of management and assist fraud examination professionals when bringing an investigation to a conclusion.

Standards for external auditors contain materiality thresholds related to auditors reporting their knowledge of frauds. Auditors may consider some minor frauds clearly inconsequential, especially when they involve misappropriations of assets by employees at low organizational levels. Auditors should report these to management at least one level above the people involved. The idea is that small matters can be kept in the management family. Having said this, fraud has often been compared to an iceberg: most of it can be hidden from sight. For this reason, auditors should be extremely cautious in deciding whether a fraud is "clearly inconsequential."

On the other hand, frauds involving senior managers or employees with significant internal control roles are never inconsequential and should be reported (along with any frauds that cause material misstatement in the financial statements) directly to those charged with governance, usually the entity's *audit committee* of its board of directors. All companies with securities traded on the exchanges (e.g., New York, American, and NASDAQ) are required to have audit committees. **Audit committees** are composed of independent, outside members of the board of directors (those not involved in the company's day-to-day operations) who can provide a buffer between the audit firm and management. *Auditing standards* set forth requirements intended to ensure that audit committees are informed about the scope and results of the independent audit.[6] External auditors are required to make oral or written communications about other topics, including the discovery of fraud.

Auditors are normally required to keep client information confidential. However, under AICPA auditing standards, limited disclosures to outside agencies of frauds and clients' noncompliance are permitted. If the audit firm resigns or is fired, the firm can cite these matters in the letter attached to SEC Form 8-K, which requires explanation of an organization's change of auditors. The predecessor auditor may tell the successor auditor about the client when the successor makes the inquiries required by auditing standards. Auditors must respond when answering a subpoena issued by a court or other agency with authority. When performing work under generally accepted government auditing standards (mandated by the Government Accountability Office), auditors are required to report frauds and noncompliance to the client agency under the audit contract.

✅ REVIEW CHECKPOINTS

4.13 What are some types of knowledge and understanding about a client's business and industry that an auditor is expected to obtain? What are some of the methods and sources of information for understanding a client's business and industry?

4.14 What is the purpose of performing preliminary analytical procedures in audit planning?

4.15 What are the five steps involved with the use of preliminary analytical procedures?

4.16 What are some of the ratios that can be used in preliminary analytical procedures?

4.17 When are analytical procedures required, and when are they optional?

AUDITORS' RESPONSIBILITIES FOR NONCOMPLIANCE WITH LAWS AND REGULATIONS (AU-C 250, AS 2405)

LO 4-6
Explain auditors' responsibilities with respect to a client's failure to comply with laws or regulations.

In addition to errors and fraud, a client's noncompliance with laws and regulations can cause financial statements to be materially misstated, and external auditors are advised to be aware of circumstances that could indicate noncompliance (Exhibit 4.13). Auditors are not required to be legal experts, but they must understand the legal and regulatory framework under which their client operates and how the entity is compliant with that framework. Auditing standards deal with two types of *noncompliance:* (1) **direct-effect noncompliance**, which produces direct and material effects on financial statement amounts (e.g., violations of pension laws or government contract regulations for revenue and expense recognition) that require the same assurance as errors and frauds (i.e., auditors must plan their work to provide reasonable assurance there are no material misstatements), and (2) **indirect-effect noncompliance**, which refers to violations of laws and regulations that are not directly connected to financial statements (e.g., occupational health and safety, food and drug administration regulations, environmental protection, and equal employment opportunity).

For direct-effect noncompliance, an auditor should consider the laws and regulations that are typically known by auditors to have a direct and potentially material effect on the financial statements. A classic example would be the corporate income tax code. Under tax law, the auditor knows that corporate taxes will impact both the accrued tax payable account and the income tax expense account in the financial statements. Another example might involve regulations that dictate the amount of revenue to be recorded by a client for a government contract. As you consider these examples and their direct effect on the financial statements, it is not surprising that (AS 2405.05) an "auditors responsibility to detect and report misstatements resulting from illegal acts having a direct and material

---

[6]Audit standards have broadened communications to include groups that serve in a similar role for private companies and refers to such groups as "those charged with governance." Audit committees serve in this role for public companies.

EXHIBIT 4.13
Indicators of
Noncompliance

The following can be indicators of a company's noncompliance:

- Investigations, fines, or penalties
- Payments for unspecified services or loans to consultants, related parties, employees, or government employees
- Excessive sales commissions or agent's fees
- Purchases significantly above or below market
- Unusual payments in cash, cashiers' checks to bearer, or transfers to numbered accounts
- Unusual transactions with companies in tax havens
- Payments to countries other than origination
- Inadequate audit trail
- Unauthorized or improperly recorded transactions
- Media comment
- Noncompliance cited in reports of examinations
- Failure to file tax returns or pay government duties or fees

effect on the determination of financial statement amounts is the same as that for misstatements caused by error or fraud."

The responsibility for detecting indirect-effect noncompliance is not the same as as the responsibility to detect a material misstatement resulting from fraud, as an auditor cannot possibly be expected to know all the relevant laws and regulations that affect their clients. As a result, the professional standards (AS 2405.06) recognize that for indirect-effect noncompliance "an auditor ordinarily does not have sufficient basis for recognizing possible violations of such laws and regulations." For example, consider an audit client who has violated environmental regulations. Ultimately, such a violation may result in a contingent liability being recorded in the financial statements. However, the auditor may not become aware of the violation until an investigation occurs or the resultant fine is reported to the auditor by the client. Thus, auditor responsibility for detecting *indirect-effect noncompliance* is limited as follows. If the auditor becomes aware of the possibility that an illegal act occurred that might have a material effect on the financial statements, the auditor should perform procedures that are directly focused on whether such an illegal act occurred. Otherwise, because the auditor cannot be considered an expert in all laws and regulations, an auditor is not required to provide assurance about indirect-effect noncompliance.

Of course, auditors must always respond to any type of noncompliance or suspected noncompliance that is identified during the audit. To do so, they must gain an understanding of the nature and circumstances of the noncompliance and then evaluate the possible effect on financial statements. The noncompliance should be discussed with management at a level above the person responsible for the noncompliance. If noncompliance is "clearly inconsequential," that may be the extent of the follow-up. Noncompliance or suspected noncompliance having financial statement effects of more than this threshold should be reported to those charged with governance such as the audit committee, and the financial statements should contain adequate disclosures about the organization's noncompliance. Discussion with the client's legal counsel may also be necessary. External auditors always have the option to withdraw from an engagement if management and directors do not take satisfactory action under the circumstances.

The Private Securities Litigation Reform Act of 1995 imposed another reporting obligation. Under this law, when auditors believe an illegal act that is more than "clearly inconsequential" has or may have occurred, the auditors must inform the organization's board of directors. When the auditors believe the illegal act has a material effect on the financial statements, the board of directors has one business day to inform the U.S. Securities and Exchange Commission (SEC). If the board decides not to inform the SEC, the auditors must (1) within one business day give the SEC the same report they gave the board of directors or (2) resign from the engagement and, within one business day, give the SEC the report. If the auditors do not fulfill this legal obligation, the SEC can impose a civil penalty (e.g., monetary fine) on them.

AUDITING INSIGHT — A Suitcase Full of Cash

In early 2003, the head of **Chiquita Brands International Inc.'s** audit committee confessed to the U.S. Department of Justice that the company had been making illegal payments to a violent Colombian terrorist group. In March 2007, Chiquita pled guilty to engaging in transactions with a terrorist group and agreed to pay $25 million in fines, marking the first time that a major U.S. company has been charged with having financial dealings with terrorists. It seems that the company continued to make illegal payments for almost a year after its confession to the Department of Justice. The company began the illegal payments (estimated at around $1.7 million over seven years) after a Colombian paramilitary organization threatened to kidnap or kill employees on Chiquita's banana farms.

Chiquita is not the only company facing charges with engaging in illegal activity. **Schnitzer Steel Industries** pleaded guilty and paid

$7.5 million in fines for offering kickbacks to its Chinese customers, **Baker Hughes Inc.** paid $21 million in fines to settle a Nigerian bribery scandal, and officials from **Siemens AG** traveled the globe with suitcases full of cash, paying more than a billion dollars in bribes to win lucrative public works contracts in countries such as Argentina, Bangladesh, and Venezuela. The German engineering company has been fined a total of $1.6 billion in fines to U.S. and German authorities. The company pleaded guilty to charges under the Foreign Corrupt Practices Act for failing to maintain proper internal controls and keeping required records. The fine is the largest ever under that statute.

Source: "Chiquita Under the Gun," *The Wall Street Journal,* August 2, 2007, p. A1; www.washingtontimes.com/news/2008/dec/16/siemens-guilty-of-global-fraud/.

 ## REVIEW CHECKPOINTS

4.18 How do the professional audit standards differ for (a) errors, (b) frauds, (c) direct-effect noncompliance, and (d) indirect-effect noncompliance?

AUDIT STRATEGY MEMORANDUM

LO 4-7
Describe the content and purpose of an audit strategy memorandum.

The *audit plan* discussed in Chapter 3, which summarizes all of the important planning information and serves to document that auditors have followed generally accepted auditing standards, includes a description of the **audit strategy memorandum**. After assessing the overall financial statement risks, determining which accounts are significant, and which assertions are relevant to those accounts, the auditor should establish an overall audit strategy that sets the scope, timing, and direction for auditing each relevant assertion. The strategy is a result of the audit risk model. If auditors believe they can rely on company controls to mitigate risks, they test the controls as described in Chapter 5. Depending on the results of such tests, the auditors determine the nature, timing, and extent of substantive procedures. If the auditors identified fraud risk or other significant risks or noncompliance with laws and regulations, they specifically address them in the strategy, including the possibility of adding fraud specialists to the team or by expanding testing.

In establishing the overall audit strategy, the auditor should take into account (1) the reporting objectives of the engagement and the nature of the communications required by auditing standards, (2) the factors that are significant in directing the activities of the engagement team, and (3) the results of preliminary engagement activities and the auditor's evaluation risk assessment. Also, various laws or regulations may require other matters to be communicated. The strategy should outline the nature, timing, and extent of *resources* necessary to perform the engagement. Planned tests of controls, substantive procedures, and other planned audit procedures required to be performed so that the engagement complies with auditing standards should be documented with specific directions about the effect on the audit.

The audit strategy memorandum becomes the basis for preparing the audit plan that lists the audit procedures to be completed for each relevant assertion related to each significant account and disclosure identified on the audit engagement. Since the audit procedures to be performed by the auditors are designed to gather sufficient appropriate evidence on which to base their audit opinion on the financial statements, the professional auditing standards require a *written* audit plan that documents the audit strategy on each engagement. An example of an audit strategy memorandum is presented in Appendix 4B.

☑ REVIEW CHECKPOINTS

4.19 What is the purpose of an audit strategy memorandum? What information should it contain?

Summary

According to AS 1101.03, "To form an appropriate basis for expressing an opinion on the financial statements, the auditor must plan and perform the audit to obtain reasonable assurance about whether the financial statements are free of material misstatement due to error or fraud. Reasonable assurance is obtained by reducing audit risk to an appropriately low level through applying due professional care, including obtaining sufficient appropriate audit evidence." In order to accomplish this objective, the auditor must take the time to carefully assess audit risk on each audit engagement. *Audit risk* is the risk assumed by the auditors that they could express an incorrect opinion on financial statements that are materially misstated as a result of errors or fraud. The audit risk model breaks down audit risk into three components: *inherent risk, control risk,* and *detection risk.* Inherent risk involves the susceptibility of accounts to misstatement (assuming that no controls are present). Control risk addresses the effectiveness (or lack thereof) of the controls in preventing or detecting misstatements. Inherent and control risk are often combined and referred to as the *risk of material misstatement.* Detection risk involves the effectiveness of the auditors' procedures in detecting fraud or misstatement. Solving for detection risk in the audit risk model yields guidance for the preparation of the audit plan and the nature, timing, and extent of further audit procedures to be performed.

Risk assessment starts with knowledge of the types of errors and frauds that can be perpetrated. It involves understanding the company, its industry, and its environment. Auditors assess risk by obtaining public and internal information, holding team brainstorming discussions, performing analytical procedures, and inquiring of management, directors, and key employees. The culmination of the auditor's risk assessment process is the identification of the risk of material misstatement for each relevant assertion for each significant account and disclosure on each audit engagement. During the engagement, auditors respond to identified risks by increasing the effectiveness of their procedures and employing specialists and experienced personnel when necessary. Audit strategies are the auditors' summaries of their assessments and how they will respond to identified risks, particularly significant risks, which include the risk of fraud. Audit strategies are documented in the audit plan.

Key Terms

accounting estimates: The approximations of financial statement numbers often included in financial statements.

analytical procedures: Procedures that allow auditors to evaluate financial information by studying relationships among both financial and nonfinancial data. When used near the end of the audit, analytical procedures allow auditors to assess the conclusions reached during the audit and evaluate the overall financial statement presentation.

audit committee: A subcommittee of the board of directors that is generally composed of three to six "outside" members of the organization's board of directors.

audit risk: The risk that the auditor will express an inappropriate audit opinion when the financial statements are materially misstated (e.g., giving an unmodified opinion on financial statements that are misleading because of material misstatements the auditors failed to discover).

audit strategy memorandum: The scope, timing, and direction for auditing each relevant assertion based on the results of the audit risk model.

business risks: Those factors, events, and conditions that could prevent the organization from achieving its business objectives.

control risk: The likelihood that the client's internal control policies and procedures fail to prevent or detect a material misstatement.

defalcation: Another name for employee fraud and embezzlement.

detection risk: The likelihood that the auditors' substantive procedures will fail to detect a material misstatement that exists within an account balance or class of transactions.

direct-effect noncompliance: The violations of laws or government regulations by the entity or its management or employees that produce direct and material effects on dollar amounts in financial statements.

embezzlement: A type of fraud involving employees or nonemployees wrongfully taking money or property entrusted to their care, custody, and control, often accompanied by false accounting entries and other forms of lying and cover-up.

employee fraud: The use of fraudulent means to take money or other property from an employer. It consists of three phases: (1) the fraudulent act, (2) the conversion of the money or property to the fraudster's use, and (3) the cover-up.

errors: The unintentional misstatements or omissions of amounts or disclosures in financial statements.

extended procedures: The audit procedures used in response to heightened fraud awareness as the result of the identification of significant risks.

fraud: The misrepresentation of facts that the individual knows to be false with the intention to deceive.

fraudulent financial reporting: The intentional or reckless conduct, whether by act or omission, that results in materially misstated financial statements.

horizontal analysis: The comparative analysis of year-to-year changes in balance-sheet and income-statement accounts.

indirect-effect noncompliance: The violation of laws and regulations that does not directly affect specific financial statement accounts or disclosures (e.g., violations relating to insider securities trading, occupational health and safety, food and drug administration regulations, environmental protection, and equal employment opportunity).

inherent risk: The probability that in the absence of internal controls, material errors or frauds could enter the accounting system used to develop financial statements.

larceny: The simple theft of an employer's property that is not entrusted to an employee's care, custody, or control.

management fraud: The deliberate fraud committed by management that injures investors and creditors through materially misleading information.

related parties: Those individuals or organizations that are closely tied to the audit client, possibly through family ties or investment relationships.

relevant assertion: A financial statement assertion that has a reasonable possibility of containing a misstatement or misstatements that would cause the financial statements to be materially misstated.

risk of material misstatement (RMM): The combined inherent and control risk; in other words, the likelihood that material misstatements may have entered the accounting system and not been detected and corrected by the client's internal control.

significant account or disclosure: An account or disclosure that has a reasonable possibility of containing a material misstatement individually or when aggregated with others regardless of the effect of controls.

significant risk: A risk of material misstatement that requires special audit consideration. Fraud risk is always considered significant risk.

vertical analysis: The common-size analysis of financial statement amounts created by expressing amounts as proportions of a common base such as sales for the income-statement accounts or total assets for the balance-sheet accounts.

white-collar crime: Fraud perpetrated by people who work in offices and steal with a pencil or from a computer terminal. The contrast is with violent street crime.

Multiple-Choice Questions for Practice and Review

LO 4-2

4.20 Auditing standards do not require auditors of financial statements to
   a. Understand the nature of errors and frauds.
   b. Assess the risk of occurrence of errors and frauds.
   c. Design audits to provide reasonable assurance of detecting errors and frauds.
   d. Report all errors and frauds found to police authorities.

LO 4-2

4.21 If sales were overstated by recording a false credit sale at the end of the year, where could you find the false "dangling debit"?
   a. Inventory.
   b. Cost of goods sold.
   c. Bad debt expense.
   d. Accounts receivable.

LO 4-2

4.22 One of the typical characteristics of management fraud is
   a. Falsification of documents in order to misappropriate funds from an employer.
   b. Victimization of investors through the use of materially misleading financial statements.
   c. Illegal acts committed by management to evade laws and regulations.
   d. Conversion of stolen inventory to cash deposited in a falsified bank account.

LO 4-2

4.23 Which of the following circumstances would most likely cause an audit team to perform extended procedures?
   a. Supporting documents are produced when requested.
   b. The client made several large adjustments at or near year-end.
   c. The company has recently hired a new chief financial officer after the previous one retired.
   d. The company maintains several different petty cash funds.

LO 4-3

4.24 The likelihood that material misstatements may have entered the accounting system and not been detected and corrected by the client's internal control is referred to as
   a. Inherent risk.
   b. Control risk.
   c. Detection risk.
   d. Risk of material misstatement.

LO 4-1

4.25 The risk of material misstatement is composed of which audit risk components?
   a. Inherent risk and control risk.
   b. Control risk and detection risk.
   c. Inherent risk and detection risk.
   d. Inherent risk, control risk, and detection risk.

LO 4-1

4.26 The risk that the auditors' own testing procedures will lead to the decision that material misstatements do not exist in the financial statements when in fact such misstatements do exist is
   a. Audit risk.
   b. Inherent risk.
   c. Control risk.
   d. Detection risk.

LO 4-1

4.27 The auditors assessed risk of material misstatement at 0.50 and said they wanted to achieve a 0.05 risk of failing to express a correct opinion on financial statements that were materially misstated. What detection risk do the auditors plan to use for planning the remainder of the audit work?

a. 0.20.

b. 0.10.

c. 0.75.

d. 0.00.

LO 4-1

4.28 If tests of controls induce the audit team to change the assessed level of control risk for fixed assets from 0.4 to 1.0 and audit risk (0.05) and inherent risk remain constant, the acceptable level of detection risk is most likely to

a. Change from 0.1 to 0.04.

b. Change from 0.2 to 0.3.

c. Change from 0.25 to 0.1.

d. Be unchanged.

LO 4-2

4.29 Which of the following is a specific audit procedure that would be completed in response to a particular fraud risk in an account balance or class of transactions?

a. Exercising more professional skepticism.

b. Carefully avoiding conducting interviews with people in areas that are most susceptible to fraud.

c. Performing procedures such as inventory observation and cash counts on a surprise or unannounced basis.

d. Studying management's selection and application of accounting principles more carefully.

LO 4-4

4.30 Analytical procedures are generally used to produce evidence from

a. Confirmations mailed directly to the auditors by client customers.

b. Physical observation of inventories.

c. Relationships among current financial balances and prior balances, forecasts, and nonfinancial data.

d. Detailed examination of external, external-internal, and internal documents.

LO 4-4

4.31 Which of the following relationships between types of analytical procedures and sources of information are most logical?

Type of Analytical Procedure	Source of Information
a. Comparison of current account balances with prior periods	Physical production statistics
b. Comparison of current account balances with expected balances	Company's budgets and forecasts
c. Evaluation of current account balances with relation to predictable historical patterns	Published industry ratios
d. Evaluation of current account balances in relation to nonfinancial information	Company's own comparative financial statements

LO 4-4

4.32 Analytical procedures can be used in which of the following ways?

a. As a means of overall review near the end of the audit.

b. As "attention-directing" methods when planning an audit at the beginning.

c. As substantive audit procedures to obtain evidence during an audit.

d. All of the above.

LO 4-4

4.33 Analytical procedures used when planning an audit should concentrate on

a. Weaknesses in the company's internal control activities.

b. Predictability of account balances based on individual significant transactions.

c. Management assertions in financial statements.

d. Accounts and relationships that can represent specific potential problems and risks in the financial statements.

LO 4-4   4.34 When a company that sells its products with a positive gross profit increases its sales by 15 percent and its cost of goods sold by 7 percent, the cost of goods sold ratio will
  a. Increase.
  b. Decrease.
  c. Remain unchanged.
  d. Not be able to be determined with the information provided.

LO 4-3   4.35 Auditors are not responsible for accounting estimates with respect to
  a. Making the estimates.
  b. Determining the reasonableness of estimates.
  c. Determining that estimates are presented in conformity with GAAP.
  d. Determining that estimates are adequately disclosed in the financial statements.

LO 4-7   4.36 An audit strategy memorandum contains
  a. Specifications of auditing standards relevant to the financial statements being audited.
  b. Specifications of procedures the auditors believe appropriate for the financial statements under audit.
  c. Documentation of the assertions under audit, the evidence obtained, and the conclusions reached.
  d. Reconciliation of the account balances in the financial statements with the account balances in the client's general ledger.

LO 4-1   4.37 It is acceptable under generally accepted auditing standards for an audit team to
  a. Assess risk of material misstatement at high and achieve an acceptably low audit risk by performing extensive substantive tests.
  b. Assess control risk at zero and perform a minimum of detection work.
  c. Assess inherent risk at zero and perform a minimum of detection work.
  d. Decide that audit risk can be 40 percent.

LO 4-6   4.38 Under the Private Securities Litigation Reform Act (the Act), independent auditors are required to first
  a. Report in writing all instances of noncompliance with the Act to the client's board of directors.
  b. Report to the SEC all instances of noncompliance with the Act they believe have a material effect on financial statements if the board of directors does not first report to the SEC.
  c. Report clearly inconsequential noncompliance with the Act to the audit committee of the client's board of directors.
  d. Resign from the audit engagement and report the instances of noncompliance with the Act to the SEC.

LO 4-3   4.39 When evaluating whether accounting estimates made by management are reasonable, auditors would be most interested in which of the following?
  a. Key factors that are consistent with prior periods.
  b. Assumptions that are similar to industry guidelines.
  c. Measurements that are objective and not susceptible to bias.
  d. Evidence of a conservative systematic bias.

LO 4-3   4.40 An audit committee is
  a. Composed of internal auditors.
  b. Composed of members of the audit team.
  c. Composed of members of a company's board of directors who are not involved in the day-to-day operations of the company.
  d. A committee composed of persons not associating in any way with the client or the board of directors.

LO 4-6

4.41   When auditors become aware of noncompliance with a law or regulation committed by client personnel, the primary reason that the auditors should obtain a better understanding of the nature of the act is to

a. Recommend remedial actions to the audit committee.

b. Evaluate the effect of the noncompliance on the financial statements.

c. Determine whether to contact law enforcement officials.

d. Determine whether other similar acts could have occurred.

LO 4-6

4.42   Which of the following statements best describes auditors' responsibility for detecting a client's noncompliance with a law or regulation?

a. The responsibility for detecting noncompliance exactly parallels the responsibility for errors and fraud.

b. Auditors must design tests to detect all material noncompliance that indirectly affects the financial statements.

c. Auditors must design tests to obtain reasonable assurance that all noncompliance with direct material financial statement effects is detected.

d. Auditors must design tests to detect all noncompliance that directly affects the financial statements.

LO 4-4

4.43   Auditors perform analytical procedures in the planning stage of an audit for the purpose of

a. Deciding the matters to cover in an engagement letter.

b. Identifying unusual conditions that deserve more auditing effort.

c. Determining which of the financial statement assertions are the most important for the client's financial statements.

d. Determining the nature, timing, and extent of further audit procedures for auditing the inventory.

LO 4-4

4.44   A primary objective of analytical procedures used in the final review stage of an audit is to

a. Identify account balances that represent specific risks relevant to the audit.

b. Gather evidence from tests of details to corroborate financial statement assertions.

c. Detect fraud that may cause the financial statements to be misstated.

d. Assist the auditor in evaluating the overall financial statement presentation.

(AICPA adapted)

LO 4-4

4.45   An auditor's analytical procedures indicate a lower than expected return on an equity method investment. This situation most likely could have been caused by

a. An error in recording amortization of the excess of the investor's cost over the investment's underlying book value.

b. The investee's decision to reduce cash dividends declared per share of its common stock.

c. An error in recording the unrealized gain from an increase in the fair value of available-for sale securities in the income account for trading securities.

d. A substantial fluctuation in the price of the investee's common stock on a national stock exchange.

(AICPA adapted)

LO 4-4

4.46   Which of the following risk types increase when an auditor performs substantive analytical audit procedures for financial statement accounts at an interim date?

a. Inherent.

b. Control.

c. Detection.

d. Sampling.

(AICPA adapted)

LO 4-3

4.47 Which of the following matters relating to an entity's operations would an auditor most likely consider as an inherent risk factor in planning an audit?

a. The entity's fiscal year ends on June 30.

b. The entity enters into significant derivative transactions as hedges.

c. The entity's financial statements are generated at an outside service center.

d. The entity's financial data is available only in computer-readable form.

(AICPA adapted)

LO 4-2

4.48 What is the primary objective of the fraud brainstorming session?

a. Determine audit risk and materiality.

b. Identify whether analytical procedures should be applied to the revenue accounts.

c. Assess the potential for material misstatement due to fraud.

d. Determine whether the planned procedures in the audit plan will satisfy the general audit objectives.

(AICPA adapted)

Exercises and Problems

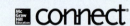 All applicable Exercises and Problems are available with *Connect.*

LO 4-4

4.49 **Analytical Procedures and Interest Expense.** Weyman Z. Wannamaker is the chief financial officer of Cogburn Company. He prides himself on being able to manage the company's cash resources to minimize the interest expense. Consequently, on the second business day of each month, Weyman pays down or draws cash on Cogburn's revolving line of credit at First National Bank in accordance with his cash requirements forecast.

You are the auditor. You find the information on this line of credit in the following table. You inquired at First National Bank and learned that Cogburn Company's loan agreement specifies payment on the first day of each month for the interest due on the previous month's outstanding balance at the rate of "prime plus 1.5 percent." The bank gave you a report that showed the prime rate of interest was 8.5 percent for the first six months of the year and 8.0 percent for the last six months.

Cogburn Company Notes Payable Balances	
Date	Balance
Jan 1	$150,000
Feb 1	200,000
Apr 1	225,000
May 1	285,000
Jun 1	375,000
Aug 1	430,000
Sep 1	290,000
Oct 1	210,000
Nov 1	172,000
Dec 1	95,000

Required:

a. Prepare an audit estimate of the amount of interest expense you expect to find as the balance of the interest expense account related to these notes payable.

b. Which of the types of analytical procedures did you use to determine this estimate?

c. Suppose that you find that the interest expense account shows expense of $23,650 related to these notes. What could account for this difference?

d. Suppose that you find that the interest expense account shows expense of $24,400 related to these notes. What could account for this difference?

e. Suppose that you find that the interest expense account shows expense of $25,200 related to these notes. What could account for this difference?

LO 4-3

4.50 **Appropriateness of Evidence and Related Parties.** Johnson & Company, CPAs, audited Guaranteed Savings & Loan Company. M. Johnson had the assignment of evaluating the collectability of real estate loans. Johnson was working on two particular loans: (1) a $4 million loan secured by Smith Street Apartments and (2) a $5.5 million construction loan on Baker Street Apartments now being built. The appraisals performed by Guaranteed Appraisal Partners Inc. showed values in excess of the loan amounts. On inquiry, Bumpus, the S&L vice president for loan acquisition, stated, "I know the Smith Street loan is good because I myself own 40 percent of the partnership that owns the property and is obligated on the loan."

Johnson then wrote in the audit documentation: (1) the Smith Street loan appears collectible as Bumpus personally attested to knowledge of the collectability as a major owner in the partnership obligated on the loan; (2) the Baker Street loan is assumed to be collectible because it is new and construction is still in progress; and (3) the appraised values all exceed the loan amounts.

Required:

a. Do you perceive any problems with related-party involvement in the evidence used by Johnson? Explain.

b. Do you perceive any problems with Johnson's reasoning or the appropriateness of evidence used in that reasoning?

LO 4-3

4.51 **Risk of Misstatement in Various Accounts.** An auditor must identify the relevant assertions about each significant financial statement account and disclosure and then gather evidence to conclude whether a material misstatement exists for each assertion. The nature of each financial statement account and disclosure contributes to the likelihood that a material misstatement exists.

a. In general, which accounts are most susceptible to overstatement? To understatement?

b. Why do you think a company could permit asset accounts to be understated?

c. Why do you think a company could permit liability accounts to be overstated?

d. Which direction of misstatement is most likely: income overstatement or income understatement?

LO 4-3

4.52 **Analysis of Accounting Estimates.** Oak Industries, a manufacturer of radio and cable TV equipment and an operator of subscription TV systems, had a multitude of problems. Subscription services in a market area, for which $12 million of cost had been deferred, were being terminated, and the customers were not paying on time ($4 million receivables in doubt). The chances are 50-50 that the business will survive another two years.

An electronic part turned out to have defects that needed correction. Warranty expenses are estimated to range from $2 million to $6 million. The inventory of this part ($10 million) is obsolete, but $1 million can be recovered in salvage, or the parts in inventory can be rebuilt at a cost of $2 million. (The selling price of the inventory on hand would then be $8 million, with 20 percent of the selling price required to market and ship the products, and the normal profit is expected to be 5 percent of the selling price.) If the inventory were scrapped, the company would manufacture a replacement inventory at a cost of $6 million, excluding marketing and shipping costs and normal profit.

The company has defaulted on completion of a military contract, and the government is claiming a $2 million refund. Company attorneys think the dispute might be settled for as little as $1 million.

The auditors had previously determined that an overstatement of income before taxes of $7 million would be material to the financial statements. These items were the only ones left for audit decisions about possible adjustment. Management has presented the following analysis for the determination of loss recognition:

Write off deferred subscription costs	$3,000,000
Provide allowance for bad debts	4,000,000
Provide for expected warranty expense	2,000,000
Lower-of-cost-or-market inventory write-down	2,000,000
Loss on government contract refund	????????

Required:

Prepare your own analysis of the amount of adjustment to the financial statements. Assume that none of these estimates have been recorded yet, and give the adjusting entry you would recommend. Give any supplementary explanations you believe necessary to support your recommendation.

LO 4-4

4.53 **Horizontal and Vertical Analysis.** *Horizontal analysis* refers to changes of financial statement numbers and ratios across two or more years. *Vertical analysis* refers to financial statement amounts expressed each year as proportions of a base such as sales for the income-statement accounts and total assets for the balance-sheet accounts. Exhibit 4.53.1 contains Retail Company's prior-year (audited) and current-year (unaudited) financial statements, along with amounts and percentages of change from year to year (horizontal analysis) and common-size percentages (vertical analysis). Exhibit 4.53.2 contains selected financial ratios based on these financial statements. Analysis of these data can enable auditors to discern relationships that raise questions about misleading financial statements.

Required:

Study the data in Exhibits 4.53.1 and 4.53.2. Write a memorandum identifying and explaining potential problem areas where misstatements in the current-year financial statements could exist. Additional information about Retail Company is as follows:

EXHIBIT 4.53.1 **Retail Company**

	Prior Year (Audited)		Current Year (Unaudited)		Change	
	Balance	Common Size	Balance	Common Size	Amount	Percent
Assets:						
Cash	$ 600,000	14.78%	$ 484,000	9.69%	$ (116,000)	−19.33%
Accounts receivable	500,000	12.32	400,000	8.01	(100,000)	−20.00
Allowance doubt. accts.	(40,000)	−0.99	(30,000)	−0.60	10,000	−25.00
Inventory	1,500,000	36.95	1,940,000	38.85	440,000	29.33
Total current assets	2,560,000	63.05	2,794,000	55.95	234,000	9.14
Fixed assets	3,000,000	73.89	4,000,000	80.10	1,000,000	33.33
Accum. depreciation	(1,500,000)	−36.95	(1,800,000)	−36.04	(300,000)	20.00
Total assets	$4,060,000	100.00%	$4,994,000	100.00%	$ 934,000	23.00%
Liabilities and equity:						
Accounts payable	$ 450,000	11.08%	$ 600,000	12.01%	$ 150,000	33.33%
Bank loans, 11%	0	0.00	750,000	15.02	750,000	NA
Accrued interest	50,000	1.23	40,000	0.80	(10,000)	−20.00
Accruals and other	60,000	1.48	10,000	0.20	(50,000)	−83.33
Total current liab.	560,000	13.79	1,400,000	28.03	840,000	150.00
Long-term debt, 10%	500,000	12.32	400,000	8.01	(100,000)	−20.00
Total liabilities	1,060,000	26.11	1,800,000	36.04	740,000	69.81
Capital stock	2,000,000	49.26	2,000,000	40.05	0	0
Retained earnings	1,000,000	24.63	1,194,000	23.91	194,000	19.40
Total liabilities and equity	$4,060,000	100.00%	$4,994,000	100.00%	934,000	23.00%
Statement of operations:						
Sales (net)	$9,000,000	100.00%	$8,100,000	100.00%	$ (900,000)	−10.00%
Cost of goods sold	6,296,000	69.96	5,265,000	65.00	(1,031,000)	−16.38
Gross margin	2,704,000	30.04	2,835,000	35.00	131,000	4.84
General expense	2,044,000	22.7	2,005,000	24.75	(39,000)	−1.91
Depreciation	300,000	3.33	300,000	3.70	0	0
Operating income	360,000	4.00	530,000	6.54	170,000	47.22
Interest expense	50,000	0.56	40,000	0.49	(10,000)	−20.00
Income taxes (40%)	124,000	1.38	196,000	2.42	72,000	58.06
Net income	$ 186,000	2.07%	$ 294,000	3.63%	$ 108,000	58.06%

"NA" means not applicable.

EXHIBIT 4.53.2
Retail Company

	Prior Year (audited)	Current Year (unaudited)	Percent Change
Balance-sheet ratios:			
Current ratio	4.57	2.0	−56.34%
Days' sales in receivables	18.40	16.44	−10.63
Doubtful accounts ratio	0.0800	0.0750	−6.25
Days' sales in inventory	85.77	132.65	54.66
Debt/equity ratio	0.35	0.56	40.89
Operations ratios:			
Receivables turnover	19.57	21.89	11.89
Inventory turnover	4.20	2.71	−35.34
Cost of goods sold/sales	69.96%	65.00%	−7.08
Gross margin %	30.04%	35.00%	16.49
Return on equity	6.61%	9.80%	48.26

- The new bank loan, obtained on July 1 of the current year, requires maintenance of a 2:1 current ratio.
- Principal of $100,000 plus interest on the 10 percent long-term note obtained several years ago in the original amount of $800,000 is due each January 1.
- The company has never paid dividends on its common stock and has no plans for a dividend.

LO 4-3

4.54 **Analysis and Judgment.** As part of your regular year-end audit of a public client, you must estimate the probability of success of its proposed new product line. The client has experienced financial difficulty during the last few years and, in your judgment, a successful introduction of the new product line is necessary for the client to remain a going concern.

Five elements are necessary for the successful introduction of the product: (1) successful labor negotiations before the strike deadline between the construction firms contracted to build the necessary addition to the present plant and the building trades unions, (2) successful defense of patent rights, (3) product approval by the Food and Drug Administration (FDA), (4) successful negotiation of a long-term raw material contract with a foreign supplier, and (5) successful conclusion of distribution contract talks with a large national retail distributor.

In view of the circumstances, you contact experts who have provided your public accounting firm with reliable estimates in the past. The labor relations expert estimates that there is an 80 percent chance of successfully concluding labor negotiations. Legal counsel advises that there is a 90 percent chance of successfully defending patent rights. The expert on FDA product approvals estimates a 95 percent chance of new product approval. The experts in the remaining two areas estimate the probability of successfully resolving (1) the raw materials contract and (2) the distribution contract talks to be 90 percent in each case. Assume that these estimates are reliable.

Required:
What is your assessment of the probability of successful product introduction? (*Hint:* You can assume that each of the five elements is independent of the others.)

LO 4-4

4.55 **Analytical Procedures.** Kelly Griffin, an audit manager, had begun preliminary analytical procedures of selected statistics related to the Majestic Hotel. Her objective was to obtain an understanding of the hotel's business in order to draft a preliminary audit plan. She wanted to see whether she could detect any troublesome areas or questionable accounts that could require special audit attention. Unfortunately, Griffin caught the flu and was hospitalized. From her sickbed, she sent you the schedule she had prepared (Exhibit 4.55.1) and has asked you to write a memorandum identifying areas of potential misstatements or other matters that the preliminary audit plan should cover.

EXHIBIT 4.55.1
Analytical Procedure
Documentation

	Majestic (percent)	Industry (percent)
Sales:		
Rooms	60.4%	63.9%
Food and beverage	35.7	32.2
Other	3.9	3.9
Costs:		
Rooms department	15.2	17.3
Food and beverage	34.0	27.2
Administrative and general	8.0	8.9
Management fee	3.3	1.1
Advertising	2.7	3.2
Real estate taxes	3.5	3.2
Utilities, repairs, maintenance	15.9	13.7
Profit per sales dollar	17.4	25.4
Rooms dept. ratios to room sales dollars:		
Salaries and wages	18.9	15.7
Laundry	1.1	3.7
Other	5.3	7.6
Profit per rooms sales dollar	74.8	73.0
Food/beverage (F/B) ratios to F/B sales dollars:		
Cost of food sold	42.1	37.0
Food gross profit	57.9	63.0
Cost of beverages sold	43.6	29.5
Beverages gross profit	56.4	70.5
Combined gross profit	57.7	64.6
Salaries and wages	39.6	32.8
Music and entertainment	—	2.7
Other	13.4	13.8
Profit per F/B sales dollar	4.7	15.3
Average annual percent of rooms occupied	62.6	68.1
Average room rate per day	$160	$120
Number of rooms available per day	200	148

Required:

Write a memorandum describing Majestic's operating characteristics compared to the industry average insofar as you can tell from the statistics. Do these analytical procedures identify any areas that could represent potential misstatements in the audit?

LO 4-4

4.56 **Preliminary Analytical Procedures.** Dunder-Mifflin Inc. wanted to expand its manufacturing and sales facilities. The company applied for a loan from First Bank, presenting the prior-year audited financial statements and the forecast for the current year shown in Exhibit 4.56.1. (Dunder-Mifflin Inc.'s fiscal year-end is December 31.) The bank was impressed with the business prospects and granted a $1,750,000 loan at 8 percent interest to finance working capital and the new facilities that were placed in service July 1 of the current year. Because Dunder-Mifflin Inc. planned to issue stock for permanent financing, the bank made the loan due on December 31 of the following year. Interest is payable each calendar quarter on October 1 of the current year and January 1, April 1, July 1, October 1 of the following year.

The auditors' interviews with Dunder-Mifflin Inc. management near the end of the current year produced the following information: The facilities did not cost as much as previously anticipated. However, sales were slow and the company granted more liberal return privilege terms than in the prior year. Officers wanted to generate significant income to impress First Bank and to preserve the company dividend ($120,000 paid in the prior year). The production managers had targeted inventory levels for a 4.0 turnover ratio and were largely successful even though prices of materials and supplies had risen about 2 percent

EXHIBIT 4.56.1
Dunder-Mifflin Inc.

	Prior Year (audited)	Forecast	Current Year (unaudited)
Revenue and Expense:			
Sales (net)	$ 9,000,000	$9,900,000	$ 9,720,000
Cost of goods sold	6,296,000	6,926,000	7,000,000
Gross margin	2,704,000	2,974,000	2,720,000
General expense	2,044,000	2,000,000	2,003,000
Depreciation	300,000	334,000	334,000
Operating income	360,000	640,000	383,000
Interest expense	60,000	110,000	75,000
Income taxes (40%)	120,000	212,000	123,200
Net income	180,000	318,000	184,800
Assets:			
Cash	600,000	880,000	690,800
Accounts receivable	500,000	600,000	900,000
Allowance for doubtful accounts	(40,000)	(48,000)	(90,000)
Inventory	1,500,000	1,500,000	1,350,000
Total current assets	2,560,000	2,932,000	2,850,800
Fixed assets	3,000,000	4,700,000	4,500,000
Accumulated depreciation	(1,500,000)	(1,834,000)	(1,834,000)
Total assets	$ 4,060,000	$5,798,000	$ 5,516,800
Liabilities and Equity:			
Accounts payable	$ 450,000	$ 450,000	$ 330,000
Bank loans, 8%	0	1,750,000	1,750,000
Accrued interest	60,000	40,000	40,000
Accruals and other	50,000	60,000	32,000
Total current liabilities	$ 560,000	$2,300,000	$ 2,152,000
Long-term debt, 10%	600,000	400,000	400,000
Total liabilities	$ 1,160,000	$2,700,000	$ 2,552,000
Capital stock	2,000,000	2,000,000	2,000,000
Retained earnings	900,000	1,098,000	964,800
Total liabilities and equity	$ 4,060,000	$5,798,000	$ 5,516,800

relative to sales dollar volume. The new facilities were depreciated using a 25-year life from the date of opening.

Dunder-Mifflin Inc. has now produced the current-year financial statements (Exhibit 4.56.1, Current Year column) for the auditors' work on the current audit.

Required:

Perform preliminary analytical procedures on the current-year unaudited financial statements for the purpose of identifying accounts that could contain errors or frauds. Use your knowledge of Dunder-Mifflin Inc. and the forecast in Exhibit 4.56.1. Calculate comparative and common-size financial statements as well as relevant ratios. (Assume that the market value of the equity for the company is $3 million.) Once your calculations are complete, identify the accounts that could be misstated. (*Note:* This assignment is available in the student section of the textbook website in Excel format.)

LO 4-1

4.57   **Audit Risk Model.** Audit risks for particular accounts and disclosures can be conceptualized in the model: Audit risk (AR) = Inherent risk (IR) × Control risk (CR) × Detection risk (DR). Use this model as a framework for considering the following situations and deciding whether the auditor's conclusion is appropriate.

a. Paul, CPA, has participated in the audit of Tordik Cheese Company for five years, first as an assistant accountant and the last two years as the senior accountant. Paul has never seen an accounting adjustment recommended and believes the inherent risk must be zero.

b. Hill, CPA, has just (November 30) completed an exhaustive study and evaluation of the internal controls of Edward Foods Inc. (fiscal year ending December 31). Hill believes the control risk must be zero because no material errors could possibly slip through the many error-checking procedures and review layers that Edward used.

c. Fields, CPA, is lazy and does not like audit jobs in Philadelphia. On the audit of Philly Manufacturing Company, Fields decided to use substantive procedures to audit the year-end balances very thoroughly to the extent that the risk of failing to detect material errors and irregularities should be 0.02 or less. Fields gave no thought to inherent risk and conducted only a very limited review of Philly's internal control system.

d. Shad, CPA, is nearing the end of a "dirty" audit of Allnight Protection Company. All of Allnight's accounting personnel resigned during the year and were replaced by inexperienced people. The comptroller resigned last month in disgust. The journals and ledgers were a mess because the one computer specialist was hospitalized for three months during the year. "Thankfully," Shad thought, "I've been able to do this audit in less time than last year when everything was operating smoothly."

(AICPA adapted)

LO 4-3

4.58 **Auditing an Accounting Estimate.** Suppose management estimated the market valuation of some obsolete inventory at $99,000; this inventory was recorded at $120,000, which resulted in recognizing a loss of $21,000. The auditors obtained the following information: The inventory in question could be sold for an amount between $78,000 and $92,000. The costs of advertising and shipping could range from $5,000 to $7,000.

Required:

a. Would you propose an audit adjustment to the management estimate? Prepare the appropriate accounting entry.

b. If management's estimate of inventory market (lower than cost) had been $80,000, would you propose an audit adjustment? Prepare the appropriate accounting entry.

LO 4-1

4.59 **Risk Assessment.** This question consists of a number of items pertaining to an auditor's risk analysis for a company. Your task is to tell how each item affects overall audit risk—that is, the probability of issuing an unmodified audit report on materially misleading financial statements.

Bond, CPA, is considering audit risk at the financial statement level in planning the audit of Toxic Waste Disposal (TWD) Company's financial statements for the year ended December 31, 2017. TWD is a privately owned company that contracts with municipal governments to remove environmental wastes. Audit risk at the overall financial statement level is influenced by the risk of material misstatements, which may be indicated by a combination of factors related to management, the industry, and the company.

Required:

Based only on the following information, indicate whether each of the following factors (items 1 through 15) would most likely increase overall audit risk, decrease overall audit risk, or have no effect on overall audit risk. Discuss your reasoning.

Company Profile

1. This was the first year TWD operated at a profit since 2012 because the municipalities received increased federal and state funding for environmental purposes.

2. TWD's board of directors is controlled by Mead, the majority stockholder, who also acts as the chief executive officer.

3. The internal auditor reports to the controller, and the controller reports to Mead.

4. The accounting department has experienced a high rate of turnover of key personnel.

5. TWD's bank has a loan officer who meets regularly with TWD's CEO and controller to monitor TWD's financial performance.

6. TWD's employees are paid biweekly.

7. Bond has audited TWD for five years.

Recent Developments

8. During 2017, TWD changed the method of preparing its financial statements from the cash basis to the accrual basis under generally accepted accounting principles.

9. During 2017, TWD sold one-half of its controlling interest in United Equipment Leasing (UEL) Co. TWD retained significant interest in UEL.

10. During 2017, the state dropped litigation filed against TWD in 2013 alleging that the company discharged pollutants into state waterways. Loss contingency disclosures that TWD included in prior-years' financial statements are being removed for the 2016 financial statements.

11. During December 2017, TWD signed a contract to lease disposal equipment from an entity owned by Mead's parents. This related-party transaction is not disclosed in TWD's notes to its 2017 financial statements.

12. During December 2017, TWD completed a barter transaction with a municipality. TWD removed waste from a municipally owned site and acquired title to another contaminated site at below-market price. TWD intends to service this new site in 2018.

13. During December 2017, TWD increased its casualty insurance coverage on several pieces of sophisticated machinery from historical cost to replacement cost.

14. Inquiries about the substantial increase in revenue that TWD recorded in the fourth quarter of 2017 disclosed a new policy. TWD guaranteed several municipalities that it would refund the federal and state funding paid to it if any municipality fails federal or state site cleanup inspection in 2018.

15. An initial public offering of TWD's stock is planned for late 2018.

LO 4-2

4.60 **Auditing Standards Review.** Management fraud (fraudulent financial reporting) is not the expected norm, but it happens from time to time. In the United States, several cases have been widely publicized. They happen when motives and opportunities overwhelm managerial integrity.

a. What distinguishes management fraud from a defalcation?

b. What are an auditor's responsibilities under auditing standards to detect management fraud?

c. What are some characteristics of management fraud that an audit team should consider to fulfill the responsibilities under auditing standards?

d. What factors might an audit team notice that should heighten the concern about the existence of management fraud?

e. Under what circumstances might an audit team have a duty to disclose management's frauds to parties other than the company's management and its board of directors?

(AICPA adapted)

LO 4-4

4.61 **Analytical Procedures: Ratio Relationships.** The following situations represent errors and frauds that could occur in financial statements.

Required:

State how the ratio in question would compare (higher, equal, or lower) to what the ratio should have been had the error or fraud not occurred.

a. The company recorded fictitious sales with credits to sales revenue accounts and debits to accounts receivable. Inventory was reduced, and cost of goods sold was increased for the profitable "sales." Is the current ratio higher than, equal to, or lower than what it should have been?

b. The company recorded cash disbursements by paying trade accounts payable but held the checks past the year-end date, meaning that the "disbursements" should not have been shown as credits to cash and debits to accounts payable. Is the current ratio higher than, equal to, or lower than what it should have been? Consider cases in which the current ratio before the improper "disbursement" recording was (1) higher than 1:1, (2) equal to 1:1, and (3) lower than 1:1.

c. The company uses a periodic inventory system for determining the balance-sheet amount of inventory at year-end. Very near the year-end, merchandise was received, placed in the stockroom, and counted, but the purchase transaction was neither recorded nor paid until the next month. What was the effect of this on inventory, cost of goods sold, gross profit, and net income? How were these ratios affected compared to what they would have been without the error: current ratio [remember three possible cases from part (b)], gross margin ratio, cost of goods sold ratio, inventory turnover, and receivables turnover?

d. The company is loath to write off customer accounts receivable even though the financial vice president makes entirely adequate provision for uncollectible amounts in the allowance for bad debts. The gross receivables and the allowance both contain amounts that should have been written off long ago. How are these ratios affected compared to what they would have been if the old receivables had been properly written off: current ratio, days' sales in receivables, doubtful account ratio, receivables turnover, return on beginning equity, and working capital/total assets?

e. Since last year, the company has reorganized its lines of business and placed more emphasis on its traditional products while selling off some marginal businesses merged by the previous management. Total assets are 10 percent less than they were last year, but working capital has increased. Retained earnings remained the same because the disposals created no gains, and the net income after taxes is still near zero, which is the same as last year. Earnings before interest and taxes (EBIT) remained the same, a small positive EBIT. The total market value of the company's equity has not increased, but that is better than the declines of the past several years. Proceeds from the disposals have been used to retire long-term debt. Net sales have decreased 5 percent because the sales' decrease resulting from the disposals has not been overcome by increased sales of the traditional products. Is the discriminant Z-score of the current year higher or lower than the one of the prior year? (See Appendix 4A for the Z-score formula.)

LO 4-7

4.62 **Audit Strategy Memorandum.** The auditor should establish an overall audit strategy that sets the scope, timing, and direction of the audit and guides the development of the audit plan. In establishing the overall audit strategy, the auditor should develop and document an audit plan that includes a description of (a) the planned nature, timing, and extent of the risk assessment procedures, (b) the planned nature, timing, and extent of tests of controls and substantive procedures, and (c) other planned audit procedures that must be performed so that the engagement complies with auditing standards.

Required:

Select a public company and determine a significant risk that could affect its financial statements. (*Hint:* Go to the EDGAR database at www.sec.gov and select the company's form 10-K. The 10-K will have a list of risk factors the company faces.) Describe the risk and how it could affect the financial statements, including what assertions might be misstated. Prepare an audit strategy memorandum for the risk describing what controls the company might use to mitigate the risk, how you could test the controls, and what substantive procedures you might use to determine whether there is a misstatement. Because this is early in your auditing class, do not worry about specific procedures; just be creative and think about a general strategy an auditor might use.

LO 4-2

4.63 **Errors and Frauds.** Give an example of an error or fraud that would misstate financial statements to affect the accounts as follows, taking each case independently. (*Note:* "Overstate" means the account has a higher value than would be appropriate under GAAP and "understate" means it has a lower value.)

a. Overstate one asset; understate another asset.

b. Overstate an asset; overstate stockholders' equity.

c. Overstate an asset; overstate revenue.

d. Overstate an asset; understate an expense.

e. Overstate a liability; overstate an expense.

f. Understate an asset; overstate an expense.

g. Understate a liability; understate an expense.

LO 4-6

4.64 **Compliance with Laws and Regulations.** Audit standards distinguish auditors' responsibility for planning procedures for detecting noncompliance with laws and regulations having a direct effect on financial statements versus planning procedures for detecting noncompliance with laws and regulations that do not have a direct effect on financial statements.

Required:

a. What are the requirements for auditors to plan procedures to detect direct-effect compliance versus indirect-effect compliance?

b. For each of the following instances of noncompliance, explain why they are either direct-effect (D) or indirect-effect (I) noncompliance:

1. A manufacturer inflates expenses on its corporate tax return.

2. A retailer pays men more than women for performing the same job.

3. A coal mining company fails to place proper ventilation in its mines.

4. A military contractor inflates the overhead applied to a combat vehicle.

5. An insurance company fails to maintain required reserves for losses.

6. An exporter pays a bribe to a foreign government official so that government will buy its products.

7. A company backdates its executive stock options to lower the exercise price.

8. A company fails to fund its pension plan in accordance with ERISA.

LO 4-4

4.65 **Preparing and Analyzing an Aging Schedule — Using IDEA.** For this exercise, your client, Bright IDEAs Inc., has provided you with a listing of sales invoices. To test whether the client appears to have a receivables collectability problem, the auditor must complete a series of related steps:

1. Import the client's database of sales invoices (pp. 28–45 of the IDEA Workbook). You may have already completed this step in Chapter 3.

2. Perform an aging analysis by following the instructions on pp. 52–56 of the IDEA Workbook.

Required Data available on *McGraw-Hill Connect*

- ACC_REC2015.ACCDB

Required:

Complete the preceding steps and answer the following questions:

a. What percentage of customers have accounts that are aged greater than 90 days?

b. What percentage of customer balances are aged greater than 90 days?

c. What effects would the findings in parts (a) and (b) have on the auditor's assessment of the risk of material misstatement? What accounts and assertions are most likely influenced by these findings?

Source: C1202 IDEA Data Analysis Workbook: IDEA Version Ten. 2016. CaseWare IDEA, Inc. Toronto, CA.

LO 4-4

4.66 **Summarizing Obsolete Inventory — Using IDEA.** For this exercise, your client, Bright IDEAs Inc., has provided you with a listing of inventory as of year end. To analyze the amount of obsolete inventory, as reported by the client, the auditor must complete a series of related steps:

1. Import the client's database of inventory on hand (pp. 187–200 of the IDEA Workbook). You may have already completed this step in Chapter 3.

2. Summarize items identified as obsolete by the client (pp. 201-204 of the IDEA Workbook).

Required Data available on *McGraw-Hill Connect*

- Inventory 2015.asc

Required:

Complete the preceding steps and answer the following questions:

a. What percentage of the dollar amount of the client's inventory has been identified as obsolete?

b. What effects would the findings in part (a) have on the auditor's assessment of the risk of material misstatement? What accounts and assertions are most likely influenced by these findings?

Source: C1202 IDEA Data Analysis Workbook: IDEA Version Ten. 2016. CaseWare IDEA, Inc. Toronto, CA.

LO 4-4

4.67 **Analyzing Profit Margins — Using IDEA.** For this exercise, your client, Bright IDEAs Inc., has provided you with a listing of inventory as of year end, which includes current selling prices. To test whether profit margins appear adequate to justify the inventory valuation provision, the auditor must complete a series of related steps:

1. Import the client's database of inventory on hand (pp. 187–200 of the IDEA Workbook). You may have already completed this step in Chapter 3 or Ex 4.69.

2. Create an analysis of selling price changes (pp. 220–225 of the IDEA Workbook).

3. Create an analysis of profit margins (pp. 226–228 of the IDEA Workbook).

Required Data available on *McGraw-Hill Connect*

- Inventory 2015.asc

Required:

Complete the preceding steps and answer the following questions:

a. What percentage of inventory items have price movements in excess of 50%? How many of these items experienced price increases? How many experienced price decreases? Which direction of change would be most concerning to the auditor?

b. What percentage of items have negative profit margins?

c. What effects would the findings in part (a) and (b) have on the auditor's assessment of the risk of material misstatement? What accounts and assertions are most likely influenced by these findings?

Source: C1202 IDEA Data Analysis Workbook: IDEA Version Ten. 2016. CaseWare IDEA, Inc. Toronto, CA.

Appendix 4A

Selected Financial Ratios

Balance-Sheet Ratios	Formula*
Current ratio	$\dfrac{\text{Current assets}}{\text{Current liabilities}}$
Days' sales in receivables	$\dfrac{\text{Ending net receivables}}{\text{Credit sales}/360}$
Doubtful account ratio	$\dfrac{\text{Allowance for doubtful accounts}}{\text{Ending gross receivables}}$
Days' sales in inventory	$\dfrac{\text{Ending inventory}}{\text{Cost of goods sold}/360}$
Debt-to-equity ratio	$\dfrac{\text{Current and long-term debt}}{\text{Stockholder equity}}$

Operations Ratios	
Receivables turnover	$\dfrac{\text{Credit sales}}{\text{Ending net receivables}}$
Inventory turnover	$\dfrac{\text{Cost of goods sold}}{\text{Ending inventory}}$
Cost of goods sold ratio	$\dfrac{\text{Cost of goods sold}}{\text{Net sales}}$
Gross margin ratio	$\dfrac{\text{Net sales} - \text{Cost of goods sold}}{\text{Net sales}}$
Return on stockholder equity	$\dfrac{\text{Net income}}{\text{Stockholder equity (beginning balance)}}$

Financial Distress Ratios (Altman)

The discriminant Z-score is an index of a company's financial health. The higher the score, the healthier the company. The lower the score, the closer financial failure approaches. The score that predicts financial failure is a matter of dispute. Research suggests that companies with scores above 3.0 never go bankrupt. Generally, companies with scores below 1.0 experience financial difficulty of some kind. The score can be a negative number.

(X_1) Working capital/Total assets	$\dfrac{\text{Current assets} - \text{Current liabilities}}{\text{Total assets}}$
(X_2) Retained earnings/Total assets	$\dfrac{\text{Retained earnings (ending)}}{\text{Total assets}}$
(X_3) Earnings before interest and taxes/Total assets	$\dfrac{\text{Net income} + \text{Interest expense} + \text{Income tax expense}}{\text{Total assets}}$
(X_4) Market value of equity/Total debt	$\dfrac{\text{Market value of common and preferred stock}}{\text{Current liabilities and long-term debt}}$
(X_5) Net sales/Total assets	$\dfrac{\text{Net sales}}{\text{Total assets}}$
Discriminant Z-score (Altman)	$1.2 * X_1 + 1.4 * X_2 + 3.3 * X_3 + 0.6 * X_4 + 1.0 * X_5$

*These ratios are shown to be calculating using year-end rather than year-average, numbers for balances such as accounts receivable and inventory. Other accounting and finance reference books could contain formulas using year-average numbers. As long as no dramatic changes have occurred during the year, the year-end numbers can have much audit relevance because they reflect the most current balance data. For comparative purposes, the ratios should be calculated on the same basis for all years being compared.

Appendix 4B

Sample Audit Memorandum

INTEGRATED CARE HEALTH INSURANCE INC
AUDIT MEMORANDUM (ABRIDGED)

OVERVIEW

Integrated Care Health Insurance Inc. (Integrated) offers a variety of valuable products and services ranging from medical, dental, and behavioral health coverage to life insurance and disability plans as well as management services for Medicaid plans. Purchasing health coverage ensures future security with respect to high and unexpected costs of health care for individuals, families, and businesses. Benefits offered by Integrated include not only coverage for medical expenses but access to a wide network of doctors, hospitals, and specialists.

PRODUCT PRICING

Integrated uses a special process to calculate premiums charged for services offered. The method involves pooling customers with similar characteristics into a single risk group based on age, gender, medical history, lifestyle, and other factors such as benefits desired, administration costs, and tax obligations. After Integrated pools customers into their respective risk groups, Integrated has the responsibility to balance projected future costs with premiums charged. The most important factor in determining financial success for Integrated is its ability to predict trends and future medical costs. Therefore, faulty forecasts can lead to huge risks and downfalls for Integrated if expectations fall short of actual results. Competing in an industry where new technology and medical breakthroughs are discovered almost daily means that sustaining profitability is an increasing concern.

GOVERNMENT INFLUENCES

Along with a great deal of risk being inherent in its business, Integrated has also been experiencing a strain in its operations due to the declining U.S. economy and increasing unemployment rate. Additionally, the health care reform legislation passed in 2009 will cause significant changes to many facets of the industry's operation according to analysts. However, certain parts of the legislation leave providers with the hope of positive changes. For example, given that the new legislation will require coverage for those who are currently uninsured, the insurance companies will acquire millions of new customers virtually overnight. Nevertheless, the total effect on the reform is still uncertain because a bulk of the legislation passed will not become effective until 2014 to 2016.

CUSTOMERS, SUPPLIERS, AND COMPETITORS

Integrated's customers include employer groups, self-employed individuals, part-time and hourly workers, governmental organizations, labor groups, and immigrants. Although there are a considerable number of companies competing, experts have noted a trend that competition is virtually disappearing due to the domination of markets by only a few providers. In a study published by the American Medical Association, 24 of 43 states have one or two insurers comprising a market share of a staggering 70 percent.[7] These statistics may suggest that there is essentially no competition in the market. However, 1,300

---

[7]D. W. Emmons, J. R. Guardado, C. K. Kane, "Competition in Health Insurance: A Comprehensive Study of U.S. Markets, 2010 Update," American Medical Association.

companies are competing in the health insurance industry, and Integrated faces significant competition in highly concentrated markets. In addition to the competition and governmental influences already present, Integrated is also facing competition from hospitals that play a pertinent role in determining the amounts billed for services provided.

RISK ASSESSMENT

The following analysis provides an overview of the identified risks and expected controls for Integrated for one accounting cycle.

REVENUE AND COLLECTION CYCLE

Risks

Due to the contract nature of the insurance industry, revenue recognition is not a high-risk area when compared to other industries. Integrated has set contracts with commercial organizations, individuals, and the government. Therefore, large fluctuations throughout the year do not typically occur. However, one area of significant risk involves the Medicare risk adjustment. The Centers for Medicare & Medicaid Services (CMS) determines Medicare and Medicaid premium payments employing a risk-based formula using coding provided by the insurance companies based on data from the diagnosis. Members with Medicare and Medicaid benefits associated with the health insurance entity are given a risk category based on their health conditions. However, because these contracts are preset for a year, patients' risk categories might fluctuate, causing an increase in needed payment from the CMS. Integrated must ensure that revenue is recognized properly by recording a risk adjustment for the difference between what CMS paid and what should have been paid based on the appropriate risk categories. CMS also performs audits known as *Risk Adjusted Data Validation (RADV) audits* to ensure CMS remits premium payments to insurance organizations appropriately.

Another area of significant risk around revenue recognition involves the Medicare Part D risk-sharing provision. With Medicare Part D, insurance entities contract with CMS for set premiums on an annual basis. The ultimate payment of total premiums, however, depends on certain thresholds that might require additional payment by CMS or reimbursement to CMS. A reconciliation (true-up) is performed after year-end to account for these differences. However, because this true-up process might occur six to nine months after year-end, Integrated must account for this process by recording receivables or payables that estimate these differences. Significant estimates are used to develop these adjustments and require the company to plan the audit procedures to provide reasonable assurance that these estimates do not include material misstatements.

Controls

The difficulty in predicting revenue adjustment amounts from these two programs concerns Integrated management's assertions of completeness, accuracy, valuation of financial statement accounts, and proper disclosure of required revenue recognition elements. To meet disclosure assertions, Integrated established a disclosure committee to determine what revenue-related disclosures should be made regarding Medicare and Medicaid. This committee meets prior to the release of each quarter's financial statements or as often as management requires. Valuation and accuracy assertions are met by requiring that qualified personnel utilize acceptable models commonly used in industry practice when estimating the amounts for the varying revenues. Appropriate supervisors review all estimates for accuracy and verify that estimates conform to the company's operational objectives.

AUDIT APPROACH

Due to the high-risk nature of the unique business and audit risks detailed here, an audit plan for Integrated must include both test of controls and substantive procedures to provide for the appropriate level of detection risk. As mentioned, significant estimates are included in the financial statements for almost every accounting cycle within the health insurance industry. The amount of management judgment needed to determine these estimates requires the use of extensive substantive testing to provide reasonable assurance that material misstatements do not exist within the financial statements. The following detailed audit plan provides guidance on the types of control testing and substantive testing that would provide reasonable assurance that material misstatements do not exist in relation to the risks outlined within this report.

AUDIT STRATEGY MEMORANDUM
Integrated Care Health Insurance Inc.

Overview

This audit strategy is intended to provide our responses to the risks identified for Integrated and generally detail the associated tests of controls and substantive procedures that will be required during the audit.

Risks

Revenue recognition related to participation in Medicare and Medicaid programs (Revenue and Collection Cycle)

Assertions	Tests of Controls	Substantive Procedures
Valuation or allocation	Test information technology and manual controls relative to calculation of revenues from Medicare and Medicaid contracts	Reperform revenue calculations for a sampling of Medicare- and Medicaid-issued contracts
	Confirm that management estimates for risk-sharing and risk-adjustment provisions (reviews include determining whether qualified personnel perform the estimates, making estimates conform to industry practices, and verifying that estimates are accurate)	Reperform estimates for risk-sharing and risk-adjustment provisions
	Confirm that assumptions and methodologies for estimates of risk-sharing and risk-adjustment provisions are documented and approved by management	Produce independent estimates for risk-sharing and risk-adjustment provisions
	Obtain an understanding of assumptions and methodology of estimates for risk-sharing and risk-adjustment provisions	
Presentation and disclosure	Confirm that a disclosure committee has been established	Review disclosure committee meeting minutes
	Confirm that comparisons of actual and budgeted Medicare and Medicaid revenues are conducted by management and significant variances are monitored	Review board of directors meeting minutes, agreements, budgets, and plans for Medicare and Medicaid revenues that should be included in financial statements
		Test whether disclosures and classifications conform to accounting principles

Source: Mark Fedewa, Emily O'Bryan, Amela Pajazetovic, and Susan Schmidt, "An Analysis of Business and Audit Risk for a Health Insurance Provider," unpublished working paper, University of Kentucky. February 28, 2011.

Risk Assessment: Internal Control Evaluation

Bernie doesn't want you to use the words "internal controls" in any more of your audit reports . . . it aggravates him.

> Cynthia Cooper, referring to the advice she was given by a colleague on how best to deal with Bernie Ebbers, then CEO of **WorldCom**, before she uncovered an $11 billion fraud that Ebbers directed. Ebbers is currently serving a 25-year prison term in connection with the fraud. (Quoted in Extraordinary Circumstances: The Journey of a Corporate Whistleblower.)

Professional Standards References

Topic	AU-C/ISA Section	AS Section
Overall Objectives of the Independent Auditor	200	1001, 1005, 1010, 1015
Audit Documentation	230	1215
Consideration of Fraud in a Financial Statement Audit	240	2401
Communications with Audit Committees	260	1301
Communicating Internal Control-Related Matters Identified in an Audit	265	1305
Consideration of Internal Control in an Integrated Audit	265	2201
Reporting on Whether a Previously Reported Material Weakness Continues to Exist	265	6115
Audit Planning	300	2101
Identifying and Assessing the Risks of Material Misstatement	315	*AS 12*
Materiality	320	2110
Auditors' Responses to Risks of Material Misstatement	330	2301
Audit Considerations Relating to an Entity Using a Service Organization	402	2601
Audit Evidence	500	1105
Audit Evidence—Specific Considerations for Selected Items	501	2503, 2505, 2510
Consideration of the Internal Audit Function in a Financial Statement Audit	610	2605
Compliance Auditing Considerations in Audits of Recipients of Governmental Financial Assistance	935	6110

An important objective of the internal control system is to help ensure that the financial statement information being presented by an organization is credible and reliable. Therefore, it is essential that an auditor take the time to understand whether an entity's internal control system has been designed and is operating effectively. In fact, the fundamental principles of auditing state that, to fulfill auditors' responsibility "[t]o obtain reasonable assurance, . . . the auditor *identifies and assesses risks of material misstatement, whether due to fraud or error, based on an understanding of the entity and its environment, including the entity's internal control*" [emphasis added]. The responsibility is even greater for most public companies because the law and professional standards require that the auditor express an opinion on management's assessment of the effectiveness of the company's internal control system. As a result, the evaluation of an entity's internal control system is a critical phase of most every public company audit engagement.

Beyond its importance in the production of reliable financial statement information and the audit, the establishment of an internal control system is an important management function to help ensure the effectiveness and efficiency of operations and the entity's compliance with laws and regulations. As a result, understanding the elements of internal control and how to evaluate their effectiveness is an important skill that every accountant should have. Even if you do not go into auditing, you probably will have responsibility for maintaining internal controls at some point in your accounting career.

This chapter presents a general introduction to the theory and definitions you will find useful for internal control evaluation and control risk assessment. The chapter uses the payroll cycle to provide specific examples of control activities and related audit procedures.

Your objectives are to be able to:

LO 5-1 Define and describe what is meant by *internal control*.

LO 5-2 Distinguish between the responsibilities of management and auditors regarding an entity's internal control.

LO 5-3 Define and describe the five basic components of internal control and specify some of their characteristics.

LO 5-4 Explain the process the audit team uses to assess control risk; understand its impact on the risk of material misstatement; and, ultimately, know how it affects the nature, timing, and extent of further audit procedures to be performed on the audit.

LO 5-5 Describe additional responsibilities for management and auditors of public companies required by Sarbanes–Oxley and PCAOB Auditing Standard No. 2201.

LO 5-6 Explain the communication of internal control deficiencies to those charged with governance, such as the audit committee and other key management personnel.

LO 5-7 List the major components of the auditors' report on internal control over financial reporting.

LO 5-8 Describe situations in which the auditors' report on internal control over financial reporting would be modified.

INTRODUCTION

In response to the significant number of major corporate accounting scandals that had rocked the financial world (e.g., **Enron,** WorldCom, **Xerox, Kmart**), Congress passed the Sarbanes–Oxley Act on July 30, 2002 (the most comprehensive financial reporting legislation since the Securities Acts of 1933 and 1934). The law was passed in direct response to the scandals and aimed to strengthen corporate financial reporting by assessing harsher criminal penalties for white-collar crimes, increasing management accountability, and enhancing public accounting firm independence.

Central among the provisions of this act is the emphasis that it places on the internal control system as an important means to prevent or detect material misstatements in the financial statements due to fraud. The feeling is that by holding both management and the auditor responsible for evaluating the effectiveness of the internal control system, the act has imposed the necessary oversight to improve the accuracy and reliability of the financial statements reported by the entity. Simply stated, the intense scrutiny on both the design and operating effectiveness of internal control systems over financial reporting should improve the reliability of the financial statements. This chapter focuses on the importance of the internal control system in the financial statement auditing process.

INTERNAL CONTROL DEFINED

LO 5-1
Define and describe what is meant by *internal control*.

In 1985, in response to a report by the National Commission on Fraudulent Financial Reporting (referred to as the *Treadway Commission* after its first chair, former SEC commissioner James Treadway), a group of professional organizations met to determine what business entities could do to improve financial reporting. Representatives from the Financial Executives Institute, the American Accounting Association, the Institute of Internal Auditors, the Institute of Management Accountants, and the American Institute of Certified Public Accountants—collectively referred to as the *Committee of Sponsoring Organizations,* or *COSO*—debated internal control theory and definitions. The resulting report, the COSO framework, issued in 1992 defined **internal control** as follows:

> Internal control is a process, effected by an entity's board of directors, management and other personnel, designed to provide reasonable assurance regarding the achievement of objectives in the following three categories:
>
> - Reliability of financial reporting.
> - Effectiveness and efficiency of operations.
> - Compliance with applicable laws and regulations.

Stated differently, internal control is a set of policies and procedures designed to achieve *management objectives* in three different categories. In the *financial reporting category,* the management objectives are related to producing reliable financial reports and safeguarding assets. In the *operations category,* some examples of management objectives are maintaining a good business reputation, ensuring a positive return on investment, increasing market share, promoting new product innovation, and using assets effectively and efficiently. In the *compliance category,* the broad management objective is to comply with laws and regulations that affect the entity. It is important to point out that external auditors are primarily concerned with a client's internal control system as it relates to the financial reporting category.

In 2013, COSO published an updated version of the framework. The updated framework acknowledges the widespread use of the original COSO framework and seeks to build upon the core tenets and definitions established in the original framework. A key goal of the updated version is to provide "enhancements and clarifications intended to ease use and application" of the framework in an ever-changing global environment. We believe that the updated version of the framework will help students as they learn about the underlying concepts and principles of an effective system of internal control. In fact, the Auditing Standards Board has even integrated important aspects of the COSO

AUDITING INSIGHT · Sarbanes–Oxley Definition of Internal Control

The Sarbanes–Oxley Act of 2002 defines internal control in a manner that is consistent with the COSO definition. However, the Sarbanes–Oxley definition focuses on the role of the internal control system over financial reporting and notes that control policies and procedures should allow:

1. Records to be maintained in reasonable detail to accurately reflect transactions.

2. Transactions to be recorded to permit financial statements to be prepared in accordance with GAAP.

3. Transactions to be executed in accordance with authorization from the entity's management.

4. Unauthorized acquisition, use, or disposition of the entity's assets to be prevented or detected on a timely basis.

Source: U.S. Congress, *Sarbanes–Oxley Act of 2002,* Pub. L. No. 107-204, 116 Stat. 745 (2002).

☑ REVIEW CHECKPOINTS

5.1 What is the Committee of Sponsoring Organizations (COSO)? Briefly describe the original COSO framework from 1992 and the improvements made in the updated COSO framework from 2013.

5.2 What are the three goals of an internal control system according to the COSO report? Which of the three is most important to auditors?

---

framework into the professional standards (i.e., AU-C 315).[1] As a result of its importance, throughout this chapter, we will highlight how the COSO 2013 report has changed the auditor's role with regards to a client's system of internal control.

MANAGEMENT VERSUS AUDITORS' RESPONSIBILITY FOR INTERNAL CONTROL

LO 5-2

Distinguish between the responsibilities of management and auditors regarding an entity's internal control.

Section 302 of the Sarbanes–Oxley Act stipulates criminal penalties for CEOs and CFOs if they issue materially misleading financial statements. A clear intention of this section of the act is to make sure that management at the top of an organization sets the proper tone for the internal control system. In fact, the act is specific about management's responsibility for the organization's internal control system: Management is responsible for establishing a control environment, assessing the risks it wishes to control, specifying information and communication channels and content (including the accounting system and its reports), designing and implementing appropriate control activities, and monitoring, supervising, and maintaining the control activities. Management must also estimate the benefits derived from specific controls and then weigh them against the costs. Management is expected to make its own judgments about the necessity of specific controls.

In addition to certifying the entity's financial statements and disclosures under Section 302, Sarbanes–Oxley requires management to assess and report on the entity's internal control over financial reporting in Section 404. Specifically, the entity's annual report must include the following:

- A statement that management is responsible for establishing and maintaining adequate internal control over financial reporting.
- A statement identifying the framework (e.g., the COSO framework) that management uses as a benchmark for evaluating the effectiveness of the entity's internal control.
- A statement providing management's assessment of the effectiveness of the entity's internal control.

Under Section 302, management must also disclose any material weaknesses in internal control. If any material weaknesses exist, management cannot conclude that the entity's internal control over financial reporting is effective. See Exhibit 5.1 for excerpts from a **Krispy Kreme** management report on internal control over financial reporting, which identified numerous material weaknesses in its internal control. This report was issued on January 28, 2007; since that time, Krispy Kreme has taken actions to improve its internal control, and the most recent report (dated March 31, 2016) does not mention material weaknesses.

Auditors' Internal Control Responsibilities

The audit team has at least three reasons for conducting an evaluation of an entity's internal control. First, Sarbanes–Oxley requires an audit of management's assessment of the effectiveness of internal control over financial reporting for public companies. The internal control audit is conducted along with the financial statement audit as part of an

---

[1]AU-C 315–Communications Between Predecessor and Successor Auditors.

EXHIBIT 5.1   Excerpts from Krispy Kreme's Management Report on Internal Control over Financial Reporting

Our *management is responsible for establishing and maintaining adequate internal control over financial reporting....* Internal control over financial reporting is a process, effected by an entity's board of directors, management and other personnel, designed to provide *reasonable assurance* regarding the reliability of financial reporting and the preparation of consolidated financial statements for external purposes in accordance with GAAP. Internal control over financial reporting includes those policies and procedures which pertain to the maintenance of records that, in reasonable detail, accurately and fairly reflect the transactions and dispositions of assets; provide reasonable assurance *that transactions are recorded as necessary* to permit preparation of consolidated financial statements in accordance with GAAP; provide reasonable assurance that *receipts and expenditures are being made only in accordance with our and/or our Board of Directors' authorization;* and provide reasonable assurance regarding *prevention or timely detection of unauthorized acquisition, use or disposition of our assets* that could have a material effect on our consolidated financial statements.

Because of its inherent limitations, internal control over financial reporting may not prevent or detect misstatements. Also, projections of any evaluation of the effectiveness of our internal control over financial reporting to future periods are subject to the risk that controls may become inadequate because of changes in conditions, or that the degree of compliance with the policies or procedures may deteriorate.

Management assessed the effectiveness of our internal control over financial reporting as of January 28, 2007, *using the criteria established in Internal Control—Integrated Framework issued by the Committee of Sponsoring Organizations of the Treadway Commission* (COSO).

A *material weakness* is a control deficiency, or combination of control deficiencies, that results in *more than a remote likelihood that a material misstatement of the annual or interim consolidated financial statements will not be prevented or detected.* As of January 28, 2007, management identified the material weaknesses described below.

We did not maintain an effective control environment based on the criteria established in the COSO framework. The following material weaknesses were identified related to our control environment:

- We did not establish a formal enterprise risk assessment process.
- We did not formalize lines of communication among legal, finance and operations personnel. Specifically, procedures were not designed and in place to ensure sharing of financial information within and across our corporate and divisional offices and other operating facilities such that significant issues are brought to the attention of appropriate level of accounting and financial reporting personnel.
- We did not maintain certain written accounting policies and procedures including those over critical accounting policies.
- We did not have an effective process for monitoring the appropriateness of user access and segregation of duties related to financial applications.

These control environment material weaknesses contributed to the material weaknesses described below.

We did not maintain effective control over our financial closing and reporting processes....
We did not maintain effective controls over the completeness and accuracy of certain franchisee revenue....
We did not maintain effective controls over the completeness and accuracy of our accounting for lease related assets, liabilities and expenses....
We did not maintain effective controls over the accuracy and completeness of our property and equipment accounts....

These control deficiencies contributed to the previously reported restatement of our consolidated financial statements for fiscal 2003 and fiscal 2004 and all quarterly periods in fiscal 2004 and the first three quarters of fiscal 2005. Management has concluded that each of the control deficiencies above could result in a misstatement of account balances or disclosures that would be material to our annual or interim consolidated financial statements that would not be prevented or detected. Accordingly, management has concluded that each of the control deficiencies listed above constitutes a material weakness as of January 28, 2007. *Because of these material weaknesses, management has concluded that we did not maintain effective internal control over financial reporting* as of January 28, 2007, based on the COSO criteria. Management's assessment of the effectiveness of our internal control over financial reporting as of January 28, 2007 has been audited by **PricewaterhouseCoopers LLP,** [emphasis added] an independent registered public accounting firm, as stated in their report which appears in this Annual Report on Form 10-K.

overall **integrated audit** that is completed at public companies. In essence, the audit firm employs one integrated process that culminates in the issuance of two opinions: one on the entity's financial statements and one on management's assessment of the effectiveness of the entity's internal control over financial reporting.

Second, for each fraud risk identified during the planning stage, the audit team should evaluate whether the client has implemented control activities that are specifically designed to address the risk of fraud that has been identified. These might include control activities that are designed to address risks of fraud to specific financial statement accounts or more generally, control activities that are designed to promote a culture of honest and ethical behavior. For example, the audit team should evaluate the controls related to the use of period-end journal entries, which have been used in the past to commit frauds at companies such as WorldCom and **Waste Management.** The Auditing Insight focused on **Dell Inc.** illustrates the use of period-end journal entries to manipulate income.

AUDITING INSIGHT · Dell Doesn't Compute

In August 2005, the SEC's Division of Enforcement notified Dell Inc. that it had commenced an investigation of the company and was seeking documents and information regarding certain accounting and financial reporting practices. The attorneys advising Dell's audit committee hired **KPMG LLP** to serve as independent forensic accountants.

Using a proprietary software tool designed to identify potentially questionable journal entries based on selected criteria (e.g., entries made late in the quarterly closing process, entries containing round dollar line items between $3 million and $50 million, and liability-to-liability transfers), KPMG selected and reviewed more than 2,600 journal entries.

The investigation raised questions relating to numerous accounting issues, most of which involved adjustments to various reserve and accrued liability accounts, and identified evidence that certain adjustments appear to have been motivated by the objective of attaining financial targets. These activities typically occurred in the days immediately following the end of a quarter when the accounting books were being closed and the results of the quarter were being compiled. KPMG found evidence that, in that timeframe, account balances were reviewed, sometimes at the request or with the knowledge of senior executives, with the goal of seeking adjustments so that quarterly performance objectives could be met. It concluded that a number of these adjustments were improper, including the creation and release of accruals and reserves that appear to have been made for the purpose of enhancing internal performance measures or reported results as well as the transfer of excess accruals from one liability account to another and the use of the excess balances to offset unrelated expenses in later periods. KPMG also found that sometimes business unit personnel did not provide complete information to corporate headquarters and, in a number of instances, purposefully incorrect or incomplete information about these activities was provided to internal or external auditors.

KPMG identified evidence that accounting adjustments were viewed at times by Dell's management team as an acceptable device to compensate for earnings shortfalls that could not be closed through operational means. Often these adjustments were for several hundred thousand or even several million dollars.

Source: Dell Inc. Form 8-K, August 13, 2007.

The final reason for evaluating an entity's internal control is to assess preliminary risk of material misstatement (RMM) for each relevant assertion. The assessment of RMM at the assertion level is completed for all financial statement audits in order to give the audit team a basis for planning the audit and determining the *nature, timing,* and *extent* of further audit procedures to be conducted for the financial statement audit. RMM is composed of *inherent risk* and *control risk.* The assessment of *inherent risk,* the susceptibility of an account to misstatement, was the focus of Chapter 4; this chapter focuses on control risk assessment. Recall that **control risk** is the probability that an entity's controls will fail to prevent or detect material misstatements due to errors or frauds that would otherwise have entered the system. The audit team assesses *control risk* to complete the preliminary determination of RMM for each relevant assertion identified in the audit plan; the higher the assessment of control risk, the higher the assessment of RMM. Most audit teams express their control risk assessment decision with descriptive terminology (e.g., high, moderate, low), which recognizes the imprecise nature of evaluating risk. An audit team's assessment of control risk as high implies that the controls are not effective at preventing or detecting material misstatements and could not be relied upon by the audit team. In this situation, the audit team would likely use substantive tests of details designed to obtain evidence (*nature*) at or near the entity's fiscal year-end (*timing*) with large sample sizes (*extent*). On the other hand, an audit team's assessment of control risk as low implies that the controls are effective at preventing or detecting material misstatements and could possibly be relied upon by the audit team. In this situation, the audit team might be able to use less time-consuming substantive analytical procedures to obtain evidence (*nature*) at an interim date before the entity's fiscal year-end (*timing*) with much smaller sample sizes (*extent*). Of course, an audit team might assess control risk as moderate (between low and high) and adjust the substantive procedures accordingly in order to obtain enough evidence to mitigate the risk of material misstatement to a low level for the relevant assertion being tested. Ultimately, the final decision about nature, timing, and extent of testing is a matter of professional judgment for the audit team. Exhibit 5.2 illustrates the trade-off between testing and relying on internal controls and how it impacts the nature, timing, and extent of further audit procedures to be performed.

EXHIBIT 5.2 **Relationship between Internal Control Reliance and Audit Procedures**

	Less Reliance on Internal Control (higher control risk; lower detection risk)	More Reliance on Internal Control (lower control risk; higher detection risk)
Nature	More effective tests (for example, use of substantive tests of detail)	Less effective tests (for example, use of substantive analytical procedures)
Timing	Testing performed at year-end	Testing can be performed at interim
Extent	Higher sample size	Lower sample size

✓ REVIEW CHECKPOINTS

5.3 What are management's and auditors' respective responsibilities regarding internal control?

5.4 Define *control risk* and explain the role of control risk assessment in audit planning.

5.5 What are the primary reasons for conducting an evaluation of an audit client's internal control?

5.6 How does control risk affect the *nature, timing,* and *extent* of further audit procedures?

COMPONENTS OF INTERNAL CONTROL

LO 5-3
Define and describe the five basic components of internal control and specify some of their characteristics.

According to the COSO framework, an internal control system that is designed and operating effectively will have met three categories of objectives within an organization (Exhibit 5.3). First, the system will allow for effective and efficient operations. Second, it will allow for reliable financial reporting. And, third, the system will allow the organization to comply with laws and regulations.

To achieve the specific objectives for each of these categories of objectives, the COSO report defines five basic components of a properly designed internal control system. The five components are (1) control environment, (2) risk assessment, (3) control activities, (4) monitoring, and (5) information and communication. It is important to point out that the five

EXHIBIT 5.3
**Internal Control—
Integrated Framework
(COSO)**

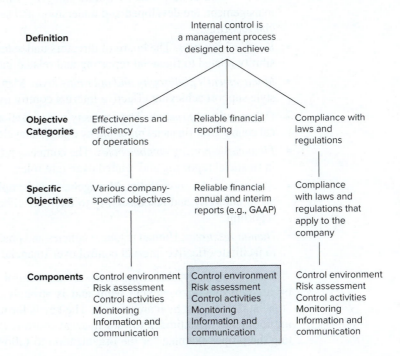

	Definition	Internal control is a management process designed to achieve	
Objective Categories	Effectiveness and efficiency of operations	Reliable financial reporting	Compliance with laws and regulations
Specific Objectives	Various company-specific objectives	Reliable financial annual and interim reports (e.g., GAAP)	Compliance with laws and regulations that apply to the company
Components	Control environment Risk assessment Control activities Monitoring Information and communication	Control environment Risk assessment Control activities Monitoring Information and communication	Control environment Risk assessment Control activities Monitoring Information and communication

components should not operate independently of each other. Instead, they should be considered as working in an interrelated manner to support the internal control system's overall effectiveness. We discuss each of the components in more detail next. As described more fully in the following Auditing Insight, a key improvement of the updated COSO framework released in 2013 is the identification of 17 principles of an effective internal control system. These principles will be used to help illustrate each of the components in this chapter.

 AUDITING INSIGHT | **COSO 2013 Features 17 Principles of Internal Control!**

In May 2013, COSO published an update to its internal control framework, originally published in 1992. While the update did not change the definition of internal control, it does attempt to provide more implementation guidance that will help organizations adapt their internal control systems to meet the needs of the current business environment. In addition, the update has been designed to help organizations extend the application of their internal control systems to better serve an increasing set of operational and reporting goals and to provide greater clarity in determining what is meant by internal control effectiveness.

Specifically, the COSO 2013 framework adds 17 explicit principles that are associated with the five components of internal control (i.e.,

control environment, risk assessment, control activities, information and communication, and monitoring). While the 17 principles were already implicit concepts in the COSO 1992 report, the updated framework now requires that each of the 17 principles be present and functioning in order for effective internal control to be achieved. As a result, the release of the COSO 2013 has helped auditors by providing concrete benchmarks to evaluate for each component.

Sources: COSO, "Internal Control—Integrated Framework Executive Summary," May 2013, New York: AICPA; K. Hoffelder, "Corporates Not Yet Ready for Internal-Controls Prime Time," *CFO.com*, August 20, 2013, available at www3.cfo.com/article/2013/8/gaap-ifrs_att-campbell-soup-coso-internal-controls.

Control Environment

The control environment sets the tone of the organization. It is the foundation for all other components of internal control. It provides discipline and structure to all participants and stakeholders. Control environment factors include the integrity, ethical values, and competence of the entity's people. According to COSO, a well-functioning internal control environment is characterized by philosophies such as the following:

- *Integrity and ethical values.* Sound integrity and ethical values, particularly of top management, are developed and understood and set the standard of conduct for financial reporting.
- *Board of directors.* The board of directors understands and exercises oversight responsibility related to financial reporting and related internal control.
- *Management's philosophy and operating style.* Management's philosophy and operating style support achieving effective internal control over financial reporting.
- *Organizational structure.* The company's organizational structure supports effective internal control over financial reporting by establishing clear and unambiguous reporting lines.
- *Financial reporting competencies.* The company retains individuals who are competent in financial reporting and related oversight roles.
- *Authority and responsibility.* Management and employees are assigned appropriate levels of authority and responsibility to facilitate effective internal control over financial reporting.
- *Human resources.* Human resource policies and practices are designed and implemented to facilitate effective internal control over financial reporting.

Most importantly, the effectiveness of the control environment is influenced heavily by a company's management team and is strongly and unquestionably related to the "tone at the top" set by management. The key is for management to be deliberate in trying to impact the attitudes toward internal controls throughout the organization by setting the proper example for the organization to follow. It has been said that the control environment has a "pervasive" effect on the reliability of financial reporting because it affects *all* other components of an organization's internal control system.

For example, in the late 1990s and up through its bankruptcy in December 2001, Enron's corporate culture was characterized by a brutal performance evaluation culture that was executed on a quarterly basis by its now infamous performance review committee (PRC) implemented by company president, Jeffrey Skilling. The PRC promoted a culture that focused inordinately on performance-based compensation where top performers earned huge bonuses and lower performers were fired. As a result, it can be said that Enron's management team seemingly selected and applied accounting procedures that were designed explicitly to improve its reported financial condition and performance and ultimately mask the company's true underlying financial condition and performance. Clearly, the tone at the top set by Skilling at Enron had an impact on the internal control system at Enron.

Because the control environment sets the overall foundation for internal control, professional auditing standards require an auditor to obtain an understanding of the control environment on all engagements. As part of this understanding, auditors also have to take the time to consider the functioning of the client's board of directors and, in particular, the impact of its audit committee on the client's control environment. The **audit committee** is a subcommittee of the board of directors that is generally composed of three to six independent members (those not involved in the entity's day-to-day management) of the organization's board of directors. Each member must be *financially literate,* and one member must be a *financial expert.* The purpose of including independent members is to provide a buffer between the audit team and the operating management team of the company. The buffer allows the audit team (and the corporate internal audit department) to report any controversial findings to members of the board of directors without fear of reprisal.

For example, should the internal auditors find wrongdoing in the CEO's office, it would do no good to report the matter to the CEO. Similarly, if management does not have control over appointing auditors, management is prevented from threatening to dismiss the auditors if they do not agree with an inappropriate accounting practice. Some of the more important duties of the audit committee are

- Appointment, compensation, and oversight of the public accounting firm conducting the entity's audit.
- Resolution of disagreements between management and the audit team.
- Oversight of the entity's internal audit function.
- Approval of nonaudit services provided by the public accounting firm performing the audit engagement.
- Oversight of the anonymous fraud hotline that is designed to provide employees a confidential and effective manner in which to report possible financial reporting issues.
- Authority to engage legal counsel in the event of management fraud.

Small and midsize entities may implement the control environment factors differently than larger entities. For example, smaller entities might not have a written code of conduct but instead develop a culture that emphasizes the importance of integrity and ethical behavior through oral communication and by management example. Similarly, a smaller entity may not have an independent or outside member on its board of directors. Regardless of the size of the entity, the COSO framework establishes five principles which, if applied properly, will result in an effective control environment component. The five principles of the control environment component are listed in Exhibit 5.4.

Risk Assessment

In recent years, entities of all sizes have increasingly recognized the need for a formalized process to identify, properly assess, and ultimately manage the full range of **business risks** that they face: factors, events, and conditions that can prevent organizations from achieving their business objectives. One way managers address these concerns is to employ an

EXHIBIT 5.4 **Five Principles of the Control Environment**

Principles of Control Environment as per COSO 2013 Report
1. The organization demonstrates a commitment to integrity and ethical values.
2. The board of directors demonstrates independence from management and exercises oversight of the development and performance of internal control.
3. Management establishes, with board oversight, structures, reporting lines, and appropriate authorities and responsibilities in the pursuit of objectives.
4. The organization demonstrates a commitment to attract, develop, and retain competent individuals in alignment with objectives.
5. The organization holds individuals accountable for their internal control responsibilities in the pursuit of objectives.

enterprise risk management (ERM) framework such as the one developed by the Committee of Sponsoring Organizations (COSO)[2] to facilitate the assessment and mitigation of business risks that the entity faces. COSO defines ERM as "a process, effected by an entity's board of directors, management and other personnel, applied in strategy setting and across the enterprise, designed to identify potential events that may affect the entity, and manage risks to be within its risk appetite, to provide reasonable assurance regarding the achievement of entity objectives."[3] In other words, management, boards, and employees have to be constantly thinking about what could go wrong with the business and how they can prevent it.

Although not all entities will employ a robust ERM framework, at a minimum, an effective internal control system will include some type of process where management takes the steps necessary to identify risks, estimate their significance and likelihood, and consider how to manage the risks. By setting management objectives, management can identify critical success factors and institute policies and procedures to ensure that they are met. (*Note:* The risk assessment element of the COSO framework is *management's* responsibility and is *not related* to an auditor's assessment of inherent risk, control risk, and the overall risk of material misstatement at the assertion level.) Although an audit client's risk assessment process should relate to all its objectives, the professional standards require the auditor to specifically gain an understanding of the process as it relates to financial reporting risks, including fraud risk. When gaining such an understanding, the auditor should determine whether management is actually assessing the likelihood of fraud risks and how it is managing such risks.

In completing their work, the audit team members seek to understand whether management is specifying financial reporting objectives with sufficient clarity and criteria to enable the identification of risks of material misstatement in financial reporting, in particular due to fraud. Once identified, the audit team also would like to see that management has a basis for determining how to manage the identified risks. For smaller entities, the risk assessment process is likely to be less formal and less structured. Although all entities should have established financial reporting management objectives, they may be recognized implicitly rather than explicitly in smaller entities. Regardless of the size of the entity, the COSO framework establishes four principles that, if applied properly, will result in an effective risk assessment component. The four principles of the risk assessment component are listed in Exhibit 5.5.

[2]The Committee of Sponsoring Organizations of the Treadway Commission (COSO) is a private sector initiative established in 1985 composed of five financial professional associations: the Institute of Internal Auditors, the American Institute of Certified Public Accountants, the American Accounting Association, the Institute of Management Accountants, and the Financial Executives Institute. COSO's stated goal is "to improve the quality of financial reporting through a focus on corporate governance, ethical practices, and internal control" (www.coso.org).

[3]COSO, "Enterprise Risk Management—Integrated Framework Executive Summary," September 2004, New York: AICPA, p. 2.

EXHIBIT 5.5   Four Principles of the Risk Assessment

Principles of Risk Assessment as per COSO 2013 Report
1. The organization specifies objectives with sufficient clarity to enable the identification and assessment of risks relating to objectives.
2. The organization identifies risks to the achievement of its objectives across the entity and analyzes the risks as a basis for determining how the risks should be managed.
3. The organization considers the potential for fraud in assessing risks to the achievement of objectives.
4. The organization identifies and assesses changes that could significantly impact the system of internal control.

☑ REVIEW CHECKPOINTS

5.7 What are the five components of management's internal control?

5.8 What is the *control environment*?

5.9 What is an *audit committee*? What are its duties?

5.10 What is the purpose of risk assessment for an entity?

Control Activities

In a well-functioning internal control system, once the risks to management's objectives have been identified, internal control activities need to be established to eliminate, mitigate, or compensate for the risks. **Control activities** are specific actions that a client's management and employees take to help ensure that management's directives are carried out. The professional standards require the audit team members to document their understanding of the internal control system on each audit, which includes their understanding of whether management has implemented control activities that are sufficient to address the risks of material misstatement for each relevant assertion.

To answer this important question, the audit team members usually begin the process by considering what they learned about the internal control activities as they were gaining an understanding of the other components of the COSO framework—in particular, the control environment and risk assessment components described earlier. The next step in the process requires the audit team members to document their understanding of the extent to which each of the client's control activities has been designed to support a relevant financial statement assertion by mitigating a risk of material misstatement. If their assessment is positive, the audit team might want to consider testing the control activity in the hopes of relying on it to reduce substantive testing for the relevant assertion that was supported. For now, see Exhibit 5.6 for several examples of this step, which will be covered in more depth later in the chapter.

EXHIBIT 5.6   Risk, Controls, and Testing of Controls

What Can Go Wrong?	Control Activity	Test of Control Activity
Sales revenue is recorded when the goods had not been shipped to the customers.	All sales invoices are matched to shipping documents before recording them in the general ledger.	For a sample of sales revenue entries made in the general ledger, compare the time/date stamp of the sales revenue entry to the time/date stamp on the shipping document.
Goods will be shipped to a new customer who is unable to pay for the goods.	The credit department performs a detailed credit check for all new customers.	For a sample of new customers, examine documentation that indicates a proper credit check was performed.
Goods will be shipped to a customer, and the revenue is not recorded.	All shipping documents are matched to sales invoices that have been recorded in the general ledger.	For a sample of shipping documents, compare the amount shipped on that day to a sales invoice recorded in the general ledger.

Importantly, when documenting their understanding of the internal control system, the audit team should keep in mind the following questions related to control activities:

- *Information technology.* Has the audit client taken full advantage of significant advances in information technology by using entirely automated control activities whenever it is efficient and effective?
- *Level of integration with their risk assessment process.* Has the audit client's management team taken the action necessary to address the identified risks to the achievement of financial reporting objectives?
- *Selection and development of control activities.* Has the audit client's management team selected and developed control activities considering their cost and their potential effectiveness in mitigating the risks identified?
- *Policies and procedures.* Have the policies related to reliable financial reporting been documented and communicated throughout the company by the audit client's management team?

In addition, regardless of the size of the entity, the COSO framework establishes three principles that, if applied properly, will result in an effective evaluation of the control activities component. The three principles of the control activities component are listed in Exhibit 5.7.

Ultimately, financial reporting control activities are imposed on the accounting system for the purpose of *preventing, detecting,* and *correcting* errors and frauds that could enter and flow through to the financial statements. Clearly, **preventive controls**, procedures that prevent misstatements before they occur (those that ensure hiring competent people, limiting access, requiring approval, separating duties, etc.), are preferable to **detective controls**, procedures that detect misstatements after they occur. In some sense, all control activities can be thought of as *preventive controls* because the possibility of being caught by a *detective control* might prevent someone from committing an error or a fraud. Control activities include performance reviews, separation of duties, physical controls, and information-processing controls.

Performance Reviews

Management has primary responsibility for ensuring that the organization's objectives are being met. Performance reviews require management's active participation in the supervision of operations. Management's study of budget variances with follow-up action is an example of a performance review. Management that performs frequent performance reviews has more opportunities to detect errors in the records than management that does not. The frequency, of course, is governed by the costs and benefits. Subsequent action to investigate or correct differences is also important. Periodic comparison and action to correct errors lowers the risk that material misstatements due to error or fraud exist in the financial statement accounts.

Separation of Duties

A very important characteristic of effective internal control is an appropriate separation of duties or functional responsibilities. Four types of functional responsibilities should be

EXHIBIT 5.7
Three Principles of the Control Activities

Principles of Control Activities as per COSO 2013 Report
1. The organization selects and develops control activities that contribute to the mitigation of risks to the achievement of objectives to acceptable levels.
2. The organization selects and develops general control activities over technology to support the achievement of objectives.
3. The organization deploys control activities through policies that establish what is expected and procedures that put policies into action.

EXHIBIT 5.8
Separation of Duties

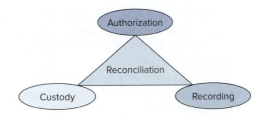

performed by different departments (see Exhibit 5.8), or at least by different persons on the entity's accounting staff:

1. *Authorization to execute transactions.* This duty belongs to people who have the authority and the responsibility for initiating or approving transactions. Authorization may be general, referring to a class of transactions (e.g., all purchases up to $100,000), or it may be specific (e.g., sale of a major asset).
2. *Recording transactions.* This duty refers to the accounting and record-keeping function, which in most organizations is delegated to a computerized information system. People who control computerized processing are the record keepers.
3. *Custody of assets involved in the transactions.* This duty refers to the actual physical possession or effective physical control of property.
4. *Periodic reconciliation of existing assets to recorded amounts.* This duty refers to making comparisons at regular intervals and taking appropriate action with respect to any differences.

Incompatible responsibilities are combinations of responsibilities that place a person alone in a position to create and conceal misstatements due to errors or frauds in her or his normal job. Duties should be divided so that no one person can control more than one of these responsibilities. If different departments or persons are forced to deal with these different facets of transactions, frauds are more difficult to commit because they would then require collusion of two or more persons, and most people hesitate to seek the help of others in order to conduct wrongful acts. A second benefit of separating duties is that by acting in a coordinated manner (handling different aspects of the same transaction), innocent errors are more likely to be found and corrected. The old saying is "Two heads are better than one."

In most computerized information processing environments, employees who have access to an application (such as payroll) might be in a position to perform incompatible functions. As a result, to achieve proper separation of duties, it is essential for an organization to have a well-thought-out plan that limits employees' access to the computerized information processing system (e.g., SAP, Oracle) to only those applications that are necessary for such employees to complete their jobs. In effect, companies must design internal control activities that will effectively limit opportunities for any one individual to both perpetrate and conceal misstatements or losses due to errors or fraud. In most situations, these often include password access controls that are designed to align the computer access rights to transactions, data, key documents, and assets with only those employees who require such access to complete their clearly defined role within the internal control system. In a sense, proper separation of duties is accomplished through appropriate system access controls.

Physical Controls

Physical access to assets and important records, documents, and blank forms should be limited to authorized personnel. Assets such as inventory and securities should not be available to persons who have no need to handle them. Likewise, access to records should be denied to people who do not have a record-keeping responsibility for them. Some blank forms are very important for accounting and control, and their availability should be restricted. For example, someone not involved in accounting for payroll should not be able to pick up blank time cards. Only authorized persons should be able to obtain blank checks after signing for them. Sometimes, access to blank forms is the equivalent of access to an important asset. For example, someone who has access to blank checks has a measure of actual custody and access to cash.

In addition, given the importance of the computerized information processing system, physical security of computer equipment and restricting access to the organization's data and computer application files are important to achieving effective internal control. Access controls help prevent the improper use or manipulation of data files, unauthorized use of computer programs, and improper use of the computer equipment. Locked doors, security passes, passwords, and check-in logs can be used to limit access to the computer system hardware. One way to detect inappropriate computer usage is by specifying a planned schedule for running large-scale computerized applications. A schedule can help detect unauthorized access because most software can produce usage reports that can be compared to the planned schedule. Applications that are being run at unauthorized times can then be investigated for inappropriate use of computer resources.

Information Processing Control Activities

Information processing control activities are essential to the effectiveness of an internal control system. Generally, all organizations employ computerized information processing on a routine basis. When entities use computerized information processing, the professional standards make clear that information technology (IT) poses specific risks to an entity's internal control system. And, although the focus of this chapter is on providing a broad understanding of internal control, you should be aware that the use of computerized information processing requires entities to implement specific control activities to enable it to support the relevant financial statement assertions (see Exhibit 5.9).

The auditing considerations that are relevant to an entity's computerized information processing environment are discussed in detail in Module H. However, before moving on, it is important to realize that even "spreadsheet goofs" can pose risks to an entity's internal control system, as shown in the following Auditing Insight. In addition, although almost all organizations employ computerized information processing, manual controls over certain information processing activities remain important in most systems. For example, as illustrated in Exhibit 5.9, important manual control activities over the purchasing and cash disbursement cycle include using purchase orders to ensure proper authorization (the *occurrence* assertion), matching vendor invoices with receiving reports and purchase orders to ensure that the quantity billed agrees with the quantity ordered and received at previously agreed-upon prices (the *accuracy* assertion), and using *and accounting for* prenumbered documents (checks, purchase orders, and receiving reports) to ensure that all transactions have been recorded (the *completeness* assertion). (*Note:* Failure to account for the numeric sequence of documents eliminates the benefit of prenumbering.) The specific control activities for each cycle are discussed in more detail in Chapters 6 through 10.

EXHIBIT 5.9
Manual Information Processing Controls

Information Processing Control	Financial Statement Assertion Supported
Purchase orders must be authorized by purchasing department before any purchase is made.	Occurrence
All invoices received from vendors for payment must be matched to receiving report and purchase order to ensure that the quantity billed agrees with the quantity ordered and received at previously agreed-upon prices.	Accuracy
Prenumbered documents (checks, purchase orders, and receiving reports) must be used and accounted for to ensure that all transactions have been recorded.	Completeness

AUDITING INSIGHT | Spreadsheet Goofs

TransAlta Corp. confessed that a "clerical error" was a costly one—$24 million, to be exact—for the power producer. The Calgary-based company said a spreadsheet goof by an employee caused the company to pay higher than intended rates to ship power in New York. CEO Steve Snyder explained via a conference call that a "cut-and-paste" foul-up within an Excel spreadsheet on a bid to New York's power grid operator led TransAlta to secure 15 times the capacity of power lines at 10 times the price. The costly human error couldn't be reversed by the grid operator, and although TransAlta has since tried to recoup the mammoth losses, it was left with a $24 million lesson.

In October 2003, about two weeks after releasing its third-quarter earnings figures, **Fannie Mae** had to restate its unrealized gains account by $1.2 billion for errors in "mark-to-market" calculations required by SFAS 149. This was apparently the result of "honest mistakes made in a spreadsheet used in the implementation of the new accounting standard."

Sources: "Cut-and-Paste Oops Costly for TransAlta," *Canadian Press,* June 4, 2003; "Fannie Mae Corrects Mistakes in Results," *The New York Times,* October 30, 2003, p. C1.

REVIEW CHECKPOINTS

5.11 What is a *control activity*?

5.12 What is the difference between preventive controls and detective controls? Give an example of each.

5.13 What kinds of functional responsibilities should be performed by different departments or persons in a control system with good separation of duties?

Information and Communication

When evaluating the information and communication component of internal control, the "auditor should obtain an understanding of the **information system** [emphasis added] including the related business processes, relevant to financial reporting. As part of that process, the auditor must seek to understand the nature of the underlying accounting records, supporting information and the accounts that are used to fully execute a transaction." The auditor should also understand "how the information system captures events and conditions, other than transactions, that are significant to the financial statements."[4] Clearly, the size of the entity will have an impact on this component. However, regardless of the entity's size. the COSO framework establishes three principles that, if applied properly, will result in an effective evaluation of the information and communication component. The three principles of the information and communication component are listed in Exhibit 5.10.

The professional standards recognize that to make effective decisions, managers must have access to *timely, reliable,* and *relevant* information. As a result, an entity's information system should be devised to identify data from reliable external sources such as suppliers, customers, economic databases, and so on, as well as internal sources. Having superior information systems can be a part of an entity's strategy and competitive advantage (e.g., **Amazon.com**). Management evaluates the quality of information by determining whether the content is appropriate and the information is timely, current, accurate, and

EXHIBIT 5.10
Three Principles of Information and Communication

Principles of Information and Communication as per COSO 2013 Report
1. The organization obtains or generates and uses relevant quality information to support the functioning of internal control.
2. The organization internally communicates information, including objectives and responsibilities for internal control, necessary to support the functioning of internal control.
3. The organization communicates with external parties regarding matters affecting the functioning of internal control.

[4]PCAOB Auditing Standard 2110, "*Identifying and Assessing Risks of Material Misstatement.*"

accessible. Note that these sometimes are contradictory. For example, waiting to ensure that information is *accurate* can cause it not to be *timely*.

Communication includes report production and distribution. The account balances are summarized in internal management reports and external financial statements. The internal reports are management's feedback for monitoring operations. The external reports are the financial information for outside investors, creditors, and others. Communication also involves expectations, responsibilities of individuals and groups, and other important matters. Specific duties must be made clear, and people need to know how their activities relate to the work of others. People also need to know what behavior is expected. In addition, personnel need a means of communicating significant information upstream in an organization. Outsiders also should know that fraudulent and unethical behavior by entity personnel is unacceptable and should be reported to management.

The information system produces a trail of activities (often referred to as an *audit trail*) from data identification to reports. You can visualize that the audit trail begins with the *source documents* (purchase orders, sales orders, etc.) and proceeds through to the financial reports. Auditors often follow this trail frontward and backward, identifying and testing relevant control activities along the way (Exhibit 5.11). They follow it backward from the financial reports to the source documents to determine whether everything in the financial reports is supported by appropriate source documents (the *occurrence* assertion). They follow it forward from source documents to reports to determine whether everything that happened (i.e., transactions) was recorded in the accounts and reported in the financial statements (the *completeness* assertion).

Information systems in small or midsize organizations are likely to be less formal than in larger organizations, but their role is just as significant. Smaller entities with active management involvement may not need extensive descriptions of accounting procedures, sophisticated accounting records, or written policies. Communication may be less formal and easier to achieve in a small or midsize company than in a larger enterprise because the smaller organization has fewer levels, and management has more visibility and availability.

One final and very important consideration made by the audit team when gaining an understanding of this component relates to the use of information produced by the company during the audit. The professional standards are clear that an auditor cannot merely rely on information produced by the company's information system without investigation. Instead, the audit team is required to perform audit procedures that are designed either to test the controls that have been designed to ensure that the information is complete and accurate or to test the completeness and accuracy of the information using substantive testing procedures. The following Auditing Insight demonstrates the focus of the PCAOB on the importance of this issue.

Monitoring

The COSO framework recognizes that in order to allow for continuous improvements and consider changes in the entity's operating environment, management needs to monitor its internal control systems. According to COSO, a well-functioning monitoring system is characterized by philosophies such as the following:

EXHIBIT 5.11

Occurrence and Completeness of a Sales Transaction

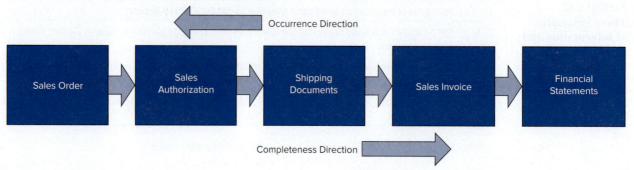

AUDITING INSIGHT	PCAOB Identifies Deficiencies Related to System-Generated Data

In a recent public report about its inspections program, the PCAOB specifically discussed a finding related to information that is produced by the entity being audited. Specifically, the PCAOB noted that certain firms failed to "test the controls over the completeness and accuracy of the system-generated data and reports used in the operation" of performance review controls executed by management. "For example, management used reports that were generated by the issuer's information system to perform its review control; however, the engagement team did not test controls over the accuracy and completeness of these reports. In addition, the engagement team did not test the reports to verify the completeness and accuracy of the individual variance calculations to determine whether the investigation of other variances was necessary." Because an entity's use of IT affects the fundamental manner in which information is produced, it is essential that an auditor is comfortable with the completeness and accuracy of all information used by management to execute control activities that are deemed important to the auditor.

Source: PCAOB Observations from 2010 Inspections of Domestic Annually Inspected Firms Regarding Deficiencies in Audits of Internal Control over Financial Reporting. PCAOB Release No. 2012-006. December 10, 2012 (available at www.pcaobus.org).

- *Ongoing and separate evaluations.* Ongoing evaluations of controls that are separate from other types of evaluations (e.g., operational) enable management to determine whether the other components of internal control continue to function over time.
- *Reporting deficiencies.* Internal control deficiencies are identified and communicated in a timely manner to those parties responsible for taking corrective action and to management and the board as appropriate.

It is important to note that monitoring does not include regular management and supervisory control activities and other actions that employees take in performing their everyday duties. Effective monitoring involves ongoing evaluation of the controls. Some common monitoring controls include

- Periodic evaluation of controls by internal audit.
- Analysis of and appropriate follow-up of operating reports or metrics that might identify anomalies indicative of a control failure.
- Supervisory review of controls, such as reconciliation reviews as a normal part of processing.
- Self-assessments by boards and management regarding the tone they set in the organization and the effectiveness of their oversight functions.
- Audit committee inquiries of internal and external auditors.
- Quality assurance reviews of the internal audit department.[5]

As you can see, some of the control activities explained earlier in this chapter also serve as monitoring activities. For example, analyzing customer complaints for follow-up is a control activity, but analyzing them to determine whether the complaints result from a weakness in other controls (e.g., a failure to compare shipping documents to customer orders) is a monitoring activity.

Although the preceding procedures provide management daily monitoring opportunities, the oversight provided to the entity by the board of directors (and, more specifically, the audit committee) provides the highest level of monitoring. In addition, management's close involvement in operations often will identify significant variances from expectations and inaccuracies in financial data. Finally, ongoing monitoring activities of small and midsize entities are more likely to be informal and are typically performed as a part of the overall management of the entity's operations. However, regardless of the entity's size, the COSO framework establishes two principles that, if applied properly, will result in an effective evaluation of the monitoring component. The two principles of the monitoring component are listed in Exhibit 5.12.

[5]*Guidance on Monitoring Internal Control Systems,* COSO, January 2009.

EXHIBIT 5.12
Two Principles of Monitoring Activities

Principles of Monitoring Activities as per COSO 2013 Report
1. The organization selects, develops, and performs ongoing and/or separate evaluations to ascertain whether the components of internal control are present and functioning.
2. The organization evaluates and communicates internal control deficiencies in a timely manner to those parties responsible for taking corrective action, including senior management and the board of directors, as appropriate.

Limitations of Internal Control

Internal control provides *reasonable* assurance, not *absolute* assurance, that management's objectives will be achieved. Because people operate the controls, breakdowns can occur. Internal control can help prevent and detect many errors, but it cannot guarantee that they will never happen. Several limitations to internal control systems prevent management from obtaining complete assurance that controls are absolutely effective:

- *Human error* due to mistakes in judgment, fatigue, and carelessness can still occur.
- Although controls are implemented to prevent and detect errors, *deliberate circumvention* by people in the system can still occur.
- Because most internal controls are directed at lower-level employees, *management override* can occur. For example, it is often possible for management to override controls by force of authority (i.e., if the CEO says to do something, most employees will).
- Although separation of duties can be extremely effective in an internal control system, *collusion* among people who are supposed to act independently can lead to a failure in the achievement of relevant internal control objectives.

In addition, one other limitation deserves special consideration. That is, an internal control system is always subject to cost–benefit considerations. Internal control could be made perfect, or nearly so, but at great expense. For example, at the lowest level of control, a company's inventory could be left completely unlocked and unguarded (i.e., with no controls at all); next, a fence could be used; locks could be installed; lighting could be used all night; television monitors could be put in place; or at the highest level of control, armed guards could be hired. Each of these successive safeguards costs additional money (as does extensive supervision of clerical personnel in an office). At some point, the cost of protecting the inventory from theft (or the cost of supervisors catching every clerical error) exceeds the benefit of the internal control activity. In the professional auditing standards, the concept of **reasonable assurance** recognizes that the costs of controls should not exceed the benefits that are expected from the controls. Hence, an entity can decide that certain controls are too costly considering the risk of loss that can occur. Finally, it is important for students to remember that internal control is a *process,* a means for management to achieve its objectives, not an end in itself. It is also dynamic, operating every day within an entity's operating structure, which can and does evolve as the entity and its operating environment change over time.

⊘ REVIEW CHECKPOINTS

5.14 What is meant by the information and communications component of an effective internal control system? How can an auditor evaluate whether a client's internal control system is functioning properly for this component?

5.15 Give some examples of everyday work an entity's management can use to enact the monitoring component of internal control. When are such activities control activities, and when are they monitoring activities?

5.16 What is the concept of reasonable assurance? What are the key limitations of an internal control system?

Chapter 5   *Risk Assessment: Internal Control Evaluation*   **191**

INTERNAL CONTROL EVALUATION

LO 5-4

Explain the process the audit team uses to assess control risk; understand its impact on the risk of material misstatement; and, ultimately, know how it affects the nature, timing, and extent of further audit procedures to be performed on the audit.

To this point, we have defined internal control, identified management's and the audit team's responsibility for internal control, and described the five components of internal control defined by COSO. These components are considered to be criteria for evaluating an entity's financial reporting controls and the bases for auditors' assessment of control and inherent risk at the financial statement assertion level. In assessing control risk, audit teams use a three-phase procedure illustrated in Exhibit 5.13. It is important to note that these phases must be completed at the relevant financial statement assertion level if the auditor plans to rely on a control activity to modify the nature, timing, and extent of further audit procedures.

EXHIBIT 5.13

Phases of Internal Control Evaluation

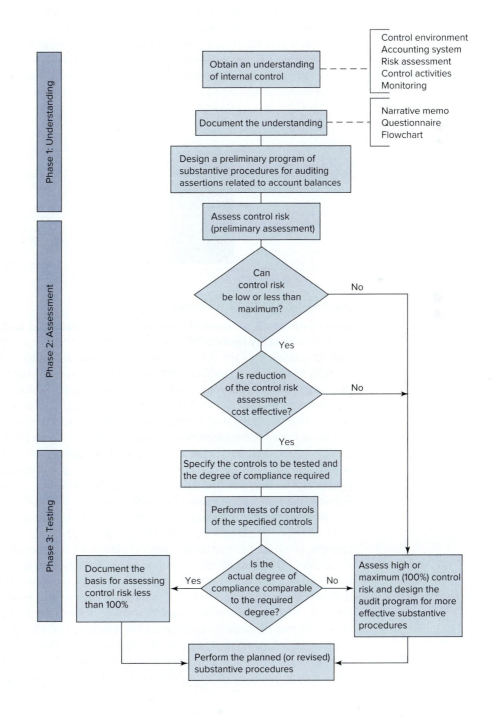

Phase 1: Understand and Document the Client's Internal Control

The process of obtaining an understanding of internal controls should occur early in the audit engagement. On every audit engagement, the audit team should evaluate the design of internal control and determine whether controls have been implemented over all relevant assertions related to each significant account and financial statement disclosure. The procedures used to gain an understanding of internal controls provide the audit team an overall acquaintance with the control environment and management's risk assessment, the flow of transactions through the accounting system, and the design of some client control activities. Gaining an understanding of internal controls should be performed in a "top-down" risk-based manner that first identifies *significant accounts* and disclosures and their *relevant assertions*. This was discussed in Chapter 4. Recall that an account's *significance* is based on its *inherent risk* (i.e., the likelihood of containing a material misstatement before the consideration of internal control). Thus, audit teams focus on likely sources of significant misstatements. This determination is not based on quantitative measures alone, but it is unlikely that a large, material account balance would ever be omitted from consideration. *Relevant assertions* are those that represent the possibility of a material misstatement. Thus, an assertion that does not represent a meaningful risk of misstatement (e.g., completeness of cash) is not relevant and should not be considered by the audit team.

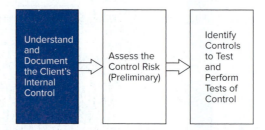

Identifying Entity-Level Controls

For all the relevant assertions for each significant account and disclosure, audit teams begin by examining **entity-level controls**, controls that are pervasive to the internal control system and the reliability of the financial statements taken as a whole. See Exhibit 5.14 for the PCAOB's list of entity-level controls from the professional standards and the audit team's methods of obtaining an understanding of such controls. Notice that the PCAOB explicitly includes parts or all of the COSO framework elements. This is deliberate. If the audit team decides that an entity-level control sufficiently reduces a specific risk of material misstatement for a relevant assertion, it may not need to delve further into transaction-level controls (discussed next) related to that risk. For example, if a chief financial officer who is very familiar with the company's payroll process performs reviews of weekly payroll reports and investigates discrepancies thoroughly, this may provide a control that is sufficient to meet the internal control objectives for payroll reporting (i.e., address or mitigate the risk of material misstatement for each of the relevant assertions for payroll expense).

In addition to entity-level controls, the audit team also identifies **transaction-level controls**, controls that pertain to specific classes of transactions, account balances, and disclosures. The most effective method used to: 1) gain an understanding of the flow of transactions; 2) the points at which a material misstatement could occur; and 3) the controls that management has implemented to mitigate each risk of material misstatement identified is by performing a *walkthrough* of a single transaction through the entire accounting system. During the walkthrough, the auditor is able to learn by observing the activities that occur and the documents that are used within an internal control process. The auditor must come to understand internal control in order to evaluate *design effectiveness*. **Design effectiveness** determines whether the controls over financial reporting, *if operating effectively,*

EXHIBIT 5.14   Entity-Level Controls and Their Assessment

Types of Entity-Level Controls	Assessment
• Controls related to the control environment • Controls related to management override • Centralized processing and controls including shared service environments • Controls to monitor results of operations • Controls to monitor other controls.	The primary evidence to test these controls is gathered through observation and inquiry and some document examination. Ultimately, the auditor needs to determine whether management's integrity, values, and operating style promote effective control consciousness throughout the entity.
• Management's risk assessment	The audit team next needs to gain an understanding of how the client assesses and responds to risk. If the client already uses enterprise risk management, inquiring and obtaining documentation of such processes is usually enough.
• Period-end financial reporting process	The auditor should assess the processes that are used to produce its annual and quarterly financial statements, including the extent to which IT is involved in the period-end process. The auditor must document who is actually participating from the management team and where the process actually takes place. Finally, the auditor needs to understand and document the types of adjusting entries that have occurred and the extent of process oversight by the management team, the board, and the audit committee.
• Policies that address significant business control and risk management practices	An entity's internal auditors and systems staff often review and evaluate this documentation. Independent auditors may review and study their work instead of doing the same tasks over again. Other sources of information include (1) previous experience with the entity as found in the prior-year audit, (2) responses to inquiries directed to client personnel, and (3) examination of documents and records.

would be expected to prevent or detect errors or fraud that could result in a material misstatement in the financial statements. A **walkthrough** consists of a combination of inquiry of personnel, observation of an entity's operations, and document examination while tracing a single transaction through the entire audit trail from the beginning or the initiation of the transaction to its final inclusion in the financial statements. Each client employee involved is asked to demonstrate the procedures that he or she follows in processing the transaction. The walkthrough is an important step in awareness because, often, the information that is contained in manuals and understood by supervisors may not be the same as the procedures actually being performed. People can change procedures to make them more efficient, they can forget to perform procedures, they may go on vacation, they may intentionally not perform procedures, or the procedures may not be understood by a new person taking over that position.

At this point, the audit team has learned the *design* of controls (or how those controls are intended to function). However, this does not inform the audit team as to the *operating effectiveness* of controls unless there is some automation that provides for the consistent application of the operation of the control. Additionally, reperformance of critical controls along the transaction trail can take place at this time to provide evidence of *operating effectiveness*. **Operating effectiveness** refers to whether the control is *operating as designed* and whether the person performing the control possesses the necessary authority and qualifications to perform the control effectively. Evidence of this nature will be obtained in a subsequent phase of the audit team's study of internal control.

Document the Internal Control Understanding

Once the audit team has learned of the design of the entity's controls, it is required to document that understanding. The understanding can be summarized and documented effectively in the form of questionnaires, narratives, and flowcharts (discussed next).

Internal Control Questionnaires   Perhaps the most efficient means to begin gathering evidence about an entity's internal control is to conduct a formal interview with knowledgeable managers using the checklist form of **internal control questionnaire** illustrated in Exhibit 5.15. This questionnaire is typically organized under headings that identify

EXHIBIT 5.15 **Internal Control Questionnaire—Payroll Processing**

	Yes/No	Comments
Control Environment		
1. Are all employees paid by check or direct deposit?		
2. Is a special payroll bank account used?		
3. Are payroll checks signed by persons who do not prepare checks or keep cash funds or accounting records?		
4. If a check-signing machine is used, are the signature plates controlled?		
5. Is the payroll bank account reconciled by someone who does not prepare, sign, or deliver paychecks?		
6. Are payroll department personnel rotated in their duties? Required to take vacations? Bonded?		
7. Is there a timekeeping department (function) independent of the payroll department?		
8. Are authorizations for deductions signed by the employees on file?		
Occurrence		
9. Are time cards or piecework reports prepared by the employee approved by her or his supervisor?		
10. Is a time clock or other electromechanical or computerized system used?		
11. Is the payroll register sheet signed by the employee preparing it and approved prior to payment?		
12. Are names of terminated employees reported in writing to the payroll department?		
13. Is the payroll periodically compared to personnel files?		
14. Are checks distributed by someone other than the employee's immediate supervisor?		
15. Are unclaimed wages deposited in a special bank account or otherwise controlled by a responsible officer?		
16. Do internal auditors conduct occasional surprise distributions of paychecks?		
Completeness		
17. Are names of newly hired employees reported in writing to the payroll department?		
18. Are blank payroll checks prenumbered and the numerical sequence checked for missing documents?		
Accuracy		
19. Are all wage rates determined by contract or approved by a personnel officer?		
20. Are timekeeping and cost accounting records (such as hours, dollars) reconciled with payroll department calculations of hours and wages?		
21. Are payrolls audited periodically by internal auditors?		
22. Are individual payroll records reconciled with quarterly tax reports?		
Classification		
23. Do payroll accounting personnel have instructions for classifying payroll debit entries?		
Cutoff		
24. Are monthly, quarterly, and annual wage accruals reviewed by an accounting officer?		

questions related to relevant themes like the control environment and relevant management assertions. Not all questionnaires are organized like this, so audit teams need to know the general objectives in order to know whether the questionnaire is complete. Likewise, if you are assigned to prepare an internal control questionnaire, you will need to be careful to include questions about each relevant assertion.

Internal control questionnaires are designed to help the audit team obtain evidence about the control environment and the accounting and control activities that are considered appropriate for normal circumstances. All organizations have unique features, and answers to the questions should not be taken as final and definitive evidence about how well controls actually function. Evidence obtained through the interview process is categorized as inquiry-level information that is not sufficient to demonstrate the operating effectiveness of a control activity. The person being interviewed could always give answers that reflect what the system should be rather than what it really is. The person can be unaware of informal ways in which duties have been changed or can be innocently ignorant of the system details. Nevertheless, interviews and questionnaires are useful for detecting control weaknesses. An auditor should always consider the possibility that a respondent admits that a control is weak.

An advantage of using internal control questionnaires is that audit teams are less likely to forget to cover some important point. Questions are worded such that a "no" answer points out a weakness or control deficiency, thus making analysis easier. However, audit teams should be aware that entity personnel often fully understand that "yes" answers are "good" and "no" answers are "bad," so they tend to tell audit teams "yes" all the time. Good auditors often change a question when they ask it, just to ensure that the interviewee is listening and not giving only "yes" answers. Also, internal control questionnaires tend to be inflexible. If a key question is not included on the list because the question is unique to a client, the auditor might not even know to ask the question. Thus, for new clients, other methods of gaining an understanding that are tailored to the client are preferable. In practice, audit teams typically use a combination of methods to document their understanding of the client's internal control.

A second method for documenting the audit team's understanding of internal control is to write a **narrative description** of each important control subsystem. Such a narrative simply describes all environmental elements, the accounting system, and all control activities. The narrative description can be efficient in audits of very small businesses. However, for a large entity, this description may be difficult to comprehend and might not readily identify potential weaknesses in internal control in a manner that "no" responses do in an internal control questionnaire.

A third method for documenting the auditors' understanding of accounting and control is to construct an accounting and control system **flowchart**. Many control-conscious companies have their own flowcharts that the audit team may use as a starting point instead of constructing their own from scratch. The advantages of flowcharts can be summarized by an old adage: "A picture is worth a thousand words." Flowcharts tend to help the audit team assess the key control points in the process and can be helpful in identifying missing controls.

Construction of a flowchart is time-consuming because an auditor must take the time to learn about the operating personnel involved in the system and gather samples of relevant documents. Thus, the information for the flowchart, like the narrative description, involves much effort and observation. When the flowchart is complete, however, the result is an easily evaluated, informative description of the system that shows the various duties performed by individuals and provides graphic evidence of any conflicting responsibilities (i.e., lack of separation of duties). Further, once a flowchart is complete, subsequent audits can easily access the flowchart and update it for changes that have been made in the process since the prior year. In recent years, flowcharting has become even more popular as a way to document an auditor's understanding of the internal control system.

For any flowcharting application, the chart must be understandable to an audit supervisor. Flowcharts are created with audit-specific flowcharting software but also can be created rather easily in Excel or PowerPoint. The flowchart should communicate all relevant information and evidence about separation of responsibilities, authorization, and accounting and control activities in an understandable, visual form. The starting point in the system, if possible, should be placed at the upper-left-hand corner. The flow of procedures and documents should be from left to right and from top to bottom as much as possible. The shapes of the symbols are commonly understood and fairly obvious. For example, rectangles are processes, circles are connectors, quadrilaterals are manual processes, and so on. Narrative explanations should be written on the face of the chart as annotations or in a readily available reference key.

Refer to Exhibit 5.16 for a partial flowchart representation of the beginning stages of a payroll processing system. The connectors shown by the circled numbers indicate

EXHIBIT 5.16 Payroll System Flowchart

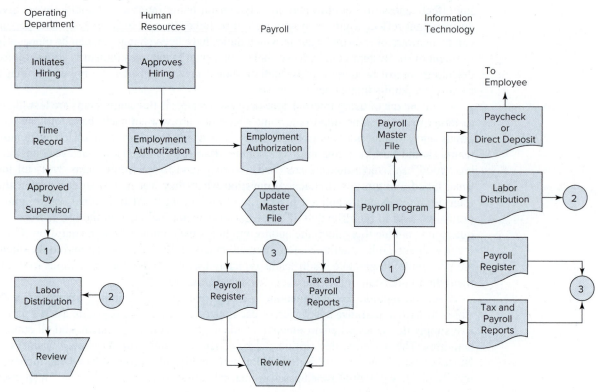

continuation on the flowchart. Ultimately, the flowchart ends showing entries in accounting journals and ledgers. In Exhibit 5.16, you can see some characteristics of both flowchart construction and this specific accounting system. By reading down the columns for each department, you can see that transaction-initiation authority (both hiring and time card preparation) and custody of checks are separated.

Key Decision: Deciding Whether to Continue to Test Controls For an integrated audit at a public company, the auditor must test controls for all relevant assertions for each significant account and disclosure. This will be discussed in detail later in this chapter. However, for audits of nonpublic companies, after the audit team members have documented their understanding of the entity's internal control, an important decision needs to be made: Should the audit team perform tests of the operating effectiveness of those controls? Audit teams may choose *not* to do so for one of two reasons. First, the audit team could conclude that the internal control system is too ineffective in preventing or detecting misstatements to rely upon justifying reductions of subsequent audit procedures for the relevant assertions. This conclusion is equivalent to assessing control risk at the highest level and specifying extensive substantive procedures such as confirmation of all customer accounts as of year-end. Consider for a moment the Krispy Kreme management report presented earlier that identified significant material weaknesses in the internal control system. In such a situation, the audit team would have to make sure that the audit is conducted in an effective manner by conducting significant substantive testing.

For private company audits, a second reason that audit teams might not test controls would be the team's decision that it would take more time to test the operating effectiveness of the control activities than it would take to perform the substantive tests necessary for a relevant assertion (even if the controls turn out to be working well). In this situation, the cost of obtaining a low control risk assessment can be high. In this case, the conclusion is also equivalent to assessing control risk at 100 percent, but this time it is because the audit team has not conducted the tests of *operating effectiveness* of control activities, not because the team has concluded that controls are ineffective.

For either reason, however, the result is the same: More extensive and effective substantive procedures are required to be completed in order to reduce the risk of material misstatement for a relevant assertion to an acceptably low level. For example, suppose the extensive testing of controls over the accuracy of payroll expenses is estimated to take 40 hours. Also suppose that, if controls were excellent, the substantive tests of payroll accuracy (e.g., confirmation sent to employees) could be reduced by 30 hours. The additional work to test controls is not economical. The decision to stop work on control risk assessment in this case is a matter of audit *efficiency*—it doesn't make sense to spend 40 hours testing controls to reduce substantive tests by 30 hours. Of course, the auditors' rationale for their final decision must be carefully documented. Before moving on, remember that this decision is appropriate only for nonpublic companies; audit teams must extensively test internal control over financial reporting for public companies.

✓ REVIEW CHECKPOINTS

5.17 What is meant by a "top-down" approach to evaluation of internal controls?

5.18 Must the overall understanding of internal control always be followed by assessment and testing phases? Explain.

5.19 Where can an auditor find a client's documentation of the accounting system?

5.20 What are the advantages and disadvantages of documenting internal control by using (1) an internal control questionnaire, (2) a narrative memorandum, and (3) a flowchart?

Phase 2: Assess the Control Risk (Preliminary)

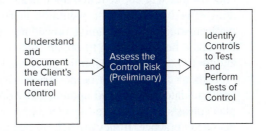

After completing phase 1—understanding and documenting internal control—the audit team should be able to make a preliminary assessment of control risk. At this preliminary stage, the audit team members also may use their internal control findings from the previous year's audit. At this stage of the process, auditors seek to identify internal control activities that are explicitly designed to support reliable financial statement reporting for the relevant financial statement assertion identified about each significant account and disclosure. It is important to remember that a well-designed internal control system will clearly link key internal control activities to the relevant financial statement assertions being supported. Exhibit 5.17 provides an illustration of this step by extending the exhibit that was developed in Chapter 4 (Exhibit 4.12) with a fourth column.

At this stage of the process, auditors are trying to identify the controls that may be relied upon as part of the overall audit process. To do so, auditors need to identify the controls that they believe will mitigate the risks of material misstatement that have been identified for each of the relevant assertions. Ultimately, these controls would have to be tested before the audit team could rely on them to reduce substantive testing. However, it is important to point out that audit teams should not perform tests of controls for those

EXHIBIT 5.17
What Can Go Wrong
and Control Activities

Significant Account	Relevant Assertions	What Can Go Wrong?	Internal Control Activity
Cash	Existence	The cash balance may not exist in the company's bank accounts.	The CFO performs a detailed review of the bank reconciliation on a monthly basis.
	Valuation	The cash balance that is held in foreign countries may not have been translated properly.	The treasurer reviews the cash translation adjustment calculation monthly and independently checks that the appropriate spot rate has been used for each foreign currency.
	Presentation and disclosure	There may be restrictions on the cash balance that were not properly disclosed.	The corporate secretary reviews the cash footnote disclosure on a quarterly basis to ensure that all legal restrictions on the cash balance have been properly disclosed.
Accounts Receivable	Existence	Accounts receivable balances are inflated and don't really exist.	Check sales order and shipping document to make sure sales were earned and a customer owes a balance.
	Completeness	Not all accounts receivable have been recorded.	Check invoices with shipping document to A/R ledger.
	Valuation	Receivables are not included in financial statements at the appropriate amount, and valuation adjustments are not recorded properly.	Management evaluates the collectability of delinquent receivables on a timely basis.

controls that will not be relied upon because there is no need to prove that they are operating effectively. Doing so would be inefficient. Instead, the audit team would have to perform additional substantive procedures to compensate for the lack of internal controls that could be relied upon to obtain sufficient appropriate evidence that would allow the auditor to reach a conclusion for the related relevant assertions.

Tests of controls must be performed to obtain evidence about whether controls that are candidates to be relied upon actually operate as described. The test of controls audit plan consists of procedures designed to produce evidence of how effectively the controls operate in practice. If they are determined to be operating effectively after testing, control risk can be assessed below the maximum. If they do not operate with the required level of effectiveness, the final conclusion is to assess a high or maximum control risk, revise the audit plan to consider the control weakness, and then proceed with additional substantive audit procedures.

The distinction between the understanding and documenting phase and the preliminary control risk assessment phase is useful for understanding the audit team's study and evaluation of internal control. However, the audit team typically performs these phases together, not as separate and distinct audit tasks. For nonpublic entities, the audit team can halt the control evaluation process for efficiency or effectiveness reasons. However, if the audit team wants to justify a low-risk assessment to reduce the substantive audit procedures, the evaluation must be continued in phase 3, the testing phase.

To summarize, then, at this stage, the audit team members have established an assessment of the level of control risk based on its understanding of internal control and identified control strengths and weaknesses. If this assessment is at a level less than the maximum level (i.e., the audit team members want to rely on internal controls to modify the nature, timing, and extent of further audit procedures), the auditors must next perform tests of controls. This final phase is discussed in the next section.

Phase 3: Identify Controls to Test and Perform Tests of Controls

When audit teams reach the third phase of an evaluation of internal control, they already have identified specific control activities for relevant assertions on which risk could be assessed below the maximum (100 percent). This is often referred to as *controls on which the audit team intends to rely.* To support the reduced control risk assessment and the reduction of related substantive procedures for each relevant assertion, audit teams must test the control activities to determine whether they are operating effectively throughout the period. The required level of effectiveness is a matter of professional judgment. Audit teams know that compliance cannot realistically be expected to be perfect. The auditors could decide, for example, that evidence such as 96 percent of recorded payroll being supported by validated time cards is sufficient to assess a "low" control risk for the occurrence assertion. Most public accounting firms have internal guidelines to determine the acceptable rate of compliance for an internal control activity to be considered effective. Generally, if a control is judged to be more important and would result in a more significant reduction in substantive testing, the level of compliance must be higher. Factors to consider in determining appropriate levels of compliance are discussed in more detail in Module F.

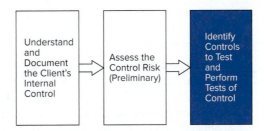

The professional standards make clear that when designing tests of controls, the auditor needs to consider the means of selecting items for testing. For tests of internal controls, there are two approaches that are commonly used: (1) testing all items in a population and (2) testing a sample from a population. The decision of which approach to use depends on the nature of the control that is being tested, along with the availability of data. For example, a control activity that is entirely automated might best be tested by an automated audit procedure that can be efficiently and effectively applied to the entire population of occurrences of that control activity. However, for a manual control activity, the auditor is likely to take a sample from the population of occurrences of that control activity. In addition, it should be noted that some manual controls (such as locking a door to safeguard assets) may have little documentation and may require other means of testing (e.g., observation and inquiry). In today's auditing environment, the increased use of computers by both the client and the auditor has dramatically increased the number of tests of control that can be effectively applied to the *entire* population of control occurrences in an efficient manner (such as exception testing).

Exception Testing

One way to subject all items in a population of occurrences for a particular control activity is to use exception testing. Exception testing is designed to identify a violation of a particular control activity through the use of an automated test procedure designed to test all items in a population. For example, consider an entirely automated control activity that is designed to compare a customer's credit limit to the sum of (1) a potential sales transaction and (2) that customer's outstanding credit balance before approval of that sales transaction. If the control activity operated effectively throughout the year, a customer's outstanding credit balance would not exceed its credit limit.

Given the nature of the control activity, one way to test the operating effectiveness would be through the use of exception testing. That is, an auditor could obtain evidence about the control's operating effectiveness by using a procedure that compares each customer's credit limit to that customer's outstanding credit balance at the end of each day for the year under audit. Such a testing strategy would not have been possible (at least economically) in previous years. However, due to advances in information technology, such testing is now possible. As a direct result, entry-level audit professionals are now expected to consider the full extent of client data available for testing purposes, before they move forward with audit tests.

USING IDEA IN THE AUDIT | Internal Control Testing

IDEA can be helpful to audit professionals when completing exception tests and conducting audit sampling. This addendum summarizes several useful assignments that are available to students in the IDEA Data Analysis Workbook: IDEA Version Ten (the IDEA Workbook). The assignments allow students to experience a hands-on application of the IDEA software to exception testing. Ultimately, exception tests provide evidence about the operating effectiveness of internal control activities by testing all items in a population. Module F provides a detailed illustration of how auditors use the sampling features of IDEA to select a representative sample from a complete population of control occurrences for a control activity to be tested.

At the end of this chapter, problems 5.72 and 5.73 can be completed to illustrate the use of IDEA during internal control testing.

Audit Sampling

Of course, there are many control activities that do not lend themselves to automated audit testing. In such situations, auditors are likely to take a sample from the population of occurrences for the control activity being tested. Most importantly, in such situations, the population being sampled must include all occurrences of the relevant control activity for the entire period of reliance, and the sample must be representative of that population to be considered appropriate audit evidence. In recent years, there has been an increased focus on the work of auditors by regulators to make sure that the sample selected is truly representative of the population of occurrences over the entire period of reliance. For example, in a recent Staff Practice Audit Alert, the PCAOB (2014) noted that its inspectors observed instances where auditors relied on controls to reduce substantive testing, but their reliance was "unsupported because the testing of controls was insufficient." The auditors failed to test the control activity over the entire period of reliance.[6] In such situations, the key is for auditors to remember that for a sample to be representative, all items in the population have an opportunity to be selected.

Tests of controls, when performed, should be applied to samples of transactions and control activities executed *throughout the period* under audit. The reason for this requirement is that the conclusions about controls will be generalized to the whole period under audit. If the auditor obtains audit evidence about the operating effectiveness of controls during an interim period, additional audit evidence should be obtained for the remaining period. There are certain situations when audit teams can rely on tests from previous periods if they have evidence that the procedure has not changed and the auditor does not believe there is a significant risk of material misstatement. However, in an annual audit, the auditor may not rely on audit evidence about the operating effectiveness of controls obtained in prior audits for controls that have changed since they were last tested or for controls that mitigate a significant risk. Audit sampling is discussed in detail in Module E.

Perform Tests of Controls

Once the items have been selected for testing, the four methods of testing controls are inquiry, observation, document examination, and reperformance. Generally, audit teams use *inquiry* about the existence of control activities and then corroborate the oral evidence by observing that the client-described control activities are actually being performed. *Observation* occurs when auditors have eyewitness observation of employees at their jobs

---

[6] From "Staff Audit Practice Alert No.12 Matters Related to Auditing Revenue in an Audit of Financial Statements," PCAOB, September 9, 2014, available at http://pcaobus.org/Standards/QandA/9-9-14_SAPA_12.pdf.

performing control activities. Observation is typically used when certain control activities, such as separation of employees' duties, leave no documentary evidence for subsequent examination. Observation also can produce evidence of access controls such as the use of password-secured access to the computerized information system, locked doors, and security guards. The limitation of observation is that this test of control is performed as of one point in time (usually near year-end), and what is observed at that point in time may not be representative of prior time periods.

Some tests of controls depend on documentary evidence such as a payroll entry supported by a time card. In these cases, *document examination* for evidence of signatures, initials, checklists, reconciliations, and the like provides better evidence than procedures that leave no documentary tracks. Document examination might be enough; the audit team may look to see whether the documents were marked with an initial, signature, or stamp to indicate they had been checked. For example, audit teams could examine canceled checks for authorized signatures, inspect voucher packets for the initials of the employee who matched vendor invoices with supporting purchase orders and receiving reports, or examine bank reconciliations to make sure that they have been performed on a timely basis.

Generally, the most effective test of controls is reperformance. *Reperformance* can involve any client internal control activity, such as the detailed review of the monthly bank reconciliation by the entity's CFO. For this control, the auditor would follow up on each reconciling item reviewed by the CFO and then reperform each of the mathematical calculations. The key difference between document examination and reperformance is that with the former, audit teams inspect documents for evidence that employees have performed the control activity; reperformance provides direct evidence that the control activity was (or was not) done correctly. Exhibit 5.18 puts control testing within the

EXHIBIT 5.18   **Relevant Assertions about Payroll Cycle Transactions**

Relevant Assertion	Control to Mitigate the Risk of Material Misstatement	Tests of Controls
Occurrence. Payroll and related events that have been recorded have occurred and pertain to the entity.	1. Payroll accounting is separated from personnel and supervision. 2. Labor usage reports are compared to job time tickets or lists of amount of time clocked. 3. Payroll supervisor approved labor usage.	1. Observe separation of duties. 2a. Vouch labor costs to labor reports. 2b. Vouch labor reports to time tickets authorized by management. 3. Examine documentary evidence of supervisor approval.
Completeness. All payroll events that occurred should have been recorded.	1. All documents are prenumbered and numerical sequence reviewed. 2. Labor costs were reviewed by supervisors and compared to budgets. 3. The personnel department notified the payroll department of new hires to include in payroll.	1. Inspect numerical sequence of selected job cost tickets and paychecks. 2. Examine documentary evidence of supervisor review of labor costs. 3. Trace a sample of employees in the personnel file to payroll time logs and the payroll register.
Accuracy. Payroll amounts and related data have been recorded accurately.	1. Payroll entries are reviewed by a person independent of preparation. 2. Budgeted payroll expenses by department are compared to actual expenses.	1. Examine evidence of review and ensure that a party independent of preparation conducted the review. 2. Examine documentary evidence of budget comparison.
Classification. Payroll-related events are recorded in the proper accounts.	1. Job cost sheets are posted weekly and summary journal entries of work-in-process and of work completed prepared monthly. 2. Payroll supervisor is required to approve distribution of payroll expense accounts and to compare payroll costs to budget.	1. Observe that payroll account distribution and job cost sheets agree. 2. Examine supervisor signature on payroll reports. Note evidence of comparison to budget.
Cutoff. Payroll-related events have been recorded in the correct accounting period.	1. Payroll reports are prepared weekly and transmitted to cost accounting.	1. Observe that the date of payroll reports agrees with dates in weekly journal entries.

perspective of the payroll function with examples of specific assertions being supported. Appendix 5A illustrates a sample audit plan for these tests.

Overall, the audit team's choice of which test of controls to use depends on the nature and importance of the control activity being tested. Not surprisingly, certain types of tests produce more evidence about the operating effectiveness of a control activity than others. The following hierarchy lists the type of control tests from the least persuasive (inquiry) to the most persuasive type of evidence:

- Inquiry of client personnel.
- Observation of the control activity being performed.
- Inspection of relevant documentation.
- Reperformance of the control activity.

Importantly, if the control activity has high risk, the audit team needs more persuasive evidence about its operating effectiveness than it would for a lower risk control in order to determine if it is operating effectively. Since gathering more persuasive evidence is typically associated with a higher cost than gathering less persuasive evidence, if the audit team wants to achieve a lower control risk assessment, it will be more costly. This is why it may be more efficient for the auditor to choose not to rely on controls and instead rely on substantive testing procedures to gain assurance for certain significant accounts.

Direction of the Tests of Controls   The tests of controls in Exhibit 5.18 are designed to test the payroll accounting cycle in two directions. One is the *completeness* direction, whereby the audit team is interested in ensuring that all valid hours are included in the entity's payroll; as a result, time logs (which represent valid hours worked) are traced to payroll department files and the payroll register (which represents hours included in the payroll). Exhibit 5.19 shows that the sample for this direction is taken from the population of time logs (including listings of electronic clock-ins).

The purpose of the *occurrence* test of payroll is to ensure that all labor hours included in the payroll (represented by the payroll register) were actually worked (represented by time logs). As a result, entries would be selected from the payroll register and vouched back to the time logs by the auditor. Because payroll provides access to cash, this cycle is highly susceptible to fraudulent activity on the part of an organization's employees. If a fictitious employee were created and added to the payroll, his or her pay could be deposited into another person's account. This is relatively difficult to detect in the era of direct deposit of paychecks.

Reassess the Control Risk

The audit team should evaluate the evidence obtained from an understanding of the client's internal control and from the related tests of control activities. If control risk

EXHIBIT 5.19
Dual-Direction Test of Payroll Controls

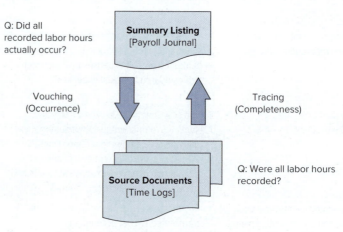

Vouching/Tracing (Payroll Cycle)

Q: Did all recorded labor hours actually occur?

Summary Listing
[Payroll Journal]

Vouching
(Occurrence)

Tracing
(Completeness)

Source Documents
[Time Logs]

Q: Were all labor hours recorded?

(and the related RMM) is assessed very low, the substantive procedures on the relevant assertions for significant account balances can be limited in cost-saving ways. For example, a surprise payroll distribution as a substantive test might be considered unnecessary or the audit team might decide it is appropriate to place considerable reliance on control activities in the payroll system. On the other hand, if tests of control activities reveal weaknesses (e.g., improper separation of duties, inaccurate cost reports, inaccurate tax returns, or lax personnel policies), the RMM would be assessed at higher levels and substantive procedures would need to be increased to lower the risk of failing to detect material misstatements in the financial statements.

Final assessment of control risk (and consequently, the RMM) is complicated. In the detailed sampling module (Module F), you will find explanations of sampling methods for performing tests of controls of the type illustrated in Exhibit 5.18. Further discussion of assessing the RMM (including control risk) is saved for those modules. However, recognize that the final evaluation of an entity's internal control is the assessment of the control risk related to each relevant assertion. These assessments are the auditors' expression of the effectiveness of control activities for preventing, detecting, and correcting specific errors and frauds in management's relevant financial statement assertions.

An assessment of control risk should be coordinated with the final audit plan, which includes the list of **substantive procedures** to detect material misstatements in account balances and financial statement disclosures for each relevant assertion. Note that the reassessment of control risk can go only one direction: upward. If the controls are not functioning as described, they cannot be relied upon. On the other hand, even if weak controls are functioning, they are still weak and do not reduce the risk of material misstatement. There is one exception: You find that you were in error during the understanding of controls phase; there are additional controls about which you were unaware. In that case, lowering control risk could be justified.

Thus far, our discussion of tests of control activities and substantive procedures has assumed that these are easily distinguishable. Be advised, however, that general audit procedures can at times be used as **dual-purpose tests**. That is, a single audit test can produce both control testing and substantive testing evidence and, thus, serve both purposes. For example, a selection of recorded payroll entries could be used to (1) vouch payroll to time cards and (2) calculate the correct dollar amount of payroll. The first procedure provides relevant information about an important control activity. The second provides dollar value information that can help offer substantive evidence to support the account balance in the financial statements.

✓ REVIEW CHECKPOINTS

5.21 What are *tests of control activities*?

5.22 What is the difference between document examination and reperformance when conducting tests of controls?

5.23 What purposes are served by a dual-purpose test?

RESPONSIBILITIES IN PUBLIC COMPANY AUDITS REQUIRED BY PCAOB AUDITING STANDARD NO. 2201

PCAOB Auditing Standard No. 2201 (AS 2201) details the work that the external audit team of public entities must perform to comply with section 404 of Sarbanes–Oxley. The audit team must plan and perform the audit to obtain *reasonable assurance* about whether the entity maintained effective control over financial reporting. The SEC understands reasonable assurance not to be absolute but a "high level of assurance" is expected.

LO 5-5
Describe additional responsibilities for management and auditors of public companies required by Sarbanes–Oxley and PCAOB Auditing Standard No. 2201.

The focus in the professional standard is to determine whether a *material weakness* exists at the *end of the year* being reported on. If a material weakness exists, the entity's internal control over financial reporting cannot be considered effective. For the audit team, this duty entails an increased amount of testing for the internal control system.

According to GAAS, when auditing nonpublic entities, the audit team must obtain an understanding of internal controls to determine the *nature, timing,* and *extent* of further audit procedures to be performed. If the team members plan to rely on controls to reduce substantive procedures, they must test the controls for operating effectiveness. However, if they do not plan to rely on controls, tests of operating effectiveness are not required. Under Sarbanes–Oxley, an audit of the internal control system over *financial reporting* is required. The audit of internal controls must be integrated with the financial statement audit and cannot be performed as a separate engagement. Thus, the procedures related to internal control in an integrated audit performed under AS 2201 are far more extensive than those in a GAAS audit for a nonpublic entity.

Requirements

Much of the initial work, including documenting and testing controls, is done by employees of the client, management, the internal audit staff, and outside parties hired by management. AS 2201 encourages the audit team to use the work of internal auditors and others, but the audit team members must evaluate the internal auditors' *competence* and *objectivity* and must perform some tests of their work. For more risky areas, audit teams should perform more of the work and the assessment of likely sources of misstatement themselves or supervise any others who assist them in the evaluation.

Another important difference between AS 2201 internal control audits and GAAS financial statement audits is that the audit of internal control is *as of the end of the fiscal year,* whereas, for audits of the financial statements, the audit team must understand and evaluate internal control for the *entire period* to determine its effect on the nature, timing, and extent of further audit procedures.

	Internal Control Audit	**Financial Statement Audit**
Scope	Test each relevant control activity each year	Test relevant control activities if relying on them
Reporting	Opinion on the effectiveness of internal control	No opinion on internal control
Timing	Evaluate effectiveness of internal control as of the fiscal year-end	Evaluate effectiveness of internal control throughout the fiscal year

AS 2201 emphasizes the use of a six-step audit process that is designed to evaluate the effectiveness of the internal control system over financial reporting:

1. *Planning the engagement.* The audit team must evaluate controls for all *relevant assertions* and for all *significant* accounts or disclosures. Thus, significant accounts, locations, and assertions must be identified. A difficult decision in auditing controls of global organizations is determining which locations are significant and must be visited. Each location is evaluated based on size, risks, and whether risks are mitigated by entitywide controls. The key to determining whether an account, location, or assertion is significant is whether there is more than a remote possibility that a material misstatement could be associated with it. Just as *control risk* is used to determine the nature, timing, and extent of further audit procedures, *inherent risk* is used to determine the nature, timing, and extent of tests of controls.

2. *Using a top-down approach.* As mentioned earlier, the top-down approach focuses on the threats to the integrity of the external financial reporting process. The audit team's first step in gaining an understanding of the client's internal control system should focus on entity-level controls (ELCs) because they can have a pervasive impact on control activities at the process, transaction, or application level. The team next moves down to the

EXHIBIT 5.20
Top-Down Process

Top-Down Process

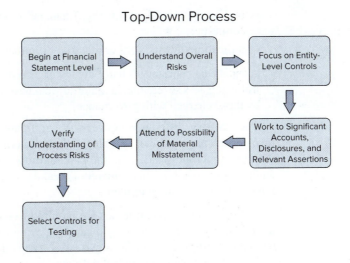

significant accounts and disclosures and their *relevant* assertions. By relevant, we mean that the assertion has a reasonable possibility of containing a material misstatement. The audit team is required to understand the internal control process over financial reporting. This aspect of the standard emphasizes performing a *walkthrough* of the internal control process by the audit team members. The top-down approach recommended in AS 2201 is illustrated in Exhibit 5.20.

3. *Testing controls.* After identifying significant controls over financial reporting in the previous step, the audit team decides which controls to test. The evaluation and testing for each assertion must be performed on an annual basis. After an understanding of internal controls is gained through inquiry, document examination, and observation, the controls are evaluated for the possibility that they would not prevent or detect a misstatement. The tests of *operating effectiveness* are similar to a test of controls discussed previously. A sample of transactions is examined using inquiry, observation, document examination, and reperformance. The more risk associated with a control, the more persuasive evidence is required for testing. Tests of controls are not performed if the internal control system design is not considered effective. Only the control activities for each relevant assertion that the auditor is relying on to mitigate the risk of material misstatement need to be tested.

4. *Evaluating identified deficiencies.* An **internal control deficiency**—whether resulting from a design or an operating deficiency—exists when either the design or the operation of the control under consideration does not allow the entity's management or employees to detect or prevent misstatements in a timely fashion. A *design deficiency* is a problem relating to either a necessary control that is missing or an existing control that is so poorly designed that it fails to satisfy the control's objective. An *operating deficiency,* on the other hand, occurs when a properly designed control is either ignored or inappropriately applied (possibly because employees are poorly trained). More serious internal control deficiencies can be categorized into one of two groups—significant deficiencies or material weaknesses—depending on their severity.

- A **material weakness** in internal control is defined as a deficiency, or combination of deficiencies, that results in a *reasonable possibility* that a *material misstatement* would not be prevented or detected on a timely basis. The following circumstances should be regarded as strong indicators that a material weakness exists:

  - Restatement of previously issued financial statements to reflect the correction of a material misstatement.
  - Evidence of material misstatements (identified by the audit team) that were not prevented or detected by the client's internal controls.

- Ineffective oversight of the financial reporting process by the entity's audit committee.
- Indication of fraud (either material or immaterial) by senior management.
- A **significant deficiency** is a deficiency or a combination of deficiencies in internal control that is less severe than a material weakness yet important enough to merit attention by those charged with governance.

The primary difference between a significant deficiency and a material weakness involves the *magnitude* of the potential misstatement that could occur and would not be detected on a timely basis. As the potential misstatement reaches overall materiality, an auditor may conclude that a material weakness exists. The final conclusion is always a matter of professional judgment.

5. *Wrapping up.* Audit teams are required to issue an opinion on the effectiveness of internal controls. They do so by evaluating evidence obtained from all sources, including the team's testing of controls, any misstatements detected during the financial statement audit, and any identified control deficiencies and material weaknesses. Audit teams then form an opinion on the effectiveness of internal control over financial reporting. Audit teams can issue one of three types of opinions on internal controls:

- *Unqualified.* No material weaknesses exist.
- *Disclaimer of opinion.* The audit team cannot perform all of the procedures considered necessary and is unable to determine whether material weaknesses exist.
- *Adverse opinion.* One or more material weaknesses exist.

Note that because the opinion on internal controls is as of the end of the fiscal year, the entity may be able to correct or remediate deficiencies or weaknesses after they have been detected. However, the audit team must have sufficient time to test the design effectiveness and operating effectiveness of the remediated control before providing an unqualified opinion.[7]

In addition to expressing an opinion on the effectiveness of the entity's internal control over financial reporting, the audit team also should evaluate the completeness and presentation of **management's annual report on internal control over financial reporting**. Among other factors, the audit team also must obtain written representations from management that explicitly acknowledges:

- It is responsible for effective internal control over financial reporting.
- It has evaluated the effectiveness of the internal control over financial reporting.
- It has disclosed all internal control deficiencies and frauds to the audit team.

6. *Reporting on internal control.* The next step in the process is reporting on internal control over financial reporting. For the auditors' report on internal control, two options are available. One option is to have two separate reports: one on the fairness of the entity's financial statements (presented earlier in Chapter 2) and a separate report on internal control over financial reporting. Each report would be separately titled, dated (although using the same date), and signed. The auditors' separate report on internal control is discussed in detail in the following section. The second option is to prepare a *combined report* that expresses one opinion on the financial statements and a second on the effectiveness of internal control over financial reporting. An example of a combined auditors' report on internal control over financial reporting and financial statements is shown in Chapter 12.

---

[7]Clients may request auditors to report separately on the elimination of material weaknesses. Guidance on preparing such a report is provided by PCAOB's *AS 4.*

AUDITING INSIGHT   The Cost of Section 404

An opinion piece published by *The Wall Street Journal* blames the excessive costs associated with the Sarbanes–Oxley Act of 2002 for the significant reduction in initial public offerings (IPOs) in recent years. In particular, the piece argues that "the pace of U.S. initial public offerings has never recovered since the enactment of Sarbox," citing that prior to the enactment, there were three times as many IPOs in the first half of the 1990s as there have been since the legislation was enacted. It specifically highlights that section 404 is primarily to blame, "chewing up more than $2.3 million each year in direct compliance costs at the average public company." Of course, in 2009, the number of financial statement restatements fell for the third consecutive year, so there appears to be some benefit to Sarbanes–Oxley as well.

Sources: "Stock Exchanges and Sarbox," *The Wall Street Journal,* May 6, 2011, p. A14; "Restatements on the Decline," *CFO.com*, March 4, 2010.

☑ REVIEW CHECKPOINTS

5.24 What is management's responsibility for reporting on internal control over financial reporting?

5.25 What steps do audit teams follow in examining internal control over financial reporting?

5.26 What are (a) an *internal control deficiency,* (b) a *significant deficiency,* and (c) a *material weakness*?

5.27 What options are available to the auditor for presenting reports on the entity's financial statements and internal control over financial reporting?

INTERNAL CONTROL COMMUNICATIONS

LO 5-6
Explain the communication of internal control deficiencies to those charged with governance, such as the audit committee and other key management personnel.

Whether auditing a nonpublic entity under GAAS or a public entity in an examination conducted under PCAOB standards, the audit team must communicate significant deficiencies and material weaknesses in internal control that come to their attention during the performance of the audit. Auditors' communications of significant deficiencies and material weaknesses are intended to help management carry out its responsibilities for internal control monitoring and change. However, external auditors' observations and recommendations are usually limited to external financial reporting matters.

For public entities, the auditors' report must be in writing and presented to those in charge of governance (usually the audit committee) before their report on internal control over financial reporting is issued to the public. The report is to be addressed to management, the board of directors, or the audit committee. See Exhibit 5.21 for an illustration of such a report. In addition, all deficiencies noted must be communicated in writing to management.

If the audit team members do not identify any significant deficiencies, they should not issue a report stating that "no significant deficiencies were noted during the audit." Doing so might be misleading because an integrated audit is not designed to detect all significant deficiencies. A manager receiving such a report could conclude (incorrectly) that the audit team is stating positively that the entity has no internal control problems.

Audit teams often issue another type of report to management called a *management letter.* This letter may contain commentary and suggestions on a variety of matters in addition to internal control matters. Examples include issues identified during the audit related to operational and administrative efficiency, business strategy, and profit-making possibilities. Auditing standards do not require management letters, but they represent a type of value-added management advice rendered as part of an audit.

EXHIBIT 5.21
Internal Control Letter

Michael Scarn, LLP, CPAs
Scranton, PA

March 7, 2018

Board of Directors
Dunder-Mifflin Inc.
Scantron, ME

In planning and performing our audit of the financial statements of Dunder-Mifflin Inc. for the year ended December 31, 2017, we considered its internal control in order to determine our audit procedures for the purpose of expressing our opinion on the financial statements as well as the effectiveness of the company's internal control over financial reporting. Our consideration of internal control would not necessarily disclose all deficiencies in internal control that might be significant deficiencies. However, we noted a certain matter involving the internal control and its operation that we consider to be a significant deficiency under standards established by the Public Company Accounting Oversight Board. A significant deficiency is a deficiency, or a combination of deficiencies, in internal control that is less severe than a material weakness, yet important enough to merit attention by those charged with governance.

   The matter noted is that shipping personnel have both transaction-initiation and alteration authority as well as custody of inventory assets. If invoice/shipping copy documents are altered to show a shipment of smaller quantities than actually shipped, customers or accomplices can receive your products without charge. The sales revenue and accounts receivable could be understated, and the inventory could be overstated. This deficiency caused us to spend more time auditing your inventory quantities.

   A material weakness in internal control is defined as a deficiency, or combination of deficiencies, that results in a reasonable possibility that a material misstatement would not be prevented or detected on a timely basis. We do not believe that the significant deficiency described above is a material weakness.

   This report is intended solely for the information and use of the board of directors and its audit committee, and is not intended to be, and should not be, used by anyone other than these specified parties.

Respectfully yours,

Michael Scarn, LLP, CPAs

✅ REVIEW CHECKPOINTS

5.28 What reports (other than auditors' report) on internal control do audit teams give to an entity's management, board of directors, or audit committee?

Summary

The purposes of the audit team's evaluation of internal control are to assess the control risk (as part of the overall assessment of the RMM) in order to make the substantive audit plan and to report control deficiencies to management and the board of directors. The PCAOB's AS 2201 defines additional responsibilities for management and public accounting firms' reports on internal control stipulated by the Sarbanes–Oxley Act.

   Internal control consists of five components: control environment, risk assessment, information and communication system, control activities, and monitoring of the control system. The auditor is required to gain an understanding of each of these components and to document this understanding in the audit files. The control environment and management's risk assessment are explained in terms of understanding the client's business. Elements of the accounting system are explained in conjunction with control activities designed to prevent, detect, and correct misstatements that occur in transactions. Documentation of an entity's internal control system is accomplished through the use of questionnaires, flowcharts, and narratives.

   Internal control is assessed in a top-down manner by which audit teams first identify accounts that may contain significant risks of material misstatement. Audit teams then identify which relevant assertions may be misstated. After determining "what can go wrong," audit teams examine entity-level controls that might mitigate the risk of material misstatement. Finally, audit teams identify transaction level controls that would mitigate any residual risks. If the audit team relies on controls, it must test the controls to ensure they are operating effectively. Where controls are not in place to reduce the risk, or if testing the controls would not be cost effective, substantive tests are designed to identify any material misstatements.

It is important to distinguish the "client's control activities" from the "audit team's tests of controls." Control activities are part of the internal control designed and operated by the entity. The audit team's procedures are the audit team's own evidence-gathering work performed to obtain evidence about the client's control activities.

Sarbanes–Oxley requires that management of public companies report on their assessments of the effectiveness of their financial reporting controls and that audit teams provide opinions on the controls over financial reporting. This may involve more extensive procedures than those required by GAAS.

Key Terms

adverse opinion on internal control over financial reporting: The opinion issued when the company has a material weakness and has not maintained an effective internal control over financial reporting.

audit committee: A subcommittee of the board of directors that is generally composed of three to six "outside" members of the organization's board of directors.

auditors' report on internal control over financial reporting: A report required by the Sarbanes–Oxley Act that provides an opinion on the effectiveness of the entity's internal control over financial reporting.

business risks: Those factors, events, and conditions that could prevent the organization from achieving its business objectives.

control activities: The specific actions taken by a client's management and employees to help ensure that management directives are carried out.

control risk: The likelihood that the client's internal control policies and procedures fail to prevent or detect a material misstatement.

design effectiveness: A condition expressing whether controls would be expected to prevent or detect errors or fraud that could result in a material misstatement in the financial statements.

detective controls: The activities that detect misstatements after they occur.

disclaimer of opinion on internal control over financial reporting: The report issued when auditors cannot provide assurance on the effectiveness of internal control over financial reporting; issued when a significant scope limitation exists.

dual-purpose test: An audit procedure used as both a test of controls and a substantive test.

enterprise risk management (ERM): A process effected by an entity's board of directors, management, and other personnel applied in strategy setting and across the enterprise that is designed to identify potential events that may affect the entity and to manage risks to be within its risk appetite to provide reasonable assurance regarding the achievement of entity objectives.

entity-level controls: The controls that are pervasive to the financial statements taken as a whole.

flowchart: The audit documentation that provides a visual display of the accounting system and control activities in an entity's internal control system.

information system: An entity's system, usually built on some type of technological platform that has been designed to produce the information necessary for the entity to operate and control its business operations.

integrated audit process: The term used to describe an audit process that is designed to provide an opinion on both the financial statements and the internal control system of an entity.

internal control: A process, effected by an entity's board of directors, management, and other personnel, designed to provide reasonable assurance regarding the achievement of objectives in the reliability of financial reporting, the effectiveness and efficiency of operations, and compliance with applicable laws and regulations.

internal control deficiency: A condition that exists when the design or operation of a control does not allow the entity's management or employees to detect or prevent misstatements in a timely fashion.

internal control questionnaire: The audit documentation that uses a checklist of internal control–related questions to gain and document an understanding of the client's internal control.

management's annual report on internal control over financial reporting: A report required by the Sarbanes–Oxley Act that states that management is responsible for establishing and maintaining adequate internal control over financial reporting, identifies the framework management uses to evaluate the effectiveness of the entity's internal control, and provides management's assessment of the effectiveness of the entity's internal control.

material weakness: A deficiency or combination of deficiencies that results in a reasonable possibility that a material misstatement would not be prevented or detected on a timely basis.

narrative description: The audit documentation that describes the environmental elements, the accounting system, and the control activities in an entity's internal control.

operating effectiveness: Description of a condition expressing whether a control is operating as designed and whether the person performing the control possesses the necessary authority and qualifications to perform the control effectively.

preventive controls: The activities that prevent misstatements before they occur.

reasonable assurance: The concept that recognizes that the costs of control activities should not exceed the benefits that are expected from the control activities.

significant deficiency: A deficiency or a combination of deficiencies in internal control that is less severe than a material weakness yet important enough to merit attention by those charged with governance.

substantive procedures: The detailed audit and analytical procedures designed to detect material misstatements in account balances and footnote disclosures.

transaction-level controls: The controls that relate to specific classes of transactions, account balances, and disclosures.

unqualified opinion on internal control over financial reporting: The report issued when no material weaknesses in internal control over financial reporting are identified and no scope limitations on the audit of internal control exist.

walkthrough: The tracing of one or more transactions through the audit trail from initiation of the transaction to its inclusion in the financial statements.

Multiple-Choice Questions for Practice and Review

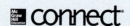 All applicable Exercises and Problems are available with *Connect*.

LO 5-3

5.33 The most important fundamental component of an entity's internal control is
 a. Effectiveness and efficiency of operations.
 b. People who operate the control system.
 c. Reliability of financial reporting.
 d. Compliance with applicable laws and regulations.

LO 5-4

5.34 The primary purpose for obtaining an understanding of a nonpublic audit client's internal control is to
 a. Provide a basis for making constructive suggestions in a management letter.
 b. Determine the nature, timing, and extent of further audit tests to be performed.
 c. Provide the rationale for the inherent risk assessment at the financial statement assertion level.
 d. Provide information for a communication of internal control–related matters to management.

LO 5-4

5.35 Effectiveness of audit procedures would be reduced by
 a. Selecting larger sample sizes for audit.
 b. Performing audit procedures at the fiscal year-end date as opposed to the interim period.
 c. Deciding to obtain external evidence instead of internal evidence.
 d. Performing procedures during the interim period as opposed to at the fiscal year-end date.

LO 5-5

5.36 According to the PCAOB, during the audit of internal controls for an issuer, the ultimate objective of testing the design effectiveness of internal controls is to
 a. Determine whether the company's controls are processing company data effectively.
 b. Determine that the company's controls will satisfy the company's control objectives and can effectively prevent or detect errors or fraud that could result in material misstatements, if they operate as prescribed.
 c. Determine that the company's employees are processing the controls according to the policy and procedures manuals at the company.
 d. None of the above.

LO 5-4

5.37 To test the operating effectiveness of a control, an audit team might use a combination of each of the following tests *except* for
a. Inquiry of client personnel.
b. Observation of company operations.
c. Confirmation of balances.
d. Inspection of documentation.

LO 5-4

5.38 Which of the following is a preventive control?
a. Reconciliation of a bank account.
b. Recalculation of a sample of payroll entries by internal auditors.
c. Separation of duties between the payroll and personnel departments.
d. Detailed fluctuation analysis completed by the CFO for revenue.

LO 5-4

5.39 In most audits of large entities, control risk assessment contributes to audit efficiency, which means that
a. The cost of substantive procedures will exceed the cost of control evaluation work.
b. Auditors will be able to reduce the cost of substantive procedures by an amount more than the control evaluation costs.
c. The cost of control evaluation work will exceed the cost of substantive procedures.
d. Auditors will be able to reduce the cost of substantive procedures by an amount less than the cost of tests of controls.

LO 5-4

5.40 Which of the following is a device designed to help the audit team obtain evidence about the accounting and control activities of an audit client?
a. A narrative memorandum describing the control system.
b. An internal control questionnaire.
c. A flowchart of the documents and procedures used by the company.
d. All of the above.

LO 5-4

5.41 Tests of controls in a GAAS audit are required for
a. Obtaining evidence about the financial statement assertions.
b. Accomplishing control over the occurrence of recorded transactions.
c. Applying analytical procedures to financial statement balances.
d. Obtaining evidence about the operating effectiveness of client control activities.

LO 5-4

5.42 A transaction-level internal control activity is best described as
a. An action taken by auditors to obtain evidence.
b. An action taken by client personnel for the purpose of preventing, detecting, and correcting errors and frauds in transactions to eliminate or mitigate risks identified by the company.
c. A method for recording, summarizing, and reporting financial information.
d. The functioning of the board of directors in support of its audit committee.

LO 5-5

5.43 When planning the audit of internal controls for an issuer, the audit team should
a. Identify significant accounts, locations, and assertions.
b. Conduct a walkthrough of the internal control process.
c. Make inquiries of employees regarding the existence of control activities.
d. Reperform control activities performed by client employees to determine their effectiveness.

LO 5-5

5.44 A material weakness is a situation in which
a. It is probable that an immaterial financial statement misstatement would not be detected on a timely basis.
b. There is a remote likelihood that a material misstatement would be detected on a timely basis.
c. It is reasonably possible that a material misstatement would not be detected on a timely basis.
d. It is reasonably possible that an immaterial misstatement would not be detected on a timely basis.

LO 5-5

5.45 When completing the audit of internal controls for an issuer, the severity of an internal control deficiency depends on

a. Whether there is a reasonable possibility that the company's controls will fail to prevent or detect a misstatement of an account balance or disclosure.

b. Whether a misstatement has actually occurred as a result of the deficiency.

c. The magnitude of the potential misstatement resulting from the deficiency or the deficiencies.

d. Both a and c are correct.

e. All of the above are correct.

LO 5-5

5.46 Which of the following does *not* accurately summarize auditors' requirements regarding internal control?

	Public Entity	Nonpublic Entity
a. Understanding	Yes	Yes
b. Documenting	Yes	Yes
c. Evaluating control risk	Yes	Yes
d. Test controls	Yes	Yes

LO 5-5

5.47 When completing the audit of internal controls for a public company, the PCAOB requires auditors to audit internal controls over

a. Operations.

b. Compliance with regulations.

c. Financial reporting.

d. All of the above.

LO 5-5

5.48 When completing the audit of internal controls for a public company, AS 2201 requires auditors to report on

Management's Report on Internal Control	An Audit of Internal Control
a. No	No
b. Yes	No
c. No	Yes
d. Yes	Yes

LO 5-5

5.49 When completing the audit of internal controls for a public company, AS 2201 requires auditors to test

a. Operating effectiveness only.

b. Design effectiveness only.

c. Both operating and design effectiveness.

d. Neither operating nor design effectiveness

LO 5-5

5.50 Which of the following would probably *not* be considered an indication of a material weakness?

a. Evidence of a material misstatement.

b. Ineffective oversight by the audit committee.

c. Immaterial fraud committed by senior management.

d. Overproduction by the manufacturing plant.

LO 5-8

5.51 Which report would *not* be appropriate for a public accounting firm to provide on financial reporting controls?

a. Unqualified—no material weaknesses found.

b. Disclaimer of opinion—unable to perform all necessary procedures.

c. Disclaimer of opinion—significant deficiencies exist.

d. Adverse—material weaknesses exist.

LO 5-4

5.52 The purpose of separating the duties of hiring personnel and distributing payroll checks is to separate the
  a. Authorization of transactions from the custody of related assets.
  b. Operational responsibility from the record-keeping responsibility.
  c. Human resources function from the controllership function.
  d. Administrative controls from the internal accounting controls.

(AICPA adapted)

LO 5-7

5.53 Which of the following statements is *not* true with respect to the auditors' report on internal control over financial reporting?
  a. The report will be dated as of the date of the financial statements.
  b. The report will express an opinion on the effectiveness of internal control over financial reporting.
  c. The auditor will issue an adverse opinion if one or more material weaknesses exist.
  d. The report may be presented with the report on the entity's financial statements as a combined report.

(AICPA adapted)

LO 5-8

5.54 If the auditors encounter a significant scope limitation in evaluating a public company's internal control over financial reporting, which of the following types of opinions on the effectiveness of the company's internal control over financial reporting would be appropriate?
  a. Unqualified opinion or adverse opinion.
  b. Qualified opinion or adverse opinion.
  c. Unqualified opinion or disclaimer of opinion.
  d. Disclaimer of opinion.

LO 5-7

5.55 Which of the following information would be included in the introductory paragraph of the auditors' report on internal control over financial reporting if the report is presented separately from the auditors' report on the entity's financial statements?
  a. The fact that the auditors conducted an audit of the entity's financial statements.
  b. The definition of a material weakness in internal control over financial reporting.
  c. Statements identifying the responsibility of the auditors and management for internal control over financial reporting.
  d. A reference to the auditors' report and opinion on the entity's financial statements.

LO 5-4

5.56 If the auditor plans to assess control risk at less than the maximum and rely on controls, and the nature, timing, and extent of further audit procedures are based on that lower assessment, the auditor must
  a. Obtain evidence that the controls selected for testing are designed effectively and operated effectively during the entire period of reliance.
  b. Assess control risk at less than the maximum for all relevant assertions.
  c. Perform only substantive procedures.
  d. Provide additional examples of responses to assessed fraud risks relating to fraudulent financial reporting.

LO 5-5

5.57 When testing a control activity's operating effectiveness, procedures the auditor performs to test operating effectiveness would likely include
  a. Inquiry of appropriate personnel.
  b. Reading over the company's code of conduct.
  c. Reperformance of the control activity.
  d. Both a and c are correct.

LO 5-5

5.58 Matters that could affect the necessary extent of testing for a control activity as it related to the degree of auditor reliance on a control activity would *not* include the following:
  a. The frequency of the performance of the control by the company during the period being audited.
  b. The length of time that the auditor is planning to rely on the operating efficiency of the control activity.
  c. The expected rate of deviation for a control activity.
  d. The relevance and reliability of the audit evidence to be obtained to test the operating effectiveness of a control activity.

LO 5-4

5.59 The auditor should assess control risk for each relevant assertion by evaluating the evidence obtained from all sources, including

a. The auditor's testing of controls for the audit of internal control on a public company.

b. Misstatements detected during the financial statement audit.

c. Any control deficiencies identified during the audit.

d. All of the above.

LO 5-5

5.60 Once the auditor detects a control deficiency, which of the following steps must he or she take first?

a. Perform tests of other controls related to the same assertion as the control deemed ineffective.

b. Evaluate the severity of the deficiency on the auditor's control risk assessment for that assertion.

c. Modify the planned substantive procedures as a result of the deficiency.

d. Test the deficient control, assuming a maximum level of risk.

Exercises and Problems

 All applicable Exercises and Problems are available with *Connect.*

LO 5-2

5.61 **Internal Control Audit Standards.** Auditors are required to obtain a sufficient understanding of each component of a client's internal control. This understanding is used to assess control risk and plan the audit of the client's financial statements.

Required:

a. For what purposes should an auditors' understanding of the internal control components be used in planning an audit?

b. What is required for an audit team to assess control risk below the maximum level?

c. What should an audit team consider when seeking to reduce the planned assessed level of control risk below the maximum?

d. What are the documentation requirements concerning a client's internal control components and the assessed level of control risk?

(AICPA adapted)

LO 5-3

5.62 **Separation of Duties.** Your small business client, Phillip's Computer Repair Shop, is experiencing financial difficulties and has to lay off one of its four employees in the accounting area. Phillip has asked you to determine what duties should be assigned to the three remaining employees—Abigail, Bryan, and Chris—to maintain the best separation of duties.

Required:

Assign the following 10 duties to each of the three employees.

a. Reconcile bank statement.

b. Open mail and list checks.

c. Prepare checks for Phillip's signature.

d. Prepare payroll checks.

e. Maintain personnel records.

f. Prepare deposit and take to bank.

g. Maintain petty cash.

h. Maintain accounts receivable records.

i. Maintain general ledger.

j. Reconcile accounts receivable records to general ledger account.

LO 5-4

5.63 **Types of Audit Tests.** Indicate whether each of the following audit procedures is a test of controls, a substantive test, or a dual-purpose test. Next, indicate the financial statement assertion most closely related to each audit procedure.

Required:

    a. Vouch recorded sales invoices to supporting shipping documents.

    b. Inspect recorded sales invoices for credit approval.

    c. Vouch recorded sales invoices prices to the approved price list.

    d. Send confirmations to all customers regarding accounts receivable.

    e. Recalculate the arithmetic accuracy of the recorded sales invoices.

    f. Compare the shipment date of recorded sales invoices with the invoice record date.

    g. Trace recorded sales invoices to posting in the general ledger control account and in the correct customer's account.

    h. Select a sample of shipping documents from the shipping department file and trace shipments to recorded sales invoices.

    i. Scan recorded sales invoices and shipping documents for missing numbers in sequence.

    j. Vouch sales invoices and shipping documents.

    k. Evaluate the adequacy of the allowance for doubtful accounts.

    l. Obtain financial statements or credit reports on large past due accounts and inquire of the credit manager about collections.

    m. Calculate an estimate of the allowance for doubtful accounts using prior relations of write-offs and sales.

LO 5-5

5.64 **Impact of Sarbanes–Oxley Act.**   Your long-time client, Central Office Supply, has been rapidly expanding, and the board of directors is considering taking the company public. CEO Terry Puckett has heard that costs of operating a public company have increased significantly as a result of the Sarbanes–Oxley Act. Puckett is particularly concerned with reports that audit fees have doubled because of internal control provisions of the act and PCAOB *Auditing Standard No. 2201.* Puckett has asked you to explain the possible effects on the audit of complying with the requirements of Sarbanes–Oxley.

Required:

Draft a letter to Puckett outlining the changes in the company's responsibilities for internal control and changes in the audit due to Sarbanes–Oxley and PCAOB *Auditing Standard No. 2201.*

LO 5-4

5.65 **Internal Control Questionnaire Items: Assertions, Tests of Controls, and Possible Errors or Frauds.**   Following is a selection of items from the payroll processing internal control questionnaire in Exhibit 5.15.

    1. Are names of terminated employees reported in writing to the payroll department?

    2. Are authorizations for deductions signed by the employee on file?

    3. Is there a timekeeping department (function) independent of the payroll department?

    4. Are timekeeping and cost accounting records (such as hours, dollars) reconciled with payroll department calculations of hours and wages?

Required:

For each of the four preceding questions:

    a. Identify the assertion to which the question applies.

    b. Specify one test of controls an auditor could use to determine whether the control was operating effectively.

    c. Provide an example of an error or fraud that could occur if the control were absent or ineffective.

    d. Identify a substantive auditing procedure that could detect errors or frauds that could result from the absence or ineffectiveness of the control items.

LO 5-4

5.66 **Obtaining a "Sufficient" Understanding of Internal Control.**   The 12 partners of a regional public accounting firm met in special session to discuss audit engagement efficiency. Jones spoke up, saying, "We all certainly appreciate the firmwide policies set up by Martin and Smith, especially in connection with the audits of the large clients that have come our way recently. Their experience with a large public accounting firm has helped build our practice. But I think the standard policy of conducting reviews and tests of internal control on all audits is raising our costs too much. We can't charge our smaller clients fees for all of the time the staff spends on this work. I would like to propose that we give engagement partners discretion to decide whether to do a lot of work on assessing control risk. I may be old-fashioned, but I think I can finish a competent audit without it." Discussion on the subject continued but ended when Martin said, with some emotion, "But we can't disregard generally accepted auditing standards like Jones proposes!"

Required:

What do you think of Jones's proposal and Martin's view of the issue? Discuss.

LO 5-4

5.67 **Fraud Opportunities.** Simon Blank Construction Company has two divisions. The president (Chris Simon) manages the roofing division. Simon delegated authority and responsibility for management of the modular manufacturing division to John Gault. The company has a competent accounting staff and a full-time internal auditor. Unlike Simon's procedures, however, Gault and his secretary handle all bids for manufacturing jobs, purchase all materials without competitive bids, control the physical inventory of materials, contract for shipping by truck, supervise the construction activity, bill the customer when the job is finished, approve all bid changes, and collect the payment from the customer. With Simon's tacit approval, Gault has asked the internal auditor not to interfere with his busy schedule.

Required:

Discuss this situation in terms of internal control and identify frauds that could occur.

LO 5-4

5.68 **Internal Control Questionnaire Items: Errors That Could Occur from Control Weaknesses.** Refer to the internal control questionnaire on a payroll system (Exhibit 5.15).

a. Assume that the answer to each question is no. Prepare a table matching the questions to errors or frauds that could occur because of the absence of the control. Your column headings should be

Question	Possible Error or Fraud Due to Weakness

b. Which controls are preventive controls and which are detective?

LO 5-7

5.69 **Reports on Internal Control over Financial Reporting (Report Modifications).** For each of the following situations, describe how the auditors' report on internal control over financial reporting would be modified from the standard, unqualified report. Do *not* write the actual reports.

a. The auditors have identified a material weakness in the processing of sales transactions.

b. Because a relatively short period of time has passed since a control weakness was remediated, the auditors do not believe that sufficient evidence can be obtained with respect to the operating effectiveness of the entity's internal control over financial reporting.

c. Component auditors have audited a significant component of the group financial statements, including internal control over financial reporting relating to that component. They did not find a material weakness in internal control, and the group auditor believes the component auditor's work can be relied on.

d. The auditors believe that the entity's management has not adequately disclosed a material weakness in its internal control over financial reporting.

LO 5-3

5.70 **Role of a Board of Directors in Internal Control.** Assume that the local newspaper just ran the following headline and article: *"Audit Results: Airport executives from Kentucky racked up $500K in lavish expenses, concert tickets, and even gentlemen's club tabs"*

LEXINGTON, Ky. (AP)—A small commercial airport in Kentucky—and the taxpayers who support it—picked up top executives' tabs in recent years for Hannah Montana concert tickets, Nintendo Wii video game bundles and even a $4,400 gentlemen club check, according to a state auditor's report.

The report released Wednesday outlines indulgences ranging from pricey electronics and exercise equipment to lavish meals and champagne. In three years, officials tallied more than

$500,000 in questionable personal expenses. [Author's note: General fund expenses were approximately $10,000,000 annually.]

Kentucky Auditor Crit Luallen said the former executive director at Lexington's **Blue Grass Airport** created a culture of wasteful spending so vast, employees sometimes were paid twice for the same expense and used airport credit cards as if they were personal checkbooks.

"I don't think we have ever seen an audit where so many different individuals involved in the management of a public agency abused the trust with such arrogance and lack of ethical standards," she said.

Luallen says she has forwarded the case to the Kentucky attorney general, the U.S. attorney's office, and the FBI.

Although the audit only covered the past three years, it does refer to one of the more glaring examples reported by the *Herald-Leader:* a $4,400 charge Michael Gobb and two other directors incurred at a Dallas strip club in 2004.

The charge, which appeared on the credit card statement of the airport's director of planning, was listed as going to Millennium Restaurant. The word "marketing" was handwritten next to the amount. The Associated Press obtained that receipt and others through an open records request.

The audit found that airport employees also used the coffers for tuxedos and other expensive clothing; more than 400 DVDs—many of them currently missing—for the internal airport library; $14,000 in holiday hams given out as gifts; and $7,400 for a NASCAR driving experience excursion for staff described as "team building."

More than 92 percent of the things Gobb charged to his airport card lacked proper documentation, Luallen said.

While Luallen acknowledged that Gobb was responsible for the free-spending culture, she said the board and its public accounting firm should have supervised the airport more closely.

Source: Excerpted from *Ky. Airport Execs Racked Up Lavish Expenses,* Jeffrey McMurray, Associated Press, February 26, 2009.

Required:

a. Discuss the role of the board of directors in monitoring the behavior of a chief executive officer.

b. If the chief executive officer has subordinates incur expenses that he or she approves, how can the board prevent abuse?

c. Should external auditors be expected to detect abuses such as these?

d. How should the use of credit cards be controlled?

LO 5-7

5.71 **Reports on Internal Control over Financial Reporting (Identify Report Deficiencies).** Sorrell, CPA, is auditing the financial statements of Van Dyke as of December 31, 2017. Sorrell's substantive procedures and other tests indicated that Van Dyke's financial statements were prepared in accordance with generally accepted accounting principles and, accordingly, Sorrell expressed an unqualified opinion on those financial statements. Because Van Dyke's securities are registered with the Securities and Exchange Commission, Van Dyke is subject to the reporting requirements of AS 2201. During its assessment of internal control over financial reporting, Van Dyke's management identified material weaknesses related to (1) the method of accounting for sales commissions and (2) separation of duties related to purchase transactions. Sorrell was able to gather sufficient evidence and did not encounter limitations with respect to the evaluation of Van Dyke's internal control over financial reporting. Sorrell prepared the following draft report on Van Dyke's internal control over financial reporting:

Required:

Identify the deficiencies in the audit report drafted by Sorrell. Group the deficiencies by paragraph and in the order in which they appear. Do not rewrite the report. Cite the relevant sections from the professional standards.

Report of Independent Registered Public Accounting Firm

To the Board of Directors and Shareholders of Van Dyke:

We have audited management's assessment, included in the accompanying Management's Report on Internal Control over Financial Reporting, that Van Dyke has not maintained effective internal control over financial reporting as of December 31, 2017, based on criteria established in Internal Control—Integrated Framework issued by the Committee of Sponsoring Organizations of the Treadway Commission (COSO criteria). Van Dyke's management is responsible for assessing the effectiveness of internal control over financial reporting. Our responsibility is to express an opinion on management's assessment and an opinion on the effectiveness of the company's internal control over financial reporting based on our audit.

We conducted our audits in accordance with the standards of the Public Company Accounting Oversight Board (United States). Those standards require that we plan and perform the audit to obtain reasonable assurance about whether effective internal control over financial reporting was maintained in all material respects. Our audit included obtaining an understanding of internal control over financial reporting, evaluating management's assessment, testing and evaluating the design and operating effectiveness of internal control, and performing such other procedures as we considered necessary in the circumstances. We believe that our audit provides a reasonable basis for our opinion.

A company's internal control over financial reporting is a process designed to provide reasonable assurance regarding the reliability of financial reporting and the preparation of financial statements for external purposes in accordance with generally accepted accounting principles. A company's internal control over financial reporting includes those policies and procedures that (1) pertain to the maintenance of records that, in reasonable detail, accurately and fairly reflect the transactions and dispositions of the assets of the company; (2) provide reasonable assurance that transactions are recorded as necessary to permit preparation of financial statements in accordance with generally accepted accounting principles and that receipts and expenditures of the company are being made only in accordance with authorizations of management and directors of the company; and (3) provide reasonable assurance regarding prevention or timely detection of unauthorized acquisition, use, or disposition of the company's assets that could have a material effect on the financial statements.

Two material weaknesses were identified in the design and operation of internal controls over the accounting for sales commissions and separation of duties related to purchases of inventory. Given the nature of the transactions and processes involved and the potential for a misstatement to occur as a result of the internal control deficiencies existing on December 31, 2017, we have concluded that there is more than a remote likelihood that a material misstatement in the annual or interim financial statements would not have been prevented or detected by internal controls.

These material weaknesses were considered in determining the nature, timing, and extent of audit tests applied in our audit of the 2017 financial statements.

In addition to the material weaknesses noted above, we identified several deficiencies in internal control over financial reporting that we deemed to be less significant than a material weakness. These deficiencies have been separately communicated to Van Dyke's management.

In our opinion, because Van Dyke has not maintained an effective internal control over financial reporting, we are unable to evaluate management's assessment that Van Dyke did not maintain effective internal control over financial reporting as of December 31, 2017. Also in our opinion, because of the effect of the material weaknesses described above on the achievement of the objectives of the control criteria, Van Dyke has not maintained, in all material respects, effective internal control over financial reporting as of December 31, 2017, based on the COSO criteria.

We have also audited, in accordance with the standards of the Public Company Accounting Oversight Board (United States), the balance sheets of Van Dyke as of December 31, 2017 and 2016, and related statements of income, shareholders' equity, and cash flows for each of the three years in the period ended December 31, 2017.

Sorrell, CPA

December 31, 2017

LO 5-4

5.72 **Authorization of Credit Tests of Controls — Using IDEA** For this exercise, your client, Bright IDEAs Inc., has provided you with data for two related files, a listing of sales invoices, and a listing of customers with credit limits. To test whether credit authorization controls are in place, the auditor must complete a series of related steps:

1. Import the client's database of sales invoices (pp. 28–45 of the IDEA Workbook).
2. Summarize the Accounts Receivable balance by customer (pp. 67–79 of the IDEA Workbook).
3. Import the client's customer credit limit data into IDEA (pp. 70–79 of the IDEA Workbook).
4. Join the Accounts Receivable balances by customer with the credit limit data (pp. 80–87 of the IDEA Workbook).
5. Extract customers with exceeded credit limits (pp. 88–89).

Required Data Available on *Connect*

- ACC_REC2015.ACCDB
- CUSTOMER.TXT

Required:

Complete the preceding steps and answer the following questions:

a. How many customers were granted credit with no indication that they had any credit limit assigned to them?
b. How many customers exceeded their credit limit?
c. What effects would the findings in parts (a) and (b) have on the auditor's assessment of the risk of material misstatement? What accounts and assertions are most likely influenced by these findings?

Source: C1202 IDEA Data Analysis Workbook: IDEA Version Ten. 2016. CaseWare IDEA, Inc. Toronto, CA.

LO 5-4

5.73 **Identifying Payments to Unauthorized Suppliers—Using IDEA**

For this exercise, your client, BrightIDEAs Inc., has provided you with data for two related files: an accounts payable history file and a supplier master file. To test the authorization of purchases to only legitimate suppliers, the auditor must complete a series of related steps:

- Import the client's database of accounts payable (pp. 98–109 of the IDEA Workbook).
- Import the client's authorized supplier list (pp. 110–113 of the IDEA Workbook).
- Merge the accounts payable and supplier databases (pp. 169–175 of the IDEA Workbook).
- Identify payments to unauthorized suppliers (pp. 175–176 of the IDEA Workbook).
- ACCPAY2015.TXT
- Supplier.xls

Required:

Complete the preceding steps and answer the following questions:

- How many different unauthorized suppliers were paid during the year?
- What was the total dollar amount of the payments to unauthorized suppliers?
- What effects would the findings in parts (a) and (b) have on the auditor's assessment of the risk of material misstatement? What accounts and assertions are most likely influenced by these findings?

Source: C1202 IDEA Data Analysis Workbook: IDEA Version Ten. 2016. CaseWare IDEA, Inc. Toronto, CA.

Appendix 5A

Audit Plan

DUNDER-MIFFLIN INC. Audit Plan for Tests of Controls in the Payroll Cycle 12/31/17		
	Performed By	**Ref.**
1. Observe the separation of duties between the personnel, timekeeping, and payroll departments.		
2. Select a sample of payments from the payroll distribution for the year.		
a. Vouch labor costs to labor reports.		
b. Vouch labor reports to time tickets or computerized listing.		
c. Examine documentary evidence of supervisor review of labor costs.		
d. Examine documentary evidence of supervisor approval.		
3. Account for numerical sequence of selected job cost tickets and paychecks. Trace a sample of employees in the personnel file to payroll department files and the payroll register.		
4. Examine documentary evidence of budget comparison.		
5. Reconcile the payroll account distribution report and the job cost sheets.		
6. Examine supervisor signature on payroll reports. Note evidence of comparison to budget.		

Appendix 5B

LO 5-7
List the major components of the auditors' report on internal control over financial reporting.

AUDITOR REPORTS ON INTERNAL CONTROL OVER FINANCIAL REPORTING

As noted earlier in this chapter, in addition to the auditors' report on the entity's financial statements, Section 404 of Sarbanes-Oxley imposes the following reporting requirements for SEC registrants related to the entity's internal control over financial reporting at the date of the financial statements:

- Management's report on its assessment of the internal control over financial reporting.
- The auditors' report on internal control over financial reporting.

The **auditors' report on internal control over financial reporting** provides an opinion on the effectiveness of the entity's internal control over financial reporting. This opinion is based on tests of the operating effectiveness of the entity's internal control policies and procedures over financial reporting. See Exhibit 5B.1 for an example of a standard, unqualified report.

EXHIBIT 5B.1 Standard Report on Internal Control over Financial Reporting

Title	Report of Independent Registered Public Accounting Firm
Address	To the Board of Directors and Shareholders Dunder-Mifflin Inc.
Introductory paragraph	We have audited Dunder-Mifflin Inc.'s internal control over financial reporting as of December 31, 2017, based on control criteria established in Internal Control—Integrated Framework issued by the Committee of Sponsoring Organizations of the Treadway Commission (COSO). Dunder-Mifflin Inc.'s management is responsible for maintaining effective internal control over financial reporting, and for its assessment of the effectiveness of internal control over financial reporting, included in the accompanying Management's Report on Internal Control over Financial Reporting. Our responsibility is to express an opinion on the company's internal control over financial reporting based on our audits.
Scope paragraph	We conducted our audits in accordance with the standards of the Public Company Accounting Oversight Board (United States). Those standards require that we plan and perform the audits to obtain reasonable assurance about whether effective internal control over financial reporting was maintained in all material respects. Our audit of internal control over financial reporting included obtaining an understanding of internal control over financial reporting, assessing the risk that a material weakness exists, and testing and evaluating the design and operating effectiveness of internal control based on the assessed risk. Our audits also included performing such other procedures as we considered necessary in the circumstances. We believe that our audit provides a reasonable basis for our opinion.
Definition paragraph	A company's internal control over financial reporting is a process designed to provide reasonable assurance regarding the reliability of financial reporting and the preparation of financial statements for external purposes in accordance with generally accepted accounting principles. A company's internal control over financial reporting includes those policies and procedures that (1) pertain to the maintenance of records that, in reasonable detail, accurately and fairly reflect the transactions and dispositions of the assets of the company; (2) provide reasonable assurance that transactions are recorded as necessary to permit preparation of financial statements in accordance with generally accepted accounting principles, and that receipts and expenditures of the company are being made only in accordance with authorizations of management and directors of the company; and (3) provide reasonable assurance regarding prevention or timely detection of unauthorized acquisition, use, or disposition of the company's assets that could have a material effect on the financial statements.
Inherent limitations paragraph	Because of its inherent limitations, internal control over financial reporting may not prevent or detect misstatements. Also, projections of any evaluation of effectiveness to future periods are subject to the risk that controls may become inadequate because of changes in conditions, or that the degree of compliance with the policies or procedures may deteriorate.

(continued)

EXHIBIT 5B.1 *(concluded)*

Title	Report of Independent Registered Public Accounting Firm
Opinion paragraph	In our opinion, Dunder-Mifflin Inc. maintained, in all material respects, effective internal control over financial reporting as of December 31, 2017, based on control criteria established in Internal Control—Integrated Framework issued by the Committee of Sponsoring Organizations of the Treadway Commission (COSO).
Paragraph on financial statement report	We have also audited, in accordance with the standards of the Public Company Accounting Oversight Board (United States), the financial position of Dunder-Mifflin Inc. as of December 31, 2017 and 2016, and the results of its operations and cash flows for each of the three years in the period ended December 31, 2017, and our report dated March 7, 2018, expressed an unmodified opinion thereon.
Signature	*Michael Scarn, LLP, CPAs* Scranton, PA
Date	March 7, 2018

As the exhibit indicates, the auditors' report includes the following key components:

- A title that includes the word *independent.*
- Statements regarding the responsibility of the auditors and management with respect to the assessment and evaluation of internal control as well as the title of management's report on internal control over financial reporting.
- A paragraph indicating that the engagement was conducted in accordance with standards established by the PCAOB with a brief description of the procedures performed in the engagement.
- The definition of internal control over financial reporting.
- An identification of the inherent limitations of internal control over financial reporting.
- The auditors' opinion on whether the entity maintained effective internal control over financial reporting. The opinion in Exhibit 5.B1 represents an **unqualified opinion on internal control over financial reporting.**
- A reference to the auditors' opinion on the financial statements, indicating the type of opinion expressed.
- The date of the report.

✔ REVIEW CHECKPOINTS

5.29 Describe the major components of the auditors' standard, unqualified report on internal control over financial reporting.

LO 5-8
Describe situations in which the auditors' report on internal control over financial reporting would be modified.

MODIFICATIONS TO THE AUDITORS' STANDARD REPORT ON INTERNAL CONTROL OVER FINANCIAL REPORTING

As noted earlier, in most situations, the audit team issues an integrated report that includes both the opinion on the financial statements and the opinion on the effectiveness of the internal control system. This report is illustrated as part of our detailed coverage of reports on audits of financial statements in Chapter 12. However, the audit team may also choose to issue separate reports for both the financial statements and the internal control system. In this chapter, we focus solely on internal control reporting.

The report in Exhibit 5.B1 expresses an unqualified opinion on the effectiveness of the entity's internal control over financial reporting. The standard unqualified report on internal control may be modified for two reasons: (1) the existence of material weaknesses in internal control over financial reporting and/or (2) the existence of a limitation in the scope of the engagement. These modifications, along with those for other factors, are discussed in the following subsections.

Material Weaknesses in the Entity's Internal Control over Financial Reporting

Recall that a *material weakness* in internal control is defined as a deficiency or combination of deficiencies that results in a reasonable possibility that a material misstatement would not be prevented or detected on a timely basis. If the audit team identifies a material weakness in internal control, the firm expresses an *adverse opinion* on the effectiveness of the entity's internal control over financial reporting. As shown in Exhibit 5B.2, the standard report on internal control over financial reporting would be modified (in the exhibit, modifications are shown in bold italic color type) as follows:

- Include a paragraph immediately following the inherent limitations paragraph that defines a material weakness.
- Describe any material weakness(es) identified during the audit as well as an identification of the material weakness(es) described in management's assessment. (*Note:* If any identified material weakness has been omitted from or not presented fairly in management's assessment, the auditors' report should so state, as well as disclose any information necessary to fairly describe the material weakness.) The description should provide specific information about the nature of the material weakness and its effect on the presentation of the company's financial statements issued during the existence of the weakness.
- Modify the opinion paragraph to indicate that because of the effect of the material weakness(es) identified, the company has *not* maintained effective internal control

EXHIBIT 5B.2   Modified Report on Internal Control over Financial Reporting if a Material Weakness Exists

Title	**Report of Independent Registered Public Accounting Firm**
Address	To the Board of Directors and Shareholders Dunder-Mifflin Inc.
Introductory paragraph	[Standard introductory paragraph]
Scope paragraph	[Standard scope paragraph]
Definition paragraph	[Standard definition paragraph]
Inherent limitations paragraph	[Standard inherent limitations paragraph]
Explanatory paragraphs	*A material weakness in internal control is defined as a deficiency, or combination of deficiencies, that results in a reasonable possibility that a material misstatement would not be prevented or detected on a timely basis.*
	During the fiscal year ended December 31, 2017, Dunder-Mifflin Inc. senior managers were able to override internal controls over financial reporting. This material weakness resulted in accounting errors that were corrected prior to the issuance of the financial statements for the year ended December 31, 2017. Given the nature of the transactions and processes involved and the potential for a misstatement to occur as a result of the internal control deficiency existing on December 31, 2017, we have concluded that there is a reasonable possibility that a material misstatement in the annual or interim financial statements would not have been prevented or detected by internal controls over financial reporting.
	This material weakness was considered in determining the nature, timing, and extent of audit tests applied in our audit of the 2017 financial statements, and this report does not affect our report dated March 7, 2018, on those financial statements.
Opinion paragraph	*In our opinion, because of the effect of the material weakness described above on the achievement of the objectives of the control criteria, Dunder-Mifflin Inc. has not maintained* effective internal control over financial reporting as of December 31, 2017, in all material respects, based on the COSO criteria.
Paragraph on financial statement report	[Standard financial statement report paragraph]
Signature	*Michael Scarn, LLP, CPAs* Scranton, PA
Date	March 7, 2018

over financial reporting. This is referred to as an **adverse opinion on internal control over financial reporting.**

The audit team also may express an adverse opinion if management's report on internal control is incomplete or improperly presents a disclosure about a material weakness. In addition to the adverse opinion, the report would include an explanatory paragraph describing the situation.

Effect of an Adverse Opinion on Internal Control on the Auditor's Opinion on the Financial Statements

One issue raised by the preceding discussion concerns how a material weakness that results in an adverse opinion on the effectiveness of the entity's internal control over financial reporting affects the opinion on the financial statements. For example, could the auditor still issue an unqualified opinion on the entity's financial statements? Assuming that no material misstatements were detected, the auditor could issue an unqualified opinion on the entity's financial statements. In addition, as shown in Exhibit 5B.2, the following language would be included in the report in the paragraph describing the material weakness(es): "This material weakness was considered in determining the nature, timing, and extent of audit tests applied in our audit of the 2017 financial statements, and this report does not affect our report dated March 7, 2018, on those financial statements."

Restriction on the Scope of the Engagement

During the engagement, audit teams could encounter scope limitations on their ability to evaluate the effectiveness of the entity's internal control over financial reporting, such as failure to obtain written management representations. An additional scope limitation related to internal control over financial reporting could arise when management has implemented new controls in response to previously identified material weaknesses. If the auditor believes the time period is not sufficient to evaluate the operating effectiveness of the new controls, a scope limitation exists.

A scope limitation may result in the issuance of a **disclaimer of opinion on internal control over financial reporting** or a withdrawal from the engagement, depending on the

EXHIBIT 5B.3 Differences in the Report on Internal Control over Financial Reporting if a Scope Limitation Exists

Title	Report of Independent Registered Public Accounting Firm
Address	To the Board of Directors and Shareholders Dunder-Mifflin Inc.
Introductory paragraph	Change "we have audited" to "we *were engaged* to audit" because an audit could not be completed. Delete the sentence describing the auditors' responsibility for internal control over financial reporting. (It is inappropriate to indicate that the auditors' responsibility is to express an opinion, and then later say that an opinion could not be expressed.)
Scope paragraph	Delete the scope paragraph.
Definition paragraph	No change
Inherent limitations paragraph	No change
Explanatory paragraphs	Provide an explanatory paragraph describing the scope limitation. If the scope limitation is related to the inability to gather sufficient evidence with respect to a potential material weakness, this paragraph also should include the definition of a material weakness.
Opinion paragraph	Modify the opinion paragraph to disclaim an opinion ("the scope of our work was not sufficient to enable us to express, and we do not express, an opinion . . .").
Signature	*Michael Scarn, LLP, CPAs* Scranton, PA
Date	March 7, 2018

significance of the limitation (Exhibit 5B.3). The standard report on internal control over financial reporting would have to be modified as well. It is important to note that the audit team can still issue an opinion on the entity's financial statements if a disclaimer of opinion is issued on internal control over financial reporting.

Other Report Modifications

AS 2201 identifies other situations that may result in modification to the auditors' report on internal control over financial reporting:

- In certain situations, an audit team may be asked to perform an audit of internal control for just one component of a larger company that is being audited by another audit firm. In those situations, the audit firm responsible for the audit of the larger company needs to determine whether to explicitly refer to the component auditors' report in its own report on internal control for the overall company.
- If management's report on internal control contains additional information (such as corrective actions taken by the entity or the entity's plan to implement new controls), the audit team members should disclaim an opinion on this information if they have not had an opportunity to evaluate the information.
- If the audit team members believe that management's annual certification (section 302 of Sarbanes–Oxley) is misstated, they should include an explanatory paragraph describing the reasons the audit team believes management's disclosures should be modified.
- If changes in internal control over financial reporting occur that materially and adversely affect the effectiveness of the entity's internal control after the financial statement date but before the issuance of the final report, the audit team should issue an adverse opinion or a disclaimer of opinion on the effectiveness of the entity's internal control over financial reporting, depending on the exacting facts and circumstances.

EXHIBIT 5B.4   Summary of Modifications to Auditors' Report on Internal Control over Financial Reporting

Situation	Effect on Opinion on Effectiveness of Internal Control
Material weaknesses in internal control over financial reporting	Issue an adverse opinion on internal control
Restriction on the scope of the engagement	Issue a disclaimer of opinion or withdraw from the engagement, depending on the severity of the scope limitation
Refer to report of component auditors as the basis for the auditors' opinion	No effect, assuming other auditors' opinion is consistent with principal auditors' opinion (would refer to report of other auditors)
Other information contained in management's report on internal control	No effect, but should disclaim an opinion on other information
Management's annual certification (section 302 of Sarbanes–Oxley) is misstated	Include an explanatory paragraph describing the reasons why management's disclosures should be modified
Significant subsequently discovered fact related to internal control	Issue either adverse opinion (if subsequently discovered fact adversely affects the effectiveness of internal control) or disclaimer of opinion (if auditor is unable to determine effects of subsequently discovered fact)

AUDITING INSIGHT

PricewaterhouseCoopers (PwC) Issues Disclaimer on Krispy Kreme

Recall the material weaknesses identified by Krispy Kreme's management in its 2007 report on internal controls in Exhibit 5.1. Things were worse in 2005. PwC found the following in its 2005 integrated audit of the company's internal control:

a. Krispy Kreme's management did not complete its assessment of internal control over financial reporting.

b. A total of 10 material weaknesses were identified, some of which represented very basic elements of the control environment.

c. The auditors acknowledged that these weaknesses resulted in financial statement restatements.

d. Krispy Kreme's management restricted PwC from completing its own assessment, resulting in a disclaimer of opinion on the effectiveness of internal control.

As a result, PwC was forced to issue the following disclaimer in its 2005 auditors' report on internal control over financial reporting at Krispy Kreme:

Since (a) the Company was unable to complete its assessment of the effectiveness of internal control over financial reporting as of January 30, 2005 and (b) management further restricted the scope of our work by directing that we not complete our (i) testing and evaluation of the effectiveness of the design of the Company's internal control over financial reporting, (ii) testing of operating effectiveness of the Company's internal control over financial reporting, and (iii) review and evaluation of the results of management's testing and of the control deficiencies noted in management's incomplete assessment, and because we were unable to complete our procedures to satisfy ourselves as to the effectiveness of the Company's internal control over financial reporting, the scope of our work was not sufficient to enable us to express, and we do not express, an opinion either on management's assessment or on the effectiveness of the Company's internal control over financial reporting, including identifying all material weaknesses that might exist as of January 30, 2005.

☑ REVIEW CHECKPOINTS

5.30 What are some major reasons for departing from the standard, unqualified report on internal control over financial reporting?

5.31 What type of opinion(s) would the audit team issue on the effectiveness of internal control over financial reporting if a material weakness in internal control exists? How would the standard report be modified?

5.32 What type of opinion would be issued by the audit team as the result of a scope limitation on the examination of internal control over financial reporting?

CHAPTER 6

Employee Fraud and the Audit of Cash

Rather fail with honor than succeed by fraud.

Sophocles, Greek playwright and scholar (496–406 BC)

Professional Standards References

Topic	AU-C/ISA Section	AS Reference
Overall Objectives of the Independent Auditor	200	1001, 1005, 1010, 1015
Supervision of the Audit Engagement	220, 300	1201
Audit Documentation	230	1215
Consideration of Fraud in a Financial Statement Audit	240	2401
Consideration of Laws and Regulations	250	2405
Communications with Audit Committees	260	1301
Audit Planning	300	2101
Consideration of Internal Control in an Integrated Audit	265	2201
Identifying and Assessing the Risks of Material Misstatement	315	2110
Materiality	320	2105
Auditors' Responses to Risks of Material Misstatement	330	2301
Audit Considerations Relating to an Entity Using a Service Organization	402	2601
Audit Evidence	500	1105
External Confirmations	505	2310
Substantive Analytical Procedures	520	2305
Auditing Accounting Estimates	540	2501
Related Parties	550	2401
Using the Work of an Audit Specialist	620	1210

LEARNING OBJECTIVES

In Chapter 5, we emphasized the important role of the internal control system in helping to ensure that the financial statement information being presented by an organization is credible and can be relied upon. Beyond its critical nature in the production of reliable financial statement information, the establishment of an internal control system is also important to help protect an organization's assets from being stolen. In this chapter, we focus on the auditor's role in helping clients prevent and/or detect the misappropriation (or theft) of assets in their organization.

Recall that in Chapter 4 we focused on the auditor's responsibilities related to fraudulent financial reporting, that is when an organization intentionally issues false or misleading financial statements to the investing marketplace. The professional standards make clear that auditors are also responsible for considering the possibility of misstatements that arise from the misappropriation of assets, otherwise known as employee theft. As a result, this chapter begins with a comprehensive discussion of this type of fraud.

Next, because cash is often the primary target of employee theft, the chapter logically transitions to a discussion of how the cash balance is audited. This discussion includes a description of the most common relevant financial statement assertions, along with a focus on the control and substantive testing procedures that are typically performed during the audit of cash balances. Importantly, our discussion of controls includes specific examples of additional internal control activities that can be put in place to help prevent or detect employee theft, also known as a misappropriation of assets fraud.

Your objectives are to be able to:

LO 6-1 Define and explain the differences among several kinds of employee frauds that might occur at an audit client.

LO 6-2 Identify and explain the three conditions (i.e., the fraud triangle) that often exist when a fraud occurs.

LO 6-3 Describe techniques that can be used to prevent employee fraud.

LO 6-4 Identify the relevant assertions and risks of material misstatement that are typically related to the cash balance.

LO 6-5 Identify important internal control activities present in a properly designed system to mitigate the risk of material misstatements for each relevant assertion related to cash and to help prevent or detect employee fraud.

LO 6-6 Give examples of substantive procedures used to test cash and relate them to the relevant assertions.

LO 6-7 Describe some extended procedures for detecting employee fraud schemes involving cash.

INTRODUCTION

LO 6-1

Define and explain the differences among several kinds of employee frauds that might occur at an audit client.

Fraud examinations can be very exciting for auditors. A fraud examination has the aura of detective work—finding things that people want to keep hidden. However, such examinations are not easy and are not activities to be pursued without special training, experience, and care. While Module D presents a more detailed discussion of fraud examinations, this chapter presents a general introduction to the theory and definitions related specifically to misappropriation of assets-type fraud. In addition, you will learn how auditors evaluate the design and operating effectiveness of internal controls that are designed to mitigate the risk of this type of employee fraud. Importantly, because cash is often the primary target of fraudsters in these schemes, we illustrate the internal controls as they relate to cash. Next, we present a discussion of the audit of the cash account on the balance sheet, with specific examples of internal control activities and related control tests and substantive audit procedures.

It is essential that auditors maintain their professional skepticism at all times throughout the engagement. In fact, professional standards require that when auditors brainstorm about the potential for all types of fraud in an engagement the activity should "occur with an attitude that includes a questioning mind, and the key engagement team members should

AUDITING INSIGHT | Let's Go for a Hike on the Appalachian Trail . . . for Life

This is exactly the plan that was put into action by James Hammes after stealing $8.7 million from his employer, a **Pepsi-Cola** bottler based in Ohio. Amazingly, his plan almost worked as he eluded capture by hiking and then living on the Appalachian Trail using an assumed name.

Hammes committed the crime while working as a controller at the company from 1998 to 2009. Because he had access to both the cash and the accounting records, he was able to divert company cash into a personal bank account and then cover up his crime by manipulating the

accounting records. When the FBI started to ask him questions about the missing cash, Hammes decided to take a hike. Eventually, another hiker became aware of his story and tipped off the authorities. Hammes was sentenced to eight years in prison and must repay the money stolen.

Source: Michael Cohn, "Accountant Who Hid on Appalachian Trail Jailed for Embezzling Millions from Pepsi Bottler," *Accounting Today,* June 23, 2016, available at: http://www.accountingtoday.com/news/audit-accounting /accountant-appalachian-trail-jailed-embezzling-pepsi-78488-1.html.

set aside any prior beliefs they might have that management is honest and has integrity."[1] Why is it so important that auditors maintain such a high degree of skepticism? Because a fraud is often committed by a person that an auditor least expects. Consider a Little League coach ripping off the league to buy expensive jewelry by using a routing number from a league payroll check.[2] Or consider an executive assistant at a large public accounting firm who wrote more than $1 million in checks to herself that were drawn on a client's bank account.[3] You just never know from where the next fraud might originate!

Not surprisingly, whenever a fraud risk exists, the professional standards require that auditors gain an understanding of the internal controls that are in place to mitigate the assessed fraud risk. At a minimum, auditors are required to document that understanding in the workpapers. In fact, auditors are also likely to evaluate the design, implementation, and operating effectiveness of identified internal control activities related to fraud risks that exist. Importantly, an entity's internal control cannot thwart or detect all fraud schemes. Inherent limitations in internal control (such as *collusion* among employees) prevent complete assurance that every fraud scheme will be detected before a loss is incurred. For this reason, the entity's auditors, accountants, and security personnel must be acquainted with the basics of fraud awareness. Although the professional auditing standards concentrate on fraudulent financial reporting—the production of materially false and misleading financial statements—the standards also require auditors to pay particular attention to employee fraud perpetrated against a client for at least two reasons. First, it is possible that employee fraud can result in a material financial statement misstatement to the extent that a crime was covered up using the financial statements. Second, audit clients always want to know if they are being robbed by their employees, regardless of the amount being stolen!

Employee Fraud Overview

Fraud consists of knowingly making material misrepresentations of fact with the intent of inducing someone to believe the falsehood and act upon it and, thus, suffer a loss or damage. This definition encompasses all ways by which people can lie, cheat, steal, and deceive other people. **Employee fraud** (often referred to as **misappropriation of assets**) is the use of fraudulent means to take money or other property from an employer. It usually involves falsifications of some kind—false documents, lying, exceeding authority, or violating an employer's policies. Employee frauds generally consist of (1) the fraudulent act itself, (2) the conversion of assets to the fraudster's use (very easy if cash is involved), and (3) the cover-up. Catching people in the fraudulent act is difficult to accomplish. The act of conversion is equally difficult to observe because it typically takes place in secret away from the entity's offices (e.g., selling stolen inventory). By noticing signs and signals of fraud and then following the trail of missing, mutilated, or false documents that are

---

[1]*PCAOB Auditing Standard No. 2110,* "Identifying and Assessing Risks of Material Misstatement."

[2]"Little League Coach Accused of Fraud," *St. Petersburg Times,* p. 3B, July 4, 2009.

[3]"Aide Gets 2 Years in Fraud Case," *San Francisco Chronicle,* p. D2, October 28, 2010.

Other Definitions Related to Fraud and Illegal Acts

Management fraud is an intentional deception that is orchestrated by management and is designed to injure investors and creditors by providing materially misleading information.

Errors are unintentional misstatements or omissions of amounts or disclosures in financial statements.

Direct-effect illegal acts are violations of laws or government regulations by the company, or its management or employees, that produce direct and material effects on dollar amounts in financial statements.

Embezzlement is a type of fraud that typically involves an employee wrongfully stealing assets that were entrusted to his or her care, custody, or control. In many situations, embezzlement is accompanied by false accounting entries or lying to try to cover up the crime.

part of the accounting records cover-up, alert auditors uncover many frauds. Being able to notice red flags, oddities, and unusual events takes some experience, but this chapter provides you with some ideas about where and when to look.

Employee Fraud Red Flags

Employee fraud can involve all types of employees from high-level executives to hourly employees in the warehouse. For most people, committing a fraudulent act is stressful. Observation of changes in a person's habits and lifestyle may reveal some red flags.[4] Fraudsters often exhibit these behaviors:

- Experience sleeplessness.
- Drink too much.
- Take drugs.
- Become irritable easily.
- Can't relax.
- Get defensive, argumentative.
- Can't look people in the eye.
- Sweat excessively.
- Go to confession (e.g., priest, psychiatrist).
- Find excuses and scapegoats for mistakes.
- Work standing up.
- Work alone.
- Work late frequently.
- Don't take vacations.

Personality red flags are difficult because (1) honest people often show them as well, (2) they often are hidden from view, and (3) auditors are not in a good position to notice these characteristics. Managers are in the best position to notice changes, especially when a person varies his or her lifestyle or spends more money than his or her salary seems to justify—for example, on homes, furniture, jewelry, clothes, boats, autos, vacations, and the like. Therefore, it is imperative that the auditor make specific inquiries of management regarding changes in an employee's demeanor and lifestyle.

Characteristics of Fraudsters

White-collar criminals are not like typical bank robbers who are often described as "young and dumb." Bank robbers and other strong-arm criminals often make comical mistakes such as writing their holdup note on the back of a probation identification card,

---

[4]Long lists of red flags can be found in G. J. Bologna and R. J. Lindquist, *Fraud Auditing and Forensic Accounting* (New York: John Wiley & Sons, 1995), pp. 49–56; W. S. Albrecht et al., in R. K. Elliott and J. J. Willingham, *Management Fraud: Detection and Deterrence* (New York: Petrocelli Books Inc., 1980), pp. 223–226; *Statement on Auditing Standards No. 99* (New York: AICPA, 2002); Auditing for Fraud courses of the Association of Certified Fraud Examiners; and courses offered by other organizations such as the AICPA and The Institute of Internal Auditors.

AUDITING INSIGHT   Are You Kidding Me?

In February 2013, investigators arrested Craig Haber, a partner in tax and advisory services in the New York City office of **Grant Thornton** for stealing payments made by clients to the firm. Allegedly, his crimes began in July 2004 and continued through July 2012. In total, he is alleged to have stolen approximately $4 million from Grant Thornton. Apparently, Haber provided instructions to his clients to send checks or wire transfers directly to him in New York instead of sending the

payments to Grant Thornton's headquarters in Chicago. He then took the checks and deposited them in a bank account that was opened "in the name of a sham business that was very similar to Grant Thornton's name." Haber then would transfer the funds from this account to his personal account.

Source: M. Cohn, "Former Grant Thornton Partner Arrested for Stealing $4 Million in Client Payments," *Accounting Today*, February 7, 2013.

leaving the getaway car keys on the convenience store counter, using a zucchini as a holdup weapon, going through a fast-food restaurant's drive-through window backward, and timing the holdup to get stuck in rush hour traffic. Then there's the classic story about the robber who ran into his own mother at the bank. (She turned him in!)

Burglars and robbers average about $400–$500 for each hit. Employee frauds often range from $20,000 up to $500,000 or even in the millions if a computer is used. Yet employee frauds are not usually the intricate, well-disguised ploys you find in espionage novels. Who are these thieves wearing ties? What do they look like? Unfortunately, they look like most everybody else, including you and me. A typical white-collar criminal:

- Has education beyond high school.
- Is likely to be married.
- Is a member of a mosque, temple, or church.
- Ranges in age from teens to over 60.
- Is socially conforming.
- Has an employment tenure from 1 to 20 years (although the scale of the fraud typically increases with tenure as the employee becomes more trusted).
- Has no arrest record.
- Usually acts alone (70 percent or more of incidents).

AUDITING INSIGHT   How Can $1.6 Billion of Cash Be Missing?

In July 2012, almost a year after **MF Global** filed for bankruptcy on October 31, 2011, investigators reported that they had located the more than $1.6 billion of customer funds that were missing from the company. The report ended a difficult process that revealed a complete lack of internal control in handling clients' funds. Scott O'Malia, a commissioner at the Commodity Futures Trading Commission,

commented that the books at MF Global "are a disaster" and its is difficult to "figure out what numbers are the real numbers."

Sources: "Inside the Hunt for MF Global Cash," *The Wall Street Journal*, November 10, 2011, p. c1; "$1.6 Billion in Missing MF Global Funds Traced," http://money.cnn.com/2012/04/24/news/companies/mf-global/index.htm.

White-collar criminals do not make themselves obvious, although they may leave telltale signs or red flags. Older individuals (usually over 50) who hold high executive positions, have long tenure, and are respected and trusted employees have often gained the trust and confidence of others and, therefore, are in a position to commit the largest frauds. After all, these are the people who have access to the largest amounts of money and have the power to give orders and override controls. When managers minimize the significance of a weak or missing control by rationalizing that the employee involved is a "long-time trusted employee," most experienced auditors will actually escalate their level of fraud risk awareness. You should as well.

AUDITING INSIGHT   Trusted Employees?

- A small business owner hired his best friend to work as his accountant. The friend was given full, unlimited access to all aspects of the business and was completely responsible for the accounting. Five years later, the owner finally terminated the friend's employment because the business was not profitable. Upon taking over the accounting responsibilities, the owner's wife found that cash receipts from customers were twice the amounts formerly recorded by the accountant "friend." An investigation revealed that the friend had stolen $450,000 in cash sales receipts from the business while the owner had never made more than $16,000 a year. (The friend had even used the stolen money to make loans to the owner to keep the business going!)

- An electrical supply company employed only one bookkeeper. She wrote the checks and reconciled the bank account. In the cash disbursements journal, she coded some checks as inventory, but she wrote the checks to herself, using her own name. When

the checks were returned with the bank statement, she simply destroyed them. Confronting continuous guilt over doing something she knew was wrong, she contacted a lawyer and turned herself in but not before she had stolen $416,000 over a five-year period. Because of the lack of separation of duties and her trusted status in the company, the fraud might have continued indefinitely (or at least until she bankrupted the company).

- Alex W. was a 47-year-old treasurer of a credit union. Over a seven-year period, he stole $160,000 from it. He was a good husband and father of six children, and he was a highly regarded credit union official. His crime came as a stunning surprise to his associates. Why did he do it? He owed significant amounts on his home, cars, college for two children, two side investments, and five credit cards. His monthly payments significantly exceeded his take-home pay.

Source: Association of Certified Fraud Examiners (ACFE), "Auditing for Fraud."

REVIEW CHECKPOINTS

6.1 What are the defining characteristics of employee fraud? Embezzlement?

6.2 What does a fraud perpetrator look like? How does one act?

THE FRAUD TRIANGLE (AU-C 315, AS 2401)

LO 6-2
Identify and explain the three conditions (i.e., the fraud triangle) that often exist when a fraud occurs.

The three conditions that are likely to be present when a fraud occurs (Exhibit 6.1) are commonly referred to as the *fraud triangle*. The first condition (incentive/pressure) recognizes that an employee or manager of a company is likely to either have incentives in place (e.g., bonus compensation) or be under significant pressure to meet specific estimates, forecasts, or expectations about net income. The second condition (opportunity) recognizes that in order for a fraud to be perpetrated, there must either be a weakness in the system of internal control or an ability to circumvent the system. Finally, the third condition (attitude/rationalization) recognizes that for an employee or a manager of a company to perpetrate a fraud, the individual must possess an "attitude" that allows her or him to rationalize why he or she is knowingly committing a crime. Each of these conditions is now discussed.[5]

EXHIBIT 6.1

Fraud Conditions

Source: W. Hillison, D. Sinason, and C. Pacini, "The Role of the Internal Auditor in Implementing SAS 82," *Corporate Controller,* July/August 1998, p. 20.

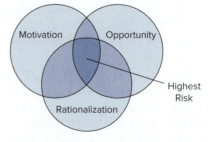

[5]For further reference, see D. R. Cressey, "Management Fraud, Accounting Controls, and Criminological Theory," pp. 117–147, and Albrecht et al., "Auditor Involvement in the Detection of Fraud," pp. 207–261, both in R. K. Elliott and J. J. Willingham, *Management Fraud: Detection and Deterrence* (New York: Petrocelli Books Inc., 1980); J. K. Loebbecke, M. M. Eining, and J. J. Willingham, "Auditors' Experience with Material Irregularities: Frequency, Nature, and Detectability," *Auditing: A Journal of Practice and Theory,* Fall 1989, pp. 1–28.

Incentive/Pressure

Incentive or pressure gives rise to a motive to commit fraud. A **motive**, in the fraud context, is essentially a reason for a person to take a fraudulent action that is believed to be unshareable with friends and confidants. Psychotic motivation is relatively rare, but it is characterized by the habitual criminal who steals simply for the sake of stealing. In general, egocentric motivations drive people to steal to achieve more personal prestige. Ideological motivations are held by people who think their cause is morally superior and they are justified in making someone else a victim. However, economic benefits are by far the most common motivations in business frauds.

AUDITING INSIGHT   I Couldn't Tell Anyone

A young unmarried woman stole $300 from her employer to pay for an abortion. Coming from a strict religious family, she felt her only alternative was to have the secret abortion. Once she realized how easy it was to steal, however, she took another $86,000 before being caught.

Source: W. S. Albrecht, "How CPAs Can Help Clients Prevent Employee Fraud," *Journal of Accountancy,* 1988, pp. 110–114.

The economic motive is simply a need or desire for money, and at times it can be intertwined with egocentric and ideological motivations. Ordinary, honest people can experience circumstances in which they have a new or unexpected need for money. If the need arises and the legitimate channels to raise the money are closed, fraud may become an option for some individuals. Consider the following needs:

- Buying a home.
- Pay uninsured medical bills.
- Pay gambling debts.
- Pay for drugs and alcohol.
- Pay alimony and child support.
- Pay for high lifestyle (vacation homes, cars, boats).
- Finance business or stock speculation losses.

AUDITING INSIGHT   When Facing Adversity, Become a Model Employee

A supervisor for a state university health service was facing great financial difficulty. Her husband had permanently injured his back and no longer worked. One of her children was in a serious automobile accident requiring large payments to cover the uninsured portion of the medical bills.

Despite these personal problems, the supervisor was considered a model employee. She would come to work early, stay late, never call in sick, and take vacation time only between semesters when the health service facility was closed. When she was ill with something contagious, she would come in to work after all other employees had left.

A newly hired director of health services noticed that although the number of students and number of services had increased, health services was having unexplained cash flow problems. An investigation revealed that the supervisor had embezzled $757,000 over a 13-year period. She was sentenced to five years in prison and ordered to repay the university $208,000 and perform 250 hours of community service.

Source: "Catching Fraudsters with Their Hands in the Till," *CPA Journal,* May 2005, pp. 13–15.

Opportunity

An opportunity is an open door for solving the unshareable problem by violating some type of trust. The violation may be a circumvention of existing internal control activities, or it may be simply taking advantage of an absence or lapse of a control activity in an entity. In general, the higher the position in an organization, the higher the degree of trust, the more likely that controls can be overridden, and, hence, the greater the opportunity for larger frauds. Here are some examples:

- Inventory is not counted on a regular basis, so inventory shortages and losses are not known.
- Proper separation of duties related to cash receipts or payments is compromised because of a termination or retirement.
- The vice president of finance has investment authority without review.
- Frequent emergency jobs leave a lot of excess material in a manufacturing plant just lying around.

 AUDITING INSIGHT No Locks on the Door

Perini Corporation kept blank checks in an unlocked storeroom to which every clerk and secretary had access. The automatic check-signing machine was also in the storeroom. The prenumbered checks were not logged when used. The bookkeeper was very surprised to open the bank statement one month and find that $1.5 million in stolen checks had been paid on the account.

Source: Association of Certified Fraud Examiners (ACFE), "Auditing for Fraud."

Attitude/Rationalization

Practically everyone, even the most violent criminal, knows the difference between right and wrong. Unimpeachable integrity is the ability to act in accordance with the highest moral and ethical values at all times. Thus, it is the lapses in integrity that permit a person's incentives or pressures to motivate fraudulent action when the opportunity presents itself. But people normally do not make deliberate decisions to "lack integrity today while I steal some money." They find a way to describe (rationalize) the act in words that make it acceptable for their self-image. Here are some of these rationalizations:

- I need it more than other people (also known as the *Robin Hood theory*).
- I am borrowing the money and will pay it back.
- Nobody will get hurt.
- The company is big enough to afford it.
- A successful image is the name of the game.
- Everybody is doing it.
- I am underpaid, so this is due compensation.

 AUDITING INSIGHT What's Your Excuse?

A manager at **Accenture** stole $240,000 by abusing the expense reimbursement procedures in her company. She claimed that she suffered from severe depression and her only remedy was shopping sprees for exorbitant jewelry and fine clothing.

Source: M. F. Zimbelman, "Student Shares Insights about Expense Fraud," *Fraud Magazine,* December 2004, pp. 15–19.

✅ REVIEW CHECKPOINTS

6.3 What are some pressures that can cause honest people to contemplate fraud? List some egocentric and ideological pressures as well as economic ones.

6.4 What conditions provide opportunities for employee fraud?

6.5 Give some examples of rationalizations that people have used to excuse fraud. Can you imagine using them?

6.6 Is capability required to commit a fraud? Is capability part of opportunity, or should it be considered a separate element of fraud?

FRAUD PREVENTION

LO 6-3

Describe techniques that can be used to prevent employee fraud.

Building a good fraud prevention program is an extremely difficult task. Most day-to-day business activities require some trust in the processes for which controls will never be absolute. For example, if we entrust an individual with check authorization, at the instant that person signs the check, he or she has physical custody of the asset. As a result, taking steps to "fraud proof" an organization is a tall order.

Accountants and auditors have often been exhorted to be the leaders in fraud prevention by employing their skills in designing "tight" control systems. This strategy is, at best, a short-run solution to a large and pervasive problem. Business activity is built on the trust that people at all levels will do their jobs properly. As a result, it is essential that management establish a strong control environment. A strong control environment and tone at the top can have a pervasive effect on the prevention of fraud at an entity because it can impact all components of an organization's internal control system. For example, a CEO who always acts with ethics and integrity sends a strong message to all employees that management is serious about internal controls and fraud prevention.

Beyond a strong control environment, management must be sensitive to the needs of the business by instituting controls that will prevent or detect fraud without impeding business activity. Control systems limit trust and, in the extreme, can strangle business in bureaucracy. The challenge is to have useful controls and to avoid picky rules that are "fun to beat." Managers and employees must have freedom to do business, which may mean giving them some freedom that can result in committing frauds. Effective long-run prevention measures are complex and difficult, involving the elimination of the causes of fraud by mitigating the effect of motive, opportunity, and lack of integrity.

Managing People and Pressures in the Workplace

From time to time, people experience financial and other pressures. The pressures cannot be eliminated, but forums and facilities for sharing such pressures can and have been created by leading organizations. Some companies have "ethics officers" to serve this purpose. Their job is to be available to talk over various ethical dilemmas faced in the workplace and help employees identify legitimate responses. However, it is important to remember that the ethics officers are not normally psychological counselors.

Many companies have anonymous hotlines for reporting ethical problems. Indeed, companies that must comply with the Sarbanes–Oxley Act of 2002 are required to maintain an anonymous employee hotline. Usually, the best kind of hotline arrangement is to have the responding party be a third-party agency outside the organization. In the United States, some external providers are in the business of being the recipients of hotline calls and coordinating their activities with the audit committee or the internal audit department of the various organizations to whom they provide this service.

Another method of long-term fraud prevention, however, lies in the treatment of people within an organization. Managers and supervisors at all levels can exhibit a genuine concern for the personal and professional needs of their subordinates and fellow managers, and subordinates can show the same concern for each other and their managers. Many companies facilitate this caring attitude with an organized employee assistance program (EAP). They offer a range of counseling referral services dealing with substance abuse, mental health issues, family problems, crisis help, legal matters, health education, retirement, career paths, job loss troubles, and family financial planning. These program types are not guaranteed to prevent fraud, but they can have a positive impact for an organization.

When external auditors are engaged in the audit of an entity's financial statements, they must obtain an understanding of and evaluate the control environment. In so doing, the audit team should consider how management addresses these types of employee issues. Using devices such as those discussed here can enhance an entity's control environment and represents the start of an effective internal control system.

Internal Control Activities and Employee Monitoring

As discussed in Chapter 5, internal control activities may include job descriptions and performance specifications that help people know the specific tasks they are supposed to accomplish. An entity whose only control is "trustworthy employees" has no control.[6] The possibility of being detected by a control activity can be an effective deterrent to a potential fraudster. Stated simply, control activities often take away the opportunity for a fraudster to commit a fraud.

As previously discussed, concealment of the crime is a distinguishing attribute of a fraud. Often, the audit team's first indication of a fraud is the identification of a control violation. Cover-up attempts generally appear in the accounting records. The key for an auditor is to be aware of and notice exceptions and oddities such as the following:

- Transactions recorded at unusual times of the day, month, or year.
- An unusual (either large or small) number or dollar amount of transactions.
- Transactions for "round" dollar amounts (e.g., $50,000).
- Transactions associated with unusual branches or locations of a multilocation entity.
- Cash shortages and overages.
- Excessive voids and credit memos.
- General ledgers that do not balance.
- An increase in past due receivables.
- Inventory shortages.
- Unexplained adjustments to inventory or accounts receivable balances, especially without adequate supporting documentation.
- Increased scrap or waste in a manufacturing plant.
- Alterations on official documents.
- Duplicate payments made to the same vendor.
- Employees who cannot be found.
- Use of copies instead of originals for supporting documentation.
- Missing documentation to support transactions.
- Unusual endorsements on checks.
- Unusual patterns in deposits in transit.
- Common names or addresses for refunds.
- Consistent customer complaints about account balances or missing shipments.

[6]W.S. Albrecht, "How CPAs Can Help Clients Prevent Employee Fraud," *Journal of Accountancy,* December 1988, pp. 110–114.

As noted previously in Chapter 5, an important feature of an effective internal control system is the separation of duties and responsibilities for (1) transaction authorization, (2) record keeping, (3) custody of or access to assets, and (4) reconciliation of actual assets to the accounting records. In general, a person acting alone or in a conspiracy who can perform two or more of these functions can commit a fraud by taking assets, converting them, and then covering up the crime. Proper separation of duties and responsibilities can prevent such fraudulent actions. For example, as it relates to cash disbursements, effective internal control begins with different people and different departments handling the cash disbursement *authorization; custody* of blank documents (checks); *record keeping* for payments; and bank *reconciliation.* Auditing with fraud awareness often involves the combination of observing client control activities that were put in place and trying to "think like a crook" and imagine ways that theft could occur. When controls are missing, the ways and means for theft may be obvious. Otherwise, it might take significant planning and collusion to figure out how to steal from an employer.

AUDITING INSIGHT   When Assessing Fraud Risk, Answer These Questions

According to fraud experts Joseph Wells and John Gill of the Association of Certified Fraud Examiners, when assessing fraud risk, answering a set of 15 questions is a good starting point for sizing up a company's vulnerability to fraud and creating an action plan for lessening the risks. Their key questions are:

1. Is the company dominated by one or two key employees?

2. Do any key employees appear to have a close association with vendors?

3. Do any key employees have outside business interests that might conflict with their job duties?

4. Does the organization conduct pre-employment background checks to identify previous dishonest or unethical behavior?

5. Does the organization educate employees about the importance of ethics and antifraud programs?

6. Does the organization have antifraud policies and provide an anonymous way to report suspected violations of ethics?

7. Is job or assignment rotation mandatory for employees who handle cash receipts and accounting duties?

8. Has the company established positive pay controls with its bank by supplying the bank with a daily list of checks issued and authorized for payment?

9. Are refunds, voids, and discounts evaluated on a routine basis to identify patterns of activity among employees, departments, shifts, or merchandise?

10. Are purchasing and receiving functions separate from invoice processing, accounts payable, and general ledger functions?

11. Is the employee payroll list periodically reviewed for duplicate or missing Social Security numbers?

12. Are there policies and procedures that address the identification, classification, and handling of proprietary information?

13. Do employees who have access to proprietary information sign nondisclosure agreements?

14. Is there a company policy that addresses the receipt of gifts, discounts, and services offered by a supplier or customer?

15. Are the organization's financial goals and objectives realistic?

Source: Joseph T. Wells and John D. Gill, "Assessing Fraud Risk," *Journal of Accountancy,* October 2007, pp. 63–65.

When collecting corroborating evidence to support the financial statements, the audit team must remain vigilant against the potential for fraud. Discrepancies in the accounting records, conflicting evidence, and missing documentation are all symptomatic of financial statement fraud. When the audit team identifies such instances, members must follow up with management to identify the source of the problems. Management's response is a key source of evidence; vague, implausible, or inconsistent responses to inquiries can be a key indicator of the pervasiveness of the fraud. Similarly, problematic or unusual relationships between the audit team and management are often present in financial statement frauds.

Module D presents a comprehensive discussion of fraud examinations and how they differ from financial statement audits. However, an example to illustrate the difference between the engagements relates to evidence. The collection of evidence in a fraud examination (which can lead to prosecution and court scrutiny) is fundamentally different from the collection of evidence to support the auditor's opinion. If the auditors do come across questionable documents or any other evidence that may indicate fraud, they should immediately work to preserve the chain of custody of evidence. The *chain of custody* is the crucial link of the evidence to the criminal suspect that bears directly on the *relevance of evidence* often referred to by attorneys and judges. If documents are lost, mutilated, coffee stained, or otherwise compromised (so a defense attorney can argue that they were altered to frame the suspect), they lose their effectiveness for the prosecution. When completing a fraud examination, auditors should learn to mark the evidence, writing an identification of the location, condition, date, time, and circumstances as soon as it appears to be a signal of fraud. This marking should be on a separate tag or page; the original document should be put in a protective (plastic) envelope for preservation and locked away for protection. Then audit work should proceed with copies of the documents instead of originals. A record should be made of the safekeeping and of all persons who use the original. Any eyewitness observations should be recorded in a timely manner in a memorandum or on tape (audio or video) with corroboration of colleagues, if possible.

Similarly, an auditor may be involved in collecting evidence that is found in computers or stored in a digital manner. This type of computer forensic work must be completed with great care, and the goal is to examine the evidence in a manner that would be appropriate in reaching the goal of "identifying, preserving, recovering, analyzing, and presenting facts and opinions about the information." Generally, the evidence that is gathered from a computer forensic investigation is subject to the same rules of evidence as manual data in the eyes of law enforcement. This brief example underscores the importance of an auditor being properly trained to conduct a fraud examination.

Tone at the Top

Establishing the right tone at the top is an essential step toward building a strong fraud prevention program. This tone is established by upper management, in large part, to demonstrate a commitment to integrity and high ethical standards in the completion of all activities throughout the organization. The upper management team is responsible for setting the tone at the top. To send the right message from the top, many organizations publish codes of conduct for employees. Some of these codes are simple, and some are very elaborate. Government agencies and defense contractors typically have the most elaborate rules for employee conduct. Sometimes these codes are effective; sometimes they are not. However, a code can be effective only if the control environment and tone at the top support it. When the chairman of the board and the president make themselves visible and living examples of the code of conduct, other people will then believe it is real. Subordinates tend to follow the boss's lead.

AUDITING INSIGHT   You're Not Supposed to Audit Me!

One of the large public accounting firms was conducting an "ethical compliance" attestation engagement of a *Fortune* 500 company. An ethical compliance attestation engagement is designed to ensure, among other things, that client personnel are following the company's code of ethical conduct. Believing that the control environment and tone at the top were the most important elements of the client's ethical compliance control system, the engagement team started in the CEO's office. They found that the CEO was using the company plane to fly his fashion designer wife and her friends back and forth to Paris on a regular basis. When confronted in a board of directors meeting with the evidence, the CEO chastised the engagement team: "You weren't supposed to check on me; you were supposed to check on the employees." The board of directors disagreed and then requested the CEO's resignation.

Hiring and firing policies are important. Background checks on prospective employees are advisable and very good business practice. A new employee who has been a fraudster in some other organization's accounting department has a higher probability of being a fraudster in a new organization. As a result, organizations have even been known to hire private investigators to make background checks. Fraudsters should be fired and, in most cases, prosecuted. Experience has shown that they have a low rate of repeat offenses if they are prosecuted, but they have a high rate if not. Prosecution has the added benefit of sending the message that management does not believe that fraudulent activity is acceptable.

AUDITING INSIGHT	Did She Really Steal from the Church?

In April 2013, a Roman Catholic nun pleaded guilty to stealing $128,000 from two different parishes in New York over a five-year period. As it turns out, the nun had a gambling addiction and apparently felt that she had nowhere else to turn to pay the debts except by committing a crime. She now faces up to six months in jail and must repay the stolen money.

Source: "NY Gambling Nun Admits Taking $128K from Churches," *The Wall Street Journal*, April 9, 2013.

Unfortunately, the accompanying Auditing Insight, while incredibly disappointing, is far more common than it should be. As a result, auditors must always be vigilant and remain skeptical about the possibility of discovering employee fraud at their audit clients. This is why we have just provided so much coverage of the topic to begin this chapter. We now turn our attention to the account that is most frequently targeted by employee thieves—cash.

 REVIEW CHECKPOINT

6.7 What are some red flags that may indicate a cover-up or concealment of a fraud?

6.8 Is there anything odd about these two situations? (a) A check to Larson Electric Supply was endorsed with "Larson Electric" above the signature of "Eloise Garfunkle." (b) Numerous checks were issued and dated December 25, January 1, and July 4.

THE AUDIT OF CASH

LO 6-4

Identify the relevant assertions and risks of material misstatement that are typically related to the cash balance.

This section of the chapter is focused on the procedures that are completed as part of the financial statement audit for cash. However, our discussion of controls also includes examples of internal control activities that are specifically put in place to help prevent or detect employee fraud. In addition, because cash is relevant to each of an audit client's accounting cycles, we also discuss cash when describing the audits of the different cycles in the following chapters. For example, the basic activities in the revenue and collection cycle (Chapter 7) are (1) receiving and processing customer orders, including credit granting; (2) delivering goods and services to customers; (3) billing customers and accounting for accounts receivable; (4) collecting and depositing cash received from customers; and (5) reconciling bank statements. The basic acquisition and expenditure activities (Chapter 8) are (1) purchasing goods and services and (2) paying the bills. Similarly, the production and conversion cycle (Chapter 9) and the investing and financing cycle (Chapter 10) also feature the collection or expenditure of cash.

Audit Evidence Used to Test Cash

There are a number of different management reports, documents, and data files that are typically used by auditors when completing work on the cash account. They are now described.

Cash Receipts Journal

The cash receipts journal contains all of the detailed entries for all receipts of cash by the entity (debits to the cash account), including cash deposits. It contains the population of credit entries that should be reflected in the credits to accounts receivable for customer payments. It also contains the adjusting and correcting entries that can result from the bank account reconciliation. These entries are important because they may signal the types of accounting errors or manipulations that occur in the cash receipts accounting.

Cash Disbursements Journal

The cash disbursements journal is the company's checkbook. It contains all detailed entries for checks written during the period being audited (cash disbursements). Because all cash disbursements (other than those from a petty cash or payroll account) should be made via check or electronic transfer, the cash disbursements journal contains the cash credit entries that provide a population for testing cash disbursements. It also contains the adjusting and correcting entries that can result from the bank account reconciliation. These entries are important because they may signal the types of accounting errors or manipulations that occur in the cash disbursements accounting. The cash disbursements journal is usually inspected for suspect items such as checks made out to "cash" or "bearer." In addition, company procedures should require that "voided" checks be retained and auditors should review these checks to ensure they were in fact actually voided and have not been recorded in bank statements.

Bank Reconciliations

The company's bank reconciliation is the primary document used to test the cash balance in the financial statements. The amount of cash in the bank is almost always different from the amount in the general ledger (financial statements), and the reconciliation is designed to explain the difference between these two amounts. In addition, a bank account reconciliation that compares the book cash balance to the bank cash balance provides management with an opportunity to monitor the separation of duties for cash receipts and cash disbursements. The timely preparation of bank reconciliations is, therefore, an important element of a company's internal control activities over cash.

Canceled Checks

Exhibit 6.2 describes the information found on a typical check. Whether the auditor examines the actual check or a scanned image obtained from the bank, knowledge of the codes for Federal Reserve districts, offices, states, and bank identification numbers could enable an auditor to spot a crude check forgery. A forger's mistake with the optional identification printing or the magnetic check number might provide a tip-off. If the amount of a check is altered after it has cleared the bank, the alteration would be noted by

AUDITING INSIGHT   Who Was That Check from Again?

Naomi, an employee at a check-cashing business in Brooklyn, New York, received only the basics of detecting check fraud from her supervisors: Look for watermarks, compare encoded check numbers, and question customers to see whether they can keep their stories straight if a check looks suspicious.

Earlier in the month, the main office of Naomi's business warned workers to look for a Roberta Kane who had been successfully passing false checks in other branches. When Roberta walked into Naomi's branch, Naomi closely examined her ID and the $200 check. The check's routing numbers were larger than they should be, the check felt softer than others, and there was no watermark. Naomi asked Roberta how she had received the check and Roberta said it was a paycheck from her employer. Naomi called the number of the company that supposedly wrote the check. When the number appeared to

be out of service, Naomi told Roberta that she had presented a false check and that the police would have to get involved. Roberta frantically ran for the door, leaving behind her fake check and ID. Even with the most basic knowledge of detecting check fraud, this teller was able to deter a thief. As you can see, it is important for auditors to review the fundamentals of check fraud detection.

In an unrelated case, four people were under investigation for an easily discovered counterfeit check-cashing scheme. Despite using high-tech computer equipment to generate the counterfeit checks, the fraudsters mistakenly misspelled the payer (Broyhill Furniture) as "Boryhill Furniture."

Sources: Suzanne Mahadeo, "Check Fraud: Separating Money from Worthless Paper," *Fraud Magazine,* September/October 2005, pp. 21–23, 50; "News of the Weird," *Funny Times,* May 2003.

EXHIBIT 6.2 **How to Read a Canceled Check and Endorsement**

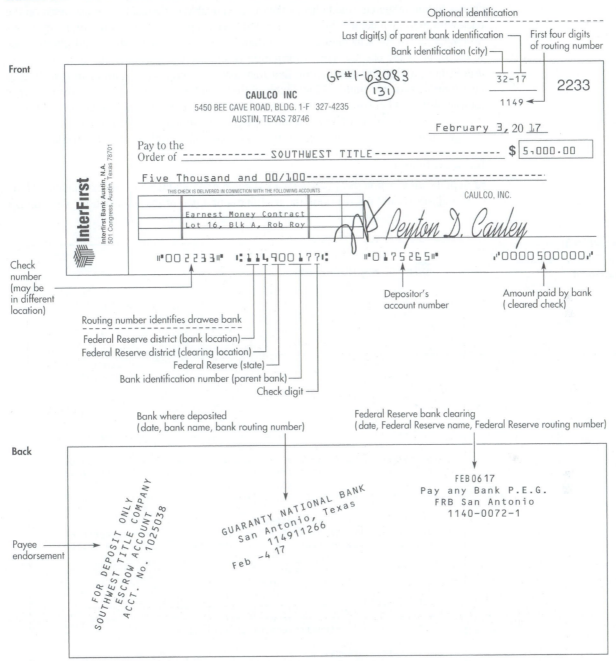

comparing the magnetic imprint of the amount paid to the amount written on the check face. The reverse side of a check carries the endorsement(s) of the payees and holders in due course; the date and the name and routing number of the bank where the check was deposited; and the date, identification of the Federal Reserve office, and its routing number for the Federal Reserve check clearing. (Sometimes, there is no Federal Reserve clearing identification when regional checks are cleared locally without going through a Federal Reserve office.) Auditors can follow the path of a canceled check by following the banks where it was deposited and cleared. This route may or may not correspond with the characteristics of the payee. (For example, ask why a check to a local business in Texas was deposited in a small Missouri bank and cleared through the St. Louis Federal Reserve office.)

Individuals engaging in fraudulent schemes involving cash often try to conceal their crimes by removing canceled checks they made payable to themselves or endorsed on the back with their own names. Missing canceled checks are a red flag. However, many banks no longer return the canceled checks to their customers. Instead, they send photocopies of the front of the checks. This information is sufficient for reconciling an account, but it does not provide the information that may assist a company or auditor in detecting or investigating possible frauds. Many banks will return the canceled checks to the company for a small fee. Other banks retain images of checks (front and back) on their Internet sites. Auditors, controllers, and CFOs should strongly recommend that their client or company pay any additional fees required to ensure that access to canceled checks is available.

Bank Statements

Most of the information shown on the bank statement in Exhibit 6.3 is self-explanatory. However, auditors should not overlook the usefulness of some of the information: The number

EXHIBIT 6.3
Small Business Bank Statement

```
                                                                          27
        ☒ First RepublicBank

             FIRST REPUBLICBANK AUSTIN, N.A.                      ACCOUNT
             P.O. BOX 908                           ---        604017-526-5
             AUSTIN, TEXAS   78781                  ---  ---

                                                    ---               PAGE
                                                    ---                  1


             CAULCO INC                                     SSN/TAX ID
             BLDG 1 OFFICE F                                74-2076251
             5450 BEE CAVE RD
             AUSTIN,  TX                                    CYC MC FREQ
             78746                                          01 01 M0000


             **  YOUR CHECKING ACCOUNT       01-29-17 THRU 02-28-17 **

      TO YOUR PREVIOUS BALANCE OF - - - - - - - - -          7,559.06
      YOU ADDED           1 DEPOSITS FOR   - - - - - -        5,654.16
      YOU SUBTRACTED    26 WITHDRAWALS FOR - - - - -         10,838.29
      GIVING YOU A CURRENT BALANCE OF - - - - - - -           7,374.93

      NUMBER OF DAYS USED FOR AVERAGES   - - - - - -                31
      YOUR AVERAGE LEDGER BALANCE - - - - - - - - -          4,014.67
      YOUR LOW BALANCE OCCURRED ON 02-22 AND WAS  -          2,374.93

                    THANK YOU


      ------------------------------------------------------------------
      ------------------------------------------------------------------
                    DEPOSITS AND OTHER ADDITIONS

          DATE      AMOUNT
          0204    5654.16
      ------------------------------------------------------------------
                    CHECKS AND OTHER WITHDRAWALS

      CHECK DATE    AMOUNT CHECK DATE    AMOUNT CHECK DATE    AMOUNT
       2201 0211     57.83  2214 0203    403.92  2225 0217    182.77
        **                  2215 0203    135.59   **
       2205 0222     16.72  2216 0216      6.16  2231 0205    254.37
       2206 0203    533.28  2217 0217    138.43  2232 0210     60.61
       2207 0203   1312.15  2218 0217    131.92
        **                  2219 0217     82.97  2234 0217     64.69
       2209 0203    247.10  2220 0217     87.49  2235 0218    279.97
       2210 0203    249.98  2221 0217     85.68   **
       2211 0203    255.26  2222 0217     84.69  2238 0219     90.00
       2212 0203    242.09   **
       2213 0203    384.91  2224 0217    449.71
```

and dollar amount of deposits and checks can be compared to the detail data on the bank statement; the account holder's federal business identification number is on the statement, and this can be used in other databases; and the statement itself can be studied for alterations.

 REVIEW CHECKPOINTS

6.9   How can you tell whether the amount on a check was altered after it was paid by a bank?

6.10 Take a closer look at Exhibit 6.3. Is there anything wrong with the bank statement? What are some ways to tell whether any of the amounts have been altered?

Significant Accounts and Relevant Assertions

According to the professional standards, an account or disclosure is significant if there is a reasonable chance that it could contain a material misstatement. The auditor identifies significant accounts and relevant assertions by applying the audit risk model.

Chapter 4 introduced the audit risk model. As noted there, this model allows auditors to control audit risk to desired levels. *Audit risk* is defined as the risk that auditors will issue an unmodified opinion on financial statements that contain a material misstatement. Audit risk is manifested when a material misstatement enters the financial reporting process (inherent risk) that the client's internal controls do not prevent or detect (control risk) and that the auditors' substantive procedures do not detect (detection risk). Recall the basic three-step approach for using the audit risk model to plan an engagement:

1. Set audit risk at desired levels (normally, low).
2. Assess risk of material misstatement, which incorporates inherent risk based on the nature of the account balance or class of significant transactions and control risk based on gaining an understanding of internal control.
3. Determine detection risk at the significant account and assertion level based on the level of audit risk and risk of material misstatement.

The components of the audit risk model are assessed for each significant account and relevant assertion. This assessment recognizes that certain accounts and assertions assume an increased level of importance and are of more interest to auditors than others. For cash, existence is always a relevant assertion in the audit plan. Other assertions may also be relevant, depending on the facts and circumstances of the engagement. For example, if an audit client has worldwide operations, valuation may be relevant because certain cash balances may be denominated in foreign currencies, necessitating a translation adjustment.

Once all of the significant accounts and disclosures have been identified, the auditor then needs to identify the relevant assertions. According to the professional standards, a financial statement assertion is relevant if it has a "reasonable possibility of containing a misstatement that would cause the financial statements to be materially misstated." Exhibit 6.4 identifies the relevant assertions that are typical for cash. Although different companies may have other risks, in general the most significant risks relate to the existence of cash and the presentation and disclosure of cash. As previously stated, depending on the nature of the audit client's operations, valuation may also be a relevant assertion for cash. Although we will focus our discussion on these assertions, other assertions may be relevant depending on the facts and circumstances at the audit client.

EXHIBIT 6.4
Significant Accounts and Relevant Assertions

Significant Account	Relevant Assertions
	Existence
Cash	Valuation
	Presentation and disclosure

Risk of Material Misstatement

As part of the planning process, the auditor must determine the source of a misstatement that could cause the financial statements to be materially misstated. One way to assess the risk of material misstatement is to use the "what can go wrong?" (WCGW) approach when thinking of each financial statement assertion. WCGW is a part of each audit firm's process and enables a thorough assessment of the risk of material misstatement.

When considering WCGW for cash, auditors consider three primary concerns: (1) Does the reported cash balance really exist? (2) Is the cash balance valued properly? (3) Is the reported cash balance presented properly and have the appropriate disclosures been made? Exhibit 6.5 summarizes the WCGW analysis for cash.

EXHIBIT 6.5   **What Can Go Wrong?**

Significant Account	Relevant Assertions	What Can Go Wrong?
Cash	Existence	The cash balance may not exist in the company's bank accounts.
	Valuation	The cash balance that is held in foreign countries may not have been translated properly.
	Presentation and disclosure	There may be restrictions on the cash balance that were not properly disclosed.

Evaluating the Design and Operating Effectiveness of Internal Controls

LO 6-5
Identify important internal control activities present in a properly designed system to mitigate the risk of material misstatements for each relevant assertion related to cash and to help prevent or detect employee fraud.

When evaluating the design of internal controls related to cash, an auditor must always consider whether the controls have been designed to mitigate the risk of material misstatement for each relevant assertion identified for the cash balance. In addition, because cash is so frequently a favorite target of employee thieves, controls over cash must be unusually strong and include special considerations related to employee fraud. As a consequence, when evaluating the design of internal controls related to cash, an auditor must also consider whether the controls have been designed to mitigate the risk of employee fraud. Clearly, there is overlap between these two goals (i.e., mitigating the risk of material misstatement *and* preventing employee fraud), meaning that certain control activities may help to achieve objectives at an audit client. However, to help improve your understanding of both objectives, we now consider these topics separately.

Internal Control Evaluation for Mitigating the Risk of Material Misstatement

Recall from the audit risk model that the auditor assesses inherent risk to determine where in the financial statements it is reasonably possible that a material misstatement could enter the process *before the consideration of any internal controls.* However, risk of material misstatement is the combination of both inherent risk and control risk.

Professional standards require auditors to first gain an understanding of the internal controls that have been designed to mitigate the risk of material misstatement for each relevant assertion identified by the auditor. In a well-designed system, the internal control activity should be explicitly designed to be aligned with this relevant assertion that was identified in a WCGW analysis.

In effect, the question an auditor should ask is, "Has the audit client designed and implemented a control that, *if operating effectively,* would mitigate the identified risk of material misstatement? Would it prevent or detect the material misstatement?" Importantly, we have already discussed how auditors would gain an understanding of the internal controls related to cash earlier in this chapter, including the control environment and tone at the top. This discussion remains relevant when auditing the cash balance.

However, when auditing the cash balance, for each WCGW identified, the auditor seeks to identify a control activity that has been placed in operation to mitigate the identified risk of material misstatement. For example, as shown in Exhibit 6.6, for the WCGW scenario related to the existence of cash (i.e., the cash does not exist in the company's bank account), the auditor must consider what management can do to prevent this misstatement from entering the financial statements or from going undetected. One control

EXHIBIT 6.6 Tests of Internal Control

Significant Account	Relevant Assertions	What Can Go Wrong?	Internal Control Activity	Test of Internal Control
Cash	Existence	The cash balance may not exist in the company's bank accounts.	The CFO performs a detailed review of the bank reconciliation on a monthly basis.	For a sample of bank reconciliations, reperform the reconciliation. Trace several reconciling items to the appropriate supporting documentation.
	Valuation	The cash balance that is held in foreign countries may not have been translated properly.	The treasurer reviews the cash translation adjustment calculation monthly and independently checks that the appropriate spot rate has been used for each foreign currency.	Inspect the monthly cash translation adjustment calculation for evidence of the treasurer's review.
	Presentation and disclosure	There may be restrictions on the cash balance that were not properly disclosed.	The corporate secretary reviews the cash footnote disclosure on a quarterly basis to ensure that all legal restrictions on the cash balance have been properly disclosed.	For a sample of cash accounts, reperfom the work completed by the corporate secretary to ensure that all cash restrictions have been properly disclosed.

that the auditor would expect management to implement involves periodic reconciliation of the bank balance to the book balance. If an employee regularly completes the reconciliation and a supervisor reviews the reconciliation, the control should mitigate the risk that a material misstatement can proceed through the accounting system undetected.

In order to rely on the design of the client's internal controls and support a reduction in control risk, the auditor must determine if each identified control is operating as designed and whether the person operating the control has the authority and competence to do so. The auditor's ultimate responsibility is to document enough support to conclude whether the control activity was operating effectively to mitigate the risk of material misstatement for the relevant assertion identified.

Auditors can perform tests of controls to determine whether company personnel are properly performing controls that are said to be in place. In general, the procedures used in tests of controls are inquiry, observation, inspection, and reperformance. Understand that if a control is missing or ineffective, the risk of a material misstatement increases, but an error or fraud may or may not exist. Thus, if controls are not in place or personnel in the organization are not performing their control activities effectively, auditors need to design substantive procedures to try to detect whether control failures have produced material misstatements in the financial statements. Exhibit 6.6 includes a column that identifies the type of test of controls that may be performed in order to support a reduction in control risk and ultimately a reduction in the amount of substantive testing.

Once the tests of control are completed, auditors must evaluate the body of evidence related to internal controls. The initial process of obtaining an understanding of the company's controls and the later process of obtaining evidence from actual tests of controls are two of the phases of control risk assessment. If the control risk is assessed to be very low, the substantive procedures on the account balances can be reduced, resulting in audit efficiency. On the other hand, if tests of controls reveal weaknesses, the substantive procedures need to be designed to lower the risk of failing to detect material misstatement in the account balances.

Internal Control Evaluation for Preventing or Detecting Employee Fraud

We now take a step back from the financial statement audit to consider how an organization can help to prevent or detect employee fraud with properly designed control activities. Recall that because cash is highly liquid, not easily identifiable as company property, and portable, it tends to be a favorite target of employee thieves. Thus, controls over cash must be unusually strong and include special considerations related to employee fraud. In that spirit, it is essential that an audit client implement control activities for both cash receipts and disbursements that are designed to help "fraud-proof" the organization. Of course, many of the control activities that we are about to discuss are also designed to help mitigate material misstatements in the financial statements. However, for now, please focus on the following control activities as they are designed to prevent the misappropriation (or theft) of cash in an organization.

Control Activities for Cash Receipts

Cash can be received in several ways—over the counter, through the mail, and by electronic funds transfer. It can also be received in a **lockbox** arrangement in which payments are remitted by customers to an external location (i.e., a lockbox). In a lockbox arrangement, a fiduciary (usually a bank) opens the box on a daily basis, lists the receipts, deposits the money, and sends the remittance advices (stubs showing the amount received from each customer) to the company. Refer to Exhibit 6.7 for some cash receipts processing procedures in a manual accounting setting.

In many situations, an individual employee initially receives cash and checks and thus has custody of the physical cash for a short time. Because this initial custody cannot be avoided, it is always a good control to (1) have two people open the mail containing customer receipts, if possible, resulting in joint custody; (2) endorse the checks immediately

EXHIBIT 6.7 **Cash Receipts Processing**

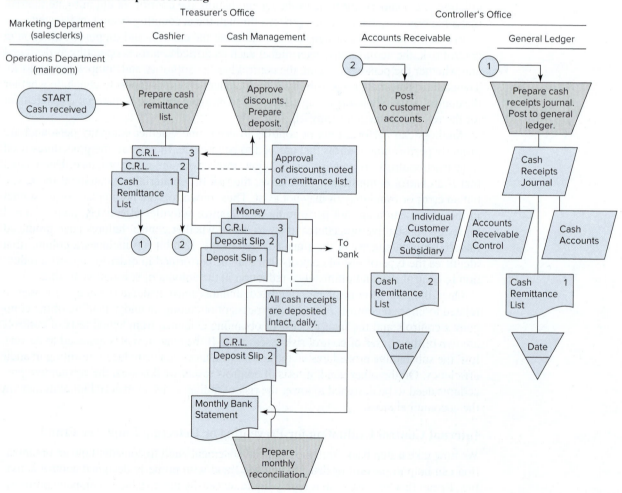

after removing them from the envelope; (3) prepare a list of the cash receipts as early in the process as possible; and then (4) separate the actual cash from the record-keeping documents. The cash should be sent to the cashier or treasurer's office where a bank deposit is prepared and the money is sent to the bank *daily* and *intact.* (No money should be withheld from the deposit.) The list or remittance advices go to the accountants (controller's office), who record the cash receipts. (You have prepared a "remittance advice" each time you write the amount enclosed on part of your credit card bill, tear it off, and enclose it with your check.)

The accountants who record cash receipts and credits to customer accounts should never handle the cash. They should use the remittance list or remittance advice to make the entries to the cash and accounts receivable control accounts and to the customers' accounts receivable subsidiary account records. A good internal control activity is to have the control account and subsidiary account entries made by different people, and later the accounts receivable entries and balances can be compared (reconciled) to determine whether they agree in total. Most computerized accounting programs post the customers' accounts automatically by keying in the customer identification number, and the computer program controls agreement.

At the end of the day, an independent employee should receive (1) a copy of the check listing, (2) a report of payments recorded in accounts receivable, and (3) a copy of the deposit slip from the bank. Commercial deposit slips have multiple copies. The bank runs these copies through the teller machine, which imprints the time, date, account, and amount on each copy. At least one copy is returned to the person making the deposit, who returns the copy to the company as evidence that the deposit was made. If the cash received during the day is maintained intact, the information on all three items should match.

Take a close look at Exhibit 6.7. Suppose that the cashier who prepares the remittance list had stolen and converted Customer A's checks to personal use. It might work for a short time until Customer A complained that the entity had not credited the account for payments. The cashier, of course, knows this. So, the cashier later puts Customer B's check in the bank deposit but shows Customer A on the remittance list; thus, the accountants give Customer A credit. So far, so good for preventing Customer A's complaint. But now Customer B needs to be covered. To detect this type of **lapping** scheme, a detailed audit should include a comparison of the checks listed on a sample of deposit slips (Customer B) to the detail of customer remittances recorded to customer accounts (Customer A). Doing so is an attempt to find credits given to customers for whom no payments were received on the day in question.

Employees outside the normal cash operations (recording and custody) should prepare bank account reconciliations on a timely basis. Deposit slips should be compared to the details on cash remittance lists, and the total should be traced to the general ledger accounts receivable entries. (This reconciliation would reveal whether money was withheld from the deposit.) This care is required to establish that all the receipts recorded in the books were deposited and that credit was given to the right customer.

A common feature of cash management is to require that persons who handle cash be insured under a **fidelity bond**, which is an insurance policy that covers most kinds of cash embezzlement losses. Fidelity bonds do not prevent or detect embezzlement, but the failure to carry the insurance exposes the company to complete loss if embezzlement occurs. Moreover, bonding companies often perform their own background checks of employees before bonding them. Auditors often recommend fidelity bonding to small companies that might not know about such coverage.

Tests of Controls over Cash Receipts

The first step in testing the controls over both cash receipts and cash disbursements (discussed later) is to gain an understanding of the controls and document that understanding. Information about a company's internal control activities can be gathered in different ways, which may include completing an internal control questionnaire. A selection of

AUDITING INSIGHT   Lapping Up the Profits

Stephan Winkler was the controller and director of accounting for a beverage distributing company in Florida. Some customers paid the route drivers by cash or check when beverages were delivered; other customers mailed payments directly to the company. Winkler performed the final accounting before the bank deposits were made and was able to skim cash collected by the route drivers by covering the customers' account with payments received in the mail from other customers. In this manner, Winkler stole approximately $350,000 from his employer.

Source: A. McNeal, "Lapping Up the Profits," *Internal Auditor,* December 2006, pp. 85–87.

these type of questionnaires for both manual and entirely automated controls over cash receipts is found in Appendix 6A at the end of this chapter. You can study these questionnaires for details related to other desirable control activities as well.

Another way to obtain general information about controls can be achieved by conducting a *walkthrough.* In conducting walkthroughs, the auditors select examples of a transaction (in this case, customer remittance advices) and "walk them through" the information-processing system from their initial receipt all the way to their recording in the accounting records. Sample documents are collected, and employees in each department are questioned about their specific duties. The walkthrough, combined with inquiries, can contribute evidence about appropriate separation of duties, which might be a sufficient basis for a preliminary assessment of control risk. However, a walkthrough is too limited in scope to provide evidence of whether the client's control activities were operating effectively during the period under audit. Rather, to justify a low control risk assessment and a reduction of substantive testing procedures, an auditor would have to conduct a test of operating effectiveness for the control activity under consideration.

An entity should establish input, processing, and output control activities to prevent, detect, and correct accounting errors. Auditors can perform tests of controls to determine whether the internal control activities related to the correct handling of cash receipts are operating effectively. If the internal control activities are not operating effectively (e.g., because personnel in the organization are not performing the cash control activities very well), auditors may need to expand substantive audit procedures to ensure that the cash balance is not materially misstated and to identify possible fraudulent acts related to cash.

Exhibit 6.8 contains a selection of tests of controls for cash receipts transactions. Many of these procedures can be characterized as steps taken to verify the content and character of sample documents from one file with the content and character of documents in another file. These steps are designed to enable the audit team to obtain objective

EXHIBIT 6.8

Tests of Controls for Cash Receipts

Internal Control	Test of Control
• Cash receipts are deposited intact and daily.	1. Observe the opening of the mail and ensure that:
	a. Two employees are opening the mail, remittance advice is received, and checks are properly endorsed.
	b. A listing of all checks is being prepared and compared to the total of the deposit ticket for the total of checks.
	c. The total amount of the deposit listed in the bank statement was recorded in the proper period.
• Deposits are reconciled with totals posted to the accounts receivable	2. For a sample of daily postings to the accounts receivable subsidiary ledger, trace the amount to the amount of cash subsidiary ledger.

evidence about the *effectiveness* of control activities and about the *reliability* of accounting records.

Control Activities for Cash Disbursements

As described in the previous section, the first step in testing the controls for cash disbursements is to gain an understanding of the controls and document that understanding. Similar to cash receipts, for cash disbursements, effective internal control begins with making sure that appropriate separation of duties has been achieved in an organization. Proper separation involves different people and different departments handling *custody* of blank documents (checks), cash disbursement *authorization, record keeping* for payments, and bank *reconciliation:*

- *Custody.* Blank documents such as blank checks should be kept secure at all times. If unauthorized persons can obtain a blank check, they can be in another country before an embezzlement is detected.
- *Authorization.* Cash disbursements are typically authorized by an accounts payable department's assembly of purchase orders, vendor invoices, and internal receiving reports to demonstrate a valid obligation to pay. This assembly of supporting documents is called a *voucher* and will be discussed in more detail in Chapter 8. (Accounts payable obligations usually are recorded when the purchaser receives the goods or services ordered.) A person authorized by management signs the checks. A company may have a policy to require two signatures on checks over a certain amount (e.g., $50,000). Vouchers should be marked "PAID" or otherwise stamped to show that they have been processed completely so they cannot be paid a second time.
- *Recording.* When checks are prepared, entries are made to debit accounts payable and credit cash. Someone without access to the check-writing function should always perform the recording function.
- *Reconciliation.* Monitoring of the internal control over cash can be provided by timely bank reconciliations made by individuals outside of the normal cash operations.

If combinations of two or more of these responsibilities are completed by one person or within the same office, there may be an opportunity for a fraudster to commit a crime. In addition, and almost more important in today's environment, is the fact that the computerized information-processing system must also provide for proper separation of duties. In practice, this is often accomplished by assigning the proper functional "permissions" to the appropriate employees through their password access credentials. Simply stated, in a computerized environment, proper separation of duties is dependent on proper password access controls. This is discussed in more detail in Module H.

Tests of Controls over Cash Disbursements

An entity should have detailed control activities in place and operating to prevent, detect, and correct accounting errors. Auditors can perform tests of controls to determine whether the internal control activities related to the correct handling of cash disbursements are operating effectively. If the internal control activities are not operating effectively (e.g., because personnel in the organization are not performing the cash control activities very well), auditors need to expand substantive audit procedures to ensure that the cash balance is not materially misstated and to identify possible fraudulent acts related to cash.

Exhibit 6.9 identifies common internal control activities that are designed to prevent or detect the misappropriation of cash and the typical test of control that would be used by auditors. As you will note, many of these procedures can be characterized as steps taken to make it difficult for a fraudster to steal cash. However, there are also controls designed to detect fraudulent activity if it occurs. The control tests are designed to enable the audit team to obtain objective evidence about the *operating effectiveness* of control activities.

EXHIBIT 6.9

Tests of Controls over Cash Disbursements

Internal Control	Test of Control
• Checks are not printed until voucher packets are prepared. • An employee compares amounts on printed checks with voucher packets prior to submission for signature. • Only authorized signers are permitted to sign checks.	1. For a sample of recorded cash disbursements from the cash disbursements journal, inspect supporting documentation for evidence of mathematical accuracy, correct classification, proper approval, authorized signature and then compare the date on the check with the date recorded in the disbursements journal.
• Checks are prenumbered and accounted for.	2. Scan checks for sequence. Look for gaps in sequence and duplicate numbers.
• Bank reconciliations are prepared on a timely basis.	3. Review bank reconciliations to ensure that they were prepared on a timely basis.

☑ REVIEW CHECKPOINTS

6.11 What is the basic sequence of activities in the cash collection process?

6.12 Why should a list of cash remittances be made and sent to the accounting department? Wouldn't it be easier to send the cash and checks to the accountants so they can enter the credits to customers' accounts accurately?

6.13 What is *lapping*? What procedures can auditors employ to detect lapping?

6.14 What feature of the acquisition and expenditure control would be expected to prevent an employee from embezzling cash by creating fictitious vouchers?

LO 6-6

Give examples of substantive procedures used to test cash and relate them to the relevant assertions.

Substantive Procedures

As you have learned previously while studying audit risk, the primary reason for evaluating the internal control system at an audit client is to reach an overall assessment of risk of material misstatement for each relevant assertion. In fact, the assessment of risk of material misstatement is completed to help form the basis for determining the nature, timing, and extent of substantive testing. Risk of material misstatement at the assertion level is comprised of both inherent risk and control risk for each relevant assertion.

If inherent risk has already been assessed as high, this means that there is high susceptibility for this account to be misstated. Recall that control risk is the "probability that an entity's controls will fail to prevent or detect material misstatements due to errors or frauds." Due to the nature of cash, the majority of audit clients have strong controls over cash, and tests of controls often support a reduction in control risk. This reduction in control risk reduces the auditor's assessment of the risk of material misstatement over cash. However, regardless of the final assessment of the risk of material misstatement, as with any significant account, the auditor will perform at least some substantive procedures over cash.

As stated previously, there are two types of substantive tests: analytical procedures and tests of detail and balances. As you may recall, a substantive analytical procedure is one where the auditor substantiates an account or disclosure by developing an independent estimate of the amount and then comparing the recorded balance to the estimate. Due to the lack of predictability of the cash balance, auditors rarely, if ever, use substantive analytical procedures to test cash. Rather, auditors typically rely exclusively on tests of detail. For example, auditors will generally test the bank reconciliations in detail, including sending confirmations to all banks in order to substantiate the existence of cash. Exhibit 6.10 presents the substantive tests that are likely to be completed to address remaining risks of material misstatement related to cash.

EXHIBIT 6.10 **Substantive Tests**

Significant Account	Relevant Assertions	Internal Control Activity	Tests of Internal Control	Possible Substantive Tests of Detail
Cash	Existence	The CFO perfoms a detailed review of the bank reconciliation on a monthly basis.	For a sample of bank reconciliations, reperform the reconciliation. Trace several reconciling items to the appropriate supporting documentation.	Test the bank reconciliation details for each significant cash account being held. Confirm the bank balance with each financial instituion.
	Valuation	The treasurer reviews the cash translation adjustment calcluation monthly and independently checks that the appropriate spot rate has been used for each foreign currency.	Inspect the monthly cash translation adjustment calculation for evidence of the treasurer's review.	For a sample of monthly cash translation adjustment calculations, trace each foreign currency spot rate to a third party pricing service.
	Presentation and Disclosure	The corporate secretary reviews the cash footnote disclosure on a quarterly basis to ensure that all legal restrictions on the cash balance have been properly disclosed.	For a sample of cash accounts, reperfom the work completed by the corporate secretary to insure that all cash restrictions have been properly disclosed.	For a sample of cash accounts, examine the legal agreements with each financial institution. Based on the examination, determine whether the audit client has properly disclosed any legal restrictions in their footnotes.

Without question, the most important test of detail completed on cash is to test the details of the entity prepared and reviewed bank reconciliation for each significant banking relationship. For that reason, our discussion of substantive procedures will focus almost exclusively on testing the bank reconciliation in detail. In effect, the auditor needs to obtain the bank reconciliation for each significant account and audit the details contained on each of them. In a well-functioning control environment, auditors should never have to perform the company's internal control activity of preparing the bank reconciliation. Always remember that the completion of the bank reconciliation is the responsibility of the client.

Bank Reconciliation

A client-prepared bank reconciliation is shown in Exhibit 6.11. When auditing the bank reconciliation, the auditor should begin by confirming the account balance listed as the "balance per bank" on the top of the bank reconciliation for each bank account from each bank that the client utilizes in the business. The auditor is required to send a confirmation letter by mail, and each bank should return it directly to the public accounting firm's office. This procedure is important because the auditor needs to make sure that the confirmation request was actually completed by an independent professional at a third-party bank. In fact, a failure to adhere to professional standards in this area was cited by the SEC and PCAOB when announcing financial statement fraud charges against **Satyam,** an information technology company based in India. A description is found in the Auditing Insight.

AUDITING INSIGHT | The Dangers of Bank Confirmations

The Securities and Exchange Commission recently charged "India-based Satyam Computer Services Limited with fraudulently overstating the company's revenue, income and cash balances by more than $1 billion over five years." The SEC's complaint states that "former senior officials at Satyam—an information technology services company based in Hyderabad, India—used false invoices and forged bank statements to inflate the company's cash balances and make it appear far more profitable to investors." In addition, "Satyam employees created bogus bank statements to reflect payment of the sham invoices. This resulted in more than $1 billion in fictitious cash and cash-related balances." In addition, the SEC instituted administrative proceedings against the auditors, **Price Waterhouse India** for "failure to properly execute third-party confirmation procedures" to test the existence of cash at Satyam.

Source: "SEC Charges Satyam Computer Services with Financial Fraud," www.sec.gov, Case 2011-81, April 5, 2011.

EXHIBIT 6.11
Bank Reconciliation

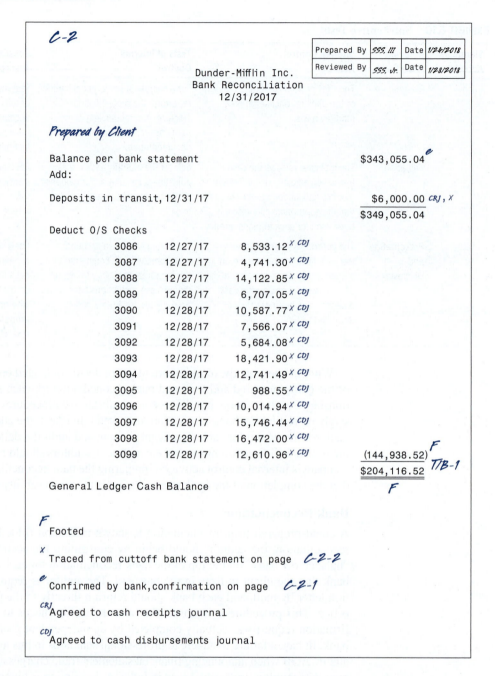

C-2

		Prepared By	*SSS, III*	Date	*1/24/2018*
		Reviewed By	*SSS, Jr.*	Date	*1/28/2018*

Dunder-Mifflin Inc.
Bank Reconciliation
12/31/2017

Prepared by Client

Balance per bank statement $343,055.04 *e*

Add:

Deposits in transit, 12/31/17 $6,000.00 *CRJ , X*
                                                          $349,055.04

Deduct O/S Checks
        3086   12/27/17   8,533.12 *X CDJ*
        3087   12/27/17   4,741.30 *X CDJ*
        3088   12/27/17   14,122.85 *X CDJ*
        3089   12/28/17   6,707.05 *X CDJ*
        3090   12/28/17   10,587.77 *X CDJ*
        3091   12/28/17   7,566.07 *X CDJ*
        3092   12/28/17   5,684.08 *X CDJ*
        3093   12/28/17   18,421.90 *X CDJ*
        3094   12/28/17   12,741.49 *X CDJ*
        3095   12/28/17   988.55 *X CDJ*
        3096   12/28/17   10,014.94 *X CDJ*
        3097   12/28/17   15,746.44 *X CDJ*
        3098   12/28/17   16,472.00 *X CDJ*
        3099   12/28/17   12,610.96 *X CDJ*   (144,938.52) *F*
                                                             TJB-1
                                                 $204,116.52
General Ledger Cash Balance   *F*

F
 Footed

X
 Traced from cuttoff bank statement on page *C-2-2*

e
 Confirmed by bank, confirmation on page *C-2-1*

CRJ
 Agreed to cash receipts journal

CDJ
 Agreed to cash disbursements journal

    The standard bank confirmation form, approved by the AICPA, the American Bankers Association, and the Bank Administration Institute, is shown in Exhibit 6.12. This form is used to obtain confirmation of deposit balances. You will note in Exhibit 6.12 that the auditor can also use the confirmation letter to confirm outstanding loan balances listed on the balance sheet. As shown, a bank's response to statement 2 would provide the auditor with evidence to test the existence assertion for liabilities. Alternatively, in regard to statement 2, the auditor may choose to leave out the detailed information about outstanding loan balances and instead ask the bank to list any loans or commitments made by the client at that bank. In this way, the auditors would be gathering evidence to test the completeness assertion for liabilities because the auditor would trace the information provided by the bank to loan balances listed on the balance sheet. We will discuss substantive tests of the loan balance in more detail in Chapter 10.

EXHIBIT 6.12 Bank Confirmation

C-2-1

**STANDARD FORM TO CONFIRM ACCOUNT
BALANCE INFORMATION WITH FINANCIAL INSTITUTIONS**

| Prepared By | SSS, III | Date | 1/24/2018 |
| Reviewed By | SSS, Jr. | Date | 1/28/2018 |

Dunder-Mifflin Inc.
CUSTOMER NAME

FINANCIAL INSTITUTION'S NAME AND ADDRESS

Twenty-First National Bank
Post Office Box 1
Shoetown, ME 00002

We have provided to our accountants the following information as of the close of business on 12/31/2017, regarding our deposit and loan balances. Please confirm the accuracy of the information, noting any exceptions to the information provided. If the balances have been left blank, please complete this form by furnishing the balance in the appropriate space below.* Although we do not request nor expect you to conduct a comprehensive, detailed search of your records, if during the process of completing this confirmation additional information about other deposit and loan accounts we may have with you comes to your attention, please include such information below. Please use the enclosed envelope to return the form directly to our accountants.

1. At the close of business on the date listed above, our records indicated the following deposit balance(s):

ACCOUNT NAME	ACCOUNT NO.	INTEREST RATE	BALANCE*	
Checking Account	604-17-526-5	n/a	343,055.04	C-2
Payroll Account	604-29-016-3	n/a	0	C-3
Savings Account	604-03-739-8	1.2%	4,150,947.95	C-4

2. We were directly liable to the financial institution for loans at the close of business on the date listed above as follows:

ACCOUNT NO./ DESCRIPTION	BALANCE*	DATE DUE	INTEREST RATE	DATE THROUGH WHICH INTEREST IS PAID	DESCRIPTION OF COLLATERAL	
Note#106316	10,000,000	1/1/2017	8.75%	11/30/2017	None	I-3
Line of Credit, Acct#7500438	44,053,000	2017 (revolving)	9.75%	11/30/2017	None	I-4

E.P. Unum   1/3/2018
(Customer's Authorized Signature)   (Date)

The information presented above by the customer is in agreement with our records. Although we have not conducted a comprehensive, detailed search of our records, no other deposit or loan accounts have come to our attention except as noted below.

I.M Rich   1/10/2018
(Financial Institution Authorized Signature)   (Date)

Account Confirmation Specialist
(Title)

EXCEPTIONS AND OR COMMENTS
No exceptions noted.

Please return this form directly to our accountants:

Smith & Smith, CPAs
31st Financial Avenue
Shoetown, ME 00002

*Ordinarily, balances are intentionally left blank if they are not available at the time this form is prepared.
Approved 1990 by American Bankers Association, American Institute of Certified Public Accountants, and Bank Administration Institute. Additional forms available from: AICPA–Order Department, P.O. Box 1003 NY, NY 10108-1003.

A couple of words of caution are in order. First, although financial institutions may note exceptions to the information typed in a confirmation and may confirm items omitted from it, the AICPA warns auditors that sole reliance on the form to satisfy the completeness assertion for cash and liabilities is inappropriate. Employees of financial institutions cannot be expected to search their information systems for balances and loans that may not be immediately evident as the client company's assets and liabilities. Second, even if the auditor properly controls the mailing and receipt of the confirmation request, she or he cannot be absolutely certain that a competent and independent professional at the bank has completed the response.

To help improve the control of both delivery and receipt of the confirmation request, to authenticate the identity of the person completing the request, and to improve efficiency, many public accounting firms now use electronic audit confirmations when confirming cash balances. In fact, almost all of the largest banks such as **Bank of America, JPMorgan Chase,** and **Wells Fargo** require auditors to use electronic audit confirmation requests and, as a result, all large audit firms now use them. When using electronic audit confirmations, auditors typically rely on a third-party intermediary (e.g., www.Confirmation.com) to provide a technological platform that allows information to be transmitted between the bank and the auditor in a safe and secure manner. In addition, the platform provides a manner to validate the authenticity of the bank employee responding to the confirmation request.[7]

AUDITING INSIGHT   More Dangers of Bank Confirmations

During the 2012 audit of **Peregrine Financial Group Inc.** (PFG), auditors from the National Futures Association requested permission to use an electronic confirmation platform, **Confirmation.com**, to confirm the cash balances at PFG. For several months, the CEO of PFG, Russell Wasendorf Sr., had adamantly resisted the authorization necessary to use Confirmation.com to confirm the company's bank balances. Ultimately, Wasendorf agreed to allow the use of the electronic platform, and within 24 hours, it was discovered that one bank account only had $6 million instead of the approximately $220 million that the company had reported to its auditors. It was later revealed

that Wasendorf had falsified bank statements and forged official letters as well as other correspondence from the bank, including letters of confirmation. Apparently, he had rented a post office box to intercept bank confirmation requests and forged the documents to conceal missing money.

Sources: "Red Flags at Failed Broker," *The Wall Street Journal,* July 12, 2012, p. C1; "Peregrine's Struggle to Stay Airborne," *The Wall Street Journal,* July 19, 2012, p. C1; "Trading Firm CEO: I Spent It," *The Wall Street Journal,* July 18, 2012, p. A1; "Peregrine CEO's Dramatic Confession," *The Wall Street Journal,* July 14, 2012, p. A1.

Once the "balance in the bank" has been confirmed and cross-referenced to the balance in the bank reconciliation, the following additional procedures are typically used in auditing the bank reconciliation:

- Test the mathematical accuracy of the reconciliation, including the listing of outstanding checks and deposits in transit.
- Examine reconciling items to ensure they are appropriately classified (e.g., that they were legitimate outstanding checks that were written but not paid by the bank at the statement date).
- Reconcile the book balance to the trial balance, which has been traced to the general ledger.

The auditors' information source for validating the bank reconciliation items is typically a **cutoff bank statement,** which is a complete bank statement including all paid checks and deposit slips. The client requests the bank to send this bank statement directly to the auditor. The cutoff bank statement usually represents a 10- to 20-day period following the

---

[7]D. Hanes, B. Porco, and J. Thibodeau, "Simply Soups Inc.: A Teaching Case Designed to Integrate the Electronic Confirmation Process into the Auditing Curriculum," *Issues in Accounting Education.* Vol. 29, No. 2: 349–369, 2014.

date of the financial statements. (It also can be the next regular monthly statement received directly by the auditors.) The cutoff bank statement is important because it (1) is sent directly to the auditors (which qualifies as *external evidence*) and (2) documents important bank transactions occurring early in the subsequent period so that the audit team does not have to wait for the normal bank statement to be sent to the client (which qualifies only as *external-internal evidence*). These transactions subsequent to the date of the financial statements are important for testing the completeness of the client's outstanding check list as well as the existence of any deposits in transit. The bank cutoff statement can also be used in a *search for unrecorded liabilities* discussed in more detail in Chapter 8.

Deposits in transit should be *vouched* from the bank reconciliation to the bank cutoff statement (*existence*) and should have been recorded by the bank in the first business days of the cutoff period. If recorded later, the inference is that the deposit may have been composed of receipts of the period after the date of the financial statements.

When auditing negative reconciling items (i.e., outstanding checks) listed on the bank reconciliation and because the audit team is most concerned about the existence of cash (i.e., overstatement) rather than the completeness of cash (i.e., understatement), the completeness of the outstanding checks listing is more critical than to support the existence of such checks. Comparably, when auditing positive reconciling items (i.e., deposits in transit) listed on the bank reconciliation, the *existence* of the deposits-in-transit on the reconciliation is more critical than their *completeness* because the audit team is most concerned about the existence of cash (i.e., overstatement) rather than the completeness of cash (i.e., understatement). As a result, the audit team *traces* outstanding checks that cleared on the cutoff bank statement (and were either returned with that statement or identified in that statement) to the client's list of outstanding checks for evidence that all checks that were written prior to the reconciliation date were included on the list of outstanding checks. Additionally, canceled checks should be traced to the cash disbursements listing (journal). For large outstanding checks not clearing in the cutoff period, other documentation supporting the disbursement may be used. These procedures are key and described by tick marks in Exhibit 6.11. As the next Auditing Insight suggests, it is important to pay close attention to possible errors in the bank reconciliation.

AUDITING INSIGHT   The Darn Stuff Is So Easy to Count

Through the use of discretionary estimates, **HealthSouth,** one of the largest health care providers in the United States, inflated its assets by $1.5 billion. In an even more bizarre twist, the company overstated its cash by more than $300 million, according to prosecutors. Because auditors use standardized forms to confirm cash balances with financial institutions, how the auditors missed the cash overstatement is a mystery. "I'm shocked that cash is manipulated and overstated, because the darn stuff is so easy to count," stated one audit expert. Nevertheless, auditors must never take the cash balance for granted when conducting the audit.

Source: "Did HealthSouth Auditor Ernst Miss Key Clues to Fraud Risks?" *The Wall Street Journal,* April 10, 2003.

Schedule of Interbank Transfers

Due to the nature of the cash balance, auditors also will often prepare a **schedule of interbank transfers** to determine whether transfers of cash from one bank to another were recorded properly (correct amount and correct date). The audit team should also be alert to the possibility of a company's practice of illegal "kiting." **Check kiting** is the deliberate floating of funds between two or more bank accounts in order to make it appear that more cash is present than is really the case. When a check is deposited in one bank, the cash receipts journal immediately includes that deposit. At the same time, the check, drawn on a different bank account, does not appear in the cash disbursements journal for several days. By this method, an entity can use the time required for checks to clear to inflate the cash amount on the entity's books. Advances in information technology and increased bank scrutiny have reduced the incidences of check kiting dramatically in recent years.

However, auditors must still be aware of the possibility; and the schedule of interbank transfers is a technique designed to detect the practice.

These are some characteristic signs of check-kiting schemes:

- Frequent deposits and checks in rounded and the same amounts.
- Frequent deposits with checks written on the same (other) banks.
- Short time lags between deposits and withdrawals.
- Frequent ATM account balance inquiries.
- Many large deposits made on Friday to take advantage of the weekend.
- Large periodic balances in individual accounts with no apparent business explanation.
- Low average balance compared to high level of deposits.
- Many checks made payable to other banks.
- Banks' willingness to pay against uncollected funds.
- "Cash" withdrawals with deposit checks drawn on another bank.
- Checks drawn on foreign banks with lax banking laws and regulations.

Auditors can detect the preceding signs of check kiting by reviewing an audit client's bank account activity. The only trouble is that criminal check kiters often destroy the banking documents. A company should provide the auditor access to all deposit slips and canceled checks. However, in today's computerized banking environment, many documents exist only in electronic form or as scanned images. The auditor may need to review the client's account activity directly on the bank's website.

Of course, if each of these cash transfers is recorded in the books, a company will show the negative balances that result from checks drawn on insufficient funds. However, perpetrators may try to hide the kiting by not recording the deposits and checks. Such maneuvers may be detected by using a schedule of interbank transfers.

Today, banks have implemented the Check Clearing for the 21st Century Act, referred to as "Check 21." In this system, checks are converted to digital images, allowing for a dramatic increase in speed in check clearing. The benefit is that the "float" on the check is virtually eliminated, and kiting becomes difficult to perform and conceal. However, in the Check 21 system, the paper check is usually destroyed, a hard copy of the check is never returned to the customer or its bank, and consequently, the nature of the audit trail is significantly different. In investigating possible fraud, the audit team is able to obtain only an electronic copy of the check and the controls over the safeguarding of the imaging files will be of great importance.

AUDITING INSIGHT   As Simple as Flying a Kite

Four employees of Detroit-based **Simplified Employment Services** were charged with defrauding banks of at least $32 million in a complex check-kiting scheme. Using seven corporate entities holding 21 separate checking accounts, the fraudsters were able to commingle legitimate company transactions with fraudulent ones to conceal overdrawn bank accounts.

Source: "4 Charged in $32 Million Check-Kiting Scheme," *Detroit News,* January 24, 2002.

☑ REVIEW CHECKPOINTS

6.15 What is a cutoff bank statement? How do auditors use it?

6.16 What is *check kiting*? How might auditors detect kiting?

6.17 How does a schedule of interbank transfers show improper cash transfer transactions?

"EXTENDED PROCEDURES" TO DETECT FRAUD

LO 6-7
Describe some extended procedures for detecting employee fraud schemes involving cash.

The auditing literature often refers to "extended procedures," which are "specific responses to fraud risk factors." Although the professional standards list a few of these procedures, an exhaustive list would be very lengthy. Moreover, authorities fear that a definitive list might limit the range of such procedures, so extended procedures are generally identified as whatever is necessary in the circumstances. This section describes some of the extended procedures and warns that (1) some auditors may consider them ordinary and (2) other auditors may consider them unnecessary in any circumstances. They are useful detective procedures in either event. Consider the following procedures.

Proof of Cash

Auditors can use another method to discover unrecorded cash transactions. It is called a *proof of cash.* You may have studied this method in your intermediate accounting course under the name of "four-column bank reconciliation." The **proof of cash** is a reconciliation in which the bank balance, the bank report of cash deposited, and the bank report of cash paid are all reconciled to the corresponding records maintained in the entity's general ledger, cash receipts journal, and cash disbursements journal. Exhibit 6.13 illustrates a proof of cash.

The proof of cash attempts to reconcile the deposits and payments reported by the bank to the deposits and payments recorded in the cash receipts and cash disbursements journals, respectively, as well as the final general ledger totals. The proof of cash is a very effective procedure to verify cash transactions but is usually used only when controls over cash are weak.

Count and Recount Petty Cash on the Same Day

A second petty cash count is unexpected, and auditors might catch an embezzling custodian who incorrectly believes that "the auditors are gone, so now it's safe!" Auditors should always make sure a client employee is present during the count and that the employee signs for the returned cash so the auditor cannot be blamed for any shortages. Another "trick of the trade" is to make sure that the auditor's pockets are empty (leave wallets locked up

EXHIBIT 6.13   Illustration of Proof of Cash—First National Bank

	Balance June 30	Month of July Deposits	Month of July Payments	Balance July 31
Bank statement amounts	$264,322	$398,406	$390,442	$272,286
Deposits in transit				
June 30	76,501	(76,501)		
July 31		79,721		79,721
Outstanding checks				
June 30	(89,734)		(89,734)	
July 31			62,958	(62,958)
Unrecorded bank interest (recorded in the next month)				
June 30	(162)	162		
July 31		(155)		(155)
Unrecorded service charges (recorded in the next month)				
June 30	118		118	
July 31			(129)	129
Unrecorded transfers received from Last National Bank		(37,000)		(37,000)
Unrecorded transfers to Last National Bank			(42,000)	42,000
General ledger amounts	$251,045	$364,633	$321,655	$294,023

safely elsewhere) when counting client cash on hand. This is especially important when counting cash at a financial services client such as a bank or credit union. All cash should be counted simultaneously to prevent embezzling employees from substituting cash from other places. If this is not possible (e.g., the employee claims that he or she does not have the safe combination), there is audit tape (similar to police tape) to seal the safe until it can be opened with the auditor present. If the seal is broken, your suspicions should be raised.

Examine Endorsements on Canceled Checks

Most business payments are deposited with one (usually stamped) endorsement. Look for handwritten endorsements and second endorsements, especially those of employees. The second endorsee indicates that the payee (possibly a "ghost employee") may not have received the benefit of the payment. Be sure to include checks payable to "cash" or to a bank for purchase of cashiers' checks.

AUDITING INSIGHT   Who Endorsed That Check?

The distribution manager called internal audit and asked why his predecessor's endorsement was on a $600 check payable to the company and why it appeared to be deposited in his personal account. Further investigation revealed that the former manager had been selling company inventory without recording the sale and keeping the payments when received. The result? More than 60 payments totaling approximately $70,000 were identified. However, a count of physical inventory revealed an inventory variance of more than $200,000. Keep an eye on those endorsements!

Source: "Purchasing Below the Radar," *Internal Auditor,* August 2003, pp. 95–97.

Retrieve Customers' Checks

If an employee has diverted customer payments for his or her own use, the canceled checks showing endorsements and deposits to a bank where the company has no account are not available because they are returned to the issuing customer. Ask the customer to give originals or copies (front and back) or to provide access for examination.

Use Marked Coins and Currency

Plant marked money in locations where cash collections should be gathered and turned over for deposit.

Analyze the Mix of Cash and Checks in Deposits

This procedure is most effective for retail operations in which cashiers receive significant amounts of both cash and checks. Unless there is a marked change in consumer behavior, one should expect the mix of cash and checks to be relatively consistent over time. A decrease in the proportion of cash in the mix is often a sign that employees may be stealing cash.

AUDITING INSIGHT   Mixing It Up

Noting a significant change in the mix of cash and checks on bank deposit slips over time, a government auditor became suspicious enough to set up a hidden camera. The camera caught a county tax clerk "skimming" cash from daily property tax deposits. The clerk would pocket most of the cash, leaving the checks to be deposited. The fraud perpetrator was able to conceal the theft by replacing the missing cash with checks written to the county for other, miscellaneous purposes for which established procedures were not closely followed.

In an unrelated fraud, **Ocean World Seafood** was charged with food stamp fraud. According to investigators, a store of Ocean World's size would normally make approximately $3,000 a month in sales paid with food stamps. Over a 13-month period, Ocean World accepted more than $1 million in food stamps. Apparently, the store would provide cash for food stamps, paying approximately 50 cents for $1 of food stamps.

Source: "Store Owner Charged in $1 Million Food Stamp Fraud," *Associated Press Wire,* April 15, 2005.

Measure Deposit Lag Time

Compare the date of the deposit slip to the date recorded as a debit in the general ledger to the date the deposit was credited in the account by the bank. Someone who takes cash and then holds the deposit for the next cash receipt to make up the difference causes a delay between the date of recording and the bank's date of deposit.

Document Examination

When performing this procedure, auditors will look for erasures, alterations, and photocopies where originals should be filed, telltale lines from a copier when a document has been pieced together, handwriting, and other oddities. Auditors should always insist on seeing original documents instead of photocopies. Importantly, while professional document examination is a technical activity that requires special training (e.g., training by the IRS, FBI), crude alterations may still be observed by the auditor when performing procedures, which should lead to a consultation with a professional document examiner when deemed necessary.

Inquiry

Be careful not to discuss fraud possibilities with the managers who might be involved. It gives them a chance to cover up their fraud or even resign from the organization prior to detecting the fraud. Described as a nonaccusatory method of asking key questions of personnel during a regular audit, *fraud audit questioning (FAQ)* provides employees an opportunity to furnish information about possible misdeeds. Fraud possibilities are addressed in a direct manner, so the FAQ approach must have the support of management. Example questions are: "Do you think fraud is a problem for business in general?" "Do you think this company has any particular problem with fraud?" "In your department, who is beyond suspicion?" "Is there any information you would like to furnish regarding possible fraud within this organization?"[9]

Covert Surveillance

When performing this procedure, auditors will observe activities while not being seen. For example, audit team members might watch employees as they punch in to a work shift, observing whether they use only one time card. Casino auditors actually get paid to gamble so they can observe cash-handling procedures. Traveling hotel auditors may check in unannounced, use the restaurant and entertainment facilities, and observe employees to determine if they are stealing cash receipts or tickets. (Trailing people on streets, undercover surveillance, and maintaining a "stake-out" should be left to trained investigators.)

Horizontal and Vertical Analyses

Horizontal and vertical ratio analysis procedures are very similar to preliminary analytical procedures explained in earlier chapters. *Horizontal analysis* refers to changes of financial statement numbers and ratios across several years. *Vertical analysis* refers to

AUDITING INSIGHT   The Case of the Extra Checkout

The district grocery store manager could not understand why receipts and profitability had fallen and inventory was hard to manage at one of the largest stores in her area. She hired an investigator who covertly observed the checkout clerks and reported that no one had shown suspicious behavior at any of the nine checkout counters. "Nine? That store only has eight," she exclaimed! As it turns out, the local store manager had installed another checkout aisle not connected to the cash receipts and inventory maintenance central computer and was pocketing all the receipts from that register.

Source: Association of Certified Fraud Examiners (ACFE), "Auditing for Fraud."

---

[9] Joseph T. Wells, "From the Chairman: Fraud Audit Questioning," *The White Paper,* National Association of Certified Fraud Examiners, May–June 1991, p. 2. This technique must be used with extreme care and practice.

financial statement amounts expressed each year as proportions of a base such as sales for the income statement accounts and total assets for the balance sheet accounts. Auditors look for relationships that do not appear logical as indicators of potential large misstatement and fraud.

Net Worth Analysis

This analysis is used when fraud has been discovered or strongly suspected and the information to calculate a suspect's net worth can be obtained (e.g., asset and liability records, bank accounts). The method involves calculating the suspect's net worth (known assets minus known liabilities) at the beginning and end of a period (months or years) and then trying to account for the difference as (1) known income less living expenses and (2) unidentified difference. The unidentified difference may be the best available approximation of the amount of a theft.

Expenditure Analysis

This analysis is similar to net worth analysis except the data are the suspect's spending for all purposes compared to known income. If spending exceeds legitimate and explainable income, the difference may be the amount of a theft.

Reasonableness Tests

Often, auditors become so involved in ticking and tying numbers that they forget to ask themselves the simplest questions: Where is the cash going? For what purpose? Is this reasonable? The answers to these questions often motivate the auditor to ask more penetrating questions of management and to dig for more evidence.

AUDITING INSIGHT · Thank Goodness It's Payday!

Five individuals were charged with tax and insurance fraud in the operation of a temporary employment agency in southeastern Massachusetts. From January 1993 through June 2001, the agency paid a large portion of its payroll in cash in order to avoid employment taxes (e.g., Social Security and Medicare) and to reduce payments for workers' compensation insurance. Why would a company pay its employees in cash? Is there a legitimate reason to do this? Even if the employees wanted cash, would there be a better way to provide it?

Source: "Five Charged in $30 Million 'Under-the-Table' Payroll Fraud, Reports U.S. Attorney," *PR Newswire*, January 27, 2005.

REVIEW CHECKPOINTS

6.18 How can a *proof of cash* reveal unrecorded cash deposit and cash payment transactions?

6.19 What is the difference between a *normal* procedure and an *extended* procedure?

6.20 What might two endorsements on a canceled check indicate?

6.21 What can an auditor find using net worth analysis? Expenditure analysis?

Summary

Although auditing standards concentrate on management fraud—the production of materially false and misleading financial statements (i.e., fraudulent financial reporting)—professional standards also require auditors to consider employee fraud perpetrated against an entity. Attention to employee fraud is important in the context that the cover-up may create financial statement misstatements (e.g., overstating inventory to disguise unauthorized removal of valuable products). The three conditions that are likely to be present when a fraud occurs (Exhibit 6.1) are commonly referred to as the "fraud triangle." The first condition (incentive/pressure) recognizes that an employee or a manager of a company is likely to either have incentives in place (e.g., bonus compensation) or be under significant pressure to meet specific estimates, forecasts, or expectations about net income. The second condition (opportunity) recognizes that in order for a fraud to be perpetrated, there must be a weakness in the system of internal control to allow the fraud to occur. Finally, the third condition (attitude/rationalization) recognizes that for an employee or a manager of a company to perpetrate a fraud, the individual must possess an "attitude" that allows her or him to rationalize that she or he is knowingly committing a crime.

Audit team members need to know about the red flags, those telltale signs and indications that have accompanied many frauds. When studying a business operation, members' ability to "think like a crook" to devise ways to steal can help in planning procedures designed to determine whether fraud has happened. Often, imaginative "extended procedures" can be employed to unearth evidence of fraudulent activity. Audit team members must always exercise technical and personal care, however, because accusations of fraud are taken very seriously. For this reason, after preliminary findings indicate fraud possibilities, the audit team should enlist the cooperation of management and assist fraud examination professionals when bringing an investigation to a conclusion.

Once the relevant assertions have been identified for cash (e.g., existence) and the tests of control activities are complete, the auditor must evaluate the evidence obtained from risk assessment activities and control tests to determine the risk of material misstatement for each relevant assertion. Cash is highly liquid, very portable, and not easily identifiable. For these reasons, cash is often the primary target of fraudulent activities and must be carefully controlled and monitored. Accordingly, controls over cash receipts and disbursements must be strong. With respect to auditing the cash balance, the detailed procedures performed on the bank reconciliation provide evidence about the existence of cash.

Additional procedures can be performed to try to detect attempts at lapping accounts receivable collections and kiting checks. For lapping, these procedures include comparing the details of customer payments listed in bank deposits to the details of customer payment postings (remittance lists). For kiting, these procedures include being alert to the signs of kiting activity and preparing a schedule of interbank transfers. If controls are weak, a proof of cash is an effective procedure to verify that recorded cash transactions have occurred and are complete.

Key Terms

check kiting: The practice of building up balances in one or more bank accounts based on uncollected (floating) checks drawn against similar accounts in other banks.

cutoff bank statement: A client bank statement (usually sent directly to the auditor) that includes all paid checks and deposit slips through a certain date, usually the middle of the month.

direct-effect illegal acts: The violations of laws or government regulations by a company or its management or employees that produce direct and material effects on dollar amounts in financial statements.

embezzlement: A type of fraud involving employees or nonemployees wrongfully taking money or property entrusted to their care, custody, and control, often accompanied by false accounting entries and other forms of lying and cover-up.

employee fraud (also called misappropriation of assets): The use of fraudulent means to take money or other property from an employer. It consists of three phases: (1) the fraudulent act, (2) the conversion of the money or property to the fraudster's use, and (3) the cover-up.

errors: The unintentional misstatements or omissions of amounts or disclosures in financial statements.

fidelity bond: An insurance policy that covers most kinds of cash embezzlement losses.

fraud: The misrepresentation of facts that the individual knows to be false with the intention to deceive.

lapping: The theft of a payment and the application of subsequent payments to cover the theft.

lockbox: An arrangement in which a fiduciary (e.g., a bank) receives the payments, lists the receipts, deposits the money, and sends the remittance advices (stubs showing the amount received from each customer) to the company.

management fraud: The deliberate fraud committed by management that injures investors and creditors through materially misleading information.

misappropriation of assets: See employee fraud.

motive: In the fraud context, is essentially a reason for a person to take a fraudulent action that is believed to be unshareable with friends and confidants.

proof of cash: A reconciliation in which the bank balance, the bank report of cash deposited, and the bank report of cash paid are all reconciled to the company's general ledger and cash receipts and disbursements journals.

schedule of interbank transfers: A document prepared for use in analyzing whether transfers of cash from one bank to another were recorded properly (correct amount and correct date).

Multiple-Choice Questions for Practice and Review

All applicable Exercises and Problems are available with *Connect.*

LO 6-2

6.22 When auditing with "fraud awareness," auditors should especially notice and follow up employee activities under which of these conditions?

a. The company always estimates the inventory but never takes a complete physical count.

b. The petty cash box is always locked in the desk of the custodian.

c. Management has published a company code of ethics and sends frequent communication newsletters about it.

d. The board of directors reviews and approves all investment transactions.

LO 6-3

6.23 The best way to enact a broad fraud prevention program is to

a. Install airtight control systems of checks and supervision.

b. Name an "ethics officer" who is responsible for receiving and acting on fraud tips.

c. Place dedicated hotline telephones on walls around the workplace with direct communication to the company ethics officer.

d. Practice management "of the people and for the people" to help them share personal and professional problems.

LO 6-3

6.24 A good fraud prevention program should address employees' motivation to steal from the company. The best method for doing this is to

a. Establish employee assistance programs.

b. Require a fidelity bond on all employees.

c. Require reconciliations of all accounts to be reviewed by a supervisor.

d. Ensure that all accounts with high inherent risk of fraud are audited.

LO 6-3

6.25 A code of ethics is an important element of a fraud prevention program. Which of the following would diminish the effectiveness of a company's code of conduct?

a. The establishment of a chief ethics officer.

b. The establishment of a hotline for reporting unethical behavior.

c. The violation of the code of ethics by senior management.

d. The posting of the code of ethics in the company workplace.

LO 6-2

6.26 Which of the following is *least* indicative of fraudulent activity?

a. Numerous cash refunds have been made to different people at the same post office box address.

b. Internal auditors cannot locate several credit memos to support reductions of customers' balances.

c. Bank reconciliation has no outstanding checks or deposits older than 15 days.

d. Three people were absent the day the auditors handed out the paychecks and have not picked them up four weeks later.

LO 6-3

6.27 Which of the following combinations is a good way to conceal employee fraud but an ineffective means of perpetrating management (financial reporting) fraud?

a. Overstating sales revenue and overstating customer accounts receivable balances.

b. Overstating sales revenue and overstating bad debt expense.

c. Understating interest expense and understating accrued interest payable.

d. Omitting the disclosure information about related-party sales to the president's relatives at below-market prices.

LO 6-5

6.28 Allison Everhart, an employee in accounts payable, believes she can run a fictitious invoice through the accounts payable system and collect the money. She knows payments are subject to an audit. Which account would be the best place to hide the fraud?

a. Inventory.

b. Wage expense.

c. Consulting service expense.

d. Property tax expense.

LO 6-1

6.29 Which of these arrangements of duties could most likely lead to an embezzlement or theft?

a. The inventory warehouse manager has responsibility for making the physical inventory observation and reconciling discrepancies to the perpetual inventory records.

b. The cashier prepared the bank deposit, endorsed the checks with a company stamp, and delivered the cash and checks to the bank for deposit (no other bookkeeping duties).

c. The accounts receivable clerk received a list of payments received by the cashier so he could make entries in the customers' accounts receivable subsidiary accounts.

d. The financial vice president received checks made out to suppliers and the supporting invoices, signed the checks, and mailed the checks.

LO 6-5

6.30 Which of the following would the auditor consider to be an incompatible operation if the cashier receives remittances?

a. The cashier prepares the daily deposit.

b. The cashier makes the daily deposit at a local bank.

c. The cashier posts the receipts to the accounts receivable subsidiary ledger cards.

d. The cashier endorses the checks.

LO 6-5

6.31 Which of the following is an effective audit procedure that an auditor might use to detect kiting between intercompany banks?

a. Review the composition of authenticated deposit slips.

b. Review subsequent bank statements.

c. Prepare a schedule of the bank transfers.

d. Prepare a year-end bank reconciliation.

LO 6-5

6.32 Immediately upon receipt of cash, a responsible employee should

a. Record the amount in the cash receipts journal.

b. Prepare a remittance listing.

c. Update the subsidiary accounts receivable records.

d. Prepare a deposit slip in triplicate.

(AICPA adapted)

LO 6-4

6.33 Each morning the controller gets the prior day's list of remittances, a copy of the payment report, and a copy of the deposit slip returned from the bank. When comparing these items, the controller would be able to determine that

a. No checks were returned for insufficient funds.

b. The cash received and remittance advice received were maintained in a single batch.

c. The accounts receivable system has controls over unauthorized access.

d. The assistant controller does not also reconcile the subsidiary accounts payable.

LO 6-4

6.34 Upon receipt of customers' checks in the mail room, a responsible employee should prepare a remittance list that is forwarded to the cashier. A copy of the list should be sent to the

a. Internal auditor to investigate the list for unusual transactions.

b. Treasurer to compare the list with the monthly bank statement.

c. Accounts receivable bookkeeper to update the subsidiary accounts receivable records.

d. Entity's bank to compare the list with the cashier's deposit slip.

(AICPA adapted)

LO 6-4

6.35 Cash receipts from sales on account have been misappropriated. Which of the following acts would conceal this defalcation and be least likely to be detected by an auditor?

a. Understating the sales journal.

b. Overstating the accounts receivable control account.

c. Overstating the accounts receivable subsidiary ledger.

d. Overstating the sales journal.

LO 6-1

6.36 Embezzlement is a type of fraud that involves

a. An employee's misappropriating an employer's money or property not entrusted to him or her.

b. A manager's falsification of financial statements for the purpose of misleading investors and creditors.

c. An employee's mistaken representation of opinion that causes incorrect accounting entries.

d. An employee misappropriating an employer's money or property entrusted to the employee's control in the employee's normal job.

LO 6-5

6.37 Which of the following control activities would best protect against the preparation of improper or inaccurate cash disbursements?

a. All checks must be signed by an officer designated by the board of directors.

b. All signed checks must be reviewed and compared with supporting documentation by the treasurer before mailing.

c. All checks must be sequentially numbered and accounted for by internal auditors.

d. All checks must be perforated or otherwise effectively canceled when they are returned with the bank statement.

LO 6-4

6.38 During an audit of cash, the auditor is most concerned with the management assertion of

a. Existence.

b. Rights and obligations.

c. Valuation or allocation.

d. Occurrence.

LO 6-6

6.39 In preparing for the audit of cash, the auditors perform analytical procedures concerning cash balances. Which of the following would be the best source of information for use in the estimate of cash?

a. Prior-years' balances.

b. Management inquiry.

c. Cash budgets.

d. Aged accounts receivable reports.

LO 6-5

6.40 Which of the following control activities could prevent a paid disbursement voucher from being presented for payment a second time?

a. Vouchers should be prepared by individuals who are responsible for signing disbursement checks.

b. Disbursement vouchers should be approved by at least two responsible management officials.

c. The date on a disbursement voucher should be within a few days of the date the voucher is presented for payment.

d. The official signing the check should compare it with the voucher and should stamp "paid" on the voucher documents.

LO 6-2

6.41 Fraud risk factors are events or conditions that indicate which of the following?

a. An opportunity to carry out a fraud.

b. An attitude or rationalization that justifies a fraudulent action.

c. An incentive or pressure to perpetrate fraud.

d. All of these are correct.

LO 6-7

6.42 If the auditor believes that a misstatement is or might be intentional and the effect on the financial statements could be material or cannot be readily determined, the auditor should do which of the following?

    a. Inquire of management as to the possibility of fraud.

    b. Discuss with the audit committee what should be done to prevent possible future misstatements.

    c. Perform procedures to obtain additional audit evidence to determine whether fraud has occurred or is likely to have occurred.

    d. Both a and b are correct.

    e. None of these is correct.

LO 6-7

6.43 In what way can audit procedures be modified to address assessed fraud risks?

    a. Obtain more reliable information.

    b. Perform procedures close to year-end.

    c. Apply computer-assisted techniques to all items.

    d. All of these are valid modifications.

LO 6-7

6.44 Incorporating elements of unpredictability in the selection of audit procedures to be performed by auditors include all of the following *except*

    a. Varying the timing of the audit procedures.

    b. Selecting items for testing that have lower amounts or are otherwise outside customary selection parameters.

    c. Performing audit procedures on an unannounced basis.

    d. Sending attorney letters to every attorney listed under the legal expense account.

    e. None of these is correct.

LO 6-2

6.45 Fraud risk factors are events or conditions that indicate

    I. An incentive or pressure to perpetrate fraud.

    II. An opportunity to carry out the fraud.

    III. An attitude or rationalization that justifies the fraudulent action.

    Which of the following statements is true?

    a. I is a fraud risk factor.

    b. I and II are fraud risk factors.

    c. II and III are fraud risk factors.

    d. None of these is a fraud risk factor.

    e. I, II, and III are fraud risk factors.

Exercises and Problems

connect All applicable Exercises and Problems are available with *Connect.*

LO 6-5

6.46 **Tests of Controls over Cash Disbursements.** The Runge Controls Corporation manufactures and markets electrical control systems: temperature controls, machine controls, burglar alarms, and the like. The company acquires electrical and semiconductor parts from outside vendors and assembles systems in its own plant. The company incurs other administrative and operating expenditures. Liabilities for goods and services purchased are entered in a vouchers payable journal, at which time the debits are classified to the asset and expense accounts to which they apply.

    The company has specified control activities for approving vendor invoices for payment, for signing checks, for keeping records, and for reconciling the checking accounts. The procedures appear to be well specified and in operation.

    You are the senior auditor on the Runge engagement and need to specify a list of test of control procedures to evaluate the effectiveness of the controls over cash disbursements.

Required:

Using management's assertions over transactions as a guide, specify two or more tests of control procedures to audit the effectiveness of typical control activities. (*Hint:* From one sample of recorded cash disbursements, you can specify procedures related to several objectives.

See Exhibit 6.9 for examples of test of control procedures over cash disbursements.) Organize your list according to the following example for the "completeness" assertion.

Completeness Assertion	Test of Controls
All valid cash disbursements are recorded and none is omitted.	Determine the numerical sequence of checks issued during the period and scan the sequence for missing numbers.

(AICPA adapted)

LO 6-5

6.47 **Internal Control Questionnaire for Book Buy-Back Cash Fund.** Taylor, a CPA, has been engaged to audit the financial statements of University Books, Incorporated. University Books maintains a large cash fund exclusively for the purpose of buying used books from students for cash. The cash fund is active all year because the nearby university offers a large variety of courses with varying starting and completion dates throughout the year.

Receipts are prepared for each purchase. Reimbursement vouchers periodically are submitted to replenish the fund.

Required:

Construct an internal control questionnaire to be used in evaluating the internal control over University Books' repurchasing process using the revolving cash fund. The internal control questionnaire should elicit a yes or no response to each question. *Do not discuss the internal controls over books that are purchased from publishers.*

(AICPA adapted)

LO 6-5

6.48 **Test of Controls over Cash Receipts.** You are the in-charge auditor examining the financial statements of the Gutzler Company for the year ended December 31. During late October, with the help of Gutzler's controller, you completed an internal control questionnaire and prepared the appropriate memoranda describing Gutzler's accounting procedures. Your comments relative to cash receipts are as follows:

- All cash receipts are sent directly to the accounts receivable clerk with no processing by the mail department. The accounts receivable clerk keeps the cash receipts journal, prepares the bank deposit slip in duplicate, posts from the deposit slip to the subsidiary accounts receivable ledger, and mails the deposit to the bank.
- The controller receives the validated deposit slips directly (unopened) from the bank. She also receives the monthly bank statement directly (unopened) from the bank and promptly reconciles it.
- At the end of each month, the accounts receivable clerk notifies the general ledger clerk by journal voucher of the monthly totals of the cash receipts journal for posting to the general ledger.
- With regard to the general ledger cash account, the general ledger clerk makes an entry each month to record the total debits to cash from the cash receipts journal. In addition, the general ledger clerk, on occasion, makes debit entries in the general ledger cash account from sources other than the cash receipts journal, for example, funds borrowed from the bank.

In the audit of cash receipts, you have already performed certain standard audit procedures:

- All columns in the cash receipts journal have been totaled and cross-totaled.
- Postings from the cash receipts journal have been traced to the general ledger.
- Remittance advices and related correspondence have been traced to entries in the cash receipts journal.

Required:

Considering Gutzler's internal control over cash receipts and the standard audit procedures already performed, list all other audit procedures that should be performed to obtain sufficient appropriate audit evidence regarding controls over cash and give the reasons for each procedure. Do not discuss the procedures for cash disbursements and cash balances. Also, do not discuss the extent to which any of the procedures are to be performed. Assume that adequate controls exist to ensure that all sales transactions are recorded. Organize your answer sheet as follows:

Other Audit Procedure	Reason for Other Audit Procedures

(AICPA adapted)

LO 6-3

6.49 **Internal Control over Sales Returns.** You are the auditor for Konerko's Office Supply Store, which is opening for business next week. The store owner has established all the controls you have recommended for ensuring that sales are recorded properly and cash is accounted for. The owner has heard from other small business owners that employees often used returned goods as means of skimming money from the register.

Required:

a. How might an employee use returned goods to skim money from the register?

b. What controls would you recommend to prevent or detect fraudulent returns?

c. What audit procedures might you perform to detect fraudulent returns?

LO 6-6

6.50 **Procedures for Auditing a Client's Bank Reconciliation.** Auditors typically will find the items lettered A–F in a client-prepared bank reconciliation.

GENERAL COMPANY
Bank Reconciliation: 1st National Bank
September 30

A. Balance per bank			$28,375
B. Deposits in transit			
Sept 29		$ 4,500	
Sept 30		1,525	6,025
			34,400
C. Outstanding checks:			
988	Aug 31	$ 2,200	
1281	Sept 26	675	
1285	Sept 27	850	
1289	Sept 29	2,500	
1292	Sept 30	7,255	(11,450)
			20,950
D. Customer note collected by the bank:			(3,000)
E. Error: Check #1282, written on Sept. 26 for $270, was erroneously charged by bank as $720; bank was notified Oct. 2			450
F. Balance per books			$20,400

Required:

Assume these facts: On October 11, the auditor received a cutoff bank statement dated October 7. The September 30 deposit in transit; the outstanding checks 1281, 1285, 1289, and 1292; and the correction of the bank error regarding check 1282 appeared on the cutoff bank statement.

a. For each of the preceding lettered items A–F, select one or more of the following procedures 1–10 that you believe the auditor should perform to obtain evidence about the item. These procedures may be selected once, more than once, or not at all. Be prepared to explain the reasons for your choices.

1. Trace to cash receipts journal.
2. Trace to cash disbursements journal.

3. Compare to the September 30 general ledger.

4. Confirm directly with the bank.

5. Inspect bank credit memo.

6. Inspect bank debit memo.

7. Ascertain reason for unusual delay, if any.

8. Inspect supporting documents for reconciling items that do not appear on the cutoff bank statement.

9. Trace items on the bank reconciliation to the cutoff bank statement.

10. Trace items on the cutoff bank statement to the bank reconciliation.

b. Auditors ordinarily foot a client-prepared bank reconciliation. If the auditors had performed this recalculation on the preceding bank reconciliation, what might they have found? Be prepared to discuss any findings.

(AICPA adapted)

LO 6-7

6.51 **Proof of Cash.** You can use the computer-based *Electronic Audit Documentation* on the textbook's website to prepare the proof of cash required in this problem.

The auditors of Steffey Ltd., decided to study the cash receipts and disbursements for the month of July of the current year under audit. They obtained the bank reconciliations and the cash journals prepared by the company accountants, which revealed the following:

June 30: Bank balance, $355,001; deposits in transit, $86,899; outstanding checks, $42,690; general ledger cash balance, $399,210.

July 1: Cash receipts journal, $650,187; cash disbursements journal, $565,397.

July 31: Bank balance, $506,100; deposits in transit, $51,240; outstanding checks, $73,340; general ledger cash balance, $484,000. Bank statement record of deposits: $835,846; of payments: $684,747.

Required:

Prepare a four-column proof of cash (see Exhibit 6.13 for an example) covering the month of July of the current year. Identify problems, if any.

LO 6-6

6.52 **Interbank Transfers.** You can use the computer-based *Electronic Workpapers* on the textbook website to prepare the schedule of interbank transfers required in this problem.

EverReady Corporation is in the home building and repair business. Construction business has been in a slump, and the company has experienced financial difficulty over the past two years. Part of the problem lies in the company's desire to avoid laying off its skilled crews of bricklayers and cabinetmakers. Meeting the payroll has been a problem.

The auditors are engaged to audit the 2017 financial statements. Knowing of EverReady's financial difficulty and its business policy, the auditors decided to prepare a schedule of interbank transfers covering the 10 days before and after December 31, which is the company's balance sheet date.

First, the auditors used the cash receipts and disbursements journals to prepare part of the schedule shown in Exhibit 6.52.1. They obtained the information for everything except the dates of deposit and payment in the bank statements (disbursing date per bank and receiving date per bank). The auditors learned that EverReady always transferred money to the payroll account at 1st National Bank from the general account at 1st National Bank. This transfer enabled the bank to clear the payroll checks without delay. The only bank accounts in the EverReady financial statements are the two at 1st National Bank.

Next, the auditors obtained the December 2017 and January 2018 bank statements for the general and payroll accounts at 1st National Bank. They recorded the bank disbursement and receipt dates in the schedule of interbank transfers. For each transfer, these dates are identical because the accounts are in the same bank. An alert auditor noticed that the 1st National Bank general account bank statement also contains deposits received from Citizen National Bank and canceled check 1799 dated January 5 payable to Citizen National Bank. This check cleared the 1st National Bank account on January 8 and was marked "transfer of funds." This led to the auditors' decision to inquire about this of EverReady's chief financial officer.

EXHIBIT 6.52.1   Schedule of Interbank Transfers

C-5

EVERREADY CORPORATION
Schedule of Interbank Transfers
December 31, 2017

Prepared _____
Date _____
Reviewed _____
Date _____

			Disbursing Account				Receiving Account	
Check	Bank	Amount	Date per Books	Date per Bank	Bank	Date per Books	Date per Bank
1417	1st National	10,463√	24-Dec	24-Dec m	1st National Payroll	24-Dec†	24-Dec n
1601	1st National	11,593√	31-Dec b	31-Dec m	1st National Payroll	31-Dec†	31-Dec n
1982	1st National	9,971√	08-Jan	08-Jan m	1st National Payroll	08-Jan†	08-Jan n

√ Traced from cash disbursements journal.
^{b} Check properly listed as outstanding on bank reconciliation.
^{m} Vouched deposit cleared in bank statement.
† Traced from cash receipts journal.
^{n} Vouched deposit cleared in bank statement.

Note: We scanned the cash disbursements and cash receipts journals for checks to and deposits from other bank accounts.

Asked about the Citizen National Bank transactions, EverReady's chief financial officer readily admitted the existence of an off-books bank account. He explained that it was used for financing transactions in keeping with normal practice in the construction industry. He gave the auditors the December and January bank statements for the account at Citizen National Bank. In it, the auditors found the following:

Citizen National Bank

Check	Payable to	Amount	Dated	Cleared Bank
4050	1st National	$10,000	23-Dec	29-Dec
4051	Chase Bank	12,000	28-Dec	31-Dec
4052	1st National	12,000	30-Dec	05-Jan
4053	Chase Bank	14,000	4-Jan	07-Jan
4054	1st National	20,000	8-Jan	13-Jan

Deposits

Received from	Amount	Date
Chase Bank	$11,000	22-Dec
Chase Bank	15,000	30-Dec
1st National	10,000	05-Jan
Chase Bank	12,000	07-Jan

When asked about the Chase Bank transactions, EverReady's chief financial officer admitted the existence of another off-books bank account, which he said was the personal account of the principal stockholder. He explained that the stockholder often used it to finance EverReady's operations. He gave the auditors the December and January bank statements for this account at Chase Bank; in it, the auditors found the following:

Chase Bank

Payments

Check #	Payable to	Amount	Dated	Cleared Bank
2220	Citizen National Bank	11,000	22-Dec	28-Dec
2221	Citizen National Bank	15,000	30-Dec	05-Jan
2222	Citizen National Bank	12,000	7-Jan	12-Jan

	Deposits	
Received from	**Amount**	**Dated**
Citizen National Bank	12,000	28-Dec
Citizen National Bank	14,000	04-Jan

An abbreviated calendar for the period is in Exhibit 6.52.2.

EXHIBIT 6.52.2

	S	M	T	W	T	F	S
December 2017	20	21	22	23	24	25	26
	27	28	29	30	31		
January 2018						1	2
	3	4	5	6	7	8	9
	10	11	12	13	14	15	16

Required:

a. Complete the Schedule of Interbank Transfers (document C-5, Exhibit 6.54.1) by entering the new information.

b. What is the actual cash balance for the three bank accounts combined, considering only the amounts given in this case information as of December 31, 2017 (before any of the December 31 payroll checks are cashed by employees)? As of January 8, 2018 (before any of the January 8 payroll checks are cashed by employees)? (*Hint:* Prepare a schedule of bank and actual balances.)

LO 6-6

6.53 **Manipulated Bank Reconciliation.** You can use the computer-based *Electronic Workpapers* on the textbook website to prepare the bank reconciliation solution.

Caulco Inc. is the audit client. The February bank statement is shown in Exhibit 6.3 in the text. You have obtained the client-prepared bank reconciliation as of February 28 (see the following).

Required:

Check 2231 was the first check written in February. All earlier checks cleared the bank, some during January and some during February. Assume that the only February-dated canceled checks returned in the March bank statement are 2239 and 2240 showing the amounts listed in the February bank reconciliation. They cleared the bank on March 3 and March 2, respectively. The first deposit on the March bank statement was $1,097.69 credited on March 3. Assume also that all checks entered in Caulco's cash disbursements journal through February 29 have either cleared the bank or are listed as outstanding checks in the February bank reconciliation.

Determine whether any errors exist in the following bank reconciliation. If errors exist, prepare a corrected reconciliation and explain the problem.

CAULCO INC.
Bank Reconciliation
February 28

Balance per bank				$7,374.93
Deposit in transit				1,097.69
Outstanding Checks				
Number	**Date**	**Payee**	**Amount**	
2239	Feb 26	Alpha Supply	500.00	
2240	Feb 28	L.C. Stateman	254.37	
Total outstanding				(754.37)
General ledger balance Feb. 28				$7,718.25

LO 6-7

6.54 **Investigating a Fraud.** Suppose you are auditing cash disbursements and discover several payments to a company you are unfamiliar with and cannot find information about this company on the Internet or in the local telephone directory. The invoices from this company have numbers very close to each other in the sequence, there is no phone number on the invoice, and each bill is for a dollar amount just under the amount that would require additional approvals before payment. Based on this information, you now suspect this may be a fraud.

Required:

Based on your suspicions, how would you change the audit procedures you would perform, and how might you change the evidence you gather?

LO 6-5

6.55 **Fraud in Purchasing.** Consider the following scenario:

Adam worked for the local hardware store as an outside sales representative. His job was to visit local companies and contractors in an attempt to identify their needs for tools and materials and provide a bid to supply those items. When a local contractor accepted a new job, Adam would get its material requirements, come back to the store, and prepare and submit a proposal for the items. After some initial success with Big Builder, a large contractor, the number of jobs awarded to Adam had decreased dramatically.

One day, Adam was back at the store after losing a bid to Big Builder when he noticed someone in the store purchasing the exact items and quantities that were in the specification for that bid. The combination of items was unusual, and it would be an unlikely coincidence for someone else to want such a combination in that exact quantity. The customer paid the retail price for the merchandise and left.

Adam decided to contact Big Builder, but he knew he could not do so and make any accusations. Adam set up a meeting with the president of Big Builder and inquired as to how Adam might "increase his business and better meet the needs of Big Builder." Eventually, the recent bid entered the conversation. Adam showed his copy of the bid to the president. The president retrieved a copy of the purchase order and recognized that the amount on it was more than the bid Adam had submitted. The company that submitted the bid was K. A. Supplies Inc. Adam had never heard of K. A. Supplies and noted its address on the purchase order. The president of Big Builder promised to investigate the bidding process.

Adam drove to the address of K. A. Supplies and found a packaging and shipping store at that address. Furthermore, Adam went to the county courthouse and inquired about K. A. Supplies. The company was listed in the county records, and one of the purchasing agents for Big Builder was listed as an officer.

Required:

a. Given the information that Adam knows, what do you believe is occurring at Big Builder?
b. What other information would you want to obtain, and how might you retrieve that information?
c. What controls might be instituted at Big Builder to prevent improprieties in the bidding and purchasing process?

LO 6-1

6.56 **The Perfect Crime?** Consider the following story of an actual embezzlement.

This was the ingenious embezzler's scheme: (a) He hired a print shop to print a private stock of Ajax Company checks in the company's numerical sequence. (b) In his job as an accounts payable clerk at Ajax, he intercepted legitimate checks written by the accounts payable department and signed by the Ajax treasurer and destroyed them. (c) He substituted the same numbered check from the private stock, payable to himself in the same amount as the legitimate check, and he "signed" it with a rubber stamp that looked enough like the Ajax Company treasurer's signature to fool the paying bank. (d) He deposited the money in his own bank account. The bank statement reconciler (a different person) was able to agree the check numbers and amounts listed in the cleared items in the bank statement to the recorded cash disbursement (check number and amount) and thus did not notice the embezzler's scheme. The embezzler was able to process the vendor's "past due" notice and the next month's statement with complete documentation, enabling the Ajax treasurer to sign another check the next month paying both the past due balance and current charges. The embezzler was careful to scatter the double-expense payments among numerous accounts (telephone, office supplies, inventory, etc.) so the double-paid expenses did not distort any accounts very much. As time passed, the embezzler was able to recommend budget amounts that allowed a large enough budget so his double-paid expenses in various categories did not often pop up as large variances from the budget.

Required:

List and explain the ways and means you believe someone might detect the embezzlement. Think first about the ordinary everyday control activities. Then think about extensive detection efforts assuming a tip or indication of a possible fraud has been received. Is this a "perfect crime"?

LO 6-7

6.57 **Select Effective Extended Procedures.** The following are some "suspicions"; you have been requested to select some effective extended procedures designed to confirm or deny the suspicions.

Required:

Write the suggested procedures for each case in definite terms so another person can know what to do.

a. The custodian of the petty cash fund may be removing cash on Friday afternoon to pay for weekend activities.

b. A manager noticed that eight new vendors were added to the purchasing department's approved vendor list after the assistant purchasing agent was promoted to chief agent three weeks ago. She suspects all or some of them might be fictitious companies set up by the new chief purchasing agent.

c. The payroll supervisor may be stealing unclaimed paychecks of employees who resigned and did not collect their last check.

d. Although no customers have complained, cash collections on accounts receivable have decreased, and the counter clerks may have stolen customers' payments.

e. The cashier may have "borrowed" cash receipts, covering this by holding each day's deposit until cash from the next day(s) collection is enough to make up the shortage from an earlier day and then sending the deposit to the bank.

LO 6-7

6.58 **Forensic Accounting: Assurance Engagement 1: Expenditure Analysis.** Expenditure analysis is used when fraud has been discovered or strongly suspected and the information to calculate a suspect's income and expenditures can be obtained (e.g., asset and liability records, bank accounts). Expenditure analysis consists of establishing the suspect's known expenditures for all purposes for the relevant period, subtracting all known sources of funds (e.g., wages, gifts, inheritances, bank balances), and identifying the difference as "expenditures financed by unknown sources of income."

The law firm of Gleckel and Morris has hired you. The lawyers have been retained by Blade Manufacturing Company in a case involving a suspected kickback by a purchasing employee, E. J. Cunningham. Cunningham is suspected of taking kickbacks from Mason Varner, a salesman for Tanco Metals. Cunningham has denied the charges, but Lanier Gleckel, the lawyer in charge of the case, is convinced the kickbacks have occurred.

Gleckel filed a civil action and subpoenaed Cunningham's financial records, including last year's bank statements. The beginning bank balance January 1 was $3,463, and the ending bank balance December 31 was $2,050. Over the intervening 12 months, Cunningham's per-month gross salary was $3,600 with a net of $2,950. His house payments were $1,377 per month. In addition, he paid $2,361 per month on a new Mercedes 500 SEL and a total of $9,444 last year toward a new Nissan Maxima (including $5,000 down payment). He also purchased new state-of-the-art audio and video equipment for $18,763 with no down payment and made total payments of $5,532 on the equipment last year. A reasonable estimate of his household expenses during the period is $900 per month ($400 for food, $200 for utilities, and $300 for other items).

Required:

Using expenditure analysis, calculate the amount of income, if any, from "unknown sources."

LO 6-7

6.59 **Forensic Accounting: Assurance Engagement 2: Net Worth Analysis.** You can use the computer-based *Electronic Workpapers* on the textbook website to prepare the net worth analysis required in this problem.

Net worth analysis is performed when fraud has been discovered or is strongly suspected and the information to calculate a suspect's net worth can be obtained (e.g., asset and liability records, bank accounts). The procedure used is to calculate the person's change in net worth (excluding changes in market values of assets) and to identify the known sources of funds to finance the changes. Any difference between the change in net worth and the known sources of funds is called *funds from unknown sources,* which might include ill-gotten gains.

Nero has worked for Bonne Consulting Group (BCG) as the executive secretary for administration for nearly 10 years. Her dedication has earned her a reputation as an outstanding employee and has resulted in increasing responsibilities. Nero is also a suspect in a fraud.

During Nero's first five years of employment, BCG subcontracted all of its feasibility and marketing studies through Jackson & Company. This relationship was terminated because Jackson & Company merged with a larger, more expensive consulting group. At the time of termination, Nero and her supervisor were forced to select a new firm to conduct BCG's market research. However, Nero never informed the accounting department that the Jackson & Company account had been closed.

Because her supervisor allowed Nero to sign the payment voucher for services rendered, she was able to continue to process checks made payable to Jackson's account. Nero was trusted to be the only signature required to authorize payments less than $10,000. The accounting department continued to write the checks and Nero took responsibility for delivering the checks. She opened a bank account in a nearby city under the name of Jackson & Company, where she made the deposits.

Nero's financial records have been obtained by subpoena. Exhibit 6.59.1 provides a summary of the data obtained from her records.

EXHIBIT 6.59.1
Nero's Subpoenaed
Records

	Year 1	Year 2	Year 3
Assets:			
Residence	$100,000	$100,000	$100,000
Stocks and bonds	30,000	30,000	42,000
Automobiles	20,000	20,000	40,000
Certificate of deposit	50,000	50,000	50,000
Cash	6,000	12,000	14,000
Liabilities:			
Mortgage balance	90,000	50,000	—
Auto loan	10,000	—	—
Income:			
Salary		34,000	36,000
Other		6,000	6,000
Expenses:			
Scheduled mortgage payments		6,000	6,000
Auto loan payments		4,800	—
Other living expenses		20,000	22,000

Required:

You have been hired to estimate the amount of loss by estimating Nero's "funds from unknown sources" that financed her comfortable life style. (*Hint:* Set up a working paper like the following:)

	End Year 1	End Year 2	End Year 3
Assets (list)			
Liabilities (list)			
Net worth (difference)			
Change in net worth			
Add total expenses			
= Change plus expenses			
Subtract known income			
= Funds from unknown sources			

LO 6-1

6.60 **Employee Embezzlement via Cash Receipts and Payment of Personal Expenses.** Assume you have received a message from an informant regarding the following case. Your assignment is to write the "audit approach" portion of the case.

 a. Write a brief explanation of desirable controls, missing controls, and especially the kinds of "deviations" that might arise from the situation described in the case. (Refer to controls explained in Chapter 5.)

 b. Develop some procedures for obtaining evidence about existing controls, especially procedures that could discover deviations from controls. If there are no controls to test, then there are no procedures to perform. Then just move on to part (c). (Refer to test of controls procedures explained in this chapter.) An audit "procedure" should instruct someone about the source(s) of evidence to obtain and the work to perform.

 c. Write some procedures for gathering evidence in this case.

 d. Write a short statement about the discovery you expect to accomplish with your procedures.

The Extra Bank Account

The Ourtown Independent School District, like all others, had formal, often bureaucratic, procedures regarding school board approval of cash disbursements. To get around the rules and to make possible timely payment of selected bills, the superintendent of schools had a school bank account that was used in the manner of a petty cash fund. The board knew about it and had given blanket approval in advance for its use to make timely payment of minor school expenses. The board, however, never reviewed the activity in this account. The business manager had sole responsibility for the account subject to the annual audit. The account received money from transfers from other school accounts and from deposit of cafeteria cash receipts. The superintendent did not like to be bothered with details and often signed blank checks so the business manager would not need to obtain a signature all the time. The business manager sometimes paid her personal **American Express** credit card bills, charged personal items to the school's Visa account, and pocketed some cafeteria cash receipts before deposit.

An informant called the state education audit agency and told the story that this business manager had used school funds to buy hosiery. When told of this story, the superintendent told the auditor to place no credibility in the informant, who was "out to get us." The business manager had, in fact, used the account to write unauthorized checks to "cash," put her own American Express bills in the school files (the school district had a Visa card, not American Express), and signed on the school card for gasoline and auto repairs during periods of vacation and summer when school was not in session. (As for the hosiery, she purchased $700 worth with school funds one year.) The superintendent was genuinely unaware of the misuse of funds. The business manager had been employed for six years, was trusted, and embezzled an estimated $25,000.

LO 6-6

6.61 **Electronic Confirmations.** As stated in the text, most of the largest banks such as Bank of America, JPMorgan Chase, and Wells Fargo require auditors to use electronic audit confirmation requests and, as a result, all large audit firms now use them. At present, Confirmation.com is the market-leading technological platform for electronic audit confirmations. Please visit their educational website at https://edu.confirmation.com/resources/mp-auditing.aspx and complete the tutorial as directed at the website address provided.

LO 6-2

6.62 **Case of the Missing Petty Cash** The case below tells the actual story of a cash embezzlement scheme. The case has two major parts: (1) problem and (2) audit approach. For the case, please consider how the auditor may have discovered the cash embezzlement scheme.

Problem

The petty cash custodian (1) brought postage receipts from home and paid them from the fund, (2) persuaded the supervisor to sign blank authorization slips the custodian could use when the supervisor was away and used them to pay for fictitious meals and minor supplies, and (3) took cash to get through the weekend, replacing it the next week. Postage receipts were from a distant post office station the company did not use. The blank authorization slips were dated on days the supervisor was absent. The fund was cash short during the weekend and for a few days the following week. The fund was small ($500), but the custodian replenished it about every two working days, stealing about $50 each time. With about 260 working days per year and 130 reimbursements, the custodian was stealing about $6,500 per year. The custodian was looking forward to getting promoted to general cashier and bigger and better things!

Audit Approach

The audit team should discuss petty cash procedures with the custodian and supervisor, especially those that relate to situations in which the custodian or supervisor is not available to provide needed petty cash. Next, a sample of petty cash reimbursement check copies with receipts and authorization slips attached should be studied for evidence of authorization and validity. On Friday, an audit team member should count the petty cash and receipts to see that they total $500. Then the fund should be recounted later in the afternoon. (The second count should be a surprise.) The custodian or supervisor should be present at all times so that the auditor will not be accused of theft.

Required

Based on the audit approach discussed, how would the auditor have caught this fraudulent scheme?

LO 6-2

6.63 **The Laundry Money Skim** The case below tells the actual story of a cash embezzlement scheme. The case has two major parts: (1) problem and (2) audit approach. For the case, please consider how the auditor may have discovered the cash embezzlement scheme.

Problem

Albert owned and operated 40 coin laundries around town. As the business grew, he could no longer visit each one, empty the cash boxes, and deposit the receipts. Each location grossed about $140 to $160 per day, operating 365 days per year—gross receipts of about $2 million per year. Each of four part-time employees visited 10 locations, collecting the cash boxes and delivering them to Albert's office where he would count the coins and currency (from the change machine) and prepare a bank deposit. One of the employees skimmed $5 to $10 from each location visited each day.

The daily theft does not seem like much, but at an average of $7.50 per day from each of 10 locations, totaled about $27,000 per year. If all four of the employees had stolen the same amount, the loss could have been over $100,000 per year.

Audit Approach

Controls over the part-time employees were nonexistent. There was no overt or covert surprise observation and no times when two people went to collect cash (thereby needing to agree, in collusion, to steal). There was no rotation of locations or other indications to the employees that Albert was concerned about control. With no controls, there is no test of control activities. Obviously, however, "thinking like a crook" leads to the conclusion that the employees could simply pocket money.

Assuming that some employees are honest, periodically rotating the stores assigned to each employee and performing revenue comparisons (analytical procedures) on a store-by-store basis may be helpful. If revenues consistently decline for stores assigned to a specific employee, further investigation may be warranted.

Required

Based on the audit approach discussed, how might an auditor devise a procedure to catch this fraudulent scheme?

Appendix 6A

Internal Control Questionnaires

EXHIBIT 6A.1 Internal Control Questionnaire—Cash Receipts Processing

	Yes	No	Comments
1. Are cash receipts deposited daily, intact, and without delay?			
2. Does someone other than the cashier or accounts receivable bookkeeper take the deposits to the bank?			
3. Are the duties of the cashier entirely separate from record keeping for notes and accounts receivable? From general ledger record keeping?			
4. Is the cashier denied access to receivables records or monthly statements?			
5. Is a bank reconciliation performed monthly by someone who does not have cash custody or record-keeping responsibility?			
6. Are the cash receipts journal entries compared to the remittance lists and deposit slips regularly?			
7. Does the person who opens the mail make a list of cash received (a remittance list)?			
8. Are currency receipts controlled by mechanical devices? Are machine totals checked by the internal auditor?			
9. Are prenumbered cash receipts listings used? Is the numerical sequence checked for missing documents?			
10. Does the accounting manual contain instructions for dating cash receipts entries the same day as the date of receipt?			
11. Is a duplicate deposit slip retained by someone other than the employee preparing the deposit?			
12. Is the remittance list compared to the deposit by someone other than the cashier?			
13. Does the accounting manual contain instructions for classifying cash receipts credits?			
14. Does someone reconcile the accounts receivable subsidiary to the control account regularly (to determine whether all entries were made to customers' accounts)?			

EXHIBIT 6A.2 Internal Control Questionnaire—Cash Disbursements Processing

	Yes	No	Comments
1. Are persons with cash custody or check-signing authority denied access to accounting journals, ledgers, and bank reconciliations?			
2. Is access to blank checks denied to unauthorized persons?			
3. Are all disbursements except petty cash made by check?			
4. Are check signers prohibited from drawing checks to cash?			
5. Are signing blank checks prohibited?			
6. Are voided checks mutilated and retained for inspection?			
7. Are invoices, receiving reports, and purchase orders reviewed by the check signer?			
8. Are the supporting documents stamped "paid" (to prevent duplicate payment) before being returned to accounts payable for filing?			
9. Are checks mailed directly by the signer and not returned to the accounts payable department for mailing?			
10. Do checks require two signatures? Is there dual control over machine signature plates?			
11. Are blank checks prenumbered and the numerical sequence checked for missing documents?			
12. Are checks dated in the cash disbursements journal with the date of the check?			
13. Are bank accounts reconciled by personnel independent of cash custody or record keeping?			

(continued)

EXHIBIT 6A.2 *(concluded)*

	Yes	No	Comments
14. Do internal auditors periodically conduct a surprise audit of bank reconciliations?			
15. Do the chart of accounts and accounting manual give instructions for determining debit classifications of disbursements not charged to accounts payable?			
16. Is the distribution of charges checked periodically by an official? Is the budget used to check on gross misclassification errors?			
17. Are special disbursements (e.g., payroll and dividends) made from separate bank accounts?			
18. Is the bank reconciliation reviewed by an accounting official with no conflicting cash receipts, cash disbursements, or record-keeping responsibilities?			

Appendix 6B

Audit Plans

EXHIBIT 6B.1   **Audit Plan—Tests of Controls—Cash**

	Documentation Reference	Performed By

1. Inquire of management concerning employees who
  a. Receive remittances from customers.
  b. Record payments in accounts payable.
  c. Prepare and deliver payments to the bank.		

2. Observe the opening of the mail and ensure that
  a. Two employees are opening the mail.
  b. Checks are restrictively endorsed.
  c. A listing of all checks is being prepared.		

3. Observe the flow of checks and remittance advices and ensure that
  a. Checks are delivered directly to the cashier.
  b. Remittance advices are delivered to the accounting department.		

4. Examine reconciliations of cash listings, accounts receivable payments, and bank deposits.		

5. Examine reconciliations of bank statements for
  a. Initials of proper review.
  b. Investigation of all outstanding items reviewed for propriety.		

EXHIBIT 6B.2   **Audit Plan—Selected Substantive Procedures—Cash**

	Documentation Reference	Performed By
1. Obtain confirmations from banks (standard bank confirmation).		

2. Obtain reconciliations of all bank accounts.
  a. Trace the bank balance on the reconciliation to the bank confirmation.
  b. Trace the reconciled book balance to the general ledger.
  c. Recompute the bank reconciliation for mathematical accuracy.		

3. Examine the bank confirmation for evidence of loans and collateral.		

4. Inquire of the client to request a cutoff bank statement for each account, to be mailed directly to the audit firm.
  a. Vouch deposits in transit on the reconciliation to the bank cutoff statement.
  b. Trace the outstanding checks that have cleared the cutoff statement back to the list of outstanding checks on the bank reconciliation.		

5. Prepare a schedule of interbank transfers for a period of 10 business days before and after the year-end date. Document dates of book entry transfer and correspondence with bank entries and reconciliation items, if any.		
6. Count cash funds in the presence of a client representative.		
7. Obtain management representations concerning compensating balance agreements.		

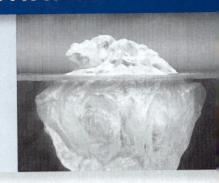

CHAPTER 7

Revenue and Collection Cycle

What at first was plunder,
assumed the softer name of revenue.

> Thomas Paine, English-American political philosopher and revolutionary
> (1737–1809)

Professional Standards References

Topic	AU-C/ISA Section	PCAOB Reference
Audit Documentation	230	AS 1215
Consideration of Fraud in a Financial Statement Audit	240	AS 2401
Audit Planning	300	AS 2101
Identifying and Assessing the Risks of Material Misstatement	315	AS 2110
The Auditor's Responses to Risks of Material Misstatement	330	AS 2301
Audit Evidence	500	AS 1105
External Confirmations	505	AS 2310
Substantive Analytical Procedures	520	AS 2305
Auditing Accounting Estimates	540	AS 2501
Related Parties	550	AS 2410
Management Representations	580	AS 2805

LEARNING OBJECTIVES

This is the first of four "cycle chapters" in which you will go through the process of evaluating the audit risks present in a specific cycle and learning how to apply the auditing standards to the identified risks. First, we give a general overview of the typical activities in the revenue and collection cycle. Next, we discuss the significant accounts and relevant assertions in the revenue cycle. After that, we discuss the risk of material misstatement in the revenue cycle. Many recent frauds have consisted of improper revenue recognition, which also results in an overstatement of assets, usually receivables. Next, we examine the appropriate design of controls normally included in the cycle and how the auditor evaluates the operating effectiveness of these controls. Finally, we discuss substantive procedures, including common analytical procedures. You will note that accounts receivable confirmations are a central part

LO 7-4 Identify important internal control activities present in a properly designed system to mitigate the risk of material misstatements for each relevant assertion in the revenue and collection cycle.

of accounts receivable auditing and are required by GAAS. You will see examples of confirmations and a discussion of procedures auditors perform when sending those confirmations. We conclude with an application of what you have learned to a specific audit issue within the revenue and collection cycle.

Your objectives are to be able to:

LO 7-1 Describe the revenue and collection cycle, including typical source documents.

LO 7-2 Identify significant accounts and relevant assertions related to the revenue and collection cycle.

LO 7-3 Discuss the risk of material misstatement in the revenue and collection cycle, with a specific focus on improper revenue recognition.

LO 7-5 Give examples of tests of controls to test the operating effectiveness of internal controls in the revenue and collection cycle.

LO 7-6 Give examples of substantive procedures in the revenue and collection cycle and relate them to assertions about significant account balances at the end of the period.

LO 7-7 Apply your knowledge to perform audit procedures in the revenue and collection cycle and evaluate the findings of your tests.

INTRODUCTION

Rather than attend an **EY** banquet honoring him as Denmark's "Entrepreneur of the Year," Stein Bagger, the dynamic CEO of the **IT Factory**, a Danish computer software company, was attempting to flee the country ahead of law enforcement officials investigating what has become known as "Denmark's Enron." Experts suggest that approximately 95 percent ($200 million) of his company's sales were fictitious. Bagger inflated his company's profits by setting up fictitious corporations that borrowed money from Danish banks. With the borrowed money, these companies "purchased" software from the IT Factory. Although audits by a Big Four firm failed to uncover the fictitious sales, red flags were apparent. In fact, a competitor had even sent out warnings that the IT Factory "simply didn't have enough known customers to explain its explosive growth."

Bagger went to great lengths to cover his tracks. To throw off a journalist who had questioned his credentials, he claimed to have a PhD in International Business from San Francisco Technological University (a bogus educational institution). He hired an actress to play an official at San Francisco State University who would disclose that San Francisco Tech had been absorbed by San Francisco State University and verify his degree.[1]

On June 11, 2009, Stein Bagger was convicted of fraud and forgery and was sentenced to seven years in prison.

REVENUE AND COLLECTION CYCLE: TYPICAL ACTIVITIES

LO 7-1
Describe the revenue and collection cycle, including typical source documents.

There is no such thing as a typical *revenue and collection cycle*. Companies come in all shapes and sizes, and the actual revenue generation process can vary greatly among industries. For example, banks and other financial services firms do not sell tangible goods. Restaurants typically do not grant credit to customers. Further, many companies accept all payments electronically. For the purposes of our discussions in the four cycle chapters, we assume a typical manufacturing company that sells products of some kind to customers—often other businesses—on credit. The basic activities in the revenue and collection cycle for a company like this are (1) receiving and processing customer orders, including credit approval; (2) delivering goods and services to customers; (3) billing customers and accounting for accounts receivable; and (4) collecting and depositing cash

EXHIBIT 7.1   Revenue and Collection Cycle

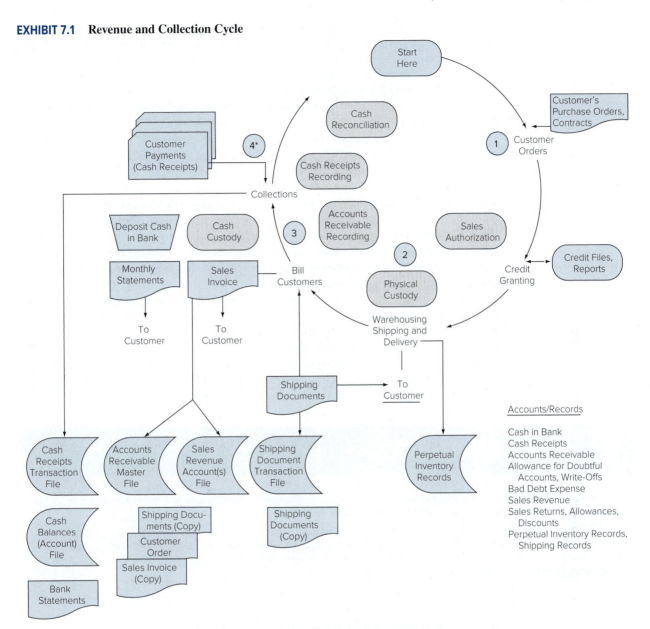

received from customers. See Exhibit 7.1 for the activities and transactions involved in a revenue and collection cycle. Note that collecting and depositing cash received from customers was covered in Chapter 6. As you follow the discussion in the text, you can track some of the highlighted elements of the cycle. The numbers listed next to the headings correspond to the numbers in Exhibit 7.1. We will discuss how different companies may vary from this "typical" cycle.

Receiving and Processing Customer Orders, Including Credit Granting ①

Customers initiate sales orders in a variety of ways. They can mail purchase orders, call or fax orders, e-mail orders, place orders on a website, or simply come to the company's place of business and buy their goods. In some cases, companies are directly linked to production schedules in their customers' computer files (via electronic data interchange, EDI), so they can ship goods automatically as the customer needs them. Electronic or Internet sales orders require special software controls that protect against unauthorized orders and protect customer information.

If a company sells its goods or services for something other than cash, it is important that someone authorize credit sales to ensure that the customer will be able to pay for the goods or services. Because various authorizations are embedded in a computerized system, access to the customer master file for additions, deletions, and other changes must be limited to responsible people. If these controls fail, orders might be processed for fictitious customers, credit might be approved for bad credit risks, and shipping documents might be created for goods that do not exist in the inventory.

Although many companies directly grant credit to customers, others rely on third-party credit, such as accepting credit cards from Visa or American Express. When a retailer accepts a third-party credit card, the authorization function is performed electronically, and the risk of nonpayment generally shifts to the third party in exchange for a processing fee. Sales such as this are considered cash sales to the retailer. Although authorization controls are minimized in this situation, data security becomes a significant issue. Retailers who accept third-party credit cards must maintain compliance with Payment Card Industry Data Security Standard requirements (PCI DSS). When companies fail to adequately protect information, they can become liable for losses to customers, as discussed in the following Auditing Insight.

Customer orders, shipping documents, and invoices should be in prenumbered sequence so the system can check the sequence and determine whether any transactions have not been recorded (*completeness* assertion) or have been duplicated (*occurrence* assertion). Prenumbered documents are an example of an internal control (i.e., control activity).

Another authorization in the system is the price list master file. This file contains the product unit prices for billing customers. Persons who have power to alter this file have the power to authorize price changes and customer billings.

AUDITING INSIGHT   Missing the Target?

Giant retailer **Target Corp.** had its customers' credit card and debit card data breached over the Black Friday weekend in 2013. The theft was not limited to any one location of the company's business and included stores nationally. Target estimates that approximately 42 million customers had their personal credit or debit card information stolen. In response to a class-action lawsuit, Target agreed to pay $10 million to the hacking victims.

Note how important it is to protect information received during the revenue cycle.

Source: *"Target Offers $10 Million Settlement in Data Breach Lawsuit,"* http://www.npr.org/sections/thetwo-way/2015/03/19/394039055/target-offers-10-million-settlement-in-data-breach-lawsuit, March 19, 2015.

Delivering Goods and Services to Customers ②

Physical custody of inventory goods starts in the storeroom or warehouse where inventory is kept. Custody is transferred to the shipping department upon the authorization of the shipping order that permits the inventory clerk to release goods to the shipping department. Proper authorization is important: Employees performing each of these steps should sign transfer documents so they are held accountable. This control procedure prevents employees from misappropriating the goods or shipping product to friends without billing them. A **bill of lading** is a form that the carrier signs to verify the goods are shipped. A **packing slip**, which describes the goods being shipped, and the quantity of goods shipped, is often included with the shipment.

Billing Customers and Accounting for Accounts Receivable ③

When a delivery or shipment is complete, the transaction is completed by filing a shipment record and preparing a final invoice for the customer (which is recorded as sales revenue and accounts receivable). A **sales invoice** is the bill sent to the customer that indicates the amount due and the payment terms. Any person who has the power to alter these transactions or to change the invoice before it is mailed to the customer should not have any custody or recording responsibilities.

Access to accounts receivable records implies the power to alter them directly or enter transactions (e.g., returns and allowance credits, write-offs) to alter them. Personnel with this power have a combination of authorization and recording responsibility. Another important facet of control is physical protection of the files. If the files are lost or destroyed, it is unlikely the accounts will be collected, so the records are truly assets. Limited access, frequent backup, and disaster recovery plans are important controls to ensure the availability of information. Moreover, customer and employee information must be protected.

The most frequent reconciliation is the comparison of the sum of customers' unpaid balances (customer database or subsidiary ledger kept in the accounts receivable department) with the accounts receivable control account total (maintained in corporate accounting). This reconciliation is accomplished by preparing a trial balance of the accounts receivable subsidiary ledger, adding it, and comparing its total with the control account balance in the general ledger. Internal auditors can perform periodic reviews of the customers' balances by sending confirmations to the customers.

Management Reports and Data Files in the Revenue and Collection Cycle

Because revenue and cash receipts transactions are generally processed using electronic systems, management is able to generate reports and data sets that can provide important information not just for management, but also for audits. Exhibit 7.2 represents a typical system for processing customer orders and accounts receivable. In this section, we discuss the client data that is typically produced in this system that will be used to evaluate the risk of material misstatement and perform audit tests.

Pending Order and Back Order Master File

Sales transactions that were initiated but are not yet completed, and thus not yet recorded as sales, are kept in the *pending order master file*. A *backorder master* file contains orders

EXHIBIT 7.2 Sales and Accounts Receivable Processing

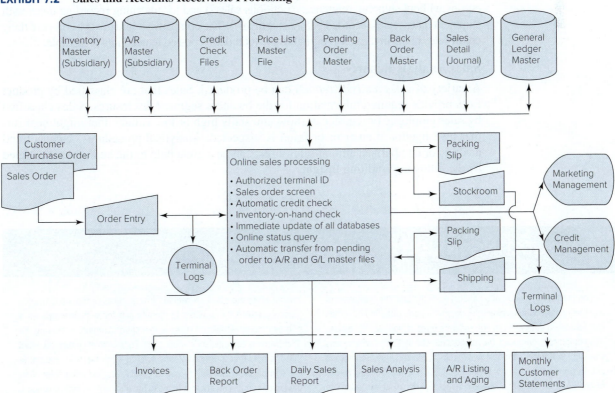

for products that are out of stock currently. Long-standing orders may represent unfilled sales to a customer, which may result in low customer satisfaction and loss of potential revenue. They also may represent shipments that actually were made but for some reason were not recorded in the sales journal or could not be matched to a customer order. Typically, a pending or backorder report will be reviewed by the company at least weekly, and exceptions should be reviewed. Auditors will review items in the pending orders file for evidence of the *completeness* of recorded sales and accounts receivable.

Customer Master File

The system may make automatic credit checks, but up-to-date maintenance of customer information is very important. Credit checks based on dated or incomplete information are not good credit checks. A sample of the *customer master file* can be tested for current status, including up-to-date credit limit information. Alternatively, the company's data change controls can be reviewed to ensure the files are accurately maintained. The company should regularly review credit limits to ensure appropriate limits are placed on customers, and auditors will often perform exception testing on credit checks. (See Application in the Field example later in this chapter.)

Price List Master File

The system may produce customer invoices automatically, but if the *price list master file* is incorrect, the billings will be incorrect. The pricing file can be compared to an official price source for accuracy. The company should perform this comparison every time it changes its prices. Remember that prices typically change over the year. Therefore, when vouching invoices and sales journal entries to price lists, the auditor must be sure to have the price list that was in effect at the time of the customer's order.

Sales Detail (Journal) File

The detailed sales entries, which should correspond with the issuance of invoices to customers and should include the shipping references and dates, should be in the *sales detail file*. The file can be scanned using computer-assisted auditing techniques (CAATs) for checking entries without shipping references (fictitious sales?) and for matching recording dates with shipment dates (sales recorded before shipment?). The company should always compare daily credit sales totals in the sales journal to the total debits posted to accounts receivable.

Sales Analysis Reports

A variety of *sales analysis reports* can be produced. Sales that are classified by product lines provide required information for the business segment disclosures. Sales classified by sales employee or region can show unusually high or low volume that might bear further investigation if an error or fraud is suspected. Analytical procedures, such as trend analysis or comparison among sales units, can be a great help to the auditor as illustrated by the following Auditing Insight.

 AUDITING INSIGHT | Peaks and Valleys

During the year-end audit of a national manufacturer, the independent auditors imported the weekly sales volume reports classified by region into Tableau, a data visualization software used in many audits. By creating graphical workbooks, the auditors noticed that sales volume was very high in Region 2 the last two weeks of March, June, September, and December. The volume was unusually low in the first two weeks of April, July, October, and January. In fact, the peaks far exceeded the volume in all the other six regions. The analysis of the sales volume reports enabled the auditors to identify and focus their efforts on a potential overstatement of revenue in a specific region, increasing the effectiveness and efficiency of the audit. Further investigation revealed that the manager in Region 2 was holding open the sales journal at the end of each quarterly reporting period (i.e., including sales from the next period) in an attempt to make the quarterly reports look good.

Accounts Receivable Listing and Aging

The *accounts receivable listing* of customers' balances contains the actual amounts specifically identified with individual customers. If the control account total is higher than the sum of the customers' balances (trial balance), it will have to be adjusted after the difference is thoroughly investigated. Remember, a receivable amount that cannot be identified with a customer cannot be collected! The trial balance is used as the starting point for selecting accounts for confirmation. The *accounts receivable aging* information is used in connection with assessing the allowance for doubtful accounts. Auditors must ensure that the calculation of the aging is accurate to verify that customer accounts are not listed as current when they are in fact past due. An example of this listing, also called an **aged trial balance**, is presented at Exhibit 7.10, which is shown later in this chapter.

Cash Receipts Listing

The cash receipts journal contains all the detail entries for cash deposits and credits to various accounts. It contains the population of entries that should be reflected in the credits to accounts receivable for customer payments. It also contains adjusting and correcting entries that can result from the bank account reconciliation. These entries are important because they might signal the types of accounting errors or manipulations that occur in the *cash receipts listing*.

Customer Statements

Probably the best control over whether cash is received and recorded is the customer. Therefore, sending *customer statements* of what has been billed, what has been paid, and ending balances on a monthly basis enables customers to spot discrepancies and notify the company. Statements should be sent if there is *any* activity in the account, even if the ending balances are zero.

✓ REVIEW CHECKPOINTS

7.1 What is the basic sequence of activities and accounting in a revenue and collection cycle?

7.2 What purpose is served by prenumbering sales orders, shipping documents, and sales invoices?

7.3 What controls should be implemented to safeguard accounts receivable files?

7.4 What computer-based files might auditors examine to find evidence of unrecorded sales? Of inadequate credit checks? Of incorrect product unit prices?

7.5 Suppose that you selected a sample of customers' accounts receivable and wanted to find supporting evidence for the entries in the accounts. Where would you go to vouch the debit entries? What would you expect to find? Where would you go to vouch the credit entries? What would you expect to find?

SIGNIFICANT ACCOUNTS AND RELEVANT ASSERTIONS

LO 7-2
Identify significant accounts and relevant assertions related to the revenue and collection cycle

According to the professional standards, an account or disclosure is significant if there is a reasonable chance that it could contain a material misstatement. The auditor identifies significant accounts and relevant assertions by applying the audit risk model.

Chapter 4 introduced the audit risk model. As noted there, this model allows auditors to control audit risk to desired levels. *Audit risk* is defined as the risk that auditors will issue an unqualified opinion on financial statements that contain a material misstatement. Audit risk is manifested when a material misstatement enters the financial reporting process (inherent risk) that the client's internal controls do not prevent or detect (control risk) and that the auditors' substantive procedures do not detect (detection risk). Recall the basic three-step approach for using the audit risk model to plan an engagement:

1. Set audit risk at desired levels (normally, low).

2. Assess risk of material misstatement, which incorporates inherent risk based on the nature of the account balance or class of significant transactions and control risk based on gaining an understanding of internal control. Remember that AS 2110 indicates that the auditor should presume that there is a fraud risk involving improper revenue recognition.

3. Set detection risk at the significant account and assertion level based on the level of audit risk and risk of material misstatement.

The components of the audit risk model are assessed for each significant account and relevant assertion. This assessment recognizes that certain accounts and assertions assume an increased level of importance and are of more interest to auditors than others. For example, because of the tendency to use fictitious sales to overstate assets and revenues, the *existence* assertion is extremely important in the audit of accounts receivable, and *occurrence* is important for sales. In addition, because material errors happen, auditors need to examine revenue and accounts receivable for completeness. However, the auditor generally presumes that management has an incentive to overstate revenues. Thus, auditors may assess inherent risk for the *existence* assertion to be higher than for the *completeness* assertion for these accounts, all other things being equal.

Once all of the significant accounts and disclosures have been identified, the auditor then needs to identify the relevant assertions. According to AS 2201.A9, a financial statement assertion is relevant if it has a "reasonable possibility of containing a misstatement or misstatements that would cause the financial statements to be materially misstated."

Exhibit 7.3 identifies the significant accounts and relevant assertions in the revenue cycle. Although different companies may have other risks, in general, the most significant risks relate to the occurrence of revenues and the existence and valuation of accounts receivable. Because of the risk of unrecorded revenue, the completeness of revenue and accounts receivable is also considered a significant risk in the revenue and collection cycle. Although we will focus our discussion on revenue and accounts receivable, we will also discuss other accounts and assertions that may require consideration in the revenue cycle.

EXHIBIT 7.3
Significant Accounts and Relevant Assertions in the Revenue and Collection Cycle

Significant Account	Relevant Assertions
Revenue	Occurrence
	Completeness
	Cutoff
Accounts Receivable	Existence
	Completeness
	Valuation

☑ REVIEW CHECKPOINTS

7.6 What makes an account significant or an assertion relevant?

7.7 Why do auditors focus on revenue as a significant account and the occurrence of revenue as a relevant assertion in the revenue cycle?

7.8 Why is inherent risk for the existence assertion for accounts receivable often set higher than inherent risk for the completeness assertion?

RISK OF MATERIAL MISSTATEMENT

LO 7-3
Discuss the risk of material misstatement in the revenue and collection cycle, with a specific focus on improper revenue recognition.

As part of the planning process, the auditor must determine the source of a misstatement that could cause the financial statements to be materially misstated. One way to assess the risk of material misstatement is to use the "what can go wrong?" (WCGW) approach when thinking of each financial statement assertion. The WCGW is a part of each audit firm's process and enables a thorough assessment of the risk of material misstatement.

When considering WCGW in the revenue and collection cycle, auditors consider three primary concerns: (1) Is revenue recognized when appropriate? (2) Is there a possibility of customers returning the goods? (3) Are the accounts receivable collectible? Exhibit 7.4 summarizes the WCGW analysis for the revenue and collection cycle.

Revenue Recognition

The IT Factory example at the beginning of this chapter is an extreme example of the violation of accounting standards related to **revenue recognition** (recording revenues in the entity's books). To be recognized, revenues must be (1) realized or realizable and (2) earned.[2]

An entity's revenue-earning activities involve delivering or producing goods, rendering services, or performing other activities that constitute its ongoing major or central operations, and revenues are considered to have been earned when the entity has substantially accomplished what it must do to be entitled to the benefits represented by the revenues.[3]

Similarly, the SEC believes that revenue generally is realized or realizable and earned when *all* of the following criteria are met:

- Persuasive evidence of an arrangement exists.
- Delivery has occurred or services have been rendered.
- The seller's price to the buyer is fixed or determinable.
- Collectability is reasonably ensured.[4]

EXHIBIT 7.4   What Can Go Wrong in the Revenue and Collection Cycle?

Significant Account	Relevant Assertions	What Can Go Wrong?
Revenue	Occurrence	Management may overstate sales by adding fictitious transactions or inflating actual sales.
		Management may fail to recognize the possibility of customer returns.
	Completeness	Not all sales are recorded.
	Cutoff	Sales have been recorded in incorrect periods.
Accounts Receivable	Existence	Accounts receivable are overstated and do not represent amounts owed from actual sales.
	Completeness	Not all accounts receivable have been recorded.
	Valuation	Receivables are not included in financial statements at the appropriate amount, and valuation adjustments are not recorded properly.

[2]*SFAC No. 5*, "Recognition and Measurement in Finance Statements."
[3]Ibid., ¶83(b).
[4]*Staff Accounting Bulletin No. 104*, "Securities and Exchange Commission."

EXHIBIT 7.5 **Revenue Recognition Rogues**

Company	Cause of Misstatement	Alleged Amount[#]
Bristol-Myers	Company offered incentives to wholesalers to build their inventories so Bristol-Meyers could meet sales forecasts (*channel stuffing*).[*]	$2.5 billion
Computer Associates	Company recognized revenue from several contracts in which it had either (1) agreed to make offsetting purchases (*round trips*) or (2) had contracts that contained undisclosed side letters that could have canceled the contracts.	$2.2 billion
Qwest Communications	Company used fiber-optic "swaps." It recorded sales of equipment when it agreed to pay hundreds of millions of dollars for Internet services. It recognized the revenue for the equipment but deferred the cost of the Internet services.	$2.2 billion
Nortel	Company prematurely recorded revenue from equipment sales before the buyer had taken title to the equipment.	$1.5 billion
SeaView Video Technology	Company prematurely recorded revenues and accounts receivable for customer orders for security camera products prior to shipping.	$1.4 billion
AOL	AOL recorded advertising revenue, some of which included one-time payments, stock sales, and "round-trip" deals in which money flowed both ways between AOL and the advertiser.	$1 billion
Royal Ahold	Company induced third parties to provide false confirmations to auditors relating to sales and accounts receivable.	$700 million
Safety-Kleen Corporation	Company recorded contingent revenues and contract claims that were not probable and recorded revenue for property not yet sold.	$534 million
Household International	Company employed incorrect timing of recognizing costs and revenues related to its MasterCard and Visa cobranding and affinity credit card relationships as well as a credit card marketing agreement with a third party.	$386 million
Xerox	Several senior managers colluded to circumvent company's accounting policies and administrative procedures. The restatement related to uncollectable long-term receivables, failure to record liabilities for amounts due to concessionaires, and, to a lesser extent, recording revenue for contracts that did not fully meet the requirements of sales-type leases.	$207 million
Interpublic	Company improperly booked credits, creating double counting; included insurance proceeds that had not been realized; and understated liabilities.	$181 million
Gemstar	Subsidiary TV Guide recorded $113 million in patent-licensing revenue from an expired Scientific-Atlanta Inc. contract.	$113 million

Channel stuffing is a deceptive business practice that inflates sales and earnings by forcing more products along a company's distribution channel without actual sales taking place.

[#]Dollar amounts represent total misstatements and may include some non-revenue items. However, revenue recognition was the major issue in each of these cases.

The SEC and the popular press have expressed concern about appropriate recognition of revenue in financial statements. A study by research firm Audit Analytics indicated that approximately 11 percent of all restatements in 2015 were related to revenue recognition. Since 2001, the percentage of restatements related to revenue recognition has varied from 10.1 percent of all restatements in 2010 to 21.3 percent of all restatements in 2003.[5] Some recent restatements are listed in Exhibit 7.5. The fact that the financial statements were restated means that the auditors missed the original misstatement or went along with the company's accounting treatment. In some cases, predecessor auditors accepted the accounting treatment, but the current auditors demanded the restatement.

[5]Ernst & Young, *Technical Line,* No. 2012–21, 7 August 2012.

AUDITING INSIGHT The Amount Isn't Always Obvious!

When a customer buys a product off a grocery store shelf, the amount of the revenue is easy to determine—the price the customer paid. Sometimes, companies enter into contracts where the amount of a revenue isn't that simple. Consider the sale of an iPad by Apple Inc. When a customer purchases an iPad, the purchase includes not just the hardware, but also a commitment from Apple to update the software included with the iPad, as well as a warranty, among other commitments. A contract such as this is referred to as a *multiple deliverable contract.* Therefore, the sales price of the iPad has to be divided among multiple revenue sources, some with obligations continuing long into the future. Until 2014, multiple deliverable contracts were subject to many different transaction and industry-specific accounting requirements. With the issuance of a new standard on revenue from contracts with customers, FASB eliminated the multiple rules and replaced it with a new principle. Per FASB ASC 606-10-05-3, "The core principle of the revenue recognition standard is that an entity should recognize revenue to depict the transfer of goods or services to customers in an amount that reflects the consideration to which the entity expects to be entitled in exchange for those goods or services."

For a company like Apple that enters into multiple deliverable contracts, this means that the revenue it recognizes on the sale of an iPad is based on some items, such as the iOS software updates, that are not sold separately and must be estimated. According to Apple, "For multi-element arrangements that include hardware products containing software essential to the hardware product's functionality, undelivered software elements that relate to the hardware product's essential software, and undelivered non-software services, the Company allocates revenue to all deliverables based on their relative selling prices." Thus, Apple's auditor (EY) must apply AS 2501, *Auditing Accounting Estimates,* to the amount of revenue that Apple distributes to each of the identifiable items sold with each iPad. This significantly increases the inherent risk in the audit of revenue.

Sources: *Apple Inc. Form 10-K, fiscal year ended September 26, 2015; FASB Accounting Standards Update 2014-09—Revenue from Contracts with Customers (Topic 606).*

Risks of improper revenue recognition are higher in high-growth companies that financial analysts often value at a multiple of total revenues. In addition, companies with complex transactions, related-party transactions, and reciprocal transactions have a higher likelihood of inflating revenues. An example of the latter occurred in the telecommunications industry in which **Global Crossing** and other companies are alleged to have traded line rights in one geographic area to other companies for rights in another area. The rights given up were recorded as revenue, while the rights received were capitalized and the expense was spread over several years. Clearly, the issues in revenue recognition and accounts receivable are complex and can be difficult for the auditors. However, not all restatements are bad, as indicated in the following Auditing Insight.

AUDITING INSIGHT It's Not Always Bad

Cubic Corp. said on Wednesday that it will restate earnings for the past three fiscal years after a review discovered errors in how the electronics company accounted for revenue from long-term development contracts as well as certain service contracts. Based on a preliminary review, the changes are expected to increase revenue and net income over the three years, Cubic said.

The company's review found that financial statements for the fiscal years ending September 30 in 2009, 2010, and 2011, and the quarters ended March 31, 2012, and December 31, 2011, can no longer be relied upon. Cubic's management recommended that adjustments be made due to errors in calculating revenue on certain long-term fixed-price development contracts, and on certain long-term service contracts with non-U.S. government customers.

The company has historically recognized development contract sales and profits using a "cost-to-cost percentage-of-completion" accounting method, with a modification that Cubic called a "formulary adjustment." Using that method, it based sales and profits on the ratio of costs incurred to estimated total costs at completion of the contract. Cubic said the formulary adjustment had the effect of deferring a portion of the revenue and profits on contracts until later in the contract period. "Cubic believed that this methodology was an acceptable variation" of the cost-to-cost percentage-of-completion method as described in accounting standards, the company said. But Cubic now believes that generally accepted accounting principles do not support the use of the formulary adjustment.

Source: *"Cubic Corp. to Restate Financial Statements," Cubic Corporation Press Release, August 1, 2012, https://www.cubic.com/News/Press-Releases/ID/423/Cubic-Corporation-to-Restate-Financial-Statements.*

Collectability of Accounts Receivable

In most companies, a portion of accounts receivable will not be collected. GAAP requires the client to provide an estimate of the amount that will likely be uncollectable and provide an allowance for this amount. Estimation of the allowance for doubtful accounts can be subjective and difficult for the client and the auditor. This is particularly true when the client has changed products, credit policies, or its customer base, causing it to have little experience on which to make estimates. Changing economic conditions also make it difficult to estimate collectability. Therefore, valuation is a high risk assertion and the auditor evaluates the reasonableness of the allowance.

Customer Returns and Allowances

In most industries, customers have a right to return unused or unsold merchandise. For example, consumers who purchase goods on **Amazon.com** typically can return the products for a full refund. Similarly, most university bookstores can return unsold textbooks to the publisher. When these agreements are in the purchase contract and disclosed to the auditor, an appropriate evaluation of revenue can be performed. However, clients may enter into informal right of return agreements with customers unknown to the auditors. Liabilities for known rights of return, warranties, and other potential obligations are often very difficult to estimate. Companies with new products or technologies have an even higher inherent risk in these areas.

 AUDITING INSIGHT Watchful Eyes

SEC Chair Mary Jo White indicated in 2014 that the SEC had increased enforcement actions on revenue recognition by more than 20 percent as a result of the new FASB revenue recognition standard. The SEC's director of enforcements, Andrew Ceresney, called revenue recognition "the New Frontier" in enforcements. The increased focus has certainly had an effect as the SEC increased independent enforcement actions overall from 341 in 2013 to 507 in 2015.

Sources: *"Revenue Recognition Changes Could Spur SEC Fraud Probes,"* http://ww2.cfo.com/gaap-ifrs/2014/12/revenue-recognition-changes-spur-sec-fraud-probes/; *"SEC Announces Enforcement Results for FY 2015,"* https://www.sec.gov/news/pressrelease/2015-245.html.

✓ REVIEW CHECKPOINTS

7.9   What do we mean by *revenue recognition*? What does GAAP say about proper revenue recognition?

7.10 Why do you think companies use revenue recognition as a primary means for inflating profits?

7.11 Why is the audit of revenue recognition riskier for a new company?

INTERNAL CONTROL ACTIVITIES AND DESIGN EVALUATION

LO 7-4
Identify important internal control activities present in a properly designed system to mitigate the risk of material misstatements for each relevant assertion in the revenue and collection cycle.

Recall from the audit risk model that the auditor assesses inherent risk to determine where in the financial statements it is reasonably possible that a material misstatement could enter the process *before the consideration of any internal controls.* However, recall that risk of material misstatement is the combination of both inherent risk and control risk.

Professional standards require auditors to first gain an understanding of the internal controls that have been designed to mitigate the risk of material misstatement for each relevant assertion identified by the auditor. In a well-designed system, the internal control activity should be explicitly designed to be aligned with this relevant assertion that was identified in a WCGW analysis.

In effect, the question an auditor should ask is, "Has the audit client designed and implemented a control that, *if operating effectively,* would mitigate the identified risk of material misstatement? Would it prevent or detect the material misstatement?"

Auditors typically achieve an understanding of controls by completing a walkthrough of the processes in the revenue and collection cycle. To do so, the auditor identifies the points in the process where a misstatement might occur and then identifies the control activities that have been placed in operation to mitigate these risks.

Just as the auditor identified existence of accounts receivable as a significant account and relevant assertion and then identified overstatement of accounts receivable through recognition of invalid revenues as a WCGW scenario, the auditor must consider what management can do to prevent this misstatement from entering the financial statements or going undetected. One control that the auditor would expect management to implement involves periodic reconciliation of debits to accounts receivable to sales invoices, customer purchase orders, and shipping documents. If management regularly evaluates the validity of recorded accounts receivable, fewer errors can proceed through the accounting system undetected.

Entity-Level Controls in the Revenue and Collections Cycle

As discussed in Chapter 5, internal control is a top-down process. Thus, prior to discussing specific control objectives in the revenue cycle in detail, the auditor must consider controls at the entity level. As part of the evaluation of internal control, the auditor typically begins in all cycles by considering the entity-level controls in place. Although the control environment is not specific to the revenue cycle, the auditor should always consider how control environment risk factors influence the assessment of control risk in the revenue cycle. For example, if the auditor is aware that the audit committee plays an active role in risk oversight, the control environment is significantly enhanced, which reduces the overall likelihood of material misstatement for all assertions. In the revenue process, overall performance review by management can serve as strong entity-level control. Management should have a process for continually reviewing revenue and comparing it to budgets and forecasts. Management should also constantly scrutinize total write-offs of accounts receivable, merchandise returns, and the timeliness of collections.

Control Considerations at the Account and Assertion Level

An initial overall control consideration auditors evaluate is the level of separation of duties in the revenue cycle. By referring to Exhibit 7.1, you can see that proper separation involves different people and different departments performing the sales and credit authorization; custody of goods and cash; and record keeping for sales, receivables, inventory, and cash receipts. Combinations of two or more of these responsibilities in one person, one office, or one computerized system might open the door for undetected errors or fraud.

It is not always possible to have complete separation of duties in a small business with few employees because the benefits of controls do not outweigh the costs involved. However, to obtain *reasonable assurance* that financial controls are intact when duties are not appropriately separated, the owner must have active involvement in the accounting process—approving credit and discounts, reviewing the aged accounts receivable listing, occasionally opening mail, and preparing bank reconciliations. The owner usually is in direct contact with customers and can ensure that shipments are received. The owner also can follow up on past due accounts.

Exhibit 7.6 describes some of the important control factors that an auditor would consider when evaluating the design effectiveness of internal control in the revenue and collection cycle.

Perhaps the most important controls in the revenue and collection cycle for many companies involve ensuring that revenues are only recorded once the revenue generation process is complete, and ensuring that all revenues that are earned are recorded once and only once. These controls primarily involve the significant accounts of revenue and accounts receivable, and the relevant assertions of occurrence (existence), completeness, and cutoff.

AUDITING INSIGHT   Rounded Up by a Lack of Controls

On February 9, 2016, Monsanto Inc. agreed to pay $80 million in penalties to the SEC for failing to appropriately account for rebates given to retailers and distributors on the purchase of the popular herbicide Roundup. The SEC accused Monsanto of having inadequate internal controls to keep track of the large number of rebates the company was giving. The company had previously restated its 2009 and 2010 financial statements as a result of the accounting fraud.

In 2009, Monsanto faced extreme pricing pressures after a generic competitor began to take away market share from Roundup. To meet sales expectations, Monsanto undertook an aggressive rebate program during the fourth quarter of 2009—but failed to account for the costs of the rebates, leading to a material overstatement of income. The $80 million settlement was one of the largest ever in an SEC investigation. A whistleblower reported the fraud to the SEC and may collect up to $24 million as a result of the settlement.

Sources: *"Monsanto to Pay $80 Million to Settle Charge of Improper Accounting,"* The New York Times, *February 9, 2016; "Monsanto Accounting Case Came from SEC Whistleblower," Accountingtoday.com, February 10, 2016.*

A primary control in the revenue cycle is ensuring that revenue is only recorded when a complete set of matched sales documents is present. A three-way match of a customer sales order, evidence of shipment, and a customer invoice provides strong evidence that a sale has been completed and a revenue has been earned. By requiring all three documents to be present before recording a revenue, a company reduces the risk of overstating revenues and accounts receivable, providing assurance related to the existence of accounts receivable, and the occurrence of revenue.

Similarly, by ensuring that all three of these primary sales documents are prenumbered, and the numerical sequence is checked, the company can ensure the completeness of recorded revenue and accounts receivable. Verifying the dates on the documents helps reduce risk of misstatement related to the cutoff assertion of revenue.

The valuation assertion of accounts receivable is also a relevant assertion in the revenue cycle. Because collectability problems can be addressed prior to making a sale, companies should have controls in place to ensure that all credit sales are authorized based on a credit limit in the customer master file. Further, collectability of delinquent receivables should be considered on a regular basis, and management should regularly evaluate the adequacy of allowances for sales returns and discounts.

In addition to the critical controls discussed previously and in Exhibit 7.6, the following control activities should generally be in place to prevent and detect errors or fraud:

- Access to inventory and the shipping area should be restricted to authorized persons.
- Access to billing terminals and blank invoice forms should be restricted to authorized personnel.
- Care should be taken to record sales and receivables as of the date the goods were shipped and the cash receipts on the date the payments were received.
- Customer invoices should be compared with bills of lading and customer orders to determine that the customer is sent the goods ordered at the proper location for the proper prices and that the quantity being billed is the same as the quantity shipped.
- Pending order files should be reviewed frequently to avoid failure to bill and record shipments.

Finally, procedures must be in place to ensure that errors noted by these steps are properly corrected. An error control log monitored by the information systems supervisor ensures that this is done. Such a log may aid in the identification of patterns that indicate either control weaknesses or possible fraudulent activities. This documentation and subsequent action is part of the information and communications aspect of internal controls.

Information about a company's controls often is gathered by completing an internal control questionnaire. Questionnaires for both manual controls and computerized controls over the revenue and collection cycle are in Appendix 7A. You can study these questionnaires for details of desirable control activities. They are organized under headings that address the

EXHIBIT 7.6   Internal Control Activities in the Revenue and Collection Cycle

Significant Account	Relevant Assertions	What Can Go Wrong?	Internal Control Activity
Revenue	Occurrence	Management may overstate sales by adding fictitious transactions or inflating actual sales.	Invoices are supported by customer purchase orders. Bill of lading or other shipping documents exist for all invoices, and recorded sales in the Sales Revenue account file are supported by invoices.
			Invoices, shipping documents, and sales orders are prenumbered, and the numerical sequence is checked.
		Management may fail to recognize the possibility of customer returns.	Management analyzes sales returns regularly and estimates an allowance for returns.
	Completeness	Not all sales are recorded.	Invoices, shipping documents, and sales orders are prenumbered, and the numerical sequence is checked.
	Cutoff	Sales have been recorded in incorrect periods.	The date of shipping document is compared to the invoice date.
Accounts Receivable	Existence	Accounts receivable are overstated and do not represent amounts from actual sales.	Check the sales order and shipping document to make sure sales were earned and a customer owes a balance.
	Completeness	Not all accounts receivable have been recorded.	Check invoices with the shipping document to the A/R ledger.
	Valuation	Receivables are not included in financial statements at the appropriate amount, and valuation adjustments are not recorded properly.	Authorize and record discounts when customers take them.
			Management evaluates the collectability of delinquent receivables on a timely basis.

assertions regarding classes of transactions. Auditors should also perform a *walkthrough* to verify that they understand each of the process activities. The revenue and collection cycle walkthrough involves following a sale from the initial customer order through credit approval, billing, and delivery of goods to the entry in the sales journal and subsidiary accounts receivable records and then its subsequent collection and cash deposit to ensure that the sale and related transactions are accurately reflected in the financial statements.

✅ REVIEW CHECKPOINTS

7.12 What are the primary control procedures to ensure completeness of recorded revenues?

7.13 Which three events should generally have occurred prior to the recognition of sales revenue?

7.14 What effect do entity level controls have on the control risk assessments of an auditor?

TESTS OF OPERATING EFFECTIVENESS OF INTERNAL CONTROL

LO 7-5
Give examples of tests of controls to verify the operating effectiveness of internal controls in the revenue and collection cycle.

In order to rely on the design of the client's internal controls and support a reduction in control risk, the auditor must determine if the control is operating as designed and whether the person operating the control has the authority and competence to do so. The auditor's ultimate responsibility is to document enough support to conclude whether the control activity was operating effectively to mitigate the risk of material misstatement for the assertion.

Auditors can perform tests of controls to determine whether company personnel are properly performing controls that are said to be in place. In general, the procedures used in tests of controls are client inquiry, observation, inspection of documents and records, reperformance, and walkthroughs. Understand that if a control is missing or ineffective, the risk of a material misstatement increases, but an error or fraud is by no means certain. For example, a person with both recordkeeping and custody of inventory has incompatible duties, but if that person is diligent and honest, no errors or frauds may exist. If controls are not in place or personnel in the organization are not performing their control activities effectively, auditors need to design substantive procedures to try to detect whether control failures have produced material misstatements in the financial statements.

Exhibit 7.7 begins with the internal control activities related to the significant accounts and relevant assertions in the revenue cycle and suggests auditor tests of controls that may be performed to support a reduction in control risk.

To be effective, auditor tests of control in the revenue cycle must be performed using dual-direction tests of controls. Exhibit 7.8 demonstrates how an auditor performs tests of control to assess control risk for both the occurrence assertion and the completeness assertion.

To ensure that the client's required three-way match is in effect and operating appropriately to ensure the occurrence assertion, the auditor will select a sample of recorded sales from the sales journal and vouch the sales to supporting customer invoices, shipping documents, and customer purchase orders. The availability of electronic client data and audit software sometimes enables auditors to perform exception testing on the entire population of sales and identify any instances where the three-way match did not occur. The auditor can then directly address the specific situations where exceptions occurred and make a more accurate assessment of control risk.

To complete the dual-direction test, the auditor performs tests of control in the completeness direction. Because shipment of goods is the event that generally leads to earned revenue, the auditor will select a sample of shipping documents and trace the documents to sales invoices and postings in the sales journal. This assures the auditor that goods shipped were invoiced and posted. The auditor will also scan data files for numerical sequence and will observe the client checking numerical sequence of shipping documents and invoices. Note, if the auditor can obtain the sales journal in electronic form, audit software (e.g., IDEA) can be employed to check the numerical sequence and duplication of invoice numbers.

One thing you may note is that these tests of controls described above also are gathering evidence on the assertions in the account balances. The audit processes to gather evidence on the assertions in account balances are called *substantive procedures.* Substantive procedures differ from tests of controls in their basic purpose. Substantive procedures are designed to obtain direct evidence about the dollar amounts in account balances, while tests of controls are designed to obtain evidence about the company's performance of its own control activities. Sometimes an audit procedure can be used for both purposes, and when it is, it is called a **dual-purpose procedure.** When the auditor tests the controls surrounding three-way matches of customer orders, shipping documents, and invoices, the items directly tested provide both evidence on controls and on the relevant assertions. Thus, these tests related to controls surrounding occurrence and completeness of revenues can be used as dual-purpose procedures.

To test the client's controls related to the valuation assertion, the auditor will discuss procedures with the credit manager and examine credit file documentation for evidence of regular evaluation of credit limits and follow-up on delinquent accounts. The auditor will also examine evidence of credit approval prior to shipment for a sample of sales.

In addition to the critical controls discussed previously and in Exhibit 7.6, the auditor might also perform other tests of controls related to assertions in the revenue cycle such as:

- *Completeness of revenue and accounts receivable*—Examine evidence of client review and follow-up of sales data related to specific classes of products or locations.
- *Accuracy of revenue and accounts receivable*—Vouch prices to approved price listing.

EXHIBIT 7.7 Tests of Controls in Revenue and Collection Cycle

Significant Account	Relevant Assertions	What Can Go Wrong/ Risk of Material Misstatement	Internal Control Activity (Mitigate Risk)	Test of Internal Control
Revenue	Occurrence	Management may overstate sales by adding fictitious transactions or inflating actual sales.	Invoices are supported by customer purchase orders. Bill of lading or other shipping documents exist for all invoices, and recorded sales in the Sales Revenue account file are supported by invoices.	Vouch sales in sales detail file to invoices, supporting shipping documents, and customer purchase orders for customer name, product description, terms, dates, and quantities.
		Management may fail to recognize the possibility of customer returns.	Management analyzes sales returns regularly and estimates an allowance for returns.	Inspect documents for evidence that management evaluates the allowance for returns regularly.
	Completeness	Not all sales are recorded.	Invoices, shipping documents, and sales orders are prenumbered, and the numerical sequence is checked.	Scan documents for numerical sequence, observe client-checking sequence, and trace shipping document to recording in sales detail file.
	Cutoff	Sales have been recorded in incorrect periods.	Date of shipping document is compared to invoice date.	Trace shipping data on shipping documents with sales invoice date, and check FOB terms.
Accounts Receivable	Existence	Accounts receivable are overstated and do not represent actual sales.	Check sales order and shipping documents to make sure sales were earned and a customer owes a balance.	When payments are received, vouch checks listed on sample deposit slips to the customer credits listed on the day's posting to customer accounts receivable.
	Completeness	Not all accounts receivable have been recorded.	Check invoices with shipping document to A/R ledger.	Inspect documents for evidence that the Billing department supervisor matches prenumbered shipping documents with entries in the sales journal.
	Valuation	Receivables are not included in financial statements at the appropriate amount, and valuation adjustments are not recorded properly.	Authorize and record discounts when customers take them.	Inspect documentation for evidence that subsequent cash receipts from the customer are reviewed. Inquire of the credit manager procedures regarding unpaid accounts. Inspect credit files for most recent review of customer creditworthiness.
			Management evaluates the collectability of delinquent receivables on a timely basis.	Inspect documentation for evidence that management evaluates the collectability of receivables.

EXHIBIT 7.8

Did all recorded sales actually occur?

Sales Invoice File (Journal)

Vouch sample of invoices to shipping documents (occurrence)

Trace sample of shipping documents to invoices (completeness)

Shipping Documents

Were all shipments invoiced?

AUDITING INSIGHT   Is Everyone Control Conscious?

Clearly, a first line of defense against accounting fraud is to ensure that everyone is control conscious—unless you work at **NutraCea.** NutraCea faked a $2.6 million sale in the second quarter of 2007 and a $1.9 million deal later that year. These deals made it look like the company had met its sales forecast when, in fact, it had not. The Securities and Exchange Commission alleges the fraud was so blatant that one executive, when told about the accounting problems by a colleague, covered his ears and said, "No, no, no, no, I don't want to hear it."

Source: *"NutraCea Ex-Execs Accused of Fraud,"* Arizona Business & Money, *January 15, 2011.*

- *Accuracy of revenue*—Observe client comparing shipping quantities to quantities recorded as sold. Examine evidence of client making the comparison.
- *Cutoff of revenue*—Trace shipping date on shipping documents to sales invoice date. Check FOB terms.
- *Classification of accounts receivable*—Trace posting of intercompany sales, sales returns, etc., to sales.

When a business receives many cash or check payments from customers on an account, a detailed audit should include a comparison of the checks listed on a sample of deposit slips to the customer credits listed on the day's posting to customer accounts receivable (daily remittance list or other record of detail postings). This procedure is a test for accounts receivable fraud—also known as *lapping* (see Chapter 6). Auditors look for credits given to customers for whom no payments were received on the day in question.

See Appendix Exhibit 7B.1 for a test of controls audit plan. These steps are designed to direct the audit team in obtaining sufficient appropriate evidence about the effectiveness of controls and about the reliability of accounting records. Thus, the tests of controls produce evidence that helps auditors determine whether the specific control was properly designed and is operating effectively.

Summary: Control Risk Assessment

Auditors must evaluate the evidence obtained from their understanding of internal control and from tests of controls. The initial process of obtaining an understanding of the company's controls and the later process of obtaining evidence from actual tests of controls are two of the phases of control risk assessment. If the control risk is assessed to be very low, the substantive procedures on the account balances can be reduced, resulting in audit efficiencies. For example, the accounts receivable confirmations can be sent on a date prior to the year-end, and the sample size can be small.

On the other hand, if tests of controls reveal weaknesses (such as posting sales without shipping documents, charging customers the wrong prices, or recording credits to customers without supporting documentation), the substantive procedures need to be designed to lower the risk of failing to detect material misstatement in the account balances (detection risk). For example, the confirmation procedure may need to be scheduled on the year-end date with a large sample of customer accounts.

✅ REVIEW CHECKPOINTS

7.15   What specific control procedures (in addition to separation of duties and responsibilities) should be in place and operating in internal controls governing revenue recognition?

7.16   What is a *walkthrough* of a sales transaction? How can the walkthrough work complement the use of an internal control questionnaire?

7.17   What types of audit procedures are typically performed in testing operating effectiveness of controls over the revenue and collection cycle?

7.18   What is *dual-direction* test of controls sampling in the revenue and collection cycle?

SUBSTANTIVE ANALYTICAL PROCEDURES AND TESTS OF DETAILS

LO 7-6
Give examples of substantive procedures in the revenue and collection cycle and relate them to assertions about significant account balances at the end of the period.

As you have learned previously while studying audit risk, the primary reason for evaluating the internal control system at an audit client is to reach an overall assessment of the risk of material misstatement for each relevant assertion. In fact, the assessment of the risk of material misstatement is completed to help form the basis for determining the nature, timing, and extent of substantive testing. Risk of material misstatement at the assertion level is comprised of both inherent risk and control risk for each relevant assertion.

If inherent risk has already been assessed as high, this means there is high susceptibility for this account to be misstated. Recall that control risk is the "probability that an entity's controls will fail to prevent or detect material misstatements due to errors or frauds." Because the revenue cycle consists of routine transactions, the majority of audit clients have strong controls in the revenue cycle, and thus tests of controls often support a reduction in control risk. This reduction in control risk reduces the auditor's assessment of the risk of material misstatement in the revenue cycle.

However, auditing standards also indicate that there is a presumptive risk of fraud in the revenue cycle. Further, according to professional standards, "for significant risks, the auditor should perform substantive procedures, including tests of details, that are specifically responsive to the assessed risks" (AS 2301, para. 11). Because revenue is a presumptive high-fraud risk and an overall significant risk, the auditor always performs *substantive procedures* in the revenue cycle. These procedures are classified as substantive analytical procedures and substantive tests of details.

A substantive analytical procedure is one in which the auditor substantiates an account or disclosure by developing an independent estimate of the amount and then comparing the recorded balance to the estimate. As we will discuss later in this chapter, the evaluation of the accounting estimate for the allowance for doubtful accounts generally involves an analytical review of the adequacy of the provision for bad debt expense.

A substantive test of details is one in which the auditor substantiates an account or disclosure by directly testing the transactions that make up the account or the items that comprise the balance of the account. For example, auditors will generally send confirmations to customers to substantiate the existence and rights and obligations assertions of accounts receivable.

Exhibit 7.9 presents common substantive tests that are performed to address remaining risks of material misstatement related to the significant accounts and relevant assertions in the revenue cycle.

EXHIBIT 7.9   Substantive Procedures in the Revenue and Collection Cycle

Significant Account	Relevant Assertions	What Can Go Wrong?	Internal Control Activity (Mitigate Risk)	Test of Internal Control	Possible Substantive Analytical Procedures	Possible Substantive Tests of Detail
Revenue	Occurrence	Management may overstate sales by adding fictitious transactions or inflating actual sales.	Invoices are supported by customer purchase orders. Bill of lading or other shipping documents exist for all invoices, and recorded sales in the Sales Revenue account file are supported by invoices.	Vouch sales in sales detail file to invoices, supporting shipping documents, and customer purchase orders for customer name, product description, terms, dates, and quantities.	Compare asset and revenue balances with recent history to help detect overstatements. Sales ratios can be compared to historical data and industry statistics for evidence of overall reasonableness.	Vouch journal entry, sales summary, sales invoice copy, shipping documents, and, finally, the customer's purchase order.
		Management may fail to recognize the possibility of customer returns.	Management analyzes sales returns regularly and estimates an allowance for returns.	Inspect documents for evidence that management evaluates the allowance for returns regularly.	Obtain a summary of sales returns subsequent to year-end, and evaluate the adequacy of the allowance.	Select a sample of sales returns subsequent to year-end, and trace to proper charging against the allowance account.
	Completeness	Not all sales are recorded.	Invoices, shipping documents, and sales orders are prenumbered, and the numerical sequence is checked.	Scan documents for numerical sequence, observe client-checking sequence, and trace shipping document to recording in sales detail file.	Compare current year's sales to last year's sales by geographic location.	Select samples of shipping documents, and trace to sales invoice and the sales journal.
	Cutoff	Sales have been recorded in incorrect periods.	The date of shipping document is compared to the invoice date.	Trace shipping date on shipping documents to sales invoice date, and check FOB terms.	Compare prior year's sales in same month to current year's sales in same month.	Trace shipping documents before and after year-end to the sales journal to ensure the sale was recorded in the proper period, credit memos for returns after year-end are vouched to receiving reports, and any goods returned after year-end that were sold during the year being audited have been deducted from sales.

Significant Account	Relevant Assertions	What Can Go Wrong?	Internal Control Activity (Mitigate Risk)	Test of Internal Control	Possible Substantive Analytical Procedures	Possible Substantive Tests of Detail
Accounts Receivable	Existence	Accounts receivable are overstated and do not represent actual sales.	Check sales order and shipping document to make sure sales were earned and a customer owes a balance.	When payments are received, vouch checks listed on sample deposit slips to the customer credits listed on the day's posting to customer accounts receivable.	Compare prior year's A/R balance in relation to sales with current year's A/R balance in relation to sales.	Confirm accounts receivable sent to bank.
	Completeness	Not all accounts receivable have been recorded.	Check invoices with shipping document to A/R ledger.	Inspect documents for evidence that the Billing department supervisor matches prenumbered shipping documents with entries in the sales journal.	Compare A/R relationship with sales to COGS relationship with inventory.	Select a sample of remittance worksheets (or bank deposits), vouch details to bank deposit slips (trace details to remittance worksheets if the sample is bank deposits), and trace to complete accounting posting in customer accounts receivable.
	Valuation	Receivables are not included in financial statements at the appropriate amount, and valuation adjustments are not recorded properly.	Authorize and record discounts when customers take them.	Inspect documentation for evidence that subsequent cash receipts from the customer are reviewed. Inquire of the credit manager procedures regarding unpaid accounts. Inspect credit files for most recent review of customer creditworthiness.	Accounts receivable write-offs should be compared with estimates of doubtful accounts. Recalculate customer discounts to make sure they are accurate.	Inspect aged trial balance, compare current year's write-off experience with prior year's allowance for bad debts.
			Management evaluates the collectability of delinquent receivables on a timely basis.	Inspect documentation for evidence that management evaluates the collectability of receivables.		

When considering relevant assertions and obtaining evidence about accounts receivable and other assets, auditors must emphasize the *existence* assertion. This emphasis on existence is appropriate because a large number of restatements of reports on financial statements involve overstated assets and revenues. When credit sales are recorded too early or fictitious sales are posted, this results in overstated accounts receivable and overstated sales revenue.

Discerning the population of assets to audit for existence is easy because the company has asserted their existence by putting them on the balance sheet. Despite the general presence of strong controls, obtaining substantive evidence supporting the existence of accounts receivable is required in audits where receivables are material. The auditor typically obtains evidence about the existence of accounts receivable through a combination of analytical procedures and confirmations.

AUDITING INSIGHT   Fraud 101?

Koss Corporation, a Milwaukee company with sales of $38 million in 2009, was the victim of a $34 million fraud. Sujata Sachdeva, vice president of finance, circumvented the books, did not record revenues, and was able to siphon the unrecorded revenue to her own personal accounts. This case could be a primer on fraud for auditors.

Sachdeva was a long-time trusted employee of Koss and was promoted to vice president of finance in 1992. Koss viewed her as such a valued an employee that when her family decided to move to Texas, Sachdeva was allowed to telecommute to her job. This is extremely unusual for someone in her position and with the type of responsibilities associated with being vice president of finance. Most auditors with fraud experience are very skeptical of any employee known to be a *long-time trusted* employee. Such a designation often comes with an ability to have controls waived or circumvented. Place this person in a remote, unsupervised situation, and trouble is likely around the corner.

Many fraud auditors will tell you that there is no such thing as an immaterial fraud. Although fraud may start as quantitatively immaterial, it can grow in nature and should be viewed as qualitatively material in all instances. Follow the numbers in the Koss fraud:

- 2005: $2,195,477
- 2006: $2,227,669
- 2007: $3,160,310
- 2008: $5,040,968
- 2009: $8,485,937
- 2010: $10,243,310 (two quarters)

Finally, there is Michael Koss, vice chairman, chief executive officer, president, and chief financial officer of Koss Corporation. Even in small companies, each of these posts is a full-time position. An auditor should not be surprised that a person with such responsibilities would have difficulty adequately supervising employees who report to him or her. In addition, each of these executive positions is instrumental in the establishment or execution of sound corporate governance, which was likely insufficient at Koss Corporation.

In the aftermath of the discovery of fraud, shareholder lawsuits have been filed against Koss Corporation, its management, and its auditor, **Grant Thornton.** A retired partner with **KPMG** stated, "The fraud is so large, in relation to the size of the company, that I have got to believe that it is going to make it difficult for Grant Thornton to prove that they conducted an audit in accordance with generally accepted auditing standards." In November 2010, Sujata Sachdeva was sentenced to 11 years in prison.

Sources: *"Koss Financial Records Will Get More Scrutiny in 2010,"* Milwaukee Journal Sentinel, *December 28, 2009; "Koss Corp: Anatomy of an Alleged $31 Million Fraud,"* www.dailyfinance.com, *January 18, 2010; "Koss Fraud May Have Been Due, In No Small Part, to Michael Koss Holding Five Executive Positions,"* goingconcern.com, *March 22, 2010; "Koss Auditor Faces Lawsuit, Questions,"* Milwaukee Journal Sentinel, *March 28, 2010; "Former Koss Corp. Executive Sachdeva sentenced to 11 years in prison,"* Milwaukee Journal Sentinel, *November 17, 2010.*

Analytical Procedures

During an audit, a variety of analytical procedures might be employed, depending on the circumstances and the nature of the business. Comparisons of asset and revenue balances with recent history might help detect overstatements. Such relationships as receivables turnover, days' sales in receivables, amount of past due receivables, gross margin ratio, and sales/asset ratios can be compared to historical data and industry statistics for evidence of overall reasonableness. Account interrelationships also can be used in analytical procedures. For example, sales returns and allowances and sales commissions generally vary directly with dollar sales volume, bad debt expense usually varies directly with credit sales, and freight expense varies with the physical sales volume. Accounts receivable write-offs may also be compared with estimates of doubtful accounts.

AUDITING INSIGHT Simple Analytical Comparison

The auditors for one company prepared a schedule of the monthly credit sales totals for the current and prior years. They noticed several variations, but one in November of the current year stood out in particular. The current-year credit sales were almost twice as large as in any prior November. Further investigation showed that a computer error had caused the November credit sales to be recorded twice in the control accounts. The accounts receivable and sales revenue were materially overstated as a result.

Confirmation of Accounts and Notes Receivable

In general, the use of confirmations for accounts receivable is considered a required audit procedure by audit standards. If auditors decide not to use them, the burden of proof is on the auditors to justify their position. Auditors should document justifications for the decision not to use confirmations for accounts receivable in a particular audit. Justifications might include (1) receivables are not material; (2) confirmations would be ineffective, based on prior-years' experience or knowledge that responses could be unreliable; and (3) analytical procedures and other substantive procedures provide sufficient, competent evidence.

AUDITING INSIGHT A Decision Not to Use Accounts Receivable Confirmations

Sureparts Manufacturing Company sold all its production to three auto manufacturers and six aftermarket distributors. All nine of these customers typically paid their accounts in full by the 10th of each following month. The auditors were able to vouch the cash receipts for the full amount of the accounts receivable in the bank statements and cash receipts records in the month following the Sureparts year-end. Confirmation evidence was not necessary in these circumstances because direct evidence of payment provided full verification of the existence and valuation of the receivables.

Confirmations provide evidence of *existence* as well as *rights and obligations* of accounts and notes receivable. However, they do not provide strong evidence on the *valuation* of accounts receivable. Remember that just because a customer owes an amount does not mean it will pay that amount. Customers in bankruptcy routinely confirm amounts owed, although the receivable's value may be only a small fraction of that amount. The accounts to be confirmed are often documented with an aged trial balance. (An aged trial balance annotated to show the auditors' work is shown in Exhibit 7.10.) Accounts for confirmation can be selected at random or in accordance with another sampling method consistent with the audit objectives. Statistical methods may be useful for determining the sample size. Audit software can be used to access computerized receivables files, select, and even print the confirmations.

There are two primary methods of confirming accounts receivable: positive confirmations and negative confirmations. A **positive confirmation** asks the customer to respond whether the balance is correct or incorrect. See Exhibit 7.11 for an example of a positive confirmation. A variation of the positive confirmation is the *blank form*. A blank confirmation does not contain the balance; customers are asked to fill it in themselves. The blank positive confirmation may produce better evidence because the recipients need to get the information directly from their own records instead of just signing the form and returning it with no exceptions noted. (However, the effort involved on the part of the recipient may cause a lower response rate.) As illustrated in several of the Auditing Insights, the auditors must follow up on all exceptions. For example, they may choose to examine the bank deposit that includes a check mentioned by the customer. The reason

EXHIBIT 7.10 Accounts Receivable Aged Trial Balance

DUNDER-MIFFLIN INC
Accounts Receivable Aged Trial Balance
For Year Ended 12/31/2017
(Prepared by Client)

C-2
Prepared *DHS 2/14/2018*
Review *ADB 2/16/2018*

	2017 Total Balance	Conf. No.	Date Mailed	Date Rec'd	Current < 30 Days	30–60 Days	Past Due 60–90 Days	>90 Days
Pay More Paper	$ 173,406.37					$ 173,406.37		
Nuke Me Office Supplies	11,630.14				$ 11,630.14			
Bet Your Life Printing	718,986.45	1 C	1/15	1/22	718,986.45			
Paper Shack	242,568.88				242,568.88		$ 461.09	
Shreadables	461.09							
Mall-Wart	6,822,725.10	2 C	1/15	1/27	γ5,765,081.85			$1,057,643.25
House of Paper	3,181.49						3,181.49	
Sunshine Office Supplies	1,644.41				1,644.41			
Imelda's Printing	32,023.89	3 E	1/15	1/21	32,023.89			
Hip Hop Invitations	230,932.95					230,932.95		
The Paper Federation	405,846.10				405,846.10			
Office Least	15,026.57	4 E	1/15	1/25	γ(1,388.75)	γ16,415.32		
Lamour Glamor Printing	127,907.18 β	5 NR	1/15a	n/a			127,907.18	
Bullseye	1,013,239.57	6 E	1/15	2/2	1,013,239.57			
Peyton's Paper	879.43				879.43			
Total	$16,410,902.71 CF				$10,233,296.72	$536,874.60	$746,034.56	$4,894,696.83
	u TB				u	u	u	u

C Confirmation received without exception.
T Tested calculation of aging.
E Confirmation received with exception. See C-2.1 for follow-up.
β Examined related invoices and shipping documents.
NR Confirmation not returned. See C-3 for application of subsequent cash receipts.

CF Crossfooted.
u Footed.
TB Agreed to trial balance.

EXHIBIT 7.11
Positive Confirmation Form

Dunder-Mifflin Inc.
Scranton, PA

Bullseye
1359 Central Boulevard
Derma, MS 39530
Attn: Accounts Payable Dept.

Our auditor, M. Chael Smith, is making his regular audit of our financial statements. Part of this audit includes direct verification of customer balances.

PLEASE EXAMINE THE DATA BELOW CAREFULLY AND EITHER CONFIRM ITS ACCURACY OR REPORT ANY DIFFERENCES DIRECTLY TO OUR AUDITORS USING THE ENCLOSED REPLY ENVELOPE.

This is not a request for payment. Please do not send your remittance to our auditors.

Your prompt attention to this request will be appreciated.

Samuel Carboy

Samuel Carboy, Controller

The balance due Dunder-Mifflin Inc. as of December 31, 2017, is
$1,013,239.57 C-2

This balance is correct except as noted below:

Our records indicate that we wrote a check to Dunder-Mifflin on 12/28 for this amount. ✓

Date: *1/21/18*   By: *Rudy Robinson*
                       Title: *Accounts Payable*

✓ *Check Received 1/3/18 RJR*

for any discrepancy will have to be investigated by the client, and the audit team will examine corroborative evidence of the client's resolution.

See Exhibit 7.12 for the **negative confirmation** form for the same request in Exhibit 7.11. The positive form asks for a response. The negative form asks for a response *only if something is wrong with the balance;* thus, lack of response to negative confirmations is considered evidence that the account is fairly stated.

The positive form is by far the more common and is used when individual balances are relatively large or when accounts are in dispute. Positive confirmations generally ask for information about the entire account balance as of a specific date. However, when customers are less likely to be able to respond to entire account balances, auditors may confirm specific invoices. The negative form is used mostly when the risk of material misstatement is considered low, when a large number of small balances is involved, and when the client's customers can be expected to consider the confirmations properly. Auditors must use these confirmations with great care. Occasionally, they use both forms by sending positive confirmations on some (large) customers' accounts and negative confirmations on others (usually smaller account balances).

EXHIBIT 7.12
Negative Confirmation Form

Dunder-Mifflin Inc.
Scranton, PA

Bullseye
1359 Central Boulevard
Derma, MS 39530
Attn: Accounts Payable Dept.

Our auditor, M. Chael Smith, is making his regular audit of our financial statements. Part of this audit includes direct verification of customer balances.

PLEASE EXAMINE THE DATA BELOW CAREFULLY AND COMPARE THEM TO YOUR RECORDS OF YOUR ACCOUNT WITH US. IF THE INFORMATION IS NOT IN AGREEMENT WITH YOUR RECORDS, PLEASE STATE ANY DIFFERENCES BELOW AND RETURN DIRECTLY TO OUR AUDITORS IN THE RETURN ENVELOPE PROVIDED. **IF THE INFORMATION IS CORRECT, NO REPLY IS NECESSARY.**

This is not a request for payment. Please do not send your remittance to our auditors.

Your prompt attention to this request will be appreciated.

Samuel Carboy
———————————————
Samuel Carboy, Controller

The balance due Dunder-Mifflin Inc. as of December 31, 2017, is $1,013,239.57 C-2

This balance is correct except as noted below:

Our records indicate that we wrote a check to Dunder-Mifflin on 12/28 for this amount. ✓

Date: *1/21/18*   By: *Rudy Robinson*
                    Title: *Accounts Payable*
✓ *Check Received 1/3/18 RJR*

Getting confirmations delivered to the intended recipient requires auditors' careful attention. Auditors need to control the mailing of the confirmations, including the addresses to which they are sent, and the confirmations should be returned directly to the auditors. The confirmations should normally be addressed to the customer's accounts payable department. There have been cases in which confirmations were mailed to company accomplices, who provided false responses. The auditors should carefully consider features of the reply, such as postmarks, fax and telephone responses, letterhead, e-mail, or other characteristics that may indicate a false response. Auditors should follow up on electronic and telephone responses to determine their origin (e.g., returning the telephone call to a known number, looking up telephone numbers to determine addresses, or using a directory to determine the location of a respondent). On the other hand, an electronic confirmation process (e.g., confirmation.com) that creates a secure confirmation environment may mitigate the risks of human intervention and misdirection. For example, encryption, electronic digital signatures, and procedures to verify website authenticity may improve the security of

EXHIBIT 7.13

Responses to Positive Confirmations (as of December 31)

Response	Follow-Up Action
"This amount was paid on December 28."	This account is probably valid because the check was likely received after year-end. However, it should be treated as an exception and the date of the receipt should be verified.
"We are unable to confirm this amount."	This is treated the same way as a nonresponse, and alternative procedures should be performed.
"We returned these items."	This is an exception that should be discussed with the client. The auditor should verify that there are no other returns included in receivables.
"We received these goods on January 3."	This is also probably valid because the shipment was likely made in late December. However, this should also be treated as an exception and the shipment should be verified. The auditor should also make sure the goods were removed from the year-end inventory.

the electronic confirmation process. Second and third requests should be sent to motivate responses to positive confirmations, and auditors should audit nonresponding customers by alternative procedures. Furthermore, the lack of response to a negative confirmation is no guarantee that the intended recipient received it or read it. Exhibit 7.13 illustrates some common confirmation responses and the appropriate follow-up action.

If an exception cannot be resolved or it appears to indicate a misstatement, auditors should (1) determine the cause of the misstatement, (2) extrapolate the misstatements over the population, and (3) consider whether fraud may have occurred. If similar misstatements could exist, additional procedures are generally necessary to determine the extent of misstatements. In the case of fraud, an extensive investigation may be necessary.[6]

Confirmation of receivables may be performed at a date other than the year-end. When confirmation is done at an interim date, the audit firm is able to spread work throughout the year and avoid the pressures of overtime that typically occur during "busy season." In addition, the audit can be completed sooner after the year-end date if confirmations have been done earlier. The primary consideration when planning confirmation of receivables before the balance sheet date is the client's internal control over transactions affecting receivables. When confirmation is performed at an interim date, the following additional procedures should be considered:

1. Obtain a summary of receivables transactions from the interim date to the year-end date, and review them for unusual items.
2. Vouch a selected sample of transactions for the period.
3. Obtain a year-end trial balance of receivables, compare it to the interim trial balance, and obtain evidence and explanations for large variations.
4. Consider the necessity for additional confirmations as of the balance sheet date if balances have significantly increased.

Alternative Procedures

Often, the client's customers are not willing or able to return the confirmation. They may not be able if, for example, they are on a voucher system that lists payables by invoice instead of by vendor account. The U.S. government is notorious for not returning confirmations because records may be kept at various agencies. In these cases, auditors

[6]"AICPA Practice Alert 03-1: Audit Confirmations," June 2007.

must perform alternative procedures to ensure existence. These include examining (1) subsequent cash receipts; (2) sales orders, invoices, and shipping documents; and (3) correspondence files for past-due accounts. Examining subsequent cash receipts is a particularly effective test because if the customer paid the account, it provides strong evidence that the receivable existed. This examination is often performed even when the customer has confirmed the account. The cash receipt should be traced to the remittance advice and the deposit into the client's cash account.

Additional Notes about Confirmations

Because of the importance of confirmations for verifying the validity of accounts receivable, the auditor should take special care to consider the sufficiency of evidence obtained. Some other considerations that auditors should make when sending confirmations follow.

- Confirmations returned by the postal service as "undeliverable" are always a red flag. The address should be double checked and evidence that the company actually exists obtained.
- Confirmations of accounts, loans, and notes receivable may not produce sufficient evidence of ownership by the client (rights assertion). Debtors may not be aware that the client sold the accounts, notes, or loans receivable to financial institutions or to the public (collateralized securities). Auditors should also consider whether their clients ever factor, or sell, receivables to third parties. Auditors need to perform additional inquiry and detailed procedures to get evidence of the ownership of the receivables and the appropriateness of disclosures related to financing transactions secured by receivables.
- Although confirmations are most often used for account balances, experienced auditors recognize that confirming a specific transaction, especially a large one, may be more effective. This is especially true if the balance consists primarily of a few large transactions. In your own life, you probably do not know what your current balance is on your credit cards, but you likely remember a recent large purchase (e.g., for textbooks).
- It is also possible for an auditor to receive an oral response to a confirmation. Such a response does not meet the definition of an external confirmation because there is no *direct written response* to the auditor. The auditor should request a written response, and, if one is not forthcoming, the auditor should determine whether alternative audit procedures are warranted.

Dual-Purpose Nature of Accounts Receivable Confirmations

Accounts receivable confirmation is a substantive procedure designed to obtain evidence of the existence and, secondarily, valuation of customers' balances directly from the customer. However, if such confirmations show numerous exceptions, auditors are concerned with the controls over the details of sales and cash receipts transactions even if previous control evaluations seemed to show little control risk.

The goal in performing substantive procedures is to detect evidence of any material misstatement due to errors or fraud. If there is a risk of material misstatement involving revenue recognition, auditors should consider confirming contract terms and investigate the presence of side agreements with customers. Items to be considered would be acceptance criteria, delivery and payment terms, future or continuing vendor obligations, rights of return, guaranteed resale, and cancellation or refund provisions.

Review for Collectability

Even if the customer confirms that the account exists, this does not necessarily mean that the customer can or will pay it! Therefore, the primary evidence gained from confirmations relates to existence. However, the audit team must review accounts for collectability and determine the adequacy of the allowance for doubtful accounts in support of the *valuation* assertion. To do this, auditors review subsequent cash receipts from the customer, discuss unpaid accounts with the credit manager, and examine the credit files. In addition, a discussion of the bankruptcy of a large customer may appear in the minutes of the board of directors meetings, the audit committee meetings, or a meeting of an executive committee. Credit files should contain the customer's financial statements, credit reports, and correspondence between the client and the customer. Based on this evidence, the audit team estimates the likely amount of nonpayment for the customer, which is included in the estimate of the allowance for doubtful accounts. In addition, an allowance should be estimated for all other customers, perhaps as a percentage of the current accounts with a higher percentage of past due accounts. The auditors then compare their estimate to the recorded balance in the allowance account and propose an adjusting entry for the difference if needed.

Cutoff and Sales Returns

The *cutoff* assertion is particularly relevant in the revenue cycle because of the significance of revenue as a benchmark for users of the financial statements. This high significance of revenues makes it highly appealing to managers for earnings management and fraud. Many questionable adjustments to revenues occur very close to year-end. As a result, auditors must make sure that sales are recorded in the proper period. To do this, they employ **sales cutoff tests**. Procedures include tracing shipping documents before and after year-end to the sales journal to ensure the sale was recorded in the proper period. Credit memos for returns after year-end are vouched to receiving reports. Any goods returned after year-end that were sold during the year being audited should be deducted from net sales.

Adjusting entries for cutoff errors (i.e., sales recorded in the current period for next month's shipments) must be considered carefully because not only are accounts receivable and sales overstated, but also inventory is understated and cost of goods sold (COGS) is overstated.

AUDITING INSIGHT   Time Doesn't Fly

The Securities and Exchange Commission filed an action alleging that **Sirena Apparel Group Inc.,** a women's swimwear manufacturer, held open the March fiscal quarter until the company had reached its sales target for that period. The fraud was accomplished by resetting the date on the company's computer clock to the end of the month. Manipulation of the computer clock allowed April shipments to be recorded as March revenue because the computer clock controlled the date that was printed on the company's invoices. The computerized system also automatically recorded revenue earned as of the date of the invoice. The bills of lading for the out-of-period shipments reflected April shipping dates. When management learned that the company's independent auditors would be testing shipping cutoff for the March 31 quarter, they instructed a subordinate to create false bills of lading to reflect March shipping dates to conceal the fraud from the auditors.

Source: *SEC Accounting and Auditing Enforcement Release No. 1325, September 27, 2000.*

In addition to the substantive tests discussed earlier and in Exhibit 7.9, the auditor often performs other substantive tests related to assertions in the revenue cycle:

- *Completeness of revenue and accounts receivable*—Include a sample of zero-balance accounts in the confirmation process.
- *Rights and obligations of accounts receivable*—Inquire whether any receivables have been sold or factored.
- *Rights and obligations of accounts receivable*—Inspect the bank confirmations, loan agreements, and minutes of the board for indications of pledged, discounted, or assigned receivables.

Companies may sell or **factor** their accounts receivable to a financial institution to obtain cash immediately. It is difficult to determine whether receivables have been sold because the customers usually do not know that someone else actually owns their account. The cash goes to the original seller, who passes it on to the financial institution. Inquiring of management and examining support for large cash receipts is the best way to detect these transactions.

- *Classification of accounts receivable*—Scan receivables ledger for negative balances for reclassification to accounts payable.
- *Presentation and disclosure of accounts receivable and revenues*—Complete a disclosure checklist and ensure completeness and accuracy of required disclosures.

When auditors are satisfied that controls have been examined and transactions and balances have been appropriately tested, the job is not over. The accounts in the revenue cycle require certain disclosures. Revenue recognition policies and the amount of the allowance for doubtful accounts are some of the items requiring specific presentation and disclosures. These disclosures must ensure that the presentation and disclosure assertions of *occurrence, rights and obligations, completeness, classification, accuracy and valuation,* and *classification and understandability* have been met. To ensure this, the auditor will often complete the audit of the revenue cycle with a disclosure checklist.

AUDITING INSIGHT   Ambassador to Fraud

The SEC has settled financial fraud charges with Raymond Green, former treasurer and principal financial accounting officer, and Barry Budilov, former president, director, and chief executive, at defunct **Ambassador Eyewear Group** (an eyeglass frame distributor), which allegedly overstated assets by as much as 35 percent. To compensate for Ambassador's large cash shortfalls, Budilov obtained an asset-based collateralized line of credit. Under the line of credit terms, Ambassador could borrow up to a percentage of the total value of accounts receivable and inventory value. Ambassador continued to encounter cash shortfalls and subsequently began to falsify accounts receivable and inventory values. On November 26, 2004, Green pleaded guilty to two counts of fraud and was sentenced to five years' probation, including eight months of home custody and an order to pay restitution of nearly $17.5 million. On July 12, 2005, Budilov pleaded guilty to four counts of fraud and was sentenced to 27 months in prison and five years' probation and was ordered to repay nearly $17.5 million.

Source: *"Mentor to Fraud? Two Former Execs Settle with SEC," www.cfo.com, September 17, 2007.*

⊘ REVIEW CHECKPOINTS

7.19 Why is it important to emphasize the *existence* assertion when auditing accounts receivable?

7.20 Which audit procedures are usually the most useful for auditing the existence assertion?

7.21 What analytical procedures might be informative regarding the existence assertion?

7.22 Distinguish between positive and negative confirmations. Under what conditions would you expect each type of confirmation to be appropriate?

7.23 What are some justifications for not using confirmations of accounts receivable on a particular audit?

7.24 What special care should be taken with regard to examining the sources (e.g., faxed copy) of accounts receivable confirmation responses?

7.25 What alternative procedures should be applied to accounts that do not return confirmations?

7.26 What procedures should be performed to determine the adequacy of the allowance for doubtful accounts?

AUDIT RISK MODEL APPLIED

Now that the inherent and control risk elements for the revenue and collection cycle along with some of the important substantive procedures have been presented, let's examine how an audit team might apply the audit risk model for the *existence* assertion.

Healthy Delights Ice Cream Inc.

Healthy Delights is a publicly held company that sells health-based ice cream to grocery store chains in the United States. Annual sales have steadily remained at around $100 million. Marsha Fields has been assigned as the senior auditor. Her firm's policy is always to set overall audit risk as low. She knows previous years' errors were few and the food industry is sound. The company is generally profitable; management's compensation is based on long-term performance, not short-term goals; and the overall economy was strong during the year under audit, so she assesses inherent risk as low to moderate. Controls have been historically strong, including hiring of competent people; maximum use of computer technology, which is reviewed by internal auditors; and careful reviews of detailed sales analyses by management. Testing of controls in accordance with AS 2201 found no design or operating deficiencies. Thus, Fields assesses the risk of material misstatement as low. In this situation, she can be comfortable setting detection risk at a moderate to high level. This will allow her to limit her sample of accounts for positive confirmations to the largest accounts with a small random sample for negative confirmations on smaller accounts. The confirmations will be sent at an interim date. She also can rely heavily on analytical procedures. In addition, a smaller sample of transactions will be selected for detail testing. This combination of low risk of material misstatement and moderate to high detection risk should lead Fields to an acceptably low overall audit risk.

APPLICATION IN THE FIELD

LO 7-7

Apply your knowledge to perform audit procedures in the revenue and collection cycle and evaluate the findings of your tests.

Historically, auditors testing the revenue cycle would select samples of items to test significant assertions and the controls that help ensure the accurate and complete processing of transactions. With an increase in the ability to handle larger amounts of data, auditors can now test all instances of some controls and transactions instead of selecting a sample.

One way to subject all items in a population of occurrences for a particular control activity in the revenue cycle is to use *exception testing*. Exception testing is designed to identify a violation of a particular control activity through the use of an automated test procedure designed to test all items in a population. For example, companies often design an automated control activity that is designed to compare a customer's credit limit to the sum of (1) a potential sales transaction and (2) that customer's outstanding credit balance before approval of that sales transaction. If the control activity operated effectively throughout the year, a customer's outstanding credit balance would not exceed its credit limit.

Given the nature of the control activity, one way for an auditor to test the operating effectiveness of this control would be through the use of exception testing. An auditor could obtain evidence about the control's operating effectiveness by using a procedure that compares each customer's credit limit to that customer's outstanding credit balance at the end of each day for the year under audit. Such a testing strategy would not have been possible (at least economically) previously. However, due to advances in information technology, such testing is now possible. Using IDEA or other audit software, the computer can make these comparisons and provide a listing of exceptions, as outlined in the following example. As a direct result, entry-level audit professionals are now expected to consider the full extent of client data available for testing purposes before proceeding with audit tests.

USING IDEA IN THE AUDIT

Credit Authorization Controls

One opportunity for auditors to take advantage of the availability of improved data analytic tools is to perform exception testing on granting credit to customers. For example, an auditor may want to test whether any customers were granted credit when they either had no approved credit limit or had exceeded their credit limit.

To accomplish this, the auditor will most likely join two related client data files—an Accounts Receivable subsidiary ledger and a Customer Master list with credit authorizations—based on customer identification. In IDEA, this can be accomplished using the **Join** command from within the **Analysis** tab.

After joining the data, the auditor can perform a direct extraction using the **Direct** command from the **Extract** group in the **Analysis** tab and create a new database of any transactions that caused a customer to exceed the credit limit. This enables the auditor to identify exceptions to authorization controls, leading to more accurate assessments of control risk and more efficient selection of substantive tests.

At the end of this chapter, you can perform this exception test in Exercise 7.77.

AUDIT CASES: EXTENDED AUDIT PROCEDURES (AS 2301)

This part of the chapter uses a set of cases that provide specific examples of tests of controls and substantive procedures (recalculation, observation, confirmation, inquiry, vouching, tracing, scanning, and analytical procedures). The case stories are better than listing schemes and detection procedures in the abstract.

The cases follow a standard format that first tells about an error or fraud situation in terms of the problem, the audit approach, and the discovery. The first part of each case gives you the "inside story" that auditors seldom know before they perform the audit work. The next part is an audit approach section, which discusses the audit objective (assertion), controls, tests of controls, and substantive procedures that could be considered in approaching the situation. The audit approach section presumes that the auditors do not know everything about the situation.

At the end of the chapter, some similar discussion cases are presented, and you can write the audit approach to test your ability to design audit procedures for detecting errors and frauds. Appendix 7B provides a substantive audit plan for reference.

Case 7.1

The Canny Cashier

PROBLEM

D. Bakel was the assistant controller of Sports Equipment Inc. (SEI), an equipment retailer. SEI maintained accounts receivable for school districts in the region; otherwise, customers received credit by using their own credit cards.

As company cashier, Bakel received all incoming mail payments on school accounts, credit card accounts, and cash and checks taken over the counter. He prepared the bank deposit, listing all checks and currency, and prepared a remittance worksheet (daily cash report) that showed amounts received, discounts allowed on school accounts, and amounts to credit to the accounts receivable. Another accountant used the remittance worksheet to post credits to the accounts receivable. Bakel delivered the deposit to the bank and reconciled the bank statement. No one else reviewed the deposits or the bank statements except the independent auditors.

Bakel opened a bank account in the name of Sport Equipment Company (SEC) after properly incorporating the company in the secretary of state's office. Over-the-counter cash, checks, and school district payments were taken from the SEI receipts and deposited in the SEC account. (None of the customers noticed the difference between the rubber stamp endorsements for the two similarly named corporations, and neither did the bank.) SEC kept the money a while, earning interest, and then Bakel wrote SEC checks to SEI to replace the "borrowed" funds, in the meantime taking new SEI receipts for deposit to SEC.

Bakel also stole payments made by the school districts, depositing them to SEC. Later he deposited SEC checks in SEI, giving the schools credit, but approved an additional 2 percent discount in the process. Thus, the schools received proper credit later, and SEC paid less by the amount of the extra discount.

SEI's bank deposits systematically showed small currency deposits. Bakel was nervous about taking too many checks, so he preferred cash. The deposit slips had to include the SEC checks because bank tellers compare the deposit slip listing to the checks submitted. The remittance worksheet showed different details: Instead of showing SEC checks, it showed receipts from school districts and currency but not many over-the-counter checks from customers.

The transactions became complicated enough that Bakel had to use the office computer to keep track of the school districts that needed to receive credit. There were no vacations for this hard-working cashier because a substitute might notice the discrepancies, and Bakel needed to give the districts credit later.

Over a six-year period, Bakel built up a $150,000 average balance in the Sport Equipment Company (SEC) account that earned a total of $67,500 interest that Sports Equipment Inc. (SEI) should have earned. By approving the "extra" discounts, Bakel skimmed 2 percent of $1 million in annual sales, for a total of $120,000. Because SEI would have had net income before taxes of about $1.6 million over these six years (about 9 percent of sales), Bakel's embezzlement took about 12.5 percent of the income.

AUDIT APPROACH

Authorization related to cash receipts, custody of cash, recording cash transactions, and bank statement reconciliation should be separate duties designed to prevent errors and frauds. Some supervision and detail review of one or more of these duties should be performed as a next-level control designed to detect errors and frauds, if they have occurred. For example, someone else should prepare the remittance worksheet, or at least the controller should approve the discounts; someone else should prepare the bank reconciliation.

Bakel performed incompatible duties. (While he did not actually perform the recording, Bakel provided the source document—the remittance worksheet—the other accountant used to make the cash and accounts receivable entries.) According to the company president, the "control" was the diligence of "our long-time, trusted, hard-working assistant controller." (*Note:* A vigilant auditor who "thought like a crook" might have been able to imagine ways Bakel could have committed fraud and thus prevented or detected this cash embezzlement and accounts receivable lapping scheme.)

Because the "control" purports to be Bakel's honest and diligent performance of the accounting and control activities that might have been performed by two or more people, the test of controls is an audit of cash receipts transactions as they relate to accounts receivable credit. The dual-direction samples and procedures are these:

- *Occurrence direction.* The auditors selected a sample of customer accounts receivable and vouched payment credits to remittance worksheets and bank deposits, including recalculation of discounts allowed in comparison to sales terms (2 percent), classification (customer name) identification, and correspondence of receipt date to recording date.
- *Completeness direction.* The auditors selected a sample of remittance worksheets (or bank deposits), vouched details to bank deposit slips (traced details to remittance worksheets if the sample is bank deposits), and traced to complete accounting posting in customer accounts receivable.

Because there was a control risk of incorrect accounting, accounts receivable were confirmed as of year-end using positive confirmations. The sample included all school district accounts.

When prompted by notice of an oddity (noted in the following discovery summary), the audit team can use the Internet, chamber of commerce directory, local crisscross directory, and a visit to the secretary of state's office to determine the location and identity of Sport Equipment Company.

DISCOVERY SUMMARY

The test of controls samples showed four cases of discrepancy, one of which is discussed here.

The auditors sent positive confirmations on all 72 school district accounts. Three of the responses stated the districts had paid the balances before the confirmation date. Follow-up procedures on their accounts receivable credit in the next period showed they had received credit in remittance reports and the bank deposits had shown no checks from the districts but had contained a check from Sports Equipment Company.

Investigation of SEC revealed the connection of Bakel, who was confronted and then confessed.

Bank Deposit Slip		Cash Remittance Report				
		Name	Amount	Discount	AR	Sales
Jones	25	Jones	25	0	0	25
Smith	35	Smith	35	0	0	35
Hill District	980	Hill District	980	20	1,000	0
Sport Equipment	1,563	Marlin District	480	20	500	0
Currency	540	Waco District	768	32	800	0
Deposit	3,143	Currency	855	0	0	855
		Totals	3,143	72	2,300	915

Case 7.2

The Taxman Always Rings Twice

PROBLEM

J. Shelstad was the tax assessor-collector in the Ridge School District, serving a large metropolitan area. The staff processed tax notices on a computerized system and generated 450,000 tax notices each October. An office copy was printed and used to check off "paid" when payments were received. Payments were processed by computer, and a master file of "accounts receivable" records (tax assessments, payments) was kept on the computer hard drive.

Shelstad was a good personnel manager and often took over the front desk at lunchtime so the teller staff could enjoy lunch together. During these times, she took payments over the counter, gave the taxpayers a counter receipt, and pocketed some of the money, which was never entered in the computerized system.

Shelstad resigned when she was elected to the Ridge school board. The district's assessor-collector office was eliminated upon the creation of a new countywide tax agency.

The computerized records showed balances due from many taxpayers who had actually paid their taxes. The book of printed notices was not marked "paid" for many taxpayers who had received counter receipts. These records and the daily cash receipts reports (cash receipts journal) were available when the independent auditors had performed the most recent annual audit in April. When Shelstad resigned in August, a power surge permanently destroyed the hard drive receivables file, and the cash receipts journals could not be found.

The new county agency managers noticed that the total of delinquent taxes disclosed in the audited financial statements was much larger than the total turned over to the county attorney for collection and foreclosure.

Shelstad had been the assessor-collector for 15 years. The "good personnel manager" pocketed 100–150 counter payments each year in amounts of $500–$2,500, stealing about $200,000 a year for a total of approximately $2.5 million. The district had assessed about $800–$900 million per year, so the annual theft was less than 1 percent. Nevertheless, the taxpayers got mad.

AUDIT APPROACH

The school district had a respectable system for establishing the initial amounts of taxes receivable. The professional staff of appraisers and the independent appraisal review board established the tax base for each property. The school board set the price (tax rate). The computerized system authorization for billing was validated on these two inputs.

The cash receipts system was well designed, calling for preparation of a daily cash receipts report (cash receipts journal that served as a source input for computerized entry). The "boss," Shelstad, always reviewed this report.

Unfortunately, Shelstad had the opportunity and power to override the controls and become both cash handler and supervisor. She made the decisions about sending delinquent taxes to the county attorney for collection and withheld the ones known to have been paid but stolen.

The auditors performed dual-direction sampling to test the processing of cash receipts.

- *Occurrence direction.* The auditors selected a sample of receivables from the computer hard disk and vouched (1) charges to the appraisal record, recalculating the amount using the authorized tax rate and (2) payments, if any, to the cash receipts journal and bank deposits. (The auditors found no exceptions.)
- *Completeness direction.* The auditors selected a sample of properties from the appraisal rolls and determined that tax notices had been sent and tax receivables (charges) recorded in the computer file. They next selected a sample of cash receipts reports, vouched them to bank deposits of the same amount and date, and traced the payments forward to credits to taxpayers' accounts. They also selected a sample of bank deposits and traced them to cash receipts reports of the same amount and date. Finally, they compared the details on bank deposits to the details on the cash receipts reports to determine whether the same taxpayers appeared on both documents. (The auditors found no exceptions.)

The auditors confirmed a sample of unpaid tax balances with taxpayers. In such cases, response rates may not be high, follow-up procedures determining the ownership (county title files) may need to be performed, and new confirmations may need to be sent.

DISCOVERY SUMMARY

Shelstad persuaded the auditors that the true receivables were the delinquencies turned over to the county attorney. The confirmation sample and other work were based on this population. Thus, confirmations were not sent to the "unpaid" balances that Shelstad knew had been paid, therefore, the auditors never had the opportunity to receive "I paid" complaints from taxpayers.

Shelstad did not influence the new managers of the countywide tax district. They questioned the discrepancy between the delinquent taxes in the audit report and the lower amount turned over for collection. Because the computer file was not usable, the managers had to use the printed book of tax notices in which paid accounts had been marked "paid." (Shelstad had not marked the stolen ones "paid," so the printed book would agree with the computer file.) Tax due notices were sent to the taxpayers with unpaid balances, and they began to show up bringing their counter receipts and loud complaints.

Acting overzealously in their documentation, the independent auditors had earlier photocopied the entire set of cash receipts reports (cash journal) and were then able to determine that the counter receipts (all signed by Shelstad) had not been deposited or entered. Shelstad was prosecuted and sentenced to a jail term.

Case 7.3

Bill Often, Bill Early

PROBLEM

McGossage Company experienced profit pressures for two years in a row. Actual profits were squeezed in a recessionary economy, but the company reported net income decreases that were not as severe as other companies' in the industry.

Sales for orders that had been prepared for shipment but not actually shipped until later were recorded in the grocery products division. Employees backdated the shipping documents. Gross profit on these "sales" was about 30 percent. Customers took discounts on payments, but the company did not record them, leaving the debit balances in the customers' accounts receivable instead of charging them to the sales discounts and allowances account. Company accountants were instructed to wait 60 days before recording discounts taken.

The division vice president and general manager knew about these accounting practices, as did a significant number of the 2,500 employees in the division. The division managers were under orders from headquarters to achieve profit objectives they considered unrealistic.

The customers' accounts receivable balances contained amounts due for discounts the customers already had taken. The cash receipts records showed payments received without credit for discounts. Discounts were entered monthly by a special journal entry.

The unshipped goods were on the shipping dock at year-end with papers showing earlier shipping dates.

As misstatements go, some of these were on the materiality borderline. Sales were overstated 0.3 percent and 0.5 percent in the prior and current years, respectively. Accounts receivable were overstated 4 percent and 8 percent, respectively. The combined effect was to overstate the division's net income by 6 percent and 17 percent. Selected data follow:

	One Year Ago*		Current Year*	
	Reported	Actual	Reported	Actual
Sales	$330.0	$329.0	$350.0	$348.0
Discounts expense	1.7	1.8	1.8	2.0
Net income	6.7	6.3	5.4	4.6

*Dollars in millions.

AUDIT APPROACH

The accounting manual should provide instructions to record sales on the date of shipment (or when title passes, if later). Management subverted this control procedure by having shipping employees date the shipping papers incorrectly.

Cash receipts procedures should provide for authorizing and recording discounts when customers take them. Management overrode this control instruction by giving instructions to delay the recording.

Questionnaires and inquiries should be used to determine the company's accounting policies. It is possible that employees and managers would lie to the auditors to conceal the policies. It is also possible that pointed questions about revenue recognition and discount recording policies would elicit answers to reveal the practices.

For detail procedures, the auditors select a sample of cash receipts, examine them for authorization, recalculate the customer discounts, and trace them to accounts receivable input for recording the proper amount on the proper date. They select a sample of shipping documents, vouch them to customer orders, and then trace them to invoices and to the accounts receivable account with proper amounts on the proper date. These tests follow the tracing direction—starting with data that represent the beginning of transactions (cash receipts, shipping) and tracing them through the company's accounting process.

The audit team should confirm a sample of customer accounts and use analytical procedures to determine relationships of past years' discount expense to a relevant base (sales, sales volume) to calculate an overall test of the discounts expense.

DISCOVERY SUMMARY

The managers lied to the auditors about their revenue and expense timing policies. The sample of shipping documents showed no dating discrepancies because the employees had inserted incorrect dates. The analytical procedures on discounts did not show the misstatement because the historical relationships were too erratic to show a deficient number. However, the sample of cash receipts transactions showed that discounts had not been calculated and recorded at time of receipt. Additional inquiry led to the discovery of the special journal entries and knowledge of the recording delay. Two customers in the sample of 65 confirmations responded with exceptions that turned out to be unrecorded discounts.

Two other customers in the confirmation sample complained that they did not owe for late invoices on December 31. Follow-up showed that the shipments were noticed on the shipping dock. Auditors taking the physical inventory noticed the goods on the shipping dock during the December 31 inventory taking. Inspection revealed the shipping documents dated December 26. When the auditors traced these shipments to the sales recording, they found them recorded **bill and hold** on December 29. (These procedures were performed and the results obtained by a new audit firm in the third year!)

Case 7.4

Thank Goodness It's Friday

PROBLEM

Alpha Brewery Corporation generally has good controls related to authorization of transactions for accounting entry, and the accounting manual has instructions for recording sales transactions in the proper accounting period. The company regularly closes the accounting process each Friday at 5 P.M. to prepare weekly management reports. The year-end date (cutoff date) is December 31, and this year, December 31 was a Monday. However, the accounting was performed through Friday as usual and the accounts were closed for the year on January 4.

AUDIT TRAIL

All entries were properly dated after December 31, including the sales invoices, cash receipts, and shipping documents. However, the trial balance from which the financial statements were prepared was dated December 31 (this year). Nobody noticed the slip of a few days because the Friday closing was normal.

Alpha recorded sales of $672,000 and gross profit of $268,800 over the January 1–4 period. Cash collections on customers' accounts were recorded in the amount of $800,000.

AUDIT APPROACH

The company had in place the proper instructions for people to date transactions on the actual date on which they occurred, to enter sales and cost of goods sold on the day of shipment, and to enter cash receipts on the day received in the company offices. An accounting supervisor should have checked the entries through Friday to make sure the dates corresponded with the actual events and that the accounts for the year were closed with Monday's transactions.

In this case, the auditors need to be aware of the company's weekly routine closing and the possibility that the December 31 date might cause a problem. Asking the question: "Did you cut off the accounting on Monday night this week?" might elicit the "Oh, we forgot!" response. Otherwise, it is normal to sample transactions around the year-end date to determine whether they were recorded in the proper accounting period.

Select transactions 7–10 days before and after the year-end date and inspect the dates on supporting documentation for evidence of accounting in the proper period.

The audit for sales overstatement is partly accomplished by auditing the cash and accounts receivable at December 31 for overstatement. Confirm a sample of accounts receivable. If the accounts are too large, the auditors expect the debtors to say so, thus leading to detection of sales overstatements.

Cash overstatement is audited by auditing the bank reconciliation to see whether deposits in transit (the deposits sent late in December) actually cleared the bank early in January. Obviously, the January 4 cash collections could not reach the bank until at least Monday, January 7. That is too long for a December 31 deposit to be in transit to a local bank.

The completeness of sales recordings is audited by selecting a sample of sales transactions (and supporting shipping documents) in the early part of the next accounting period (January next year). One way this year's sales could be incomplete would be to postpone recording December shipments until January, and this procedure will detect those deferred sales if the shipping documents are dated properly.

The completeness of cash collections (and accounts receivable credits) is examined by auditing the cash deposits early in January to see whether there is any sign of holding cash without entry until January.

In this case, the existence objective is more significant for discovery of the problem than the completeness objective. After all, the January 1–4 sales, shipments, and cash collections did not "exist" in December this year.

DISCOVERY SUMMARY

The test of controls sample from the days before and after December 31 quickly revealed the problem. Company accounting personnel were embarrassed, but there had been no effort to misstate the financial statements. This was a simple error. The company readily made the following adjustment:

	Debit	Credit
Sales	$672,000	
Inventory	403,200	
Accounts receivable	800,000	
Accounts receivable		$672,000
Cost of goods sold		403,200
Cash		800,000

✅ REVIEW CHECKPOINTS

7.27 What are the goals of dual-direction testing regarding an audit of the accounts receivable and cash collection system?

7.28 In the case of The Canny Cashier, name one control that could have revealed signs of the embezzlement.

7.29 What feature(s) could SEI have installed in its cash receipts internal controls that would have been expected to prevent the cash receipts journal and recorded cash sales from reflecting more than the amount shown on the daily deposit slips?

7.30 In the case of The Taxman Always Rings Twice, what information could have been obtained from confirmations directed to the real population of delinquent accounts?

7.31 In the case of Bill Often, Bill Early, what information might have been obtained from inquiries? From tests of controls? From observations? From confirmations?

7.32 With reference to the case of Thank Goodness It's Friday, what contribution could an understanding of the business and the management reporting system have made to discovery of the open cash receipts journal cutoff error?

AUDITING INSIGHT — PCAOB Inspections and the Revenue and Collections Cycle

- In this audit, the Firm failed to obtain sufficient appropriate audit evidence to support its audit opinion on the financial statements, as its procedures to test revenue and cost of sales for a significant portion of the issuer's business were insufficient. To test the revenue and cost of sales for this portion of the issuer's business, the Firm performed several substantive analytical procedures, using revenue and cost of sales data disaggregated by month and by product line. The Firm, however, failed to test the accuracy of certain of the disaggregated data that it used in the performance of these analytical procedures.

- For two of the issuer's segments, the Firm failed to perform sufficient procedures related to certain revenue that represented a significant portion of total revenue. Specifically—

  - For one of these segments, the Firm identified a fraud risk related to the timing of revenue recognition. To address the fraud risk, the Firm selected for testing a control that consisted of the review of adjustments to revenue for shipments that were in transit at the end of each period; however, the Firm's testing of this control was insufficient. Specifically, the Firm's procedures were limited to determining that the analysis used in the control had been prepared, inquiring of certain individuals involved in the process, inspecting documents with comments that indicated reviews that were part of the control had occurred, and comparing certain amounts to the general ledger. The Firm, however, failed to sufficiently test an important aspect of the control related to the specific review procedures performed by the control owner, as its procedures to test this aspect were limited to inquiry. (AS No. 5, paragraphs 42 and 44)

  - For this same segment, the Firm selected for testing a control that consisted of the approval of negotiated contract terms, including prices in the contracts that were used to calculate revenue; the Firm, however, failed to test any controls over the consistency of the prices in the issuer's accounting system with the prices in the contracts. (AS No. 5, paragraph 39)

- For the other segment, which included a category of revenue that was recognized on shipment and another category of revenue that was recognized on delivery, the Firm failed to test controls that sufficiently addressed the risks of material misstatement related to revenue recognition. Specifically, the controls that the Firm PCAOB Release No. 104-2015-121 Inspection of Ernst & Young LLP June 16, 2015 Page 10 identified and tested were limited to (1) a control related to the review of the accounts receivable aging and (2) a control related to the review of the journal entries made to record revenue; neither of these controls addressed the risks related to improper revenue recognition. (AS No. 5, paragraph 39)

- The Firm failed to identify and test any controls over the accuracy and completeness of data that the issuer used in the performance of certain of the controls described above. (AS No. 5, paragraph 39)

- The issuer generated revenue at numerous locations where certain types of routine transactions were initiated and entered for processing. In performing inquiries as part of planning the audit, the Firm obtained information that indicated there could be an opportunity to carry out a potential fraud, but the Firm did not take this into account when determining its fraud risks and, as a result, did not design procedures that were intended to specifically address this risk.

- This issuer's most significant category of revenue typically consisted of arrangements that included multiple deliverables. The Firm failed in the following respects to perform sufficient procedures related to this category of revenue.

  - The Firm failed to identify and test any controls over the allocation of the consideration among the separate units of accounting.

  - With respect to one of the issuer's segments, which reported approximately eighty percent of this revenue, the Firm failed to perform any substantive procedures to test the allocation of the consideration among the separate units of accounting.

- The Firm failed to identify and test any controls over the recognition of routine revenue transactions; the adequacy of the allowances for doubtful accounts, claims, and rebates; and the factoring of the issuer's accounts receivable.
- The Firm's sample size to test revenue was too small to provide sufficient evidence because it did not appropriately consider tolerable misstatement for the population.
- The Firm tested the existence of accounts receivable as of an interim date. The Firm's procedures to extend its conclusion to

year-end were not sufficient. Specifically, these procedures were limited to (1) comparing sales activity to system-generated reports, (2) comparing the year-end balance to the subsidiary ledger and also to the balance at the date of its interim testing, and (3) comparing certain percentages and ratios, which were based on the balances at the interim date and year-end, and noting that the amounts were consistent with prior periods.

Source: 2014 PCAOB Inspection of BDO USA LLP; 2014 PCAOB Inspection of Deloitte & Touche LLP; 2014 PCAOB Inspection of Ernst & Young LLP; 2014 Inspection of KPMG LLP; and 2014 Inspection of PricewaterhouseCoopers LLP. All reports can be found on the PCAOB's website, https://pcaobus.org/Inspections/Reports/Pages/default.aspx.

Summary

The revenue and collection cycle consists of customer order processing, credit checking, shipping goods, billing customers, accounting for accounts receivable, and collecting and accounting for cash receipts. Companies reduce control risk by having a suitable separation of authorization, custody, recording, and periodic reconciliation duties. Error-checking activities of comparing customer orders and shipping documents are important for billing customers the correct prices for the delivered quantities. Otherwise, many things could go wrong—ranging from making sales to fictitious customers or customers with bad credit to erroneous billings for the wrong quantities at the wrong prices at the wrong time.

Confirmation is the primary substantive audit procedure accompanied by analytical procedures, application of subsequent cash receipts, and other alternative procedures. Confirmations of loans, accounts receivable, and notes receivable are required unless auditors can justify substituting other procedures in the circumstances of a particular audit. Confirmations for accounts and notes receivable can be in positive or negative form, and the positive form may be a blank confirmation. Confirmations yield evidence about *existence* and gross *valuation*. Other procedures must be undertaken to audit the collectability of the accounts. Nevertheless, confirmations can give some clues about collectability when customers tell about balances in dispute. Confirmations of accounts, notes, and loans receivable should not be used as the only evidence of the ownership (*rights* assertions) of these financial assets.

Although these procedures may seem to be common sense, auditing the revenue and collection cycle is not straightforward. The Auditing Insight on pages 316–317 discusses some deficiencies the PCAOB noted in its inspections of registered public accounting firms regarding audits of this cycle. Note that these issues can involve more than a slap on the wrist and added staff training. In December 2007, the PCAOB fined Deloitte & Touche $1 million for failing to exercise due professional care and obtain sufficient evidential matter regarding revenues in the audit of **Ligand Pharmaceuticals.**

Key Terms

aged trial balance: A schedule that lists each receivable and indicates whether it is current or past due and if past due, for how long; the total should equal the accounts receivable general ledger balance.

bill and hold: A fraudulent financial reporting activity by which a company recognizes a sale even though it does not ship the merchandise to the customer but holds it in its own warehouse.

bill of lading: A contract between the shipper and the carrier; includes shipping information such as ship dates and origination, purchase order number, and signatures for receipt of merchandise.

dual-purpose procedure: An audit procedure that simultaneously serves the substantive purpose (obtain direct evidence about the dollar amounts in account balances) and the test of controls purpose (obtain evidence about the company's performance of its own control activities).

factor: The action to sell accounts receivable to another party (the factor) at a discount from face value.

negative confirmation: A form sent to a customer by auditors requesting that the customer respond only if the balance shown on it is incorrect.

packing slip: A document included with a shipment that shows the description and quantity of the goods being shipped.

positive confirmation: A letter sent to a customer by auditors requesting that the customer respond whether the balance shown on it is correct or not.

revenue recognition: The recording of revenues in the general ledger, often done fraudulently by schemes such as bill and hold.

sales cutoff tests: The tests that ensure that sales are recorded in the proper period—generally, when they are shipped—and that the cost of sales is recorded and removed from inventory.

sales invoice: A bill sent to customers for payment showing the amount due and payment terms.

Multiple-Choice Questions for Practice and Review

connect All applicable Exercises and Problems are available with *Connect*.

LO 7-1

7.33 Revenues are normally considered to have been earned when
   a. All possibility of return has expired.
   b. The company has substantially accomplished what it must to be entitled to the benefits.
   c. The cash is collected.
   d. Goods have been shipped.

LO 7-3

7.34 Sales are normally recorded on the date of the
   a. Customer purchase order.
   b. Bill of lading.
   c. Sales invoice.
   d. Payment check.

LO 7-6

7.35 When auditing the revenue and collection cycle, auditors normally select balances to confirm from the
   a. Sales journal.
   b. Accounts receivable listing.
   c. General ledger.
   d. Cash receipts listing.

LO 7-2

7.36 Which of the following accounts is *not* normally part of the revenue and collection cycle?
   a. Sales.
   b. Accounts Receivable.
   c. Cash.
   d. Purchases Returns and Allowances.

LO 7-4

7.37 The control procedure "credit sales approved by credit department" is directed toward which assertion?
   a. Existence/Occurrence.
   b. Completeness.
   c. Valuation/Accuracy.
   d. Cutoff.

LO 7-4

7.38 Which of the following would be the best protection for a company that wishes to prevent the "lapping" of trade accounts receivable?
   a. Separate duties so that the bookkeeper in charge of the general ledger has no access to incoming mail.
   b. Separate duties so that no employee has access to both checks from customers and currency from daily cash receipts.
   c. Have customers send payments directly to the company's depository bank.
   d. Request that customer's payment checks be made payable to the company and addressed to the treasurer.

LO 7-4

7.39 Which of the following internal control activities will most likely prevent the concealment of a cash shortage by improperly writing off a trade account receivable?

a. Write-offs must be approved by a responsible officer after review of credit department recommendations and supporting evidence.

b. Write-offs must be supported by an aging schedule showing that only receivables overdue several months have been written off.

c. Write-offs must be approved by the cashier who is in a position to know whether the receivables have, in fact, been collected.

d. Write-offs must be authorized by company field sales employees who are in a position to determine customers' financial standing.

LO 7-3

7.40 Auditors sometimes use comparisons of ratios as audit evidence. An unexplained decrease in the ratio of gross profit to sales may suggest which of the following possibilities?

a. Unrecorded purchases.

b. Unrecorded sales.

c. Merchandise purchases being charged to selling and general expense.

d. Fictitious sales.

LO 7-6

7.41 An audit team is auditing sales transactions. One step is to vouch a sample of debit entries from the accounts receivable subsidiary ledger back to the supporting sales invoices. The purpose of this audit procedure is to establish that

a. Sales invoices represent bona fide sales.

b. All sales have been recorded.

c. All sales invoices have been properly posted to customer accounts.

d. Entries in the accounts receivable subsidiary ledger were properly invoiced.

Use the following information to answer questions 7.42 and 7.43:

An auditor noted that client sales increased 10 percent for the year. At the same time, Cost of Goods Sold as a percentage of sales had decreased from 45 percent to 40 percent and year-end accounts receivable had increased by 8 percent.

LO 7-3

7.42 Based on this information, the auditor is most likely concerned about

a. Unrecorded costs.

b. Improper credit approvals.

c. Improper sales cutoff.

d. Fictitious sales.

LO 7-6

7.43 Based on this information, the auditor interviewed the sales manager, who stated that the increase in sales without a corresponding increase in cost of goods sold was due to a price increase enacted by the company during the year. How would the auditor test the sales manager's representation?

a. Perform additional inquiries with sales personnel.

b. Obtain copies of all price lists in use during the year and vouch the prices to sales invoices.

c. Send confirmations asking customers about unit prices paid for product.

d. Vouch vender invoices to payments made after year-end.

LO 7-3

7.44 To conceal a theft involving receivables, a dishonest bookkeeper might charge which of the following accounts?

a. Miscellaneous income.

b. Petty cash.

c. Miscellaneous expense.

d. Sales returns.

LO 7-6

7.45 Which of the following responses to an accounts receivable confirmation at December 31 would cause an audit team the most concern?

a. "This amount was paid on December 30."

b. "We received this shipment on January 2."

c. "These goods were returned for credit on November 15."

d. "The balance does not reflect our sales discount for paying by January 5."

LO 7-6   7.46 A client has a separate sales group for its largest "preferred" customers, a select group of customers who normally make purchases in excess of $250,000 and often have accounts receivable balances in excess of $1 million. Which of the following audit procedures would the auditor most likely perform?

a. Prepare a schedule of purchases and payments for these customers.

b. Send out negative confirmations on a large sample of these customers.

c. Inquire of the sales manager regarding the accounts receivable terms.

d. Send out positive confirmations on a large sample of these customers.

LO 7-6   7.47 Audit documentation often includes a client-prepared, aged trial balance of accounts receivable as of the balance sheet date. The audit team uses this aging primarily to

a. Evaluate internal control over credit sales.

b. Test the accuracy of recorded charge sales.

c. Estimate credit losses.

d. Verify the existence of the recorded receivables.

LO 7-6   7.48 Which of the following might be detected by auditors' cutoff review and examination of sales journal entries for several days prior to the balance sheet date?

a. Lapping year-end accounts receivable.

b. Inflating sales for the year.

c. Kiting bank balances.

d. Misappropriating merchandise.

LO 7-6   7.49 Confirmation of individual accounts receivable balances directly with debtors will, of itself, normally provide the strongest evidence concerning the

a. Collectability of the balances confirmed.

b. Ownership of the balances confirmed.

c. Existence of the balances confirmed.

d. Internal control over balances confirmed.

LO 7-4   7.50 Which of the following is the best reason for prenumbering in numerical sequence documents such as sales orders, shipping documents, and sales invoices?

a. Enables company personnel to determine the accuracy of each document.

b. Enables personnel to determine the proper period recording of sales revenue and receivables.

c. Enables personnel to check the numerical sequence for missing documents and unrecorded transactions.

d. Enables personnel to determine the validity of recorded transactions.

LO 7-6   7.51 When a sample of customer accounts receivable is selected for vouching debits, auditors will vouch them to

a. Sales invoices with shipping documents and customer sales invoices.

b. Records of accounts receivable write-offs.

c. Cash remittance lists and bank deposit slips.

d. Credit files and reports.

LO 7-2   7.52 In the audit of accounts receivable, the most important emphasis should be on the

a. Completeness assertion.

b. Existence assertion.

c. Rights and obligations assertion.

d. Presentation and disclosure assertion.

LO 7-6   7.53 When accounts receivable are confirmed at an interim date, auditors need not be concerned with

a. Obtaining a summary of receivables transactions from the interim date to the year-end date.

b. Obtaining a year-end trial balance of receivables, comparing it to the interim trial balance, and obtaining evidence and explanations for large variations.

    c. Sending negative confirmations to all customers as of the year-end date.

    d. Considering the necessity for some additional confirmations as of the balance sheet date if balances have increased materially.

LO 7-6

7.54 The negative request form of accounts receivable confirmation is useful particularly when the

Assessed Level of Risk of Material Misstatement Relating to Receivables Is	Number of Small Balances Is	Proper Consideration by the Recipient Is
a. Low	Many	Likely
b. Low	Few	Unlikely
c. High	Few	Likely
d. High	Many	Likely

(AICPA adapted)

LO 7-5

7.55 When an audit team traces a sample of shipping documents to the related sales invoice copies, they are trying to find relevant evidence that

    a. Shipments to customers were invoiced.

    b. Shipments to customers were recorded as sales.

    c. Recorded sales were shipped.

    d. Invoiced sales were shipped.

(AICPA adapted)

LO 7-4

7.56 Write-offs of doubtful accounts should be approved by

    a. The salesperson.

    b. The credit manager.

    c. The treasurer.

    d. The cashier.

LO 7-6

7.57 When an audit team does not receive a response on a positive accounts receivable confirmation, auditors should do all of the following *except*

    a. Send a second request.

    b. Do nothing for immaterial balances.

    c. Examine shipping documents.

    d. Examine client correspondence files.

LO 7-3

7.58 Cash receipts from sales on account have been misappropriated. Which of the following acts would conceal this defalcation and be *least likely* to be detected by an auditor?

    a. Understating the sales journal.

    b. Overstating the accounts receivable control account.

    c. Overstating the accounts receivable subsidiary ledger.

    d. Understating the cash receipts journal.

(AICPA adapted)

LO 7-4

7.59 Which of the following internal control activities most likely would deter lapping of collections from customers?

    a. Independent internal verification of dates of entry in the cash receipts journal with dates of daily cash summaries.

    b. Authorization of write-offs of uncollectable accounts by a supervisor independent of credit approval.

    c. Separation of duties between receiving cash and posting the accounts receivable ledger.

    d. Supervisory comparison of the daily cash summary with the sum of the cash receipts journal entries.

(AICPA adapted)

LO 7-6

7.60 The financial records of the Movitz Company show that R. Dennis owes $4,100 on an account receivable. An independent audit is being carried out, and the auditors send a positive confirmation to R. Dennis. What is the most likely reason as to why a positive confirmation rather than a negative confirmation was used here?

 a. Control risk was particularly low for accounts receivable.

 b. Inherent risk was particularly high for accounts receivable.

 c. Dennis's account was not yet due.

 d. Dennis's account was not with a related party.

LO 7-3

7.61 An audit client sells 15 to 20 units of product annually. A large portion of the annual sales occur in the last month of the fiscal year. Annual sales have not materially changed over the past five years. Which of the following approaches would be most effective concerning the timing of audit procedures for revenue?

 a. The auditor should perform analytical procedures at an interim date and discuss any changes in the level of sales with senior management.

 b. The auditor should inspect transactions occurring in the last month of the fiscal year and review the related sale contracts to determine that revenue was posted in the proper period.

 c. The auditor should perform tests of controls at an interim date to obtain audit evidence about the operational effectiveness of internal controls over sales.

 d. The auditor should review period-end compensation to determine whether bonuses were paid to meet earnings goals.

(AICPA adapted)

LO 7-3

7.62 An auditor is required to confirm accounts receivable if the accounts receivable balances are

 a. Older than the prior year.

 b. Material to the financial statements.

 c. Smaller than expected.

 d. Subject to valuation estimates.

(AICPA adapted)

LO 7-6

7.63 During the confirmation of accounts receivable, an auditor receives a confirmation via the client's fax machine. Which of the following actions should the auditor take?

 a. Not accept the confirmation and select another customer's balance to confirm.

 b. Not accept the confirmation and treat it as an exception.

 c. Accept the confirmation and file it in the working papers.

 d. Accept the confirmation but verify the source and content through a telephone call to the respondent.

(AICPA adapted)

Exercises and Problems

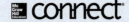 All applicable Exercises and Problems are available with *Connect.*

LO 7-4

7.64 **Control Objectives and Procedures Associations.** Exhibit 7.64.1 contains an arrangement of examples of transaction errors (lettered a–g) and a set of client control procedures and devices (numbered 1–15). Make a copy of the exhibit page and complete the following requirements.

Required

 a. Opposite the examples of transaction errors lettered a–g, write the name of the transaction assertion clients wish to achieve to prevent, detect, or correct the error.

 b. Opposite each numbered control procedure, place an "X" in the column that identifies the error(s) the procedure is likely to control by prevention, detection, or correction.

LO 7-4

7.65 **Assertion Associations.** Exhibit 7.64.1 contains an arrangement of examples of transaction errors (lettered a–g) and a set of client control procedures and devices (numbered 1–15).

Required:

For each error/control objective, identify the assertion about classes of transactions and events most benefited by the control.

EXHIBIT 7.64.1

a.	Sales recorded, goods not shipped
b.	Goods shipped, sales not recorded
c.	Goods shipped to a bad credit risk customer
d.	Sales billed at the wrong price or wrong quantity
e.	Product line A sales recorded as Product line B
f.	Failure to post charges to customers for sales
g.	January sales recorded in December

CONTROL PROCEDURES

1. Sales order approved for credit
2. Prenumbered shipping doc prepared, sequence checked
3. Shipping document quantity compared to sales invoice
4. Prenumbered sales invoices, sequence checked
5. Sales invoice checked to sales order
6. Invoiced prices compared to approved price list
7. General ledger code checked for sales product lines
8. Sales dollar batch totals compared to sales journal
9. Periodic sales total compared to same period accounts receivable postings
10. Accountants have instructions to date sales on the date of shipment
11. Sales entry date compared to shipping doc date
12. Accounts receivable subsidiary totaled and reconciled to accounts receivable control account
13. Intercompany accounts reconciled with subsidiary company records
14. Credit files updated for customer payment history
15. Overdue customer accounts investigated for collection

LO 7-5

7.66 **Client Control Procedures and Audit Tests of Controls.** Exhibit 7.64.1 contains an arrangement of examples of transaction errors (lettered a–g) and a set of client control procedures and devices (numbered 1–15).

Required:

For each client control procedure numbered 1–15, write a test of controls that could produce evidence on the question of whether the client's control procedure has been implemented and is in operation.

LO 7-6

7.67 **Confirmation of Trade Accounts Receivable.** L. King, CPA, is auditing the financial statements of Cycle Company, a client that has receivables from customers arising from the sale of goods in the normal course of business. King is aware that the confirmation of accounts receivable is a generally accepted auditing procedure.

Required:

a. Under what circumstances could King justify omitting the confirmation of Cycle's accounts receivable?

b. In designing confirmation requests, what factors are likely to affect King's assessment of the reliability of confirmations that King sends?

c. What alternative procedures could King consider performing when replies to positive confirmation requests are not received?

(AICPA adapted)

LO 7-6

7.68 Audit Objectives and Procedures for Accounts Receivable. In the audit of accounts receivable, auditors develop specific audit assertions related to the receivables. They then design specific substantive procedures to obtain evidence about each of these assertions. Here is a selection of accounts receivable assertions:

a. Accounts receivable represent all amounts owed to the client company at the balance sheet date.

b. The client company has a legal right to all accounts receivable at the balance sheet date.

c. Accounts receivable are stated at net realizable value.

d. Accounts receivable are properly described and presented in the financial statements.

Required:

For each of these assertions, select the following audit procedure (numbered 1–7) that is best suited for the audit plan. Select only one procedure for each audit objective. A procedure may be selected once, not at all, or more than once.

1. Analyze the relationship of accounts receivable and sales and compare with relationships for preceding periods.

2. Perform sales cutoff tests to obtain assurance that sales transactions and corresponding entries for inventories and cost of goods sold are recorded in the same and proper period.

3. Review the aged trial balance for significant past due accounts.

4. Obtain an understanding of the business purpose of transactions that resulted in accounts receivable balances.

5. Review loan agreements for indications of whether accounts receivable have been factored or pledged.

6. Review the accounts receivable trial balance for amounts due from officers and employees.

7. Analyze unusual relationships between monthly accounts receivable and monthly accounts payable balances.

LO 7-4

7.69 Overstated Sales and Accounts Receivable. This case is designed like the ones in the chapter. Your assignment is to write the "audit approach" portion of the case, organized around these sections:

Objective. Express the objective in terms of the facts supposedly asserted in financial records, accounts, and statements.

Control. Write a brief explanation of desirable controls, missing controls, and especially the kinds of "deviations" that might arise from the situation described in the case.

Tests of controls. Write some procedures for getting evidence about existing controls, especially procedures that could discover deviations from those controls. If there are no controls to test, then there are no procedures to perform; go then to the next section. A "procedure" should instruct someone about the source(s) of evidence to tap and the work to do.

Audit of balance. Write some procedures for getting evidence about the existence, completeness, valuation, ownership, or disclosure assertions identified in the objective section you wrote.

Discovery summary. Write a short statement about the discovery you expect to accomplish with your procedures.

Ring around the Revenue

Mattel toy manufacturing company had experienced several years of good business. Income had increased steadily, and the common stock was a favorite among investors. Management had confidently predicted continued growth and prosperity. However, business turned worse instead of better. Competition became fierce.

In earlier years, Mattel had accommodated a few large retail customers with the practice of field warehousing coupled with a "bill and hold" accounting procedure. These large retail customers executed noncancelable written agreements, asserting their purchase of toys and their obligation to pay. The toys were not actually shipped because the customers did not have available warehouse space. The toys were set aside in segregated areas on the Mattel premises and identified as the customers' property. Mattel would later ship the toys to various retail locations upon instructions from the customers. The "field warehousing" was explained as Mattel's serving as a temporary warehouse and storage location for the customers' toys. In the related bill and hold accounting procedure, Mattel prepared invoices billing the customers, mailed the invoices to the customers, and recorded the sales and accounts receivable.

When business took a downturn, Mattel expanded its field warehousing and its bill and hold accounting practices. Invoices were recorded for customers who did not execute the written agreements used in previous arrangements. Some customers signed the noncancelable written agreements with clauses permitting subsequent inspection, acceptance, and determination of discounted prices. The toys were not always set aside in separate areas, and this failure later gave shipping employees problems with identifying shipments of toys that had been "sold" earlier and those that had not.

Mattel also engaged in overbilling. Customers who ordered closeout toys at discounted prices were billed at regular prices, even though the customers' orders showed the discounted prices to which Mattel sales representatives had agreed.

In a few cases, the bill and hold invoices and the closeout sales were billed and recorded in duplicate. In most cases, the customers' invoices were addressed and mailed to specific individuals in the customers' management instead of the routine mailing to the customers' accounts payable departments.

Audit trail. The field warehousing arrangements were well known and acknowledged in the Mattel accounting manual. Related invoices were stamped "bill and hold." Customer orders and agreements were attached in a document file. Sales of closeout toys also were stamped "closeout," indicating the regular prices (basis for salespersons' commissions) and the invoice prices. Otherwise, the accounting for sales and accounts receivable was unexceptional. Efforts to record these sales in January (last month of the fiscal year) caused the month's sales revenue to be 35 percent higher than the January of the previous year.

In the early years of the practice, inventory sold under the field warehousing arrangements (both regular and closeout toys) was segregated and identified. The shipping orders for these toys left the "carrier name" and "shipping date" blank, even though they were signed and dated by a company employee in the spaces for the company representative and the carrier representative signatures.

The lack of inventory segregation caused problems for the company. After the fiscal year-end, Mattel solved the problem by reversing $6.9 million of the $14 million bill and hold sales. This caused another problem because the reversal was larger than the month's sales, causing the sales revenue for the first month of the next year to be a negative number!

Amount. Company officials gave persuasive reasons for the validity of recognizing sales revenue and receivables on the bill and hold procedure and field warehousing. After considering the facts and circumstances, the company's auditors agreed that the accounting practices appropriately accounted for revenue and receivables.

Mattel's abuse of the practices caused financial statements to be materially misstated. In January of the year in question, the company overstated sales by about $14 million, or 5 percent of the sales that should have been recorded. The gross profit of $7 million on these sales caused the income to be overstated by about 40 percent.

LO 7-6

7.70 **CAATs Application—Receivables Confirmation.** You are using computer audit software to prepare accounts receivable confirmations during the annual audit of the Eastern Sunrise Services Club. The company has the following data files:

Master file—debtor credit record.

Master file—debtor name and address.

Master file—account detail:

> Ledger number.
>
> Sales code.
>
> Customer account number.
>
> Date of last billing.
>
> Balance (gross).
>
> Discount available to customer (memo account only).
>
> Date of last purchase.

The discount field represents the amount of discount available to the customer if the customer pays within 30 days of the invoicing date. The discount field is cleared for expired amounts during the daily updating. You have determined that this is properly executed.

Required:

From the data files shown, list the information that you would include on the confirmation requests. Identify the file from which the information can be obtained.

LO 7-5

7.71 **Rock Island Quarry—Evidence Collection in an Online System.** Your firm has audited the Rock Island Quarry Company for several years. Rock Island's main revenue comes from selling crushed rock to construction companies from several quarries owned by the company in Illinois and Iowa. The rock is priced by weight, quality, and crushed size.

Past procedure. Trucks owned by purchasing contractors or by Rock Island needed to display a current certified empty weight receipt or be weighed in. The quarry yard weigh master recorded the empty weight on a handwritten "scale ticket" along with the purchasing company name, the truck number, and the date. After the truck was loaded, it was required to leave via the scale where the loaded weight and rock grade were recorded on the scale tickets. The scale tickets were sorted weekly by grade and manually recorded on a summary sheet that was forwarded to the home office. Scale tickets were prenumbered and an accountant in the home office checked the sequence for missing numbers.

Audit procedures for revenue (and receivables) involved evaluating the controls at selected quarries (rotated each year) and vouching a statistical sample of scale tickets to weekly summaries. Weekly summaries were traced through pricing and invoicing to the general ledger on a sample basis, and general ledger entries were vouched back to weekly summaries on a sample basis. Few material discrepancies were found.

New procedures. At the beginning of the current year, Rock Island converted to a local area network of personal computers to gather the information formerly entered manually on the scale ticket. This conversion was done with your knowledge but without your advice or input. Now all entering trucks must weigh in. The yard weigh master enters "NEW" on the terminal keyboard and a form appears on the screen that is similar to the old scale ticket except that the quarry number, transaction number, date, and incoming empty weight are automatically entered. Customer and truck numbers are keyed in. After the weigh-in, the weigh master enters "HOLD" through the terminal. The weight ticket record is stored in the computer until weigh-out.

When a truck is loaded and stops on the scale, the weigh master enters "OLD" and a directory of all open transactions appears on the screen. The weigh master selects the proper one and enters "OUT." The truck out-weighs and the rock weights are computed and entered automatically. The weigh master must enter the proper number for the rock grade but cannot change any automatically entered field. When satisfied that the screen weight ticket is correct, the weigh master enters "SOLD," and the transaction is automatically transmitted to the home office computer, and the appropriate accounting database elements are updated. One copy of a scale ticket is printed and given to the truck driver. Rock Island keeps no written evidence of the sale.

Required:

It is now midyear for Rock Island, and you are planning for this year's audit.

a. What control procedures (manual and computerized) should you expect to find in this system for recording quarry sales?

b. The computer programs that process the rock sales and perform the accounting reside at the home office and at the quarries. What implication does this have for your planned audit procedures?

c. What are you going to do to gather substantive audit evidence now that there are no written scale tickets?

LO 7-3

7.72 **Organizing a Risk Analysis.** You are the director of internal auditing of a large municipal hospital. You receive monthly financial reports prepared by the accounting department, and your review of them has shown that total accounts receivable from patients has steadily and rapidly increased over the past eight months.

Other information in the reports shows the following conditions:

a. The number of available hospital beds has not changed.

b. The bed occupancy rate has not changed.

c. Hospital billing rates have not changed significantly.

d. The hospitalization insurance contracts have not changed since the last modification 12 months ago.

Your internal audit department audited the accounts receivable 10 months ago. The audit file for that assignment contains financial information, a record of the risk analysis, documentation of the study and evaluation of management and internal risk mitigation controls, documentation of the evidence-gathering procedures used to produce evidence about the existence and collectability of the accounts, and a copy of your report, which commented favorably on the controls and collectability of the receivables.

However, the current increase in receivables has alerted you to a need for another audit so that things will not get out of hand. You remember news stories last year about the manager of the city water system who got into big trouble because his accounting department double-billed all the residential customers for three months.

Required:

You plan to perform a risk analysis to get a handle on the problem if one indeed exists. Write a memo to your senior auditor listing at least eight questions to use to guide and direct the risk analysis. (*Hint:* The questions used last year were organized under these headings: (1) Who does the accounts receivable accounting? (2) What information processing procedures and policies are in effect? and (3) How is the accounts receivable accounting done? This time, you will add a fourth category: What financial or economic events have occurred in the past 10 months?)

(AICPA adapted)

LO 7-4

7.73 **Study and Evaluation of Management Control.** The study and evaluation of management risk mitigation control is not easy. First, auditors must determine the risks and the controls subject to audit. Then they must find a standard by which performance of the control can be evaluated. Next they must specify procedures to obtain the evidence on which an evaluation can be based. Insofar as possible, the standards and related evidence must be quantified. The following description gives certain information (in italics) that internal auditors would know about or be able to determine on their own. Fulfilling the requirement thus amounts to taking some information from the scenario and figuring out other things by using accountants' and auditors' common sense.

The Scenario

Ace Corporation ships building materials to more than a thousand wholesale and retail customers in a five-state region. The company's normal credit terms are net/30 days, and no cash discounts are offered. Fred Clark is the chief financial officer, and he is concerned about risks related to maintaining control over customer credit. In particular, he has stated two management control principles for this purpose.

1. Sales are to be billed to customers accurately and promptly. *Clark knows that errors will occur but thinks company personnel ought to be able to hold quantity, unit price, and arithmetic errors down to 3 percent of the sales invoices. He considers an invoice error of $1 or less not to matter.* He believes prompt billing is important because customers are expected to pay within 30 days. *Clark is very strict in thinking that a bill should be sent to the customer one day after shipment.* He believes he has staffed the billing department well enough to be able to handle this workload. The relevant company records consist of an accounts receivable control account; a subsidiary ledger that enters customers' accounts by billing (invoice) date and credits and by date of payment receipts; a sales journal that lists invoices in chronological order; and a file of shipping documents cross-referenced by the number on the related sales invoice copy kept on file in numerical order.

2. Accounts receivable are to be aged and followed up to ensure prompt collection. *Clark has told the accounts receivable department to classify all customer accounts in categories of (a) current, (b) 31–59 days overdue, (c) 60–90 days overdue, and (d) more than 90 days overdue. He wants this trial balance to be complete and to be transmitted to the credit department within five days after each month-end. In the credit department, prompt follow-up means sending a different (stronger) collection letter to each category, cutting off credit to customers over 60 days past due (putting them on cash basis), and giving the over-90-days accounts to an outside collection agency. These actions are supposed to be taken within five days after receipt of the aged trial balance.* The relevant company records, in addition to the others listed, consist of the aged trial balance, copies of the letters sent to customers, copies of notices of credit cutoff, copies of correspondence with the outside collection agent, and reports of results—statistics of subsequent collections.

Required:

Take the role of a senior internal auditor and write a memo to the internal audit staff to inform them about comparison standards for the study and evaluation of these two management control policies. You also need to specify two or three procedures for gathering evidence about performance of the controls. The body of your memo should be structured as follows:

1. Control: Sales are billed to customers accurately and promptly.
   a. Accuracy.
      (1) Policy standard . . .
      (2) Audit procedures . . .
   b. Promptness.
      (1) Policy standard . . .
      (2) Audit procedures . . .
2. Control: Accounts receivable are aged and followed up to ensure prompt collection.
   a. Accounts receivable aging.
      (1) Policy standard . . .
      (2) Audit procedures . . .
   b. Follow-up prompt collection.
      (1) Policy standard . . .
      (2) Audit procedures . . .

LO 7-3

7.74 **Cash Receipts and Billing Control.** The following narrative description of a company's cash receipts and billing system is in the auditors' audit files:

Rural Building Supplies Inc. is a single-store retailer that sells a variety of tools, garden supplies, lumber, small appliances, and electrical fixtures. About half of the sales are to walk-in customers and about half to construction contractors. Rural employs 12 salaried sales associates, a credit manager, three full-time clerical workers, and several part-time cash register clerks and assistant bookkeepers. The full-time clerical workers are the cashier who handles the cash and the bank deposits, the accounts receivable supervisor who prepares invoices and does the accounts receivable work, and the bookkeeper who keeps journals and ledgers and sends customer statements. Their work is described more fully in the narrative.

Control Narrative

Rural's retail customers pay for merchandise by cash or credit card at cash registers when they purchase merchandise. A building contractor can purchase merchandise on account if approved by the credit manager. The credit manager bases approvals on general knowledge of the contractor's reputation. After credit is approved, the sales associate files a prenumbered charge form with the accounts receivable (A/R) supervisor to set up the contractor's account receivable.

The A/R supervisor independently verifies the pricing and other details on the charge form by reference to a management-authorized price list, corrects any errors, prepares the sales invoice, and supervises a part-time employee who mails the invoice to the contractor. The A/R supervisor electronically posts the details of the invoice in a customer database, and the computerized system simultaneously transmits the transaction details to the bookkeeper. The A/R supervisor also prepares (1) a monthly computer-generated A/R subsidiary ledger without reconciliation to the A/R control account and (2) a monthly report of overdue accounts.

The cashier performs the cash receipts functions, including supervising the cash register clerks. The cashier opens the mail, compares each check with the enclosed remittance advice, stamps each check "for deposit only," and lists the checks on the deposit slip. The cashier then gives the remittance advices to the bookkeeper for recording. The cashier deposits the checks each day and prepares a separate deposit of the cash from the cash registers. The cashier retains the verified bank deposit slips (stamped and dated at the bank) to use in reconciling the monthly bank statements. The cashier sends to the bookkeeper a copy of the daily cash register summary. The cashier does not have access to the bookkeeper's journals or ledgers.

The bookkeeper receives information for journalizing and posting to the general ledger from the A/R supervisor (details of credit transactions) and from the cashier (cash reports). After recording the remittance advices received from the cashier, the bookkeeper electronically transmits the information to the A/R supervisor for subsidiary ledger updating. Upon receipt of the A/R supervisor's report of overdue balances, the bookkeeper sends monthly statements of account to contractors with unpaid balances. The bookkeeper authorizes the A/R supervisor to write off accounts as uncollectable six months after sending the first over-due notice. At this time, the bookkeeper notifies the credit manager not to approve additional credit to that contractor.

Required:

Take the role of the supervising auditor on the Rural engagement. Your assistants pre-pared the narrative description. Now you must analyze it and identify the internal control weaknesses. Organize them under the heading of employee job functions: credit manager, accounts receivable supervisor, cashier, and bookkeeper. (Do not give advice about correct-ing the weaknesses.)

Optional Requirement:

Discuss the possibilities for fraud you notice in this control system.

LO 7-5

7.75 **Tests of Controls and Errors/Frauds.** The following four questions are taken from an internal control questionnaire. For each question, state (a) one test of controls procedure you could use to find out whether the control technique was really functioning and (b) what error or fraud could occur if the question were answered "no" or if you found the control was not effective.

1. Are blank sales invoices available only to authorized personnel?
2. Are sales invoices prenumbered and are all numbers accounted for?
3. Are sales invoices checked for the accuracy of quantities billed? Prices used? Mathemati-cal calculations?
4. Are the duties of the accounts receivable bookkeeper separate from all cash functions?
5. Are customer accounts regularly balanced with the control account?
6. Do customers receive a monthly statement even when the ending balance on the account is zero?

LO 7-1

7.76 **Revenue Recognition and Ethics.** The following article was published in *Newsday* on Feb-ruary 9, 2009:

Call for Probe of Ticket Sales

Bruce Springsteen fans were victims of a "classic bait and switch" scam by the nation's largest concert ticket seller, Senator Charles Schumer said yesterday, as he called for a federal investigation into the company, Ticketmaster. Schumer wants the Federal Trade Commission to look into whether the Ticketmaster website withheld the best tickets from the public and then shuttled fans to TicketsNow, a fully owned subsidiary. TicketsNow had the best seats available immediately—at sky-high prices—after Springsteen tickets went on sales at 10 A.M. on February 2.

A federal investigation would look into whether Ticketmaster was instantly scalping the tickets, never giving fans a chance to buy them at face value, Schumer said. Customers who tried to buy tickets originally priced at $95 on Ticketmaster's website were directed to TicketsNow where they were priced at more than $2,000.

Since buying TicketsNow in February, Ticketmaster has faced similar criticism for its handling of Elton John tickets in Canada and numerous U.S. concert tours, including Radiohead. Law enforcement agencies in Connecticut and New Jersey have also launched investigations.

Required:

a. During the course of an audit, do you believe that the auditor should look into how rev-enues are being generated? Do you think the auditors should have looked at the business practices of Ticketmaster?
b. Assume that Ticketmaster had properly accounted for the revenue it received from the Springsteen concert. Should the auditors have asked Ticketmaster to make adjustments or disclosures regarding its sales practices?
c. Should Ticketmaster disclose the investigations being conducted in Connecticut and New Jersey?

LO 7-7

7.77 Authorization of Credit Tests of Controls—Using IDEA

For this exercise, your client, Bright IDEAs Inc., has provided you with data for two related files, a listing of sales invoices, and a listing of customers with credit limits. To test whether credit authorization controls are in place, the auditor must complete a series of related steps:

1. Import the client's database of sales invoices (pp. 28–45 of the IDEA Workbook).
2. Summarize the Accounts Receivable balance by customer (pp. 67–79 of the IDEA Workbook).
3. Import the client's customer credit limit data into IDEA (pp. 70–79 of the IDEA Workbook).
4. Join the Accounts Receivable balances by customer with the credit limit data (pp. 80–87 of the IDEA Workbook).
5. Extract customers with exceeded credit limits (pp. 88–89).

Required Data available on *Connect*

- ACC_REC2015.ACCDB

- CUSTOMER.TXT

Required:

Complete the preceding steps and answer the following questions:

a. How many customers were granted credit with no indication that they had any credit limit assigned to them?

b. How many customers exceeded their credit limit?

c. What effects would the findings in parts (a) and (b) have on the auditor's assessment of the risk of material misstatement? What accounts and assertions are most likely influenced by these findings?

Source: C1202 IDEA Data Analysis Workbook: IDEA Version Ten. 2016. CaseWare IDEA, Inc. Toronto, CA.

Applying IDEA to the Revenue Cycle—Elm Manufacturing Company

Exercises 7.78, 7.79, and 7.80 require the application of IDEA in the revenue cycle audit. Elm Manufacturing Company (ELM) is a small manufacturer of backpacks located in Rochelle, Illinois. You have access to ELM's electronic records on Connect. The appropriate file for these exercises is the Sales 2017 – 4th Q dataset. Detailed information about ELM, instructions for accessing datasets, and a data directory for data sets can be found on Connect.

LO 7-5, 7-7

7.78 Tests of Control Exceptions with IDEA. You have identified relevant controls for several assertions within the revenue cycle, and you must use IDEA to perform several tests of controls.

Required:

a. ELM has a policy of using prenumbered customer order forms to help control for the completeness assertion. Inquiry of the client determined that order forms 17001–17405 were used during the quarter. Using IDEA, create a schedule of missing customer order forms. How many missing order forms were there?

b. Each customer order should be entered into the system once and only once. Using IDEA, search for duplicate customer order forms. What is the total dollar amount of duplicate orders?

c. To assist with the collectability of accounts receivable, ELM has a policy that all customer orders must be approved and marked as approved in the order system. Create a schedule of exceptions to this policy.

d. To ensure the posting of sales in a timely manner and increase the collectability of accounts receivable, ELM has a policy to always invoice customers within two days of shipping. Create a schedule of exceptions to the invoicing policy.

e. Draft a memo outlining the findings of your tests of controls. Address not only your findings, but also the effects of your findings on your assessment of control risk related to specific financial statement assertions.

LO 7-5, 7-7

7.79 Tests of Controls with IDEA—Payment Receipts. Use the information related to ELM's payment and discount policy (referenced earlier) to analyze the company's discount program and late payments. All dates for payments are based off the date the customer is invoiced.

Required:

a. Are there any companies that made their payments after the stated due date? How many companies, and what is the total dollar amount of the payments? (*Hint:* Each company has a two-day grace period beyond the stated due date.)

b. Refer to ELM's discount policy. Are any companies receiving discounts when the invoice terms indicate they should never be eligible for discounts? What is the total dollar amount of the discounts taken by these companies? (*Hint:* This refers to the terms of the invoices, not whether these companies paid too late to receive discounts.)

c. Refer to ELM's discount policy. Are there any companies receiving discount percentages greater than the amount accounting to the policy?

d. Are any companies taking the discount even if they are not paying within the 10-day period? (*Hint:* Each company has a two-day grace period beyond the stated discount period.)

LO 7-6, 7-7

7.80 Testing the Valuation Assertion with IDEA—Aging Accounts Receivable. You have been instructed to create an aging schedule for ELM's accounts receivable using IDEA. For the purposes of this exercise, assume the aging begins on the date that the customer is invoiced and should only include valid accounts receivable (e.g., amounts not yet fully paid by the customer). You can assume that rounding differences on discounts taken by customers are considered to be fully paid. Your senior has instructed you to create a schedule with the following tranches: Current, 0–30 days delinquent, 31–60 days delinquent, 60+ days delinquent.

Required:

a. Create an aged accounts receivable according to your senior's instructions. Assume there are no receivables still outstanding prior to January 1, 2017. Note that the data set includes all orders received between January 1, 2017, and March 31, 2017. This includes orders that have already been paid for, orders received at the end of March that were shipped but have not been invoiced, and orders that have been received that have not shipped. These orders would not be considered a receivable as of March 31; therefore, these items need to be excluded from the data for this schedule and in other requirements within this assignment.

b. What is the total amount of accounts receivable as of March 31, 2017?

c. What is the total amount of accounts receivable that are past due less than 30 days? Recall that invoices are due n/30, thus they become past due 30 days after invoice date.

d. What is the total amount of accounts receivable that are more than 30 days past due?

Appendix 7A

Internal Control Questionnaires

EXHIBIT 7A.1 Internal Control Questionnaire—Revenue and Collection Cycle

	Yes/No	Comments
Occurrence		
1. Is the customer database maintained by someone who does *not* have access to cash?		
2. Is access to sales invoice blanks restricted?		
3. Are prenumbered bills of lading or other shipping documents prepared or completed in the shipping department?		
4. Are customers' statements mailed monthly by the accounts receivable department?		
5. Are direct confirmations of accounts and notes obtained periodically by the internal auditor?		
6. Are differences reported by customers routed to someone outside the accounts receivable department for investigations?		
7. Are returned goods checked against receiving reports?		
8. Are returned sales credits and other credits supported by documentation as to receipt, condition, and quantity and approved by a responsible officer?		
9. Are write-offs, returns, and discounts allowed after discount date subject to approval by a responsible officer?		
10. Are large loans or advances to related parties approved by the directors?		
Completeness		
11. Are sales invoice forms prenumbered?		
12. Is the sequence checked for missing invoices?		
13. Is the numerical sequence for shipping documents checked for missing bills of lading numbers?		
14. Are credit memo documents prenumbered and the sequence checked for missing documents?		
Accuracy		
15. Is customer credit approved before orders are shipped?		
16. Are delinquent accounts listed periodically for review by someone other than the credit manager?		
17. Is the credit department separated from the sales department?		
18. Are sales prices and terms based on approved standards?		
19. Are shipped quantities compared to invoice quantities?		
20. Are sales invoices checked for error in quantities, prices, extensions and footings, and freight allowances and checked with customers' orders?		
21. Do the internal auditors confirm customer accounts periodically to determine accuracy?		
22. Does someone reconcile the accounts receivable subsidiary to the control account regularly?		
Cutoff		
23. Does the accounting manual contain instructions to date sales invoices on the shipment date?		
Classification		
24. Does the accounting manual contain instructions for classifying sales?		
25. Are summary journal entries approved before posting?		
26. Are sales of the following types controlled by the same procedures described: sale to employees, cash-on-delivery sales, disposals of property, cash sales, and scrap sales?		
27. Are receivables from officers, directors, and affiliates identified separately in the accounts receivable records?		

EXHIBIT 7A.2   **Internal Control Questionnaire—Sales and Accounts Receivable Computerized Controls**

	Yes/No	Comments
1. Does each terminal perform only designated functions? For example, the terminal at the shipping dock cannot be used to enter initial sales information or to access the payroll database.		
2. Are an identification number and password (issued on an individual person basis) required to enter the sale and each command that a subsequent action has been completed? Unauthorized entry attempts are logged and immediately investigated. Furthermore, certain passwords have "read-only" (cannot change any data) authorization. For example, the credit manager can determine the outstanding balance of any account or view online "reports" summarizing overdue accounts receivable but cannot enter credit memos to change the balances.		
3. Is all input information immediately logged to provide restart processing should any terminal become inoperative during the processing?		
4. Does a transaction code call up on the terminals a full-screen "form" that appears to the operator in the same format as the original paper documents? Each clerk must enter the information correctly or the computer will not accept the transaction. This is called *online input validation* and utilizes validation checks such as missing data, check digit, and limit tests.		
5. Are all documents prepared by the computer numbered with the number stored as part of the sales record in the accounts receivable database?		
6. Is a daily search of the pending order database made by the computer with sales orders outstanding more than seven days listed on the terminal in marketing management?		

Appendix 7B

Audit Plan

EXHIBIT 7B.1

	Performed By	Ref.
DUNDER-MIFFLIN INC. **Audit Plan for Tests of Controls in the Revenues and Collection Cycle** **12/31/17**		
Sales		
1. Select a sample of recorded sales from the sales journal.		
a. Vouch to supporting shipping documents.		
b. Vouch to supporting sales order.		
c. Inspect sales orders for credit approval.		
d. Vouch prices to the approved price list.		
e. Vouch the quantity billed to the quantity shipped. Recalculate the invoice arithmetic.		
g. Compare the shipment date with the sales journal record date.		
h. Trace the invoice to posting in the general ledger control account and in the correct customer's account.		
i. Inspect for proper revenue account classification.		
2. Select a sample of shipping documents from the shipping department file and trace shipments to entries in the sales journal.		
3. Scan recorded sales invoices and shipping documents for missing numbers in sequence.		
Accounts Receivable		
1. Select a sample of customers' accounts from the accounts receivable database.		
a. Vouch recorded sales to supporting sales invoices.		
b. Vouch recorded payments to supporting cash receipts documents.		
2. Select a sample of credit memos.		
a. Inspect for proper approval.		
b. Trace to posting in customers' accounts.		
3. Scan the accounts receivable control for postings from sources other than the sales and cash receipts journals (e.g., general journal adjusting entries, credit memos). Vouch a sample of such entries to supporting documents.		

EXHIBIT 7B.2

DUNDER-MIFFLIN INC. Audit Plan for Accounts and Notes Receivable and Revenue 12/31/17	**Performed By**	**Ref.**

A. Accounts and Notes Receivable
1. Obtain an aged trial balance of individual customer accounts. Recalculate the total and trace to the general ledger control account.
2. Review the aging for large and unusual items.
3. Send confirmations to all accounts over \$X.* Select a random sample of all remaining accounts for confirmation.
  a. Investigate exceptions reported by customers.
  b. Investigate any confirmations returned by the post office as undeliverable.
  c. Perform alternative procedures on accounts that do not respond to positive confirmation requests.
    (1) Vouch cash receipts after the confirmation date for subsequent payment.
    (2) Vouch sales invoices and shipping documents.
4. Review the adequacy of the allowance for doubtful accounts.
  a. Inquire of management regarding assumptions used in calculating the allowance for doubtful accounts.
  b. Vouch a sample of current amounts in the aged trial balance to sales invoices to determine whether amounts aged current should be aged past due.
  c. Compare the current-year write-off experience to the prior-year allowance.
  d. Vouch cash receipts after the balance sheet date for collections on past due accounts.
  e. Obtain financial statements or credit reports and inquire of the credit manager about collections on large past due accounts.
  f. Calculate an allowance estimate using prior relations of write-offs and sales, taking under consideration current economic events.
5. Inspect the bank confirmations, loan agreements, and minutes of the board for indications of pledged, discounted, or assigned receivables.
6. Inspect or obtain confirmation of notes receivable.
7. Recalculate interest income and trace to the income account.
8. Obtain management representations regarding pledge, discount, or assignment of receivables, and about receivables from officers, directors, affiliates, or other related parties.
9. Review the adequacy of control over recording all charges to customers (completeness) audited in the sales transaction test of controls audit plan.
 	
B. Revenue
1. Select a sample of sales recorded in the sales journal and vouch to underlying shipping documents.
2. Select a sample of shipping documents and trace to sales invoices.
3. Obtain production records of physical quantities sold and calculate an estimate of sales dollars based on average sale prices.
4. Compare revenue dollars and physical quantities with prior-year data and industry economic statistics.
5. Select a sample of sales invoices prepared a few days before and after the balance sheet date and vouch to supporting documents for evidence of proper cutoff.		

*The auditor will determine a threshold for large accounts based on performance materiality.

CHAPTER 8

Acquisition and Expenditure Cycle

Show those numbers to the damn auditors and I'll throw you out the $%@@ window.*

—Buddy Yates, director of WorldCom Inc. general accounting, to an employee asking for an explanation of a large accounting discrepancy

Professional Standards Reference

Topic	AU-C/ISA Section	PCAOB Reference
Consideration of Internal Controls in an Integrated Audit	265	AS 2201
Audit Documentation	230	AS 1215
Auditors' Responses to Risks of Material Misstatement	240	AS 2301
Audit Planning	300	AS 2101
Identifying and Assessing the Risks of Material Misstatement	315	AS 2110
Materiality	320	AS 2105
Audit Considerations Relating to an Entity Using a Service Organization	402	AS 2601
Audit Evidence	500	AS 1105
External Confirmations	505	AS 2310
Substantive Analytical Procedures	520	AS 2305
Auditing Accounting Estimates	540	AS 2501
Written Representations	580	AS 2805

LEARNING OBJECTIVES

This chapter contains a concise overview of the cycle for the acquisition of goods and services as well as the expenditure of cash in connection with paying for the purchases and acquisitions. This cycle affects more general ledger accounts than any other cycle.

Major accounts discussed include accounts payable, expenses, and long-term assets. For accounts payable, the focus shifts to the *completeness* assertion. A series of short cases is used to show the application of audit procedures when errors or fraud might be discovered. Payroll is a subcycle related to the acquisition and expenditure cycle and to the production cycle. A discussion of payroll controls and audit tests is included in Appendix 8C.

Your objectives are to be able to:

LO 8-1 Describe the acquisition and expenditure cycle, including typical source documents.

LO 8-2 Identify significant accounts and relevant assertions related to the acquisition and expenditure cycle.

LO 8-3 Discuss the risk of material misstatement in the acquisition and expenditure cycle.

LO 8-4 Identify important internal control activities present in a properly designed system to mitigate the risk of material misstatements

for each relevant assertion in the acquisition and expenditure cycle.

LO 8-5 Give examples of tests of controls to test the operating effectiveness of internal controls in the acquisition and expenditure cycle.

LO 8-6 Give examples of substantive procedures in the acquisition and expenditure cycle and relate them to assertions about significant account balances at the end of the period.

LO 8-7 Apply your knowledge to perform audit procedures in the acquisition and expenditure cycle and evaluate the findings of your tests.

LO 8-8 Describe the payroll cycle including risks, source documents, and controls (Appendix 8C).

INTRODUCTION

Rita Crundwell was the treasurer of Dixon, Illinois, a small town about two hours west of Chicago best known as the birth place of Ronald Reagan. Crundwell started working for the city in 1970 while still in high school. By 1983, she had gained such trust from city officials that they appointed her Dixon's comptroller/treasurer. By the late 1980s, she controlled every aspect of the city's money. She wrote the checks, made the deposits, requested the funds, and advised the city on the availability of funds for projects. Bank statements were sent to the city's post office box that Crundwell controlled. On February 14, 2013, she was sentenced to more than 19 years in prison for embezzling more than $53 million using a special capital account that she established and only she knew existed.

In 1990, Crundwell created at First Bank South (now Fifth Third Bank) a special account called the Reserve Sewer Capital Development Account (RSCDA) on which she was the only authorized signer. The bank, which handled the other accounts for the city of Dixon, thought nothing of it. Crundwell was the treasurer and controller and, as such, was authorized to do the banking. She created false invoices for work requiring payments from the city's capital development fund. The payments for these fictitious invoices were made payable to "Treasurer" and deposited in the RSCDA. Crundwell then wrote checks from the RSCDA to pay for all types of personal items. The fraud started in 1991 with a theft of $181,000. In 2008, the fraud netted Crundwell $5.8 million. During this time period, Crundwell consistently counseled the city government on the need for spending cuts because of the lack of sufficient funds. For example, she turned down requests for additional police equipment and slashed the budget for the municipal band (a city favorite) while she looted the town coffers.

Furthermore, the city of Dixon is governed by a commissioner form of government. In this system, members of the city council are not elected by district but to oversee a segment of the government (e.g., parks commissioner). The individual elected finance commissioner (a job paying $2,700 per year in 2012) has oversight responsibilities for the financial management and operations of the city. This is clearly a part-time position and may be filled with a person who does not have the required background to understand proper finance and accounting policies and procedures. So Crundwell, acting as treasurer, controller, check writer, authorizer of funds, and keeper of the post office box, had little competent supervision.

The bulk of the stolen money went to fund Crundwell's horse business, which, at the time of her arrest, had grown to 400 quarter horses. In addition, Crundwell had a stable on

6.9 acres of land; purchased an additional 88 acres for $540,000; built a 20,000-square-foot showing barn with an arena, office, and stall; purchased a $2 million motor home; and spent hundreds of thousands of dollars on jewelry. All on a salary that never exceeded $83,000. Townspeople thought the money came from the horse business.

At the time of her sentence, the judge commented, "You have much better compassion for your horses than the people of Dixon you were supposed to represent."[1] In a remarkable rarity, the city of Dixon was able to gain 100 percent restitution by selling the assets of Crundwell and by settling lawsuits against the bank, the CPA firm that performed the compilations, and the audit firm. The city used the money to pay down its debt. According to the mayor, the city did not want any assets for which someone might say "we bought that with the Rita Crundwell money."

As you can see from the Dixon example, manipulating expense accounts and payments can lead to significant misstatements and frauds. GAAP prescribes that expenses be charged to income to reflect the consumption of economic benefits. The FASB *Statement of Concepts* discusses three ways to recognize expenses:

1. When they can be matched with related revenues (e.g., cost of goods sold with sales) and those revenues are recognized.
2. In the period in which they are incurred.
3. When they are allocated to the future periods benefited by a "systematic and rational" process (e.g., depreciation).[2]

It is imperative that the auditor understand these concepts of expense recognition and ascertain that the client is correctly applying the appropriate concept to the expense at hand and is properly valuing the expense.

ACQUISITION AND EXPENDITURE CYCLE: TYPICAL ACTIVITIES

LO 8-1

Describe the acquisition and expenditure cycle, including typical source documents.

The basic acquisition and expenditure activities include (1) purchasing goods and services, (2) receiving the good or service, (3) recording the asset or expense and related liability, and (4) paying the vendor. (Note that paying the vendor was covered in Chapter 6.) See Exhibit 8.1 for the activities and transactions involved in an acquisition and expenditure cycle. The exhibit also lists the accounts and records typically found in this cycle. As you follow the exhibit, you can track the elements of internal control described in the following sections.

Purchasing Goods and Services ①

The expenditure cycle begins when an individual or department needs supplies, materials, equipment, or services. The individual or department requests these items by sending a **purchase requisition** to the purchasing department. The purchase requisition will include the name of the department asking for the items, a listing of the items being requested, an account number where the cost of the material is to be charged when received, and an authorization signature from someone with the authority to commit the department to that amount of expense. The requisition may also include a recommended vendor.

The purchasing department reviews the purchase requisition and, if everything is in order, seeks to order the items where the best price, quality, and appropriate delivery can be obtained. Generally, the vendor must be on the approved vendor list. The **approved vendor list** includes only vendors that have been inspected by the organization and are authorized for purchases. It often requires several departments to approve a vendor. Purchasing usually approves the vendor for appropriate pricing, payment terms, and delivery; quality control may approve a vendor for both the quality of the product it makes and its system of quality

[1]www.forbes.com/sites/walterpavlo/2013/02/14/fmr-dixon-il-comptroller-rita-crundwell-sentenced-to-19-12-years-in-prison/; www.chicagomag.com/Chicago-Magazine/December-2012/Rita-Crundwell-and-the-Dixon-Embezzlement/.
[2]*SFAC No. 5,* "Recognition and Measurement in Finance Statements."

EXHIBIT 8.1   Acquisition and Expenditure Cycle

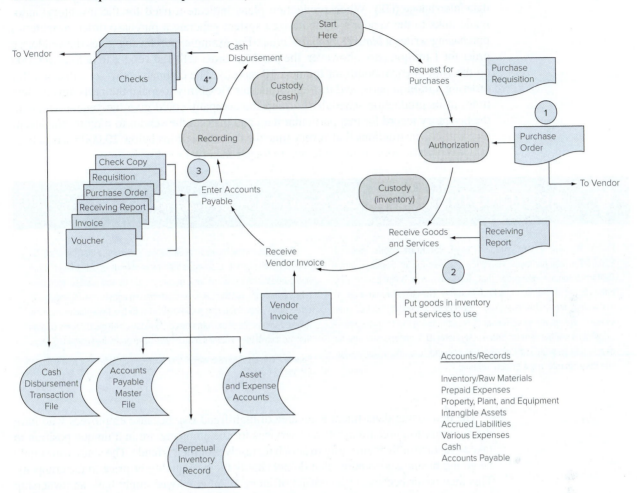

*Paying the vendor is discussed in the "Cash Disbursements" section of Chapter 6.

control used during the vendor's manufacturing process; and production (or engineering) may approve the items as appropriate for its purposes on the purchasing company's production line. There have been several frauds where only one person approved a vendor for inclusion on the approved vendor list. The individual was able to add to the list fictitious companies or disreputable firms willing to provide kickbacks to the individual.

There may be instances where material must be purchased from a vendor not on the approved vendor list. For example, the current vendors cannot deliver the needed material or a new part is required that cannot be manufactured by existing approved vendors. In this instance, there should be a process where multiple individuals and departments approve the purchase and steps must be taken to approve the vendor as soon as possible.

Once purchasing identifies the appropriate vendor for the purchase, a **purchase order** is sent to the selected vendor. In most companies, if a purchase or series of purchases from a vendor exceed a certain dollar amount, there is a requirement to receive bids from several vendors (usually at least three). The bidding process ensures that the company gets the best price, delivery, and payment terms. However, because of the large amounts at stake in this process (often multimillion-dollar orders), vendors may wish to get "an edge" in the process. To control for kickbacks, information leaks, and corruption, bids should come to someone other than the purchasing agent and be secured until the bidding process is complete. As a manager (or auditor), what would you think if one company was always the last bidder and its bids were always just below the second lowest bidder?

Often inventory is automatically ordered from approved vendors through **electronic data interchange (EDI)**. When production plans indicate a need for the inventory, automatic links to the vendor's computerized system generate a purchase order. Sometimes purchasing writes a *blanket purchase order*. For example, purchasing gives the vendor an order for 1 million parts; however, the purchase order tells the vendor to deliver 100,000 on the 10th of each month for the next 10 months. The company may get a discount for ordering a million parts, and the vendor has the flexibility to make the parts during slow times in its production schedule. Further, the company could give the vendor access to the inventory record for that particular item and instruct the vendor to monitor the inventory with the instructions that "every time the inventory drops below 10,000 parts deliver 100,000 parts as soon as possible but no longer than two weeks."

AUDITING INSIGHT — Do You Want Tomatoes on Your Salad?

Robert Watson, a top ingredient buyer for **Kraft Foods,** needed $20,000 to pay his taxes. He called a broker for **SK Foods,** a large California tomato processor that, for years, had been paying him bribes to get its products into Kraft factories. The check would soon be in the mail, the broker promised. "We'll have to deduct it out of your commissions as we move forward," he said, using the term "commissions" as a euphemism for bribes. Days later, U.S. government agents descended on Kraft's offices near Chicago and confronted Watson. He admitted his role in the bribery scheme.

Prosecutors next took aim at SK Foods. They stated that, for years, SK Foods had shipped its customers millions of pounds of bulk tomato paste and puree that fell short of basic quality standards and falsified documentation to hide the practice. Bribes to purchasing agents at Kraft Foods and three other large food companies, along with the false documentation, masked shipments of old tomatoes or tomatoes with mold counts so high that the sale of the tomatoes should have been prohibited under U.S. laws.

Source: "Bribes Let Tomato Vendor Sell Tainted Food," *The New York Times,* February 24, 2010.

The purchasing department is an area of high-fraud risk because employees who have the authority to purchase assets and services for the company are in a unique position to take advantage of their authority to enrich themselves or their friends. The abuse can simply be giving business to vendors that do not supply the best quality or price to the company. This may occur because of a conflict of interest. An employee might have an ownership interest in a supplier, might receive a kickback (the vendor provides the purchasing agent a gift or payment), or the employee might set up a "shell" company (a company created by the employee to provide fictitious invoices and receipt of payment). The abuse can extend to misdirecting purchases for the employee's personal benefit. These abuses are difficult to detect because vendors are often reluctant to lose favor with purchasing decision makers.

AUDITING INSIGHT — Where's My Milk Money?

Joseph J. DeRusso , a food service buyer for Roman Catholic school-children in New York, demanded commissions in cash from vendors providing milk and juice to various schools. At first DeRusso took a 5 percent "commission" but later upped the amount to 10 percent. Over the course of six years, he collected at least $240,000 in bribe money.

In an example of corporate culture, three other purchasing agents were also found to be receiving bribes.

Source: Julia Preston, "4 Purchasing Agents Accused of Skimming School Money," *The New York Times,* January 6, 2006.

Receiving the Goods or Services ②

When goods arrive at a company, the trucker will have a **bill of lading** that should include the purchase order number of the company receiving the delivery. It is imperative that the bill of lading be matched to the purchase order on file at receiving. If a company obtains a reputation for receiving any goods that show up at its receiving department, any "undeliverable" item on a truck may find its way to the company's receiving docks.

After the delivery is verified as the company's purchase, the receiving department inspects the goods received for quantity and quality and prepares a **receiving report**. The items are sent to the area designated by the department that originally requisitioned the material (e.g., engineering may order a piece of equipment but want it delivered to the production facility). A receiving report is completed to indicate the quantity and description of the item. Receiving departments should receive a "blind" purchase order that has all purchase information except the quantity, which is left blank for the receiving department to fill in after an independent inspection and count. Services are not "received" in this manner, but responsible persons indicate that the service was satisfactorily performed by signing the invoice or some other form that can be used like a receiving report to verify that the service was completed.

Recording the Asset or Expense and Related Liability ③

Accounts payable usually are recorded when the purchaser receives the goods or services ordered. The accounts payable department attaches a **voucher** to the purchase order, a **vendor's invoice**, and a receiving report. The combined documents are often called the **voucher package**. The voucher shows the accounts that are debited and indicates who checked the invoice for proper date, price, math, and reconciled the purchase order, receiving report, and vendor invoice. After the voucher package has been completed, accountants enter the accounts (or vouchers) payable with debits to proper inventory, fixed asset, or expense accounts with a corresponding credit to accounts payable.

✅ REVIEW CHECKPOINTS

8.1 What is a *voucher*? What is a *voucher package*?

8.2 How can purchasing managers use their position to defraud the company? What can be done to prevent it?

8.3 Why is a "blind" purchase order used as a receiving report document?

SIGNIFICANT ACCOUNTS AND RELEVANT ASSERTIONS

LO 8-2

Identify significant accounts and relevant assertions related to the acquisition and expenditure cycle.

STAGES OF AN AUDIT

Obtain (or Retain) Engagement	Engagement Planning	Risk Assessment	Reporting	Audit Evidence

Remember that an account or disclosure is significant if there is a reasonable chance that it could contain a material misstatement. The auditor identifies significant accounts and relevant assertions by applying the audit risk model.

We introduced the audit risk model in Chapter 4 and reviewed it in Chapter 7. Therefore, this chapter and subsequent chapters will not review the components of the model again. Instead, these chapters will focus on the use of the audit risk model in assessing risk and planning the engagement in the specific areas addressed in these chapters.

Exhibit 8.2 identifies the significant accounts and assertions in the expenditure cycle. In this cycle, the most significant risks usually relate to the completeness of expenditures and the valuation of acquisitions. It is also possible that individuals will attempt to run personal expenses through accounts payable and receive reimbursement for the purchase of these items. Therefore, the validity of expenses is also a significant risk in the expenditure cycle.

EXHIBIT 8.2 **Significant Accounts and Assertions in the Expenditure and Acquisition Cycle**

Significant Account	Relevant Assertions	Assertion Risk
Accounts Payable	Completeness	High
	Cutoff	High
	Existence	Moderate
	Rights and obligations	Moderate
	Valuation	Moderate
Expenses*	Completeness	High
	Cutoff	High
	Accuracy	High*
	Classification	High

* Expense valuation risk is especially high for services.

Accounts Payable

In many ways, the purchasing process, including accounts payable, is the most important to the organization. If purchasing is not done well, manufacturers may need to cease production because of raw material shortages, retailers may have insufficient inventory for customer needs, and needed services may not be obtained. Purchasing and the subsequent receipt of goods and services gives rise to an accounts payable—the obligation to pay the vendor for the goods and services acquired. If accounts payable does not pay the vendor on time and for the proper amount, vendors may raise the price charged to that client to cover the cost of capital in the delayed payment, ask for orders to be C.O.D. (cash on delivery), or cease to provide products or services to the organization. We have already learned that audit firms will not do business with clients if the relationship is improper. Vendors may also decide not to do business with a customer who does not appropriately honor his or her obligations.

AUDITING INSIGHT   Give Me All Your Money

Aeropostale, a large fashion retailer, filed for Chapter 11 bankruptcy protection in a New York court and quickly closed 113 of its 739 U.S. stores and all 41 of its Canada stores. The bankruptcy filing comes after a dispute with one of its largest suppliers, MGF Sourcing, which demanded cash on delivery **(C.O.D.).**

Source: Nathan Bomey, "Aeropostale Files for Chapter 11 Bankruptcy" *USA Today,* May 5, 2016.

There are three important assertions for accounts payable: completeness, cutoff, and valuation. Completeness and cutoff go hand-in-hand because management may desire to improve the books by not recording an obligation in the correct period. An incomplete listing of accounts payable at the end of the period lowers current liabilities (and corresponding expenses). Because vendors do need to be paid eventually, management may accomplish this by delaying the recording of accounts payable until the subsequent period—in other words, by closing the books early so end-of-period obligations become the obligations of the subsequent period. Accounts payable may also be understated. Obligations may not reflect the total cost of the purchase such as freight, tariff, and taxes. On large purchases, this may be substantial and may be the result of an error or an intentional act to reduce the accounts payable liability.

AUDITING INSIGHT | Would You Like Me to Pay Your Credit Card Bill?

Nathan Mueller's wife was pregnant, and his $80,000 salary was not allowing him to pay all his bills. He believed if he could just catch up with the bills, then everything would be all right.

Mueller had the authority to approve checks up to $250,000 for his company ING. He had the ability to log onto the accounts payable system as someone else and issued checks made out to *Universal.* ING did business with an insurance company that had *Universal* as part of its name, and Mueller's credit card company had *Universal* as part of its name. In June 2003, he ran a check for $1,100 to pay his credit card bill in order to "test his scheme." Once that check went through and his credit card was paid, he transferred all his outstanding debt to that credit card and, over several months, paid $88,000 in credit card debt.

According to Mueller, "in our small accounting department, we knew everyone else's system passwords. This was a practical workaround

for when we needed to get something done when someone was out of the office. We logged in as someone else to get the job done." Eventually, Mueller logged on to the system as someone else and requested a check for *Ace Business Consulting.* (Remember, service expenses are easier for fraudsters.) The check request was routed to Mueller for approval. He received his first check for $27,000 a few days later and deposited it in a bank account he opened in the name of *Ace Business Consulting.* Using this method, he stole approximately $8 million from 2004 to 2007. According to Mueller, after getting his $88,000 "bonus" he couldn't help himself. "I wanted to do it again, even though I didn't really need the money like before."

Source: Mark J Nigrini, and Nathan J. Mueller, "Lessons from an $8 Million Fraud: What the Criminal Was Thinking and What Can Be Done to Prevent or Uncover Similar Crimes," *Journal of Accountancy,* August 2014, pp. 32–37.

Auditors should be cautious not to discount other assertions. While management would not intentionally create a fictitious accounts payable, the item may not reflect an obligation of the company. A vendor account may have been paid, but the payment has not been recorded in the proper account. The liability remains on the books but no longer reflects an obligation. Individuals may try to run personal expenses through the payable system. This is especially true in companies where blank purchase orders or receiving reports can be obtained. If this is the case, the payable does not represent an obligation of the firm and may be fictitious or an obligation of an employee.

Expenses

The corresponding entry to the accounts payable is often an expense account. Because expenses affect the income statement, the misstatement of expenses is often the objective of misstating a purchase or payable. Again, not recording expenses in the current period or delaying the recognition of expenses to the subsequent period is often the method for financial statement fraud. Closing the books early for expenses (say, December 22 for December 31 year-end clients) forces ensuing expenses into the next period. Further, an unethical controller might lock in her desk several large bills received near the year-end and place them into the payables system after year-end, thereby violating the cutoff assertion.

Another issue for expenses is classification. There may be many reasons to classify expenses in the wrong account. **WorldCom Inc.** is an example of a company that simply placed ordinary expenses in capital accounts, thus lowering expenses and increasing assets by billions of dollars. While capitalizing expenses increases net income in the year in which they should have been completely expensed, the expenses do not go away. (Amounts would be expensed over a number of years as depreciation or amortization expense.) When forced to restate these expenses, WorldCom recorded nearly $5 billion in immediate recognition of expenses. WorldCom is just one of many companies that used expenses to inflate their financial statements. Exhibit 8.3 shows some of the more egregious misstatements in recent years.

Other reasons may exist for improper classification of expenses. For example, some projects are performed under cost-plus contracts. These are often large construction projects, such as military ship building, where changes to the contract specifications are expected during construction. Here, the construction company submits bills for material and labor and is reimbursed for all expenses and paid a set percentage over the costs (say, an 8 percent profit). There may be little incentive for a disreputable contractor to restrain costs and few restrictions for a dishonest contractor to place costs from one project to another as in the following Auditing Insight.

AUDITING INSIGHT   My Money Went to Higher Education

Auston International Group's former chief financial officer, Chua Peck Wee, was sentenced to seven months in jail for playing a part in the falsification of the company's accounts four years ago. Chua is the first to be convicted and sentenced out of three parties who have been charged in connection with the Auston accounting fraud.

The former CFO admitted creating false documents and sending them to the Auston accounts staff, with instructions to record a payment of $268,525 as "academic cooperation fees" to Upper Iowa University for FY2003. This amount was actually a payment made by Auston to the University of Wollongong for university fees for FY2002.

By falsely recording the amount as academic cooperation fees instead of university fees, Auston could classify it as a development cost and amortize the amount over three to five years instead of having to record the full amount as an expense in FY2002. The falsification reduced the amount of expenses recorded for FY2002 and increased the net profit Auston reported in its initial public offer (IPO) prospectus in 2003.

Source: Michelle Quah, "Ex-Auston CFO Gets Seven Months' Jail; This Comes after Chua Pleaded Guilty to One Charge of Abetting Fraud," *The Business Times Singapore*, January 12, 2007.

✓ REVIEW CHECKPOINTS

8.4 Why do auditors focus on completeness of expenditures as a significant account and relevant assertion in the expenditure cycle?

8.5 Why is inherent risk for the existence of inventory an issue in the expenditure cycle audit?

8.6 Why is a service expense a good account for recording a fictitious expense?

RISK OF MATERIAL MISSTATEMENT

LO 8-3
Discuss the risk of material misstatement in the acquisition and expenditure cycle.

Audit Analytics reported that, for 2014, there were 96 financial statement restatements for expenses (including general and administrative expenses, payroll, and related accounts payable). This accounted for 11.5 percent of all restatements and ranked as number 5 on the list of reasons for financial statement restatements. The *Audit Analytics* report indicates that although restatements as a whole have declined since 2007 (a finding attributed to the PCAOB rigorous inspections), expense recognition errors had increased over the past three years (60 in 2012; 76 in 2013).[3]

EXHIBIT 8.3   Cost and Expense Capers

Company	Alleged Fraud Strategy	Restatement Amount
MCI (WorldCom)	The telecommunications company improperly capitalized expense items.	$11 billion
Waste Management Inc.	The waste disposal giant used "top-level adjustments" to improperly eliminate and defer current-period expenses and avoided depreciation on garbage trucks by assigning unsupported, inflated, and arbitrary salvage values and extending the useful lives.	$1.1 billion
Adelphia Communications Corporation	The cable company did not report off-balance-sheet liabilities.	$210.0 million
Orbital Sciences Corporation	The satellite manufacturer improperly capitalized costs.	$124.0 million
Aurora Food, Inc.	The food company did not record trade-marketing expenses (e.g., case discounts to induce grocery stores to stock its goods).	$81.5 million
Dixon, Illinois	The treasurer/controller created a fictitious account that she used to pay for her personal expenses.	$53.0 million
Collins and Aikman	The automotive supply company booked rebates as lump sums that should have been spread out over time.	$16.0 million

---

[3] Audit Analytics, "2014 Financial Restatements: A Fourteen Year Comparison," April 2015.

In many accounting systems, liabilities are not recorded until receiving reports have been matched to purchase orders and invoices. This is often referred to as a "three-way match." Often, when there is a problem in matching the documents, the recording of the liability is delayed or not recorded, thus understating costs and overstating profits. Further, in an attempt to make the financial statements appear better, management may decide to delay the recording of expenses and related liabilities until after the fiscal year-end. Additionally, noncancelable purchase agreements may exist where goods are ordered for future delivery (as with blanket purchase orders). If market forces or technology causes a permanent decline in the value of those goods, the company must recognize any related losses immediately, even though no liability or expense exists because the goods have not been received. Therefore, risks in the acquisition and expenditure cycle include *unrecorded liabilities* and *noncancelable purchase agreements.*

Remember from Chapter 7 that as part of the planning process, the auditor must determine the source of a misstatement that could cause the financial statements to be materially misstated. We established the idea of assessing the risk of material misstatement by using the "what can go wrong?" approach when thinking of each financial statement assertion. The WCGW is a part of each audit firm's process and enables a thorough assessment of the risk of material misstatement.

When considering WCGW in the expenditure and acquisition cycle, auditors consider five primary concerns:

1. Have liabilities and corresponding expenses or assets been recorded (completeness)?
2. Have liabilities and corresponding expenses or assets been recorded in the proper period (cutoff)?
3. Do liabilities reflect the actual needs and obligations of the company (occurrence and obligation)?
4. Have liabilities and corresponding expenses or assets been recorded at their proper amount (valuation)?
5. Have expenses been recorded in the proper account (classification)?

Exhibit 8.4 summarizes the WCGW analysis for the expenditure and acquisition cycle.

We have seen in several of the Audit Insights multimillion-dollar accounts payable schemes perpetrated to enhance the financial statements or for an employee's benefit.

EXHIBIT 8.4 **Assertions and What Could Go Wrong**

Significant Account	Relevant Assertions	What Can Go Wrong?
Accounts Payable	Completeness	Liabilities are not recorded.
	Cutoff	Liabilities have been recorded in incorrect periods.
	Existence	Liabilities may not represent actual obligations of the company.
	Presentation	Liabilities are not recorded in the proper accounts and properly disclosed in the footnotes.
	Valuation	Payables are recorded at an incorrect amount.
Various Expenses	Completeness	Not all expenses are recorded.
	Cutoff	Expenses have not been recorded in incorrect periods.
	Accuracy	Expenses are recorded at an incorrect amount.
	Classification	Expenses have been improperly recorded as capitalized expenses.

Clearly, these frauds can result in material misstatements. Remember, while large dollar frauds and errors that occur in well-known companies are widely reported in the financial news, most frauds are perpetrated in smaller companies where $100,000 may be the difference between success and bankruptcy.

REVIEW CHECKPOINTS

8.7 What are the short-term effect and the long-term effect of improperly capitalizing expenditures on the financial statements?

8.8 If an account payable is left off the end of the period balance, what are the possible other accounts that may be misstated?

INTERNAL CONTROL ACTIVITIES AND DESIGN EVALUATION

LO 8-4
Identify important internal control activities present in a properly designed system to mitigate the risk of material misstatements for each relevant assertion in the acquisition and expenditure cycle.

Control risk assessment is important because it governs the nature, timing, and extent of substantive procedures that will be applied in the audit of account balances in the acquisition and expenditure cycle. The primary accounts discussed in this chapter are accounts payables and expenses, and the assertions and significant internal control activities are summarized in Exhibit 8.5. However, you should not lose sight of the fact that many other accounts are affected by activities in this cycle. These accounts include the following:

- Prepaid expenses.
- Fixed assets.
- Inventory.
- Accrued liabilities.
- Supplies.

Entity-Level Controls

It is important that auditors consider entity-level controls in all processes and procedures. In the expenditure process, management should have a process for continually reviewing expenses and comparing them to budgets and forecasts. Proper authorization for all expenditures should be established and included in company policy and procedures. Corporate values and ethics that have been established should be communicated to suppliers and other partners of the entity along with a place where inappropriate behavior (such as the solicitation of a bribe or kickback) may be reported. The security of items such as blank purchase orders and blank receiving reports is an important control, as are the proper delivery and safeguarding of all material received by the entity.

Control Considerations

Control activities for proper separation of responsibilities should be in place and operating. By referring to Exhibit 8.1, you can see that proper separation involves different people and different departments performing the purchasing, receiving, and cash disbursement authorization; custody of inventory, fixed assets, and cash; record keeping for purchases and payments; and reconciliation of assets, cash, and accounts payable. Combinations of two or more of these responsibilities in one person, one office, or one computerized system can open the door for errors and frauds. Specifically, the persons authorizing purchases should not be responsible for recording them. Persons who actually handle the receipt and storage of goods should neither authorize nor account for them.

EXHIBIT 8.5 Internal Control Activities in the Expenditure and Acquisition Cycle

Significant Account	Relevant Assertion	What Can Go Wrong?	Internal Control Activity
Accounts Payable	Completeness	Liabilities are not recorded	Receiving reports should be prenumbered and used in order. All receiving reports completed by the end of the period should be accounted for in that period.
	Cutoff	Liabilities are recorded in the incorrect period.	Payables recorded in the first weeks of a period should be compared to receiving reports and bills of lading for the recording period.
	Existence	Liabilities may not represent actual obligations of the company.	Voucher packages for payments to vendors should include purchase orders and receiving reports. A three-way match should be performed for purchase orders, receiving reports, and vendor invoices. Vendors should be on the approved vendor list.
	Valuation	Payables recorded at an incorrect amount.	Payables should be matched with the vendor invoice.
Expenses	Completeness	Not all expenses are recorded.	Items recorded as an expense in the first weeks of a period should be matched to the underlying receipt of goods or service to indicate the proper period of recording.
	Cutoff	Expenses have been recorded in the incorrect period.	Items recorded as an expense in the first weeks of a period should be matched to the underlying receipt of goods or service to indicate the proper period of recording.
	Accuracy	Expenses are recorded at an incorrect amount.	Expenses should be matched with vendor invoices or work orders for the proper cost of items or service performed.
	Classification	Expenses have been improperly recorded.	Expenses should be reviewed to determine that they have been recorded in the proper account.

The persons who sign checks should not prepare the vouchers, nor should they mail the checks.

In addition, the internal controls should provide for detailed control-checking activities. For example, purchase requisitions and purchase orders should be signed or initialed by authorized personnel. Computer-generated purchase orders should come from a system where master file specifications for reordering and vendor identification are restricted to changes by authorized persons.

Nowhere in the company is proper recording of accounts more important than in the recording of expenses. Improper recording of expenses may occur intentionally, as illustrated by the following Auditing Insight, or may be due to a mistake in judgment as to the proper accounting for invoices. Accountants should be instructed to record accounts payable only when all supporting documentation is in order, and care should be taken to record purchases and payables as of the date goods and services are received. Vendor invoices should be compared to purchase orders and receiving reports to determine that the vendor is charging the approved price and that the quantity being billed is the same as the quantity received.

AUDITING INSIGHT   What Were Those Charges Again?

A headline in the March 14, 2003, issue of *The New York Times* announced that WorldCom Inc. was going to write down assets by more than $70 *billion* to correct the company's accounting records for a massive fraud that had been uncovered. To put this number in perspective, the amount of the write-off almost equaled the entire gross domestic product for the country of Ireland.

A large part of the restatement was a result of the company's practice of capitalizing (rather than properly expensing) certain transactions to fixed asset accounts. The improper charges were not part of the regular system but were hidden in computerized files of adjusting entries to intercompany receivables. Only the determined pursuit of the facts led by the company's director of internal audit and 2002 *Time*

Person of the Year Cynthia Cooper uncovered the massive fraud. The internal auditors' search included midnight hacking into the computerized system to sort through hundreds of thousands of transactions—a process that discovered $2 billion of questionable items in the first week! When **Andersen**, the company's public accounting firm, was first apprised of the problems, the firm allegedly told Cooper that it had approved some of the very accounting practices she questioned. At the time of its discovery, the WorldCom fraud represented the largest fraud ever perpetrated in the United States.

Source: Simon Romero, "WorldCom to Write Down $79.8 Billion of Good Will," *The New York Times,* March 14, 2003.

Custody

Access to inventory and other physical assets must be restricted by placing them in locked areas when possible. Responsibility must be established by having someone sign for receipt of the assets when they are moved. Cash "custody" rests largely in the hands of the person or persons authorized to sign checks.

Another aspect of custody involves access to blank documents such as purchase orders, receiving reports, and checks. If unauthorized persons can obtain blank copies of these internal business documents, they can forge a false purchase order to a fictitious vendor, forge a false receiving report, send a false invoice from a fictitious supplier, and receive a company check, thereby accomplishing embezzlement. In addition, a blank purchase order can be used to order merchandise, material, or services for personal use. If this material can be diverted and if sound controls are not in place, the company may end up paying for an employee's home improvement project.

Periodic Reconciliation

A periodic comparison or reconciliation of existing assets to recorded amounts is not shown in Exhibit 8.1, but it occurs in several ways, including the following:

- Preparing an accounts payable trial balance and comparing it to the accounts payable control account.
- Comparing accounts payable records to vendors' monthly statements.
- Reviewing unmatched purchase orders, receiving reports, and invoices.
- Taking a physical inventory and comparing it to inventory records.
- Inspecting fixed assets and comparing them to detailed fixed asset records.

Information about the control system is often gathered by completing an *internal control questionnaire.* Appendix 8A provides examples of questionnaires for both manual controls and computer controls. These questionnaires can be studied for details of desirable control activities. They are organized under headings that identify the management assertions.

 REVIEW CHECKPOINTS

8.9   What primary functions should be separated in the acquisition and expenditure cycle?

8.10 What feature of the acquisition and expenditure control would be expected to prevent an employee's embezzling cash through creation of fictitious vouchers?

TESTING OF OPERATING EFFECTIVENESS OF INTERNAL CONTROL

LO 8-5

Give examples of tests of controls to verify the operating effectiveness of internal controls in the acquisition and expenditure cycle.

Tests of Controls

An organization should have controls in place and operating to prevent, detect, and correct accounting errors. Arguably, the most risks in the expenditure cycle are in the purchasing activity. Purchasing itself is not an account (except in government accounting), but it does affect the occurrence and valuation of other accounts. Exhibit 8.6 delineates some important controls in the purchasing activity and relates the test of controls to what could go wrong.

Auditors can perform tests of controls to determine whether company controls actually are in place and operating effectively. Tests of controls consist of identification of (1) the control that will be relied on to reduce assessed control risk and (2) the data population from which a sample of items will be selected for audit. In general, the actions in tests of controls involve inspecting, inquiry, observing, scanning, matching, and recalculating.

An auditor might select a sample of voucher packages and inspect the documents for indications that reconciliations and approvals for payment are evident. If personnel in the organization are not performing control activities effectively, auditors need to design substantive procedures to try to detect whether control failures have produced materially incorrect account balances. Procedures such as matching, recalculating, and scanning for unusual items often can be performed electronically using computer-assisted audit techniques (CAATs). For example, CAATs can scan the accounts payable balances for debit balances.

Tests of controls over occurrence involve tests of the additions to the expense accounts. The chart in Exhibit 8.7 shows the direction of the test for tests of controls in the acquisition and expenditure cycle. Selecting a sample of closed purchase orders, receiving reports, or vendor invoices and tracing them to the accounts payable journal provides evidence of completeness. At the same time, the auditor can inspect these documents for proper authorization. Taking a sample of payments to vendors and vouching those payments to the receiving report and purchase order provides evidence that the delivery occurred and the purchase existed. Further, vouching payments to receiving reports and purchase orders may find fictitious vendors (there is usually no receiving report because fictitious vendors don't deliver product) or payments for employee personal use (often, the purchase order is missing or lacks the proper approval).

Summary: Control Risk Assessment

The auditor should evaluate the evidence obtained from understanding internal controls and from the tests of controls. This evaluation of control risk along with the auditor's understanding of the inherent risk leads to the auditor's determination of the risk of material misstatement (RMM). If the control risk is assessed below the maximum, the substantive procedures can be reduced in cost-saving ways. For example, if *completeness* controls are strong, only large items in purchases, accounts payable, cash disbursements, and fixed assets need to be examined in the search for unrecorded liabilities in accounts

EXHIBIT 8.6 **Purchasing Transactions and Events: Acquisition and Expenditure Cycle**

What Could Go Wrong	Controls	Tests of Control
Purchases received have not been properly recorded.	• Separation of duties between purchasing, receiving, and accounting • Use of prenumbered vouchers, receiving reports, purchase orders, and checks and the numerical sequence checked • Purchase orders supported by authorized requisitions. • Purchases received are matched with receiving report and vendor invoices • Purchases from approved vendors listed on an approved vendor list • Overall comparisons of purchases by a statistical or product line analysis made periodically • Comparison by managers of actual expenses with budgeted amounts	• Observe separation of duties. • Trace receiving reports to recording in purchases journal. • Scan purchases journal for numerical sequence of purchase orders and receiving reports. • Scan cash disbursements journal for client checking sequence. • Vouch purchase orders to requisitions and review requisitions for authorizations. • Review and reconcile voucher packages for three-way match of purchase order, receiving reports, and invoice. • Vouch purchase order to the approved vendor list, and review the purchase order for correct customer name, address, product description, terms, dates, and quantities. • Examine evidence that managers review statistical analyses, and follow up on unusual relationships. • Examine evidence that managers review actual versus budget, and follow up on unusual items.
Purchase amounts and other data related to significant purchase transactions and events have not been recorded properly.	• Purchase contracts authorized at the appropriate level • Comparison of invoice quantities and prices with purchase orders and receiving reports • Vendor statements reviewed and approved by appropriate personnel • Prices and mathematical accuracy independently checked before approving voucher for payment • Journal entries reviewed at the appropriate level • Individual accounts payable reconciled to general ledger	• Examine contracts for authorization. Inquire how accounting is notified of pending contracts. • Observe client comparing receiving quantities, and inspect documentary evidence of comparison. • Vouch prices to approved price listing. • Review reconciliation and support for reconciling items. • Recalculate price extensions and discounts. • Inspect evidence of approval for payment. • Inspect evidence of client checking.
Purchases have been recorded in the incorrect period.	• Date of receiving report compared with invoice date	• Trace the date of receipt to date recorded in voucher journal. • Inspect evidence of client comparison of dates. • Inspect purchases occurring near year-end for recording in appropriate period.
Purchases have not been recorded in the proper accounts.	• Chart of accounts used for classifying purchase entries • Purchases from subsidiaries and affiliates classified as intercompany purchases and payables • Purchase returns and allowances properly classified • Journal entries reviewed at the appropriate level	• Observe use of charts of accounts. • Observe correct account classification. • Inspect evidence of journal entry review.

payable, and if *occurrence* controls are strong, vouching of expenses can be limited to significant items. On the other hand, if the tests of controls reveal weaknesses, the substantive procedures need to be designed to lower the detection risk for the account balances. For example, if *completeness* controls are weak, the auditor might send confirmation letters to vendors with small or zero balances. If *occurrence* controls are weak, the auditor may

EXHIBIT 8.7
Direction of Tests

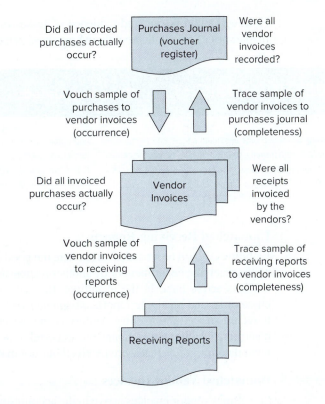

have to perform substantive tests of significant transactions by recalculating and testing a sample of payments for the period for monetary errors rather than just evidence of control effectiveness. Other substantive procedures that can be affected include vouching of debits to assets and expenses.

> ☑ **REVIEW CHECKPOINTS**
>
> 8.11 How should an auditor test for proper authorization in the expenditure cycle?
>
> 8.12 Where would an auditor find the proper authorization that indicates it is okay to pay a vendor?

SUBSTANTIVE ANALYTICAL PROCEDURES AND TESTS OF DETAILS

LO 8-6
Give examples of substantive procedures in the acquisition and expenditure cycle and relate them to assertions about significant account balances at the end of the period.

STAGES OF AN AUDIT

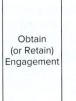   

| Obtain (or Retain) Engagement | Engagement Planning | Risk Assessment | Audit Evidence | Reporting |

Computerized processing of acquisition and payment transactions enables management to generate several reports that can provide important audit evidence.

Open Purchase Orders

Purchase orders are "open" from the time they are issued until all goods and services have been received. They are held in an *open purchase order file*. Generally, no liability exists until the transactions have been completed (i.e., the merchandise or services are received).

However, auditors can find evidence of losses on purchase commitments in this file if market prices have fallen below the purchase price shown in purchase orders.

AUDITING INSIGHT · Thinking Ahead

Lone Moon Brewing purchased bulk aluminum sheets and manufactured its own cans. To ensure a source of raw materials supply, the company entered into a long-term purchase agreement for 6 million pounds of aluminum sheeting at 40 cents per pound. At the end of the year, it had purchased and used 1.5 million pounds, but the market price had fallen to 32 cents per pound. Lone Moon was on the hook for a $360,000 (4.5 million pounds at 8 cents) purchase commitment in excess of current market prices that should be recognized as a loss in the period.

Unmatched Receiving Reports

Liabilities should be recorded on the date the goods and services are received and accepted by the receiving department or by another responsible person. Sometimes, however, vendor invoices arrive later. In the meantime, the accounts payable department holds the purchase order and receiving reports *unmatched* with invoices, awaiting enough information to record an accounting entry. Auditors can inspect the unmatched receiving report file to determine whether the company has material unrecorded liabilities on the financial statement date for goods that were received but not matched to invoices.

Unmatched Vendor Invoices

Sometimes vendor invoices arrive in the accounts payable department before the receiving activity is complete. Such invoices are held *unmatched* with receiving reports, awaiting information that the goods and services were actually received and accepted. Auditors can inspect the *unmatched invoice file* and compare it with the *unmatched receiving report file* to determine whether liabilities that have been incurred are unrecorded. Systems failures and human coding errors can cause unmatched invoices and related unmatched receiving reports to sit around unnoticed when all of the information for recording a liability is actually in hand. Sometimes, however, unmatched invoices are indicators of fraudsters looking for an easy score, as noted in the following Auditing Insight.

AUDITING INSIGHT · Paying for Nothing

A Toronto man received more than $7 million by mailing thousands of phony invoices to companies around the world. Emanuel Medeiros mailed fake "renewal notices" in the amount of $297.83 and received payments from more 25,000 companies. Medeiros hired a commercial mailing company in New York to send out 200 to 400 bills stamped "RENEWAL" in large, bold letters every two weeks. The bills were sent in the name of two companies, Bradstreet International and Boom Global Media. One company tried to contact Boom to cancel the service. When the next bill arrived for twice the amount and threatened that the account would be turned over for collection, the company immediately sent a check for $595.66.

After receiving complaints, the U.S. Postal Service stopped the mailing, and after some communications, Medeiros agreed to come to New York. He pleaded guilty to fraud, agreed to pay $300,000, and was sentenced to 46 months in prison. In addition, the U.S. Attorney's Office in New York notified victim companies who may file for restitution.

Source: "Fake Invoices Net $7M and Four Years," *National Post,* January 29, 2009.

Accounts (Vouchers) Payable Trial Balance

This trial balance is a list of payable amounts by vendor, and the total should agree with the accounts payable control account. (Some organizations keep records by individual vouchers instead of vendor names, so the trial balance is a list of unpaid vouchers. The total still should agree with the control account balance.) The best type of trial balance for audit purposes is one that contains the names of all vendors with whom the organization has done business, even those whose balances are zero. The search for unrecorded liabilities should emphasize accounts with small and zero balances, especially for regular vendors, because these accounts can be the places where unrecorded liabilities may exist.

Purchases Journal

A list of all purchases may or may not be printed. It may exist only in a computer transaction file. In either event, it provides information for (1) the analysis of purchasing patterns that can exhibit characteristics of errors and frauds and (2) the sample selection of transactions for tests of controls. (A company could have already performed analyses of purchases that auditors can use for analytical procedures, provided the analyses are produced under reliable control activities.)

Fixed Asset Reports

Many large purchases are for fixed assets. Auditors should trace large purchases to the fixed asset reports and ensure that the details of fixed assets in control accounts are consistent with purchase orders. Furthermore, additions to fixed assets should be vouched to the purchasing documents to ensure that items were acquired in accordance with policy and procedure.

 REVIEW CHECKPOINTS

8.13 Where could an auditor look to find evidence of (a) losses on purchase commitments or (b) unrecorded liabilities to vendors?

8.14 List the management reports and computer files that can be used for audit evidence. What information in them can be useful to auditors?

The Completeness Assertion

When considering assertions and obtaining evidence about accounts payable and other liabilities, auditors must emphasize the *completeness* assertion. (Remember from Chapter 7 that the emphasis is on the *existence* assertion for asset and occurrence for revenue accounts.) This emphasis on completeness is rightly placed because financial statement users are typically more concerned if a company understates expenses and liabilities than if management overstates those accounts.

Evidence is much more difficult to obtain to support the *completeness* assertion than the *existence* assertion. Auditors cannot rely entirely on a management assertion of *completeness,* even in combination with a favorable assessment of the risk of material misstatement. The **search for unrecorded liabilities** is the set of procedures designed to yield audit evidence of liabilities that were not recorded in the reporting period. Such a search normally should be performed from the audit client's balance sheet date to the date of the auditors' report.

The following is a list of procedures useful in the *search for unrecorded liabilities*. The audit objective is to search all places where evidence of liabilities could exist.

- Inquire of client personnel about their procedures for ensuring that all liabilities are recorded.
- Scan the open purchase order file at year-end for indications of material purchase commitments at fixed prices. Obtain current prices, and determine whether any adjustments for loss and liability for purchase commitments are needed.
- Examine the unmatched vendor invoices, and determine when the goods were received, focusing on the unmatched receiving reports and receiving reports prepared around year-end. Determine which invoices, if any, should be recorded by tracing them to the payables listing.
- Review the unmatched receiving reports, and determine whether entries are recorded in the proper accounting period.
- Select a sample of cash disbursements from the accounting period following the balance sheet date. Vouch them to supporting documents (invoice, receiving report) to determine whether the related liabilities were recorded in the proper accounting period.

- Confirm accounts payable with vendors, especially those most likely to be understated (regular suppliers showing small or zero balances in the year-end accounts payable ledger). Unlike accounts receivable confirmations, accounts payable confirmations are not required by auditing standards. Such confirmations are not commonly used because they are primarily directed at the *existence* assertion, and the main concern regarding liabilities is *completeness*. However, accounts payable confirmations might be used under the following circumstances:
  - Internal controls are weak.
  - The company is in a tight cash position, and bill paying is slow.
  - Physical inventories exceed general ledger inventory balances by significant amounts.
  - Certain vendors do not send statements.
  - Vendor accounts are pledged by assets.
  - Vendor accounts include unusual transactions.
- Perform analytical procedures appropriate in the circumstances. In general, accounts payable volume and period-end balances should increase when the company experiences increases in physical production volume or engages in inventory stock-piling. Some liabilities can be functionally related to other activities; for example, sales taxes are functionally related to sales dollar totals, payroll taxes to payroll totals, excise taxes to sales dollars or volume, and income taxes to income.
- Purchase cutoff must be tested both at year-end and in conjunction with the observation of the physical inventory count. Receiving reports issued and unissued at the end of the period are examined and listed. Later, auditors check to ensure that the goods received on the issued reports are included in inventory and payables and to ensure that no goods are recorded for the unissued receiving reports.

Additional procedures are included in a sample audit plan in Appendix 8B.

✓ REVIEW CHECKPOINTS

8.15 How would substantive procedures for accounts payable be affected by (a) a low risk of material misstatement or (b) a high risk of material misstatement?

8.16 Describe the purpose and give examples of audit procedures in the search for unrecorded liabilities.

8.17 In substantive procedures, why is the emphasis on the *completeness* assertion for liabilities instead of on the *existence* assertion as in the audit of assets?

There are other accounts affected by the expenditure and acquisition cycle that the auditor needs to review. We have not covered inventory in this chapter because inventory is a main focus of Chapter 9.

Prepaid Expenses and Accrued Liabilities

Some of the other accounts affected by the acquisition and expenditure cycle are listed in Exhibit 8.1. Performing substantive procedures for cash and inventory accounts are discussed in other chapters. Many accounts, particularly expense accounts, can be tested using analytical procedures, such as horizontal and vertical analyses. Other accounts such as prepaid expenses can be analyzed by a schedule similar to Exhibit 8.8. In addition to vouching payments, related expense accounts are cross-referenced to expense workpapers (X-10, 11, 12 in Exhibit 8.8). A sample audit plan for prepaid, deferred, and accrued expenses is shown at Appendix Exhibit 8B.2.

Accrued Income Taxes

Income taxes are a special audit area because the accounting and underlying federal tax laws are so complex. State and local tax differences add to the complexity. Approximately one-third

EXHIBIT 8.8 **Account Analysis for Prepaid Expenses**

		DUNDER-MIFFLIN INC. Prepaid Expenses For Year Ended 12/31/2017 Prepared by Client			E-1

					Prepared by RJR	1/16/18
					Reviewed by TJL	1/18/18

Acct #	Account Title	(Audited) Balance 12/31/2016	Additions	Amortization/ Disposals	Unaudited Balance 12/31/2017
14100	Prepaid insurance	$706,148.66PY	$941,531.55v	$904,365.83C X-10	$743,314.38
14200	Prepaid rent	190,000.00PY	760,000.00v	750,000.00C X-11	200,000.00
14300	Office supplies	7,036.48PY	26,025.00v	25,654.66C X-12	7,406.82
		$903,185.14	$1,727,556.55	$1,680,020.49	$950,721.20CF
		F	F	F	F TB

PY = Agreed to prior-year documentation.
v = Vouched to policies or agreements and vendor invoice.
F = Footed.

CF = Crossfooted.
C = Calculated.
TB = Carried forward to the Trial Balance.

of the first round of adverse opinions on internal controls under Sarbanes–Oxley requirements cited tax accounting control weaknesses.[4] In addition, income tax expense is one of the largest items on the income statement. *Accounting Standard Codification 740* (ASC 740) requires companies to estimate deferred income tax assets and liabilities, both of which are very subjective. An important aspect of ASC 740 requires a higher standard for tax benefits before they can be recognized in a company's financial statements. Public accounting firms normally include tax specialists on the audit team to assess tax liabilities and estimates. The procedures for auditing estimates (discussed in detail in Chapter 10) are generally followed, including evaluating controls over management's procedures for determining assumptions and calculating the amounts. Basic audit procedures are similar to those discussed for accrued liabilities: Auditors vouch payments, test the expense, and recalculate the liability. All tax returns and government communications are carefully reviewed.

AUDITING INSIGHT   H&R Block Is Taxing

As part of its ongoing work to remediate control weaknesses in its corporate tax function, **H&R Block** restated its results for fiscal years 2005 and 2004 as well as previously reported quarterly results for fiscal 2006. The restatement pertains principally to errors in determining the company's state income tax rate, resulting in a cumulative understatement of its state income tax liability of approximately $32 million as of April 30, 2005.

Source: H&R Block press release, February 23, 2006.

Property, Plant, and Equipment and Intangible Assets

Management makes assertions about *existence, completeness, rights and obligations,* and *valuation and allocation.* Typical specific assertions relating to property, plant, and equipment (PP&E) and intangible assets include these:

- Recorded PP&E exist.
- All PP&E are recorded (completeness).

[4]K. Frieswick, *CFO Magazine*, November 7, 2005, www.cfo.com/article.cfm/5077959/c_2984354/?f5archives.

- PP&E are owned (rights).
- Repair and maintenance expense does not include items that should have been capitalized (completeness).
- Freight-in is included as part of purchase and added to equipment costs (valuation).
- Purchased goodwill is properly valued (valuation).
- Goodwill is not impaired (valuation).
- Capitalized intangible costs relate to intangibles acquired in exchange transactions (existence).
- Amortization and depreciation expenses are properly allocated (valuation).
- Items listed in PP&E are used in operations (classification).

The two primary means of gathering evidence supporting management's assertions with respect to PP&E are physical inspection and vouching. The principal goal of the physical inspection of PP&E is to determine actual *existence* and condition of the property (*valuation*). The auditor should compare the inspection of equipment to the detailed PP&E records. Unlike current assets, most of the items in PP&E were also in the account in the previous year. Therefore, if the company was audited last year, the audit team can trace existing items to the previous-year audit documentation. The cost of newly acquired PP&E can be vouched to invoices, purchase documents, or physically inspected (*existence, valuation*), and title documents (for items such as land, buildings) may be inspected (*rights and obligations*). Disposals of items that were on last year's list should also be traced to cash receipts records if they were sold or to other documentation if they were traded in, donated, or abandoned. Auditors also should prepare or obtain a schedule of casualty insurance on buildings and equipment and determine the adequacy of insurance in relation to asset market values. Auditors should always keep their eyes open for buildings or equipment not in use. Equipment not in use with no intention of being used in the future (e.g., held for disposal or sale) should not be included in PP&E.

The depreciation schedule is audited by recalculating the depreciation expense (*valuation or allocation*), using the company's methods, estimates of useful life, and estimates of residual value. Auditors also must evaluate the useful lives and residual values assigned by the client for reasonableness. Industry groups often publish tables of useful lives of assets commonly found in the industry. The asset acquisition and disposition information in the schedule gives auditors some key information for auditing the asset additions and disposals. When the schedule covers hundreds of assets and numerous additions and disposals, auditors can use (1) CAATs to recalculate the depreciation expense and (2) sampling to choose additions and disposals for tests of controls and substantive procedures. See Exhibit 8.9 for an abbreviated illustration of audit documentation for PP&E and depreciation. Note that the ending balances of PP&E, accumulated depreciation, and depreciation expense are carried forward to the trial balance.

AUDITING INSIGHT   The Sign of the Credit Balance

Auto Parts & Repair Inc. kept perpetual inventory records and equipment records on a computerized system. Because of the size of the files (8,000 parts in various locations and 1,500 asset records), the company never printed reports for visual inspection. Auditors ran a computer-audit "sign test" on inventory balances and equipment net book balances that called for a printed report for all balances less than zero. The auditors discovered 320 negative inventory balances that were caused by employees' failure to record purchases and 125 negative net asset balances caused by depreciating assets more than their cost.

[5]"Goodwill Impairment Slide Continues in U.S., Says KPMG Study," Press Release, www.kpmg.com/us/en/issuesandinsights/articlespublications/press-releases/pages/goodwill-impairment-slide-continues-2011-study.aspx.

EXHIBIT 8.9   Sample PP&E and Depreciation

				DUNDER-MIFFLIN INC. **Building and Land Improvements** **for Year Ended 12/31/2017** **Prepared By Client**			**F-1**	
							Prepared by RJR	2/18/18
							Reviewed by TJL	2/20/18

	Asset Cost ($)				Accumulated Depreciation ($)			
Description	**Beginning Balance**	**Added**	**Sold**	**Ending Balance**	**Beginning Balance**	**Depreciation Expense**	**Sold**	**Ending Balance**
Building 1	$218,367 PY	$ 0	$ 0	$218,367	$54,591 PY	$10,918 C	$ 0	$65,509
Building 2	0	155,976 v	0	155,976	0	1,050 C	0	1,050
Building 1 improvements	149,737 PY	109,825 v	10,000 E	249,562	37,434 PY	10,232 C	2,500 C	45,166
Total buildings and improvements	$368,104	$265,801	$10,000	$623,905	$92,025	$22,200	$2,500	$111,725
	F	F	F	F/CF	F	F	F	F/CF

PY = Agreed to prior-year documentation.
v = Vouched to purchase contract.
E = Examined sales agreement and related cash receipts.
F = Footed.

CF = Crossfooted.
C = Recalculated.
TB = Carried forward to the Trial Balance.

With respect to intangible assets, official documents of patents, copyrights, and trademark rights can be inspected to see that they are recorded in the client's name. Goodwill is of special interest to companies and auditors. A 2011 study by **KPMG** indicates $39 billion in goodwill impairment for U.S. companies in 2010.[5] The client must review goodwill for impairment, and the auditors must review and evaluate management's calculations and decisions to ensure that goodwill is correctly valued and impairments are properly recorded. Amortization of other intangibles should be recalculated. Similar to depreciation expense, this expense owes its existence to a calculation, and recalculation based on audited costs and rates is sufficient appropriate audit evidence.

Auditors inquire of company counsel about knowledge of any lawsuits or defects relating to patents, copyrights, trademarks, or trade names. Questions about lawsuits challenging patents, copyrights, or trade names can produce early knowledge of problem areas for further investigation. Likewise, discussions and questions about research and development successes and failures can alert the audit team to problems of valuation of intangible assets and related amortization expenses. Responses to questions about licensing of patents can be used in the audit of related royalty revenue accounts. Auditors can confirm royalty income from patent licenses received from a single licensee and review licensing and royalty contracts. However, such income amounts usually are audited by vouching the licensee's reports and the related cash receipt.

Vouching may be extensive in the areas of research and development (R&D) and deferred software development costs. The principal evidence problem is to determine whether costs are properly classified as assets or as R&D expenses. Recorded amounts generally are selected on a sample basis and the purchase orders, receiving reports, payroll records, authorization notices, and management reports are compared with them. Some R&D costs can resemble non-R&D costs (such as supplies, payroll costs), so auditors must be very careful in the vouching to be alert for costs that appear to relate to other operations.

Merger and acquisition transactions should be reviewed in terms of the appraisals, judgments, and allocations used to assign portions of the purchase price to tangible assets, intangible assets, liabilities, and goodwill. In the final analysis, nothing really substitutes for the inspection of transaction documentation, but verbal inquiries can help auditors to understand the circumstances of a merger. An illustrative plan of substantive procedures for PP&E and related accounts can be found in Appendix Exhibit 8B.3.

AUDITING INSIGHT · How Good Is Goodwill?

Northrop Grumman Corporation announced a fourth-quarter non-cash, after-tax charge of $3.0 to $3.4 billion for impairment of goodwill in accordance with *Accounting Standards Codification 350* (ASC 350), "Goodwill and Other Intangible Assets." Because of this charge, the company reported a net loss for the fourth quarter and in 2008. The company performed its required annual testing of goodwill as of November 30, 2008, using a discounted cash flow analysis supported by comparative market multiples to determine the fair values of its businesses versus their book values. Testing as of November 30, 2008, indicated that book values for shipbuilding and space technology exceeded the fair values of these businesses. The charge is attributable to goodwill recorded in connection with acquisitions made in 2001 and 2002.

Source: Northrop Grumman press release, January 22, 2009, www.irconnect.com/noc/press/pages/news_releases.html?d5158124.

Other Expenses

As mentioned earlier, most expense accounts can be tested in conjunction with tests of related assets and liabilities (e.g., depreciation) or through analytical procedures. However, if risk of material misstatement is high, expenses can be tested by **tests of details**, by which a sample of significant transactions is tested much like a test of controls except that auditors look for evidence that the significant transactions are properly recorded rather than that controls are operating. Payroll expense is usually audited by testing controls or using substantive tests of transactions and performing analytical procedures (see Appendix 8C). Some expenses should be examined separately because of their unique nature. For example, the client should list legal and professional expenses, and significant amounts should be vouched so the auditors can determine what legal and professional services the client is using. Miscellaneous expenses likewise should be listed and examined for significant unusual items. Finally, maintenance and repairs should be examined to determine whether any items should be capitalized.

Presentation and Disclosure

Once auditors are satisfied that controls have been examined and significant transactions and balances have been appropriately tested, the job is not over. The accounts in the acquisition and expenditure cycle require many disclosures. Depreciation methods, asset impairments, leases, and details about income taxes are only a few of the essential items with specific presentation and disclosure requirements. These disclosures must ensure that the presentation and disclosure assertions of *occurrence and rights and obligations, completeness, classification and understandability,* and *accuracy and valuation* are all met.

☑ REVIEW CHECKPOINTS

8.18 How do audit procedures for prepaid expenses and accrued liabilities also provide audit evidence about related expense accounts?

8.19 What assertions found in PP&E, investments, and intangibles accounts are of interest to an auditor during the examination of the expenditure and acquisition cycle?

8.20 What items in a client's PP&E and depreciation schedule give auditors points of departure (assertions) for audit procedures?

8.21 What methods are used to audit other expense accounts?

AUDIT RISK MODEL APPLIED

LO 8-7

Apply your knowledge to perform audit procedures in the acquisition and expenditure cycle and evaluate the findings of your tests.

Now that the elements of risk of material misstatement for the acquisition and expenditure cycle as well as some of the important substantive procedures have been presented, let's examine how auditors might apply the audit risk model for the completeness and classification assertions.

Chi-Chi's Clothing Stores Inc. Example

Chi-Chi's Clothing Stores Inc. is a chain of women's clothing stores that sells upscale fashions, mostly in the northeastern United States. Chi-Chi's is a public company with annual sales increasing at a rate of almost 30 percent per year. David Escobar has been assigned as the senior auditor. The policy of his firm is to always set overall audit risk as low. Chi-Chi's accounting department and systems have not kept up with the rapid growth. As a result, numerous audit adjustments have been required every year, and the company received an adverse report on internal controls in the previous year. One problem has been that invoices do not come from the stores on a timely basis. The company has been very profitable, causing enormous increases in management stock options, which are a significant part of management compensation. Although the economy has taken a downturn, management and analyst forecasts still project a 30 percent growth rate. Escobar is concerned that management could be biased toward understating costs and liabilities and therefore sets inherent risk at high.

As mentioned, controls have not kept pace with company growth. Chi-Chi's has been working to improve the systems, but the accounting department and internal audit department are overworked. Their staff members have not had time to sufficiently test new systems or train new personnel. Thus, Escobar assesses control risk as high and plans to test only year-end controls sufficiently to comply with AS 2201. In this situation, Escobar believes he must set risk of material misstatement as high and set detection risk at low. He will perform an extensive search for unrecorded liabilities, examining a large sample of disbursements after the balance sheet date, and he will send confirmations to vendors that historically have had activity but have small or zero year-end balances. Escobar also will vouch a sample of additions to PP&E accounts to ensure they are not items that should be expensed. The combination of high inherent risk, high control risk, and low detection risk should lead Escobar to an acceptably low overall audit risk.

Finding Fraud Signs in Accounts Payable

Fraudsters can have a field day generating false payments through a company's acquisition and expenditure systems. A common scheme is to send false invoices on the letterhead of a fictitious vendor to the company and have an insider manipulate supporting documents or controls to make payments. Sometimes, a company's own employees engage in unauthorized "business" as suppliers to their employers. In these cases, the perpetrators receive company payments from these "vendors" for personal use.

These frauds can proceed undetected for a long time as long as auditors and managers do not identify the signs and signals the perpetrators leave behind. If the review for fraud risk indicates that a potential significant risk of fraud exists in the acquisition and

AUDITING INSIGHT   Did We Take Him to the Hospital?

Olaronke Fakunle pleaded guilty to defrauding **Star Air Ambulance Service** of $210,000 between September 7, 2007, and October 9, 2008. Fakunle was able to divert money from the organization by setting up Blackbaud, a false corporation, and creating fictitious invoices for that company. A week after the controller at Star began an internal investigation into payments to Blackbaud, Fakunle gave her two weeks' notice. She then went to work for **Rosen Canada Ltd.,** where she fraudulently received $54,885 using a similar fictitious vendor scheme.

Source: "Stars Bilked for $210,000," *The Daily Herald-Tribune* (Grande Prairie, Alberta, Canada), November 9, 2010.

expenditure cycle, auditors can try several types of searches and matches in the company's records. These searches and matches are often performed using CAATs.

- *Inspect the invoices in the files for photocopies.* Fraudsters alter real invoices for false or duplicate payments and make photocopies to hide whiteout and cut-and-paste changes.
- *Inspect vendor's invoices submitted in numerical order.* False vendors sometimes use the same pad of prenumbered invoices (easily purchased at an office supply store) to send bills to the company. Either the company is the vendor's only customer, or the company is a victim of a false billing scheme.
- *Inspect vendor's invoices for invoices that always are in round numbers.* Prices, shipping charges, and taxes too often come in penny amounts, making a vendor's invoice in even dollars an unusual occurrence.
- *Scan vendor's invoices for invoices that are always slightly lower than a review threshold.* Insiders know that a company gives special attention and approval to invoices over a specified dollar amount (e.g., $10,000). Therefore, the fraudster always avoids invoices for more than that amount.
- *Scan vendor files for vendors with only post office box addresses.* Although many businesses use post office box addresses for receiving payments, files also should show a street address location.
- *Scan vendor invoices for invoices with no listed telephone number.* Legitimate businesses normally do not hide behind unlisted telephone numbers. In addition, cheap fraudsters sometimes do not buy a phone line for their false companies.
- *Match vendor and employee addresses and telephone numbers.* Many companies have policies that their employees cannot also be vendors. Insiders (employees) often know how to circumvent controls when their business with the employer could be suspicious.
- *Scan multiple vendors at the same address and telephone number.* Many invoices from the same location, especially invoices for different kinds of products and services, could simply come from a front organization conducting a false invoice scheme. However, legitimate suppliers often operate under several company names and conduct business from the same location and office parks with multiple offices at the same street address exist. This procedure can be done quickly with CAATs and is a red flag that should be investigated.
- *Vouch a sample of vendor invoices to the approved vendor list.* All vendors should be approved. If a company is doing business with a vendor not on the approved vendor list, this relationship should be investigated. Look for names that are similar, but not the same. For example, the company may be doing business with Dan's Hardware Supply and a fraudster may submit invoices for Don's Hardware Service (an account the fraudster has established at a bank).
- *Review invoices for addresses of the local mail drops (e.g., shipping and packaging stores that accept client mail).* These stores provide a street address for fraudulent companies, adding false legitimacy to their fraudulent invoices. However, legitimate companies use these services as well. The use of such a mail drop is a red flag that needs further investigation.

✔ REVIEW CHECKPOINTS

8.22 What items could indicate a significant risk of fraud in the acquisition and expenditure cycle (i.e., be red flags)?

8.23 Describe the purpose and give examples of specific fraud detection procedures in the acquisition and expenditure cycle.

8.24 Are these specific fraud detection procedures designed to detect fraudulent financial reporting or misappropriation of assets? Explain.

AUDITING INSIGHT | Using IDEA in the Audit
Credit Authorization Controls

Significant issues in accounts payable occur when vendors that are not on the approved vendor list are paid. Auditors can take advantage of CAATs by comparing all vendor payments to the approved vendor list. In the past, such a complete test was virtually impossible, and the best the auditors could do was to test a sample of payments. In addition, auditors can search for duplicate payments to vendors. Only a few vendor payments should reoccur each month for the exact amount (e.g., loan payments, insurance payments, rents). A vendor being paid for goods or services repeatedly for the exact amount of money may indicate a fraud.

To gather evidence in these situations, an auditor will most likely join the approved vendor list with the cash disbursements list or purchase journal. In addition, the auditor can request the program to provide a listing of identical payments to the same vendor. The resulting reports should be carefully reviewed by the auditor and evidence gathered as to the propriety of the items.

At the end of this chapter, you can perform this exception test in Exercise 8.59.

FRAUD CASES: EXTENDED AUDIT PROCEDURES (ISA/AS 2301)

The audit of account balances consists of making procedural efforts to detect errors and frauds that could exist in the balances, thus making them misleading in financial statements.

Case 8.1

Printing (Copying) Money

PROBLEM

Argus Productions Inc., a motion picture and commercial production company, assigned M. Welby the authority and responsibility for obtaining copies of scripts used in production. Established procedures permitted Welby to arrange for outside script-copying services, receive the copies, and approve the bills for payment. In effect, Welby was the "purchasing department" and the "receiving department" for this particular service. To a certain extent, he was also the "accounting department" by virtue of approving bills for payment and coding them for assignment to projects. Welby did not make the actual accounting entries or sign the checks.

Welby set up a fictitious company under the registered name Quickprint Company with himself as the incorporator and stockholder complete with a post office box number, letterhead stationery, and nicely printed invoices but no printing equipment. Legitimate copy services were "subcontracted" by Quickprint to perform the actual printing and then billed Quickprint. Welby then prepared Quickprint invoices billing Argus, usually at the legitimate shop's rate, but for a few extra copies each time. Welby also submitted Quickprint bills to Argus for fictitious copying jobs on scripts for movies and commercials that never went into production. As the owner of Quickprint, Welby endorsed Argus's checks with a rubber stamp and deposited the money in the business bank account, paid the legitimate printing bills, and took the rest for personal use.

Argus's production cost files contained all of the Quickprint bills sorted under the names of the movie and commercial production projects. Welby even created files for proposed films that never went into full production and thus should not have had script-copying costs. There were no copying service bills from any shop other than Quickprint Company.

Welby conducted this fraud for five years, embezzling $475,000 in false and inflated billings. (Argus's net income was overstated a modest amount because copying costs were capitalized as part of production cost and then amortized over a two- to three-year period.)

AUDIT APPROACH

Management should assign the authority to request copies and the purchasing authority to different responsible employees. Other persons also should perform the accounting, including coding cost assignments to projects. Managerial review of production results could result in notice of excess costs.

The request for the quantity (number) of copies of a script should come from a person involved in production who knows the number needed. This person also should sign off for the receipt (or approve the bill) for this requested number of copies, thus acting as the "receiving department." This procedure could prevent waste (excess cost), especially if the requesting person also were held responsible for the profitability of the project. A company agent always performs actual purchasing, and in this case, the agent was Welby. Purchasing agents generally have latitude to seek the best service at the best price with or without bids from competitors. A requirement to obtain bids is usually a good idea, but much legitimate purchasing is done without bid. However, an approval process should be employed before vendors are placed on the approved vendor list.

Someone in the accounting department should be responsible for coding invoices for charges to authorized projects, thus making it possible to detect costs charged to projects not actually in production. Someone with managerial responsibility should review project costs and the purchasing practices. However, this is an expensive use of executive time. It was not spent in the Argus case.

In gaining an understanding of the internal controls, auditors could learn of the trust and responsibility vested in Welby. Because the embezzlement was about $95,000 per year, the total copying cost under Welby's control must have been around $1 million or more. (It might attract unwanted attention to inflate a cost more than 10 percent.)

Controls were very weak, especially in the combination of duties performed by Welby and in the lack of managerial review. For all practical purposes, there were no controls to test other than to see whether Welby had approved the copying cost bills and coded them to active projects. This provides an opportunity because proper classification is a control objective.

The auditors should select a sample of project files and vouch costs charged to them to support source documents (*occurrence* direction of the test). Select a sample of expenditures and trace them to the project cost records shown coded on the expenditures (*completeness* direction of the test).

Substantive procedures are directed at obtaining evidence about the *existence* of film projects, *completeness* of the costs charged to them, *valuation* of the capitalized project costs, *rights* in copyright and ownership, and proper *disclosure* of amortization methods. The most important procedures are the same as the tests of control activities; thus, when performed at the year-end date on the capitalized cost balances, they are dual-purpose audit procedures. Either of the procedures described earlier as tests of controls should show evidence of projects that had never gone into production. (Auditors should be careful to obtain a list of actual projects before they begin the procedures.) Chances are good that the discovery of bad project codes with copying cost will reveal a pattern of Quickprint bills.

Knowing that controls over copying cost are weak, auditors could be tipped off to the possibility of a Welby-Quickprint connection. Efforts to locate Quickprint should be taken (telephone book, chamber of commerce, other directories). Inquiry with the secretary of state for names of the Quickprint incorporators should reveal Welby's connection. The audit findings can then be turned over to a trained investigator to arrange an interview and confrontation with Welby.

DISCOVERY SUMMARY

In this case, internal auditors performed a review of project costs at the request of the manager of production, who was worried about profitability. The auditors performed the procedures described earlier, noticed the dummy projects and the Quickprint bills, investigated the ownership of Quickprint, and discovered Welby's association. They had first tried to locate Quickprint's shop but could not find it in the telephone, chamber of commerce, or other city directories. They were careful not to direct any mail to the post office box for fear of alerting the then-unknown parties involved. A sly internal auditor already had used a ruse at the post office and learned that Welby rented the box, but the auditors did not know whether anyone else was involved. Alerted, the internal auditors gathered all Quickprint bills and determined the total charged for nonexistent projects. Carefully, under the covert observation of a representative of the local district attorney's office, Welby was interviewed and readily confessed.

Case 8.2

Real Cash Paid to Phony Doctors

PROBLEM

As manager of the medical claims processing department, Martha Lee was considered one of Beta Magnetic's best employees. She had never missed a day of work in 10 years, and her department had one of the company's best efficiency ratings. Controls were considered good, including the verification by a claims processor that (1) the patient was a Beta employee, (2) medical treatments were covered in the plan, (3) the charges were within approved guidelines, (4) the cumulative claims for the employee did not exceed $50,000 (paid all claims less than $50,000 but submitted claims more than $50,000 to an insurance company), and (5) the calculation for payment was correct. After verification processing, claims were sent to the claims payment department to pay the doctor directly. No payments ever went directly to employees.

Lee prepared false claims on real employees, forging the signatures of various claims processors, adding her own review approval, and naming bogus doctors who would be paid by the payment department. The payments were mailed to various post office box addresses and to her husband's business address.

Nobody ever verified claims information with the employees. The employees received no reports of medical benefits paid on their behalf. Although the department had performance reports by claims processors, these reports did not show claim-by-claim details. No one verified the credentials of the doctors. As noted, Martha never missed a day of work for vacation or sickness. She was considered an ideal employee.

The falsified claim forms were in Beta's files, containing all fictitious data on employee names, processor signatures, doctors' bills, and phony doctors and addresses. The canceled checks were returned by the bank and were kept in Beta's files, containing "endorsements" by the doctors. Lee and her husband were clever: They deposited the checks in various banks in accounts opened in the names of the "doctors."

Lee did not stumble on the audit trail. She drew the attention of an auditor who saw her take her 24 claims processing employees out to an annual staff appreciation luncheon in a fleet of stretch limousines.

Over the seven years, Lee and her husband had stolen $3.5 million and, until the last, no one noticed anything unusual about the total amount of claims paid.

AUDIT APPROACH

The controls were good as far as they went. The claims processors used internal data in their work: employee files for identification, treatment descriptions submitted by doctors with comparisons with plan provisions, and mathematical calculations. This work amounted to all approval necessary for the claims payment department to prepare a check. No controls connected the claims data with outside sources such as employee acknowledgment or doctor investigation. Employees certainly should be notified of any payments made on their behalf.

By never taking a day off, Lee was able to make sure she saw all documents related to her scheme. The company needed an enforced vacation and employee rotation policy.

The processing and control work in the claims payment department can be audited for deviations from controls. The auditors should select a sample of paid claims and re-perform the claims processing procedures to verify the employee status, coverage of treatment, proper guideline charges, cumulative amount of less than $50,000, and accurate calculation. However, this procedure would not help answer the question, "Does Martha Lee steal the money to pay for the limousines?"

"Thinking like a crook" points out the holes in the controls. Nobody seeks to verify data with external sources. However, the audit team must be careful in an investigation not to cast aspersions on a manager by letting rumors start when interviewing employees to find out whether they actually had the medical attention whose claim is paid on their behalf. If money is being taken, the company check must be intercepted in some manner.

The balance under audit is the sum of the charges in the employee medical benefits expense account, and the objective relates to the valid existence of the payments.

The first procedure can be as follows: Obtain a list of doctors paid by the company and look them up in the state medical society directory. Look up their business addresses and determine whether they are valid. You could try comparing claims processors' signatures on various forms, but this is difficult and requires training. An extended procedure would be as follows: Compare the doctors' addresses to addresses known to be associated with Lee and other claims processing employees.

DISCOVERY SUMMARY

The comparison of doctors to the medical society directory showed eight "doctors" who were not licensed in the current period. Five of these eight had post office box addresses, and discrete inquiries and surveillance showed that Lee rented them. The other three had the same mailing address as her husband's business. Further investigation involving the district attorney and police was necessary to obtain personal financial records and reconstruct the thefts from prior years.

 REVIEW CHECKPOINTS

8.25 What key control concept was missing at Argus Productions?

8.26 What evidence could the *verbal inquiry* audit procedure provide in "Printing (Copying) Money"?

8.27 If Lee had not been seen taking employees out in a limousine, how else could she have been caught?

8.28 How would a policy of mandatory vacations have helped discover the Beta fraud?

AUDIT ISSUES IN THE EXPENSE AND ACQUISITION CYCLE

Auditing the acquisition and expenditure cycle is not straightforward. Because it is ripe for fraud, an auditor must be aware that inappropriate policies and procedures or poor execution of processes can lead to problems for the client as illustrated by the following Auditing Insight.

 AUDITING INSIGHT | **It's Not a Fraud—It's Just a Mess**

When Jim Farrelly took over as executive director of the **Pasco Hernando Early Learning Coalition,** arranging for an audit was at the top of his to-do list. The CPA firm of **Woodruff, Wardlow, Nelson & Cash** found the following:

- Purchases costing more than $5,000 were made without board approval in violation of the agency's policy.
- An American Express card used by staffers was in the name of a director rather than the Coalition.
- Invoices submitted to the State Office of Early Learning did not match amounts on invoices submitted for payment.
- The financial records used to report expenditures incurred for services provided for school readiness and voluntary prekindergarten programs could not be relied upon and were inaccurate.
- Sloppy record keeping did not reflect employees' paid leave time.
- Methods of recording fixed assets were inadequate.
- Backup documentation for transactions in accounts payable was lacking.
- One staffer handled bills *and* paid them.

- No staffers were qualified in applying generally accepted accounting practices to record financial transactions and prepare financial statements.

The CPA firm's recommendations included the following:

- Accounts payable should be coordinated by the fiscal manager, office manager, and executive director.
- Invoices should not be paid without purchase documentation.
- All transactions exceeding $5,000 should be noted with the date of board approval.
- A computer-based system of inventory control using bar codes should be established.
- A computer system should be established for tracking employees' accrued time off.
- Invoices submitted for state reimbursement should require paperwork showing that the amount matches the invoices.

Source: "Board 'Disturbed' by Audit Findings," *Tampa Bay-Times,* May 17, 2008, p. 8.

Even with proper diligence and due professional care, it may be difficult to identify all issues related to expenses, purchases, and unrecorded items. This is illustrated in the Auditing Insight that lists matters identified by the Public Company Accounting Oversight Board (PCAOB) during its annual inspections for audits conducted by the Big Four firms.

AUDITING INSIGHT	PCAOB Inspections and the Expenditure and Acquisition Cycle

- The Firm's analytical procedures to test operating expenses did not meet the requirements for substantive analytical procedures because, in one procedure, the Firm did not set a threshold for investigation and evaluation that allowed it to achieve the desired level of assurance and, in another procedure, there was no evidence in the audit documentation, and no persuasive other evidence, that the Firm had obtained corroboration of management's explanations for significant differences from the Firm's expectations.

- The issuer completed a significant acquisition during the year. The Firm failed to perform audit procedures regarding the revenues and expenses of the acquired company from the date of acquisition to year-end.

- The Firm failed to perform sufficient substantive procedures to test certain long-lived assets and related accounts payable because it designed its procedures based on a level of reliance on internal control that was excessive due to the deficiencies in the Firm's testing of controls.

- [For the control], which consisted of management's review of certain expense calculations, the Firm's procedures were limited to inquiring of management and inspecting email correspondence as evidence that the reviews had occurred. The Firm's procedures to test these controls did not include evaluating whether the controls operated at a level of precision that would prevent or detect material misstatements, as it failed to evaluate the criteria used by the control owner to identify matters for investigation and the process for investigating and resolving such matters. In addition, the Firm failed to evaluate whether misstatements that had not been prevented by the issuer's controls should have had an effect on its conclusion about the effectiveness of controls.

Sources: 2005, 2008, 2011 PCAOB Inspection of Deloitte & Touche (November 30, 2006; April 16, 2009, November 28, 2012); 2011 PCAOB Inspection of Ernst & Young (December 6, 2012); 2006, 2014 Inspection of KPMG (January 11, 2007; October 15, 2015); and 2008 PCAOB Inspection of Pricewaterhouse Coopers (March 25, 2009). All reports can be found on the PCAOB's website, http://pcaobus.org/Inspections/Reports/Pages/default.aspx.

Summary

The acquisition and expenditure cycle consists of purchase requisitioning, purchase ordering, receiving goods and services, recording vendors' invoices, recording accounts payable, and making cash disbursements. Companies reduce control risk by having a suitable separation of authorization, custody, recording, and periodic reconciliation duties. Error-checking procedures requiring the comparison of purchase orders, receiving reports, and vendor invoices are important for recording proper amounts of accounts payable liabilities. Having a separation of duties between preparing cash disbursement checks and actually signing them provides supervisory control. Otherwise, many things—ranging from processing false or fictitious purchase orders to failing to record liabilities for goods and services received—could go wrong.

Purchases are executed for a myriad of items, including inventory; property, plant, and equipment; supplies; and all other items necessary for a business to operate. Large purchases for capital equipment may be significant items requiring the auditors' inspection and review. Reviewing the accruals for income taxes may be complex, especially if the organization is operating in multiple tax jurisdictions. The use of a tax specialist may be appropriate in auditing income tax expense.

The *completeness* assertion is important in the audit of liabilities because misleading financial statements often have involved unrecorded liabilities and expenses. The search for unrecorded liabilities is an important set of audit procedures.

Key Terms

approved vendor list: A record of vendors that have been vetted to ensure that vendors meet company policy and procedure in terms of price, quality, delivery, etc. This control activity provides evidence of vendor existence to auditors.

bill of lading: A contract between the shipper and the carrier; includes shipping information such as ship dates and origination, purchase order number, and signatures for receipt of merchandise.

capitalizing: The recording of expenditures as assets and charging them to expense by a systematic allocation over a number of years.

clearing accounts [Appendix 8C]: The temporary storage places for transactions awaiting final accounting that should eventually have zero balances.

electronic data interchange (EDI): The transfer of data between/among different companies using networks such as the Internet.

ghost employees [Appendix 8C]: The fictitious or separated employees fraudulently maintained on the payroll to obtain checks.

imprest bank account [Appendix 8C]: An account used for special purposes such as payroll or branch banking that is maintained at a zero or fixed balance in the general ledger. Checks written on the account are offset by deposits of the same amount.

matching: The recognition of expenses in the same period as associated revenues.

purchase order: A formal contractual document (may be a computer document) between a buyer and seller issued by the buyer establishing price, delivery point, delivery dates, and other information pertinent to the purchase.

purchase requisition: An internal document initialed by a department or person within the entity asking the purchasing department to buy specific goods or services.

receiving report: The documentation completed by the receiving department that includes receiving date and time, purchase order number, condition of material received, and amount of material received; provides evidence regarding the receipt of materials by the entity.

search for unrecorded liabilities: A substantive procedure to test the completeness assertion for liability accounts.

tests of details: The tests of a sample of transactions during the period for monetary errors.

vendor's invoice: A bill sent from the vendor to the entity purchasing the goods or services.

voucher/voucher package: A document used as a source for recording payables. It shows approvals, accounts, and amounts to be recorded, usually attached to the supporting purchase order, receiving report, and vendor invoice.

W-2 [Appendix 8C]: The annual report of gross salaries and wages and the income, Social Security, and Medicare taxes withheld.

Multiple-Choice Questions for Practice and Review

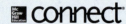 All applicable Exercises and Problems are available with *Connect*.

LO 8-1

8.29 Which of the following accounts does *not* appear in the acquisition and expenditure cycle?
 a. Cash.
 b. Purchases returns.
 c. Sales returns.
 d. Prepaid insurance.

LO 8-1

8.30 For which of the following accounts would the matching concept be the most appropriate?
 a. Cost of goods sold.
 b. Research and development.
 c. Depreciation expense.
 d. Sales.

LO 8-1

8.31 Which of the following would *not* overstate current-period net income?
 a. Capitalizing an expenditure that should be expensed.
 b. Failing to record a liability as an expense.
 c. Failing to record a check paying an item in Vouchers Payable.
 d. All of the above would overstate net income.

LO 8-2

8.32 A client's purchasing system ends with the recording of a liability and its eventual payment. Which of the following best describes auditors' primary concern with respect to liabilities resulting from the purchasing system?
 a. Accounts payable are not materially understated.
 b. Authority to incur liabilities is restricted to one designated person.
 c. Acquisition of materials is not made from one vendor or one group of vendors.
 d. Commitments for all purchases are made only after established competitive bidding procedures are followed.

LO 8-4   8.33   Which of the following is an internal control activity that could prevent a paid disbursement voucher from being presented for payment a second time?

    a. Vouchers should be prepared by individuals who are responsible for signing disbursement checks.

    b. Disbursement vouchers should be approved by at least two responsible management officials.

    c. The date on a disbursement voucher should be within a few days of the date the voucher is presented for payment.

    d. The official who signs the check should compare the check with the voucher and should stamp "PAID" on the voucher documents.

LO 8-4   8.34   Budd, the purchasing agent of Lake Hardware Wholesalers, has a relative who owns a retail hardware store. Budd arranged for hardware to be delivered by manufacturers to the retail store on a cash-on-delivery (C.O.D.) basis, thereby enabling his relative to buy at Lake's wholesale prices. Budd was probably able to accomplish this because of Lake's poor internal control over

    a. Purchase requisitions.

    b. Cash receipts.

    c. Perpetual inventory records.

    d. Purchase orders.

LO 8-6   8.35   Which of the following is the *best* audit procedure for determining the existence of unrecorded liabilities?

    a. Examine confirmation requests returned by creditors whose accounts are on a subsidiary trial balance of accounts payable.

    b. Examine a sample of cash disbursements in the period subsequent to year-end.

    c. Examine a sample of invoices a few days prior to and subsequent to the year-end to ascertain whether they have been properly recorded.

    d. Examine unusual relationships between monthly accounts payable and recorded purchases.

LO 8-6   8.36   Which of the following procedures is *least* likely to be performed before the balance-sheet date?

    a. Observation of inventory.

    b. Review of internal control over cash disbursements.

    c. Search for unrecorded liabilities.

    d. Confirmation of receivables.

LO 8-6   8.37   To determine whether accounts payable are complete, auditors perform a test to verify that all merchandise received has been recorded. The population for this test consists of all

    a. Vendors' invoices.

    b. Purchase orders.

    c. Receiving reports.

    d. Canceled checks.

                                                (AICPA adapted)

LO 8-6   8.38   When verifying debits to the perpetual inventory records of a nonmanufacturing company, auditors would be most interested in examining a sample of purchase

    a. Approvals.

    b. Requisitions.

    c. Invoices.

    d. Orders.

LO 8-4   8.39   A furniture company ordered 84 tables from a supplier. The supplier accidentally sent only 48 tables, but the receiving department at the furniture company accepted the tables. The invoice was eventually received but was for the original 84 tables. The furniture company paid the entire amount. Which of the following controls would have been *least* likely to have prevented this erroneous payment?

    a. The copy of the purchase order sent to the furniture company's receiving department should not have shown an expected quantity.

    b. Personnel in the furniture company's accounts payable department should compare the receiving report to the purchase invoice before creation of the voucher.

c. Personnel in the furniture company's cash disbursements department should compare the check that is prepared to all of the backup documentation.

d. Personnel in the furniture company's purchasing department should compare the purchase requisition with the purchase order.

LO 8-4

8.40 Curtis, a maintenance supervisor, submitted maintenance invoices from a phony repair company and received the checks at a post office box. This should have been prevented by

a. Comparison of the company name to the approved vendor list by the check signer.

b. Recognition of the excess maintenance costs by Curtis's supervisor.

c. Refusal by the purchasing department to approve the vendor.

d. All of the above.

LO 8-6

8.41 An audit team would most likely examine the detail support for charges to which of the following accounts?

a. Payroll expense.

b. Cost of goods sold.

c. Supplies expense.

d. Legal expense.

LO 8-6

8.42 Which of the following accounts would most likely be audited in connection with a related balance-sheet account?

a. Property Tax Expense.

b. Payroll Expense.

c. Research and Development.

d. Legal Expense.

LO 8-6

8.43 When auditing account balances of liabilities, auditors are most concerned with management's assertion about

a. Existence.

b. Rights and obligations.

c. Completeness.

d. Valuation and allocation.

LO 8-5

8.44 In a test of controls, auditors may trace receiving reports to vouchers recorded in the voucher register. This is a test for

a. Occurrence.

b. Completeness.

c. Classification.

d. Cutoff.

LO 8-4

8.45 A company employs three accounts payable clerks and one treasurer. Their responsibilities are as follows:

Employee	Responsibility
Clerk 1	Reviews vendor invoices for proper signature approval.
Clerk 2	Enters vendor invoices into the accounting system and verifies payment terms.
Clerk 3	Posts entered vendor invoices to the accounts payable ledger for payment and mails checks.
Treasurer	Reviews the vendor invoices and signs each check.

Which of the following would indicate a weakness in the company's internal control?

a. Clerk 1 opens all of the incoming mail.

b. Clerk 2 reconciles the accounts payable ledger with the general ledger monthly.

c. Clerk 3 mails the checks and remittances after they have been signed.

d. The treasurer uses a stamp for signing checks.

(AICPA adapted)

LO 8-6

8.46 Which of the following tests of details most likely would help an auditor determine whether accounts payable have been misstated?

a. Examining reported purchase returns that appear too low.

b. Examining vendor statements for amounts not reported as purchases.

c. Searching for customer-returned goods that were not reported as returns.

d. Reviewing bank transfers recorded as cash received from customers.

(AICPA adapted)

Exercises and Problems

All applicable Exercises and Problems are available with *Connect*.

LO 8-1, LO 8-2, LO 8-5

8.47 Payable ICQ Items: Assertions, Tests of Controls, and Possible Errors or Frauds. Following is a selection of items from internal control questionnaires.

1. Are purchase orders above a certain level approved by an officer?

2. Are the quantity and quality of goods received determined at the time of receipt by receiving personnel independent of the purchasing department?

3. Are vendors' invoices matched against purchase orders and receiving reports before a liability is recorded?

4. Are journal entries authorized at appropriate levels?

Required:

For each preceding item:

a. Identify the management assertion to which it applies.

b. Specify one test of controls auditors could use to determine whether the control was operating effectively.

c. Give an example of an error or fraud that could occur if the control were absent or ineffective.

d. Write a substantive procedure that could find errors or frauds that could result from the absence or ineffectiveness of the control items.

LO 8-6

8.48 Unrecorded Liabilities Procedures. You are in the final stages of your audit of the financial statements of Ozine Corporation for the year ended December 31, 2017, when the corporation's president consults you. The president believes there is no point to your examining the 2015 voucher register and testing data in support of 2018 entries. She stated that any bills pertaining to 2017 that were received too late to be included in the December voucher register were recorded by a year-end journal entry and the internal auditor tested for unrecorded liabilities after the year-end. The president will provide you a letter certifying that there are no unrecorded liabilities.

Required:

a. Should your procedures for unrecorded liabilities be affected by the fact that the client made a journal entry to record 2017 bills that were received later? Explain.

b. Should your test for unrecorded liabilities be affected by the fact that a letter is obtained in which a responsible management official certifies that, to the best of that person's knowledge, all liabilities have been recorded? Explain.

c. Should your test for unrecorded liabilities be eliminated or reduced because of the internal audit work? Explain.

d. What sources, in addition to the 2018 voucher register, should you consider for locating possible unrecorded liabilities?

(AICPA adapted)

LO 8-3, LO 8-6

8.49 Accounts Payable Confirmations. Partners Clark and Kent, both CPAs, are preparing their audit plan for the audit of accounts payable on Marlboro Corporation's annual audit. Saturday afternoon they reviewed the thick file of last year's documentation, and they both remembered too well the six days they spent last year on accounts payable.

Last year, Clark had suggested that they mail confirmations to 100 of Marlboro's suppliers. The company regularly purchases from about 1,000 suppliers, and these account payable balances fluctuate widely, depending on the volume of purchase and the terms Marlboro's purchasing agent is able to negotiate. Clark's sample of 100 was designed to include accounts with large balances. In fact, the 100 accounts confirmed last year covered 80 percent of the total dollars in accounts payable. Both Clark and Kent had spent many hours tracking down minor differences reported in confirmation responses. Nonresponding accounts were investigated by comparing Marlboro's balance with monthly statements received from suppliers.

Required:

    e. Identify the accounts payable audit objectives that auditors must consider in determining the audit procedures to be performed.

    f. Identify situations when auditors should use accounts payable confirmations, and discuss whether they are required to use them.

    g. Discuss why the use of large dollar balances as the basis for selecting accounts payable for confirmation is not the most effective approach, and indicate a more effective sample selection procedure that could be followed when choosing accounts payable for confirmation.

LO 8-6

8.50 **Search for Unrecorded Liabilities.** C. Marsh, CPA, is the independent auditor for Compufast Corporation, which sells personal computers, peripheral equipment (printers, data storage), and a wide variety of programs for business and games. From experience on Compufast's previous audits, Marsh knew that the company's accountants were very much concerned with timely recording of revenues and receivables and somewhat less concerned with keeping up-to-date records of accounts payable and other liabilities. Marsh knew that the control environment was strong in the asset area and weak in the liability area.

Required:

List substantive procedures that Marsh and the audit staff can perform to obtain reasonable assurance that Compufast's unrecorded liabilities are discovered and adjusted in the financial statements currently under audit.

LO 8-4, LO 8-5, LO 8-6

8.51 **Fictitious Vendors, Theft, and Embezzlement.** The following case is designed like the ones in the chapter. Your assignment is to write the audit approach portion of the cases organized around these sections:

    Objective. Express the objective in terms of the facts supposedly asserted in financial records, accounts, and statements.

    Control. Write a brief explanation of desirable controls, missing controls, and especially the kinds of "deviations" that could arise from the situation described in the case.

    Tests of controls. Write some procedures for getting evidence about existing controls, especially procedures that could discover deviations from controls. If there are no controls to test, then there are no procedures to perform; go to the next section. A "procedure" should instruct someone about the source(s) of evidence to tap and the work to do.

    Audit of balance. Write some procedures for getting evidence about the existence, completeness, valuation or allocation, or rights and obligations assertions identified in your objective section.

    Discovery summary. Write a short statement about the discovery you expect to accomplish with your procedures.

    Bailey Books Inc. is a retail distributor of upscale books, periodicals, and magazines. Bailey has 431 retail stores throughout the southeastern states. Three full-time purchasing agents work at corporate headquarters. They are responsible for purchasing all inventory at the best prices available from wholesale suppliers. They can purchase with or without obtaining competitive bids. The three purchasing agents are R. McGuire in charge of purchasing books, M. Garza in charge of purchasing magazines and periodicals, and L. Collins (manager of purchasing) in charge of ordering miscellaneous items such as paper products and store supplies.

    One of the purchasing agents is suspected of taking kickbacks from vendors. In return, Bailey is thought to be paying inflated prices, which first are recorded in inventory and then in cost of goods sold and other expense accounts as the assets are sold or used.

    The duties of Collins, the manager in charge, do not include audit or inspection of the performance of the other two purchasing agents. No one audits or reviews Collins's performance.

    The purchasing system is computerized and detail records are retained. An extract from these records is in Exhibit 8.47.1.

    This kickback scheme has been going on for two or three years. Bailey Books could have overpaid by several hundred thousand dollars.

(ACFE adapted)

LO 8-1, LO 8-4

8.52 **Bidding Process.** Maine Construction builds office buildings. The buildings generally cost between $5 million and $8 million to build, and the plumbing can cost between $300,000 and $600,000 depending on the building requirements. Therefore, Maine always sends the

EXHIBIT 8.51.1   BAILEY BOOKS, INC

Selected Purchases 2015–2017

Vendor	Items Purchased	2015	2016	2017	Date of Last Bid	Percent of Purchases Bid (3-yr. period)
Armour	Books	$ 83,409	$ 02,929	$ 810,103	12/01/13	87%
Burdick	Sundries	62,443	70,949	76,722	—	—
Canon	Magazines	1,404,360	1,947,601	2,361,149	11/03/15	94
DeBois, Inc.	Paper	321,644	218,404	121,986	06/08/15	57
Elton Books	Books	874,893	781,602	649,188	07/21/15	91
Fergeson	Books	921,666	1,021,440	1,567,811	09/08/15	88
Guyford	Magazines	2,377,821	2,868,988	3,262,490	10/08/15	81
Hyman, Inc.	Supplies	31,640	40,022	46,911	10/22/15	—
Intertec	Books	821,904	898,683	949,604	11/18/15	86
Jerrico	Paper	186,401	111,923	93,499	10/04/15	72
Julian-Borg	Magazines	431,470	589,182	371,920	02/07/15	44
King Features	Magazines	436,820	492,687	504,360	11/18/15	89
Lycorp	Sundries	16,280	17,404	21,410	—	—
Medallian	Books	—	61,227	410,163	12/15/15	99
Northwood	Books	861,382	992,121	—	12/07/14	—
Orion Corp.	Paper	86,904	416,777	803,493	11/02/14	15
Peterson	Supplies	114,623	—	—	N/A	N/A
Quick	Supplies	—	96,732	110,441	11/03/15	86
Robertson	Books	2,361,912	3,040,319	3,516,811	12/01/15	96
Steele	Magazines	621,490	823,707	482,082	11/03/15	90
Telecom	Sundries	81,406	101,193	146,316	—	—
Union Bay	Books	4,322,639	4,971,682	5,368,114	12/03/15	97
Victory	Magazines	123,844	141,909	143,286	06/09/15	89
Williams	Sundries	31,629	35,111	42,686	—	—

plumbing work out for bid before deciding on whom to use as a subcontractor. The company has had 21 projects over the past five years with $10 million dollars in plumbing contracts being sent out for bids.

Over the past five years, Maine has asked for bids from three contractors: Beltran Plumbing, Delgado Plumbing Services, and Wright Contracting–Plumbing Specialists. Each vendor has been reviewed by Maine and is on Maine's approved vendor list.

Required:

For each of the following situations (each situation is independent), determine whether the auditor should be concerned about the controls over the bidding process. If yes, what control would you recommend to Maine to ensure a fair and honest bidding process?

a. Of the 21 projects sent out for bid, Wright had the winning bid on 12 of the projects.

b. Of the 21 projects sent out for bid, Wright had the winning bid on 12 of the projects. In each of these bidding processes, Wright's bid was the last bid received.

c. Of the 21 projects sent out for bid, each vendor had the winning bid on 7 of the projects.

d. Of the 21 projects sent out for bid, Delgado was awarded 5 contracts even though he did not have the lowest bid.

LO 8-7

8.53 **Grounds for Dismissal.** This case is designed like the ones in the chapter. Your assignment is to write the "audit approach" portion of the case organized around these sections: *Objective.* Express the objective in terms of the facts supposedly asserted in financial records, accounts, and statements.

Control. Write a brief explanation of desirable controls, missing controls, and especially the types of "deviations" that might arise from the situation described in the case.

Tests of controls. Write some audit procedures for getting evidence about existing controls, especially procedures that could discover deviations from controls. If there are no controls to test, then there are no procedures to perform; go to the next section. A "procedure" should instruct someone about the source(s) of evidence to tap and the work to do.

e. Determine whether corresponding retirements of replaced PP&E have occurred and have been properly entered in the detail records.

f. Select major additions for the year and a random sample of other additions, and inspect the physical assets.

g. Vouch a sample of charges in the Repairs account, and determine whether they are proper repairs, not capital items.

h. Review the useful lives, depreciation methods, and salvage values for reasonableness. Recalculate depreciation.

i. Study loan documents for terms and security of loans obtained for purchase of PP&E.

j. Inspect title documents for automotive and real estate assets.

k. Analyze the productive economic use of PP&E to determine whether any other-than-temporary impairment is evident.

(AICPA adapted)

LO 8-6

8.57 **CAATs Application—PP&E.** You are supervising the audit fieldwork of Sparta Springs Company and need certain information from Sparta's equipment records, which are maintained on a computer file. The particular information is (1) net book value of assets so that your assistant can reconcile the subsidiary ledger to the general ledger control accounts (the general ledger contains an account for each asset type at each plant location) and (2) sufficient data to enable your assistant to find and inspect selected assets. The record layout of the master file follows:

Asset number.
Description.
Asset type.
Location code.
Year acquired.
Cost.
Accumulated depreciation, end of year (includes accumulated depreciation at the beginning of the year plus depreciation for year to date).
Depreciation for the year to date.
Useful life.

From the data file described earlier,

a. List the information needed to verify correspondence of the subsidiary detail records with the general ledger accounts. Does this work complete the audit of PP&E?

b. What additional data are needed to enable your assistant to inspect the assets?

LO 8-7

8.58 **Search for Unrecorded Liabilities.** The list of vouchers payable for Potter's Magic Shoppe at December 31 is as follows:

Vendor	Invoice Date	Amount
Hagrid Cleaning Services	11/15	$ 4,322.43
Hermione's Hats	12/02	2,167.76
Lockhart Magic Books	12/31	6,489.11
Malfoy Financial Consultants	12/28	23,752.63
McGonagall Veterinary Supplies	12/23	4,590.60
Moaning Myrtle's Mystical Capes	10/14	11,529.88
Nicholas Fancy Headwear	12/29	51,268.62
Snape's Snakes	12/28	36,152.45
Weasley's Wands	12/28	6,400.55
Hogwart's Rentals	12/15	53,000.00
Total vouchers payable		$199,674.03

Checks written in the following January are:

Check Number	Payee	Description	Invoice Date	Amount
1842	Malfoy Financial Consultants	Professional services	12/28	$23,752.63
1843	Hagrid Cleaning Services	October monthly cleaning	11/15	4,322.43
1844	Hogwart's Rentals	January rent	12/15	53,000.00
1845	Lockhart Magic Books	Inventory	12/31	6,489.11
1846	Dudley Pastries	Catering for office Christmas party	1/15	6,300.00
1847	Weasley's Wands	Inventory	12/28	6,400.55
1848	Rowlin' Enterprises	Trademark	1/1	10,000.00
1849	McGonagall Veterinary Supplies	Inventory	12/23	4,590.60
1850	Nicholas Fancy Headwear	Inventory	12/29	51,268.62
1851	Weasley's Wands	Inventory	12/31	6,400.55
1852	Hermione's Hats	Inventory	12/02	2,167.76
1853	Lockhart Magic Books	Inventory	12/31	5,932.89
1854	Hagrid Cleaning Service	November monthly cleaning	12/15	4,322.43
1855	Malfoy Financial Consultants	Professional services	1/28	13,888.56

Required

    a. Prepare an audit plan for the audit of unrecorded liabilities for Potter's Magic Shoppe.

    b. Prepare an adjusting journal entry to correct accounts payable. Potter's maintains perpetual inventory records, and the inventory was counted and adjusted on December 31.

LO 8-7

8.59 **Identifying Payments to Unauthorized Suppliers**

For this exercise, your client, BrightIDEAs Inc., has provided you with data for two related files, an accounts payable history file and a supplier master file. To test the authorization of purchases to only legitimate suppliers, the auditor must complete a series of related steps:

1. Import the client's database of accounts payable (pp. 102–111 of the IDEA Workbook).
2. Import the client's authorized supplier list (pp. 112–115 of the IDEA Workbook).
3. Merge the accounts payable and supplier databases (pp. 171–177 of the IDEA Workbook).
4. Identify payments to unauthorized suppliers (pp. 177–178 of the IDEA Workbook).

Required Data available on *Connect*

- ACCPAY2012.txt
- Supplier.xls

Applying IDEA to the Purchasing Cycle—Elm Manufacturing Company

Exercises 8.60, 8.61, and 8.62 require the application of IDEA in the purchasing cycle audit. Elm Manufacturing Company (ELM) is a small manufacturer of backpacks located in Rochelle, Illinois. You have access to ELM's electronic records in Connect. The appropriate files for these exercises are the Purchases 2017–4th Q dataset, as well as the Cash Disbursements 2017–4th Q dataset. You will also require the Approved Vendors dataset to complete these assignments. Detailed information about ELM, instructions for accessing datasets, and a data directory for data sets can be found in Connect.

LO 8-7

8.60 **Summarizing Purchasing Data with IDEA.** You have been assigned the task of understanding the client's purchasing habits, including their use of authorized vendors and payment time frames, and you must use IDEA to gather this information.

Required:

    a. Determine the total dollar amount ordered from each vendor. What companies are the three largest vendors by dollar amount? How would this information assist an auditor in planning the audit?

    b. Determine what products are ordered most often. What item is ordered most often? How might this information affect the audit?

    c. Determine the accounts payable amount for each vendor as of March 31. What companies have the three largest accounts payable balances? How would this information assist an auditor in planning the audit?

    d. Were any orders made to vendors not on the approved vendor list? How would this information assist an auditor in planning the audit?

    e. Were there any discounts available that were not taken? Why is this important?

    f. Were there any vendors paid late? Why is this important?

    g. Were there any items that did not pass inspection? Why is this information important to the auditor?

LO 8-7

8.61 **Tests of Controls in the Purchasing Cycle with IDEA.** You have identified relevant controls for several assertions within the purchasing cycle, and you must use IDEA to perform several tests of controls.

Required:

    a. Are all checks accounted for? If there are checks that are not accounted for, how would this affect the audit?

    b. Are there any duplicate check numbers? If there are duplicate checks, how would this affect the audit?

    c. Are there any payments to vendors not on the approved vendor list? If there are checks to such vendors, how would this affect the audit?

    d. Were any checks voided? Were any checks written to at cash or bearer? How would this affect the audit?

LO 8-7

8.62 **Testing for Unmatched Invoices.** A concern in all audits is the risk that payments are made that do not represent valid expenses. One common test is to match payments to valid invoices, and you must use IDEA to perform this test.

Required:

Match the paid invoice numbers in the purchases data set with the invoice numbers in the cash disbursements data set. Are there unmatched invoices from the purchase data? Are there any disbursements with invoices that do not match to the purchase data? What are the possible causes for discrepancies between these data sets? How would the auditor address these discrepancies?

Appendix 8A

Internal Control Questionnaires

APPENDIX EXHIBIT 8A.1 Internal Control Questionnaire—Acquisitions and Expenditures

	Yes/No	Comments
Occurrence		
1. Are the purchasing department, accounting department, receiving department, and shipping department independent of each other?		
2. Are receiving reports prepared for each item received and copies transmitted to inventory custodians? To purchasing? To the accounting department?		
3. Are purchases made by employees authorized through standard purchases procedures?		
4. Are quantity and quality of goods received determined at the time of receipt by receiving personnel independent of the purchasing department?		
5. Are vendors' invoices reconciled against purchase orders and receiving reports before a liability is recorded?		
6. Do managers compare actual expenses to budget?		
7. Are all documents in the vouchers package canceled with a PAID stamp when paid?		
8. Are shipping documents authorized and prepared for goods returned to vendors?		
9. Are invoices approved for payment by a responsible officer?		
Completeness		
1. Are the purchase order forms prenumbered and the numerical sequence checked for missing documents?		
2. Are receiving report forms prenumbered and the numerical sequence checked for missing documents?		
3. Is the accounts payable department notified of goods returned to vendors?		
4. Are vendors' invoices recorded immediately on receipt?		
5. Are unmatched receiving reports reviewed frequently and investigated for proper recording?		
6. Is statistical analysis used to examine overall purchasing levels?		
7. Are vendors' monthly statements reconciled with individual accounts payable accounts?		
Accuracy		
1. Are competitive bids received and reviewed for certain items?		
2. Are all purchases made only on the basis of approved purchase requisitions?		
3. Are all purchases, whether for inventory or expense, routed through the purchasing department for approval?		
4. Does the accounts payable department check invoices against purchase orders and receiving reports for dates, quantities, prices, and terms?		
5. Does the accounting department check invoices for mathematical accuracy?		
6. Is the accounts payable listing balanced periodically with the general ledger control account?		
7. Are purchase prices approved by a responsible purchasing officer?		
8. Is accounts payable reconciled to the general ledger every period?		
9. Are monthly statements reviewed by senior officials?		
Classification		
1. Do the chart of accounts and the accounting manual give instructions for classifying debit entries when purchases are recorded?		
2. Are journal entries authorized at appropriate levels?		
Cutoff		
1. Does the accounting manual give instructions to date purchase/payable entries on the date of receipt of goods?		

APPENDIX EXHIBIT 8A.2 Selected Computerized Questionnaire Items—General and Application Controls

	Yes/No	Comments
General Controls		
1. Are computer operators and programmers excluded from participating in the input and output control functions?		
2. Are programmers excluded from entering transactions or performing other routine computer operations?		
3. Is there a database administrator who is independent of computer operations, systems, programming, and users?		
4. Are computer personnel restricted from initiating, or authorizing, transactions or adjustments to the general ledger master database or the subsidiary ledger master database?		
5. Is access to the computer room restricted to authorized personnel?		
6. Is online access to data and programs controlled with the use of department account codes, personal ID numbers, and passwords?		
7. Are systems, programs, and documentation stored in a fireproof area?		
8. Can current files, particularly master files, be reconstructed from files stored in an offsite location?		
Application Controls		
1. Are process manuals for purchasing and accounts payable current?		
2. Are process documents (e.g., purchase requisitions, purchase orders, bills of lading) signed as evidence of review and authorization?		
3. Are all data fields subject to input validation tests—missing data tests, limit and range tests, check digits, valid codes, and so forth?		
4. Are input error reports generated daily? Are they returned to the accounting department for correction of errors?		
5. Is an accounting department person assigned the responsibility for promptly correcting input errors and reentering the data for inclusion with the next report?		
6. Are controls used to reconcile computerized output to input control data?		
7. Are reports reviewed for reasonableness, accuracy, and legibility by the responsible department personnel?		

APPENDIX EXHIBIT 8A.3 Acquisitions and Expenditures—Computerized Controls

	Yes/No	Comments
1. Is each terminal restricted to designated functions? For example, the receiving clerk's terminal cannot accept a purchase order entry.		
2. Are identification numbers and passwords required to enter purchase orders, vendors' invoices, and the receiving report information?		
3. Are certain personnel authorized to determine the status of various records, such as an open voucher, but not authorized to enter data? Do these personnel have "read only" authorization?		
4. Is all input immediately logged to provide restart processing should any terminal become inoperative during the processing?		
5. Do transaction codes call up a full screen "form" on the terminals that appears to the operators in the same format as the original paper documents?		
6. Does the system reject incomplete or incorrect information (online input validation)?		
7. Are all printed documents computer numbered, and are the numbers stored as part of the record?		
8. Do all records in the open databases have the vendor's number as the primary search and matching field key?		
9. Can status searches be made by another field? For example, the inventory number can be the search key to determine the status of a purchase of an item in short supply.		
10. Is a daily search of the open databases made—for example, open purchase orders more than 10 days past the delivery date?		
11. Is the check signature printed using a signature plate that is installed on the computer printer only when checks are printed?		
12. Does a designated person in the treasurer's office maintain custody of this signature plate and take it to the computer room to be installed when checks are printed?		
13. Is this person restricted from access to blank check stock?		
14. Are the printed checks taken immediately from the computer room for mailing?		

APPENDIX EXHIBIT 8A.4   **Acquisitions and Expenditures—Computerized Controls**

	Yes/No	Comments
Occurrence		
1. Is the accounting department notified of actions of disposal, dismantling, or idling a productive asset? For terminating a lease or rental?		
2. Are assets inspected periodically and physically counted?		
Completeness		
1. Are detailed property records maintained for the various assets included in PP&E?		
2. Are property tax assessments periodically analyzed? When was the last analysis?		
3. Are purchase contracts for major assets provided to the accounting department?		
Accuracy		
1. Are capital expenditure and leasing proposals prepared for review and approval by the board of directors or by responsible officers?		
2. When actual expenditures exceed authorized amounts, is the excess approved?		
3. Is there a uniform policy for assigning depreciation rates, useful lives, and salvage values?		
4. Are depreciation calculations checked by internal auditors or other officials?		
5. Are subsidiary records periodically reconciled to the general ledger accounts?		
Classification		
1. Does the accounting manual contain policies for capitalization of assets and expensing repair and maintenance?		
2. Are memorandum records of leased assets maintained?		
Cutoff		
1. Does the accounting manual give instructions for recording PP&E additions on a proper date of acquisition?		

Appendix 8B

Audit Plans

APPENDIX EXHIBIT 8B.1

DUNDER-MIFFLIN, INC. Audit Plan for Accounts Payable 12/31/17		
	Performed by	**Ref.**

1. Obtain a trial balance of recorded accounts payable as of year-end.
  a. Foot and trace the total to the general ledger account.
  b. Vouch a sample of balances to vendors' statements. Review the trial balance for related-party payables.
2. Send confirmations to creditors, especially those with small or zero balances and those with which the company has done significant business.
3. Inquire of client personnel about their procedures for ensuring that all liabilities are recorded.
4. Scan the open purchase order file at year-end for indications of material purchase commitments at fixed prices. Obtain current prices and determine whether any adjustments for loss are needed.
5. Obtain a list of unmatched vendor invoices, and review receiving reports for receipt of goods.
6. For goods received before year-end, trace the unmatched receiving reports to accounts payable, and determine whether items recorded in the next accounting period need to be adjusted.
7. Select a sample of cash disbursements from the accounting period following the balance-sheet date. Vouch them to supporting documents (invoice, receiving report) to determine whether the related liabilities were recorded in the proper accounting period.		

APPENDIX EXHIBIT 8B.2

DUNDER-MIFFLIN, INC. Audit Plan for Prepaid Expenses, Accrued Expenses, Deferred Costs 12/31/17		
	Performed by	**Ref.**

1. Obtain a schedule of all prepaid expenses, deferred costs, and accrued expenses.
2. Review documentation to determine whether each item is properly allocated to the current or future accounting periods.
3. Select significant additions to deferred and accrued amounts, and vouch them to supporting invoices, contracts, or calculations.
4. Examine documentation for the basis for deferral and accrual, and recalculate the recorded amounts.
5. Review the nature of each item, inquire of management, and determine whether the remaining balance will be recovered from future operations.
6. Scan income and expense items for items that should be considered prepaid, deferred, or accrued and allocated to current or future accounting periods.
7. Scan the expense accounts in the trial balance and compare to prior year.
  a. Investigate an unusual difference that could indicate failure to account for a prepaid or accrual item.
  b. Review each item to determine the proper current or noncurrent balance sheet classification.		

APPENDIX EXHIBIT 8B.3

			Performed by	Ref.
DUNDER-MIFFLIN, INC. **Audit Plan for Property, Plant and Equipment** **12/31/17**				

Property, Plant, and Equipment

1. Summarize and foot detailed asset subsidiary records, and reconcile to general ledger control account(s).
2. Select a sample of detail asset subsidiary records:
    a. Perform a physical observation (inspection) of the assets recorded.
    b. Inspect title documents, if any, to ensure ownership by the client.
3. Prepare, or have client prepare, a schedule of asset additions and disposals for the period:
    a. Vouch to documents indicating proper approval.
    b. Vouch costs to invoices, contracts, or other supporting documents.
    c. Review all costs of shipment, installation, testing, and other appropriate costs for proper capitalization.
    d. Vouch proceeds (on dispositions) to cash receipts or other asset records.
    e. Recalculate gain or loss on dispositions.
    f. Trace amounts to detail asset records and general ledger control account(s).
4. Observe the taking of a physical inventory of the assets, and compare with detailed asset records.
5. Obtain written representations from management regarding pledge of assets as security for loans and leased assets.
6. Select a sample of repair and maintenance expense entries, and vouch them to supporting invoices for evidence of property that should be capitalized.

Depreciation

1. Review depreciation expense for overall reasonableness with reference to costs of assets and average depreciation rates.
2. Prepare, or have client prepare, a schedule of accumulated depreciation showing beginning balance, current depreciation, disposals, and ending balance.
    a. Review the schedule for appropriate asset costs, useful life, and salvage value.
3. Trace equipment listed to depreciation expense and asset disposition analyses.
4. Recalculate depreciation expense and trace to general ledger account(s).
5. Trace amounts to general ledger account(s).

Other Accounts

1. Review prepaid insurance for proper recording and adequacy of coverage.
2. Review accrued property taxes to determine whether taxes due on assets have been paid or accrued.
3. Recalculate prepaid and/or accrued insurance and tax expenses.
4. Select a sample of rental expense entries and vouch to rent/lease contracts to determine whether any leases qualify for capitalization.

Intangibles and Related Expenses

1. Review merger documents for proper calculation of purchased goodwill.
2. Inquire of management about legal status of patents, leases, copyrights, and other intangibles.
3. Review documentation of new patents, copyrights, leaseholds, and franchise agreements.
4. Select a sample of recorded research and development expenses. Vouch to supporting documents for evidence of proper classification.
5. Recalculate amortization of goodwill, patents, and other intangibles.
6. Perform tests for goodwill impairment.

Appendix 8C

LO 8-8

Describe the payroll cycle, including typical source documents and controls.

The Payroll Cycle

Martin Bodner, the former finance chief of **Tommy Hilfiger Group Handbags and Small Leather Goods Inc.,** pleaded guilty to mail fraud and wire fraud for allegedly stealing more than $19 million, according to Michael Garcia, U.S. Attorney for the Southern District of New York. According to Garcia, Bodner began working at the Hilfiger licensee in March 2000, eventually rising to CFO. Among his responsibilities was to supervise the company's payroll. Beginning in 2000, Bodner began stealing money from his employer by secretly increasing the amount of money that he was to be paid in salary and bonus and arranging to be reimbursed by the handbag and leather goods unit for phony expenses he purportedly had incurred. In addition, during 2004 and 2005, Bodner added one of his sons, who did not work for the company, to the company's payroll. He arranged for his son to be paid about $225,500 during those years. Bodner was fired on December 21, 2007.

Bodner entered into a plea deal in which he agreed to forfeit a home in Sands Point, New York, along with a Manhattan apartment, three cars, and various other properties. Bodner also was accused of causing hundreds of checks to be issued to various recipients for the purpose of paying off his personal credit card bills; purchasing a luxury automobile for himself; paying for insurance for a home, apartments, and automobiles owned by Bodner; and paying for decorating services.[6]

Every company has payroll. It can include manufacturing labor, research scientists, administrative personnel, or all of these. Payroll may take different forms. Personnel management and the payroll accounting cycle not only include transactions that affect the wage and salary accounts, but also the transactions that affect pension benefits, deferred compensation contracts, compensatory stock option plans, employee benefits (such as health insurance), payroll taxes, and related liabilities for these costs. An important aspect of the payroll cycle is that it is self-policing. If employees are not paid, they will complain. If someone commits fraud by overpaying an employee and then diverts the difference, the employee will complain because his or her W-2 will be overstated and the employee will owe too much tax. As a result, company employees report many misstatements (both intentional and unintentional).

Typically, balance sheet accounts such as accrued payroll and accrued taxes are not material to companies' financial position. In addition, because of the self-policing nature of the accounts and the regulatory restrictions of the Internal Revenue Service and the Department of Labor, controls over payroll are normally stronger than over other areas. Therefore, most audit procedures related to payroll consist of evaluation of internal control and analytical procedures.

THE PAYROLL CYCLE: TYPICAL ACTIVITIES

Appendix Exhibit 8C.1 shows a payroll cycle. It starts with hiring (and firing) people and determining their wage rates and deductions, proceeds to attendance and work (timekeeping), and ends with payment followed by preparation of governmental (tax) and internal reports.

The elements that follow are part of the payroll internal control system.

Personnel ①

A human relations department that is independent of the other functions should have authority to add new employees to the payroll, delete terminated employees, obtain

---

[6]"Hilfiger Unit Ex-CFO Pleads Guilty to $19M Fraud," CFO.com, September 16, 2008.

EXHIBIT 8C.1   Typical Activities in the Payroll Cycle

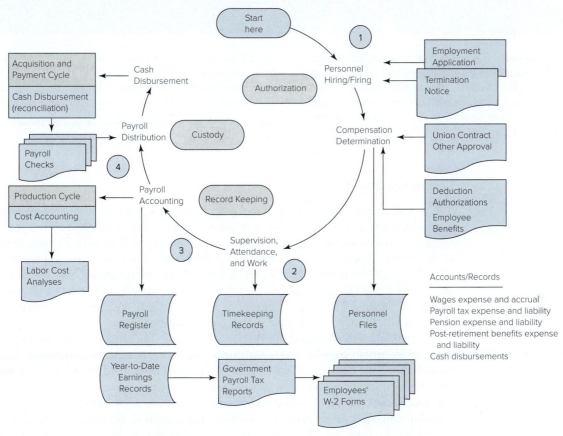

authorizations for deductions, and transmit authority for pay rate changes to the payroll department. A process should exist to ensure that terminated employees are removed from the payroll. This is often done in conjunction with an exit interview performed by human resources. Final checks and W-2s should be mailed to the employee's home.

Supervision ②

Supervisors assign the employees to their jobs and approve any overtime. The immediate supervisor should approve all employee activity data (number of hours worked, job number, absences, time off allowed for emergencies, and the like). Finally, supervisors compare production plans and budget reports to actual employee costs for discrepancies.

Timekeeping ③

Employees paid by the hour or on various incentive systems require records of time, production, piecework, or other measures of the basis for their pay. (Salaried employees do not require such detailed records.) Timekeeping or similar records are collected in a variety of ways. The traditional time clock is still used in many organizations. More sophisticated computerized systems perform the same function without the paper time card. Production employees may clock in for various jobs or production processes in the system for assigning labor cost to various stages of production.

Supervisors should approve timekeeping records. In computerized systems, this approval may be automatic by virtue of the supervisory passwords used to input data into a computerized payroll system.

AUDITING INSIGHT   Nurse, I Need You?

Hospital Corporation of America (HCA) runs more than 160 facilities across the United States and in London and treats millions of people a year. In 2006, HCA was bought by a consortium including its management, the family of former Senate majority leader Bill First (Tennessee), and three major financial firms for about $33 billion in the largest leveraged buyout ever at the time. The Securities and Exchange

Commission has opened a probe into whether HCA violated securities laws by manipulating books and records. Part of the investigation has focused on HCA's London subsidiary and whether the company fabricated tens of thousands of payments for phantom nursing shifts.

Source: "SEC Probing Biggest Hospital Company: Nursing Shifts Examined in HCA London Unit," *The Washington Post,* October 7, 2009.

Record Keeping ④

The payroll accounting function should prepare individual paychecks, pay envelopes, or make electronic transfers using rate and deduction information supplied by the personnel function and data supplied by the timekeeping–supervision functions. Persons in charge of the hiring, supervision, and timekeeping functions should not also prepare the payroll. They could be tempted to get checks for fictitious or terminated employees. Payroll accounting maintains individual year-to-date earnings records and prepares the state and federal tax reports. The payroll tax returns and the annual W-2 report to employees are useful records for audit recalculation and analytical procedures.

The main feature of custody in the payroll cycle is the possession of the paychecks, cash, or electronic transfer codes for direct payments. A payroll distribution function should control the delivery of pay to employees so that unclaimed checks, cash, or incomplete electronic transfers are not returned to persons involved in any of the other functions. The functional duties and responsibilities just described relate primarily to nonsalaried (hourly) employees. For salaried employees, the system is simplified by not having to collect timekeeping data. In non-manufacturing businesses, the cost accounting operations can be very simple or even nonexistent.

Direct deposit is an excellent control for payroll distribution. Employees on vacation, ill, or otherwise not at the facility will still have their check delivered, and unclaimed paychecks are almost non-existent. Further, there is no opportunity for employees to alter a paycheck in any manner. Be aware that some individuals do not have (and do not want) a bank account. Also, the client cannot require an employee to have a bank account. Therefore, even if the client has a direct deposit system, the auditor should make inquires as to those employees paid by check.

The relative importance of each of these four areas should be determined for each engagement in light of the nature and organization of the company's operations.

AUDITING INSIGHT   Why Am I Underpaid?

Leonid Fridman, 60, owned and operated **Millennium Commercial Corp.,** a Brooklyn-based company that performed tile work for the Port Authority of New York and New Jersey. The defendant and his company performed tile restoration work as a subcontractor on the renovation of the TWA Flight Center at John F. Kennedy Airport in 2009 and 2010. Under the Port Authority contract for the project and labor law, the defendant was required to pay his laborers and mason tenders more than $50 per hour and more than $70 per hour for tile setters.

According to court records, Fridman was aware that he was required to pay the prevailing wages but still paid his workers only

$10 to $30 per hour. To avoid detection, Fridman filed false certified payroll reports stating he paid his workers the prevailing wages and issued paychecks to the workers that matched those payroll reports. Fridman then made his workers cash the checks at his bank and kick back, or return, a majority of the cash to him, according to the New York Attorney General's office.

Prosecutors say that Fridman then hid more than $100,000 of the money he stole by moving it into the account of a Florida corporation, Green Investments Inc., that he controlled.

Source: "NYC Contractor Charged with Payroll Fraud, Larceny, and Laundering," CPA Practice Advisor, February 6, 2013.

✅ REVIEW CHECKPOINTS

8C.1 What functional responsibilities are associated with the payroll cycle?

8C.2 Which duties should be separated in the payroll cycle?

8C.3 How does a company ensure that terminated employees are removed from the payroll?

8C.4 Describe a walkthrough of the payroll transaction flow from hiring authorization to payroll check disbursement. (a) What document copies would be collected? (b) What controls should be noted?

Significant Accounts and Relevant Assertions

The major risks in the payroll cycle include

- Paying **ghost employees**, employees who do not exist (invalid transactions).
- Paying terminated employees (who have not been removed from payroll) whose paychecks are then endorsed with forged signatures by their supervisors.
- Overpaying for time or production (inaccurate transactions, improper valuation).
- Accounting incorrectly for costs and expenses (incorrect classification, improper or inconsistent presentation and disclosure).
- Not ensuring that related taxes and third parties (e.g., insurance providers) are appropriately paid.

Because of these risks, and the desire of employees to obtain more money, the valuation of payroll is the most relevant assertion. This is illustrated in the next Auditing Insight. The potential for ghost employees makes existence a key assertion as well. Management may also gain from misclassifying payroll so the auditor must consider the classification assertion a risk. Certainly, if an employee was left off the payroll, the employee would make that known to the organization, therefore, completeness is a very low risk.

 AUDITING INSIGHT A Dedicated Employee

Prosecutors told the Winchester Crown Court in southern England that Jaswinder Bains, 45, was "blatantly dishonest" on the time cards for his job as a social worker on at least 24 occasions. In one instance, Bains allegedly claimed he worked 23 hours in one day on 29 case files, even though his credit card records show he was on a shopping spree in Paris that day. Bains testified that he did not falsify his work hour records. "I was working very long hours without sleep," he said. "I do not need a lot of sleep." He did not explain what was behind his records on another day, when he claimed he worked 28 hours.

Source: "Social Worker 'Claimed for 28-Hour Day,'" *The Guardian*, www.theguardian.com.

Payroll systems produce numerous reports. Some are internal reports and bookkeeping records. Others are government tax reports.

Personnel Files

The personnel, human relations, or labor relations department keeps individual employee files. The files usually include an employment application, a background investigation report, a notice of hiring, a job classification with pay rate authorization, and employee authorizations for deductions. When employees retire, resign, or are otherwise dismissed, appropriate notices of termination are filed.

A personnel file should establish a person's existence and employment. The background investigation report is important for employees in such sensitive areas as accounting, finance, and asset custody positions. News reports are rich with reports of errors and frauds perpetrated by people who falsified their credentials.

Payroll Register

The *payroll register* is a special journal. It typically contains a row for each employee with columns for the gross regular pay, gross overtime pay, income tax withheld, Social Security and Medicare tax withheld, other deductions, and net pay. The net pay amount usually is transferred from the general bank account to a special **imprest bank account** that maintains a zero or fixed balance.

Payroll department records contain the canceled checks (or a similar computerized deposit record). The checks have the employees' endorsements on the back.

AUDITING INSIGHT \ Who Signed That?

Marsha Marston, an assistant accountant, was instructed to look at the endorsements on the back of a sample of canceled payroll checks. She noticed three occurrences of the payee's signature followed by a second signature. Although scrawled almost illegibly, the second signatures were identical and were later identified as the handwriting of Fred Holmes (the payroll accountant). Holmes had taken unclaimed checks and converted (stole) them. When cashing these "third-party checks," banks and stores had required him to produce identification and endorse the checks that already had been "endorsed" by the employee payee. The lesson is that second endorsements are a red flag.

Labor Cost Analysis

One of the internal reports in the payroll cycle is a report of labor cost to the cost accounting department, thus linking the payroll cycle with cost accounting in the production cycle. The cost accounting department can receive its information in more than one way. Some companies have systems that independently report time and production work data from the production floor directly to the cost accounting department. Other companies let their cost accounting department receive labor cost data from the payroll department. When the data are received independently, they can be reconciled with a report from the payroll department.

The cost accounting department (or a similar accounting function) is responsible for labor distribution. This is the most important part of the classification assertion with respect to payroll. Labor distribution is an assignment of payroll to the accounts where it belongs for internal and external reporting.

Payroll data flow from the hiring process, through the timekeeping function, into the payroll department, then to the cost accounting department, and finally to the accounting entries that record the payroll for inventory cost determination and financial statement presentation. The same data are used for various governmental and tax reports.

Beware the "Clearing Account"

Clearing accounts are temporary storage places for transactions awaiting final accounting. All clearing accounts should have zero balances after the accounting is completed. A balance in a clearing account means that some amounts have not been classified properly in the accounting records. When the dollars in the clearing account are material, auditors usually investigate the nature of the account with a great deal of skepticism.

Governmental and Tax Reports

One of the main objectives of a payroll system is to calculate the payments due to third parties, including insurance fees, union dues, retirement funds, and so on. Of most importance is the calculation of payroll taxes due to the federal, state, and local governments. Large fines, mounting interest, or business closure is a possible ramification if these taxes are not paid timely and accurately. These issues cause payroll systems to be complicated and change almost every year as tax law and tax rates change. The payroll system produces several reports. Auditors can use these reports in tests of controls and substantive procedures produced by accumulating numerous payroll transactions.

Companies in financial difficulty have been known to try to postpone payment of employee taxes withheld. However, the consequences can be serious. The IRS can and will padlock the business and seize its assets for nonpayment.

Year-to-Date Earnings Records

The year-to-date (YTD) earnings records are the cumulative subsidiary records of each employee's gross pay, deductions, and net pay. Each time a periodic payroll is produced, the YTD earnings records are updated for the new information. The YTD earnings records are a subsidiary ledger of the wages and salaries cost and expense in the financial statements. Like any subsidiary and control account relationship, their sum (i.e., the gross pay amounts) should be equal to the costs and expenses in the financial statements. These YTD records provide the data for periodic governmental tax forms. They can be reconciled to the tax reports. Details can be compared to the company's YTD earnings records.

Employee W-2 Reports

The W-2 is the annual report of gross salaries and wages and the income, Social Security, and Medicare taxes withheld. Copies are filed with the Social Security Administration and the IRS, and copies are sent to employees for use in preparing their income tax returns. The W-2s contain the annual YTD accumulations for each employee. Auditors can use the name, address, Social Security number, and dollar amounts in certain procedures to obtain evidence about the existence of the employees. The W-2s can be reconciled to the payroll tax reports.

W-2s should be mailed directly to employees' homes so if someone has been collecting additional pay in an employee's name (e.g., if an employee leaves and the supervisor continues to send in a time card), the employee can spot the added income.

The assessment of payroll-cycle control risk normally takes on added importance because most companies have fairly elaborate and well-controlled personnel and payroll functions. The significant transactions in this cycle are numerous during the year yet result in small amounts in balance-sheet accounts at year-end. Therefore, in most audit engagements, the review of controls, tests of controls, and substantive tests of transactions constitute the major portion of the evidence gathered for these accounts. On most audits, the substantive procedures devoted to auditing the payroll-related account balances are limited.

Internal Control Activities and Evaluation

In the payroll function, auditors pay special attention to the controls that have been put in place. In a large company, tens of thousands of payroll checks or direct deposit payments may be made during the year. While auditors may test the detail of some transactions, it is the evaluation of internal controls that is deemed most important.

Control activities for proper separation of responsibilities should be in place and operating. By referring to Exhibit 8C.1, you can see that proper separation involves authorization (personnel department hiring and termination, pay rate, and deduction authorizations) by persons who do not have payroll preparation, paycheck distribution, or reconciliation duties. Payroll distribution (custody) is in the hands of persons who do not authorize employees' pay rates or time or prepare the payroll checks. Record keeping is performed by payroll and cost accounting personnel who do not make authorizations or distribute pay. Combinations of two or more of the duties of authorization, payroll preparation and record keeping, and payroll distribution in one person, one office, or one computerized system can open the door for errors and frauds.

In addition, the internal controls should provide for detailed control checking procedures. Examples of these controls follow:

- Periodic comparison of the payroll register to the personnel department files to check hiring authorizations and any terminated employees who have not been deleted.
- Periodic rechecking of wage rate and deduction authorizations.

- Reconciliation of time and production material to cost accounting calculations.
- Quarterly reconciliation of YTD earnings records with tax returns.
- Payroll bank account reconciliation.

Some companies send each supervisor a copy of the payroll register, showing the employees paid under the supervisor's authority and responsibility. The supervisor has a chance to reapprove the payroll after it has been completed. Managers also should receive a comparison of actual labor costs to standards to review any unusual differences. The payroll report sent to cost accounting can be reconciled to the labor records used to charge labor cost to production. The cost accounting function should determine whether the labor paid is the same as the labor cost used in the cost accounting calculations. Finally, the payroll bank account can be reconciled like any other bank account.

Information about the payroll cycle control often is gathered initially by completing an internal control questionnaire (ICQ). An example of an ICQ for payroll controls is in Exhibit 5.25. You can study this questionnaire for details of desirable controls. It is organized with headings that identify the important assertions.

COMPUTERIZED PAYROLL

Complex computerized systems that gather payroll data, calculate payroll amounts, print checks, and transfer computerized deposits are found in many companies. Even though the technology is complex, the basic management and control functions of ensuring a flow of data to the payroll department should be in place. Various paper records and approval signatures may not exist. They may be embedded in computerized payroll systems. Companies often use service organizations to process their payroll because it is a specialized function that can be performed effectively and efficiently by an organization whose specialty is to keep up with and apply changes in tax laws and rates. Thus, auditors should refer to the requirements of AU-C 402 ("Service Organizations") in addressing this function.

Service Organizations

Service organizations are widely used for payroll preparation. This process can range from the calculation of payroll including the amounts due to third parties and to the actual payment of the payroll to individuals and third parties. Even when service bureaus are used to process payroll, the client is still responsible for payroll. For example, if the calculation for

AUDITING INSIGHT Who Is Your Help Helping?

Robert Kenneth Dromm, owner of **Pay 1 Plus Payroll Administrators,** admitted to siphoning money from clients who hired his company to process quarterly payroll tax payments. Dromm's firm processed quarterly payroll tax payments for hundreds of clients around the Tampa Bay area. The clients would send Dromm's company their estimated tax payments. Pay 1 Plus Payroll was supposed to handle the paperwork and send the money to the IRS. Between 1999 and 2004, Dromm submitted false, understated filings to the IRS but gave many clients what appeared to be correct payroll tax returns. That allowed him to skim off money and direct it to his personal accounts. According to the plea deal concerning this, Dromm used these accounts for personal and business expenses as well as real estate investments.

Defense attorney Anthony LaSpada said the diversion began as a way to pay off old tax debts, not to defraud anyone. Some of Dromm's clients had financial needs (to pay debts, rents, wages, taxes, etc.) According to LaSpada, in the mid-1990s, Dromm advanced them money. When a number of these clients went out of business, Pay 1 Plus Payroll was left in a precarious position, and Dromm began to divert funds. During that time, he paid $1.3 million in old tax debts to the IRS, LaSpada added that the company hit another snag in 2003 with the discovery that chief bookkeeper Robert M. Crawford Jr. had embezzled $1.5 million to $2 million on his own. "I strongly believe that had it not been for that embezzlement by Mr. Crawford, that he would have been able to pay," LaSpada said. Dromm pleaded guilty and was sentenced to four years in federal prison and ordered to pay $1.6 million in restitution.

Source: "Payroll Tax Scam Nets 4-Year Term," *Tampa Bay Times,* November 3, 2007.

federal taxes is incorrect, the IRS will be auditing the client, not the service bureau payroll provider. Therefore, the auditor must review the payroll controls both at the client and the service organization for processing payroll. This would include getting a report on controls from the service bureau's auditor and ensuring that controls at the client are in place. The client should verify that the number of checks issued by the service bureau equals the number of employees eligible for compensation during the period. The client should review reports from the third party such as a payroll register (a listing of changes made to the payroll file), and a report of payments due to third parties should be reviewed by the client. The auditor should ensure that payroll numbers are reasonable given the activity level at the client. Analytical procedures can be a powerful test in these situations.

Substantive Analytical Procedures and Tests of Details

As stated, for the payroll process, auditors rely heavily on tests of controls. However, there are substantive tests that can be performed. If the workforce is stable, payroll from one period to the next will be relatively consistent. If a weekly payroll significantly declines or increases, the auditor should inquire of management about the inconsistency. Layoffs, overtime, or seasonality may explain the discrepancy, and the auditor can review the payroll register for that period to corroborate the change in the number of paychecks or the increase in overtime.

There are times when the auditor is concerned about payroll controls or inexplicable changes in payroll expenses. In these cases, the auditor may select a sample of items from the payroll register (remember completeness is low risk so the register should include all employees) and vouch the information to the timecards (hours worked), payroll master file (wage), and the personnel file for authorizations for deductions (insurance, withholding, pension) and wage rate. Personnel files are excellent sources of information when ghost employees are expected. Few ghost employees have life or health insurance. Auditors may scan the payroll register looking for employees with no voluntary deductions from their paycheck and vouch the employee information to the personnel files in human resources.

⊘ REVIEW CHECKPOINTS

8C.5 What documents should be included in an employee's personnel file?

8C.6 What features of a payroll system could be expected to prevent or detect the (a) payment of a fictitious employee and (b) omission of payment to an employee?

8C.7 What are the most common errors and frauds in the personnel and payroll cycle? Which control characteristics are auditors looking for to prevent or detect these errors and frauds?

FRAUD CASE: EXTENDED AUDIT PROCEDURES (AU-C/ISA 240, AS 2301)

Case 8C.1

Time Card Forgeries

PROBLEM

A personnel agency that leased employees to hospitals assigned Nurse Jane Kent to work at County Hospital. She claimed payroll hours on agency time cards that showed approval signatures of a hospital nursing shift supervisor. The hospital had terminated the shift supervisor several months prior to the periods covered by the time cards in question. Kent worked one or two days per week but submitted time cards for a full 40-hour workweek. The personnel agency paid Kent and then billed County Hospital for the wages and benefits. Supporting documents were submitted with the personnel agency's bills.

Each hospital workstation keeps ward shift logs, which are sign-in sheets showing nurses on duty at all times. Nurses sign in and sign out when going on and going off duty. County Hospital maintains personnel records showing, among other things, the period of employment of its own nurses, supervisors, and other employees.

Kent's wages and benefits were billed to the hospital at $22 per hour. False time cards overcharging about 24 extra hours per week cost the hospital $528 per week. Kent was assigned to County Hospital for 15 weeks during the year, so she caused overcharges of about $7,900. However, she told three of her friends about the procedure, and they over-charged the hospital another $24,000.

AUDIT APPROACH

Control activities should include a hiring authorization to put employees on the payroll. When temporary employees are used, this authorization includes contracts for nursing time, conditions of employment, and terms including the contract reimbursement rate. Control records of attendance and work should be kept (ward shift log). Supervisors should approve time cards or other records used by the payroll department to prepare paychecks. In this case, the contract with the personnel agency provided that approved time cards had to be submitted as supporting documentation for the agency billings.

Although the activities and documents for control were in place, the controls did not operate because no one at the hospital ever compared the ward shift logs to time cards, and no one examined the supervisory approval signatures for their validity. The fraud was easy in the personnel agency situation because the nurses submitted their own time cards to the agency for payment. The same fraud could be operated by the hospital's own employees if they, too, could write their time cards and submit them to the payroll department.

Auditors should make inquiries (e.g., internal control questionnaire) about the error-checking activities performed by hospital accounting personnel. Tests of controls are designed to determine whether control activities are followed properly by the organization. Because the comparison and checking activities were not performed, there is nothing to test.

Select a sample of personnel agency billings and their supporting documentation (time cards). Vouch rates billed by the agency to the contract for agreement to proper rate. Vouch time claimed to hospital work attendance records (ward shift logs). Obtain handwriting examples of supervisors' signatures and compare them to the approval signatures on time cards. Use personnel records to determine whether supervisors were actually employed by the hospital at the time they approved the time cards. Use available work attendance records to determine whether supervisors were actually on duty at the time they approved the time cards.

DISCOVERY SUMMARY

The auditors quickly found that Kent (and others) had not signed in on ward shift logs for days they claimed to have worked. Further investigation showed that the supervisors who supposedly signed the time cards were not even employed by the hospital at the time their signatures were used for approvals. Handwriting comparison showed that the signatures were not those of the supervisors.

The personnel agency was informed and refunded the $31,900 overpayment that the auditors had proved. The auditors continued to comb the records for more!

Source: Adapted from vignette published in *Internal Auditor*.

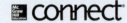 All applicable Exercises and Problems are available with *Connect.*

8C.8 An audit team most likely would assess control risk at the maximum if the payroll department supervisor is responsible for

a. Examining authorization forms for new employees.

b. Comparing payroll registers with original batch transmittal data.

c. Authorizing payroll rate changes for all employees.

d. Hiring all subordinate payroll department employees.

(AICPA adapted)

LO 8-8   8C.9   Which of the following departments most likely would approve changes in pay rates and deductions from employee salaries?

    a. Personnel.

    b. Treasurer.

    c. Controller.

    d. Payroll.

    (AICPA adapted)

LO 8-8   8C.10   Matthew Corp. has changed from a system of recording time worked on clock cards to a computerized payroll system in which employees record time in and out with magnetic cards. The computerized system automatically updates all payroll records. Because of this change

    a. A generalized computer audit plan must be used.

    b. Part of the audit trail is altered.

    c. The potential for payroll-related fraud is diminished.

    d. Transactions must be processed in batches.

    (AICPA adapted)

LO 8-8   8C.11   Effective control over the cash payroll function would mandate which of the following?

    a. The payroll clerk should fill the envelopes with cash and a computation of the net wages.

    b. Unclaimed payroll envelopes should be retained by the paymaster.

    c. Each employee should be asked to sign a receipt.

    d. A separate checking account for payroll should be maintained.

LO 8-8   8C.12   A large retail enterprise has established a policy that requires the paymaster to deliver all unclaimed payroll checks to the internal audit department at the end of each payroll distribution day. This policy was most likely adopted to

    a. Ensure that employees who were absent on a payroll distribution day are not paid for that day.

    b. Prevent the paymaster from cashing checks that are unclaimed for several weeks.

    c. Prevent a bona fide employee's check from being claimed by another employee.

    d. Detect any fictitious employee who may have been placed on the payroll.

    (AICPA adapted)

LO 8-8   8C.13   Auditors ordinarily ascertain whether payroll checks are properly endorsed during the audit of

    a. Clock cards.

    b. The voucher system.

    c. Cash in bank.

    d. Accrued payroll.

    (AICPA adapted)

LO 8-8   8C.14   In determining the effectiveness of an entity's policies and procedures relating to the occurrence assertion for payroll transactions, auditors most likely would inquire about and

    a. Observe the separation of duties concerning personnel responsibilities and payroll disbursement.

    b. Inspect evidence of accounting for prenumbered payroll checks.

    c. Recompute the payroll deductions for employee benefits.

    d. Verify the preparation of the monthly payroll account bank reconciliation.

    (AICPA adapted)

LO 8-8   8C.15   Which of the following activities most likely would be considered a weakness in an entity's internal control over payroll?

    a. A voucher for the amount of the payroll is prepared in the general accounting department based on the payroll department's payroll summary.

    b. Payroll checks are prepared by the accounts payable department and signed by the treasurer.

c. The employee who distributes payroll check returns unclaimed payroll checks to the payroll department.

d. The personnel department sends employees' termination notices to the payroll department.

LO 8-8

8C.16 Which of the following payroll control activities would most effectively ensure that payment is made only for work performed?

a. Require all employees to record arrival and departure by using the time clock.

b. Have a payroll clerk recalculate all time cards.

c. Require all employees to sign their time cards.

d. Require employees to have their direct supervisors approve their time cards.

(AICPA adapted)

LO 8-8

8C.17 Which of the following activities performed by a department supervisor most likely would help to prevent or detect a payroll fraud?

a. Distributing paychecks directly to department employees.

b. Setting the pay rate for departmental employees.

c. Hiring employees and authorizing them to be added to payroll.

d. Approving a summary of hours each employee worked during the pay period.

(AICPA adapted)

Exercises and Problems

 All applicable Exercises and Problems are available with *Connect*.

LO 8-8

8C.18 **Major Risks in Payroll Cycle.** Prepare a schedule of the major risks in the payroll cycle. Identify the financial statement assertions related to each. Create a two-column schedule like this:

Payroll Cycle Risk	Assertion

LO 8-8

8C.19 **Payroll Authorization in a Computerized System.** Two accountants were discussing control activities and tests of controls for payroll systems. The senior accountant in charge of the engagement said: "It is impossible to determine who authorizes transactions when the payroll account is computerized."

Required:

Evaluate the senior accountant's statement about control in a computerized payroll system. List the points in the flow of payroll information where authorization takes place.

LO 8-8

8C.20 **Payroll Processed by a Service Organization.** Assume that you are the audit senior conducting a review of a new client's payroll system. In the process of interviewing the payroll department manager, she makes the following statement: "We don't need many controls because our payroll is done outside the company by Automated Information Processing, a service bureau."

Required:

Evaluate the payroll department manager's statement and describe how a service organization affects an auditor's review of controls.

LO 8-8

8C.21 **Payroll Audit Procedures, Computers, and Sampling.** You are the senior auditor in charge of the annual audit of Onward Manufacturing Corporation for the year ending December 31. The company is of medium size with only 300 employees. All 300 employees are union members paid by the hour at rates set forth in a union contract, a copy of which is furnished to you. Job and pay rate classifications are determined by a joint union–management conference, and a formal memorandum is placed in each employee's personnel file.

Every week, clock cards prepared and approved in the shop are collected and transmitted to the payroll department. The total of labor hours is summed on a calculator and entered on each clock card. Batch and hash totals are obtained for the following: (1) labor hours and (2) last four digits of Social Security numbers. These data are input into a disk file, batch balanced, and batch processed. The clock cards (with cost classification data) are sent to the cost accounting department.

The payroll system is computerized. As each person's payroll record is processed, the Social Security number is matched to a table (in a separate master file) to obtain job classification and pay rate data, then the pay rate is multiplied by the number of hours, and the check is printed. (Ignore payroll deductions for the following requirements.)

Required:

What audit procedures would you recommend to obtain evidence that payroll data are accurately totaled and transformed into machine-readable records? What deviation rate might you expect? What tolerable deviation rate would you set? What "items" would you sample? What factors should you consider in setting the size of your sample?

What audit procedures would you recommend to obtain evidence that the pay rates are appropriately assigned and used in figuring gross pay? In what way, if any, would these procedures be different if the gross pay were calculated by hand instead of on a computer?

LO 8-8

8C.22   Payroll Tests of Controls. The diagram in Exhibit 8C.22.1 describes several payroll tests of controls. It shows the direction of the tests, leading from samples of clock cards, payrolls, and cumulative year-to-date earnings records to blank squares.

Required:

For each blank square in Appendix Exhibit 8C.22.1, write a payroll test of controls procedure and describe the evidence it can produce. (*Hint:* Refer to Exhibit 5.12.)

EXHIBIT 8C.22.1
Diagram of Payroll Tests of Controls

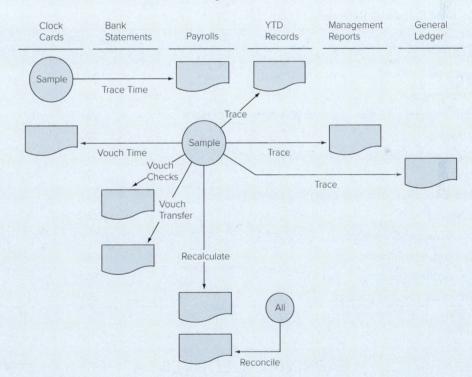

CHAPTER 9

Production Cycle

> *There is one rule for industrialists and that is: Make the best-quality of goods possible at the lowest cost possible, paying the highest wages possible.*
>
> *Henry Ford*

Professional Standards References

Topic	AU-C/ISA Section	PCAOB Reference*
An Audit of Internal Control over Financial Reporting	*Various*	AS 2201
Audit Documentation	230	AS 1215
Auditors' Responses to the Risks of Material Misstatements	240	AS 2301
Audit Planning	300	AS 2101
Identifying and Assessing the Risks of Material Misstatement	315	AS 2110
Materiality	320	AS 2105
Audit Considerations Relating to an Entity Using a Service Organization	402	AU 2601
Audit Evidence	500/501	AS 1105
Substantive Analytical Procedures	520	AS 2305
Auditing Accounting Estimates	540	AU 2501
Management Representations	580	AU 2805
Using the Work of an Audit Specialist	620	AU 1210

LEARNING OBJECTIVES

In the production cycle, materials, labor, and overhead are converted into finished goods (inventory) and services. Even companies that do not sell products sell services generated solely from the labor of employees. These services still represent costs that have to be accounted for and recovered by revenues. This chapter covers the production cycle, focusing on determining inventory valuation and cost of goods sold. Observation of the client's physical inventory count is such an important audit procedure that auditing standards require it. This chapter discusses procedures to be followed in observing the physical inventory count. It also discusses procedures for auditing the accumulation and pricing of inventory and recording it in the financial statements.

This chapter includes several short cases to illustrate the application of audit procedures in situations in which errors and frauds can be discovered.

Your objectives are to be able to:

LO 9-1 Describe the production cycle, including typical source documents.

LO 9-2 Identify significant accounts and relevant assertions related to the production cycle.

LO 9-3 Discuss the risk of material misstatement in the production cycle.

LO 9-4 Identify important internal control activities present in a properly designed system to mitigate the risk of material misstatements for each relevant assertion in the production cycle.

LO 9-5 Give examples of tests of controls to test the operating effectiveness of internal controls in the production cycle.

LO 9-6 Give examples of substantive procedures in the production cycle and relate them to assertions about significant account balances at the end of the period.

LO 9-7 Apply your knowledge to perform audit procedures in the production cycle and evaluate the findings of your tests.

PHAR-MOR INC.

From his childhood, Mickey Monus loved all sports, especially basketball. However, with limited talents and height (five feet nine on a good day), he would never play on a professional team. Monus did have one trait, however, shared by top athletes: an unquenchable thirst for winning.

Monus transferred his boundless energy from the basketball court to the boardroom. He acquired a single drugstore in Youngstown, Ohio, and, within 10 years, he had built 299 more stores and formed the national chain **Phar-Mor.** Unfortunately, it was all built on nonexistent inventory and phony profits that eventually would be the downfall of Monus and his company and would cost the company's auditors millions of dollars. Here is how it happened.

After acquiring the first drugstore, Monus dreamed of building his modest holdings into a large pharmaceutical empire using *power buying,* that is, offering products at deep discounts. First, he took his one unprofitable, unaudited store and increased the profits with the stroke of a pen by adding phony inventory figures. Armed only with his gift of gab and a set of inflated financials, Monus bilked money from investors, bought eight stores within a year, and began the mini-empire that grew to 300 stores. Monus became a financial icon, and his organization gained near-cult status in Youngstown.

With his newly found wealth, Monus decided to fulfill a sports fantasy by starting the World Basketball League (WBL) in which no players would be more than six feet five inches tall. He pumped $10 million of Phar-Mor's money into the league. However, the public did not like short basketball players and were not buying tickets, so Monus poured more Phar-Mor money into the WBL. One day, a travel agent who booked flights for league players received a $75,000 check for WBL expenses, but it was disbursed from a Phar-Mor bank account. The employee thought it odd that Phar-Mor would be paying the team's expenses. Because she was an acquaintance of one of Phar-Mor's major investors, she showed him the check. Alarmed, the investor began conducting his own investigation into Monus's illicit activities and helped expose an intricate financial fraud that caused losses of more than $1 billion.

Generating phony profits over an entire decade was no easy feat. Phar-Mor's CFO said the company was losing serious money because it was selling goods for less than it had paid for them. A significant mantra of Phar-Mor was "We will not be undersold by Walmart." (Remember that a highly competitive industry can be an important red flag for management fraud.) Nevertheless, Monus argued that through Phar-Mor's *power buying,* it would become so large that it could sell its way out of trouble. Eventually, the CFO caved in—under extreme pressure from Monus—and for the next several years, he and some of his staff kept two sets of books: the ones they showed the auditors and the ones that reflected the awful truth.

Phar-Mor's management dumped the losses into the "bucket account" and then used "blow-out" entries to reallocate the sums to the company's hundreds of stores in the form of increases in inventory costs. They issued fake invoices for merchandise purchases, made phony journal entries to increase inventory and decrease cost of sales, recognized inventory purchases but failed to accrue a liability, and overcounted and double-counted merchandise. The finance department was able to conceal the inventory shortages because the auditors, **Coopers & Lybrand,** observed inventory in only four of 300 stores and informed Phar-Mor months in advance which stores they would visit. Phar-Mor executives fully stocked the four selected stores and allocated the phony inventory increases to the other stores. Regardless of the accounting tricks, Phar-Mor was heading for collapse. During its last audit, cash was so tight suppliers threatened to cut the company off for nonpayment of bills. The auditors never uncovered the fraud, for which they paid dearly. This failure cost the audit firm more than $300 million in civil judgments. The CFO, who did not profit personally, was sentenced to 33 months in prison. Monus himself went to jail for 10 years.[1]

PRODUCTION CYCLE: TYPICAL ACTIVITIES

LO 9-1
Describe the production cycle, including typical source documents.

When auditing a manufacturer, whether it is a small entity producing specialty goods or a *Fortune* 100 corporation manufacturing millions of units each year, it is paramount that an auditor understand all stages involved with converting raw materials into finished goods. If this process is not properly controlled, not only are financial statement misstatements likely, but also mismanagement can quickly put a company out of business.

The production cycle links the acquisition cycle in which goods and services are purchased to the revenue cycle, in which the inventory is sold (see Exhibit 9.1). These cycles, along with the payroll cycle, account for all additions and reductions of inventory items. Thus, the production cycle (Exhibit 9.2) is mostly concerned with accounting for inventory as it moves through the production stages from raw materials to work-in-process to finished goods and for accumulating accurate costs of the inventory items.

Sales Forecasts ①

Production activities start with a **sales forecast**, a marketing projection of product sales, based on past performance and marketing initiatives. Based on this forecast and other pertinent factors (e.g., production setup costs, scheduled equipment maintenance, finished goods inventories, and raw material inventories), the production planner can determine both the type and the quantity of products that need to be produced to meet anticipated demand and can schedule the products in a production plan. The sales forecast is one of the most important documents in any organization. If it is incorrect and underestimates the company's production requirements, hundreds of thousands of dollars of potential profits may be unattainable. However, if it is incorrect and overstates the product demand,

EXHIBIT 9.1
Relationship of Business Cycles

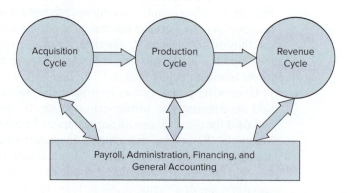

[1]J. T. Wells, "Ghost Goods: How to Spot Phantom Inventory," *Journal of Accountancy,* June 2001

EXHIBIT 9.2
Production cycle

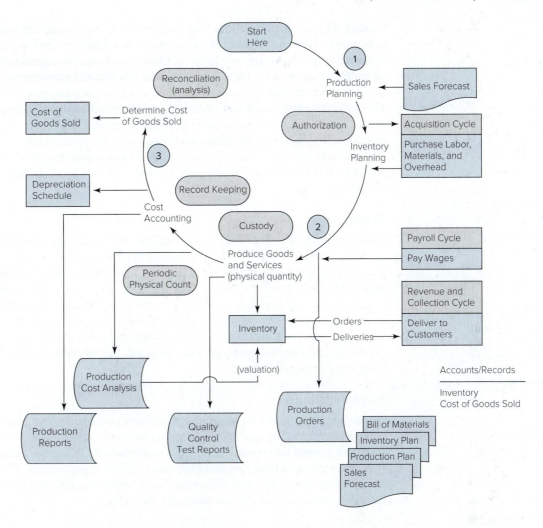

millions of dollars of raw material and finished goods inventory may needlessly utilize corporate assets and warehouse space.

Production Planning ①

The goal of production planning is to provide a schedule for manufacturing, called the **production plan**, so that quality products will be available at the appropriate time for the lowest cost. For example, production planners must balance the finished goods warehousing costs associated with making large (high-quantity) production runs with the changeover costs of making several smaller (low-quantity) production runs. In addition, production planners must integrate corporate strategies such as long-range plans and just-in-time (JIT) inventory management. Refer to Exhibit 9.2 for the activities and accounting involved in a production cycle. As you follow the exhibit, you can track the elements of a control system that are described in the following sections.

The physical output of a production cycle is inventory (starting with raw materials, proceeding to work-in-process, and then moving through to finished goods). Exhibit 9.2 shows the connection of inventory to the revenue and collection cycle in terms of orders and deliveries. Most of the transactions in a production cycle are cost accounting allocations, unit cost determinations, and standard cost calculations. These are internal transactions produced entirely within the company's accounting system. Exhibit 9.2 also includes the elements of depreciation cost calculation, cost of goods sold determination, and production cost analysis as examples of these transactions.

The job of the production planner is one of the most critical in any manufacturing operation. The production planner not only creates a production plan, but also must identify the total quantity of raw materials necessary for production based on the production plan and the **bill of materials** (a specification of the type and quantity of component materials required for the production). Once raw materials requirements (from the bill of materials) are known, the planner uses the **raw material inventory status report** to determine whether enough raw materials are in stock to complete production. If insufficient raw materials exist, additional materials must be purchased and, if required, the planner must send a purchase requisition to purchasing (which begins the expenditure cycle as discussed in Chapter 8). Purchase lead times must be factored into the production plan. The production planner must also be aware of labor requirements. If the production plan identifies a change in total production, human resources must be aware of the impact on the labor force.

Production ②

Once the production plan has been finalized, it is generally shared with managers in the sales/marketing department, production department, and possibly human resources who may be required to "sign off" as evidence of their approval of the plan. Managers may request adjustments to the schedule or may need to adjust personnel, maintenance schedules, even overtime, to ensure that production operates efficiently. As you can see, an error in the production plan may mean insufficient raw materials and personnel, excessive warehousing of finished goods, an oversupply of raw materials, unnecessary personnel, or insufficient finished goods to meet demand. All of these conditions represent real, substantial costs to the entity.

Inventory Control

As the time for production nears, the production planner issues a **production order** to the appropriate production personnel including inventory control and production managers. Inventory control will receive a **materials requisition** or **materials transfer ticket** that authorizes inventory to release raw materials and supplies to production. These documents are the inventory record keepers' authorizations to update the raw materials inventory files to record the reductions of the raw materials inventory.

Cost Accounting ③

When production is completed, production orders and the related records of materials and labor used are sent to the cost accounting department. Labor is reported by various means from time sheets to computerized clocks. Employees designate what job or product they worked on, or the labor is automatically assigned based on the department or machinery to which the employee is assigned. Because these accounting documents may come from the production workers, it may require an independent verification of hours worked from other sources (e.g., notifications of materials from the inventory custodian or labor costs assigned from the payroll department).

Cost accounting generally records finished goods at **standard costs**. Developing standard costs is a difficult, time-consuming process, even for relatively simple products. All materials, supplies, labor, and overhead that go into the product must be measured based on the bill of materials and accumulated into the production cost. Differences between standard costs and actual costs are recorded in variance accounts and reviewed by supervisors. (*Note:* GAAP recognizes specific-item, first-in, first-out [FIFO], last-in, first-out [LIFO], and weighted-average costing but does not recognize standard costs per se. The auditor must ensure that standard costs are not materially different from the GAAP method that the client has adopted.)

The cost accounting department produces analyses of actual cost per unit, standard cost, and variances. Cost accounting also may determine the **overhead allocation** to production in general, to production orders, and to finished units. Depending on the design of the company's cost accounting system, these costs are used to value inventory and ultimately to determine the cost of goods sold. In addition, production reports are authorization for the finished goods inventory custodian to place the units in the finished goods inventory. The reports also authorize the inventory record keepers to update the finished goods inventory. In many cases, the cost accounting department is also responsible for calculating the depreciation of fixed assets and the amortization of intangibles.

It would be wrong to think of the production cycle as only applying to manufacturing companies. With only some modification, the events depicted apply equally to a retail organization. Clearly, **Target** has a sales forecast, and its product managers (their equivalent of a production manager) need to determine what products are available in stores and in the warehouses and compare that with the forecasted needs. Purchase requisitions are issued to buy additional product and have it available at the appropriate time. Production may be viewed as the process of getting items from the warehouse to the store and into the appropriate retail space for sale.

AUDITING INSIGHT   Overhead Allocation

The cost accounting department at Pointed Publications Inc. routinely allocated overhead to book printing runs at the rate of 40 percent of materials and labor cost. The debit was made initially to the finished goods (books) inventory, and the credit went to an "overhead allocated" account that was offset against other entries in the cost of goods sold calculation, which included all actual overhead incurred. During the year,

the company produced 10 million books, to which $40 million of overhead were allocated. The auditors noticed that actual overhead expenditures were $32 million and that 3 million books remained in the ending inventory. This finding resulted in the conclusion that inventory was overstated by $2.4 million, the cost of goods sold was understated by $2.4 million, and the income before taxes was overstated by 8.2 percent.

Overhead Allocation

	Company Accounting	Proper Accounting
Books produced	10 million	10 million
Books sold	7 million	7 million
Labor and materials cost	$100 million	$ 100 million
Overhead allocated	$40 million	$32 million (actual cost)
Cost per book	$14.00	$13.20
Cost of goods sold:		
Labor and materials cost	$100 million	$ 100 million
Overhead allocated to books	40 million	
Overhead incurred	32 million	32 million
Overhead credited to cost	(40 million)	
Ending inventory	(42 million)	(39.6 million)
Total cost of goods sold	$ 90 million	$92.4 million

☑ REVIEW CHECKPOINTS

9.1 What functions are normally associated with the production cycle?

9.2 What inventory costing methods does GAAP recognize?

9.3 Describe a walkthrough of a production transaction from receiving production orders to making an entry in the finished goods perpetual inventory records. What document copies would be collected? What controls noted? What duties separated?

9.4 How might an auditor use a client's sales forecast for general familiarity with the production cycle or for evaluation of slow-moving inventory?

SIGNIFICANT ACCOUNTS AND RELEVANT ASSERTIONS

LO 9-2
Identify significant accounts and relevant assertions related to the production cycle.

STAGES OF AN AUDIT

| Obtain (or Retain) Engagement | Engagement Planning | Risk Assessment | Reporting | Audit Evidence |

Exhibit 9.3 identifies the significant accounts and assertions in the production cycle. In this cycle, the most significant risks usually relate to the existence and valuation of inventory and the correct valuation of labor, which was discussed in Appendix 8C. In addition, because the primary components of cost of goods sold are direct labor and direct material, this account also has significant risk. If management wants to inflate sales by creating fictitious sales or inflating sales amounts, there must be a corresponding debit. Expenses can be used for this purpose as explained in Chapter 8. However, inventory has been a favorite place to hide fraud for many infamous frauds (e.g., Phar-Mor, Crazy Eddie's).

Unethical managers might prefer to manipulate inventory instead of other expenses because of the double effect on the financial statements. When ending inventory is overstated, assets are overstated and cost of goods sold is understated, thereby increasing both total assets and income. Analysts often look at a company's profit margins to determine how well it is managing costs and to determine whether the company can maintain sufficient markup to cover other operating and nonoperating costs and be competitive.

Another reason that inventory is an inviting target for manipulation is the complexity and subjectivity involved in accounting for it. Because there are many large purchases of inventory, fraudsters believe that fictitious or overstated transactions may be hard to catch or the audit of inventory can be controlled to the extent that such inflated inventory numbers can be obscured from the auditors. Further, even if the inventory account is correct, the manipulation of the cost by only a few cents on many items can result in a multi-million dollar misstatement. Therefore, the audit of inventory is especially important to ensure that the financial statements are not materially misstated.

The Phar-Mor case illustrates how even a relatively simple inventory process can be manipulated and misstated. Many other corporate frauds such as those at **Crazy Eddie's, Leslie Fay,** and **Health Management** were concealed by creating nonexistent or overvalued inventory. Inventory is often the largest current asset on a company's balance sheet, and it is likely to be a complex account. Imagine trying to value the cars at **General Motors,** the computers at **IBM,** or the oil reserves at **ExxonMobil.** How about the $952 million

EXHIBIT 9.3 **Significant Accounts and Assertions in the Production Cycle**

Significant Account	Relevant Assertions	Assertion Risk
Inventory*	Existence	High
	Valuation & Allocation	High
	Cutoff	High
	Presentation	Moderate
	Rights	Moderate
	Completeness	Low
Wages and salary expense	Completeness	Moderate
	Accuracy	High
Cost of goods sold	Valuation	High

* Detailed relevant risks for inventory are shown in more detail in Exhibit 9.4.

in livestock listed as inventory by **Tyson Foods**? Even inventories of simple commodities present issues of measurement and valuation. Inventories of more complex items such as electronics or biochemicals can require the use of specialists by the auditors.

A number of problems can arise in accounting for inventory. Some inventories are very susceptible to theft. Others require complex cost build-ups (especially if they are valued at LIFO). GAAP require inventory to be stated at the lower of cost or **net realizable value (NRV)**. Cost is the total price paid, including freight-in, or estimates of actual costs using LIFO, FIFO, or an average. Net realizable value is the selling price of the goods less all costs to complete and to sell the goods (e.g., sales commissions). Items should be added to inventory when the company has title to them and included in cost of goods sold when the related revenue is recognized.[2] In addition, work-in-process inventory may be especially difficult because each item has different amounts of materials and labor incorporated into the product at the inventory date. These multiple and often subjective evaluations make inventory a high-risk area that management often uses to overstate assets. Because of the multiple and complex risks for inventory, there are several relevant risks, as shown in Exhibit 9.4.

EXHIBIT 9.4   **Relative Assertion Risks for Inventory Accounts**

AICPA Assertions	Raw Materials Inventory	Work-in-Process Inventory	Finished Goods Inventory	Explanation
Transaction assertions				Management may overstate all inventories: *Raw material* and *finished goods inventories* are most often overstated by adding numbers to counts or stating that items' costs are higher than actual costs. *Work-in-process* inventory is difficult to value and may be overstated by adding labor and material that have not been actually applied to the product. In addition, it might be easy to miss items within the manufacturing process.
• Occurrence	High	Low	High	
• Completeness	Low	Medium	Low	
• Cutoff	Medium	Low	Medium	
• Accuracy	Medium	High	High	
• Classification	Low	Low	Low	
Balance assertions				As stated, fictitious inventory may exist in *raw materials* and *finished goods inventory*. *Raw material inventory* may contain goods not owned by the client. *Finished goods inventory* may include consignment goods. Inventory costs may be overstated in all three inventories. Significant disclosures are required for inventory balances that may be manipulated to management's advantage.
• Existence	High	Low	High	
• Rights and obligations	Medium	Low	Medium	
• Completeness	Low	Low	Low	
• Valuation and allocation	High	High	High	
Presentation and disclosure assertions				Inventory disclosures concerning valuation method as well as lower of cost or net realizable value are required. Disclosures concerning inventory returns and obsolescence may also be required.
• Occurrence	Medium	Low	Medium	
• Rights and obligations	Medium	Medium	Medium	
• Completeness	Low	Low	Low	
• Accuracy, valuation, and allocation	High	High	High	
• Classification and understandability	Low	Medium	Low	

Note: These risks are for a typical entity engaged in manufacturing, retail, and other similar industries. Some specialized industries may have risks that vary from those indicated in this table.

✓ REVIEW CHECKPOINTS

9.5 If the actual sales for the year are substantially lower than the sales forecasted at the beginning of the year, what potential valuation problems could arise in the production cycle accounts?

9.6 What information is used in the cost accounting department to calculate cost of goods sold for a production operation? What are the significant risks that would make this calculation inaccurate?

9.7 The balance sheet of a company lists $25 million of inventory. What assertions is management making regarding inventory?

[2]FASB, Revenue Recognition, ASC 606, May 2014.

RISK OF MATERIAL MISSTATEMENT

LO 9-3

Discuss the risk of material misstatement in the production cycle.

When considering what could go wrong (WCGW) in the production cycle, auditors consider six primary concerns:

1. All inventory items have been included (completeness).
2. Inventory has been properly accounted for and properly valued using an acceptable GAAP accounting method (valuation).
3. Items included in inventory were in inventory on the balance sheet date (existence and cutoff).
4. Items included in inventory were the property of the client (rights).
5. Proper presentation and disclosures have been provided for inventory (presentation and disclosure).
6. Cost of goods sold includes all applicable materials, labor, and overhead properly valued (accuracy).

Exhibit 9.5 summarizes the WCGW analysis for the production cycle.

As previously discussed in this chapter, inventory is a significant account, with a pervasive effect on the financial statements and combined with its volume and its complexity, a misstatement may be probable if sufficient internal controls are not in place. In order for inventory to be proper disclosed, all items comprising inventory must be included and properly valued. Consider the balance sheet and inventory footnote for **Target Corporation**'s 2015 fiscal year (January 30, 2016) shown in Exhibit 9.6. Note that Target asserts that it has $8.6 billion in inventory, which represents 61 percent of its current assets and

EXHIBIT 9.5   **Assertions and What Could Go Wrong**

Significant Account	Relevant Assertions	What Can Go Wrong?
Inventory	Existence	Items included in inventory records are not actual items in inventory.
	Valuation	1. Inventory is not accurately recorded. 2. Proper amounts are not allocated to inventory. 3. Inventory is old or obsolete and has declined in value.
	Cutoff/Existence	Items are included in inventory even when received in the subsequent period.
	Presentation & Disclosure	Inventory pledged as collateral is not disclosed.
	Rights	Items held on consignment are included in inventory.
	Completeness	Some items are not included in inventory.
Wages and salary expense	Completeness	Some employees are paid off the books.
	Accuracy	Wages and salaries are not recorded at the proper amount.
Cost of goods sold	Accuracy	Direct material, labor, and overhead have not been properly included.

EXHIBIT 9.6   Excerpts from Target Corporation's 10-K

Panel A

Consolidated Statements of Financial Position (millions, except footnotes)

	January 30, 2016	January 31, 2015
Assets		
Cash and cash equivalents, including short-term investments of $3,008 and $1,520	$4,046	$2,210
Inventory	8,601	8,282
Assets of discontinued operations	322	1,058
Other current assets	1,161	2,074
Total current assets	14,130	13,624
Property and equipment		
Land	6,125	6,127
Buildings and improvements	27,059	26,613
Fixtures and equipment	5,347	5,329
Computer hardware and software	2,617	2,552
Construction-in-progress	315	424
Accumulated depreciation	(16,246)	(15,093)
Property and equipment, net	25,217	25,952
Noncurrent assets of discontinued operations	75	717
Other noncurrent assets	840	879
Total assets	$40,262	$41,172

Panel B

Inventory Footnote

12. Inventory

The majority of our inventory is accounted for under the retail inventory accounting method (RIM) using the last-in, first-out (LIFO) method. Inventory is stated at the lower of LIFO cost or market. The cost of our inventory includes the amount we pay to our suppliers to acquire inventory, freight costs incurred in connection with the delivery of product to our distribution centers and stores, and import costs, reduced by vendor income and cash discounts. The majority of our distribution center operating costs, including compensation and benefits, are expensed in the period incurred. Inventory is also reduced for estimated losses related to shrink and markdowns. The LIFO provision is calculated based on inventory levels, markup rates, and internally measured retail price indices.

Under RIM, inventory cost and the resulting gross margins are calculated by applying a cost-to-retail ratio to the inventory retail value. RIM is an averaging method that has been widely used in the retail industry due to its practicality. The use of RIM will result in inventory being valued at the lower of cost or market because permanent markdowns are taken as a reduction of the retail value of inventory.

Certain other inventory is recorded at the lower of cost or market using the cost method. The valuation allowance for inventory valued under a cost method was not material to our Consolidated Financial Statements as of the end of fiscal 2015 or 2014.

We routinely enter into arrangements with vendors whereby we do not purchase or pay for merchandise until the merchandise is ultimately sold to a guest. Activity under this program is included in sales and cost of sales in the Consolidated Statements of Operations, but the merchandise received under the program is not included in inventory in our Consolidated Statements of Financial Position because of the virtually simultaneous purchase and sale of this inventory. Sales made under these arrangements totaled $2,261 million, $2,040 million, and $1,833 million in 2015, 2014, and 2013, respectively.

Source: Target 10-K, January 30, 2016.

21 percent of its total assets. Other than buildings and improvements, it is the largest single asset that Target owns. Further, consider the difficulties in establishing this number in its 1,792 stores and 37 distribution centers in the United States. Consider that if Target has 1,000 pairs of socks in each store and 10,000 in each warehouse and the cost was misstated by 10 cents, the balance sheet error would be more than $116,000. While this is not a material amount to an inventory of more than $8.6 billion, it illustrates how a small error or misstatement can result in a large inventory valuation error. Phar-Mor used this technique across hundreds of items to cover up its fraud.

An additional review of Target's inventory footnote reveals several other issues. Note the second paragraph speaks of using a cost-to-retail method to value inventory and discusses that some items have been marked down in value. Further, the fourth paragraph indicates that there are items that Target does not own and are paid for only after the merchandise is sold (items on consignment). Without good internal controls, a small error in the application of the cost estimation could produce a substantial inventory misstatement. Also, inventory on consignment might inappropriately end up as part of the inventory Target asserts that it owns. Clearly, Target must take great care in establishing the value of its inventory in its entire system, and auditors must take care that the accumulation of inventory misstatements does not lead to a material misstatement in its financial statements.

Now let's look at how an inventory misstatement might affect the overall financial statements. The following table provides numbers for 2015 for inventory, sales, cost of sales, earnings from continuing operations, and net income reported by Target in its January 30, 2016, 10-K report (all amounts in millions of dollars). While Target does an excellent job of preparing financial statements and we have no reason to suspect that the numbers presented are inaccurate in any way, for our purposes, let's suppose that inventory is overstated by 5 percent, or $430 million. The third column shows how this hypothetical misstatement affects each of the accounts presented. Ignoring tax effects, this 5 percent inventory misstatement has resulted in a 13 percent error in net income. When auditors identify inventory as a pervasive error, they are referring to this cascading effect of the error.

Account	Actual Amount as Reported for Target 2015	Account as Affected by a 5% Inventory Error
Inventory	$8,601	$8,171
Sales	$73,785	$73,785
Cost of sales	$51,997	$52,427
Earnings from continuing operations	$5,530	$5,100
Net income	$3,363	$2,933

✅ REVIEW CHECKPOINTS

9.8 What makes the recording of inventory at its proper amount difficult on the financial statements?

9.9 Why do auditors consider inventory errors pervasive?

INTERNAL CONTROL ACTIVITIES AND DESIGN EVALUATION

In order to properly assess control risk, the auditor must understand the internal control system, assess the design of the controls, and assess whether the controls are in operation. Control risk assessment is important because it governs the *nature, timing,* and *extent*

LO 9-4

Identify important internal control activities present in a properly designed system to mitigate the risk of material misstatements for each relevant assertion in the production cycle.

of substantive procedures that will be performed in the audit of account balances in the production cycle. These account balances include:

- Raw materials inventory.
- Work-in-process inventory.
- Finished goods inventory.
- Cost of goods sold.

With respect to inventory valuation, this chapter discusses the cost accounting function and its role in determining the cost valuation of manufactured finished goods.

Entity-Level Controls

It is important that auditors consider entity-level controls in all processes and procedures. In the production cycle, controls over access to the production facility, including inventory, are essential. The prevention of theft of inventory and equipment begins with a facility that requires escorts for visitors and ensures that only authorized personnel have access to inventory and production areas. Furthermore, adequate security must be enforced when the facility is not in operation. Finally, production reports should be adequate to ensure that only authorized operations are performed and that performance statistics are reviewed on a timely basis and anomalies are investigated promptly.

Control Considerations

Control activities for proper separation of responsibilities should be in place and operating. By referring to Exhibit 9.2, you can see that proper separation involves authorization (production planning, inventory planning, and purchase requisitions) by persons who do not have custody, record-keeping, cost accounting, or reconciliation duties. Custody of inventories (raw materials, work-in-process, and finished goods) is in the hands of persons who do not authorize the amount or timing of production or the purchase of materials and labor, perform the cost accounting record keeping, or prepare cost analyses (reconciliations). Persons who do not authorize production or have custody of assets in the production process perform cost accounting (a recording function). Combinations of two or more of the duties of authorization, custody, and accounting in one person, one office, or one computerized system could open the door for errors and frauds.

In addition, the controls should provide for detailed checking activities, for example:

- Production orders should contain a list of materials and their quantities, and they should be approved by a production planner/scheduler.
- Material should not be issued to the production floor without an authorized material requisition.
- Material requisitions should be compared in the cost accounting department with the list of materials on the production orders, and the production operator and the materials inventory storekeeper should sign the materials requisitions.
- All material requisitions should be accounted for. Material requisitioned is used in production, is unusable (scrap), or excess material returned to raw material inventory.
- Documentation for material returned to raw material inventory should accompany the returned items with a copy going to inventory control for use in adjusting the perpetual raw material inventory.
- Production supervisors should sign (or review if the time is kept electronically) labor time records on jobs, and the cost accounting department should reconcile these cost amounts with the labor report from the payroll department.
- The production supervisor and finished goods inventory custodian should review production reports of finished units and then forward them to cost accounting.
- Inventory should be periodically counted with the counts agreed to perpetual inventory records.

These control activities track the raw materials and labor from the beginning of production to completion of the production process. With each internal transaction, the responsibility and accountability for assets are passed from one person or location to another.

Many entities have complex computer systems to manage production and materials flow. Even though the technology is complex, the basic management and control functions of ensuring the flow of labor and materials to production and the control of waste should be in place. Manual signatures, paper production orders, and paper requisitions might not exist, but computer system equivalents should be in place.

Custody

Supervisors and production workers have physical custody of materials and labor documents (time cards, job tickets, etc.) while the production work is being performed. Authorized employees can requisition materials from the raw materials inventory, assign people to jobs, and control the pace of work. In a sense, they have custody of a "moving inventory." The work-in-process (WIP) is literally "moving" and changing form in the process of being transformed from raw materials into finished goods.

Inventory warehouses and fixed asset locations should be under adequate physical security (storerooms, fences, locks, and the like). However, control over goods in process is more difficult than control over a warehouse of raw materials or finished goods where unauthorized individuals cannot gain access. Control over WIP can be exercised by holding supervisors and workers accountable for the use of materials specified in the production orders, for the timely completion of production, and for the quality of the finished goods. This accountability can be achieved with effective cost accounting, cost analysis, performance reviews, and quality control testing. Accountability may be evident by ensuring that supervisors and management are analyzing the costs of production orders, comparing the costs to prior experience or to standard costs, and determining lower-of-cost-or-NRV valuations. When costs of material or labor, scrap rates for materials, or production numbers do not meet expectations, management should require a documented assessment by cost accounting or internal audit to determine the cause and corrective action required.

AUDITING INSIGHT

The Securities and Exchange Commission has charged the Jacksonville, Florida-based retail chain **Stein Mart Inc.** with materially misstating its pre-tax income due to improper valuation of inventory subject to price discounts and for having inadequate internal accounting controls.

An SEC investigation found the retailer often offered its merchandise to customers at retail price reductions referred to as Perm POS markdowns and that merchandise subject to such a markdown never reverted back to its original retail price. Stein Mart reduced the value of inventory subject to these markdowns at the time the item was sold rather than immediately at the time the markdown was applied.

As a result, according to the SEC, Stein Mart materially misstated its pre-tax income in certain quarterly public filings with the SEC, including an overstatement of almost 30 percent in the first quarter of 2012.

"Inventory is one of the most significant assets for retail companies, and as a result, it is critical that companies have effective internal accounting controls to ensure that inventory is valued properly," said Michael Maloney, chief accountant of the SEC's Enforcement Division, in a statement. "Stein Mart failed in this regard as its internal accounting controls to ensure proper inventory valuations were inadequate in various ways."

According to the SEC's order instituting a settled administrative proceeding, Stein Mart's internal accounting controls over Perm POS markdowns were inadequate. For example, until at least the middle of 2011, the retailer's decision to characterize a markdown as Perm POS resided solely with Stein Mart's merchandising department, which did not understand the impact that Stein Mart's markdowns could have on inventory valuation accounting, according to the SEC.

In the fall of 2012, Stein Mart raised its accounting treatment of Perm POS markdowns with its external auditor, and the external auditor informed Stein Mart that its accounting for Perm POS markdowns was not acceptable under GAAP. In May 2013, Stein Mart restated its financial results for the first quarter of 2012, all reporting periods in fiscal year 2011, and its annual reporting period in fiscal year 2010. According to the SEC's order, Stein Mart also had inadequate internal accounting controls in the areas of software assets, credit card liabilities, and other inventory-related issues.

In agreeing to settle the charges without admitting or denying the SEC's findings, Stein Mart consented to the SEC's order imposing an $800,000 penalty and requiring the company to cease and desist from committing or causing any violations or any future violations of the reporting, books and records, and internal controls provisions of the federal securities laws.

Source: Michael Cohn, "Stein Mart Settles with SEC for $800,000 on Inventory Valuation and Accounting Controls," *Accounting Today,* September 22, 2015.

Internal Control Questionnaire

Information about the production cycle control often is gathered initially by completing an *internal control questionnaire (ICQ)*. An ICQ for control activities commonly found in the production cycle is included in Appendix Exhibit 9A.1. You can study this questionnaire for details of desirable control activities. The ICQ is organized with headings that identify the important transaction assertions: *existence, completeness, accuracy, cutoff,* and *classification.*

Exhibit 9.7 shows the significant accounts in the production cycle and the related important assertions, what could go wrong in the related assertions, and the control activity that should be in place to mitigate the risk.

EXHIBIT 9.7   Internal Control Activities in the Expenditure and Acquisition Cycle

Significant Account	Relevant Assertion	What Can Go Wrong?	Internal Control Activity
Inventory	Existence	Items may be included in the inventory that do not exist.	Inventory areas should be secure to prevent theft. Inventory is only provided to production with proper documentation. A physical count of inventory is performed and compared to the inventory records.
	Completeness	Items may not be recorded in the inventory account.	A physical inventory count should be taken and compared to the inventory record.
	Cutoff/Existence	Inventory received in the subsequent period may be included in current year's inventory.	Receiving reports should be prenumbered and used in consecutive order. Receiving report dates should be traced to inventory records to ensure inventory was recorded in the proper period.
	Rights	Items included in inventory belong to the company.	Documentation for inventory items should clearly state the ownership of the items. A separate account number should be used to track inventory on consignment.
	Valuation	Items in inventory are not properly valued or may have declined in value.	Inventory items should be reviewed for usability or salability. Valuation calculations should be reviewed by management.
Cost of goods sold (COGS)	Completeness	Labor or material may be omitted from COGS.	Cost sheets should be reviewed for all projects and production runs to ensure all items are included.
	Accuracy	Items included in COGS may not be properly valued.	Cost sheets should be reviewed for all projects and production to ensure labor and material assigned are properly valued.

TESTING OF OPERATING EFFECTIVENESS OF INTERNAL CONTROL

LO 9-5

Give examples of tests of controls to test the operating effectiveness of internal controls in the production cycle.

Tests of Controls

An entity should have detailed control activities in place and operating to prevent, detect, and correct accounting errors. While production activities vary widely from one company to another, there are some specific controls that an auditor may evaluate. Observation of the physical controls over inventory may be of particular interest, especially if either raw materials or finished goods have significant value. Further, the auditor can observe the movement of inventory from raw materials to finished goods, specifically noting that proper authorization and documentation have been provided to the inventory custodian. The auditor should obtain evidence of proper separation of duties (custody of the inventory, inventory record keeping, authorization for inventory movement) in the inventory area through observation. Documentation in the production and cost accounting areas should be inspected to determine that labor and material costs are properly recorded and allocated to the correct production run. Exhibit 9.8 puts controls in the perspective of production activity with examples of specific assertions. This exhibit identifies the transaction assertions in specific examples related to production.

Auditors can perform tests of controls to determine whether company personnel are effectively performing control activities that are said to be in place and operating properly. Exhibit 9.8 includes a selection of tests of controls for the accumulation of costs for WIP inventory. This is the stage of inventory that is in the production process. Upon completion, the accumulated costs become the value of the finished goods inventory. The illustrative procedures presume the existence of production cost reports that are updated as production takes place. Reports such as labor reports that assign labor cost to the job, material reports that charge raw materials to the production orders, and reports that provide overhead allocation calculations. Some or all of these documents may be in the form of computerized records.

It is important for the auditor performing tests of controls in the production cycle to recognize that most of the company's documentation is internal. The entity's reporting system generates production reports, inventory reports, material and labor distribution reports, and other documents auditors rely on. The auditor must pay close attention to general and application controls over the production reporting system in order to have some assurance that reports can be relied on for testing.

Direction of Tests of Controls

The tests of controls in Exhibit 9.8 are designed to test production accounting in two directions. One is the *completeness* direction, in which the auditors are interested in determining that all production that was started was recorded. Exhibit 9.9 shows that the sample for this direction is taken from the population of production orders found in the production-planning department. The procedures trace the cost accumulation forward to the production cost reports in the cost accounting department.

Testing the other direction relates to the *occurrence* of production. The auditors are interested in determining that items composing WIP and finished goods inventories

EXHIBIT 9.8   **Assertions about Classes of Transactions and Events: Production Cycle**

What Could Go Wrong?	Controls	Tests of Controls
Production and related events that have been recorded have not actually occurred.	• Cost accounting is separated from production, payroll, and inventory control. • Material usage reports are reconciled with raw material stores' issue slips, scrap reports, and documentation of unused material returned to inventory.	• Observe separation of cost accounting function from production, payroll, and inventory control. • Inspect evidence of reconciliations.
All production documents have not been recorded.	• All documents are prenumbered and numerical sequence reviewed. • Periodic count of inventory is compared to perpetual records. • Open production cost reports are reconciled to the WIP inventory cost report. • Receiving reports and material usage are posted to perpetual inventory records. • Job cost sheets are posted weekly, and summary journal entries of work-in-process and work completed are prepared monthly.	• Inspect evidence of review of numerical sequence. Select a sample of documents and examine numerical sequence. • Inspect evidence that inventory counts are compared to perpetual records. • Inspect reconciliation of production cost reports to WIP inventory control report. • Trace receiving reports to perpetual inventory. Trace materials used reports to production cost reports. • Inspect journal entries and agree with approved cost sheets. Compare costs to standard cost listing.
Production information, including costs, has been improperly calculated and recorded.	• Labor usage reports are compared to job time tickets. • Material usage and labor usage reports are prepared by floor supervisor and approved by production supervisor. • Periodic count of inventory is compared to perpetual records. • Receiving reports are posted to perpetual inventory on a timely basis.	• Inspect evidence of comparison by client. • Inspect evidence of approval of material and labor usage reports. • Reconcile inventory counts with perpetual records. • Trace dates on receiving reports to posting in perpetual inventory records.
Production events have not been recorded in the correct accounting period.	• Receiving reports are posted to perpetual inventory in the proper period. • Finished goods are recorded in the proper period. • Production reports of material and labor are prepared weekly and transmitted to cost accounting.	• Vouch the dates of inventory records to receiving reports. • Inspect production data and agree with finished goods inventory status reports. • Inspect production reports and agree dates with dates in weekly journal entries.
Production material has been not been recorded in the proper accounts.	• Production supervisor is required to account for all material and labor as direct or indirect and to identify appropriate job classifications.	• Observe supervisor allocation. Test allocation. Examine supervisor signature.

recorded in the inventory accounts were produced. Exhibit 9.10 shows that the sample for this test is from the inventory accounts. This sample is vouched to the production reports (quantity and cost) recorded in the inventory accounts. Additional testing may include vouching from the production reports to the recorded material, labor, and payroll reports. Potential findings include errors in the *accuracy* of the recorded inventory cost. Of course, CAATs could be used to perform a 100 percent match that would accomplish both goals.

Summary: Control Risk Assessment

The audit team should evaluate the evidence obtained from an understanding of the internal controls and from the tests of controls. The evaluation of control risk with the assessment of inherent risk provides the auditors an assessment of the risk of material misstatement. If the risk of material misstatement is relatively low, the substantive procedures on the account balances can be reduced. For example, if inventory observation test counts are performed on a date prior to the year-end, fewer counts would be made,

EXHIBIT 9.9
**Test of Production
Cost Controls:
Completeness Direction**

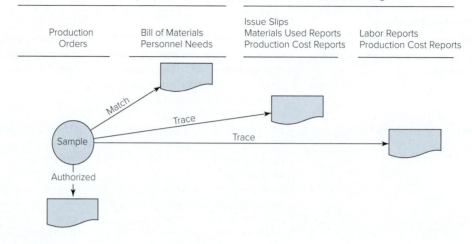

EXHIBIT 9.10
**Test of Production Cost
Controls: Occurrence
Direction**

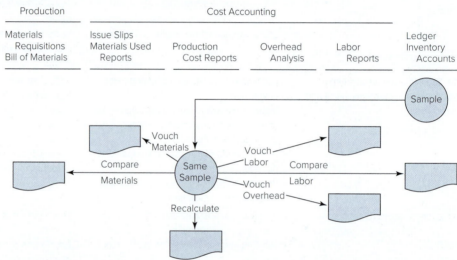

and the inventory valuation procedures could be reduced in scope (i.e., smaller sample size). Furthermore, substantive analytical procedures could be used with more confidence in detecting material misstatements not otherwise evident in the accounting details.

On the other hand, if tests of controls reveal weaknesses and the risk of material misstatement is higher, the substantive procedures need to be designed to lower detection risk in the inventory and cost of goods sold account balances. For example, a large number of inventory production reports may be selected for valuation calculations, and the inventory observation may be scheduled nearer the year-end date with the audit team making a large number of test counts. Descriptions of significant deficiencies, control weaknesses, and inefficiencies may be incorporated in a letter to the client and must be communicated to the audit committee.

✓ REVIEW CHECKPOINTS

9.13 What population of documents would an auditor examine to determine whether (a) all authorized production was completed and placed in inventory or recorded as scrap and (b) finished goods inventory was actually produced and the costs were accounted for properly?

9.14 Why should receiving reports be prenumbered? What assertion would an auditor test using the receiving reports, and how would the auditor do this?

SUBSTANTIVE ANALYTICAL PROCEDURES AND TESTS OF DETAILS

LO 9-6
Give examples of substantive procedures in the production cycle and relate them to assertions about significant account balances at the end of the period.

See Exhibit 9.11 for the assertions and primary substantive procedures used for accounts in the production cycle. In this cycle, inventory is the primary account balance for substantive procedures. When inventory is significant, GAAS requires auditors to be present to observe the client's physical inventory count. After the inventory has been counted, the client summarizes the count by item number and then applies standard costs to determine the total amount of inventory owned on that date, which is compared with the amount in the general ledger. This step is normally referred to as the *compilation and pricing procedure,* which the auditors also test. Differences between the inventory count and the perpetual records are adjusted by increasing or decreasing cost of goods sold.

Analytical Procedures

The production cycle is an excellent area for auditors to employ analytical procedures. Inventory turnover, days' sales in inventory, and simple trend analysis can indicate whether the client is able to sell the inventory or whether inventory is slow moving and in danger of becoming obsolete. In addition, an unexpected increase in raw material inventory may be a red flag indicating bribes and kickbacks in purchasing or production. Increased scrap rates may be used to conceal theft of finished product at the end of the production process (prior to the transfer to finished goods inventory). The gross margin percentage reveals whether the client is able to price the inventory to earn an acceptable profit. Moreover, comparing current-year gross margin to that of prior years can uncover fraudulent inventory accounting. These ratios should be disaggregated to specific product lines or geographic regions to make them more meaningful. The results can be compared to the amounts budgeted, results in previous years, results of competitors, and industry averages.

EXHIBIT 9.11   **Account Balance Substantive Procedures in the Production Cycle**

What Could Go Wrong?	Substantive Procedures
Inventory included in inventory records does not exist.	• Observe client's physical inventory count. • Confirm inventory held by others on consignment. • Vouch items on inventory listing to inventory count tags. • Analytical procedures. Compare inventory turnover and gross margin to budget and previous periods and discuss differences with client personnel.
The entity records inventory that is owned by other parties.	• Inquire whether any inventory is on consignment. • Inquire whether inventory has been pledged as collateral or security. • Inspect loans and other agreements for the use of inventory as collateral.
Inventory that should have been recorded has been omitted from the inventory account.	• Trace inventory subsidiary accounts to inventory control account. • Observe physical inventory to ensure all items were counted. • Trace test inventory counts to inventory subsidiary accounts and control account.
Inventory is included in the financial statements at incorrect amounts and any valuation adjustments are not properly recorded.	• Perform lower-of-cost-or-NRV. • Review cost of goods sold calculations. • Trace inventory cost to standard costs or purchase invoices. • Inquire whether any inventory is obsolete or unsalable. • Analytical procedures. Compare inventory turnover and gross margin to budget and previous periods and discuss differences with client personnel.

Substantive Evidence in Management Reports

Most production systems produce timely reports that managers need for monitoring and controlling production. Auditors can use these reports as supporting evidence for assertions about raw materials inventories, work-in-process inventories, finished goods inventories, and cost of goods sold.

Sales Forecast

Management's sales forecast provides the basis for several aspects of business planning, notably of production and inventory levels. Forecasts can be used in gaining an understanding of management's plans for the year under audit, some of which will have already been completed when the audit work begins. Forecasts help auditors understand the nature and volume of production orders and management's strategy and rationale for inventory levels. Forecasts for the following year can be used in valuing the inventory at lower of cost or NRV (e.g., identifying slow-moving and potentially obsolete inventory). Special care must be taken when using the forecast for the next year in valuing inventory because an overly optimistic forecast can lead to a failure to write down inventory, accelerate the depreciation of fixed assets, and account for more cost of goods sold.

If the auditors want to use the forecast for audit decisions, they should perform some work to obtain assurance about its reasonableness. For example, the auditors can inquire about how the forecast was prepared, what assumptions were made, and how the client ensures its accuracy. The auditors also can compare previous forecasts with actual results. In addition, some work on the mechanical accuracy of the forecast should be performed to avoid relying on faulty calculations. This work can usually be limited to overall tests for reasonableness.

AUDITING INSIGHT · The SALY Forecast

The auditors were reviewing the inventory items that had not been issued for 30 days or more, considering the need to write some items down to market lower than cost. The production manager showed them the SALY forecast that indicated continuing need for the materials in products that are expected to have reasonable demand. The auditors agreed that the forecasts supported the prediction of future sales of products at prices that would cover the cost of the slow-moving material items. Unfortunately, the auditors neglected to ask the meaning of *SALY* in the designation of the forecast and therefore did not learn that it meant "same as last year." It was not a forecast at all. The products did not sell at the prices expected, and the company experienced losses the following year that should have been charged to cost of goods sold earlier.

Inventory Reports

Companies can produce a wide variety of inventory reports useful to auditors in conducting analytical procedures. These reports should include a list of the items in inventory and their costs and should agree with the inventory control account. Auditors can use this list (1) to scan for unusual conditions (e.g., negative item balances, overstocking, and valuation problems) and (2) as a population for sample selection for a physical inventory observation. The scanning and sample selection may be performed by computer-assisted audit techniques (CAATs) on the computerized inventory report file.

Production Plans and Reports

Based on the sales forecast, management should develop a plan for the amount and timing of production. The production plan provides general information to the auditors, but the production orders and inventory plan associated with the production plan are even more important. The production orders carry the information about requirements for raw materials, labor, and overhead, including the requisitions for purchase and use of materials and labor. These documents are the initial authorizations for control of the inventory and production.

Production reports record the completion of production quantities. When coupled with the related cost accounting reports, they are the company's record of the cost of goods placed into the finished goods inventory. In most cases, auditors examine the cost reports in connection with determining the cost valuation of inventory and cost of goods sold.

AUDITING INSIGHT | Do You Want a Lamborghini Cheap?

Viken Keuylian's once sold 5 percent of the world's Lamborghinis to a star-studded clientele that included NBA star Kobe Bryant. In 2007, he appeared at fund-raisers with actress Sharon Stone and singer-songwriter Elton John. In April of that year, Keuylian gave actors Eric Roberts and Luke Perry a helicopter ride to one of his dealership parties. Photos of the grand opening of the Calabasas (California) store show him with Natalie Maines of the Dixie Chicks and actors Kristen Bell, Hayden Panettiere, and Milo Ventimiglia. In May 2008, Keuylian told *The Orange County Register,* "Other dealers are turning down cars, and we're picking them up and selling them at a profit."

In fact, by the fall of 2007, Keuylian had become "financially overextended" and could not meet his debt obligations. So he began selling super-luxury cars without reporting the transactions to his floor planner. (*Floor plan* is the industry term that refers to the dealer's inventory.) He pleaded guilty to bilking **Volkswagen Credit Inc.** of at least $6 million in floor plan loans by keeping sold items on the floor plan. Keuylian used the proceeds from sales to pay for his southern California vineyard, Newport Beach commercial property, and a Lotus dealership in Beverly Hills. In October 2008, in a desperate move to stay afloat, Keuylian sold 54 vehicles in two weeks, mostly to other

dealers and auto auctions. He steeply discounted most of the vehicles, which included 45 Lamborghinis, four Bentleys, two Mercedes, a Ferrari, a Jaguar, and a Dodge Sprinter van. As an example, Volkswagen Credit had loaned $336,320 to buy a 2008 Lamborghini Murcielago, which he sold for $90,000. He had a $387,720 floor plan loan for a 2009 Lamborghini LP640, which he sold for $60,430. Seventeen other vehicles had discounts of at least $100,000. Keuylian showed Volkswagen Credit inventory reports that included these sold vehicles. Records show that Keuylian received $8.1 million for vehicles that Volkswagen Credit had financed for $12.6 million.

In an agreement with the district attorney, Keuylian pleaded guilty to numerous charges and was sentenced to five years in prison. The FBI impounded 14 of the vehicles sold in connection with the scheme. The cars were either returned to their new owners or were given to Volkswagen Credit, depending on the circumstances surrounding each car's sale. "You can draw your own conclusions about whether someone getting a Lamborghini at $60,000 would get suspicious or not," said Andrew Stolper, the assistant U.S. attorney handling the case.

Source: "Star Lambo Dealer Played Fast, Loose with Funds," *Automotive News,* April 20, 2009.

Physical Inventory Observation

The auditing procedures for inventory and related cost of sales accounts frequently are extensive in an audit engagement. Remember, a material error or fraud in inventory has a pervasive effect on financial statements. Although analytical procedures may indicate inventory misstatements, the auditor's best opportunity to detect inventory errors and frauds is during a **physical inventory observation**, an observation of the client's **physical inventory count** taken by company personnel. Auditors observe the inventory taking and make test counts, but they seldom actually count the entire inventory.

AUDITING INSIGHT | Do You Want Mushrooms on That?

Apparently, quite a bit of money can be made from gourmet mushrooms (no, not that kind). So much so that Gino Silva and Steven Perei, both employees with **D'Artagnan,** a mushroom distributor, set up their own company in direct competition with their employer.

Starting in December 2007, Silva and Perei made sales on behalf of their own company, Mediterra, and then stole D'Artagnan's inventory to complete the sale. To conceal the inventory, Silva enlisted the help of D'Artagnan's inventory control specialist to manipulate purchase order records and alter inventory records. This scheme was simple yet quite brilliant—by using their employer's inventory for their new company, top-line sales essentially equaled bottom-line profit.

Why pay for something when someone else can foot the bill? The mushroom scheme lasted just over 12 months.

In April 2011, Silva pleaded guilty to interstate theft of property while on release pending sentencing in another federal criminal matter. Silva was sentenced to 28 months in prison. Perei pleaded guilty in April 2010 to one count of selling and receiving stolen goods and was sentenced to two years of probation in June 2011.

Sources: "Payroll and Inventory Fraud—Are You Next?" March 13, 2012; "Former Employee of New Jersey-Based Gourmet Mushroom Distributor Sentenced to Prison for Stealing Mushrooms for Rival Company," www.fbi.gov, March 12, 2012.

The auditor's first task is to review the client's inventory-taking instructions, which should include the following:

1. Names of client personnel responsible for the count.
2. Dates and times of inventory taking.
3. Names of client personnel who will participate in the inventory taking.
4. Instructions for recording accurate descriptions of inventory items, for counting and double-counting, and for measuring physical quantities (such as counting by measures of gallons, barrels, feet, dozens).
5. Instructions for making notes of obsolete or worn items.
6. Instructions for the use of tags, punched cards, count sheets, computers, or other media devices and for their collection and control. (A typical inventory count sheet is illustrated at Exhibit 9.12.)
7. Plans for shutting down plant operations or for taking inventory after store closing hours and plans for having goods in proper places (such as on store shelves instead of on the floor, or of raw materials in a warehouse rather than in transit to a job).
8. Plans for counting or controlling movement of goods in receiving and shipping areas if those operations are not shut down during the count.
9. Instructions for computer compilation of the count media (such as tags, count sheets) into final inventory lists or summaries.
10. Instructions for review and approval of the inventory count; supervisory personnel notations of obsolescence or other matters.
11. Instructions for making changes and corrections to count tickets.

EXHIBIT 9.12
Inventory Count Sheet

DUNDER-MIFFLIN INC.
Inventory Count Sheet
12/31/2017

SHEET NO. 3

COUNT TEAM

J. Morris, T. Peters
ENTERED BY

H.R. Samuels
REVIEWED BY

A. Jacobs

Pallet Location	SKU#	Style	Type	Size	Quantity Counted
A10	10030	Siren	Men's	8	1080
A11	10030	Siren	Men's	8	1080
A12	10030	Siren	Men's	8	1080
A13	10030	Siren	Men's	8	890

These instructions characterize a well-planned counting operation. As the plan is carried out, the auditors should be present to hear the count instructions being given to the client's count teams and to observe the instructions being followed. In addition, the auditor should make selected test counts and record these in the audit documentation.

Manual Physical Inventory

Refer to Appendix Exhibit 9B.1 for an example of an audit plan for observing a physical inventory count. Note the requirement for obtaining tag numbers. It is critically important to know which tag numbers or count sheets were and were not used to prevent the client from simply adding inventory items by creating more tags at a later date. Also, note the cutoff procedures of examining shipping and receiving documents issued immediately before and after the count. The items that are included in the count must be the same as those recorded in the inventory records, and any items that have been sold or are not yet received must be excluded from the count and the records.

The auditors can perform dual-direction testing by (1) selecting inventory items from a perpetual inventory record, going to the location, and obtaining a test count, which produces evidence for the *existence* balance assertion (vouching from the inventory record to the actual items in inventory), and (2) selecting inventory from locations on the warehouse floor, obtaining a test count, and tracing the count to the final inventory compilation, which produces evidence for the *completeness* balance assertion (tracing items from the inventory to the inventory records). If the company does not have perpetual records and a file to test for *existence,* the auditors must be careful to obtain a record of all counts and use it for the existence-direction tests. In addition to the test counts, the auditor should document whether: client personnel were following the inventory instructions, the tag or count sheet numbers used and unused, the last shipping and receiving reports issued before the inventory count, the condition of the inventory, any inventory on hand that the client does not own, and any unusual items noticed during the count.

Bar Codes and Computers in Physical Inventory Counts   Most organizations are now using bar codes located on product to improve the efficiency and effectiveness of monitoring and counting the physical inventory. Perhaps on a trip to the grocery store or department store you have seen an individual with a handheld device scanning the store shelves. This device (see Exhibit 9.13) is designed to scan the bar code located on the front of the shelf. That bar code records the product type, manufacturer, and size in the hand unit. Once the individual counts the number of units in inventory, the count can be entered and stored in the scanner by using the number pad located on the top of the scanner. When the counts are completed, the unit can be brought back to the physical inventory supervisor, who can download the data to the computer program being used to manage the physical inventory.

EXHIBIT 9.13

Example of Inventory Bar Code Scanners

© Paul Bradbury/Getty Images RF

Although the use of scanners and computers greatly improves the accuracy (all product descriptions are identical) and efficiency (product descriptions and counts do not need to be written), there is still a need to follow the basic elements of a physical inventory count. For example, all items still should be counted twice. However, the computer program can match first and second counts and, if they are identical, accept and record the count. If the counts are not identical, the item can be flagged for review by the physical inventory supervisor.

RFID Physical Inventory   Many people driving in cities with toll roads and bridges now bypass the toll booths by using the technology of radio-frequency identification (RFID). Its devices send a signal to an RFID reader that identifies the automobile or truck as it travels and charges the driver's account for the toll. This same technology is being used in some warehouses and stores around the world. As more and more products are tagged with RFID chips, most about the size of a nickel, companies will automatically scan each product as it enters or leaves the warehouse or store or count the inventory by using portable RFID readers. For example, **Sam's Club** uses an electronic product code (EPC) system designed to track goods using RFID technology. When a case of products tagged with RFID labels arrives in a warehouse, it is detected by readers on the door. A staff member can then use a handheld RFID reader to trace the case and process the product. If every product is tagged with individual RFID labels, inventory levels can be recorded automatically and out-of-stock situations reduced. **Walmart** has been using RFID technology for about a decade, resulting in numerous benefits—including more efficient inventory management.

Will this eliminate the need for a physical inventory? Probably not. But it will change the focus of the audit of the physical inventory. If the RFID reader is connected to a computer, a completely accurate count of the RFID signals can be made without the need for a second count. The major focus may be on sampling items to ensure the actual goods are contained in the shipping container, not just an empty container with only an RFID chip.

AUDITING INSIGHT   Using RFID in Inventory Management

Radio-frequency identification (RFID) was up and running when the new 63,000-square-foot shoe department opened in **Macy's** Herald Square (New York City) store. RFID, a technology that has been around for about 10 years, has become much more economical to apply to track merchandise. The first phase launched in August 2012 with 300,000 pairs of shoes for sale on any given day. RFID made it much easier to track such a large quantity of shoes and, importantly, made it possible to serve the customer faster and more efficiently.

Installing RFID in the shoe department is the first broad use of this technology by Macy's. From shoes, RFID will be expanded into other departments next year. Merchandise that is basic, always in stock, and always in need of replenishment will follow. About one-third of the full replenishment assortment at Macy's will be on RFID. As a result, merchandise in stock levels will rise, and customers will be happier. For example, shoes inventory will be monitored by size, width, and color, and eventually, polo shirts will be monitored by color and size. The cost

of RFID technology and the chips on each garment have come down dramatically in price, making it possible for Macy's to take this first step.

Recently, Macy's has implemented a new program that employs RFID to allow omnichannel fulfillment of consumer purchases, right down to its last available unit of in-store merchandise. The program, which Macy's has named Pick to the Last Unit (P2LU), enables the retailer to list goods for sale online even when there is only one such item available at the store. In the past, inventory counts were simply not precise enough to ensure that a unit of a particular product was actually in stock and available for sale. However, Macy's says it has proven that by using RFID technology to perform inventory counts, it can be certain of what it has available and can, therefore, put it up for sale.

Sources: "Macy's Wins with Technology," *Forbes*, www.forbes.com, July 7, 2012; Claire Swedberg, "Macy's Launches Pick to the Last Unit Program for Omnichannel Sales," *RFID Journal*, www.rfidjournal.com/articles/view?13990, January 26, 2016.

Inventory Circumstances

The following are some inventory issues that often present difficulties for the auditors.

Physical Inventory Not on Year-End Date   Clients usually count the inventory before or after the balance-sheet date. When the auditors are present to make their physical observation, they follow the procedures outlined for observation of the physical count.

However, with an intervening period between the count date and the year-end, additional **inventory roll-forward** auditing procedures must be performed on transactions during that period. The inventory on the count date is reconciled to the year-end inventory by appropriate addition or subtraction of the subsequent receiving and shipping transactions.

Cycle Inventory Counting   **Cycle counts** are physical counts of selected inventory throughout the year (i.e., different parts of the inventory throughout the year). They are most appropriate when internal control over inventory is effective (i.e., a low level of control risk is present). Other companies use a statistical counting plan. In these circumstances, the auditors must understand the cycle or sampling plan and evaluate its appropriateness. In this situation, the auditors are present for only some of the physical inventory counts. Only under unusual circumstances and as an "extended procedure" are auditors present every month (or more frequently) to observe all counts. Businesses that count inventory using cycle counts purport to have accurate perpetual records and carry out the counting as a means of testing the records and maintaining their accuracy.

When counts go on all year long, the auditors are present for only a few counts. Auditors should review annual inventory schedules and carefully select the inventories to observe. These observations may be performed during interim periods, but good inventory observation procedures should always be followed. The auditors must be present during some counting operations to evaluate the counting plans and their execution. The same procedures enumerated for an annual count are used, test counts are made, and the audit team is responsible for making a determination concerning the accuracy of perpetual records.

Professional Inventory Teams

Some clients with large numbers of operating facilities (e.g., retail store chains) may have a professional inventory team(s) or hire a professional inventory company. These teams go from one facility to another performing physical inventory counts all year long. In addition, these inventory companies may have their own standard inventory procedures, minimum qualification requirements, and substantial training for inventory count supervisors and employees. These types of operations add an air of professionalism and expertise to the physical inventory count. Auditors should review inventory team qualifications, training requirements, and standard policies and procedures.

Auditors Not Present for Client's Inventory Count   This situation can arise on a first audit when the accounting firm is appointed after the beginning inventory already has been counted. Because the beginning inventory amount affects cost of goods sold, the auditors must disclaim an opinion on the income statement and may have substantial concerns with stockholders' equity, the statement of cash flows, and additional items affected by net income if they are unable to perform alternative procedures. The auditor can utilize alternative procedures to provide sufficient, appropriate evidence that the beginning inventory number is not materially misstated. For example, the auditors must review the client's plan for the already completed count as described earlier. Some test counts of current inventory should be made and traced to current records to determine the reliability of perpetual records. If the actual count was recent, intervening transaction activity might be reconciled back to the inventory count. The reconciliation of more than a few months' transactions to unobserved beginning inventories could be very difficult. The auditors can employ analytical procedures using such interrelationships as sales activity, physical volume, price variation, standard costs, and gross profit margins for the decision about beginning inventory reasonableness. Nevertheless, much care must be exercised in "backing into" the audit of inventory previously taken.

Inventories Located Off the Client's Premises   The auditors must determine where and in what dollar amounts inventories are located off the client's premises, in the custody of consignees, or in public warehouses. If amounts are material and if control activities are not exceptionally strong, the audit team may wish to visit these locations and conduct onsite test counts. However, if amounts are not material, if alternative evidence (such as periodic reports, cash receipts, receivables records, shipping records) is adequate, or if control risk is low, then direct confirmation with the custodian may be considered sufficient appropriate evidence of the existence of quantities.

After the observation is complete, auditors should have sufficient appropriate evidence of the following physical quantities and valuations:

- Goods in the perpetual records but not owned were excluded from the inventory compilation.
- Goods on hand were counted and included in the inventory compilation.
- **Consignment (consigned-out) goods** or goods stored in outside warehouses (goods owned but not on hand) were included in the inventory compilation.
- Goods in transit (goods actually purchased and recorded but not received) were added to the inventory count and included in the inventory compilation.
- Goods on hand that have been sold and by agreement are being held by the client were excluded from the inventory compilation.
- Consignment (consigned-in) goods were excluded from the inventory compilation.

 REVIEW CHECKPOINTS

9.15 What characteristics should be considered in reviewing a client's inventory-taking instructions?

9.16 Explain dual-direction sampling in the context of inventory test counts.

9.17 Why is it important for auditors to obtain control information over inventory count sheets or tickets?

9.18 What inventory information should auditors document?

Pricing and Compilation

The physical observation procedures are designed to audit for *existence* and *completeness* (physical quantities). The **pricing and compilation** tests examine *valuation* (recalculation of appropriate FIFO, LIFO, or other pricing at cost, and lower of cost or NRV, and write-down of obsolete or worn inventory).

The compilation and pricing stage starts by listing all inventory items counted. The auditor foots[3] the list and tests the mathematical accuracy by multiplying the quantities and the price to get the total value for each item. Test counts taken by the auditor during

 AUDITING INSIGHT   Whose Inventory Is It?

James E. Lorenz, former corporate controller of **Electro Scientific Industries (ESI),** pleaded guilty to federal charges that he lied to auditors in connection with a scheme to falsely increase the company's profits. Lorenz, who was charged in a 17-count indictment in September 2004, pleaded guilty to one count of making false statements to a public company's accountants in connection with his role in the scheme. He faces a maximum penalty of 20 years in prison and a $5 million fine.

According to the indictment, on December 10, 2002, Lorenz lied on a quarterly review questionnaire that **KPMG** had asked him to complete. Lorenz knew that he had recently changed the way in which consignment inventory was valued on the books of ESI. Before the second quarter of fiscal 2003, consignment inventory was not recorded as an asset, but in the second quarter of 2003, Lorenz changed ESI's accounting practice to treat the inventory as an asset. The change, which was concealed from the auditors, falsely increased quarterly net income by $650,564. Lorenz admitted to lying to auditors by telling them that he had made no changes in company accounting practices in the second quarter of fiscal 2003. Former ESI CEO James T. Dooley also pleaded guilty to lying to auditors about a separate accounting transaction.

Source: "Electro Scientific's Ex-Controller Pleads Guilty," *CFO,* www.cfo.com, August 8, 2007.

---

[3]Foots is an accounting term meaning to add up a column.

the physical count are traced to the list, and other items from the list are vouched back to inventory count tags. The unit price is vouched to the vendor invoices for the purchase price for raw materials and to standard cost for in-process and finished goods. Many of these tests can be performed automatically using CAATs.

Lower-of-cost-or-NRV testing is an important step toward the *valuation* assertion. NRV can be obtained by examining the client's catalogue and actual sales in the subsequent period and reviewing the costs associated with product sales. Items that are slow moving or obsolete can be spotted during the inventory observation if they demonstrate evidence of unsalability (e.g., old inventory tags, dust, and rust). Appendix Exhibit 9B.2 illustrates an audit plan for inventory pricing and compilation tests.

AUDITING INSIGHT   Sometimes Things Aren't Worth What They Were

Worthington Industries is a diversified metals processing company focused on steel processing and manufactured metal products. On December 3, 2008, Worthington announced that market weakness and decline in steel pricing have left it with inventories in excess of demand with reduced market values. As a result, Worthington wrote down the value of its inventories by approximately $100 million.

Source: "Worthington Industries Announces Inventory Write-Down and Declares Quarterly Dividend," www.worthingtonIndustries.com, December 3, 2008.

Inventory—A Ripe Field for Fraud

These problems have occurred in entities' inventory frauds:

- Auditors were fooled as a result of taking a small sample for test counting, thus missing important information.
- Entities included inventory they pretended to have ordered.
- Entities stacked inventory on pallets in such a manner that "empty spaces" were not visible to auditors, resulting in overstatements of inventory.
- Auditors permitted company officials to follow them and note their counts. Then the managers falsified counts for inventory the auditors did not count.
- Shipments between plants (transfers) were reported as inventory at both plant locations.
- Auditors spotted a barrel whose contents management had valued at thousands of dollars, but it was filled with sawdust. The auditors required management to exclude the value from the inventory, but it never occurred to them that they had found just one instance in an intentional and pervasive overstatement fraud.
- Auditors observed inventory at five store locations and told the management in advance of the specific stores. Management took care not to make fraudulent entries in these 5 stores but, instead, made fraudulent adjustments in many of the other 236 stores.
- After counting an inventory of computer chips, the auditors received a call from the client's controller: "Just hours after you left the plant, 2,500 chips arrived in a shipment in transit." The auditors included them in inventory but never checked to see whether the chips were actually received.[4]

Accounting Firm Tips

To help detect inventory fraud, **Grant Thornton,** a large national accounting firm, advises its audit personnel:

- Focus test counts on high-value items and sample lower-value items. Test count a sufficient dollar amount of the inventory.
- If all locations will not be observed, do not follow an easily predictable pattern. Advise client personnel as late as possible of the locations to be visited.

[4]Examples cited in this list have been taken from *The Wall Street Journal*.

tells a structured story about the audit objective, controls, tests of controls, substantive procedures, and discovery summary. At the end of the chapter, some similar discussion cases are presented, and you can prepare the audit approach to test your ability to design audit procedures for the detection of errors and frauds.

Case 9.1

The Players Weren't All That Was Short![5]

PROBLEM

Mickey Monus, the CEO of Phar-Mor, stated on many occasions that he would "not let Walmart undersell Phar-Mor." To that end, Phar-Mor would actually sell many products at a loss resulting in corporate net losses. Phar-Mor dumped these losses in a "bucket account" and spread them over the individual stores by increasing inventory amounts. When company personnel found out which stores the auditors would be visiting for inventory observation, they simply moved goods from the stores that were not visited to make up for shortages. Phar-Mor used an outside service for inventory counting, but after receiving the results, Phar-Mor personnel would inflate the amounts during the pricing and compilation process. In some cases, the compilations were altered after the auditors tested them. When Phar-Mor rolled forward the inventory from the count date, the inventory showed large increases right at year-end. These increases were due to the "blow-out" entries allocating the losses in the bucket account to stores' inventory. One entry was as high as $139 million. Finally, Phar-Mor did not have perpetual records but used the retail inventory method instead. Employees used distorted margin percentages to increase the estimated cost of the inventory on hand.

Phar-Mor issued fictitious invoices for purchases, made fictitious journal entries to increase inventory and decrease cost of sales, recognized purchases but failed to record the liabilities, and overcounted the merchandise.

The fraud lasted over a 10-year period, resulting in a financial statement fraud of more than $1 billion.

AUDIT APPROACH

The primary control should have been an environment that discouraged false accounting. However, this clearly was not the case. Other controls that should have prevented or detected these misstatements include a review of nonstandard journal entries, comparison of inventory records to actual periodic counts, and management analysis of gross margins and cash flows. Senior management can easily override any controls. Doing so requires only employees who can be bribed, threatened, or intimidated into going along.

How does one test the control environment? In the client acceptance/continuation stage of planning, the auditors should obtain evidence about management's reputation for integrity. In this case, many vendors were complaining because they were "squeezed" by Phar-Mor to provide rebates and promotion allowances, and some were threatening to cut the company off for nonpayment of bills. Many employees, including the controller, were very concerned about the company's practices and might have been persuaded to come clean had the auditors approached the audit with skepticism. However, because the client's chief financial officer was a former partner of the audit firm, the auditors appeared to lack skepticism.

It is not practical to observe inventory at all stores. However, because the auditors had identified inventory valuation as a high-risk area, they probably should have visited more than four stores! Moreover, the actual stores that the auditors visited for inventory observation should have been kept secret until the day of the count and randomized from one year to the next.

The auditors performed only a reasonableness test of the margins used in the retail method. They selected a sample of items in a "haphazard" method that turned out not to be representative. When the sample margins differed from the company's margins, the auditors explained the difference away without expanding their sample. In vouching the costs of inventory, the auditors should have been alert to phony documentation. Finally, large nonstandard journal entries at the end of the year should have been thoroughly scrutinized.

[5]Additional data taken from D. Cottrell and S. Glover, "Finding Auditors Liable for Fraud: What the Jury Heard in the Phar-Mor Case," *CPA Journal*, July 1997, pp. 14–21.

DISCOVERY SUMMARY

When a travel agent noticed that a bill for the World Basketball League (WBL) was paid with a Phar-Mor check, she asked a neighbor, who was a major shareholder, why Phar-Mor would pay the WBL's expenses. The neighbor phoned a board member, who initiated the investigation that uncovered the fraud.

AUDITING INSIGHT | Using IDEA in the Audit

INVENTORY TESTING

Significant issues in inventory occur when amounts in the physical inventory do not match the amounts in the accounting records. Auditors are aware of the beginning inventory for the year, (the audited value for ending inventory form the previous year) and using computer software can calculate inventory received from receiving reports and inventory used from production reports. Using these numbers, the auditor can obtain an approximation of inventory that should be in this year's ending inventory, as follows:

Beginning inventory + inventory purchases – inventory usage = ending inventory.

If we adjust the ending inventory for scrap, the number is even more accurate.

The recorded ending inventory and the inventory account should not be materially misstated from the preceding calculation. Major discrepancies should be investigated and may be the result of poor record keeping or theft of inventory. Further, audit software like IDEA can compare physical counts with actual inventory. The use of such a program is extremely important when inventory includes tens of thousands of items. (*Note:* A typical Walmart store has approximately 140,000 SKUs.)

Further, inventory valuation is critical to reaching an audit conclusion about inventory, and audit software can assist the auditor in identifying unusual and potentially obsolete inventory items.

At the end of this chapter, you can perform testing related to the valuation assertion in Exercise 8.63, and tests related to inventory summarization in Exercises 8.64–8.66.

 REVIEW CHECKPOINTS

9.23   What steps should auditors take if the client has multiple locations being counted?

9.24   What is an inventory roll-forward? What roll-forward tests should be performed?

Summary

Production involves production planning; inventory planning; acquiring labor, materials, and overhead (acquisition and payment cycle); custody of assets; and cost accounting. Production information systems produce many internal documents, reports, and files that are sources of audit information as described in the chapter. The production cycle is characterized by having mostly internal documentation as evidence and having relatively little external documentary evidence; therefore, the systems that produce these documents must be evaluated to ensure the validity of the information.

Companies reduce control risk by having a suitable separation of authorization, custody, recording, and periodic reconciliation duties. Error-checking procedures, including analyzing production orders and finished production cost reports, are important for the proper determination of inventory values and proper valuation of cost of goods sold. Otherwise, many things could go wrong, ranging from overvaluing the inventory to understating costs of production by deferring costs that should be expensed.

Cost accounting is a central feature of the production cycle. The illustrative case in the chapter tells the stories of financial reporting manipulations and the audit procedures that will detect them. The physical inventory observation audit work was discussed because actual contact with inventories provides auditors direct eyewitness evidence of important tangible assets.

It may appear that production and related activities offer little risk, especially if the nature of inventory does not lend itself to high risk (e.g., steel I-beams) or when production material is not highly susceptible to theft, but many frauds have been hidden in the inventory accounts. Therefore, the auditors should pay attention to the inventory balance assertions of *existence* and *valuation and allocation.* The accompanying Auditing Insight presents deficiencies noted in the PCAOB inspection reports of some of the largest audit firms regarding audits of this cycle.

AUDITING INSIGHT | PCAOB Inspection and Production Cycle

In this audit of a manufacturer, the Firm failed in the following respects to obtain sufficient appropriate audit evidence to support its audit opinions on the financial statements and on the effectiveness of ICFR:

- The Firm failed to perform sufficient procedures to test controls over inventory. The Firm selected for testing controls that consisted of reviews of inventory variances and the inventory allowance. The Firm's procedures to test these controls were limited to inquiring of management, obtaining certain documents that were reviewed during the operation of the controls, and inspecting signatures as evidence that reviews had occurred. The Firm's testing did not include (1) ascertaining the nature of the review procedures that the control owners performed or (2) ascertaining and evaluating the criteria used by the control owners to identify matters for investigation and whether those matters were appropriately investigated and resolved. As a result, the Firm failed to evaluate whether the controls operated at a level of precision that would prevent or detect material misstatements. In addition, the Firm failed to identify and test any controls over the accuracy and completeness of certain data and reports used in the performance of these controls, and also in a control over adjustments to inventory quantities that the Firm tested.

- The Firm failed to perform sufficient substantive procedures to test the existence of inventory. The issuer performed a physical count of all inventory at an interim date more than four months before year-end. The issuer also performed a physical count of all raw materials and work-in-process inventory after year-end; the Firm's planned procedure to test the existence of this inventory was to roll back these inventory balances from the date of the subsequent count to year-end. The Firm's roll-back procedures were insufficient, as the Firm limited its procedures to comparing a very small sample of items counted to the quantities at year-end. In addition, the Firm failed to perform any procedures to roll forward the finished goods inventory balance from the date of the interim count to year-end.

The Firm's procedures to test controls over the valuation of inventory were insufficient. Specifically:

- The Firm failed to perform sufficient procedures to test the one control it had identified over the valuation of inventory that the issuer accounted for using the retail method, which represented a significant portion of total inventory, as its procedures were limited to performing a walkthrough of the process, without evaluating whether the control operated at a level of precision that would prevent or detect material misstatements.

- The Firm failed to perform sufficient substantive procedures to test the valuation of the inventory that was calculated using the retail method of accounting. Specifically, the Firm's procedures were limited to testing only one input used in that calculation, without testing other important inputs or the accuracy of the calculation.

- The Firm's procedures to test the existence of, and controls over the existence of, the issuer's inventory were insufficient. Specifically, there was no evidence in the audit documentation, and no persuasive other evidence, that the Firm had tested whether the issuer's cycle-count procedures addressed that inventory items were counted in accordance with the frequency schedule established by management.

- The Firm's procedures related to inventory were insufficient. Specifically:

  - The Firm's procedures to test controls over vendor incentives were insufficient. The Firm tested two controls, which consisted of (a) verifying whether vendor incentive agreements existed, determining whether approvals existed for certain amounts, and comparing calculated vendor incentives to the amounts recorded in the general ledger, and (b) approving inventory price changes. The Firm, however, failed to identify and test any controls over the calculation of the amount of vendor incentives recorded.

  - For one control, consisting of the automated calculation of inventory costs, the Firm's procedures were limited to reviewing the recalculation of one inventory cost. This review, however, was insufficient to support a conclusion that the system was operating effectively to calculate all inventory costs, as the Firm failed to obtain an understanding of, and test, how the system was configured to perform this control. The Firm failed to identify and test any controls over (1) the accuracy of shipping terms, quantities shipped, and shipment dates that were entered into the system and (2) the classification of costs for raw materials inventory.

The Firm's procedures related to inventory were insufficient, as follows:

- The Firm failed to perform sufficient procedures related to the existence and completeness of inventory held at external locations, consisting of outside warehouses and manufacturers. This inventory was multiple times the Firm's established level of materiality and represented a significant proportion of current assets. The Firm failed to identify and test any controls over the existence and completeness of this inventory. In addition, to substantively test this inventory, the Firm inappropriately limited its procedures to confirming a sample of inventory balances with the warehouses and manufacturers.

- The Firm failed to perform sufficient procedures related to inventory held at the issuer's warehouses. The Firm selected for testing a control over the inventory cycle counts at the issuer's warehouses and planned for its testing of this control to provide both substantive and control assurance. The Firm, however, failed to test whether the issuer's cycle-count procedures addressed that sufficient inventory items were counted.

- The issuer disclosed that it had experienced a decline in its inventory turnover, and the Firm identified a number of inventory items that had had no sales within the past 12 months, but the Firm failed to consider whether this evidence should have affected its conclusion that the issuer's inventory reserve was appropriate.

- The Firm failed to perform sufficient procedures to test the existence of the majority of the inventory held at the external warehouses. Specifically, for this portion of the inventory, which represented a significant proportion of the issuer's current assets,

(continued)

AUDITING INSIGHT   *(concluded)*

the Firm failed to perform any procedures beyond obtaining confirmations from certain of the custodians.

- The Firm understood that certain inventory, for which the recorded value was several times the Firm's established materiality level, was in-transit between the issuer's receiving facilities and some of its other facilities at year-end. The Firm failed to perform sufficient substantive procedures to test this inventory. Specifically, the Firm's procedures to test the existence of this inventory were limited to comparing the quantity, shipping date, and order identification numbers, for a sample of items, from the issuer's inventory ledger to the issuer's system that contained shipping information received from its suppliers. In addition, the Firm failed to perform any procedures to test the valuation of this inventory.

The Firm failed to perform sufficient tests related to the valuation of inventory for one of the issuer's segments, which held a significant portion of total inventory. Specifically:

- For a portion of inventory that was valued using the average cost method, the Firm failed to identify and test any controls over the calculation of the average cost.
- For a portion of inventory that was accounted for using standard costs, the Firm selected for testing a control that consisted of man-

agement's review of variances between actual and standard costs, but it failed to identify and test any controls over the accuracy and/or completeness of certain data and a schedule that were used in the performance of this control.

- With respect to the reserve for excess and obsolete inventory, the Firm selected for testing a control that consisted of the calculation of the reserve. The Firm, however, failed to identify and test any controls over the accuracy and completeness of certain data used in the performance of this control.

- The Firm failed to perform sufficient substantive procedures to test the valuation of inventory for this segment. The Firm designed its substantive procedures—including sample sizes—based on a level of control reliance that was not supported due to the deficiencies in the Firm's testing of controls that are discussed above. As a result, the sample sizes the Firm used in its testing were too small to provide sufficient evidence.

Sources: 2015 PCAOB Inspection Report BDO Seidman (December 12, 2015); 2015 PCAOB Inspection of Grant Thornton (December 16, 2015); 2015 PCAOB Inspection Report of Ernst & Young (June 16, 2015); 2015 PCAOB Inspection of PricewaterhouseCoopers (June 30, 2015); 2015 PCAOB Inspection of KPMG (October 15, 2015).

Key Terms

bill of materials: A list of raw materials and supplies used to build a product that is used to develop standard costs.

consignment goods: The goods that are given by one party, the consignor, to another party, the consignee, to sell; however, the consignee retains title until the goods are sold.

cycle counts: A method of physically counting different areas of inventory throughout the year.

inventory roll-forward: An accounting process from date of physical inventory count to the end of the period; includes additions for purchases and production and reductions for sales, scrap, and so on.

material requisition (materials transfer ticket): A form used to obtain raw materials and supplies from inventory custodian.

net realizable value (NRV): The selling price less costs to sell (e.g., sales commissions).

overhead allocation: An accounting procedure used to assign indirect costs to various products.

physical inventory count: The client's procedure for determining actual amount of inventory on hand.

physical inventory observation: The auditor's procedures during client's physical inventory count; includes observing inventory procedures and performing test counts on selected inventory items.

pricing and compilation: The procedure for translating units counted in the physical inventory count to amounts recorded in the accounting records, including gains or losses for shortages or overages; involves mathematically accumulating counts and applying standard costs.

production order: A document that communicates to production personnel the specific product, product quantity, and date a product is to be produced.

production plan: A schedule of goods to be produced for a period based on sales forecasts.

raw material inventory status report: A periodic report (usually daily or weekly) that includes a list of all raw materials and the inventoried quantity of each material.

sales forecast: A report, usually prepared by marketing, predicting future sales of product.

standard costs: The estimates of cost to produce a product; used for transferring products between departments and to finished goods and to record cost of goods sold; compared to actual costs to obtain variances.

Multiple-Choice Questions for Practice and Review

Mc Graw Hill Education **connect**   All applicable Exercises and Problems are available with *Connect*.

LO 9-1   9.23   Which cycle is *not* directly linked to the production cycle?
  a. Acquisition and expenditure cycle.
  b. Payroll cycle.
  c. Revenue and collection cycle.
  d. Finance and investment cycle.

LO 9-1   9.24   To determine the client's planned amount and timing of production of a product, the auditor reviews the
  a. Sales forecast.
  b. Inventory reports.
  c. Production plan.
  d. Purchases journal.

LO 9-1   9.25   An auditor reviews job cost sheets to test which *transaction assertion*?
  a. Occurrence.
  b. Completeness.
  c. Accuracy.
  d. Classification.

LO 9-4   9.26   Which of the following is an internal control weakness for a company whose inventory of supplies consists of a large number of individual items?
  a. Supplies of relatively little value are expensed when purchased.
  b. The cycle basis is used for physical counts.
  c. The warehouse manager is responsible for maintenance of perpetual inventory records.
  d. Perpetual inventory records are maintained only for items of significant value.

LO 9-2   9.27   To make a year-to-year comparison of inventory turnover *most* meaningful, the auditor performs the analysis
  a. For the company as a whole.
  b. By division.
  c. By product.
  d. All of the above.

LO 9-4   9.28   Which of the following procedures would best prevent or detect the theft of valuable items from an inventory that consists of hundreds of different items selling for $1 to $10 and a few items selling for hundreds of dollars?
  a. Maintain a perpetual inventory of only the more valuable items with frequent periodic verification of the accuracy of the perpetual inventory record.
  b. Have an independent accounting firm prepare an internal control report on the effectiveness of the controls over inventory.
  c. Have separate warehouse space for the more valuable items with frequent periodic physical counts and comparison to perpetual inventory records.
  d. Require a manager's signature for the removal of any inventory item with a value of more than $50.

LO 9-6   9.29   An auditor usually traces the details of the test counts made during the observation of physical inventory counts to a final inventory compilation. This audit procedure is undertaken to provide evidence that items physically present and observed by the auditor at the time of the physical inventory count are
  a. Owned by the client.
  b. Not obsolete.
  c. Physically present at the time of the preparation of the final inventory schedule.
  d. Included in the final inventory schedule.

LO 9-3

9.30   A retailer's physical count of inventory was higher than that shown by the perpetual records. Which of the following could explain the difference?

    a.   Inventory items had been counted, but the tags placed on the items had not been taken off and added to the inventory accumulation sheets.

    b.   Credit memos for several items returned by customers had not been recorded.

    c.   No journal entry had been made on the retailer's books for several items returned to its suppliers.

    d.   An item purchased FOB shipping point had not arrived at the date of the inventory count and had not been reflected in the perpetual records.

(AICPA adapted)

LO 9-6

9.31   From the auditors' point of view, inventory counts are more acceptable prior to the year-end when

    a.   Internal control is weak.

    b.   Accurate perpetual inventory records are maintained.

    c.   Inventory is slow moving.

    d.   Significant amounts of inventory are held on a consignment basis.

LO 9-4

9.32   Which of the following internal control activities most likely addresses the completeness assertion for inventory?

    a.   The work-in-process account is periodically reconciled with subsidiary inventory records.

    b.   Employees responsible for custody of finished goods do not perform the receiving function.

    c.   Receiving reports are prenumbered, and the numbering sequence is checked periodically.

    d.   There is a separation of duties between the payroll department and inventory accounting personnel.

LO 9-6

9.33   When auditing inventories, an auditor would *least* likely verify that

    a.   All inventory owned by the client is on hand at the time of the count.

    b.   The client has used proper inventory pricing.

    c.   The financial statement presentation of inventories is appropriate.

    d.   Damaged goods and obsolete items have been properly accounted for.

(AICPA adapted)

LO 9-6

9.34   A client maintains perpetual inventory records in quantities and in dollars. If the assessed control risk is high, an auditor would probably

    a.   Apply gross profit tests to ascertain the reasonableness of the physical counts.

    b.   Increase the extent of tests of controls relevant to the inventory cycle.

    c.   Request the client to schedule the physical inventory count at the end of the year.

    d.   Insist that the client perform physical counts of inventory items several times during the year.

(AICPA adapted)

LO 9-6

9.35   An auditor selected items for test counts while observing a client's physical inventory. The auditor then traced the test counts to the client's inventory listing. This procedure *most likely* obtained evidence concerning management's balance assertion of

    a.   Rights and obligations.

    b.   Completeness.

    c.   Existence.

    d.   Valuation and allocation.

(AICPA adapted)

LO 9-6

9.36   Which of the following auditing procedures probably would provide the most reliable evidence concerning the entity's assertion of rights and obligations related to inventories?

    a.   Trace test counts noted during the entity's physical count to the entity's summarization of quantities.

    b.   Inspect agreements to determine whether any inventory is pledged as collateral or subject to any liens.

c. Select the last few shipping documents used before the physical count and determine whether the shipments were recorded as sales.

d. Inspect the open purchase order file for significant commitments that should be considered for disclosure.

(AICPA adapted)

LO 9-6

9.37 An auditor *most* likely would analyze inventory turnover rates to obtain evidence concerning management's balance assertions about

a. Existence.

b. Rights and obligations.

c. Completeness.

d. Valuation and allocation.

LO 9-2

9.38 An auditor would vouch inventory on the inventory status report to the vendor's invoice to obtain evidence concerning management's balance assertions about

a. Existence.

b. Rights and obligations.

c. Completeness.

d. Valuation.

LO 9-5

9.39 When evaluating inventory controls, an auditor would be *least* likely to

a. Inspect documents.

b. Make inquiries.

c. Observe procedures.

d. Consider policy and procedure manuals.

LO 9-5

9.40 When testing a company's cost accounting system, the auditor uses procedures that are primarily designed to determine that

a. Quantities on hand have been computed based on acceptable cost accounting techniques that reasonably approximate actual quantities on hand.

b. Physical inventories agree substantially with book inventories.

c. The system is in accordance with generally accepted accounting principles and is functioning as planned.

d. Costs have been properly assigned to finished goods, work-in-process, and cost of goods sold.

LO 9-6

9.41 The auditor tests the quantity of materials charged to work-in-process by vouching these quantities to

a. Cost ledgers.

b. Perpetual inventory records.

c. Receiving reports.

d. Material requisitions.

LO 9-6

9.42 Your client counts inventory three months before the end of the fiscal year because controls over inventory are excellent. Which procedure is *not* necessary for the roll-forward?

a. Check that shipping documents for the last three months agree with perpetual records.

b. Trace receiving reports for the last three months to perpetual records.

c. Compare gross margin percentages for the last three months.

d. Request the client to recount inventory at the end of the year.

LO 9-5

9.43 An auditor is examining a nonpublic company's inventory procurement system and has decided to perform tests of controls. Under which of the following conditions do GAAS require tests of controls be performed by an auditor?

a. Significant weaknesses were found in the company's internal control.

b. The auditor hopes to reduce the amount of work to be done in assessing inherent risk.

c. The auditor believes that testing the controls could lead to a reduction in overall audit time and cost.

d. Tests of controls are always performed when the auditor begins to assess control risk.

LO 9-6

9.44 Which of the following management assertions is an auditor *most* likely testing if the audit objective states that all inventory on hand is reflected in the ending inventory balance?

a. The entity has rights to the inventory.

b. Inventory is properly valued.

c. Inventory is properly presented in the financial statements.

d. Inventory is complete.

(AICPA adapted)

LO 9-6

9.45 A portion of a client's inventory is in public warehouses. Evidence of the existence of this merchandise can most efficiently be acquired through which of the following methods?

a. Observation.

b. Confirmation.

c. Calculation.

d. Inspection.

(AICPA adapted)

LO 9-6

9.46 The purpose of tracing a sample of inventory tags to a client's computerized listing of inventory items is to determine whether the inventory items

a. Represented by tags were included on the listing.

b. Included on the listing were properly counted.

c. Represented by tags were reduced to the lower of cost or market.

d. Included in the listing were properly valued.

Exercises and Problems

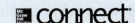 All applicable Exercises and Problems are available with *Connect.*

LO 9-4

9.47 **Internal Control Questionnaire Items: Possible Error or Fraud Due to Weakness.** Refer to the internal control questionnaire for the production cycle (Appendix Exhibit 9A.1) and assume that the answer to each question is "no." Prepare a table matching questions to errors or frauds that could occur because of the absence of the control. Your column headings should be as follows:

Question	Possible Error or Fraud Due to Weakness

LO 9-5

9.48 **Tests of Controls Related to Controls and Assertions.** Each of the following tests of controls could be performed during the audit of the controls in the production cycle.

Required:

For each procedure, identify (a) the internal control activity (strength) being tested and (b) the assertion(s) being addressed.

1. Balance and reconcile detailed production cost sheets to the work-in-process inventory control account.

2. Scan closed production cost sheets for missing numbers in the sequence.

3. Vouch a sample of open and closed production cost sheet entries to (a) labor reports and (b) issue forms and materials used reports.

4. Locate the material issue forms and determine whether they are (a) prenumbered, (b) kept in a secure location, and (c) available to unauthorized persons.

5. Select several summary journal entries in the work-in-process inventory and (a) vouch them to weekly labor and material reports and to production cost sheets and (b) trace them to the control account.

6. Select a sample of the material issue forms in the production department file. Examine them for

a. Issue date and materials used report date.

b. Production order number.

c. Floor supervisor's signature or initials.

d. Name and number of material.

  e. Raw material stores clerk's signature or initials.

  f. Material requisition in raw material stores file, noting the date of requisition.

7. Determine by inquiry and inspection whether cost clerks review dates on reports of units completed for accounting in the proper period.

LO 9-4

9.49 **Cost Accounting Tests of Controls.** The diagram in Exhibit 9.51.1 describes several cost accounting tests of controls. It shows the direction of the tests, leading from samples of cost accounting analyses, management reports, and the general ledger to blank squares.

Required:

For each blank square in Exhibit 9.51.1, write a cost accounting test of controls procedure and describe the evidence it can produce. (*Hint:* Refer to Exhibits 9.4 and 9.6.)

LO 9-6

9.50 **Inventory Count Observation: Planning and Substantive Procedures.** Sammy Smith is the partner in charge of the audit of Blue Distributing Corporation, a wholesaler that owns one warehouse containing 80 percent of its inventory. Smith is reviewing the audit documentation that was prepared to support the firm's opinion on Blue's financial statements and wants to be certain that essential audit procedures are well documented.

Required:

a. What evidence should Smith expect to find indicating that the observation of the client's physical count of inventory was well planned and that assistants were properly supervised?

b. What substantive procedures should Smith find in the audit documentation of management's balance assertions about existence and completeness of inventory quantities at the end of the year? (Refer to Appendix 9B for the audit plan's procedures.)

(AICPA adapted)

LO 9-6

9.51 **Sales/Inventory Cutoff.** Your client took a complete physical inventory count under your observation as of December 15 and adjusted the inventory control account (perpetual inventory method) to agree with the physical inventory. After considering the count adjustments as of December 15 and after reviewing the transactions recorded from December 16 to December 31, you are almost ready to accept the inventory balance as fairly stated. However, your review of the sales cutoff as of December 15 and December 31 disclosed the following items not previously considered:

Sales		Date		
Cost	Price	Shipped	Billed	Credited to Inventory Control
$28,400	$36,900	12/14	12/16	12/16
39,100	50,200	12/10	12/19	12/10
18,900	21,300	1/2	12/31	12/31

EXHIBIT 9.51.1

Diagram of Cost Accounting Tests of Controls

Required:

What adjusting journal entries, if any, would you make for each of these items? Explain why each adjustment is necessary.

(AICPA adapted)

LO 9-6

9.52 **Purchasing Cutoff.** When tracing using the cutoff information from the December 31 inventory count of Thermo-Tempur Mattresses, you note the following information:

Receiving Report Number	Date Received	Total Cost
	12/28	$12,433.61
1180	12/28	8,923.34
1181	12/29	15,448.22
1182	12/31	14,109.33
1183	12/31	11,482.57
1184	1/2	17,852.56
1185	1/3	8,753.95

The purchases list shows that the following items were recorded in December.

Receiving Report Number	Date Received	Total Cost
1179	12/28	$12,433.61
	12/28	8,923.34
1181	12/29	15,448.22
1182	12/31	14,109.33
1184	1/2	17,852.56

The documentation indicates that the last receiving report included in the inventory count was Receiving Report 1182. Receiving Reports 1183 and 1184 were for goods received on the company's truck but not unloaded. Receiving report 1185 was for goods received on January 3.

Required:

Prepare a correcting journal entry assuming that Thermo-Tempur uses (a) a periodic inventory system and (b) a perpetual inventory system that was updated for the inventory count.

LO 9-6

9.53 **Statistical Sampling Used to Estimate Inventory.** ACE Corporation does not conduct a complete annual physical count of purchased parts and supplies in its principal warehouse but uses statistical sampling to estimate the year-end inventory. ACE maintains a perpetual inventory record of parts and supplies. Management believes that statistical sampling is highly effective in determining inventory values and is sufficiently reliable, making a physical count of each item of inventory unnecessary.

Required:

a. List at least 10 normal audit procedures that should be performed to verify physical quantities whenever a client conducts a periodic physical count of all or part of its inventory. (See Appendix Exhibit 9B.1 for procedures.)

b. Identify the audit procedures you should use that change or are in addition to normal required audit procedures [in addition to those listed in your solution to part (a)] when a client utilizes statistical sampling to determine inventory value and does not conduct a 100 percent annual physical count of inventory items.

LO 9-6

9.54 **Inventory Procedures Using Computer-Assisted Audit Techniques (CAATs).** You are conducting an audit of the financial statements of a wholesale cosmetics distributor with an inventory consisting of thousands of individual items. The distributor keeps its inventory in its own distribution center and in two public warehouses. A perpetual inventory computer database is maintained on a computer disk. The database is updated at the end of each business day. Each record of the perpetual inventory database contains the following data:

Item number.
Location of item.
Description of item.
Quantity on hand.
Cost per item.
Date of last purchase.
Date of last sale.
Quantity sold during year.

You are planning to observe the distributor's physical count of inventories as of a given date. The client will provide a computer file of the preceding items taken from its database as of the date of the physical count. Your firm has a computer audit plan that will be ideal for analyzing the inventory records.

Required:

List the basic inventory auditing procedures and, for each, describe how the use of CAATs and the computerized perpetual inventory database might be helpful to the auditor in performing such auditing procedures. (See Appendix 9B for substantive procedures for inventory.)

Organize your answer as follows:

Basic Inventory Auditing Procedures	How CAATs and Copy of the Inventory Data File Might Be Helpful
Conduct an observation of the company's physical count.	Determine which items are to be test counted by selecting a random sample of a representative number of items from the inventory file as of the date of the physical count.

(AICPA adapted)

LO 9-6

9.55   **CAATs Application: Inventory.** Your client, Boos & Becker Inc., is a medium-size manufacturer of products for the leisure-time activities market (camping equipment, scuba gear, bows and arrows, and the like). During the past year, a computer system was installed, and inventory records of finished goods and parts were converted to computerized processing. Each record of the inventory master file contains the following information:

Item or part number.
Description.
Size.
Quantity on hand.
Cost per unit.
Total value of inventory on hand at cost.
Date of last sale or usage.
Quantity used or sold this year.
Reorder point (quantity).
Economic order quantity.
Code number of major vendor or code number of secondary vendor.

In preparation for year-end inventory, the client has two identical sets of preprinted inventory cards prepared from the master file. One set is for the client's inventory counts, and the other is for your use to make audit test counts. The following information has been included on the preprinted cards:

Item or part number.
Description.
Size.
Unit of measure code.

In taking the year-end count, the client's personnel will write the actual counted quantity on the face of each card. When all counts are complete, the counted quantity will be processed against the master file, and quantity-on-hand figures will be adjusted to reflect the actual count. A computer list will be prepared to show any missing inventory count cards and all quantity adjustments of more than $100 in value. Client personnel will investigate these items and will make all required adjustments. When adjustments have been completed, the final year-end balances will be computed and posted to the general ledger.

Your firm has available an audit software package that will run on the client's computer and can process both cards and disk master files.

Required:

a. In general, and without regard to the preceding facts, discuss the nature of CAATs and list the various audit uses of such packages.

b. List and describe at least five ways CAATs can be used to assist in all aspects of the audit of the inventory of Boos & Becker Inc. (For example, CAATs can be used to read the inventory master file and list items and parts with a high unit cost or total value. Such items can be included in the test counts to increase the dollar coverage of the audit verification.) (*Hint:* Think of the normal audit procedures in gathering evidence on inventory when the client makes a periodic count; then think of how these could help in this particular client situation.)

(AICPA adapted)

LO 9-6

9.56 **Inventory Evidence and Long-Term Purchase Contracts.** During the audit of Mason Company Inc. for the calendar year 2014, you noted that the company produces aluminum cans at the rate of about 40 million units annually. On the plant tour, you noticed a large stockpile of raw aluminum in storage. Your inventory observation and pricing procedures showed this stockpile to be the raw materials inventory of 400 tons valued at $240,000 (LIFO cost). Inquiry with the production chief yielded the information that 400 tons was about a four-month supply of raw materials.

Suppose you learn that Mason had executed a firm long-term purchase contract with All Purpose Aluminum Company to purchase raw materials on the following schedule:

Delivery Date	Quantity	Total Price
January 30, 2013	500	$300,000
June 30, 2013	700	420,000
December 30, 2013	1,000	500,000

Because of recent economic conditions, principally a decline in the demand for raw aluminum and a consequent oversupply, the price stood at 20 cents per pound as of January 15, 2015. Commodities experts predict that this low price will prevail for 12 to 15 months or until there is a general economic recovery.

Required:

a. Describe the procedures you would employ to gather evidence about this contract (including its initial discovery).

b. What facts recited in the problem would you have to discover for yourself in an audit?

c. Discuss the effect this contract has on the financial statements.

LO 9-6

9.57 **Tracing the Inventory Count.** You have been assigned to trace the results of the observation of Brightware China's physical inventory count to its pricing and compilation. You note the following conditions.

1. The last inventory tag documented by Mark Hulse, the auditor who observed the inventory, was 1732, but you notice a number of items with count ticket numbers higher than 1732. You contact the client's controller, Marcia Vines, who tells you the client found a storage room full of a new product that Brightware had just produced and added it to the inventory.

2. The count tickets recorded by Hulse agree to the inventory list, but some of the other count tickets you select are substantially different from it. Vines tells you these are input errors and she will have them corrected.

3. Hulse described several boxes of goods as being dusty and even broken. They are included in the inventory at cost. Vines's explanation is that china never "goes bad" and the goods themselves were not broken.

Required:

a. Prepare an audit plan for tracing the information from the inventory count to the compilation.

b. What might have caused the conditions you found? What effect might they have on the financial statements?

c. What steps will you take to follow up on Vines's explanations?

LO 9-6

9.58 **FIFO Inventory Pricing.** You are auditing Martha's Prison Clothes Inc. as of December 31, 2014. The inventory for orange jumpsuits shows 1,263 suits at $782 for a total of $987,666. When you look at the invoices for the jumpsuits, you see the following:

Inventory Number	Date	Quantity	Unit Price	Total
12732	11/22/13	1,000	$765	$765,000
12844	12/03/13	800	777	621,600
12905	12/28/13	600	782	469,200

Required:

a. Determine the adjusting entry, if any, for the cost of inventory at December 31, 2014.

b. Would your answer to part (a) be different if you saw an invoice dated January 9, 2015, for 500 suits at $750?

Instructions for Problems 9.61, 9.62, and 9.63

The cases in Problems 9.61, 9.62, and 9.63 are similar to the one in the chapter. They give the problem and the amount. Your assignment is to write the audit approach portion of the case organized around these sections:

Objective. Express the objective in terms of the facts supposedly asserted in the financial records, accounts, and statements.

Control. Write a brief explanation of desirable controls, missing controls, and especially the types of deviations that might arise from the situation described in the case.

Tests of controls. Write some procedures for obtaining evidence about controls, especially procedures that could discover control deviations. If there are no controls to test, there are no procedures to perform; go to the next section. A *procedure* should instruct someone about the source(s) of evidence to tap and the work to do.

Audit of balance. Write some procedures for obtaining evidence about the balance assertions of existence, rights and obligations, completeness, valuation, and accuracy identified in your objective section.

Discovery summary. Write a short statement about the discovery you expect to accomplish with your procedures.

Inventory and deferred cost overstatement. Follow the preceding instructions. Write the audit approach section following the cases in the chapter.

LO 9-7

9.59 **Toying around with the Numbers. Mattel Inc.,** a manufacturer of toys, failed to write off obsolete inventory, thereby overstating inventory and improperly deferred tooling costs, both of which understated cost of goods sold and overstated income.

"Excess" inventory was identified by comparing types of toys (wheels, general toys, dolls, and games), parts, and raw materials with the forecasted sales or usage; lower-of-cost-or-market (LCM) determinations then were made to calculate the obsolescence write-off. Obsolescence was expected and the target for the year was $700,000. The first comparison computer run showed $21 million "excess" inventory! The company "adjusted" the forecast by increasing the quantities of expected sales for many toy lines. (Forty percent of items had forecasted sales more than their actual recent sales.) Another "adjustment" was to forecast toy closeout sales not at reduced prices but at regular prices. In addition, certain parts were labeled "interchangeable" without the normal reference to a new toy product. These adjustments to the forecast reduced the excess inventory exposed to LCM valuation and write-off. The cost of setting up machines, preparing dies, and other preparations for manufacture are tooling costs. They benefit the lifetime run of the toy manufactured. The company capitalized them as prepaid expenses and amortized them in the ratio of current-year sales to expected product lifetime sales (much like a natural resource depletion calculation).

To lower the amortization cost, the company transferred unamortized tooling costs from toys with low forecasted sales to ones with high forecasted sales. This caused the year's amortization ratio to be lower, the calculated cost write-off lower, and the cost of goods sold lower than it should have been.

The computerized forecast runs of expected usage of interchangeable parts provided a space for a reference to the code number of the new toy where the part would be used. Some of these references contained the code number of the part itself, not a new toy. In other business cases, the forecast of toy sales and parts usage contained the quantity on hand, not a forecast number.

In the tooling cost detailed records, unamortized cost was classified by lines of toys (similar to classifying asset cost by asset name or description). Unamortized balances were carried forward to the next year. The company changed the classifications shown at the prior year-end to other toy lines that had no balances or different balances. In other words, the balances of unamortized cost at the end of the prior year did not match the beginning balances of the current year except for the total prepaid expense amount.

For lack of obsolescence write-offs, inventory was overstated at $4 million. The company recorded a $700,000 obsolescence write-off. It should have been about $4.7 million, as later determined. The tooling cost manipulations overstated the prepaid expense by $3.6 million.

The company reported net income (after taxes) of $12.1 million in the year before the manipulations took place. If pretax income were in the $20 to $28 million range in the year of the misstatements, the obsolescence and tooling misstatements alone amounted to about 32 percent income overstatement.

LO 9-7

9.60 **No Defense for These Charges.** Follow the instructions preceding Problem 9.61. Write the audit approach section following the case in the chapter.

SueCan Corporation manufactured electronic and other equipment for private customers and government defense contracts. It deferred costs under the heading of defense contract claims for reimbursement and deferred tooling labor costs, thus overstating assets, understating cost of goods sold, and overstating income.

Near the end of the year, the company used a journal entry to remove $110,000 from cost of goods sold and defer it as deferred tooling cost. This $110,000 was purported to be labor cost associated with preparing tools and dies for large production runs.

The company opened a receivables account for "cost overrun reimbursement receivable" as a claim for reimbursement on defense contracts ($378,000).

The company altered the labor time records for the tooling costs in an effort to provide substantiating documentation. Company employees prepared new work orders numbered in the series used late in the fiscal year and attached labor time records dated much earlier in the year. The production orders originally charged with the labor cost were left completed but with no labor charges!

The claim for reimbursement on defense contracts did not have documentation specifically identifying the labor costs as being related to the contract. There were no work orders. (Auditors know that Defense Department auditors insist on documentation and justification before approving such a claim.)

SueCan reported net income of about $442,000 for the year, an overstatement of approximately 60 percent.

LO 9-7

9.61 **Chips Ahoy.** Follow the instructions preceding Problem 9.61. Write the audit approach section following the cases in the chapter.

The following is an excerpt from an article, "Memory Chip Trader Gets 14 Years for Bank Fraud," *The Straits Times* (Singapore), February 13, 2009:

Through most of the 1990s, entrepreneur Kelvin Ang Ah Peng rode the crest of a wave as his company traded in memory chips and recycled used ones for sale at a good price. His story, which follows the ebb and flow of the integrated circuit (IC) chip business, started at **EC–Asia International (ECI)** in 1993. Computer chips were expensive, so his business did well. A major earthquake in Taiwan in 1999 totaled the computer chip factories there. Production halted and the market price of computer chips soared even higher. The bubble burst the following year, when the Taiwan factories recovered and several computer chip businesses folded. In 2001, as ECI struggled to keep afloat, Ang started abusing its credit facilities. Between that year and early 2007, he bought and sold worthless memory chips and created fake orders and invoices to receive payment from banks.

He was charged in October 2008 on 687 charges involving US$290 million; last month, he pleaded guilty to 30 charges—28 for cheating and 2 for money laundering and falsifying revenues in ECI's initial public offering (IPO) prospectus. Deputy Public Prosecutor David Chew Siong Tai said that, to secure credit in the absence of incoming orders, Ang fashioned an elaborate scheme with the help of Hong Kong firms. He got ECI's partners to issue the necessary trade documents and to circulate computer chips and money between Hong Kong and Singapore. Chips were actually shipped in these sham transactions as if they were bona fide trades. In reality these were worthless, defective chips due for scrapping by ECI. In November 2006 when asked about ECI's unusually large inventory in Hong Kong and the huge debts owed by the firm's Hong Kong "customers," Ang confessed to an ECI subsidiary's director that 90 percent of the inventory did not exist and that its billings were all faked.

Yesterday, Ang, 44, was jailed for 14 years for having swindled banks of US$23 million (US$35 million) and laundering these proceeds through Hong Kong. The Australian-listed ECI is now being liquidated, and Ang was declared bankrupt last year.

LO 9-7

9.62 **Detection of Errors and Fraud.** For each of the following independent events, indicate the (1) effect of the error or fraud on the financial statements and (2) what auditing procedures could have detected the misstatement resulting from error or fraud.

a. The physical inventory count of J. Payne Enterprises, which has a December 31 year-end, was conducted on August 31 without incident. In September, the perpetual inventory was not reduced for the cost of sales.

b. Holmes Drug Stores counted its inventory on December 31, which is its fiscal year-end. The auditors observed the count at 20 of Holmes's 86 locations. The company falsified the inventory at 20 of the locations not visited by the auditors by including fictitious goods in the counts.

c. Pope Automotive inadvertently included in its inventory automobiles that it was holding on consignment for other dealers.

d. Peffer Electronics Inc. overstated its inventory by pricing wiring at $200 per hundred feet instead of $200 per thousand feet.

e. Goldman Sporting Goods counted boxes of baseballs as having one dozen baseballs per box when they had only six per box.

LO 9-7

9.63 **Identifying Obsolete Inventory and Proposing Provisions**

For this exercise, your client, BrightIDEAs Inc., has provided you with a listing of inventory on hand as of the end of the year. You have been assigned the task of performing procedures to identify unusual or potentially obsolete inventory items and propose a valuation allowance.

Required:

a. Import the client's database of inventory and reconcile it to the general ledger (pp. 193–202 of the IDEA Workbook).

b. Use data extraction techniques to identify client-identified obsolete inventory items in the client's inventory listing or items showing negative amounts or quantities (pp. 203–206 of the IDEA Workbook).

c. Calculate inventory usage ratios to identify inventory items not flagged by the client that may nonetheless be obsolete. (pp. 206–213 of the IDEA Workbook).

d. Use your calculations from the above steps to estimate a provision for obsolete inventory. (pp. 214–218 of the IDEA Workbook).

e. Do you consider the difference between what the client proposed and your proposed provision to be a material difference?

Required Data available on *Connect*

- Inventory 2015.asc

Applying IDEA to the Production Cycle—Elm Manufacturing Company

Exercises 9.64–9.67 require the application of IDEA in the production cycle audit in summarizing client data and recalculating inventory balances using client records. Elm Manufacturing Company (ELM) is a small manufacturer of backpacks located in Rochelle, Illinois. You have access to ELM's electronic records on Connect. The appropriate files for these exercises are the Sales 2017 4th Q data set, the Purchases 2017-4th Q data set, the Inventory Count data set, the Ending Inventory Balances 2017-3rd Q data set, the Finished Goods Production 2017-4th Q data set, the Production Bill of Raw Materials data set, and the Combined Materials and Supplies Vendor Price List data set. You will also require the 2017 ELM Production Cycle Supplementary Information document. Detailed information about ELM, instructions for accessing data sets, and a data directory for data sets can be found on Connect.

LO 9-7

9.64   Summarizing Direct Materials Production Costs Using IDEA

ELM reports that the following is the total cost for each product:

Product	Direct material	Direct Labor	Overhead*	Total Cost
SP001	$ 5.91	$ 1.99	$ 0.16	$ 8.06
HB005	$ 13.40	$ 4.96	$ 0.40	$ 18.76
CB008	$ 56.39	$ 8.11	$ 0.65	$ 65.15

*Overhead is allocated at 8% of direct labor costs (rounded)

Required:

Assume that the cost of Direct Labor and Overhead has been separately verified. Use the Bill of Materials and the Materials Unit Cost sheet to recalculate the Direct Materials cost per unit for the three products. Do you find any differences in calculated materials costs?

LO 9-7

9.65   Summarizing Finished Goods Quantities Using IDEA

You have been assigned the task of recalculating the client's Finished Goods ending inventory quantity based on sales and manufacturing records and comparing it to the year-end inventory count. You may assume there is no Work-in-Process inventory as of year-end.

Required:

a. Perform an inventory roll-forward and calculate the total year end quantity for each of the three items in Finished Goods inventory (Hints: Beginning Balance + Finished Goods Manufactured – Sales = Ending Balance. Don't forget that you should only consider sales that have shipped during the quarter and that the company sells products in cases of 12. You may assume there were no shipments of outstanding orders from prior quarters.).

b. Compare the ending inventory balances from part a. to the quantity based on the year-end inventory count. Are there any significant discrepancies between the calculated ending inventory and the inventory counts?

c. What are some of the reasons that could cause these discrepancies? How would you resolve these issues?

d. What would you propose as the final inventory quantity?

LO 9-7

9.66   Summarizing Raw Materials Quantities Using IDEA

You have been assigned the task of recalculating the client's Raw Materials ending inventory quantity based on purchase and manufacturing records and comparing it to the year-end inventory count. You may assume there is no Work-in-Process inventory as of year-end.

Required:

a. Calculate the total year end quantity for Raw Materials Inventory (Hint: Beginning Balance + Purchases – Used in Production = Ending Balance. Don't forget that you should only include purchases that have been received in calculating purchases. Column "TYPE" in 3rd q inventory database will be helpful for extracting relevant records.)

b. Are there any significant discrepancies between the calculated ending inventory and the inventory counts? Identify possible reasons for such discrepancies.

c. How would you proceed to resolve these issues?

d. What would you propose as the final raw materials inventory quantity?

LO 9-7

9.67   Testing Supplies Inventory and Expense Using IDEA

You have been assigned the task of testing the client's Supplies Expense based on purchase records and the year-end inventory count. ELM's unaudited Trial Balance shows a recorded amount of $33,650 for Supplies Expense during the 4th quarter. Per the client, Supplies Expense consists of the all supplies indirectly used in the factory, but which do not get included in the cost of the manufacturing process. These products are all inventory units beginning with E, Q, or J. Assume that the cost of supplies remained constant throughout the quarter.

Required:

a. Using the information given about beginning balances, purchases, ending counts, and the vendor price list, recalculate Supplies Expense. For the purposes of this exercise, ignore any taxes or shipping charges and base costs solely on the price list.

b. Does ELM's recorded Supplies Expense appear reasonable? Would the auditor perform any further detail testing on Supplies Expense? Explain your reasoning.

Internal Control Questionnaires

APPENDIX EXHIBIT 9A.1 Production Cycle

	Yes/No	Comment
Occurrence		
1. Is cost accounting separate from production, payroll, and inventory control?		
2. Is access to blank production order forms restricted to authorized persons?		
3. Is access to blank bills of materials and labor needs forms restricted to authorized persons?		
4. Is access to blank material requisition forms restricted to authorized persons?		
5. Are production orders prepared by authorized persons?		
6. Are bills of materials and labor needs prepared by authorized persons?		
7. Are material usage reports compared to raw material stores issue forms?		
8. Are labor usage reports compared to job time tickets?		
9. Are material requisitions and job time tickets reviewed by the production supervisor after the floor supervisor prepares them?		
10. Are the weekly direct labor and materials used reports reviewed by the production supervisor after preparation by the floor supervisor?		
Completeness		
1. Are production orders prenumbered and the numerical sequence checked for missing documents?		
2. Are bills of materials and labor needs forms prenumbered and the numerical sequence checked for missing documents?		
3. Are material requisitions and job time tickets prenumbered and the numerical sequence checked for missing documents?		
4. Are inventory issue forms prenumbered and the numerical sequence checked for missing documents?		
5. Is accounting notified of terms on purchase agreements?		
6. Is accounting notified of orders received on consignment?		
Accuracy		
1. Are differences between inventory issue forms and materials used reports recorded and reported to the cost accounting supervisor?		
2. Are differences between job time tickets and the labor report recorded and reported to the cost accounting supervisor?		
3. Are standard costs used? If so, are they reviewed and revised periodically?		
4. Are reports for materials issued to production reconciled with finished goods reports?		
Cutoff		
1. Does the accounting manual give instructions to date cost entries on the date of use?		
2. Does an accounting supervisor review monthly, quarterly, and year-end cost accruals?		
Classification		
1. Are summary entries reviewed and approved by the cost accounting supervisor?		
2. Does the accounting manual give instructions for proper classification of cost accounting transactions?		

APPENDIX EXHIBIT 9A.2 **Inventory Transaction Processing**

	Yes/No	Comment
Occurrence		
1. Are perpetual inventory records kept for raw materials? Supplies? Work-in-process? Finished goods?		
2. Is merchandise or materials held on consignment (not the property of the company) physically segregated from goods owned by the company?		
3. Are additions to inventory quantity records made only on receipt of a receiving report copy?		
4. Do inventory custodians notify inventory record keepers of reductions of inventory?		
Completeness		
1. Are reductions of inventory record quantities made only on receipt of inventory issuance documents?		
2. Do inventory custodians notify the records department of additions to inventory?		
3. Are separate records maintained for consignment inventory?		
Accuracy		
1. Are perpetual records reconciled to general ledger control accounts?		
2. Do the perpetual records show both quantities and prices?		
3. Are inventory records maintained by someone other than the inventory stores custodian?		
4. Are the inventory records compared to physical counts?		
5. Are production reports of material and labor prepared weekly and transmitted to cost accounting?		
6. Are job cost sheets posted weekly and summary journal entries of work-in-process and work completed prepared monthly?		
7. Are job cost sheet entries reviewed by a person independent of the preparer?		
8. If standard costs have been used for inventory pricing, have they been reviewed for reasonableness and current applicability?		
9. Is there a periodic review for overstocked, slow-moving, or obsolete inventory? Have any adjustments been made during the year?		
10. Are periodic counts of physical inventory made to correct errors in the individual perpetual records?		
Cutoff		
1. Does the accounting manual give instructions to record inventory additions on the date of the receiving report?		
2. Does the accounting manual give instructions to record inventory issues on the issuance date?		
Classification		
1. Are perpetual inventory records kept in dollars periodically reconciled to general ledger control accounts?		

Appendix 9B

Audit Plans

DUNDER-MIFFLIN, INC
Audit Plan for Physical Inventory Observation
December 31, 2017

	Performed by	Ref.
1. Obtain client's inventory-counting instructions and review for completeness.		
2. Tour facility before the inventory count looking for out-of-the-way items, obsolete items, and patterns of inventory flow.		
3. Observe client personnel taking inventory counts for compliance with instructions.		
4. Test count a selection of items throughout the facility, and record a sample of your test counts. Note description, stage of completion, counting unit, and condition.		
5. Obtain and record tag numbers used and ensure all tag numbers are accounted for.		
6. Select sample of used tags and trace them to the items on the floor.		
7. Record the last five receiving reports and last five shipping documents and the numbers of next five unused items in sequence. Vouch the recorded items to inventory count to determine that the item was appropriately included (or excluded) from the inventory count.		
8. Tour facilities to ensure all items have been counted.		

DUNDER-MIFFLIN, INC
Audit Plan for Inventory Observation and Cost of Goods Sold
December 31, 2017

	Performed by	Ref.
Inventory		
1. Obtain client's inventory list, recalculate, and check it against the general ledger.		
2. Trace test counts from inventory observation to the final inventory compilation.		
3. Select a sample of inventory items.		
a. Vouch unit prices to vendors' invoices or other cost records.		
b. Recalculate the inventory valuation for sampled items.		
4. Scan the inventory compilation for items added from sources other than the physical count and items that appear to be large round numbers or systematic fictitious additions.		
5. Recalculate the extensions and footings of the final inventory compilation for mathematical accuracy. Reconcile the total to the adjusted trial balance.		
6. For selected inventory items and categories, determine the replacement cost and the applicability of lower-of-cost-or-NRV valuation.		
7. Inspect inventory for evidence of obsolete or damaged goods. Trace identified obsolete or damaged goods to inventory records for write-down.		
8. Inquire about obsolete, damaged, slow-moving, and overstocked inventory.		
9. Scan the perpetual records for slow-moving items.		
10. During the physical observation, be alert to notice damaged or scrap inventory.		
11. Compare the list of obsolete, slow-moving, damaged, or unsalable inventory from last-year's audit to the current inventory compilation.		
12. At year-end, identify the numbers of the last shipping and receiving documents for the year. Compare these to the sales, inventory/cost of sales, and accounts payable entries for proper cutoff.		
13. Read bank confirmations, debt agreements, and minutes of the board and make inquiries about pledge or assignment of inventory to secure debt.		
14. Inquire about inventory held by third parties on consignment and inventory on hand on consignment from vendors.		

(continued)

APPENDIX EXHIBIT 9B.2 *(concluded)*

	Performed by	Ref.
DUNDER-MIFFLIN, INC **Audit Plan for Inventory Observation and Cost of Goods Sold** **December 31, 2017**		
15. Confirm or inspect inventories held in public warehouses.		
16. Recalculate the amount of intercompany profit to be eliminated in consolidation.		
17. Obtain management representations concerning pledging of inventory as collateral, intercompany sales, and other related-party transactions.		
Cost of Sales		
1. Select a sample of recorded cost of sales entries and vouch to supporting documentation.		
2. Select a sample of basic transaction documents (such as sales invoices, production reports) and determine whether the related cost of goods sold was figured and recorded properly.		
3. Review the accounting costing method used by the client (such as FIFO, LIFO, standard cost) for proper application.		
4. Compute the gross margin rate and compare to prior years.		
5. Compute the ratio of cost elements (such as labor, material) to total cost of goods sold and compare this ratio to that for prior years.		

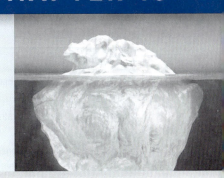

CHAPTER 10

Finance and Investment Cycle

Credit has done a thousand times more to enrich mankind than all the goldmines in the world. It has exalted labor, stimulated manufacture, and pushed commerce over every sea.

Daniel Webster, American statesman, lawyer, and orator (1782–1852)

Professional Standards References

Topic	AU-C/ISA Section	PCAOB Reference
Consideration of Internal Control in an Integrated Audit	N/A	AS 2201
Audit Documentation	230	AS 1215
Consideration of Fraud in a Financial Statement Audit	240	AS 2401
Audit Planning	300	AS 1201
Identifying and Assessing Risks of Material Misstatement	315	AS 2110
Materiality	320, 330	AS 2105
Audit Evidence	332, 500	AS 1105
Audit Evidence—Specific Consideration for Selected Items	501	AS 2503
External Confirmations	505	AS 2310
Analytical Procedures	520	AS 2305
Auditing Accounting Estimates	540	AS 2501
Auditing Fair Value Measurements and Disclosures	540	AS 2502
Related Parties	550	AS 2410
Written Representations	580	AS 1301, AS 2805
Using the Work of an Audit Specialist	620	AS 1210

LEARNING OBJECTIVES

The finance and investment cycle consists of planning for capital requirements and raising the required money by borrowing, selling stock, and entering into acquisitions and joint ventures. The finance part of the cycle involves obtaining money through stock or debt issues. The investment portion of the cycle encompasses using the funds for investments in property, plant, and equipment (covered in the acquisition and expenditure cycle in Chapter 8); marketable securities; joint ventures and partnerships; and subsidiaries. The transactions discussed in this chapter generally involve large dollar amounts and

EXHIBIT 10.2

Finance and Investment Cycle

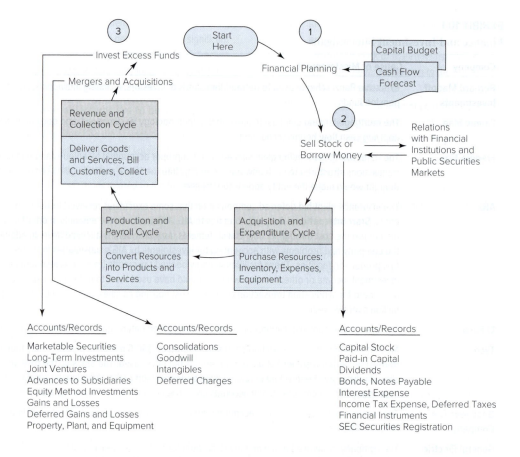

Accounts/Records	Accounts/Records	Accounts/Records
Marketable Securities	Consolidations	Capital Stock
Long-Term Investments	Goodwill	Paid-in Capital
Joint Ventures	Intangibles	Dividends
Advances to Subsidiaries	Deferred Charges	Bonds, Notes Payable
Equity Method Investments		Interest Expense
Gains and Losses		Income Tax Expense, Deferred Taxes
Deferred Gains and Losses		Financial Instruments
Property, Plant, and Equipment		SEC Securities Registration

topics in accounting: equity method accounting for investments, consolidation accounting, goodwill, income taxes, and derivatives, to name a few. The purpose of this chapter is to focus on the auditing issues associated with each of these accounting topics, not to explain how to account for these balances and transactions. Further, we will focus on the more general characteristics of assets, liabilities, and equity accounts in this cycle.

You may recall that an entity's operations and accounting records consist of routine transactions, nonroutine transactions, and accounting estimates. Auditors typically approach audits of routine transactions with a reliance approach—evaluate internal controls and rely on the operation of controls found to be in place. In contrast, audits of nonroutine transactions generally take a substantive approach. In the large majority of audits that do not require an audit of internal controls, auditors may do very few tests of controls related to nonroutine transactions and rely on substantive tests. Similarly, auditors apply a more substantive approach with accounting estimates. Because the financing and investment cycle generally involves large, infrequent, significant transactions—often with some degree of estimation—auditors usually employ more substantive testing procedures in this cycle and rely less on tests of controls.

Exhibit 10.2 is an illustration of the finance and investment cycle, which interacts with all of the other cycles. Its major functions are financial planning; raising capital; and entering into mergers, acquisitions, and other investments. As you follow the exhibit, you can use the numbers to track the elements of internal control described in the following sections.

Financing the Entity through Debt and Stockholder Equity

Transactions in debt and stockholder equity are normally few in number but large in monetary amount, and with a high level of management involvement. The highest levels of corporate governance authorize and execute these transactions. The control-related duties and responsibilities reflect this high-level attention.

Financial Planning ①

The purpose of financial planning is to ensure that the entity has enough cash to operate the business. Entities can fund capital needs through their operations, but any additional needs must be fulfilled through financing activities. Financial planning starts with the cash flow forecast by the chief financial officer (CFO). This forecast informs the board of directors and management of the business plans, the prospects for cash inflows, and the needs for cash outflows. The cash flow forecast usually is integrated with the capital budget, which contains the plans for asset purchases and business acquisitions. A **capital budget** approved by the board of directors constitutes the authorization for major capital asset acquisitions (acquisition cycle) and investments. Cash flow planning and capital budgeting are important controls over major management decisions.

Raising Capital ②

The board of directors usually authorizes sales of capital stock and debt financing transactions. All directors must sign registration documents for public securities offerings. However, authority normally is delegated to the CFO or treasurer to complete other significant transactions (e.g., periodic renewals of notes payable and other ordinary types of significant financing transactions without specific board approval of each transaction). Auditors should expect to find the authorizing signatures of the CEO, CFO, treasurer, chair of the board of directors, and perhaps other high-ranking officers on financing documents. Because financing transactions are typically authorized and executed by top management and directors, it is much more difficult to rely on segregation of duties to ensure that these transactions flow properly through the accounting system using only internal employees. As a result, most entities rely on external parties to process debt and equity transactions involving multiple investors.

Company bonds and stocks are normally handled by an intermediary called a **transfer agent**, generally a bank or trust company. The transfer agent tracks securities' owners for payment of interest or dividends. The certificate records are kept by a **registrar** who updates the records based on information from the transfer agent. Often, the registrar and transfer agent are the same company.

In the past, many financing transactions have been off the balance sheet. Companies entered into obligations and commitments that did not require entries in the accounting system. Examples of transactions that did not necessitate reporting on the balance sheet include operating leases and endorsements on discounted notes or on other companies' obligations, letters of credit, guarantees, repurchase or remarketing agreements, commitments to purchase at fixed prices, commitments to sell at fixed prices, and certain kinds of stock options. As noted previously, the Enron debacle was a case of using SPEs to keep certain large transactions off the company's balance sheet. Off-balance-sheet transactions often cause problems in financial reporting and disclosure. Although new accounting standards will reduce the number of off-balance-sheet transactions (e.g., new rules make it harder to create SPEs and have mandated more disclosure), auditors must still be aware of their existence and ensure their proper use and adequate disclosure. Because of the complexity of the transactions, often the most difficult task for the auditor is discovery and understanding of the transactions.

Record Keeping for Long-Term Liabilities

The accounting department and the CFO or controller maintain records of notes and bonds payable. The record-keeping procedures should be similar to those used to account for vendor accounts payable: comparing payment notices from lenders to the accounting records, monitoring due dates, setting up interest in vouchers for payment, and making accruals for unpaid interest on financial reporting dates. If the company has only a few bonds and notes outstanding, it usually does not keep subsidiary records of them. All information is in the general ledger accounts. However, many large companies, especially in industries such as utilities, have large numbers of bonds and notes and may keep control and subsidiary accounts as is done for accounts payable. Exhibit 10.3 shows

EXHIBIT 10.3
Consolidated Edison Inc. 2015 Financial Statements

Consolidated Edison Company of New York, Inc.
Consolidated Statement of Capitalization

LONG-TERM DEBT (Millions of Dollars)   At December 31,

Maturity	Interest Rate	Series	2015	2014
DEBENTURES:				
2015	5.375%	2005C	$ —	$ 350
2016	5.50	2006C	400	400
2016	5.30	2006D	250	250
2018	5.85	2008A	600	600
2018	7.125	2008C	600	600
2019	6.65	2009B	475	475
2020	4.45	2010A	350	350
2024	3.30	2014B	250	250
2033	5.875	2003A	175	175
2033	5.10	2003C	200	200
2034	5.70	2004B	200	200
2035	5.30	2005A	350	350
2035	5.25	2005B	125	125
2036	5.85	2006A	400	400
2036	6.20	2006B	400	400
2036	5.70	2006E	250	250
2037	6.30	2007A	525	525
2038	6.75	2008B	600	600
2039	5.50	2009C	600	600
2040	5.70	2010B	350	350
2042	4.20	2012A	400	400
2043	3.95	2013A	700	700
2044	4.45	2014A	850	850
2045	4.50	2015A	650	—
2054	4.625	2014C	750	750
TOTAL DEBENTURES			10,450	10,150
TAX-EXEMPT DEBT – Notes issued to New York State Energy Research and Development Authority for Facilities Revenue Bonds*:				
2032	0.42%	2004B Series 1	127	127
2034	0.34	1999A	293	293
2035	0.44	2004B Series 2	20	20
2036	0.27	2001B	98	98
2036	0.01	2010A	225	225
2039	0.36	2004A	98	98
2039	0.01	2004C	99	99
2039	0.01	2005A	126	126
TOTAL TAX-EXEMPT DEBT			1,086	1,086

(continued)

Maturity	Interest Rate	Series	2015	2014
Unamortized debt expense			(78)	(76)
Unamortized debt discount			(21)	(22)
TOTAL			11,437	11,138
Less: Long-term debt due within one year			650	350
TOTAL LONG-TERM DEBT			10,787	10,788
TOTAL CAPITALIZATION			$22,202	$21,976

The accompanying notes are an integral part of these financial statements.
*Rates are to be reset weekly or by auction held every 35 days; December 31, 2015 rates shown.

debentures of **Consolidated Edison Inc.** as disclosed in its 2015 financial statements. With 24 debentures totaling more than $10 billion as of the end of 2015, record keeping and auditing records represent a formidable task. But add to this eight additional tax-exempt items, and the total debt exceeds $11 billion. Also, when all or parts of the notes become due within the next year, the CFO and controller must have the necessary information for properly classifying current and long-term amounts. As shown in Exhibit 10.3, long-term debt accounts for nearly half of Consolidated Edison Inc.'s total capitalization, making this a significant audit issue.

Another class of credit balances for which the functions of authorization, custody, and reconciliation are not easy to describe are the "calculated liabilities and credits": lease obligations, deferred income taxes, pension and postretirement benefit liabilities, and foreign currency translation gains and losses, to name a few. These are accounting transactions calculated according to accounting rules using basic data from company plans and operations. Management usually has considerable discretion in structuring leases, tax strategies, pension plan and employee benefit terms, foreign holdings, and the like. These accounting calculations often involve significant accounting estimates made by management. Company accountants try to capture the economic reality of these calculated liabilities by following generally accepted accounting principles, which are often complex and difficult to understand. Auditors need to discuss these transactions at length and ensure that the fundamental economic and business assumptions underlying significant transactions are reasonable.

Periodic Reconciliation

Most public entities use registrars and transfer agents to issue certificates and track stock ownership. Reports can be obtained from registrars and transfer agents to verify that the company's record of the number of shares outstanding agrees with the registrar's number. (Without this reconciliation, counterfeit shares handled by the transfer agent and recorded by the registrar might go unnoticed.) A **trustee** having duties and responsibilities similar to those of registrars and transfer agents can handle ownership of bonds. Confirmations and reports from bond trustees can be used to reconcile the trustee's records to the company's records.

Some small, especially closely held, corporations may issue stock certificates themselves. These companies utilize a stock certificate book to issue certificates as authorized by the board of directors. A responsible independent person should periodically inspect the stock certificate book to determine whether all certificates are recorded and in the possession of bona fide owners. If necessary, officials in very small companies can confirm the ownership of shares with the holders of record.

Investing Transactions: Investments and Intangibles ③

Company investments can take many shapes. Management invests company resources through the purchase or lease of PP&E, which was discussed in Chapter 8. Investments in intangible assets may be in the form of purchased assets (e.g., patents, trademarks) or accounting allocations (e.g., goodwill, deferred charges). Finally, a company can have a variety of types of investments in marketable securities. The following sections are phrased in the context of a manufacturing or service company; however, financial institutions (banks, thrifts), investment companies (mutual funds, small business investment companies), and insurance companies have more elaborate systems for managing their investments and intangibles.

Authorization

Those in the entity charged with governance (e.g., board of directors or investment committee) should approve all investment policies. It is not unusual to find board or executive committee approval required for major investment transactions. However, auditors should expect to find a great deal of variation across companies about the nature and amount of transactions that must have specific high-level approval. It is imperative that auditors understand the approval process and vouch major acquisitions to the appropriate documented approval.

AUDITING INSIGHT   Authorization: Here Today, Gone Tomorrow

The chief financial officer of Travum County invested several million dollars of county funds with a California-based investment money manager. Soon thereafter, news stories of the money manager's expensive personal lifestyle and questionable handling of clients' funds began to circulate, indicating that clients could lose much of their investments. At the same time, news stories about the county treasurer's own credit card spending habits were published locally, indicating that she had obtained a personal credit card by using the county's name. Although no county funds were lost and no improper credit card bills were paid, the county commissioners temporarily suspended the treasurer's authority to choose investment vehicles for county funds.

Custody

Negotiable certificates such as stocks and bonds may be kept in a brokerage account. Other negotiable certificates (such as titles to real estate) may be in the actual possession of the client. If the company keeps them, they should be in a safe or a bank safe deposit box. Only high-ranking officers (e.g., CFO, CEO, president, and chairman of the board) should have access, which should require two people (**dual control**) to access these documents. This may require two signatures to access a safe deposit box or ensure that no one person knows the complete combination to the safe. When it is not possible for one person to access a safe, cabinet, or drawer, as in two locks and no one has both keys, or no one knows the entire combination, a strict form of dual custody, known as **joint custody,** is implemented as a control.

Patents, trademarks, copyrights, and similar legal intangible rights can be evidenced in legal documents and contracts. These seldom are negotiable, and they usually are kept in ordinary company files. However, these intangible assets are highly valued, and entities make every effort to protect these assets as indicated in the following Auditing Insight.

AUDITING INSIGHT   Don't Use Our Logo

The University of Texas at Austin has trademark rights over the "longhorn" symbol and a particular school color (burnt orange). The university actively prohibits businesses from using these symbols without permission. For example, a local cleaning business and a trash-hauling business were informed that they must cease and desist using the longhorn head logo on their buildings, signs, and trucks. The businesses complied by repainting and finding other ways to promote their business.

The **Coalition to Advance the Protection of Sports Logos** (CAPS), whose members are colleges and the professional leagues (NFL, NBA, MLB, and NHL), uses a national network of investigators to scour flea markets, customs ports, and parking lots on game days to ferret out unlicensed T-shirts, caps, and other gear. Since 1993, CAPS, working with local law enforcement, has seized more than 9 million illegal products valued at more than $329 million.

Source: *"Stopping Knockoffs an Elusive Goal for Flyers,"* The Philadelphia Inquirer, *May 15, 2008, p. C01.*

Record Keeping for Investments

The procedures for purchase of most investments involve the voucher system previously described in Chapter 8. Unauthorized transactions can be a major risk for investments and intangibles. The board of directors or other responsible officials should authorize large transactions. These authorizations provide the approval for the purchasing department to acquire the assets and for the accounting department to prepare the voucher and the check. The treasurer or CFO signs the check to purchase the investment.

The record keeping for many types of investments and intangibles can be complicated. The complications arise not so much from the original recording of transactions, but from the maintenance of the accounts over time. This is where complex accounting standards for marketable securities, equity method accounting, consolidations, goodwill, intangibles' amortization and valuation, depreciation, deferred charges, deferred taxes, pension and postretirement benefit liabilities, and various financial instruments enter the picture. High-level accountants who prepare financial statements are involved with the accounting rules and the management estimates required to account for such investments and intangibles. Management plans and estimates of future events and interpretations of the accounting standards often become elements of the accounting maintenance of these balances. These decisions are ripe areas for overstatement of assets, understatement of liabilities, and understatement of expenses.

Periodic Reconciliation

Investment accounts may be overstated by recording marketable securities that the entity does not own (this represents a violation of the rights assertion). When a brokerage firm holds the securities, the inspection is accomplished with a written confirmation, which is the most typical situation. However, when a company physically holds marketable securities in its possession, a reconciliation performed through inspection and count of negotiable securities certificates is a critical control. This reconciliation is similar to a physical inventory count consisting of an inspection of certificates on hand and comparison with the information recorded in the accounts.

A securities count is not a mere handling of bits of paper. A securities count should include a record of the name of the company represented by the certificate, the interest rate for bonds, the dividend rate for preferred stocks, the due date for bonds, the serial numbers on the certificates (known as the *CUSIP number*), the number of stock shares or face amount of bonds, and notes on the name of the owner shown on the face of the certificate or on the endorsements on the back (should be the client company). Companies should perform this reconciliation reasonably often and not wait for an annual visit by the independent auditors. A securities count in a financial institution that holds thousands of shares in multibillion-dollar asset accounts is a major undertaking. A surprise count by the auditors may be done during the interim testing. As with other assets, the auditor should insist that client personnel are present during the entire count.

✅ REVIEW CHECKPOINTS

10.1   Who is normally responsible for the authorization of investment activities? Why is the authorization normally performed at this level?

10.2   What constitutes the authorization for notes payable? What documentary evidence could auditors examine to confirm this authorization?

10.3   What documents would a company need to correctly account for its investment securities, and what information would they obtain from these documents?

10.4   Describe the activities a company should perform to ensure appropriate reconciliation of marketable securities.

INTERNAL CONTROL ACTIVITIES AND DESIGN EVALUATION

LO 10-4

Identify important internal control activities present in a properly designed system to mitigate the risk of material misstatements for each relevant assertion in the finance and investment cycle.

In the finance and investment cycle, auditors look for control activities such as authorization, appropriate custody, record keeping, and periodic reconciliation. They especially look for information about the level of management that is involved in these functions. Tests of controls generally begin with inquiries and observations related to these features. Inspection of documents, primarily looking for proper authorizations, and a walkthrough of controls over the determination of the fair value of assets should also be performed.

Because finance and investment transactions are often individually material, each transaction usually is audited using substantive procedures. Auditors do not normally examine samples of significant transactions for tests of controls as they do in the other cycles because reliance on controls does not normally reduce the extent of substantive procedures on finance and investment cycle accounts. However, lack of controls can lead to performance of significant extended procedures. Of particular importance are the entitywide controls that restrict access to systems, documents, and assets—many of which are key in the performance of investment cycle activities. Establishing appropriate procedures, including adequate controls, for determining the fair market value of investments, derivatives, hedges, and other investment instruments is imperative in accessing the overall control structure for any company that maintains a material amount of such instruments. Of course, for public companies in which the auditors must issue a report on the effectiveness of controls over the financial reporting process, evaluation of controls over these transactions is essential. However, for the majority of nonpublic clients, tests of controls may be limited to entity level in the finance and investment cycle. Exhibit 10.6 outlines some of the primary control considerations in the finance and investment cycle that entities use to mitigate risk.

EXHIBIT 10.6

Significant Account	Relevant Assertions	What Can Go Wrong?	Internal Control Activity (Mitigate Risk)
Investments	Existence/occurrence	Management may sell company-owned securities for their own benefit.	Broker transaction confirmations should be periodically reviewed by the investment committee of the board of directors (BOD).
			Investment purchases and sales should be approved by the BOD.
		Investment securities held by the entity may be stolen.	Securities should be held in lockboxes, and responsibility for custody should be separated from responsibility for record keeping.
		Management may record fictitious interest income.	The investment committee of the BOD should regularly compare investment performance to expectations.
	Completeness	Investment transactions from the current period may be recorded in the subsequent period.	The responsibility for authorization of purchases of securities should be separated from recording purchases in the securities ledger.
	Valuation	Management fails to mark marketable equity securities to fair market value.	Qualified staff is responsible for end-of-period fair value estimates.

(continued)

Significant Account	Relevant Assertions	What Can Go Wrong?	Internal Control Activity (Mitigate Risk)
		Equity method investments are not accurately adjusted for investee income and dividends.	Ensure accurate financial statements for investees are obtained on a timely basis.
		Impairments to investment securities are not properly recorded.	Management reviews investment securities for evidence of other than temporary declines in value.
			Separate the duty of investment acquisition from the duty of investment valuation.
	Presentation and disclosure	Management fails to appropriately account for derivative transactions that do not qualify for hedge treatment.	Properly trained employees supervise the estimation process for derivative securities.
		Available for Sale Debt securities are misclassified as Held to Maturity.	Ensure the investment committee of the BOD has a written policy on investment classification.
Long-Term Debt	Existence/occurrence	Fully-paid notes are not properly removed from schedule of long-term debt.	The BOD authorizes all issuances of long-term notes and bonds.
	Completeness	Management fails to record capital lease obligations.	Separate the duties of authorization of lease agreements from accounting for lease agreements.
	Valuation	Amortization of long-term debt is calculated incorrectly.	Hire qualified personnel and review their work.
	Presentation and disclosure	Management fails to reclassify current portions of long-term debt.	Ensure active oversight by independent financial experts from the audit committee.
		Management fails to disclose future minimum required debt payments.	Ensure active oversight by independent financial experts from the audit committee.
		Violations of restrictive loan covenants are not properly disclosed.	Ensure active oversight by independent financial experts from the audit committee.
Capital Stock	Completeness	Some issued stock is not recorded.	Management regularly obtains register of issued stock from third-party registrar and compares with recorded capital stock.
		Treasury stock repurchases are not recorded.	Require authorization of BOD for treasury stock repurchases.
	Presentation and disclosure	Exercises of stock options are not allocated correctly between capital stock accounts.	Hire qualified accounting staff and review their work.
Retained Earnings	Completeness	Declared dividends are not recorded.	Management should periodically review equity accounts.
		Prior-period error corrections are not recorded appropriately.	Hire qualified personnel and review their work.

Control Considerations

Control activities for suitable handling of responsibilities should be in place and operating. By referring to the discussion accompanying Exhibit 10.2, you may notice that these responsibilities are primarily in the hands of senior management officials. You also can surmise that different companies may have widely different policies and activities.

It is difficult to have a strict separation of functional responsibilities when the principal officers of a company authorize, execute, and control finance and investment activities. It is not realistic to have the CEO authorize investments but not have access to stockholder records, securities certificates, and the like. Real separation of duties can be found in middle management and lower ranks, but it is difficult to create and enforce among upper managers.

Because of this control problem, a company should have *compensating control activities*. A **compensating control** is a control activity used because a specific standard control activity is not in place. The compensating control reduces the risk due to the missing control. For example, the board of directors may authorize the purchase of an investment and delegate the execution of investment purchases to the CFO. The CFO would call the company's broker to execute the authorized transaction. Because the CFO is authorized to instruct the broker to buy and sell securities, the CFO is in a position to sell company securities for personal use. A compensating control might be an agreement with the broker to mail transaction confirmations to other company personnel or to use electronic transfer directly into the company's account for all proceeds from the sale of investments. In the area of finance and investment, the compensating control feature often involves two or more persons in each area of important functional responsibility.

If involvement by multiple persons is not specified, an oversight or review can be substituted. For example, the board of directors can authorize the purchase of securities or the creation of a partnership. The CFO or CEO can carry out the transactions, have custody of certificates and agreements, manage the partnership or the portfolio of securities, oversee the record keeping, and make the decisions about valuations and accounting (authorizing the journal entries). These are normal management activities, and they combine several responsibilities. The compensating control can exist in the form of periodic reports to the board of directors, oversight by the investment committee of the board, and internal audit involvement in making a periodic reconciliation of securities certificates in a portfolio with the amounts and descriptions recorded in the accounts.

Auditors considering the design of internal controls in the finance and investment cycle typically perform a walkthrough, which involves starting with an inquiry of management about how the processes are completed. For example, the auditor may ask management who initiates an investment transaction, how the transaction is approved, and how the transaction is executed. The auditor may then inspect and document a sample investment transaction to obtain a clear understanding of the design of the controls put into action. Based on the understanding, the auditor will then often discuss the resulting flowchart or narrative with management and document a preliminary risk assessment related to the purchase or sale of an investment transaction. A similar process can be repeated for other significant accounts and assertions within the finance and investment cycle.

TESTS OF OPERATING EFFECTIVENESS OF INTERNAL CONTROL

LO 10-5
Give examples of tests of controls to verify the operating effectiveness of internal controls in the finance and investment cycle.

Following an assessment of the design effectiveness of internal controls in the finance and investment cycle, the auditor may consider testing the operating effectiveness of internal control. Of course, recall that auditors performing an integrated audit must always test the operating effectiveness of internal controls. Exhibit 10.7 outlines some of the tests of controls that an auditor may perform in the finance and investment cycle. A scan of the exhibit likely shows you that tests of controls in this cycle are very different from the ones covered

EXHIBIT 10.7

Significant Account	Relevant Assertions	What Can Go Wrong?	Internal Control Activity (Mitigate Risk)	Test of Internal Control
Investments	Existence/ occurrence	Management may sell company-owned securities for their own benefit.	Broker transaction confirmations should be periodically reviewed by the investment committee of the board of directors (BOD).	Inspect documents for evidence of periodic board review of purchase transactions.
			Investment purchases and sales should be approved by the BOD.	Review BOD minutes for evidence of authorization of investment purchases.
		Investment securities held by the entity may be stolen.	Securities should be held in lockboxes, and responsibility for custody should be separated from responsibility for record keeping.	Inquire about proper segregation of duties and about lockbox security procedures.
		Management may overstate current-period interest income.	The investment committee of the BOD should regularly compare investment performance to expectations.	Inspect documents for evidence of periodic board review of investment performance.
	Completeness	Investment transactions from the current period may be recorded in the subsequent period.	The responsibility for authorization of purchases of securities should be separated from recording purchases in the securities ledger.	Inquire about proper segregation of duties.
	Valuation	Management fails to mark marketable equity securities to fair market value.	Qualified staff is responsible for end-of-period fair value estimates.	Inquire about the estimation process, and observe evidence that process is being followed.
		Equity method investments are not accurately adjusted for investee income.	Ensure accurate financial statements for investees are obtained on a timely basis.	Inquire about the process of obtaining investee financial statement information, and inspect evidence of timeliness.
		Impairments to investment securities are not properly recorded.	Management reviews investment securities for evidence of other than temporary declines in value.	Inspect documentation for evidence of management review of investment valuation.
			Separate the duty of investment acquisition from the duty of investment valuation.	Inquire of personnel about impairment process, and observe separation of duties.
	Presentation and disclosure	Management fails to appropriately account for derivative transactions that do not qualify for hedge treatment.	Properly trained employees supervise the estimation process for derivative securities.	Inquire about the client's policies and procedures for determining hedge treatment of derivative securities.
		Available for Sale Debt securities are misclassified as Held to Maturity.	Ensure the investment committee of the BOD has a written policy on investment classification.	Review entity's investment classification policy.

(continued)

EXHIBIT 10.7 (*Continued*)

Significant Account	Relevant Assertions	What Can Go Wrong?	Internal Control Activity (Mitigate Risk)	Test of Internal Control
Long-Term Debt	Existence/ occurrence	Fully-paid notes are not properly removed from schedule of long-term debt.	The BOD authorizes all issuances of long-term notes and bonds.	Inspect BOD meeting minutes for evidence of approval of debt.
	Completeness	Management fails to record capital lease obligations.	Separate the duties of authorization of lease agreements from accounting for lease agreements.	Inquire of personnel about lease contracting process, and observe separation of duties.
	Valuation	Amortization of long-term debt is calculated incorrectly.	Hire qualified personnel and review their work.	Inspect documents for evidence of management review of debt schedules.
	Presentation and disclosure	Management fails to reclassify current portions of long-term debt.	Ensure active oversight by independent financial experts from the audit committee.	Obtain minutes of audit committee meetings, and inspect for evidence of appropriate oversight.
		Management fails to disclose future minimum required debt payments.	Ensure active oversight by independent financial experts from the audit committee.	Obtain minutes of audit committee meetings, and inspect for evidence of appropriate oversight.
		Violations of restrictive loan covenants are not properly disclosed.	Ensure active oversight by independent financial experts from the audit committee.	Obtain minutes of audit committee meetings, and inspect for evidence of appropriate oversight.
Capital Stock	Completeness	Some issued stock is not recorded.	Management regularly obtains register of issued stock from third-party registrar and compares with recorded capital stock.	Inspect documents for evidence that management periodically reviews stock registers.
		Treasury stock repurchases are not recorded.	Require authorization of board of directors for treasury stock repurchases.	Inspect BOD meeting minutes for evidence of approval of treasury stock repurchases.
	Presentation and disclosure	Exercises of stock options are not allocated correctly between capital stock accounts.	Hire qualified accounting staff and review their work.	Inquire about hiring process, and inspect evidence of management review of capital stock transactions.
Retained Earnings	Completeness	Declared dividends are not recorded.	Management should periodically review equity accounts.	Inquire of management about process for ensuring accuracy and completeness of equity accounts.
		Prior-period error corrections are not recorded appropriately.	Hire qualified accounting staff and review their work.	Inquire about hiring process, and inspect evidence of management review of error corrections.

in the other cycle chapters. Auditors do not typically vouch or trace transactions as control tests in this cycle. The primary reason is that there are often so few transactions, and they are likely material, so the auditor tests the transactions as substantive tests, not tests of controls for the purpose of assessing control risk. In fact, tests of controls in the finance and investment cycle primarily deal with determining whether there is sufficient board oversight in practice, proper authorization and review of transactions, and sufficient documentation of finance and investment policies. In this section, you will learn about some of the more difficult evaluations auditors must make in assessing control risk in the finance and investment cycle. First, you will learn about tests of controls surrounding accounting estimates, and then you will read a discussion about tests of controls surrounding authorization, record-keeping, and custody.

Control over Accounting Estimates

An **accounting estimate** is an approximation of a financial statement element, item, or account. Estimates often are included in basic financial statements because (1) the measurement of some amount of valuation is uncertain, perhaps depending on the outcome of future events, or (2) relevant data cannot be accumulated on a timely, cost-effective basis (AS 2501.01). Some examples of accounting estimates in the finance and investment cycle include the following:

- *Plant and equipment depreciation.* Useful lives, salvage values.
- *Financial instruments.* Valuation of securities, including fair values assigned to debt and equity securities; classification into held-to-maturity, available-for-sale, and trading securities investment portfolios; probability of a correlated hedge; sales of securities with puts and calls; investment model assumptions; and impairments. The issue of valuation may be especially difficult if the investment was received in a noncash transaction and is not readily marketable. Appraisals, financial modeling, or other methods may be necessary to estimate the investment's value.
- *Accruals.* Compensation in stock option plans, actuarial assumptions in pension costs.
- *Leases.* Initial direct costs, useful lives, executory costs, and residual values; capitalization interest rate.
- *Rates.* Imputed interest rates on receivables and payables.
- *Other.* Losses and net realizable value on segment disposal and business restructuring, fair values in nonmonetary exchanges, and impairment of goodwill.

A client's management is responsible for making estimates and should have processes and controls designed to reduce the likelihood of material misstatements in them. According to auditing standards (AS 2501.06), specific relevant aspects of such controls include the following:

- Management communication of the need for proper accounting estimates.
- Accumulation of relevant, sufficient, and reliable data for estimates.
- Preparation of estimates by qualified personnel.
- Adequate review and approval by appropriate levels of authority.
- Comparison of prior estimates with subsequent results to assess the reliability of the process used to develop estimates.
- Consideration by management of whether particular accounting estimates are consistent with the company's operational plans.

Auditors' tests of controls over the estimation process include making inquiries and observations. Inquiries would include such questions as: Who prepares estimates? When are they prepared? What data are used? Who reviews and approves the estimates? Have prior estimates been compared with subsequent actual events? The auditor also will assess the involvement of the audit committee of the board of directors in evaluating the estimation process. If the audit committee is more heavily involved in risk assessment and process evaluation, control risk may be reduced for relevant assertions in the finance and investment cycle. Observations in tests of controls over accounting estimates include study of data documentation, study of comparisons of prior estimates with subsequent actual experience, and study of intercompany correspondence concerning estimates and operational plans. The audit of a valuation estimate starts with the tests of controls, many of which have a bearing on the quality of the estimation process and of the estimate itself.

AUDITING INSIGHT   OOPS!

A large television manufacturer decided to extend its 90-day warranty on labor to one year. Because the company had no experience with such an extended warranty, it devised a complex formula to take into account the increased likelihood of repair and the associated cost.

While going through the pages and pages of calculations with the warranty accountant to obtain an understanding, the auditor noticed that one fraction used in the calculation was inverted. The error resulted in a $20 million understatement of the warranty reserve.

Authorization

Most of the transactions in the financing and investing cycle involve large amounts of cash or other assets. Therefore, authorization is a critical issue when examining these transactions. The issuance, sale, or purchase of company stock and bonds, the obtaining of large bank loans, and the purchase or sale of large assets generally are discussed at the highest levels of the organization. Auditors must review minutes of the board of directors meetings, finance committee meetings, or other appropriate committee meetings for the authorization of significant transactions, including dividends, treasury stock repurchases, issuance of stock options, and acquisitions, among many others. In addition, the authorization for the purchase of large assets may reside in the capital budget, which should have been approved by senior management and the board. Absent tangible evidence of the authorization of significant transactions, the auditor should make inquiries at the highest levels to ensure that these major transactions have been approved.

Record Keeping

Transactions that occur on a daily basis are usually recorded in a journal designed especially for those transactions (e.g., sales journals, purchase journals, payroll journals). Usually, the transactions in this cycle occur infrequently and are recorded in the general journal. In addition, because the transactions are infrequent, vary greatly in type, and are for large dollar amounts, controls over the proper recording of the transaction must be implemented. The competency of the individuals making these journal entries and the review and reconciliation of the general ledger are essential controls that the auditor should test. Assessing the competency of client employees can be difficult but should begin with inquiry of management regarding the qualifications of employees responsible for record keeping in the finance and investment cycle. Auditors will also often evaluate the hiring process of employees in an audit of the company's human resources and payroll accounts. The auditor also can use evidence obtained from prior audits as an indication of the competency/lack thereof of a company's employees. For this reason, employee turnover is deemed a significant risk factor when considering controls over complex transactions.

Custody

In large companies, custody of **stock certificate books** is not a significant management problem because of the use of registrars and transfer agents. Small companies often keep their own stockholder records. A stock certificate book looks like a checkbook. It has perforated stubs for recording the number of shares, the owner's name and other identification, and the date of issue. Actual unissued share certificates are attached to the stubs, like blank checks in a checkbook. The company should have a record of certificates that are outstanding in the possession of owners. Custody of the stock certificate book is important because the unissued certificates are like money or collateral. If improperly removed, they can be sold to buyers who think they are genuinely issued or can be used as collateral with unsuspecting lenders. Auditors should test controls surrounding the physical security of stock certificate books and should test the process for issuance of stock certificates.

Lenders have custody of debt instruments (e.g., leases, bonds, and notes payable). However, when a company repurchases its bonds or pays off its debt, the debt instruments are returned to the company. These documents could be misused by improperly reselling them to unsuspecting investors. Auditors should inspect documentation indicating the extinguishment of debt and should inspect returned bonds or notes for appropriate cancelation or evidence of destruction.

AUDITING INSIGHT   A New Meaning for "Recycling"

Something strange must have happened on the way to the dump. Hundreds of long-term bonds were redeemed early and presented to **Citibank** in New York, which acted as the agent for the issues. Many of the bonds still had not reached the maturity date marked on them. Citibank sent about $1 billion of the canceled U.S. corporate bonds to a landfill dump in New Jersey, but some of them turned up at banks in Europe and the United States. Although the bonds are worthless, they still might look genuine to a layperson or even to some bankers. The FBI traced the canceled bonds to a defunct company in New Jersey that had a contract to destroy the bonds. (*Note:* Companies obtain a destruction certificate when bonds and stock certificates are canceled. The certificates obtained by Citibank apparently were fraudulent.)

Source: *Securities Exchange Act Release No. 31612, December 17, 1992, www .sec.gov/news/digest/1992/dig121792.pdf.*

Summary: Control Risk Assessment

From the preceding discussion, you can tell that tests of controls take a variety of forms: inquiries, observations, inspection of documentation, comparisons with related data, and detail audits of some significant transactions. However, because of the nature of finance and investment transactions (i.e., few in number and high in dollar amount), auditors often focus on substantive tests rather than tests of controls. For example, a company may have only 10 significant security investment transactions during the year. The most efficient use of audit time may be to review all 10 significant transactions for all relevant assertions. Conversely, some companies may have numerous debt-financing transactions and a more detailed evaluation of control risk may be pertinent, including the selection of a sample of significant transactions for control risk assessment evidence.

See Appendix 10A for internal control questionnaires for the finance and investment cycle. They illustrate typical questions about the assertions. These inquiries give auditors insights into the client's specifications for review and approval of major investing and financing transactions, the system of accounting for them, and the provision for error-checking review activities.

The audit team should evaluate the evidence obtained from an understanding of the design of internal control and from tests of the operating effectiveness of controls.

These tests can take many forms because management systems for finance and investment accounts can vary a great deal among clients. The involvement of senior officials in a relatively small number of high-dollar transactions makes control risk assessment a process tailored specifically to the company's situation. Some companies enter into complicated financing and investment transactions while others keep to the simple transactions.

AUDITING INSIGHT   Blockwhat?

Many companies, particularly companies that have significant international and online businesses, are beginning to accept payments in bitcoin, a digital asset and payment system first introduced by Satoshi Nakamoto in 2008. As of 2016, more than 100,000 merchants were accepting bitcoins as payment. Bitcoin transactions are peer-to-peer and do not require an intermediary, thus reducing transaction costs considerably. In addition, bitcoin transactions are permanently recorded in blockchain, a distributed database of transactions that cannot be tampered with or revised. Blockchain technology has the potential to lead to better electronic audit trails, but with it comes potential issues. As **EY** recently tweeted, "With blockchain what comes first, opportunity or threat?" However, from an auditing standpoint, bitcoins

present potential issues both for valuation and for controls. Because they are not a currency, they are not treated as cash, but more like a mark-to-market investment. Unlike investment securities, however, bitcoins are not backed by any asset. Further, they are maintained in digital wallets, and anyone with access to the wallet can immediately steal the bitcoins. Thus, both existence and valuation of bitcoins represent significant risks of material misstatement, and tests of controls must be performed on clients with material bitcoin assets or transactions.

Sources: A. Cuthbertson, "Bitcoin Now Accepted by 100,000 Merchants Worldwide," *International Business Times* February 4, 2015; EY, "Implementing Blockchains and Distributed Infrastructure," 2016; https://twitter.com/EYnews/status/747468816641200128.

✓ REVIEW CHECKPOINTS

10.5 What is a compensating control? Give some examples for finance and investment cycle accounts.

10.6 What are some of the specific relevant aspects of management's control over the estimation process? What are some inquiries auditors can make?

10.7 What are some specific transactions that an auditor would expect to be approved by the board of directors? How would it affect the audit if these transactions were not required to be approved by the board?

10.8 What documentation should an auditor inspect when a client has paid off a bank note? How could an employee defraud the company if the bank note has no indication of being paid?

SUBSTANTIVE ANALYTICAL PROCEDURES AND TESTS OF DETAILS

LO 10-6
Give examples of substantive procedures in the finance and investment cycle and relate them to assertions about significant account balances at the end of the period.

As discussed earlier, the finance and investment cycle is primarily audited with a substantive approach. When the auditor uses a reliance approach in the operating cycle, reductions in control risk enable the use of less detailed substantive testing. For example, an auditor may choose to use analytical procedures to assess the reasonableness of certain current liabilities without testing the transactions or balances in detail. However, because the finance and investment cycle consists of infrequent and significant transactions, the auditor relies less on tests of controls and more on direct substantive tests of details. This section addresses the typical types of substantive tests an auditor uses to obtain sufficient, appropriate evidence in the finance and investment cycle. As in previous chapters, the section concludes with some cases illustrating errors and frauds to describe useful audit approaches.

Exhibit 10.8 completes the audit approach for the finance and investment cycle. In the exhibit, substantive analytical procedures and substantive tests of details that are often used to obtain evidence about significant accounts and relevant assertions are presented.

EXHIBIT 10.8

Significant Account	Relevant Assertions	What Can Go Wrong?	Internal Control Activity (Mitigate Risk)	Test of Internal Control	Possible Substantive Analytical Procedures	Possible Substantive Tests of Details
Investments	Existence/ occurrence	Management may sell company-owned securities for their own benefit.	Broker transaction confirmations should be periodically reviewed by the investment committee of the board of directors (BOD).	Inspect documents for evidence of periodic board review of purchase transactions.		Confirm investments with brokerage.
			Investment purchases and sales should be approved by the BOD.	Review BOD minutes for evidence of authorization of investment purchases.		Vouch purchases and sales of securities to broker's advices.
		Investment securities held by the entity may be stolen.	Securities should be held in lockboxes, and responsibility for custody should be separated from responsibility for record keeping.	Inquire about proper segregation of duties and about lockbox security procedures.		Physically inspect all investment securities held by entity.
		Management may overstate current-period interest income.	The investment committee of the BOD should regularly compare investment performance to expectations.	Inspect documents for evidence of periodic board review of investment performance.	Recalculate interest income on debt securities based on principal balances and interest rates.	Vouch recorded interest income to cash receipts journal and premium/discount amortization.
	Completeness	Investment transactions from the current period may be recorded in the subsequent period.	The responsibility for authorization of purchases of securities should be separated from recording purchases in the securities ledger.	Inquire about proper segregation of duties.	Compare current-year investment account balances with expected balances based on prior-year balances and current-year operating and financing activities.	Scan cash disbursements ledger for large purchases surrounding year-end.
	Valuation	Management fails to mark marketable equity securities to fair market value.	Qualified staff is responsible for end-of-period fair value estimates.	Inquire about the estimation process, and observe evidence that process is being followed.	Inspect client budgets, and compare with actual investment returns.	Vouch market values of marketable investment securities to *The Wall Street Journal*.

(Continued)

467

EXHIBIT 10.8 (*Continued*)

Significant Account	Relevant Assertions	What Can Go Wrong?	Internal Control Activity (Mitigate Risk)	Test of Internal Control	Possible Substantive Analytical Procedures	Possible Substantive Tests of Details
		Equity method investments are not accurately adjusted for investee income.	Ensure accurate financial statements for investees are obtained on a timely basis.	Inquire about the process of obtaining investee financial statement information, and inspect evidence of timeliness.		Obtain financial statements of investments accounted for by the equity method, and recalculate recorded amounts.
		Impairments to investment securities are not properly recorded.	Ensure management reviews investment securities for evidence of other than temporary declines in value.	Inspect documentation for evidence of management review of investment valuation.		Inspect client documentation for calculations of possible impairments and test.
			Separate the duty of investment acquisition from the duty of investment valuation.	Inquire of personnel about impairment process, and observe separation of duties.		
	Presentation and disclosure	Management fails to appropriately account for derivative transactions that do not qualify for hedge treatment.	Properly trained employees supervise the estimation process for derivative securities.	Inquire about the client's policies and procedures for determining hedge treatment of derivative securities.		Inspect documentation supporting client classification of derivative securities.
		Available for Sale Debt securities are misclassified as Held to Maturity.	The investment committee of the BOD has a written policy on investment classification.	Review entity's investment classification policy.		Obtain representations from management regarding intent of debt investments.
Long-Term Debt	Existence/ occurrence	Fully-paid notes are not properly removed from schedule of long-term debt.	The BOD authorizes all issuances of long-term notes and bonds.	Inspect BOD meeting minutes for evidence of approval of debt.	Compare expected debt balances to actual debt balances based on understanding of client's financing needs and prior-year balances.	Confirm long-term debt with debtors, including terms and interest rates.

EXHIBIT 10.8 *(Continued)*

Significant Account	Relevant Assertions	What Can Go Wrong?	Internal Control Activity (Mitigate Risk)	Test of Internal Control	Possible Substantive Analytical Procedures	Possible Substantive Tests of Details
	Completeness	Management fails to record capital lease obligations.	Separate the duties of authorization of lease agreements from accounting for lease agreements.	Inquire of personnel about lease contracting process, and observe separation of duties.		Inspect lease agreements, and evaluate appropriate accounting treatment.
	Valuation	Amortization of long-term debt is calculated incorrectly.	Hire qualified personnel and review their work.	Inspect documents for evidence of management review of debt schedules.		Obtain debt amortization schedules, and recalculate balances.
	Presentation and disclosure	Management fails to reclassify current portions of long-term debt.	Ensure active oversight by independent financial experts from the audit committee.	Obtain minutes of audit committee meetings, and inspect for evidence of appropriate oversight.		Inspect schedule of long-term debt, and evaluate appropriate classification of debt.
		Management fails to disclose future minimum required debt payments.	Ensure active oversight by independent financial experts from the audit committee.	Obtain minutes of audit committee meetings, and inspect for evidence of appropriate oversight.		Complete disclosure checklist, and agree footnote disclosures to debt instruments.
		Violations of restrictive loan covenants are not properly disclosed.	Ensure active oversight by independent financial experts from the audit committee.	Obtain minutes of audit committee meetings, and inspect for evidence of appropriate oversight.		Inspect debt agreements, and recalculate ratios for compliance with debt covenants.
Capital Stock	Completeness	Some issued stock is not recorded.	Management regularly obtains register of issued stock from third-party registrar and compares with recorded capital stock.	Inspect documents for evidence that management periodically reviews stock registers.	Compare current-year capital stock accounts with expectations based on review of board minutes and prior-year balances.	Confirm capital stock with third-party registrar.
						Inspect cash receipts ledger for presence of equity transactions surrounding year-end.

(Continued)

469

EXHIBIT 10.8 *(Concluded)*

Significant Account	Relevant Assertions	What Can Go Wrong?	Internal Control Activity (Mitigate Risk)	Test of Internal Control	Possible Substantive Analytical Procedures	Possible Substantive Tests of Details
		Treasury stock repurchases are not recorded.	Require authorization of BOD for treasury stock repurchases.	Inspect BOD meeting minutes for evidence of approval of treasury stock repurchases.		Inspect schedule of treasury stock repurchases, and trace to general ledger.
	Presentation and disclosure	Exercises of stock options are not allocated correctly between capital stock accounts.	Hire qualified accounting staff and review their work.	Inquire about hiring process, and inspect evidence of management review of capital stock transactions.		Inspect BOD minutes for approval of stock options.
						Obtain schedule of stock options, and test for accuracy. Trace to capital stock ledger and general ledger.
Retained Earnings	Completeness	Declared dividends are not recorded.	Management should periodically review equity accounts.	Inquire of management about process for ensuring accuracy and completeness of equity accounts.		Inspect BOD minutes for evidence of dividend declarations, and trace to general ledger.
		Prior-period error corrections are not recorded appropriately.	Hire qualified accounting staff and review their work.	Inquire about hiring process, and inspect evidence of management review of error corrections.		Trace schedule of known prior period adjustments to retained earnings.

In general, substantive procedures on finance and investment accounts are extensive. Nevertheless, control deficiencies and unusual or complicated transactions can cause auditors to adjust the nature and timing of audit procedures. For example, if separation of duties is lacking in the execution of investment transactions, the auditor may move most testing of investment securities and related accounts to year-end. Complicated financial instruments, pension plans, exotic equity securities, related-party transactions, and nonmonetary exchanges of investment assets call for procedures designed to find evidence of errors and frauds in the finance and investment accounts.

As shown in Exhibit 10.8, the auditor's primary concerns surrounding typical marketable investment securities mostly involve the existence of the securities and the valuation of the securities. For this reason, auditors typically rely on either positive external confirmation with a broker or direct physical examination of security certificates to ensure the existence of the investments, and they verify ownership through confirmation or inspection to determine that the client is listed as the owner. Similarly, the auditor relies on vouching the reported market value of securities to a public source such as *The Wall Street Journal*. Auditors also evaluate disclosures and recalculate both realized and unrealized gains and losses on marketable investment securities, as well as consider the reasonableness of management's classification of the securities within the relevant financial accounting standard. However, companies can have a wide variety of investments and relationships with affiliates. Investment accounting may be on the market value method, cost method, equity method, or full consolidation, depending on the nature, size, and influence represented by the investment. Consolidations usually create problems of accounting for the fair value of acquired assets and the related goodwill. Auditors must identify the appropriate accounting method for each investment and ensure that investments are properly valued. The next section discusses some of the more complex issues auditors may face in auditing investment securities. The section concludes with two specific valuation and classification issues: auditing fair value measurements and derivative securities.

Trouble Spots in Audits of Investments and Intangibles   To some, it might appear that the audit of investments and intangibles presented in this chapter is straightforward. After all, in many instances, we have stated that the auditor can test most, if not all, of the significant transactions in these areas; finding documentation for authorization is the key control. The following are some of the complex issues in the audit of investments and intangibles:

- Valuation of investments at cost or market or impairment that is other than temporary.
- Determination of significant influence relationship for equity method investments.
- Impairment of goodwill.
- Capitalization and continuing valuation of intangibles and deferred charges.
- Propriety, effectiveness, and risk disclosure of derivative securities used as hedges of exposure to changes in fair value (fair value hedge), variability in cash flows (cash flow hedge), or fluctuations in foreign currency.
- Determination of the fair value of derivatives and securities, including valuation models and the reasonableness of key assumptions.
- Realistic distinctions of research, feasibility, and production milestones for capitalization of software development costs.
- Adequate disclosure of restrictions, pledges, or liens related to investment assets.

Investment costs should be vouched to brokers' confirmations, monthly statements, or other documentary evidence of cost. At the same time, the amounts of investment sales should be traced to gain or loss accounts, and the amounts of sales prices and proceeds should be vouched to the brokers' statements and the cash receipts journal. Auditors should determine what method of cost-out assignment was used (i.e., FIFO, specific identification, or average cost) and whether it is consistent with prior-years' transactions.

Market valuation of securities is required for securities classified in trading portfolios and available-for-sale portfolios. Although management may assert that an investment valuation is not impaired, subsequent sale at a loss before the end of audit fieldwork will indicate otherwise. Auditors should review significant investment transactions subsequent to the balance-sheet date for this kind of evidence about value impairment.

Classification of marketable securities is another management judgment that auditors must evaluate. If management classifies securities as trading securities, net income includes unrealized gains. When the market is doing well, these gains can provide significant additions to the bottom line. When the market is down, management can classify the securities as available for sale, which removes the losses from net income. However, management is required to make transfers between trading and available-for-sale securities at fair value, thus the auditor must verify consistent classification of securities. Similar management judgments can move securities from noncurrent to current, thus affecting current ratios. Auditors must use their professional judgment to ensure that management is basing its classifications on sound business judgments, not their financial statement effect. However, there is often little tangible evidence in support of management responses to these audit inquiries. By consulting quoted market values for securities, auditors can calculate market values and determine whether investments should be written down in value. If quoted market values are not available, financial statements related to investments must be obtained and analyzed for evidence of basic value. If such financial statements are unaudited, they provide extremely weak evidence.

Income amounts can be verified by consulting published or online dividend records for quotations of dividends actually declared and paid during a period (e.g., Moody's and Standard & Poor's dividend records). Because auditors know the holding period of securities, dividend income can be calculated and compared to the amount in the account. Any difference could indicate a cutoff error, misclassification, defalcation, or failure to record a dividend receivable. In a similar manner, application of interest rates to bond or note investments produces a calculated interest income figure (considering amortization of premium or discount if applicable).

Inquiries should deal with the nature of investments and the reasons for holding them, especially derivative securities used for hedging activities. The classification affects the accounting treatment of market values and the unrealized gains and losses on investments. Due to the complexity of ASC 815, "Derivatives and Hedging," auditors may need special skills or knowledge to understand clients' hedging transactions, to ensure that effective controls are in place to monitor them, and to audit the significant transactions.

When equity method accounting is used for investments, auditors need to obtain financial statements of the investee company. These should be audited statements. The inability to obtain financial statements from a closely held investee could indicate that the client investor does not have the significant controlling influence required by *APB Opinion No. 18.* When available, these statements are used as the basis for recalculating the amount of the client's share of income to recognize in the accounts. In addition, these statements can be used to audit the disclosure of investees' assets, liabilities, and income presented in footnotes, a disclosure recommended when investments accounted for by the equity method are material.

Auditing Fair Value Measurements (AS 2502)

GAAP pronouncements increasingly require the use of fair value for measurement of transactions and disclosure amounts. In addition, recent FASB pronouncements have required more stringent determination and more complete disclosures for investments, derivatives, and other assets and liabilities that are measured at fair value on a recurring basis. A fair value hierarchy has been established at three different levels as explained in Exhibit 10.9.

Disclosure is required not only as to the level for assets and liabilities, but also as to specific information if an item is moved between levels. For level 3 assets and liabilities, a reconciliation of the beginning and ending balances is required. These additional disclosure requirements increase the risk for assets and liabilities measured at fair value.

Auditing fair value measurements is similar to auditing accounting estimates. Substantive procedures for auditing accounting estimates include determining whether (1) the valuation principles are acceptable under the financial reporting framework, (2) the valuation principles are consistently applied, (3) the valuation principles are supported by the underlying documentation, and (4) the method of estimation and the significant assumptions are properly disclosed according to GAAP.

EXHIBIT 10.9   Fair Market Value Measurement Hierarchy

The Financial Accounting Standards Board (FASB) and International Accounting Standards Board (IASB) have established a three-level hierarchy in dealing with the problem of fair values that do not result from market prices:

Level 1: Fair values are derived from quoted market prices for identical assets or liabilities from an active market to which an entity has immediate access.

Level 2: Market prices are available for similar (as opposed to identical) assets or liabilities.

Level 3: If values for levels 1 or 2 are not available, fair value is estimated using valuation techniques.

As with other estimates, management has primary responsibility for determining fair value in accordance with GAAP. Observable market-based values are generally preferred (level 1). However, if market prices are not readily available, clients should incorporate assumptions that would have been used by the marketplace (level 2). If information about the assumptions is not readily available, management can use their own assumptions "as long as there are no contrary data . . . " (AS 2502.06) (level 3). Thus, auditors first must determine whether a market-based value is available; if not, they must evaluate whether clients' assumptions would have been used by the marketplace or there are data contrary to what the client used—very murky waters, indeed. The auditor must take considerable care when auditing fair value calculations for level 3. These calculations use a considerable amount of judgment and estimates resulting in an increased risk of improper valuation. Appendix Exhibit 10B.1 provides an example of an audit plan for the fair market value of assets and liabilities.

AUDITING INSIGHT   Impossible to Audit?

In 2008, **Lehman Brothers** was the fourth largest investment bank in the United States. The company, originally founded in 1850, had boomed in the mid-2000s with the acquisition of five large mortgage lenders, several making loans to borrowers with poor credit or no documentation requests. The risky strategy led to record profits, including $4.2 billion net income in 2007. Even though housing defaults were on the rise, Lehman's CFO indicated that the risks posed to Lehman were minimal and would have little impact on the firm's earnings.

However, Lehman's estimates of the valuation of its portfolio of mortgage-backed securities (MBSs) proved to be based on default assumptions that were not nearly conservative enough, and as the housing market crashed, so did Lehman's ability to generate cash flow from loan repayments and, in turn, its stock price, losing more than $46 billion of market value.

When Lehman Brothers filed for bankruptcy on September 15, 2008, it was the largest bankruptcy in history with $619 billion of debt, blowing away the bankruptcies of previous widely covered collapses of Enron and WorldCom.

Ernst & Young, Lehman Brothers' auditor, was quickly hit with civil fraud cases claiming that it stood by watching while Lehman used shady accounting gimmicks to hide its problems. Ernst & Young

vigorously defended the accusations claiming that, "Lehman's audited financial statements clearly portrayed Lehman as a highly leveraged entity operating in a risky and volatile industry." However, institutional investors questioned the audit work performed and asked specifically whether the firm had misrepresented Lehman's financial condition, "artificially inflating the value of its securities." Perhaps because of the high costs of defending lawsuits, Ernst & Young settled two separate lawsuits in 2013 and 2015 for $99 million with investors and $10 million with the state of New York without admitting to any flaws in the audits.

The Lehman Brothers failure demonstrates how fair values of investment securities can be difficult, or maybe impossible, to audit in some situations. It is important to note that the valuations used by Lehman were based on the same assumptions used at many other large investment bankers who failed concurrently with Lehman Brothers. This again demonstrates the importance of maintaining a skeptical attitude in all aspects of the audit.

Sources: G. McCool, *"Ernst & Young Accused of Hiding Lehman Troubles,"* Reuters, *December 21, 2010;* A. Harris, *"Ernst & Young Settles Lehman Investor Lawsuit for $99 Million,"* Accounting Today, *December 2, 2013;* C. Smythe Bloomburg, *"Ernst & Young Will Pay $10 Million to End N.Y. Lehman Suit,"* Accounting Today, *April 15, 2015.*

Derivative Instruments, Hedging Activities, and Investments in Securities (AS 2503)

Derivative instruments are those that take their value from another asset or index. For example, an option to buy Disney stock is a derivative instrument. Interest rate swaps, options, futures contracts, and foreign currency options are also derivatives. Derivatives can be used as **hedging instruments** to protect companies from uncertainties in the marketplace. For example, a clothing manufacturer could buy futures contracts on cotton to lock the price of its main raw material so that it can predict the future cost of goods sold. Likewise, companies selling overseas use currency futures to lock in the exchange rate for their sales. Accounting for derivatives is extremely complex, and new ones are constantly being developed. There are even derivatives to protect against bad weather!

Depending on why a company engages in derivative activities, the company may have only a few derivatives (e.g., foreign currency hedges to protect a few large contracts where foreign currency is the method of payment) or a large number of derivatives (commodity options to protect the company from price swings in essential raw materials). In the latter case, the auditor may need to focus on control activities and adjust the substantive testing based on the control risk assessment. When derivative activity is characterized by few significant transactions, the auditor likely focuses on the transaction authorization and performs substantive tests on most or all of the significant transactions. Auditors must ensure that derivatives are recorded at their fair market value at the balance-sheet date and should review derivative activities after the balance-sheet date in a search for unrecorded derivatives. Because of the risk of misclassifying derivative securities, auditors must also test management's evaluation of the successfulness of the hedges.

AUDITING INSIGHT   Trimming the Hedge?

J.M. Smucker Company, the maker of Smucker's jams and Jif peanut butter, saw a strong first quarter on higher volumes in its key brands and expects the momentum to continue into the second quarter, helped by its hedging activities taken in response to increasing coffee prices. The company said it has protected itself against exposure to coffee price fluctuations for the second quarter very well. Indeed, Smucker, whose coffee brands include Folgers and Dunkin' Donuts,

said the coffee segment, which accounts for about 38 percent of its revenue, surpassed its expectations with a 7 percent increase in sales for the quarter, but the margin took a beating due to higher green coffee costs. Coffee futures have rallied about 40 percent since the beginning of March.

Source: *"JM Smucker Sees Strong Q2 on Coffee Price Hedging," Reuters, August 20, 2010.*

An illustrative audit plan of substantive procedures for investments and related accounts is presented in Appendix Exhibit 10B.2. Part B of this audit plan covers portfolio classification, fair value determination, and evidence about impairment.

☑ REVIEW CHECKPOINTS

10.9   What are some of the important assertions found in investment accounts?

10.10 What are some of the typical areas of concern to auditors involving investment accounts?

10.11 How can confirmations be used in auditing investments in stocks?

10.12 How can auditors gain assurance about fair value estimates in the investment cycle?

Long-Term Liabilities and Related Accounts

Exhibit 10.8 also presents substantive procedures for audits of long-term debt. The primary audit concerns with the verification of long-term liabilities is that all of them are recorded, that the interest expense is properly paid or accrued, and that they are classified and disclosed appropriately. Therefore, the balance-sheet assertions of *completeness* and *presentation and disclosure* are paramount. Alertness to the possibility of unrecorded liabilities during the performance of procedures in other areas frequently uncovers liabilities that have not been recorded. For example, when PP&E are acquired during the year under audit, auditors should inquire about the source of funds to finance the new assets. Auditors also should be alert for large cash disbursements and maintenance expenses for upgrades of electrical, plumbing, and air-conditioning systems. Often, all of these are indicators of the purchase and installation of equipment.

When auditing long-term liabilities, auditors usually obtain independent written confirmations for notes and bonds payable. In the case of notes payable to banks, the standard bank confirmation may be used and should include a request to list any banking relationships not listed on the confirmation request. The amount and terms of bonds payable, mortgages payable, and other formal debt instruments can be verified by reading the bond **indenture**, the written agreement with the bondholders, and confirmed by requests to bondholders or the bond trustee. The confirmation request should include questions not only of amount, interest rate, and due date, but also of collateral, restrictive covenants, and other items of agreement between lender and borrower. Confirmation requests should be sent to lenders with whom the company has done business in the recent past, even if no liability balance is shown at the confirmation date. Such extra coverage is a part of the search for unrecorded liabilities. An illustration of typical audit documentation for auditing long-term debt and interest expense is in Exhibit 10.10. Note that the interest expense consists of additions to the accrual account as well as amortization of premiums or discounts on long-term debt. An illustrative audit plan of substantive procedures for notes payable and long-term debt is in Appendix Exhibit 10B.3.

Confirmation and inquiry procedures may be used to obtain responses on a class of items loosely termed *off-balance-sheet information*. Within this category are terms of loan agreements, leases, endorsements, guarantees, and insurance policies (whether issued by a client insurance company or owned by the client). Among these items is the difficult-to-define set of commitments and contingencies that often pose evidence-gathering problems. See Exhibit 10.11 for some common types of commitments.

EXHIBIT 10.10 Audit Documentation—Long-Term Debt and Interest Expense

DUNDER-MIFFLIN INC.
Long-Term Debt, Accrued Interest Payable, and Interest Expense
For Year Ended 12/31/2017
Prepared by Client

Prepared by	RJR
	3/10/2018
Reviewed by	DHS
	3/12/2018

		Long-Term Debt				Accrued Interest Payable			
	Date Due	Balance 12/31/2016	Additions	Amortization/ Payments	Balance 12/31/2017	Balance 12/31/2016	Interest Expense	Payments	Balance 12/31/2017
5.25% senior subordinated debt	6/30/23	$2,500,000 PY	0	$250,000 v	$2,250,000 CF/ TB	$66,750	$ 131,437 C	$143,750 v	$54,437 CF
4% note payable— Bank One	9/30/16	0	$500,000ᵘ	0	$ 500,000 CF/ TB	$ 5,000	$ 20,000 C	$ 20,000 v	$ 5,000 CF
Premium on long-term debt		$ 354,128 PY	0	$ 18,266 C	$ 335,862 CF/ TB		$ 18,266 C		
						$71,750	$169,703	$163,750	$59,437 CF
						F PY	F/TB	F	F/TB

EXHIBIT 10.11   Off-Balance-Sheet Commitments

Type of Commitment	Typical Audit Procedures
Repurchase or remarketing agreements	Vouching of contracts, confirmation by customer, and inquiry of client management
Commitments to purchase at fixed prices	Vouching of open purchase orders, inquiry of purchasing personnel, and confirmation by supplier
Commitments to sell at fixed prices	Vouching of sales contracts, inquiry of sales personnel, and confirmation by customer
Guaranteed obligations of unconsolidated subsidiaries	Vouching of contracts, confirmation with debtors, and inquiry of client management
Loan commitments (as in a savings and loan association)	Vouching of open commitment file, inquiry of loan officers
Lease commitments	Vouching of lease agreement, confirmation with lessor or lessee

Footnote disclosure should be considered for the types of commitments shown in Exhibit 10.11. Some of them can be estimated and valued and, thus, can be recorded in the accounts and shown in the financial statements themselves (such as losses on fixed-price purchase commitments and losses on fixed-price sales commitments). Interest expense generally is related item by item to interest-bearing liabilities. Based on the evidence of long-term liability transactions (including those that have been retired during the year), the related interest expense amounts can be recalculated. The amount of debt, the interest rate, and the time period are used to determine whether the interest expense and accrued interest are properly recorded. Interest expense also may be estimated by the analytical procedure of multiplying average debt outstanding by the average interest rate.

Stockholders' Equity: Substantive Procedures

Stockholders' equity transactions usually are well documented in the minutes of the meetings of the board of directors, proxy statements, and securities offering registration statements. For publicly traded companies, stock transactions usually require a filing with the SEC (e.g., an offering of stock to raise capital). Transaction authorization can be vouched to these documents, and the cash proceeds can be traced to the bank accounts. Capital stock may be subject to confirmation when independent registrars and transfer agents are employed. Such agents are responsible for knowing the number of shares authorized and issued and for keeping lists of stockholders' names. The basic information about capital stock—such as number of shares, classes of stock, preferred dividend rates, conversion terms, dividend payments, shares held in the company name, expiration dates, and terms of warrants and stock dividends and splits—can be confirmed with the independent agents. The audit team's own inspection and reading of stock certificates, charter authorizations, directors' minutes, and registration statements can corroborate many of these items. However, when the client company does not use independent agents, most audit evidence is gathered by inspecting and vouching stock record documents (such as certificate book stubs). When circumstances call for extended procedures, information on outstanding stock in very small corporations having only a few stockholders may be confirmed directly with the holders.

Auditing Stock-Based Compensation Plans

ASC 718 requires that employee stock-based compensation must be recorded using a fair value–based method at the date the award is granted and must be credited to paid-in-capital and expensed over the compensation period. The definition of fair value accounting in ASC 718 is different from the general definition of fair value in ASC 820 and often requires the application of complex option pricing models. As a result, auditing stock-based compensation can be a risky area. There are many types of employee stock-based compensation, and some, such as employee stock options, require appropriate allocation between common stock and paid-in-capital accounts upon exercise.

When auditing employee share options, auditors must follow the standards for auditing accounting estimates (AS 2501) and auditing fair value estimates (AS 2502) as discussed earlier. However, because employee share options are complex financial instruments, and no market value is available, companies typically use option-pricing models, which have assumptions that can be difficult to evaluate. Some of these assumptions include a stock price volatility rate and a risk-free interest rate that are assumed to be constant. In auditing employee share option plans, auditors focus on valuation of the options as well as presentation and disclosure of the options. The auditor should obtain copies of any employee stock-based compensation plans and vouch to approval by the board of directors. In addition, auditors should test the accounting for the valuation estimates and recalculate compensation expense. The PCAOB has specifically addressed auditing of employee share options and focuses on auditors' understanding of the process used by management for valuing and accounting for share options.[2]

With the exception of stock-based compensation plans, audits of stockholders' equity are considered to be low risk. See Appendix Exhibit 10B.4 for an illustrative audit plan of substantive procedures for stockholders' equity.

☑ REVIEW CHECKPOINTS

10.13 What are some of the important assertions found in stockholders' equity account balances and disclosures?

10.14 What are some of the important assertions found in the long-term liability accounts?

10.15 How can confirmations be used in auditing (a) stockholder capital accounts and (b) notes and bonds payable?

10.16 What information about capital stock could be confirmed with outside parties? How could the auditors corroborate this information?

10.17 Define and give examples of off-balance-sheet information. Why should auditors be concerned with such items?

10.18 If a company does not monitor notes payable for due dates and interest payment dates in relation to financial statement dates, what misstatements can appear in the financial statements?

FRAUD CASES: EXTENDED AUDIT PROCEDURES (AS 2301)

LO 10-7
Apply your knowledge to perform audit procedures in the revenue cycle and evaluate the findings of your tests.

These cases first set the stage with a story about an accounting error or fraud. The problem section of each case gives you the "inside story," which auditors seldom know before they perform this audit work. The second part of the case is the audit approach, which tells a structured story about the audit objective, desirable controls, test of control activities, and audit of balance procedures. The third part wraps up the case with a discovery summary. You will have an opportunity to develop your own audit approach for similar cases in Exercises 10-60 through 10-62 at the end of this chapter.

Case 10.1

Unregistered Sale of Securities

PROBLEM

A.T. Bliss & Company (Bliss) salespeople contacted potential investors and sold limited partnership interests in the company. The setup deal called for these limited partnerships

---

to purchase solar hot-water heating systems for residential and commercial use from Bliss. All partnerships entered into arrangements to lease the equipment to Nationwide Corporation, which then rented the equipment to end users. The limited partnerships were, in effect, financing conduits for obtaining investors' money to pay for Bliss's equipment. The investors depended on Nationwide's business success and ability to pay under the lease terms for their return of capital and profit.

Bliss published false and misleading financial statements, which used a non-GAAP revenue recognition method and failed to disclose cost of goods sold. Bliss overstated Nationwide's record of equipment installation and failed to disclose that Nationwide had little cash flow from end users (resulting from rent-free periods and other inducements). Bliss knew—and failed to disclose to prospective investors—the fact that numerous previous investors had filed petitions with the U.S. tax court to contest the disallowance by the IRS of all their tax credits and benefits claimed in connection with their investments in Bliss's tax-sheltered equipment lease partnerships.

All of the money put up by the limited partnership investors was at risk but was not disclosed to investors.

AUDIT APPROACH

Management should employ experts—attorneys, underwriters, and accountants—who can determine whether securities and investment contract sales require registration. Auditors should learn the business backgrounds and securities industry expertise of the client's senior managers. They should study the minutes of board of directors meetings for authorization of the fund-raising method, obtain and study opinions rendered by attorneys and underwriters about the legality of the fund-raising methods, and inquire about management's interaction with the SEC in any presale clearance. (The SEC gives advice about the necessity for registration.)

Auditors should study the offering documents and literature used in the sale of securities to determine whether financial information is being used properly. In this case, the close relationship with Nationwide and the experience of earlier partnerships give reasons for extended procedures to obtain evidence about the representations concerning Nationwide's business success (in this case, lack of success).

DISCOVERY SUMMARY

The auditors gave unmodified reports on Bliss's materially misstated financial statements. The auditors apparently did not question the legality of the sales of the limited partnership interests as a means of raising capital. They apparently did not perform procedures to verify representations made in offering literature reflecting Bliss or Nationwide finances. Two partners in the audit firm were enjoined because of violations of the securities laws. The partners resigned from practice before the SEC and were ordered not to perform any attest services for companies making filings with the SEC. According to SEC Litigation Release 10274, AAER 20, and AAER 21, they later were expelled from the AICPA as reported in *The CPA Letter,* for failure to cooperate with the Professional Ethics Division in its investigation of alleged professional ethics violations.

Case 10.2

Off-Balance-Sheet Inventory Financing

PROBLEM

Verity Distillery Company's president incorporated the Veritas Corporation, making him and two other Verity officers the sole stockholders. The president arranged to sell $40 million of Verity's inventory of whiskey in the aging process to Veritas, showing no gain or loss on the transaction. The officers negotiated a 36-month loan with a major bank to get the money Veritas used for the purchase, pledging the inventory as collateral. Verity pledged to repurchase the inventory for $54.4 million, which amounted to the original $40 million plus 12 percent interest for three years.

The contract of sale was in the files, specifying the name of the purchasing company, the $40 million amount, and the cash consideration. Nothing mentioned the relationship of Veritas to the officers. Nothing mentioned the repurchase obligation. However, the sale amount was unusually large for a company the size of Verity.

The $40 million amount was 40 percent of the normal inventory. Veritas's cash balance increased 50 percent. The current asset total was not changed, but the inventory ratios (e.g., inventory turnover, days' sales in inventory) and quick ratio were materially altered. Long-term liabilities were understated by not recording the liability. The ploy was actually a secured loan with inventory pledged as collateral, but this reality was neither recorded nor disclosed. The total effect would be to keep debt off the books, to avoid recording interest expense, and later to record inventory at a higher cost. Subsequent sale of the whiskey at market prices would not affect the ultimate income results, but the unrecorded interest expense would be buried in the cost of goods sold. The net income in the first year when the "sale" was made was not changed, but the normal relationship of gross margin to sales was distorted by the zero-profit transaction.

	Before Transaction	Recorded Transaction	Pro Forma
Assets	$530 million	$530 million	$570 million
Liabilities	390	390	430
Stockholder equity	140	140	140
Debt/equity ratio	2.79	2.79	3.07

AUDIT APPROACH

The relevant control in this case would rest with the integrity and accounting knowledge of the senior officials who arranged the transaction. Remember, competent individuals in key positions is an element of the control environment at the entity level. Authorization in the board minutes might detail the arrangements, but, if the officials wanted to hide it from the auditors, they also would suppress the telltale information in the board minutes.

Inquiries should be made about large and unusual financing transactions. This might not elicit a response because the event is a sales transaction according to Veritas. Other audit work on controls in the revenue and collection cycle might reveal the large sale. Fortunately, this one sticks out as a large one.

Analytical procedures to compare monthly or seasonal sales probably will identify the sale as large and unusual. This identification should lead to an examination of the sales contract. Auditors should discuss the business purpose of the transaction with knowledgeable officials. If being this close to discovery does not result in an admission of the loan and repurchase arrangement, the auditors nevertheless should investigate further. Even if the "customer" names were not a give-away, a quick inquiry of the corporation records office at the secretary of state will show the names of the officers, and the auditors will know the related-party nature of the deal. A request for the financial statements of Veritas should, therefore, be made.

DISCOVERY SUMMARY

The auditors found the related-party relationship between the officers and Veritas. Confronted, the president admitted the attempt to make the cash position and the debt/equity ratio look better than they were. The financial statements were adjusted to reflect the pro forma set of figures shown earlier.

Case 10.3

Go for the Gold

PROBLEM

In 2009, Alta Gold Company was a public shell corporation that was purchased for $1,000 by the Blues brothers. Operating under the corporate names of Silver King and Pacific Gold, the brothers purchased numerous mining claims in auctions conducted by the U.S. Department of the Interior. They invested a total of $40,000 in 300 claims. Silver King sold limited partnership interests in its 175 Nevada silver claims to local investors, raising $20 million to begin mining production. Pacific Gold then traded its 125 Montana gold mining claims for all of the Silver King assets and partnership interests, valuing the silver claims at $20 million. (Silver King valued the gold claims received at $20 million as the fair value in the exchange.) The brothers then put $3 million obtained from dividends into Alta Gold and, with the aid of a bank loan, purchased half of the Silver King gold claims for $18 million. The Blues brothers then obtained another bank loan of $38 million to merge the remainder of Silver King's assets and all of Pacific Gold's mining claims by purchase. They paid off the limited partners. At the end of 2009, Alta Gold had cash of $16 million, mining assets valued at $58 million, and liabilities on bank loans of $53 million.

Alta Gold had in its files the partnership-offering documents, receipts, and other papers showing partners' investment of $20 million in the Silver King limited partnerships. The company also had Pacific Gold and Silver King contracts for the exchange of mining claims. The $20 million value of the exchange was justified in light of the limited partners' investments.

Appraisals in the files showed one appraiser's report that there was no basis for valuing the exchange of Silver King claims other than the price limited partner investors had been willing to pay. The second appraiser reported a probable value of $20 million for the exchange based on proved production elsewhere, but no geological data on the actual claims had been obtained. The $18 million paid by Alta to Silver King also had similar appraisal reports.

The transactions occurred over a period of 10 months. The Blues brothers had $37 million of cash in Silver King and Pacific Gold as well as the $16 million in Alta (all of which was the gullible bank's money, which the bank had loaned to Alta with the mining claims and production as security). The mining claims that had cost $40,000 were now in Alta's balance sheet at $58 million, the $37 million was about to flee, and the bank was about to be left holding the bag containing 300 mining claim papers.

AUDIT APPROACH

Alta Gold, Pacific Gold, and Silver King had no internal controls. The Blues brothers engineered all transactions and hired friendly appraisers. The only control that might have been effective was at the bank in a more diligent loan process.

The most likely control would have been the engagement of competent, independent appraisers. Because the auditors need to use (or try to use) the appraisers' reports, the procedures involve investigating the reputation, engagement terms, experience, and independence of the appraisers. The auditors can use local business references, local financial institutions that keep lists of approved appraisers, membership directories of the professional appraisal associations, and interviews with the appraisers themselves (AU-C 620).

The procedures for auditing the asset values include analyses of each of the transactions through all of the complications, including obtaining knowledge of the owners and managers of the several companies and the identities of the limited partner investors. If the Blues brothers did not disclose their connection with the other companies (and perhaps with the limited partners), the auditors need to inquire at the secretary of state's offices where Pacific Gold and Silver King are incorporated and try to discover the identities of the players in this flip game. Numerous complicated premerger transactions in small corporations and shells often signal manipulated valuations.

Loan applications and supporting papers should be examined to determine the representations Alta made in connection with obtaining the bank loans. These papers may reveal some contradictory or exaggerated information.

Ownership of the mining claims might be confirmed with the Department of Interior auctioneers or be found in the local county deed records (spread all over Nevada and Montana).

DISCOVERY SUMMARY

The inexperienced audit staff was unable to unravel the Byzantine exchanges and never questioned the relation of Alta Gold to Silver King and Pacific Gold. They never discovered the Blues brothers' involvement in the other side of the exchange, purchase, and merger transactions. They accepted the appraisers' reports because they had never worked with appraisers before and thought all appraisers were competent and independent. The bank lost $37 million. The Blues brothers changed their names.

Case 10.4

No Treasure in This Treasure Planet[3]

PROBLEM

In 2002, **Disney** had to take a last-minute write-down of motion picture production costs for the movie *Treasure Planet*. The set-in-space version of Robert Louis Stevenson's *Treasure Island* cost $140 million to make, but opening five-day revenues were only $16.7 million, compared to relatively successful *Lilo & Stitch*, which grossed $35.3 million in its first weekend.

Revenue forecasts are based on many factors, including facts and assumptions about number of theaters, ticket prices, receipt-sharing agreements, domestic and foreign reviews, and moviegoer tastes. Several publications track the box-office records of movies. You can find them in newspaper entertainment sections and in industry trade publications. Of course, the production companies themselves are the major source of the information. However, company records also show the revenue realized from each movie. Revenue forecasts can be checked against actual experience, and the company's history of forecasting accuracy can be determined by comparing actual to forecast over many films and many years.

The write-down in 2002 was $74 million.

AUDIT APPROACH

Revenue forecasts should be prepared in a controlled process that documents the facts and underlying assumptions built into the forecast. Forecasts should break down the revenue estimate by years, and the accounting system should produce comparable actual revenue data so that forecast accuracy can be assessed after the fact. Forecast revisions should be prepared in as much detail and documentation as original forecasts.

The general procedures and methods used by personnel responsible for revenue forecasts should be studied (inquiries and review of documentation), including their sources of information, both internal and external. Procedures for review of mechanical aspects (arithmetic) should be tested. Select a sample of finished forecasts and recalculate the final estimate.

Specific procedures for forecast revision also should be studied in the same manner. A review of the accuracy of forecasts for other movies with hindsight on actual revenues helps in a circumstantial way, but past accuracy on different film experiences does not directly influence the forecasts on a new, unique product.

The audit of motion picture development costs concentrates on the content of the forecast itself. The preparation of forecasts used in the impairment calculation should be studied to distinguish underlying reasonable expectations from hypothetical assumptions. A hypothetical assumption is a statement of a condition that is not necessarily expected to occur but nonetheless is used to prepare an estimate. For example, a hypothetical assumption is like an "if-then" statement: "If *Treasure Planet* sells 15 million tickets in the first 12 months of release, then domestic revenue and product sales will be $40 million, and foreign revenue can eventually reach $10 million." Auditors need to assess the reasonableness of the basic 15-million-ticket assumption. It helps to have some early actual data from the film's release in hand before the financial statements need to be finished and distributed. For actual data, auditors should review industry publications and pay special attention to competing films and critics' reviews (yes, movie reviews!).

DISCOVERY SUMMARY

The company was too optimistic in its revenue forecasts, and management did not weigh unfavorable actual/forecast history comparisons heavily enough. Apparently, management let itself be convinced that the movie was comparable to recent animated hits from other studios such as *Shrek* and *A Bug's Life*. One of the possible problems was the long development time—17 years from conception. The audit of forecasts and estimates used in accounting determinations is very difficult, especially when company personnel have incentives to hype the numbers, seemingly with conviction about the artistic and commercial merit of their productions. The high production costs finally came home to roost in big write-offs when the film was released.

[3]F. Ahrens, "Is Disney Losing Its Boy Appeal?" *The Washington Post*, December 19, 2002.

☑ REVIEW CHECKPOINTS

10.19 What unfortunate lesson did the auditors learn from the situation in the Unregistered Sale of Securities case? What should auditors do when a violation of U.S. securities laws is suspected?

10.20 How could auditors have discovered the off-balance-sheet financing described in the Off-Balance-Sheet Inventory Financing case?

10.21 What effect can related-party transactions have in some cases of asset valuation? (Refer to the Go for the Gold case.)

10.22 How should an audit team assess the reasonableness of a film studio's estimate of film revenues? (Refer to the No Treasure in This Treasure Planet case.)

Summary

The finance and investment cycle contains a wide variety of accounts: Capital Stock, Dividends, Long-Term Debt, Interest Expense, Income Tax Expense and Deferred Taxes, financial instruments, marketable securities, equity method investments, related gains and losses, consolidated subsidiaries, goodwill, and other intangibles. These accounts involve some of the most technically complex accounting standards. They create many of the difficult judgments for financial reporting.

Senior officials generally authorize these transactions and maintain control of them in these accounts. Therefore, internal control is centered on the integrity and accounting knowledge of these officials. The procedural controls over details of transactions are not very effective because senior managers can override them and order their own desired accounting presentations. As a consequence, auditors' work on the assessment of control risk is directed toward the senior managers and the board of directors, focusing on authorization and design of finance and investment activities. Because of the threat of management override and the high dollar value of many of these transactions, auditors ensure the occurrence and valuation of transactions as well as the existence and valuation of year-end balances. Many accounts consist of relatively few high-dollar transactions; therefore, the auditor often relies on substantive testing of most, if not all, of the transactions that occurred during the audit period. See the following Auditing Insight for some deficiencies the PCAOB noted in its inspections of the registered public accounting firms regarding audits of this cycle.

 AUDITING INSIGHT | **PCAOB Inspections and the Finance and Investment Cycle**

- The Firm's substantive procedures to test the valuation of the business that the issuer deconsolidated and the goodwill for the reporting unit noted above were insufficient. Specifically, the issuer used certain significant assumptions, consisting of projections related to revenue, capital expenditures, and profit margins, in its analyses. The Firm's procedures to test these assumptions consisted of inquiry of management and a comparison of the assumptions to historical rates or industry data. These procedures were not sufficient to evaluate the reasonableness of these assumptions, as the Firm failed to consider the differences between certain of these assumptions and the issuer's historical rates or the industry data used for comparison. In addition, the Firm failed to evaluate whether the industry data that it used to evaluate the reasonableness of certain of these assumptions related to companies that were comparable to the issuer.

- The issuer owned interests in several entities that it accounted for using the equity method. For the majority of these investments, the issuer asserted that the related real estate investments were under development; therefore, the issuer reported no equity income or loss. The Firm's testing of the issuer's equity-method investments was insufficient, as follows

  1. The Firm limited its substantive procedures and its tests of controls to those investments for which the issuer recognized equity income or loss during the year, which represented less than 40 percent of the issuer's total equity-method investments.

  2. The Firm selected for testing two controls over the issuer's accounting for investments but failed to sufficiently test these controls with respect to the equity-method investments

for which the issuer recognized equity income or loss. Specifically, the Firm selected its samples to test the operating effectiveness of these controls without taking into account its assessment of the risk associated with these controls and the number of investments for which the controls operated, and the samples that the Firm selected were too small to provide sufficient appropriate evidence.

- The issuer performed its annual analysis of the possible impairment of goodwill as of an interim date and recorded a goodwill impairment loss for one of its reporting units. The Firm's procedures related to the issuer's analysis for that reporting unit were insufficient. Specifically:

1. The Firm selected for testing certain controls that consisted of management's review of certain assumptions used in the analysis but limited its procedures to test those controls to inquiring of management and comparing information used in the analysis to supporting documentation. The Firm's testing did not include (1) ascertaining the nature of the review procedures that the control owners performed to assess the reasonableness of these assumptions or (2) evaluating the criteria used by the control owners to identify matters for follow-up and whether those matters were appropriately addressed. As a result, the Firm failed to evaluate whether the controls operated at a level of precision that would prevent or detect material misstatements. In addition, the Firm failed to evaluate whether the controls that it selected for testing were also designed to address the reasonableness of other significant assumptions used in the analysis.
2. The Firm failed to sufficiently evaluate the reasonableness of certain significant assumptions underlying the cash-flow projections that the issuer used to determine the fair value of the reporting unit and the amount of the goodwill impairment loss. Specifically:

   - The Firm limited its procedures for one assumption to verifying that the assumption was consistent with the information in a presentation that management had given to the issuer's board of directors in the prior year.
   - The issuer's assumptions related to certain costs and selling prices were based on market information. For the costs, the Firm failed to evaluate whether the forecasted market information was relevant to the issuer. For certain selling prices, the issuer used market information as of four months before the date of the goodwill impairment analysis, but the Firm failed to evaluate the reasonableness of the use of this information in light of significant price declines throughout the year.
   - The Firm failed to perform any procedures to evaluate the reasonableness of another of the issuer's significant assumptions.
   - The Firm failed to consider the implications of a significant shortfall in the issuer's actual results for the first nine months of the year compared to its forecast on the reliability of the issuer's projections.

- The Firm identified a fraud risk related to the issuer's identification and disclosure of existing or potential debt covenant violations. The Firm selected for testing a control over the issuer's liquidity

model, which the issuer used to assess the likelihood of a debt covenant violation. This control included management's review of the liquidity model, and the Firm concluded that this control addressed the accuracy and completeness of the data used in the model. The Firm's procedures to test this control were not sufficient. Specifically, the Firm failed to test the specific steps that the control owners performed to address the accuracy and completeness of the data used in the liquidity model or, in the alternative, test any other controls over the accuracy and completeness of such data.

- The Firm failed to perform sufficient procedures related to the valuation of investment securities. Specifically:

1. The issuer recorded the fair values of investment securities based on the prices received from an external pricing service and then compared the recorded fair values to prices received from another external pricing service. The Firm selected for testing a control that consisted of the preparation and review of the comparison. The Firm's procedures to test this control were limited to inquiring of management, reading a memorandum prepared as part of the control, and inspecting signatures as evidence that a review had occurred. The Firm's testing did not include ascertaining and evaluating the criteria used by the control owner to identify matters for investigation and whether such matters were appropriately investigated and resolved. As a result, the Firm failed to evaluate whether this control operated at a level of precision that would prevent or detect material misstatements. In addition, the Firm failed to identify and test any controls over the accuracy and completeness of a report used in the performance of this control.
2. As described in the first paragraph regarding this audit, the Firm used a sample to test the investment securities that was designed using an inappropriate level of materiality. In addition, the Firm determined the sample based on a level of control reliance that was not supported due to the deficiencies in the Firm's testing of controls that are discussed above. For both of these reasons, the sample that the Firm used to test investment securities was too small to provide sufficient evidence.

- Regarding the issuer's off-balance-sheet structures, the Firm failed to perform adequate tests of controls over, or perform other procedures (beyond inquiry of management), to test the issuer's process for identifying events affecting continued off-balance-sheet accounting treatment and the completeness of the issuer's inventory of off-balance-sheet structures. Specifically, the controls tested were entity-level controls that were not precise enough to identify all such events or structures. In addition, the Firm failed to test the issuer's ongoing compliance with certain of the qualifications for the off-balance-sheet accounting used for Qualifying Special Purpose Entities, including servicing activities, clean-up calls, limits on asset sales, amendments, and events of default.

Sources: 2014 PCAOB Inspection of Ernst & Young LLP; 2014 PCAOB Inspection of PricewaterhouseCoopers LLP; 2014 PCAOB Inspection of Deloitte & Touche LLP; 2014 PCAOB Inspection of BDO USA, LLP; 2009 PCAOB Inspection of KPMG.

Key Terms

accounting estimate: An approximation of a financial statement element, item, or account.

capital budget: A listing of the proposed expenditures for property, plant, and equipment or other capital items for a period of time (usually annually). The capital budget is submitted to senior management with corporate governance responsibilities for approval; is often a part of the annual budget.

compensating control: A control activity instituted by a company to offset the risk imposed by a weakness in another activity.

derivative instrument: A financial instrument whose value is based on an index or value of another financial instrument.

dual control: Having two people perform a task (e.g., open the mail) as a control over the process.

hedging instrument: An investment made to reduce the risk of adverse price movements in a security or future transaction by taking an offsetting position in a related security such as an option or a short sale.

indenture: A written agreement between the issuers of bonds and the bondholders, usually specifying interest rate, maturity date, convertibility, and other terms.

joint custody: The safeguarding of assets by placing them in a secured area that requires two people to access (e.g., a cabinet with two locks to which no individual has both keys).

loan covenant: A provision in a loan agreement that requires the borrower to undertake or refrain from specified actions and to maintain specified financial levels and ratios.

registrar: A financial institution appointed to record issue and ownership of company securities.

related party: A relationship between two businesses that have a personal or other association that might destroy the self-interest of one of the parties to an extent that one of them might be prevented from fully pursuing its own separate interests.

special purpose entity (SPE): A partnership formed by a company to pursue particular lines of business, often used to keep risky enterprises off the company's books. QSPE (qualified special purpose entity) is the newer term used by the FASB.

stock certificate book: A book (similar to a checkbook) with prenumbered stock certificates. These certificates are issued to investors with the custodian of the book recording the number of shares, the owner's name, the date of issue, and other identification information; basically used only by small companies that are not traded publicly.

transfer agent: A bank or other company employed by a corporation to maintain shareholder records, including purchases, sales, and account balances.

trustee: Agent of a bond issuer who handles the administrative aspects of a loan and ensures that the borrower complies with the terms of the bond indenture.

Multiple-Choice Questions for Practice and Review

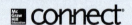 All applicable Exercises and Problems are available with *Connect*.

LO 10-1

10.23 Which of the following approaches is most suitable for auditing the finance and investment cycle?

    a. Perform extensive tests of controls and limit substantive procedures to analytical procedures.

    b. Ignore internal controls and perform extensive substantive procedures.

    c. Gain an understanding of internal controls and perform extensive substantive procedures.

    d. Ignore internal controls and limit substantive procedures to analytical procedures.

LO 10-1

10.24 Loan covenants are used for which of the following reasons?

    a. To protect the lender from the borrower's substantially weakening of the latter's financial position.

    b. To protect the borrower from the lender's calling the loan early.

    c. To protect the auditors from false information by the borrower.

    d. To protect shareholders from management taking on too much debt.

LO 10-1

10.25 A related party is a person or entity that
   a. Has a family tie to a management member.
   b. Does business with the company.
   c. Can exert significant influence over or be influenced by the company.
   d. Is a member of the company's management team or board of directors.

LO 10-6

10.26 Jones was engaged to examine the financial statements of Gamma Corporation for the year ended June 30. Having completed an examination of the investment securities, which of the following is the *best* method of verifying the accuracy of recorded dividend income?
   a. Tracing recorded dividend income to cash receipts records and validated deposit slips.
   b. Performing analytical procedures and statistical sampling.
   c. Comparing recorded dividends with amounts appearing on federal information Form 1099.
   d. Comparing recorded dividends with a standard financial reporting service's record of dividends.

LO 10-4

10.27 When the client holds a large amount of negotiable securities, auditors need to plan to guard against
   a. Unauthorized negotiation of the securities before they are counted.
   b. Unrecorded sales of securities after they are counted.
   c. Substitution of securities already counted for other securities that should be on hand but are not.
   d. Substitution of authentic securities with counterfeit securities.

LO 10-6

10.28 In connection with the audit of an issue of long-term bonds payable, the audit team should
   a. Determine whether bondholders are persons other than owners, directors, or officers of the company issuing the bond.
   b. Calculate the effective interest rate to see whether it is substantially the same as the rates charged for similar issues.
   c. Decide whether the bond issue was made without violating state or local laws or regulations.
   d. Ascertain that the client has obtained the opinion of counsel on the legality of the issue.

LO 10-6

10.29 Which of the following is the most important audit consideration when examining the stockholders' equity section of a client's balance sheet?
   a. Changes in the capital stock account are verified by an independent stock transfer agent.
   b. Stock dividends and stock splits during the year under audit were approved by the stockholders.
   c. Stock dividends are capitalized at par or stated value on the dividend declaration date.
   d. Entries in the capital stock account can be traced to resolutions in the minutes of meetings of the board of directors.

LO 10-6

10.30 If the auditors discover that the carrying amount of a client's investments is overstated because of a loss in value that is other than a temporary decline in market value, they should insist that
   a. The approximate market value of the investments be shown in parentheses on the face of the balance sheet.
   b. The investments be classified as long term for balance-sheet purposes with full disclosure in the footnotes.
   c. The loss in value be recognized in the financial statements.
   d. The equity section of the balance sheet separately show a charge equal to the amount of the loss.

LO 10-6

10.31 The primary reason for preparing a reconciliation between interest-bearing obligations outstanding during the year and interest expense in the financial statements is to
   a. Evaluate internal control over securities.
   b. Determine the validity of prepaid interest expense.
   c. Ascertain the reasonableness of imputed interest.
   d. Detect unrecorded liabilities.

LO 10-6

10.32 The auditors should insist that a representative of the client be present during the inspection and count of securities to
  a. Lend authority to the auditors' directives.
  b. Detect forged securities.
  c. Coordinate the return of all securities to proper locations.
  d. Acknowledge the receipt of securities returned.

LO 10-4

10.33 When independent stock transfer agents are not employed and the corporation issues its own stock and maintains stock records, canceled stock certificates should
  a. Be defaced to prevent reissuance and attached to their corresponding stubs.
  b. Not be defaced but be segregated from other stock certificates and retained in a canceled certificates file.
  c. Be destroyed to prevent fraudulent reissuance.
  d. Be defaced and sent to the secretary of state.

LO 10-6

10.34 When a client company does not maintain its own capital stock records, the auditors should obtain written confirmation from the transfer agent and registrar concerning
  a. Restrictions on the payment of dividends.
  b. The number of shares issued and outstanding.
  c. Guarantees of preferred stock liquidation value.
  d. The number of shares subject to agreements to repurchase.

(AICPA adapted)

LO 10-6

10.35 All corporate capital stock transactions should ultimately be traced to the
  a. Minutes of the meetings of the board of directors.
  b. Cash receipts journal.
  c. Cash disbursements journal.
  d. Numbered stock certificates.

LO 10-6

10.36 An audit plan for the examination of the retained earnings account should include a step that requires verification of the (choose *two* steps)
  a. Market value used to charge retained earnings to account for a 2-for-1 stock split.
  b. Approval of the adjustment to the beginning balance as a result of a write-down of account receivables.
  c. Authorization for both cash and stock dividends declared and paid.
  d. Gain or loss resulting from disposition of treasury shares.

LO 10-4

10.37 When an entity uses a trust company as custodian of its marketable securities, the possibility of concealing fraud *most likely* would be reduced if the
  a. Trust company has no direct contact with the entity employees responsible for maintaining investment accounting records.
  b. Securities are registered in the name of the trust company rather than the entity itself.
  c. Interest and dividend checks are mailed directly to an entity employee who is authorized to sell securities.
  d. The trust company places the securities in a bank safe deposit vault under the custodian's exclusive control.

(AICPA adapted)

LO 10-6

10.38 An audit team would *most likely* verify the interest earned on bond investments by
  a. Vouching the receipt and deposit of interest checks.
  b. Confirming the bond interest rate with the issuer of the bonds.
  c. Recomputing the interest earned on the basis of face amount, interest rate, and period held.
  d. Testing internal controls relevant to cash receipts.

(AICPA adapted)

LO 10-6

10.39 A client has a large and active investment portfolio that is kept in a bank safe deposit box. If the auditors are unable to count securities at the balance sheet date, they *most likely* will
  a. Request the bank to confirm to the auditors the contents of the safe deposit box at the balance-sheet date.
  b. Examine supporting evidence for transactions occurring during the year.

c. Count the securities at a subsequent date and confirm with the bank whether securities were added or removed since the balance-sheet date.

d. Request the client to have the bank seal the safe deposit box until the auditors can count the securities at a subsequent date.

(AICPA adapted)

LO 10-6

10.40 An audit team testing long-term investments would ordinarily use analytical procedures to ascertain the reasonableness of the

a. Existence of unrealized gains or losses.

b. Completeness of recorded investment income.

c. Classification as available-for-sale or trading securities.

d. Valuation of trading securities.

(AICPA adapted)

LO 10-6

10.41 In auditing for unrecorded long-term bonds payable, an audit team *most likely* will

a. Perform analytical procedures on the bond premium and discount accounts.

b. Examine documentation of assets purchased with bond proceeds for liens.

c. Compare interest expense with the bond payable amount for reasonableness.

d. Confirm the existence of individual bondholders at year-end.

(AICPA adapted)

LO 10-6

10.42 An audit plan to examine long-term debt *most likely* would include steps that require

a. Comparing the carrying amount of held-to-maturity securities with their year-end market values.

b. Correlating interest expense recorded for the period with outstanding debt.

c. Verifying the existence of the holders of the debt by direct confirmation.

d. Inspecting the accounts payable subsidiary ledger for unrecorded long-term debt.

(AICPA adapted)

LO 10-4

10.43 Which of the following questions would auditors *most likely* include on an internal control questionnaire for notes payable?

a. Are assets that collateralize notes payable critically needed for the entity's continued existence?

b. Are two or more authorized signatures required on checks that repay notes payable?

c. Are the proceeds from notes payable used to purchase noncurrent assets?

d. Are direct borrowings on notes payable authorized by the board of directors?

(AICPA adapted)

LO 10-6

10.44 An audit team's purpose in reviewing the documentation concerning the renewal of a note payable shortly after the balance-sheet date *most likely* is to obtain evidence concerning management's assertions about

a. Existence.

b. Valuation.

c. Completeness.

d. Classification.

(AICPA adapted)

LO 10-6

10.45 Which of the following audit procedures would *not* likely be performed for audits of investments?

a. Read board of directors' minutes for authorization of investment strategies.

b. Confirm investments with registrar.

c. Confirm investments with broker or trustee.

d. Compare valuation to published market prices.

LO 10-6

10.46 Which of the following audit procedures would *not* likely be performed for audits of shareholders' equity?

a. Read board of directors' minutes for authorization of equity transactions.

b. Confirm outstanding common and preferred stock with stock registrar.

c. Compare valuation of stock to published market prices.

d. Obtain management representation about number of shares issued and outstanding.

LO 10-6

10.47 ABC Company has 100 shares of IBM stock that it holds as an investment. The stock was purchased three years ago and has been in the client's safe deposit box along with other investment securities. During an inspection of securities held by the client, the auditor noted the 100 shares of IBM stock had a different CUSIP number than the number listed when purchased and the number verified during the previous audit. Which of the following would be the auditor's main concern about this discovery?

a. The certificates in the safe deposit box were forgeries.

b. There had been unauthorized buying and selling of investment securities.

c. The securities may be misclassified on the balance sheet.

d. ABC Company no longer owns the securities.

Exercises and Problems

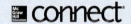 All applicable questions are available with *Connect.*

LO 10-4

10.48 **Internal Control Questionnaire for Equity Investments.** Cassandra Corporation, a manufacturing company, periodically invests large sums in marketable equity securities. The investment committee of the board of directors established the investment policy. The treasurer is responsible for carrying out the investment committee's directives. All securities are stored in a bank safe deposit vault. Your internal control questionnaire with respect to Cassandra's investments in equity securities contains the following three questions:

1. Is investment policy established by the investment committee of the board of directors?

2. Is the treasurer solely responsible for carrying out the investment committee's directive?

3. Are all securities stored in a bank safe deposit vault?

Required:

In addition to these three questions, what questions should your internal control questionnaire include with respect to the company's investment in marketable equity securities? (*Hint:* Prepare questions to cover management's transaction assertions of *occurrence, completeness, cutoff, accuracy, classification.*)

(AICPA adapted)

LO 10-6, 10-7

10.49 **Investment Securities.** You are engaged in the audit of the financial statements of Bass Corporation for the year ended December 31 and you are about to begin an audit of the investment securities. Bass's records indicate that the company owns various bearer bonds as well as 25 percent of the outstanding common stock of Commercial Industrial Inc. All securities in Bass's portfolio are actively traded in a broad market. You are satisfied with evidence that supports the presumption of significant influence over Commercial Industrial Inc. The various securities are at two locations as follows:

1. Recently acquired securities are in the company's safe in the custody of the treasurer.

2. All other securities are in the company's bank safe deposit box.

Required:

a. Assuming that the internal controls over securities are satisfactory, what are the objectives (specific assertions) for the audit of the held-to-maturity securities?

b. What audit procedures should you undertake with respect to obtaining audit evidence for the existence and cost valuation of Bass's securities in the held-to-maturity classification?

c. What audit procedures should you undertake with respect to obtaining audit evidence against Bass's investment in Commercial Industrial Inc.?

d. What audit procedures should you undertake with respect to obtaining audit evidence about the classification of held-to-maturity securities in the Bass portfolio? (*Hint:* Review the audit plan in Appendix Exhibit 10B.1.)

e. Suppose that the held-to-maturity portfolio (excluding the investment in Commercial Industrial Inc.) is carried at cost in the amount of $3,450,000. What audit procedures should you undertake with respect to obtaining audit evidence about the fair market value of this portfolio?

f. Suppose that the auditors determine that the held-to-maturity portfolio (excluding the investment in Commercial Industrial Inc.) has an aggregate fair market value of $2,970,000. What audit procedures should they undertake with respect to obtaining audit evidence regarding a value impairment that might be "other than temporary"? (*Hint:* Review the audit plan in Appendix Exhibit 10B.1.)

(AICPA adapted)

LO 10-6, LO 10-7

10.50 **Lease Accounting. Union Pacific Corp.** opened its new 19-story, $260 million headquarters in Omaha, Nebraska. The railroad operator is the owner of the city's largest building, the Union Pacific Center. Under an initial operating lease, Union Pacific guaranteed 89.9 percent of all construction costs through the building's completion date. After completing the building, the company signed a new operating lease, which guarantees 85 percent of the building's costs. Both were "synthetic" leases, which allow the company to take income tax deductions for interest and depreciation while maintaining complete operational control (Jonathan Weil, "Open Secrets: How Leases Play a Shadowy Role in Accounting," *The Wall Street Journal,* September 22, 2004).

Required:

a. Explain why Union Pacific would want to structure the lease to be an operating lease.

b. What audit evidence would you require for testing the appropriate accounting for this lease?

LO 10-6, 10-7

10.51 **Securities Examination and Count.** You are in charge of the audit of the financial statements of Demot Corporation for the year ended December 31. The corporation has a policy of investing its surplus funds in marketable securities. Its stock and bond certificates are kept in a safe deposit box in a local bank. Only the president and the treasurer of the corporation have access to the box.

You were unable to obtain access to the safe deposit box on December 31 because neither the president nor the treasurer was available. Arrangements were made for your assistant to accompany the treasurer to the bank on January 11 to examine the securities. Your assistant should be able to inspect all securities on hand in an hour. Your assistant has never examined securities in the safe deposit box and requires instructions.

Required:

a. List the instructions that you should give to your assistant regarding the examination of the stock and bond certificates kept in the safe deposit box. Include in your instructions the details of the securities to be examined and the reasons for examining these details.

b. After returning from the bank, your assistant reports that the treasurer had entered the box on January 4 to remove an old photograph of the corporation's original building. The photograph was loaned to the local chamber of commerce for display purposes. List the additional audit procedures that are required because of the treasurer's action.

(AICPA adapted)

LO 10-6, LO 10-7

10.52 **Audit Objectives and Procedures for Investments.** In the audit of investment securities, auditors develop specific audit assertions related to the investments. They then design specific substantive procedures to obtain evidence about each of these assertions. Following is a selection of investment securities assertions:

1. Investments are properly described and classified in the financial statements.

2. Recorded investments represent investments actually owned at the balance-sheet date.

3. Investments are properly valued at the balance-sheet date.

Required:

For each of these assertions, select the following audit procedure that is best suited for the audit plan. Select only one procedure for each assertion. A procedure may be selected once or not at all.

a. Trace opening balances in the general ledger to prior-year audit documentation.

b. Determine whether employees who are authorized to sell investments have access to cash.

c. Examine supporting documents for a sample of investment transactions to verify that prenumbered documents are used.

d. Determine whether any other-than-temporary impairments in the carrying value of investments have been properly recorded.

e. Verify that transfers from the trading portfolio to the held-to-maturity investment portfolio have been properly recorded.

f. Obtain positive confirmations as of the balance sheet date of investments held by independent custodians.

g. Trace investment transactions to minutes of the board of directors meetings to determine that transactions were properly authorized.

(AICPA adapted)

LO 10-6, 10-7

10.53 **Intangibles.** Sorenson Manufacturing Corporation was incorporated on January 3, 2016. The corporation's financial statements for its first year's operations were not examined by a CPA. You have been engaged to audit the financial statements for the year ended December 31, 2017, and your work is substantially completed. A partial trial balance of the company's accounts follows:

SORENSON MANUFACTURING CORPORATION
Trial Balance
At December 31, 2017

	Debit	Credit
Cash	$11,000	
Accounts receivable	42,500	
Allowance for doubtful accounts		$500
Inventories	38,500	
Machinery	75,000	
Equipment	29,000	
Accumulated depreciation		10,000
Patents	85,000	
Leasehold improvements	26,000	
Prepaid expenses	10,500	
Organization expenses	29,000	
Goodwill	24,000	
Licensing Agreement No. 1*	50,000	
Licensing Agreement No. 2*	49,000	

*An intangible asset representing the right to use a patent.

The following information relates to accounts that may yet require adjustment:

1. Patents for Sorenson's manufacturing process were purchased January 2, 2017, at a cost of $68,000. An additional $17,000 was spent in December 2016 to improve machinery covered by the patents and charged to the Patents account. The patents had a remaining legal term of 17 years.

2. On January 3, 2014, Sorenson purchased two licensing agreements; at that time they were believed to have unlimited useful lives. The balance in the Licensing Agreement No. 1 account included its purchase price of $48,000 and $2,000 in acquisition expenses. Licensing Agreement No. 2 also was purchased on January 3, 2016, for $50,000, but it has been reduced by a credit of $1,000 for the advance collection of revenue from the agreement.

3. In December 2016, an explosion caused a permanent 60 percent reduction in the expected revenue-producing value of Licensing Agreement No. 1 and, in January 2017, a flood caused additional damage, which rendered the agreement worthless.

4. A study of Licensing Agreement No. 2 made by Sorenson in January 2017 revealed that its estimated remaining life expectancy was only 10 years as of January 1, 2017.

5. The balance in the Goodwill account includes $24,000 paid December 30, 2016, for an advertising program, which it is estimated will assist in increasing Sorenson's sales over a period of four years following the disbursement.

6. The Leasehold Improvement account includes (a) the $15,000 cost of improvements with a total estimated useful life of 12 years, which Sorenson, as tenant, made to leased premises in January 2016; (b) movable assembly-line equipment costing $8,500, which was installed in the leased premises in December 2017; and (c) real estate taxes of $2,500 paid by Sorenson, which, under the terms of the lease, should have been paid by the landlord. Sorenson paid its rent in full during 2017. A 10-year nonrenewable lease was signed January 3, 2016, for the leased building that Sorenson used in manufacturing operations.

7. The balance in the Organization Expenses account includes preoperating costs incurred during the organizational period.

Required:

For each of the items 1–7:

a. Prepare adjusting entries as necessary.

b. Identify the substantive audit procedures you would perform to test the transactions.

(AICPA adapted)

LO 10-1, 10-6

10.54 Loan Covenants. A *loan covenant* is a condition requiring the borrower to comply with the terms of a loan agreement. If the borrower does not act in accordance with the covenants, the loan can be considered in default and the lender has the right to demand payment (usually in full).

Required:

a. Why do banks add covenants to loan agreements?

b. The following is a list of common loan covenants. For each covenant, indicate what the bank is trying to accomplish by requiring it.
   (1) Maintain hazard insurance/content insurance.
   (2) Maintain key-person life insurance.
   (3) Make all payments of taxes/fees/licenses.
   (4) Provide financial information on borrower and guarantor.
   (5) Maintain a certain level in key financial ratios such as
       (a) Minimum quick and current ratios (liquidity).
       (b) Minimum return on assets and return on equity (profitability).
       (c) Minimum equity and minimum working capital.
       (d) Maximum debt to worth (leverage).
   (6) Make no change of management or merger without prior approval.
   (7) Obtain no more loans without prior approval.
   (8) Make no dividends/withdrawals or limited dividend withdrawals.

c. For each item 1–7, indicate where the auditor would be *most likely* to find evidence of the company's adherence with the covenant.

d. Why is it important for an auditor to review the covenants and review documents related to each item listed in part (b)?

LO 10-6

10.55 Long-Term Financing Agreement. You have been engaged to audit the financial statements of Broadwall Corporation for the year ended December 31, 2017. During the year, Broadwall obtained a long-term loan from a local bank pursuant to a financing agreement, which provided the following:

1. The loan is to be secured by the company's inventory and accounts receivable.

2. The company is to maintain a debt:equity ratio not to exceed 2:1.

3. The company is not to pay dividends without permission from the bank.

4. Monthly installment payments are to commence July 1, 2017. In addition, during the year, the company also borrowed, on a short-term basis, substantial amounts just prior to the year-end from the president of the company.

a. For the purposes of your audit of the Broadwall Corporation's financial statements, what procedures should you employ in examining the described loans? Do not discuss internal control.

b. What are the financial statement disclosures that you should expect to find with respect to the loan from the president?

LO 10-6

10.56 **Bond Indenture Covenants.** The following covenants are extracted from the indenture of a bond issue. The indenture provides that failure to comply with its terms in any respect automatically advances the due date of the loan to the date of noncompliance (the stated date is 20 years hence).Give any audit steps or reporting requirements you believe should be taken or recognized in connection with each of the following:

1. "The debtor company shall endeavor to maintain a working capital ratio of 2:1 at all times and, in any fiscal year following a failure to maintain said ratio, the company shall restrict compensation of officers to a total of $500,000. Officers for this purpose shall include the board chair, president, all vice presidents, secretary, and treasurer."

2. "The debtor company shall keep all property that is security for this debt insured against loss by fire to the extent of 100 percent of its actual value. Policies of insurance comprising this protection shall be filed with the trustee."

3. "The debtor company shall pay all taxes legally assessed against property that is security for this debt within the time provided by law for payment without penalty and shall deposit receipted tax bills or equally acceptable evidence of payment of same with the trustee."

(AICPA adapted)

LO 10-6

10.57 **Common Stock and Treasury Stock: Substantive Audit Procedures.** You are the continuing auditor of Sussex Inc. and are beginning the audit of the common stock and treasury stock accounts. You have decided to design substantive procedures with reliance on internal controls.

Sussex has no-par, no-stated-value common stock and acts as its own registrar and transfer agent. During the past year, Sussex both issued and reacquired shares of its own common stock, some of which the company still owned at year-end. Additional common stock transactions occurred among the shareholders during the year.

Common stock transactions can be traced to individual shareholders' accounts in a subsidiary ledger and to a stock certificate book. The company has not paid any cash or stock dividends. There are no other classes of stock, stock rights, warrants, or option plans.

What substantive procedures should you apply in examining the common stock and treasury stock accounts? Organize your answer as a list of audit procedures organized by the financial statement assertions. (See Appendix Exhibit 10B.4 for examples of substantive procedures for stockholders' equity.)

(AICPA adapted)

LO 10-6

10.58 **Stockholders' Equity.** You are a CPA engaged in an audit of the financial statements of Pate Corporation for the year ended December 31. The financial statements and records of Pate Corporation have not been audited by a CPA in prior years. The stockholders' equity section of Pate Corporation's balance sheet at December 31 follows:

Pate Corporation was founded in 1985. The corporation has 10 stockholders and serves as its own registrar and transfer agent. No capital stock subscription contracts are in effect.

a. Prepare the detailed audit plan for the examination of the three accounts composing the stockholders' equity section of Pate Corporation's balance sheet. Organize the audit plan under broad financial statement assertions. (Do not include in the audit plan the audit of the results of the current-year operations.)

b. After every other figure on the balance sheet has been audited, it might appear that the retained earnings figure is a balancing figure and requires no further audit work. Why do auditors audit retained earnings as they do the other figures on the balance sheet? Discuss.

(AICPA adapted)

LO 10-6

10.59 Intercompany and Interpersonal Investment Relations. You have been engaged to audit the financial statements of Hardy Hardware Distributors Inc., as of December 31. In your review of the corporate nonfinancial records, you have found that Hardy Hardware owns 15 percent of the outstanding voting common stock of Hardy Products Corporation. Upon further investigation, you learn that Hardy Products Corporation manufactures a line of hardware goods, 90 percent of which is sold to Hardy Hardware.

James L. Hardy, president of Hardy Hardware, has supplied you objective evidence that he personally owns 30 percent of the Hardy Products voting stock and the remaining 70 percent is owned by Juana Hardy Lewis, his sister and president of Hardy Products. Hardy also owns 20 percent of the voting common stock of Hardy Hardware Distributors, another 20 percent is held by an estate of which Hardy and Lewis are beneficiaries, and the remaining 60 percent is publicly held. The stock is listed on the American Stock Exchange.

Hardy Hardware consistently has reported operating profits higher than the industry average. Hardy Products Corporation, however, has a net return on sales of only 1 percent. The Hardy Products investment always has been reported at cost, and no dividends have been paid by the company. During the course of your conversations with the Hardy siblings, you learn that you were appointed as auditor because they had a heated disagreement with the former auditors over the issues of accounting for the Hardy Products investment and the prices at which goods have been sold to Hardy Hardware.

Required:

Discuss the following.

a. Identify the issues in this situation as they relate to (1) conflicts of interest and (2) controlling influences among individuals and corporations.

b. Should the investment in Hardy Products Corporation be accounted for using the equity method?

c. What evidence should the auditor seek with regard to the prices paid by Hardy Hardware for products purchased from Hardy Products Corporation?

d. What information would you consider necessary for adequate disclosure in the financial statements of Hardy Hardware Distributors?

Instructions for Discussion Cases 10.60–10.62

These cases are designed to be similar to the ones in the chapter. They give the problem, and your assignment is to write the audit approach portion of the case organized around these sections:

- *Objectives.* Express the objective in terms of the facts supposedly asserted in financial records, accounts, and statements.
- *Control.* Write a brief explanation of control considerations, especially the kinds of manipulations that could arise from the situation described in the case.
- *Tests of controls.* Write some procedures for getting evidence about existing controls, especially procedures that could discover management manipulations. If there are no controls to test, there are no procedures to perform; go on then to the next section. A *procedure* should instruct someone about the source(s) of evidence to tap and the work to do.
- *Audit of balance.* Write some procedures for getting evidence about the *existence, completeness, valuation, rights,* and *disclosure* assertions identified in your objectives section.
- *Discovery summary.* Write a short statement about the discovery you expect to accomplish with your procedures.

LO 10-1, 10-6, 10-7

10.60 Related-Party Transaction "Goodwill." Write the audit approach section like the cases in the chapter.

Hide the Loss under the Goodwill

Gulwest Industries, a public company, decided to discontinue its unprofitable line of business of manufacturing sporting ammunition. Gulwest had capitalized the startup cost of the business, and with its discontinuance, the $7 million deferred cost should have been written off. Instead, Gulwest formed a new corporation, Amron, and transferred the sporting ammunition assets (including the $7 million deferred cost) to it in exchange for all Amron stock. In the Gulwest accounts, the Amron investment was carried at $12.4 million, which was the book value of the assets transferred (including the $7 million deferred cost).

Gulwest and a different public company (Big Industrial) created another company (Big-Shot Ammunition). Gulwest transferred all Amron assets to BigShot in exchange for (1) common and preferred stock of Big Industrial valued at $2 million and (2) a note from BigShot in the amount of $3.4 million. Big Industrial thus acquired 100 percent of the stock of BigShot. Gulwest management reasoned that it had "given" Amron stock valued at $12.4 million to receive stock and notes valued at $5.4 million, so the difference must be good-will. Thus, the Gulwest accounts carried amounts for Big Industrial Stock ($2 million), BigShot's note receivable ($3.4 million), and Goodwill ($7 million).

Gulwest directors included in the minutes of board meetings an analysis of the sporting ammunition business's lack of profitability. The minutes showed approval of a plan to dispose of the business, but they did not use the words *discontinue the business.* The minutes also showed approval of the creation of Amron, the deal with Big Industrial, the formation of BigShot, and the acceptance of Big's stock and BigShot's note in connection with the final exchange and merger.

LO 10-1, 10-6, 10-7   10.61   **Related-Party Transaction Valuation.** Follow the instructions preceding the case in problem 10.60. Write the audit approach section like the cases in the chapter.

In Plane View

Whiz Corporation owned 160,000 shares of Wing Company stock, carried on the books as an investment in the amount of $6,250,000. Whiz bought a used airplane from Wing, giving in exchange (1) $480,000 cash and (2) the 160,000 Wing shares. Even though the quoted market value of the Wing stock was $2,520,000, Whiz valued the airplane received at $3,750,000, indicating a stock valuation of $3,270,000. Thus, Whiz recognized a loss on disposition of the Wing stock in the amount of $2,980,000.

Whiz justified the airplane valuation with another transaction. On the same day it was purchased, Whiz sold the airplane to the Mexican subsidiary of one of its subsidiary companies (two layers down, but Whiz owned 100 percent of the first subsidiary, which in turn owned 100 percent of the Mexican subsidiary). The Mexican subsidiary paid Whiz with US$25,000 cash and a promissory note for US$3,725,000 (market rate of interest).

The transaction was within the authority of the chief executive officer, and company policy did not require a separate approval by the board of directors. A contract of sale and correspondence with Wing detailing the terms of the transaction were in the files. Like-wise, a contract of sale to the Mexican subsidiary, a copy of the deposit slip, and a memo-randum of the promissory note were on file. The note itself was kept in the company vault. None of the Wing papers cited a specific price for the airplane.

Whiz overvalued the Wing stock and justified it with a related-party transaction with its own subsidiary company. The loss on the disposition of the Wing stock was understated by $750,000.

LO 10-6, 10-7   10.62   **Lack of Controls over Investments.** Follow the instructions preceding the case in problem 10.60. Write the audit approach section like the cases in the chapter.

Rogue Trader

In February 1989, 22-year-old Nicholas Leeson joined **Barings Investment Bank.** In 1993, he began trading on behalf of the Barings group as a "proprietary trader" on the Singapore International Monetary Exchange (SIMEX). By 1995, he had wiped out the 233-year-old bank, which had counted Queen Elizabeth as a client. He left behind liabilities totaling $1.3 billion. As a proprietary trader, Leeson was to arbitrage or take advantage of differences between the prices quoted for identical contracts on SIMEX and on other exchanges. This was supposed to be achieved by entering into matching purchase and sale contracts simultaneously to capture favorable price differences. Unfortunately, Leeson entered into very large contracts that were not matched with offsetting contracts, exposing the bank to enormous potential losses from even small market movements. These trades were hidden in a separate account: 88888. Transactions were transferred from other Barings accounts into account 88888 to artificially generate a profit for the other accounts.

During the period, Barings was reorganizing and Leeson reported to local managers in Singapore and product managers in London. Neither set of managers checked Leeson's activities. An internal audit report had criticized the reporting structure, but its recommendations were never implemented. Funds to finance Leeson's trades were requested from him to ostensibly fund client positions and were recorded as receivables from clients. The credit control group never reviewed the creditworthiness of the clients because they said they were never informed of the remittances.

Leeson's managers accepted reports of his profitability with admiration. They did not question the unusually large profits from his trading that would have been unlikely from an arbitrage operation.

Appendix 10A

Internal Control Questionnaires

EXHIBIT 10A.1   Internal Control Questionnaire: Investments

	Yes/No	Comments
Environment		
1. Does the board of directors authorize investment strategies?		
2. Are investment structures based on legitimate business goals?		
3. Are trading guidelines and limits established by company policy?		
4. Are derivatives used for legitimate company objectives?		
5. Are brokerage relationships reviewed for potential conflicts of interests?		
6. Are personnel recording investments competent and appropriately trained to ensure the accuracy and appropriateness of journal entries?		
Existence/Occurrence		
7. Are brokerage statements reconciled to the general ledger monthly?		
Completeness		
8. Are company traders monitored in their discussions with brokers?		
Valuation		
9. Does accounting review all significant transactions?		
10. Are purchases and sales of investments listed on brokerage statements compared to changes in the investment account?		
11. Are purchases and sales of investments listed on brokerage statements compared to receipts and disbursements?		
12. Are changes in investments accounted for on the equity method monitored and recorded in the financial statements?		
13. Are accounting personnel trained in standards for hedge accounting?		
Cutoff		
14. Are purchases and sales of investments listed on brokerage statements compared to changes in the investment account to ensure they were recorded in the proper period?		
Presentation and disclosure		
15. Are investment classifications based on legitimate management intentions?		
16. Are disclosures reviewed by senior management?		

EXHIBIT 10A.2   Internal Control Questionnaire: Notes Payable

	Yes/No	Comments
Environment		
1. Are notes payable records kept by someone who cannot sign notes or checks?		
2. Are direct borrowings on notes payable authorized by the directors? By the treasurer or by the chief financial officer?		
3. Are two or more authorized signatures required on notes?		
Existence/Occurrence		
4. Are paid notes canceled, stamped PAID, and filed?		
Completeness		
5. Is all borrowing authorized by the directors checked to determine whether all notes payable are recorded?		
Valuation		
6. Are loan documents forwarded to accounting for review?		
7. Are bank due notices compared with records of unpaid liabilities?		
8. Is the subsidiary ledger of notes payable periodically reconciled with the general ledger control account(s)? Are interest payments and accruals monitored for due dates and financial statement dates?		
Cutoff		
9. Are new notes recorded in the appropriate period?		
Presentation and disclosure		
10. Is sufficient information available in the accounts to enable financial statement preparers to classify current and long-term debt properly?		

Appendix 10B

Substantive Audit Plans

DUNDER-MIFFLIN INC. Audit Plan for Fair Market Value of Assets and Liabilities December 31, 2017		
	Performed By	**Ref.**
A. Review Details of Management's Valuation Approach		
1. Assess the completeness of management assumptions (i.e., whether management has considered all relevant issues).		
2. Determine the reasonableness of significant assumptions, including whether these assumptions reflect		
a. The general economic environment.		
b. The specific industry's economic and regulatory environment.		
c. Other market information.		
d. Assumptions made in prior periods.		
e. Past experience with the entity.		
f. The potential variability in the amount and timing of cash flows and related effect on the discount rate.		
g. Results of other audit procedures.		
3. Obtain data used in reaching these assumptions including		
a. Recency of data.		
b. Source of data.		
c. Consistency of data (i.e., assumptions used in one calculation are consistent with assumptions used in other calculations).		
4. Reperform computations.		
5. Trace data to source documents for accuracy.		
6. Identify possible bias or misapplication of assumptions.		
B. Reperform the Valuation Process to Provide an Auditor's Estimate of the Value Estimate and Compare That Value to Management's Estimate		
C. Review Transactions That Have Occurred since Year-End That Provide Evidence		
1. Determine whether the assumptions underlying management's valuation supports (or refutes) that valuation.		
2. Review the valuation itself.		
D. Document All Management Assumptions and Audit Procedures Used to Substantiate Those Assumptions		

DUNDER-MIFFLIN INC. Audit Plan for Investments and Related Accounts December 31, 2017		
	Performed By	**Ref.**
A. Investments and Related Accounts		
1. Obtain a schedule of all investments, including purchase and disposition information for the period. Reconcile with investment accounts in the general ledger.		
2. Inspect or confirm with a trustee or broker the name, number, identification, interest rate, and face amount (if applicable) of securities held as investments.		
3. Vouch the cost of recorded investments to brokers' reports, contracts, canceled checks, and other supporting documentation.		
4. Vouch recorded sales to brokers' reports and bank deposit slips and recalculate gain or loss on disposition.		
5. Recalculate interest income and verify dividend income from a dividend-reporting service (such as Moody's or Standard & Poor's annual dividend record).		
6. Obtain market values of investments and determine whether any write-down or write-off is necessary. Scan transactions soon after the client's year-end to see whether any investments were sold at a loss. Recalculate the unrealized gains and losses required for fair value securities accounting.		

(continued)

EXHIBIT 10B.2 *(concluded)*

<table>
<tr><td colspan="3" align="center">**DUNDER-MIFFLIN INC.**
Audit Plan for Investments and Related Accounts
December 31, 2017</td></tr>
<tr><td></td><td>**Performed By**</td><td>**Ref.**</td></tr>
<tr><td>

7. Read loan agreements and minutes of the board of directors and inquire of management about pledges of investments as security for loans.
8. Obtain audited financial statements of joint ventures, investee companies (equity method of accounting), subsidiary companies, and other entities in which an investment interest is held. Evaluate indications of significant controlling influence. Inspect documents for proper balance sheet classification and conformity with accounting principles.
9. Obtain management representations concerning pledge of investment assets as collateral.

B. Investments in Debt and Equity Securities

1. Review the proper classification of securities in the categories of held-to-maturity, available-for-sale, and trading securities.
   a. Inquire about management's intent regarding classifications.
   b. Inspect written records of investment strategies.
   c. Inspect documentation for investment activities and transactions.
   d. Review instructions to portfolio managers.
   e. Inspect minutes of the investment committee of the board of directors.
2. Review whether facts support management's intent to hold securities to maturity.
   a. Inquire of management concerning the company's financial position, working capital requirements, results of operations, debt agreements, guarantees, and applicable laws and regulations.
   b. Inspect documentation and review for compliance with working capital requirements, debt agreements, guarantees, and applicable laws and regulations.
   c. Inspect the company's cash flow forecasts.
   d. Obtain management representations confirming proper classification with regard to intent and ability.
3. Review the value of debt and equity securities by performing the following:
   a. Obtain published market quotations.
   b. Obtain market prices from broker-dealers who are market makers in particular securities.
   c. Obtain valuations from expert specialists.
   d. Inspect documentation and review proprietary market valuation models for reasonableness and evaluate the data and assumptions in them are appropriate.
4. Review whether value impairments are "other than temporary," considering evidence of the following:
   a. Fair market is materially below cost.
   b. The value decline is due to specific adverse conditions.
   c. The value decline is industry or geographically specific.
   d. Management does not have both the intent and the ability to hold the security long enough for a reasonable hope of value recovery.
   e. The fair value decline has existed for a long time.
   f. A debt security has been downgraded by a rating agency.
   g. The financial condition of the issuer has deteriorated.
   h. Dividends of interest payments have been reduced or eliminated.

</td><td></td><td></td></tr>
</table>

EXHIBIT 10B.3

DUNDER-MIFFLIN INC. Audit Plan for Notes Payable and Long-Term Debt December 31, 2017		
	Performed By	**Ref.**
1. Obtain a schedule of notes payable and other long-term debt (including capitalized lease obligations) showing beginning balances, new notes/issuances, repayment, and ending balances. Trace to general ledger accounts. 2. Confirm liabilities with creditor: amount, interest rate, due date, collateral, and other terms. Some of these confirmations may be standard bank confirmations. 3. Review the standard bank confirmation for evidence of assets pledged as collateral and for unrecorded obligations. 4. Review loan agreements for terms and conditions that need to be disclosed and for pledge of assets as collateral. 5. Recalculate the portion of long-term debt classified as a current liability and trace to the trial balance. 6. Inspect lease agreements for indications of need to capitalize leases. Recalculate the capital and operating lease amounts for required disclosures. 7. Recalculate interest expense on debts and trace to the interest expense and accrued interest accounts. 8. Obtain written representations from management concerning notes payable, collateral agreements, and restrictive covenants.		

EXHIBIT 10B.4

DUNDER-MIFFLIN INC. Audit Plan for Stockholders' Equity December 31, 2017		
	Performed By	**Ref.**

1. Obtain an analysis of stockholders' equity transactions. Trace additions and reductions to the general ledger.
  a. Vouch additions to directors' minutes and cash receipts.
  b. Vouch reductions to directors' minutes and other supporting documents.
2. Read the directors' minutes for stockholders' equity authorization. Trace to entries in the accounts. Review related disclosures for completeness and accuracy.
3. Confirm outstanding common and preferred stock with stock registrar.
4. Vouch stock option and profit-sharing plan disclosures to contracts and plan documents.
5. Vouch treasury stock transactions to cash receipts and cash disbursement records and to directors' authorization. Inspect treasury stock certificates.
6. When the company keeps its own stock records:
  a. Inspect the stock record stubs for certificate numbers and number of shares.
  b. Inspect the unissued certificates.
7. Obtain management representations about the number of shares issued and outstanding.		

CHAPTER 11

Completing the Audit

It ain't over till it's over.

> "Yogi" Berra, former American Major League Baseball catcher, coach, and manager

Professional Standards References

Topic	AU-C/ISA Section	AS Section
Terms of Engagement	210	1301
Quality Control for an Audit Engagement	220	1220
Communication with Those Charged with Governance	260	1301
Communicating Internal Control-Related Matters Identified in an Audit	265	1305
Evaluation of Misstatements	450	2810
Inquiry of a Client's Lawyer	501	2505
Analytical Procedures	520	2305
Accounting Estimates	540	2501
Subsequent Events and Subsequently Discovered Facts	560	2801, 2905
Going Concern	570	2415
Written Representations	580	2805
Omitted Procedures	585	2901

LEARNING OBJECTIVES

This chapter discusses the completion of the audit examination and identifies major events and auditors' responsibilities in the completion stage of the audit.

Your objectives are to be able to:

LO 11-1 Identify major activities performed by auditors in completing the substantive procedures following the date of the financial statements.

LO 11-2 Understand the role of attorney letters in evaluating litigation, claims, and assessments.

LO 11-3 Explain why auditors obtain written representations and identify the key components of written representations.

LO 11-4 Identify the final steps in the completion of an audit.

LO 11-5 Understand auditors' responsibility for subsequent events and subsequently discovered facts.

LO 11-6 Identify important activities and communications following the completion of the audit and audit report release date.

INTRODUCTION[1]

Canadian pharmaceutical giant **Valeant** appeared to be on top of the world. The hedge fund darling experienced significant growth through the acquisition of other pharmaceutical companies and their portfolios of prescription drugs. Valeant would then raise the prices for those drugs it thought were underpriced.

Everything came to a screeching halt for Valeant in early 2016. First, just after the company's December 31, 2015 year-end, the company announced that CEO Michael Pearson was taking an indefinite leave of absence for health reasons. At the same time, public outrage over price increases (some as high as 525 percent) for commonly used prescription drugs brought unwanted congressional attention to the company's operations. Questions also began to circulate about the company's revenue recognition practices, especially those involving drug distributor **Philidor**; critics alleged that Philidor coerced insurers to pay reimbursements for Valeant's drugs over cheaper alternatives.

Under current rules, large public companies are required to file audited financial statements with the SEC within 60 days of their fiscal year-ends. This deadline requires auditors to complete their work within a relatively short time period and ensure that all important matters are addressed and promptly resolved with clients. Failing to file its Form 10-K on time with the SEC raised concerns as to whether Valeant would be able to meet its debt covenants with its lenders; violating its debt covenants might force the company into bankruptcy.

With all of these issues facing its client, Valeant's auditor, **PwC**, was faced with a dilemma. With the SEC filing deadline looming, should the public accounting firm issue its audit report on time to allow Valeant to meet the deadline or delay until more information was available to address remaining concerns? In this chapter, we discuss the many issues an engagement team faces when wrapping up an audit. Although the Valeant case is obviously unusual, it illustrates that the completion of an audit is not necessarily a straight-forward, "check-the-boxes" activity.

Thus far in this text, we have discussed auditors' use of the audit risk model to limit exposure to audit risk, auditors' tests of controls to determine the operating effectiveness of internal control and to assess control risk (and the risk of material misstatement), and auditors' substantive procedures to determine the fairness of the account balances and classes of transactions. At this point, it seems as though little work remains to be done! Although the audit is concluding, the potential for audit failure is at its highest. Consider just a few of the questions that Valeant's auditors may have been asking as the audit was concluding:

- Have year-end misstatements that significantly affect the financial statements been identified?
- What events that occurred after the date of the financial statements could have affected the current-year financial statements?
- What potential exposure does the client have for pending litigation?
- Has the client provided all relevant information to auditors during the engagement?
- What matters need to be discussed with the individuals charged with governance of the client (normally, the audit committee)?

Valeant finally filed its Form 10-K in late April, two months after the SEC filing deadline, but the company was able to get debt covenant waivers from its lenders. An internal investigation, however, found a material weakness in internal control over financial reporting that allowed the company to prematurely recognize revenue of almost $60 million in sales to Philidor. The company's stock price, once trading at more than $250 per share, was trading in the low $30s by June 2016.

[1]Much of the background in this section is drawn from "Valeant Could have Trouble Getting Clean Opinion from Auditor," *CFO Journal*, March 21, 2016.

As shown in the following Auditing Insight, the completion of the audit involves significant auditor judgment and attention. The Public Company Accounting Oversight Board (PCAOB) identified these matters during its annual inspections for audits conducted by the Big Four firms (**Deloitte, Ernst & Young [EY], KPMG**, and PwC). In this excerpt, "the firm" refers to one of these firms.

AUDITING INSIGHT · PCAOB Inspections and Completing the Audit

- The Firm identified known errors that it concluded did not warrant further investigation, discussion, or adjustment to the financial statements. Some of these errors were left in the audit documentation without final disposition, despite the fact that they exceeded the Firm's posting threshold.

- The Firm's analytical procedures for testing operating expenses did not appropriately set a threshold for investigation of significant differences between the recorded balance and the firm's expectations; further, the Firm did not document its corroboration of management's explanations for significant differences between the recorded balance and the Firm's expectations.

- The Firm did not perform sufficient audit procedures with respect to income tax contingencies (assessing the likelihood of occurrence, testing the amount of the estimate accrued by the client, evaluating whether the client's policy on establishing reserves was consistent with GAAP, and evaluating the client's conclusion that no reserve was required for items that were disallowed in a report received in connection with an Internal Revenue Services' audit).

- While the Firm tested certain revenue transactions that occurred during the first seven months of the year, it failed to perform roll-forward procedures for the remaining five months of the year or otherwise adequately test revenues at year-end.

- While the Firm obtained responses to attorneys' letters, the responses did not include an evaluation from the attorneys regarding the probability of an unfavorable outcome and the Firm failed to perform additional procedures to evaluate the contingency.

- Firms did not sufficiently test or challenge management's forecasts, views, or representations that constituted critical support for amounts recorded in the financial statements.

- Deficiencies raised questions about the sufficiency, rigor, and effectiveness of the review of audit documentation, including engagement quality review. In some of these instances, the amount of time committed to an engagement quality review did not appear sufficient, given the difficulty and complexity of the engagement.

All four of the firms performed additional auditing procedures in response to PCAOB inspection findings; in all but one instance, the additional procedures did not affect the firms' conclusions, the client's financial statements, or the firms' reports on the financial statements. In the one exception, the firm's failure to identify departures from GAAP resulted in the client restating its financial statements.

Sources: 2005-2015 PCAOB Inspection of Deloitte, EY, KPMG, and PwC. All reports can be found on the PCAOB website.

AUDIT TIMELINE

This chapter discusses the completion (or wrap-up) of the audit. During this time, many important issues arise, and many other issues that have served as the focus of the auditors' work need to be documented. To provide an overview of the general time frame of the audit and the potential emergence of issues and matters for the auditors' consideration, consider the following broad timeline:

Beginning of Year January 1, 2017	Year-End Date (date of the financial statements) December 31, 2017	Date of the Auditor's Report (audit completion date) February 15, 2018	Audit Report Release Date February 17, 2018
Interim testing Test of controls Substantive procedures	Completing substantive procedures Attorneys' letters Written representations Going-concern assessment Adjusting journal entries Audit documentation review Subsequent events	Subsequently discovered facts	Subsequently discovered facts Omitted audit procedures Management letter Communications with those charged with governance

The preceding timeline suggests four important periods, beginning with the period under audit. Auditors often do a significant amount of tests of controls and substantive procedures prior to year-end to "spread" the audit work over a more extended period. This *interim testing* occurs between the beginning of the year (January 1, 2017) and the year-end date under audit (December 31, 2017), also referred to as the **date of the financial statements**.

The second period of interest begins on the date of the financial statements (December 31, 2017) and runs through the completion of the audit (February 15, 2018). Although a significant amount of audit evidence is typically gathered prior to the date of the financial statements, auditors will continue to perform other procedures and gather evidence following this date. At some point, auditors will have gathered sufficient, appropriate evidence on which to base their reports on the financial statements and internal control over financial reporting; this includes the review of audit documentation, preparation of the financial statements and related disclosures, and management's assertion that they take responsibility for the financial statements and disclosures. We refer to this as the **date of the auditor's report**, which is the date auditors use for their reports on the client's financial statements and internal control over financial reporting. (This date is also referred to as the *audit completion date* and, in our example, would be February 15, 2018.) Recall that the auditor's report on the entity's financial statements covers all events that occur up to this date, and, as a result, auditors need to continue to be alert for developments affecting the client.

In some instances, auditors become aware of a development affecting the client *after* the date of the auditor's report (in our example, February 15, 2018) but *prior* to the **audit report release date** (date on which auditors allow the client to use the auditor's reports in conjunction with the financial statements, in our example, February 17, 2018).[2] This is the third period of interest to the auditor. Although this period normally is fairly short, events occurring between the date of the auditor's report and audit report release date present significant challenges to auditors—they are no longer actively obtaining audit evidence—however, their reports have yet to be issued. The auditors' dilemma is simple: how to report on the new development without increasing the responsibility for other (unknown) developments. As discussed later in this chapter, auditors may consider dual dating the report on the financial statements to limit responsibility to specifically identified developments.

Finally, some issues can come to auditors' attention after the audit report release date and the issuance of the client's financial statements (in our example, February 17, 2018); this is the fourth period of interest.[3] Although Form 10-K and auditor's reports have been released, information may come to the auditor's attention that could cause the auditor to take steps to ensure that third parties do not inappropriately rely on auditors' reports that are no longer reliable. In addition, following the audit report release date, auditors make other communications to the client and individuals charged with governance based on observations during the audit examination.

This chapter focuses on a number of the topics addressed in the preceding timeline. Regarding auditors' responsibility for various matters, it is important to consider the timing of these topics in the timeline discussed.

✓ REVIEW CHECKPOINT

11.1 Identify four primary periods in an audit examination and the tasks and activities that occur in each.

---

[2]These reports include opinions on the financial statements and the effectiveness of internal control over financial reporting. As noted in Chapter 12, both auditors' reports are dated on the audit completion date and included with the 10-K filed with the U.S. Securities and Exchange Commission (SEC).

[3]Larger public entities must file annual reports with the SEC within 60 days after the date of the financial statements. Thus, audit fieldwork must be completed and auditors' reports for these companies must be dated earlier than 60 days after the date of the financial statements.

PROCEDURES PERFORMED DURING FIELDWORK

LO 11-1
Identify major activities performed by auditors in completing the substantive procedures following the date of the financial statements.

Completing Substantive Procedures

Roll-Forward Procedures

From earlier chapters, you know that auditors often test account balances at an interim point for efficiency reasons. For example, if relevant internal controls are effective, accounts receivable can be confirmed at November 30 for a December 31 year-end client. Similarly, although most inventory observations occur near year-end, they actually can be performed at an earlier time. In such cases, auditors use **roll-forward procedures** to *roll* the conclusions *forward* to the year-end date under audit. Common roll-forward procedures include examining material account transactions that occur between the interim testing date and the date of the financial statements.

Analytical Procedures and Review of Accounts

Throughout the text, we have discussed the use of **analytical procedures**, which allow auditors to evaluate financial information by studying relationships among both financial and nonfinancial data. Professional standards state that analytical procedures can be used throughout the audit:

1. During planning to assist auditors in planning the nature, timing, and extent of other auditing procedures (*required*).
2. As part of substantive testing, to obtain audit evidence about particular assertions related to account balances or classes of transactions (*optional*).
3. Near the end of the audit as an overall review of the financial information to assess the conclusions reached and evaluate the overall financial statement presentation (*required*).

This latter use of analytical procedures is of interest to auditors in completing the audit. In this use, auditors review the financial statements and footnotes to the financial statements to evaluate (1) the adequacy of evidence gathered in response to unexpected account balances or relationships among account balances identified during the audit and (2) unusual or unexpected account balances or relationships among account balances that were not previously identified in other parts of the audit. To illustrate, in the early 2000s, **WorldCom**'s ratio of line expenses to revenues (an important metric in the telecommunications industry) was stable despite the fact that the industry was experiencing a significant downturn and industry ratios were increasing (becoming less favorable). An overall review of WorldCom's ratios, along with the auditors' knowledge of the economic conditions facing the industry, would have suggested a potential issue and triggered the need to gather additional audit evidence. In hindsight, had WorldCom's auditor (**Arthur Andersen**) performed this relatively simple analytical procedure near the end of the audit, one of the largest corporate frauds in history could have been averted!

In addition to the preceding, auditors should be alert for "miscellaneous," "other," and "clearing" accounts classified as revenues or expenses, particularly when they result from adjustments made at the end of the year or quarter. These items can be identified by scanning accounts for large and unusual entries. In many cases, these items reflect adjustments made to meet analysts' earnings expectations (known as *earnings management*) and should be more appropriately classified as *deferred items, assets, liabilities, contra-assets,* or *contra-liabilities.* **HealthSouth, Sunbeam**, and WorldCom used adjustments (which did not comply with generally accepted accounting principles) near the end of a reporting period to improve their reported earnings. If items of this nature are identified, auditors should examine related documentation and inquire of the client to verify that classification as a revenue or expense is appropriate. More recently, inquiries into **Lehman Brothers**' practice of using "Repo 105s" (accounting maneuvers that involve the sale and subsequent repurchase of debt within a short period of time) to reduce reported debt near the end of fiscal quarters further illustrate the importance for auditors to evaluate carefully significant transactions occurring near the end of the year or quarter.[4]

Review of Accounting Estimates

Chapters 6 through 10 discuss auditing procedures performed in the examination of various cycles. As noted in these chapters, the entity's account balances and financial statements are affected by many significant estimates that must be made by management. For example, **Best Buy** (a retailer of consumer electronics, home office products, entertainment software, appliances, and related services) identifies the following as some of the critical accounting estimates necessary in preparing its financial statements:

- Future markdown and loss reserves for valuing its inventories.
- Future cash flows from long-lived assets for evaluating potential impairment.
- Sales returns for recognizing net revenues.
- Allowance for doubtful accounts for determining the balance of accounts receivable.
- Potential benefits earned by customers under loyalty programs for accruing potential liabilities related to those programs.
- Gift card usage for determining revenue earned from the sale of gift cards.

Because estimates, by their very nature, reflect uncertainty and future outcomes, auditors cannot "audit," "corroborate," or "verify" accounting estimates. However, auditors should consider whether estimates are *reasonable* in the circumstances. For example, it is not likely that assigning computer equipment a 20-year useful life for purposes of depreciation would be considered reasonable. Although the reasonableness of accounting estimates is assessed to some extent on an account-by-account basis throughout the audit, auditors will evaluate management's process for developing estimates as well as the overall *reasonableness* of management's estimates near the end of the audit. With respect to reasonableness, auditors should ensure that estimates are consistent with one another, historical data, and industry data. In addition, auditors should consider how events occurring after the date of the financial statements may affect the reasonableness of accounting estimates. For example, a significant economic downturn may suggest that previous estimates related to uncollectible accounts are insufficient and a higher percentage of uncollectible accounts should be estimated. In a sense, this overall review of the reasonableness of accounting estimates is similar in nature and purpose to the role of analytical procedures conducted near the end of the audit.

☑ REVIEW CHECKPOINTS

11.2 What are roll-forward procedures? Provide some examples.

11.3 How are analytical procedures used near the end of the audit?

11.4 What additional issues are involved with miscellaneous, other, and clearing accounts?

11.5 What are auditors' responsibilities with respect to accounting estimates made by management?

LO 11-2

Understand the role of attorney letters in evaluating litigation, claims, and assessments.

Attorney Letters

For financial statements to be presented according to an applicable financial reporting framework (such as GAAP), all material contingencies (contingent gains or losses) must be properly accounted for and disclosed in the financial statements. According to *Accounting Standards Codification 450 (ASC 450)*, a **contingency** is

---

[4]"Debt 'Masking' Under Fire," *The Wall Street Journal*, April 21, 2010, p. A1.

Part Two *The Financial Statement Audit*

an existing condition, situation, or set of circumstances involving uncertainty as to possible gain or loss to an enterprise that will ultimately be resolved when one or more future events occur or fail to occur.

Examples of contingent liabilities include potential payments related to warranties for products and services sold by the entity, income taxes in disputes with the Internal Revenue Service, and guarantees of debt on behalf of another party. With respect to contingencies, auditors should ensure that (1) all contingencies have been appropriately identified and (2) any client disclosure of contingencies reflects the most current information and all recent developments, both favorable and unfavorable to the client. These contingencies are normally evaluated as part of the audit of the related account balances and classes of transactions and have been discussed in previous chapters of this text.

A contingent liability that requires special consideration by auditors is the uncertain outcome of litigation, claims, and assessments pending against the entity. From the auditors' standpoint, two important issues relating to pending litigation, claims, and assessments are ensuring that all pending litigation, claims, and assessments (1) have been disclosed to auditors and (2) are properly presented and disclosed in the client's financial statements. Because the client's attorneys are most familiar with the existence and classification of pending litigation, claims, and assessments, they play a very important role in auditors' evaluation of these matters.

Auditors should inquire of management and discuss potential litigation, claims, and assessments. Once this inquiry has identified litigation, claims, and assessments, auditors perform the following procedures:

- Obtain from management a description and evaluation of litigation, claims, and assessments.
- Examine documents in the client's possession concerning litigation, claims, and assessments, including correspondence and invoices from attorneys.
- Obtain assurance from management that it has disclosed all material unasserted claims the attorney has advised them are likely to be litigated.
- Read minutes of meetings of stockholders, directors, and appropriate committees.
- Read contracts, loan agreements, leases, and correspondence from taxing or other governmental agencies.
- Obtain information concerning guarantees from bank confirmations.
- Review the legal expense account, cash disbursements records, and invoices related to legal services.

The client's responsibility is to respond to auditors' inquiries and provide auditors with a description and evaluation of litigation, claims, and assessments. When auditors assess a risk of material misstatement from pending litigation, claims, and assessments, they will request that the client send an **attorney letter** (or letter of inquiry) to all attorneys who worked for the client during the period under audit. It is important to note that the client should make this request because it informs the attorney that the client is waiving the attorney-client privilege and is authorizing the attorney to provide information to auditors. The attorney letter (see Exhibit 11.1) should contain the following information (prepared from the client's perspective):

- A list of pending or threatened litigation, claims, or assessments.
- A description of each item, including the nature of the case and management responses or intended responses to the case.
- An evaluation of the likelihood of an unfavorable outcome.
- An estimate of the range of potential loss.

Review the following diagram for the flow of correspondence related to the attorney letter. The process begins when auditors request the client to *prepare* a letter to its attorney(s) (step 1). In step 2, the attorney receives the letter *mailed by the auditor* asking

EXHIBIT 11.1 Sample Attorney Letter

The Bluth Company
1725 Slough Avenue
Newport Beach, CA 92660

March 2, 2018

Bob Loblaw
1728 Slough Avenue
Newport Beach, CA 92660

> Information is provided by management

In connection with an audit of our financial statements at December 31, 2017, and for the year then ended, management of The Bluth Company has prepared, and furnished to Michael Scarn, LLP, P.O. Box 10024, Scranton, PA 18501, a description and evaluation of certain contingencies, including those set forth below involving matters with respect to which you have been engaged and to which you have devoted substantive attention on behalf of The Bluth Company in the form of legal consultation or representation. These are regarded by the management of The Bluth Company as material for this purpose. Your response should include matters that existed at December 31, 2017, and during the period from that date to the date of your response.

[Add description of pending or threatened litigation]

Please furnish to our auditors such explanation, if any, that you consider necessary to supplement the foregoing information, including an explanation of those matters as to which your views may differ from those stated and an identification of the omission of any pending or threatened litigation, claims, and assessments or a statement that the list of such matters is complete.

> Attorneys indicate whether view differs from management's views

[Add description of unasserted claims and assessments]

Please furnish to our auditors such explanation, if any, that you consider necessary to supplement the foregoing information, including an explanation of those matters as to which your views may differ from those stated.

We understand that whenever in the course of performing legal services for us with respect to a matter recognized to involve an unasserted possible claim or assessment that may call for financial statement disclosure, if you have formed a professional conclusion that we should disclose or consider disclosure concerning such possible claim or assessment, as a matter of professional responsibility to us, you will so advise us and will consult with us concerning the question of such disclosure and the applicable requirements of Financial Accounting Standards Board (FASB) *Accounting Standards Codification (ASC) 450, Contingencies.* Please specifically confirm to our auditors that our understanding is correct.

Please specifically identify the nature of and reasons for any limitation on your response.

Signed:
GOB Bluth
G.O.B. Bluth, Chief Executive Officer

Source: Adapted from AU-C 501.A69

the attorney to respond to the letter (step 3). The *attorney's response* should be provided *directly* to auditors for purposes of control and should explain any matters noted in the attorney letter in which the attorney's view differs from the information in the letter. For example, the client may indicate that the likelihood of an unfavorable outcome is "remote," but the attorney may believe that it is higher than "remote." In addition, the attorney may inform auditors of pending litigation, claims, or assessments not included in the attorney letter.

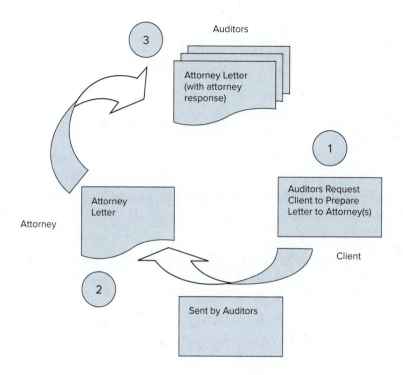

EXHIBIT 11.2

Role of Various Parties in Audit of Litigation, Claims, and Assessments

Party	Responsibilities
Auditors	• Inquire of client regarding the existence of litigation, claims, and assessments. • Perform various procedures regarding litigation, claims, and assessments. • Initiate request to the client for attorney letter. • Mail attorney letter prepared by client.
Client	• Respond to auditors' inquiries regarding litigation, claims, and assessments. • Provide auditors a list, description, and evaluation of litigation, claims, and assessments. • Prepare letter to attorney (attorney letter) that includes information related to litigation, claims, and assessments.
Attorney	• Respond to auditors regarding client's description of litigation, claims, and assessments contained in the attorney letter.

The general roles of the client, auditors, and attorney(s) in this process are summarized in Exhibit 11.2.

Unasserted claims raise additional issues for attorney letters. An **unasserted claim** represents that no formal lawsuit or claim has been filed or threatened on behalf of others but that circumstances such as a catastrophe, accident, or other physical occurrence could result in a suit or claim being filed in the future. In these cases, attorneys must consider the likelihood that a lawsuit or claim will be filed as well as the possibility of an unfavorable outcome when responding to the attorney letter.

Because unasserted claims have not been filed, the issue of client disclosure of these matters to auditors is less clear. Attorneys should encourage their clients to disclose this information to auditors when the assertion of a claim is at least *probable.* However, the American Bar Association's guidelines to attorneys do not require them to disclose unasserted claims to auditors unless the client specifically lists them in the attorney letter. Thus, auditors must rely on the attorney to inform the client (not the auditors) if an unasserted claim must be disclosed. As shown in Exhibit 11.1, the attorney letter explicitly asks that this understanding be communicated to the client's auditors through the attorney's response.

AUDITING INSIGHT   Microsoft's Contingencies

In its 2010 10-K, **Microsoft,** a company that develops, manufactures, licenses, and supports software and other computer-related products, disclosed the following contingencies in its footnotes to the financial statements:

- The appeal of a fine paid to the European Commission related to pricing terms on Microsoft's products licensed to competitors.

- An investigation by the European Commission related to the interoperability of Microsoft Office products.

- Numerous antitrust and unfair competition lawsuits related to sales of Microsoft's operating system and other software products.

- An appeal by Novell on dismissals of antitrust claims against Microsoft related to Novell's ownership of a competing product (WordPerfect).

- Various patent and intellectual property claims (a total of 54, 10 of which were set for trial in the upcoming year).

In response to these contingencies, Microsoft accrued more than $1.2 billion in liabilities. However, Microsoft notes that adverse outcomes that "we could estimate" could result in an additional $800 million of liabilities. To the extent that external auditors are involved in this litigation, issues related to these actions would be included in attorney letters.

Source: Microsoft 2010 10-K, July 30, 2010.

✅ REVIEW CHECKPOINTS

11.6   What are the responsibilities of (a) client management, (b) auditors, and (c) the client's attorneys with respect to obtaining evidence regarding litigation, claims, and assessments?

11.7   What is the typical content of attorney letters?

11.8   In addition to obtaining responses to attorney letters, what other procedures can be used to gather audit evidence regarding litigation, claims, and assessments?

LO 11-3

Explain why auditors obtain written representations, and identify the key components of written representations.

Written Representations

Under section 302 of the Sarbanes–Oxley Act of 2002, all 10-Q and 10-K filings with the SEC are required to include certifications from the chief executive officer and chief financial officer related to the fairness of the financial statements and effectiveness of the internal control over financial reporting. However, these are only some representations that the client makes. As noted in previous chapters, an important source of audit evidence is inquiries of client personnel. Many of the responses to these inquiries are very important. To the extent that additional evidence is obtainable through other procedures, auditors should corroborate these representations.

Professional standards require that auditors obtain **written representations** (also known as *management representations* or *client representations*) to confirm certain matters and support other evidence obtained during the audit. The representations take the form of a letter on the client's letterhead addressed to auditors and signed by responsible officers of the client (normally the chief executive officer [CEO], chief financial officer [CFO], and other appropriate officers). These representations are dated as of the date of the auditor's reports, which is when the audit is completed (in fact, the completion of the audit depends on auditors' receipt of assertions from management regarding its responsibility for the fairness of the financial statements and related disclosures through written representations). Thus, written representations cover events and representations running beyond the date of the financial statements up to this date.

It is important to note that written representations are not substitutes for corroborating evidence obtained by applying other substantive procedures. That is, auditors cannot substitute client inquiry (and representations regarding that inquiry) for substantive procedures. For example, the representation that "management told us that the inventory costing method was FIFO and adequate allowance for obsolescence was provided" is not a good excuse for failing to obtain the evidence from the records and other sources.

However, in some cases, written representations are the only available evidence about important matters of management intent. For example, the following representations (written by the client's management) provide auditors important audit evidence regarding presentation and disclosure matters:

- "We will discontinue the parachute manufacturing business, wind down the operations, and sell the remaining assets" (classification of the parachute manufacturing business as a discontinued operation).
- "We will exercise our option to refinance the maturing debt on a long-term basis" (classification of the maturing debt as long-term debt).

Exhibit 11.3 is a sample of written representations in the form of a letter from the client to auditors. As noted earlier, it is written by the client (specifically, key officers) to auditors and is dated March 2, 2018 (the date of the auditor's report). Notice from Exhibit 11.3 that the representations are organized into three sections that discuss:

1. The entity's financial statements, including:

   - Management's responsibilities for the financial statements and internal control over financial reporting.
   - The appropriate disclosure, presentation, and reasonableness of certain items (accounting estimates, related parties, subsequent events, and litigation and claims).
   - A statement that uncorrected misstatements are immaterial to the financial statements taken as a whole.

2. Information provided to the auditors, both in general and related to sensitive areas (fraud, noncompliance with laws and regulations, litigation, and related-party transactions).

3. Internal control over financial reporting (for audits of public entities).

Although representations should be limited to matters that are material, professional standards note that materiality guidelines do not apply for representations not related to amounts included in the financial statements (such as management's responsibility for the financial statements) or for management's acknowledgement regarding its responsibility for designing, implementing, and maintaining internal control to prevent and detect fraud.

Clearly, written representations provide an important part of auditors' overall ability to support the opinion on the financial statements. As a result, management's refusal to furnish representations constitutes a scope limitation, which requires a qualification in the auditor's report on the entity's financial statements or a disclaimer of opinion. Auditors should be very skeptical of any situation in which the client's management refuses to furnish representations.

In addition to those discussed, auditors may obtain representations related to specific transactions or activities, particularly if they have a material effect on the companies'

 AUDITING INSIGHT   Can You Trust Written Representations?

Gemstar-TV Guide International Inc., a media, entertainment, and technology company headquartered in Los Angeles, California, engaged in a massive scheme to inflate its revenue; the most significant fraudulent transaction was $100 million in revenue from an expired contract with **Scientific-Atlanta Inc.** Gemstar's auditor (KPMG) raised specific questions about the Scientific-Atlanta transaction and received written assurance from Henry Yuen (then CEO of Gemstar) and Elsie Leung (then CFO) that the revenue from Scientific-Atlanta was legitimate and would be received. Brian Palbaum, the KPMG partner involved with this audit, indicates that Yuen and Leung "may have misled [him] about the status of the settlement negotiations with Scientific-Atlanta."

Source: "As Fraud Case Unravels, Executive Is at Large," *The Wall Street Journal,* April 25, 2007, pp. A1, A9.

EXHIBIT 11.3

Sample Written Representations

DUNDER-MIFFLIN INC.
1725 Slough Avenue
Scranton, PA 18501

[Callout: Representations addressed to auditors]

March 2, 2018

To: Michael Scarn, LLP

   This representation letter is provided in connection with your audit of the financial statements of Dunder-Mifflin Inc., which comprise the balance sheet as of December 31, 2017, and the related statements of income, changes in stockholders' equity and cash flows for the year then ended, and the related notes to the financial statements, for the purpose of expressing an opinion as to whether the financial statements are presented fairly, in all material respects, in accordance with accounting principles generally accepted in the United States (U.S. GAAP).

   Certain representations in this letter are described as being limited to matters that are material. Items are considered material, regardless of size, if they involve an omission or misstatement of accounting information that, in the light of surrounding circumstances, makes it probable that the judgment of a reasonable person relying on the information would be changed or influenced by the omission or misstatement.

   Except where otherwise stated below, immaterial matters are not considered to be exceptions that require disclosure for the purpose of the following representations. This amount is not necessarily indicative of amounts that would require adjustment to or disclosure in the financial statements.

   We confirm that, to the best of our knowledge and belief, having made such inquiries as we considered necessary for the purpose of appropriately informing ourselves as of March 2, 2018:

Financial Statements

- We have fulfilled our responsibilities, as set out in the terms of the audit engagement dated March 1, 2017, for the preparation and fair presentation of the financial statements in accordance with U.S. GAAP.
- We acknowledge our responsibility for the design, implementation, and maintenance of internal control relevant to the preparation and fair presentation of financial statements that are free from material misstatement, whether due to fraud or error.
- We acknowledge our responsibility for the design, implementation, and maintenance of internal control to prevent and detect fraud.

Detail omitted; see AU-C 580.A36

[Callout: Representations related to financial statements and disclosures]

Information Provided

- We have provided you with:
  — Access to all information, of which we are aware that is relevant to the preparation and fair presentation of the financial statements such as records, documentation and other matters;
  — Additional information that you have requested from us for the purpose of the audit; and
  — Unrestricted access to persons within the entity from whom you determined it necessary to obtain audit evidence.
- All transactions have been recorded in the accounting records and are reflected in the financial statements.
- We have disclosed to you the results of our assessment of the risk that the financial statements may be materially misstated as a result of fraud.

Detail omitted; see AU-C 580.A36

Internal Control over Financial Reporting [for audits of public entities under *AS 2201*]:

- We have performed an assessment of the effectiveness of internal control over financial reporting based on criteria established in Internal Control — Integrated Framework issued by the Committee on Sponsoring Organizations of the Treadway Commission (COSO criteria).
- Based on this assessment, we conclude that we have maintained an effective internal control over financial reporting as of December 31, 2017.
- We have disclosed to you all deficiencies in the design or operation of internal control over financial reporting, including separate disclosure of any deficiencies that we believe to be significant deficiencies or material weaknesses.
- There are no subsequent changes in internal control over financial reporting or other factors that may significantly affect internal control over financial reporting.

[Callout: Representations related to internal control over financial reporting]

Signed:

Cosmo Kramer
Cosmo Kramer, Chief Executive Officer

Newman Post
Newman Post, Chief Financial Officer

[Callout: Representations provided and signed by management]

Source: AU-C 580.A36.

financial statements. See the accompanying Auditing Insight for an example of such a representation (although in this case, some questions as to the validity of the representation were raised).

⊘ REVIEW CHECKPOINTS

11.9 What are the major categories of information contained in written representations?

11.10 If the entity is subject to PCAOB requirements regarding communication about control deficiencies *(AS 1305)*, what written representations should auditors obtain from the client with respect to internal control over financial reporting?

11.11 Why are written representation and attorney letters obtained near the end of the evidence-gathering process and dated on the date of the auditor's report?

11.12 How should auditors respond if the client refuses to furnish written representations?

LO 11-4

Identify the final steps in the completion of an audit.

Ability to Continue as a Going Concern

As auditors gather evidence throughout the engagement, they may encounter information that raises questions as to the client's ability to continue as a going concern, such as

- Negative trends, including recurring operating losses, working capital deficiencies, and negative cash flow from operations.
- Indications of financial difficulties, including default on loans, denial of trade credit from suppliers, restructuring of debts, or arrearages in dividends.
- Internal matters, including work stoppages or substantial dependence on the success of a particular project or activity.
- External matters, including legal proceedings; loss of a key franchise, license, or patent; or loss of a major customer or supplier.

Auditors are not expected to design and perform procedures solely for the purpose of identifying conditions that indicate going-concern uncertainties. However, procedures performed during the normal course of the audit might reveal such situations. For example, performing analytical procedures may reveal deteriorating profitability and cash flows, which may indicate the client's inability to continue as a going concern. Also, communications received from client attorneys (discussed earlier in this chapter) might reveal litigation that could significantly threaten the client's ability to continue to exist.

Auditors are required to consider whether any evidence that comes to their attention during the examination provides "substantial doubt" about the client's ability to continue as a going concern for a period of time not to exceed one year beyond the date of the financial statements being audited. Once again, auditors are not required to perform additional procedures during the completion stages designed to assess going-concern status. However, they are required to consider evidence obtained and accumulated throughout the audit and make an overall evaluation as to whether substantial doubt exists with respect to the ability of the client to continue as a going concern.

If the auditors' evaluation suggests going-concern uncertainties, auditors should obtain information about management's plans to mitigate the effect of these factors and assess the likelihood that these plans can be effectively implemented. For example, clients may have the ability to delay or reduce expenditures, restructure existing debt on more favorable terms, or access additional sources of financing. If so, and these actions would allow the client to continue in operations, auditors may conclude that the likelihood of going-concern uncertainties is low. In this instance, auditors would likely conclude that substantial doubt about going concern *does not* exist and no further financial statement disclosures or audit report modifications would be necessary.

In contrast, if after this evaluation, auditors still believe that substantial doubt exists about the client's ability to continue as a going concern, they should ensure that appropriate disclosures related to going concern are provided in the financial statements and modify their opinion on the client's financial statements. Depending upon the severity of the going-concern uncertainty, an unmodified opinion, qualified opinion, or disclaimer of opinion may be issued; the specific report modifications for going-concern uncertainties are discussed in Chapter 12.

In all cases, audit documentation should include information related to the (1) conditions or events that suggested going-concern uncertainties, (2) management's plans to mitigate going-concern uncertainties and the audit procedures performed to evaluate management's plans, and (3) the auditors' conclusion as to whether substantial doubt exists about the client's ability to continue as a going concern and whether the audit report needs to be modified to reflect that substantial doubt.

AUDITING INSIGHT   Going Concerns at Borders

In early 2011, **Borders Group Inc.** (the second-largest bookstore chain in the United States at the time) announced it was seeking to delay payments to some of its publishers as part of efforts to refinance its debt. Borders indicated that "there can be no assurance" that their refinancing efforts would be successful and, if they were not, they could experience a liquidity shortfall in the first quarter of 2011. Borders had also experienced net losses in 9 of the preceding 11 quarters. Both issues suggested potential going-concern uncertainties. On April 13, 2011, Borders notified the SEC that, because of these financial difficulties, it would delay filing its 2010 financial statements; these statements were ultimately filed on April 29, 2011, and Borders' auditor (EY) modified its opinion to acknowledge Borders' going-concern uncertainties. On July 19, 2011, Borders announced that it would liquidate and close its remaining 399 stores.

Sources: "Borders Delays Payments to Publishers," *The Wall Street Journal,* December 31, 2010, p. B1; "Borders to Ask Publishers to Agree to Longer IOUs," *The Wall Street Journal,* January 5, 2011, p. B1; "Borders Forced to Liquidate, Close All Stores," *The Wall Street Journal,* July 19, 2011, p. B1.

✅ REVIEW CHECKPOINTS

11.13 What responsibility do auditors have for evaluating a client's ability to continue as a going concern?

11.14 What factors may indicate that substantial doubt exists about the client's ability to continue as a going concern?

11.15 What actions should auditors take if evidence suggests that substantial doubt exists about the client's ability to continue as a going concern?

Adjusting Entries and Financial Statement Disclosure

The financial statements, including the accompanying footnotes, are the responsibility of the client's management. Thus, although auditors could detect some misstatements in the financial statements during the examination, it is the client's responsibility to adjust the financial statements. Even when the failure to adjust the financial statements would result in materially misstated financial statements, it is the client's decision as to whether to accept auditors' proposed adjustments.

Exhibit 11.4 is a summary worksheet ("score sheet") showing the effect of proposed adjusting journal entries. In this example, three potential adjustments were noted during the audit: (1) recording payments on account to vendors made prior to year-end, (2) reversing sales entries that were incorrectly recorded in the current year, and (3) recording items discovered during the auditors' search for unrecorded liabilities. In addition, a fourth adjustment reflects the income tax effects of these adjustments (if recorded by the client). These adjustments are considered to be *proposed* to indicate the responsibility of management for the financial statements. This summary indicates how the proposed adjustments would affect the financial statements and helps auditors decide which adjustments must be made to support an unmodified opinion on the financial statements and which adjustments may be waived (or not corrected). An **uncorrected misstatement** is a misstatement that the auditors have identified and accumulated during the audit that the client has not corrected (or adjusted), often because of materiality or cost/benefit considerations. Prior to the issuance of Sarbanes–Oxley, evidence suggests that a large number of misstatements were not corrected.[5]

As shown in Exhibit 11.4, the misstatements have a current-year $7,410 debit (decrease) effect on net income and a $7,410 credit (decrease) effect on net assets. In addition, note that $18,000 of uncorrected misstatements was identified in previous audits. If performance materiality were established at $100,000, auditors could decide not to require adjustment of these misstatements because doing so would not result in materially misstated financial statements. However, *Staff Accounting Bulletin No. 99* notes that auditors and clients should not simply decline to adjust "apparently" immaterial misstatements without giving consideration to a number of other factors (such as the effect of adjusting the misstatement on debt covenants).

An important issue with respect to the auditors' adjustment recommendation is whether a number of uncorrected misstatements in previous years will accumulate over time to have a material effect on an entity's financial statements in a future year. For example, if performance materiality is $100,000 and an entity fails to accrue a $25,000 liability for unused sick pay (which will not be paid until employees retire) each year for four years, this matter will not have a material effect on the income statement in any individual year. However, assuming this obligation has not been paid, at least in part, by the end of year 4, the cumulative effect on the entity's balance sheet would become material ($100,000).

Auditors may use either of two methods to evaluate the materiality of uncorrected misstatements. The **rollover method** considers only the current-period income effect(s); when using the rollover method as in the example shown in Exhibit 11.4, auditors would consider the misstatement to be $7,410. In contrast, the **iron curtain method** considers the aggregate effect of the misstatements on the entity's balance sheet; when using the iron curtain method, auditors would consider the misstatement to be $25,410 (the $7,410 of current-year adjustments and the $18,000 of uncorrected prior-year adjustments). In September 2006, the Securities and Exchange Commission issued *Staff Accounting Bulletin No. 108,* which requires auditors to evaluate misstatements using both methods and propose an adjustment if either method indicates that the misstatement is material. Because neither the amount of the current-year uncorrected misstatement in Exhibit 11.4 ($7,410) nor the cumulative effect of uncorrected misstatements ($25,410) exceeds performance materiality of $100,000, the auditors would conclude that the financial statements are not materially misstated (see conclusion in Exhibit 11.4). Although auditors could recommend the client adjust its financial statements for all known adjustments, no adjustment is required in this situation.

Auditors are required to communicate all misstatements detected during the audit to the client's audit committee (or other individuals charged with governance). These should be communicated regardless of whether they have a material effect on the financial statements. A report issued by the PCAOB noted that a common deficiency observed by inspection teams was the failure of audit teams to accumulate all uncorrected misstatements and communicate these to the audit committee.[6] Auditors' identification

[5]For example, an academic study of audits performed by Deloitte & Touche (then Deloitte, Haskins & Sells) reported that 75 percent of all detected errors were not corrected; see C. Houghton and J. Fogarty, "Inherent Risk," *Auditing: A Journal of Practice & Theory,* Spring 1991, pp. 1–21. A similar study of audits conducted by an unnamed international public accounting firm found a corresponding rate of 65 percent; see A. Wright and S. Wright, "An Examination of Factors Affecting the Decision to Waive Audit Adjustments," *Journal of Accounting, Auditing, & Finance,* Winter 1997, pp. 15–36. However, J. Joe et al. concluded that the additional scrutiny faced by auditors from the Sarbanes–Oxley Act may, in part, account for a much lower percentage of uncorrected misstatements in their study (24.2 percent); see "The Impact of Client and Misstatement Characteristics on the Disposition of Proposed Audit Adjustments," *Auditing: A Journal of Practice and Theory,* May 2011, pp. 103–124.

[6]*Report on the PCAOB's 2004, 2005, 2006, and 2007 Inspections of Domestic Annually Inspected Firms,* PCAOB Release No. 2008-008, December 5, 2008.

EXHIBIT 11.4

Proposed Adjusting Journal Entries (Score Sheet)

	Income Statement	Balance Sheet		
	Increase (Decrease) Net Income	Increase (Decrease) Assets	Increase (Decrease) Liabilities	Increase (Decrease) Equity
(1) Unrecorded cash disbursements				
Accounts payable			($42,000)	
Cash		($42,000)		
(2) Improper sales cutoff				
Sales	($13,000)			($13,000)
Inventory		7,800		
Cost of goods sold	7,800			7,800
Accounts receivable		(13,000)		
(3) Unrecorded liabilities				
Utilities expense	(700)			(700)
Commissions expense	(3,000)			(3,000)
Wage expense	(2,500)			(2,500)
Accounts payable			700	
Accrued expenses payable			5,500	
Net effect before taxes	($11,400)	($47,200)	($35,800)	($11,400)
(4) Reduction in income taxes ($11,400 X 0.35)				
Income tax expense	3,990			3,990
Income taxes payable			(3,990)	
Current-year effects	($7,410)	($47,200)	($39,790)	($7,410)
Uncorrected misstatements from prior audits	($18,000)			($18,000)
Cumulative effect of uncorrected misstatements	($25,410)			($25,410)

Conclusion: Uncorrected misstatements from previous audits had a net debit effect of $18,000 on the income statement (decrease in net income) and a net credit effect on the balance sheet (decrease in net assets, or equity). When considered with the $7,410 effect noted in the current year, the cumulative uncorrected misstatements ($25,410) are less than performance materiality ($100,000). As a result, no adjustment to the financial statements is considered necessary.

of material misstatements is normally considered to be a "strong indicator" of a material weakness in internal control over financial reporting even if these misstatements are ultimately adjusted by the client.

AUDITING INSIGHT   Auditors and Restatements

XEROX

In 2003, the Securities and Exchange Commission filed suit against KPMG for civil fraud and accused the firm of "knowingly and recklessly" misleading investors on its audits of **Xerox.** However, when it came to adjustments, KPMG's main partner on the Xerox audit (Ronald Safan) was

extremely stringent. Safan insisted that virtually every audit adjustment be recorded, including immaterial amounts that were not required for the financial statements to be prepared in conformity with generally accepted accounting principles. In fact, during 2001, Xerox had to delay filing its annual report due to a disagreement with KPMG over accounting issues.

Epilogue: On April 11, 2002, Xerox agreed to a $10 million fine with the SEC and restated its financial statements from 1997 to 2001; on April 21, 2005, KPMG agreed to pay $22.5 million to the SEC to settle charges related to its audits of Xerox. On March 28, 2008, Xerox agreed to pay $670 million and KPMG $80 million to settle shareholder lawsuits.

Sources: "KPMG's Auditing with Xerox Tests Toughness of SEC," *The Wall Street Journal,* May 6, 2002, p. A10; "Xerox: New Lease on Life," *CFO.com,* October 24, 2003; "KPMG Settles Xerox Charges with SEC," *CFO.com,* April 21, 2005; "Xerox to Pay $670 Million to Settle Securities Suit," *The Wall Street Journal,* March 28, 2008, p. B3.

ACADEMIC INSIGHTS

A significant amount of academic research has evaluated the process through which auditors and clients "negotiate" with respect to adjustments identified during the audit examination. These studies demonstrate that this process is prevalent; Gibbins et al. (2001) found that 67 percent of audit partners entered into some level of negotiation with more than one-half of their clients and that all partners have negotiated with at least one client. Some interesting conclusions in these studies include:

- While approximately one-third of surveyed chief financial officers (CFOs) and audit partners indicated they "won" the negotiation (34 percent for CFOs and 32 percent for auditors), both groups indicated that negotiations resulted in a compromise (26 percent

for CFOs and 41 percent for auditors) or a new solution generated during the negotiation (17 percent for CFOs and 16 percent for auditors) (Gibbins et al., 2005). (Each group was asked to recall an auditor–client negotiation and was not necessarily considering the same negotiation.)

- Factors considered as important by CFOs in the outcome of the negotiation include accounting and disclosure standards, the prior relationship with the audit partner, the organization's (client's) accounting expertise, and the audit firm's accounting expertise; auditors primarily considered accounting and disclosure standards and the audit firm's accounting expertise as important in influencing the outcome of the negotiation (Gibbins et al., 2005).

- The (income-decreasing) adjustments proposed by auditors are smaller in cases in which the magnitude of the audit difference is higher and when the client has previously conceded with respect to an audit issue (Hatfield et al., 2010).

Sources: M. Gibbins, S. Salterio, and A. Webb, "Evidence about Auditor-Client Management Negotiation Concerning Client's Financial Reporting," *Journal of Accounting Research,* December 2001, pp. 535–563; M. Gibbins, S. McCracken, and S. Salterio, "Negotiations over Accounting Issues: The Congruency of Audit Partner and Chief Financial Officer Recalls," *Auditing: A Journal of Practice & Theory,* Supplement 2005, pp. 171–193; R.C. Hatfield, R.W. Houston, C.M. Stefaniak, and S. Usrey, "The Effect of Magnitude of Audit Differences and Prior Client Concessions on Negotiations of Proposed Adjustments," *The Accounting Review,* September 2010, pp. 1647–1668.

☑ REVIEW CHECKPOINTS

11.16 Why are adjusting entries and note disclosures labeled "proposed"?

11.17 What is an uncorrected misstatement? What is the auditors' responsibility for communicating misstatements detected during the audit?

11.18 Identify the two methods of evaluating the performance materiality of uncorrected misstatements. What are the requirements of *Staff Accounting Bulletin No. 108* for evaluating the performance materiality of these misstatements?

Audit Documentation Review

During fieldwork, the audit supervisor—and sometimes the audit manager—reviews the audit documentation soon after the audit staff complete it. The general purpose of this review is to ensure that all appropriate steps in the audit plan were performed, the referencing among audit documentation is clear, and the explanations contained in the audit documentation are understandable. In general, the supervisor is attempting to determine that the work was performed with due care and that, if necessary, the work can be reperformed or verified by another party. A common outcome of this review is a set of "review notes" prepared by the audit supervisor that are to be completed or addressed by the audit staff; these notes address the procedures performed, the referencing among audit documentation, and the appropriateness of the audit staff member's conclusions based upon the procedures performed. This review process provides evidence of compliance with the performance principle, which requires proper planning and supervision.

When this initial review has been completed, the audit manager and audit partner review the audit documentation. This review focuses more on the overall scope of the audit and whether the overall conclusions in the audit documentation are sufficient to provide support for the opinion on the financial statements.

Current GAAS requires the audit documentation to be reviewed by an additional person (normally, a partner or equivalent with the firm) who has not been involved with the audit (known as an *engagement quality reviewer*). This review focuses on the significant judgments made by the engagement team and the conclusions reached by the engagement team in preparing the auditor's report. AS 1220 notes that this **engagement quality review** (formally known as a *second-partner review* or *concurring-partner review*) is undertaken to ensure that the quality of audit work and reporting is in keeping with the public accounting firm's quality standards. In addition, the engagement quality review provides a very-high-level review of whether the evidence obtained during the audit is sufficient to support the opinion on the client's financial statements. The use of electronic audit documentation and the accompanying search capabilities has enhanced the efficiency and effectiveness of audit documentation review. Audit documentation review provides a number of benefits to the firm, including these:

- Because audit documentation is the primary evidence of the audit procedures performed and conclusions reached by auditors, the review ensures that the audit is conducted in accordance with GAAS.
- Audit documentation review provides the firm an opportunity to evaluate the overall quality of the firm's audit practices as a method of quality control.
- Audit documentation review often serves as an important component of the training and evaluation of audit staff members.
- Audit documentation review allows the firm to adhere to the performance principle, which requires that auditors adequately plan the work and properly supervise any assistants.

☑ REVIEW CHECKPOINTS

11.19 Describe the audit documentation review process in a public accounting firm.

11.20 What is an engagement quality review?

11.21 What are some of the benefits of audit documentation review to a public accounting firm?

SUBSEQUENT EVENTS AND SUBSEQUENTLY DISCOVERED FACTS

LO 11-5

Understand auditors' responsibility for subsequent events and subsequently discovered facts.

What is the auditors' responsibility for events occurring after the date of the financial statements but before the audit report is released? In early 2008, after the company's fiscal-year end, real estate investments held by **UBS** (a global financial services firm) declined in value by 19 billion Swiss francs (US $16 billion). On one hand, because this decline in value occurred *after* December 31, 2007 (the date of UBS's financial statements), it did not affect the financial position or results of operations as of December 31, 2007. However, it would clearly be misleading for UBS to fail to disclose this decline in market value if it occurred and was known prior to the issuance of its financial statements. As a result, auditors not only should evaluate the fairness of the entity's financial statements based on facts and circumstances that exist as of the date of the financial statements but also should consider the impact of events occurring after the date of the financial statements.

Subsequent Events

Events occurring between the date of the financial statements and the date of the auditor's report are referred to as **subsequent events**. The auditors' primary objective with respect to subsequent events is to ensure that any material events that affect the fairness of the client's financial statements and disclosures are properly identified and disclosed in the client's financial statements. Professional standards (specifically AU-C 560) identifies the following two types of subsequent events; examples of these events from SEC filings are shown in the accompanying Auditing Insight:

- Events that provide additional evidence of conditions that existed *at the date of the financial statements* (for example, the deteriorating financial condition of the client's customer that had a large accounts receivable balance at the date of the financial statements).
- Events that provide evidence of conditions that arose *following the date of the financial statements* (for example, a major acquisition occurring after the date of the financial statements).

 AUDITING INSIGHT The Real World of Subsequent Events

The following are examples of subsequent events disclosed by companies in their footnotes to the financial statements.

- In early 2010, **Citigroup, DuPont, Praxair,** and **Federal Mogul** disclosed the decision by the Venezuelan government to devalue its currency (the bolivar) and the potential financial statement impacts of this devaluation.
- In 2010, **Hewlett-Packard** disclosed that it sold land and buildings, which resulted in a $280 million gain.

- In January 2009, **Kellogg Company** announced a hold on sales of products and recall of a number of products because of potential salmonella contamination; it estimated total costs associated with this recall of $34 million, or $0.06 per share.
- In January 2009, **Pfizer** announced a merger agreement to acquire **Wyeth** for $68 billion.

Sources: Citigroup, DuPont, Praxair, Federal Mogul, Hewlett-Packard, Kellogg, and Pfizer 10-K filings.

Auditors may learn of subsequent events through audit procedures performed in obtaining evidence related to account balances or classes of transactions. For example, the deterioration of a customer's financial condition may be identified through accounts receivable confirmations obtained after the date of the financial statements. Other procedures performed during the completion stage of the audit (such as attorney letters and written representations) may provide auditors information about the existence of subsequent events. Professional standards identify the following procedures that should be specifically performed to identify the existence of material subsequent events:

- Obtain an understanding of procedures management performed to identify material subsequent events.
- Inquire of management and those charged with governance as to the existence of subsequent events. (This inquiry should subsequently be corroborated through written representations.)
- Read minutes of meetings of owners, management, or those charged with governance held after the date of the financial statements.
- Review the entity's latest interim financial statements, if applicable.

When material subsequent events are identified, auditors are required to ensure that the financial statement disclosure of these events reflects all current information and is according to GAAP. This might require adjustment to the financial statements to reflect new information (for conditions existing at the date of the financial statements) or disclosure of the information in the financial statements or footnotes accompanying the financial statements (for conditions that arose after the date of the financial statements).

Subsequently Discovered Facts

In the preceding discussion, we assumed that auditors identified material subsequent events prior to the date of the auditor's report. This assumption is noteworthy because the auditors are still conducting fieldwork and can obtain evidence regarding the appropriate presentation and disclosure of the subsequent events. However, in some situations, auditors learn of events or facts following the date of the auditor's report. The dilemma for auditors in these situations is that the fieldwork is complete and, in some cases, the financial statements and auditor's report may have been issued. Facts that become known to auditors after the date of the auditor's report that, had they been known at that time, may have caused the auditors to revise their report, are known as **subsequently discovered facts**.

The auditors' response to subsequently discovered facts depends on when the facts are identified. In some circumstances, auditors could learn of these facts *after the date of the auditor's report* but *prior to the audit report release date*. The issue this raises for the auditors is that auditing procedures have been performed only through the date of the auditor's report, yet the facts are discovered prior to the release of the financial statements and auditor's report. As a result, the financial statements, or auditor's report, or both could still be revised prior to issuance. If these facts require revision of the financial statements or footnote disclosures, auditors should perform additional procedures and evaluate the appropriateness of the disclosure of these events. One option would be to do so and change the date on the auditor's report to reflect the new (later) date. However, a disadvantage of this approach is that the auditors' responsibility for *all events* is now extended to this later date.

When facts are discovered following the date of the auditor's report but prior to the audit report release date, auditors normally choose to **dual date** the report (that is, to give it two dates). For example, EY completed the fieldwork of its 2001 audit of Hewlett-Packard on November 13, 2001. (Hewlett-Packard had an October 31 year-end.) On December 6, 2001, Hewlett-Packard made an offering of $1 billion of debt, which it disclosed in Note 19 to its financial statements. The date used by EY in its 2001 auditor's report of Hewlett-Packard was as follows:

> November 13, 2001, except for Note 19, as to which the date is December 6, 2001.

As this report dating noted, EY has taken full responsibility for all material subsequent events through November 13, 2001, except for the issuance of debt. EY has responsibility for this event through December 6, 2001.

Dual dating serves two important functions. First, it provides a way to modify the financial statements and disclosures for information discovered by auditors after the date of the auditor's report. This gives financial statement users the most complete and current set of information about the entity. Second, it limits auditors' liability for events after the date of the auditor's report to the event(s) specifically identified in the report date. In some cases (particularly if facts become known immediately before a filing deadline), auditors may choose not to evaluate the effect of subsequently discovered facts on the financial statements. For example, in January 2011, **American International Group (AIG)** disclosed the impact of the recapitalization of AIG through the distribution of 92.2 percent of its outstanding shares of common stock to the **U.S. Department of the Treasury.** This event was disclosed in the footnotes to AIG's financial statements and was marked as "unaudited."

Alternatively, auditors may learn of facts following the issuance of the financial statements and auditor's report. Obviously, this situation presents additional challenges because the financial statements and auditor's report have already been issued to financial statement users. If these facts would result in either the revision of the auditor's report or the financial statements and individuals continuing to rely on these financial statements, the client should take the following actions:

For *Fortune* 100 companies in 2010, the average lag between the date of the financial statements and the date of the auditor's report is 52.8 days and from the date of the auditor's report to the filing of the 10-K with the SEC is 0.44 days. Interestingly, 87.4 percent of the *Fortune* 100 companies file their 10-K with the SEC on the same date as the date of the auditor's report. Clearly, the length of the period between the date of the auditor's report and the audit report release

date is quite short for the largest companies; this same period is 0.38 days for the *Fortune* 500 and 0.34 days for the *Fortune* 1000. (This may be a conservative measure because the auditor's report may be released even earlier than this through inclusion in an 8-K or other filing.)

Source: Drawn from Wharton Research Data Services *Audit Analytics* database.

1. Notify individuals known to be relying on the financial statements or likely to rely on the financial statements that (a) the financial statements should not be relied upon and (b) revised financial statements and a new auditor's report will be issued.
2. Issue revised financial statements as soon as practicable with appropriate disclosure of the matter related to the subsequently discovered facts.

In the event that management refuses to take either of these actions, auditors should notify management, regulatory agencies, or any individuals known to be relying on the financial statements that the auditor's report cannot be relied upon. If auditors determine that the subsequently discovered facts would require revision to the financial statements, the nature of the matter and effect on the financial statements should also be included in the auditor's notification.

The audit timeline and actions for subsequent events and subsequently discovered facts follow:

Year-End Date **(December 31, 2017)**	**Date of the Auditor's Report** **(audit completion date)** **(February 15, 2018)**	**Audit Report Release Date** **(February 17, 2018)**
• Perform procedures related to subsequent events • Adjust financial statements or disclose subsequent events	• Perform procedures related to subsequently discovered facts • Adjust financial statements or disclose subsequently discovered facts • Extend date of the auditor's report or dual date auditor's report on financial statements	• Request client to take action to reduce reliance on financial statements and auditor's report and reissue financial statements • If client refuses to take above actions, notify client, regulatory agencies, and users that auditor's report is not to be relied upon

On August 13, 2007, Dell filed a Form 8-K with the Securities and Exchange Commission indicating that its previously issued financial statements for fiscal 2003, 2004, 2005, and 2006 (including interim financial statements) should no longer be relied upon because of certain accounting errors and irregularities in those financial statements.

Source: *Dell Form 8-K,* August 13, 2007.

In June 2011, EY notified the Securities and Exchange Commission that it was withdrawing its opinion on **Life Partners Holdings Inc.**'s

2010 financial statements because they were "no longer able to rely on management's representations" and are not willing to be associated with Life Holdings' financial statements. This decision was based, in part, on disagreements related to Life Partners' recognition of revenue and the potential need for a restatement of prior results that arose following the audit report release date.

Source: "Auditor Is Exiting from Life Partners," *The Wall Street Journal,* June 9, 2011, p. C3.

REVIEW CHECKPOINTS

11.22 What is a *subsequent event*?

11.23 What procedures do auditors perform to identify subsequent events?

11.24 Identify the two types of subsequent events. How should information about these events be reflected in the financial statements?

11.25 What are *subsequently discovered facts*?

11.26 What are auditors' responsibilities for subsequently discovered facts if these are identified (a) prior to the audit report release date and (b) following the audit report release date?

11.27 What is the purpose of dual dating the auditor's report?

RESPONSIBILITIES FOLLOWING THE AUDIT REPORT RELEASE DATE

LO 11-6

Identify important activities and communications following the completion of the audit and audit report release date.

Omitted Procedures

Although auditors have no responsibility to continue to review their work after the audit report release date, auditor's reports and audit documentation may be subjected to a PCAOB inspection, external peer review, or the firm's own internal inspection program as part of its system of quality control. Section 104 of Sarbanes–Oxley requires inspections to be conducted annually by the PCAOB (if the firm provides services for more than 100 public audit clients) or every three years (if the firm provides services for 100 or fewer public audit clients). These inspections could reveal situations in which an audit was not performed in accordance with generally accepted auditing standards. In particular, auditors could have failed to perform necessary audit procedures prior to the audit report release date. This situation is referred to as **omitted procedures**.

Professional standards provide guidance for such situations. If (1) the omitted procedures are important in supporting the auditor's opinion and (2) individuals are currently relying on the client's financial statements (and auditor's reports), auditor's should perform the omitted procedure or alternative procedure(s), if practicable. Assuming that the procedures allow auditors to support the previously expressed opinion, no further action is necessary. However, if they do not, auditors should formally withdraw the original report, issue revised reports, and inform persons currently relying on the financial statements. This course of action is illustrated in actions by PwC (or an affiliate firm's actions) in its audits of **OAO Yukos** and **Satyam Computer Services** included in the accompanying Auditing Insight.

 AUDITING INSIGHT   Discovering Facts . . . 10 Years Later

In 2007, a Russian unit of PwC withdrew its audits and reports from 1995–2004 for oil company OAO Yukos, indicating that Yukos's management may have provided inaccurate information to the engagement team. PwC indicated that its decision to formally withdraw the reports "was influenced by the fact that some former shareholders and management of Yukos are continuing to encourage others to rely on PwC's audit reports."

In 2009, following the revelation of a $1 billion accounting scandal at India's Satyam Computer Services, Price Waterhouse India (an affiliate of PwC's international network) notified the company's board that, while the firm followed appropriate audit procedures, its reports from 2000 through 2008 could no longer be relied upon.

Sources: "PwC Withdraws a Decade of Yukos Audits," *The Wall Street Journal*, June 25, 2007, p. A3; "Satyam Overlooked Oversight," *CFO.com*, January 20, 2009.

Communications with Individuals Charged with Governance

During the engagement, matters can arise that are of such importance that they must be communicated with "individuals charged with governance." **Individuals charged with governance** are the person(s) responsible for overseeing the client's financial reporting process, including the internal control over financial reporting. Although this phrase can include the client's management and full board of directors, for public entities it is typically the audit committee of the board of directors. Audit committees are required for registrants under Sarbanes–Oxley and must be composed of only independent directors. Audit committees are an important element in the governance process because they are directly responsible for the appointment, compensation, and oversight of auditors and the audit examination.

Sections 204 and 404 of Sarbanes–Oxley both address required communications between auditors and the client's audit committee. Professional standards require auditors to communicate (*in writing*) *all* significant internal control deficiencies and material weaknesses to the client and individuals charged with governance. For public entities, the communication must be made prior to the audit report release date. For nonpublic entities, it is preferable to provide this communication prior to the audit report release date, but it should be made no later than 60 days following the audit report release date. Although auditors may decide to communicate significant deficiencies and material weaknesses to the client as they are discovered during the audit, if the client has not corrected (or remediated) these deficiencies or weaknesses, they must be communicated again in writing near the end of the audit.

For nonpublic entities, auditors' communication would acknowledge that the purpose of the audit is to express an opinion on the financial statements, not on internal control over financial reporting; furthermore, the communication would explicitly state that auditors are not expressing an opinion on internal control over financial reporting. For public entities subject to the reporting requirements of Sarbanes–Oxley, this communication would parallel the form and content of the auditor's report on internal control over financial reporting, which expresses an opinion on internal control over financial reporting.

In addition to internal control deficiencies, professional standards require auditors to communicate various other matters to the client. As with internal control communications, auditors ordinarily make these communications with individuals charged with governance after the audit; however, if the matters are particularly significant, they should be communicated during the audit. These communications may be made either orally or in writing (however, because of the important nature of these matters, one would anticipate that they be made in writing).

Auditors should communicate the following information to individuals charged with governance:

- Auditors' responsibility under generally accepted auditing standards.
- An overview of the planned scope and timing of the audit.
- Auditors' judgment about the quality of the client's critical accounting policies, accounting estimates, and financial statement disclosures.
- Any significant difficulties encountered during the audit.
- Any uncorrected misstatements identified during the audit other than those auditors believe to be trivial and a request to correct the misstatements.
- Any disagreements with management.
- Material, corrected misstatements that were brought to the attention of management.
- Representations requested from the client's management.
- Any management consultations with other auditors or any contentious matters about which the auditor consulted outside the engagement team that may be relevant to the oversight of the financial reporting process.
- Any significant issues arising from the audit that were discussed with management.
- The auditor's understanding of the business rationale for significant unusual transactions.
- Other findings or issues that are significant and relevant to individuals charged with governance.

Auditors also should determine that individuals charged with governance have received copies of written communications regarding material issues between auditors and management such as engagement letters, written representations, and reports on deficiencies in internal control over financial reporting. Because of its important role, auditors communicate frequently with the audit committee throughout the engagement. However, as the accompanying Auditing Insight reveals, such communication does not ensure that all relevant issues will be handled appropriately.

AUDITING INSIGHT   Meetings with Audit Committees?

Based on interviews with auditors, an academic study by Cohen et al. provided the following insights into auditors' meetings with client audit committees:

- The frequency of meetings has increased from two to three times per year prior to Sarbanes–Oxley to more than six times per year.
- The most frequent issues discussed in audit committee meetings relate to accounting/auditing issues encountered in the engage-

ment, the audit plan, the results of the audit, and other mandated disclosures (discussed in this section).

- A relatively small percentage of auditors (52 percent) indicated that audit committees played an important role in resolving auditor disputes with management.

Source: J. Cohen, G. Krishnamoorthy, and A. Wright, "Corporate Governance in the Post-Sarbanes–Oxley Era: Auditors' Experiences," *Contemporary Accounting Research*, (Fall 2010), pp. 751–786.

Management Letter

During the engagement (particularly the study and evaluation of the client's internal control, assessment of the risk of material misstatement, and evaluation of the effectiveness of internal control over financial reporting), auditors note matters that can be made as recommendations to the client. These recommendations may allow the client to improve the efficiency and effectiveness of their operations. Near the end of the audit, these matters are summarized in a letter (commonly referred to as the **management letter**) that is delivered to and discussed with the client. Management letters are not required by generally accepted auditing standards but are considered an important method of adding value to clients beyond that provided by the audit examination. In this spirit, some firms encourage consulting and tax professionals to participate in preparing the management letter.

Management letters are a service provided as a by-product of the audit. The management letter is an excellent opportunity to develop rapport with the client and to make the client aware of other business services offered by the public accounting firm.

Summary of Audit Communications

This text has mentioned many types of formal communications. Because you are learning the final procedures to complete the audit, this is a good place to summarize these various communications. See Exhibit 11.5 for a summary of audit correspondence other than auditor's reports on the financial statements (discussed in Chapter 12) and internal control over financial reporting (discussed in Chapter 5).

✓ REVIEW CHECKPOINTS

11.28 What steps should auditors take if, after the audit report release date, they discover that an important audit procedure was omitted?

11.29 Identify information that auditors are required to communicate to individuals charged with governance of the client.

11.30 What is a *management letter*? Are management letters required by generally accepted auditing standards?

EXHIBIT 11.5   **Audit Communications**

Type	From	To	Timing	Reference	Method
Engagement letter	Auditors	Client	Before engagement	AU-C 210; AS 1301	Written
Acceptance letter (signed copy of engagement letter)	Client	Auditors	Before engagement	AU-C 210; AS 1301	Written
Attorney letter response	Attorney	Auditors	Near date of the auditor's reports	AU-C 501; AS 2505	Written
Written representations	Client	Auditors	Date of the auditor's reports (audit completion date)	AU-C 580; AS 2805	Written
Internal control deficiencies	Auditors	Individuals charged with governance (audit committee)	Prior to audit report release date (for public entities) or within 60 days of audit report release date (for large nonpublic entities)	AU-C 265; AS 1305	Written
Communications with individuals charged with governance	Auditors	Individuals charged with governance (audit committee)	After audit	AU-C 260; AS 1301	Oral or written
Management letter	Auditors	Client	After audit	None	Oral or written

Summary

This chapter began by identifying four major periods during an audit: (1) prior to the date of the financial statements, (2) between the date of the financial statements and the date of the auditor's report, (3) between the date of the auditor's report and the audit report release date, and (4) following the audit report release date. As various matters are discussed, it is important to determine the time period in which auditors identify issues because this will affect auditors' responsibility for these matters.

Within the context of the four periods, the chapter discussed several aspects of completing an audit. These events include (1) completing substantive procedures, (2) obtaining responses to attorney letters, (3) obtaining written representations, (4) evaluating the entity's ability to continue as a going concern, (5) summarizing proposed adjustments to the financial statements, (6) reviewing audit documentation, (7) considering the effects of subsequent events and subsequently discovered facts, (8) evaluating omitted audit procedures identified following the audit examination, and (9) providing communications near the end of the audit. The purpose of these procedures is to enable auditors to issue and support opinions on financial statements and internal control over financial reporting.

Key Terms

analytical procedures: Procedures that allow auditors to evaluate financial information by studying relationships among both financial and nonfinancial data. When used near the end of the audit, analytical procedures allow auditors to assess the conclusions reached during the audit and evaluate the overall financial statement presentation.

attorney letter: A communication prepared by the client but sent by the auditors to the client's attorneys that details all pending litigation, claims, and assessments against the client and that requests the attorneys to comment on these matters directly to the client's auditors.

audit report release date: The date on which auditors allow the client to use their reports in conjunction with the financial statements; also the date on which the client's financial statements are issued.

contingency: An existing condition, situation, or set of circumstances involving uncertainty as to possible gain or loss to an enterprise that will ultimately be resolved when one or more future events occur or fail to occur.

date of the auditor's report: The date on which auditors have gathered sufficient appropriate evidence on which to base their opinions on the financial statements and internal control over financial reporting; the date that will be used for auditors' reports on the client's financial statements and internal control over financial reporting.

date of the financial statements: The year-end date of the latest period covered by the client's financial statements.

dual date: The use of two dates in the auditor's report to limit the responsibility beyond the date of the auditor's report to a specific subsequent event identified in the report.

engagement quality review: A review of audit documentation by an additional person (normally, a partner or equivalent with the firm who has not been involved with the audit) to ensure that the quality of the audit work and reporting is consistent with the quality standards of the public accounting firm.

individual(s) charged with governance: The person(s) responsible for overseeing the client's financial reporting process, including the internal control over financial reporting; individuals charged with governance may include the client's management and full board of directors, but typically refers to public entities' audit committee of the board of directors.

iron curtain method: The process used when evaluating the effect of uncorrected misstatements that considers the aggregate effect of current and prior misstatements in the entity's balance sheet.

management letter: A communication that provides a summary of auditors' recommendations resulting from the audit engagement that allows the client to improve the effectiveness and efficiency of its operations.

omitted procedures: The inadvertent failure of auditors to perform necessary audit procedures prior to the audit report release date.

roll-forward procedure(s): The procedure(s) performed by auditors to extend the conclusions from an interim date to the date of the financial statements.

rollover method: The process used when evaluating the effect of uncorrected misstatements that considers only the current-period income effect(s) of the potential adjustment.

subsequent events: Events occurring between the date of the financial statements and the date of the auditor's report.

subsequently discovered fact: Information that becomes known to auditors after the date of their report that, had it been known at that time, may have caused the auditors to revise their report.

unasserted claim: A representation that no formal lawsuit or assertion has been filed or threatened on behalf of others against the audit client but that circumstances such as a catastrophe, accident, or other physical occurrence could result in a suit or assertion being filed in the future.

uncorrected misstatement: A misstatement that the auditor identified and accumulated during the audit that has not been corrected (or adjusted) by the client.

written representation: A written assertion provided by management to auditors related to the entity's financial statements, the information provided to the auditors, and management's internal control over financial reporting to confirm certain matters and support other evidence obtained during the audit.

Multiple-Choice Questions for Practice and Review
LO 11-1

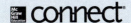 All applicable questions are available with *Connect.*

11.31 Which of the following best describes the role of analytical procedures near the end of the audit engagement?

a. To identify possible deficiencies in the client's internal control over financial reporting.

b. To identify accounts that appear to be misstated with the intention of planning the nature, timing, and extent of other substantive procedures.

c. To gather evidence to support one or more assertion(s) related to the account balance or class of transactions.

d. To provide an overall review of the financial information and assessment of the adequacy of evidence gathered during the audit engagement.

LO 11-3

11.32 A major objective of written representations is to
a. Shift responsibility for financial statements from the management to auditors.
b. Provide a substitute source of audit evidence for substantive procedures that auditors would otherwise perform.
c. Provide management an opportunity to make assertions about the quantity and valuation of the physical inventory.
d. Impress on management its ultimate responsibility for the financial statements and disclosures.

LO 11-2

11.33 Which of these substantive procedures is *not* used to obtain evidence about contingencies?
a. Scanning expense accounts for credit entries.
b. Obtaining a letter from the client's attorney.
c. Reading the minutes of the board of directors' meetings.
d. Examining terms of sale in sales contracts.

LO 11-5

11.34 Subsequent knowledge of which of the following would cause the entity to adjust its December 31 financial statements?
a. Sale of an issue of new stock for $500,000 on January 30.
b. Settlement of a damage lawsuit for a customer's injury sustained February 15 for $10,000.
c. Settlement of litigation in February for $100,000 that had been estimated at $12,000 in the December 31 financial statements.
d. Storm damage of $1 million to the entity's buildings on March 1.

LO 11-5

11.35 A. Griffin audited the financial statements of Dodger Magnificat Corporation for the year ended December 31, 2017. She completed gathering sufficient appropriate evidence on January 30 and later learned of a stock split voted by the board of directors on February 5. The financial statements were changed to reflect the split, and she now needs to dual date the report on the entity's financial statements. Which of the following is the proper form?
a. December 31, 2017, except as to Note X, which is dated January 30, 2018.
b. January 30, 2018, except as to Note X, which is dated February 5, 2018.
c. December 31, 2017, except as to Note X, which is dated February 5, 2018.
d. February 5, 2018, except for the date of the auditor's report, for which the date is January 30, 2018.

LO 11-5

11.36 Auditors have a responsibility related to management's disclosure of new information related to subsequent events until
a. The date of the financial statements.
b. The date of the auditor's report.
c. The audit report release date.
d. The following year's date of the financial statements.

LO 11-5

11.37 The auditing standards regarding subsequently discovered facts refers to knowledge obtained after
a. The date the fieldwork began.
b. The date of the auditor's report.
c. The date of the financial statements.
d. The date interim audit work was complete.

LO 11-6

11.38 Which of the following is *not* required by generally accepted auditing standards?
a. Written representations.
b. Attorney letter.
c. Management letter.
d. Engagement letter.

LO 11-6

11.39 Which of these persons generally does *not* participate in writing the management letter?
a. Client's outside attorneys.
b. Client's accounting and production managers.
c. Public accounting firm's audit team on the engagement.
d. Public accounting firm's consulting and tax experts.

LO 11-1

11.40   Which of the following is ordinarily performed *last* in the audit examination?

a.   Securing a signed engagement letter from the client.

b.   Performing tests of controls.

c.   Performing a review for subsequent events.

d.   Obtaining signed written representations.

LO 11-1

11.41   Which of the following normally occurs *earliest* in the audit examination?

a.   Discovery of an omitted audit procedure.

b.   Dual dating the auditor's report on the entity's financial statements for subsequent events that exist at the date of the financial statements.

c.   Preparation of the management letter.

d.   Review of audit documentation.

LO 11-5

11.42   Ambrose is auditing the financial statements of Mays (dated December 31, 2017). The date of the auditor's report is February 17, 2018, and the audit report release date is February 20, 2018. For which of the following matters would Ambrose have the *least* responsibility?

a.   The obsolescence of inventory held on December 31, 2017, that was identified on January 20, 2018.

b.   A customer's deteriorating financial condition that was identified on February 19, 2018.

c.   A merger that was announced by Mays and known by Ambrose on February 12, 2018.

d.   A major loss due to a catastrophe that occurred and was known by Ambrose on March 1, 2018.

LO 11-2

11.43   Which of the following statements is *most likely* to be included in an attorney letter?

a.   "Certain representations in this letter are described as being limited to matters that are material."

b.   "If any unasserted claims or assessments are omitted from this disclosure, please provide this information directly to our auditors."

c.   "Our work enabled us to notice some actions that could enhance the profitability of the Company."

d.   "Please furnish to our auditors such explanation, if any, that you consider necessary to supplement the foregoing information."

LO 11-6

11.44   After the audit report release date, auditors determine that an important auditing procedure was omitted. Which of the following initial courses of action is most appropriate?

a.   Perform the omitted procedure or an alternative procedure.

b.   Notify the board of directors and regulatory agencies that are currently relying on auditor's reports.

c.   Determine whether the omitted procedure is important in supporting the auditor's opinion on the entity's financial statements.

d.   Engage another public accounting firm to conduct a quality assurance review.

LO 11-3

11.45   Which of the following statements is *not* true with respect to written representations?

a.   The failure of management to furnish them is a significant scope limitation, resulting in either an adverse opinion or a disclaimer of opinion.

b.   They should address management's responsibility for designing internal control to prevent and detect fraud.

c.   Auditors use them to corroborate information received during the audit from the client and its employees.

d.   They are dated the same date as the auditor's reports.

LO 11-3

11.46   Hall accepted an engagement to audit the year 1 financial statements of XYZ Company. XYZ completed the preparation of the year 1 financial statements on February 13, year 2, and its auditors began the fieldwork on February 17, year 2. Hall completed gathering sufficient appropriate evidence on March 24, year 2; Hall's report and XYZ's financial statements were released on March 28, year 2. The written representations normally would be dated

a.   February 13, year 2.

b.   February 17, year 2.

c.   March 24, year 2.

d.   March 28, year 2.

(AICPA adapted)

LO 11-2

11.47 What is an auditor's *primary* method to corroborate information on litigation, claims, and assessments?

    a. Examining legal invoices sent by the client's attorney.

    b. Verifying attorney–client privilege through interviews.

    c. Reviewing the response from the client's lawyer to a letter of audit inquiry.

    d. Reviewing the written representation letter obtained from management.

(AICPA adapted)

LO 11-5

11.48 Which of the following substantive procedures should auditors ordinarily perform regarding subsequent events?

    a. Compare the latest available interim financial statements with the financial statements being audited.

    b. Send second requests to the client's customers who failed to respond to initial accounts receivable confirmation requests.

    c. Communicate material weaknesses in internal control to the client's audit committee.

    d. Review the cutoff bank statements for several months after the date of the financial statements.

(AICPA adapted)

LO 11-5

11.49 Which of the following substantive procedures would auditors most likely perform to obtain evidence about the occurrence of subsequent events?

    a. Recompute a sample of large-dollar transactions occurring after the date of the financial statements for arithmetic accuracy.

    b. Investigate changes in shareholders' equity occurring after the date of the financial statements.

    c. Send confirmations to vendors with whom the client normally does business but for which no balance in accounts payable is noted.

    d. Confirm bank accounts established after the date of the financial statements.

(AICPA adapted)

LO 11-2

11.50 The primary reason auditors request responses to attorney letters is to provide auditors

    a. The probable outcome of asserted claims and pending or threatened litigation.

    b. Corroboration of the information furnished by management about litigation, claims, and assessments.

    c. The attorney's opinions of the client's historical experiences in recent similar litigation.

    d. A description and evaluation of litigation, claims, and assessments that existed at the date of the financial statements.

(AICPA adapted)

LO 11-2

11.51 The scope of an audit is *not* restricted when an attorney letter limits the response to

    a. Matters to which the attorney has given substantive attention in the form of legal representation.

    b. An evaluation of the likelihood of an unfavorable outcome of the matters disclosed by the entity.

    c. The attorney's opinion of the entity's historical experience in recent similar litigation.

    d. The probable outcome of asserted claims and pending or threatened litigation.

(AICPA adapted)

Exercises and Problems

connect All applicable questions are available with *Connect.*

LO 11-3

11.52 **Written Representations.** Hart, an assistant accountant with the firm of Better & Best, CPAs, is auditing the financial statements of Tech Consolidated Industries Inc. The firm's audit plan calls for the preparation of written representations.

Required:

a. In an audit of financial statements, in what circumstances are auditors required to obtain written representations?

b. What are the major categories of items covered by written representations?

c. To whom should the representations be addressed and as of what date should they be dated?

d. Who should sign the representations, and what would be the effect of a refusal to sign them?

e. In what respects may auditors' other responsibilities be relieved by obtaining written representations?

(AICPA adapted)

LO 11-3 11.53 **Written Representations Omissions.** During the audit of the annual financial statements of Amis Manufacturing Inc., the company's president, Vance Molar, and Wanda Dweebins, the engagement partner, reviewed matters that were supposed to be included in written representations. Amis Manufacturing is a private company. Upon receipt of the following representations, Dweebins contacted Molar to state that they were incomplete.

To John & Wayne, CPAs:

In connection with your examination of the balance sheet of Amis Manufacturing Inc., as of December 31, 2017, and the related statements of income, retained earnings, and cash flows for the year then ended, for the purpose of expressing an opinion on whether the financial statements present fairly the financial position, results of operations, and cash flows of Amis Manufacturing Inc., in conformity with generally accepted accounting principles, we confirm, to the best of our knowledge and belief, the following representations made to you during your audit. There were no

- Plans or intentions that could materially affect the carrying value or classification of assets or liabilities.
- Communications from regulatory agencies concerning noncompliance with, or deficiencies in, financial reporting practices.
- Agreements to repurchase assets previously sold.
- Violations or possible violations of laws or regulations whose effects should be considered for disclosure in the financial statements or as a basis for recording a contingent liability.
- Unasserted claims or assessments that our lawyer has advised are probable of assertion that must be disclosed in accordance with *Accounting Standards Codification (ASC) 450.*
- Capital stock purchase options or agreements or capital stock reserved for options, warrants, conversions, or other requirements.
- Compensating balance or other arrangements involving restrictions on cash balances.

Vance Molar, President
Amis Manufacturing Inc.
March 14, 2018

Required:

Identify the other matters that Molar's representations should specifically confirm.

(AICPA adapted)

LO 11-3 11.54 **Written Representations.** Each of the following statements is a communication from management. Indicate whether the inclusion of each statement in written representations is appropriate. Provide your rationale for any statements whose inclusion in written representations is *not* appropriate.

a. "Certain representations in this letter are described as being limited to matters that are material."

b. "No frauds involving management, employees who have significant roles in internal control, or other frauds that could have a material effect on the financial statements have occurred during the year under audit."

c. "Based on our assessment, we conclude that the Company has maintained an effective internal control over financial reporting as of December 31, 2017."

d. "We have prepared a description and evaluation of certain contingencies for which our attorneys have devoted substantive attention on our behalf in the form of legal representation."

e. "There are no significant deficiencies, including material weaknesses, in the design or operation of internal controls that could adversely affect our ability to record, process, summarize, and report financial data."

f. "Summarized below are important actions taken in response to comments provided by you in the management letter dated March 22, 2018, based on your prior audit."

g. "Our assessment of internal control over financial reporting provides us absolute assurance that no material misstatements will occur and be undetected by our internal control."

h. "We have made available to you all financial records and related data."

LO 11-3

11.55 **Written Representations.** Classify each of the following issues according to whether they will be (1) included in written representations in all audits, (2) included in written representations in audits of public entities (under PCAOB standards), or (3) not included in written representations:

a. Management acknowledgment of its responsibility for the fairness of the financial statements in accordance with U.S. GAAP.

b. A list of pending or threatened litigation, claims, or assessments currently outstanding against the client.

c. A description of recommendations that allow the client to improve the efficiency and effectiveness of its operations.

d. Availability of all financial records and related data.

e. Information related to the presentation and disclosure of items within the financial statements.

f. Disclosure of all significant deficiencies and material weaknesses in internal control.

g. Information concerning fraud involving management and employees who have significant roles in internal control.

h. Auditors' judgment about the quality of the client's accounting principles.

i. Management's conclusion about the effectiveness of its internal control over financial reporting.

j. A statement that the financial statements are prepared according to U.S. generally accepted accounting principles.

LO 11-2

11.56 **Client Request for Attorney Letter.** The firm of Cole & Cole, CPAs, is auditing the financial statements of Consolidated Industries Co. for the year ended December 31, 2017. On March 6, 2018, C. R. Brown, Consolidated's chief financial officer, gave the auditors a draft of an attorney letter for Cole's review before mailing it to J. J. Young, Consolidated's outside counsel. This letter is intended to elicit the attorneys' responses to corroborate information furnished to the auditors by management concerning pending and threatened litigation, claims, assessments, and unasserted claims and assessments.

March 6, 2018
J. J. Young, Attorney at Law
123 Main Street, Anytown, USA
Dear J. J. Young:

In connection with an audit of our financial statements at December 31, 2017, and for the year then ended, management of the Company has prepared, and furnished to our auditors, Cole & Cole, CPAs, a description and evaluation of certain contingencies, including those set forth below, involving matters with respect to which you have been engaged and to which you have devoted substantive attention on behalf of the Company in the form of legal consultation or representation. Your response should include matters that existed at December 31, 2017. Because of the confidentiality of all these matters, your response may be limited.

In November 2017, an action was brought against the Company by an outside salesman alleging breach of contract for sales commissions and asking an accounting with respect to claims for fees and commissions. The causes of action claim damages of $3,000,000, but the Company believes it has meritorious defenses to the claims. The possible exposure of the Company to a successful judgment on behalf of the plaintiff is slight.

In July 2017, an action was brought against the Company by Industrial Manufacturing Company (Industrial) alleging patent infringement and seeking damages of $20,000,000. On October 16, 2017, the U.S. District Court decided that the Company had infringed on seven Industrial patents and awarded damages of $14,000,000. The Company vigorously denies these allegations and has filed an appeal with the U.S. Court of Appeals. The appeal process is expected to take approximately two years, but there is some chance that Industrial may ultimately prevail.

Please furnish to our auditors such explanation, if any, that you consider necessary to supplement this information, including an explanation of those matters as to which your views may differ from those stated, and an identification of the omission of any pending or threatened litigation, claims, and assessments or a statement that the list of such matters is complete. Your response may be quoted or referred to in the financial statements without further correspondence with you.

You also consulted on various other matters considered to be pending or threatened litigation. However, you may not comment on these matters because publicizing them may alert potential plaintiffs to the strengths of their cases. In addition, various other matters probable of assertion that have some chance of an unfavorable outcome, as of December 31, 2017, are presently considered unasserted claims and assessments.

Respectfully,

C. R. Brown

Chief Financial Officer

Required:

Describe the omissions, ambiguities, and inappropriate statements and terminology in Brown's letter. Remember that this is Brown's letter requesting a response to auditors, but it must request responses in the manner most useful to auditors.

(AICPA adapted)

LO 11-2

11.57 **Attorney Letters.** Faye Jaworski, CPA, is auditing the financial statements of Fulbright Company. As she is nearing the audit completion date, Jaworski realizes that she needs to evaluate whether all material contingencies are properly accounted for and disclosed in Fulbright's financial statements. Because of its size, Fulbright has retained external counsel (Vinson, LLP) to handle its various legal matters.

Required:

a. List some common procedures that Jaworski will perform with respect to Fulbright's litigation, claims, and assessments.

b. What are the responsibilities of Jaworski, Fulbright, and Vinson with respect to litigation, claims, and assessments?

c. Attorney letters are used to provide corroboration of litigation, claims, and assessments against the client. Briefly describe the process through which attorney letters are prepared, sent, and used in the audit examination.

d. What information is normally included in an attorney letter?

LO 11-4

11.58 **Uncorrected Misstatements and Performance Materiality.** Aaron Rivers, CPA, is auditing the financial statements of Charger Company, a client for the past five years. During past audits of Charger, Rivers identified some immaterial misstatements (most of which relate to isolated matters and do not have common characteristics). A summary of these misstatements follows. (To illustrate, in 2012, the misstatements would have reduced net income by $13,200 if corrected:)

Year	Effect on Net Income	Effect on Assets	Effect on Liabilities	Effect on Equity
2012	($13,200)	($20,000)	($6,800)	($13,200)
2013	5,000	12,000	7,000	5,000
2014	(9,250)	(11,000)	(1,750)	(9,250)
2015	(2,000)	(5,500)	(3,500)	(2,000)
2016	1,000	1,000	0	1,000

During the most recent audit, Rivers concluded that sales totaling $11,000 were recognized as of December 31, 2017, that did not meet the criteria for recognition until 2018. When Rivers discussed these sales with Chris Turner, Charger Company's chief financial officer, Turner asked Rivers about the performance materiality level used in the audit, which was $25,000. Upon learning of this, Turner remarked, "Then there's no need to worry . . . it's not a material amount. Why should we bother with this item?"

Required:

a. How does the misstatement identified in 2017 affect net income, assets, liabilities, and equity in 2017? (Assume a 35 percent tax rate for Charger.)

b. Comment upon Turner's remark to Rivers. Is Turner's reasoning correct?

c. Upon doing some research, Rivers learned of the rollover method and iron curtain method for evaluating the performance materiality of misstatements. Briefly define each of these methods.

d. How would Rivers evaluate the performance materiality of the $11,000 sales cutoff error in 2017 under the *rollover method* and *iron curtain method?*

e. Based on your response to part (d), what adjustments (if any) would Rivers propose to Charger Company's financial statements under the rollover method and iron curtain method?

LO 11-4

11.59 Uncorrected Misstatements and Performance Materiality. During the conduct of an audit, auditors may identify misstatements as a result of the completion of their substantive procedures. An important activity performed in the completion stages of the audit is considering the materiality of misstatements identified during the audit.

Required:

a. What is an *uncorrected misstatement*? What is the auditors' responsibility for uncorrected misstatements during the completion stage of the audit engagement?

b. How do auditors use the *rollover method* and *iron curtain method* to evaluate uncorrected misstatements?

c. Assume that auditors have identified misstatements during the current audit that had a net impact of $100,000 on expenses and payables (both were understated). If the cumulative effect of prior uncorrected misstatements was $120,000 (overstatement of net income and understatement of liabilities) and materiality was $150,000, what would the auditors' conclusion be with respect to the misstatements under the rollover method and iron curtain method?

d. Based on your response to part (c), what adjustments (if any) would the auditors propose to the client's financial statements?

e. What requirements do auditors have for communicating uncorrected misstatements identified during the audit engagement?

LO 11-4

11.60 Uncorrected Misstatements and Performance Materiality. Pat Colt is auditing the financial statements of Manning Company. The following is a summary of the uncorrected misstatements that Colt has identified during the past three years. These misstatements are immaterial and have related to isolated matters. In this summary, parentheses imply that the misstatements would have reduced balances if they had been corrected (e.g., in 2014, the misstatements would have reduced net income by $82,500, assets by $100,000, liabilities by $17,500, and equity by $82,500 if corrected).

Year	Effect on Net Income	Effect on Assets	Effect on Liabilities	Effect on Equity
2014	$(82,500)	$(100,000)	$(17,500)	$(82,500)
2015	(22,000)	(25,500)	(3,500)	(22,000)
2016	30,000	30,000	0	30,000

During the most recent audit, Colt concluded that expenses totaling $130,000 were recognized in January 2018 (when Manning paid them) but should have been recognized in 2017.

Required:

a. How does the misstatement identified in 2017 affect net income, assets, liabilities, and equity? (Assume a 35 percent tax rate for Manning.)

b. Describe the *rollover method* of evaluating uncorrected misstatements. Assume that performance materiality was set at $170,000. How would Colt evaluate the materiality of the misstatement under the rollover method? What adjustments (if any) would Colt propose to Manning's financial statements?

c. Describe the *iron curtain method* of evaluating uncorrected misstatements. Assume that performance materiality was set at $170,000. How would Colt evaluate the materiality of the $130,000 misstatement in 2017 under the iron curtain method? What adjustments (if any) would Colt propose to Manning's financial statements?

d. If performance materiality were established at $100,000 for Manning, how would Colt evaluate the materiality of the misstatement in 2017 under the rollover method and iron curtain method?

e. Based on your response to part (d), what adjustments (if any) would Colt propose to Manning's financial statements under the rollover method and the iron curtain method?

LO 11-5

11.61 Subsequent Events—Internet Exercise. The following subsequent event was disclosed in **Dole Food Company**'s 2009 annual report:

Note 24: Subsequent Event
On February 27, 2010, a significant earthquake struck the country of Chile. Although Dole's Chilean operations resumed business after the earthquake in a matter of days, Dole is currently evaluating its impact, if any, to its financial results. Preliminary reports indicate no major structural damage to the Dole facilities. Dole maintains customary insurance for its properties, including business interruption and extra related expense.

Required:

a. What is a subsequent event?

b. Access Dole's 2009 10-K (filed in 2010) from the SEC's website (www.sec.gov).
1. What is Dole's fiscal year-end?
2. What is the date of the auditor's report?
3. When was Dole's 10-K filed with the SEC?

c. Given your answers in part (b), does it appear that this event meets the definition of a "subsequent event"? Why or why not?

d. Assuming that this event did meet the definition of a subsequent event, would you classify it as a subsequent event that relates to a condition that existed at the date of the financial statements or one that arose after the date of the financial statements?

e. Given the preceding disclosure, what procedures do you think Dole's auditors (Deloitte & Touche) performed with respect to this event?

LO 11-2

11.62 Attorney Letters and Litigation—Internet Exercise. From the SEC's website (www.sec.gov), access any company's 10-K and review its footnote disclosures related to pending litigation.

Required:

a. Briefly summarize the nature of pending litigation facing the company you selected.

b. From the auditors' perspective, what is the primary concern with respect to the disclosure of pending litigation?

c. Identify the responsibility of the company, the auditor, and its attorneys with respect to the presentation and disclosure of this pending litigation.

d. What information included in the disclosure you selected would have been included in attorney letters? What is the attorney's responsibility with respect to this information?

LO 11-5 11-6

11.63 Omitted Procedures and Subsequently Discovered Facts—Internet Exercise. From the "Inspections" section of the PCAOB's website, access the most recent inspection reports for each of the Big Four firms (Deloitte, EY, KPMG, and PwC). Each inspection report contains the following information:

- An introductory preface.
- Inspection procedures and observations, which include specific findings related to issuers (clients) (Part I).
- A summary of the inspection process.
- The firm's response to the inspection report.

Occasionally, the PCAOB's inspection process identifies situations in which necessary audit procedures were not performed or in which the auditors did not identify departures from GAAP.

Required:

a. What is the auditors' responsibility with respect to subsequently discovered facts and omitted procedures?

b. If one is provided, review and briefly summarize the firm's response to the inspection report. Comment on whether you believe the firm's response to omitted procedures and subsequently discovered facts was consistent with generally accepted auditing standards.

LO 11-5

11.64 Subsequent Events and Subsequently Discovered Facts. Michael Ewing is auditing the financial statements of Dallas Company for the year ended December 31, 2017. In concluding the process of gathering sufficient appropriate evidence, Ewing has asked to meet with his supervisor on the audit (John Ross) to discuss responsibility for events occurring after the date of the financial statements.

Required:

a. What is a *subsequent event*? During what time period is Ewing responsible for subsequent events?

b. List some procedures that Ewing may perform to assist him in identifying subsequent events.

c. What are two types of subsequent events? How should information related to these types of subsequent events be reflected in Dallas's financial statements?

d. Assume that on January 8, 2018, Dallas Company agreed to acquire Houston Inc. in a significant transaction. The date of Ewing's report was February 7, 2018, and Dallas issued its financial statements (and Ewing's reports on its financial statements and internal control over financial reporting) on February 14, 2018. How would Ewing proceed if he became aware of this subsequent event on the following dates?

1. January 10, 2018.
2. February 10, 2018.
3. February 20, 2018.

e. On March 2, 2018, Dallas announced that it also will acquire San Antonio Company in a significant transaction. What is Ewing's responsibility with respect to this acquisition in the audit of Dallas's financial statements for the year ended December 31, 2017?

LO 11-2, 11-5

11.65 Subsequent Events and Contingent Liabilities. Crankwell Inc. is preparing its annual financial statements and annual report to stockholders. Management wants to be sure that all of the necessary and proper disclosures have been incorporated into the financial statements and the annual report. Two classes of items that have an important bearing on the financial statements are subsequent events and contingent liabilities. The financial statements could be materially inaccurate or misleading if proper disclosure of these items is not made.

Required:

a. With respect to subsequent events

1. Define what is meant by a *subsequent event.*
2. Identify two types of subsequent events and explain the appropriate financial statement presentation of each type.
3. What are the procedures that should be performed to ascertain the existence of subsequent events?

b. With respect to contingent liabilities

1. Identify the essential elements of a contingent liability.
2. Explain how a contingent liability should be disclosed in the financial statements.

c. Explain how a subsequent event may relate to a contingent liability. Give an example to support your answer.

(CMA adapted)

LO 11-5

11.66 Subsequent Events Procedures. You are in the process of completing the gathering of sufficient appropriate evidence for Top Stove Corporation, a company engaged in the manufacture and sale of kerosene space heaters. To date, there has been every indication that the financial statements of the client present fairly the position of the company at

December 31 and the results of its operations and cash flows for the year then ended. Top Stove had total assets at December 31 of $4 million and a net profit for the year (after deducting federal and state income taxes) of $285,000. The principal records of the company include a general ledger, cash receipts record, voucher register, sales register, check register, and general journal. Financial statements are prepared monthly. Your audit report is dated February 20, and you plan to deliver the reports to the client by March 12.

Required:

a. Write a brief statement about the purpose and period to be covered in a review of subsequent events.

b. Outline the program you would follow to determine what transactions involving material amounts, if any, have occurred since the date of the financial statements.

(AICPA adapted)

LO 11-5

11.67 **Subsequent Events—Cases.**   In connection with your examination of the financial statements of Olars Manufacturing Corporation for the year ended December 31, your post-balance-sheet substantive procedures disclosed the following items:

1. *January 3.* The state government approved a plan for the construction of an express highway. The plan will result in the appropriation of a portion of the land area owned by Olars. Construction will begin late next year. No estimate of the condemnation award is available.

2. *January 4.* Yang Olars (president of Olars Manufacturing Corporation) loaned the company $25,000. He obtained these funds on July 15 by borrowing against a personal life insurance policy. The loan from Olars to Olars Manufacturing Corporation was recorded in the account Loan Payable to Officers. Olars's source of the funds was not disclosed in the company records. The corporation pays the premiums on the life insurance policy, and the president's wife is the owner and beneficiary of the policy.

3. *January 7.* The mineral content of a shipment of ore in transit on December 31 was determined to be 72 percent. The shipment was recorded at year-end at an estimated content of 50 percent by a debit to Raw Materials Inventory and a credit to Accounts Payable in the amount of $20,600. The final liability to the vendor is based on the actual mineral content of the shipment.

4. *January 15.* A series of personal disagreements have arisen between Olars and Zane Tweedy, his brother-in-law, the treasurer. Tweedy resigned, effective immediately, under an agreement whereby the corporation would purchase his 10 percent stock ownership at book value as of December 31. Payment is to be made in two equal amounts in cash on April 1 and October 1. In December, the treasurer had obtained a divorce from Olars's sister.

5. *January 31.* As a result of reduced sales, production was curtailed in mid-January and some workers were laid off. On February 5, all remaining workers went on strike. To date the strike is unsettled.

Required:

Assume that the preceding items came to your attention prior to completion of your audit work on February 15. For each item

a. Give the substantive procedures, if any, that would have brought the item to your attention. Indicate other sources of information that could have revealed the item.

b. Discuss the disclosure that you would recommend for the item, listing all details that should be disclosed. Indicate those items or details, if any, that should not be disclosed. Give your reasons for recommending or not recommending disclosure of the items or details.

(AICPA adapted)

LO 11-5

11.68 **Subsequently Discovered Facts.**   On June 1, Sidney Faultless of A. J. Faultless & Co., CPAs, noticed some disturbing information about the firm's client, Hopkirk Company. A story in the local paper mentioned the indictment of Tony Baker, whom Faultless knew as the assistant controller at Hopkirk. The charge was mail fraud. Faultless made discreet inquiries with the controller at Hopkirk's headquarters and learned that Baker had been speculating in foreign currency futures. In fact, part of Baker's work at Hopkirk involved managing the company's foreign currency. Unfortunately, Baker had violated company policy, lost a small amount of money, and then decided to speculate some more, lost some more, and eventually lost $7 million of company funds.

The mail fraud was involved in Baker's attempt to cover his activity until he recovered the original losses. Most of the events were in process on March 1, when Faultless had signed and dated the unmodified opinion on Hopkirk's financial statements for the year ended on the previous December 31.

Faultless determined that the information probably would affect the decisions of external users and advised Hopkirk's chief executive to make the disclosure. She flatly refused to make any disclosure, arguing that the information was immaterial. On June 17, Faultless provided the subsequent information in question to a news reporter, and it was printed in *The Wall Street Journal* with a statement that the financial statements and accompanying auditor's report on the company's financial statements could not be relied on.

Required:

Evaluate the actions of Faultless & Co., CPAs, with respect to the information discovered. What other action could Faultless & Co. have taken? What are the possible legal effects of the firm's actions, if any?

LO 11-6

11.69 **Omitted Audit Procedures.** The following are independent situations that have occurred in your public accounting firm, Arthur Hurdman[7]:

Case 1

During the internal inspection by a regional office of Arthur Hurdman, one of its clients, Wildcat Oil Suppliers, was selected for review. The reviewers questioned the thoroughness of inventory obsolescence procedures, especially in light of the depressed state of the oil exploration industry at the time. They believed that specific substantive procedures, which they considered appropriate, were not performed by your audit team.

Case 2

Top Stove, one of your clients, installed an automated system in July 2017 to process part of its accounting transactions. You completed the audit of Top Stove's December 31, 2017, statements on February 15, 2018. During the April 2018 review work on Top Stove's first-quarter financial information, you discovered that during the audit of the 2017 statements, only the manual records had been investigated in the search for unrecorded liabilities.

Required:

a. Without regard to the specific situation given, answer the following questions:
   1. What are the proper steps auditors should take if it is discovered, after the report date, that an important substantive procedure was omitted?
   2. How are auditors' decisions affected if, after review of the audit documentation, they determine that other substantive procedures produced the sufficient appropriate audit evidence?
   3. If, in subsequently applying the omitted procedure, auditors become aware of material new information that should have been disclosed in the financial statements, how should they proceed?

b. Describe the proper action to take in each of the preceding situations, given the following additional information:

   Case 1. You thoroughly consider the scope of the audit of Wildcat Oil Suppliers and have made a detailed review of the audit documentation. You have concluded that sufficient compensating procedures were conducted to support the valuation of inventory.

   Case 2. Your subsequent investigation of the information system's records of Top Stove revealed that material liabilities were not recorded as of December 31.

LO 11-5, 11-6

11.70 **Subsequent Events, Subsequently Discovered Facts, and Omitted Procedures.** Jay Ralph completed the December 31, 2017, audit of Raider Company on February 3, 2018; Raider's financial statements and Ralph's reports on Raider's financial statements and internal control over financial reporting were released on February 12, 2018. During April 2018, Ralph's firm conducted a quality review over selected audits that had been completed during the most recent year, and the audit of Raider Company was randomly selected for

[7]Situation derived from examples given in Thomas R. Weirich and Elizabeth J. Ringelberg, "Omitted Audit Procedures," *CPA Journal,* March 1984, pp. 34–39.

review. The reviewer identified the following matters that Ralph had not addressed during the audit of Raider:

a. On February 9, 2018, Ralph learned of the following events during his postaudit meeting with Raider's chief operating officer.

1. A class-action lawsuit was brought against Raider Company by some of its former employees for workplace discrimination. An attorney on behalf of a class of employees filed the lawsuit on January 10, 2018. The letter from Raider's attorneys did not identify this lawsuit.

2. One of Raider's major customers is experiencing significant financial difficulties; this customer's account receivable balance on December 31, 2017, was $1.2 million, which represented 2 percent of Raider's total accounts receivable on that date.

   Because of an important deadline for submitting the financial statements to lenders for evaluation, Raider did not modify its financial statements for the preceding events despite the fact that they were material. Raider's justification was that because the events occurred after the date of the financial statements, they were not required to be disclosed in the financial statements. Ralph acquiesced to Raider's wishes and did not modify the report on Raider's financial statements.

b. On March 16, 2018, Ralph initially learned of the following events affecting Raider Company, neither of which was disclosed in Raider's financial statements:

1. Raider Company declared a significant dividend payable to its shareholders. This dividend was declared on March 14, 2018, to be paid to Raider's shareholders of record on May 16, 2018.

2. Raider Company activated a portion of its line of credit on February 1, 2018, by borrowing $2.5 million. This additional obligation increased Raider Company's long-term liabilities by 10 percent.

c. Reviewing Ralph's audit documentation, it does not appear that any tests were conducted to evaluate the need for impairment of the carrying value of Raider Company's property, plant, and equipment.

Required:

For each of the preceding items, describe what actions Ralph should take after the firm's quality review identified these issues.

LO 11-3, 11-4, 11-5, 11-6

11.71 **Various Completion Matters.** For each of the following independent situations, describe the most appropriate course of action that the auditors should take.

a. Drew Allison is conducting the audit of Anderson Inc. as of December 31, 2017. At the beginning of the evidence gathering, Allison becomes aware that one of Anderson's major customers (Jones) is experiencing significant financial difficulties. Jones normally accounts for 5 percent of Anderson's net sales. After performing the necessary procedures, Allison believes that $2.8 million of Jones's receivable balance will ultimately become uncollectible. Allison further believes this amount is material to Anderson's financial condition and results of operations.

b. Nagan Carmelo is completing the December 31, 2017, audit of Nugget Company. As part of the final procedures, Carmelo has requested representations from Nugget's management regarding their assertion as to the fairness of the financial statements and other important matters addressed by professional standards. Because Nugget's management is attending an analyst briefing in the upcoming week, Carmelo receives these signed representations dated February 6, 2018. Carmelo has a few remaining items to complete, does so, and dates the auditor's report February 9, 2018.

c. Pat Colt completed the December 31, 2017, audit of Manning and issued an unmodified opinion on Manning's financial statements dated March 15, 2018. Colt's opinion was released, along with Manning's financial statements, on March 21, 2018. During a review of Manning's first quarter 10-Q in late April, Colt became aware of the company's settlement with a customer over a product warranty lawsuit; this case had been settled on March 13, 2018. Although Colt had received the necessary letter from Manning's attorneys, the letter arrived prior to the settlement of the case and did not mention this development. After reviewing the information related to the settlement, Colt does not believe that the settlement is material to Manning's financial condition or results of operations and believes the opinion on Manning's financial statements is still supportable.

d. Cameron Alta completed the December 31, 2017, audit of Saxe Company on February 10, 2018. Saxe is planning to release its financial statements, along with Alta's opinion on these financial statements and internal control over financial reporting, on February 17, 2018. On February 12, 2018, a flood in one of Saxe's warehouses located in the Gulf Coast region destroyed more than $10 million of inventory. Although the extent to which this loss is recoverable through Saxe's insurance is uncertain at this time, Alta believes that this loss could have a material impact on Saxe's financial condition and results of operations.

e. During the audit of Glomco, Angel Myron identified a number of misstatements. These misstatements are not material in dollar amount, do not appear to represent any discernable pattern, and do not represent fraudulent activity. As a result, Myron has decided that Glomco's financial statements do not need to be adjusted to reflect the effect of these misstatements.

f. Following the completion of the 2017 audit of Blankenship Corporation and release of the financial statements and auditor's reports, Reese Jill met with the manager to conduct a postmortem on the engagement and identify how changes in Blankenship's operations noted during the most recent audit may affect future audits. During this review, Jill became aware that Blankenship's process for evaluating goodwill related to an acquisition made by Blankenship during the most recent year for potential impairment had not been considered. Jill believes that the omitted procedure is important in supporting the opinion on Blankenship's financial statements and that users continue to rely on the financial statements and the auditor's reports.

LO 11-2

11.72 **Attorney Letter Responses.** Omega Corporation is involved in a lawsuit brought by a competitor for patent infringement. The competitor is asking $14 million actual damages for lost profits and unspecified punitive damages. The lawsuit has been in progress for 15 months, and Omega has worked closely with its outside counsel preparing its defense. Omega recently requested its outside attorneys with the firm of Wolfe & Goodwin to provide information to its auditors.

The managing partner of Wolfe & Goodwin asked four different lawyers who have worked on the case to prepare a concise response to auditors. The auditors received these responses from the lawyers:

1. The action involves unique characteristics in which authoritative legal precedents bearing directly on the plaintiff's claims do not seem to exist. We believe the plaintiff will have serious problems establishing Omega's liability; nevertheless, if the plaintiff is successful, the damage award may be substantial.

2. In our opinion, Omega will be able to defend this action successfully, but, if not, the possible liability to Omega in this proceeding is nominal in amount.

3. We believe the plaintiff's case against Omega is without merit.

4. In our opinion, Omega will be able to assert meritorious defenses and has a reasonable chance of sustaining an adequate defense with a possible outcome of settling the case for less than the damages claimed.

Required:

a. Interpret each of the four responses separately. Decide whether each is (1) adequate to conclude that the likelihood of an adverse outcome is "remote," requiring no disclosure in financial statements or (2) too vague to serve as adequate information for a decision, requiring more information from the lawyers or from management.

b. What response do you think auditors would receive if they asked the plaintiff's counsel about the likely outcome of the lawsuit? Discuss.

LO 11-2

11.73 **Accounting for a Contingency: Attorney Letter Information.** Central City was involved in litigation brought by Mexican American Legal Defense and Educational Fund (MALDEF) over the creation of single-member voting districts (which require candidates to receive only the highest number of votes, even if not a majority) for city council positions. Auditors were working on the financial statements for the year ended December 31, 2017, and had almost completed gathering sufficient appropriate evidence by February 12, 2018.

The court heard final arguments on February 1 and rendered its judgment on February 10. The ruling was in favor of MALDEF and required the creation of certain single-member voting districts. This ruling did not impose a monetary loss on Central City, but the court also ruled that MALDEF would be awarded a judgment of court costs and attorney fees to be paid by Central City.

Local newspaper reports stated that MALDEF would seek a $250,000 recovery from the city. Auditors obtained an attorney letter dated February 15 that stated the following: In my opinion, the court will award some amount for MALDEF's attorney fees. In regard to your inquiry about an amount or range of possible loss, I estimate that such an award could be anywhere from $30,000 to $175,000.

Required:

a. What weight should be given to the newspaper report of the $250,000 amount that MALDEF might ask? What weight should be given to the attorney's estimate?

b. How should this subsequent event be reflected in the 2014 financial statements of Central City?

CHAPTER 12

Reports on Audited Financial Statements

In our opinion, the financial statements referred to above present fairly, in all material respects, the financial position of Enron Corp. and subsidiaries as of December 31, 2000 and 1999, and the results of their operations, cash flows, and changes in shareholders' equity for each of the three years in the period ended December 31, 2000, in conformity with accounting principles generally accepted in the United States.

> Opinion paragraph from Arthur Andersen's final audit of Enron, February 23, 2001

Professional Standards References

Topic	AU-C/ISA Section	AS Section
Going Concern	570	2415
Audits of Group Financial Statements	600	1205
Reporting on Financial Statements	700	3101
Modifications to Reports on Financial Statements	705	3101
Emphasis-of-Matter and Other-Matter Paragraphs	706	3101
Consistency	708	2820
Other Information	720	2710
Supplementary Information	725	2701
Required Supplementary Information	730	2705
Summary Financial Statements	810	3315

LEARNING OBJECTIVES

Management has the primary responsibility for the presentation of financial statements in accordance with generally accepted accounting principles (GAAP) or other applicable reporting frameworks. Following the substantive procedures, auditors express an opinion on the fairness of these financial statements, which represent the culmination of the audit examination.

Your objectives are to be able to:

LO 12-1 Understand the types of reports that accompany an entity's financial statements and the content of the auditors' standard (unmodified) report.

LO 12-2 Identify situations in which language in the standard (unmodified) report is modified and the type of opinion issued in those situations.

LO 12-3 Identify situations in which auditors add explanatory language to an unmodified opinion.

LO 12-4 Identify other circumstances affecting auditors' reporting responsibilities and explain how they affect auditors' reports on an entity's financial statements.

INTRODUCTION

In Chapter 2, we presented **EY**'s 2016 report related to its audit of **McDonald's Corporation.** This report was prepared under the provisions of U.S. generally accepted auditing standards (specifically, standards of the PCAOB) and expressed EY's opinion that McDonald's financial statements were fairly presented in accordance with generally accepted accounting principles.

An emerging concern regarding U.S. audit reporting is that the reports provide little information as to major risks or issues related to the company and its financial statements. In 2013, the United Kingdom's Financial Reporting Council (FRC) expanded existing reporting requirements (which were similar to those of the PCAOB) for certain entities to include the following elements:[1]

- A description of the risks of material misstatement that had the greatest impact on overall audit strategy, the allocation of resources in the audit, and the efforts of the engagement team.
- An explanation of how the auditor applied the concept of materiality in planning and performing the audit.
- An overview of the scope of the audit, including an explanation of how the scope was affected by the risks of material misstatement.

KPMG's audit report on **Rolls-Royce**'s 2013 financial statements created quite a stir in audit reporting circles. This report addressed the expanded requirements of the FRC but went a step further by including KPMG's audit response and findings related to the following risks:

- Basis of accounting for revenue and profit in Rolls-Royce's civil aerospace business.
- Measurement of revenue and profit in Rolls-Royce's civil aerospace business.
- Recoverability of intangible assets and amounts recoverable on contracts in Rolls-Royce's civil aerospace business.
- Accounting for the consolidation of **Rolls-Royce Power Systems** and valuation of **Daimler AG'**s put option to purchase an interest in Rolls-Royce Power Systems.
- Revenue recognition related to nonrefundable cash payments under risk and revenue sharing arrangements.
- Ongoing investigations of bribery and corruption related to contracting arrangements.
- The presentation of "underlying" profit (presented as a complement to IFRS financial statements).[2]

When contrasting the Rolls-Royce report with that of McDonald's, the former uses more than 5,300 words (approximately 4,300 of which are related to the preceding risks) included in six pages of the annual report while the latter uses approximately 300 words occupying one-half page. In addition to information about the risks of material

[1] *Financial Reporting Council, Internal Standard on Auditing (UK and Ireland) 700,* "The Independent Auditor's Report on Financial Statements," June 2013.
[2] http://ar.rolls-royce.com/2013/. KPMG's reports on Rolls-Royce's 2014 and 2015 financial statements contained a similar level of detail and disclosures.

misstatement, the Rolls Royce report provided the following materiality- and scope-level disclosures:

- Overall materiality level of £86 million ($52.3 million based on exchange rates on December 31, 2013), representing 4.9 percent of income before taxes.
- Materiality levels for reporting components ranging from £0.5 million to £50 million.
- Any uncorrected misstatements in excess of £4 million (income statement) and £8 million (balance sheet) would be communicated to the audit committee.
- Audit procedures covered 98 percent of revenue, 99 percent of income before taxes, and 94 percent of total assets.

While the impact of the FRC's expanded reporting requirements cannot yet be determined, it is clear from KPMG's audit report that expanded reporting requirements have the potential to significantly impact information provided by auditors in their reports.[3] A proposed PCAOB standard would require similar disclosures (referred to as "critical audit matters") in its reports (the AICPA is also considering similar revisions to its auditors' reports).[4] An academic study has concluded that disclosure of critical audit matters in researcher-developed auditor reports does influence nonprofessional investors' decisions.[5] Clearly, audit reporting will continue to evolve to provide important information to investors, lenders, and others who rely on audited financial statements in making economic decisions.

OVERVIEW OF AUDITORS' REPORTS

LO 12-1

Understand the types of reports that accompany an entity's financial statements and the content of the auditors' standard (unmodified) report.

Because the entity's management is responsible for preparing its financial statements, the auditors' examination (and report on that examination) plays an important role in users' ability to rely on the financial statements when making economic decisions. Public entities (those entities that offer registered securities for sale to the general public) are required to file certain financial information with the Securities and Exchange Commission (SEC) within 60 to 90 days (depending upon their size) of their fiscal year-end. This information, which includes audited financial statements, footnotes, and other required disclosures related to the financial statements, is filed using Form 10-K.

In contrast, nonpublic entities are not subject to these filing or audit requirements. However, third-party users may demand audited financial statements as a condition for certain lending or investing activities or for use in monitoring the entity's activities. In addition, regulatory bodies other than the SEC may require audits for governmental and other types of nonpublic entities.

For both public and nonpublic entities, the auditors' report on financial statements and related disclosures provides (or disclaims) an opinion on whether the entity's financial statements and related disclosures are presented in accordance with GAAP. This opinion is based on the tests of controls and substantive procedures that have been performed during the audit engagement and discussed throughout this text.

In addition to the auditors' report on financial statements and related disclosures, public entities are subject to additional reporting requirements. The Sarbanes–Oxley Act of 2002 and Auditing Standard 3101 (AS 3101) have mandated two additional types of reports:

1. A report, prepared by the entity's management, on the effectiveness of the entity's internal control over financial reporting.
2. A report, prepared by the auditors, on the effectiveness of the entity's internal control over financial reporting.

[3] A recent study concluded that the FRC's expanded reporting requirements did not affect audit quality (as measured by discretionary accruals) or investor reaction to the release of the auditors' report in the first two years after adoption. In addition, this same study found that total audit fees were influenced by the length of the report, the length of discussion of significant risks of material misstatement, and the number of identified risks. See E. Gutierrez, M. Minutti-Meza, K. W. Minutti-Meza, K. W. Tatum, and M. Vulcheva, "Consequences of Changing the Auditor's Report: Evidence from the U.K.," Unpublished working paper.

[4] See *Proposed Auditing Standard-The Auditor's Report on the Audit of Financial Statements when the Auditor Expresses an Unqualified Opinion and Related Amendments to PCAOB Standards*, PCAOB Release No. 2016-003, May 11, 2016 and "Bid to Make Audit Reports More Useful to Investors is Rebooted," *The Wall Street Journal Online,* May 11, 2016.

[5] B. E. Christensen, S. M. Glover, and C. J. Wolfe, "Do Critical Audit Matter Paragraphs in the Audit Report Change Nonprofessional Investors' Decision to Invest?," *Auditing: A Journal of Practice & Theory,* November 2014, pp. 71–93.

The following is a summary of the reports that accompany an entity's financial statements. The focus of this chapter is on the auditors' report on financial statements and related disclosures; reports on the effectiveness of the entity's internal control over financial reporting were previously discussed in Chapter 5.

Type of Entity	Report(s)
Public entity	Mandatory reports on • Effectiveness of internal control over financial reporting (prepared by management) • Effectiveness of internal control over financial reporting (prepared by auditors) • Fairness of financial statements and related disclosures (prepared by auditors)
Nonpublic entity	Fairness of financial statements and related disclosures based on user demand (prepared by auditors)

✅ REVIEW CHECKPOINTS

12.1 Identify the reports that accompany the financial statements of public entities and nonpublic entities.

12.2 What are the audit requirements for nonpublic and public entities?

The Standard Report

The auditors' report on the financial statements expresses an opinion on whether the financial statements present the entity's financial position, results of operations, and cash flows in accordance with GAAP (or other applicable financial reporting framework). The report should be titled *independent auditor's report* (or other suitable title stressing the independence of the auditors). The report is typically addressed to the board of directors and shareholders but may also be addressed to an individual lender, creditor, or investor who requested the audit.

Because the Auditing Standards Board (ASB) prescribes the format and contents of the report for nonpublic entities, these reports are sometimes referred to as the *Auditing Standards Board* (or *ASB*) *report.* See Exhibit 12.1 for an example of a standard (unmodified) report issued for a nonpublic entity. This report is appropriate when no material issues are encountered during the audit and the financial statements are prepared in accordance with GAAP.

All standard (unmodified) reports contain four major sections:

1. *Introduction.* The **introductory paragraph** identifies the financial statements and years examined by the audit team. The report in Exhibit 12.1 identifies the balance sheet, income statement, statement of changes in shareholders' equity, and statement of cash flows for the year ended December 31, 2017, as the financial statements and years examined.

2. *Management's Responsibility for the Financial Statements.* The paragraph in this section explicitly indicates that the entity's management is responsible for both the fairness of the financial statements and the design, implementation, and maintenance of internal control under which those statements are prepared.

3. *Auditor's Responsibility.* This section includes three paragraphs that (a) identify the audit team's responsibility to conduct an audit under generally accepted auditing standards (GAAS), (b) provide a brief description of an audit, and (c) indicate that the audit evidence provides a basis for the audit team's opinion.

4. *Opinion.* This section expresses the audit team's opinion on whether the financial statements present the financial condition, results of operations, and cash flows in accordance with an appropriate financial framework. The conclusion of the report in Exhibit 12.1 indicates that the financial statements are prepared in accordance with accounting principles generally accepted in the United States of America (GAAP). Because this section consists of a single paragraph, it is also referred to as the **opinion paragraph**.

EXHIBIT 12.1 **Standard (Unmodified) Report for Nonpublic Entity**

Independent Auditor's Report	Title
To the Board of Directors and Shareholders of Dunder-Mifflin Inc.	Addressee
We have audited the accompanying financial statements of Dunder-Mifflin Inc., which comprise the balance sheet as of December 31, 2017, and the related statements of income, changes in shareholders' equity, and cash flows for the year then ended, and the related notes to the financial statements.	Introductory Paragraph
Management's Responsibility for the Financial Statements Management is responsible for the preparation and fair presentation of these financial statements in accordance with accounting principles generally accepted in the United States of America; this includes the design, implementation, and maintenance of internal control relevant to the preparation and fair presentation of financial statements that are free from material misstatement, whether due to fraud or error.	Management's Responsibility Section
Auditor's Responsibility Our responsibility is to express an opinion on these financial statements based on our audit. We conducted our audit in accordance with auditing standards generally accepted in the United States of America. Those standards require that we plan and perform the audit to obtain reasonable assurance about whether the financial statements are free from material misstatement. An audit involves performing procedures to obtain audit evidence about the amounts and disclosures in the financial statements. The procedures selected depend on the auditor's judgment, including the assessment of the risks of material misstatement of the financial statements, whether due to fraud or error. In making those risk assessments, the auditor considers internal control relevant to the entity's preparation and fair presentation of the financial statements in order to design audit procedures that are appropriate in the circumstances, but not for the purpose of expressing an opinion on the effectiveness of the entity's internal control. Accordingly, we express no such opinion. An audit also includes evaluating the appropriateness of accounting policies used and the reasonableness of significant accounting estimates made by management, as well as evaluating the overall presentation of the financial statements. We believe that the audit evidence we have obtained is sufficient and appropriate to provide a basis for our audit opiton.	Auditor's Responsibility Section
Opinion In our opinion, the financial statements referred to above present fairly, in all material respects, the financial position of Dunder-Mifflin Inc. as of December 31, 2017, and the results of its operations and its cash flows for the year then ended in accordance with accounting principles generally accepted in the United States of America.	Opinion Paragraph
Michael Scarn, LLP Scranton, PA January 29, 2018	Signature and Date

Following the opinion paragraph, the auditors' report should

- Be signed using the firm's name.
- Be dated using the date when the auditors have obtained sufficient appropriate evidence to support the opinion (the **date of the auditors' report**).

Auditors' Reports for Public Entities

The preceding discussion relates to audits of nonpublic entities, which serve as the focus of this chapter. For public entities, Auditing Standard 3101 (AS 3101) prescribes a different form of report, shown in Exhibit 12.2 (this version is sometimes referred to as the PCAOB report).[6] Although the length of the report and format slightly varies from the

[6]Public entities are required to present two years of comparative balance sheets and three years of comparative statements of income, changes in shareholders' equity, and cash flows. Thus, a report on a single year (such as that shown in Exhibit 12.2) would not be appropriate for a public entity. This report is illustrated to compare this report with that for a nonpublic entity in Exhibit 12.1.

AUDITING INSIGHT | Signing and Dating

- In **Hertz Global Holdings'** 10-K filed with the SEC on February 26, 2010, PricewaterhouseCoopers' audit report was dated March 3, 2009 (almost 10 months *before* the date of the financial statements covered by the report!). Without identifying the reason for the discrepancy (other than the report contained a "typographical error in the opinion date"), Hertz subsequently filed an amended 10-K that contained the correct report date of February 26, 2010.

- The PCAOB issued a rule that requires firms to disclose the name of the engagement partner for each audit in a separate filing (one version of an original proposal required this disclosure in the auditors' report itself). This issue initially received attention with the revelation of a KPMG partner's involvement in an insider-trading

scandal and the lack of publicly available information regarding the audits on which he participated. An academic study revealed that higher-quality audit partners are associated with more favorable market reactions and perceptions in the Taiwanese markets, indicating that partner identity may provide useful information.

Sources: Hertz Global Holdings 2010 10-K; *Improving the Transparency of Audits:Rules to Require Disclosure of Certain Audit Participants on a New PCAOB Form and Related Amendments to Auditing Standards,* PCAOB Release No. 2015-008, December 15, 2015; "Looking for KPMG's Mystery Man," *The Wall Street Journal,* April 10, 2013, p. C12; D. Aobdia, C-J. Lin, and R. Petacchi, "Capital Market Consequences of Audit Partner Quality," *The Accounting Review,* November 2015, pp. 2143–2176.

---

report shown Exhibit 12.1, you should see many similarities in the general content and message communicated by the two reports. Some noteworthy differences are:

- In describing the standards under which the audit is conducted, the AS 3101 report references "standards of the Public Company Accounting Oversight Board (United States)" (because these audits are conducted under PCAOB standards) rather than "auditing standards generally accepted in the United States of America."

- The AS 3101 report has a paragraph that references the audit team's report and opinion on the entity's internal control over financial reporting, which is required in the audit of a public entity (a similar requirement does not exist for the audit of a nonpublic entity).

EXHIBIT 12.2   Standard Report for Public Entity

Report of Independent Registered Public Accounting Firm	Title
To the Board of Directors and Shareholders of Dunder-Mifflin Inc.	Addressee
We have audited the accompanying balance sheet of Dunder-Mifflin Inc. as of December 31, 2017, and the related statements of income, stockholders' equity, and cash flows for the year then ended. These financial statements are the responsibility of Dunder-Mifflin Inc.'s management. Our responsibility is to express an opinion on these financial statements based on our audit.	Introductory Paragraph
We conducted our audit in accordance with the standards of the Public Company Accounting Oversight Board (United States). Those standards require that we plan and perform the audit to obtain reasonable assurance about whether the financial statements are free of material misstatement. An audit includes examining, on a test basis, evidence supporting the amounts and disclosures in the financial statements, assessing the accounting principles used and significant estimates made by management, and evaluating the overall financial statement presentation. We believe that our audit provides a reasonable basis for our opinion.	Scope Paragraph
In our opinion, the financial statements referred to above present fairly, in all material respects, the financial position of Dunder-Mifflin as of December 31, 2017, and the results of its operations and its cash flows for the year then ended in conformity with accounting principles generally accepted in the United States of America.	Opinion Paragraph
We have also audited, in accordance with the standards of the Public Company Accounting Oversight Board (United States), the effectiveness of Dunder-Mifflin's internal control over financial reporting as of December 31, 2017, based on criteria established in *Internal Control—Integrated Framework* issued by the Committee of Sponsoring Organizations of the Treadway Commission and our report dated January 29, 2018, expressed an unqualified opinion thereon.	Internal Control Paragraph
Michael Scarn, LLP Scranton, PA January 29, 2018	Signature and Date

Because of the audit requirement for public entities, the report is addressed to the entity's board of directors and shareholders. As shown in Exhibit 12.2, the auditors' report on the financial statements references their report and opinion on internal control. Similarly, when separate reports on internal control are provided, their report on internal control will reference their report and opinion on the financial statements.

As an alternative to issuing separate reports on the financial statements (as shown in Exhibit 12.2) and internal control over financial reporting, the audit team could choose to issue a single report that expresses opinions on Dunder-Mifflin Inc.'s financial statements and internal control over financial reporting. This report (sometimes referred to as an **integrated report**) essentially combines the report on Dunder-Mifflin Inc.'s financial statements (shown in Exhibit 12.2) with a report on its internal control (for examples, see Chapter 5).

Information on the audit reports of *Fortune* 500 companies (largest 500 U.S. companies based on revenues) available on the Audit Analytics database indicates that 36 percent used an integrated report and 64 percent used two separate reports.

Types of Opinions

Users of audited financial statements are generally most interested in the opinion paragraph, which contains the conclusions about the financial statements. This conclusion is in the form of an *opinion* on whether the entity's financial statements present its financial condition, the results of operations, and cash flows in accordance with GAAP.

Auditors may issue four types of opinions:

1. An **unmodified opinion** in which the conclusion is that the financial statements present the financial condition, results of operations, and cash flows in accordance with GAAP. (Until recently, this type of opinion was referred to as an *unqualified opinion*). The *auditors' standard (unmodified) report* in Exhibit 12.1 is an example of an unmodified opinion; however, unmodified opinions can be issued in forms other than the standard (unmodified) report.

2. A **qualified opinion** in which the conclusion is that, with the exception of one or more issues, the financial statements present the financial condition, results of operations, and cash flows in accordance with GAAP. Qualified opinions use the phrase *except for* in describing the issues that give rise to the qualification. Interestingly, although the term "qualified" normally has a positive connotation, qualified opinions are issued when one or more issues are encountered during the audit.

3. An **adverse opinion**, in which the conclusion is that the financial statements *do not* present the financial condition, results of operations, and cash flows in accordance with GAAP.

4. A **disclaimer of opinion**, in which the auditors do not express an opinion on the fairness of the entity's financial statements.

AU-C 705 refers to qualified opinions, adverse opinions, and disclaimers of opinion as **modified opinions**.

REVIEW CHECKPOINTS

12.3 To whom is the auditors' report addressed?

12.4 Identify the four major sections of the auditors' standard (unmodified) report for a nonpublic entity and the major contents of each section.

12.5 What date should be used on the auditors' report?

12.6 What are the major differences in the auditors' report for nonpublic and public entities?

12.7 What alternatives are available to auditors for reporting on the financial statements and internal control over financial reporting in the audit of public entities?

12.8 What are the types of opinions and the conclusion of each type of opinion?

CONDITIONS THAT REQUIRE MODIFICATIONS TO THE AUDITORS' STANDARD (UNMODIFIED) REPORT

LO 12-2
Identify situations in which language in the standard report is modified and the type of opinion issued in those situations.

In some cases, auditors encounter situations that require them to modify the language in the standard (unmodified) report shown in Exhibit 12.1 as well as the conclusion with respect to the entity's financial statements. These situations include departures from GAAP, scope limitations, and the involvement of component auditors in the audit of group financial statements and are discussed as follows.

Departures from GAAP[7]

Audit examinations may identify transactions that have not been recorded according to GAAP. In most of these situations and assuming that the results are material to the financial statements, entities adjust their financial statements to reflect the proper accounting treatment for the transactions. The process through which auditors propose adjustments to financial statements for misstatements identified during the audit was discussed in Chapter 11.

An entity's management may decide to present financial statements containing an accounting treatment or disclosure that is not in accordance with GAAP. Situations in which an entity does not follow GAAP in preparing its financial statements are referred to as **departures from GAAP**. Exhibit 12.3 summarizes auditors' reporting options when departures from GAAP are noted.

As with any issue, a departure from GAAP may not be material to the entity's financial statements. Recall the wording of the opinion paragraph in the auditors' standard (unmodified) report: "In our opinion, the financial statements referred to above present fairly, *in all material respects . . .*" [emphasis added]. As a result, if a departure from GAAP is immaterial, the auditors would treat the departure as if it did not exist. In this case, they can express an unmodified opinion and issue the standard (unmodified) report.

If the departure is sufficiently material to affect users' decisions that are based on the financial statements but the departure can be compartmentalized, the auditors must *qualify* the opinion. By "compartmentalized," we mean that the departure can be isolated to a particular account group (e.g., accounts receivable not valued at net realizable value)

EXHIBIT 12.3
GAAP Departures

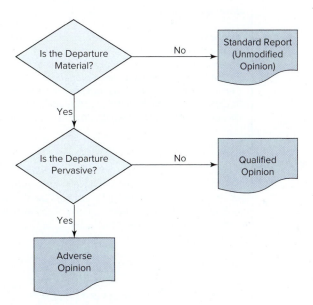

---

[7]The discussion in this section does not refer to situations in which departures from GAAP are undertaken to prevent the financial statements from being misleading. In such cases, auditors should modify the standard (unmodified) report to describe the departure, its impact, and the reasons why compliance with GAAP would result in misleading financial statements (AU-C 700.A15). These cases (referred to as Rule 203 reports) are extremely rare and no guidance is provided in the clarified standards for appropriate report wording.

or transactions (e.g., failure to capitalize leases) without affecting other accounts to a material extent. In other words, this departure would not be considered *pervasive*. This qualification identifies a particular departure but indicates that the financial statements are otherwise in accordance with GAAP. The nature of the GAAP departure must be explained in a separate paragraph in the report, as shown in Exhibit 12.4.[8]

On the other hand, if the GAAP departure is pervasive, affecting numerous accounts and financial statement relationships, or is material to the point that the financial statements as a whole are misleading, the auditors must issue an adverse opinion. As noted earlier, in an adverse opinion, auditors conclude that the financial statements *do not present fairly* the financial position, results of operations, and cash flows in accordance with GAAP. As with the qualified opinion, all substantive reasons must be disclosed in the report.

The example in Exhibit 12.5 assumes that the same departure in GAAP that served as the focus of the qualified opinion in Exhibit 12.4 reached a level of materiality and pervasiveness to warrant an adverse opinion.

The following summarizes modifications to the auditors' standard (unmodified) report for departures from GAAP (assuming such departures are material). Referring to Exhibits 12.4 and 12.5, notice that the paragraph describing the GAAP departure is labeled as "Basis for Qualified (Adverse) Opinion" and the opinion paragraph is labeled as "Qualified (Adverse) Opinion" to emphasize the modified nature of the opinion.

EXHIBIT 12.4

Departure from GAAP Report (Qualified Opinion)

Independent Auditor's Report

Addressee (no revisions)

Introductory Paragraph (no revisions)

Management's Responsibility for the Financial Statements (no revisions)

Auditor's Responsibility (no revisions)

Basis for Qualified Opinion

As discussed in Note 16, an additional provision in the amount of $30,000,000 for possible uncollectible receivables at December 31, 2016, was charged to operations during the year ended December 31, 2017, which, in our opinion, should have been reflected in the financial statements for 2016. Had this provision been properly recorded in the 2016 financial statements, Dunder-Mifflin Inc. would have reported net earnings of $700,000 for the year ended December 31, 2017, rather than the net loss of $29,300,000 as reflected in the statements of income, changes in shareholders' equity, and cash flows for that period.

Qualified Opinion

In our opinion, *except for the effects of the matter described in the Basis for Qualified Opinion paragraph,* the financial statements referred to above present fairly, in all material respects, the financial position of Dunder-Mifflin Inc. as of December 31, 2017, and the results of its operations and its cash flows for the year then ended in accordance with accounting principles generally accepted in the United States of America.

Michael Scarn, LLP
Scranton, PA
January 29, 2018

---

[8]For easier reference, all revisions to the auditors' standard (unmodified) report in Exhibit 12.1 are shown in color and italicized in reports presented throughout this chapter.

	Qualified Opinion	Adverse Opinion
Introductory Paragraph	No modification	No modification
Management's Responsibility for the Financial Statements Section	No modification	No modification
Auditor's Responsibility Section	No modification	No modification
Opinion Paragraph	Modified to note "except for" a specific departure, financial statements are presented according to GAAP	Modified to note that financial statements are not presented according to GAAP
Additional Paragraph	Identifies departure from GAAP	Identifies departure from GAAP

Although the reports shown in Exhibits 12.4 and 12.5 reflect the appropriate wording if departures from GAAP necessitate the issuance of qualified and adverse opinions, under the provisions of Regulation S-X, public companies are not permitted to file financial statements with the SEC if these statements would be false or misleading. As a result, if a material departure from GAAP is noted during an audit examination of a public entity, the auditors' report must be modified to identify that departure as noted in the preceding subsections. However, the entity's financial statements and accompanying auditors' report would be classified as a "deficient" filing by the SEC and would not satisfy its reporting requirements.

⊘ REVIEW CHECKPOINTS

12.9 Explain the effect of pervasiveness on the auditors' report when the entity uses an accounting method that departs from GAAP.

12.10 What are the major differences in wording for qualified opinions and adverse opinions issued as a result of departures from GAAP?

12.11 How is the auditors' standard (unmodified) report modified for qualified or adverse opinions issued as a result of departures from GAAP?

Scope Limitations

A GAAS audit presumes that auditors are able to gather sufficient appropriate evidence on which to base their opinion. Two situations may create **scope limitations** when auditors are unable to obtain sufficient appropriate evidence. The two arise from (1) management's deliberate refusal to provide auditors access to evidence or to otherwise limit the auditors' application of auditing procedures (known as a **client-imposed scope limitation**) and (2) circumstances beyond the auditors' and client's control such as the late appointment of the auditors that lead to auditors' inability to perform certain auditing procedures (known as a **circumstance-imposed scope limitation**). The auditors' reporting options depend on the nature and materiality of the scope limitation (see Exhibit 12.6).

Exhibit 12.6 notes the following:

- If the scope limitation is not material or the auditors can perform alternative procedures, the standard (unmodified) report can be issued. This report does not need to reference the inability to perform certain procedures or the alternative procedures performed.
- If the scope limitation is material and alternative procedures cannot be performed, auditors issue either a qualified opinion or disclaimer of opinion, depending upon the materiality and pervasiveness of the scope limitation.

Refer to Exhibits 12.7 and 12.8 for examples of reports when scope limitations are encountered. The failure to take physical counts of inventory could have been based on a request from the client's management *(client imposed)*, or it could have resulted from other circumstances such as the entity not anticipating the need for an audit and appointing the auditors after the latest year-end *(circumstance imposed)*.

EXHIBIT 12.5
Departure from GAAP Report (Adverse Opinion)

Independent Auditor's Report

Addressee (no revisions)

Introductory Paragraph (no revisions)

Management's Responsibility for the Financial Statements (no revisions)

Auditor's Responsibility (no revisions)

Basis for Adverse Opinion

As discussed in Note 16, an additional provision in the amount of $30,000,000 for possible uncollectible receivables at December 31, 2016, was charged to operations during the year ended December 31, 2017, which, in our opinion, should have been reflected in the financial statements for 2016. Had this provision been properly recorded in the 2016 financial statements, Dunder-Mifflin Inc. would have reported net earnings of $700,000 for the year ended December 31, 2017, rather than the net loss of $29,300,000 as reflected in the statements of income, changes in shareholders' equity, and cash flows for that period.

Adverse Opinion

In our opinion, *because of the significance of the matter discussed in the Basis for Adverse Opinion paragraph,* the financial statements referred to above *do not* present fairly the financial position of Dunder-Mifflin Inc. as of December 31, 2017, or the results of its operations or its cash flows for the year then ended in accordance with accounting principles generally accepted in the United States of America.

Michael Scarn, LLP
Scranton, PA
January 29, 2018

EXHIBIT 12.6
Scope Limitations

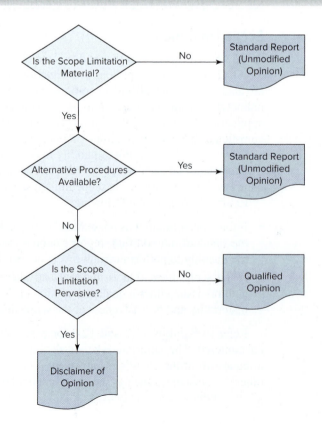

EXHIBIT 12.7
Scope Limitation Report (Qualified Opinion)

Independent Auditor's Report

Addressee (no revisions)

Introductory Paragraph (no revisions)

Management's Responsibility for the Financial Statements (no revisions)

Auditor's Responsibility (no revisions)

Basis for Qualified Opinion

Dunder-Mifflin Inc. did not make a count of its physical inventory in 2017, stated in the accompanying financial statements at $10,000,000 at December 31, 2017, and we were unable to observe the physical quantities on hand. Dunder-Mifflin Inc.'s records do not permit the application of other auditing procedures to the audit of inventories.

Qualified Opinion

In our opinion, *except for the possible effects of the matter described in the Basis for Qualified Opinion paragraph,* the financial statements referred to above present fairly, in all material respects, the financial position of Dunder-Mifflin Inc. as of December 31, 2017, and the results of its operations and its cash flows for the year then ended in accordance with accounting principles generally accepted in the United States of America.

Michael Scarn, LLP
Scranton, PA
January 29, 2018

In Exhibit 12.7, the opinion is qualified. In this case, the lack of evidence is considered material but not pervasive to the financial statements. Note that the qualification is based on the fact that the auditors were not able to determine whether the inventory is fairly stated, not the inability to perform the procedure *per se*. The report "compartmentalizes" the scope limitation to inventories.

In Exhibit 12.8, the situation has a more significant impact on the auditors' opinion; that is, the scope limitation is pervasive. The auditors believe that the inventories are too material to even be able to express an opinion on the financial statements. The report then must express a disclaimer of opinion. Notice that the introductory paragraph differs from the introductory paragraph in the standard (unmodified) report. This paragraph indicates "[w]e *were engaged to audit* . . ." instead of "[w]e have audited. . . ." Also notice that the section on auditor's responsibility has been modified to indicate that the auditor was not able to obtain sufficient appropriate evidence and refers to the Basis for Disclaimer of Opinion paragraph.

One additional consideration in evaluating reporting options when scope limitations exist is the nature of the limitation. Auditors should carefully consider the implications of a *client-imposed scope limitation* because such restrictions on the audit may cast doubt on management's integrity. (Why would management restrict the auditor's engagement?) Because of these implications, auditors normally disclaim an opinion or even withdraw from the engagement in these situations. Any client-imposed scope limitation should be communicated to those charged with the entity's governance.

The following summarizes modifications to the auditors' standard (unmodified) report for scope limitations (assuming that such limitations are material and alternative auditing procedures are not available). In addition, similar to departures from GAAP, the paragraphs describing the scope limitation and expressing the opinion are labeled to indicate the type of opinion expressed by the auditors (either qualified or a disclaimer of opinion).

	Qualified Opinion	Disclaimer of Opinion
Introductory Paragraph	No modification	Modified to note auditor was "engaged" to audit the financial statements
Management's Responsibility for the Financial Statements Section	No modification	No modification
Auditor's Responsibility Section	No modification	First paragraph modified to note auditor was not able to obtain sufficient appropriate evidence Paragraphs describing an audit and indicating that the audit provides a basis for the opinion are deleted
Opinion Paragraph	Modified to note "except for" the effects of adjustments that might have been identified, financial statements are presented according to GAAP	Modified to indicate that an opinion cannot be expressed on the financial statements
Additional Paragraph	Identifies scope limitation	Identifies scope limitation

EXHIBIT 12.8
Scope Limitation Report (Disclaimer of Opinion)

Independent Auditor's Report

Addressee (no revisions)

We *were engaged* to audit the accompanying financial statements of Dunder-Mifflin Inc., which comprise the balance sheet as of December 31, 2017, and the related statements of income, changes in shareholders' equity, and cash flows for the year then ended, and the related notes to the financial statements.

Management's Responsibility for the Financial Statements (no revisions)

Auditor's Responsibility

Our responsibility is to express an opinion on these financial statements *based on conducting the audit in accordance with auditing standards generally accepted in the United States of America. Because of the matter described in the Basis for Disclaimer of Opinion paragraph, however, we were not able to obtain sufficient appropriate audit evidence to provide a basis for an audit opinion.*

[Remainder of section deleted]

Basis for Disclaimer of Opinion

Dunder-Mifflin Inc. did not make a count of its physical inventory in 2017, stated in the accompanying financial statements at $10,000,000 at December 31, 2017, and we were unable to observe the physical quantities on hand. Dunder-Mifflin Inc.'s records do not permit the application of other auditing procedures to the audit of inventories

Disclaimer of Opinion

Because of the significance of the matter described in the Basis for Disclaimer of Opinion paragraph, we have not been able to obtain sufficient appropriate audit evidence to provide a basis for an audit opinion. Accordingly, we do not express an opinion on these financial statements.

Michael Scarn, LLP
Scranton, PA
January 29, 2018

⊘ REVIEW CHECKPOINTS

12.12 Distinguish between client-imposed scope limitations and circumstance-imposed scope limitations. Which of these scope limitations is generally of more concern to auditors?

12.13 If a scope limitation exists but auditors are able to perform alternative procedures, how is the standard (unmodified) report modified to reflect the scope limitation?

12.14 If a scope limitation exists and auditors cannot perform alternative procedures, what are the auditors' reporting options?

12.15 When a scope limitation exists, how would the standard (unmodified) report be modified to express (a) a qualified opinion and (b) a disclaimer of opinion?

AUDITS OF GROUP FINANCIAL STATEMENTS

Many large entities prepare consolidated financial statements that include more than one component (division, subsidiary, or other segment); these financial statements are referred to as **group financial statements**. In some cases, principal auditors (known as the *group engagement team* or **group auditors**) perform the audit of a material portion of the consolidated entity's assets, liabilities, revenues, and expenses, and other independent auditors (known as **component auditors**) may be engaged to audit divisions, subsidiaries, or components that are included in the group financial statements.[9]

Situations such as this may occur if clients have significant remote subsidiaries or if clients have an investment in another entity that is accounted for using the equity method. Because the group engagement partner's signature appears in the report on the financial statements of a consolidated or parent entity, the group auditors must make decisions regarding the use of the work and reports of the component auditor(s).

The group auditors must first obtain information about the independence and professional reputation of the component auditors. If the group auditors are satisfied with these qualities, they must next communicate with the component auditors and decide whether to refer to their work in the group auditors' report. As shown in Exhibit 12.9, the group

EXHIBIT 12.9

Reporting Options for Audits of Group Financial Statements

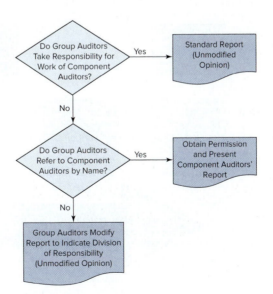

[9] The PCAOB recently issued a proposal that amends existing guidelines related to the supervision, planning, documentation, and engagement quality review by group auditors (referred to by the PCAOB as "lead auditors") of the work of component auditors (referred to as "other auditors"). See *Proposed Amendments Relating to the Supervision of Audits Involving Other Auditors* and *Proposed Auditing Standard—Dividing Responsibility for the Audit with Another Accounting Firm,* PCAOB Release No. 2016-002, April 12, 2016.

auditors may decide to make no reference and issue the standard (unmodified) report. In this case, the group auditors assume full responsibility for the component auditors' work.

On the other hand, the group auditors may decide to refer to the work and reports of the component auditors; this is referred to as a **division of responsibility**. Such a reference is not in itself a scope limitation and the report should not be considered to be inferior to a standard (unmodified) report that does not contain such a reference. The explanation should disclose the extent of the component auditors' work by indicating the percent or amount of assets, revenues, and expenses related to their work.

When the group auditors refer to the component auditors' work, the component auditors are ordinarily not identified by name. In fact, the component auditors may be named in the group auditors' report only by express permission and with publication of their report along with the group auditors' report. Refer to Exhibit 12.9 for a summary of the options available to group auditors for reporting when component auditors are involved in the audit of group financial statements.[10]

Exhibit 12.10 is an example of a group auditors' report that has been modified to express an unmodified opinion on financial statements and referencing the work of component auditors. Note in this report that the group auditors do not identify the "other auditors" by name.

Shown below is a summary of reporting options for the three situations described in this section (departures from GAAP, scope limitations, and audits of group financial statements). Notice that unmodified opinions are issued for matters that are not material, qualified opinions for matters that are material but less pervasive, and adverse opinions and disclaimers of opinions for matters that are material and more pervasive. A recent academic study found that the initial disclosure of the use of component auditors resulted in negative market reaction, but this negative reaction was not observed in following audits.[11]

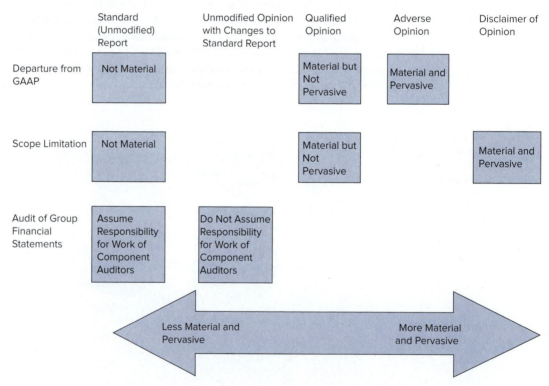

[10] *Improving the Transparency of Audits: Rules to Require Disclosure of Certain Audit Participants on a New PCAOB Form and Related Amendments to Auditing Standards,* PCAOB Release No. 2015-008, December 15, 2015, requires group auditors to disclose specific information regarding any component auditors whose work constituted at least five percent of the total audit hours.
[11] C.C. Dee, A. Lulseged, and T. Zhang, "Who Did the Audit? Audit Quality and Disclosures of Other Audit Participants in PCAOB Filings," *The Accounting Review,* September 2015, pp. 1939–1967.

EXHIBIT 12.10
Report on Audit of Group Financial Statements

Independent Auditor's Report

Addressee (no revisions)

Introductory paragraph (no revisions)

Management's Responsibility for the Financial Statements (no revisions)

Auditor's Responsibility

Our responsibility is to express an opinion on these financial statements based on our audit. *We did not audit the financial statements of B Company, a wholly-owned subsidiary, which statements reflect total assets constituting 20 percent of total assets at December 31, 2017, and total revenues constituting 18 percent of total revenues for the year then ended. Those statements were audited by other auditors whose report has been furnished to us, and our opinion, insofar as it relates to the amounts included for B Company, is based solely on the report of the other auditors.* We conducted our audit in accordance with auditing standards generally accepted in the United States of America. Those standards require that we plan and perform the audit to obtain reasonable assurance about whether the financial statements are free from material misstatement.

(No revisions to remainder of the section)

Opinion

In our opinion, *based on our audit and the report of other auditors,* the financial statements referred to above present fairly, in all material respects, the financial position of Dunder-Mifflin Inc. as of December 31, 2017, and the results of its operations and its cash flows for the year then ended in accordance with accounting principles generally accepted in the United States of America.

Michael Scarn, LLP
Scranton, PA
January 29, 2018

AUDITING INSIGHT | Penske Automotive Group and Component Auditors

In its 2016 auditors' report on **Penske Automotive Group, Deloitte & Touche** disclosed that other auditors audited the financial statements of **UAG UK Holdings Limited** (an entity whose assets and revenues account for 41 percent and 39 percent of Penske's consolidated totals for 2015, respectively).

 REVIEW CHECKPOINTS

12.16 Define *group auditors* and *component auditors*. What issues are introduced when component auditors examine a division, subsidiary, or segment of group financial statements?

12.17 What options are available to group auditors when component auditors are involved in the examination of group financial statements?

12.18 Is the reference in the auditors' report to work performed by component auditors a scope limitation? Explain.

AUDITORS' REPORTS REFERENCING OTHER MATTERS ENCOUNTERED DURING THE AUDIT

LO 12-3
Identify situations in which auditors add explanatory language to an unmodified opinion.

The preceding section illustrated reporting options for situations in which the language in the auditors' standard (unmodified) report was modified; in many cases, these situations required an opinion other than an unmodified opinion (qualified opinion, adverse opinion, or disclaimer of opinion) to be issued. In other cases, situations encountered during the audit involve adding a paragraph to the standard (unmodified) report shown in Exhibit 12.1 to describe the matter. These paragraphs are labeled as follows:

- Paragraphs that provide information fundamental to users' understanding of the entity's financial statements are known as **emphasis-of-matter paragraphs**.
- Paragraphs that provide information relating to users' understanding of the audit, auditors' responsibility, or auditors' report are known as **other-matter paragraphs**.

Emphasis-of-matter and other-matter paragraphs may be collectively referred to as **explanatory paragraphs**. In most cases, the auditors' reporting responsibility is exception-based reporting, which means that the report will refer only to these matters if an issue is noted during the audit.

Consistency

The concept of *consistency* is based on the importance of permitting users to appropriately compare an entity's financial statements across years. GAAS require that the auditors' report be modified by adding an *emphasis-of-matter paragraph* (following the opinion paragraph) for the following issues related to consistency:

1. Changes in accounting principles (from one GAAP method to another GAAP method).
2. Changes in the form of the reporting entity (other than that resulting from a transaction or event).
3. Changes in an accounting principle that is not a generally accepted accounting principle to one that is a generally accepted accounting principle (which is considered to be an adjustment to correct a misstatement in previously issued financial statements).
4. Changes in accounting principles inseparable from changes in estimates.

The following is an excerpt from EY's 2013 report on **The Coca-Cola Company**'s financial statements related to consistency.

> As discussed in Note 1 to the consolidated financial statements, The Coca-Cola Company has elected to change its method of calculating the market-related value of plan assets related to certain of its pension plans in 2012.

Changes in accounting principles may result from the issuance of new accounting standards or from management's selection of alternatives provided under existing accounting standards (as noted in the preceding example). When evaluating a change in accounting principle, auditors should be satisfied that (1) the newly adopted accounting principle is a generally accepted accounting principle, (2) the method of accounting for the change is appropriate, (3) disclosures relating to the change are appropriate, and (4) the newly adopted principle is preferable to the previously used principle. If these criteria are not met, the audit team should treat the change in principle as a departure from GAAP and modify the report accordingly.

"Going-Concern" Uncertainties

GAAP are based on the *going-concern* principle, which means the entity is expected to continue in operation and meet its obligations as they become due without substantially disposing of its assets outside the ordinary course of business, restructuring its debt, or taking similar actions. Hence, an opinion that financial statements are in accordance with

GAAP means that continued existence may be presumed for a "reasonable time" not to exceed one year beyond the date of the financial statements. As noted in Chapter 11, one of the activities performed by auditors during the completion of the audit is assessing the entity's ability to continue as a going concern for a period not to exceed one year beyond the date of the financial statements.

Questions raised about the entity's ability to continue in operation and meet its obligations as they become due are known as **going-concern uncertainties**. The most common report issued when going-concern uncertainties exist is an unmodified opinion with an *emphasis-of-matter paragraph* following the opinion paragraph that directs users' attention to management's disclosures about going-concern uncertainties and specifically includes the words "substantial doubt" and "going concern." For very severe going-concern uncertainties, professional standards (AU-C 570.18) indicate that auditors may issue a disclaimer of opinion with the auditors' report providing all substantive reasons for the disclaimer. The following is an excerpted paragraph from Deloitte & Touche's 2016 report on **Caesars Entertainment Corporation**'s financial statements:

> The accompanying consolidated financial statements have been prepared assuming that the Company will continue as a going concern. As discussed in Note 1 to the consolidated financial statements, . . . The uncertainty of the outcome of these matters raises substantial doubt about the Company's ability to continue as a going concern. Management's plans concerning these matters are discussed in Notes 1, 3, and 4 to the consolidated financial statements.

These reporting options assumed that the entity has properly disclosed matters related to the going-concern uncertainty. If they have not done so, auditors would issue a qualified or adverse opinion on the entity's financial statements, similar to actions taken for other departures from GAAP.

A research report by Audit Analytics examining the time period 2000-2014 revealed the following with respect to going-concern reports.[12]

- The percentage of auditors' reports indicating going-concern uncertainties ranged from 14.2% to 21.1% per year (the latter in 2008 concurrent with the financial crisis).
- The most frequent issues raised in 2014 reports (percentage of going-concern reports in parentheses) were net/operating losses (62%), working capital/current ratio deficiencies (31%), negative cash flow from operations (29%), net losses since inception (24%), and insufficient revenues (22%) (more than one issue was mentioned in some reports).
- Smaller companies are more likely to receive a going-concern report; the percentage of auditors' reports indicating going-concern uncertainties were lowest for large accelerated filers (public equity of $700 million or more) (average of 0.4%), followed by accelerated filers (public equity of between $75 million and $700 million) (average of 3.5%), then by smaller companies (average of 23.4%).

Using the Audit Analytics database, only three going-concern reports have been received by *Fortune* 500 companies since 2011: **American Airlines Group Inc.** (2012 and 2013) and **Caesars Entertainment Corporation** (2016).

Other Information Accompanying Audited Financial Statements

In many cases, audited financial statements include a variety of information that accompanies the financial statements. For example, all annual reports to shareholders and SEC filings contain such sections as a president's letter and management's discussion and analysis (MD&A) of operations. Auditors have an obligation to read the other information and determine whether this information is consistent with the audited financial statements or contains material misstatements.

[12] *2014 Going Concerns: A Fifteen Year Review* (Audit Analytics), 2015.

AUDITING INSIGHT | Research on Going-Concern Reports

The following academic studies have examined going-concern reports:

- Menon and Williams found that the stock market's reaction to a going-concern report was more negative if the report mentioned difficulties in obtaining financing and if the company had debt covenants that were related to the receipt of a going-concern report.

- Kaplan and Williams found that auditors were more likely to issue going-concern reports for clients with a high risk of litigation. In addition, the authors concluded that the issuance of going-concern reports reduced the likelihood of litigation and, in cases where litigation occurred, reduced the likelihood of large financial settlements.

- Chen et al. concluded that going-concern reports are less likely to be issued by auditors following large "insider sales" of a company's stock by its management. They attribute this finding to the possibility that management may pressure auditors not to reference going-concern matters to reduce the likelihood of shareholder litigation resulting from management sales of stock in advance of an opinion referencing going concern.

- Geiger et al. found that auditors were more likely to issue going-concern reports to financially stressed companies following the onset of the 2008 global financial crisis than prior to the crisis.

- Carson et al. examined audit opinions issued from 2000–2010 and found that going-concern reports were more likely to be issued for companies with smaller market capitalizations and that more than 60 percent of bankruptcies are preceded by the issuance of a going-concern report.

- Chen et al. found that going-concern reports affected various aspects of loan decisions (higher interest rates, increased use of general loan covenants, reduced loan sizes and shorter maturities, and increased collateral requirements).

Sources: K. Menon and D. D. Williams, "Investor Reaction to Going Concern Audit Reports," *The Accounting Review,* November 2010, pp. 2075–2105; S. E. Kaplan and D. D. Williams, "Do Going Concern Audit Reports Protect Auditors from Litigation? A Simultaneous Equations Approach," *The Accounting Review,* January 2013, pp. 199–232; C. Chen, X, Martin, and X. Wang, "Insider Trading, Litigation Concerns, and Auditor Going-Concern Opinions," *The Accounting Review,* March 2013, pp. 365–393; M. A. Geiger, K. Raghunandan, and W. Riccardi, "The Global Financial Crisis: U.S. Bankruptcies and Going-Concern Audit Opinions," *Accounting Horizons,* March 2014, pp. 59–75; E. Carson, N. L. Fargher, M. A. Geiger, C. S. Lennox, K. Raghunandan, and M. Willekens, "Audit Reporting for Going-Concern Uncertainty: A Research Synthesis," *Auditing: A Journal of Practice & Theory,* Supplement 1, 2013, pp. 353–384; P. F. Chen, S. He, Z. Ma, and D. Stice, "The Information Role of Audit Opinions in Debt Contracting," *Journal of Accounting and Economics,* February 2016, pp. 121–144.

Similar to consistency and going-concern uncertainties, other information accompanying audited financial statements is subject to "exception-based" reporting (i.e., auditors' reports mention the other information only if inconsistencies or misstatements exist). If misstatements or inconsistencies exist with respect to other information and the entity chooses not to revise the other information, the auditors should (1) notify the client in writing of their views, (2) consult with legal counsel about appropriate action to take, and (3) consider whether this inconsistency affects the opinion on the financial statements. If it does affect the opinion, the auditors should revise their opinion on the financial statements; if not, the auditors should expand their report to add an *other-matter paragraph* identifying the misstatement or inconsistencies of the other information.

Required Supplementary Information

In addition to the financial statements and footnotes accompanying the financial statements, accounting standard-setting bodies may require companies to provide supplementary information that is not part of the basic financial statements. For example, the FASB requires energy companies to present oil, gas, and other mineral reserve information as supplementary information. Other examples of such information related to specific industries or types of companies (construction, development-stage entities, financial services, and real estate) can be found in *ASC 235.*

Auditors are required to perform limited procedures (inquiring of management, comparing information for consistency with the financial statements, and obtaining written representations from management) with respect to the required supplementary information. When companies present required supplementary information, auditors are required to expand their report on the financial statements to include an *other-matter paragraph* that identifies the supplementary information, describes any procedures performed with respect to this information, and identifies any issues related to this information. However, the paragraph specifically disclaims an opinion or any form of assurance on the supplementary information.

Other Modifications

Beyond the wording in the standard (unmodified) report, auditors can enrich the information content in their reports by adding one or more paragraphs to emphasize something they believe readers should consider important or useful. Although auditing standards place no official limits on the content of these paragraphs, auditors often use them to describe circumstances that present some business or information risk. Matters that may be emphasized include a warning that a bankruptcy filing may be imminent, a description of the auditee as a subsidiary of a larger entity, the effects of business events on the comparability of financial statements, the interaction of the auditee with related parties, and the effect of events that occur after the date of the financial statements (commonly referred to as *subsequent events*). For example, during the 2008-2009 financial crisis, both **American International Group (AIG)** and **Fannie Mae**'s auditors' reports mentioned issues encountered by these firms during this time.

Some recent examples include

- Modifications to and changes in accounting for consideration received related to **Alaska Air**'s affinity card agreement (2015 auditors' report).
- **Abbott Laboratories**' spin-off of **ABBVie, Inc.** (2014 auditors' report).
- **SoftBank Corp.**'s merger with **Sprint Communications** (2014 auditors' report).
- The change in **Best Buy Co., Inc.**'s fiscal year end from February to January (2015 auditors' report).
- The exclusion of **Harris Teeter Supermarkets, Inc.** from **The Kroger Co.**'s management's assessment of internal control over financial reporting (2014 auditors' report).

Summary: Emphasis-of-Matter and Other-Matter Paragraphs

Assuming that the matters discussed in this section are properly accounted for and disclosed by the entity, the auditors' report is modified by adding a paragraph labeled "Emphasis of Matter" or "Other Matter" to the report. It is important to reiterate that the opinion on the financial statements would still be unmodified.

A recent academic study analyzing audit opinions with explanatory paragraphs that were issued between 2000 and 2009 identified the following most common disclosures (as a percentage of all opinions with explanatory paragraphs): (1) adoption of new accounting principles (80 percent); (2) financial distress (including going-concern) (7 percent); (3) financial statement restatements (5 percent); (4) mergers (4 percent); and, (5) consistency (2 percent).[13]

✓ REVIEW CHECKPOINTS

12.19 Define *emphasis-of-matter* and *other-matter* paragraphs. What type of information do auditors provide in these paragraphs?

12.20 What types of matters would result in the auditors' report being modified for consistency?

12.21 What are *going-concern uncertainties*? What is the auditors' responsibility for evaluating going-concern uncertainties?

12.22 What are auditors' reporting options when going-concern uncertainties are noted?

12.23 What is the auditors' reporting responsibility for (a) other information accompanying the audited financial statements and (b) required supplementary information?

[13] K. Czerney, J.J. Schmidt, and A.M. Thompson, "Does Auditor Explanatory Language in Unqualified Audit Reports Indicate Increased Financial Misstatement Risk?," *The Accounting Review*, November 2014, pp. 2115–2149.

OTHER REPORTING TOPICS

LO 12-4

Identify other circumstances affecting auditors' reporting responsibilities and explain how they affect auditors' reports on an entity's financial statements.

To this point, we have focused on situations in which auditors have examined and reported on a single year's financial statements. Additional issues are introduced when companies provide multiple years of financial statements in comparative form, auditors are engaged to examine and report on information other than the financial statements and related disclosures, and auditors' involvement in the financial reporting process might be misunderstood by users. These situations are the focus of this section.

Comparative Financial Statements

The SEC requires public entities to present balance sheets for two years and statements of income, changes in shareholders' equity, and cash flows for three years in comparative (side-by-side) format. Financial statement footnotes also contain disclosures in comparative form. Together, these comparative financial statements and footnotes are the subject of the auditors' work and report. Although nonpublic companies are not subject to similar requirements, users may request that entities provide multiple years of financial statements in comparative form.

The issue introduced when financial statements are presented in comparative form is that users may assume that the auditor has examined all comparative years presented. Therefore, it is important that the auditor's report specifically identify the responsibility assumed for all financial statements presented in comparative form.

Same Auditors, Same Opinions for Comparative Years

When auditors issue a report on the current-year financial statements, they are required to update their report on the prior years' financial statements by considering whether the opinions on the prior years' financial statements are still appropriate. The **updated report** is based not only on the prior-year audits, but also on information that has come to the auditors' attention since then (particularly in the course of the most recent audit). An updated report carries the most recent date of the auditors' report, and the auditors' responsibility for the comparative financial statements now extends to this date.

Recall the standard (unmodified) report shown in Exhibit 12.1. Assume that Dunder-Mifflin Inc. presented balance sheets for 2016 and 2017 and statements of income, changes in shareholders' equity, and cash flows for 2015, 2016, and 2017. If Michael Scarn had audited Dunder-Mifflin all three years and concluded that an unmodified opinion was appropriate in all three years, a "plural" form of the standard (unmodified) report would be issued which expresses an opinion on the financial condition for 2016 and 2017 and the results of operations and cash flows for 2015, 2016, and 2017.

An updated report differs from a **reissued report**. When auditors reissue a report, they simply provide additional copies of a previously issued report or grant entities permission to use a previously issued report in another document sometime after its original date. However, auditors do not attempt to update the report or otherwise consider events that have occurred since the date of the original report. The date of a reissued report is the same as that for the original report, indicating a cutoff date for the auditors' responsibility.

Same Auditors, Different Opinions for Comparative Years

Auditors can express different opinions on comparative years' financial statements in the same report. For example, assume that Dunder-Mifflin incorrectly recorded a $30 million provision for uncollectible receivables in the 2016 financial statements instead of in 2015. As a result, both years' financial statements were not prepared in accordance with GAAP, so Michael Scarn issued an adverse opinion in those two years. However, Scarn concluded that an unmodified opinion was appropriate in 2017. The report shown in Exhibit 12.11 would be appropriate in the circumstances.

EXHIBIT 12.11
Different Opinions in Comparative Year Financial Statements

Independent Auditor's Report

Addressee (no revisions)

Introductory Paragraph (no revisions, refer to 2015, 2016, and 2017)

Management's Responsibility for the Financial Statements (no revisions)

Auditor's Responsibility (no revisions)

Basis for Adverse Opinion on 2015 and 2016 Financial Statements

As discussed in Note 16, an additional provision in the amount of $30,000,000 for possible uncollectible receivables at December 31, 2015, was charged to operations during the year ended December 31, 2016, which, in our opinion, should have been reflected in the financial statements for 2015. Had this provision been properly recorded in the 2015 financial statements, net income and shareholders' equity for 2015 would have been $30,000,000 lower than that reported and net income for 2016 would have been $30,000,000 higher than that reported, as reflected in the balance sheets and statements of income, changes in shareholders' equity, and cash flows for those years.

Adverse Opinion on 2015 and 2016 Financial Statements

In our opinion, because of the significance of the matter discussed in the Basis for Adverse Opinion on 2015 and 2016 Financial Statements paragraph, the financial statements referred to above do not present fairly the financial position of Dunder-Mifflin Inc. as of December 31, 2016 and 2015, or the results of its operations or its cash flows for the two-year period then ended in accordance with accounting principles generally accepted in the United States of America.

Opinion

In our opinion, the financial statements referred to above present fairly, in all material respects, the financial position of Dunder-Mifflin Inc. as of December 31, 2017, and the results of its operations and its cash flows for the year then ended in accordance with accounting principles generally accepted in the United States of America.

Michael Scarn, LLP
Scranton, PA
January 29, 2018

Essentially, the report in Exhibit 12.11 combines an adverse opinion on Dunder-ww financial statements for 2015 and 2016 with an unmodified opinion on its financial statements for 2017.

Same Auditors with Modification of Previously Issued Opinion

Auditors should modify the opinion expressed on prior years' financial statements if circumstances have changed in the intervening period. For example, consider the departure from GAAP shown in Exhibit 12.11 and discussed in the preceding section. In 2017, if Dunder-Mifflin restated its 2015 and 2016 financial statements to record the provision in the appropriate year (2015), all three years of financial statements would now be in accordance with GAAP. Therefore, an unmodified opinion (standard report) on all three years would now be appropriate.

One concern with not referring to the previous opinions is that Michael Scarn's updated opinion on the 2015 and 2016 financial statements is now different from the originally issued opinion. To alert readers to this fact, an explanatory other-matter paragraph such as the following one would be added to the report (following the opinion paragraph):

Other Matter

In our report dated January 30, 2017, we expressed an opinion that the 2016 and 2015 financial statements did not fairly present the financial position, results of operations, and cash flows in accordance with principles generally accepted in the United States of America because Dunder-Mifflin Inc. incorrectly recorded a $30,000,000 provision for uncollectible receivables in 2016 rather than in 2015. As described in Note 2, Dunder-Mifflin Inc. has restated its 2016 and 2015 financial statements to conform with accounting principles generally accepted in the United States of America. Accordingly, our present opinion on the restated 2016 and 2015 financial statements, as presented herein, is different from that expressed in our previous report.

Different Auditors in Comparative Years

Assume that Michael Scarn became the auditor of Dunder-Mifflin in 2017 and another (predecessor) firm had examined the 2015 and 2016 financial statements and issued an unmodified opinion (standard report) on these statements. In this case, Michael Scarn's report should indicate that he audited the 2017 financial statements and expressed an opinion on the 2017 financial statements. However, how should the results of the other firm's audit of the 2015 and 2016 financial statements be communicated?

One option would be to add an other-matter paragraph (following the introductory paragraph) that summarizes the predecessor auditors' responsibility and report. An example of this type of paragraph follows. If the predecessor auditors issued an opinion other than the standard (unmodified) opinion, the paragraph should be expanded to provide information about the report modification. The predecessor auditors' report would also be included along with the comparative financial statements.

Other Matter

The financial statements of Dunder-Mifflin Inc. as of December 31, 2016 and 2015, were audited by other auditors whose report dated February 4, 2017, expressed an unmodified opinion on those statements.

AUDITING INSIGHT   Changing Their Mind (and Auditor)

Dillard's Inc. has employed three different auditors since 2009 and presented the following auditors' reports along with their financial statements (two years of balance sheets and three years of income statements, statements of changes in stockholders' equity, and statements of cash flows were presented in comparative form).

2011 (2009–2011): Deloitte & Touche opinion on 2009 financial statements, PwC opinion on 2010 and 2011 financial statements

2012 (2010–2012): PwC opinion on 2010 and 2011 financial statements, KPMG opinion on 2012 financial statements

2013 (2011–2013): PwC opinion on 2011 financial statements, KPMG opinion on 2012 and 2013 financial statements

Beginning in 2014 through 2016, only reports issued by KPMG were presented, as they were the auditors during the entire three-year period.

Summary Financial Statements

Published financial statements are lengthy and often complex. Entities sometimes have occasion to present the financial statements in considerably less detail (e.g., summary totals of current assets, current liabilities, long-term liabilities, operating income, or other subtotals). Generally, such summary financial statements (sometimes referred to as *condensed financial statements*) are derived directly from the full audited financial statements. However, summary financial statements are not fair presentations of financial position, results of operations, and cash flows in accordance with GAAP.

In some cases, users may engage auditors to examine and report on summary financial statements. Auditors can do so only if they have audited the full financial statements. The report on summary financial statements parallels the auditors' report on the financial statements illustrated throughout this chapter and must refer to the auditors' report on the full financial statements, giving the date and the type of opinion expressed. The auditors' conclusion on summary financial statements will not express an opinion on the summary financial statements but will indicate whether the information in the summary financial statements is fairly stated in all material respects in relation to the complete financial statements.

Supplementary Information

Earlier, we discussed supplementary information that standard-setting bodies (such as the FASB) require entities to present along with their financial statements and related footnote disclosures (known as *required supplementary information*). Other types of supplementary information may be presented outside the basic financial statements; this information differs in that there is no expressed requirement for presenting it or any authoritative guidelines for presenting or preparing this information.

Similar to summary financial statements, users may engage auditors to examine and report on supplementary information. The auditors' conclusion will not express an opinion on the supplementary information but will indicate whether it is fairly stated, in all material respects, in relation to the financial statements as a whole. Auditors may report on this information either by adding an other-matter paragraph to their report on the financial statements (following the opinion paragraph) or by preparing a separate report on the supplementary information. For example, KPMG added a paragraph to its 2016 report on its audit of **General Electric** that references ". . . consolidating information appearing on pages 129, 133, and 135 [of General Electric's annual report]" and indicates that this information ". . . is fairly stated in all material respects in relation to the consolidated financial statements taken as a whole."

Disclaimers of Opinion

In addition to the situations described in the previous sections of this chapter, other circumstances may result in auditors issuing disclaimers of opinion. Auditors may be engaged to conduct an audit but subsequently discover a relationship involving the firm that results in a lack of independence. In other cases, auditors may consent to the use of their name in some form of communication containing the entity's financial statements or submit to their clients or others (such as third-party users) financial statements they have prepared or assisted in preparing. These situations are referred to as being **associated with financial statements.**

In these situations, auditors will issue a single paragraph report shown in Exhibit 12.12. Note that this report is not addressed to any specific users, nor does it reference any procedures performed on Dunder-Mifflin's financial statements.

When auditors are not independent, the report in Exhibit 12.12 would begin with the phrase "We were not independent with respect to Dunder-Mifflin Inc." The report should not mention any reasons for not being independent because readers may erroneously interpret them as unimportant.

EXHIBIT 12.12
Disclaimer of Opinion on Unaudited Financial Statements

The accompanying balance sheet of Dunder-Mifflin Inc. as of December 31, 2017, and the related statements of income, changes in shareholders' equity, and cash flows for the year then ended were not audited by us and, accordingly, we do not express an opinion on them.

Michael Scarn, LLP
Scranton, PA
January 29, 2018

Summary

This chapter has discussed a wide range of reporting issues. The array and variety of reports may seem confusing, but several simple rules will enable you to remember the basics of auditors' reports on financial statements. First, begin with the standard (unmodified) report in Exhibit 12.1. Keeping the four sections in mind, remember that the following basic rules apply:

- The introductory paragraph is modified when the financial statements examined or responsibility assumed by auditors changes (e.g., for a pervasive scope limitation).
- The Management's Responsibility section is not modified for any of the issues discussed in this chapter because they are not related to management's responsibility for the financial statements and internal control.
- The Auditor's Responsibility section is modified for matters that affect the auditors' responsibility for the financial statements (scope limitations or audits of group financial statements).
- The opinion paragraph is modified when an opinion other than an unmodified opinion is issued.
- Additional paragraphs are added to the report when an opinion other than an unmodified opinion is issued or when some other matter arises.

Like all general guidelines, exceptions to these rules can be found. For example, when component auditors are involved in the audit of group financial statements, an additional paragraph *would not* be added, which contradicts the general rule related to additional paragraphs; in addition, the opinion paragraph is modified despite the fact that an unmodified opinion is issued. See Exhibit 12.13 for a comprehensive summary of auditors' reports discussed in this chapter. In reviewing Exhibit 12.13, it is important to note that if any of the issues does not have a material effect on the financial statements, auditors can issue the standard (unmodified) report without any reference to the issue (except for a lack of independence, which is always considered to be material).

EXHIBIT 12.13   Summary of Reporting Issues

	Significance of the Matter		Paragraphs/Sections Modified				Other Comments
	Material	Pervasive	Introductory	Auditor's Responsibility	Opinion	Additional	
Departure from GAAP	Qualified opinion	Adverse opinion			X	X	
Scope limitation	Qualified opinion	Disclaimer of opinion	X	X	X	X	• Auditors can issue standard (unmodified) report if alternative procedures are available and performed • Should consider disclaimer if client-imposed limitation • Introductory paragraph and Auditor's Responsibility section modified only for disclaimer
Audit of group financial statements	Unmodified opinion	Unmodified opinion		X	X		Auditors can issue a standard (unmodified) report if group auditors assume responsibility for component auditors' work
Consistency	Unmodified opinion	Unmodified opinion				X	
Going-concern uncertainty	Unmodified opinion	Disclaimer of opinion			X	X	The opinion paragraph is modified only if a disclaimer is issued
Other information	Unmodified opinion	Unmodified opinion				X	Paragraph added only if other information is inconsistent with the financial statements
Required supplementary information	Unmodified opinion	Unmodified opinion				X	
Emphasis of a matter	Unmodified opinion	Unmodified opinion				X	
Lack of independence	Disclaimer of opinion	Disclaimer of opinion					Auditors would issue single-paragraph disclaimer of opinion
Association with unaudited financial statements	Disclaimer of opinion	Disclaimer of opinion					Auditors would issue single-paragraph disclaimer of opinion

Key Terms

adverse opinion: The opinion issued when the auditors conclude that the financial statements do not present the financial condition, results of operations, and cash flows in accordance with GAAP.

associated (association) with financial statements: Situations in which auditors consent to the use of their name in some form of communication containing the entity's financial statements or submit to their clients or others (such as third-party users) financial statements they have prepared or assisted in preparing. Auditors should issue a one-paragraph disclaimer when they are associated with (but did not audit) financial statements

circumstance-imposed scope limitation: A restriction on auditors from gathering sufficient appropriate evidence because of a situation beyond control of both the auditors and client, such as late appointment of the auditors.

client-imposed scope limitation: A restriction on auditors from gathering sufficient appropriate evidence because of the client's deliberate refusal to provide them access to evidence or to otherwise limit the auditors' application of auditing procedures.

component auditor: The auditor who audits divisions, subsidiaries, or components that are included in the group financial statements.

date of the auditors' report: The date on which auditors have obtained sufficient appropriate evidence to support their opinion.

departure from GAAP: Situation in which an entity does not follow GAAP in preparing its financial statements. Auditors can issue qualified or adverse opinions for material departures from GAAP.

disclaimer of opinion: A report issued when auditors do not express an opinion on the fairness of the entity's financial statements. Disclaimers of opinion are issued for pervasive going-concern uncertainties, pervasive scope limitations, situations in which auditors' are associated with (but did not audit) financial statements, and situations in which the auditors are not independent.

division of responsibility: Situation in which the component auditors are involved with the examination of a subsidiary, branch, component, or investment that is included in the financial statements audited by group auditors.

emphasis-of-matter paragraph: A paragraph added to an auditors' report that provides information fundamental to users' understanding of the financial statements (such as consistency or going-concern uncertainties).

explanatory paragraph: A paragraph added to an auditors' report that either provides information fundamental to users' understanding of the financial statements (emphasis-of-matter paragraph) or is relevant to users' understanding of the audit, the auditor's responsibility, or auditors' report (other-matter paragraph).

going-concern uncertainty: Situation in which questions are raised about an entity's ability to continue operations and meet its obligations as they become due.

group auditors: The auditors who perform the audit of a material portion of the assets, liabilities, revenues, and expenses of an entity's group financial statements; also known as *principal auditors*.

group financial statements: The financial statements of more than one component (division, subsidiary, or other segment).

integrated report: A single report issued by auditors expressing their opinion on the fairness of the financial statements and effectiveness of internal control over financial reporting.

introductory paragraph: The paragraph in the auditors' report that identifies the financial statements examined by the auditors and the responsibility of auditors and management with respect to the financial statements.

modified opinion: Any opinion other than an unmodified opinion on an entity's financial statements (qualified opinion, adverse opinion, or disclaimer of opinion).

opinion paragraph: A paragraph in the auditors' report that expresses their opinion on whether the financial statements are presented in accordance with GAAP.

other-matter paragraph: A paragraph added to the auditors' report that is relevant to users' understanding of the audit, the auditor's responsibility, or the auditors' report.

qualified opinion: An opinion issued when the auditors conclude that, with the exception of one or more issue(s), the financial statements present the financial condition, results of operations, and cash flows in accordance with GAAP. Qualified opinions can be issued for material departures from GAAP and material scope limitations.

reissued report: A copy of a previously issued report that auditors provide or grant entities permission to use in another document after its original date; the report is not modified to consider events occurring subsequent to the date of the original report.

scope limitation: A situation in which the auditors are unable to obtain sufficient appropriate evidence. If material, a scope limitation results in the issuance of either a qualified opinion or disclaimer of opinion.

unmodified opinion: An opinion issued when the auditors conclude that the financial statements present the financial condition, results of operations, and cash flows in accordance with GAAP (until recently, known as an *unqualified opinion*).

updated report: The auditors' report on prior-year financial statements that is based on both the prior-year audit and information that has come to the auditors' attention in the most recent audit.

Multiple-Choice Questions for Practice and Review

All applicable questions are available with Connect.

LO 12-1

12.30 When reporting under GAAS, certain statements are required in all auditors' reports ("explicit") and others are required only under certain conditions ("implicit"). Which combination that follows correctly describes the auditors' responsibilities for reporting?

	(a)	(b)	(c)	(d)
1. GAAP	Explicit	Explicit	Implicit	Implicit
2. Consistency	Implicit	Explicit	Explicit	Implicit
3. Going concern	Implicit	Implicit	Explicit	Explicit
4. Opinion	Explicit	Explicit	Implicit	Implicit

LO 12-2

12.31 Auditors found that the entity has not capitalized a material amount of leases in the financial statements. When considering the materiality of this departure from GAAP, the auditors would choose between which reporting options?

a. Unmodified opinion or disclaimer of opinion.

b. Unmodified opinion or qualified opinion.

c. Unmodified opinion with an emphasis-of-matter paragraph or an adverse opinion.

d. Qualified opinion or adverse opinion.

LO 12-3

12.32 The auditors determined that the entity is suffering financial difficulty and its going-concern status is seriously in doubt. Assuming that the entity adequately disclosed this matter in the financial statements, the auditors must choose between which of the following auditors' report alternatives?

a. Unmodified opinion with a reference to going-concern or disclaimer of opinion.

b. Standard (unmodified) report or a disclaimer of opinion.

c. Qualified opinion or adverse opinion.

d. Standard (unmodified) report or adverse opinion.

LO 12-1

12.33 Which of the following statements is *not* true with respect to the audit examinations and reports for public and nonpublic entities?

a. Audit examinations for nonpublic entities are based on user demand but based on legislative requirements for public entities.

b. The reports for both public and nonpublic entities express an opinion on the entity's financial statements.

c. Auditors are required to express an opinion on internal control in the audit of nonpublic entities but not in the audit of public entities.

d. Management is responsible for the fairness of the financial statements for both public entities and nonpublic entities.

LO 12-3

12.34 Which of these situations would require auditors to append an emphasis-of-matter paragraph about consistency to an otherwise unmodified opinion?

a. Entity changed its estimated allowance for uncollectible accounts receivable.

b. Entity corrected a prior mistake in accounting for interest capitalization.

c. Entity sold one of its subsidiaries and consolidated six subsidiaries this year compared to seven last year.

d. Entity changed its inventory costing method from FIFO to LIFO.

LO 12-4   12.35   R. Wolfe became the new auditor for Royal Corporation, succeeding C. Mason, who audited the financial statements last year. Wolfe needs to report on Royal's comparative financial statements and should disclose in the report an explanation about other auditors having audited the prior year

a. Only if Mason's opinion last year was qualified.

b. To describe the prior audit and the opinion but not name Mason as the predecessor auditor.

c. To describe the audit but not reveal the type of opinion issued by Mason.

d. To describe the audit and the opinion and name Mason as the predecessor auditor.

LO 12-2   12.36   When component auditors are involved in the audit of group financial statements, the group auditors may issue a report that

a. Refers to the component auditors, describes the extent of the component auditors' work, and expresses an unmodified opinion.

b. Does not consider or evaluate the component auditors' work but expresses an unmodified opinion in a standard report.

c. Places primary responsibility for the reporting on the component auditors.

d. Names the component auditors, describes their work, and presents only the group auditors' report.

LO 12-3   12.37   When auditors wish to issue an unmodified opinion but highlight that the entity changed its method of accounting for software development costs, they would most appropriately identify the change in accounting method in which of the following?

a. The introductory paragraph.

b. The opinion paragraph.

c. An emphasis-of-matter paragraph.

d. An other-matter paragraph.

LO 12-2   12.38   Under which of the following conditions can a disclaimer of opinion *never* be issued?

a. The entity's going-concern problems are highly material and pervasive.

b. The entity does not allow the auditors access to evidence about important accounts.

c. The auditors own stock in the entity.

d. The auditors have determined that the entity uses the NIFO (next-in, first-out) inventory costing method.

LO 12-1   12.39   How is the auditors' responsibility for expressing the opinion on financial statements disclosed in the standard (unmodified) report for a nonpublic company?

a. Stated explicitly in the Auditor's Responsibility section.

b. Unstated but understood in the Auditor's Responsibility section.

c. Stated explicitly in the opinion paragraph.

d. Stated explicitly in the introductory paragraph.

LO 12-1   12.40   Company A hired Samson & Delilah, CPAs, to audit the financial statements of Company B and deliver the report to Megabank. Who is the client?

a. Megabank.

b. Samson & Delilah.

c. Company A.

d. Company B.

LO 12-1   12.41   Which of the following is *not* included in the standard (unmodified) report on the financial statements?

a. An identification of the financial statements that were audited.

b. A general description of an audit.

c. An opinion that the financial statements present financial position in accordance with GAAP.

d. An emphasis-of-matter paragraph commenting on the effect of economic conditions on the entity.

LO 12-1

12.42 If the auditors decide to present separate reports on the entity's financial statements and internal control over financial reporting, which of the following should be modified to refer to the other report?

	Report on Financial Statements	Report on Internal Control over Financial Reporting
a.	Yes	Yes
b.	Yes	No
c.	No	Yes
d.	No	No

LO 12-4

12.43 When financial statements are presented in comparative form and another firm audited the prior years' financial statements (but the other firm's report is not presented with the financial statements), the auditors' report on the current-year financial statements should

  a. Disclaim an opinion on the prior years' financial statements.

  b. Not refer to the prior years' financial statements.

  c. Refer to any procedures performed by the current auditor to verify the opinion on the prior years' financial statements.

  d. Refer to the report and type of opinion issued by the other firm on the prior years' financial statements.

LO 12-4

12.44 If the opinion issued on prior years' financial statements is no longer appropriate and financial statements are presented in comparative form, the auditors' current report should

  a. Not reference the prior years' financial statements.

  b. Indicate that the opinion on the prior years' financial statements cannot be relied upon.

  c. Reference the type of opinion issued on the prior years' financial statements and indicate that the current opinion on these financial statements differs from that expressed in the prior years.

  d. Express the revised opinion on the prior years' financial statements without referencing the previously issued opinion.

Exercises and Problems

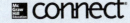 All applicable questions are available with Connect.

LO 12-2

12.45 **Basic Reports.** The concepts of materiality and pervasiveness are important to auditors in examinations of financial statements and expressions of opinion on these statements.

Required:

How will materiality influence auditors' reporting decisions in the following circumstances? In your response, consider both the matter's materiality and pervasiveness.

  a. The entity prohibits confirmation of accounts receivable, and sufficient and appropriate evidence cannot be obtained using alternative procedures.

  b. The entity is a gas and electric utility company that follows the practice of recognizing revenue when it is billed to customers. At the end of the year, amounts earned but not yet billed are not recorded in the accounts or reported in the financial statements.

  c. The entity leases buildings for its chain of transmission repair shops under terms that qualify as capital leases under *ASC 840*. These leases are not capitalized as leased property assets and lease obligations.

  d. The entity has lost a lawsuit in federal district court. The case is on appeal in an attempt to reduce the amount of damages awarded to the plaintiffs. No loss amount is recorded.

LO 12-2

12.46 **Departures from GAAP.** For each of the following departures from GAAP, indicate the type of opinion that the auditors would issue as well as any modifications that would be made to the standard (unmodified) report.

a. A departure that had an immaterial effect on the financial statements.

b. A departure that had a material effect on the financial statements (this effect was not pervasive and affected only one account).

c. A departure that had a material effect on the financial statements and was pervasive (affected a number of accounts on both the balance sheet and income statement).

LO 12-2

12.47 **Scope Limitations.** Situations in which auditors are unable to obtain sufficient appropriate evidence necessary to support their opinion on the entity's financial statements are referred to as *scope limitations*.

Required:

a. Distinguish between *client-imposed* scope limitations and *circumstance-imposed* scope limitations. Which of these is generally of more concern to auditors?

b. Why do scope limitations impact the auditors' ability to express an opinion on the entity's financial statements?

c. Assume that a circumstance-imposed scope limitation prevented auditors from performing procedures they considered to be necessary. How would each of the following factors independently influence the opinion expressed on the entity's financial statements?

1. The account balances affected by the scope limitation are not material to the entity's financial position, results of operations, or cash flows.

2. The account balances affected by the scope limitation are material to the entity's financial position, results of operations, and cash flows. However, the auditors are able to perform alternative procedures that provide evidence supporting the accounts affected by the scope limitation.

3. The account balances affected by the scope limitation are material to the entity's financial position, results of operations, and cash flows. Because of a lack of supporting documentation and key accounting records, auditors are unable to perform alternative procedures that provide evidence supporting the accounts affected by the scope limitation.

d. For each of the situations in part (c), briefly describe how the auditors' report on the entity's financial statements would be affected. (Do *not* rewrite or draft the report that would be issued in each of these circumstances.)

LO 12-2

12.48 **Scope Limitations.** Following are four possible scenarios that reflect scope limitations encountered by J. Bruce, CPA, during the audit of Weaver Inc. In all cases, assume that the ending balance in inventory is material to Weaver's financial position, results of operations, and cash flows.

- *Scenario A.* Because of the late appointment to the audit engagement, Bruce is unable to observe Weaver's physical inventory for the year ended December 31, 2017. However, Weaver maintains extensive perpetual inventory records, and Bruce has been able to perform other substantive procedures and is satisfied as to the fairness of the ending inventory balance for December 31, 2017.

- *Scenario B.* Because of the late appointment to the audit engagement, Bruce is unable to observe Weaver's physical inventory for the year ended December 31, 2017. Because Weaver's accounting records are not complete, Bruce is unable to perform other substantive procedures and is not satisfied as to the fairness of the ending inventory balance for December 31, 2017.

- *Scenario C.* Because of a direct request by Weaver's management, Bruce did not observe Weaver's physical inventory for the year ended December 31, 2017. However, Weaver maintains extensive perpetual inventory records, and Bruce has been able to perform other substantive procedures and is satisfied as to the fairness of the ending inventory balance for December 31, 2017.

- *Scenario D.* Because of a direct request by Weaver's management, Bruce did not observe Weaver's physical inventory for the year ended December 31, 2017. Weaver's accounting records are not complete, so Bruce is unable to perform other substantive procedures and is not satisfied as to the fairness of the ending inventory balance for December 31, 2017.

Required:

For each of these scenarios, indicate what reporting option(s) and factors Bruce should consider in deciding which type of opinion to issue in the circumstances. (Do *not* draft Bruce's report on Weaver Inc.'s financial statements for the year ended December 31, 2017.)

LO 12-2

12.49   **Scope Limitations.**   D. Brady has been engaged as the auditor of Patriot Company and is currently planning the year-end physical inventory counts. Patriot is a retailer that holds significant inventories in its warehouses and stores in six regions across the United States. Because of timing and logistics, Brady is able to observe the physical inventory at only one of Patriot's warehouses, which accounts for 20 percent of Patriot's inventories.

In Brady's professional judgment, the fact that inventories held at only one warehouse can be observed does not provide sufficient evidence with respect to Patriot's inventory balances at the date of the financial statements. Although physical inventory counts could be delayed at the remaining warehouses for Brady to observe the counts, the flow of goods in and out of the warehouses would result in a discrepancy between the inventory quantities on hand at year-end and the inventory quantities on hand at the date of the count.

Required:

a. Assume that Brady observes physical inventory at only the one warehouse and does not perform alternative procedures related to inventories held at the other warehouses. Does this cause a scope limitation? If so, is this a client-imposed or circumstance-imposed scope limitation?

b. What type of opinion would Brady likely issue for the situation in part (a)? How would the wording in the standard (unmodified) report be modified to reflect this opinion?

c. What alternative procedures might be available to Brady with respect to this scope limitation? (*Hint:* You may wish to refer to Chapter 9 to identify alternative procedures for inventory.)

d. Assume that Brady performs one or more of the alternative procedures in part (c) and is able to gather evidence to support the recorded balance in inventory. What type of opinion would Brady issue on Patriot's financial statements (assuming that no other issues were identified in the audit examination)?

LO 12-2

12.50   **Audit of Group Financial Statements.**   Lando Corporation is a domestic company with two wholly owned subsidiaries. Michaels, CPA, has been engaged to audit the financial statements of the parent company and one of its subsidiaries and to serve as the group auditor. Thomas, CPA, has audited the financial statements of the other subsidiary whose operations are material in relation to the consolidated financial statements.

The work performed by Michaels is sufficient for serving as the group auditor and to report as such on the financial statements. Michaels has not yet decided whether to refer to the part of the audit performed by Thomas.

Required:

a. What responsibilities does Michaels have with respect to Thomas when deciding whether to rely on the work of Thomas?

b. What are the reporting requirements with which Michaels must comply in naming Thomas and referring to the work done by Thomas?

c. What report should be issued if Michaels does not wish to assume responsibility for Thomas's work or refer to Thomas's work?

LO 12-2, 12-3

12.51   **Various Reporting Situations.**   Assume that the auditors encountered the following separate situations when deciding on the report to issue for the current-year financial statements.

1. The auditors decided that sufficient appropriate evidence could not be obtained to complete the audit of significant investments the entity held in a foreign entity.

2. The entity failed to capitalize lease assets and obligations but explained them fully in the notes to the financial statements. These lease obligations meet the criteria for capitalization under *ASC 840.*

3. The entity is defending a lawsuit on product liability claims. (Customers allege that power saw safety guards were improperly installed.) All facts about the lawsuit are disclosed in the notes to the financial statements, but the auditors believe the entity should record a loss based on a probable settlement mentioned by the entity's attorneys.

4. The entity hired the auditors after taking inventory on December 31. The accounting records and other evidence are not reliable enough to enable the auditors to have sufficient evidence about the proper inventory amount.

5. The FASB requires the energy company to present supplementary oil and gas reserve information outside the basic financial statements. The auditors find that this information, which is not required as a part of the basic financial statements, has been omitted.

6. The auditors are group auditors of the parent company, but they reviewed the component auditors' work and reputation, and decided not to take responsibility for the work of the component auditors on three subsidiary companies included in the consolidated financial statements. The component auditors' work amounts to 32 percent of the consolidated assets and 39 percent of the consolidated revenues.

7. The entity changed its depreciation method from units of production to straight line, and its auditors believe the straight-line method is the more appropriate method in the circumstances. The change, fully explained in the notes to the financial statements, has a material effect on the year-to-year comparability of the comparative financial statements.

8. Because the entity has experienced significant operating losses and has had to obtain waivers of debt payment requirements from its lenders, the auditors decide that there is substantial doubt that the entity can continue as a going concern. The entity has fully described all problems in a note in the financial statements and the auditors believe that, while material, the uncertainty is not serious enough to warrant a disclaimer of opinion.

Required:

a. What kind of opinion should the auditors express in each separate case?

b. What other modification(s) or addition(s) to the standard (unmodified) report is (are) required for each separate case?

LO 12-2, 12-3, 12-4

12.52 **Various Reporting Situations.** Assume that Stanford CPAs encountered the following issues during its various audit engagements in 2017:

1. It conducted the audit of Luck, a new client this past year. Last year, Luck was audited by another CPA, who issued an unmodified opinion on its financial statements. Luck is presenting financial statements for 2016 and 2017 in comparative form.

2. One of Stanford's clients is RealCo, a real estate holding company. Assume that RealCo experienced a significant decline in the value of its investment properties during the past year because of a downturn in the economy and has appropriately recognized that decline in market value under GAAP. Stanford wishes to emphasize the decline in the economy and its impact on RealCo's financial position and results of operations for 2017 in its audit report.

3. For the past five years, Stanford has conducted the audits of TechTime, a company that provides technology consulting services, and has always issued unmodified opinions on its financial statements. Based on its 2017 audit, Stanford believes that an unmodified opinion is appropriate; however, Stanford did note that TechTime reported its third consecutive operating loss and has experienced negative cash flows because of the inability of some of its customers to promptly pay for services received.

4. Stanford has assisted Cardinal Inc. with the preparation of its financial statements but has not audited, compiled, or reviewed those financial statements. Cardinal wishes to include these financial statements in a communication that would describe Stanford's involvement in the preparation of the financial statements. Stanford believes that Cardinal's communication is adequate and appropriately describes Stanford's limited role in the preparation of the financial statements.

5. Trees Inc. presents summary financial information along with its financial statements. The summary financial information has been derived from the complete set of financial statements that Stanford has audited (and issued an unmodified opinion on the complete financial statements). A lender has engaged Stanford to evaluate and report on Trees' summary financial information; Stanford believes that the summary financial information is fairly stated in relation to Trees' complete financial statements.

6. Stanford believes that some of the verbiage in Plunkett's Management Discussion & Analysis section is inconsistent with the firm's financial statements. Stanford has concluded that Plunkett's financial statements present its financial position, results of operations, and cash flows in accordance with GAAP and has decided to issue an unmodified opinion on Plunkett's financial statements.

7. Oil Patch is a client in the energy industry that is required to present supplementary oil and gas reserve information. Stanford has performed certain procedures regarding this information and concluded that it is presented in accordance with FASB presentation guidelines and does not appear to depart from GAAP. Based on Stanford's audit, it plans to issue an unmodified opinion on Oil Patch's financial statements.

Required:

How would each of these issues affect Stanford's report on the client's financial statements? (Do *not* draft the report that Stanford would issue in each situation).

LO 12-2, 12-3, 12-4

12.53 **Various Reporting Situations.** For each of the following situations, indicate the type of opinion(s) that auditors could issue (more than one opinion may be appropriate in each circumstance). Unless otherwise noted, assume that no departures from GAAP were identified in the audit engagement. In addition, indicate how the standard (unmodified) report would be modified, if appropriate.

1. Auditors have identified an immaterial departure from GAAP in their examination, but the entity has not adjusted its financial statements for this departure or disclosed this departure in its financial statements or related disclosures.

2. Because they were appointed to the engagement after the date of the financial statements, the auditors have experienced a significant scope limitation and were unable to perform standard auditing procedures used in their engagements. The account(s) affected by this scope limitation were material and pervasive. However, the auditors have been able to completely satisfy themselves as to the fairness of the related account balances and classes of transaction by performing alternative procedures.

3. During the year, the entity changed its method of accounting for inventories from FIFO to LIFO and has disclosed this change in the footnotes to the financial statements and accounted for the change properly. However, the auditors do not agree with the rationale for the change and believe that it was made to report a higher level of earnings.

4. Subsequent to accepting the audit engagement, the auditors determined that they are not independent with respect to the client because of a financial interest in the client held by a newly admitted partner to the audit firm.

5. Evidence gathered during the audit examination and inquiry of the client's management revealed substantial doubt about the client's ability to continue in existence. The auditors believe that the client has appropriately disclosed the going-concern uncertainties in its financial statements and footnotes.

6. The auditors wish to emphasize the company's acquisition of two large subsidiaries during the most recent year.

7. The auditors have engaged component auditors to conduct a portion of the audit but do not wish to assume responsibility for their work. The auditors have not approached the component auditors about presenting their reports with the company's financial statements and do not plan to do so.

8. The client has not recognized a material loss related to a decline in the market value of its investments. Because the auditors believe this decline in value is not temporary, they believe the financial statements do not present the client's financial position and results of operations in accordance with GAAP.

9. The auditors have experienced a significant scope limitation and are unable to satisfy themselves as to the fairness of the affected account balances through alternative procedures.

LO 12-2, 12-3

12.54 **Audit Report Deficiencies.** On September 23, 2018, Betsy Ross drafted the following report on Continental Corporation's financial statements.

To Whom It May Concern:

We have audited the accompanying financial statements of Continental Corporation, which comprise the balance sheet as of July 31, 2018, and the related statements of income and changes in shareholders' equity for the year then ended, and the related notes to the financial statements.

Management's Responsibility for the Financial Statements

Management is responsible for the preparation and fair presentation of these financial statements in accordance with accounting principles generally accepted in the United States of America; this includes the design, implementation, and maintenance of internal control relevant to the preparation and fair presentation of financial statements that are free from material misstatement, whether due to fraud or error.

Auditor's Responsibility

In accordance with instructions by Continental's management, we have conducted a complete audit. An audit involves performing procedures to obtain audit evidence about the amounts and disclosures in the financial statements. The procedures selected depend on the auditor's judgment, including the assessment of the risks of material misstatement of the financial statements, whether due to fraud or error. In making those risk assessments, the auditor considers internal control relevant to the entity's preparation and fair presentation of the financial statements in order to design audit procedures that are appropriate in the circumstances, but not for the purpose of expressing an opinion on the effectiveness of the entity's internal control. Accordingly, we express no such opinion. An audit also includes evaluating the appropriateness of accounting policies used and the reasonableness of significant accounting estimates made by management, as well as evaluating the overall presentation of the financial statements.

We believe that the audit evidence we have obtained is sufficient and appropriate to provide a basis for our audit opinion.

Opinion

In our opinion, with the explanation given below and with the exception of some minor errors we consider immaterial, the financial statements referred to above present the financial position of Continental Corporation as of July 31, 2018, and the results of its operations and its cash flows for the year then ended in accordance with pronouncements of the Financial Accounting Standards Board.

Emphasis of Matter

In many respects, this was an unusual year for Continental Corporation. The weakening of the economy in the early part of the year and the strike of plant employees in the summer led to a decline in sales and net income. After making several tests of the sales records, nothing came to our attention that would Indicate sales have not been properly recorded.

Betsy Ross & Co, CPA
July 31, 2018

Required:

List and explain the deficiencies and omissions in the report prepared by Ross on Continental Company's financial statements.

LO 12-2

12.55 **Audit Report Deficiencies: Adverse Opinion.** The board of directors of Cook Industries Inc. engaged Brown & Brown, CPAs, to audit the financial statements for the year ended December 31, 2017.

Independent Auditor's Report

To the President of Cook Industries Inc.:

We have audited the accompanying financial statements of Cook Industries Inc. for the year ended December 31, 2017, and the related notes to the financial statements. Our responsibility is to express an opinion on these financial statements based on our audit. We conducted our audit in accordance with auditing standards generally accepted in the United States of America. Those standards require that we plan and perform the audit to obtain reasonable assurance about whether the financial statements are free from material misstatement.

Auditor's Responsibility
An audit involves performing procedures to obtain audit evidence about the amounts and disclosures in the financial statements. The procedures selected depend on the auditor's judgment, including the assessment of the risks of material misstatement of the financial statements, whether due to fraud or error. In making those risk assessments, the auditor considers internal control relevant to the entity's preparation and fair presentation of the financial statements in order to design audit procedures that are appropriate in the circumstances, but not for the purpose of expressing an opinion on the effectiveness of the entity's internal control. Accordingly, we express no such opinion. An audit also includes evaluating the appropriateness of accounting policies used and the reasonableness of significant accounting estimates made by management, as well as evaluating the overall presentation of the financial statements.

We believe that the audit evidence we have obtained is sufficient and appropriate to provide a basis for our audit opinion.

Basis for Adverse Opinion
As discussed in Note G to the financial statements, the Company carries its property and equipment at appraisal values and provides depreciation on the basis of such values. Furthermore, the Company does not provide for income taxes with respect to differences between financial income and taxable Income arising from the use, for income tax purposes, of the installment method of reporting gross profit from certain types of sales.

Opinion
In our opinion, the financial statements referred to above present fairly, in all material respects, the financial position of Cook Industries Inc. as of December 31, 2017, and the results of its operations and its cash flows for the year then ended in accordance with accounting principles generally accepted in the United States of America.

Brown & Brown, CPAs
March 14, 2018

Required:

Identify the deficiencies in the following draft of the report. Do *not* rewrite the report.

(AICPA adapted)

LO 12-4

12.56 **Audit Report Deficiencies: Comparative Reporting.** An assistant drafted the following auditors' report at the completion of the audit of Cramdon Inc. on March 5, 2018. The partner in charge of the engagement has decided the opinion on the 2017 financial statements should be modified only with reference to the change in the method of computing the cost of inventory. In 2016, Cramdon used the next-in, first-out (NIFO) method, which is not permissible under GAAP, but in 2017 changed to FIFO and restated the 2016 financial statements. The auditors' report on the 2016 financial statements was prepared by the same firm and dated March 5, 2017.

Independent Auditor's Report

To the Board of Directors of Cramdon Inc.:

We have audited the accompanying financial statements of Cramdon Inc. as of December 31, 2017 and 2016, and the related notes to the financial statements.

Management's Responsibility for the Financial Statements
Management is responsible for the preparation and fair presentation of these financial statements in accordance with accounting principles generally accepted in the United States of America; this includes the design, implementation, and maintenance of internal control relevant to the preparation and fair presentation of financial statements that are free from material misstatement, whether due to fraud or error.

Auditor's Responsibility
Our responsibility is to express an opinion on these financial statements based on our audits. We conducted our audits in accordance with auditing standards generally accepted in the United States of America. Those standards require that we plan and perform the audit to obtain reasonable assurance about whether the financial statements are free from material misstatement.

An audit involves performing procedures to obtain audit evidence about the amounts and disclosures in the financial statements. The procedures selected depend on the auditor's judgment, including the assessment of the risks of material misstatement of the financial statements, whether due to fraud or error. In making those risk assessments, the auditor considers internal control relevant to the entity's preparation and fair presentation of the financial statements in order to design audit procedures that are appropriate in the circumstances, but not for the purpose of expressing an opinion on the effectiveness of the entity's internal control. Accordingly, we express no such opinion. An audit also includes evaluating the appropriateness of accounting policies used and the reasonableness of significant accounting estimates made by management, as well as evaluating the overall presentation of the financial statements.

We believe that the audit evidence we have obtained is sufficient and appropriate to provide a basis for our audit opinion.

Opinion
In our opinion, based upon the following, the financial statements referred to above present fairly, in all material respects, the financial position of Cramdon Inc. as of December 31, 2017, and the results of its operations and its cash flows for the year then ended in accordance with accounting principles generally accepted in the United States of America, consistently applied, except for the changes in the method of computing inventory cost as described in Note 7 to the financial statements.

Other Matter
As discussed in Note 7 to the financial statements, the company changed its method of accounting for inventory cost from NIFO to FIFO. The 2016 financial statements have been restated to reflect this change in accordance with accounting principles generally accepted in the United States of America. Accordingly, our present opinion on the 2016 financial statements, as presented herein, is different from the opinion we expressed in our previous report.

George Constanza, CPA
March 5, 2018

Required:
Identify the deficiencies and errors in the draft report and write an explanation of the reasons they are errors and deficiencies. Do *not* rewrite the report.

LO 12-2

12.57   **Audit Report Deficiencies: Audits of Group Financial Statements and Other Operating Matters.**   Following is Rex Wolf's report on Bonair Corporation's financial statements. Bonair publishes general-purpose financial statements for distribution to owners, creditors, potential investors, and the general public.

Independent Auditor's Report

To the Board of Directors and Shareholders of Bonair Corporation:

We have audited the accompanying financial statements of Bonair Corporation, which comprise the balance sheet as of December 31, 2017, and the related statements of income, changes in shareholders' equity, and cash flows for the year then ended, and the related notes to the financial statements.

Management's Responsibility for the Financial Statements

Management is responsible for the preparation and fair presentation of these financial statements in accordance with accounting principles generally accepted in the United States of America; this includes the design, implementation, and maintenance of internal control relevant to the preparation and fair presentation of financial statements that are free from material misstatement, whether due to fraud or error.

Auditor's Responsibility

Our responsibility is to express an opinion on these financial statements based on our audit. We did not examine the financial statements of Caet Company, a wholly-owned subsidiary. Those statements were audited by Nero Stout, CPA, whose report has been furnished to us, and our opinion insofar as it relates to the amounts included for Caet Company, is based solely on the report of other auditors. With the exception of this matter, we conducted our audit in accordance with auditing standards generally accepted in the United States of America. Those standards require that we plan and perform the audit to obtain reasonable assurance about whether the financial statements are free from material misstatement.

An audit involves performing procedures to obtain audit evidence about the amounts and disclosures in the financial statements. The procedures selected depend on the auditor's judgment, including the assessment of the risks of material misstatement of the financial statements, whether due to fraud or error. In making those risk assessments, the auditor considers internal control relevant to the entity's preparation and fair presentation of the financial statements in order to design audit procedures that are appropriate in the circumstances, but not for the purpose of expressing an opinion on the effectiveness of the entity's internal control. Accordingly, we express no such opinion. An audit also includes evaluating the appropriateness of accounting policies used and the reasonableness of significant accounting estimates made by management, as well as evaluating the overall presentation of the financial statements.

We believe that the audit evidence we have obtained is sufficient and appropriate to provide a basis for our audit opinion.

Opinion

In our opinion, except for the matter of the report of the component auditors, the financial statements referred to above present fairly, in all material respects, the financial position of Bonair Corporation as of December 31, 2017, and the results of its operations and its cash flows for the year then ended.

Other Matter

As noted in the Auditor's Responsibility section of this report, Nero Stout, CPA, audited the financial statements of Caet Company, a wholly-owned subsidiary.

Rex Wolf, CPA

March 5, 2018

Describe the reporting deficiencies and explain why they are considered deficiencies. Organize your response according to each of the paragraphs or sections in the standard (unmodified) report.

LO 12-4

12.58 **Audit Report Deficiencies: Disclaimer of Opinion.** Your partner drafted the following auditors' report yesterday. You need to describe the reporting deficiencies, explain the reasons for them, and discuss with the partner how the report should be corrected. You have decided to prepare a three-column worksheet showing the deficiencies, reasons, and corrections needed. Your partner's report follows:

I made my examination in accordance with auditing standards generally accepted in the United States of America. However, I am not independent with respect to Mavis Corporation because my wife owns 5 percent of the company's outstanding common stock. The accompanying balance sheet as of December 31, 2017, and the related statements of income, changes in shareholders' equity, and cash flows for the year then ended were not audited by me. Accordingly, I do not express an opinion on them.

Required:

Prepare the three-column worksheet described.

LO 12-3, 12-4

12.59 **Audit Report Deficiencies: Accounting Change and Uncertainty.** The following auditors' report was drafted by Quinn Moore, a staff auditor with Tyler & Tyler, CPAs, at the completion of the audit of the financial statements of Park Publishing Company for the year ended September 30, 2017. The engagement partner reviewed the audit documentation and properly decided to issue an unmodified opinion. In drafting the report, Moore considered the following:

- During fiscal year 2017, Park changed its depreciation method. The engagement partner concurred with this change in accounting principles and its justification, and Moore included an emphasis-of-matter paragraph in the report.
- The 2017 financial statements are affected by an uncertainty concerning a lawsuit, the outcome of which cannot presently be estimated. Moore included an emphasis-of-matter paragraph in the report to disclose this uncertainty.
- The financial statements for the year ended September 30, 2016, are to be presented for comparative purposes. Tyler & Tyler previously audited these statements and expressed an unmodified opinion.

Independent Auditor's Report

To the Board of Directors of Park Publishing Company:

We have audited the accompanying financial statements of Park Publishing Company, which comprise the balance sheet as of September 30, 2017 and 2016, and the related statements of income, changes in shareholders' equity, and cash flows for the years then ended, and the related notes to the financial statements.

Management's Responsibility for the Financial Statements
Management is responsible for the preparation and fair presentation of these financial statements; this includes the design, implementation, and maintenance of internal control relevant to the preparation and fair presentation of financial statements that are free from material misstatement, whether due to fraud or error.

Auditor's Responsibility
We conducted our audits in accordance with auditing standards generally accepted in the United States of America. Those standards require that we plan and perform the audit to obtain reasonable assurance about whether the financial statements are fairly presented.

An audit involves performing procedures to obtain audit evidence about the amounts and disclosures in the financial statements. The procedures selected depend on the auditor's judgment, including the assessment of the risks of material misstatement of the financial statements, whether due to fraud or error. In making those risk assessments, the auditor considers internal control relevant to the entity's preparation and fair presentation of the financial statements in order to design audit procedures that are appropriate in the circumstances, but not for the purpose of expressing an opinion on the effectiveness of the entity's internal control. Accordingly, we express no such opinion. An audit also includes evaluating the appropriateness of accounting policies used and the reasonableness of significant accounting estimates made by management, as well as evaluating the overall presentation of the financial statements.

We believe that the audit evidence we have obtained is sufficient and appropriate to provide a basis for determining whether any material modifications should be made to the financial statements.

Emphasis of Matter
As discussed in Note X to the financial statements, the company changed its method of computing depreciation in fiscal 2017.

Opinion
In our opinion, except for the accounting change, with which we concur, the financial statements referred to above present fairly, in all material respects, the financial position of Park Publishing Company as of December 31, 2017, and the results of its operations and its cash flows for the year then ended in accordance with accounting principles generally accepted in the United States of America.

Emphasis of Matter
As discussed in Note Y to the financial statements, the company is a defendant in a lawsuit alleging infringement of certain copyrights. The company has filed a counteraction, and preliminary hearings on both actions are in progress. Accordingly, any provision for liability is subject to adjudication of this matter.

Tyler & Tyler, CPAs
November 5, 2018

Required:

Identify the deficiencies in the auditors' report as drafted by Moore. Group the deficiencies by section or paragraph and in the order in which they appear. Do *not* rewrite the report.

(AICPA adapted)

LO 12-1

12.60 **Internet Exercise: Reports on Financial Statements (Public Companies).** One of the great resources for auditors is the SEC's Electronic Data Gathering, Analysis and Retrieval (EDGAR) system database at www.sec.gov. Public companies file SEC-required documents electronically. The SEC makes this information available on its web page.

Required:

The following are the largest five companies in the United States, based on the *Fortune* 500, along with their ticker symbols. After accessing the EDGAR database, download copies of auditors' reports from the Form 10-K filings and complete the following table (Wal-Mart Stores has been done as an example). (*Hint:* Search the 10-K filing by using the key word "independent," as in Report of Independent Registered Public Accounting Firm.) Use the following responses in completing the table.

- Opinion: Unmodified, Qualified, Adverse, Disclaimer
- Additional Paragraphs/Issues: Identify by Type
- Internal Control Report: Combined or Separate
- Auditor: Identify Name of Firm

Company	Opinion	Additional Paragraph(s)	Internal Control Report	Auditor
Wal-Mart Stores (WMT)	Unmodified	None	Separate	EY
Exxon Mobil (XOM)				
Apple (AAPL)				
Berkshire Hathaway (BRK-A)				
McKesson (MCK)				

Preparing Auditors' Reports

Cases 12.61 through 12.67 require you to draft auditors' reports. A Word file (AUDIT REPORT) containing the standard (unmodified) report can be found in Connect. This report can be modified (as necessary) for the conditions noted in the following cases. Unless instructed otherwise, assume the following in drafting your reports: (1) your firm, Anderson, Olds, & Watershed (AOW), conducted the audit examination of the identified client; (2) the fiscal year-end is December 31, 2017; (3) the date of the auditors' report is February 10, 2018; and (4) the client is not publicly traded and, therefore, not subject to the auditing and reporting requirements of AS 3101.

LO 12-3

12.61 **Financial Difficulty: The "Going-Concern" Problem.** Pitts Company has experienced significant financial difficulty. Current liabilities exceed current assets by $1 million, cash has decreased to $10,000, the interest on the long-term debt has not been paid, and a customer has brought a lawsuit against Pitts for $500,000 on a product liability claim. Significant questions concerning the going-concern status of the company exist. The lawsuit and information about the going-concern status have been appropriately described in footnote 3 to the financial statements.

Required:

a. Draft AOW's report, assuming that the auditors decide that an unmodified opinion instead of a disclaimer of opinion is appropriate in the circumstances.

b. Draft AOW's report, assuming that the auditors decide the uncertainties are so serious that they do not wish to express an opinion on Pitts' financial statements.

LO 12-4

12.62 **Disagreement with Auditors.** Officers of Richnow Company do not wish to disclose information about a product liability lawsuit filed by a customer seeking $500,000 in damages. They believe the suit is frivolous and without merit. Outside counsel is more cautious. The auditors insist on disclosure. Angered, Richnow's chair of the board threatens to sue AOW if a standard (unmodified) report is not issued within three days.

Required:

Draft AOW's report appropriate under the circumstances.

LO 12-2

12.63 **Late Appointment of Auditors.**   AOW has completed the audit of the financial statements of Musgrave Company for the year ended December 31, 2017, and is now preparing the report.

AOW has audited Musgrave's financial statements for several years, but this year Musgrave delayed the start of the audit work, so AOW was not present to observe the taking of the physical inventory on December 31, 2017. The inventory balance is $194,000, which represents 39 percent of Musgrave's total assets and 69 percent of its current assets. However, AOW performed alternative procedures including (1) examination of shipping and receiving documents with regard to transactions since the date of the financial statements, (2) extensive review of the inventory count sheets, and (3) discussion of the physical inventory procedures with responsible company personnel. AOW also is satisfied about the propriety of the inventory valuation calculations and the consistency of the valuation method. Musgrave determines year-end inventory quantities solely by means of physical count.

Required:

Draft AOW's report on the balance sheet at the end of the current year and on the statements of operations, changes in shareholders' equity, and cash flows for the year then ended. (*Hint:* Did the alternative procedures produce sufficient appropriate evidence?)

LO 12-2

12.64 **Audits of Group Financial Statements.**   AOW is the group auditor for the December 31, 2017, consolidated financial statements of Ferguson Company and subsidiaries. However, component auditors perform the work on certain subsidiaries for the year under audit amounting to 29 percent of total assets and 36 percent of total revenues.

AOW investigated the component auditors, as required by auditing standards, and they furnished AOW their reports. AOW has decided to rely on their work and to refer to the component auditors in their report. None of the audit work revealed any issues with respect to Ferguson Company or its subsidiaries.

Required:

Draft AOW's report.

LO 12-3

12.65 **Other Information in a Financial Review Section of an Annual Report.**   Gustav Humphreys (chair of the board) and Ingrid VanEns (vice president, finance) prepared the draft of the financial review section of the annual report. You are reviewing it for consistency with the audited financial statements. The draft contains the following explanation about income coverage of interest expense:

Last year, operating income before interest and income taxes covered interest expense by a ratio of 6:1. This year, on an incremental basis, the coverage of interest expense increased to a ratio of 6.59:1.

The relevant portion of the audited financial statements showed the following:

	Current Year	Prior Year
Operating income	$400,000	$360,000
Extraordinary gain from realization of tax benefits	100,000	0
Interest expense	(81,250)	(60,000)
Income taxes	(127,500)	(120,000)
Net income	$291,250	$180,000

Required:

a. Determine whether the financial review section statement about coverage of interest is or is not consistent with the audited financial statements. Be able to show your conclusion with calculations.

b. Assume that you find an inconsistency and the officers disagree with your conclusions. Draft the other-matter paragraph you should include in your auditors' report.

LO 12-2

12.66 **Departures from GAAP.** On January 1, Graham Company purchased land (the site of a new building) for $100,000. Soon thereafter, the state highway department announced that a new feeder road would run next to the site. The effect was a dramatic increase in local property values. Comparable land located nearby sold for $700,000 in December of the current year. Graham presents the land at $700,000 in its accounts and, after reduction for implicit taxes at 33 percent, the fixed asset total is $400,000 higher than historical cost with the same amount shown separately in the shareholder equity account Current Value Increment. The valuation is fully disclosed in a footnote to the financial statements with a letter from a certified property appraiser attesting to the $700,000 value.

Required:

a. Draft the appropriate auditors' report, assuming that you believe the departure from GAAP is material but not pervasive enough to cause you to issue an adverse opinion.

b. Draft the appropriate auditors' report, assuming that you believe an adverse opinion is necessary.

LO 12-2, 12-3

12.67 **Reporting on an Accounting Change.** In December of the current year, Williams Company changed its method of accounting for inventory and cost of goods sold from LIFO to FIFO. The account balances shown in the trial balance have already been recalculated and adjusted retroactively as required by *ASC 250*. The accounting change and the financial effects are described in Note 2 in the financial statements.

Required:

a. Assume that you believe the accounting change is justified as required by *ASC 250*. Draft the report appropriate in the circumstances.

b. Assume that you believe the accounting change is not justified and causes the financial statements to be materially misstated. Inventories that would have been reported at $1.5 million (LIFO) are reported at $1.9 million (FIFO); operating income before tax that would have been $130,000 is reported at $530,000. As a result of this change, current assets, total assets, and shareholders' equity have increased by 17 percent, 9 percent, and 14 percent, respectively. Draft the report appropriate in the circumstances.

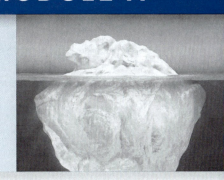

MODULE A

Other Public Accounting Services

> *There's no business like show business, but there are several businesses like accounting.*
>
> David Letterman, American comedian and television host

Professional Standards References

Topic	AU-C/ISA Section*	PCAOB Reference
Attestation Engagements		
Attestation Engagements	AT-C 105	AT 101
Agreed-Upon Procedures Engagements	AT-C 215 ISAE4400	AT 201
Prospective Financial Information	AT-C 305 ISAE4400	AT 301
Reporting on Pro Forma Financial Information	AT-C 310	AT 401
An Examination of an Entity's Internal Control in an Audit of Its Financial Statements	AT 501	AS 2201
Compliance Attestation	AT-C 315	AT 601
Examination Engagements Regarding Compliance Reports of Brokers and Dealers	N/A	AT 1
Review Engagements Regarding Exemption Reports of Brokers and Dealers	N/A	AT 2
Management's Discussion and Analysis	AT 701	AT 701
Reporting on Controls at a Service Organization	AT-C 320 ISAE3402	AS 2601
Reporting on Greenhouse Gas Information	ISAE 3410 SOP 3-2	N/A
Review and Compilation of Unaudited Financial Statements		
General Principles for Engagements Performed in Accordance with Statements on Standards for Accounting and Review Services	AR-C 60	N/A
Preparation of Financial Statements	AR-C 70	N/A
Compilation Engagements	AR-C 80 ISRS 4410	N/A
Review of Financial Statements	AR-C 90 ISRE 2400	N/A

Special Reports

Special Considerations—Audits of Financial Statements Prepared in Accordance with Special-Purpose Frameworks	AU-C 800	AS 3310
Special Considerations—Audits of Single Financial Statements and Specific Elements, Accounts, or Items of a Financial Statement	AU-C 805	AS 3101 AS 3305
Reporting on Compliance with Aspects of Contractual Agreements or Regulatory Requirements in Connection with Audited Financial Statements	AU-C 806	AS 3305
Reports on Application of Requirements of an Appropriate Financial Reporting Framework	AU-C 915	AS 6105
Other Information	AU-C 720	AS 2710
Interim Financial Information	AU-C 930 ISRE 2410	AS 4105

*References other than AU-C are as follows: *ISAE* (International Standards on Assurance Engagements), *ISRE* (International Standards for Review Engagements), *SOP* (Statements of Position—Auditing and Attestation). ISRSs (International Standards on Related Services).

LEARNING OBJECTIVES

Certified public accountants (CPAs) are trusted professionals with a reputation for objectivity and integrity. The reputation has its foundation in a long history of service to the business community and the general public. Despite recent problems (such as the Madoff scandal and the banking crisis), individuals and businesses still view their CPAs as trusted business professionals who add value to their businesses and provide valuable guidance concerning difficult business decisions. In this tradition, CPAs and other accountants offer numerous assurance and attestation services on information other than audited financial statements. These services result from consumer demand for assurance by objective experts. This module covers several areas of public accounting practice related to accountants' association with information other than audited historical financial statements discussed in Chapter 12.

Your objectives are to be able to:

LO A-1 Explain and provide examples of attestation engagements.

LO A-2 Describe reviews, compilations, and preparation of unaudited financial statements and prepare appropriate reports given specific factual circumstances.

LO A-3 Explain auditors' responsibilities related to reporting on interim financial information.

LO A-4 Define, explain, and give examples of other special reports provided by auditors, including specified elements of financial statements, special-purpose frameworks, and application of requirements of appropriate financial reporting frameworks.

LO A-5 Explain and provide examples of assurance services engagements.

INTRODUCTION

The "green" movement is "sweeping" the world. Fueled by an increased emphasis on corporate social responsibility (CSR), companies are paying more attention to their impact on the natural world. To prove their commitment to environmental sustainability to their stakeholders, companies are voluntarily reporting on such items as carbon emissions, greenhouse gases, and other potentially detrimental effects that their operations may be generating. According to a 2015 report from the AICPA, 72 percent of S&P companies published sustainability reports in 2013, up from only 20 percent in 2011.[1] Given the public's skepticism when **BP** and other large companies report on the positive impact that they have on the environment, the public has turned to third-party assurors to verify the company's results. According to research on CSR, professional accounting firms are among the most trusted assurors of such information. Although some might question whether accountants can audit these highly technical areas, a recent *Journal of Accountancy*[2] article argues otherwise:

> CPAs are well-suited to provide assurance on sustainability reports and greenhouse gas emissions information. They possess strong assurance methodology; experience with numerous systems, information processes, and control frameworks; the capability to identify weaknesses and other risks of misstatement; and the capability to learn new subject matters and develop new specializations.

To provide accounting professionals with guidance in these engagements, the IAASB issued ISAE 3410, "Assurance Engagements on Greenhouse Gas Statements" in June 2012; similarly, the ASB issued SOP No. 03-2, "Attest Engagements on Greenhouse Gas Emissions Information." This type of engagement may be a growing opportunity for professional accountants—independent research firm Verdantix projected an annual growth rate in sustainability assurance revenues of 11 percent from 2013 to 2017[3]—but it is only one of many needed services that accountants can provide to businesses beyond examining financial statements or preparing tax returns. Many of these other professional services will be discussed in this module.

ATTESTATION ENGAGEMENTS

LO A-1

Explain and provide examples of attestation engagements.

Introduction to Attestation Engagements

Although the majority of this textbook is devoted to the audit of financial statements, audit services are really a subset of a larger group of services referred to as *attestation services* or simply *attestation engagements*. An **attestation** is defined as an engagement

> in which a practitioner is engaged to issue or does issue an examination, a review, or an agreed-upon procedures report on subject matter, or an assertion about the subject matter . . . that is the responsibility of another party. [AT-C 105.01]

The subject matter of an attest engagement may take many forms, including the following:

a. Historical or prospective performance or condition (for example, backlog data).

b. Physical characteristics (for example, narrative descriptions, square footage of facilities).

c. Historical events (for example, the price of a market basket of goods on a certain date).

d. Analyses (for example, break-even analyses).

---

[1] AICPA, "The State of Sustainability Assurance and Related Advisory Services in the U.S.: Two Market Assessments," June 2015, p. 2.

[2] Beth A. Schneider, "Assurance Opportunities Broaden," *Journal of Accountancy*, May, 2013.

[3] AICPA, "The State of Sustainability Assurance and Related Advisory Services in the U.S.: Two Market Assessments," June 2015, p. 2.

e. Systems and processes (for example, internal control).

f. Behavior (for example, corporate governance, compliance with laws and regulations, and human resource practices).

The subject matter of an attest engagement may be as of a point in time or for a period of time. The **responsible party** is the person at the client who is accountable for the information (e.g., the company's controller for financial information.). The accountant[4] should obtain written acknowledgment or other evidence of the party's responsibility for the subject matter or the written assertion. The responsible party can acknowledge responsibility in a number of ways, for example, in an engagement letter or a representation letter. If the accountant is not able to directly obtain written acknowledgment, the practitioner should obtain other evidence of the party's responsibility for the subject matter (e.g., by reference to legislation, a regulation, or a contract).

The preceding definition of attestation identifies three types of engagements:

- An **examination** is similar in substance to an audit but may be limited in terms of the focus of the engagement. Accountants evaluate internal controls and assess the risk of material misstatement, gather evidence in support of the assertions, and render opinions that represent a high level of assurance.

- A **review** provides only a limited level of assurance. The procedures performed in a review engagement are generally limited to making inquiries and performing analytical procedures, although the accountants may decide that other procedures are necessary.

- In an **agreed-upon procedures** engagement, the client delineates exactly what procedures it wants accountants to perform. Therefore, the level of assurance provided by such an engagement varies depending on the procedures requested.

The purpose of differentiating attestation engagements from audits is to provide accountants a framework that allows them to perform other services often requested by their clients. For example, clients may want a public accounting firm to lend its name to a report on compliance with a contract or an environmental regulation. Public accounting firms have even attested to success rates at fertility clinics!

Professional standards for performing attest engagements are provided by *Statements on Standards for Attestation Engagements* (SSAEs) in the AT section of the AICPA's Professional Standards. SSAE 10 lists standards similar to the fundamental auditing principles on which *Statements on Auditing Standards* (SASs) are based (see Exhibit A.1 for a comparison).

Attestation standards are similar to the fundamental auditing principles; however, some important differences exist. The general standards concern the *practitioner's* knowledge about the *subject matter* of the engagement and having suitable *criteria by which to measure* the subject matter. To be suitable, the criteria must be objective, measurable, complete, and relevant. The attestation standards do not require an evaluation of internal controls, although such an evaluation may be necessary, particularly in an examination engagement. In financial statement audits, the measurement criteria or **appropriate financial reporting framework** is the financial reporting framework adopted by management and, when appropriate, those charged with governance in the preparation of the financial statements that is acceptable in view of the nature of the entity and the objective of the financial statements, or that is required by law or regulation. They include generally accepted accounting principles (GAAP), international financial reporting standards (IFRS), and special-purpose frameworks (discussed later in this module); therefore, the determination of suitable measurement criteria has already been established. In engagements in which GAAP, IFRS, or special-purpose frameworks are not suitable measurement criteria, the identification of the appropriate criterion may be difficult and time-consuming. The reporting standards restrict the distribution of the reports to persons who will understand the subject matter.

---

[4]Because this module discusses a wide variety of engagements, the word *accountant* is used to refer to practitioners performing nonaudit engagements rather than the word *auditor,* which has been used to this point in the text.

EXHIBIT A.1   Comparison of Attestation Standards and Principles

Attestation Standards	Principles
General Standards	
1. The practitioner must have adequate technical training and proficiency to perform the attest engagement.	Auditors are responsible for having appropriate competence and capabilities to perform the audit.
2. The practitioner must have adequate knowledge of the subject matter.	Not applicable
3. The practitioner must have reason to believe that the subject matter is capable of evaluation against criteria that are suitable and available to users.	Not applicable
4. The practitioner must maintain independence in mental attitude in all matters relating to the engagement.	Auditors are responsible for complying with appropriate ethical requirements.
5. The practitioner must exercise due professional care in the planning and performance of the engagement and the preparation of the report.	Auditors are responsible for maintaining professional skepticism and exercising professional judgment throughout the planning and performance of the audit.
Standards of Fieldwork	
1. The practitioner must adequately plan the work and must properly supervise any assistants.	To obtain reasonable assurance . . . the auditor plans the work and properly supervises any assistants.
[Depending upon the subject matter, determination of materiality may not be required for an attestation engagement.]	To obtain reasonable assurance . . . the auditor determines and applies appropriate materiality level or levels throughout the audit.
[Depending upon the subject matter, assessment of the risk of material misstatement may not be required for an attestation engagement.]	To obtain reasonable assurance . . . the auditor identifies and assesses risks of material misstatement, whether due to fraud or error, based on an understanding of the entity and its environment, including the entity's internal control.
2. The practitioner must obtain sufficient evidence to provide a reasonable basis for the conclusion that is expressed in the report.	To obtain reasonable assurance . . . the auditor obtains sufficient appropriate evidence about whether material misstatements exist, through designing and implementing appropriate responses to the assessed risks.
Standards of Reporting	
1. The practitioner must identify the subject matter or the assertion being reported on and state the character of the engagement in the report.	The financial statements are the subject matter of audits (which are a subset of attestation engagements).
2. The practitioner must state the practitioner's conclusion about the subject matter or the assertion in relation to criteria against which the subject matter was evaluated in the report.	. . . the auditor expresses . . . an opinion . . . [which] states whether the financial statements are presented fairly . . . in accordance with the applicable financial reporting framework.
3. The practitioner must state all of the practitioner's significant reservations about the engagement, the subject matter, and if applicable, the assertion related thereto in the report.	Not applicable
4. The practitioner must state in the report that the report is intended solely for the information and use of the specified parties under the following circumstances [detail omitted].	Not applicable

Attestation engagements include those related to

- Agreed-upon procedures.
- Financial forecasts and projections.
- Pro forma financial information.
- An entity's internal control over financial reporting.
- Compliance attestation.
- Management's discussion and analysis.
- Service organizations.

We briefly discuss these types of attestation engagements in the following sections.

Applying Agreed-Upon Procedures

Clients sometimes engage accountants to perform specified procedures, known as *agreed-upon procedures,* to examine a particular element, account, or item in financial statements or to perform a special engagement. For example, restaurant managers may ask their accountants to classify and summarize customer comment cards, or a composer might ask an accountant to verify the mathematics on a royalty report. Such engagements should not be considered audits because the specified sets of agreed-upon procedures are usually not sufficient to be considered as audits in accordance with auditing standards. Agreed-upon procedures engagements have a limited scope, so the performance principles (assessing the risk of material misstatement and obtaining sufficient appropriate evidence for an opinion) and the reporting principle do not apply.

Under attestation standards for agreed-upon procedures engagements, accountants must reach a clear understanding with the client and the report users about the users' needs and the procedures to be performed. For these types of engagements, clearly worded engagement letters specifically delineating the desired procedures to be performed are of utmost importance. Reports are to be restricted to the specified users who participate in and take responsibility for defining the work on the engagement.

A report on an agreed-upon procedures engagement is quite different from the standard audit report. In particular, the report should identify the specified users and describe in detail the procedures the users decided were necessary, state that the work is not an audit or review that results in an overall opinion or assurance, and describe each of the agreed-upon procedures and the specific findings related to each procedure. No overall "opinion" or "negative assurance" is given as a conclusion to the report. Instead, the report provides the accountant's findings based on the procedures performed. An example agreed-upon procedures report is provided in Exhibit A.2.

Prospective Financial Information and Pro Forma Financial Information

Prospective financial information is financial information representing the financial position, results of operations, and cash flows for some period of time in the future. A **financial forecast** is prospective financial information based on *expected* conditions and courses of action. A **financial projection** is prospective financial information based on the occurrence of one or more *hypothetical* events that change the entity's existing business structure (e.g., possible addition of a new distribution center, potential new product line). In contrast, **pro forma** financial information shows the effect of a proposed or consummated transaction on the *historical* financial statements "as if" that transaction had occurred by a specific date.

In many cases, the entity is negotiating directly with a single user (*limited use*) that has requested prospective financial information for use in making economic decisions (e.g., for a bank loan). Both financial projections and financial forecasts can be used for limited purposes because users directly requested the information and are aware of the nature of this information. In other instances, the entity may be preparing financial statements that it intends to present to a large number of users (*general use*), none of whom it is negotiating with at the current time. Only financial forecasts can be provided for general use because the users may not be familiar with the hypothetical event(s) underlying a financial projection.

The prospective financial information may contain amounts similar to historical financial statements (single-point estimates, e.g., forecast revenues of $10 million) or ranges of amounts (e.g., $10 million to $14 million). If ranges are used, care should be taken to indicate that the endpoints of this range do not represent best- and worst-case scenarios. In addition, the prospective financial information should disclose the significant accounting policies and procedures used to generate the statements. If the basis in the prospective financial information is different from that used in the historical financial statements, a reconciliation of the two bases must be shown. In addition, the entity must disclose all

EXHIBIT A.2   Example Agreed-Upon Procedures Report

GRABOWSKI, SPARANO & VINCELETTE

Certified Public Accountants
1814 Newport Gap Pike
Wilmington, Delaware 19808

TELEPHONE (302) 999-7300
TELEFAX (302) 999-7183

Thomas J. Grabowski, CPA
Joseph C. Sparano, CPA
Charles J. Vincelette, CPA

Member American Institute of CPA's
Delaware Society of CPA's

INDEPENDENT ACCOUNTANT'S REPORT ON APPLYING AGREED-UPON PROCEDURES

Town of Ocean View
32 West Avenue
Ocean View, Delaware

We have performed the procedures enumerated below, which were agreed to by the Town of Ocean View, State of Delaware's Office of the Auditor of Accounts, Department of Homeland Security, and the Office of the State Treasurer, solely to assist the specified parties with respect to determining the Town's compliance with Delaware's applicable laws, regulations, financial reporting and the effectiveness of the internal control structure related to the municipal grant funds received for the year ended June 30, 2008. The Town of Ocean View's management is responsible for compliance with those requirements.

This agreed-upon procedures attestation engagement was performed in accordance with *Government Auditing Standards*, issued by the Comptroller General of the United States and the attestation standards established by the American Institute of Certified Public Accountants. The sufficiency of these procedures is solely the responsibility of those parties specified in this report. Consequently, we make no representation regarding the sufficiency of the procedures described below either for the purpose for which this report has been requested of for any other purpose.

Our procedures and findings were as follows:

1. Complete the State of Delaware Office of Auditor of Accounts municipal grants agreed-upon procedures program to determine the Town of Ocean View's compliance with applicable laws, regulations and financial reports related to municipal grant funds received for the year ended June 30, 2008, and detail any instances of noncompliance.

    The Town of Ocean View received municipal grant funds under the following programs for the year ended June 30, 2008:

    Municipal Street Aid
    Police Pension
    State Aid to Local Law Enforcement

    During the completion of the agreed-upon procedures checklists as provided by the State of Delaware Auditor of Accounts, there were no findings or recommendations relating to any of the municipal grant funds indicated above.

2. Address the status of any findings and recommendations disclosed in previous reports.

    There were no findings or recommendations relating to any municipal grant funds administered by the Town of Ocean View in previous reports.

We were not engaged to and did not conduct an examination, the objective of which would be the expression of an opinion on compliance with specified laws. Accordingly, we do not express such an opinion. Had we performed additional procedures, other matters might have come to our attention that would have been reported to you.

This report is intended solely for the information and use of the Town of Ocean View's management and council members, the State of Delaware's Office of Auditor of Accounts, Department of Homeland Security, and the Office of the State Treasurer and should not be used by those who have not agreed to the procedures and have not taken responsibility for the sufficiency of the procedures for their purposes. However, this report is a matter of public record, and its distribution is not limited.

Grabowski, Sparano & Vincelette, CPA's

Wilmington, Delaware
January 9, 2009

significant assumptions used to prepare prospective financial statements; indicate that actual events or conditions may not be consistent with these assumptions; and, for financial projections, indicate the limited usefulness of the projection.

To perform an attestation engagement on either prospective financial information or pro forma information, accountants must evaluate the preparation of the financial information, the support underlying the assumptions, and the presentation of the information. To accomplish these objectives, accountants must (1) obtain knowledge about the entity's business, accounting principles, and factors affecting the events and transactions in question; (2) obtain an understanding of the process through which the information was developed (e.g., determine whether all relevant information was considered in developing assumptions); (3) evaluate the assumptions (and their underlying support) used to prepare the information; (4) identify key factors affecting the information; and (5) evaluate the preparation and presentation of the financial information (e.g., consistency with AICPA guidelines).

Understanding the purposes of forecasts, projections, and pro forma engagements can be challenging. Exhibit A.3 presents a summary of the key differences between the attestation engagements discussed in this section.

EXHIBIT A.3 **A Comparison of Prospective and Pro Forma Engagements**

Engagement	Accountants Report on . . .	Example Key Question Addressed
Financial forecast	Prospective information based upon future expected conditions	What will things look like if we continue along our expected path?
Financial projection	Prospective information based upon hypothetical ("what-if?") events	What will things look like if we choose a different path(s)?
Pro forma	Financial information based on historical information "as if" the event had previously occurred	What would things look like if actual events (e.g., a merger) occurred as of December 31 instead of January 15?

AUDITING INSIGHT   Attestation Expectation Gap?

The results of an academic study indicate significant differences in beliefs among accountants, users, and preparers of prospective financial information concerning forecast reliability and the role and responsibilities of accountants and management. Contrary to the usual published studies on the expectation gap between accountants and the public, researchers found that accountants believe that forecasts are *more* reliable than users or preparers do. Accountants also believe that they have a higher level of responsibility and accountability than is attributed to them by users or preparers.

Source: P. Schelluch and G. Gay, "Assurance Provided by Auditors' Reports on Prospective Financial Information: Implications for the Expectation Gap," *Accounting and Finance,* 46 (December 2006), p. 653.

An Examination of an Entity's Internal Control over Financial Reporting That Is Integrated with an Audit of Its Financial Statements (AT 501)

Auditing Standard 2201 (AS 2201) requires the management of public companies to assess and report on their internal control over financial reporting and the auditors to express an opinion on the effectiveness of internal control based on established criteria (generally, based on criteria established by the Committee of Sponsoring Organizations, or COSO) in conjunction with the financial statement audits. These reports are covered in Chapter 5.

Regulators, boards, or management of *nonpublic* companies may engage accountants to examine and report on the effectiveness of internal controls over financial reporting in their organization in conjunction with their financial statement audit. Accountants should not accept an engagement to *review* an entity's internal control. The attestation standard (AT 501) that governs accountants' examination of an entity's internal control is very similar to AS 2201. It calls for an examination of internal controls using a top-down, risk-based approach and control testing comparable to the approach discussed in Chapter 5. The following conditions must be met before accountants can conduct an examination on an entity's internal control:

- Management accepts responsibility for the effectiveness of its internal control.
- Management's evaluation of control is based on suitable and available criteria (e.g., COSO Report; see Chapter 5).
- Management's evaluation of control is supported by sufficient evidence.
- Management presents its assertion about the effectiveness of its internal control in a written report that accompanies the accountants' report.

Reports on examination of internal controls under AT 501 are also similar to those required by AS 2201. A material weakness requires an adverse report. The inability to complete the engagement requires a disclaimer of opinion. A written report of significant deficiencies and material weaknesses must also be given to those charged with governance.

Compliance Attestation

Management often must report its compliance with contractual obligations to third parties. For example, entities may have restrictive covenants in loan agreements, and lenders may require a periodic report on whether the entity has complied with these covenants. Contractual agreements could include dividend limitations, loan limitations, prescribed debt/equity ratios, or limitations on geographic operations. In addition, companies and governmental agencies must comply with applicable laws and regulations. Accountants may accept engagements to attest to (1) an entity's compliance with the requirement of the laws, regulations, rules, and so forth, and (2) the effectiveness of an entity's internal controls that ensure compliance with the requirements. In addition to these examination engagements, accountants can perform *agreed-upon procedures* regarding compliance. (*Reviews* of compliance are not appropriate engagements.)

For a compliance attestation, three conditions must be met: (1) management accepts responsibility for compliance, (2) compliance or the controls over compliance is/are capable of evaluation and measurement against reasonable criteria, and (3) sufficient evidence must be available to support management's evaluation. Management may make an assertion in either a written report or as a written representation to the accountants. The accountants then *examine* or perform *agreed-upon procedures* that evaluate management's written assertion about the entity's compliance with the criteria.

Attestation standards require accountants to consider inherent risk, control risk, and detection risk in connection with *examination* engagements for compliance. These considerations are very similar to the risk elements in financial statement audits. However, consideration of materiality in compliance engagements may be difficult; sometimes monetary measures can be applied; sometimes they cannot. Nevertheless, risk and materiality are as important in compliance attestation as they are in financial statement audits.

Exercise of due care and professional skepticism about noncompliance are prerequisites for a compliance examination. Otherwise, the major steps in a compliance examination are these:

- Understand the specific compliance requirements and assess planning materiality.
- Plan the engagement and assess inherent risk.
- Understand relevant controls over compliance, assess control risk, and design tests of compliance with detection risk in mind.
- Obtain sufficient evidence of compliance with specific requirements, including a written letter of management representations.

EXHIBIT A.4 **Standard Unmodified Compliance Attestation Report**

> Independent Accountant's Report
>
> To the Agency:
>
> We have examined the Agency's compliance with Department of Employment Regulation JR-52 during the year ended December 31, 2017. Management is responsible for the Agency's compliance with those requirements. Our responsibility is to express an opinion on the Agency's compliance based on our examination.
>
> Our examination was conducted in accordance with attestation standards established by the American Institute of Certified Public Accountants and, accordingly, included examining, on a test basis, evidence about the Agency's compliance with those requirements and performing such other procedures as we considered necessary in the circumstances. We believe that our examination provides a reasonable basis for our opinion. Our examination does not provide a legal determination on the Agency's compliance with specified requirements.
>
> In our opinion, the Agency complied, in all material respects, with the aforementioned requirements for the year ended December 31, 2017.
>
> *Michael Scarn, LLP*
> Scranton, PA
> February 15, 2018

- Consider subsequent events: subsequent information that bears on the management assertion and subsequent events of noncompliance after the assertion date.
- Form an opinion and prepare the report.

These standards call for work that is directly parallel to that in financial statement audits. The standard unmodified report in a compliance examination engagement (Exhibit A.4) expresses the accountant's opinion as to compliance. Accountants can issue an unmodified report or, if findings dictate (1) a report modified to disclose a noncompliance event, (2) a qualified report stating material noncompliance, or (3) an adverse report stating that the entity is not in compliance.

Accountants may also be asked to provide similar assurance with regard to federal and state regulatory requirements. Examples include limitations on investments for mutual funds or state insurance department regulations about the nature of insurance company investments. Regulatory agencies may seek assertions in prescribed report language that go beyond acceptable professional reporting responsibilities and involve accountants in areas outside their function and responsibility. In such cases, accountants should insert additional wording in the prescribed report language or write a completely revised report that adequately reflects their position and responsibility.

Broker–Dealer Compliance

In 2010, in response to several high-profile **broker–dealer** collapses, including Madoff Investment Securities (see Auditing Insight, page 48), the *Dodd-Frank Wall Street Reform and Consumer Protection Act* gave the PCAOB the authority to oversee audits of broker–dealers. The SEC responded in 2011 with Rule 17a-5, outlining reporting, audit, and notification requirements for broker–dealers. To address the SEC's rules, the PCAOB established AT 1 and AT 2 to guide examinations of broker–dealer compliance with the SEC requirements.

Broker–dealers are not subject to audits of internal controls under AS 2201; however, broker–dealers who clear investment transactions or carry customer assets are required to file a report with the SEC addressing their compliance with net capital requirements (Rule 15c3-1), reserves and custody of securities (Rule 15c3-c), quarterly security counts (Rule 17a-13), and compliance with rules on customer statements. These compliance reports must be audited in accordance with PCAOB AT 1.

AT 1 requires auditors to obtain sufficient, appropriate evidence to provide reasonable assurance on the following assertions from the broker–dealer's compliance report:

- The broker–dealer was in compliance with the net capital rule and the reserve requirement rule at fiscal year-end.
- The broker–dealer had effective internal control over compliance during the year and at year-end.
- The broker–dealer based its assertions on information from its accounting records.

The AT 1 engagement is an examination similar to other attestation engagements. Auditors must have adequate technical proficiency, follow ethical requirements, exercise due professional care, and have an adequate understanding of the rules relevant to broker–dealer regulations. Further, the examination should be coordinated with the audit of the financial statements and the audit procedures performed on supplemental broker–dealer information under AS 2701.

In planning the examination engagement, the auditor should:

- Evaluate the nature of noncompliance identified during previous examinations.
- Obtain an understanding of the entity's processes (including relevant controls) regarding compliance with financial responsibility rules (including assessing management's competence).
- Obtain an understanding of instances of noncompliance identified by management during the current fiscal year.
- Assess the risks associated with related parties.
- Read the Financial and Operational Combined Uniform Single reports (FOCUS report).
- Read reports of internal auditors that are relevant to the assertions.
- Inquire about regulator examinations and correspondence with the SEC that are relevant to the assertions.
- Obtain an understanding of the nature and frequency of customer complaints relevant to the assertions.
- Assess the risk of fraud (including misappropriate of customer assets) relevant to compliance.

The auditor must test both the design and the operating effectiveness of the entity's internal control over compliance. The procedures proscribed by AT 1 to test the design and operating effectiveness of internal control over compliance are similar to the requirements of AS 2201 (covered in Chapter 5). Similar to AS 2201, the evidence obtained depends upon the risk associated with the control. However, there are two primary differences:

1. The examination of Internal Control under AT 1 only covers controls over compliance with the SEC regulations. The auditor of a broker–dealer is *not* required to perform a full audit of ICFR under AS 2201.
2. The examination of internal control over compliance under AT covers controls as of fiscal year-end *and* throughout the fiscal period. The audit of ICFR under AS 2201 only is as of the fiscal year-end. The auditor should communicate all deficiencies identified to management.

Auditors must also perform sufficient procedures to support whether the broker–dealer was in compliance with the net capital and reserve requirements rules as of the end of the fiscal year. The tests should be planned and performed to be responsive to risks (including fraud risks) associated with noncompliance. Inquiry alone does not provide sufficient appropriate evidence. In conjunction with performing net capital and reserve requirements testing, the auditor must perform procedures to obtain evidence about the existence of customer funds or securities held for customers. Auditors must also obtain a representation letter from management and communicate with both management and the audit committee any identified instances of noncompliance with financial responsibility rules, identified material weaknesses, or instances where information used to determine compliance was not derived from the broker–dealer's financial records.

AUDITING INSIGHT   This Isn't Reassuring . . .

In 2012, the **North American Securities Administrators Association** (NASAA) identified the top broker–dealer compliance violations. In an examination of 236 companies, more than 450 violations were found, including nearly 150 involving the books and records of the entity. The most common violation involved maintenance of records for new customer accounts. Also included were problems with supervisory

approval and customer statements/confirmations. AT 1 was designed to help prevent these issues.

Source: B. Singer, "Top Broker-Dealer Compliance Issues Disclosed by State Securities Regulators," www.forbes.com/sites/billsinger/2012/09/10/top-broker-dealer-compliance-issues-disclosed-by-state-securities-regulators/.

An auditor must issue an adverse opinion for any instance of noncompliance or a single material weakness in internal control over compliance at any time during the fiscal year, even if the entity has completed remediation efforts. It does not matter whether the issue was discovered by the auditor or management. In that situation, the report reflects both the identification of the matter that led to the adverse opinion and an indication that the issue had been adequately resolved. The report should be dated no earlier than the date on which the auditor obtains sufficient appropriate evidence, but it should not be earlier than the date of the auditor's report on the financial statements.

Some broker–dealers perform all their trading on their own behalf and do not hold customer funds. These entities are exempt from filing compliance reports, and instead file an exemption report. The exemption report is subject to a review engagement under AT 2. The SEC concluded that because safeguarding customer assets is so important, some degree of assurance is required. The review standard requires auditors to obtain moderate assurance whether conditions exist that would indicate that the broker-dealer should not have claimed an exemption.

Management's Discussion and Analysis

Accountants also can examine or review **management's discussion and analysis (MD&A)** that usually accompanies the audited financial statements in corporate annual reports. Under existing audit standards, auditors are required to read the MD&A section to ensure that this information accompanying the audited financial statements is consistent with them. For example, MD&A should not indicate that operating income increased by 10 percent from the prior year if this is not consistent with information in the company's audited income statement. Attestation standards allow accountants to undertake engagements to additionally *examine* or *review* the MD&A section. The performance of the attestation engagement and subsequent reporting responsibilities are similar to other attestation engagements and result in accountants issuing an opinion on the MD&A based on the engagement performed.

Service Organizations

Often, a **service organization** that provides services to *user entities* processes clients' transactions that are likely to be relevant to user entities' internal control over financial reporting. Examples of service organizations include payroll processing companies, computerized information processing service centers, trust departments of banks, insurers that maintain the accounting records for reinsurance transactions, mortgage bankers and savings and loan associations that service loans for owners, and transfer agents that handle the shareholder accounting for mutual and money market investment funds. The fact that management is *outsourcing* some of its noncore functions does not absolve management of its responsibility for internal control over those functions. Management (as well as the audit team) of *user entities* must somehow gain comfort that controls are in place and effective. The solution to this dilemma is a special-purpose report on internal control (formerly referred to as an SAS 70 report) in which the service organization's auditors report on the effectiveness of the service organization's internal control to the user entities (and their auditors).

There are three categories of *service organization control (SOC) reports* that serve different purposes for organizations.

- SOC 1 is the report (illustrated in Exhibit A.5) for controls over financial reporting, now referred to as the SSAE 16 report.
- The SOC 2 report is a "report on controls at a service organization relevant to security, availability, processing integrity, confidentiality, or privacy," which may be requested by a user but does not apply directly to the user's financial statements. The report contents are the same as SOC 1 reports.
- SOC 3 is a trust services report. It is used in marketing organizations' control effectiveness. An SOC 3 report basically covers the same subject matter as SOC 2 does but in less detail and in a format that lends itself to a general-use report.

Within each category, there are two types of SOC reports:

- A *type 1 report* describes the service organization's internal controls placed in operation at a specific point in time but does not report on the effectiveness of the controls.
- A *type 2 report* not only includes a description of the controls but also reports on the service organization's auditors' *testing* of the controls over a minimum six-month period.

Only the type 2 reports are useful with respect to meeting Sarbanes–Oxley's rigorous internal control requirements. Ordinarily, service auditors' reports are not public reports on internal controls but are used only by user entities' auditors to assess internal controls at the service organization.

AUDITING INSIGHT   Increase in SSAE 16 Reports Tied to Sarbanes–Oxley

With increased outsourcing of activities that are not company core competencies, the emphasis on SSAE 16 reports takes on greater significance. Take, for example, **Service Corporation International (SCI)**, the largest provider of funeral, cemetery, and cremation services in North America. SCI's funeral homes are spread across 48 states, Canada, and Puerto Rico. The company outsources both generic activities (e.g., payroll) and some activities specific to its industry (e.g., the management of trust accounts held for future funeral and cremation services). Although it would not be cost effective for the company's management to examine the controls over all of these activities (as required by Sarbanes–Oxley), management relies on service auditors to do the work for them—the company collects more than 40 SSAE 16 reports a year.

Source: "*SAS 70* Reports Continue to Grow in Demand and Utility for Sarbanes–Oxley Compliance," www.proviti.com

As a condition of the engagement, management of the service organization is required to provide the auditor with a written assertion about (1) the fairness of the presentation of the description of the service organization's system; (2) the suitability of the design controls to achieve the related control objectives; and, in a type 2 engagement, (3) the operating effectiveness of those controls. In a type 2 report, the service auditor expresses an opinion on the fairness of the description and on the suitability of the design and operations of the controls throughout the period covered by the report. The service auditor should inquire whether management is aware of any subsequent events that could have a significant effect on the controls at the service organization or on the service auditor's report. The service auditor also should modify the report if information comes to the service auditor's attention that causes him or her to conclude that (1) design deficiencies exist and (2) user organizations would not be expected to have controls in place to mitigate such design deficiencies.

EXHIBIT A.5
Service Auditor's
SOC 1 Type 2 Report

Service Organization's Controls

Independent Service Auditor's Report on a Description of a Service Organization's System and the Suitability of the Design and Operating Effectiveness of Controls

To XYZ Service Organization:

We have examined XYZ Service Organization's description of its Global Development Center system for processing user entities' transactions throughout the year ended December 31, 2017, and the suitability of the design and operating effectiveness of controls to achieve the related control objectives stated in the description.

On page 22 of the description, XYZ Service Organization has provided an assertion about the fairness of the presentation of the description and suitability of the design and operating effectiveness of the controls to achieve the related control objectives stated in the description. XYZ Service Organization is responsible for preparing the description and for the assertion, including the completeness, accuracy, and method of presentation of the description and the assertion, providing the services covered by the description, specifying the control objectives and stating them in the description, identifying the risks that threaten the achievement of the control objectives, selecting the criteria, and designing, implementing, and documenting controls to achieve the related control objectives stated in the description.

Our responsibility is to express an opinion on the fairness of the presentation of the description and on the suitability of the design and operating effectiveness of the controls to achieve the related control objectives stated in the description based on our examination. We conducted our examination in accordance with attestation standards established by the American Institute of Certified Public Accountants. Those standards require that we plan and perform our examination to obtain reasonable assurance about whether, in all material respects, the description is fairly presented and the controls were suitably designed and operating effectively to achieve the related control objectives stated in the description throughout the year ended December 31, 2017.

An examination of a description of a service organization's system and the suitability of the design and operating effectiveness of the service organization's controls to achieve the related control objectives stated in the description involves performing procedures to obtain evidence about the fairness of the presentation of the description and the suitability of the design and operating effectiveness of those controls to achieve the related control objectives stated in the description. Our procedures included assessing the risks that the description is not fairly presented and that the controls were not suitably designed or operating effectively to achieve the related control objectives stated in the description. Our procedures also included testing the operating effectiveness of those controls that we consider necessary to provide reasonable assurance that the related control objectives stated in the description were achieved. An examination engagement of this type also includes evaluating the overall presentation of the description and the suitability of the control objectives stated therein, and the suitability of the criteria specified by the service organization and described at page 22. We believe that the evidence we obtained is sufficient and appropriate to provide a reasonable basis for our opinion.

Because of their nature, controls at a service organization may not prevent, or detect and correct, all errors or omissions in processing or reporting transactions. Also, the projection to the future of any evaluation of the fairness of the presentation of the description, or conclusions about the suitability of the design or operating effectiveness of the controls to achieve the related control objectives, is subject to the risk that controls at a service organization may become inadequate or fail.

In our opinion, in all material respects, based on the criteria described in XYZ Service Organization's assertion on page 22

a. the description fairly presents the system that was designed and implemented throughout the year ended December 31, 2017.

b. the controls related to the control objectives stated in the description were suitably designed to provide reasonable assurance that the control objectives would be achieved if the controls operated effectively throughout the year ended December 31, 2017.

c. the controls tested, which were those necessary to provide reasonable assurance that the control objectives stated in the description were achieved, operated effectively throughout the year ended December 31, 2017.

The specific controls tested and the nature, timing, and results of those tests are listed on pages 10-20.

This report, including the description of tests of controls and results thereof on pages 10–20, is intended solely for the information and use of XYZ Service Organization, the user entities of XYZ Service Organization's system during some or all of the year ended December 31, 2017, and the independent auditors of such user entities, who have a sufficient understanding to consider it, along with other information including information about controls implemented by user entities themselves when assessing the risks of material misstatements of user entities' financial statements. This report is not intended to be and should not be used by anyone other than these specified parties.

Michael Scarn, LLP
Scranton, PA
March 15, 2018

Exhibit A.5 is an example of a SOC 1 type 2 report addressing both the design and operating effectiveness of the service organization's controls.

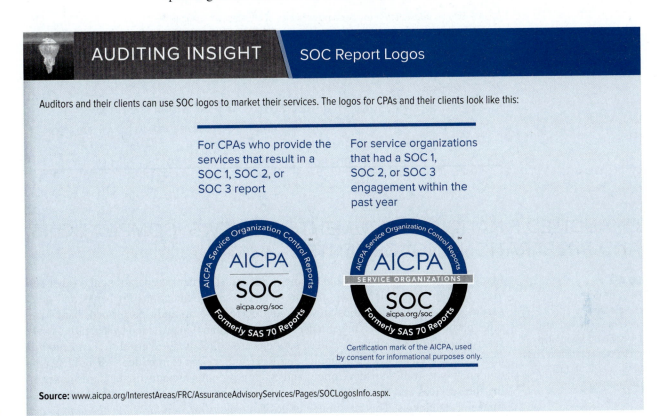

AUDITING INSIGHT   SOC Report Logos

Auditors and their clients can use SOC logos to market their services. The logos for CPAs and their clients look like this:

For CPAs who provide the services that result in a SOC 1, SOC 2, or SOC 3 report

For service organizations that had a SOC 1, SOC 2, or SOC 3 engagement within the past year

Certification mark of the AICPA, used by consent for informational purposes only.

Source: www.aicpa.org/InterestAreas/FRC/AssuranceAdvisoryServices/Pages/SOCLogosInfo.aspx.

This section discussed engagements and reports related to attestation services. A brief summary of these services is shown in Exhibit A.6.

EXHIBIT A.6
Summary of
Attestation Reports

Services	Description	Type(s) of Engagements	Report Distribution
Agreed-upon procedures engagement	Perform procedures requested by specified users	Agreed-upon procedures	Distribution limited to users participating in determining scope of the engagement
Financial forecast	Expected conditions	Examination or agreed-upon procedures	General or limited use
Financial projections	Hypothetical conditions	Examination or agreed-upon procedures	Limited use
Pro forma	Historical statements "as if" a transaction had occurred	Examination or review	General use
Internal control	Similar to AS 2201	Examination	General use
Compliance	Compliance or controls over compliance	Examination or agreed-upon procedures	General use for examinations
Management's discussion and analysis	Compared to rules and regulations of the SEC	Examine or review	General or limited use
Service organizations	Examine controls over financial information	Type 1—design effectiveness Type 2—operating effectiveness	Limited to user organizations and their auditors

UNAUDITED FINANCIAL STATEMENTS: REVIEWS, COMPILATIONS, AND PREPARATION ENGAGEMENTS

LO A-2

Describe reviews, compilations, and preparation of unaudited financial statements and prepare appropriate reports given specific factual circumstances.

Many accountants perform bookkeeping, financial statement preparation, and other services to help nonpublic entities prepare financial communications for banks and other parties. Because these entities are not required to have an audit performed, banks and other parties may request a lower level of assurance than that provided by an audit. A subset of *attestation engagements,* these services are collectively referred to as *accounting and review services.* The Accounting and Review Services Committee (ARSC) has continuing responsibility for developing and issuing pronouncements of standards concerning the services and reports that accountants may render in connection with unaudited financial statements. This committee issues *Statements on Standards for Accounting and Review Services* (SSARS), which apply to accountants' services on unaudited financial statements of *nonissuers.*[5] The AICPA's Code of Professional Conduct and Statements on Quality Control Standards also govern these engagements. Accountants who perform accounting and review services should possess a level of knowledge of the accounting principles and practices of the industry. Their reports should compare financial statements to the *appropriate financial accounting framework.* All three SSARS engagements require a written engagement letter specifying the services provided.

Review Services

A review is a service performed by accountants to obtain limited assurance that no material modifications should be made to the financial statements in order for the statements to be in conformity with the applicable reporting framework (usually GAAP). Because some assurance is provided in a review engagement, accountants must be independent in order to perform review services.

Procedures performed during a review of unaudited financial statements consist primarily of obtaining **review evidence** by

1. Obtaining a written understanding with management about the nature and limitations of a review engagement (engagement letter).

2. Obtaining knowledge of the entity's business, accounting principles in the entity's industry, and the entity's organization and operations.

3. Inquiring of management about the entity's accounting system; actions taken at meetings of shareholders, directors, and other important executive committees; and issues surrounding the preparation and presentation of the financial statements, such as accounting

---

[5]According to SSARS, nonissuers are all entities except those whose securities are registered under the Securities Exchange Act of 1934 or are required to file reports under the Securities Act of 1933.

principles used, unusual or complex transactions, significant transactions near the end of the period, subsequent events, and communications with regulatory agencies.

4. Conducting analytical procedures.
5. Reconciling the financial statements to the underlying records.
6. Obtaining written representations from management.

Professional standards require accountants to provide adequate documentation for the review engagement. Accountants are required to describe the procedures they performed and the results obtained. Although the information gained through these procedures is similar to audit evidence, they are much more limited in scope than the typical auditing procedures for assessing the risk of material misstatement, conducting physical observation of tangible assets, sending confirmations, or examining documentary details of transactions. In addition, a review does not contemplate obtaining an understanding of internal control. As a result, a review engagement does *not* provide a basis for expressing an opinion on financial statements. In a standard unmodified report for an *audit* engagement, auditors provide *positive assurance* (a forthright and factual statement of the auditors' opinion based on an audit) that the financial statements are fairly presented.

For engagements that are less than an audit, accountants instead provide *negative assurance* through a phrase such as "we are not aware of any material modifications" that is necessary for the financial statements to be in conformity with an appropriate financial reporting framework. While *auditing* standards prohibit the use of negative assurance in reports on audited financial statements (because it is considered too weak a conclusion for the audit effort), negative assurance is permitted in reviews of unaudited financial statements, in letters to underwriters, and in reviews of interim financial information. Understand that, although the assurance provided is less than in an audit engagement, the accountant should exercise professional judgment when conducting a review engagement, recognizing that circumstances may cause the financial statements to be materially misstated.

When accountants perform a review engagement, each page of the company's financial statements should be marked "See independent accountants' review report." This clearly indicates to users that an audit engagement was not performed.

Similar to an audit report, the accountant should include an emphasis-of-matter paragraph in the review report after the conclusion paragraph when it is necessary to draw users' attention to a matter appropriately presented or disclosed in the financial statements that is fundamental to users' understanding (e.g., the client used a basis of accounting other than GAAP). The accountant should also include an other-matter paragraph if the accountant considers it necessary to communicate a matter other than those presented or disclosed in the financial statements. An example of a review report is provided in Exhibit A.7. Note that the review was done on financial statements prepared using a special-purpose framework (tax basis) rather than GAAP.

Review Services and Fraud

SSARS require accountants to establish an understanding with the entity in an engagement letter that management is responsible for preventing and detecting fraud for all accounting and review services provided. However, for a review, the accountant has the additional responsibility to obtain written representations from management that specifically acknowledge responsibility for designing internal control to prevent and detect fraud. Further, management should acknowledge disclosure to the accountant of any fraud or suspected fraud or noncompliance with laws and regulations whose effects should be considered when preparing financial statements. In a review engagement, if the accountant becomes aware that fraud may have occurred, the accountant should communicate the matter to the appropriate level of management (at a level above those suspected of fraud). If management does not provide sufficient information that supports that the financial statements are not materially misstated due to fraud, the accountant should consider withdrawing from the engagement.

EXHIBIT A.7

Example Review Report (Income Tax Basis)

Independent Accountant's Review Report

To the Board of Directors and Shareholders of the Dunder-Mifflin, Inc.

We have reviewed the accompanying statement of assets, liability, and equity—income tax basis of the Dunder-Mifflin, Inc. as of December 31, 2017, and the related statement of revenue and expenses—income tax basis for the year then ended. A review includes primarily applying analytical procedures to management's financial data and making inquiries of company management. A review is substantially less in scope than an audit, the objective of which is the expression of an opinion regarding the financial statements as a whole. Accordingly, we do not express such an opinion.

Management's Responsibility for the Financial Statements

Management is responsible for the preparation and fair presentation of the financial statements in accordance with the basis of accounting the company uses for income tax purposes; this includes determining that the basis of accounting the company uses for income tax purposes is an acceptable basis for the preparation of financial statements in the circumstances. Management is also responsible for the design, implementation, and maintenance of internal control relevant to the preparation and fair presentation of financial statements that are free from material misstatement, whether due to fraud or error.

Accountants' Responsibility

Our responsibility is to conduct the review engagement in accordance with Statements on Standards for Accounting and Review Services promulgated by the Accounting and Review Services Committee of the AICPA. Those standards require us to perform procedures to obtain limited assurance as a basis for reporting whether we are aware of any material modifications that should be made to the financial statements for them to be in accordance with the basis of accounting that the company uses for income tax purposes. We believe that the results of our procedures provide a reasonable basis for our conclusion.

Accountant's Conclusion

Based on our review, we are not aware of any material modifications that should be made to the accompanying financial statements in order for them to be in accordance with the basis of accounting the partnership uses for income tax purposes.

Basis of Accounting

We draw attention to Note 1 of the financial statements, which describes the basis of accounting. The financial statements are prepared in accordance with the basis of accounting the company uses for income tax purposes, which is a basis of accounting other than accounting principles generally accepted in the United States of America. Our conclusion is not modified with respect to this matter.

Michael Scarn, LLP
Scranton, PA
March 1, 2018

Comparative Financial Statements

Review reports often are presented with comparative financial statements. Similar to an audit, when comparative financial statements are presented, the accountant's report should refer to each period for which financial statements are presented. However, because of the lower level of assurance, there are several issues that can arise in a review that are distinct from an audit.

If the accountant's report on the financial statements contains a change from a prior-period report related to a departure from the applicable financial reporting framework, the accountant's review report should include an other-matter paragraph. This additional paragraph should reference the date of the previous review report; the circumstances that cause the reference to change; and if applicable, that the financial statements of the prior period have been changed. Similarly, if the prior period was audited and the auditor's report on the prior period is not reissued, the review report should include an other-matter paragraph indicating that the financial statements of the prior period were audited, the date of the auditor's report, and the type of opinion issued.

Change from an Audit to a Review

Occasionally, a client may engage an accountant to perform an audit but request a change to a review engagement. The client may want to make this change for a number of reasons: a creditor no longer requires an audit; the client misunderstood the difference between an audit and a review; or a scope limitation, such as inability to count inventory at year-end, prevented the completion of the audit. Professional Standards require that the accountant decide whether to agree to the change after considering the reason given, as well as how much additional effort and cost would be required to be able to complete the audit engagement. If the audit procedures are substantially complete, it may not be appropriate to accept the change. Generally, if the reason for the requested change is revised needs of the client or a misunderstanding about the services, a change would be acceptable. If a scope limitation led to the change, the auditor may consider the possibility that information affected by the scope limitation may be incomplete, inaccurate, or otherwise unsatisfactory. The accountant is specifically precluded from accepting a change from an audit to a review engagement, except in rare circumstances, when the scope limitation results from management's refusal to allow the accountant to correspond with the entity's legal counsel.

Other Issues Relevant to Review Engagements

1. An accountant may be engaged to review a single financial statement as long as the scope of the accountant's procedures were not restricted. Similarly, an accountant may also review specific elements or accounts of a financial statement, supplementary information (including required information), or financial information included in a tax return.

2. Sometimes, an accountant will review information that is only intended or suitable for certain parties. For example, an accountant may review certain complex valuation estimates as part of a business combination. In situations where restrictions are necessary, an accountant's review report should include an alert, in a separate paragraph, restricting the use of the report when the accountant determines that the measurement or disclosure criteria are only suitable or available to certain parties.

3. When performing a review, certain analytical procedures are considered presumptively mandatory. The accountant should compare the financial statements with comparable information for the prior period. The accountant should also compare recorded amounts or ratios developed from recorded amounts to expectations developed based on an understanding of the entity and its industry, as well as comparing disaggregated revenue data. In making these comparisons, the accountant should determine the amount of difference that is acceptable without further investigation.

4. When performing a review, certain inquiries of management are also considered presumptively mandatory. These include inquires about whether the financial statements have been prepared and fairly presented in accordance with the applicable financial reporting framework, including unusual or complex situations, significant transactions, uncorrected misstatements identified during the previous review, subsequent events, knowledge of fraud or suspected fraud, noncompliance with laws and regulations, significant journal entires, related party transactions, litigation, the reasonableness of significant estimates, and actions taken at board and committee meetings. The accountant should also inquire about any other matters considered relevant.

5. Subsequent events and subsequently discovered facts in a review are treated similarly to how they are treated in an audit.

6. When supplementary information (such as MD&A) is included with the financial statements, the accountant should clearly indicate the degree of responsibility taken for the information in either an other-matter paragraph or a separate report. If the supplementary information is required, the other-matter paragraph should also discuss if the accountant is aware of omissions or departures from the prescribed guidelines and whether the accountant has any unresolved doubts about whether the information is presented in accordance with guidelines.

Compilation Services

Compilation is a synonym for an older term, *write-up.* Both terms refer to accountants helping clients summarize (or "write up") their financial information in the form of financial statements. The purpose of a **compilation** engagement is to assist management in presenting financial information that is the representation of management in the form of financial statements—without providing any assurance on the accuracy or completeness of that information but with an accountant's report attached that explicitly describes the service.

When performing a compilation engagement, the accountant has no responsibility to assess the conformity of the entity's financial statements with GAAP. However, accountants should obtain an engagement letter; understand the entity's business and applicable accounting standards; read the financial statements looking for obvious clerical or accounting principle errors; and follow up on information that is incorrect, incomplete, or otherwise unsatisfactory. Accountants are *not* required to assess control risk or to perform any other evidence-gathering procedures. Documentation should provide a clear understanding of the work performed, the engagement letter, significant findings or issues, the resolution of those issues, and any oral or written communications with management regarding fraud or illegal acts.

In a compilation engagement, given the very limited procedures performed, accountants explicitly state that no opinion and no assurance are expressed, thus taking no responsibility for a report on the fair presentation of financial statements in conformity with GAAP. Because no assurance is provided, accountants are *not* required to be independent to perform compilation engagements or issue compilation reports. However, accountants must assess whether they are independent and state in the compilation report whether they are not.

Each page of the financial statements should be marked "See accountants' compilation report." An example report for a compilation engagement is presented in Exhibit A.8.

Three primary types of reports on compiled financial statements can be issued:

1. The management or owners may not wish to present all footnote disclosures required by GAAP (believing such disclosures are not needed for their purposes). Accountants can issue a compilation report that notifies users of the omission and states that if they were included, they might influence users' conclusions about the business (provided the accountant has no reason to believe the footnotes were omitted to mislead the financial statement user).

2. If accountants are not independent, their report should specifically state their lack of independence. Unlike audits or reviews, accountants may provide a general description of the reason for impaired independence (e.g., providing internal control services) in their compilation report if they choose.

3. The management or owners can also choose to present the financial statements complete with all disclosures required by GAAP.

EXHIBIT A.8

Example Compilation Report

> Management is responsible for the accompanying financial statements of Dunder-Mifflin, Inc., which comprise the balance sheet as of December 31, 2017 and the related statements of income, changes in stockholders' equity, and cash flows for the years then ended, and the related notes to the financial statements in accordance with accounting principles generally accepted in the United States of America. We have performed a compilation engagement in accordance with Statements on Standards for Accounting and Review Services promulgated by the Accounting and Review Services Committee of the AICPA. We did not audit or review the financial statements, nor were we required to perform any procedures to verify the accuracy or completeness of the information provided by management. Accordingly, we do not express an opinion, a conclusion, or provide any form of assurance on these financial statements.
>
> *Michael Scarn, LLP*
> Scranton, PA
> March 1, 2018

Preparation of Financial Statements

In your first principles of accounting course, you were probably given a list of account balances and accounting information and asked to prepare basic financial statements. If you had been a CPA at the time and had submitted the financial statements to a client, you may have unknowingly triggered a compilation engagement when neither you nor your client wanted a report attached to the financial statements. Many doctors, lawyers, and other small businesses want assistance from accountants with financial statements but have no need for an accountant's report or any form of assurance.

To allow accountants to perform simple services without requiring an accountant's report, the AICPA created a new type of engagement known as *preparation of financial statements*. When performing a preparation of financial statements engagement, the accountant should prepare an engagement letter, but he or she does not need to even assess independence. The accountant should prepare the financial statements using the client's records and should include a statement on each page of the financial statements indicating that "no assurance is provided."

Because the accountant does not prepare a report, disclosure in the financial statements is the primary means of communicating information to users. For example, if the client uses a non-GAAP method of accounting or substantially omits all disclosures, the accountant should make sure that this is disclosed either on the face of the financial statements or in a note to the financial statements. Similarly, if the accountant becomes aware that the financial statements are incomplete, inaccurate, or otherwise unacceptable, the accountant should inform management and request additional or corrected information. However, even if management does not correct the information, the accountant need only disclose the material misstatements in the notes to the financial statements.

A preparation engagement is not performing bookkeeping for a client, nor does it qualify as many other services an accountant may perform. Exhibit A.9 outlines examples that are and are not preparation engagements.

EXHIBIT A.9
Preparation of Financial Statements vs. Assistance in Preparing Financial Statements

Examples of Services That Are Preparation Engagements	Examples of Services That Are Not Preparation Engagements
Preparation of financial statements prior to audit or review by another accountant	Preparation of financial statements when the accountant is engaged to perform an audit, review, or compilation of such financial statements
Preparation of financial statements to be presented alongside the entity's tax return	Preparation of financial statements solely for submission to taxing authorities
Preparation of personal financial statements for presentation alongside a financial plan	Personal financial statements that are prepared for inclusion in written personal financial plans prepared by the accountant
	Financial statements prepared in conjunction with litigation services that involve pending or potential legal or regulatory proceedings
	Financial statements prepared in conjunction with business valuation services
	Maintaining depreciation schedules
	Preparing or proposing certain adjustments, such as those applicable to deferred income taxes, depreciation, or leases
Preparation of single financial statements, such as a balance sheet, income statement, or financial statements with substantially all disclosures omitted	Drafting financial statement notes
Using the information in a general ledger to prepare financial statements outside of an accounting software system	Entering general ledger transactions or processing payments (general bookkeeping) in an accounting software system

Source: AR-C 70.

| | AUDITING INSIGHT | Do Plain-Paper Financial Statements Have Any Value? |

A survey of practicing CPAs and bankers found that both groups reported confidence and were likely to place some reliance on plain-paper statements. This confidence was even greater when a CPA was involved with the financial statements.

Source: A. Reinstein, B. P. Green, and C. L. Miller, "Evidence of Perceived Quality of 'Plain-Paper Statements,'" *Auditing: A Journal of Practice & Theory*, November 2006, pp. 85–94.

Summary of Audits, Reviews, and Compilations

Exhibit A.10 summarizes the differences among audits, reviews, and compilations.

EXHIBIT A.10
Summary of Differences among Audits, Reviews, and Compilations

	Audit	Review	Compilation
Objective	To provide a reasonable basis for expressing an opinion regarding the financial statements taken as a whole	To provide a reasonable basis for expressing limited assurance that there are no material modifications that should be made to the financial statements in order for the statements to be in conformity with GAAP or, if applicable, special-purpose framework	To present in the form of financial statements information that is the representation of the management or owners
Procedures	Audit procedures required by generally accepted auditing standards (GAAS)	Make inquiries Perform analytical procedures Obtain management representation letter	Read the financial statements and look for obvious errors
Assurance	Positive	Limited (negative)	No assurance
Independence required?	Yes	Yes	No
Professional standards	PCAOB *Auditing Standards* (ASs) and ASB *Statements on Auditing Standards* (SASs)	AICPA *Statements on Standards for Accounting and Review Services* (SSARS)	

✅ REVIEW CHECKPOINTS

A.7 In what area(s) of practice is (are) the Accounting and Review Service Committee pronouncements applicable?

A.8 What is the difference between a review service engagement and a compilation service engagement regarding historical financial statements? Compare both of these with an audit engagement.

RESPONSIBILITIES RELATED TO REPORTING ON INTERIM FINANCIAL INFORMATION

LO A-3
Explain auditors' responsibilities related to reporting on interim financial information.

Interim financial information refers to financial information or statements covering a period less than a full year or for a 12-month period ending on a date other than the entity's fiscal year-end. Entities often provide interim financial information to owners and other financial statement users or include such information in documents containing their audited annual financial statements. Companies that are under the jurisdiction of the SEC are required to engage independent accountants to review internal control over financial reporting and interim financial information filed with the SEC. In addition, when a nonissuer entity is required to file financial information with a regulatory agency in preparation for a public offering or listing, the interim information included in the filing must be reviewed. In each case, the accountants performing the review must also be engaged to perform the audit of the annual financial statements for the current year. (If they audited the financial statements in the previous year, they need only *expect* to be engaged to audit the current year.)

A review of interim financial information differs considerably from an audit. According to professional standards, the objective of a review of interim financial information is to provide the accountants a basis for communicating whether material modifications should be made to interim financial information to ensure conformity with GAAP. In this respect, the interim information review is very similar to a review of unaudited financial statements of a nonissuer. The interim review does not require a complete assessment of control risk each quarter or gathering sufficient appropriate evidential matter on which to base an opinion on interim financial information. The objective of an interim review of *internal controls* for public companies is to provide a basis for determining whether material modifications should be made to management's quarterly certifications about changes in internal control, which are required by the Sarbanes–Oxley Act.

In reviewing interim financial information, the accountants need to acquire a sufficient knowledge of the entity's business and its internal control. This information helps the accountants identify the types of potential misstatements and select the inquiries and analytical procedures that allow the accountants to communicate any modifications that must be made for the information to conform to GAAP. Basically, the extent of review procedures depends on the accountants' professional judgment about deficiencies in the internal control, the severity of unique accounting problems, and the errors that have occurred in the past. With knowledge of these areas, the accountants can direct and fine-tune the review procedures. Procedures include performing analytical procedures; reading minutes; inquiring of management and obtaining written representation about accounting issues, changes in internal controls, and the entity's ability to continue as a going concern; and reconciling the financial statements with accounting records. Procedures for reviews of internal controls include inquiring of management about significant changes in internal control, evaluating the implications of any misstatements found through other procedures that relate to internal control, and determining through observation and inquiry whether any change might materially affect internal control over financial reporting.

A written report is not required unless the entity refers to the accountant's review in writing; however, accountants may report on interim information presented separately from audited financial statements provided that a review has been satisfactorily completed. If a report is prepared, each page of the financial statements should be marked "Unaudited."

A report on reviewed interim information presented in a quarterly report (not within an annual report) is shown in Exhibit A.11.

EXHIBIT A.11
Report on Interim Financial Statements

Independent Accountant's Report

We have reviewed the accompanying unaudited condensed balance sheets of Dunder-Mifflin Inc. as of March 31, 2017, and the related consolidated statements of income and comprehensive income for the three-month period then ended. This interim financial information is the responsibility of the company's management.

We conducted our review in accordance with standards established by the American Institute of Certified Public Accountants. A review of interim financial information consists principally of applying analytical procedures and making inquiries of persons responsible for financial and accounting matters. It is substantially less in scope than an audit conducted in accordance with auditing standards generally accepted in the United States, the objective of which is the expression of an opinion regarding the financial information taken as a whole. Accordingly, we do not express such an opinion.

Based on our review, we are not aware of any material modifications that should be made to the accompanying interim financial information for it to be in conformity with accounting principles generally accepted in the United States of America.

Michael Scarn, LLP
May 1, 2017

The preceding section relates to auditors' responsibilities for interim financial information filed throughout the year with the SEC in Form 10-Q. In addition, in their Form 10-Ks, companies provide interim information for their fourth quarter as well as a summary of interim information for the entire year. This information may be presented as supplementary information accompanying audited financial statements or in a note to audited annual financial statements and should be clearly labeled "Unaudited." The auditor's report for the entity's financial statements need not refer to the reviewed information unless this information

- Has not been marked "Unaudited." (In this case, the auditor should disclaim an opinion on the interim financial information.)
- Is not in conformity with GAAP. (In this case, the opinion on the audited statements is not modified, but the departure is discussed in a separate paragraph.)
- Is required and has been omitted.
- Has not been reviewed by the accountant.

☑ REVIEW CHECKPOINTS

A.9 In what respects is a review of interim financial information similar to a review of the unaudited annual financial statements of a nonissuer?

A.10 Is interim financial information required to be presented by (a) U.S. GAAP and (b) SEC filing requirements?

OTHER TOPICS: SPECIAL AND RESTRICTED-USE REPORTS

LO A-4
Define, explain, and give examples of other special reports provided by auditors, including specified elements of financial statements, special-purpose frameworks, and application of requirements of appropriate financial reporting frameworks.

Auditors may issue special reports in connection with the following:

- Conducting engagements to report on specified elements, accounts, or items of a financial statement.
- Reporting on accounting using a special-purpose framework.
- Reporting on the requirements of appropriate financial reporting frameworks.

Specified Elements, Accounts, or Items

Entities may have a lender or another user request an audit of an element, account, or item within the financial statements. Auditors may be requested to render special reports on a single financial statement (e.g., balance sheet only) or such elements as rentals, royalties, profit participations, or a provision for income taxes. These engagements are different from attestation engagements in that the accountant follows the fundamental auditing principles instead of attestation standards and should consider any disclosures related to the element.

The auditor's report on a single statement or elements, accounts, or items is very similar to the auditor's standard (unmodified) report on the complete set of financial statements. The auditors express an opinion on whether the element, account, or item is fairly stated in accordance with GAAP. Refer to Exhibit A.12 for an illustrative report on a company's accounts receivable. If an adverse opinion or disclaimer of opinion is issued for the financial statements taken as a whole, the public accounting firm may separately report only on an element, account, or item in the financial statements if that report is *not* published with the report containing the adverse or disclaimer of opinion, and the element is not a major portion of the financial statements and is not related to stockholders' equity or net income. Auditors cannot express an unmodified opinion on a single financial statement if they expressed a disclaimer or adverse opinion on the complete set of financial statements.

EXHIBIT A.12
Report on a Financial Element

Independent Auditor's Report

The Board of Directors and Stockholders
Dunder-Mifflin Inc.

We have audited the accompanying schedule of accounts receivable of Dunder Mifflin Inc. as of December 31, 2017, and the related notes (the schedule).

Management's Responsibility for the Financial Statements

Management is responsible for the preparation and fair presentation of this schedule in accordance with accounting principles generally accepted in the United States of America; this includes the design, implementation, and maintenance of internal control relevant to the preparation and fair presentation of the schedule that is free from material misstatement, whether due to fraud or error.

Accountants' Responsibility

Our responsibility is to express an opinion on the schedule based on our audit. We conducted our audit in accordance with auditing standards generally accepted in the United States of America. Those standards require that we plan and perform the audit to obtain reasonable assurance about whether the schedule is free from material misstatement. An audit involves performing procedures to obtain audit evidence about the amounts and disclosures in the schedule. The procedures selected depend on the auditor's judgment, including the assessment of the risks of material misstatement of the schedule, whether due to fraud or error. In making those risk assessments, the auditor considers internal control relevant to the entity's preparation and fair presentation of the schedule in order to design audit procedures that are appropriate in the circumstances, but not for the purpose of expressing an opinion on the effectiveness of the entity's internal control. Accordingly, we express no such opinion. An audit also includes evaluating the appropriateness of accounting policies used and the reasonableness of significant accounting estimates made by management, as well as evaluating the overall presentation of the schedule. We believe that the audit evidence we have obtained is sufficient and appropriate to provide a basis for our audit opinion.

Accountant's Conclusion

In our opinion, the schedule referred to above presents fairly, in all material respects, the accounts receivable of Dunder-Mifflin Inc. as of December 31, 2017, in accordance with accounting principles generally accepted in the United States of America.

We have audited, in accordance with auditing standards generally accepted in the United States of America, the financial statements of Dunder-Mifflin Inc. as of and for the year ended December 31, 2017, and our report thereon, dated March 11, 2018, expressed an unmodified opinion on those financial statements.

Michael Scarn, LLP
Scranton, PA
March 11, 2018

Special-Purpose Frameworks

Often, small companies choose to report on a framework other than U.S. GAAP or IFRS, using instead **special-purpose frameworks**, also known as *other comprehensive bases of accounting* or *OCBOA*. A special-purpose framework in this context refers to a coherent accounting treatment in which substantially all important financial measurements are governed by criteria other than GAAP. Some examples include (1) statements conforming to regulatory agency accounting rules, (2) tax basis accounting, (3) **cash basis framework** accounting (i.e., no accruals) or **modified cash basis framework** accounting (i.e., limited accruals such as long-term assets and liabilities or inventory), and (4) some other method required for contractual purposes.

The Private Companies Practice Section (PCPS) of the AICPA Division for Firms has promoted special-purpose frameworks to its members as a way to accomplish simplified reporting. The position is that special-purpose framework financial statements can be less expensive to produce and easier to interpret than full GAAP statements. Surveys report that 50 percent of special-purpose framework financial statements are on the tax basis of accounting, and 49 percent are on the cash basis. However, PCPS also notes that special-purpose frameworks are appropriate *only* when they meet user needs. Companies that are not subject to SEC regulations and filing requirements can choose to present financial information in accordance with special-purpose frameworks.

Professional Standards warn that special-purpose framework financial statements should not use the titles normally associated with GAAP statements such as balance sheet, statement of financial position, statement of operations, income statement, statement of comprehensive income, and statement of cash flows. Even the titles are said to suggest GAAP financial statements. Instead, special-purpose framework statements should use titles such as statement of assets and liabilities and statement of revenue and expenses, with a designator for the basis used (regulatory, cash, income tax, etc.):

- Statement of assets and liabilities—regulatory basis.
- Statement of admitted assets, liabilities, and surplus—statutory basis required by the insurance department of the state of (name).
- Statement of income—regulatory basis.
- Statement of revenue collected and expenses paid—cash basis.
- Statement of changes in partners' capital accounts—income tax basis.

Special-purpose framework statements can be audited, reviewed, or compiled like any other financial statements. All auditing standards apply, and the standards for review and compilation apply just as they do for GAAP financial statements. Special-purpose frameworks do not reduce disclosure requirements. The only difference introduced is that a basis of accounting different from GAAP is used in the preparation of the financial statements. The standard requires that auditors of special-purpose framework statements

- Obtain an understanding of (1) the purpose for which the financial statements are prepared, (2) the intended users, and (3) the steps taken by management to determine that the special-purpose framework is acceptable in the circumstances.
- Obtain the agreement of management that it acknowledges and understands its responsibility to include all informative disclosures that are appropriate for the special-purpose framework used to prepare the financial statements, including, but not limited to, additional disclosures beyond those required by GAAP that may be necessary to achieve fair presentation. The auditor is required to evaluate whether such disclosures are necessary.
- In the case of special-purpose financial statements prepared in accordance with a contractual basis of accounting, obtain an understanding of any significant interpretations of the contract that management made in the preparation of those financial statements and to evaluate whether the financial statements adequately describe such interpretations.
- When management has a choice of financial reporting frameworks in the preparation of the financial statements, explain management's responsibility for the financial statements in the auditor's report and refer to management's responsibility for determining that the applicable financial reporting framework is acceptable in the circumstances.
- In the case of financial statements prepared in accordance with a regulatory or contractual basis of accounting, describe in the auditor's report the purpose for which the financial statements are prepared or refer to a note in the special-purpose financial statements that contains that information.

When special-purpose frameworks are audited, the auditor's report is modified as follows: (1) The introductory paragraph of the report includes a sentence that identifies the special-purpose framework basis of accounting; (2) the scope paragraph is modified to "auditing standards generally accepted in the United States of America," not PCAOB standards; and (3) the opinion sentence refers to the special-purpose framework instead of GAAP. Unless the financial statements are prepared under a regulatory basis for general use, the report should include an emphasis-of-matter paragraph under an appropriate heading that, among other things, states that the financial statements are prepared in accordance with a special-purpose framework, which is a basis of accounting other than

GAAP and refers to the note to the financial statements that describes the framework. If the special-purpose framework relates to a contractual or a regulatory basis of accounting, it also should be restricted to those within the entity, parties to the agreement, or a regulatory agency. If the financial statements are prepared on a regulatory basis for general use, the emphasis of a matter paragraph is not required, but the auditor should provide two opinion paragraphs—one about whether the financial statements are prepared in accordance with GAAP and another about whether the financial statements are prepared in accordance with the special-purpose framework. Exhibit A.13 summarizes the reporting requirements.

Disclosures in the financial statements should (1) contain an explanation of the special-purpose framework and (2) describe in general how the special-purpose framework differs from GAAP. However, the differences between GAAP and the special-purpose framework do not have to be quantified; that is, the special-purpose framework does not need to be reconciled to GAAP with dollar amounts. For all practical purposes, GAAP criteria are replaced by criteria applicable to the special-purpose framework. See Exhibit A.14 for an example of an auditor's report on modified cash basis statements.

Reports on Application of Requirements of an Appropriate Financial Reporting Framework

The subject of reporting on the application of requirements of an appropriate financial reporting framework touches a sensitive nerve in the public accounting profession. The issue arose from entities searching for a public accounting firm that would agree to give an unmodified audit report on a questionable accounting treatment. *Opinion shopping* often involved auditor–client disagreements, after which the client said, "If you won't agree with my accounting treatment, then I'll find an auditor who will." These disagreements often involved early revenue recognition and unwarranted expense or loss deferral. A few cases of misleading financial statements occurred after opinion shopping resulted in clients switching to more agreeable auditors. On the other hand, obtaining "second opinions" on complex accounting matters may be helpful to both clients and auditors in resolving these issues.

EXHIBIT A.13   *Overview of Reporting Requirements*

	Cash Basis	Tax Basis	Regulatory Basis	Regulatory Basis (general use)	Contractual Basis
Opinion(s)	Single opinion on special-purpose framework	Single opinion on special-purpose framework	Single opinion on special-purpose framework	Dual opinion on special-purpose framework and generally accepted accounting principles	Single opinion on special-purpose framework
Description of purpose for which special-purpose financial statements are prepared	No	No	Yes	Yes	Yes
Emphasis of matter paragraph alerting readers as to the preparation in accordance with a special-purpose framework	Yes	Yes	Yes	No	Yes
Other matter paragraph restricting the use of the auditor's report	No	No	Yes	No	Yes

610 Part Three Stand-Alone Modules

EXHIBIT A.14
Special Report on Special-Purpose Framework (cash basis statements)

Independent Auditor's Report

The Board of Directors and Stockholders
Dunder-Mifflin, Inc.

Report on the Financial Statements

We have audited the accompanying financial statements of Dunder-Mifflin, Inc., which comprise the statement of assets and liabilities arising from cash transactions as of December 31, 2017, and the related statement of revenue collected and expenses paid for the year then ended, and the related notes to the financial statements.

Management's Responsibility for the Financial Statements

Management is responsible for the preparation and fair presentation of these financial statements in accordance with the cash basis of accounting described in Note 1; this includes determining that the cash basis of accounting is an acceptable basis for the preparation of the financial statements in the circumstances. Management is also responsible for the design, implementation, and maintenance of internal control relevant to the preparation and fair presentation of financial statements that are free from material misstatement, whether due to fraud or error.

Accountants' Responsibility

Our responsibility is to express an opinion on these financial statements based on our audit. We conducted our audit in accordance with auditing standards generally accepted in the United States of America. Those standards require that we plan and perform the audit to obtain reasonable assurance about whether the financial statements are free from material misstatement.

An audit involves performing procedures to obtain audit evidence about the amounts and disclosures in the financial statements. The procedures selected depend on the auditor's judgment, including the assessment of the risks of material misstatement of the financial statements, whether due to fraud or error. In making those risk assessments, the auditor considers internal control relevant to the partnership's preparation and fair presentation of the financial statements in order to design audit procedures that are appropriate in the circumstances, but not for the purpose of expressing an opinion on the effectiveness of the partnership's internal control. Accordingly, we express no such opinion. An audit also includes evaluating the appropriateness of accounting policies used and the reasonableness of significant accounting estimates made by management as well as evaluating the overall presentation of the financial statements. We believe that the audit evidence we have obtained is sufficient and appropriate to provide a basis for our audit opinion.

Accountant's Conclusion

In our opinion, the financial statements referred to above present fairly, in all material respects, the assets and liabilities arising from cash transactions of Dunder-Mifflin, Inc. as of December 31, 2017, and its revenue collected and expenses paid during the year then ended in accordance with the cash basis of accounting described in Note 1.

We draw attention to Note 1 of the financial statements, which describes the basis of accounting. The financial statements are prepared on the cash basis of accounting, which is a basis of accounting other than accounting principles generally accepted in the United States of America. Our opinion is not modified with respect to this matter.

Michael Scarn, LLP
Scranton, PA
March 1, 2018

The auditing standards establish procedures for dealing with requests for consultation from parties other than auditors' own clients. These parties can include other companies (nonclients who are shopping), attorneys, and investment bankers. This standard is applicable in these situations:

- When preparing a written report or giving oral advice on specific transactions, either completed or proposed.
- When preparing a written report or giving oral advice on the type of audit opinion that might be rendered on specific financial statements.

Providing a written report on a hypothetical transaction (as opposed to a specific proposal) is prohibited. Also, the standard does not apply to conclusions about accounting requirements offered in connection with litigation support engagements or expert witness work, nor does it apply to advice given to another CPA in public practice. Nor does it apply to an accounting firm's expressions of positions in newsletters, articles, speeches, lectures, and the like, provided that the positions do not give advice on a specific transaction or apply to a specific company.

When auditors evaluate the requirements of GAAP, they are not required to issue written reports. However, a written report or oral advice that is provided to an entity regarding the requirements of an appropriate financial reporting framework should

- Describe the engagement and state that it was performed in accordance with appropriate standards.
- Identify the entity and describe the significant transactions, circumstances, and sources of information.
- Provide the conclusion about the requirements of the appropriate financial reporting framework or the type of audit report, including reasons for the conclusions, if appropriate.
- State that the entity's management is responsible for proper accounting treatments in consultation with its own auditors.
- State that any differences in facts, circumstances, or assumptions might change the conclusions.
- Include a separate paragraph that indicates (1) the report is for the sole use of specified parties, (2) the specified parties for whom the report is intended, and (3) the restriction that the information should not be used by anyone else.

The purpose of this standard is to impose some discipline on the process of shopping/consultation and to erect a barrier to some companies' quest for willing auditors. The reporting accountant should always consult with the continuing auditor of the entity to ascertain all the available facts relevant to forming a professional judgment.

✅ REVIEW CHECKPOINTS

A.11 Why would a client ask an accountant to report on a financial statement element?

A.12 Regarding special-purpose frameworks, (a) why do they exist, and (b) can financial statements prepared using special-purpose frameworks be audited?

A.13 What are some examples of special-purpose framework?

A.14 How could "opinion shopping" be (a) suspect or (b) helpful?

A.15 What must an accountant do when reporting on the application of requirements of an appropriate financial reporting framework?

ASSURANCE SERVICES

LO A-5

Explain and provide examples of assurance services engagements.

Why Develop New Assurance Services?

Auditing courses focus on the role of auditors in the financial reporting process, but students should not lose sight of the fact that accountants require sufficient revenue to cover expenses, provide profit, and provide funds for continued growth. One of the objectives of the AICPA has been to identify additional niche services that accountants might offer to enhance their value to clients, attract new clients, and improve the potential for growth as a business. Such services include tax and consulting, personal financial planning, forensic, and valuation services. One broad area of services falls under the heading of assurance services.

The AICPAs Assurance Services Executive Committee (ASEC) identified five mega-trends that can affect accountants' business. Each presents opportunities to provide assurance service products, and each presents business risks:

1. *The shift from the industrial age to the knowledge age.* The current knowledge-based economy emphasizes management of intangible assets and decreases the focus on physical assets, measured largely in terms of historical cost. Market values may significantly differ from book values, hindering optimal capital allocation.

2. *Information technology.* The proliferation of tools (e.g., cloud technology, file sharing, notepads, and smartphones) that make data digital, mobile, personal, and virtual will amplify and empower collaboration. These tools should make open-source innovation more open because they will enable more individuals to collaborate with one another in more ways and from more places than ever before. These tools will enhance outsourcing because they will make it much easier for a single department of any company to collaborate with another company. They will enhance supply chaining because headquarters will be able to be connected in real time with every individual employee stocking the shelves, every individual package, and every factory manufacturing the goods. The tools will enhance insourcing—having a company such as **UPS** come deep inside a retailer and manage its whole supply chain using drivers who can interact with its warehouses and with every customer carrying a smartphone. And most obviously, they will enhance informing—the ability to manage your own knowledge supply chain.[6]

3. *Globalization.* One consequence of the globalization of capital markets is that organizations have facilities in different jurisdictions with different cultural principles, affiliations, ownership, accountability, and auditing standards. Domestic demand for international capital sources drives demand for a common language and global consistency in accounting and auditing standards—hence, the recent focus on convergence of international auditing and accounting standards.

4. *Demands for transparency and new focus on corporate governance.* The call for more relevant information echoes externally from investors, creditors, analysts, regulatory agencies, and standards setters and internally from boards of directors and management. Regulatory bodies around the world are also facing pressure for, and consequently demanding, more granular levels of assessment.

5. *New social structures.* The final category of change involves new socioeconomic structures, such as the democratization of the capital markets, the aging population, and the increasing social pressures. Increasing social pressures have manifested themselves in a growing global focus on corporate social responsibility and sustainability whereby investors are demanding increased accountability from companies via regular responsibility or sustainability business reports and are often basing investment decisions on them.[7]

Definition: Assurance Services

Assurance services are "independent professional services that improve the quality of information, or its context, for decision makers."[8] A large group of activities can fit within this definition. In addition, although attestation and audit services are highly structured and intended to be useful for large groups of decision makers (e.g., investors,

[6]T. L. Friedman, *The World Is Flat* (New York: Farrar, Straus & Giroux, 2005).

[7]AICPA Assurance Services Executive Committee White Paper, "The Shifting Paradigm in Business Reporting and Assurance," 2008.

[8]Ibid.

lenders), assurance services are more customized and intended to be useful to smaller, targeted groups of decision makers. In this sense, assurance services resemble consulting services.

Although there are many potential assurance services, several have been featured by the AICPA as offering potential for providing value to clients and improving the quality and transparency of information entities provide to their constituents.

eXtensible Business Reporting Language (XBRL)

The SEC has mandated financial reporting using **eXtensible Business Reporting Language (XBRL)**, which provides a computer-readable identifying tag for each item of data. For example, "company net profit" has its own unique tag. The introduction of XBRL tags enables automated processing of business information by computer software. Computers can treat XBRL data "intelligently": They can recognize the information in an XBRL document, select it, analyze it, store it, exchange it with other computers, and present it automatically in a variety of ways for users. XBRL greatly increases the speed of handling financial data, reduces the chance of error, and permits automatic checking of information.

XBRL can handle data in different languages and prepared according to different accounting standards. It is flexible and can be adapted to meet different requirements and uses. Data can be transformed into XBRL by suitable mapping tools or can be generated in XBRL by appropriate software.

Although the SEC does not require auditor involvement with the XBRL tagged data or related controls, at some point it may be necessary for auditors to provide some degree of assurance on XBRL-coded data. Issues to be addressed will include the appropriate levels of assurance for various scenarios and the subject matter of assurance.[9] The ASEC has established the *XBRL Assurance Task Force* to develop guidance that will assist CPAs in public practice who are requested to provide assurance on XBRL-related documents, and the ASEC and the Auditing Standards Board have released *Statement of Position 09-1,* "Performing Agreed-Upon Procedures Engagements That Address the Completeness, Accuracy, or Consistency of XBRL-Tagged Data" that provides recommendations and guidance for practitioners who perform an attest engagement under AT-C 215 to provide assurance on XBRL reports. In addition, the Center for Audit Quality issued Alert 2009-55, "Potential Audit Firm Service Implications Raised by the SEC Final Rule on XBRL," to raise auditors' level of awareness of the implications of XBRL, including potential services that may be provided.

Enhanced Business Reporting

Enhanced business reporting focuses on improving business reporting by developing an internationally recognized, voluntary framework for presentation and disclosure of value drivers, nonfinancial performance measures, and qualitative information.[10] Benefits would include better allocation of capital by investors, reduced financing costs of companies and more efficient and effective regulatory processes, strengthened global competitiveness, and stability in the capital markets.

Integrated Reporting

The International Integrated Reporting Council (IIRC) was formed to "enhance and consolidate existing reporting practices to move towards a reporting framework that provides the information needed to develop the global economic model to meet the

---

[9]Ibid.

[10]http://www.aicpa.org/INTERESTAREAS/FRC/ACCOUNTINGFINANCIALREPORTING/ENHANCEDBUSINESSREPORTING/Pages/EnhancedBusinessReporting.aspx.

challenges of the 21st century."[11] The first <IR> standards were issued in 2013 to encourage a more complete set of reporting, including not only financial information, but also information about a wide range of factors that affect an entity's ability to create value over time.

Trust Services

Electronic commerce (or e-commerce), the sale of goods and services via the Internet, is exploding. According to the U.S. Census Bureau, U.S. e-commerce revenues represented 6.8 percent of all retail sales in the first quarter of 2015, up from 2.8 percent in 2006 and 5.6 percent in 2013.[12] Although the growth of e-commerce continues unabated, security issues, both real and perceived, have prevented many potential customers from purchasing goods and services via the Internet. Many customers and business owners distrust the Internet as a medium of conducting business. Indeed, a general lack of security is the top reason nonbuyers give for not purchasing products online and the top concern among current online buyers. Specifically, prospective buyers have expressed concerns about ascertaining whether an e-commerce company is authentic, is trustworthy (the e-tailer will do what it says it will do), and will safeguard buyers' personal information. Customers also want to be reassured that they can get their products, services, and repairs on a timely basis. Despite growing familiarity with doing business on the Internet, these security issues have not diminished for potential customers.

For significant customer–supplier business relationships, company computers are often directly linked through Internet-based virtual private networks. Purchase orders for goods are made and sent via computer, and payment is made automatically through electronic funds transfer directly to the vendors bank. The primary benefit of such a relationship is an increase in the timeliness of the process; transactions that once took several weeks to complete manually (from customer purchase order generation to final payment being deposited to the suppliers bank account) now take only as long as it takes to ship and receive the goods. However, just as Internet customers are wary of purchasing online, business customers are often cautious about entering into such relationships with other businesses.

The AICPA and the Canadian Institute of Chartered Accountants (CICA) developed WebTrust Services to provide assurance to the consumer on the reliability of Internet websites and SysTrust Services to focus on a company's systems as a means of increasing the reliability of business-to-business (B-to-B) computer transactions. Because these two services have a common framework to address risks and technological opportunities, the AICPA has adopted the term **trust services** to define a set of professional attestation and advisory services based on a core set of principles and criteria that address the risks and opportunities of IT-enabled systems and privacy programs.[13] The ASEC Trust Information Integrity Task Force is focused on updating and maintaining the Trust Services Principles and Criteria (TSPC) and creating a framework of principles and criteria to provide assurance on the integrity of information, with new standards codified as TSP Section 100 effective for years ending on or after December 15, 2014.

[11]The International <IR> Framework, http://integratedreporting.org/wp-content/uploads/2015/03/13-12-08-THE-INTERNATIONAL-IR-FRAMEWORK-2-1.pdf.

[12]Quarterly Retail E-Commerce Sales, 1st Quarter 2015, https://www.census.gov/retail/mrts/www/data/pdf/ec_current.pdf.

[13]AICPA TSP 100 2015, para. 1.

Trust Services comprise a set of professional attestation and advisory services based on a core set of principles and criteria that address the risks and opportunities of IT-enabled systems and privacy programs. Practitioners use the following principles and related criteria in the performance of trust services engagements:

- *Security.* The system is protected against unauthorized access (both physical and logical).
- *Availability.* The system is available for operation and use as committed or agreed.
- *Processing integrity.* System processing is complete, accurate, timely, and authorized.
- *Confidentiality.* Information designated as confidential is protected as committed or agreed.
- *Privacy.* Personal information is collected, used, retained, disclosed, and destroyed in conformity with the commitments in the entity's privacy notice and with criteria set forth in generally accepted privacy principles issued by the AICPA and CICA.[14]

Accountants offering **WebTrust Services** and **SysTrust Services** can issue opinions and corresponding "seals of assurance" on individual principles or a combination of the principles.

Sustainability Reporting

Sustainability (also called *corporate social responsibility*) is defined by the AICPA as "the triple-bottom-line of (1) economic viability, (2) social responsibility, and (3) environmental responsibility."[15] EY reports that 95 percent of the Global 250 issue sustainability reports.[16] Nearly all companies have adopted the reporting standards of the Global Reporting Initiative (GRI). The GRI G4 guidelines offer entities two options to report "in accordance" with standards. The Core option communicates the essential elements of a company's economic, environmental, social, and governance performance. The Comprehensive option expands these disclosures to provide additional information about the organization's strategy, governance, ethics, and integrity.

Various assurance approaches are currently being used for sustainability reports by CPA firms, engineering firms, stakeholder panels, external review committees, and other groups. Standard setters have also developed assurance standards. The AICPA and CICA have developed SOP 13-1, "Attest Engagements on Greenhouse Gas Emissions Information," and IFAC has adopted a similar standard, ISAE 3410. See Exhibit A.15 for an illustration of an assurance report on **Starbucks'** sustainability.

☑ REVIEW CHECKPOINTS

A.16 What makes accountants qualified to perform the assurance services discussed here?

A.17 Briefly describe the two trust services in terms of those provided and of intended customers.

A.18 What is *sustainability reporting*? Why would a company choose to provide a sustainability report? Why would it pay for independent assurance?

---

[14]http://www.aicpa.org/interestareas/businessindustryandgovernment/resources/sustainability/pages/sustainabilityfaqs.aspx.

[15]http://www.aicpa.org/InterestAreas/InformationTechnology/Resources/SOC/TrustServices/DownloadableDocuments/TrustServicesPrinciples-TSP100.pdf.

[16]http://www.ey.com/US/en/Services/Specialty-Services/Climate-Change-and-Sustainability-Services/Value-of-sustainability-reporting.

Required:

These supervisor's review notes may or may not be correct. For each item a–o, indicate whether Stone is correct (C) or incorrect (I) in the criticism of Kent's draft.

a. The report should contain no reference to the prior-year audited financial statements in the first (introductory) paragraph.

b. All current-year basic financial statements are not properly identified in the first (introductory) paragraph.

c. The report should contain no reference to the American Institute of Certified Public Accountants in the first (introductory) paragraph.

d. The accountants' review and audit responsibilities should follow management's responsibilities in the first (introductory) paragraph.

e. The report should contain no comparison of the scope of a review to an audit in the second (scope) paragraph.

f. Negative assurance should be expressed on the current-year reviewed financial statements in the second (scope) paragraph.

g. The report should contain a statement that no opinion is expressed on the current-year financial statements in the second (scope) paragraph.

h. The report should contain a reference to "conformity with generally accepted accounting principles" in the second paragraph.

i. The report should *not* express a restriction on the distribution of the accountants' review report in the third paragraph.

j. The report should *not* contain a reference to "material modifications" in the third paragraph.

k. The report should indicate the type of opinion expressed on the prior-year audited financial statements in the last paragraph.

l. The report should indicate that no auditing procedures were performed after the date of the report on the prior-year financial statements in the fourth (separate) paragraph.

m. The report should not contain a reference to "updating the prior-year auditor's report for events and circumstances occurring after that date" in the fourth (separate) paragraph.

n. The description of procedures performed in a review engagement in the second (scope) paragraph is incomplete.

o. The review report should have paragraph headings similar to those in an audit report.

(AICPA adapted)

LO A-1

A.44 **Review of Forecast Assumptions.** Dodd Manufacturing Corporation has engaged you to attest to the reasonableness of the assumptions underlying its forecast of revenues, costs, and net income for the next calendar year, 2018. Four of the assumptions follow.

1. The company intends to sell certain real estate and other facilities held by Division B at an after-tax profit of $600,000; the proceeds of this sale will be used to retire outstanding debt.

2. The company will call and retire all outstanding 9 percent subordinated debentures (callable at 108). The debentures are expected to require the full call premium given present market interest rates of 8 percent on similar debt. A rise in market interest rates to 9 percent would reduce the loss on bond retirement from the projected $200,000 to $190,000.

3. Current labor contracts expire on September 1, 2018, and the new contract is expected to result in a wage increase of 5.5 percent. Given the forecasted levels of production and sales, after-tax operating earnings would be reduced approximately $50,000 for each percentage point of wage increase in excess of the expected contract settlement.

4. The sales forecast for Division A assumes that the new Portsmouth facility will be complete and operating at 40 percent of capacity on February 1, 2018. It is highly improbable that the facility will be operational before January 2018. Each month's delay would reduce Division A sales by approximately $80,000 and operating earnings by $30,000.

Required:

For each assumption, state the evidence sources and procedures you would use to determine the reasonableness of that assumption.

LO A-1

A.45 **Internet Exercise: Reporting on Service Organization Controls.** Search for a service organization auditor's report on internal controls on the web. (*Hint:* You may have to look under the old name "SAS 70 reports.") If you cannot find an auditor's report, find a company's news release describing its auditor's service organization report.

Required:

  a. Why do you think it is so difficult to find an actual report?

  b. If you found an auditor's report, were any deficiencies noted? If so, what were they?

  c. Why would a service organization publicize the results of its auditor's report?

LO A-2

A.46 **Accounting and Review Services.** Henry Horkheimer, MD, is considering expansion of his office as a result of adding a new doctor to his family medical practice. Dr. Horkheimer knows that his business is profitable, but he does not produce regular financial statements, nor does he possess the technical knowledge to do so. Although he is financially savvy enough to know that he needs financial statements to obtain financing to expand his business, he is completely unsure as to what services he needs or even what is available. He has asked you for advice.

Required:

Consider Dr. Horkheimer's need for financing and write a memo outlining the pros and cons of four services an accountant could provide: audit, review, compilation, and preparation of financial statements. Conclude your memo with a recommendation for what you believe would best suit Dr. Horkheimer's needs.

LO A-2

A.47 **Compilation and Review Procedures.** The following numbered items 1–10 state procedures accountants should consider in review engagements and compilation engagements on the annual financial statements of nonissuers (performed in accordance with AICPA *Statements on Standards for Accounting and Review Services*).

Required:

For each item (taken separately), tell whether the item is required in all review engagements and/or required in all compilation engagements. For each item, give two responses, one regarding review engagements and the other regarding compilation engagements.

  1. The accountants should establish an understanding in writing with the entity's management regarding the nature and limitations of the services to be performed.

  2. The accountants should make inquiries concerning actions taken at the board of directors' meetings.

  3. The accountants, as the entity's successor accountants, should communicate with the predecessor accountants to obtain access to the predecessors' audit documentation.

  4. The accountants should obtain a level of knowledge of the accounting principles and practices of the entity's industry.

  5. The accountants should obtain an understanding of the entity's internal control.

  6. The accountants should perform analytical procedures designed to identify relationships that appear to be unusual.

  7. The accountants should assess the risk of material misstatement.

  8. The accountants should obtain a letter from the entity's attorney to corroborate the information furnished by management concerning litigation.

  9. The accountants should obtain management representations from the entity.

  10. The accountants should study the relationship of the financial statement elements that would be expected to conform to a predictable pattern.

(AICPA adapted)

LO A-2

A.48 **Compilation Presentation Alternatives.** Jimmy C. operates a large service station, garage, and truck stop on Interstate 95 near Plainview. His brother, Bill, has recently joined him as a partner, even though he will continue his small CPA practice. One slow afternoon, they were discussing financial statements with Bert, the local CPA who operates the largest public practice in Plainview.

  • **Jimmy:** The business is growing, and sometimes I need to show financial statements to parts suppliers and the loan officers at the bank.

  • **Bert:** That so?

  • **Bill:** Heck, Jimmy, I know all about that. I can compile a jim-dandy set of financial statements for us.

  • **Bert:** Bill can't do compiled financial statements for you. He's not independent.

  • **Jimmy:** I know. Momma didn't let him outa the house 'til he was 24. The neighbors complained.

  • **Bert:** That so?

  • **Bill:** Shucks.

Required:

Think about the financial disclosure problems of Jimmy and Bill's small business.

a. Why does Jimmy need a compilation service?

b. What types of compiled financial statements can be prepared for them and by whom?

LO A-2

A.49 Negative Assurance in Review Reports. One portion of the report on a review services engagement is the following: "Based on my review, I am not aware of any material modifications that should be made to the accompanying financial statements in order for them to be in conformity with generally accepted accounting principles [or another framework for financial reporting]."

Required:

a. Is this paragraph a "negative assurance" given by the accountants?

b. Why is negative assurance generally prohibited in audit reports?

c. What justification is there for permitting negative assurance in a review services report on unaudited financial statements and on interim financial information?

(AICPA adapted)

LO A-4

A.50 Reporting on a Special-Purpose Framework. The following abstracted report is a report on a trust fund that refers to a statutory basis of accounting (special-purpose framework) as well as to generally accepted accounting principles (GAAP).

Independent Auditor's Report

To Natalia National Bank Association (Trustee)
and the Unit Holders of the Mega Offshore Trust:

We have audited the accompanying statements of assets, liabilities, and trust corpus—cash basis, of the Mega Offshore Trust as of December 31, 2017 and 2016, and the related statements of changes in trust corpus—cash basis, for each of the three years in the period ended December 31, 2017. These financial statements are the responsibility of the Company's management. Our responsibility is to express an opinion on these financial statements based on our audits.

(Standard scope and responsibility paragraphs here)

As described in Note 2, these financial statements were prepared on the cash receipts and disbursements basis of accounting, which is a comprehensive basis of accounting other than generally accepted accounting principles.

In our opinion, the financial statements referred to above present fairly, in all material respects, the assets, liabilities, and trust corpus arising from cash transactions of the Mega Offshore Trust as of December 31, 2017 and 2016, and the related changes in trust corpus arising from cash transactions for each of the three years in the period ended December 31, 2017, on the basis of accounting described in Note 2.

George Costanza, CPA
March 18, 2018

Required:

Write Note 2 to Mega Offshore Trust's 2017 financial statements.

LO A-2

A.51 Prepare a Compilation Report. The Coffin brothers have engaged you to compile their financial schedules from books and records maintained by James Coffin. The brothers own and operate three auto parts stores in Central City. Even though their business is growing, they have not wanted to employ a full-time bookkeeper. James specifies that all he wants is a balance sheet, a statement of operations, and a statement of cash flows. He does not have time to write up footnotes to accompany the financial statements.

James directed the physical count of inventory on June 30 and adjusted and closed the books on that date. You find that he actually is a good accountant, having taken some night courses at the community college. The accounts appear to have been maintained in conformity with generally accepted accounting principles. At least you have noticed no obvious errors.

Required:

You are independent with respect to the Coffin brothers and their Coffin Auto Speed Shop business. Prepare a report on your compilation engagement.

LO A-2

A.52 **Reporting on Comparative Unaudited Financial Statements.** A. Jones, CPA, performed a review service for the Independence Company in 2017. He wants to present comparative financial statements. However, the 2016 statements were compiled by Able and Associates, CPAs, and Able does not want to cooperate with Jones by reissuing the prior-year compilation report. Jones has no indication that any adjustments should be made to either the 2017 or the 2016 statements, which are to be presented with all necessary disclosures. However, he does not have time to perform a review of the 2016 statements. Jones completed his work on January 15, 2018, for the statement dated December 31, 2017.

Required:

Write Jones's review report and include the paragraph describing the report on the 2016 statements. List any assumptions you need to make to write the report.

LO A-3

A.53 **Interim Financial Information.** June's Java provides coffee services (coffee, cups, cream, sugar, and coffee makers) to local companies for use in their offices. Each of five drivers has a truck with inventory and has a different route each day to replenish coffee supplies to the companies on the route. In past audits, the accountant found that June's Java was having difficulty properly recognizing revenue, usually due to timing issues. In addition, the internal control over inventory on each driver's truck was weak.

June's Java has prepared its third-quarter financial statements, and the owners want a review of the information. The accountants have audited the financial statements for the past three years but have never been asked to review any interim financial information until now.

Required:

Prepare a review plan that lists the procedures that accountants should perform to do a professional review in accordance with professional standards. Be as specific as possible in planning your procedures.

LO A-3

A.54 **Erroneous Reporting on Interim Financial Information.** Baker & Baker, CPAs, prepared the following report on the interim financial information of Micro Mini Company. The interim financial information was presented in the first quarterly report for the three-month period ended March 31, 2018. No comparative quarterly information of the first quarter of the prior year was presented. Baker & Baker completed a review on April 15, 2018 in accordance with standards established by the AICPA and found that, to the best of their knowledge, the information was presented in conformity with GAAP. In an audit report dated January 21, 2018, Baker & Baker had given a standard unmodified audit report on Micro Mini's 2017 and 2016 annual financial statements.

Report of Independent Auditors

To the Board of Directors and Stockholders,
Micro Mini Company:

We have made a review of the balance sheet of Micro Mini Company at March 31, 2018, the related statement of income and comprehensive income for the three-month period ended March 31, 2018, and the statement of cash flows for the three-month period ended March 31, 2018, in accordance with standards established by the American Institute of Certified Public Accountants.

A review of interim financial information consists principally of obtaining an understanding of the system for the preparation of the interim financial information, applying analytical review procedures to financial data, and making inquiries to persons responsible for financial and accounting matters.

In our opinion, the accompanying interim financial information presents fairly, in all material respects, the financial position of Micro Mini Company at March 31, 2018, and the results of its operations and its cash flows for the three-month period then ended in conformity with generally accepted accounting principles.

Baker & Baker, CPAs
March 31, 2018

Required:

a. Review the report and list, with explanation, the erroneous portions in it.

b. Rewrite the report.

LO A-4

A.55 **Report on Special-Purpose Framework.** Brooklyn Life Insurance Company prepares its financial statements on a statutory basis in conformity with the accounting practices prescribed and permitted by the Insurance Department of the State of New York. This statutory basis produces financial statements that differ materially from statements prepared in conformity with generally accepted accounting principles. On the statutory basis, for example, agents' first-year commissions are expensed instead of being partially deferred.

The company engaged its auditors, Major and Major Associates, to audit the statutory basis financial statements and report on them. Footnote 10 in the statements contains a narrative description and a numerical table explaining the differences between the statutory basis and GAAP accounting. Footnote 10 also reconciles the statutory basis assets, liabilities, income, expense, and net income (statutory basis) to the measurements that would be obtained using GAAP.

Required:

Write the audit report appropriate in the circumstances. The year-end date is December 31, 2017, and the audit fieldwork was completed on February 20, 2018. (The company plans to distribute this report to persons other than the department of insurance regulators, so the auditors need to follow AU-C 800.)

LO A-5

A.56 **Internet Exercise: CPA WebTrust.** Visit the AICPA WebTrust site (www.webtrust.org). Required:

a. What is WebTrust?

b. Why is WebTrust needed?

c. How does an Internet user know that a website has received the WebTrust service?

d. Where can a person obtain copies of the Trust service principles?

LO A-5

A.57 **Assurance Services.** In 2008, the AICPA Assurance Services Executive Committee identified five global "mega trends" that can affect a CPA's business.

Required:

a. Review the mega trends that were identified. Are these trends still viable in today's society and economy? Which trends, if any, need to be reconsidered because of current conditions in society and the economy?

b. Are there additional trends in the marketplace that could affect a public accounting firm's business?

LO A-5

A.58 **Assurance Services.** Davis has a store that sells old baseball cards. To expand the business, he has decided to open an Internet site where potential customers can view the cards and place orders. Davis hires Johnson, who is an expert in constructing websites for small businesses. She explains that even with a quality website and pictures of the merchandise for sale, customers may be reluctant to purchase baseball cards from Davis's website.

Required:

a. Explain the reasons for Johnson's concerns.

b. What steps can Davis and Johnson take to reduce customer's reluctance to make purchases on the Internet?

LO A-5

A.59 **Assurance Services.** Henry's Health Food Store maintains a perpetual inventory on its computer. The sales representative from A-Plus Vitamins has recommended the following to Henry:

- All the files should have password protection.

- A-Plus Vitamins should be given the URL and the password for Henry's inventory file on the computer, which can be accessed from outside.

- A-Plus Vitamins will search the inventory for items that fall below an established reorder point and will automatically ship a set amount of product to Henry's.

Required:

a. What are the advantages of this arrangement for Henry's? For A-Plus Vitamins?

b. What concerns might Henry's have in this arrangement?

c. How might these concerns be addressed?

LO A-5

A.60 **Internet Assignment: Global Reporting.** Go to the Global Reporting Initiative website (www.globalreporting.org) and obtain the G4 Reporting Principles and Standard Disclosures.

Required:

a. Identify the three primary categories of sustainability indicators identified in the G4 reporting standards. For each category, define the types of indicators included and list several aspects of the category as described in Section 5 of the standard.

b. How can accountants provide assurance for sustainability reporting as a service to their clients?

LO A-1

A.61 **Attestation Evaluation Criteria.** The local high school experienced trouble two years ago. Its graduation rates had declined to the bottom 10 percent in the state, college admission rates were low, and graduates had a high unemployment rate. The school board and administration have notified the state Department of Education and the taxpayers in the school district that these problems have been fixed. Graduation rates have increased, a higher percentage of students are continuing with their education, and a higher percentage of graduates have jobs. The Department of Education wants an independent attestation to these assertions. It is concerned not only about the numbers claimed by the school board and administration but also about the underlying process and means used to obtain these numbers.

Required:

Establish a list of criteria you would use to validate the claim of the school board and administration and to determine the processes and means used to obtain these numbers.

Professional Ethics

Auditors must approach their jobs with independence and skepticism. How do we instill those necessary traits in auditors? This may be the most important auditing question of our time.

James R. Doty, PCAOB Chairman, in remarks made at SEC Reporting Conference, June 2, 2011

To educate a person in mind and not in morals is to educate a menace to society.

Theodore Roosevelt, 26th President of the United States (1858–1919)

Always do right—this will gratify some and astonish the rest.

Mark Twain (pseudonym of Samuel L. Clemens), famous American writer (1835–1910)

Professional Standards References

Topic	AU-C/ISA Section	AS Section
Overall Objectives of the Independent Auditor	**200**	**1001**
Quality Control for an Audit Engagement	220	1220
Responsibility Not to Knowingly or Recklessly Contribute to Violations		Rule 3502
Auditor Independence		Rule 3520
Contingent Fees		Rule 3521
Tax Transactions		Rule 3522
Tax Services for Persons in Financial Reporting Oversight Roles		Rule 3523
Audit Committee Preapproval of Certain Tax Services		Rule 3524
Audit Committee Preapproval of Nonaudit Services Related to Internal Control over Financial Reporting		Rule 3525
Communication with Audit Committees Concerning Independence		Rule 3526
	ET Section†	
Members in Public Practice	ET 1.000–1.800	
Members in Business	ET 2.000–2.400	
Other Members	ET 3.000–3.400	
AICPA Council Resolution Designating Bodies to Promulgate Technical Standards	ET Appendix A	
AICPA Council Resolution Concerning Form of Organization and Name (Rule 505)	ET Appendix B	
AICPA Code of Conduct Revision History Table	ET Appendix C	
AICPA Code of Conduct Mapping Document	ET Appendix D	

†ET references represent sections in the AICPA Code of Professional Conduct. BL references represent sections of the AICPA bylaws.

As described in Chapter 2, the responsibilities principle identifies three specific responsibilities. Two of the responsibilities—(1) having appropriate competence and capabilities to perform the audit and (2) maintaining professional skepticism and exercising professional judgment throughout the planning and performance of the audit—have been focused on in other chapters of this book. This module focuses on the third responsibility: complying with relevant ethical requirements. In this spirit, this module is designed to teach you about the AICPA Code of Professional Conduct and demonstrate why it is so important to your success as a professional accountant. As you will soon learn, regulation of the profession, including any discipline for violations, depends on the prevailing published codes of ethics and enforcement practices. As a result, we believe this module is essential to your success.

Your objectives are to be able to:

LO B-1   Understand general ethics and a series of steps for making ethical decisions.

LO B-2   Reason through an ethical decision problem using the imperative, utilitarian, and virtue theories of moral philosophy.

LO B-3   Identify the different entities that make ethics rules for CPAs and public accounting firms.

LO B-4   With reference to American Institute of Certified Public Accounting (AICPA), Government Accountability Office (GAO), Public Company Accounting Oversight Board (PCAOB), and Securities and Exchange Commission (SEC) rules, analyze factual situations and decide whether an accountant's conduct does or does not impair independence.

LO B-5   With reference to AICPA rules on topics other than independence, analyze factual situations and decide whether an accountant's conduct does or does not conform to the AICPA Code of Professional Conduct.

LO B-6   Explain the types of penalties that can be imposed on accountants.

INTRODUCTION

Scott London seemed to have it all. One of three sons of a Los Angeles certified public accountant, he followed his father into the accounting business. He graduated in 1984 from California State University–Northridge, and soon landed a job at a firm that later became part of **KPMG.** From an outsider's perspective, London appeared to have an ideal personal life. He and his wife Michele had two children and lived in an expensive home at the end of a cul-de-sac in a Los Angeles suburb known as the gateway to the Santa Monica Mountains. Professionally, as the KPMG partner in charge of the firm's Pacific Southwest Audit practice, he had more than 50 partners and 500 employees reporting to him. After 29 years with the firm, he seemed to be set financially. However, with all this going for him, he plead guilty to passing confidential client information to a golf buddy who then traded on the information to make more than $1 million in illegal gains. Although the information was initially passed "innocently" in casual conversation on the golf course, London began accepting payments of cash and jewelry in exchange for the tips. Bryan Shaw, the recipient of the information who profited from the illegal trades, cooperated with authorities, including agreeing to wear a wire to gain evidence against his benefactor. In return for the confidential information, London received more than $50,000 in cash and gifts, including a $12,000 Rolex watch; however, the amount of these "gifts" are seemingly immaterial given London's estimated seven-figure annual salary.

The sting operation that nabbed London was the result of a joint investigation by the FBI, SEC, and Department of Justice. When first notified of the allegations, KPMG acted immediately and decisively, firing London, who the firm said "violated the firm's rigorous policies and protections, betrayed the trust of clients as well as colleagues, and acted with deliberate disregard for KPMG's long-standing culture of professionalism and integrity." The firm also took legal action against London. Due to independence concerns, the firm resigned as auditor of **Skechers** and **Herbalife**, companies whose audits London over-saw. KPMG also announced that it would reassess its quality control standards, which include employee training, monitoring key employees' personal investments, and a whis-tleblowing hot line.

In addition to losing his job and being sued by his former employer, London ended up serving 14 months in prison and paying $100,000 in fines. He is still on probation and performing community service. He has openly confessed to his misconduct and has expressed his remorse: "I cannot begin to apologize for my incredibly stupid actions. There is no excuse for my wrongful conduct." However, even in hindsight, London has trouble explaining his behavior: "I felt guilt about it regularly—I can't explain it to be honest with you. . . . I look back at when this started and I can't explain it. . . . I guess [the] best way to describe it is that humans make mistakes."[1]

We may never know the true motives behind his actions, but we do know that London made a conscious decision to betray his employer, his clients, and his profession, violat-ing a number of rules from the AICPA Code of Professional Conduct in the process. In this module, we discuss the AICPA Code of Professional Conduct and many of the rules that London violated when sharing stock tips on the golf course.

GENERAL ETHICS

LO B-1

Understand general ethics and a series of steps for making ethical decisions.

What is ethics? Wheelwright defined *ethics* as "that branch of philosophy which is the systematic study of reflective choice, of the standards of right and wrong by which it is to be guided, and of the goods toward which it may ultimately be directed."[2] In this definition, you can detect three key elements: ethics (1) involves questions requiring reflective choice (*decision problems*), (2) involves guides of right and wrong (*moral principles*), and (3) is concerned with the consequences (*good or bad*) of decisions.

What is an ethical problem? A *problem situation* exists when an individual must make a choice among alternative actions and the right choice is not absolutely clear. An *ethical problem situation* may be described as one in which the choice of alternative actions affects the well-being of other persons. Although these are technical definitions of ethical dilemmas, we are often faced with situations in which what we want to do conflicts with what we know is the right course of action. Ethicists may argue that these are not ethical dilemmas, but that fact does not make the decisions any easier.

What is *ethical behavior*? You can find three standard philosophical answers to this question: Ethical behavior is that which (1) produces the greatest good, and/or (2) conforms to moral rules and principles, and/or (3) best demonstrates the virtues you value most. The most difficult problem situations arise when two or more rules conflict or when a rule and the criterion of "greatest good" conflict. However, as a professional auditor, you must always conform to the code of ethical behavior that applies to your jurisdiction or face the possibility of being formally sanctioned by the profession.

Why does an individual or group need a code of ethical conduct? A *code* makes explicit some of the criteria for conduct unique to the profession. *Codes of professional ethics* provide guidance in addressing situations that may not be specifically available in general ethics theories. An individual is better able to know what the profession expects. From the viewpoint of the organized profession, a *code* is a public declaration of principled conduct and a means of facilitating *enforcement* of standards of conduct. Once again, you can see the value of ethical behavior. Remember that accounting is the only business

---

[1]"Insider Trader Is Identified," *The Wall Street Journal*, April 11, 2013, p. C1.

[2]Philip Wheelwright, *A Critical Introduction to Ethics*, 3rd ed. (Indianapolis, IN: Odyssey Press, 1959).

discipline that is considered a profession similar to those of doctors and lawyers. As a student of auditing, you must commit yourself to knowing and understanding the AICPA *Code of Professional Conduct.* Understanding the Code of Professional Conduct will allow you to be better prepared to handle difficult situations like the one posed in the following ethical example.

A Shocking Example of Unethical Behavior

In a famous experiment conducted by Stanley Milgram (a psychologist at Yale University), subjects were told to ask questions of an individual in another room. If the individual answered incorrectly, the subjects were told to inflict an electric shock as punishment. In reality, no shock was actually administered; however, the subjects believed they were administering one and could hear shouts, cries, and appeals to stop emanating from the next room. The experimenter ordered the subjects to continue to apply the shocks at ever-increasing amounts. Many subjects increased the voltage to intensities labeled as dangerous and continued even after the individual in the next room asked for a doctor. Why do you think the subjects continued to apply shocks? What would you have done in this circumstance? Many have used the Milgram study result as an explanation for how good people often get caught up in wide-reaching frauds such as **Enron** and **WorldCom**, by subordinating their judgments to authority figures.

AN ETHICAL DECISION PROCESS

LO B-2
Reason through an ethical decision problem using the imperative, utilitarian, and virtue theories of moral philosophy.

When considering general ethics, your primary goal is to arrive at a personal framework for making ethical decisions. Consequently, an understanding of some of the general principles of ethics can provide background for a detailed consideration of standards for professional conduct.

In the earlier definition of ethics, one of the key elements was *reflective choice.* This involves engaging in an important sequence of events beginning with the recognition of a decision problem. Collection of evidence, in the ethics context, refers to thinking about rules of behavior and outcomes of alternative actions. The process ends with analyzing the situation and taking an action. Ethical decision problems almost always involve projecting yourself into the future to live with your decisions. Professional ethics decisions usually turn on these questions: "What written and unwritten rules govern my behavior?" and "What are the possible consequences of my choices—whom will my decision affect?" *Principles of ethics* can help you think about these two questions in real situations.

A good way to approach ethical decision problems is to think through several steps:

1. Define all facts and circumstances known at the time you need to make the decision. They are the "who, what, where, when, and how" dimensions of the situation. Identify the actor who needs to decide what to do.

   a. Because ethical decision problems are defined in terms of their effects on people, identify the people involved in the situation or affected by it. These are the "stakeholders"; be careful not to expand the number of stakeholders beyond the bounds of reasonable analysis.

   b. Identify and describe the stakeholders' rights and responsibilities in general and to each other.

2. Specify the actor's major alternative decision actions and their consequences (good, bad, short-run, long-run).

3. The actor must choose among the alternative actions.

   Let's apply the preceding ethical framework to an ethical decision.

An Example of an Ethical Decision Process

Step 1: Define the Problem Kathy Ellis (the chief financial officer) ordered Jorge Santos (a staff accountant) to "enhance" the financial statements in a loan application to Spring National Bank by understating the allowance for uncollectible accounts receivable saying, "It's an estimate anyway and we need the loan for a short time to keep from laying off loyal employees." What should Santos do?

Step 1a: Define the Stakeholders The stakeholders include the direct participants—Ellis, Santos, and Luis Perez (Spring National Bank's loan officer)—and some indirect participants—bank stockholders and loyal employees. Other people may be affected—Santos's mother, citizens who depend on the solvency of the banking system as a whole, taxpayers who may eventually need to bail out the insolvent banking system, and others—but identifying them probably will not improve the analysis.

Step 1b: Define the Responsibilities of the Individuals Ellis and Santos should act with integrity, and Ellis should not pressure Santos to cut corners with financial statements. Perez should make careful loan approval decisions. *Rights:* Santos should not be subject to pressures to cut corners with "enhanced financial statements." Perez should receive information that is not materially misstated or manipulated. (Some rights of employees and bank stockholders also could be identified.)

Step 2: Determine the Consequences (a) Santos can follow orders: Ellis is happy, he keeps his job, Perez gets fooled and approves the loan, the employees keep their jobs, the company may fail, the bank may be unable to collect the loan, the employees are laid off anyway, and Ellis and Santos are prosecuted and convicted of making false statements to a federal institution and go to federal prison. (b) Santos can refuse to "enhance" the financial statements: Ellis is not happy, Santos is fired, Ellis prepares the financial statements herself, and so on. (c) Santos persuades Ellis of the potential problems and Perez refuses the loan, and the company must find another way to survive, or Perez approves the loan anyway and the bank takes the risk; or Ellis does not agree, and Santos must again face alternatives (a) and (b) anyway. There is a fourth alternative (d): Santos could resign. This alternative may seem like an ideal way for Santos to extricate himself from the situation, but the problem facing others in this scenario does not go away.

In addition to weighing the consequences, Santos also should consider general and professional rules. If he is a CPA, some of the relevant professional rules relate to maintaining integrity (AICPA Rule 102), application of accounting standards (AICPA Rule 203), and the prohibition of discreditable acts (AICPA Rule 501). Santos needs to decide whether to follow rules or balance the expected consequences in the particular situation.

Step 3 Choose a Course of Action: As the actor, Santos must choose one of the alternative actions and justify it by presenting a convincing argument for its superiority. He can base the argument on rules, consequences, or a combination of both.

PHILOSOPHICAL PRINCIPLES IN ETHICS

We could skip a discussion of ethical theories if we were willing to accept a simple rule: "Let your *conscience* be your guide." Such a rule is appealing because it calls on an individual's own judgment, which may be based on wisdom, insight, adherence to custom, or an authoritative code. However, it also might be based on caprice, immaturity, ignorance, stubbornness, or misunderstanding. Often, as in the Milgram experiments, undue pressures might cause us to act in a way that we will later regret. The problem with using conscience as a guide is that it tells you about a wrong decision *after* you act!

In a similar manner, reliance on the opinions of others or on the weight of opinions of a particular social group is not always enough. Another person or a group of persons may perpetuate a custom or habit that is wrong. To adhere blindly to custom or to group habits is to abdicate individual responsibility. Titus and Keeton summarized this point succinctly: "Each person capable of making moral decisions is responsible for making his own decisions. The ultimate locus of moral responsibility is in the individual."[3] This does not mean you should not consult with friends, colleagues, or family members when facing a dilemma, but that only *you* have the final responsibility.

There are several philosophies, often referred to as *ethic principles*, that may be used to guide the ethical decision process. Thus, the function of ethical principles is not to provide a simple and sure rule but to provide some guides for your individual decisions and actions. Of course, as a professional auditor, you are required to follow the code of professional conduct. So, in that sense, professional auditors must always first apply the imperative principle. However, because many decisions go beyond the code, the principle of utilitarianism and the generalization argument are also considered. Finally, the decision must align with your own character (or virtue).

The Imperative Principle

The *imperative principle* directs a decision maker to act according to the requirements of an ethical rule. Strict versions of imperative ethics maintain that a decision should be made without trying to predict whether an action will create the greatest balance of good

[3]H. H. Titus and M. Keeton, *Ethics for Today,* 4th ed. (New York: American Book–Stratford Press, 1966), p. 131.

over evil. Ethics in the *imperative* sense is a function of moral rules and principles and does not involve a situation-specific calculation of the consequences.[4]

The philosopher Immanuel Kant (1724–1804) was perhaps the foremost advocate of the imperative school. Kant maintained that *reason* and the strict *duty to be consistent* should govern our actions. He believed that individuals should act only as they think everyone should act all of the time. This law of conduct (in moral philosophy) is known as Kant's **categorical imperative**, meaning that it specifies an *unconditional obligation*. One such maxim (rule), for example, is "Lying is wrong."

Suppose you believe that Santos (from our earlier ethical decision process example) should agree with Ellis and do everything she asked for "enhancing the financial statements," thus participating in a lie (knowingly misrepresenting the facts about the allowance for uncollectible accounts receivable). The Kantian test of the morality of such a lie is this: Can this maxim be a moral rule that should be followed without exception by all persons who have the opportunity to fool a bank loan officer for a good cause? If Santos refuses to manipulate the financial statements and the loan is refused, the result may be economic hardship and employee layoffs. Kant maintained that motive and duty alone define a moral act, not the consequences of the act. This reasoning places the highest value on the duty to be consistent and a lower value on the consequences, in this case the fate of the employees.

The general objection to the imperative principle is the belief that so-called universal rules always turn out to have exceptions. The general response to this objection is that if the rule is stated properly to include the exceptional cases, the principle is still valid. The problem with this response, however, is that human experience is complicated, and extremely complex universal rules would have to be constructed to try to cover all possible cases.[5]

Most professional codes of ethics have characteristics of the imperative type of theory. As a general matter, professionals are expected to act in a manner in conformity with the rules. As it relates to your work as an audit professional, this principle would lead you to follow the code of professional conduct to the letter of the law. This, of course, is what you must do to avoid being sanctioned by the profession. However, society frequently questions not only conduct itself, but also the rules on which conduct is based. Thus, a dogmatic imperative approach to ethical decisions may not be completely sufficient for the maintenance of professional standards. Society may question the rules, and conflicts among them are always possible. A means of estimating the consequences of alternative actions may be useful.

An Ethical Conflict

Consolidata Inc. was a tax client of **Alexander Grant & Company, CPAs** (AG). Consolidata prepared payrolls for 38 customers, received the customers' money, and then paid the payrolls. AG learned that Consolidata was in serious financial difficulty and advised the company to inform its customers, but company officials did not do so. When AG learned that the company's officers and directors had resigned, AG telephoned 12 Consolidata customers who were also AG clients, told them of the situation, and advised them not to entrust further payroll funds to Consolidata. The 12 were spared the risk of losing their money when Consolidata went out of business one month later.

Consolidata accused AG of breach of contract for breaking an obligation of confidentiality required by the AICPA Code of Professional Conduct (discussed later in this module). One SEC attorney said she thought AG should have alerted all 38 customers, not just the 12 AG clients. Accountants and SEC officials viewed the situation as a balancing of confidentiality (AICPA rule) against the public interest (Consolidata customers who needed a warning). Ethicists would view this dilemma as a conflict between an imperative principle (client confidentiality) and utilitarianism (what action benefits the most parties).

---

[4]I. Kant, *Foundations of the Metaphysics of Morals*, trans. Lewis W. Beck (Indianapolis, IN: Bobbs-Merrill, 1959; originally published in 1785).
[5]Several rules in the AICPA Code of Professional Conduct are explicitly phrased to provide for exceptions to the general rules, notably Rules 203 and 301. Imperative rules also seem to generate borderline cases, so the AICPA Ethics Division issues interpretations and rulings to explain the applicability of the rules.

The Principle of Utilitarianism (or Consequentialism)

The *principle of utilitarianism* emphasizes examining the *consequences* of action rather than following some rules. The criterion of producing the greater good is made an explicit part of the decision process. The *principle* is very useful, but be sure to notice that it does not specify the *values* that enable you to determine the good or evil of an action. In **act-utilitarianism**, the center of attention is the *individual act* as it is affected by the specific circumstances of a situation. The general difficulty with act-utilitarianism is that it seems to permit too many exceptions to well-established rules. By focusing attention on individual acts, the long-run effect of setting examples for other people appears to be ignored. If an act-utilitarian decision is to break a moral rule, the decision's success usually depends on everyone else's adherence to the rule, which is highly unlikely in auditing.

Rule-utilitarianism, on the other hand, emphasizes the centrality *of rules for ethical behavior* while still maintaining the criterion of the greatest universal good. This kind of utilitarianism means that decision makers must first determine the rules that will promote the greatest general good for the largest number of people. The initial question is not which *action* has the greatest utility but which *rule*.

The Generalization Argument

The generalization argument may be considered a judicious combination of the imperative and utilitarian principles. Basically, the **generalization argument** considers the consequences of a decision made by similar persons acting under similar circumstances.[6] A more everyday expression of the argument is this question: "What would happen if everyone acted in that certain way?" If the answer to the question is that the consequences would be undesirable, the conclusion, according to the generalization test, is that the way of acting is unethical and should not be done.

In our ethical decision example, Santos's problem as a professional accountant and as an employee arose when Ellis asked him to "enhance the financial statements" and he saw the enhancement as a lie. His generalization question may be something like this: "What if all accountants fudged financial statements and fooled loan officers when their companies needed to obtain loans?" Most people will see an easy answer: The result would be undesirable (because it might succeed often and cause considerable losses to banks along with other undesirable personal consequences for the actors in addition to the problem of having broken a rule that requires truth telling). Another kind of conflict subject to the generalization test is illustrated by a public accounting firm's desire for service and need for independence. (See the Auditing Insight "Service versus Independence".)

Virtue Ethics

Virtue ethics can be traced not only to the Greek philosophers Aristotle and Plato (his *Republic* discusses the Four Cardinal Virtues: wisdom, justice, fortitude, and temperance), but also to Buddhist ethical tradition. Rather than a focus on following rules or weighing outcomes, virtue ethics emphasizes the role of one's character in the decision-making process. Questions that may be asked include, "What action will help me become my ideal self?" or, "What action would I be the proudest of?"

To contrast the different approaches, consider the example of cheating on a class assignment. A utilitarian approach might weigh the potential positive outcome of cheating ("I need to pass this class") against the negatives ones (hurting others' grades, possibly getting caught). Under Kant's categorical imperative approach, cheating is always wrong, no matter what positive outcomes may come from it. Under the Aristotelian virtue ethics approach, one would consider whether cheating was most aligned with the person the student aspired to be.

This brief review of ethical principles provides some important background to the ways that many people approach difficult ethical decision problems. As a professional auditor, you are required to adhere to the prevailing code of conduct in all your duties. However, there will be times in your career when the code does not go far enough. In those situations,

[6]M. G. Singer, *Generalization in Ethics* (New York: Atheneum, 1961, 1971), esp. pp. 5, 10–11, 61, 63, 73, 81, 105–122.

AUDITING INSIGHT   Service versus Independence

For many years, a national public accounting firm encouraged its professionals to become active members of the boards of directors of corporations. The purpose was to provide expertise to businesses in the metropolitan area and to enable the public accounting firm to become well known and well respected. The public accounting firm changed its policy to prohibit such service after it had to refuse the opportunity to obtain some of these corporations as audit clients because of independence concerns. The public accounting firm's audit independence was considered impaired when a member of the firm had served in a director or management capacity during the period covered by the financial statements the corporations wanted the firm to audit. The generalization test was this: If members of the firm serve on the boards of directors of all corporations that may become audit clients, none of these corporations can be accepted as audit clients—a result that is undesirable.

it is important to consider the three major approaches to ethical decision making—the categorical imperative's focus on rules, utilitarianism's focus on outcomes, and virtue ethics' focus on character—and apply them to decisions. Deciding how you will behave (i.e., what ethical principle you will follow) *before* you find yourself in an ethical dilemma can prepare you for the kind of pressures the Milgram subjects and our hypothetical Santos experienced and allow you to make decisions of which you will be proud.

 REVIEW CHECKPOINTS

B.1 What roles must a professional accountant be prepared to perform in regard to ethical decision problems?

B.2 When might the rule "Let your conscience be your guide" *not* be a sufficient basis for (a) your personal ethical decisions and (b) your professional ethical decisions?

B.3 Assume that you accept the following ethical rule: "Failure to tell the whole truth is wrong." In the textbook illustration about Santos's problem with Ellis's instructions, (a) what would this rule require Santos to do and (b) why is an unalterable rule such as this classified as an element of imperative ethical theory?

B.4 How do utilitarian ethics differ from imperative ethics?

ETHICAL CODES OF CONDUCT

LO B-3
Identify the different entities that make ethics rules for CPAs and public accounting firms.

Independence, professionalism, and integrity have long been concerns of the accounting profession, but the accounting scandals of **Enron, WorldCom**, and the financial crisis have brought renewed cries and placed additional emphasis on these issues. The PCAOB was created, in part, to help bring a new level of independence and integrity to the profession. In that spirit, the PCAOB has issued a number of rules that apply to auditors that serve clients that are public entities. Furthermore, public accounting firms and CPAs also must follow rules set forth by the SEC and the AICPA Professional Ethics Executive Committee (PEEC). Public accounting firms and CPAs completing multinational audits also must comply with the International Federation of Accountants (IFAC) Code of Ethics for Professional Accountants. If you are an internal auditor, you will be expected to observe the rules of conduct of the Institute of Internal Auditors (IIA). As a management accountant, the standards of ethical conduct for management accountants of the Institute of Management Accountants (IMA) will apply to you. Certified fraud examiners are expected to observe the Association of Certified Fraud Examiners (ACFE) Code of Ethics. If you find this "alphabet soup" of ethics rule makers confusing, imagine those CPAs who have to deal with complex and often conflicting rules on a daily basis. As a CPA, you will be expected to observe rules of conduct published in several codes of ethics, depending on the jurisdiction. In summary, if you join the AICPA and a state society of CPAs and practice before the U.S. Securities and Exchange Commission (SEC) on a multinational audit client, you will be subject to the following:

Source of Rules of Conduct	Applicable to
U.S. Securities and Exchange Commission (SEC)	Persons who practice before the SEC as accountants and auditors for SEC-registered companies
Public Company Accounting Oversight Board (PCAOB)	Registered firms and individuals who perform audits of companies under the jurisdiction of the PCAOB
International Federation of Accountants (IFAC)	Public accounting firms and CPAs performing audits of multinational companies
American Institute of CPAs (AICPA)	AICPA members
Applicable state society of CPAs	Members of a state society of CPAs
Applicable state board of accountancy	Persons licensed by the state to practice accounting

AUDITING INSIGHT · Fraud Auditor Expelled for Committing Fraud

A trial board of the ACFE found that a member had wrongfully represented himself as a *certified internal auditor* when in fact he did not hold the CIA designation. Such conduct is in violation of Article 1.A.4 of the Certified Fraud Examiners Code of Professional Ethics, and the member was summarily expelled from the organization.

L. Jackson Shockey, CFE, CPA, CISA, chairperson of the board of regents, said: "We are saddened that a member has been expelled for such conduct. However, in order to maintain the integrity of the CFE program, the trial board vigorously investigates violations of the Code of Professional Ethics. When appropriate, the board of regents will not hesitate to take necessary action."

Source: *CFE News.*

U.S. Securities and Exchange Commission (SEC)

The SEC has federal statutory authority to regulate the public accounting profession for the purposes of (1) protecting the reliability and integrity of the financial statements of public companies and (2) promoting investor confidence in financial statements and the securities markets. The SEC's jurisdiction covers only public companies that are required by federal securities laws to file financial statements audited by independent accountants. In addition to the duties outlined earlier, the passage of the Sarbanes–Oxley Act in 2002 requires the SEC to oversee the PCAOB.

The Public Company Accounting Oversight Board (PCAOB)

The PCAOB has been given the responsibility to set standards for public accounting firms and to oversee quality control, ethics, and independence issues for accounting professionals who audit financial statements of public companies. Students are urged to review the PCAOB website (www.pcaobus.org) for the latest standards and rules issued by the PCAOB.

Although the PCAOB has almost the same level of authority as the SEC, the SEC must approve all PCAOB proposed rules before they are final. Also, even though the PCAOB has authority over the audits of only public entities, it would be a mistake to believe that the PCAOB's influence ends there. Indeed, several states (e.g., California) have passed legislation that incorporates PCAOB rules into state law applicable to audits of all companies, both public and private.

The International Federation of Accountants (IFAC)

For audits of multinational companies, auditors must follow the guidelines promulgated by the IFAC. IFAC's International Ethics Standards Board for Accountants is responsible for the Code of Ethics for Professional Accountants (IESBA Code), which is the code of conduct that governs the audits of multinational companies.[7] Although there are differences between the IESBA Code and the AICPA Code of Professional Conduct used to govern the audits of U.S. companies (which will be described later in this module), the codes are actually quite similar. In general, a CPA should always comply with the more restrictive standard that is applicable on a particular audit engagement. Not surprisingly, with the dramatic increase in audits of multinational companies by public accounting firms from the United States, the importance of the IESBA Code has increased. Indeed, the AICPA has just completed a convergence and codification project designed to align the AICPA and IESBA codes and simplify the overall structure of the AICPA Code.

The Professional Ethics Executive Committee (PEEC) of the American Institute of CPAs (AICPA)

The PEEC is the AICPA committee that makes and enforces all rules of conduct for CPAs (i.e., the AICPA Code of Professional Conduct) who are AICPA members. You might think that if you were not in public accounting and not a member of the AICPA, the rules would not apply. However, state and federal court proceedings and disciplinary bodies have consistently upheld that CPAs must adhere to professional ethical standards even if they are not members of the AICPA. Furthermore, most states incorporate the AICPA Code of Professional Conduct into their own accounting statutes.

As mentioned earlier, the PEEC has recently undertaken a project to recodify the AICPA's ethics standards to increase its accessibility and usefulness to members. The new code (http://pub.aicpa.org/codeofconduct), effective as of December 15, 2014, is structured into topical areas and has been revised to reflect more of a conceptual framework approach. Importantly, the new recodified standards closely follow the IESBA ethical standards. The revised AICPA Code of Professional Conduct contains four parts. The first section, referred to as the Preface, includes a discussion of the Principles of Professional Conduct, a set of six positive essays expressing the profession's high ideals:

I. *Responsibilities.* In carrying out their responsibilities as professionals, members should exercise sensitive professional and moral judgments in all of their activities.

II. *The public interest.* Members should accept the obligation to act in a way that will serve the public interest, honor the public trust, and demonstrate commitment to professionalism.

III. *Integrity.* To maintain and broaden public confidence, members should perform all professional responsibilities with the highest sense of integrity.

IV. *Objectivity and independence.* A member should maintain objectivity and be free of conflicts of interest in discharging professional responsibilities. A member in public practice should be independent in fact and appearance when providing auditing and other attestation services.

V. *Due care.* A member should observe the profession's technical and ethical standards, strive continually to improve competence and quality of services, and discharge professional responsibility to the best of the member's ability.

VI. *Scope and nature of services.* A member in public practice should observe the Principles of the Code of Professional Conduct in determining the scope and nature of services to be provided.

The responsibility to the public interest clearly sets accountants apart from other business professionals. It is the reason that accounting is considered a profession even beyond other professionals such as doctors and lawyers whose primary responsibility is to their patients/clients. However, this *responsibility to the public interest* demands that CPAs' work must reflect high levels of moral judgment, true commitment to the public interest, and excellent performance. The *scope and nature of services* refer to the issue of balancing

---

[7]The most recent edition of the IESBA Code of Ethics was published on June 3, 2013, and is available at www.ifac.org/publications-resources/2013-handbook-code-ethics-professional-accountants.

public accounting firms' commitment to clients (giving business advice and consulting) and commitment to the public (giving opinions on financial statements).

Although the first section of the AICPA Code of Professional Conduct embodies principles to which CPAs should adhere, they are very general in nature, and thus are difficult, if not impossible, to enforce on their own. The three remaining parts contain enforceable rules that were derived from the six Principles of Professional Conduct. Part 1 applies to members practicing public accounting; Part 2 does the same for those CPAs working in business; and Part 3 applies to all other members, including those who are retired or are between jobs.

AICPA Code of Professional Conduct

AICPA Code of Professional Conduct			
Preface: Applicable to All Members			
0.100	Overview of the Code of Professional Conduct	1.500	Fees and Other Types of Remuneration
0.200	Structure and Application of the AICPA Code	1.600	Advertising and Other Forms of Solicitation
0.300	Principles of Professional Conduct	1.700	Confidential Information
0.400	Definitions	1.800	Form of Organization and Name
0.500	Nonauthoritative Guidance	Part 2 – Members in Business	
0.600	New, Revised, and Pending Interpretations and Other Guidance	2.000	Introduction
0.700	Deleted Interpretations and Other Guidance	2.100	Integrity and Objectivity
Part 1 – Members in Public Practice		2.300	General Standards
1.000	Introduction	2.310	Compliance with Standards
1.100	Integrity and Objectivity	2.320	Accounting Principles
1.200	Independence	2.400	Acts Discreditable
1.300	General Standards	Part 3 – Other Members	
1.310	Compliance with Standards	3.000	Introduction
1.320	Accounting Principles	3.400	Acts Discreditable
1.400	Acts Discreditable		

The PEEC also publishes interpretations of the Code of Professional Conduct, which are detailed explanations of specific rules necessary to help members understand particular applications. Finally, the PEEC also publishes "rulings" on the applicability of rules in specific situations.[8]

Principles		**Rules**		**Interpretations**
Aspirational goals of behavior	$\longrightarrow$	Enforceable ethical regulations that CPAs must follow	$\longrightarrow$	Applications of rules to specific business situations

✅ REVIEW CHECKPOINTS

B.5 In regard to ethics rules, what are the jurisdictions of the (a) AICPA PEEC, (b) SEC, (c) PCAOB, and (d) IFAC?

B.6 What organizations and agencies have rules of conduct that you must observe when you practice (a) public accounting, (b) internal auditing, (c) management accounting, and (d) fraud examination?

[8]The full text of the interpretations and rules are available on the AICPA website (www.aicpa.org).

AN EMPHASIS ON INDEPENDENCE

LO B-4

With reference to American Institute of Certified Public Accounting (AICPA), Government Accountability Office (GAO), Public Company Accounting Oversight Board (PCAOB), and Securities and Exchange Commission (SEC) rules, analyze factual situations and decide whether an accountant's conduct does or does not impair independence.

At the time the U.S. Senate passed the Sarbanes–Oxley Act in July 2002 (by a vote of 99–0), the investing public was outraged by the magnitude of the financial statement frauds at both Enron and WorldCom (among many other frauds). The audacity of these frauds is mind boggling. Consider that in 2000, Enron was the seventh largest company on the *Fortune* 500 with reported assets of $65 billion and sales revenues of $100 billion. However, just a year later, Enron filed for bankruptcy, and billions of shareholder dollars were lost. In June 2002, WorldCom announced that it would be restating its financial statements due to improper accounting that took two major forms: the over-statement of revenue by at least $958 million and the understatement of line costs, its largest category of expenses, by more than $7 billion. The passage of Sarbanes–Oxley was a direct response to these financial statement frauds. Indeed, a number of the sections of the act are specifically targeted to prevent the threats to auditor independence that existed on both the Enron and WorldCom audit engagements. For example, Section 201 of Sarbanes–Oxley makes it unlawful for a public accounting firm to provide most consulting type services to its audit clients, including information systems design and implementation (e.g., SAP) and internal audit outsourcing. This regulation was clearly designed to prevent the type of relationship that existed between Enron and **Arthur Andersen** (Andersen). In 2000, Enron paid Andersen $25 million for financial state-ment audit services and $27 million for consulting and other services, such as internal audit services. The significant amount of revenue generated on consulting services was considered a threat to independence by many, especially considering that the com-pensation of audit partners at Andersen depended, in part, on consulting sales to its audit clients.

As you will soon learn, the AICPA Code of Professional Conduct (the Code) is crys-tal clear about the importance of independence. The responsibilities principle requires auditors to maintain independence *in mental attitude;* that is, auditors are expected to be unbiased and impartial with respect to all professional judgments and to the financial statements they audit. This "state of mind" is often referred to as the auditor's possess-ing independence in fact. It is important for auditors not only to be unbiased but also to appear to be unbiased. *Independence in appearance* relates to financial statement users' perceptions of auditors' independence. For example, even if the auditors do not have any direct or indirect financial interest or obligation with the audit client, they must ensure that no part of their behavior or actions appears to affect their independence in the opin-ion of the public. Simply stated, audit quality and the value of the profession depend on independence. If an auditor's independence is doubted, users of audited financial state-ments are likely to question the motives of the public accounting firm in completing the audit, greatly diminishing the value of the audit. As a result of its importance, public accounting firms now spend a substantial amount of time making sure they maintain their independence at all times.

American Institute of Certified Public Accountants[9]

The PEEC makes independence rules for CPAs that are applicable not only for audits of public companies but also for all other audits (audits of nonpublic companies, not-for-profit organizations, and government units) and attestation engagements. Independence is required for audit as well as attestation engagements, including reviews of financial statements. However, attestation engagements are governed by *Statements on Standards for Attestation Engagements (SSAEs)* dealing with assertions other than financial statements in which some form of assurance is provided. The Independence Rule is

---

[9]The AICPA annually publishes a "Plain English Guide to Independence," which is designed to increase understanding of the complex independence rules. The guide can be downloaded from the AICPA website, www.aicpa.org/interestareas/professionalethics/resources/tools/downloadabledocuments/plain%20english%20guide.pdf.

derived from the AICPA Code of Professional Conduct's objectivity and independence principle.

Independence Rule

> A member in public practice shall be independent in the performance of professional services as required by standards promulgated by bodies designated by Council. (1.200.001)[10]

The Independence Rule itself has very little substantive content. Instead, it incorporates PEEC interpretations that are explained in the following paragraphs. The fundamental thrust of these interpretations is that auditors preserve **independence**, the mental attitude and appearance that auditors are not influenced by others in making judgments and decisions, by (1) avoiding financial connections that make it appear that the auditor's wealth depends on the outcome of the audit and (2) avoiding managerial connections that make it appear that the auditors are involved in management decisions for the audit client (thus auditing their own work).

Essentially, **covered members** are prohibited from having any financial interest in clients that could affect their audit judgment (*independence in fact*) or would appear to others to have an influence on their judgment (*independence in appearance*). In addition, immediate family members are under the same restrictions as the auditor. Again, the appearance of independence would be jeopardized if the auditor's child owned stock in a client. Similarly, if a close relative or immediate family member worked for a client in a position that could influence the audit (e.g., a controller), independence in appearance, if not in fact, is impaired. Exhibit B.1 provides important definitions (both AICPA and SEC) used in delineating these issues. Exhibit B.2 summarizes the PEEC interpretations and other independence matters.

So, what do all of the definitions presented in Exhibit B.2 mean for applying the independence rules? For most practical purposes, the people who are prohibited from having financial and managerial relationships with the client are the audit engagement team, the people in the chain of command, the covered persons in the public accounting firm, their close family members, and immediate family members.

EXHIBIT B.1 Comparison of SEC and AICPA Selected Definitions

	AICPA Definition	SEC Definition
Engagement Team	Professionals participating in the audit or attest engagement, including those who perform reviews. The audit or attest engagement team includes all professionals and contractors who participate in the audit or attest engagement, irrespective of their functional classification (for example, audit, tax, or management consulting services). The audit or attest engagement team excludes specialists and individuals who perform only routine clerical functions.	All partners, principals, shareholders, and professional employees participating in an audit, review, or attestation engagement of an audit client, including those conducting reviews and all persons who consult with others on the audit engagement team during the audit, review, or attestation engagement regarding technical or industry-specific issues, transactions, or events.
Chain of Command	**Partner:** A proprietor, shareholder, equity or nonequity partner, or any individual who assumes the risks and benefits of firm ownership or who is held out by the firm to be the equivalent of an owner or partner. **Manager:** A professional employee of the firm who has either of the following responsibilities: 1. Continuing responsibility for the overall planning and supervision of engagements for specified clients. 2. Authority to determine that an engagement is complete subject to final partner approval.	All persons who (1) supervise or have direct management responsibility for the audit, (2) evaluate the performance or recommend the compensation of the audit engagement partner, or (3) provide quality control or other oversight of the audit.

---

[10]The "bodies designated by Council" refers to the PEEC.

	AICPA Definition	SEC Definition
Covered Person	The following are considered covered members: (1) An individual on the audit or attest engagement team; (2) An individual in a position to influence the audit or attest engagement; (3) A partner or manager who provides nonattest services to the audit or attest client beginning once he or she provides 10 hours of nonattest services to the audit or attest client within any fiscal year and ending on the later of the date (i) the firm signs the report on the financial statements for the fiscal year during which those services were provided or (ii) he or she no longer expects to provide 10 or more hours of nonattest services to the audit or attest client on a recurring basis; (4) A partner in the office in which the lead audit or attest engagement partner primarily practices in connection with the audit or attest engagement; (5) The firm, including the firm's employee benefit plans; or (6) An entity whose operating, financial, or accounting policies can be controlled (as defined by generally accepted accounting principles [GAAP] for consolidation purposes) by any of the individuals or entities described in (1) through (5) or by two or more such individuals or entities if they act together.	The following partners, principals, shareholders, and employees of an accounting firm are considered covered members: (1) An individual on the audit engagement team, (2) An individual in the chain of command, (3) Any other partner, principal, shareholder, or managerial employee of the firm who has provided 10 or more hours of nonaudit services to the audit client for the period beginning on the date such services are provided and ending on the date the accounting firm signs the report on the financial statements for the fiscal year during which those services are provided, or who expects to provide 10 or more hours of nonaudit services to the audit client on a recurring basis, and (4) Any other partner, principal, or shareholder from an office of the accounting firm in which the lead audit engagement partner primarily practices in connection with the audit. *Authors' Note:* In essence, the "covered members" are the firm's professionals closely connected to the audit engagement and the firm's owners who are located in the office where the lead engagement partner practices. However, the SEC added the category of manager-level professionals and owners who provide nonaudit (tax, consulting) services for the audit client. Therefore, almost everyone who provides services of any type for an audit client must observe the independence rules.
Close Family Member	Parent, sibling, or nondependent child.	Person's spouse, spousal equivalent, parent, dependent child, nondependent child, or sibling.
Immediate Family Member	Spouse, spousal equivalent, or dependents (whether or not related).	Person's spouse, spousal equivalent, or dependents.

EXHIBIT B.2
Summary of Independence Rule Interpretations

A covered member cannot
- Have a direct financial interest in a client.
- Have a material indirect financial interest in a client.
- Be a trustee or administrator of an estate that has a direct or material indirect financial interest in a client.
- Have a joint investment with a client that is material to the covered member.
- Have a loan to or from a client, any officer of the client, or any individual owning more than 10 percent of the client (except as specifically described in *Interpretation 101-5*).
- Participate on an attest engagement if she or he was formally employed by the client in a position to influence the audit or acted as an officer, director, promoter, underwriter, or trustee of a pension or profit-sharing trust of the client.

A covered member's immediate family cannot
- Have a direct financial interest in a client.
- Have a material indirect financial interest in a client.
- Have vested retirement benefits at a client.

A covered member's close relatives cannot
- Have a key management level position with a client.
- Have a material financial interest in a client that is known to the covered member.
- Have a financial interest in a client that allows the relative to have significant influence in a client.
- Be in a position to influence the audit.

A partner or a professional employee cannot
- Be associated with a client as a director, officer, employee, promoter, underwriter, voting trustee, or trustee of a pension or profit-sharing trust of the client.

EXHIBIT B.3
AICPA Code of
Conduct Conceptual
Framework

Source: www.aicpa.org.

Conceptual Framework
Ethics Codification

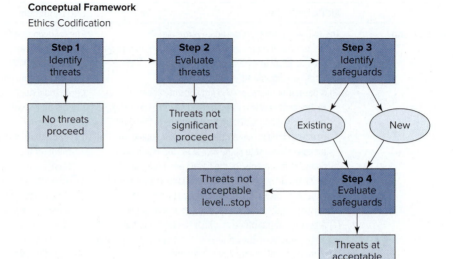

When a questionable practice or relationship arises, the CPA must evaluate whether the practice or relationship poses an unacceptable risk to a CPAs' independence.[11] Because there is not a rule or interpretation for every ethical dilemma a CPA might face, there is a Conceptual Framework (Exhibit B.3) that CPAs can use when facing a situation not covered in the Code of Conduct.

The Conceptual Framework uses a three-step risk-based approach that involves (1) identifying and evaluating threats to independence, (2) determining whether safeguards eliminate or sufficiently mitigate the identified threats, and (3) determining whether independence is impaired.

Identified threats to independence include the following:

1. *Adverse interest threat.* CPAs acting in opposition to clients (e.g., through litigation).
2. *Undue influence threat.* Attempts to coerce or otherwise influence the CPA member (e.g., significant gifts or threats to replace the auditor over an accounting principles disagreement).
3. *Advocacy threat.* CPAs promoting a client's interests or position.
4. *Management participation threat.* CPAs taking on the role of client management or otherwise performing management functions.
5. *Familiarity threat.* CPAs becoming too sympathetic to client interests because of long-standing or close relationships.
6. *Self-interest threat.* CPAs having a financial relationship with a client.
7. *Self-review threat.* CPAs reviewing their own work.

Next we take a closer look at threats to independence and their related interpretations that address those threats.

Adverse Interest and Undue Influence Threats

Conditions can arise when a public accounting firm and a client move into an adversary relationship instead of the cooperative relationship needed in an attest engagement. Public accounting firm independence is considered impaired when the firm is involved in threatened or actual litigation involving an audit. Such cases may be rare, but the AICPA has provided auditors a way out of the difficult audit situation by this rule requiring them to

---

[11]In April 2006, the PEEC adopted the *Conceptual Framework for AICPA Independence Standards,* which describes the PEEC's risk-based approach to analyzing independence issues that arise.

declare "nonindependence" and the ability to give only a disclaimer on financial statements or other information. Essentially, the CPA–client relationship ends and the litigation begins a new relationship.

Occasionally, the public accounting firm may find that it is a defendant in a lawsuit initiated by a third party or parties. Normally, this type of litigation is not considered to adversely impact the independence of the public accounting firm. However, sometimes these lawsuits result in claims from the client's management that existing problems are the result of audit deficiencies or claims from the auditor that deficiencies are the result of fraud or deceit on the part of management. When such cross-claims are threatened or filed, independence may be impaired.

Advocacy and Management Participation Threats

In addition to prohibitions against financial relationships with clients, a covered member is prohibited from acting in the capacity of a manager, employee, promoter, or trustee of a client. Generally, independence is impaired if the public accounting firm even *appears* to outside observers to be working in the capacity of management or employees of the client. The client management (including its board of directors and audit committee) must understand that they are responsible for establishing and maintaining internal control and directing the internal audit function, if any. The board of directors and/or audit committee (i.e., those charged with governance) must understand their roles and responsibilities with regard to extended audit services including the establishment of guidelines for both management and the public accounting firm to follow in carrying out these responsibilities and monitoring how well the respective responsibilities have been met.

In addition to the guidance discussed in the previous paragraphs, the following additional activities would impair independence:[12]

- Performing ongoing monitoring or control activities.
- Determining which, if any, recommendations for improving internal control should be implemented.
- Reporting to the board of directors or audit committee on behalf of management or the individual responsible for the internal audit function.
- Authorizing, executing, or consummating transactions or otherwise exercising authority on behalf of the client.
- Preparing source documents for transactions.
- Having custody of assets.
- Approving or being responsible for the overall internal audit work plan including the determination of the internal audit risk and scope project priorities and the frequency of performance of audit procedures.
- Performing forensic accounting services, litigation support work, or any other service in which it appears that the CPA is taking an advocacy position on the client's behalf. Although performing tax compliance work would not normally impair independence, certain tax work in which an advocacy position is required does (e.g., representing a client in court to resolve a tax dispute).
- Being connected with the client as an employee or in any capacity equivalent to a member of client management (for example, being listed as an employee in client directories or other client publications, permitting himself or herself to be referred to by title or description as supervising or being in charge of the client's internal audit function, or using the client's letterhead or internal correspondence forms in communications).

---

[12]Although the following information does not prohibit auditors from providing internal audit and a variety of other services, it should be emphasized that the interpretation covers client companies that are public and private. Audits of public companies must comply with the rules of the SEC, the appropriate stock exchange, and the PCAOB. These agencies have rules that prohibit auditors from providing internal audit services to audit clients in most cases and have more stringent requirements regarding extended services.

Although this list is not all-inclusive, a prohibited activity is any that would force the CPA to act either in the capacity of management or as an advocate for management.

As noted, independence is ordinarily impaired if a CPA serves on an organization's board of directors. However, members can be *honorary* directors of organizations such as charity hospitals, fund drives, symphony orchestra societies, and similar not-for-profit organizations so long as (1) the position is purely honorary, (2) the CPA is identified as an honorary director on letterheads and other literature, (3) the only form of participation is the use of the CPA's name, and (4) the CPA does not vote with the board or participate in management functions. When all of these criteria have been satisfied, the CPA/board member can perform audit and attest services because the appearances of independence will have been preserved.

Familiarity Threat

An immediate family member may not hold a position of influence (key position) in an audit client. The close family member's definition comes into play in connection with (1) ownership or control of an audit client or (2) employment with an audit client. An example of (1) is the impairment of the public accounting firm's independence when a close family member of a covered person in the firm owns a material investment in an audit client or is in a position to exert significant influence over an audit client. An example of (2) is the impairment of the public accounting firm's independence when a close family member works in an accounting or financial reporting role at an audit client or was in such a role during any period covered by an audit for which the person in the firm is a covered person. (Neither an immediate family member nor a close family member can work in a capacity such as a member of the board of directors, chief executive officer, president, chief financial officer, chief operating officer, general counsel, chief accounting officer, controller, director of internal audit, director of financial reporting, treasurer, or vice president of marketing.)

Independence problems do not end when owners (partners, shareholders) and professional employees retire, resign, or otherwise leave a public accounting firm. A former owner or professional can cause independence to be impaired if a relationship continues with a client of the former firm. However, the problems are solved and independence is not impaired if (1) the person's retirement benefits are fixed, (2) the person is no longer active in the public accounting firm (sometimes retired owners remain "active"), and (3) the former owner is not held out to be associated with the public accounting firm.

In addition to the preceding considerations, the public accounting firm must ensure that appropriate consideration is given to any increase in risks that may exist due to the former partner's or professional's knowledge of the firm's audit plan and procedures. The firm must consider the following:

- The interaction with the former partner or professional.
- The ability of audit team members to manage the interaction with the former partner or professional employee.
- Modification of the engagement procedures.
- The appropriateness of the review to determine that an appropriate level of skepticism was maintained.

Financial Self-Interest Threat

Any direct financial interest (e.g., ownership of common or preferred stock) is prohibited. This requirement is the strictest one in the code. There are no exceptions; indirect financial interests, on the other hand, are allowed up to the point of materiality (with reference to the member's wealth). This provision permits members to have some limited business transactions with clients so long as they do not reach material proportions. Other provisions define certain specific types of prohibited and allowed indirect financial interests. Immediate family members are subject to the same provisions that prescribe the acceptable actions of the covered person. Like the covered person, an immediate family member may not have a direct financial or material indirect financial interest in a client.

We already understand that a covered member cannot have a financial relationship with a client. However, suppose the client is an investor in another company and the covered member has invested in that company. Has independence been impaired? If the covered member's investment is a direct or materially indirect financial interest in a non-client investee, independence is considered to be impaired. The reasoning for the basic rule is that the client investor, through its ability to influence a nonclient investee, can increase or decrease the CPA's financial stake in the investee by an amount material to the CPA, and therefore, the CPA may not appear to be independent. If the investment by the client is not material to the nonclient (i.e., there does not appear to be any influence over the investee), then independence is not impaired unless the covered member's investment allows the member to exercise significant influence over the nonclient.

Material cooperative arrangements with clients (i.e., joint participation in a business activity) also impair independence. Examples include joint ventures to develop or market products or to market a package of client and CPA services or one party working to market the products or services of the other.

Most loans to or from audit clients are prohibited: "Independence is considered impaired if a covered member has a loan from a client, officer, director, or any individual owning 10 percent or more of a client." Similarly, independence is impaired if there are unpaid fees or a note receivable arising from unpaid fees from the client outstanding for more than a year. The only loans permitted are "grandfathered loans" and "other permitted loans."

Grandfathered loans are those loans that were obtained either (1) before the independence rules changed (but met the requirements of the Independence Rule in effect at that time) or (2) from a financial institution before it became a client for services requiring independence. These grandfathered loans must at all times be current under all of their terms, and the terms shall not be renegotiated. The specific types of loans that are grandfathered are home mortgages, loans not material to the CPA's net worth, and secured loans for which the collateral value must exceed the balance of the loan at all times.

Other permitted loans include

- Auto loans and leases collateralized by the automobile.
- Insurance policy loans based on policy surrender value.
- Loans collateralized by cash deposits at the same financial institution.
- Credit card balances and cash advances of $10,000 or less.

Ethics rules do not cover all circumstances in which the appearance of independence might be questioned. It is the member's responsibility to determine whether the personal and business relationships would lead a reasonable person aware of all the relevant facts to conclude that there is an unacceptable threat to the member's and the firm's independence.

Self-Review Threat

Independence is impaired if the public accounting firm performs the bookkeeping or makes accounting or management decisions for a company whose management does not know enough about the financial statements to take primary responsibility for them. The problem in this situation is the appearance of the public accounting firm having both prepared the financial statements or other information and provided the auditors' report or other attestation on its own work. In the final analysis, the management must be able to say, "These are our financial statements (or other information); we made the choices of accounting principles; we take primary responsibility for them." The auditors cannot authorize transactions, control assets, sign checks or reports, prepare source documents, supervise the client's personnel, or serve as the client's registrar, transfer agent, or general counsel.

Other Threats?

Other Independence Rule interpretations include relationships with governmental entities and alternative practice structures. The full list of interpretations, with accompanying detail, can be found on the AICPA's website (pub.aicpa.org/codeofconduct).

As you can see, the detail is substantial, yet you have no choice but to understand the full details of the AICPA independence requirements. Lack of knowledge of the appropriate jurisdiction's ethical requirements is not a defense when facing severe sanctions and penalties.

We have examined a number of threats that have been identified that impair independence. What about those not specifically covered? When those situations arise, the Conceptual Framework guides the CPA to make the best decision to address the threats. Note that the Conceptual Framework is to be used only when specific guidance is not in the Code. It cannot be used to override existing rules or interpretations.

In addition to identifying and considering the significance of each threat, the CPA should identify *safeguards* that might eliminate or reduce the threat to an acceptable level. Safeguards can be client or firm-specific, including policies and procedures in place to prevent ethical problems. Examples include training on the importance of independence, threats of disciplinary action, hotlines to discuss ethical dilemmas, tone at the top, and the use of different offices (or different firms) to perform parts of the engagement.

Lastly, whenever the CPA runs into ethical issues, especially those in which safeguards are identified to eliminate or reduce significant threats, the CPA must document the decisions reached. Failure to do so would be a violation of the Compliance with Standards Rule (discussed later in this module).

SEC and PCAOB Independence Rules

Prior to the issuance of Sarbanes–Oxley in 2002, the SEC accepted most of the independence rules established by the PEEC. However, the SEC became concerned about the public accounting profession's emphasis on consulting fees and the resulting effect on public accounting firm independence. In fact, the SEC issued a comprehensive independence rule in November 2000. The rule is based upon two premises: (1) *independence in fact* is a mental state of objectivity and lack of bias and (2) *independence in appearance* depends on whether a reasonable investor, with knowledge of all relevant facts and circumstances, can conclude that the auditor is not capable of exercising objective and impartial judgment. Hence, an auditor's independence depends on auditors both having the proper mental state and passing the appearance test.

In a preface to the rule, the SEC stated four principles for determining whether a public accounting firm is independent of an audit client, factors the SEC will first consider when making independence determinations in controversial cases. Auditors are *not* independent if they have a relationship that

- Creates a mutual or conflicting interest between the public accounting firm and the audit client.
- Places the public accounting firm in the position of auditing its own work.
- Results in the public accounting firm personnel acting as management or employees of the audit client.
- Places the public accounting firm in a position of being an advocate for the audit client.

The SEC independence rules relating to financial relationships are very similar to the AICPA Code of Professional Conduct Rule 101 Interpretations explained earlier. The most significant categories addressed by the SEC rules are in the areas of financial and employment relationships, nonaudit services (e.g., taxation, consulting), and disclosure of fees.

Nonaudit Services

The SEC is very concerned about the fact and appearance of independence when public accounting firms perform consulting services for audit clients. A major issue in the Enron case was that more than half of the fee it paid to Arthur Andersen was for consulting services. This fact exacerbated the concern that auditors would allow a client's improper financial reporting for the sake of preserving lucrative fees from other services. The SEC's concern in this regard is controversial, but the PCAOB has reinforced it. The SEC and PCAOB independence rules prohibit or place restrictions on the following types of nonaudit services provided to *audit* clients:

- Bookkeeping or other services related to the audit client's accounting records or financial statements (including maintaining or preparing the accounting records, preparing the financial statements, or preparing or originating source data underlying the financial statements *except* in emergency situations).
- Financial information systems design and implementation (including operating or supervising the client's information system, designing or implementing a hardware or software system that generates information that is significant to the client's financial statements *unless* the audit client's management takes full and complete responsibility for all design, implementation, internal control, and management decisions about the hardware and software).
- Appraisal or valuation services or fairness opinions (including any such services material to the financial statements when the auditor might audit the results of the public accounting firm's own work, *but* the public accounting firm's valuation experts may audit actuarial calculations, perform tax-oriented valuations, and perform nonfinancial valuations for audit clients).
- Actuarial services (including determination of actuarial liabilities *unless* the audit client management first uses its own actuaries and accepts responsibility for significant actuarial methods and assumptions).
- Internal audit services (including those related to the client's internal accounting controls, financial systems, or financial statements).
- Management functions (including acting temporarily or permanently as a director, officer, or employee of an audit client, or performing any decision-making, supervisory, or ongoing monitoring function for the audit client).
- Human resources (including all aspects of executive search activities, reference checking, status and compensation determination, and hiring advice).
- Broker–dealer services (including acting as a broker–dealer, promoter, or underwriter on behalf of an audit client; making investment decisions or otherwise having discretionary authority over investments; executing a transaction to buy or sell investments; or having custody of assets).
- Legal services (including any service under circumstances in which the person providing the service must be admitted to practice before the courts of a U.S. jurisdiction).
- Expert services (including providing expert opinions or other services to an audit client or legal representative of an audit client for the purpose of advocating the audit client's interests in litigation, regulatory, or administrative investigations or proceedings; the auditor may perform internal investigations at the direction of the audit committee or its legal counsel).
- Any service performed for an audit client where the auditor is paid a contingent fee or commission.
- Tax services that are based on judicial proceedings or aggressive interpretations of tax law.
- Planning or opining on the tax consequence of a transaction.
- Tax services for key company executives.

The PCAOB's Rule 3526 (*Communication with Audit Committees Concerning Independence*) requires public accounting firms to discuss any independence issues with the audit committee (or those charged with governance) *prior* to accepting an initial engagement. This discussion must be documented (usually in the engagement administrative file workpapers).

AUDITING INSIGHT — EY, PeopleSoft, and a Loss of Independence

An administrative law judge recommended that **Ernst & Young** (EY) pay the government $1.7 million and be barred from taking new auditing clients for six months for violating SEC conflict-of-interest regulations involving a joint marketing agreement with **PeopleSoft**, a former audit client. The judge found that EY had "engaged in improper professional conduct because it violated applicable professional standards for auditors by conduct that was both reckless and negligent." Furthermore, the Big Four firm had displayed "an utter disdain for

the commission's rules and regulations of auditor independence." Although no wrongdoing was alleged in its auditing of the software company, the joint marketing agreement violated SEC rules against having anything more than a "consumer" relationship with audit clients. The firm sold its consulting arm that created the conflict of interest.

Source: "Ernst & Young Hit Hard in PeopleSoft Case," April 16, 2004, available at www.thestreet.com.

Disclosures about Fees

The SEC believes that investors who use financial statements and auditors' reports can be enlightened with information about auditors' fee arrangements with clients. Hence, SEC rules require that companies (not auditors) disclose the following in proxy statements delivered to their shareholders:

- Total audit fees paid to the public accounting firm for the annual audit and the reviews of quarterly financial information.
- Total fees paid to the public accounting firm for tax and other advisory work (over and above the audit fees).
- Whether the audit committee or the board of directors considered the public accounting firm's advisory work to be compatible with maintaining the auditor's independence.
- The percentage of the audit hours performed by persons other than the principal auditor's full-time, permanent employees, if greater than 50% of the total audit hours. (This disclosure refers to "leased employees" in an "alternative practice structure" arrangement.)

Other Effects of Sarbanes–Oxley on Auditor Independence

Sarbanes–Oxley required the SEC to modify its position on auditor independence in several ways. Perhaps the most important change in independence arises from the changing role of the audit committee. Since the inception of the principle of the independence for auditors, it has been the auditor who was responsible for evaluating and determining the independence of the individual and firm. Auditors still must be vigilant in establishing and monitoring independence policy to ensure that they are in fact independent, but Sarbanes–Oxley has placed the responsibility for the determination of independence in appearance at the door of the audit committee. This is particularly evident by the fact that the audit committee bears the responsibility for determining the scope of services provided by the auditor and reviewing independence issues prior to the appointment of the auditor. The audit committee may do this on a case-by-case basis or may establish a set of policies and procedures that establish acceptable and unacceptable services.

In addition, Sarbanes–Oxley limits the engagement partners and concurring audit partners on an engagement to five-year terms. Other partners associated with the engagement are limited to seven-year terms with that client. Partners also are deemed as not independent if they receive compensation that is based on selling services to an audit client other than audits, reviews, or attestations.

In the past, it was not unusual for a member of an audit team, usually a manager or higher, to leave the public accounting firm to take a financial management position with a client. Under the rules established by Sarbanes–Oxley, a public accounting firm cannot perform an audit of a company in which an individual with financial reporting oversight responsibilities was a member of the audit engagement team for the audit period, up to the audit date.

Government Accountability Office (GAO) Independence Requirements

Many state agencies and local municipalities use public accounting firms to perform audits required by government charters, laws, or contractual obligations (usually as part of a grant). During these audits, the public accounting firm is required to follow all GAO standards included in the Government Auditing Standards manual (also called the *Yellow Book;* see Module D). These standards require the auditor to be independent with respect to the government entity. These standards differ from the SEC, AICPA, and Sarbanes–Oxley requirements in the following ways. Nonaudit services are allowed providing that the audit organization does not perform management functions, make management decisions, or audit its own work. However, the audit organization must employ the following safeguards:

1. Personnel who provide nonaudit services are prohibited from planning, conducting, or reviewing audit work related to the nonaudit services.
2. The audit organization may not reduce the scope or extent of work performed on the audit because a member of the firm performed the nonaudit work. The extent of the audit work may be reduced by an amount consistent with a reduction had the nonaudit been performed by another public accounting firm.
3. The audit organization must document its reasons that the nonaudit services do not affect the firm's independence.
4. The audit organization must document an understanding with the client regarding the objectives, scope, and work product for the nonaudit service.
5. The audit organization must have established policies and procedures to ensure that effects of nonaudit services on the present and future audits are considered.
6. The audit organization must communicate to the government entity any situation in which the nonaudit service would prohibit it from performing the audit.
7. When subjected to a peer review, the audit organization must identify all nonaudit services provided to the audited entity.

✅ REVIEW CHECKPOINTS

B.7 Yolanda is the executive in charge of the Santa Fe office of Best & Co, an international public accounting firm. She is responsible for the practice in all areas of audit, tax, and consulting, but she does not serve as a field audit partner or a reviewer. Javier is the partner in charge of the Besame Inc. audit (an SEC filing). Is Best & Co independent if (a) Yolanda owns common stock of Besame or (b) her brother owns 10 shares of the common stock of Besame?

B.8 Can audit managers on the audit engagement team, who are also attorneys admitted to the state bar, assist in the defense of a lawsuit against an audit client for product liability defects?

B.9 Why do you think the SEC requires companies to disclose fees paid to independent accounting firms for audit and consulting services? What must be disclosed?

B.10 What do the SEC disclosure rules and PCAOB Rule 3526 have in common with auditors' relations with an audit client's board of directors and its audit committee?

B.11 Given what you have learned about independence, do you believe that there would be a perceived independence problem concerning members of an audit engagement team entertaining employment offers from audit clients? Why or why not?

AICPA RULES OF CONDUCT: INTEGRITY AND OBJECTIVITY, RESPONSIBILITIES TO CLIENTS, AND OTHER RESPONSIBILITIES

LO B-5

With reference to AICPA rules on topics other than independence, analyze factual situations and decide whether an accountant's conduct does or does not conform to the AICPA Code of Professional Conduct.

Now that we have discussed the Independence Rule, we can turn to the other AICPA rules of conduct.

Integrity and Objectivity Rule

In the performance of any professional service, a member shall maintain objectivity and integrity, shall be free of conflicts of interest, and shall not knowingly misrepresent facts or subordinate his or her judgment to others. (1.100.001 and 2.100.001)

The Integrity and Objectivity Rule applies not only to CPAs in public practice but also to CPAs working in business. (Santos, the staff accountant in the decision process illustration in Ethical Example 2, is a business CPA.) The rule requires integrity and objectivity in all types of professional work—tax practice and consulting practice as well as audit practice for public accountants—and all types of accounting work performed by CPAs employed in corporations, not-for-profit organizations, governments, and individual practices. In addition to integrity and objectivity, this rule emphasizes (1) being free from conflicts of interest between CPAs and others, (2) representing facts truthfully in reports and discussions, and (3) not letting other people dictate or influence the CPA's judgment and professional decisions.

Conflicts of interest refer to the need to avoid having business interests in which the accountant's personal financial relationships or the accountant's relationships with other clients might tempt the accountant to fail to serve the best interests of a client or the public. Some examples of conflicts of interest are those in which the CPA:

- Is engaged to perform litigation support services for a plaintiff in a lawsuit filed against a client.
- Recommends that a client makes an investment in a business in which the CPA has a financial interest.
- Performs management consulting for a client and has a financial or managerial interest in a major competitor.

The phrases "shall not knowingly misrepresent facts" and "shall not subordinate his or her judgment to others" emphasize conditions people ordinarily identify with the concepts of integrity and objectivity. Accountants who know about a client's fraudulent tax return, about false journal entries, about material misrepresentations in financial statements, and yet do nothing have violated both the spirit and the letter of the Integrity and Objectivity Rule.

The prohibition of misrepresentations in financial statements applies to the management accountants who prepare companies' statements. Business CPAs should not subordinate their professional judgment to superiors who try to produce materially misleading financial statements and fool their external auditors. They must be candid and not knowingly misrepresent facts or fail to disclose material facts when dealing with their employer's external auditor. They also cannot have conflicts of interest in their jobs and their outside business interests that are not disclosed to their employers and approved. The importance of integrity and objectivity for business CPAs cannot be overemphasized. Too often, CPAs relate the Code of Professional Conduct only to CPAs in public practice. In fact, one of the objectives of the recodification of the AICPA Code of Conduct is to emphasize the importance of business CPAs adhering to ethics rules that relate to them.

The Integrity and Objectivity Rule has two other applications. One concerns serving as a client advocate, which occurs frequently in taxation and rate regulation practice as well as in supporting clients' positions in FASB and SEC proceedings. Client advocacy in support or advancement of client positions is acceptable only so long as the member acts with integrity, maintains objectivity, and does not subordinate judgment to others. (Accountants-as-advocates do not adopt the same attitude as defense attorneys in a courtroom.) The other application is directed specifically to your college professors: They are supposed to maintain integrity and objectivity, be free of conflicts of interest, and not knowingly misrepresent facts to students.

General Standards Rule

A member shall comply with the following standards and with any interpretations thereof by bodies designated by Council:

A. *Professional competence.* Undertake only those professional services that the member or the member's firm can reasonably expect to be completed with professional competence.

B. *Due professional care.* Exercise due care in the performance of professional services.

C. *Planning and supervision.* Adequately plan and supervise the performance of professional services.

D. *Sufficient relevant data.* Obtain sufficient relevant data to afford a reasonable basis for conclusions or recommendations in relation to any professional services performed. (1.300.001 and 2.300.001)

The General Standards Rule is a comprehensive statement of general standards that accountants are expected to observe in all areas of practice. This is the rule that enforces the various series of professional standards. The AICPA Council has authorized the following agencies, boards, and committees to issue enforceable standards under this rule:

- Public Company Accounting Oversight Board (PCAOB).
- Auditing Standards Board.
- Accounting and Review Services Committee.
- Tax Executive Committee.
- Management Consulting Services Executive Committee.

The General Standards Rule effectively prohibits the acceptance of any engagement that the CPA cannot competently complete. Such engagements may involve audits that require specialized industry knowledge or technical expertise the practitioner does not possess. Practitioners are allowed to accept an engagement if, through education, hiring of additional staff, or contracting with auditors' specialists, the practitioners can obtain the required knowledge *prior to the conclusion* of the engagement. As a result, a practitioner can accept an engagement for which he or she does not possess knowledge as long as this knowledge can be obtained prior to the conclusion of the engagement. This rule covers all areas of public accounting practice except personal financial planning and business valuation. Of course, a CPA may have to do some research to learn more about a unique problem or technique and may need to engage a colleague as a consultant.

Compliance with Standards Rule

> A member who performs auditing, review, compilation, management consulting, tax, or other professional services shall comply with standards promulgated by bodies designated by Council. (1.310.001 and 2.31.001)

The Compliance with Standards Rule requires adherence to duly promulgated technical standards in all areas of professional service. These areas include the ones cited in the rule: auditing, review and compilation (unaudited financial statements), consulting, tax, or "other" professional services. The "bodies designated by Council" are the Auditing Standards Board, the Accounting and Review Services Committee, the Tax Executive Committee, and the Consulting Services Executive Committee. The practical effect of this rule is to make noncompliance with technical standards (in addition to the general standards) subject to disciplinary proceedings. Therefore, failure to follow auditing standards, accounting and review standards, tax standards, and consulting standards is a violation of the Compliance with Standards Rule.

Accounting Principles Rule

> A member shall not (1) express an opinion or state affirmatively that the financial statements or other financial data of any entity are presented in conformity with generally accepted accounting principles or (2) state that he or she is not aware of any material modifications that should be made to such statements or data in order for them to be in conformity with generally accepted accounting principles, if such statements or data contain any departure from an accounting principle promulgated by bodies designated by Council to establish such principles that has a material effect on the statements or data taken as a whole. If, however, the statements or data contain such a departure and the member can demonstrate that due to unusual circumstances the financial statements or data would otherwise have been misleading, the member can comply with the rule by describing the departure, its approximate effects, if practicable, and the reasons why compliance with the principle would result in a misleading statement. (1.320.001 and 2.320.001)

The AICPA Council has designated three rule-making bodies to pronounce accounting principles under the Accounting Principles Rule. The Financial Accounting Standards Board (FASB) is designated to pronounce standards in general, the Governmental Accounting Standards Board (GASB) has the responsibility to pronounce accounting standards for state and local government entities, and the Federal Accounting Standards Advisory Board (FASAB) is charged with respect to statements of federal accounting standards.

The Accounting Principles Rule requires adherence to official pronouncements unless such adherence would be misleading. The consequences of misleading statements to outside decision makers would be financial harm, so presumably the greater good would be realized by explaining a departure and thereby "breaking the rule of officially promulgated accounting principles." Such an instance occurs in very rare situations, and the burden of proving that following pronouncements would be misleading is the responsibility of the auditor.

CPAs in business also can be subject to the Accounting Principles Rule. These accountants produce and certify financial statements and sign written management representation letters for their external auditors. They also present financial statements to regulatory authorities and creditors. Business accountants generally "report" that the company's financial statements conform to GAAP, and this report is taken as an expression of opinion (or negative assurance) of the type governed by the Accounting Principles Rule. The result is that accountants who present financial statements containing any undisclosed departures from official pronouncements face disciplinary action for violating the rule.

Confidential Client Information Rule

> A member in public practice shall not disclose any confidential information without the specific consent of the client. (1.700.001)

Confidential information is any information that is not available to the public (or in the public domain). As Scott London in this module's opening vignette was well aware, such information should not be disclosed to outside parties unless demanded by a court or an administrative body having subpoena or summons power. *Privileged information* is information that cannot even be demanded by a court. Common-law privilege exists for husband–wife and attorney–client relationships. While physician–patient and priest–penitent relationships have obtained the privilege through state statutes, no accountant–client privilege exists under federal law, and no state-created privilege has been recognized in federal courts. In all recognized privilege relationships, the professional person is obligated to observe the privilege, which can be waived only by the client, patient, or penitent. (These persons are said to be the *holders of the privilege.*)

The rules of privileged and confidential communication are based on the belief that they facilitate a free flow of information between parties to the relationship. The nature of accounting services makes it necessary for the accountant to have access to information about salaries, products, contracts, merger or divestment plans, tax matters, and other information required for the best possible professional work. Managers would be less likely to reveal such information if they could not trust the accountant to keep it confidential. If accountants were to reveal such information, the resulting reduction of the information flow might be undesirable, so no accountant should break the confidentiality rule without a good reason.

AUDITING INSIGHT Spies, Lies, and Client Confidentiality

What would you do if a government intelligence agent approached you to assist him in a "top secret" assignment involving national security? Guy Enright, an accountant with KPMG's Financial Advisory Services Ltd. in Bermuda, said "yes" to Nick Hamilton, a British intelligence officer, and agreed to deposit confidential audit documents in plastic containers at "dead drop" sites located throughout Bermuda. Unfortunately for Enright, KPMG, and its client, **IPOC International Growth Fund Ltd.** (IPOC), "Nick Hamilton" was in fact Nick Day, a cofounder of **Diligence Inc.**, a Washington-based private intelligence firm that was gathering information for one of IPOC's business competitors.

The setup was quite elaborate. "Hamilton" required Enright to undergo a detailed background check, even producing an official-looking questionnaire with a British government seal at the top, before he could participate on "Project Yucca." The undercover mission came to an abrupt end when someone (still unknown) dropped off a package of Diligence business records and e-mails involving "Project Yucca" at KPMG's Montvale office. After KPMG sued, Diligence ended up paying $1.7 million.

Source: "Spies, Lies, and KPMG," www.businessweek.com, February 26, 2007.

Difficult problems arise over auditors' obligations to "blow the whistle" about clients' shady or illegal practices. For all practical purposes, information is not considered confidential if its disclosure is necessary to prevent financial statements from being misleading. If a client refuses to accept an auditors' report that has been modified because of the inability to obtain sufficient appropriate evidence about a suspected illegal act, failure to account for or disclose properly a material amount connected with an illegal act, or inability to estimate amounts involved in an illegal act, the public accounting firm should withdraw from the engagement and give the reasons in writing to the board of directors. In such an extreme case, the withdrawal amounts to whistleblowing, but the action results from the client's decision not to disclose the information.

Auditors are not, in general, legally *obligated* to blow the whistle on clients. However, circumstances in which auditors are legally *justified* in making disclosures to a regulatory agency or a third party may exist. Such circumstances include when (1) a client has intentionally and without authorization associated or involved a CPA in its misleading conduct (e.g., used the CPA's name on financial statements), (2) a client has distributed misleading draft financial statements prepared by a CPA for internal use only, or (3) a client prepares and distributes in an annual report or prospectus misleading information for which the CPA has not assumed any responsibility. In addition, the Private Securities Litigation Reform Act of 1995 imposed another reporting requirement in connection with clients' illegal acts (see Module C).

The Confidential Client Information Rule possibly provides accountants the most difficulties and may be the most violated procedure. First, in its strictest interpretation, the principle of confidentiality applies to the communication of information to anyone who is not involved in the audit except as noted by the rule. Over lunch or after hours, however, you might find auditors discussing the day's work with other members of the firm or company. Second, CPAs should not view the Confidential Client Information Rule as an excuse for inaction when action may be appropriate to right a wrongful act committed or about to be committed by a client. In some cases, auditors' inaction may be viewed as part of a conspiracy or willingness to be an accessory to a wrong. A useful initial course of action is to consult an attorney about possible legal pitfalls of both whistleblowing and silence.

Accountants can permit other accountants to review confidential audit documentation and other information about clients in connection with arrangements to sell or merge an accounting practice. The AICPA advises accountants to have an agreement among themselves that extends the confidentiality safeguard to the prospective purchasing accountant as it existed with the original accountant.

CPAs also may disclose confidential information without the client's permission to remain in compliance with applicable laws (e.g., responding to a subpoena), as part of an ethics investigation (*of a CPA*), or as part of a peer review or PCAOB investigation of *public accounting firm* practices. The exception related to ethics violations applies only to investigative or disciplinary bodies under the AICPA's jurisdiction, namely the AICPA Professional Ethics Division, the ethics enforcement committees in the various state societies of CPAs, and state boards of accountancy.

While the Client Confidential Information Rule specifically addresses CPA's responsibilities to clients, CPAs (both in public practice and in business) must also keep their employers' proprietary information confidential. Failure to do so would be a violation of the Acts Discreditable Rule, discussed later in this module.

AUDITING INSIGHT — Crimes of the Heart?

An Ernst & Young partner was convicted of six counts of securities fraud related to insider trading arising from a relationship that began on an extramarital dating website. The principal witness against the partner was a woman who had befriended him online, and through a guessing game they played from their respective offices, guessed the impending mergers he was working on. She then traded 18 times on the insider information, netting approximately $400,000 on the transactions. Her trading was funded by another man she met on the same website. Her suspicious trading just before the mergers were announced caused her name to repeatedly appear on SEC watch lists. When confronted, she cut a deal, pleading guilty to 15 counts of securities fraud and agreeing to testify against the E&Y partner who apparently was unaware of the insider trading scheme and did not make a cent off the trades.

Source: "Insider Affair: An SEC Trial of the Heart," *The Wall Street Journal,* July 28, 2009, p. C1.

Fees and Other Types of Remuneration

Contingent Fees

A member in public practice shall not:

(1) Perform for a contingent fee any professional services for, or receive such a fee from, a client for whom the member or the member's firm performs:

(a) an audit or review of a financial statement; or

(b) a compilation of a financial statement when the member expects, or reasonably might expect, that a third party will use the financial statement and the member's compilation report does not disclose a lack of independence; or

(c) an examination of prospective financial information; or

(2) Prepare an original or amended tax return or claim for a tax refund for a contingent fee for any client. (1.510.001)

Suppose you are a shareholder in New Medical Corporation. You have some concerns about the company's revenue practices, but the fact that New Medical received an unmodified audit opinion reassures you. Now let's assume that you discover that the New Medical contract with its auditor paid the auditor more for an unmodified opinion than a qualified opinion. How might that affect the value you placed on the auditor's report?

A **contingent fee** is a fee established for the performance of any service in an arrangement in which no fee will be charged unless a specific finding or result is attained or the fee otherwise depends on the result of the service. (Fees are not contingent if they are fixed by a court or other public authority or, in tax matters, determined as a result of the findings of judicial proceedings or the findings of government agencies; nor are fees contingent when they are based on the complexity or time required for the work.) CPAs can charge contingent fees for work such as representing a client in an IRS tax audit and certain other tax matters, achieving goals in a consulting service engagement, or helping a person obtain a bank loan in a financial planning engagement. However, the PCAOB has issued an independence rule that prohibits all contingent fees for audit clients of registered public accounting firms. CPAs are allowed to receive contingent fees *except* from clients for whom the CPAs perform attest services when users of financial information may be relying on the CPAs' work. The prohibitions in items 1(a), 1(b), and 1(c) all refer to attest engagements in which independence is required. Acceptance of contingent fee arrangements during the period in which the member or the member's firm is engaged to perform any of these attestations or during the period covered by any historical financial statements involved in any of these engagements is considered an impairment of independence.

Contingent fees are also prohibited in connection with the everyday tax practice of preparing original or amended tax returns. This prohibition arose from an interesting conflict of government agencies. The Federal Trade Commission (FTC) wanted to see contingent fees permitted, but the IRS objected on the grounds that such fees might induce accountants and clients to "play the audit lottery"—understate tax improperly in the hope of escaping audit. The IRS asserted that if the AICPA permitted such contingent fees, the IRS would make its own rules prohibiting them. The FTC agreed that the AICPA rule could contain this prohibition.

Commissions and Referral Fees

A. Prohibited Commissions
A member in public practice shall not recommend or refer to a client any product or service for a commission, or recommend or refer any product or service to be supplied by a client for a commission, or receive a commission, when the member or the member's firm also performs for that client:
(a) an audit or review of a financial statement; or
(b) a compilation of a financial statement when the member expects, or reasonably might expect, that a third party will use the financial statement and the member's compilation report does not disclose a lack of independence; or
(c) an examination of prospective financial information.

This prohibition applies during the period in which the member is engaged to perform any of the services listed above and the period covered by any historical financial statements involved in such listed services.

B. Disclosure of Permitted Commission
A member in public practice who is not prohibited by this rule from performing services for, or receiving a commission from, and who is paid or expects to be paid a commission, shall disclose that fact to any person or entity to whom the member recommends or refers a product or service to which the commission relates.

C. Referral Fees
Any member who accepts a referral fee for recommending or referring any service of a CPA to any person or entity or who pays a referral fee to obtain a client shall disclose such acceptance or payment to the client. (1.520.001)

A **commission** is generally defined as a percentage-based fee charged for professional services in connection with executing a transaction or performing some other business activity. Examples are insurance sales commissions, real estate sales commissions, and securities sales commissions. A CPA can earn commissions except in connection with any client for whom the CPA performs attestation services.

Commissions are an impairment of independence similar to contingent fees. Recall that *contingent fees* are based on attaining a specific finding or result and are prohibited for attestation clients. When involved in an attest engagement with a client, the CPA cannot receive a commission from anyone for (1) referring a product or service to the client or (2) referring to someone else a product or service supplied by the client. It does not matter which party actually pays the commission.

Commissions are permitted provided that the engagement *does not involve attestation* of the types cited in part A of the rule. This permission is tempered by the requirement that the CPA must disclose to clients an arrangement to receive a commission.

Most of the commission fee activity takes place in connection with personal financial planning services. CPAs often recommend insurance and investments to individuals and families. Some critics point out that clients cannot always trust commission agents (e.g., insurance salespersons, securities brokers) to have clients' best interests in mind when the agents' own compensation depends on clients' buying the product that produces commissions.

Referral fees are fees (1) a CPA receives for recommending another CPA's services or (2) a CPA pays to obtain a client. Referral involves the practice of sending business to another CPA and paying other CPAs or outside agencies for drumming up business. Some CPAs have hired services that solicit clients on their behalf, paying a fixed or percentage fee. Many CPAs frown on these arrangements, but they are permitted. However, CPAs must disclose such fees to clients.

Acts Discreditable Rule

> A member shall not commit an act discreditable to the profession. (1.400.001, 2.400.001, and 3.400.001)

The Acts Discreditable Rule may be called the *moral clause* of the code, but it is only occasionally the basis for disciplinary action. Penalties normally are invoked automatically under the AICPA bylaws, which provide for expulsion of members found by a court to have committed any fraud, filed false tax returns, been convicted of any criminal offense, or found by the AICPA Trial Board to have been guilty of an act discreditable to the profession.

AICPA interpretations have determined the following to be discreditable acts:

- Withholding a client's books and records and important documentation when the client has requested his or her return.
- Being found guilty by a court or administrative agency as having violated employment antidiscrimination laws, including ones related to sexual and other forms of harassment.
- Failing to follow government audit standards and guides in governmental audits when the client or the government agency expects such standards to be followed.
- Failure to follow the requirements of governmental bodies, commissions, or other regulatory bodies including the PCAOB.
- Soliciting or disclosing CPA Examination questions and answers from the CPA Examination.
- Failing to file tax returns or remit payroll and other taxes collected for others (e.g., employee taxes withheld).
- Making, or permitting others to make, false and misleading entries in records and financial statements.

This last item is specifically applicable to all CPAs, whether in public practice, in business, between jobs, or in retirement. Any management accountant who participates in the production of false and misleading financial statements commits a discreditable act.

AUDITING INSIGHT `Discreditable Act?

The Enforcement Committee found that Respondent drew a gun from his desk drawer during a dispute with a client in his office in contravention of Section 501.41 [discreditable acts prohibition] of the [Texas] Rules of Professional Conduct. Respondent agreed to accept a private reprimand to be printed . . . in the Texas State Board Report.

Source: Texas State Board of Accountancy Report.

Advertising and Other Forms of Solicitation Rule

> A member in public practice shall not seek to obtain clients by advertising or other forms of solicitation in a manner that is false, misleading, or deceptive. Solicitation by the use of coercion, overreaching, or harassing conduct is prohibited. (1.600.001)

Advertising consists of messages designed to attract business that are broadcast widely to an undifferentiated audience (e.g., print, radio, television, billboards). Advertising is permitted with only a few limitations. The current rule applies only to CPAs practicing public accounting and relates to their efforts to obtain clients. The guidelines basically prohibit false, misleading, and deceptive messages:

- Advertising may not create false or unjustified expectations of favorable results.
- Advertising may not imply the ability to influence any court, tribunal, regulatory agency, or similar body or official.
- Advertising may not contain a fee estimate when the CPA knows it is likely to be substantially increased unless the client is notified.
- Advertising may not contain any other representation likely to cause a reasonable person to misunderstand or be deceived.

Most CPAs carry out only modest advertising efforts, and many do no advertising at all. Public practice is generally marked by decorum and a sense of good taste. However, there are exceptions, and they tend to get much negative attention from other CPAs and the public in general. The danger in bad advertising lies in creating the image of a professional huckster, which may backfire on efforts to build a practice.

Solicitation generally refers to direct contact (e.g., in person, mail, telephone) with a specific potential client. In regard to solicitation, Rule 502 basically prohibits extreme bad behavior (coercion, overreaching, or harassing conduct). Many CPAs abhor solicitation, and many state boards of accountancy try to prohibit direct, uninvited approaches to prospective clients, especially when the client already has a CPA. Nevertheless, the U.S. Supreme Court has struck down state solicitation prohibitions, declaring them to be an infringement of personal and business rights to free speech and due process.

AUDITING INSIGHT Felicity and Solicitations

CPA Fane moved to Florida and conducted face-to-face meetings to obtain clients. The Florida Board of Accountancy brought suit to enforce its antisolicitation rule but lost in a Supreme Court decision. As a result, some state boards try to discourage solicitation with restrictive rules they hope will not run afoul of the Supreme Court decision. Other state boards are trying to put antisolicitation rules into their state laws when they think they will be shielded from the U.S. Supreme Court. Currently, solicitation is legal, but be aware that your local state board may have rules or laws prohibiting it.

Source: *Edenfield v. Fane*, 507 U.S. 761 (1993).

CPAs sometimes hire marketing firms to obtain clients. The AICPA permits such arrangements but warns that all such "practice development" activity is subject to the Advertising and Other Forms of Solicitation Rule because members cannot do through others things what they are prohibited from doing themselves.

Form of Organization and Name Rule

A member may practice public accounting only in a form of organization permitted by law or regulation whose characteristics conform to resolutions of Council. A member shall not practice public accounting under a firm name that is misleading. Names of one or more past owners may be included in the firm name of a successor organization. A firm may not designate itself as "Member of the American Institute of Certified Public Accountants" unless all of its CPA owners are members of the Institute. (1.800.001)

The Form of Organization and Name Rule allows CPAs to practice public accounting in any form of organization permitted by a state board of accountancy and authorized by law. Organization forms include sole proprietorship, partnership, limited partnership, limited liability partnership (LLP), professional corporation (PC), limited liability corporation (LLC), and ordinary corporation (Inc.). You may have noticed that the large international accounting firms now place LLP after their firm names. Many small accounting firms include PC in their names.

CPAs in public practice cannot use misleading firm names. For example, suppose CPAs Stone and Thompson, who are not in partnership, agree to share expenses for office support, advertising, and continuing education. They cannot put up a sign that states "Stone & Thompson CPAs" because this name suggests a partnership where there is none.

A member who practices public accounting also can participate in the operation of another business organization (e.g., a consulting or tax preparation firm) that offers professional services of the types offered by public accounting firms. If this business is permitted to practice public accounting under state law, the member also is considered to be in the practice of public accounting in it and must observe all rules of conduct. CPAs who work in alternative practice structures occupy an odd position. They can prepare compiled (unaudited) financial statements, which is considered a form of public accounting practice. In such a case, CPA employees of the alternative practice structure (e.g., "PublicCo") must take final responsibility for the accountants' compilation report and must sign it with their own personal names (not the name of PublicCo).

The last paragraph of the Form of Organization and Name Rule permits a mixed accounting organization consisting of CPA and non-CPA owners to designate itself "Members of the AICPA" if all of the CPA owners are actually AICPA members. However, the AICPA Council limits this privilege of organizational form by expressing certain requirements for ownership and control, especially regarding non-CPAs who have ownership interests in an organization that practices public accounting. (See the Council Resolution provisions in the feature "Council Resolution: Form of Organization and Name." The purpose of the Council Resolution is to conform the operations of an accounting organization as closely as possible to the traditional accounting firm and to ensure control of professional services in the hands of CPAs.)

Council Resolution: Form of Organization and Name

(EXCERPTS)

The characteristics of an accounting organization under the Form of Organization and Name Rule are as follows:

- A majority (50 percent or more) ownership and voting rights must belong to CPAs.
- Non-CPA owners must be active in the firm, not passive investors.
- A CPA must have ultimate responsibility for the firm's services.
- Non-CPA owners can use titles such as "principal, owner, officer, member, and shareholder" but cannot hold out to be a CPA.

- Non-CPA owners must abide by the AICPA Code of Professional Conduct.
- Non-CPA owners must hold a bachelor's degree, and after the year 2010, must have 150 semester hours of college education.
- Non-CPA owners must complete the same continuing education requirements as CPAs who are members of the AICPA.
- Non-CPA owners are not eligible to be members of the AICPA.

The International Ethics Standards Board for Accountants (IESBA) Code

The IESBA Code must be followed by auditors whenever an audit engagement is completed for a multinational client. As a result, the importance of the IESBA Code has increased dramatically in recent years. Although there are some differences between the IESBA Code and the AICPA Code of Ethics, the codes are quite similar. For example, each code is highly focused on the possible threats to auditor independence, and each code provides many safeguards to mitigate these threats. However, there are differences in the way that these threats and safeguards are described.[13] Given the increased importance of the international standards, the AICPA revised its Code of Conduct to better align ("converge") the two codes.

✔ REVIEW CHECKPOINTS

B.12 What ethical responsibilities do members of the AICPA have for acts of nonmembers who are under their supervision (e.g., recent college graduates who are not yet CPAs)?

B.13 What rules of conduct apply specifically to members in government and industry?

B.14 What provisions of the AICPA Council Resolution on form of organization place control of accounting services in the hands of CPAs?

B.15 What is the primary difference between commissions and referrals?

CONSEQUENCES OF VIOLATING THE CODE OF PROFESSIONAL CONDUCT

LO B-6
Explain the types of penalties that can be imposed on accountants.

Public accounting firms and responsible professional accountants understand the importance of ethics to the profession and seek to ensure that the organization and all employees are acting in an ethical manner. Unethical behavior by an auditor can have financial implications (e.g., fines, lawsuits) and reputation implications that may be difficult to remedy. Quality control practices and disciplinary proceedings provide the mechanisms of *self-regulation*. **Self-regulation** refers to the quality control reviews and disciplinary actions conducted by fellow CPAs—professional peers.

Self-Regulatory Discipline

Individual persons (not accounting firms) are subject to the rules of conduct of state CPA societies and the AICPA only if they choose to join these organizations. The AICPA and most of the state societies have entered into a Joint Ethics Enforcement Program through which the AICPA can refer complaints against CPAs to state societies or state societies can refer them to the AICPA. Both organizations have ethics committees to hear complaints. They can (1) acquit an accused CPA, (2) find the CPA in violation of rules and issue a letter of required corrective action, or (3) refer serious cases to an AICPA trial board. The letter of required corrective action ordinarily admonishes the CPA and requires specific continuing education courses to bring the CPA up to date in technical areas.

The trial board panel has the power to (1) acquit the CPA, (2) admonish the CPA, (3) suspend the CPA's membership in the state society and the AICPA for up to two years, or (4) expel the CPA from the state society and the AICPA. The AICPA bylaws (not the Code of Professional Conduct) provide for automatic expulsion of CPAs judged to have committed a felony, failed to file their tax returns, or aided in the preparation of a

[13]For a summary of the specific differences between the IESBA and the AICPA codes, please consult C. Allen, "Comparing the Ethics Codes: AICPA and IFAC," *Journal of Accountancy,* October 2010, pp. 24–32.

AUDITING INSIGHT — The AICPA Joint Trial Board in Action

The following is the AICPA's report on cases investigated and their resolutions for 2014 and 2013 cases:

	2014	2013
Total cases at beginning of period (including 141 and 140, respectively, deferred due to pending litigation)	734	827
Cases opened during period	708	437
Cases completed during period	(530)	(530)
Total cases at end of period (including 133 and 141, respectively, deferred due to pending litigation)	912	734
Summary of Disposition of Completed Cases		
Expelled or suspended	113	90
Admonished	66	76
Corrective action required	113	167
No violation/dismissed	81	69
No further action	100	85
Subsequent monitoring completed satisfactorily	32	30
Other	25	13
	530	530

Source: AICPA website (www.aicpa.org).

false and fraudulent income tax return. The trial board panels are required to publish the names of the CPAs disciplined in their proceedings.

The expulsion penalty, while severe, does not prevent a CPA from continuing to practice accounting. Membership in the AICPA and state societies, while beneficial, is not required. However, a CPA must have a valid state license in order to practice. Most state boards of accountancy are the agencies that can suspend or revoke the license to practice.

Public Regulation Discipline

State boards of accountancy are government agencies consisting of CPA and non-CPA officeholders. In most states, the state board of accountancy issues licenses to practice accounting in their jurisdictions. Most state laws require a license to use the designation CPA or certified public accountant and limit the attest (audit) function to license holders only.

State boards have rules of conduct and trial board panels. They can admonish a license holder; perhaps more importantly, most can suspend or revoke the license to practice. Suspension and revocation are severe penalties because a person no longer can use the CPA title and cannot sign auditors' reports. When candidates have successfully passed the CPA examination and are ready to become CPAs, some state boards administer an ethics examination or require taking an ethics course intended to familiarize new CPAs with the state rules.

The SEC and the PCAOB also conduct public disciplinary actions. Their authority comes from their rules of practice, of which Rule 102(e) provides that the SEC can deny, temporarily or permanently, the privilege of practice before the SEC to any person found to have engaged in unethical or improper professional conduct. When conducting a "Rule 102(e) proceeding," the SEC acts in a quasi-judicial role as an administrative agency.

AUDITING INSIGHT — Be Audit You Can Be

The PCAOB instituted disciplinary proceedings against **Deloitte & Touche LLP** and a former Deloitte audit partner, James L. Fazio, CPA, for violations of the board's interim auditing standards in connection with the firm's 2003 audit for **Ligand Pharmaceuticals Incorporated.** Without admitting or denying the board's findings, Deloitte consented to an order imposing a $1 million civil penalty. In addition to the monetary fine, as described in the order, Deloitte has implemented changes to its system of quality control for identifying and addressing potential audit quality concerns regarding the performance and deployment of its audit partners. The order requires Deloitte to undertake certain documentation practices relating to these additional quality control policies and procedures. The firm also was censured. The PCAOB also sanctioned accountants with **BDO Seidman** and **Geisler & Oppenheimer** for failing to review the audit work of a junior member of the firm and then trying to cover up by backdating documents (including backdating initials and signatures) and independence violations, respectively.

Sources: "PCAOB Sanctions Three Auditors," *CFO.com*, December 18, 2007; "Ex-BDO Seidman Auditors Disciplined by PCAOB" *WebCPA*, December 18, 2007.

The SEC penalty bars an accountant from signing any documents filed by an SEC registered company. The penalty effectively stops the accountant's SEC practice. In a few severe cases, Rule 102(e) proceedings have resulted in settlements barring not only the individual accountant but also her or his accounting firm or certain of its practice offices from accepting new SEC clients for a period of time.

The PCAOB's Division of Enforcement and Investigations (DEI) handles disciplinary actions involving accountants (and their firms) who are engaged to audit public companies (also known as "issuers"). The DEI's role is to identify matters (often from tips) for further investigation, conduct an investigation, and recommend disciplinary proceedings (if considered necessary). Common investigations include violations of the PCAOB's *Auditing Standards,* independence violations, and failures to cooperate with inspections/investigations. If violations are found, the DEI makes recommendations for sanctions to the Board. The Board may decide to suspend or permanently bar an accountant from auditing any public companies, suspend or revoke an accounting firm's registration, appoint a monitor to oversee a firm's practice, impose monetary penalties, require additional continuing professional education, or impose other sanctions permitted under PCAOB rules.

AUDITING INSIGHT — What Do Other Countries Do?

Different countries have different penalties for accountants caught not honoring the public trust. In China, the *death sentences* for Zhou Limin, the former head of the China Construction Bank, and Liu Yibing, an accountant, were upheld by China's State Supreme Court. The pair was found guilty of stealing more than $60 million by offering fake accounts with high interest rates.

Source: "Accountant Gets Death Penalty," *CFO.com*, December 14, 2006.

☑ REVIEW CHECKPOINTS

B.16 What penalties can be imposed by the AICPA and the state societies on CPAs in their "self-regulation" of ethics code violators?

B.17 What penalties can the SEC and PCAOB impose on CPAs who violate rules of conduct?

Summary

This module begins with philosophers' considerations of moral philosophy, explains the AICPA Code of Professional Conduct as well as the SEC and PCAOB rules related to auditors' independence, provides an overview of the IESBA Code of Ethics, and ends with a review of enforcement actions against those CPAs who choose not to follow the rules. It is important to remember that accounting is the only business discipline that is considered a profession as are medicine and the law. As a result, professional ethics for accountants is not simply a matter covered by a few rules in a formal code of professional conduct. Concepts of proper professional conduct permeate all areas of practice. Ethics and accompanying sanctions for ethical failures provide the foundation for public accountants' value in the marketplace.

The spirit of the AICPA Code of Professional Conduct is that, although independence is required for audit and attest services, integrity and objectivity are required in connection with all professional services. In this context, integrity and objectivity are the larger concepts and "independence" is a special condition largely defined by the matters of appearance specified in the interpretations of the Independence Rule. The ethics rules may appear to be restrictive, but they are intended to benefit the public, protect the profession, and allow for sanctions to those CPAs choosing not to comply with the rules. The AICPA Code of Professional Conduct was recently reorganized to address situations faced by accountants in varying business environments; the following graphic illustrates how the different rules affect the varying roles that accountants play, whether in public practice, in business, or in other situations (e.g., between jobs).

Applicability of the New AICPA Code of Ethics to CPAs

CPAs in Business
Integrity and Objectivity
General Standards
Compliance with Standards
Accounting Principles

CPAs in Public Pratice
Independence
Fees and Other Types of Remuneration
Advertising and Other Forms of Solicitation
Confidential Information
Form of Organization and Name

All CPAs
(including those unemployed and retired)
Acts Discreditable

Specific rules in the AICPA Code of Professional Conduct may not necessarily be classified under one of the ethics principles. Decisions based on a rule may involve imperative, utilitarian, or personal virtue considerations, or elements of all three. The rules have the form of imperatives because that is the nature of a code. However, elements of utilitarianism and generalization seem to be apparent in the underlying rationale for most of the rules. If this perception is accurate, auditors may use these two principles in difficult decision problems for which adherence to a rule could produce an undesirable result. Your knowledge of philosophical principles in ethics—the imperative, utilitarian, and virtue theories—will help you make decisions about the AICPA, SEC, and PCAOB rules. This structured approach to thoughtful decisions is important not only when you are employed in public accounting but also when you work in government, industry, and education.

Public accountants must be careful in all areas of practice. As an accountant, you must not lose sight of the nonaccountants' perspective. No matter how complex or technical a decision may be, a simplified view of it always tends to cut away the details of special technical issues to get directly to the heart of the matter. A sense of professionalism coupled with sensitivity to the effect of decisions on other people is invaluable in the practice of accounting and auditing. Remember that when you face an ethical dilemma, you are not alone. The AICPA, other professional organizations, and most accounting firms have anonymous hotlines for you to ask questions, and you always have your colleagues, friends, and family members to talk to.

Key Terms

act-utilitarianism: The emphasis on an individual act as it is affected by the specific circumstances of a situation.

categorical imperative: Kant's specification of an unconditional obligation to act as one thinks others should act regardless of circumstances.

commission: A percentage fee charged for professional services in connection with executing a transaction or performing some other business activity.

contingent fee: A type of compensation established for the performance of any service in an arrangement in which no amount will be charged unless a specific finding or result is attained or the fee otherwise depends on the result.

covered member: Broadly defined, any individual who might be in a position to compromise the integrity of an audit. In the AICPA Code of Professional Conduct, the term is defined as any individual, among others, who is (1) on the audit engagement team, (2) in a position to influence the audit engagement, (3) a partner or manager of a nonaudit client service team, or (4) a partner from the local office of the public accounting firm.

generalization argument: A judicious combination of the imperative and utilitarian principles; to act as one thinks others should act in a similar circumstance.

independence: A mental attitude and the appearance that the auditor is not influenced by others in judgments and decisions.

referral fee: The (1) compensation that a CPA receives for recommending another CPA's services and (2) that a CPA pays to obtain a client; may or may not be based on a percentage of the amount of any transaction.

rule-utilitarianism: The emphasis on the centrality of rules for ethical behavior while still maintaining the criterion of the greatest universal good.

self-regulation: The quality control reviews and disciplinary actions conducted by fellow CPAs—professional peers.

virtue ethics: The focus on the role of one's character in the decision-making process.

Multiple-Choice Questions for Practice and Review

All applicable questions are available with *Connect.*

LO B-4

B.18 Auditors are interested in having independence in appearance because
a. They want to impress the public with their independence in fact.
b. They want the public at large to have confidence in the profession.
c. They need to comply with the fundamental principles of GAAS.
d. Audits should be planned and properly supervised.

LO B-4

B.19 Under Sarbanes–Oxley and PCAOB rules, ensuring that the auditor is independent in appearance is the responsibility of
a. The public accounting firm.
b. Senior management.
c. The audit committee.
d. The PCAOB.

LO B-2

B.20 If a public accounting firm says it always follows the rule that requires adherence to FASB pronouncements in order to give a standard unmodified auditors' report, it is following a philosophy characterized by
a. The imperative principle.
b. The utilitarian principle.
c. Virtue ethics.
d. Reliance on members' collective conscience.

LO B-3

B.21 Which of the following agencies issues independence rules for the auditors of public companies?

a. Financial Accounting Standards Board (FASB).

b. Government Accountability Office (GAO).

c. Public Company Accounting Oversight Board (PCAOB)

d. AICPA Accounting and Review Services Committee (ARSC).

LO B-4

B.22 Audit independence in fact is most clearly lost when

a. A public accounting firm audits competitor companies in the same industry (e.g., Coca-Cola and Pepsi).

b. An auditor agrees to the argument made by the client's financial vice president that deferring losses on debt refinancing is in accordance with generally accepted accounting principles.

c. An audit team fails to discover the client's misleading omission of disclosure about permanent impairment of asset values.

d. A public accounting firm issues a standard unmodified report, but the reviewing partner fails to notice that the assistant's observation of inventory was woefully incomplete.

LO B-4

B.23 The audit committee's responsibility for auditor independence concerns

a. Ensuring that partners of the public accounting firm are not stockholders in the company.

b. Ensuring that nonaudit services provided by the auditor do not impair independence.

c. Reporting on auditor independence to the PCAOB.

d. Ensuring that all nonaudit services are provided by auditors who do not perform the financial statement audit.

LO B-5

B.24 AICPA members who work in industry and government must always uphold which *two* of the following AICPA rules of conduct?

a. The Independence Rule.

b. The Integrity and Objectivity Rule.

c. The Confidential Client Information Rule.

d. The Acts Discreditable Rule.

LO B-4

B.25 A public accounting firm's independence is not impaired when members of the audit engagement team does which of the following for a public company audit client?

a. Prepares special purchase orders for active plutonium in secure national defense installations.

b. Completes operational internal audit assignments under the directions of the client's director of internal auditing.

c. Prepares outsourced internal audit work on the client's financial accounting control monitoring.

d. Prepares actuarial assumptions used by the client's actuaries for life insurance actuarial liability determination.

e. All of the above would impair the public accounting firm's independence.

LO B-4

B.26 When a public accounting firm audits FUND-A in a mutual fund complex that has sister funds FUND-B and FUND-C, independence for the audit of FUND-A is *not* impaired when

a. Managerial-level professionals located in the office where the engagement audit partner is located but who are not on the engagement team own shares in FUND-B, which is not an audit client.

b. The wife of the FUND-A audit engagement partner owns shares in FUND-C (an audit client of another of the firm's offices), and these shares are held through the wife's employee benefit plan funded by her employer, the AllSteelFence Company.

c. Both (a) and (b).

d. Neither (a) nor (b).

LO B-4

B.27 Which of the following is considered a close relative (but not an immediate family member) as defined by the AICPA?

a. Spouse.

b. Spousal equivalent.

c. Parent.

d. Uncle.

LO B-5

B.28 Which of the following is true if an auditor performs nonaudit services for a government entity?

a. The scope of the audit must be reduced so that the auditor does not audit the area for which the nonaudit work was performed.

b. The auditor is prohibited from providing nonaudit work in areas directly related to the production of accounting information.

c. The senior members of the government entity must document their review of the nonaudit service and indicate why it is appropriate for the auditors to perform this service.

d. The scope of the audit cannot be reduced because the nonaudit work was performed by the public accounting firm.

LO B-4

B.29 Which of the following is true?

a. Members of an audit engagement team cannot speak with audit client officers about matters outside the scope of the audit while the audit engagement is in progress.

b. Audit team members who leave the public accounting firm for employment with audit clients can provide audit efficiencies (next year) because they are very familiar with the firm's audit plans.

c. Audit team partners who leave the public accounting firm for employment with audit clients can retain variable annuity retirement accounts established in the person's former firm retirement plan.

d. The public accounting firm must discuss with the audit client's board or its audit committee the independence implications of the client's having hired the audit engagement team manager as its financial vice president.

LO B-3

B.30 Which of the following "bodies designated by Council" have been authorized to promulgate general standards enforceable under the General Standards Rule of the AICPA Code of Professional Conduct?

a. AICPA Division of Professional Ethics.

b. Financial Accounting Standards Board.

c. Government Accounting Standards Board.

d. Accounting and Review Services Committee.

LO B-5

B.31 Which of the following "bodies designated by Council" have been authorized to promulgate accounting principles enforceable under the Accounting Principles Rule of the AICPA Code of Professional Conduct?

a. Auditing Standards Board.

b. Federal Accounting Standards Advisory Board.

c. Consulting Services Executive Committee.

d. Accounting and Review Services Committee.

LO B-5

B.32 Phil Greb has a thriving practice in which he assists attorneys in preparing litigation dealing with accounting and auditing matters. He is "practicing public accounting" if he

a. Uses his CPA designation on his letterhead and business card.

b. Is in partnership with another CPA.

c. Practices in a professional corporation with other CPAs.

d. Never lets his clients know that he is a CPA.

LO B-5

B.33 The AICPA removed its general prohibition of CPAs taking commissions and contingent fees because

a. CPAs prefer more price competition to less.

b. Commissions and contingent fees enhance audit independence.

c. Nothing is inherently wrong about the form of fees charged to nonaudit clients.

d. Objectivity is not always necessary in accounting and auditing services.

LO B-4

B.34 CPA Kara Rambo is the auditor of Ajax Corporation. Her audit independence will *not* be considered impaired if she

a. Owns $1,000 worth of Ajax stock.

b. Has a husband who owns $1,000 worth of Ajax stock.

    c. Has a sister who is the financial vice president of Ajax.

    d. Owns $1,000 worth of the stock of Pericles Corporation, which is controlled by Ajax as a result of Ajax's ownership of 40 percent of Pericles' stock, and Pericles contributes 3 percent of its total assets and income in Ajax's financial statements.

LO B-5

B.35 When a client's financial statements contain a material departure from an FASB *Statement on Accounting Standards* and the public accounting firm believes the departure is necessary to ensure that the statements are not misleading,

    a. The public accounting firm must qualify the auditors' report for a departure from GAAP.

    b. The public accounting firm can explain why the departure is necessary and then give an unmodified opinion paragraph in the auditors' report.

    c. The public accounting firm must give an adverse auditors' report.

    d. The public accounting firm can give the standard unmodified auditors' report with an unmodified opinion paragraph.

LO B-5

B.36 Which of the following would *not* be considered confidential information obtained in the course of an engagement for which the client's consent would be needed for disclosure?

    a. Information about whether a consulting client has paid the CPA's fees on time.

    b. The actuarial assumptions used by a tax client in calculating pension expense.

    c. Management's strategic plan for next year's labor negotiations.

    d. Information about material contingent liabilities relevant for audited financial statements.

LO B-5

B.37 Which of the following would probably *not* be considered an "act discreditable to the profession"?

    a. Numerous moving traffic violations.

    b. Failing to file the CPA's own tax return.

    c. Filing a fraudulent tax return for a client in a severe financial difficulty.

    d. Refusing to hire Asian Americans in an accounting practice.

LO B-5

B.38 According to the AICPA Code of Conduct, which of the following acts is generally forbidden to CPAs in public practice?

    a. Purchasing bookkeeping software from a high-tech development company and reselling it to tax clients.

    b. Being the author of a "TaxAid" newsletter promoted and sold by a publishing company.

    c. Having a commission arrangement with an accounting software developer to receive 4 percent of the price of programs recommended and sold to audit clients.

    d. Engaging a marketing firm to obtain new financial planning clients for a fixed fee of $1,000 for each successful contact.

LO B-6

B.39 A CPA's legal license to practice public accounting can be revoked by the

    a. American Institute of Certified Public Accountants.

    b. State society of CPAs.

    c. Auditing Standard Board.

    d. State board of accountancy.

LO B-5

B.40 According to the Acts Discreditable Rule for accountants in public practice, which of the following is *not* a "discreditable act"?

    a. Withholding a client's sales records.

    b. Failing to file or remit tax payments.

    c. Failing to follow requirements of the PCAOB during the audit of an SEC client.

    d. Advertising that indicated the firm can reduce IRS penalties.

LO B-4

B.41 An auditor's independence would *not* be considered impaired if she or he had

    a. Owned common stock of the audit client but sold it before the company became a client.

    b. Sold short the common stock of an audit client while working on the audit engagement.

    c. Served as the company's treasurer for six months during the year covered by the audit but resigned before the company became a client.

    d. Performed the bookkeeping and financial statement preparation for the company, which had no accounting personnel and for which the president had no understanding of accounting principles.

LO B-5

B.42 When a CPA knows that a tax client has skimmed cash receipts and not reported the income in the federal income tax return but signs the return as a CPA who prepared the return, the CPA has violated which of the following AICPA rules of conduct?

a. The Confidential Client Information Rule.

b. The Integrity and Objectivity Rule.

c. The Independence Rule.

d. The Accounting Principles Rule.

LO B-5

B.43 An accountant recommends a local computer company to a client that is trying to upgrade its computerized sales records. The client purchases $25,000 worth of equipment and sends a check to the accountant for 5 percent of the total sales. This is an example of a

a. Commission.

b. Contingent fee.

c. Referral fee.

d. Nonaudit fee.

LO B-5

B.44 Which of the following ownership situations is permissible for a public accounting firm?

a. A partner of the firm is responsible for fraud issues related to audits and audit clients. He owns 20 percent of the firm and is not a CPA.

b. Because the firm now specializes in fraud auditing and fraud investigation, the managing partner of the firm has a background in law enforcement and fraud investigation but is not a CPA.

c. A partner of the firm who owns 50 shares of stock in an audit client of the firm is responsible for fraud issues related to audits and audit clients.

d. A partner of the firm who has 20 years of experience in law enforcement and fraud investigation is responsible for fraud issues related to audits and audit clients. The partner's career began as a police officer after receiving a law enforcement degree from a local community college.

Exercises and Problems

Mc Graw Hill Education **connect** All applicable questions are available with *Connect.*

LO B-4

B.45 **SEC Independence Rules.** Is independence impaired for the individual or the public accounting firm on these SEC filing audits according to SEC independence rules?

a. CPA Yolanda is the Best & Co engagement partner on the Casa Construction Company (CCC) audit supervised from the Santa Fe office of the firm. Yolanda owns 100 shares of CCC.

b. CPA Yolanda sold the 100 CCC shares to CPA Javier, who is another partner in the Santa Fe office but who is not involved in the CCC audit.

c. CPA Javier transferred ownership of the 100 CCC shares to his wife.

d. CPA Javier's wife gave the shares to their 12-year-old son.

e. CPA Javier's son sold the shares to Javier's father.

f. CPA Javier's father was happy to combine the 100 CCC shares with shares he already owned because now he owns 25 percent of CCC and can control many decisions of the board of directors.

g. CPA Javier's father declared personal bankruptcy and sold his CCC stock. CCC then hired him to fill the newly created position of director of financial reporting.

LO B-4

B.46 **SEC Independence and Nonaudit Services.** Is independence impaired on these SEC filing audits according to SEC independence rules regarding nonaudit services?

a. CPA Dakota Tidrick is a staff assistant II auditor on the Section Co. audit. Upon the audit completion date in January, Tidrick drafted the balance sheet, income statement, comprehensive income statement, statement of cash flows, and notes for review by the engagement partner before the auditors' report was finalized.

b. CPA Mel Carnes is a manager in the firm's consulting division. He spent 100 hours with the Section Co. audit client on an accounts payable information system study, which involved selecting the preferred software and supervising Section Co.'s employees in startup operations.

c. CPA Nicky Webber, working in the public accounting firm's asset valuation consulting division located in Chicago, prepared for Section Co. an appraisal of the fair value of assets purchased in Section's merger with the Group Co. These valuations were then audited by the engagement team located in Dallas in connection with the purchase accounting for the merger.

d. CPA Fran Young is the engagement partner on the Section Co. audit and is an actuarial consultant in the firm's consulting division. Young personally audited the client's post-templyoment benefits calculations, which had been prepared by Section's actuaries.

e. Section Co. appointed its own employee, certified internal auditor (CIA) Pat Mumta, to be director of internal auditing with complete responsibility for planning, management, and review of all internal audit work. Mumta engaged Section Co.'s independent public accounting firm to supply staff to perform all operational audit studies of efficiency and effectiveness in Section's domestic subsidiary companies. The public accounting firm used half of these same staff professionals to work on the audit of Section's financial statement audit.

f. CPA Dale Churyk is the partner in charge of the Dallas office where the Section Co. audit is managed (by engagement partner Jack). Churyk has no direct role on the audit engagement team. However, Section relies on Churyk to prepare the confidential papers for the board of directors' stock options and sign the release forms for option grants.

g. CPA Robin Mantzke works in the executive search department of the public accounting firm's consulting division, located in New York City. In connection with Section Co.'s hiring of its new vice president for marketing, Mantzke checked the references on the lead candidate Smith and performed a thorough background investigation that led to the firm's advice that Smith was the best person for the appointment. Section Co. board members investigated other candidates and hired Smith in Dallas without further interaction with Mantzke.

h. Section Co. completed a private placement of long-term bonds during the year under audit. The bonds were distributed to 40 qualified-exempt investors through the brokerage firm of Amalgamated Exchange Inc., which is 50 percent owned by the public accounting firm and 50 percent owned by Lynch Merrill Investment Corporation.

i. The public accounting firm's tax consulting division prepared Section Co.'s export-import tax reports, which involved numerous interpretations of complicated export-import tax law provisions.

LO B-4

B.47 **Independence, Integrity, and Objectivity Cases.** Read the following cases.

Required:

For each case, state whether the action or situation shows a violation of the AICPA Code of Professional Conduct, explain why if it does, and cite the relevant rule.

a. CPA Ellen Stout performs the audit of the local symphony society. Because of her good work, she was elected an honorary member of the board of directors.

b. CPA Darcy Wolfe practices management consulting in the area of computerized information systems under the firm name of Wolfe & Associates. The "associates" are not CPAs, and the firm is not an accounting firm. However, Wolfe shows "CPA" on business cards and uses these credentials when dealing with clients.

c. CPA Alex Goodwin performs significant day-to-day bookkeeping services for Harper Corporation and supervises the work of the one part-time bookkeeper employed by Hadley Harper. This year, Harper wants to engage CPA Goodwin to perform an audit.

d. CPA H. Poirot bought a home in 1989 and financed it with a mortgage loan from Farraway Savings and Loan. Farraway was merged into Nearby S&L, and Poirot became the manager in charge of the Nearby audit.

e. Poirot inherited a large sum of money from old Mr. Giraud in 2000. Poirot sold his house, paid off the loan to Nearby S&L, and purchased a much larger estate. Nearby S&L provided the financing.

f. Poirot and Mala Lemon (a local real estate broker) formed a partnership to develop apartment buildings. Lemon is a 20 percent owner and managing partner. Poirot and three partners in the accounting firm are limited partners. They own the remaining 80 percent of the partnership but have no voice in everyday management. Lemon obtained permanent real estate financing from Nearby S&L.

g. Lemon won the lottery and purchased part of the limited partners' interests. She now owns 90 percent of the partnership and remains general partner while the CPAs remain limited partners with 10 percent interest.

h. CPA Justin Shultz purchased a variable annuity insurance contract that offered the option to choose the companies in which this contract will invest. As directed, the insurance company purchased common stock in one of Shultz's audit clients.

LO B-4

B.48 **Independence, Integrity, and Objectivity Cases.** Read the following cases.

Required:

For each separate case, state whether the action or situation shows a violation of the AICPA Code of Professional Conduct; if so, explain why and cite the relevant rule or interpretation.

a. Your client, Contrary Corporation, is very upset over the fact that your audit last year failed to detect an $800,000 inventory overstatement caused by employee theft and falsification of the records. The board discussed the matter and authorized its attorneys to explore the possibility of a lawsuit for damages.

b. Contrary Corporation filed a lawsuit alleging negligent audit work, seeking $1 million in damages.

c. In response to the lawsuit by Contrary, you decided to bring litigation against certain officers of the company alleging management fraud and deceit. You are asking for a damage judgment of $500,000.

d. The Allright Insurance Company paid Contrary Corporation $700,000 under a fidelity bond covering an inventory theft by employees. Allright is suing your public accounting firm for damages on the grounds of negligent performance of the audit, claiming that a proper audit would have uncovered the theft sooner and the amount of loss would have been considerably less.

e. Your audit client, Science Tech Inc., installed a cost accounting system devised by the consulting services department of your firm. The system failed to account properly for certain product costs (according to management), and the system had to be discontinued. Science Tech management was very dissatisfied and filed a lawsuit demanding return of the $10,000 consulting fee. The audit fee is normally about $50,000, and $10,000 is not an especially large amount for your firm. However, you believe that Science Tech management operated the system improperly. You are willing to do further consulting work at a reduced rate to make the system operate, but you are unwilling to return the entire $10,000 fee.

f. A group of dissident shareholders filed a class-action lawsuit against both you and your client, Amalgamated Inc., for $30 million. They allege there was a conspiracy to present misleading financial statements in connection with a recent merger.

g. CPA Ellis Lisa, a shareholder in the firm of Eden, Benjamin, and Block, P.C. (a professional accounting corporation), owns 25 percent of the common stock of Dove Corporation (not a client of Eden, Benjamin, and Block). This year, Dove purchased a 32 percent interest in Tale Company and is accounting for the investment using the equity method of accounting. The investment amounts to 11 percent of Dove's consolidated net assets. Tale Company has been an audit client of Eden, Benjamin, and Block for 12 years.

h. CPAs Mark and Ben Saliba are the father-and-son partners of Queens, LLP. They have a 12 percent joint private investment in ownership of the voting common stock of Hydra Corporation, which is not an audit client of Queens, LLP. However, the firm's audit client, Howard Company, owns 46 percent of Hydra, and this investment accounts for 20 percent of Howard's assets (using the equity method of accounting).

i. Drew Francie and Madison Brian, CPAs, regularly perform the audit of the First National Bank, and the firm is preparing for the audit of the financial statements for the year ended December 31, 2017.

(1) Two directors of the First National Bank became partners in Francie and Brian, CPAs, on July 1, 2017, resigning their directorship on that date. They will not participate in the audit.

(2) During 2017, the former controller of the First National Bank, now a partner in Francie and Brian, was frequently called on for assistance regarding loan approvals and the bank's minimum checking account policy. In addition, the former controller conducted a computer feasibility study for First National.

j. The Cather Corporation is indebted to a CPA for unpaid fees and has offered to give the CPA unsecured interest-bearing notes. Alternatively, Cather Corporation offered to give the CPA two shares of its common stock, after which 10,002 shares would be outstanding.

k. May Debra is not yet a CPA but is doing quite well in her first employment with a large public accounting firm. She has been on the job two years and has become an "experienced assistant." If she passes the CPA exam this year, she will be promoted to senior accountant. This month, during the audit of Row Lumber Company, Debra told the controller that she is remodeling an old house. The controller likes Debra and had a load of needed materials delivered to the house, billing Debra at a 70 percent discount—a savings over the normal cash discount of about $300. Debra paid the bill and was happy to have the materials that she otherwise could not afford on her meager salary.

l. Groaner Corporation is in financial difficulty. You are about to sign the report on the current audit when your firm's office manager informs you the audit fee for last year has not yet been paid.

m. CPA Aubrey Rowan prepared Goodwin's tax return this year. Last year, Goodwin prepared the return and paid too much income tax because the tax return erroneously contained "income" in the amount of $300,000 from an inheritance received when dear Aunt Martha died. This year, Goodwin sold the inherited property for $500,000. Goodwin argued with Rowan, who agreed to omit the sale of the property and the $200,000 gain this year on the grounds that Goodwin had already overpaid tax last year and this omission would make things even.

n. CPA Sage Watson is employed by Baker Street Company as its chief accountant. Lee Lestrade, also a CPA and the financial vice president of Baker, owns a trucking company that provides shipping services to Baker in a four-state area. The trucking company needs to buy 14 new trailers, and Lestrade authorized a payment to finance the purchase in the amount of $750,000. The related document cited repayment in terms of reduced trucking charges for the next seven years. Lestrade created the journal entry for this arrangement, charging the $750,000 to prepaid expenses. Watson and Lestrade signed the representation letter to Baker's external auditors and stated that Baker had no related-party transactions that were not disclosed to the auditors.

LO B-5

B.49 **Integrity and Objectivity.** In 1997, a disagreement arose between **Livent Inc.** and its auditor, Deloitte and Touche. Livent, which operated several theaters for live stage production, had sold the naming rights to one of its theaters to **AT&T** for $12.5 million. The agreement was oral, and one of the theaters was under construction. The auditors for Deloitte believed that only a portion of the deal should be included in revenue, but Livent wanted to book the entire $12.5 million. Livent retained Ernst & Young (EY) to provide an opinion on the transaction. EY's report indicated that all $12.5 million could be recorded as revenue. Deloitte hired **Price Waterhouse** (currently **PricewaterhouseCoopers**) to review the transaction. Price Waterhouse agreed with E&Y and Livent, and Deloitte allowed Livent to book the $12.5 million. In 1998, Livent issued a series of press releases indicating the discovery of significant account irregularities and, later in 1998, declared bankruptcy.

Required:

Comment on the decision to engage EY and Price Waterhouse concerning the $12.5 million transaction. What would your position be on the need for other opinions? What would your position be for the disposition of the transaction?

LO B-5

B.50 **General and Technical Rule Cases.** Read the following cases. For each, state whether the action or situation shows a violation of the AICPA Code of Professional Conduct; if so, explain why and cite the relevant rule.

a. CPA Jerry Cheese became the new auditor for Python Insurance Company. Cheese knew a great deal about insurance accounting but had never conducted an audit of an insurance company. Consequently, Cheese hired CPA Tate Gilliam, who had six years of experience with the State Department of Insurance Audit. Gilliam managed the audit, and Cheese was the partner in charge.

b. CPA Mackenzie Palin practices public accounting and is a director of Comedy Company. Palin's firm performs consulting and tax services for Comedy. Palin prepared unaudited financial statements on Comedy's letterhead and submitted them to First National Bank in support of a loan application. Palin's accounting firm received a fee for this service.

c. CPA Ellery Idle audited the financial statements of Monty Corporation and gave an unmodified report. Monty is not a public company, so the financial statements did not contain the SEC-required reconciliation of deferred income taxes.

d. CPA Gwyn Chapman audited the financial statement of BTV Ltd. These financial statements contain capitalized leases that do not meet FASB criteria for capitalization. They resemble more closely the criteria for operating leases. The effect is material, adding $4 million to assets and $3.5 million to liabilities. However, BTV has a long experience with acquiring such property as its own assets after the "lease" terms end. Chapman and BTV management believe the financial statements should reflect the operating policy of the management instead of the technical requirements of the FASB. Consequently, the auditors' report explains the accounting and gives an unmodified opinion.

LO B-5

B.51 **Responsibilities to Clients' Cases.** Read the following cases. For each case, state whether the action or situation shows a violation or potential for violation of the AICPA Code of Professional Conduct, explain why, and cite the relevant rule.

a. CPA Sal Colt has discovered a way to eliminate most of the boring work of processing routine accounts receivable confirmations by contracting with the Cohen Mail Service. After the auditor has prepared the confirmations, Cohen stuffs them in envelopes, mails them, receives the return replies, opens the replies, and returns them to Colt.

b. Cadentoe Corporation, without consulting Jora Cramer, its CPA, has changed its accounting so that it is not in conformity with GAAP. During the regular audit engagement, Cramer discovers that the statements based on the accounts are so grossly misleading that they might be considered fraudulent. Cramer resigns the engagement after a heated argument. Cramer knows that the statements will be given to Sandy Panzer, a friend at the Last National Bank, and that Panzer is not a very astute reader of complicated financial statements. Two days later, Panzer calls Cramer and asks some general questions about Cadentoe's statements and remarks favorably on the very thing that is misrepresented. Cramer corrects the erroneous analysis and Panzer is very much surprised.

c. A CPA who had reached retirement age arranged to sell the practice to another certified public accountant. Their agreement called for the review of all audit documentation and business correspondence by the accountant purchasing the practice.

d. Martha Jacoby, CPA, withdrew from the audit of Harvard Company after discovering irregularities in Harvard's income tax returns. One week later, Jacoby received a phone call from Jake Henry, CPA, who explained that he had just been retained by Harvard Company to replace her. Henry asked Jacoby why she withdrew from the Harvard engagement, and she told him.

e. CPA Chen Wallace has two audit clients: Willingham Corporation owned by Jayden Willingham and Ward Corporation owned by Bailey Ward. Willingham Corp. sells a large proportion of its products to Ward Corp., which amounts to 60 percent of Ward Corp.'s purchases in most years. Willingham and Ward are also Wallace's tax clients as individuals. This year, while preparing Ward's tax return, Wallace discovered information that suggested Ward Corporation is in a failing financial position. In consideration of the fact that the companies and individuals are mutual clients, Wallace discussed Ward Corporation's financial difficulties with Willingham.

f. Ashley Fiddle, CPA, prepared an uncontested claim for a tax refund on Faddle Corporation's amended tax return. The fee for the service was 30 percent of the amount the IRS rules to be a proper refund. The claim was for $300,000.

g. After Faddle had won a $200,000 refund and Fiddle collected the $60,000 fee, Jordan Faddle, the president, invited Fiddle to be the auditor for Faddle Corporation.

h. Burgess Company engaged CPA Kim Philby to audit Maclean Corporation in connection with a possible initial public offering (IPO) of stock registered with the SEC. Burgess

Company established a holding company named Cairncross Inc. and asked Philby to issue an engagement letter addressed to Cairncross stating that Cairncross would receive the auditors' report. Cairncross has no assets, and Philby agreed to charge a fee for the audit of Maclean only if the IPO is successful.

LO B-5

B.52 **Other Responsibilities and Practices Cases.** Read the following cases. For each, state whether the action or situation shows a violation or potential for violation of the AICPA Code of Professional Conduct; if so, explain why, and cite the relevant rule.

a. CPA Ron Stout completed a review of the unaudited financial statements of Wolfe Gifts. Arvida Wolfe was very displeased with the report. An argument ensued, and she told Stout never to darken her door again. Two days later, she telephoned Stout and demanded that he return (1) Wolfe's cash disbursement journal, (2) Stout's documentation schedule of adjusting journal entries, (3) Stout's inventory analysis documentation, and (4) all other documentation prepared by Stout. Wolfe had not yet paid her bill, so Stout replied that state law gave him a lien on all of the records and he would return them as soon as she paid his fee.

b. CPA O'Dell May teaches a CPA review course at the university. He needs problem and question material for students' practice, but the CPA examination questions and answers are no longer published. He pays $5 to students who take the exam for each question they can "remember" after taking the examination.

c. CPA Kelsey Blitz has been invited to conduct a course in effective tax planning for the City Chamber of Commerce. The chamber's president said a brochure would be mailed to members giving the name of Blitz's firm, Blitz's educational background and degrees held, professional society affiliations, and testimonials from participants in the course held last year comparing Blitz's excellent performance with other CPAs who have offered competing courses in the city.

d. CPA Reece Philby is a member of the state bar whose practice is a combination of law and accounting and is heavily involved in estate planning engagements. Philby's letterhead has the following: Member, State Bar of Illinois, and Member, AICPA.

e. The public accounting firm of Burgess & Maclean (B&M) has made a deal with Brit & Company, a firm of management consulting specialists, for mutual business advantage. B&M agreed to recommend Brit to clients who need management consulting services. Brit agreed to recommend B&M to clients who need improvements in their accounting systems. During the year, both firms would keep records of fees obtained by these mutual referrals. At the end of the year, Brit and B&M would settle the net differences based on a referral rate of 5 percent of fees.

f. Jack Robinson and Archie Robertson (both CPAs) are not partners, but they have the same office, the same employees, and a joint bank account and work together on audits. A letterhead they use shows both their names and the description "Members, AICPA."

g. CPA Lou Dewey retired from the two-person firm of Dewey & Cheatham (D&C). One year later, D&C merged practices with Howe & Company to form a regional firm under the name of Dewey, Cheatham, & Howe Company.

LO B-4

B.53 **AICPA Independence and Other Services.** The Independence Rule of the AICPA Code of Conduct cites several "other services" that do and do not impair audit independence.

Required:

Go to the AICPA website (www.aicpa.org) and find whether the following items impair independence (Yes) or do not impair independence (No) when performed for audit clients.

a. Post the client-approved entries to a client's trial balance.

b. Authorize the client's customer credit applications.

c. Use CPA's information-processing facilities to prepare the client's payroll and generate checks for the client treasurer's signature.

d. Sign the client's quarterly federal payroll tax return.

e. Advise client management about the application or financial effect of provisions in an employee benefit plan contract.

f. Have emergency signature authority to cosign cash disbursement checks in connection with a client's hospital benefit plan.

g. As an investment advisory service, provide analyses of a client's investments in comparison to benchmarks produced by unrelated third parties.

h. Take temporary custody of a client's investment assets each time a purchase is made as a device to reduce cash float expense.

LO B-1

B.54 **General Ethics.** Is there any moral difference between a disapproved action in which you are caught and the same action that never becomes known to anyone else? Do many persons in business and professional society make a distinction between these two circumstances? If you respond that you do (or do not) perceive a difference while persons in business and professional society do not (or do), how do you explain the differences in attitudes?

LO B-2

B.55 **Competition and Audit Proposals.** Accounting firms are often asked to present "proposals" to companies' boards of directors. These proposals are comprehensive booklets, accompanied by oral presentations, telling about the firm's personnel, technology, special qualifications, and expertise in the hope of convincing the board to award the work to the firm.

Kourtney Dena has a new job as staff assistant to Selby Michael, chairman of the board of Granof Grain Company. The company has a policy of engaging new auditors every seven years. The board will hear oral proposals from 12 accounting firms. This is the second day of the three-day meeting. Dena's job is to help evaluate the proposals. During the first day of meetings, the proposal presented by Eden, Benjamin, and Block was clearly the best.

At the end of the day, Dena sees Michael's staff chief slip a copy of Eden, Benjamin, and Block's written proposal into an envelope. He then tells Dena to take it to a friend who works for Hunt and Hunt, a public accounting firm scheduled to make its presentation tomorrow, saying, "I told him we'd let him glance at the best proposal." Michael is absent from the meeting and will not return for two hours.

Required:

What should Dena do? What should CPA Hunt do if he receives the Eden, Benjamin, and Block proposal, assuming he has time to modify the Hunt and Hunt proposal before tomorrow's presentation?

LO B-2

B.56 **Engagement Timekeeping Records.** A time budget is always prepared for audit engagements. Numbers of hours are estimated for various segments of the work, for example, internal control evaluation, cash, inventory, and report review. Audit supervisors expect the work segments to be completed "within budget" and evaluate staff accountants' performance in part on the ability to perform audit work efficiently within budget. Jessica Sara is an audit manager who has worked hard to get promoted. She hopes to become a partner in two or three years. Finishing audits on time is heavily weighted on her performance evaluation. She assigned the cash audit work to Paul Ed, who has worked for the firm for 10 months. Ed hopes to get a promotion and salary raise this year. Twenty hours were budgeted for the cash work. Ed is efficient, but it took 30 hours to finish because the company had added seven new bank accounts. Ed was worried about his performance evaluation, so he recorded 20 hours for the cash work and put the other 10 hours under the internal control evaluation budget.

Required:

What do you think about Ed's resolution of his problem? Was his action a form of lying? What would you think of his action if the internal control evaluation work was presently under budget because it was not yet complete and another assistant was assigned to finish that work segment later?

LO B-2

B.57 **Audit Overtime.** The performance evaluation of all accountants is based in part on their ability to do audit work efficiently and within the time budget planned for the engagement. New staff accountants, in particular, usually have some early difficulty learning speedy work habits, which demand that no time be wasted. Cynthia Elizabeth started work for Julie and Jacob CPAs in September. After attending the staff training school, she was assigned to the Rising Sun Company audit. Her first work assignment was to complete the extensive recalculation of the inventory compilation using the audit test counts and audited unit prices for several hundred inventory items. Her time budget for the work was six hours. She started at 4 P.M. and was not finished when everyone left the office at 6 P.M. Not wanting to stay downtown alone, she took all necessary audit documentation home. She resumed work at 8 P.M. and finished at 3 A.M. The next day, she returned to the CPA offices, put the completed documentation in the file, and recorded six hours in the time budget/actual schedule. Her supervisor was pleased, especially about her diligence in taking the work home.

Required:

a. What do you think about Elizabeth's diligence and her understatement of the time she took to finish the work?

b. What would you think of the case if she had received help at home from her husband Paul?

c. What would you think of the case if she had been unable to finish and had left the work at home for her husband to finish?

LO B-5

B.58 **Conflict of Client's Interests.** Jon Williams, CPA, is in the middle of the real-life soap opera, *Taxing Days of Our Lives.*

The Cast of Characters

Oneway Corporation is Williams's audit and tax client. The three directors are the officers and the only three stockholders, each owning exactly one-third of the shares. President Raul Jack founded the company and is now nearing retirement. As an individual, he is also Williams's tax client. Vice President Jana Jill manages the day-to-day operations. She has been instrumental in increasing the business and its profits. Jill's individual tax work is done by CPA Corin Phil. Treasurer Chris Bill has been a long-term, loyal employee and has been responsible for many innovative financial transactions and reports of great benefit to the business. He is Williams's close personal friend and an individual tax client.

The Conflict

President Jack discussed with CPA Williams the tax consequences to him as an individual of selling his one-third interest in Oneway Corporation to Vice President Jill. Later, meeting with Bill to discuss his individual tax problems, Williams learns that Bill fears that Jack and Jill will make a deal, put him in a minority position, and force him out of the company. Bill says, "Jon, we've been friends a long time. Please keep me informed about Jack's plans, even rumors. My interest in Oneway Corporation represents my life savings and my resources for the kid's college. Remember, you're little Otto's godfather."

Thinking back, Williams realized that Vice President Jill has always been rather hostile. Chances are that Phil would get the Oneway engagement if Jill acquires Jack's shares and controls the corporation. Nevertheless, Bill will probably suffer a great deal if he cannot learn about Jack's plans, and Williams's unwillingness to keep him informed will probably ruin their close friendship.

Later, on a Dark and Stormy Night

Williams ponders the problem. "Oneway Corporation is my client, but a corporation is a fiction—only a form. The stockholders personify the real entity, so they are collectively my clients, and I can transmit information among them as though they were one person. Right? On the other hand, Jack and Bill engage me for individual tax work, and information about one's personal affairs is really no business of the other. What to do? What to do?"

Required:

Give Williams advice about alternative actions, considering the constraints of the AICPA Code of Professional Conduct.

LO B-4

B.59 **AICPA Code of Professional Conduct.** Reread the Module B introduction about Scott London, CPA.

Required:

a. What code violations have occurred in this case?

b. What is the range of penalties that the PCAOB could levy against London? By the California State Board of Accountancy?

c. What do you think is the appropriate penalty?

LO B-6

B.60 **Disciplinary Action.** Go to the PCAOB website (www.pcaobus.org) and find settled disciplinary orders. Review the cases and the penalties indicated for each case.

Required:

What did Susan Birkert do to get in trouble, and what was her sanction?

LO B-6

B.61 **Ethics Case.**[14] Sandy Sally is a sole proprietor CPA who runs a successful practice with five employees. Several years ago, Sally purchased an office building and relocated the practice in about 20 percent of the space and rented out the remaining portion. Things went well for the first few months, but then two of Sally's tenants ran into financial difficulties and had to vacate the building. Sally was unable to quickly find new tenants for the space.

Sally struggled to keep current with the mortgage payments for a few months, but the loss of tenant income combined with the expense of operating a building became a large burden. Cash flow became very tight, and Sally stopped remitting the employee payroll taxes withheld.

The IRS filed a lien for nonpayment of employee payroll taxes, which was published in a local newspaper. A concerned citizen filed an ethics complaint.

Investigation found that, although the company had been delinquent in remitting employee payroll taxes and a federal tax lien had been filed, Sally had brought the tax liabilities into current status and produced evidence that the IRS lien had been released.

Required:

a. What code violation(s) have occurred in this case?

b. What is the range of penalties that could be levied against Sally?

c. What do you think is the appropriate penalty?

---

[14]The following information was obtained from the *Pennsylvania CPA Journal* and is adopted from a case brought before the Pennsylvania Ethics Committee; see R. J. DePasquale and C. Williams, "The CPA's Taxes and the Code of Ethics," *Pennsylvania CPA Journal,* Winter 2004.

Legal Liability

> *When men are pure, laws are useless; when men are corrupt, laws are broken.*
>
> Benjamin Disraeli, British prime minister and author (1804–1881)

Professional Standards References

Topic	AU-C/ISA Section	AS Section
Audit Documentation	230	1215
Letters for Underwriters and Certain Other Requesting Parties	920	6101
Filings Under the Securities Act of 1933	925	4101

LEARNING OBJECTIVES

Module B on professional ethics dealt mainly with auditors' self-regulation. This module focuses on public regulation enforced by the Securities and Exchange Commission (SEC) and state and federal court systems. The discussion will help you understand auditors' legal liability for professional work.

Your objectives are to be able to:

LO C-1 Identify and describe auditors' exposure to lawsuits and loss judgments.

LO C-2 Specify the characteristics of auditors' liability under common law and cite specific case precedents.

LO C-3 Describe auditors' liability to third parties under statutory law.

LO C-4 Specify the civil and criminal liability provisions of the Securities Act of 1933.

LO C-5 Specify the civil and criminal liability provisions of the Securities Exchange Act of 1934.

LO C-6 Understand recent developments that affect auditors' liability to clients and third parties.

BDO is one of the nation's largest accounting firms, with revenues of more than $1 billion in 2016. In 2007, investors of **E.S. Bankest** (a Miami, Florida, factoring firm) brought a $170 million lawsuit against BDO for losses the investors incurred because of BDO's alleged failure to detect a fraud that led to E.S. Bankest's collapse. BDO was not willing to settle the case out of court but risked a trial that could lead to the demise of the entire firm. Scott Univer, BDO's general counsel, noted that "we do settle cases. But there are situations where, if we're accused of fraud or collaboration or misconduct, we have to draw a line. We'll see you in court."[1] Prior to the Bankest case, BDO had taken six cases to trial over the preceding 12 years and had prevailed in each one.

[1]"BDO Prepares to Fight Lawsuit, with Survival Possibly at Stake," *The Wall Street Journal,* January 24, 2007, p. C2.

On June 16, 2007, a Florida jury concluded that BDO had exhibited gross negligence in its audits of Bankest; subsequently, BDO was ordered to pay $521 million ($170 million in compensatory damages plus $351 million in punitive damages). In 2010, following an appeal by BDO, a Florida state appeals court overturned this verdict and ordered a new trial. BDO's chief executive, Jack Weisbaum, stated that BDO "acted at all times consistent with its professional obligations."[2] An attorney for the original claimant (**Banco Espirito Santo)** contradicted Weisbaum's comments, indicating that "the evidence of BDO failures of even the most basic auditing procedures is so overwhelming that we expect a new jury will reach the same conclusion as the original jury."[3]

BDO's track record in court is unusual simply because most legal actions against auditors and accounting firms do not actually make it to trial. Accounting firms have generally found it preferable to settle cases out of court instead of risking a trial and significant monetary judgments. As Michael Young, an attorney who has represented the Big Four firms as well as BDO, noted, "The practical reality is that our system of justice breaks down when you're talking about the Big Four. The damages sought are often so big that a rational approach is to settle."[4] In addition to the potential monetary damages, firms consider the opportunity costs of their professionals' time as well as negative publicity surrounding an extensive legal proceeding when making decisions whether to risk a trial. Ironically, on May 5, 2011, BDO entered into a confidential settlement with the plaintiffs in the Bankest case.

Legal liability continues to be an important consideration for auditors and accounting firms as they conduct business. Recent settlements involving the largest accounting firms reveal that our litigious society has significantly impacted the auditing profession:[5]

- **Deloitte & Touche** (Deloitte): **Adelphia Communications** ($167.5 million in 2007), **Delphi** ($38 million in 2008), **Fortress Re** ($250 million in 2006), **General Motors** ($26 million in 2008), **Parmalat, SpA** ($159 million in 2007).
- **EY: Bank of New England** ($84 million in 2005), **Cendant** ($335 million in 1999), **HealthSouth** ($143 million in 2009), **Lehman Brothers** ($99 million in 2013).
- **KPMG: Countrywide** ($24 million in 2010), **Xerox** ($80 million in 2008), **New Century** ($44.8 million in 2010).
- **PricewaterhouseCoopers (PwC): American International Group (AIG)** ($97.5 million in 2008), **Amerco** ($50 million in 2004), **Safety-Kleen** ($48 million in 2005), **Tyco** ($225 million in 2007), **MF Global** ($65 million in 2015).
- **BDO: Le-Nature's Inc.** ($285 million in 2012), **Grand Court Lifestyles** ($91 million in 2011).
- **Grant Thornton:** Parmalat (6.5 million in 2009).

[2]"Florida Court Overturns Seidman Jury Verdict," *The Wall Street Journal,* June 24, 2010, p. C3.
[3]Ibid.
[4]"BDO Prepares to Fight Lawsuit," p. C2.
[5]"Deloitte to Be Latest to Settle in Accounting Scandals," *The Wall Street Journal,* April 26, 2005, p. B1; "Deloitte Pays Insurers More than $200 Million," *The Wall Street Journal,* January 6, 2006, p. C3; "Big Accounting Firms Still Pay for Scandals," *The Wall Street Journal,* January 13, 2007, p. B5; "PwC Sets Accord in Tyco Case," *The Wall Street Journal,* July 7–8, 2007, p. A3; "Deloitte to Pay $167.5M in Adelphia Case," *CFO.com,* August 6, 2007; "Deloitte to Pay $38 Million in Delphi Case," *CFO.com,* January 2, 2008; "PwC Zapped in $97.5 Million Settlement," *CFO.com,* October 6, 2008; "GM Reaches Settlement in Securities-Fraud Case," *The Wall Street Journal,* August 9, 2008, p. B5; "Xerox to Pay $670 Million to Settle Securities Suit," *The Wall Street Journal,* March 28, 2008, p. B3; "N.Y. Funds Reach Settlement with Countrywide, KPMG," *The Wall Street Journal* (Online), May 7, 2010; "$91M BDO Seidman Verdict Highlights Malpractice Lawsuits," *South Florida Business Journal,* February 4, 2011; "BDO Seidman Settles New York Lawsuit Over Le-Nature's Loan," *Bloomberg News,* April 5, 2012; "Ex-Parmalat Auditors Settle US Investor Lawsuit," Reuters, November 19, 2009; "Judge OKs $125 Mln New Century Lawsuit Settlement," Reuters, August 10, 2010. "Ernst & Young Settles Lehman Investor Lawsuit for $99 Million," *Accounting Today,* December 2, 2013; "Ernst & Young will pay $10 Million to End N.Y. Lehman Suit," *Accounting Today,* April 15, 2015; "PwC Settles MF Global Lawsuit for $65 Million," *Accounting Today,* April 20, 2015.

AUDITING INSIGHT   Did Auditors Play a Role in the Subprime Crisis?

The charges filed against Ernst & Young for its audit of Lehman Brothers raised further questions about the role auditors could have played in averting the recent financial crisis. Lynn Turner, former chief accountant at the SEC, noted that, while auditors' performance improved following Sarbanes–Oxley, the slowing economy resulted in auditors "... reversing course, heading down the same old road they've been on before the corporate scandals." In contrast, Michael Young, an attorney at Willkie Farr & Gallagher, noted that auditors forced many of their financial institution clients to justify their valuations and eventually, take write-downs on assets and concluded that "by and large, the accountants rose to the occasion." Both literally and figuratively, the jury remains out on the issue. Recently, the SEC sued two KPMG auditors individually for their role in the audit of TierOne, a Nebraska bank that filed for bankruptcy after hiding millions in troubled loan losses. To date, this is the first action the regulatory agency has taken against auditors relating to the subprime lending crisis.

Sources: "Auditors Role in Crisis Gets Fresh Scrutiny," *The Wall Street Journal,* December 23, 2010, p. C1, C2; "Two Auditors Charged Over Bank Failure," *The Wall Street Journal,* January 9, 2013, p. C1.

These settlements and the related litigation costs (including insurance) have been staggering. A 2008 report noted that "litigation and practice protection costs" were as high as 15.1 percent (!) of the largest firms' revenues.[6]

The largest firms are not the only targets of lawsuits. Recently, singer Rihanna sued her former accountants, blaming them for mismanagement of her 2009 "Last Girl on Earth" tour, negligent bookkeeping, and problems with the IRS due to their errors. The defendants managed to pocket 22 percent of tour revenues by paying themselves commissions on revenue, leaving the singer with only 6 percent after other expenses.[7] This chapter summarizes the legal liability of auditors and the burden of care they owe to various parties who rely upon their work.

THE LEGAL ENVIRONMENT

LO C-1
Identify and describe auditors' exposure to lawsuits and loss judgments.

How does legal liability arise? Consider the following schematic that summarizes the relationship between auditors and two key parties: the client and third-party users. As the graphic here shows, auditors owe clients a responsibility to conduct an audit in

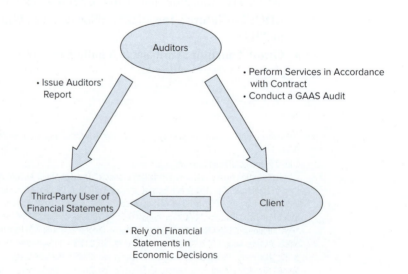

[6]*Final Report of the Advisory Committee on the Audition Profession,* October 6, 2008.
[7]"Rihanna Sues Ex-Accountants for Millions in Losses," *The Wall Street Journal,* July 5, 2012.

accordance with generally accepted auditing standards (GAAS) consistent with the terms in the *engagement letter* that serves as a contract between auditors and their clients. Clients may suffer losses related to these responsibilities for two reasons.

1. A breach of contract between auditors and the client (e.g., auditors' failure to complete the engagement by a specified deadline) may cause economic losses to the client resulting from delays, such as failing to receive funding through loans or investments, issuing its shares through a public offering at a less favorable price, or paying fines or penalties for missed deadlines.

2. Clients may suffer economic losses from acts of fraud or other misappropriation of assets by employees that a GAAS audit *should have identified.*

In either case, whether the client's loss is caused by the breach of contract or failure to exercise the appropriate level of professional care (substandard performance) by auditors, the client may seek legal action.

With respect to third-party users, auditors are responsible for issuing a report based on a GAAS audit that provides reasonable assurance that the financial statements on which these users base their economic decisions (lending decisions and investment decisions) are presented according to generally accepted accounting principles (GAAP). For third-party users, economic losses are either related to the client's inability to repay loans or other obligations or to a decline in the value of the user's investment in the client (in the form of a partnership interest or publicly traded shares of stock). If the user's loss is caused by reliance on financial statements and those financial statements were not presented according to GAAP, users may seek legal action against auditors.

The main defense for auditors is that they followed GAAS and performed their audits with due professional care. In many cases, lawsuits are brought against auditors not because they are necessarily at fault, but in the case of client failure, they are the only party with resources against which recovery can be made (the **"deep pockets" theory**). As Bill Thompson, president of **CPA Mutual Insurance Company of America,** noted, auditors are ". . . the last men standing—and they carry insurance, which, to the attorneys, equals deep pockets."[8]

Many users of auditors' reports expect auditors to detect and report fraud, theft, and illegal acts despite the fact that a GAAS audit cannot be expected to identify all items of this nature. Some financial statement users' expectations are very high; for this reason, an **expectation gap** often exists between the diligence that users expect and the diligence that auditors are able (and required) to provide. For example, in performing an audit on a multibillion-dollar corporation, auditors may choose to exclude testing transactions of $50,000, $100,000, $500,000, or more as immaterial. Certainly, a $1 million error in the financial statements of **General Electric** (2015 revenues of $116 billion) would be immaterial to auditors. However, it would be difficult to convince an individual investor with $25,000 of retirement money invested that $1 million is not a significant amount of money. Clearly, many financial statement users believe auditors are looking at most, if not every, transaction; are evaluating each transaction, event, person, and department for fraud; and are certifying that financial statements are accurate. No auditors would, however, accept an engagement for which any of these objectives was required.

When auditors do not meet the expectations of clients or financial statement users, they may be held liable under common law or statutory law, depending on the nature of the action and relationship of the party to the auditors. **Common law** uses legal precedent to identify the fault and responsibility of parties when there is no violation of a written law or statute. When no legal precedent can be found, the judge follows a sense of justice or morality, considering the prevailing customs and moral standards. Common law liability against auditors is available to clients and nonshareholder third parties; the

[8]"Target: CPAS," *Accounting Today,* July 1, 2011, p. 53.

jurisdiction for common law actions is typically a court in the state in which the alleged action occurred.

Statutory law is based on laws passed by legislative bodies and compiled in federal, state, and municipal codes. In a statutory case, the primary basis for a decision is whether the party's actions have violated the law as written in the code. A lawsuit claiming that auditors did not perform the audit in an appropriate manner is a common law action. The primary statutory laws relevant to the audit of financial statements are laws governing the purchase and sale of securities; as a result, auditors' liability under statutory law is primarily to third-party shareholders for securities issued by public entities. The Securities Act of 1933 and Securities and Exchange Act of 1934 (discussed later in this module) provide U.S. district courts with jurisdiction for violations of these acts.

✅ REVIEW CHECKPOINTS

C.1 Identify the general responsibilities auditors owe to clients and third parties.

C.2 Distinguish between *common law* liability and *statutory law* liability. Which parties generally bring suit against auditors under common law and under statutory law liability?

LIABILITY UNDER COMMON LAW

LO C-2
Specify the characteristics of auditors' liability under common law, and cite specific case precedents.

Under common law, lawsuits may be brought against auditors based on the law of contracts or as tort actions for failure to exercise the appropriate level of professional care.

- **Breach of contract** is a claim that accounting or auditing services were not performed in the manner described in the contract. Although auditors may have contractual relationships with third parties, cases involving breach of contract are most frequently brought against auditors by their clients.

- **Tort** actions cover other civil complaints (e.g., fraud, deceit, injury) arising from auditors' failure to exercise the appropriate level of professional care (substandard performance). Clients or users of financial statements can bring tort actions against auditors.

Suits for damages under common law usually result when someone suffers a financial loss after relying on financial statements later found to be materially misstated. The popular press calls such unfortunate events *audit failures*. **Plaintiffs** in legal actions involving auditors (clients or third-party users of financial statements) generally assert all possible causes of action, including breach of contract, tort, deceit, fraud, and whatever else may be relevant to the claim. Various legal terms that will be used throughout this module are summarized in the accompanying feature for reference.

Liability to Clients

Clients may bring a lawsuit for breach of contract and other tort actions. The relationship of direct involvement between parties to a contract is known as **privity of contract**. When privity exists, plaintiffs must demonstrate all of the following:

1. They suffered an economic loss.
2. Auditors did not perform in accordance with the terms of the contract (for breach of contract).
3. Auditors failed to exercise the appropriate level of professional care (for tort actions).
4. The breach of contract or failure to exercise the appropriate level of professional care caused the loss.

The first case in the United States involving an auditor and client dispute (*Smith v. London Assurance Corp.*) established auditors' obligation for breach of contract.

Legal Precedent

SMITH V. LONDON ASSURANCE CORP. (1905)
This was the first U.S. case involving auditors. Smith, the auditor, sued the client (**London Assurance Corp.**) for an unpaid fee. In a countersuit, London Assurance Corp. brought suit against Smith for losses resulting from employee embezzlement, which London claimed would not have occurred except for the auditors' breach of contract. The evidence indicated that Smith had indeed failed to audit the cash accounts at one branch office as stipulated in an engagement contract. The court recognized auditors as skilled professionals and held Smith liable for the embezzlement losses that could have been prevented by appropriate performance under the terms of the contract.

In addition to breach of contract, auditors may be liable to clients for tort liability. Three levels of substandard performance that may lead to tort liability include (listed from least severe to most severe):

1. **Ordinary negligence**: An unintentional breach of duty owed to another party because of a lack of reasonable care.
2. **Gross negligence**: A breach of duty owed to another party because of a lack of minimal care.
3. **Fraud**: A misrepresentation of facts that the individual knows to be false with the intention to deceive.

Because of the very close relationship between auditors and their clients, auditors have a high level of responsibility to their clients. This responsibility is to conduct an audit in accordance with GAAS; if auditors exhibit *ordinary negligence,* clients will typically prevail in their legal actions against auditors. (Auditors are also liable to their clients for *gross negligence* and *fraud.*)

Auditors' Defenses for Client Claims

Auditors may attempt to mitigate clients' claims by using one of the following three defenses:

1. Auditors exercised the appropriate level of professional care (tort) or performed the engagement in accordance with terms of the contract (breach of contract).
2. The client's economic loss was caused by a factor other than auditors' failure to exercise appropriate levels of professional care or breach of contract (the **causation defense**).
3. Actions on the part of the client were, in part, responsible for the loss (for example, failure of the client to establish effective internal control to prevent embezzlement losses). This is referred to as **contributory negligence** and is available to auditors in certain jurisdictions.

Liability to Third Parties

In the early part of the 20th century, parties other than clients had difficulty succeeding in lawsuits against auditors. Parties not in privity of contract have no cause of action for breach of contract. However, these parties can bring lawsuits against auditors for failure to exercise appropriate levels of professional care (tort action). In these cases, third parties suffer an economic loss because they relied on the audited financial statements and auditors' reports on those statements. Recall that the three levels of failure to exercise the appropriate level of professional care that have emerged through various cases are

defenses available against clients, except for the unavailability of the contributory negligence defense in cases brought by third parties:)

1. The third party did not have appropriate standing to sue in that jurisdiction (for example, bringing suit for ordinary negligence if the appropriate relationship between auditors and third party does not exist). Recall that auditors' liability to third parties for ordinary negligence differs significantly depending on the jurisdiction in which the action is brought.

2. The third party's loss was caused by events other than the financial statements and auditors' examination (causation defense). For example, the failure of an entity (and losses incurred by parties providing capital to that entity) may result from poor business practices and decisions, not misstated financial statements.

3. Auditors' work was performed in accordance with professional standards (e.g., GAAS for audits of financial statements), which is generally interpreted to mean that auditors were not negligent (ordinary negligence).

Liability for Compilation and Review Services

People find it easy to think about common law liability in connection with audited financial statements. Do not forget, however, that accountants also render compilation and review services and are associated with the resultant *unaudited* financial information. Users expect public accountants to perform these services in accordance with professional standards, and courts can impose liability for accounting work found to be substandard. Accountants have been assessed damages for work on such statements, as shown in the *1136 Tenants' Corporation v. Max Rothenberg & Co.* case. In this case, the court concluded that accountants engaged to perform "write-up" (compilation) work had a duty to inform clients of indicators of fraud that were identified during the engagement.

One significant risk involved with compilation and review engagements is that the client may fail to understand the nature of the service being given. Accountants should use a conference and an engagement letter to explain clearly that a compilation engagement (write-up) does not involve gathering sufficient appropriate evidence and is lesser in scope than a review engagement. Similarly, a review service should be explained in terms of being less extensive than an audit engagement conducted in accordance with GAAS. Clear understandings at the outset (along with clearly worded engagement letters) can enable accountants and clients to avoid later disagreements. In *Iselin v. Landau* (1992), the court decided that the lack of an opinion on reviewed financial statements precluded the third party (**William Iselin & Company**) from bringing a lawsuit against the auditors (**Mann Judd Landau**) because of losses suffered from the bankruptcy of one of Iselin's customers. (Mann Judd Landau had performed a review engagement on the financial statements of Iselin's customer.)

✅ REVIEW CHECKPOINTS

C.3 For what type of actions can clients bring suit against auditors under common law? What must clients prove prior to bringing suit in each case?

C.4 In terms of tort liability, what level of responsibility do auditors owe clients under common law?

C.5 What must third parties prove in a common law action seeking recovery of damages from auditors?

C.6 What legal theory is derived from the *Ultramares* decision? Can auditors rely on the *Ultramares* decision today?

C.7 Define and explain *privity, primary beneficiary, foreseen party,* and *foreseeable party* in terms of the degree of failure to exercise the appropriate level of professional care on the part of auditors that would trigger the liability.

C.8 What defenses are available to auditors against suits brought by clients under common law? Against suits brought by third parties under common law?

C.9 What additional defenses can accountants use in lawsuits related to compilation and review engagements?

LIABILITY UNDER STATUTORY LAW

LO C-3

Describe auditors' liability to third parties under statutory law.

Auditors can be liable to individuals when they violate a specific law or statute when performing professional services; this is referred to as *statutory liability*. Several federal statutes provide sources of potential liability for auditors, including the Federal False Statements Statute, the Federal Mail Fraud Statute, the Federal Conspiracy Statute, the Securities Act of 1933 (Securities Act), the Securities Exchange Act of 1934 (Securities Exchange Act), and the Sarbanes–Oxley Act. Federal securities regulation in the United States was enacted in the 1930s not only as a reaction to the events of the early years of the Great Depression but also as a culmination of attempts at "blue-sky" regulation by states.[12] The Securities Act and the Securities Exchange Act require registrants to disclose important financial and nonfinancial information required for making informed investment decisions. The securities acts and the SEC operate for the protection of investors and for the facilitation of orderly capital markets. Even so, no federal government agency, including the SEC, rules on the *quality* of investments. The securities acts have been characterized as "truth-in-securities" law. Their spirit favors the otherwise uninformed investing public, and caveat vendor—let the seller beware of violations—is applied to the issuer.

As the following graphic shows, auditors are exposed to liability under the Securities Act and the Securities Exchange Act when investors purchase or sell securities ([1] in the graphic). If an economic loss is suffered [2] and if the financial statements contain a material misstatement [3], auditors may be held liable for failure to detect the material misstatement.

Although not involving an auditor, the following Auditing Insight demonstrates the need for shareholders to prove they suffered an economic loss to successfully bring suit.

AUDITING INSIGHT   Who Needs to Show a Loss?

In a federal judge's decision to overturn a jury award of $5.55 per share to shareholders of Apollo Group Inc. (owner of the University of Phoenix), the judge did not dispute the contention that Apollo may have misled investors by withholding a negative report on student recruitment policies contained in a Department of Education Review.

However, he indicated that "[the plaintiffs] failed to prove that Apollo's actions caused investors to suffer any harm."

Source: "Verdict Against Apollo Group Overturned," *The Wall Street Journal*, August 6, 2008, p. B5.

Because of the availability of class action litigation and the wide dissemination and use of financial information filed with the SEC, litigation against auditors under the Securities Act and Securities and Exchange Act is the highest growing area of concern for auditors. The following sections discuss auditors' liability under these acts in more detail.

✓ REVIEW CHECKPOINT

C.10 How does auditors' liability under statutory law arise?

[12]The term *blue sky* comes from a state judge's remark during a securities fraud case: "These securities have no more substance than a piece of blue sky."

THE SECURITIES ACT OF 1933 (SECURITIES ACT)

LO C-4
Specify the civil and criminal liability provisions of the Securities Act of 1933.

The Securities Act of 1933 regulates the initial issuance of securities by registrants to the investing public through a market (including **initial public offerings [IPOs]**). The Securities Act provides that no person may lawfully buy, sell, offer to buy, or offer to sell any security by means of interstate commerce unless a **registration statement** is *effective* (a legal term essentially meaning *filed and accepted by the SEC*). A registration statement is a set of documents filed with the SEC prior to the offering of securities. An important component of the registration statement is a **prospectus**, which is a legal document offering securities for sale and includes significant information about the issuing entity, including its historical financial statements and other necessary disclosures. Certain exemptions exist for limited offerings, offerings by small investors, and offerings involving financially sophisticated investors; these exemptions can be found in section 3, section 4, and Regulation D of the Securities Act.

The general point concerning the Securities Act is that, with some minor exceptions, *all* issuances of securities to the public must be registered with the SEC. Importantly for the auditor, the Securities Act requires that the registration statement include financial statements and required disclosures that ". . . shall be certified by an independent public or certified accountant"; this language requires an audit examination. Auditors are required not only to audit the financial statements as of the most recent date of the financial statements but also to ensure that these statements are fairly stated up to the date the registration statement becomes effective, which could possibly be up to one year beyond the date of the financial statements. This audit requirement provides the basis for auditors' liability to investors under the Securities Act.

Section 11: Civil Liability

Section 11 of the Securities Act is of great interest to auditors because of the duties and responsibilities it establishes. This section discusses the principal criteria defining civil liabilities under the statute.

Section 11. Securities Act of 1933

The following excerpts from Section 11 are of particular importance in identifying the responsibilities of auditors under this Act.

Section 11(a): . . . any person acquiring such security [in a registered offering] . . . may sue:

- Every person who signed the registration statement.
- Every person who was a director of . . . or partner in, the issuer.
- Every *accountant*, engineer, or appraiser.
- Every underwriter with respect to such security.

Section 11(b): Notwithstanding the provisions of subsection (a), no person, other than the issuer, shall be liable as provided therein who shall sustain the burden of proof that . . . as regards any part of the registration statement purporting to be made upon his authority as an expert . . . he had, after reasonable investigation, reasonable grounds to believe . . . that the statements therein were true and that there was no omission to state a material fact. . . .

Although section 11(a) notes that a number of parties involved in the registration and sale process might be liable to persons acquiring securities, section 11(b) generally limits the liability to the issuers of securities with some exceptions. Because auditors are considered to be the "experts" regarding the fairness of the financial statements and must perform a "reasonable investigation" (an audit in accordance with GAAS), section 11(b) is of great importance to auditors. This requirement imposes liability for auditors for acts representing *ordinary negligence*.

Auditors commonly provide assurance to underwriters, who act as intermediaries between the offering entity and investing public by purchasing securities for investment or resale. Auditors provide **comfort letters** to underwriters that address, among other information, the independence of auditors and the fairness of the registrant's financial statements.

Section 11 includes two other very important implications for auditors. First, reviewing the first two words in section 11(*a*), "*any person*" [emphasis added] may bring suit against auditors. Essentially, the Securities Act treats *all* persons as being *reasonably foreseeable* and holds auditors liable to these persons. In addition, section 11 shifts the major burden of proof from the plaintiff (investor) to the auditors; essentially, plaintiffs must prove each of the following:

1. They suffered an economic loss.
2. The financial statements contained a material misstatement.

Recall that under common law liability, plaintiffs had to also allege and prove some level of failure to exercise the appropriate level of professional care and that the loss was caused by reliance on the misstated financial statements. Thus, under the Securities Act, the plaintiff is *not* required to demonstrate that the misstated financial statements caused the loss; the burden of proof regarding professional care rests with auditors. Section 11 has the following major implications for auditors:

• Auditors are liable for ordinary negligence.
• Auditors have potential liability to a large class of parties (investors in securities).
• Auditors (not others) have the burden of proof, in this case, proving that a reasonable investigation under section 11(*b*) was conducted.

The final implication is particularly important because it presumes that auditors are "guilty until proven innocent" and has increased auditors' exposure to investors. However, section 11 was written with the protection of the investing public in mind, not the protection of the expert auditors. The first significant court case under section 11 was *Escott v. BarChris Construction Corporation.*

Legal Precedent

ESCOTT V. BARCHRIS CONSTRUCTION CORP. (1968)

BarChris Construction Corporation built bowling alleys. In 1961, BarChris engaged in a public offering of convertible bonds that was subject to the provisions of the Securities Act. BarChris issued a registration statement that included financial statements audited by **Peat, Marwick, Mitchell & Co.** (now KPMG). The financial statements included material overstatements of revenues, current assets, gross profit, and backlog of sales orders and material understatements of contingent liabilities, loans to company officers, and potential liability for customer delinquencies. BarChris's worsening financial condition resulted in a default on interest payments (the economic loss), and BarChris eventually declared bankruptcy. Investors sued BarChris's executive officers, directors, and auditor (Peat, Marwick, Mitchell & Co.) under the provisions of the Securities Act, citing lack of appropriate level of professional care during the conduct of the audit.

The judge ruled that the auditors had failed to perform a diligent and reasonable investigation [section 11(*b*)]. The judge found that the auditor had spent "only" 20.5 hours on the subsequent events review, had read no important documents, and "He asked questions, he got answers that he considered satisfactory, and he did nothing to verify them. . .. He was too easily satisfied with glib answers to his inquiries." The judge also said, "Accountants should not be held to a standard higher than that recognized in their profession. I do not do so here. The senior accountant's review [of subsequent events] did not come up to that standard. He did not take some of the steps which [the] written program prescribed. He did not spend an adequate amount of time on a task of this magnitude."

Case conclusion: The auditors' failure to perform a reasonable investigation of subsequent events did not satisfy section 11(*b*) and resulted in their liability to investors in BarChris's bonds.

Auditors' Defenses under the Securities Act

Section 11 provides two possible defenses to auditors, assuming that purchasers of securities are able to demonstrate they suffered a loss and the financial statements are materially misstated. Note that these defenses are similar to two defenses available to auditors for actions brought by clients and third parties under common law.

purchase or sale of securities. Rule 10(*b*)-5, made by the SEC staff under their authority to create administrative rules related to the statute, is more explicit than section 10 in identifying auditors' specific responsibilities.

Rule 10(*b*)-5. Securities Exchange Act of 1934

Rule 10(*b*)-5. Employment of Manipulative and Deceptive Devices. It shall be unlawful for any person, directly or indirectly, by the use of any means or instrumentality of interstate commerce, or of the mails, or of any facility of any national securities exchange,

1. To employ any device, scheme, or artifice to defraud.
2. To make any untrue statement of material fact or to omit to state a material fact necessary in order to make the statements made,

in the light of the circumstances under which they were made, not misleading.

3. To engage in any act, practice, or course of business that operates or would operate as a fraud or deceit upon any person in connection with the purchase or sale of any security.

An important point about Rule 10(*b*)-5 liability is that plaintiffs must prove **scienter** (a mental state embracing the intent to deceive, manipulate, or defraud) to impose liability under the rule. Mere failure to exercise the appropriate level of professional care is not enough cause for liability. Two cases (*Ernst & Ernst v. Hochfelder* and *Denise L. Nappier et al. v. PricewaterhouseCoopers*) illustrate the need for purchasers and sellers of securities to prove scienter on the part of auditors and confirm the inability for these parties to bring suit against auditors for ordinary negligence. The *Hochfelder* case was also significant in providing exposure for auditors in cases of gross negligence, even in the absence of scienter.

Legal Precedent

ERNST & ERNST V. HOCHFELDER (1976)

In this case, **Hochfelder** represented investors in an escrow account with **First Securities of Chicago**; this account was maintained by Lester Nay (president of First Securities), who diverted funds for his own personal use through a fraudulent scheme that was revealed in a suicide note prepared by Nay. When the escrow accounts proved worthless (the economic loss), the investors (through Hochfelder) brought suit against the auditor (**Ernst & Ernst**), alleging that their negligence prevented them from uncovering the scheme and preventing their losses. Hochfelder specifically disclaimed any allegations of fraud or intentional misconduct on the part of Ernst & Ernst but wanted to sue for liability under section 10(*b*) imposed for ordinary negligence in the auditors' failure to uncover the fraudulent scheme.

The Court reasoned that section 10(*b*) in its reference to "employment of any manipulative and deceptive device" meant that intention to deceive, manipulate, or defraud is necessary to support a private cause of action under section 10(*b*), and failure to exercise the appropriate level of professional care is not sufficient. This decision is considered a landmark for auditors because it relieved them of liability for ordinary negligence under section 10(*b*) of the Securities Exchange Act and its companion SEC Rule 10(*b*)-5.

However, footnote 12 in this opinion noted that "[in] certain areas of the law recklessness is considered to be a form of intentional conduct for purposes of imposing liability for some act. We need not address here the

question whether, in some circumstances, reckless behavior is sufficient for civil liability under 10(*b*) and Rule 10(*b*)-5."

Case conclusion: This case established precedent for the plaintiff's need to prove scienter to impose section 10(*b*) liability under the Securities Exchange Act. In addition, the reference to "recklessness" in the footnote to the opinion provides potential exposure to auditors for gross negligence under the Securities Exchange Act.

DENISE L. NAPPIER ET AL. V. PRICEWATERHOUSECOOPERS (2002)

Denise L. Nappier (treasurer of the state of Connecticut) successfully brought suit on behalf of shareholders (including Connecticut Retirement Plans and Trust Funds) against **Campbell Soup Company** and its directors for losses incurred upon declines in Campbell's stock price (the economic loss). In this suit, Nappier demonstrated that the purchase of these shares was influenced by audited financial statements that were shown to contain material misstatements. The shareholders then attempted to assert an additional claim against Campbell's auditor (**Pricewaterhouse Coopers**), alleging that it violated the provisions of the Securities Exchange Act by being a party to the preparation and certification of fraudulent financial statements.

Case conclusion: The case was dismissed when the shareholders could not prove the allegation that PricewaterhouseCoopers operated with scienter in conducting its audits of Campbell's financial statements.

Section 18: Civil Liability

Section 18 sets forth the pertinent civil liability under the Securities Exchange Act. Under Rule 10(*b*)-5 and section 18, plaintiffs have the same burden of proof as under common law. (That is, they must demonstrate that the loss was caused by reliance on the materially misstated financial statements and that the auditors failed to exercise the appropriate level of professional care.) However, under the Securities Exchange Act, plaintiffs must demonstrate scienter on the part of auditors. Thus, plaintiffs must demonstrate all of the following:

1. They suffered an economic loss.
2. The financial statements contained a material misstatement.
3. The loss was caused by reliance on the materially misstated financial statements.
4. Auditors were aware that the financial statements contained a material misstatement. (Recall that, under *Hochfelder,* auditors may be held liable for gross negligence.)

Of note, two key differences in liability under the Securities Exchange Act and Securities Act are that, under the former (1) plaintiffs have the burden of proof and (2) auditors cannot be held liable for ordinary negligence. The importance of placing the burden of proof on the plaintiffs is illustrated by cases summarized in the accompanying Auditing Insight. Clearly, the shift of burden of proof from auditors (in the Securities Act) to plaintiffs (in the Securities Exchange Act) is an important distinction and determinant in plaintiffs' ability to successfully prevail in securities actions.

AUDITING INSIGHT   Prove It!

The importance of placing the burden of proof on plaintiffs is demonstrated by two decisions. The U.S. Court of Appeals for the Seventh Circuit (*Tricontinental Industries v. Pricewaterhouse Coopers, LLP*) and the U.S. Court of Appeals for the Second Circuit *(Lattanzio v. Deloitte & Touche, LLP)* dismissed charges against the accounting firms because plaintiffs failed to demonstrate that their losses were caused by materially misstated financial statements. The following excerpt from the Seventh Circuit Court in the former case is of particular note:

Although we agree with the district court that Tricontinental's scienter allegations are problematic, we believe that Tricontinental's claim for pre-closing fraud suffers from a more fundamental infirmity. . . . Tricontinental's claim falls short with respect to the last requirement: Tricontinental does not allege how PwC's fraud caused its losses.

Sources: *Tricontinental Industries v. PricewaterhouseCoopers LLP,* 2007, U.S. App. LEXIS 7247 (7th Cir., 2007); *Lattanzio v. Deloitte & Touche LLP,* 476 F.3d 147 (2d Cir. 2007).

Section 18 of the Securities Exchange Act establishes a statute of limitations of one year after discovery of the violation of the Act or within three years after the violation of the Act itself; for cases involving fraud, Sarbanes–Oxley extends these dates to two and five years, respectively.

Auditors' Defenses under the Securities Exchange Act

As a defense, auditors can attempt to demonstrate that they acted in "good faith" and had no knowledge of the material misstatement. (Causation is not a defense because it is presumed that the plaintiff has already demonstrated this in bringing suit.) Although this would seem to imply that auditors are liable only for fraudulent actions under the Securities Exchange Act (by demonstrating they had no knowledge of the material misstatement), the *Hochfelder* decision has resulted in some uncertainty as to auditors' liability in the absence of scienter (specifically, for acts that may be considered to represent gross negligence). Importantly, in contrast to the Securities Act, auditors are not liable to shareholders for actions representing ordinary negligence under the Securities Exchange Act.

Section 32: Criminal Liability

Section 32 states the criminal penalties for violation of the Securities Exchange Act. Like that pertaining to section 24 of the Securities Act, the critical test is whether the violator acted "willfully and knowingly." Therefore, to be subject to criminal liability, auditors must be shown to be guilty of fraud. Sarbanes–Oxley markedly increased the criminal penalties for violating the Securities Exchange Act; currently, violators may be fined up to $5 million and imprisoned for up to 20 years. In addition, Sarbanes–Oxley provides that if the "person" was not a natural person (for example, an accounting firm), fines of up to $25 million can be assessed. The *United States v. Natelli* (better known as the "National Student Marketing" case) illustrates potential criminal liability for auditors charged with violations of section 32. (It is important to note that this case occurred prior to the increased liability imposed by Sarbanes–Oxley.)

Legal Precedent

UNITED STATES V. NATELLI ("NATIONAL STUDENT MARKETING" CASE) (1975)

In this case, two auditors were convicted because of their involvement with materially misstated financial statements included in the proxy statement of **National Student Marketing Corporation.** These financial statements failed to reveal a $1 million write-off of "sales" (about 20 percent of the amount previously reported) and a corresponding large adjustment to National Student Marketing's operating income. The court stated:

- It is hard to probe the intent of a defendant. . . . When we deal with a defendant who is a professional accountant, it is even harder at times

to distinguish between simple errors of judgment and errors made with sufficient criminal intent to support a conviction, especially when there is no financial gain to the accountant other than his legitimate fee.

Case conclusion: Both the audit partner in charge of the engagement (Anthony Natelli) and his supervisor were fined and received jail sentences of one year each. Although a federal appeals court reversed the supervisor's conviction, it upheld Natelli's conviction because of his apparent motive and action to conceal the effect of some accounting adjustments. Natelli's sentence was eventually reduced to 60 days.

Foreign Corrupt Practices Act (FCPA)

In 1977, Congress passed the FCPA, which

- Made it illegal for corporations or their officers to knowingly bribe foreign officials or participate in bribery schemes involving foreign officials to obtain or retain business.
- Required entities to develop and maintain effective internal controls.

In 1988, the FCPA became codified as an amendment to the Securities Exchange Act. As a result, auditors may be liable for violations of this act if they should have identified these violations during their examination. In a 2008 settlement, German conglomerate **Siemens AG** agreed to pay $800 million to settle bribery investigations involving payment to foreign government officials; Siemens did not admit to the bribery allegations, but it did acknowledge having inadequate controls and maintaining improper accounting records. This was the largest fine ever imposed under the FCPA.[13] More recent investigations involving alleged payments made by **Hewlett-Packard** to secure a contract for the delivery and installation of an information network to Russia's prosecutor general, offers by **Goldman Sachs** and other financial institutions for payments to a Libyan investment authority, and **Oracle's** software sales to government agencies in Western and Central Africa indicate that increasing scrutiny is being placed on potential violations of FCPA, as noted in the accompanying Auditing Insight.[14]

---

[13]"Siemens to Pay Huge Fine in Bribery Inquiry," *The Wall Street Journal,* December 15, 2008, p. B1.
[14]"H-P Bribe Probe Widens," *The Wall Street Journal,* September 10, 2010, p. B1; "SEC Probes Goldman Over Libyan Dealings," *The Wall Street Journal,* August 10, 2011, p. C1; "U.S. Probes Oracle Dealings," *The Wall Street Journal,* August 31, 2011, pp. B1, B2.

AUDITING INSIGHT   Increased Focus on FCPA

The U.S. Department of Justice is increasing its enforcement of potential FCPA violations, as evidenced by the following:

- Nearly 80 percent of corporate acquisitions have either ended or been renegotiated because of anticorruption issues or potential violations of the FCPA. These decisions are likely driven by the experiences of companies such as General Electric, which was required to pay $23.4 million in fines to settle FCPA violations at **Ionics** and **Amersham** that occurred prior to General Electric's acquisition of these entities.

- All of the 10 largest settlements for violations of FCPA have occurred since 2008; 8 occurred in 2010 alone.

- In 2000, prosecutors brought no charges in FCPA criminal actions; in 2009, they pursued 34 actions with an additional 150 open investigations in process.

- In 2016, the SEC settled almost two dozen FCPA allegations, including agreeements with J.P. Morgan ($264 million), Embraer ($205 million), and Annheuser-Busch InBev ($6 million).

Sources: "The Bribery Law Racket," *Forbes*, May 24, 2010, pp. 70–77; "Deal-Breaker: Fear of the FCPA," *CFO.com*, February 15, 2011; "SEC Enforcement Actions: FCPA Cases," www.sec.gov/spotlight/fcpa/fcpa-cases/shtml.

✓ REVIEW CHECKPOINTS

C.18 Identify the contents of Form 10-K, Form 10-Q, and Form 8-K. How are auditors involved with the information in these filings?

C.19 What are (a) Regulation S-X, (b) Regulation S-K, (c) Financial Reporting Releases, and (d) Staff Accounting Bulletins?

C.20 Who may bring suit against auditors under the Securities Exchange Act? What must these parties demonstrate in order to bring suit?

C.21 What defenses are available to auditors under the Securities Exchange Act?

C.22 What are the criminal penalties associated with violations of the Securities Exchange Act?

C.23 What is *scienter*? How do the findings in *Ernst & Ernst v. Hochfelder* and *Denise L. Nappier et al. v. PricewaterhouseCoopers* relate to scienter?

C.24 What are the major differences in auditors' liability under the Securities Act of 1933 and the Securities Exchange Act of 1934?

SUMMARY OF AUDITORS' LIABILITY TO CLIENTS AND THIRD PARTIES

Thus far, we have discussed auditors' potential liability to clients and third parties under both common law and statutory law (Securities Act of 1933 and Securities Exchange Act of 1934, respectively). Exhibit C.2 summarizes various elements of this liability, including (1) the level of professional care (performance) owed to various parties by auditors, (2) the burden of proof, and (3) various defenses available to auditors. Most noteworthy in Exhibit C.2 is the fact that plaintiffs have the burden of proving that auditors' failure to exercise the appropriate level of professional care caused the loss ("burden of proof") under common law and the Securities Exchange Act of 1934; however, the burden of proof is with auditors under the Securities Act of 1933. See Exhibit C.3 for a summary of important cases that have either developed auditor liability (common law) or clarified various provisions of the Securities Acts.

It is important to note that auditors' liability will continue to evolve over time. In a 2007 case (*Tellabs Inc. v. Makor Issues & Rights Ltd.*), the U.S. Supreme Court held that trial courts must consider all plausible inferences of scienter and that cases should be permitted to proceed only if the possibility of scienter is "cogent and at least as compelling as any opposing inference."[15] Some cases have been dismissed using this standard, but other cases have taken the view that the burden of proof regarding scienter still remains with the defendant. Future cases and rulings will likely provide further clarification as to the relative burden of proof in cases involving accusations of scienter.

---

[15] *Tellabs Inc. v. Makor Issues & Rights Ltd.*, 127 S. Ct. 2499 (2007).

EXHIBIT C.2 **Summary of Auditors' Liability**

Source of Liability	Party(ies) Involved	Plaintiff Proof	Type of Offense	Auditors' Defenses
Common law	Client	• Economic loss • Auditors' breach of contract or failure to exercise the appropriate level of professional care • Loss caused by breach of contract or failure to exercise appropriate level of professional care	• Breach of contract • Ordinary negligence • Gross negligence • Fraud	• No breach of contract or no failure to exercise the appropriate level of professional care • Economic loss caused by other factors (causation) • Clients partially responsible for loss (contributory negligence)
	Third parties	• Economic loss • Auditors' failure to exercise the appropriate level of professional care • Material misstatements in financial statements • Loss caused by reliance on materially misstated financial statements	• Ordinary negligence (depends on jurisdiction and standing of party) • Gross negligence • Fraud	• Lack of appropriate standing (relationship) between third party and auditors • Loss caused by factors other than financial statements and auditors' examination • Work performed in accordance with GAAS or other professional standards
Securities Act of 1933	Purchasers of securities in an initial registration	• Economic loss • Material misstatements in financial statements	• Ordinary negligence • Gross negligence • Fraud	• Due diligence (auditors conducted a GAAS audit) • Loss caused by factors other than financial statements and auditors' examination
Securities Exchange Act of 1934	Purchasers and sellers of securities through subsequent transactions	• Economic loss • Material misstatements in financial statements • Loss caused by reliance on materially misstated financial statements • Auditors were aware of material misstatements and acted with intent (scienter)	• Gross negligence • Fraud	• Auditors acted in good faith • Auditors had no knowledge of material misstatements

EXHIBIT C.3 **Significant Cases Affecting Auditors' Liability**

Smith v. London Assurance Corp. (1905)	• Established auditors' liability to clients for breach of contract
Ultramares Corp. v. Touche (1931)	• Established rights of third parties not in privity with auditors to bring legal action • Concluded that auditors are generally not liable to third parties not in privity for ordinary negligence but could be liable for gross negligence
Credit Alliance v. Arthur Andersen (1985)	• Established auditors' liability to primary beneficiaries for ordinary negligence
Rusch Factors v. Levin (1968); *Fleet National Bank v. Gloucester Co. (1994)*	• Established auditors' liability to foreseen parties for ordinary negligence *(restatement of torts doctrine)*
Rosenblum Inc. v. Adler (1983)	• Established auditors' liability to foreseeable parties for ordinary negligence
Escott v. BarChris Construction Corp. (1968)	• Confirmed auditor liability for ordinary negligence to investors under the Securities Act • Established importance of auditors' review of subsequent events
Ernst & Ernst v. Hochfelder (1976)	• Confirmed auditors' liability to shareholders under the Securities Exchange Act if scienter is demonstrated • Provided potential exposure to auditors for gross negligence even in absence of scienter

THE CHANGING LANDSCAPE OF AUDITORS' LIABILITY

LO C-6
Understand recent developments that affect auditors' liability to clients and third parties.

The preceding discussion identifies the significant exposure of auditors to legal liability for their actions to various parties. Most people would argue that auditors performing substandard work *should* be held liable for that work, but a number of factors have increased auditors' exposure to litigation brought by plaintiffs:

- Increased pressure to hold auditors accountable in light of a number of highly publicized audit failures in the early 2000s (e.g., **Enron** and **WorldCom**) and the significant losses of billions of dollars to investors in those companies.
- Investors' and other individuals' awareness of litigation against auditors as an avenue to recover losses, regardless of the actual reason for and cause of those losses.
- The existence of highly complex accounting standards and difficulty in interpreting and evaluating financial statements prepared under those standards (e.g., Audit Analytics, a financial statement analysis tracking company, reports that there have been over 500 annual financial report restatements per year since 2002).
- The doctrine of joint and several liability, which may expose auditors to extensive and unreasonable losses when they are only partially at fault.
- The availability of class action suits, which makes it attractive for a small number of individuals to bring suit on behalf of a larger number of others.
- The availability of joint and several liability, class action suits, and contingent fee arrangements make litigation against auditors an attractive opportunity for plaintiff attorneys.

AUDITING INSIGHT · Are CPAs a Target?

In addition to the number of factors listed here that have increased auditors' exposure to litigation brought by plaintiffs, a recent article identified the following additional factors that are providing auditors increased exposure for liability claims:

- A reduced likelihood of judges dismissing charges against auditors.
- The availability of insurance, which makes auditors a desirable target for attorneys for recovery.

- Mergers of smaller firms and larger firms and difficulties during the transition period of these mergers because of the lack of effective risk management practices for smaller firms.
- Reductions in staff by accounting firms in response to the economic 2008–2010 downturn.
- Clients' increased interest in pursuing professional liability claims to recoup losses during the economic downturn.

Source: "Target CPAs," *Accounting Today,* July 1, 2011, pp. 1, 53.

The auditing profession considers the U.S. tort liability system a crisis of expanding liability exposure in need of reform. Some important reforms that have been implemented or are currently being discussed in response to these damages are summarized in the remainder of this section. Some of these reforms influence auditors' liability under common law and statutory law described in the preceding sections.

Sarbanes–Oxley

The corporate scandals of Enron and WorldCom were the impetus for the creation and passage of the *U.S. Public Company Reform and Investor Protection Act of 2002,* better known as the *Sarbanes–Oxley Act.* This act seeks to strengthen corporate accountability and governance of public entities. Although the more publicized aspects of Sarbanes–Oxley affect corporate officers and directors, some of its provisions affect auditors' statutory liability under the securities acts by increasing the penalties for auditors' involvement in financial statement fraud. Many of the aspects of Sarbanes–Oxley that affect auditors' planning, implementation, and reporting processes are discussed in other chapters in this book. Sarbanes–Oxley has impacted auditors' liability as follows:

- Extended the statute of limitations for bringing suit under the Securities Exchange Act to the earlier of (1) two years after the discovery of facts relating to violations of the act or (2) five years following the violation of the act. In addition, as noted earlier, the penalties for securities fraud have been increased to provide for fines of up to $5 million and imprisonment of up to 20 years for violations of the Securities Exchange Act.
- Increased penalties for mail fraud and wire fraud from 5 years to 20 years of imprisonment.
- Addressed the destruction, alteration, or falsification of records in federal investigations and bankruptcies. Although these issues are addressed in laws regarding obstruction of justice and were the means by which the Department of Justice successfully prosecuted **Arthur Andersen**, Sarbanes–Oxley adds another avenue to pursue actions against accounting firms that fail to cooperate with federal investigations.[16] Firms and individuals found to have altered or destroyed documents with the intent to impede an investigation may be subject to fines and imprisonment for up to 20 years. In addition, under PCAOB standards, accountants performing an audit of a public company must maintain all engagement documentation for a period of seven years. Firms that do not comply with the record-retention provision are subject to fines and imprisonment of individual violators within the firm for up to 10 years. This provision of Sarbanes–Oxley has forced many firms to review and revise their record-retention policies.

In addition to the preceding items, Sarbanes–Oxley amended federal sentencing guidelines that increase financial and criminal penalties when securities fraud, obstruction of justice, and criminal fraud exist. This means not only that auditors face a higher liability risk but also that Sarbanes–Oxley may influence the courts in decisions regarding awards in civil cases. These provisions are considered a setback for the accounting profession's initiative to reduce auditors' liability.

AUDITING INSIGHT When Does the Auditor's Responsibility End?

A recent case may expand liability under the Securities Exchange Act by requiring auditors to evaluate the appropriateness of previously issued opinions. In *Overton v. Todman & Co, CPAs PC,* plaintiffs alleged that **Todman & Co.** (auditors) became aware of misstatements in the financial statements of **Direct Brokerage** following the issuance of their unmodified opinion on Direct Brokerage financial statements in 2002. (These misstatements existed at the date of Todman & Co.'s opinion, but Todman & Co. was unaware of them at that time.) David Overton subsequently used these financial statements to invest and loan more than $2 million to Direct Brokerage;

Overton suffered an economic loss when Direct Brokerage ceased operations in 2004.

The U.S. Court of Appeals for the Second District ruled that Todman & Co.'s failure to correct or withdraw its previously issued opinion resulted in liability under section 10(*b*) and Rule 10(*b*)-5. The court did note that its findings required auditors to correct only previous opinions for facts existing at the date of these opinions, not update these opinions based on subsequent developments.

Source: *David Overton and Jerome Kransdorf v. Todman & Co., CPAs, PC, and Trien, Rosenberg, Rosenberg, Weinberg, Ciulo & Fazzari,* 478 F.3d 479 (2d Cir. 2007).

Racketeer Influenced and Corrupt Organizations Act

The Racketeer Influenced and Corrupt Organizations Act (RICO) was enacted to combat organized crime in businesses and other organizations by providing for extended criminal penalties and civil courses of action for various offenses. RICO targeted members of organized crime, but an unintended consequence of this legislation was exposure of its provisions to auditors, whom attorneys threatened to classify as "racketeers" and impose

---

[16]Arthur Andersen was indicted and convicted of obstruction of justice, which resulted in the firm's collapse. This conviction was subsequently reversed by the U.S. Supreme Court, but it was too late to save Andersen. See "KPMG Faces Indictment Risk on Tax Shelters: Justice Officials Debate Whether to Pursue Case; Fears of 'Andersen Scenario,'" *The Wall Street Journal,* June 16, 2005, p. A1.

the threat of penalties for treble (triple) damages under the law. In 1988, **Laventhol & Horwath** (at the time, the seventh-largest accounting firm) became the first firm to lose a jury trial under RICO statutes related to its role in a cattle-breeding venture in which almost 3,000 investors lost more than $20 million. (Laventhol & Horwath subsequently filed for bankruptcy in 1990.)[17]

In 1993, the U.S. Supreme Court (in *Reeves v. Arthur Young*) ruled that auditors are not subject to RICO complaints unless they "actively participate" in the management or operation of a corrupt business. Thus, failure to exercise the appropriate level of professional care (i.e., ordinary negligence) is not sufficient to use the provisions of RICO in a lawsuit against auditors.

Aiding and Abetting

Under the legal doctrine of aiding and abetting, plaintiffs have the ability to include parties in legal actions who were indirectly involved with particular offenses. In the past, shareholders argued that auditors' failure to exercise the appropriate level of professional care exposed them to liability through this legal doctrine. In *Central Bank v. First Interstate Bank* (1994), the U.S. Supreme Court severely limited the extent to which the aiding and abetting doctrine could be used against auditors. More recently, in *Stoneridge Investment Partners v. Scientific-Atlanta,* the Supreme Court ruled that investors who suffer losses because of corporate fraud can typically recover losses only from the entity, its officers, and its directors, not from others who are engaged in business with the corporation. Although *Stoneridge* did not directly address involvement of auditors, the court's decision has been viewed as making it more difficult for plaintiffs to recover damages in civil actions from bankers, attorneys, and accountants under the so-called legal theory of scheme liability.[18] However, members of the Senate recently have introduced legislation that would allow civil actions to be brought against a participating party (such as an auditor) who "knowingly or recklessly provides substantial assistance" to anyone violating securities laws.[19]

Organization of Accounting Firms as Limited Liability Partnerships

Almost all of the major accounting firms have names that end with the designation LLP (limited liability partnership). Prior to 1990, accounting firms were organized as partnerships. One of the major disadvantages of the partnership form of organization is that the personal assets of all partners within the firm were at risk (i.e., were subject to loss via litigation) for the actions of all others within the firm. In the early 1990s, decisions in New York and Hawaii to permit and recognize limited liability partnerships to practice within their jurisdictions led to accounting firms reorganizing themselves as limited liability partnerships.

A limited liability partnership combines the advantages of the traditional partnership form of organization (taxation of partnership income to the partners, limited ownership of partnership interests) with the liability protection afforded to corporations. Specifically, in a limited liability partnership, any claims against the partnership are limited to partnership assets unless an individual partner directly participated in the action giving rise to the claim. After the Department of Justice indicted Arthur Andersen over the audits of Enron, some partners of the firm expressed concern about whether their limited liability partnership agreement would shield nonparticipating partners from claims. (This was never strictly tested in the courts.)[20] It is important to note that organization of a firm as a limited liability partnership does not affect the firm's legal liability but only the extent to which the individual partners' assets were subject to loss via litigation.

[17]"Laventhol to Pay $15 Million in Suit," http://articles.philly.com/1988-05-10/business/26262663_1_laventhol-horwath-rico-suits-rico-statute.
[18]"You Can't Sue the Bean Counters," *BusinessWeek,* January 28, 2008, p. 30; "Can Shareholders Sue Third Parties?" *The Wall Street Journal,* October 6–7, 2007, p. A19.
[19]"Could New Regs Bring More Lawsuits?" *CFO.com,* January 11, 2010.
[20]"Partners Forever? Within Andersen, Personal Liability May Bring Ruin," *The Wall Street Journal,* April 2, 2002, pp. C1, C16.

Proportionate Liability

One significant concern for auditors is the doctrine of **joint and several liability**, which allows a successful plaintiff to recover the full amount of a damage award from any defendant found to have failed to exercise the appropriate level of professional care regardless of the relative guilt of this defendant compared to other defendant(s). Stated another way, if both the auditors and the client are found to have been responsible for misstatements in the client's financial statements, plaintiffs can seek recovery from either or both parties. Often in cases of business failures, auditors are the only parties with "deep pockets" of financial resources to pay damages. Thus, when a group of defendants (auditors, management, and client) is found liable for damages, auditors may be required to pay the entire amount even though they may be only partially at fault. In contrast, under **proportionate liability**, a defendant is required to pay a proportionate share of the court's damage award depending on the degree of fault determined by a judge and jury (e.g., 20 percent, 30 percent, but not 100 percent).

Proportionate liability was largely accomplished at the federal level in 1995 with the passage of the *Private Securities Litigation Reform Act*. Civil lawsuits for damages now are governed by these proportionate liability terms:

- The total responsibility for loss is divided among all parties responsible for the loss.
- If other defendant(s) are insolvent, a solvent defendant's liability is extended to 50 percent more than the proportion found at trial. (For example, if an accounting firm is found 20 percent responsible for a loss and the client and its managers are insolvent, the accounting firm will have to pay 30 percent of the loss but not 100 percent as before.)
- Only the defendants who knowingly committed a violation of securities laws remain jointly and severally liable for all of the plaintiffs' damages. (This is the imposition of penalty for actively participating in an actual fraud.)

The Private Securities Litigation Reform Act includes an exception to these provisions to compensate smaller investors. If plaintiffs have a net worth of less than $200,000 and lost 10 percent or more of the net worth because of auditors' failure to exercise appropriate levels of professional care, auditors remain jointly and severally liable.

 AUDITING INSIGHT | Joint and Several Liability

In July 2005, a federal jury found **Coopers & Lybrand** (which has since merged with **Price Waterhouse** to form PricewaterhouseCoopers) and the president of the client (**Ambassador Insurance Company**) to be jointly liable for losses incurred by policyholders of Ambassador, which became insolvent in 1983. The jury assigned the liability as 60 percent against Arnold Chait (president of Ambassador) and 40 percent against Coopers & Lybrand, but Chait died during the 1990s with insufficient assets in his estate. As a result, PricewaterhouseCoopers was required to pay the entire $182.9 million settlement for an audit conducted more than 20 years earlier! (This judgment was upheld at the appellate level in September 2008.)

Sources: "PwC to Pay $182.9M for Coopers Audit," *CFO.com*, October 3, 2005; "Pricewaterhouse Is Ordered to Pay $182.9 Million," *The Wall Street Journal*, October 5, 2005, p. B6.

Class-Action Suits

It is not unusual for shareholders or investors who have suffered losses to band together and bring legal action against entities or auditors. In a **class action**, a relatively small number of aggrieved plaintiffs with small individual claims can bring suit for large damages in the name of an extended class. After a bankruptcy, for example, 50 bondholders who lost $40,000 might decide to sue and can do so on behalf of the entire class of bondholders for *all* of their alleged losses (say $40 million). Attorneys take these cases on a contingency fee basis (a percentage of the judgment, if any). The size of the claim and the zeal of the attorneys can make the class-action suit a serious matter. For example, an appeals court's decision to "certify" a class-action suit against **Wal-Mart Stores Inc**. for sexual discrimination had the potential to expose the retailer to liability and potential damages to 1.6 million past and present female employees.[21] In what is being viewed as a significant victory for defendants, the U.S. Supreme Court (in a 5–4 vote) ruled that the plaintiffs in this case could not establish the "common injury" necessary for class action consideration.[22]

In the past, most class-action lawsuits were adjudicated in state courts, and a great deal of "jurisdiction shopping" was performed to find a court that might be more sympathetic to the plaintiffs. Some of the large corporate failures (e.g., **Lincoln Savings and Loan**, Enron, WorldCom) have resulted in class-action lawsuits that have proven costly for defendants to defend and difficult for them to win. In February 2005, the *Class Action Fairness Act* was signed into law. This act is designed to expand federal jurisdiction over class-action lawsuits and is estimated to result in the movement of 40 percent of class-action lawsuits from various state courts to federal court. Federal courts are preferable venues for defendants in class-action lawsuits because:

- Class-action lawsuits come under more scrutiny in federal court compared to state courts.
- Federal courts have more resources at their disposal in managing class-action cases than state courts.
- State courts have been alleged to unfairly discriminate against defendants from other jurisdictions.
- State court verdicts often affect plaintiffs in other jurisdictions (states). A verdict in federal court is regarded as more appropriate when it is applied to multiple jurisdictions.

It is important to note that not all class-action lawsuits will come under federal jurisdiction, and the rules for determining whether a state or federal court has jurisdiction over a case are complex. It is too early to determine the exact effects of the Class Action Fairness Act on lawsuits against auditors, but initial perceptions are that it may reduce class-action lawsuits and provide a more impartial venue for auditors in defending themselves against class-action lawsuits.

In addition to the Class Action Fairness Act, Congress enacted the *Securities Litigation Uniform Standards Act* in 1998. The most significant provision of this legislation requires class-action lawsuits with 50 or more parties to be filed in the federal courts. As noted earlier, federal courts are generally more favorable venues for class-action lawsuits for the defendants (auditors).

AUDITING INSIGHT   How Big Is the Class?

In 2015, the number of class-action settlements (80) and total settlement dollars (over $3 billion) increased over the past year. The increase in settlement dollars was primarily due to a large increase in "mega settlements," including AIG's $970.5 million settlement, the largest class action settlement in which no criminal or regulatory charges were ever pursued.

Source: *Securities Class Action Settlements—2015 Review and Analysis* (Cornerstone Research, 2016).

---

[21]"Wal-Mart Wants to Skip This Class," *CFO.com*, October 15, 2004; "Wal-Mart Ruling Has Wide Reach on Discrimination," *The Wall Street Journal*, March 23, 2009, p. A2.
[22]"Justices Curb Class Actions," *The Wall Street Journal*, June 21, 2011, pp. A1, A2.

Auditors' Liability Caps

A final development in the legal liability arena is related to various measures of limiting (or "capping") auditors' liability to both clients and third parties. In their engagement letters, auditors are attempting to limit their potential liability to clients through wording such as the following (excerpted from **United Rental**'s 2006 proxy statement):

> In connection with the audit of the 2005 financial statements, the company entered into an engagement agreement with Ernst & Young LLP. . . . That agreement is subject to alternative dispute resolution procedures and an exclusion of punitive damages.

A strict reading of this language suggests that United Rental is barred from bringing suit against Ernst & Young and would need to seek redress through mediation and arbitration; furthermore, it suggests that Ernst & Young would be liable only for compensatory (not the often more costly punitive) damages. Although the effectiveness of this language in limiting auditors' liability has not been legally tested, some negative publicity over these agreements has resulted in Ernst & Young's deciding no longer to include language related to exclusion of punitive damages in its engagement letters. (It continues to include the language related to alternative dispute resolution.)[23]

In addition to liability to clients, some other actions have been taken to potentially limit auditors' liability to third parties. In late 2006, the Committee on Capital Markets Regulation (a group of business, financial, investor, legal, and accounting leaders) was formed in response to evidence that the U.S. public markets were losing registrants to foreign and private equity markets. Among other areas, their report addressed liability issues facing public entities and other parties (including auditors). This group did not provide a specific recommendation, but its report suggested dollar liability caps and safe harbors against certain types of auditing activities as a possible mechanism for protecting accounting firms against large monetary losses.[24] In addition, Conrad Hewitt (at the time, the SEC's chief accountant) called for limiting the exposure of accounting firms to lawsuits citing concerns if one of the remaining Big Four were to be forced out of business because of litigation.[25]

Other Developments

Auditor liability continues to change along with the landscape of the auditing profession. In 2009, a U.S. judge denied **Deloitte Touche Tohmatsu**'s motion for a summary judgment that would relieve the firm of any liability for audits of Parmalat conducted by its Italian member firm (**Deloitte & Touche SpA**). This action clearly expands liability for international accounting firms in cases in which the firm itself provides little actual service to the client. Speaking on behalf of the plaintiffs, attorney Stuart Grant noted, "Judge Kaplan has finally made the law reflect reality. These accounting firms sell themselves as worldwide, seamless organizations. Now they are going to be held responsible in the same fashion. In essence, Judge Kaplan has said that the parent can't hide from the misdeeds of its children."[26] In more recent auditor-friendly rulings, the concept of *in pari delicto* has been strengthened as an auditor defense. Basically, this legal concept means that the court should not intercede between two wrongdoers. To put this in context, a corporation whose officers committed fraud cannot later sue the auditors for not catching the fraud; note, however, that innocent shareholders may still proceed with litigation against the auditors.[27]

---

[23]"More Companies Are Disclosing Pacts with Auditors on Liability Caps," *The Wall Street Journal,* June 22, 2006, p. C4.

[24]"Panel Seeks Cap on Liability of Accounting Firms," *The Wall Street Journal,* November 30, 2006, p. C3. The report of the committee can be found at www.capmktsreg.org/pdfs/11.30Committee_Interim_ReportREV2.pdf.

[25]"SEC's Hewitt: Indemnify the Big Four," *CFO.com,* January 29, 2007.

[26]"A Parmalat Ruling May Broaden Liability," *The Wall Street Journal,* January 29, 2009, p. C4; "Judge: OK to Sue Deloitte over Parmalat," *CFO.com,* January 30, 2009.

[27]S. Benson, "Shielding the Auditor from Corporate Fraud Liability," *The CPA Journal,* April, 2012, pp. 58–65.

AUDITING INSIGHT   What Affects Litigation?

Three recent studies have examined factors influencing litigation.

- Schmidt concluded that litigation against auditors related to financial statement misstatements is more likely when the misstatement is associated with (1) financial fraud, (2) a regulatory investigation, (3) a large decline in stock price, and (4) a higher number of errors in applying GAAP. In addition, the results of this study showed that litigation against an auditor/firm resulted in that office's demonstrating more conservative behavior with respect to other clients (such as lower levels of positive financial statement accruals and a longer time period for issuing the audit reports). In a follow-up study, Schmidt found that the perception that auditors' independence has been impaired by the amount of nonaudit services provided also influences the auditor's decision to settle and increases the amount of the settlement.

- Casterella et al. found that in comparison with smaller firms, larger accounting firms, firms experiencing significant growth, firms with

a higher number of claims outstanding against them, and firms that have been investigated or disciplined by a professional oversight body had higher levels of litigation risk.

- Boone et al. found that auditors involved with engagements having higher litigation risk were less likely than auditors with lower risk to acquiesce to client earnings management behavior and that the Private Securities Litigation Reform Act reduced the risk of litigation against auditors.

Sources: J. Schmidt, "Perceived Auditor Independence and Audit Litigation: The Role of Nonaudit Service Fees, *The Accounting Review,* May, 2012, pp. 1033–1065; J. R. Casterella, K. L. Jensen, and W. R. Knechel, "Litigation Risk and Audit Firm Characteristics," *Auditing: A Journal of Practice & Theory,* November 2010, pp. 71–82.; J. P. Boone, I. K. Khurana, and K. K. Raman, "Litigation Risk and Abnormal Accruals," *Auditing: A Journal of Practice & Theory,* May 2011, pp. 231–256.

REVIEW CHECKPOINTS

C.25 List some of the major changes in auditors' liability provided by Sarbanes–Oxley.

C.26 What is the difference between *joint and several liability* and *proportionate liability*?

C.27 What major changes did the Private Securities Litigation Reform Act provide? What major changes did the Class Action Fairness Act provide?

C.28 What new requirement was enacted in the Securities Litigation Uniform Standards Act that affected class-action lawsuits?

Summary

This module summarizes the potential liability auditors have to clients and third parties who rely on their work. Auditors can be liable under either common law (based on prior legal decisions and precedents) or statutory law (violating a written law). Auditors' liability to clients arises through an economic loss suffered because of failure to perform the engagement in accordance with the contract (breach of contract) or because of auditors' failure to exercise the appropriate level of professional care (tort liability). Because of the close relationship between auditors and clients, auditors owe their clients a very high degree of performance and are liable when they commit ordinary negligence (lack of reasonable care), gross negligence (lack of minimal care), or fraud (knowledge and intent to deceive).

Auditors' liability to third-party investors or creditors under common law arises because of economic decisions made by these parties using audited financial statements. Under common law, auditors are liable to all third-party users for levels of failure to exercise the appropriate level of professional care representing gross negligence or fraud. With respect to ordinary negligence, three separate approaches to liability are for third parties who are primary beneficiaries (*Credit Alliance v. Arthur Andersen*), foreseen third parties (*restatement of torts doctrine, Fleet National Bank v. Gloucester Co.*), or foreseeable third parties (*Rosenblum Inc. v. Adler*). The legal precedent in the jurisdiction in which the action is brought determines auditors' liability to third parties for ordinary negligence.

Under statutory liability, the Securities Act of 1933 and the Securities Exchange Act of 1934 dictate liability to investors in securities. These acts differ based on both the burden of proof and the level of failure to exercise the appropriate level of professional care required to bring suit. Under the Securities Act, the burden of proof is on auditors; purchasers of securities may bring suit for ordinary negligence, gross negligence, or fraud. Under the Securities Exchange Act, the burden of proof is on purchasers or sellers of securities, and suit can be brought only for gross negligence or fraud. Clearly, the Securities Act imposes the highest degree of care on auditors and the lowest barriers for plaintiffs to bring suits against auditors.

Although Sarbanes–Oxley has expanded the statute of limitations as well as the penalties to auditors under the Securities Exchange Act, other recent developments have reduced (or advocate a reduction in) auditors' exposure to legal liability. These developments include the Private Securities Litigation Reform Act, the Class Action Fairness Act, and various calls for liability limitations (or caps).

Key Terms

breach of contract: A claim that accounting or auditing services were not performed in the manner described in the contract.

causation defense: An argument available to auditors who can show that a plaintiff's economic loss was caused by a factor other than the auditors' failure to exercise the appropriate level of professional care or breach of contract.

class action: A situation in which a group of plaintiffs comes together in a legal action against another party.

comfort letter: A letter issued by auditors to underwriters of securities that provides an opinion on the fairness of the issuers' financial statements.

common law: The liability for injuries that is based on reasons other than violation of a written law or statute. Under common law, legal precedent is used in assessing the degree of responsibility or fault of the parties; auditors have common law liability to clients and nonshareholder third parties.

constructive fraud: A failure to provide any care in fulfilling a duty owed to another including a reckless disregard for the truth (similar to gross negligence).

contributory negligence: A legal defense theory in which the plaintiff's own failure to perform with the appropriate level of professional care bars recovery from auditors.

"deep pockets" theory: The concept that lawsuits may be brought against auditors not because they are necessarily at fault but because they are the only party with resources against which recovery can be made.

expectation gap: The difference between the actual work and assurance required by GAAS and the expectation of that work by the general public.

Financial Reporting Releases (FRRs): Reports prepared by SEC staff that express new rules and policies about disclosure.

foreseeable party: The individuals or organizations whose decisions normally rely on audited financial statements and opinions on those financial statements.

foreseen party: A limited class of individuals or organizations that could be reasonably expected to rely on auditors' work.

Form 8-K: The "current events" report filed periodically at the occurrence of major events, such as earnings releases, major asset sales, acquisitions, and auditor changes.

Form 10-K: The form to use for annual filing of financial statements and related disclosures by public companies with the SEC.

Form 10-Q: The form to use for quarterly filing of financial statements and related disclosures by public companies with the SEC.

fraud: The misrepresentation of facts that the individual knows to be false with the intention to deceive.

gross negligence: The breach of duty owed to another party because of a lack of minimal care (similar to constructive fraud).

initial public offering (IPO): The initial issuance of securities by a registrant entity to the investing public through a market that is subject to the provisions of the Securities Act of 1933.

joint and several liability: The legal doctrine that when multiple defendants are named, the full amount of a damage award may be collected from any of the defendants named in the lawsuit even though they may be only partially at fault.

limited liability partnership: A form of organization adopted by most large accounting firms that combines the advantages of a traditional partnership with the liability protection afforded to corporations.

ordinary negligence: The unintentional breach of duty owed to another as a result of a lack of reasonable care.

plaintiff: The person or organization that initiates a lawsuit (client or third-party user of financial statements).

primary beneficiary: A person known by name to the auditor for whose primary benefit the audit or other accounting service is performed.

privity of contract: A situation in which parties have a contractual relationship.

proportionate liability: The legal doctrine that payment of a share of the court's damage award be based on the extent (or proportion) of fault exhibited by a convicted defendant.

prospectus: A legal document offering securities for sale; includes significant information about the issuing entity, including its historical financial statements and other necessary disclosures.

registration statement: A set of documents, including a prospectus, that a company files with the SEC prior to an initial public offering.

Regulation S-K: The SEC requirements relating to all business, analytical, and supplementary financial disclosures other than financial statements themselves.

Regulation S-X: The SEC accounting requirements for annual and interim financial statements filed under both the Securities Act and the Securities Exchange Act.

scienter: A mental state embracing the intent to deceive, manipulate, or defraud prior to committing those actions (for example, auditors' knowledge of a misstatement in the financial statements and the intentional failure to disclose this misstatement in their report).

Staff Accounting Bulletins (SABs): The unofficial but important interpretations of Regulation S-X and Regulation S-K by SEC staff.

statutory law: The legal rules affecting liability based on violations of written laws or statutes. Auditors have statutory liability to third-party investors under the securities acts.

tort: A civil complaint charging that the action of one person caused injury (personal or financial) to another; such action against auditors is normally initiated by users of financial statements.

Multiple-Choice Questions for Practice and Review

All applicable questions are available with *Connect.*

LO C-2

C.29 A lack of reasonable care that may be characterized by the failure of auditors to follow GAAS in the conduct of the audit is known as

 a. Constructive fraud.

 b. Fraud.

 c. Gross negligence.

 d. Ordinary negligence.

LO C-6

C.30 From the auditors' point of view, which of the following is a preferable provision for imposition of civil liability in a lawsuit for financial damages?

 a. Joint and several liability.

 b. Reasonably foreseeable users' approach to privity.

 c. Foreseen third parties' approach to privity.

 d. Proportionate liability.

LO C-1

C.31 Users of financial statements have a different perception concerning the nature of auditors' services than the actual objectives of an audit. This difference is known as

 a. Diverse liability perception.

 b. Reasonable foreseeable third parties.

    c. Insurance hypothesis.

    d. Expectations gap.

LO C-2   C.32 Individuals who believe they relied on misstated financial statements to make a decision and have suffered losses as a result will issue an action known as a

    a. Breach of contract.

    b. Tort.

    c. Securities litigation.

    d. Constructive fraud.

LO C-6   C.33 Assume that auditors lost a civil lawsuit for damages and the court found total losses of $5 million. If the auditors were determined to be 30 percent at fault and were the only solvent defendants, what is the auditors' likely obligation under proportionate liability?

    a. $5,000,000.

    b. Zero.

    c. $2,250,000.

    d. $1,500,000.

LO C-6   C.34 Suppose that the auditors in the preceding question participated knowingly in commission of violations of securities laws (with managers and directors of the audit client). What is the auditors' likely obligation?

    a. $5,000,000.

    b. Zero.

    c. $2,250,000.

    d. $1,500,000.

LO C-2   C.35 When a client sues an accountant for failure to perform consulting work properly, the accountants' best defense is probably based on the doctrine of

    a. Lack of privity of contract.

    b. Contributory negligence on the part of the client.

    c. Lack of any measurable dollar amount of damages.

    d. No negligence on the part of the consultant.

LO C-2   C.36 When creditors who relied on an entity's audited financial statements suffer monetary losses after a customer (the auditors' client) goes bankrupt, what must the plaintiff creditors in a lawsuit for damages show in a court that follows the doctrine in *Credit Alliance*?

    a. The auditors knew and specifically acknowledged identification of the creditors.

    b. The auditors could reasonably foresee them as beneficiaries of the audit because entities such as this client use financial statements to obtain credit from vendors.

    c. The plaintiffs were foreseen users of the audited financial statements because they were vendors of long standing.

    d. All of the above.

LO C-2   C.37 When accountants agree to perform a compilation or review of unaudited financial statements, the best way to avoid clients' misunderstanding the nature of the work is to describe it completely in

    a. An engagement letter.

    b. The auditors' opinion.

    c. A report to the clients' board of directors at the close of the engagement.

    d. A management letter to the board of directors' audit committee.

LO C-4   C.38 Entities desiring to issue equity or debt must provide a set of financial statements to any prospective purchaser. This set of financial statements and other information for prospective purchasers is known as a

    a. Prospectus.

    b. Review.

    c. Patron's acquisition statement.

    d. Projected audited financial information.

LO C-3   C.39 The Securities Act of 1933 and Securities Exchange Act of 1934 contain

    a. Civil liability provisions applicable to auditors.

b. Criminal liability provisions applicable to auditors.

c. Neither *a* nor *b*.

d. Both *a* and *b*.

LO C-2

C.40 Which of the following third parties is known by name to auditors as the audit is conducted?

a. Foreseeable third party.

b. Foreseen third party.

c. General third party.

d. Primary beneficiary.

LO C-5

C.41 Which of the following would be the auditors' most likely defense in an action brought under the Securities Exchange Act of 1934?

a. The investor did not have privity with auditors.

b. The investor did not suffer a loss based on the materially misstated financial statements.

c. The auditors acted in good faith and were not aware of the materially misstated financial statements.

d. The financial statements were not filed with the Securities and Exchange Commission.

LO C-4

C.42 Which of the following statements regarding auditors' liability under the Securities Act of 1933 is *not* true?

a. The act relates to the initial issuance of securities to the public, normally through an initial public offering.

b. Auditors' liability arises because of audited financial information filed with the SEC.

c. Third parties must demonstrate that they relied on misstated financial statements that were examined by auditors.

d. Auditors may be liable if they are found to have engaged in ordinary negligence.

LO C-5

C.43 Under the Securities Exchange Act of 1934, entities are required to report to the public about changing auditors on

a. Form 10-K.

b. Form S-a.

c. Form 10-Q.

d. Form 8-K.

LO C-4

C.44 Section 11(*b*) of the Securities Act of 1933 provides that individuals can be sued and may be liable for investors' losses in connection with a public securities offering under which of these circumstances?

a. The chairman of the board of directors performed a reasonable investigation of facts in connection with preparing the section in the registration statement concerning the specification of the use of the proceeds of the offering.

b. A consulting engineer performed a reasonable investigation and reported in the registration statement on the feasibility of construction of a roadway to be financed with the offering proceeds.

c. The president of the issuing entity had no reason to doubt the report of the consulting engineer, although the president did not perform a separate reasonable investigation of her own.

d. The officers of the issuing entity were relieved that the independent auditors did not make an issue about the excessive valuation of inventory held to support construction in progress.

LO C-5

C.45 In comparison to the burden of proof required of plaintiffs in civil lawsuits against independent auditors under common law, section 10(*b*) of the Securities Exchange Act of 1934

a. Is the same regarding plaintiffs' need to prove damages or losses.

b. Is the same regarding plaintiffs' need to establish privity or a beneficiary relationship with auditors.

c. Does not require that plaintiffs prove their reliance on materially misstated financial statements.

d. Does not require that plaintiffs prove that relying on the materially misstated financial statements caused their losses.

LO C-2

C.46 Which of the following cases provides auditors the broadest exposure for liability to third parties for ordinary negligence under common law?

a. *Credit Alliance v. Arthur Andersen.*

b. *Fleet National Bank v. Gloucester Co.*

c. *Rosenblum Inc. v. Adler.*

d. *Ultramares.*

LO C-4, C-5

C.47 Which of the following is a major difference in auditors' liability under the Securities Act of 1933 and the Securities Exchange Act of 1934?

a. The burden of proving reliance on misstated financial statements and the relationship between these financial statements and the economic loss.

b. The auditors' required degree of professional care.

c. Both of the above.

d. Neither of the above.

LO C-4

C.48 When an entity registers a security offering under the Securities Act of 1933, the law provides an investor

a. An SEC guarantee that the information in the registration statement is true.

b. Insurance against loss from the investment.

c. Financial information examined by independent auditors.

d. Inside information about the entity's trade secrets.

LO C-2

C.49 A group of investors sued Anderson, Olds, and Watershed, CPAs (AOW) for alleged damages suffered when the entity in which they held common stock went bankrupt. To avoid liability under the common law, AOW must demonstrate which of the following?

a. The investors actually suffered a loss.

b. The investors relied on the financial statements audited by AOW.

c. The investors' loss was a direct result of their reliance on the audited financial statements.

d. The audit was conducted in accordance with generally accepted auditing standards and with due professional care.

LO C-5

C.50 The Securities and Exchange Commission document that governs accounting in financial statements filed with the SEC is

a. Regulation D.

b. Form 8-K.

c. Form SB-l.

d. Regulation S-X.

LO C-5

C.51 Which of the following cases upheld the requirement that plaintiffs demonstrate scienter when bringing action under the Securities Exchange Act of 1934?

a. *Ernst & Ernst v. Hochfelder.*

b. *Escott v. BarChris Construction Corp.*

c. *Smith v. London Assurance Corp.*

d. *Ultramares.*

LO C-5

C.52 A public entity subject to the periodic reporting requirements of the Securities Exchange Act of 1934 must file an annual report with the SEC known as the

a. Form 10-K.

b. Form 10-Q.

c. Form 8-K.

d. Regulation S-X.

LO C-4

C.53 When investors sue auditors for damages under section 11 of the Securities Act of 1933, they must allege and prove

a. Scienter on the part of auditors.

b. The audited financial statements contained a material misstatement.

c. They relied on the materially misstated financial statements.

d. Their reliance on the materially misstated financial statements was the direct cause of their loss.

LO C-6

C.54 Which of the following is *not* part of Sarbanes–Oxley?

  a. An increased duty on the part of auditors to identify financial statement fraud.

  b. A requirement that the CEO and CFO certify the financial statements.

  c. Increased penalties for destruction of records in federal investigations.

  d. Increased penalties for mail fraud and criminal violations of the Securities Exchange Act of 1934.

LO C-2

C.55 If a CPA firm is being sued for common law fraud by a third party based upon materially false financial statements, which of the following is the best defense the auditors could assert?

  a. Lack of privity.

  b. Lack of reliance.

  c. A disclaimer contained in the engagement letter.

  d. Contributory negligence on the part of the client.

(AICPA adapted)

LO C-2

C.56 Locke, CPA, was engaged by Hall Inc. to audit Willow Company. Hall purchased Willow after receiving Willow's audited financial statements, which included Locke's unmodified auditors' opinion. Locke was negligent in the performance of the Willow audit engagement; this negligence was caused by failure to perform the engagement in accordance with terms of the engagement letter. As a result of Locke's negligence, Hall suffered damages of $75,000. Hall appears to have grounds to sue Locke for

	Breach of Contract	Negligence
a.	Yes	Yes
b.	Yes	No
c.	No	Yes
d.	No	No

(AICPA adapted)

LO C-4

C.57 An investor seeking to recover stock market losses from a CPA firm associated with an initial offering of securities based on an unmodified opinion on financial statements that accompanied a registration statement must establish that

  a. The audited financial statements contain a false statement or omission of material fact.

  b. The investor relied on the financial statements.

  c. The CPA firm did not act in good faith.

  d. The CPA firm would have discovered the false statement or omission if it had exercised due care in its examination.

(AICPA adapted)

LO C-5

C.58 Donalds & Company, CPAs, audited the financial statements included in the annual report submitted by Markum Securities Inc. to the Securities and Exchange Commission. The audit was improper in several respects. Markum is now insolvent and unable to satisfy the claims of its customers. Customers have instituted legal action against Donalds based on Section 10(*b*) and Rule 10(*b*)-5 of the Securities Exchange Act of 1934. Which of the following is likely to be Donalds' best defense?

  a. The firm did not intentionally certify the false financial statements.

  b. Section 10(*b*) does not apply to the case.

  c. The firm was not in privity of contract with the creditors.

  d. The engagement letter specifically disclaimed any liability to any party that resulted from Markum's fraudulent conduct.

(AICPA adapted)

Problems C.59 and C.60 are based on the following information:

West & Co., CPAs, rendered an unmodified opinion on the financial statements of Pride Corp., which were included in Pride's registration statement filed with the SEC. Subsequently, Hex purchased 500 shares of Pride's preferred stock as part of a public offering subject to the Securities Act of 1933. Hex has commenced an action against West based on the

Securities Act of 1933 for losses resulting from misstatements of facts in the financial statements included in the registration statement.

LO C-4

C.59 Which of the following elements must Hex prove to hold West liable?

a. West rendered its opinion with knowledge of material misstatements.

b. West performed the audit negligently.

c. Hex relied on the financial statements included in the registration statement.

d. The misstatements were material.

(AICPA adapted)

LO C-4

C.60 Which of the following defenses would be *least* helpful to West in avoiding liability to Hex?

a. West was not in privity of contract with Hex.

b. West conducted the audit in accordance with GAAS.

c. Hex's losses were caused by factors other than the misstatements.

d. Hex knew of the misstatements when Hex acquired the preferred stock.

(AICPA adapted)

Exercises and Problems

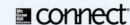 All applicable questions are available with *Connect.*

LO C-2

C.61 **Breach of Contract.** Although large-dollar lawsuits brought by shareholders grab the headlines, auditors are most often sued by the client for breach of contract.

Required:

a. How can auditors be in breach of contract with a client?

b. How can a client be in breach of contract with auditors?

c. What are the best defenses for auditors against breach of contract lawsuits brought by their clients?

LO C-2

C.62 **Liability to Clients.** Thomas, CPA, is a regional firm that provides a variety of services to its clients. The following summarizes some issues that it has encountered with three of its audit clients during the most recent year:

- Thomas was engaged by Brown Company to conduct an audit of its financial statements. Brown is a nonpublic entity that is seeking financing and is having the audit conducted because of user demand for audited financial statements. Because this was an initial audit, it took Thomas longer to conduct the audit than anticipated. During this time, economic conditions resulted in a general increase in interest rates, and Brown's costs of obtaining financing were higher than it had anticipated.

- Green Stores has been an audit client of Thomas for more than 10 years. Following the most recent audit (which resulted in an unmodified opinion on Green's financial statements), Green Stores learned that its treasurer had been engaged in a significant embezzlement scheme, resulting in Green's losses in excess of $2 million. Throughout Thomas's 10-year relationship with Green Stores, it had issued unmodified opinions on Green's financial statements and had not identified any weaknesses in Green's internal control or other evidence that suggested the existence of this defalcation scheme.

- Fuchsia Inc. has been an audit client of Thomas for the past five years. During the most recent audit, Thomas identified misstatements that understated Fuchsia's liabilities; Thomas believed that these misstatements should be corrected in order to fairly present Fuchsia's financial condition, results of operations, and cash flows in conformity with GAAP. Fuchsia refused to make these misstatements, and Thomas resigned from the engagement. Fuchsia has engaged another auditor, but the delays associated with this change in auditors may result in accelerated payments to Fuchsia's lenders for failure to provide them audited financial statements on a timely basis.

Required:

a. Without specific reference to any of the preceding situations, on what basis/general areas of liability may clients bring suit against auditors?

b. Without specific reference to any of the preceding situations, what facts must clients demonstrate to bring suit against auditors?

c. Without specific reference to any of the preceding situations, what defenses might be available to auditors for suits brought against them by their clients?

d. For each of the preceding clients, identify the potential basis or bases for legal action that might be brought against Thomas.

e. In your opinion, is Thomas likely to be liable to these clients for its actions? What factors should be considered in assessing Thomas' potential liability in these situations?

LO C-2

C.63   Common Law Responsibility for Errors and Fraud.   Huffman & Whitman (H&W), a large regional accounting firm, was engaged by Ritter Tire Wholesale Company to audit its financial statements for the year ended January 31. H&W had a busy audit engagement schedule from December 31 through April 1 and decided to audit Ritter's purchase vouchers and related cash disbursements on a sample basis. The firm instructed staff members to select a random sample of 130 purchase transactions and gave directions about important deviations, including missing receiving reports. Boyd, the assistant in charge, completed the audit documentation, properly documenting the fact that 13 of the purchases in the sample had been recorded and paid without including the receiving report (required by stated internal control procedures) in the file of supporting documents. Whitman, the partner in direct charge of the audit, showed the findings to Lock, Ritter's chief accountant. Lock appeared surprised but promised that the missing receiving reports would be inserted into the files before the audit was over. Whitman was satisfied, noted in the audit documentation that the problem had been solved, and did not say anything to Huffman about it.

Unfortunately, H&W did not discover the fact that Lock was involved in a fraudulent scheme in which he diverted shipments of tires to a warehouse leased in his name and sent the invoices to Ritter for payment. He then sold the tires for his own profit. Internal auditors discovered the scheme during a study of slow-moving inventory items. Ritter's inventory was overstated by about $500,000 (20 percent), the amount Lock had diverted.

Required:

a. Do you believe H&W has any further audit responsibility with respect to the missing receiving reports? Explain.

b. Do you believe H&W failed to exercise the appropriate level of professional care? Why or why not?

LO C-2

C.64   Common Law Responsibility for Errors and Fraud.   Herbert McCoy is the president of McCoy Forging Corporation. For the past several years, Donovan & Company, CPAs, has performed the company's compilation and some other accounting and tax work. McCoy decided to have Donovan & Company conduct an audit. He had recently received a disturbing anonymous letter that stated, "Beware; you have a viper in your nest. The money is literally disappearing before your very eyes! Signed: A friend." He told no one about the letter.

McCoy Forging engaged Donovan & Company, CPAs, to render an opinion on the financial statements for the year ended June 30. McCoy told Donovan he wanted to verify that the financial statements were "accurate and proper." He did not mention the anonymous letter. The usual engagement letter providing for an audit in accordance with generally accepted auditing standards (GAAS) was drafted by Donovan & Company and signed by both parties.

The audit was performed in accordance with GAAS. The audit did not reveal a clever defalcation plan. Harper, the assistant treasurer, was siphoning off substantial amounts of McCoy Forging's funds. The defalcations occurred both before and after the audit. Harper's embezzlement was discovered by McCoy's new internal auditor in October after Donovan had delivered the auditors' opinion. Although the scheme was fairly sophisticated, it could have been detected if Donovan & Company had performed additional procedures. McCoy Forging demands reimbursement from Donovan for the entire amount of the embezzlement, some $40,000 of which occurred before the audit and $65,000 after. Donovan has denied any liability and refuses to pay.

Required:

Discuss Donovan's responsibility in this situation. Do you think McCoy Forging could prevail in whole or in part in a lawsuit against Donovan under common law? Explain your conclusions.

(AICPA adapted)

LO C-2

C.65 Auditors' Liability for Fraud.   Auditors may be liable to third parties for fraud in several ways.

Required:

    a. Identify auditors' liability for fraud to third parties.

    b. Distinguish between fraud and constructive fraud.

    c. What is auditors' liability for constructive fraud to third parties?

    d. In your opinion, is auditors' liability to third parties for fraud and constructive fraud appropriate (or "fair")?

LO C-2

C.66 Accusation of Fraud.   (This exercise is based on the actual case of **Health Management Inc.**) During the audit of the Health Management's 1995 financial statements, $1.8 million of inventory in transit was included on the entity's balance sheet. The auditors never obtained evidence of the existence of this inventory even though several questions had been raised concerning the excessively large amount of inventory in transit at year-end. In 1996, Health Management announced that it had discovered a series of accounting irregularities.

Required:

    a. Do legal grounds exist to claim that the auditors committed fraud?

    b. What would be the auditors' defense if such grounds exist?

LO C-2

C.67 Common Law Liability Exposure.   An accounting firm was engaged to examine the financial statements of Martin Manufacturing Corporation for the year ending December 31. Martin needed cash to continue its operations and agreed to sell its common stock investment in a subsidiary through a private placement. The buyers insisted that the proceeds be placed in escrow because of the possibility of a major contingent tax liability that could result from a pending government claim against Martin's subsidiary. The payment in escrow was completed in late November. Martin's president told the audit partner that the proceeds from the sale of the subsidiary's common stock, held in escrow, should be shown on the balance sheet as an unrestricted current account receivable. The president held the opinion that the government's claim was groundless and that Martin needed an "uncluttered" balance sheet and a "clean" auditors' opinion to obtain additional working capital from lenders. The audit partner agreed with the president and issued an unmodified opinion on Martin's financial statements, which did not refer to the contingent liability and did not properly describe the escrow arrangement.

    The government's claim proved to be valid, and pursuant to the agreement with the buyers, the purchase price of the subsidiary was reduced by $450,000. This adverse development forced Martin into bankruptcy. The accounting firm is being sued for deceit (fraud) by several of Martin's unpaid creditors who extended credit in reliance on the accounting firm's unmodified opinion on Martin's financial statements.

Required:

    a. What deceit (fraud) do you believe the creditors are claiming?

    b. Is the lack of privity between the accounting firm and the creditors important in this case?

    c. Do you believe the accounting firm is liable to the creditors? Explain.

(AICPA adapted)

LO C-2

C.68 Common Law Liability Exposure.   Risk Capital Limited, a Delaware corporation, was considering the purchase of a substantial investment in Florida Sunshine Corporation, a closely held corporation. Initial discussions with the Florida Sunshine Corporation began late in 2017.

    Wilson and Wyatt, Florida Sunshine's auditor, regularly prepared quarterly and annual unaudited financial statements. The most recently prepared financial statements were for the year ended September 30, 2017.

    On November 15, 2017, after extensive negotiations, Risk Capital agreed to purchase 100,000 shares of no par, class A capital stock of Florida Sunshine at $12.50 per share. However, Risk Capital insisted on audited statements for 2017. The contract that was made available to Wilson and Wyatt specifically provided that Risk Capital shall have the right to rescind the purchase of said stock if the audited financial statements of Florida Sunshine show a material adverse change in the financial condition of the corporation.

The audited financial statements furnished to Florida Sunshine by Wilson and Wyatt showed no such material adverse change. Risk Capital relied on the audited statements and purchased the investment in Florida Sunshine. It was subsequently discovered that, as of the date of the financial statements, the audited statements were misstated and that in fact there had been a material adverse change in the corporation's financial condition. Florida Sunshine is insolvent, and Risk Capital will lose virtually its entire investment.

Risk Capital seeks recovery against Wilson and Wyatt.

Required:

Assuming that only ordinary negligence is proved, will Risk Capital prevail

a. Under a privity of contract standard?

b. Under a primary beneficiary standard?

c. Under a foreseen parties standard?

LO C-2

C.69 Common Law Liability Exposure.   Smith, CPA, is the auditor for Juniper Manufacturing Corporation, a nonpublic entity that has a June 30 fiscal year. Juniper arranged for a substantial bank loan, which depended on the bank receiving audited financial statements showing a debt-to-equity ratio of no more than 2 to 1. The bank's deadline for receiving these financial statements was September 30. On September 25, just before the auditors' opinion was to be issued, Smith received an anonymous letter on Juniper's letterhead indicating that Juniper's five-year lease of a factory building that was classified in the financial statements as an operating lease was in fact a capital lease. The letter stated that Juniper had a secret written agreement with the lessor modifying the lease and creating a capital lease.

Smith confronted the president of Juniper, who admitted that a secret agreement existed but said it was necessary to treat the lease as an operating lease to meet the debt-to-equity ratio requirement of the pending loan and that nobody would ever discover the secret agreement with the lessor. The president said that if Smith did not issue a report by September 30, Juniper would sue Smith for substantial damages that would result from not getting the loan. Under this pressure and because the audit documentation contained a copy of the five-year lease agreement supporting the operating lease treatment, Smith issued the report with an unmodified opinion on September 29. In spite of the fact that it received the loan, Juniper went bankrupt. The bank is suing Smith to recover its losses on the loan, and the lessor is suing Smith to recover uncollected rents.

Required:

Answer the following, setting forth reasons for any conclusions stated.

a. Is Smith liable to the bank?

b. Is Smith liable to the lessor?

c. Was Smith independent?

(AICPA adapted)

LO C-2

C.70 Common Law Liability to Third Parties.   Flacco, CPA, conducted the audit of Raven Company and issued an unmodified opinion that concluded that the financial statements presented its financial condition, results of operations, and cash flows according to GAAP. As part of the preaudit conference, Flacco was informed by Raven's management that its audited financial statements would be presented to Baltimore National Bank to secure financing for a significant expansion opportunity.

Using these financial statements, as well as Flacco's opinion on those statements, Raven obtained financing from the following parties: (1) Baltimore National Bank, (2) Regional State Bank, and (3) Maryland Equity Partners (a private equity firm). Each of these parties specifically requested audited financial statements and relied on these statements in providing financing to Raven. Six months after obtaining financing, Raven's financial condition worsened, and it declared bankruptcy, forcing Raven to default on its payments to Baltimore National Bank and Regional State Bank. In addition, Maryland Equity Partners' investment in Raven became worthless.

After the bankruptcy, the parties that had provided financing to Raven determined that Raven had intentionally misstated its financial statements by recording fictitious revenues and accounts receivable. These parties decided to file suit against Flacco for failure to identify the fictitious revenues and accounts receivable.

Required:

a. Define the following type of third parties: (1) *primary beneficiary,* (2) *foreseen third parties,* and *(3) foreseeable third parties.*

b. Considering the three types of third parties identified in (a), how would you classify (1) Baltimore National Bank, (2) Regional State Bank, and (3) Maryland Equity Partners?

c. Assume that court proceedings concluded that Flacco's work failed to comply with generally accepted auditing standards but that Flacco was neither aware of the misstatements nor grossly negligent in his performance. Which of the parties would be likely to prevail in its claim against Flacco?

d. Assume that court proceedings concluded that Flacco failed to send confirmations to Raven's customers and simply mathematically verified the summary listing of accounts receivable provided to him by Raven. Which of the parties would be likely to prevail in its claim against Flacco?

LO C-2

C.71 **Common Law Liability to Third Parties.** Madeoff is a small, nonpublic retailer seeking capital for expansion. To obtain necessary capital, Madeoff engaged Allen, CPAs to audit its annual financial statements. In discussing the engagement, Madeoff explicitly informed Allen that the purpose of the audit was to obtain additional financing for expansion into new markets.

Madeoff obtained $3 million from lenders. These lenders included the following:

- First Trust and Bank provided $2 million. When engaging Allen, Madeoff indicated that it would use the audited financial statements and Allen's opinion on these statements to seek financing from First Trust and Bank; also, First Trust and Bank was specifically named in the engagement letter. Prior to committing the capital, First Trust and Bank had reviewed Madeoff's financial statements and, based on the financial condition reflected in its balance sheet, deemed Madeoff to be a qualified loan candidate.
- MoonTrust Bank provided $800,000 of capital to Madeoff. Although not named in the engagement letter or identified to Allen, Madeoff had previous business dealings with MoonTrust and maintained several accounts at MoonTrust. Based primarily on its prior relationships with Madeoff, MoonTrust approved the additional financing to Madeoff prior to receiving the audited financial statements or Allen's report on those financial statements.
- Alice Lay, a local philanthropist, provided $200,000 of capital to Madeoff. Although her decision was primarily motivated by Madeoff's role in the community and its corporate citizenship, she did request and review Madeoff's audited financial statements and Allen's report on those financial statements prior to providing funding. Alice had never entered into a loan agreement of this nature in the past but felt personal ties to Madeoff and was interested in its continued success.

Approximately six months following these loans, Madeoff declared bankruptcy.

Following the bankruptcy, lenders discovered that Allen's audit failed to disclose several material financial statement misstatements that, if corrected, would have presented a less favorable depiction of Madeoff's financial condition, results of operations, and cash flows. These lenders are exploring potential litigation against Allen to recover the funds they provided to Madeoff.

Required:

a. Would these third parties more likely pursue litigation against Madeoff under common law or statutory law?

b. How would each of the lenders likely be classified based on their relationship with Allen and the potential use of Madeoff's financial statements and Allen's report?

c. Assume that Allen's audit did not comply with generally accepted auditing standards but that it did not demonstrate a lack of minimum care or actual knowledge of the misstatements. Given the circumstances noted, how would you assess each of these parties' ability to prevail against Allen in a potential claim?

d. Repeat part (c), assuming that the parties could prove that Allen was aware that Madeoff's financial statements contained a material misstatement.

LO C-2

C.72 **Liability in a Review Engagement.** Mason & Dilworth (M&D), CPAs, were auditors for Hotshot Company, a closely held corporation owned by 30 residents of the area. Hotshot had previously engaged M&D to perform some compilation and tax work. Bubba Crass,

Hotshot's president and holder of 15 percent of the stock, said he needed something more than these services. He told Mason, the partner in charge, that he wanted financial statements for internal use, primarily for management purposes but also to obtain short-term loans from financial institutions. Mason recommended a "review" of the financial statements and did not prepare an engagement letter.

During the review work, Mason had some reservations about the financial statements. Mason told Dilworth at various times he was "uneasy about certain figures and conclusions," but he would "take Crass's word about the validity of certain entries since the review was primarily for internal use in any event and was not an audit."

M&D did not discover a material act of fraud committed by Crass. The fraud would have been detected had Mason not relied so much on the unsupported statements Crass made concerning the validity of the entries about which he had felt so uneasy.

Required:

a. What potential liability might M&D have to Hotshot Company and other stockholders?

b. What potential liability might M&D have to financial institutions that used the financial statements in connection with making loans to Hotshot Company?

(AICPA adapted)

LO C-4, C-5   C.73   **Liability under the Securities Acts.**   Orange is a public entity whose shares are traded on a national exchange. A Public Company Accounting Oversight Board inspection revealed a deficiency in audits conducted by Orange's auditor, LeGrow. LeGrow had failed to perform important auditing procedures; after performing these procedures in response to the inspection, LeGrow identified several material misstatements and requested that Orange restate its financial statements. These restatements had the effect of reducing Orange's reported income and cash flow from operations and increasing its liabilities.

Upon the disclosure of these restatements, Orange's stock price declined more than 40 percent. Angered over this decline, investors are contemplating bringing legal action against LeGrow for failing to detect the misstatements.

Required:

a. Assume that investors are bringing suit under the Securities Act of 1933. What would investors need to demonstrate to bring suit against LeGrow under this act?

b. What is LeGrow's potential liability to investors if LeGrow's audit was characterized as demonstrating (1) ordinary negligence, (2) gross negligence, or (3) fraud?

c. Repeat parts (a) and (b), assuming that investors are bringing suit under the Securities Exchange Act of 1934.

d. What are the primary differences in LeGrow's liability to investors under the Securities Act of 1933 and the Securities Exchange Act of 1934?

LO C-4, C-5   C.74   **Liability under the Securities Acts.**   Jones, CPA, audits a number of public companies. During the past year, some deficiencies with respect to audits conducted for two of Jones's clients in the software industry (SoftWare and ExternalDrive) were identified. These deficiencies related to Jones's audit procedures used to evaluate the revenue recognized by these clients. Some pertinent facts in each of these audits are summarized as follows:

SoftWare. In 2014, SoftWare issued securities to investors in an initial public offering with an average offering price of $50 per share. Jones audited the financial statements, which were later determined to have overstated revenues through premature revenue recognition. The net effect on SoftWare's operations was an overstatement of revenue by 25 percent and an overstatement of net income by 63 percent. Following the issuance, the market value of SoftWare's shares declined to $15 per share.

ExternalDrive. ExternalDrive has been a client of Jones for five years and has been publicly traded throughout that entire period. In 2014, ExternalDrive's Form 10-K revealed revenues of $25 million, net income of $8.5 million, and earnings per share of $1.40, all of which exceeded prior-years' results and analysts' estimates. ExternalDrive's financial statements were subsequently found to have overstated revenues by $2.25 million, which reduced reported revenues and earnings per share by 11 percent and 24 percent, respectively. Following the revelation of these misstatements, ExternalDrive's stock price declined from $18 per share to $9 per share.

You have been asked to defend Jones in legal actions involving shareholders of both companies and have engaged an auditing expert to evaluate Jones's performance. After reviewing the audit documentation and related professional literature, she concluded that Jones's performance was likely in violation of generally accepted auditing standards; however, it did not rise to the level of being considered "reckless," and it does not appear that Jones was aware of the departures from GAAP. In addition, although unrelated to Jones's audit, she observed that the market price of software companies had declined in a similar manner to that of SoftWare and ExternalDrive because of overall economic conditions.

Required:

a. Which statute would govern Jones's liability to shareholders of SoftWare? ExternalDrive?

b. What would shareholders of SoftWare and ExternalDrive need to demonstrate prior to bringing suit against Jones?

c. Based on the case facts as described, what possible defense(s) would you recommend to Jones in each of these situations?

d. Assume that these two cases went to trial and Jones's performance was deemed to be "reckless" in nature and that Jones possessed scienter. How does this change the likelihood of a favorable outcome for Jones?

LO C-6

C.75 **Class-Action Lawsuits.** In the United States, it has become common to seek recovery of financial losses from other parties, often even if that other party is not at fault. Frequently, this occurs by means of a class-action lawsuit.

Required:

a. What is a class-action lawsuit?

b. What advantages does a class-action lawsuit have for the plaintiffs?

c. What disadvantages does a class-action lawsuit have for the defendant?

d. How has recent legislation affected class-action lawsuits?

e. Perform an Internet search for information regarding class-action lawsuits against auditors. What are the (1) particulars of the lawsuit and (2) auditors' defenses?

LO C-2, C-4

C.76 **Liability under Common Law and the Securities Act of 1933.** Butler Manufacturing Corporation raised capital for a plant expansion by borrowing from a bank and making a stock offering. Butler engaged Weaver, CPA, to audit its December 2014 financial statements. Butler told Weaver that the financial statements would be given to Union Bank and certain other named banks and included in a registration statement for the stock offering.

In performing the audit, Weaver did not confirm accounts receivable and, therefore, failed to discover a material overstatement. Weaver also was aware of a pending class-action product liability lawsuit that was not disclosed in Butler's financial statements. Despite being advised by Butler's legal counsel that the entity's potential liability under the lawsuit would result in material losses, Weaver issued an unmodified opinion on Butler's financial statements.

In May 2018, Union Bank relied on the financial statements and Weaver's opinion to grant Butler a $500,000 loan.

Butler raised additional funds in November 2018 with a $14,000,000 unregistered offering of preferred stock. This offering was sold directly by the entity to 40 nonaccredited private investors during a one-year period.

Shortly after obtaining the Union Bank loan, Butler experienced financial problems but was able to stay in business because of the money raised by the stock offering. Butler lost the product liability suit, resulting in a judgment that the entity could not pay. Butler also defaulted on the Union Bank loan and was involuntarily petitioned into bankruptcy. This caused Union Bank to sustain a loss, and Butler's stockholders' investments became worthless.

Union Bank sued Weaver for failure to provide the appropriate level of professional care and for common law fraud. The stockholders who purchased Butler's stock through the offering sued Weaver, alleging fraud under section 17 of the Securities Act of 1933.

These transactions took place in a jurisdiction providing for auditors' liability for ordinary negligence to known and intended users of financial statements.

Required:

Answer the following questions and give the reasons for your conclusions.

a. Will Union Bank be successful in its suit against Weaver under common law for (1) ordinary negligence and (2) fraud?

b. Will the stockholders who purchased Butler's stock through the offering succeed against Weaver under the antifraud provisions of section 17 of the Securities Act of 1933?

(AICPA adapted)

LO C-4, C-5

C.77 **Liability under the Securities Acts.** One of your firm's clients, Fancy Fashions Inc., is a highly successful, rapidly expanding entity. It is owned predominantly by the Munster family and key corporate officials. Although additional funds would be available on a short-term basis from its bankers, they would represent only a temporary solution of the entity's need for capital to finance its expansion plans. In addition, the interest rates being charged are not appealing. Therefore, Chris Munster, Fancy's chairman of the board, in consultation with the other shareholders, has decided to explore the possibility of raising additional equity capital of approximately $15 million to $16 million. This will be Fancy's first public offering.

At a meeting of Fancy's major shareholders, its attorneys and a member of your firm spoke about the advantages and disadvantages of "going public" and registering a stock offering. One of the shareholders suggested that Regulation D under the Securities Act of 1933 might be a preferable alternative.

Required:

a. Assume that Fancy makes a public offering for $16 million and, as a result, more than 1,000 persons own shares of the entity. Following the public offering, what are the implications with respect to the Securities Exchange Act of 1934? (*Hint:* You can identify the thresholds for being subject to the reporting requirements of the Securities Exchange Act of 1934 through reference to the SEC's website, www.sec.gov.)

b. What federal civil and criminal liabilities under the Securities Act of 1933 could apply in the event that Fancy sells the securities without registration and a registration exemption is not available?

c. Using the SEC's website (www.sec.gov) as a reference, define "accredited investor" and discuss the exemption applicable to offerings made under Regulation D for accredited investors.

(AICPA adapted)

LO C-4

C.78 **Section 11 of Securities Act of 1933: Liability Exposure.** Chriswell Corporation decided to raise additional long-term capital by issuing $20 million of 12 percent subordinated debentures to the public. May, Clark & Company, CPAs, the company's auditors, were engaged to examine the June 30, 2018, financial statements, which were included in the bond registration statement.

May, Clark & Company completed its examination and submitted an unmodified auditors' report dated July 15, 2018. The registration statement was filed and became effective on September 1, 2018. On August 15, one of the partners of May, Clark & Company called on Chriswell Corporation and had lunch with the financial vice president and the controller. He questioned both officials on the company's operations since June 30 and inquired whether there had been any material changes in the company's financial position since that date. Both officers assured him that everything had proceeded normally and that the financial condition of the company had not changed materially.

Unfortunately, the officers' representation was not true. On July 30, a substantial debtor of the company failed to pay the $400,000 due on its account receivable and indicated to Chriswell that it would probably be forced into bankruptcy. This receivable was shown as a collateralized loan on the June 30 financial statements. It was secured by stock of the debtor corporation, which had a value in excess of the loan at the time the financial statements were prepared but was virtually worthless at the effective date of the registration statement. This $400,000 account receivable was material to the financial condition of Chriswell Corporation, and the market price of the subordinated debentures decreased by nearly 50 percent after the foregoing facts were disclosed.

The debenture holders of Chriswell are seeking recovery of their loss against all parties connected with the debenture registration.

Required:

Are May, Clark & Company liable to the Chriswell debenture holders under section 11 of the Securities Act of 1933? Explain. (*Hint:* Review the *BarChris* case in this chapter.)

(AICPA adapted)

LO C-5

C.79 **Rule 10(*b*)-5 Liability under the Securities Exchange Act of 1934.** Gordon & Groton (G&G), CPAs, were auditors of Bank & Company, a brokerage firm and member of a national stock exchange. G&G examined and reported on the financial statements of Bank, which were filed with the Securities and Exchange Commission.

Several of Bank's customers were swindled by a fraudulent scheme perpetrated by Bank's president, who owned 90 percent of the voting stock of the company. The facts establish that G&G failed to perform the audit with the appropriate level of professional care but neither participated in the fraudulent scheme nor knew of its existence.

The customers are suing G&G under the antifraud provisions of section 10(*b*) and Rule 10*b*-5 of the Securities Exchange Act of 1934 for aiding and abetting the president's fraudulent scheme. The customers' suit for fraud is predicated exclusively on G&G's failure to conduct a proper audit, thereby failing to discover the fraudulent scheme.

Required:

Answer the following, setting forth reasons for any conclusions stated.

a. What is the probable outcome of the lawsuit?

b. What might be the result if plaintiffs had sued under common law for ordinary negligence? Explain.

(AICPA adapted)

LO C-5

C.80 **Independence and Securities Exchange Act of 1934.** Anderson, Olds, and Watershed (AOW) have been the independent auditors for Accord Corporation since 1990. Accord is a public entity obligated to file periodic reports under the Securities Exchange Act of 1934.

Beginning in January 2017, the AOW litigation support consulting division performed a special engagement for Accord. The work involved a lawsuit that Accord had filed against Civic Company for patent infringement on microchip manufacturing processes. AOW personnel compiled production statistics—costs and lost profits—under various volume assumptions and then testified in court about the losses to Accord that had resulted from Civic's improper use of patented processes. The amounts at issue were very large, with claims of $50 million for lost profits and a plea for $150 million punitive damages. Accord won a court judgment for a total of $120 million, and Civic has appealed the damage award. The case remained pending throughout 2017 and into 2018. By March 1, 2018, AOW had billed Accord $265,000 for the litigation support work.

In November 2017, AOW started the audit work on Accord's financial statements for the fiscal year ending December 31, 2017. During this work, AOW auditors found that Accord's management and board of directors did not fully disclose the stage of the appeal of the Civic Company case, had improperly deferred a material loss on new product start-up costs as an element of its inventory, and had accrued sales revenue for promotional chip sales that carried an unconditional right of return. As partner in charge of the engagement, D. Ward agreed with the president that the accounting and disclosure were suitable to protect Accord's shareholders from adverse business developments, and he issued a standard unmodified opinion that was included in the entity's 10-K annual report filed with the SEC and dated April 1, 2018.

On April 2, 2018, AOW then billed Accord for the $200,000 audit fee and sent a reminder for payment of the $265,000 consulting fee.

Required:

a. Was AOW independent for the audit of Accord for the fiscal year ended December 31, 2017? Explain.

b. Did Ward and AOW follow generally accepted auditing standards in the audit? Cite any specific standards that might have been violated, and explain your reasoning.

c. Did Ward and AOW violate any section(s) of the Securities Exchange Act of 1934? Explain.

LO C-5

C.81 **Auditors' Liability under Securities Exchange Act of 1934.** Adam, an Illinois resident, was interested in purchasing stock in Joshua Foods Inc. Joshua Foods has corporate headquarters in Fond du Lac, Wisconsin, and is incorporated in Delaware. Adam accessed Joshua Foods' 2017 annual report including the financial statements on its corporate website. Adam also reviewed several analysts' opinions on the Internet, including the opinions provided from his Internet broker, Matthew & Co. ExpressTrade. Adam received the annual report in the mail. Based on the increasing revenues, the $8 million net income indicated on the financial statements, and the other information received from the analysts, Adam purchased $350,000 worth of stock.

Three months later, Joshua Foods announced that over the past three years, the company had included $25 million of fictitious revenue and had capitalized more than $30 million of charges that should have been expensed. These irregularities will result in a restatement of the fiscal 2017 financial statements, resulting in a $1,250,000 loss for fiscal 2017. The press release from the company says that it will likely declare bankruptcy in the next few weeks. In the following two weeks, the value of Adam's holdings in the stock declined to $50,000.

Required:

a. You are Adam's attorney. List the various legal issues and precedents that you will use in trying to recover the losses Adam sustained.

b. You are the attorney for Joshua Foods' auditors. It is apparent that Adam will try to recover losses from your firm. List the defenses you would prepare to protect the auditors from liability.

c. How does Sarbanes–Oxley affect the position of either Adam's attorney or the auditors' attorney? You may find www.soxlaw.com helpful.

Internal Audits, Governmental Audits, and Fraud Examinations

You have a chance to really learn and improve the business. You build relationships with the board and the major business leaders. You can move internal audit to more value-added processes. And it builds your ability to manage people and work with cross-functional teams.

Michael Fung, former CFO, Walmart North American stores division, on his four years spent in internal audit[1]

Professional Standards References

Topic	AU-C/ISA Section	AS Section
Consideration of Fraud in a Financial Statement Audit	240	2401
Consideration of Laws and Regulations	250	2405
An Audit of Internal Control Over Financial Reporting That Is Integrated with an Audit of Financial Statements		2201
Consideration of the Internal Audit Function in a Financial Statement Audit	610	2415
Compliance Auditing Considerations in Audits of Governmental Entities and Recipients of Governmental Financial Assistance	801	6110
		ET/AT Standard[†]
Compliance Attestation		AT-C 315
Independence, Integrity, and Objectivity		ET 101-191
		IIA Standard
Independence and Objectivity		IIA 1100
Organizational Objectivity		IIA 1110
Individual Objectivity		IIA 1120
Proficiency		IIA 1210
Managing the Internal Audit Activity		IIA 2000
Nature of Work		IIA 2100
Governance		IIA 2110
Risk Management		IIA 2120

[1]*CFO.com*, June 10, 2008.

Control	IIA 2130
Engagement Planning	IIA 2200
Planning Considerations	IIA 2201
Engagement Objectives	IIA 2210
Engagement Scope	IIA 2220
Performing the Engagement	IIA 2300
Communicating Results	IIA 2400
Criteria for Communicating	IIA 2410
Quality of Communications	IIA 2420
Resolution of Senior Management's Acceptance of Risks	IIA 2600

†ET indicates ethics standard.

LEARNING OBJECTIVES

This module explores governmental audits, internal audits, and fraud examination. These fields differ in important respects from financial statement auditing practiced by independent accountants in public accounting. However, you will find that all fields of auditing share many elements. Fraud examination can be very exciting. It has the aura of detective work—finding things people want to keep hidden. The explanations and examples in this module will help you understand the working environment, objectives, and procedures that characterize governmental, internal, and fraud examination.

Your objectives are to be able to:

LO D-1 Define *internal auditing,* describe internal audit institutions (e.g., the IIA), describe how internal auditors interact with independent auditors, explain internal auditors' independence problems, and list features of internal audit reports.

LO D-2 Define *governmental auditing,* describe governmental audit institutions (e.g., the GAO), describe how governmental auditors interact with independent auditors, explain governmental auditors' independence problems, and list features of governmental audit reports.

LO D-3 Explain the function of standards and measurements in economy, efficiency, and program results audits.

LO D-4 Describe the Single Audit Act of 1984 in relation to audits of governmental fund recipients.

LO D-5 Define *fraud examination* and describe various engagements performed by fraud examiners.

LO D-6 Describe the elements necessary for a successful fraud examination and explain the differences in the way fraud examiners and external auditors handle evidence.

LO D-7 Describe the ways accountants can assist in prosecuting fraud perpetrators.

INTRODUCTION

In the summer of 2002, **WorldCom** announced that its financial statements were misstated by more than $7 billion. The misstatement was the result of capitalizing ordinary expenses. WorldCom's vice president of internal audit, Cynthia Cooper, discovered the accounting fraud. Despite opposition from WorldCom's chief financial officer, Cooper took her findings to the chairman of the audit committee of WorldCom's board of directors. The actions of WorldCom's internal auditors led to the disclosure of one of the largest financial statement frauds in history. Cooper was subsequently named one of *Time* magazine's three "Persons of the Year" in 2002.

"EXTERNAL," GOVERNMENTAL, AND INTERNAL AUDITS

In today's environment of Sarbanes–Oxley, the Public Company Accounting Oversight Board (PCAOB), and increased public scrutiny, organizations are asking public accounting firms for more assistance. Public accounting firms are no longer able to provide internal audit services to their publicly traded audit clients. However, organizations that need assistance with internal audit, investigation, and other related services can turn to public accounting firms that do not serve as their financial statements auditor. One of the main segments in most large public accounting firms is outsourced and cosourced internal audit services, and this opportunity has led to several business ventures focused primarily on providing internal audit and other nonaudit services to clients (e.g., **Protiviti Inc.**).

AUDITING INSIGHT   Taking Care of Business

The following is an excerpt from the Protiviti website:

Protiviti is a global business consulting and internal audit firm composed of experts specializing in risk, advisory, and transaction services. We help solve problems in finance and transactions, operations, technology, litigation, governance, risk, and compliance. Our highly trained, results-oriented professionals provide a unique perspective on a wide range of critical business issues for clients in the Americas, Asia-Pacific, Europe, and the Middle East.

Source: *http://www.protiviti.com/en-US/Pages/About-Us.aspx*

Many of the tasks and processes that internal auditors and governmental auditors perform are similar to those that financial statement auditors perform. However, services performed by governmental and internal auditors do vary considerably. When internal and governmental auditors perform audits of financial information, the scope of the engagement typically is wider than the scope performed by an external auditor. Internal auditors and governmental auditors often have objectives that go beyond the fair presentation of the financial statements, such as the efficiency of the financial reporting process. Furthermore, government and internal auditors often perform audits of monthly financial statements or other internal financial reports to ensure that information for management decisions is reliable. In this module, we explore the services provided by internal auditors and governmental auditors and gain an understanding of the elements that help to define what is meant by a *quality audit*.

A discussion of internal auditing, governmental auditing, and financial statement auditing performed by public accounting firms is often confusing. Many governmental and internal auditors are CPAs and perform services similar to those performed by public accounting firms. Indeed, several state audit organizations are considered independent auditors and issue opinions on the financial statements of government agencies. At the same time, many public accounting firms are employed to audit the financial statements of government entities such as counties, cities, and school districts. To further complicate the discussion, many public accounting firms offer internal audit services to non-SEC clients and non-financial statement audit clients alike. It is important to note that although the PCAOB prohibits auditors of public companies from providing internal audit services to their financial statement audit clients, auditors of privately held and not-for-profit (NFP) entities may still provide both internal and external audit services to their clients. For purposes of this module, therefore, *external* auditing refers to financial statement auditing performed by CPAs in public accounting firms and thereby distinguishes that public practice from governmental and internal practices.

INTERNAL AUDITS

LO D-1
Define *internal auditing,*
describe internal audit
institutions (e.g., the IIA),
describe how internal
auditors interact with
independent auditors,
explain internal auditors'
independence problems,
and list features of internal
audit reports.

In the past, *internal auditors* have been defined as auditors working for the organization they were auditing. Internal auditors were employed by an organization such as a bank, hospital, city government, or industrial company. However, in recent years, many professional services firms are providing internal audit services to the business community. Therefore, internal auditors may now be employed by either the organization they are auditing or an independent professional services firm.[2] Many corporations believe that they gain expertise and improve control over audit costs when the internal audit function is outsourced to an external audit firm. Conversely, other companies believe that an in-house internal audit function is better aligned with the company's goals and objectives and auditors gain more experience and expertise with the company's organization and business. Currently, we are seeing more firms implementing a co-sourcing strategy in which the company retains an in-house internal audit department augmented by auditors from an outside firm. This strategy allows the company to have a core audit group dedicated to the company with specialized "institutional knowledge" in company policy, procedure, and strategy, yet the company can obtain expertise and audit knowledge from the professional services firm for specific engagements or projects.

The Institute of Internal Auditors (IIA), the organization that sets standards and governs the internal audit profession, defines **internal auditing** and states its objective as follows:

> Internal auditing is an independent, objective, assurance and consulting activity designed to add value and improve an organization's operations. It helps an organization accomplish its objectives by bringing a systematic, disciplined approach to evaluate and improve effectiveness of risk management, control, and governance processes.

Several key elements in this definition warrant further evaluation.

Independence

You may be wondering how in-house internal auditors employed by the company being audited can classify themselves as independent and objective. Although internal auditors employed by the entity under audit cannot be disassociated from their employers in the eyes of the public, they seek organizational and individual independence. Internal auditors achieve independence during the audit process when they are free from direction or constraint by the managers of the business unit under audit. To establish this organizational independence, many internal audit organizations report directly to the audit committees of the board of directors. Such a reporting relationship reduces management's influence over the audit scope and reporting.

An element that greatly assists the internal audit department in establishing an independent and objective organization is the **audit charter**. Many departments and organizations have charters, and it is particularly important for the internal audit department to have one. An internal audit charter approved by senior management and the board of directors provides:

- A commitment from management to the establishment of an independent and objective audit organization.
- A definition of the authority and responsibility of the audit department.
- A definition of the scope of the audit department's activities.
- The department's authorization to perform audits, request materials, and gather evidence.
- The performance and reporting requirements for the audit department.

These elements provide an essential foundation for building an independent department. The audit charter for the South Bank Corporation is provided in Exhibit D.1.

---

[2]Professional services firms include public accounting firms that offer a variety of auditing, accounting, and consulting services and some consulting firms that do not perform financial statement audit services but do provide other services including internal audit services (e.g., Protiviti).

EXHIBIT D.1 **Internal Audit Charter of South Bank Corporation**

South Bank Corporation

Internal Audit Charter

1. *POLICY STATEMENT*

   It is the policy of South Bank Corporation to establish and support an Internal Audit function as an independent appraisal function to examine and evaluate the Corporation's activities as a service to management and the Board of Directors.

2. *DEFINITION*

   Internal auditing is an independent, objective assurance and consulting activity designed to add value and improve an organisation's operations. It helps an organisation accomplish its objectives by bringing a systematic, disciplined approach to evaluate and improve the effectiveness of risk management, control, and governance processes. (*International Standards for the Professional Practice of Internal Auditing, October 2008*)

3. *OBJECTIVE*

   The primary objective of Internal Audit is to assist members of management and the Board of Directors in the effective discharge of their responsibilities. To this end, Internal Audit will furnish management with analyses, recommendations, counsel, and information concerning the activities reviewed.

   A strategic audit plan shall be developed, which ensures coverage of the Corporation as a whole over a 3-year period. The strategic audit plan is to be risk based and is to be reviewed annually at the time of development of the annual audit plan. Internal Audits of South Bank Corporation will be conducted by Internal Audit based upon an annual audit plan drawn from the strategic audit plan (both approved by the Audit Committee) or by special request of management or the Audit Committee. The following objectives will be satisfied through the completion of audit work for a specific function or area:

   - Appraise adequacy and soundness of internal accounting controls and operating procedures. Review controls for cost effectiveness and relevance to the current operating environment.
   - Determine compliance with applicable regulatory or contractual requirements.
   - Recommend operating improvements and ensure that operations are in line with organisational goals.
   - Assess the reliability of management information utilised in decision-making processes.
   - Evaluate the effectiveness of existing policies or provide assistance in the formulation thereof, when necessary.
   - Determine whether appropriated funds are used efficiently and for the purposes for which they were appropriated.
   - Ensure that South Bank Corporation assets are properly recorded and adequately safeguarded against loss.
   - Identify opportunities for cost savings and make recommendations for improved cost efficiencies.

4. *AUTHORITY*

   Authorization is granted for full and complete access to records (manual or automated), physical property, and personnel of South Bank Corporation that relate to areas under audit. Internal Audit is expected to follow the standards of confidentiality with regard to sensitive information as it applies to staff in the particular area.

5. *INDEPENDENCE*

   The Internal Audit function shall have direct access to the Audit Committee of the Board of Directors. Internal Audit shall take directly to the Chairman of the Audit Committee matters that are of significant magnitude or concern to require immediate attention of the Committee.

6. *RESPONSIBILITY*

   Internal Audit has no direct responsibility for the operations and functions within audited areas. It can, however, make recommendations regarding the quality of those operations or adequacy of internal controls in the normal course of audits. Internal Audit may take an active role in the formulation of policy or development of new systems; it will be in an advisory capacity, with final decisions and implementation being the responsibility of South Bank Corporation management.

7. *RELATIONSHIP WITH EXTERNAL AUDITORS*

   The responsibilities and objectives of the internal and external auditing groups are generally different. However, at those times when objectives of both groups coincide, the completion of specific work will be coordinated to ensure that maximum audit coverage is provided at a minimum cost to South Bank Corporation.

8. *STANDARDS OF AUDIT PRACTICE*

   Internal Audit will comply with and acknowledges the mandatory nature of both the *International Standards for the Professional Practice of Internal Auditing*, as adopted by the Institute of Internal Auditors (IIA), and the Code of Ethics of the IIA.

   AUDIT REPORTS

9. Audit Reports shall be provided to management for comment within 7 days of the completion of each audit—management shall provide written response to the audit matters raised within a further 14 days, and a final audit report shall be finalised within a further 7 days. Should there be disagreement with the audit findings from management, Internal Audit shall include a further comment to assist the Audit Committee in its deliberations.

   ANNUAL REPORTS

10. Annually a report outlining the performance of Internal Audit in undertaking the annual audit plan shall be submitted to the Audit Committee together with information on any significant issues or major concerns, which Internal Audit believes should be brought to the attention of the Audit Committee.

The other key aspect of independence and objectivity concerns the attitude of the individuals engaged in the audit. An internal auditor must have an impartial, unbiased attitude in performing the audit. In addition, individual auditors must not have any conflicts of interests. Such conflicts may result when the same company employs family members or outside business interests appear to affect audit judgments.

As previously mentioned, many public accounting firms are performing internal audit work for clients. Although Sarbanes–Oxley, the PCAOB, and the Securities and Exchange Commission strictly prohibit this for public companies, public accounting firms can provide internal audit services to clients that are not publicly traded and to publicly traded companies that are not financial statement audit clients. However, great care should be given concerning independence issues—both independence in fact and independence in appearance. Auditors should take great care to avoid even the appearance that they are auditing their own work or are biased in their audit judgments due to revenue and relations emanating from internal audit work.

AUDITING INSIGHT   Does Everyone Know What They're Doing?

An auditor was reviewing the mortgage procedures at a large bank including a discussion with a clerk in charge of escrow accounts. The clerk knew about receiving funds and placing them in the escrow account. The clerk knew to pay for surveys, inspections, title investigations, and other fees from the escrow account. However, the clerk was not aware that once the property sale was completed, any remaining funds were to be taken by the bank as revenue. The auditor found $77,000 in unrecorded revenue.

Source: Personal experience of author.

Value-Added Audit

The objectives of an internal audit and an external audit are vastly different. Generally speaking, internal auditors perform little of their work on the financial statements. In-house internal auditors audit their companies all year, often months removed from both the previous or the subsequent issue of annual financial statements. Internal auditors are primarily concerned with affecting the company's bottom line; hence, the definition of internal auditing includes the phrase *to add value and improve an organization's operations*. Internal auditors add value to a company primarily by achieving the following four audit objectives:

1. Recognizing and analyzing industry, business, and operational risks.
2. Improving the economy and efficiency of the operations.
3. Ensuring compliance with management directives.
4. Serving as management's representative.

Recognizing and Analyzing Industry, Business, and Operational Risks

A major goal of an internal audit organization is to gain as much expertise as possible concerning the industry, business, and operational areas of the company. This expertise allows the internal auditors to recognize and evaluate changes in the economy, business environment, technology, regulatory environment, and management. These types of changes often result in additional risks for the organization. The internal audit department must take a proactive approach to reduce or eliminate these risks. By reducing or eliminating risks that might create potential losses, the internal audit organization adds value to the company.

Improving Economy and Efficiency of the Operations

Over a period of a few years, an internal auditor will have evaluated almost every department and almost every aspect of a company's business. This experience makes the auditor a valuable asset to the organization. Indeed, many organizations use internal audit as a training ground for management, and entities highly value the experience gained as a member of the internal audit organization. (Note the quote by Michael Fung, former CFO of **Wal-Mart Stores Inc.** at the beginning of this module.) This experience also enables the internal auditor to evaluate many aspects regarding the performance of a particular department or process. For example, an internal auditor for **Sears** may visit five or six distribution centers in a given year. A particular distribution center may have developed a procedure that enables orders to be processed faster. The internal auditor may be able to recommend this "best practice" to other facilities.

An important ingredient in successfully recommending changes in a company's operations is for the auditor to have a complete business and technical perspective of the operation under evaluation. For example, auditors are not successful in implementing meaningful change in a marketing department without completely considering the marketing perspective on the processes and procedures used in that specialty. Many internal audit organizations enhance this critical element of internal audit by adding personnel with backgrounds in production, engineering, computer science, and other relevant disciplines to the internal audit staff. Further, it is extremely important that the internal auditor understand the industry. Compliance audits require a knowledge of the laws, regulations, and reporting requirements imperative to high-quality company performance.

Ensuring Compliance with Management Directives

Management provides all departments and operations with directives regarding the desired performance of the company's business. These directives are designed to ensure that the company complies with laws and regulations; that departments are operating efficiently and effectively; and that risks are minimized. Many of these directives are found in the policy and procedure manuals maintained by each functional area. Internal audit is charged with reporting on departments' compliance with these directives. Often, these directives delineate the internal controls established by management to reduce or eliminate risk within a functional area.

It is important to recognize the distinction between the compliance issues of internal auditors and those of external auditors. External auditors review compliance with internal controls that are relevant to the financial reporting process. The internal auditors are concerned with any noncompliance that (1) increases the risk faced by the company or (2) diminishes the efficiency or effectiveness of the company's operations. Basically, internal auditors are concerned with any noncompliance, both financial and nonfinancial in nature, that might adversely affect the company's likelihood of meeting its goals and objectives.

Serving as Management's Representative

The complexities of managing a large organization often prohibit senior management from visiting locations and departments critical to the success of the organization. For example, because of the number of distribution centers operated by Sears, it may not be feasible for the vice president of materials management to personally visit and review every individual operation at each distribution center. Therefore, the reports from the internal audit department may be the only critical objective evaluations received by management regarding certain distribution centers and other key operations.

It should be evident that the four audit objectives discussed here are not mutually exclusive. For example, the evaluation of compliance with company policies and procedures includes elements of reducing risk, evaluating economy and efficiency, and being management's representative.

Scope of Service

Internal auditors make recommendations that result in additional profits or cost savings for their companies. In this capacity, they function as management consultants. Within the IIA definition of "to evaluate and improve effectiveness of risk management, control, and governance processes," almost any type of assessment of any aspect of the organization is feasible. In fact, it is difficult to define the variety of audits that the modern internal audit department performs.

The stated objective of internal auditing is phrased in terms of "helping the organization accomplish its objectives." To achieve this goal, internal auditors provide services including (1) financial audits of financial reports and accounting control systems; (2) compliance audits that ensure conformity with company policies, plans, and procedures and with laws and regulations; (3) operational audits that evaluate the economy and efficiency of business process; and (4) audits of effectiveness in achieving program results in comparison to established objectives and goals (IIA Standards 2100 and 2210).

Financial Audits

Internal auditors usually do not audit quarterly or year-end financial statements in the same manner as external auditors. However, internal auditors may evaluate areas that management believes may be of concern to the external auditors, such as areas that were found to have problems in the prior audit. Such a preliminary evaluation may allow for correction of errors prior to the arrival of the external auditors.

Internal auditors perform audits of financial reports for internal use. This type of audit provides managers assurance that the information they are using in the decision-making process is relevant and reliable. Such an assurance function reduces management's risk in making daily operating decisions or in determining appropriate action to address a unique problem. This type of auditing is similar to the auditing described elsewhere in this textbook.

AUDITING INSIGHT   Did I Take That Trip?

Toni McEwen, an internal auditor at Deerfield College, was auditing expense accounts. To her surprise, an expense report of Bruce Livingstone, a supervisor at the Deerfield College School of Dentistry's business office, listed her as a traveling partner on a recent business trip. Livingstone (who was married) took his girlfriend on a business trip at the college's expense but needed to list another college employee if the college was to pay for her expenses. Listing an auditor as his traveling partner was probably not the best way to cover this fraud!

Because fraudulent behavior in management often leads to additional fraudulent behavior (tone at the top), the auditors launched an investigation of the business office. The auditors uncovered $63,000 in fictitious vendor payments, perpetrated by Cheryl Brown, an administrative assistant working for Livingstone.

Source: "One Fraud Leads to Another," *Internal Auditor,* December 2008.

Compliance Audits

In many functional areas, management's primary concern is compliance with policies, procedures, laws, and regulations—thus, the definition of **compliance audits**. The degree of management's concern for such audits may vary by industry or by functional area. For example, compliance with laws will be of more concern in the banking, insurance, and health care industries as compared with a company in the retail industry. Also, in an audit of the human resources department, the main audit objective may be compliance with policies and procedures designed to ensure conformity with laws regarding fair hiring and proper dismissals of employees.

AUDITING INSIGHT   How Hard Did You Study for Your Last Exam?

Internal auditors evaluate an organization's compliance with every aspect of policy and procedure. An internal audit at Auburn University found that a grade for a scholarship athlete had been changed without the professor's knowledge from an incomplete to an A, raising the athlete's average for the semester just over the 2.0 minimum for graduation.

Source: "An Audit Reveals More Academic Questions at Auburn," *The New York Times,* December 10, 2006.

Operational Audits

In the past, the terms *internal auditing* and *operational auditing* were used almost interchangeably because the vast majority of audits performed by internal auditors were operational audits. The internal auditing activity known as **operational auditing** refers to auditors' study of business operations for the purpose of making recommendations about economic and efficient use of resources, effective achievement of business objectives, and compliance with company policies. The goal of operational auditing is to help managers perform their management responsibilities and improve profitability. Therefore, operational auditing is included in the definition of internal auditing given previously. In a similar context, an AICPA committee defined operational auditing performed by independent public accounting firms as a distinct type of consulting service having the goal of helping a client improve the use of its capabilities and resources to achieve its objectives. So, internal auditors consider operational auditing an integral part of internal auditing, and external auditors define it as a type of consulting service offered by public accounting firms.

Governance Audits

The definition of internal auditing includes evaluating the *governance process.* According to **MetricStream,** a quality and risk management consulting organization,

> There is a widespread call for greater [Board of Directors] (BoD) accountability and transparency—the twin key issues that engage boards are—What are the risks? and How are they managed? An Internal Audit function addresses both concerns. Internal Audit supports the BoD and its committees by independently assessing the effectiveness of an organization's system of internal controls as well as compliance with statutory, legal and regulatory requirements. Given the importance the BoD attaches to this role, organizations are making every effort to adopt Internal Audit across the enterprise for better management of risk and effective compliance with regulation.[3]

> As Internal Audit adopts new roles—provide assurance and establish trust through assessment of design, implementation, and application of internal controls across all disciplines—organizations are looking for ways to make the Internal Audit function an integral part of governance and an instrument to improve business performance.

> In this role as an integral part of governance, the auditor reports on a wide variety of critical information. It is essential that management understands the risks that the business and industry are facing. It is also imperative that management receives objective, timely feedback concerning corporate strategies and initiatives in order to effectively guide the corporation and fulfill their fiduciary responsibilities. **Governance audits** ensure that senior management receives accurate and timely information concerning management and leadership throughout the organization as well as the proper implementation and execution of company strategy and plans. This function of internal audit is continuing to grow in both scope and importance.

 AUDITING INSIGHT | Internal Auditors Produce Interest Income

During an audit of the cash management operations at branch offices, internal auditors found that bank deposits were not made until several days after cash and checks were received. Company policy was to complete the bookkeeping before making the deposit.

The auditors showed branch managers a cost-efficient way to capture the needed bookkeeping information that would permit the release of the cash and checks. Management agreed to implement the timely deposit of checks and transfers of cash through an electronic funds transfer system from local banks to the headquarters bank, performing the bookkeeping afterward.

The change resulted in additional interest income in the first year in the amount of $150,000.

Other Audits

Internal auditors may perform audits that are specific to the nature of the business they serve.

Quality Control Audits   Auditors who work with manufacturing companies may provide **quality control audits** designed specifically to determine whether the product meets the standards established by management. Customer service departments also may be subject to a quality audit to ensure that customers are being served in the manner prescribed by the company. The auditors are not a substitute for the quality control department, but they can review the work of quality control, quality control reports, and the responses of management to issues raised by quality control.

Environmental Audit   Another type of audit performed in some organizations is an **environmental audit.**[4] Many organizations deal with materials that must be handled in manners prescribed by law (e.g., what does Walmart do with those old batteries, tires, and oil?). Auditors can review procedures, record keeping, liability issues, and compliance as they relate to the organization's environmental issues. In addition, auditors can make recommendations for reducing waste (e.g., reusable shipping containers) and making products that are more environmentally friendly (e.g., recyclable packaging materials).

Sustainability Audits   In other chapters, we have discussed sustainability as an assurance service. That is, management may report on sustainability issues such as carbon emissions and instruct the auditors to attest to the validity of the numbers in the report provided. However, as sustainability accounting and reporting gain more acceptance, especially in the United States, internal auditors are being asked to provide sustainability service beyond an assurance of numbers. Many organizations need audit assistance in establishing a sustainability program, measurement criteria, reporting standards, and other issues that require the internal auditor's knowledge of the company and sustainability issues.

The IIA includes sustainability under a broad context of corporate social responsibility (CSR). In this context, auditors assist management in areas of

- Governance.
- Ethics.
- Environment issues.
- Health, safety, and security.
- Human rights and work conditions.

Clearly, we have seen the impact on corporate image and reputation as well as the questioning of the social morality of corporations whose products have been reported as having been manufactured in facilities with substandard conditions. According to the IIA:

> Internal auditors should understand the risks and controls related to CSR objectives. Where appropriate, the CAE [chief audit executive] should plan to audit, facilitate control self-assessments, verify results, and/or consult on the various subjects. Internal auditors should maintain the skills and knowledge necessary to understand and evaluate the governance, risks, and controls of CSR strategies.[5]

Because of the newness of sustainability, many companies have found that this area is best served through outsourced internal audit services. At this time, most large CPA firms have more expertise than some of their clients (especially when they can rely on knowledge transferred from European offices that have been working on sustainability issues for a long period of time). Over time, it is expected that an in-house internal audit department will gain sufficient expertise to service more of the sustainability issues within the company.

[4]Many organizations are engaged in *sustainability accounting* that includes an environmental component. However, due to the highly technical nature of environmental laws and policy, most organizations that have significant exposure have an environmental audit function.

[5]Institute of Internal Auditors, *Practice Guide, Evaluating Corporate Social Responsibility/Sustainable Development*, p. 1; www.theiia.org/bookstore/product/evaluating-corporate-social-responsibilitysustainable-development-practice-guide-download-pdf-1483.cfm.

AUDITING INSIGHT   The Prince Speaks

The following is an excerpt from a speech by His Royal Highness The Prince of Wales given to Parliament in December 2006. Prince Charles has been a major advocate of sustainability reporting worldwide.

In the 20th century, accountancy made a number of modifications to include new costs which had begun to take on more significance in modern business and, for example, pensions costs are now included, as are the costs of foreign exchange trading.

In our current century, we appear to have reached a point when further costs need to be measured and accounted for. The value of dwindling natural resources, and the cost of increasing atmospheric pollution, should surely be included in the price we are all paying for what we buy and consume?

At the moment, these costs often do not appear in anyone's books. Apparently, therefore, the cost of draining a wetland or destroying a rain-forest is zero. If a company exhausts an oil field, it appears to cost the planet 'nothing'. The cost of pumping tons of carbon into the atmosphere can be—depending where you are in the world—zero. . . . At one level, it appears that no-one is accounting for these costs. Yet, at another level . . . we are all paying for them. . . . . To put it another way, we are running up the biggest global credit card debt in history, but with little or no thought for how the bill will ever be paid.

The Accounting for Sustainability project . . . has been established to try to help address this issue.

Sources: HRH The Prince of Wales, "Time to Account for Our Actions," November 2007, www.princeofwales.gov.uk/media/speeches/speech-hrh-the-prince-of-wales-the-accounting-sustainability-forum; http://ehis.ebscohost.com/ehost/pdfviewer/pdfviewer?sid=db7c9889-7ad6-4fe9-9499-7a8235053970%40sessionmgr114&vid=2&hid=116.

Internal Audit Standards

The IIA is the international organization that governs the standards, continuing education, and general rules of conduct for internal auditors as a profession. The IIA also sponsors research and development of practices and procedures designed to enhance the work of internal auditors wherever they are employed.

The IIA issues *International Standards for the Professional Practice of Internal Auditing* (IIA *Standards*). (See the IIA website at www.theiia.org.) The IIA standards are classified in three major categories:

1. Attribute standards.
2. Performance standards.
3. Implementation standards.

Aptly named, the attribute standards address the *characteristics of internal auditors* (e.g., independence, objectivity) *and organizations* performing internal audit activities. Performance standards relate to *conducting internal audit activities* and provide a *measure of quality* against which the performance of internal audit activities can be measured. The attribute and the performance standards apply to internal audit services in general. Implementation standards, on the other hand, are specific applications of the attribute and performance standards to specific types of engagements (e.g., assurance or consulting engagements).

Internal auditors are expected to comply with the IIA's standards of professional conduct. IIA audit standards are recommended and encouraged, but compliance with them depends on their acceptance, adoption, and implementation by practicing internal auditors. Many internal audit organizations include compliance with IIA standards in their department charters and in their audit reports. (Note the reference to the IIA standards in the audit charter of South Bank Corporation in Exhibit D.1.) The IIA standards require internal auditors to be skilled in dealing with people and in communicating effectively. Such a requirement may be considered implicit in GAAS related to training and proficiency, but little is said in GAAS about effective communication, perhaps because the audit report language is so standardized. External auditors tend to believe the public has the responsibility to learn how to understand their audit reports, while internal auditors believe it is their responsibility to see that management and the audit committee understand the audit findings and recommendations.

The IIA also issues practice advisories. Because of the diversity of entities serviced by internal auditors, guidance from practice advisories is not mandatory. They suggest "best practices" in internal audit, and internal audit organizations are encouraged to implement those practices that are applicable to the business and industry they serve.

Many of the IIA standards deal with the organization and management of the internal audit department. CPAs in public practice have similar standards, but their standards are included in the AICPA quality control standards rather than in GAAS. However, observance of quality control standards is considered essential for proper auditing practice in accordance with GAAS. The AICPA quality control standards are incorporated by reference in GAAS and enforced through the peer reviews and monitoring activities of accounting firms.

Although AICPA standards for financial statements are comprehensive, the related IIA standards are very brief. It would be extremely difficult to provide detailed specifications on internal audit reports because the reports vary by entity and audit objective. The best the IIA can provide is an outline of desirable audit report characteristics.

The IIA also administers the certified internal auditor (CIA) program. This certification is a mark of professional achievement that has gained international acceptance. To become a CIA, a candidate must hold a college degree and pass an examination on internal auditing and related subjects. The exam has three parts:

- **Part 1**—Internal audit basics.
- **Part 2**—Internal audit practice.
- **Part 3**—Internal audit knowledge elements.

Candidates also must have two years of audit experience (internal audit or public accounting audit) obtained before or after passing the examination. Holders of master's degrees need only one year of experience. You can sit for the CIA exam prior to completion of your bachelor's degree. For more details, consult the IIA's website (www.theiia.org).

Internal Audit Reports

Internal audit reports are not standardized as are external auditors' reports on financial statements. Each report is different because internal auditors need to communicate findings on a variety of assignments and audit objectives. The key criterion for an internal audit report is clear and concise communication of findings and recommendations.

The reporting stage is the internal auditors' opportunity to capture management's undivided attention. To be effective, a report cannot be unduly long, tedious, technical, or laden with minutiae. It must be accurate, concise, clear, and timely. It must speak directly to the risks the auditors evaluated. Most quality audit reports ensure that significant issues are described by five elements:

1. The *condition* the auditor identified.
2. The *criteria* that renders the condition inappropriate.
3. The *cause* of the condition.
4. The *effect* the condition may have on the company.
5. The *recommendation* that may eliminate or mitigate the condition.

For example, let's say that during a compliance audit of the human resource area you notice that a recent candidate for an accounting position was asked several inappropriate questions on the employment application. An inappropriate question might be, "have you ever been arrested?" (Questions may ask only whether someone has ever been convicted because a person is considered innocent until proven guilty.) After further investigation, you discover that the human resource department ran out of current job applications and decided to use some old applications kept in storage. The auditor needs to report the following for this audit finding:

1. Condition—inappropriate questions asked of job candidates.
2. Criteria—fair hiring laws and company policies.

3. Cause—use of old job applications due to out of stock of current applications.
4. Effect—possible lawsuits and adverse publicity.
5. Recommendation—destroy obsolete job applications to prevent further use and maintain a copy of the current form on the computer (to be printed if another "stock out" situation occurs).

Generally, internal auditors meet with the business unit's management team to review the audit report before it is distributed to senior management. This meeting is called the **exit conference**. Its purpose is to inform the business unit's management of the audit results, reach an agreement on the correctness of the findings, and learn of the corrective action management plans. Sometimes disagreements concerning audit findings occur. In the interest of fair and complete disclosure, many auditors include management's reasons for disagreement in the audit report.

Internal audit reports are sent to the highest level of management in the organization, often including the CEO and the audit committee. Usually the senior manager overseeing a business unit (e.g., the vice president of materials management for distribution centers and purchasing) would receive audit reports and respond to senior management and the audit committee regarding which recommendations will be implemented. The manager also must explain why certain recommendations will not be implemented. Top management and the audit committee may compel management to reconsider selected actions.

Once senior management agrees with acceptance or rejection of audit recommendations, the business unit is obligated to implement the accepted recommendations. The IIA standards include a requirement for a **follow-up** to ascertain that appropriate action is being taken on accepted recommendations. Only after the follow-up is completed is the audit considered closed. External auditors do not have a similar follow-up requirement.

☑ REVIEW CHECKPOINTS

D.1 How can internal auditors achieve practical independence?
D.2 What auditing services do internal auditors provide?
D.3 What special professional certification is available for internal auditors?
D.4 Who is responsible for enforcing compliance with laws and regulations in the business?

GOVERNMENTAL AUDITS

LO D-2
Define *governmental auditing,* describe governmental audit institutions (e.g., the GAO), describe how governmental auditors interact with independent auditors, explain governmental auditors' independence problems, and list features of governmental audit reports.

Government officials and recipients of federal monies are responsible for carrying out public functions efficiently, economically, effectively, ethically, and equitably while achieving desired public objectives. High-quality auditing is essential for government accountability to the public and transparency regarding linking resources to related program results.[6]

Many federal agencies (e.g., Army, Navy, Department of Transportation) have governmental auditors who are charged with ensuring compliance with agency and department policies and procedures. The accounting, auditing, and investigative agency of the federal government is the Government Accountability Office (GAO). It audits the departments, agencies, and programs of the federal government (even if they are subject to audits by their own internal audit staffs) to determine whether the laws passed by the U.S. Congress are followed and to determine whether programs are being implemented with economy and efficiency and are achieving desired results. The U.S. Congress always receives copies of GAO reports.

[6]*Government Auditing Standards,* January 2011, p. 1.

Congress Relies on the GAO

- "Senator Richard (Dick) Blumenthal (D-CT) sent a letter to the Government Accountability Office (GAO) requesting an investigation of drug shortages. In his letter, Senator Blumenthal requests that the GAO investigation "examine the extent of hospital shortages of pharmaceutical products and the prevalence of these shortages in recent years, the impact of such shortages on patient care, possible explanations, and potential legislative or administrative approaches to addressing this problem."[a]

- "Sen. Susan Collins, R-Maine, has asked the Government Accountability Office to review the statutory framework for federal agency chief information officers and potential modifications that could further enhance CIOs' authorities."[b]

- Sen. Susan Collins (R-ME) has asked the Government Accountability Office (GAO) to audit a program that helps federal employees who suffer on-the-job injuries. The ranking member of the Senate Homeland Security panel, Collins wrote in a letter to the GAO that she is concerned that the Federal Employees' Compensation Act program has "potential for waste, fraud, and abuse."[c]

- When approving the Katrina Housing Tax Relief Act of 2007, the U.S. House Ways and Means Committee included an amendment requiring the GAO to report on any waste, fraud, or abuse.[d]

- "Congress did not write a blank check for spending in Iraq. We need to know funds are being used appropriately, which is what the GAO will do," Senator Tom Harkins.[e]

- "Every time we open these GAO reports we find more outrageous spending," Senator Chuck Grassley.[f]

- "Concerned that the IRS whistleblower program does not process awards in a timely fashion, Senate Finance Committee Leaders are asking the Government Accountability Office to look into the IRS processes and resources devoted to administrator the program."[g]

- A spokesman for Oregon Sen. Ron Wyden says the senator will ask the GAO to investigate a monitoring and maintenance program for underground waste tanks at the nation's most contaminated nuclear site. The request follows news Friday that six tanks at the Hanford Nuclear Reservation are leaking.[h]

- The Senate has passed a bill that would direct the GAO to examine the economic benefits large banks receive for being "too big to fail."[i]

- Several senators have requested that the GAO look for ways to coordinate the efforts of law enforcement and public health agencies at various levels and nonprofit organizations to address prescription drug abuse.[j]

- Senate Homeland Security and Governmental Affairs Ranking Member Tom Coburn, M.D. (R-OK), Chairman Tom Carper (D-DE), Financial and Contracting Oversight Subcommittee Chairwoman Claire McCaskill (D-MO), Senator Susan Collins (R-ME), and House Committee on Oversight and Government Reform Chairman Darrell Issa highlighted a report from the GAO entitled *Federal Employees' Compensation Act: Case Examples Illustrate Vulnerabilities That Could Result in Improper Payments of Overlapping Benefits*. The report examines improper and overlapping payments in the Federal Employees Compensation Act (FECA) and unemployment insurance programs. In its report, the GAO outlined steps to lower the risk of improper payments, including actions by the Department of Labor, as well as necessary action by Congress to allow the Department of Labor and state governments to perform more effective oversight and payment controls.[k]

[a]"Senator Requests GAO Study of Drug Shortages," *American Society of Anesthesiologists*, March 14, 2011.

[b]"Senator Requests GAO Review of CIO Roles," *Washington Business Journal*, March 8, 2011.

[c]"Senator Asks for GAO Audit of Compensation Program," *The Hill*, January 11, 2011.

[d]"Katrina Relief Bill Contains Hulshof Provision," *States News Service*, March 29, 2007.

[e]"Harkin Calls on State Department to Allow GAO Auditors in Baghdad," *States News Service*, March 12, 2007.

[f]"Grassley: Time for Waste, Fraud and Abuse of Government," Capitol Hill Press Releases, March 7, 2007.

[g]"Wyden and Hatch Ask GAO to Look into IRS Whistleblower Program," Taxanalysts, June 24, 2014.

[h]"U.S. Senators Johnson and Lankford Call on GAO to Review Administration's Executive Actions," WDI News and Opinion, March 30, 2015.

[i]"Oregon Senator to Ask for GAO Probe of Hanford," *The Washington Times*, February 22, 2013.

[j]"Senate Passes Bill to Require GAO Study on TBTF," *American Banker*, December 22, 2012.

[k]"Senators Encourage GAO to Investigate Ways to Collaborate on Prescription Drug Abuse," *Drug Store News*, March 5, 2013; "GAO Report Outlines Improper Federal Employees Compensation Payments," May 6, 2013, Tom Coburn, U.S. Senate press release.

The U.S. Comptroller General heads the GAO. In one sense, GAO auditors are the highest level of internal auditors for the federal government. State and federal agencies and other local government units use the GAO's *generally accepted government auditing standards (GAGAS)* to guide their audits. These standards are published in a book with a yellow cover, referred to as the **Yellow Book**.

Many states also have audit agencies similar to the GAO. They answer to state legislatures and perform the same types of work described here as GAO auditing. In another sense, the GAO and many state agencies are really external auditors with respect to government agencies they audit because they are organizationally independent.

Many government agencies have their own internal auditors and inspectors general. Well-managed local governments also have internal audit departments. For example, most federal agencies (e.g., Department of Defense, Department of the Interior), state agencies (e.g., education, welfare, controller), and local governments (e.g., cities, counties, tax districts) have internal audit staffs. Governmental auditors are charged with looking for projects that do not spend the taxpayers' money wisely. If you were a governmental auditor looking at the project in the following Auditing Insight, would you raise any issues?

AUDITING INSIGHT   Million-Dollar Pen

During the heat of the space race in the 1960s, the U.S. National Aeronautics and Space Administration decided it needed a ballpoint pen to write in the zero gravity confines of its space capsules. After considerable research and development, the Astronaut Pen was developed at a cost of approximately $1 million. The pen worked and also enjoyed some modest success as a novelty item back here on Earth.

The Soviet Union, faced with the same problem, used a pencil. In a follow-up to this story, NASA issued a statement that it had considered the use of a pencil but deemed the risk of a broken pencil point floating in the capsule too great a risk.

Types of Governmental Audits

The GAO shares with internal auditors many of the same elements of expanded-scope services. The GAO, however, emphasizes the accountability of public officials for the efficient, economical, and effective use of public funds and other resources. The GAO defines and describes *expanded-scope governmental auditing* in terms of three types of governmental audits:

1. Financial statement audits.
2. Attestation engagements.
3. Performance audits.

Financial Statement Audits

Financial statement audits determine whether the financial statements of an audited entity present fairly the financial position, results of operations, and cash flows in conformity with generally accepted accounting principles. In addition, financial audits can have other objectives, including:

- Issuing special reports for specified elements, accounts, or items of a financial statement.
- Reviewing interim financial statements.
- Issuing letters for underwriters.
- Reporting on the processing of transactions by service organizations.
- Auditing compliance with regulations relating to federal award expenditures and other governmental financial assistance.

Attestation Engagements

Attestation engagements involve providing an opinion on subject matter or an assertion about the subject matter that is the responsibility of another party. The subject matter of an attestation engagement may take many forms, including historical or prospective performance or condition, physical characteristics, historical events, analyses, systems and processes, or behavior. Examples of such engagements include reporting on

- Internal control over financial reporting or compliance with specified requirements.
- Compliance with requirements of specified laws, regulations, rules, contracts, or grants.
- Management's discussion and analysis presentation.

- Prospective or pro forma financial information.
- The reliability of performance measures.
- The reasonableness and allowability of proposed contract amounts.
- Performance of specified procedures on a subject matter.

Performance Audits

Performance audits provide objective analysis so that management and those charged with governance and oversight can rely on information to improve program performance and operations, reduce costs, facilitate decision making by corrective action, and contribute to public accountability.[7]

Performance audits may be requested by management or a legislative body or may be mandated by the law, grant, or contract under which an agency or company is operating or receiving money. Performance audits provide an objective and systematic examination of evidence of the performance and management of a program against objective criteria. Performance audits provide information to improve program operations and facilitate decision making by those with oversight responsibility. Examples of performance audits include assessing:

- The extent to which legislative, regulatory, or organizational goals and objectives are being achieved.
- The relative ability of alternative approaches to provide better program performance or eliminate factors that inhibit program effectiveness.
- The relative cost and benefits or cost effectiveness of program performance.
- The degree to which, if at all, a program produced the intended results.
- The degree to which, if at all, a program produced unintended effects.
- The extent to which programs duplicate, overlap, or conflict with other related programs.
- The degree to which, if at all, the audited entity is using sound procurement practices.
- The validity and reliability of performance measures or financial information related to the program.

The audit of a governmental organization, program, activity, or function may involve one or more of these audit types. The scope of the work is determined by the needs of the users of the audit results.

Audit Procedures—Economy, Efficiency, and Program Results Audits

LO D-3
Explain the function of standards and measurements in economy, efficiency, and program results audits.

The general evidence-gathering procedures used during the audit of financial statements in governmental audits are basically the same as the ones used by external auditors. These procedures are explained in other chapters in this textbook. However, the audit problems are usually different in audits of *economy, efficiency,* and *program results.* Also, although internal auditors occasionally perform audits of this nature, the vast majority of these audits are performed in the governmental sector.

Governmental and internal auditors must be as objective as possible when developing conclusions about efficiency, economy, and program results. This objectivity is achieved by (1) finding standards for evaluation, (2) determining the actual results of the program, and (3) comparing the actual results to the standards. Finding standards and deciding on relevant measurements is often difficult.

Students are often surprised by the difficulty in establishing standards and measurement criteria because these issues are not prominent during a financial statement audit. In a financial statement audit, the standards (which are the objective criteria) have already been set in the establishment of GAAP.

---

[7]*Government Auditing Standards,* January 2011.

AUDITING INSIGHT Establishing Standards

In the mid-1990s, the Florida state legislature gave millions of dollars to school districts to improve education for the next millennium. The program was called "Blueprint 2000." The legislature asked the Office of the Auditor General to monitor the use and performance of these funds. It took a team of auditors almost a year to establish standards and measurement criteria so that successful audits could begin.

Source: Personal experience of author.

When dealing with standards, measurements, and comparisons, auditors must keep inputs and outputs in perspective. Evidence about inputs—personnel hours and cost, material quantities and costs, asset investment—are most important in connection with reaching financial audit conclusions. For economy, efficiency, and program results, output measurements are equally important. Management has the responsibility for devising information systems to measure output. Such measurements should correspond to program objectives set forth in laws, regulations, administrative policies, legislative reports, or other such sources. Auditors must realize that output measurements are usually not expressed in financial terms (e.g., water quality improvement, educational progress, weapons effectiveness, materials-inspection time delays, and test program reporting accuracy).

Many economy and efficiency audits, and most program audits, are output oriented. Auditors need to be careful not to equate program activity with program success without measuring program results. These features are significantly different from auditors' roles with respect to financial statement audits for which the primary concern is with the reporting on the accounting for inputs.

An Example of Setting Performance Audit Criteria

Kinerville has instituted a new program in its school system. The program provides a healthy balanced breakfast for underprivileged students in grades K–12. You have been asked to audit the program's effectiveness. In planning this audit, the following issues must be resolved:

First, what is the goal of the program? If you said, "to feed hungry children," you would be only partially correct. The actual goal of school breakfast programs is based on the assumption that children do better in school when they have a good breakfast. Therefore, the main purpose of the program is to improve the educational experience for underprivileged children.

Second, by what standard would you measure success? A comparison to other students in the school who are not in the program? If these students are not "underprivileged," is this a fair measure? Should Kinerville's school district withhold breakfasts from some underprivileged children so there is a comparison group? Is there a moral issue with this type of evaluation? (This is an ethical question that the medical profession wrestles with on a regular basis because in studies of a new medicine, placebos are given to ill patients.) Would a comparison with other schools in other districts be appropriate? Maybe, but the comparison group would have to be carefully selected and matched on many demographic factors.

Third, what is the measure that will be used for comparison? Increased grades? Higher standardized test scores? What are the problems with these measures? Will teachers change their teaching methods and focus exclusively on test preparation? Can there be other reasons for an increase in test scores?

Lastly, how large an improvement is required for the program to be successful?

You may want answers to all of these questions, but real concrete answers do not exist. Most of these issues can be resolved with tests and measures that have some positive aspects and some negative aspects, and the audit team may need to have several measures and make many difficult judgments.

✓ REVIEW CHECKPOINTS

D.5 What auditing services do governmental auditors provide?

D.6 What difficulties do auditors find when conducting a performance audit?

D.7 How can governmental and internal auditors try to achieve objectivity when developing conclusions about economy, efficiency, or program results?

GAO Government Auditing Standards

The GAO establishes GAGAS that guide all audits for federal government agencies and facilities and all audits of entities receiving federal funds. Note that these standards must be adhered to even if an accounting firm is engaged to perform one of these audits. (Rule 501 of the AICPA Code of Conduct makes the *failure to follow government standards during a government audit* an act discreditable; see Module B.) In addition, many state and local governments have adopted GAGAS as the audit standards for agencies, municipalities, and government districts (e.g., school districts).

In many areas, GAGAS are similar to the AICPA *Statements on Auditing Standards.* However, GAGAS go beyond the AICPA standards in several respects. Government auditing standards impose additional rules and regulations about handling government funds and accounts.[8] A sample of this literature includes the following:

- Single Audit Act of 1984. This is the federal law that established uniform requirements for audits of federal financial assistance provided to state and local governments (discussed later in the module).
- *OMB Circular A-133,* "Audits of States, Local Governments, and Non-Profit Organizations." This Office of Management and Budget guidance helps auditors implement the Single Audit Act of 1984 for governmental units and a wide range of nonprofit organizations (e.g., colleges, universities, and voluntary health and welfare organizations, hospitals).
- *OMB Circular A-122,* "Cost Principles for Nonprofit Organizations."
- *OMB Circular A-110,* "Uniform Requirements for Grants to Universities, Hospitals, and Other Nonprofit Organizations."
- *OMB Circular A-102,* "Uniform Requirements for Grants to State and Local Governments."
- *OMB Circular A-87,* "Cost Principles for State and Local Governments."
- *OMB Circular A-21,* "Cost Principles for Educational Institutions."
- *AICPA Audit and Accounting Guide,* "Audits of State and Local Governments."

Because most governmental programs are created by grants and operate under laws and regulations, GAGAS explicitly require review and testing for compliance with applicable laws and regulations. Governmental auditors must be especially diligent when noncompliance with laws and regulations could result in errors or frauds that could be material to the financial statements.

GAGAS have more elaborate specifications for audit documentation and reporting than GAAS require. The GAO standards require the following written reports in financial statement audits:

1. An audit report on financial statements.
2. A report on the auditee's compliance with applicable laws and regulations, including a report of irregularities, frauds, illegal acts, material noncompliance, and internal control deficiencies.
3. A report on the auditee's internal control and the control risk assessment.

GAGAS also contain an elaborate set of guidelines for reports on performance audits. These audits cover such a wide range of subjects (from food programs to military contracts) that no "standard" report is possible. The details of these standards can be found on the GAO website (www.gao.gov). These GAO standards are good guides for internal

---

[8]Extensive government audit literature can be found at three important websites: (1) the OMB website (www.whitehouse.gov/omb), (2) the AICPA website (www.aicpa.org/InterestAreas/GovernmentalAuditQuality/Pages/GaQC.aspx), and (3) the GAO website (www.gao.gov).

EXHIBIT D.2
Significant Revisions to Government Auditing Standards

Area	Emphasis or Nature of Revision
Ethics	Heightened emphasis on ethics principles
Nonaudit services	Additional guidance on the acceptance of professional services other than audit services and the impact on audit work
Recent developments in auditing and internal control	Revised standards that increase transparency concerning restatements, uncertainties, and unusual events
Performance auditing	Additional guidance on the overall framework for high-quality performance auditing including reasonable assurance and its relationship to risk and level of evidence used to support findings and conclusions
Audit language	Standardized audit language throughout the standards
Auditor responsibilities	Reinforcement of the auditors' role in accountability and improvements for government operations

audit reports and for operational audit reports (consulting services engagements) prepared by CPAs in public practice.

In January 2007 and 2011, the GAO updated the government auditing standards. A review of these changes indicates six specific issues designed to increase the transparency and accountability of audits. A review of these changes (see Exhibit D.2) indicates that the GAO (1) believes these issues to be significant in increasing audit consistency and quality and (2) is moving in a manner consistent with the Public Company Accounting Oversight Board (PCAOB).

✅ REVIEW CHECKPOINTS

D.8 How does the scope of practice differ for governmental audits?

D.9 Why do GAGAS require a review for compliance with laws and regulations in conjunction with financial audits?

Single Audit Act of 1984 and Amendments of 1996

LO D-4
Describe the Single Audit Act of 1984 in relation to audits of governmental fund recipients.

The federal government requires audits of state and local governments that receive federal financial assistance through appropriations, grants, contracts, cooperative agreements, loans, loan guarantees, property, interest subsidies, and insurance. Prior to 1985, audit teams from several federal agencies often visited state and local governments. The Single Audit Act of 1984 (the Act) replaced the system of expensive and duplicative grant-by-grant audits with an organizationwide **single audit** encompassing all federal funds that a government unit receives. When a state or local government, university, or community organization receives federal financial assistance from several federal agencies, all of these agencies are supposed to rely on the single audit report instead of requiring other auditors to enter the same unit to audit various grants.

The Act established an annual audit requirement for all governments, agencies, and nonprofit organizations that expend $750,000 or more of federal funds. A single audit, conducted in accordance with GAGAS, covering financial statements, compliance with laws and regulations, and internal control is required. The Act does not require expanded scope audits of economy, efficiency, or program results. However, federal agencies may require, and pay for, additional audits of economy, efficiency, and program results to monitor the benefits of federal fund expenditures.

The auditors can be from public accounting firms or from state and local agencies provided they meet the GAO independence and proficiency requirements. In a single audit, the auditors are expected to determine and report whether:

1. The financial statements present fairly the financial position and results of operations in accordance with GAAP.

2. The organization has internal controls to provide reasonable assurance that it is managing federal financial assistance programs in compliance with applicable laws and regulations.

3. The organization has complied with laws and regulations that may have a material effect on its financial statements and on each major federal assistance program.

OMB *Circular A-133* imposes additional audit and reporting requirements. These reports provide the following information about the accountability of agencies that receive federal funds:

- A supplementary schedule of federal financial assistance programs showing expenditures for each program.
- A report of the compliance audit procedures showing the extent of testing and the amount and explanation of questioned expenditures.
- A report on internal control, identifying significant controls designed to provide reasonable assurance that federal programs are being managed in compliance with laws and regulations and identifying material weaknesses.
- A report of fraud, abuse, or illegal acts that become known to the auditors.

Government audits under the Yellow Book and the Single Audit Act Amendments of 1996 (including OMB *Circular A-133*) are difficult and time consuming. The GAO requires auditors to have 24 hours of continuing education in governmental auditing to qualify for planning an audit, conducting fieldwork, and preparing reports. The GAO also imposes requirements for continuing education and participation in a peer review program.[9]

Governmental audits require more work on compliance and reporting on internal control than external auditors normally perform in an audit of financial statements of a private business. The reason is the federal government's concern for laws, regulations, and control of expenditures. More than $450 billion of federal funds are used by state and local governments for various programs, so the stakes are high. See Exhibit D.3 for the Single Audit Report for the Louisville Metro Council for the fiscal year ended June 30, 2012.

GAO Audit Reports

GAGAS have three sets of reporting standards: one for financial audits, one for attestation engagements, and another for performance audits.

Financial audit reports start with an audit report similar to the external auditors' standard report except that the description of the audit in the scope paragraph must include a reference to GAGAS. The report on financial statements contains an opinion regarding conformity with GAAP, just as the reports that independent auditors in public practice give on nongovernmental organizations. In addition, GAGAS require reports on internal control, fraud, illegal acts, violations of provisions of contracts, grant agreements, abuse of government assets, and tests of compliance with laws and regulations as part of the financial reporting requirements.

Governmental auditors, like their public accounting firm counterparts, may be asked to perform attestation engagements. Attestation engagements provide an opinion or conclusion concerning a specific subject or an assertion about a subject. It is important when reporting on attestation engagements to clearly specify the subject matter or assertion, the conclusions, and any significant reservations concerning the subject matter or assertion addressed in the report.

---

[9]Most CPAs in public practice have similar continuing education and peer review requirements in connection with their state licenses and voluntary membership in the AICPA but not specific to governmental auditing. However, the GAO makes the requirements even for CPAs who do not have similar demands from their state boards or who choose not to belong to the AICPA. In this manner, the GAO exercises its own control over government audit quality.

EXHIBIT D.3 Single Audit Report for the Louisville Metro Council Fiscal Year Ended June 30, 2013

INDEPENDENT AUDITOR'S REPORT ON INTERNAL
CONTROL OVER FINANCIAL REPORTING AND ON
COMPLIANCE AND OTHER MATTERS BASED ON AN
AUDIT OF FINANCIAL STATEMENTS PERFORMED IN
ACCORDANCE WITH GOVERNMENT AUDITING STANDARDS

Honorable Mayor Greg Fischer and
The Louisville Metro Council
Louisville, Kentucky

We have audited the financial statements of the governmental activities, the aggregate discretely presented component units, each major fund, and the aggregate remaining fund information of Louisville/Jefferson Country Metro Government ("Metro Government") as of and for the year ended June 30, 2012, which collectively comprise Metro Government's basic financial statements and have issued our report thereon dated December 14, 2012, which cited reliance on the reports of other auditors. We conducted our audit in accordance with auditing standards generally accepted in the United States of America and the standards applicable to financial audits contained in Government Auditing Standards, issued by the Comptroller General of the United States.

Internal Control over Financial Reporting

Management of Metro Government is responsible for establishing and maintaining effective internal control over financial reporting. In planning and performing our audit, we considered Metro Government's internal control over financial reporting as a basis for designing our auditing procedures for the purpose of expressing our opinion on the financial statements, but not for the purpose of expressing an opinion on the effectiveness of Metro Government's internal control over financial reporting. Accordingly, we do not express an opinion on the effectiveness of Metro Government's internal control over financial reporting.

A deficiency in internal control exists when the design or operation of a control does not allow management or employees, in the normal course of performing their assigned functions, to prevent, or detect and correct, misstatements on a timely basis. A material weakness is a deficiency, or a combination of deficiencies, in internal control such that there is a reasonable possibility that a material misstatement of the entity's financial statements will not be prevented, or detected and corrected on a timely basis.

Our consideration of the internal control over financial reporting was for the limited purpose described in the first paragraph and was not designed to identify all deficiencies in internal control that might be deficiencies, significant deficiencies, or material weaknesses. We did not identify any deficiencies in internal control over financial reporting that we consider to be material weaknesses, as defined above.

Compliance and Other Matters

As part of obtaining reasonable assurance about whether Metro Government's financial statements are free of material misstatement, we performed tests of its compliance with certain provisions of laws, regulations, contracts, and grant agreements; noncompliance with which could have a direct and material effect on the determination of financial statement amounts. However, providing an opinion on compliance with those provisions was not an objective of our audit and accordingly, we do not express such an opinion. The results of our tests disclosed no instances of noncompliance or other matters that are required to be reported under Government Auditing Standards.

Purpose of this Report

The purpose of this report is solely to describe the scope of our testing of internal control over financial reporting and compliance and the results of that testing, and not to provide an opinion on the effectiveness of the entity's internal control or on compliance. This report is an integral part of an audit performed in accordance with Government Auditing Standards in considering the entity's internal control and compliance. Accordingly, this communication is not suitable for any other purpose.

Crowe Horwath LLP
Crowe Horwath LLP

Louisville, Kentucky
December 14, 2012

Both attestation engagement reports and performance audit reports are completely different from financial audit reports. Like that for internal audit reports, the GAO objective is clear communication for the purpose of making recommendations and improving operations. Hence, the Yellow Book's performance audit reporting standards require timely, well-written communications of findings and recommendations for action. The managers of an audited entity are expected to respond to the report, and this response is usually included in the final version of the report. Unlike internal audit reports, most GAO reports are available to the public and can be requested from the Government Printing Office.

However, performance audits have another side. GAGAS require the reports to relate illegal acts, abuse of public money and property, noncompliance with laws and regulations, and internal control weaknesses. These matters reflect negatively on an organization's management.

AUDITING INSIGHT   Which Side Is Supplying?

A report from the GAO states that U.S. military officials do not know what happened to 30 percent of the weapons the United States distributed to Iraqi forces from 2004 through early 2007 as part of the effort to train and equip Iraqi forces. The latest estimate is that more than 14,000 weapons are unaccounted for!

Source: "Weapons Given to Iraq are Missing," *The Washington Post*, August 6, 2007.

✓ REVIEW CHECKPOINTS

D.10 What audit fieldwork requirements do GAGAS and the Single Audit Act of 1984 impose that AICPA generally accepted auditing standards do not?

D.11 What are the major differences between independent auditors' reports on financial statements and internal and governmental reports on efficiency, economy, and program results audits?

D.12 Why do you think GAGAS reporting standards permit performance audit reports to include the views of responsible officials concerning the auditors' findings, conclusions, and recommendations?

FRAUD EXAMINATIONS

LO D-5
Define *fraud examination* and describe various engagements performed by fraud examiners.

The responsibilities of external auditors, internal auditors, and governmental auditors often require the identification of suspected fraud. AU-C 240 requires auditors to use information obtained during the planning and performance of the audit to identify risks that may result in a material misstatement due to fraud. In addition, auditors need to be aware of the various types of frauds, their signs (red flags), and the need to follow up to determine whether a suspicion is justified. If justified, auditors need to alert management and call in the experts.

> A focused effort by internal auditors on the prevention, deterrence, and detection of financial statement misstatements arising from asset misappropriation is consistent with their broad mission of maximizing owners' wealth (which requires safeguarding the entity's assets). In carrying out their mission, internal auditors should be aware of the risks and warning signs of fraud.[10]

As illustrated in Exhibit D.4, most frauds are found through anonymous tips (42.2 percent) or management review (16.0 percent). Internal auditors uncover about 14.1 percent of

---

[10]W. Hillison, D. Sinason, and C. Pacini, "The Role of the Internal Auditor in Implementing *SAS 82*," *Corporate Controller*, July/August 1998, p. 21. Although SAS 82 has been superseded by SAS 99, the content of the quote is still valid.

discovered fraud, and external auditors get credit for finding about 3.0 percent of the frauds (see Exhibit D.4).[11] Once a fraud is suspected, a fraud examiner may be called to investigate further. Although it is technically correct to call these engagements *fraud investigations* or *examinations,* many firms and companies use the term *fraud audit.*

For governmental auditors, the basic requirements are to know the applicable laws and regulations, to design the audit to detect abuse and illegal acts, and to report their findings to the proper level of authority. All governmental auditors are required to prepare a written report on their tests of compliance with applicable laws and regulations, including all material instances of noncompliance and all instances or indications of illegal acts that could result in criminal prosecution. Reports are directed to the top official of an organization and, in some cases, to an appropriate oversight body, including other government agencies and audit committees. Persons receiving the audit reports are responsible for reporting to law enforcement agencies.

Compliance auditing in governmental audits is a matter of considerable concern to the AICPA. AU-C 200, 210, 220, 230, 250, 260, and 265 all have sections that outline auditor responsibilities regarding errors, frauds, and illegal acts. GAO standards, and certain government bulletins delineate special requirements of government entities and other recipients of government financial assistance.

EXHIBIT D.4
Finding Fraud

Source: Association of Certified Fraud Examiners, "Report to the Nation," 2012.

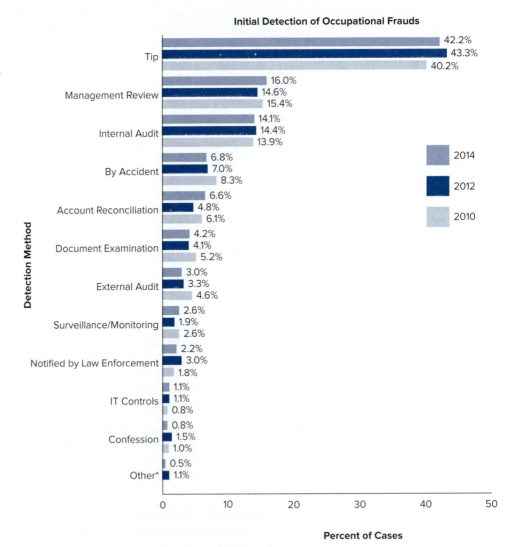

*"Other" category was not included in the 2010 Report.

[11]Association of Certified Fraud Examiners, *2014 Report to the Nation: Occupational Fraud and Abuse.*

The Art of Fraud Examinations

LO D-6
Describe the elements necessary for a successful fraud examination and explain the differences in the way fraud examiners and external auditors handle evidence.

Auditors are required to provide reasonable assurance that financial statements are free of material misstatements due to fraud. During an audit, auditors may uncover facts or circumstances indicating that fraud may exist. At this point, a fraud examination may commence and may require the assistance of a certified fraud examiner (CFE).[12]

Fraud examinations combine the expertise of auditors and criminal investigators. Fraud examiners are fond of saying that their successes are the result of accident, hunches, or luck. Nothing can be further from reality. Successes come from experience, logic, and the ability to see things that are not obvious. (As for Sherlock Holmes, famous detective of literature, sometimes it is "the dog that did not bark" that is the clue.) Fraud examinations, broadly speaking, involve familiarity with many elements: the human factor, organizational behavior, common fraud schemes, evidence and its sources, standards of proof, and red flags.

[12]The CFE designation is offered by the Association of Certified Fraud Examiners. Information concerning the designation and requirements can be found on its website (www.acfe.com).

Benford's Law

Frank Benford made a simple observation while working as a physicist at the GE Research Laboratories in Schenectady, New York, in the 1920s. He noticed that the first few pages of his logarithm tables books were more worn than the last few and from this he surmised that he was consulting the first pages—which gave the logs of numbers with low digits—more often. The first digit of a number is leftmost—for example, the first digit of 45,002 is 4. (Zero cannot be a first digit.)

Benford extrapolated that he was looking up the logs of numbers with low first digits more frequently because there were more numbers with low first digits in the world. Benford then tested this idea by looking at the first digits of 20 lists of numbers with a total of 20,229 observations. His lists came from varied sources, such as geographic, scientific, and demographic data. One list contained all the numbers in an issue of the *Reader's Digest*. He found that about 31 percent of the numbers had 1 as the first digit, 19 percent had 2, and only 5 percent had 9 as a first digit.

Benford then made some physics-related assumptions about the distribution of naturally occurring data and, using integral calculus, computed the expected frequencies of the digits and digit combinations. Not all data sets follow Benford's law. Those data sets that most likely follow Benford's law have the following characteristics: (1) The numbers describe the sizes of similar phenomena (e.g., market values of corporations); (2) the numbers do not contain a built-in maximum or minimum value (such as deductible IRA contributions or hourly wage rates); and (3) assigned numbers, such as Social Security numbers, zip codes, or bank account numbers, will not conform to Benford's law.

Benford's law has been applied to many sets of financial data, including income tax or stock exchange data, corporate disbursements and sales figures, demographics, and scientific data. Since the 1940s, more than 150 academic papers on Benford's law have been published by mathematicians, statisticians, engineers, physicists, and—recently—accountants.

EXAMPLE 1: Fraudulent checks. In 1993, in *State of Arizona v. Wayne James Nelson* (CV92-18841), the accused was found guilty of trying to defraud the state of nearly $2 million. Nelson, a manager in the office of the Arizona State Treasurer, argued that he had diverted funds to a bogus

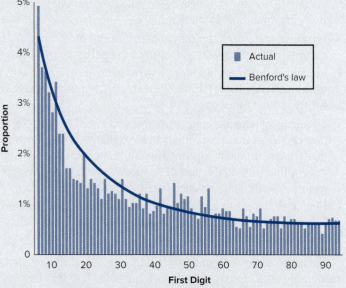

First two digits of an accounts payable file of a NASDAQ-listed software company

vendor to demonstrate the absence of safeguards in a new computer system.

Because human choices are not random, invented numbers are unlikely to follow Benford's law. Most of the amounts were just below $100,000. It's possible that higher dollar amounts received additional scrutiny or that checks above that amount required human signatures instead of automated check writing. By keeping the amounts just below an additional control threshold, the manager tried to conceal the fraud. The result was that the digit patterns of the check amounts were almost opposite to those of Benford's law. More than 90 percent had 7, 8, or 9 as a first digit. The numbers appear to have been chosen to give the appearance of randomness.

Benford's law is quite counterintuitive; people do not naturally assume that some digits occur more frequently. None of the check amounts was duplicated, there were no round numbers, and all the amounts included cents. However, subconsciously, the manager repeated some digits and digit combinations. Among the first two digits of the invented amounts, 87, 88, 93, and 96 were all used twice. For the last two digits, 16, 67, and 83 were duplicated. There was a tendency toward the higher digits (7 through 9 were the most frequently used digits), in contrast to Benford's law. A CPA familiar with Benford's law could have easily spotted the fact that these numbers—invented to seem random by someone ignorant of Benford's law—fall outside expected patterns and thus merit closer examination.

Example 2: On-the-job applications. Corporate accounts payable data are a favorite target of digital analysis technology. The first- and second-digit tests are used as high-level examinations of reasonableness (data authenticity). The graph of the first two digits of an accounts payable file of a NASDAQ-listed software company is shown in the exhibit on page 743.

The line plots Benford's law and the bars show the actual proportions. When the bars extend above the Benford's law line, the actual proportion exceeds the Benford's law predicted proportion, creating an abnormal level of duplication for that first-two digit combination. An analysis of the actual dollar amounts showed that the numbers $25, $30, and $10 occurred most frequently. The follow-up audit showed that invoices with these amounts were mainly for courier charges. Repeated low dollar amounts highlight inefficiencies if they are being processed for the same type of purchase. At one company, the follow-up audit showed that accounts payable was processing about 12,000 invoices annually for employee business card purchases from the same vendor. Monthly billing could make steep reductions in processing costs.

Other problems that have been found include:

- *Biases in corporate data.* In one company's accounts payable data, there was a large first-two-digit spike (excess of actual over expected) at 24. An analysis showed that the amount $24.50 occurred abnormally often. The audit revealed that these were claims for travel expenses and that the company had a $25 voucher requirement. Employees were apparently biased toward claiming $24.50.

- *Ducking authorization levels.* Sometimes managers concentrate their purchases just below their authorization levels so their choices won't be scrutinized. Managers with $3,000 purchasing levels might have a lot of invoices for $2,800 to $2,999, which would show up in data analysis by spikes at 28 and 29. During one bank audit, the auditors analyzed the first two digits of credit card balances written off as uncollectible. The graph showed a large spike at 49. An analysis of the related dollar amounts (i.e., from $480 to $499 and from $4,800 to $4,999) showed that the spike was caused mainly by amounts between $4,800 and $4,999, and that one officer was responsible for the bulk of these write-offs. The write-off limit for internal personnel was $5,000. It turned out that the officer was operating with a circle of friends who would apply for credit cards. After they ran up balances of just under $5,000, he would write the debts off.

Source: Mark J. Nigrini, "I've Got Your Number," *Journal of Accountancy* 187, no. 5 (May 1999), pp. 79–83.

Independent auditors of financial statements and fraud examiners approach their work differently. Some of the most important differences are as follows:

- Financial statement auditors follow a program/procedural approach designed to accomplish a fairly standard job; fraud examiners work in unique and unusual situations in which little is standard.

- Financial statement auditors note errors and omissions; fraud examiners also focus on exceptions, but they must be aware of peculiarities and patterns of conduct as well.

- Financial statement auditors assess control risk to design audit procedures; fraud examiners habitually "think like a crook" to imagine ways controls could be subverted for fraudulent purposes.

- Financial statement auditors use the concept of materiality (dollar size large enough to matter). Most fraud examiners believe that "immaterial fraud" is an oxymoron. Fraud is often larger than it appears, fraud left unchecked tends to grow, and fraud indicates a lack of integrity on the part of the person or persons involved. For these reasons, fraud examiners often pursue even small frauds.

- Financial statement audits are based on theories of financial accounting and auditing logic; fraud examination is grounded in a theory of behavioral motive, opportunity, and rationalization.

Financial statement auditors often use inductive reasoning—that is, they sample accounting data, derive audit findings, and project ("induct") the finding to a conclusion about the population of data sampled. Fraud examiners often enjoy the expensive luxury of using deductive reasoning—that is, after being tipped off that a certain type of loss occurred or probably occurred, they can identify the suspects, make clinical observations (e.g., stakeouts), conduct interviews and interrogations, eliminate dead-end results, and establish a legal case against the alleged fraudster. They can conduct covert activities that usually are not used in the financial audit. The "expensive luxury" of the deductive approach involves surveying a wide array of information and information sources, eliminating the extraneous, and retaining the selection that proves the fraud.

Successfully identifying and catching fraud perpetrators often depends on the auditors' awareness. The identification of evidence that may indicate a fraud, the handling of that evidence, and the timely involvement of the fraud examiner may mean the difference between stopping a fraud and recovering stolen assets or continuing the expansion of fraud in the client's business.

AUDITING INSIGHT   What Car Are You Driving?

A government fraud examiner uncovered a fraud while driving into the parking lot of the city hall of a small town. The auditor always parked in the employee lot (saving the customer parking for residents conducting business with city hall). In the parking lot, along with the Fords and Chevrolets, was a candy-apple red Porsche. After parking his car, the auditor went over to the Porsche and began to look the car over. When someone from city hall came out, the auditor began a conversation.

- **Auditor:** This is certainly a beautiful car!
- **City hall employee:** Yes, it is.
- **Auditor:** Do you know how much horsepower it has?

- **City hall employee:** Not a clue. The car belongs to Bob. I'm certain he'd tell you.
- **Auditor:** Great. I would love to find out more about this car. Where would I find Bob?
- **City hall employee:** Oh. Bob's a city inspector. You'll find him in the inspector's office.
- **Auditor:** Thanks!

Further investigation revealed that Bob had been taking kickbacks.

Source: Story told by a government fraud examiner at an Association of Certified Fraud Examiners seminar.

 ## REVIEW CHECKPOINTS

D.13 Compare and contrast the type of work performed by external auditors (auditing financial statements to render an opinion) and fraud examiners.

Fraud Examiner Responsibilities

When a fraud examiner is called, fraud is strongly suspected or already recognized. The Association of Certified Fraud Examiners (ACFE) indicates that assignments are initiated only with **predication**, which means a reason to believe fraud may have occurred.[13]

Fraud examiners' attitudes and responsibilities differ from those of other auditors in two additional respects: internal control and materiality. Fraud examiners' interest in internal control policies and procedures involves less evaluation of strengths and more evaluation of weaknesses. Fraud examiners "think like crooks" to imagine fraud schemes that get around an organization's internal controls.

Fraud examiners have four main objectives in performing an investigation. First, fraud examiners must determine whether a fraud does exist. Second, once fraud examiners determine that a fraud does exist, the examiner must determine the scope of the fraud. For organizations that received an external audit, the median fraud, when discovered, had been in operation for more than 18 months.[14] Therefore, fraud examiners must attempt

---

[13]The Professional Standards and Practices for Certified Fraud Examiners can be found on the association's website at www.acfe.com.
[14]Association of Certified Fraud Examiners, *2012 Report to the Nation: Occupational Fraud and Abuse.*

to determine when the fraud started and what assets have been misappropriated. Third, fraud examiners must identify the perpetrators. The examiners must take great care not to falsely accuse employees and not to solicit help from management personnel who might be involved in the fraud. Finally, examiners must determine how the fraud occurred and whether changes in controls or policy can eliminate this type of fraud in the future.

Fraud examiners' attitude about *materiality* differs from that of auditors. Auditors have a large-dollar amount as a criterion for an error that is big enough to matter, but fraud examiners have a much lower threshold, and many operate under the theory that there is no such thing as an immaterial fraud. In fact, fraud is sometimes compared to an iceberg in the sense that most of it is hidden and only a small part may be visible. A fraud loss of $20,000 this year may not be material to an external auditor, but $20,000 each year for a 15-year fraud career amounts to $300,000 in the fraud examiner's eyes—and it is big enough to matter!

✅ REVIEW CHECKPOINTS

D.14 Internal auditors have one of the highest incidents of fraud detection (higher then external auditors). Why might this be true? To what extent would you think internal auditors include fraud detection responsibility in their normal audit assignments?

D.15 In fraud examiners' terminology, what is *predication?*

D.16 Why might fraud examiners' attitudes about control systems and materiality differ from that of other auditors?

A Fraud Examination Example

Alice, a fraud examiner, has been called into Bulldog Corporation because an accounts payable fraud is suspected. Several vendor invoices were paid to Longhorn Enterprises, a vendor not on the approved vendor list. Although this may indicate a fictitious vendor set up by someone in the company as a fraud, it also may be an indication of someone not following procedure. It is possible that the purchases from this vendor were valid, but the vendor was not put on the approved vendor list. The fraud examiner must determine whether this is a fraud or just a case of not following procedure. The fraud examiner may take several steps to identify whether Longhorn Enterprises exists.

DOES FRAUD EXIST?

Alice has called the secretary of state's office, checked the telephone directory, and searched the Internet but has not found any indication of a company called Longhorn Enterprises. In addition, the invoices from Longhorn Enterprises have no telephone number and only a post office box as an address. Finally, there are no creases on the invoices in the file, indicating they were probably not mailed to the company.

HOW LARGE IS THE FRAUD?

Convinced that Longhorn Enterprises does not exist, Alice sets out to determine the extent of the fraud and searches the cash disbursements journal and accounts payable records looking for checks paid to Longhorn Enterprises. After finding 32 invoices paid over the last two years, Alice has Bulldog obtain copies of the canceled checks, front and back. Alice makes copies of all of the invoices and places the originals in a plastic bag. (They are evidence and may have fingerprints or other forensic information.) All the originals are locked up for safekeeping. The total of the checks is $67,245.

WHO COMMITTED THE FRAUD?

Alice notices that the checks are endorsed by hand (most companies endorse checks with a stamp) and that the checks are deposited in Smalltime Regional Bank. Because Bulldog pays its employees through direct deposit, Alice can compare the banks used by employees with the bank used to deposit Longhorn Enterprises' checks. Alice compares that list with the list of employees who are involved in the purchasing and payables process and finds three purchasing and payable employees who use the Smalltime Regional Bank. Alice takes this information to an attorney, who assists in getting a subpoena for the bank records and postal information concerning the post office box. Alice finds that both the post office box and bank account are registered to Dallas Fry, an accounts payable clerk who uses Smalltime Regional Bank for payroll deposits. The bank records also show transfers of money from the bank account, listed as LE Inc., to Fry's personal bank account.

Next, Alice talks with other employees in the accounts payable area and discovers that Fry has purchased a new car and took an expensive vacation last year. Alice is now ready to confront Fry with the evidence and obtain a confession.

HOW COULD THIS FRAUD HAPPEN?

Finally, from Fry's confession, Alice determines that the assistant treasurer routinely approves small payments without scrutinizing the supporting documentation. Fry inserted fictitious invoices in stacks of other invoices for the assistant treasurer to sign. Alice's final report included the fact that the assistant treasurer's failure to follow procedure allowed the fraud to occur.

LO D-7
Describe the ways CPAs can assist in prosecuting fraud perpetrators.

Building a Fraud Case

Building a case against a fraudster is a task for trained investigators who know how to conduct interviews and interrogations, perform surveillance, use informants, and obtain usable confessions. In almost all cases, the postdiscovery activity proceeds with a special prosecutorial attitude and with management cooperation or leadership. The district attorney and police officials also may be involved. Prosecution of fraudsters is advisable because, if left unpunished, they often go on to steal again. In addition, failure to prosecute sends a negative message to other potential fraudsters in the organization.

Protecting the Evidence

While engaged in audit work, auditors should know how to preserve the *chain of custody* of evidence. The chain of custody is the crucial link of the evidence to the suspect, called the *relevance* of evidence by attorneys and judges. If documents are lost, mutilated, coffee soaked, or compromised (so a defense attorney can argue that they were altered to frame the suspect), they can lose their effectiveness for the prosecution. Auditors should learn to mark evidence, writing an identification of the location, condition, date, time, and circumstances as soon as it appears to be a signal of fraud. This marking may be on a separate tag or page, or the original may be marked in a manner that preserves the integrity of the document. The original document should be put in a protective envelope (plastic) for preservation, and investigative work should proceed with copies of the documents instead of originals. A record should be made of the safekeeping and of all persons who used the original. Any eyewitness observations should be promptly recorded in a memorandum or on tape (audio or video) with corroboration of colleagues if possible. Other features of the chain of custody relate to interviews, interrogations, confessions, documents obtained by subpoena, and other matters, but auditors usually do not conduct these activities.

Obtaining Litigation Support

Independent CPAs often accept engagements for litigation support and expert witnessing. This work is often referred to as **forensic accounting**, which means applying accounting and auditing evidence to legal problems, both civil and criminal. Litigation support can take several forms, but it usually amounts to consulting in the capacity of helping attorneys document cases and determine damages. Expert witness work involves testifying to findings determined during litigation support and testifying about accounting principles and auditing standards applications. The AICPA, ACFE, and IIA conduct continuing education courses for auditors who want to become experts in these fields.

✓ REVIEW CHECKPOINTS

D.17 Why is prosecution of fraud perpetrators generally a good idea?

D.18 Why do fraud examiners handle information in a different manner than auditors? Why is this important?

Summary

Governmental and internal auditing standards include the essence of the AICPA's generally accepted auditing standards (GAAS) but also include standards for audits of economy, efficiency, and program results. In addition, the internal auditing standards contain guidance for the management of an internal audit department within a company. The auditor's responsibilities, professional organizations, and standards are summarized in Exhibit D.5.

EXHIBIT D.5 Summary of Auditor Information

Auditor	Primary Functions	Professional Organization	Certification	Standards
Internal auditor	Evaluate departments and functions (1) to determine operational efficiency and effectiveness and compliance with laws, regulations, policies, and procedures and (2) to provide consulting services to management.	Institute of Internal Auditors www.theiia.org	Certified Internal Auditor (CIA) Various specialty certifications such as certified financial services auditor (CFSA)	International Standards for the Professional Practice of Internal Auditing
Governmental auditor	Evaluate government entities to (1) determine compliance with laws, regulations, and policies as well as efficiency and effectiveness in the performance of programs and (2) investigate government operations as mandated or directed by government oversight bodies.	Association of Government Accountants www.agacgfm.org	The certified government financial manager (CGFM) and certified government auditing professional (CGAP) (offered through the IIA)	Government auditing standards (The Yellow Book)
Fraud auditor	Provide investigative services to auditors and management when the predication of fraud exists.	Association of Certified Fraud Examiners www.acfe.com	Certified fraud examiner (CFE)	CFE Code of Professional Standards

All auditors hold independence as a primary goal, but internal auditors must establish an internal organizational independence from the managers and executives whose areas they audit. Governmental auditors must be concerned about factual independence with regard to social, political, and level-of-government influences.

Governmental auditing is complicated by the special context of audit assignments intended to accomplish accountability by agencies that handle federal funds—grants, subsidies, entitlement programs, and the like. The requirements of the GAO standards and the Single Audit Act of 1984 impose on the audit function the responsibility for compliance audit work designed to determine agencies' observance of laws and regulations, of which there are many. Auditors must report not only on financial statements but also on internal control, violations of laws and regulations, fraud, abuse, and illegal acts. These elements are all part of the federal oversight of federal spending facilitated by auditors.

Governmental and internal audit reports are not standardized as are the GAAS reports on audited financial statements. Auditors must be very careful that their reports communicate their conclusions and recommendations in a clear and concise manner. The variety of assignments and the challenge of reporting in such a free-form setting contribute to making governmental auditing, internal auditing, and consulting services exciting fields for career opportunities.

Auditors must have knowledge of the types of errors, frauds, and illegal acts that can be perpetrated in any audit. External, internal, and governmental auditors all have standards for care, planning, detection, and reporting of errors, frauds, and illegal acts. Fraud examiners, on the other hand, have little in the way of standard programs or materiality guidelines because of the unlimited nature of frauds. However, auditors must exercise technical and personal care because accusations of fraud are always taken very seriously. For this reason, after preliminary findings indicate fraud possibilities, auditors should enlist the support of management and assist fraud examination professionals in bringing an investigation to a conclusion.

Key Terms

Audit charter: The internal audit charter is a formal document that defines the internal audit activity's purpose, authority, and responsibility. The internal audit charter establishes the internal audit activity's position within the organization, including the nature of the chief audit executive's functional reporting relationship with the board; authorizes access to records, personnel, and physical properties relevant to the performance of engagements; and defines the scope of internal audit activities.

compliance audit: An examination designed to ensure that an organization is following applicable laws, regulations, and management directives; usually performed by internal auditors but may be performed by governmental or external auditors as well.

environmental audit: An examination designed to ensure that an organization is following environmental standards established by laws, regulations, and management directives; may recommend methods of reducing environmental problems by reducing or reusing waste or by-products of an organization's processes.

exit conference: A meeting that occurs at the end of an internal audit between the auditors and management of the organization being audited in many external audits and is a required part of an internal audit.

follow-up: A process required of internal auditors to ensure that significant audit findings have been addressed by the auditee in accordance with the agreement between the auditor and management.

forensic accounting: The application of accounting and auditing evidence to resolve legal issues in civil and criminal law.

governance audit: An examination designed to provide management the information required to make governance decisions or to ensure that high-quality information is provided for these decisions.

internal auditing: An examination service provided to a company to assist the company to meet its corporate goals and objectives by evaluating and recommending risk management, control, and governance processes.

operational auditing: An examination designed to evaluate the processes and procedures of an organization or an area within an organization to ensure the process or area is operating efficiently and effectively.

performance audit: An examination designed to ensure that the resources of an organization are being used appropriately and that its objectives are being met.

predication: A suspicion that a fraud may have occurred.

quality control audit: An examination designed to ensure that an organization is meeting its quality control standards; usually involves determining that personnel responsible for performing quality control are meeting the goals and objectives established and that quality information is being reported to appropriate members of management.

single audit: A governmental examination standard that allows an entity to receive one audit of its financial statements, compliance with laws and regulations, and internal control that will be utilized by multiple agencies granting money to the entity.

Yellow Book: The common name used to refer to the generally accepted government auditing standards (GAGAS).

Multiple-Choice Questions for Practice and Review

LO D-1

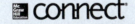 All applicable Exercises and Problems are available with *Connect.*

D.19 Which of the following would be considered in determining whether an internal audit department is independent?

a. The organizational level of the chief audit officer and the objectivity of the audit staff.

b. A requirement for the auditors to report to the audit committee and for the composition of that committee.

c. The organizational status of the audit committee and the individual independence of internal auditors in the department.

d. The nature of the audit charter and the objectivity of the audit staff.

LO D-1

D.20 Which of the following would be considered the most significant problem for internal audit if the chief audit executive reports to the controller?

a. The controller would amend the audit schedule so more audit time was spent on accounting issues.

b. The controller may have no training as an internal auditor.

c. During times when the budget needs to be cut, internal audit would likely be the first to lose funding.

d. The controller can control the scope of audits and censor audit reports before being sent to management and the audit committee.

LO D-1

D.21 Which of the following is *not* an internal audit objective designed to add value to a purchasing department?

a. A review of the bidding process indicates that a vendor company may be operating under two different names; therefore, purchasing is not getting the three independent bids required by policy.

b. The purchasing process is causing unnecessary delays in ordering product.

c. The purchasing department is not following a new human resource policy requiring a six-month performance review for new employees.

d. The director of purchasing is new to the organization and has made several decisions regarding vendor approvals with which the auditor does not agree.

LO D-1

D.22 In an internal auditor's report, audit findings would include all of the following *except*

a. The effect of audit finding on the auditee or the company.

b. The cause of the audit finding.

c. The relevance of the audit finding on the audit.

d. The recommendation to correct the audit finding.

LO D-1

D.23 Governmental auditors' independence and objectivity are enhanced when they report the results of an audit assignment directly to

a. Managers of the government agency under audit and in which the auditors are employed.

b. The audit committee of directors of the agency under audit.

c. Political action committees of which they are members.

d. The congressional committee that ordered the audit.

LO D-2

D.24 In all audits of governmental units performed according to GAGAS, the most important work is

a. Compliance auditing.

b. Obtaining a sufficient understanding of internal control.

c. Documentation of the audit.

d. Exit interviews with managers in the governmental unit.

LO D-1

D.25 Which of the following is considered different and more limited in objectives than the others?

a. Operational auditing.

b. Performance auditing.

c. Management auditing.

d. Financial statement auditing.

LO D-3

D.26 A typical objective of an operational audit is for the auditor to

a. Determine whether the financial statements fairly present the company's operations.

b. Evaluate the feasibility of attaining the company's operational objectives.

c. Make recommendations for achieving company objectives.

d. Report on the company's relative success in attaining profit maximization.

LO D-2

D.27 A governmental auditor assigned to audit the financial statements of the state highway department would not be considered independent if the auditor

a. Also held a position as a project manager in the highway department.

b. Was the state audit official elected in a general statewide election with responsibility to report to the legislature.

c. Normally works as a state auditor employed in the department of human services.

d. Was appointed by the state governor with responsibility to report to the legislature.

LO D-2

D.28 Governmental auditing can extend beyond audits of financial statements to include audits of an agency's efficient and economical use of resources and

a. Constitutionality of laws and regulations governing the agency.

b. Evaluation of the personal managerial skills shown by the agency's leaders.

c. Correspondence of the agency's performance with public opinion regarding the social worth of its mission.

d. Evaluations concerning the agency's achievements of the goals set by the legislature for the agency's activities.

LO D-1

D.29 Which of the following best describes how the detailed audit plan of a financial statement auditor compares with the audit client's comprehensive internal audit plan?

a. The comprehensive internal audit plan covers areas that an external auditor would normally not review.

b. The comprehensive internal audit plan is more detailed, although it covers fewer areas than an external audit would normally cover.

c. The comprehensive internal audit plan is substantially identical to the audit plan used by an external auditor because both review substantially identical areas.

d. The comprehensive internal audit plan is less detailed and covers fewer areas than an external auditor would normally review.

LO D-1

D.30 Which of the following is usually *not* part of an internal audit department's audit charter?

a. A commitment from management to ensure the independence of the internal audit department.

b. A definition of the scope of the audit department's activities.

c. The organizational structure of the internal audit department.

d. The reporting requirements of the internal audit department.

LO D-2

D.31 Which of the following would you *not* expect to see in an auditor's report(s) on the financial statements of an independent government agency?

a. A statement that the audit was conducted in accordance with generally accepted government audit standards.

b. A report on the agency's compliance with applicable laws and regulations.

c. Commentary by the agency's managers on the audit findings and recommendations.

d. A report on the agency's internal controls.

LO D-4

D.32 The federal Single Audit Act of 1984 requires auditors to determine and report several things about state and local governments that receive federal funds. Which of the following is *not* normally required to be reported?

a. An opinion on the fair presentation of the financial statements in accordance with generally accepted accounting principles.

b. A report on the government's internal control related to federal funds.

c. The government's performance in meeting goals set in enabling legislation.

d. A report on the government's compliance with applicable laws and regulations.

LO D-2

D.33 The Government Accountability Office (GAO) describes expanded-scope governmental auditing to include all of the following *except*

a. Financial statement audits.

b. Attestation engagements.

c. Compliance audits.

d. Performance audits.

LO D-1–D-3

D.34 In government and internal performance auditing, which of the following is the *least* important consideration when performing the fieldwork?

a. Determining the applicable generally accepted government accounting principles pronounced by the GASB.

b. Defining problem areas or opportunities for improvement and defining program goals.

c. Selecting and performing procedures designed to obtain evidence about operational problems and production output.

d. Evaluating evidence in terms of economy, efficiency, and achievement of program goals.

LO D-2

D.35 Which of the following is the *least* important consideration for a governmental auditor who needs to be objective when auditing and reporting on an agency's achievement of program goals?

a. Measure the actual output results of agency activities.

b. Compare the agency's actual output results to quantitative goal standards.

c. Perform a comprehensive review of management controls.

d. Determine quantitative standards that describe goals the agency was supposed to achieve.

LO D-4

D.36 Compliance auditing performed under the Single Audit Act of 1984 in accordance with GAGAS is necessary for an auditor's

a. Report on the auditee's internal control, including reportable conditions and material weaknesses.

b. Opinion on the auditee's observance, or lack thereof, of applicable laws and regulations.

c. Opinion on the auditee's financial statements.

d. Report of a supplementary schedule of federal assistance programs and amounts.

LO D-6

D.37 Which *two* of the following characterize the work of fraud examiners?

a. Analysis of control weaknesses for determination of acceptable fraud risk.

b. Analysis of control strengths as a basis for planning other audit procedures.

c. Determination of a materiality amount that represents a significant misstatement of the financial statements.

d. Consideration of a materiality amount in cumulative terms—that is, becoming large over a number of years.

LO D-6

D.38 When auditing with "fraud awareness," auditors should especially notice and review employee activities under which of these conditions?

a. The company always estimates the inventory but never takes a complete physical count.

b. The petty cash box is always locked in the desk of the custodian.

c. Management has published a company code of ethics and sends frequent communication newsletters about it.

d. The board of directors reviews and approves all investment transactions.

LO D-6

D.39 The *best* way to enact a broad fraud prevention program is to

a. Install airtight control systems of checks and supervision.

b. Name an ethics officer who is responsible for receiving and acting upon fraud tips.

c. Place dedicated hotline telephones on walls around the workplace with direct communication to the company ethics officer.

d. Establish a corporate culture conducive to ethical behavior in the workplace.

LO D-6

D.40 A reason to believe that a fraud has occurred is called

a. Deliberation.

b. Forensics.

c. Predication.

d. Restitution.

LO D-7

D.41 In a fraud examination, original documents must be protected from damage and tampering to

a. Establish motive.

b. Develop documentation for employee dismissal.

c. Protect the chain of custody.

d. Ensure that suspects are unaware of an investigation in progress.

LO D-1

D.42 An environmental audit might include all of following *except*

a. Determining that proper tracking of waste material is being maintained by the organization.

b. Reviewing the liability account established for pending environmental claims against the company.

c. Reviewing the environmental history of another company that the internal auditor's organization is interested in purchasing.

d. All of the above are appropriate issues for an environmental audit.

Exercises and Problems

connect   All applicable Exercises and Problems are available with *Connect.*

LO D-1, D-2, D-5

D.43   **Identification of Audits and Auditors.** Audits may be characterized as (a) financial statement audits, (b) compliance audits, (c) economy and efficiency audits, and (d) program audits. The work can be done by independent (external) auditors, internal auditors, or governmental auditors (including IRS auditors and federal bank examiners). Following is a list of the purpose or products of various audit engagements. [Students may need to refer to Chapter 1.]

a. Analyze proprietary schools' spending to train students for oversupplied occupations.

b. Determine the fair presentation in conformity with GAAP of an advertising agency's financial statements.

c. Study the Department of Defense's expendable launch vehicle program.

d. Determine costs of municipal garbage pickup services compared to comparable service subcontracted to a private business.

e. Audit tax shelter partnership financing terms.

f. Study a private aircraft manufacturer's test pilot performance in reporting on the results of test flights.

g. Periodically have U.S. comptroller of currency examine a national bank for solvency.

h. Evaluate the promptness of materials inspection in a manufacturer's receiving department.

i. Report on the need for the states to consider reporting requirements for chemical use data.

j. Render a public report on the assumptions and compilation of a revenue forecast by sports stadium/racetrack complex.

Required:

Prepare a three-column schedule showing (1) each of the engagements listed, (2) the type of audit (financial statement, compliance, economy and efficiency, or program), and (3) the kind of auditors you would expect to be involved.

LO D-1

D.44   **Organizing a Risk Analysis.** You are the director of internal auditing of a large municipal hospital. You receive monthly financial reports prepared by the accounting department, and your review of them has shown that total accounts receivable from patients has steadily and rapidly increased over the past eight months.

Other information in the reports shows the following conditions:

• The number of available hospital beds has not changed.

• The bed occupancy rate has not changed.

• Hospital billing rates have not changed significantly.

• The hospitalization insurance contracts have not changed since the last modification 12 months ago.

Your internal audit department audited the accounts receivable 10 months ago. The audit documentation file for that assignment contains financial information, a record of the risk analysis, documentation of the study and evaluation of management and internal risk mitigation controls, documentation of the evidence-gathering procedures used to produce evidence about the validity and collectability of the accounts, and a copy of your report, which commented favorably on the controls and collectability of the receivables. However, the current increase in receivables has alerted you to a need for another audit so any existing problem will not get out of hand. You remember news stories last year about the manager of the city water system who got into big trouble because his accounting department double-billed all residential customers for three months.

Required:

You plan to perform a risk analysis to understand the problem if indeed one exists. Write a memo to your senior auditor listing at least eight questions to use to guide and direct the risk analysis. (*Hint:* The questions used last year were organized under these headings: (1) Who does the accounts receivable accounting? (2) What data processing procedures and policies are in effect? and (3) How is the accounts receivable accounting done? This time, you will add a fourth category: (4) What financial or economic events have occurred in the last 10 months?)

(CIA adapted)

LO D-1

D.45 **Study and Evaluation of Management Control.** The study and evaluation of management risk control in a governmental or internal audit is not easy. First, auditors must determine the risks and the controls subject to audit. Then they must find a standard by which performance of the control can be evaluated. Next they must specify procedures to obtain the evidence on which an evaluation can be based. Insofar as possible, the standards and related evidence must be quantified.

Students working on this case usually do not have the experience or theoretical background to determine control standards and audit procedures, so the following scenario gives certain information (in italics) that internal auditors would know about or be able to learn on their own. Fulfilling the requirement thus amounts to taking some information from the scenario and learning other things by using accountants' and auditors' common sense.

The Scenario

Ace Corporation ships building materials to more than a thousand wholesale and retail customers in a five-state region. The company's normal credit terms are net/30 days; it offers no cash discounts. Jerry Clark is the chief financial officer and is concerned about risks related to maintaining control over customer credit. In particular, Clark has stated two management control principles for this purpose.

1. Sales are to be billed to customers accurately and promptly. Clark knows that errors will occur but thinks company personnel should be able to hold quantity, unit price, and arithmetic errors down to 3 percent of the sales invoices. Clark considers an invoice error of $1 or less not to matter and believes that prompt billing is important because customers are expected to pay within 30 days. Clark is very strict in thinking that a bill should be sent to the customer one day after shipment and believes the billing department is staffed well enough to be able to handle this workload. *The relevant company records consist of an accounts receivable control account, a subsidiary ledger of customers' accounts in which charges are entered by billing (invoice) date and credits are entered by date of payment receipts, a sales journal that lists invoices in chronological order, and a file of shipping documents cross-referenced by the number on the related sales invoice copy kept on file in numerical order.*

2. Accounts receivable are to be aged and followed up to ensure prompt collection. Clark has told the accounts receivable department to classify all customer accounts in categories of (a) current, (b) 31–59 days overdue, (c) 60–90 days overdue, and (d) more than 90 days overdue. Clark wants this trial balance to be complete and to be transmitted to the credit department within five days after each month-end. In the credit department, prompt follow-up means sending a different (stronger) collection letter to each category, cutting off credit to customers that are more than 60 days past due (putting them on cash basis), and giving the over-90-days accounts to an outside collection agency. These actions are supposed to be taken within five days after receipt of the aged trial balance. *The relevant company records, in addition to the ones listed, consist of the aged trial balance, copies of the letters sent to customers, copies of notices of credit cutoff, copies of correspondence with the outside collection agent, and reports of results—statistics of subsequent collections.*

Required:

Take the role of a senior internal auditor. You are to write a memo to the internal audit staff to inform them about comparison standards for the study and evaluation of these two management control policies. You also need to specify two or three procedures for gathering evidence about performance of the controls. The body of your memo should be structured as follows:

1. Control: Sales are billed to customers accurately and promptly.

    a. Accuracy.

        (1) Policy standard . . .

        (2) Audit procedures . . .

    b. Promptness.

        (1) Policy standard . . .

        (2) Audit procedures . . .

2. Control: Accounts receivable are aged and followed up to ensure prompt collection.

    a. Accounts receivable aging.

        (1) Policy standard . . .

        (2) Audit procedures . . .

    b. Follow-up prompt collection.

        (1) Policy standard . . .

        (2) Audit procedures . . .

LO D-1

D.46 **Quality Control Audit of a University.**   In a quality audit, defining the measurement criteria is often difficult and time consuming. You have been a student at a college or university for several years and should have a basic understanding of its academic operations. You have been engaged to perform a quality audit of your university.

Required:

    a. How would you measure quality in a university environment? What departments are responsible for measuring quality?

    b. What audit evidence would you look for in performing the quality audit?

LO D-1

D.47 **Internal Audit of Inventory.** External auditors usually calculate inventory turnover (cost of goods sold for the year divided by average inventory) and use the ratio as a broad indication of inventory age, obsolescence, or overstocking. External auditors are interested in evidence relating to the material accuracy of the financial statements taken as a whole. Internal auditors, on the other hand, calculate turnover by categories and classes of inventory to detect problem areas that might otherwise be overlooked. This kind of detailed analytical audit might point to conditions of buying errors, obsolescence, overstocking, and other matters that could be changed to save money.

The data shown in Exhibit D.47.1 are for turnover, cost of sales, and inventory investment for a series of four historical years and the current year. In each of the years, the external auditors did not recommend any adjustments to the inventory valuations.

EXHIBIT D.47.1
Inventory Data

	Inventory				Current-Year Inventory ($000)	
	2014	2015	2016	2017	Beginning	Ending
Total inventory	2.1	2.0	2.1	2.1	$3,000	$2,917
Materials and parts	4.0	4.1	4.3	4.5	1,365	620
Work-in-process	12.0	12.5	11.5	11.7	623	697
Finished products:						
Computer games	6.0	7.0	10.0	24.0	380	500
Flash drives	8.0	7.2	7.7	8.5	64	300
Semiconductor parts	4.0	3.5	4.5	7.0	80	400
Chargers and cables	3.0	2.5	2.0	1.9	488	400

Additional Information Current Year ($000)					
	Transfers	Sales	Cost of Goods Sold	Gross Profit	Compared to Prior Year
Materials and parts	$3,970[*]	NA	NA	NA	
Work-in-process	7,988[†]	NA	NA	NA	
Computer games	2,320[‡]	$2,000	$2,200	$<200>	Sales volume declined 60%[§]
Flash drives	2,236[‡]	3,000	2,000	1,000	Sales volume increased 35%
Semiconductor parts	2,720[‡]	4,000	2,400	1,600	Sales volume increased 40%
Chargers and cables	712[‡]	1,000	800	200	Sales volume declined 3%

NA means not applicable.
[*]Cost of materials transferred to Work-in-Process.
[†]Cost of materials, labor, and overhead transferred to Finished Goods.
[‡]Cost of goods transferred from Work-in-Process to Finished Product Inventories.
[§]Selling prices also were reduced and the gross margin declined.

Required:

Calculate the current-year inventory turnover ratios. Interpret the ratio trends and identify what conditions might exist. As an internal auditor, write a memo to the vice president for production explaining your findings, possible causes related to problems, and additional investigation that should be conducted.

LO D-1

D.48 **Internal Auditors in the Fast-Food Industry.** Internal auditors perform risk-based audits that go beyond the risks of the financial statements. Assume you are on the internal audit staff of **McDonald's.**

Required:

a. Identify the risks in the fast-food industry associated with
   I.   Competition.
   II. Customer preference.
   III. The economy.
   IV. Technology.
   V.   Regulation.
   VI. Other risks.

b. Explain how each of the risks you identified could affect McDonald's.

c. Explain how these risks might affect the internal audits performed by the internal audit staff for McDonald's.

LO D-2

D.49 **CPA Involvement in an Expanded-Scope Audit.** A public accounting firm has been engaged to audit a local food distribution program funded by the U.S. Department of Agriculture. The engagement is to encompass both financial and performance audits that constitute the expanded scope of a GAGAS audit and is to be conducted in accordance with the audit standards published by the Government Accountability Office (GAO).

Required:

a. The accountants should perform sufficient audit work to satisfy the financial and compliance element of GAGAS. What is the objective of such audit work? (*Hint:* Go to the Generally Accepted Government Auditing Standards at www.gao.gov.)

b. The accountants should be aware of general and specific kinds of uneconomical or inefficient practices in such a program. What are some examples?

c. What might be some standards and sources of standards for judging program results?

LO D-6

D.50 **Selection of Effective Extended Procedures.** The following lettered items are some "suspicions," and you have been requested to select some effective procedures designed to confirm or repudiate the suspicions.

a. The custodian of the petty cash fund may be removing cash on Friday afternoon to pay for weekend activities.

b. A manager noticed that eight new vendors had been added to the purchasing department's approved list after the assistant purchasing agent was promoted to purchasing manager three weeks ago. The manager suspects all or some of them might be fictitious companies set up by the new purchasing manager.

c. The payroll supervisor may be stealing unclaimed paychecks of people who quit work and do not pick up the last check.

d. Although no customers have complained, cash collections on accounts receivable are down. The counter clerks may have stolen customers' payments.

e. The cashier may have "borrowed" money, covered it by holding each day's deposit until cash from the next day(s)'s collection is enough to make up the shortage from an earlier day, and then send the deposit to the bank.

Required:

Write the suggested procedures for each case in definite terms so another person will know what to do.

LO D-1

D.51 **Internet Exercise: Audit Charters.** Most universities have internal audit departments, and most of them have audit charters that are available on the university website (although you may need to hunt to find it). Go to the website of your college or university and find the internal audit department. Find and print the audit charter or its equivalent. If you are having trouble finding it, call or e-mail the internal audit department and ask whether someone can provide a copy of the audit charter. If your university does not have an internal audit department or does not make its charter available, check the website of one of the larger public universities in your state.

Required:

As described in the audit charter:

a. What are the responsibilities of the internal audit department?

b. What authority does the internal audit department have?

c. To whom does the internal audit department report?

d. When the internal audit department issues a report, who gets it?

e. Are there any items described in the audit charter that you find surprising or interesting?

LO D-1

D.52 **Internet Exercise: Governmental Audit Reports.** Go to the website of the town where you reside and find the Comprehensive Annual Financial Report (CAFR). Find and print the auditor's report. *Warning:* Be careful! CAFRs can be more than 100 pages, so make certain you're printing only the auditor's report.

Required:

a. Who audited the financial statements in the CAFR?

b. How does the auditor's report compare to the three-paragraph standard report used when auditing for-profit companies' financial statements?

c. What additional paragraphs were added to the report?

LO D-6

D.53 **Collecting Evidence in a Fraud Examination.** A fraud examiner was called into a business because of a suspicion of fraud. An assistant manager in a bookstore is taking books off the shelf, bringing them to the return book area, completing a customer return form, and pocketing the money. This is done late in the day when few other employees are in the store and are involved in closing activities that occupy them in other areas.

Required:

a. What are the objectives of the fraud examiner in performing a fraud examination?

b. What evidence could the fraud examiner obtain that would help reach the objectives of the audit?

c. How should the fraud examiner handle the evidence obtained?

LO D-2

D.54 **Auditing the Effectiveness of a Loan Program.** The following problem is based on an actual program and situation.

The Office of Economic Opportunity (OEO) designed special programs to have a major impact on unemployment, dependency, and community tensions in urban areas with large concentrations of low-income residents or in rural areas having substantial migration to such urban areas. The purpose of these experimental programs—combining business, community, and personnel development—is to offer poor people an opportunity to become self-supporting through the free enterprise system. The programs are intended to create training and job opportunities, improve the living environment, and encourage development of local entrepreneurial skills.

Assume that the OEO has identified Mayville as a participant in the special impact program. The Mayville program received more than $50 million in federal funds and obtained another $10 million from private foundations.

Problems

Mayville is a three-square-mile section of Mega City with a population of approximately 200,000. This area has serious problems of unemployment and underemployment and inadequate housing.

Mayville's problems are deeply seated and have resisted rapid solution. They stem primarily from the fact that local residents, to a considerable degree, lack the education and training required for the jobs available elsewhere in the city and from the lack of jobs in the area. Unemployment and underemployment, in turn, reduce buying power, which has a depressing effect on the area's economy.

The magnitude of the Mayville problems is indicated by the following data disclosed by the U.S. census:

1. Of the total civilian labor force, 8.9 percent was unemployed compared with unemployment rates of 7.1 percent for Mega City and 6.8 percent for the standard metropolitan statistical area (SMSA).

2. Per capita income was $14,106, compared with $22,720 for New York City and $29,909 for the SMSA.

3. Families below the poverty level made up 27.8 percent of the population, compared with 12.4 percent in New York and 9.2 percent in the SMSA.

4. Families receiving public assistance made up 25.4 percent of the population, compared with 9.6 percent in New York and 7.5 percent in the SMSA.

A number of factors aggravate the area's economic problems and make them more difficult to solve. Some of these are

- A reluctance of industry to move into Mega City.
- A net outflow of industry from Mega City.
- High city taxes and a high crime rate.
- A dearth of local residents possessing business managerial experience.

The area's housing problems resulted from the widespread deterioration of existing housing and are, in part, a by-product of below-average income levels resulting from unemployment and underemployment. These problems were aggravated by a shortage of mortgage capital for residential housing associated with a lack of confidence in the area on the part of financial institutions, which, as discussed later, seems to have been somewhat overcome.

Mayville was the target of several special impact programs. Included were programs designed to stimulate private business, to improve housing, to establish community facilities, and to train residents in marketable skills. There were two programs to stimulate private business: a program to loan funds to local businesses and a program to attract outside businesses to the area.

Under the business loan program begun five years ago, the sponsors proposed to create jobs and stimulate business ownership by local residents. At first, investments in local businesses were made only in the form of loans. Later, the sponsors adopted a policy of making equity investments in selected companies to obtain the sponsors' voice in management. Equity investments totaling about $159,000 were made in four companies.

Loans were to be repaid in installments over periods of up to 10 years, usually with a moratorium on repayment for six months or longer. Repayment was to be made in cash or by applying subsidies allowed by the sponsors for providing on-the-job training to unskilled workers. Loans made during the first two years of the program were interest free. Later, the sponsors revised the policy to one of charging below-market interest rates. Rates charged were from 2 to 5 percent. This policy change was made to (1) emphasize to borrowers their obligations to repay the loan and (2) help the sponsors monitor borrowers' progress toward profitability.

Prospective borrowers learned of the loan program through (1) information disseminated at neighborhood centers, (2) advertisements on radio and television and in a local newspaper, and (3) word of mouth. Those who wished to apply for loans were required to complete application forms providing information relating to their education, business and work experience, and personal financial statements and references. The sponsors set up a management assistance division, which employed consultants to supplement its internal marketing assistance efforts and to provide management, accounting, marketing, legal, and other assistance to borrowers.

The sponsors proposed to create at least 1,700 jobs during the first four years of the loan program by making loans to some 73 new and existing businesses.

Required:

Put yourself in the position of the GAO manager in charge of all audits pertaining to the Office of Economic Opportunity. The Mega City field office has been assigned to conduct a detailed review of the special impact program described here. Prepare a memo to the Mega City field office in which you indicate, in as much detail as is possible from the information provided, the specific steps the field office should perform in evaluating the effectiveness of the special impact loan program.

LO D-1

D.55 **Operational Audit: Customer Complaints.** Danny Deck, the director of internal auditing for Rice Department Stores, was working in his office one Thursday when Chris McMurray, president of the company, burst in to tell Deck about a problem. According to McMurray, "Customer complaints about delays in getting credit for merchandise returns are driving

Sally Godwin up the wall! She doesn't know what to do because she has no control over the processing of credit memos."

Godwin is the manager in charge of customer relations and tries to keep everybody happy. Upon her recommendation, the company had adopted an advertising motto: "Satisfaction Guaranteed and Prompt Credit When You Change Your Mind." The motto is featured in newspaper ads and on large banners in each store.

Deck performed a preliminary review and found the following:

1. Godwin believes customers will be satisfied if they receive a refund check or notice of credit on account within five working days.

2. The chief accountant described the credit memo processing procedure as follows: When a customer returns merchandise, the sales clerks give a smile, a "returned merchandise receipt," and a promise to send a check or a notice within five days. The store copy of the receipt and the merchandise are sent to the purchasing department, where buyers examine the merchandise for quality or damage to decide whether to put it back on the shelves, return it to the vendor, or hold it for the annual rummage sale. The buyers then prepare a brief report and send it with the returned merchandise receipt to the customer relations department for approval. The buyer's report is filed for reference and the receipt, marked for approval in Godwin's department, is sent to the accounting department. The accounting department sorts the receipts in numerical order, checking the numerical sequence, and files them in preparation for the weekly batch processing of transactions other than sales and cash receipts, both of which are processed daily. When the customer has requested a cash refund, the checks and canceled returned merchandise receipts are approved by the treasurer, who signs and mails the check. When the credit is on a customer's charge account, it is shown on the next monthly statement sent to the customer.

3. The processing in each department takes two or three days.

Required:

   a. Analyze the problem. How much time does it take the company to process the merchandise returns?

   b. Formulate a recommendation to solve the problem. Write a brief report explaining your recommendation.

LO D-2

D.56 **GAO Auditor Independence.** The GAO reporting standards for performance audits state that each report should include "recommendations for action to correct the problem areas and to improve operations." For example, an audit of the Washington Metropolitan Area Transit Authority found management decision deficiencies affecting some $230 million in federal funds. The GAO auditors recommended that the transit authority could improve its management control over rail car procurement through better enforcement of contract requirements and development of a master plan to test cars.

Suppose the transit authority accepted and implemented specific recommendations made by the GAO auditors.

Required:

Do you believe these events would be enough to impair the independence of the GAO auditors in a subsequent audit of the transit authority? Explain and tell whether it makes any difference to you that the same or different person performs both the first and subsequent audits.

LO D-3

D.57 **Efficiency Standards.** The U.S. Postal Service (USPS) advertises prompt delivery schedules for express mail (overnight delivery) and priority mail (two-to–three-day delivery). The USPS knows various risks that may arise to thwart a timely (as advertised) delivery but believes that systems and controls are in place and operating to mitigate the risks. The USPS advertised that 94 percent of express mail and 87 percent of priority mail was delivered on time from the time the mail was postmarked to the time it reached the destination post office. However, a consulting firm studied the USPS operations and determined that the express mail arrived at the recipients' addresses on time 81 percent of the time (not 94 percent) and the priority mail arrived timely 75 percent of the time (not 87 percent).

Required:

What can account for the difference in these performance statistics between the USPS delivery rates and the consultant's rates? (*Hint:* Think in terms of orientation to customers and standards for measuring performance.)

LO D-6

D.58 **The Perfect Crime.** Embezzlers often try to cover up by removing canceled checks they made payable to themselves or endorsed on the back with their own names. Missing canceled checks are a signal (red flag). However, people who reconcile bank accounts may not notice missing checks if the bank reconciliation is performed using only the numerical listing printed in the bank statement. Now consider the case of truncated bank statements for which the bank does not even return the canceled checks to the payer. All of the checks are "missing," and the person performing the bank reconciliation has no opportunity to notice anything about canceled checks. Consider the following story of a real embezzlement.

The embezzler hired a print shop to print a private stock of Ajax Company checks in the company's numerical sequence. In his job as an accounts payable clerk, he intercepted legitimate checks written by the accounts payable department and signed by the Ajax treasurer and then destroyed them. He substituted the same-numbered check from the private stock, made it payable to himself in the same amount as the legitimate check, and "signed" it with a rubber stamp that looked enough like the Ajax Company treasurer's signature to fool the paying bank. He deposited the money in his own bank account.

The bank statement reconciler (a different person) was able to agree the check numbers and amounts listed in the cleared items in the bank statement to the recorded cash disbursement (check number and amount) and thus did not notice the trick. The embezzler was able to process the vendor's "past due" notice and next month statement with complete documentation, enabling the Ajax treasurer to sign another check the next month paying both the past due balance and current charges. The embezzler was careful to scatter the double-expense payments among numerous accounts (telephone, office supplies, inventory, etc.) so the double-paid expenses did not distort accounts very much. As time passed, the embezzler was able to recommend budget figures that allowed a large enough budget so his double-paid expenses in various categories did not often pop up as large variances from the budget.

Required:

List and explain the ways and means you believe someone might detect this fraud scheme. Think first about the ordinary everyday control procedures. Then think about extensive detection efforts assuming a tip or indication of a possible fraud has been received. Is this a "perfect crime"?

LO D-1

D.59 **Impact of Changing Rules.** Many companies outsource their internal audit function to CPA firms.

Required:

a. What benefits might be gained from having a CPA firm provide its internal audit services?
b. What benefits might be gained from having an in-house internal audit department?
c. What concerns might arise from having a CPA firm provide its internal audit services?

LO D-1, D-6

D.60 **Looking for Evidence of Fraud.** Wen-Li is an internal auditor for Main Electrical Supply in Springfield, Illinois. During her audit, she came across the invoice shown in Exhibit D.60.1. The invoice is in almost pristine condition with few marks and no creases. The invoice was properly filed in a vendor folder marked Best Office Supply, which is on the approved vendor list, but the vendor review sheet, which is required to place a vendor on the approved vendor list, is missing from the file.

Three other invoices were in the file:

June 14, 2016	Invoice 0076	$238.99
July 17, 2016	Invoice 0081	324.55
August 16, 2016	Invoice 0085	386.82

Required:

a. Is this a legitimate invoice? What information might lead you to suspect that this invoice may indicate a fraud?
b. What type(s) of fraud might this indicate?

EXHIBIT D.60.1   Vendor Invoice

September 15, 2016

Best Office Supply Company
P.O. Box 1934
Springfield, Illinois 62705

Invoice #0089

Bill to:
Main Electrical Supply
506 Commerce Avenue
Springfield, IL 62707
217-555-2230

Product	Quantity	Price per Unit	Total Cost
Pens	10 boxes	$3.65	$36.50
Copy paper	15 cases	$15.76	$236.40
Toner cartridges	8 units	$22.56	$180.48
Total			$453.38

Payment is due immediately upon receipt

The remainder of this module discusses sampling in a generic (nonaudit) context. In addition, we provide a broad overview of the use of sampling in these two audit contexts. The next two modules provide detailed illustration of the use of sampling in the audit team's study of internal control (Module F) and the audit team's substantive procedures (Module G).

When Should Sampling Be Used?

To illustrate the basic concepts associated with sampling, assume that a regional fitness chain (Healthy Bodies) was interested in determining whether a six-month aerobic program would lower the resting heart rate of members who participated in this program. Healthy Bodies has determined that if a member's heart rate would decrease by 15 beats per minute (bpm), it can reliably claim that aerobic programs are effective in reducing the resting heart rate of a "typical" individual.[4] (It is not important for you to know how the 15 bpm was determined, but it incorporates a margin for error or randomness.) Healthy Bodies wants to publicize the results of this study and hires a local public accounting firm to provide assurance on their measurement process.

One possible way to test this claim is to measure the resting heart rate of every member of Healthy Bodies prior to the aerobic program and then following the aerobic program. (In this case, note that the population is defined as all members of Healthy Bodies and not all human beings.) The differences in heart rates would be determined and, assuming that no computational errors were made in the calculations, Healthy Bodies would know the average resting heart rate (if any) with certainty.

Would an engagement team consider using sampling to answer this question? Sampling is typically used when the question of interest has the following two characteristics:

1. *The need for exact information is not important.* Considering the preceding example, the engagement team would be more interested in testing all members if it wanted to know an exact change in resting heart rates (e.g., does an aerobic program lower heart rates by 16 bpm as opposed to 15 bpm or more?).
2. *The number of items comprising the population is large.* If the number of members was 50, the engagement team would be more likely to test all 50 members than if the number of members were 2,500.

Essentially, sampling trades *effectiveness* for *efficiency*. That is, sampling allows an individual to obtain information about a population of interest in a fraction of the time it would take to examine the entire population. In other words, *sampling is more efficient*. However, because the individual is not examining all items in the population, there is a chance that sampling will not provide the correct answer to the question being examined. (*Sampling is less effective.*) Sampling is used when the gains associated with efficiency exceed the losses associated with effectiveness.

Sampling Risk versus Nonsampling Risk

As noted, sampling can result in the loss of effectiveness; that is, basing a conclusion about a population on a sample drawn from that population could fail to provide the correct conclusion. For example, assume that the engagement team tested 50 members, calculated the resting heart rates, and concluded that the average reduction was 17 bpm. Recall that the engagement team is interested in determining whether the reduction is greater than 15 bpm. If the true decrease (which the engagement team would not know unless it tested all members) is 18 bpm, the use of sampling has provided the engagement team the correct conclusion.

Now assume that the measurements provided an average reduction of 11 bpm. In this case, the engagement team's conclusion that an aerobic program was not effective in reducing the resting heart rate would be incorrect because the true average reduction (unknown

---

[4] The American Heart Association notes that the average heart rate of a well-trained athlete is 40 beats per minute and that of a less active person ranges from 60 to 100 beats per minute. See http://www.heart.org/HEARTORG/HealthyLiving/PhysicalActivity/FitnessBasics/Target-Heart-Rates_UCM_434341_Article.jsp#.V4vgmTXKt80.

AUDITING INSIGHT Sampling's OK, Sampling's Not OK

MBIA Inc. can use statistical sampling to pursue repurchase demands against **Bank of America Corporation,** a judge said in a lawsuit claiming MBIA was fraudulently induced to insure $21 billion in mortgage-backed securities. MBIA asked New York State Supreme Court Judge Eileen Bransten to allow company lawyers to develop evidence using samples from 368,000 mortgages in 15 securitized pools to establish its fraud claims rather than go through each loan. Proceeding loan by loan might lead to "a delay of several years before trial," Philippe Z. Selendy, an attorney for Armonk, New York-based MBIA, said in an October 13 letter to the judge.

On December 22, 2010, Bransten ruled that "the court does not find any prejudice in deciding the motion before it and allowing the use of statistically significant samples of the securitizations at issue." She said the defendants could also choose to use their "own sampling chosen in a statistically valid manner" to rebut MBIA's arguments.

Source: "Bank of America Loses Evidence Ruling in MBIA Suit," *Bloomberg Businessweek,* December 29, 2010; "Bank of America Loses Bid to Stop MBIA Using Statistics in Fraud Lawsuit," http://www.bloomberg.com/news/articles/2010-12-22/bofa-loses-evidence-ruling-in-mbia-fraud-suit-over-21-billion-in-coverage.

President Barack Obama's nominee to head the Census Bureau ruled out using statistical sampling to adjust the results of the 2010 census, apparently easing Republican concerns and making his confirmation likely. Robert Groves, director of the University of Michigan's Survey Research Center and a former Census Bureau official, is an expert on statistical sampling. Proponents of sampling say it helps produce a more accurate count of the population, especially when it comes to traditionally undercounted groups, such as minorities living in urban areas. But many Republican lawmakers insist that sampling violates the Constitution.

During his confirmation hearing, Groves said he wouldn't use sampling to adjust the 2010 count. Asked whether he would consider using it in a future census, he said: "There are no plans to do that for 2020."

Source: "Census Pick Rules Out Using Sampling in 2010," *The Wall Street Journal,* May 16, 2009, p. A2.

to the engagement team) is 18 bpm.[5] This situation is an example of **sampling risk**, which is the likelihood that the decision made based on the sample differs from the conclusion that would have been made if the entire population had been examined. This relationship is shown in Exhibit E.1. Sampling risk occurs because of a **nonrepresentative sample**, which is a sample that differs substantially on one or more key characteristics of interest from the population from which the sample is drawn. The Auditing Insight "Polling Problems" illustrates how sampling risk is introduced when predicting election results.

Sampling risk can never be eliminated (unless, of course, the engagement team were to test all members of the Healthy Bodies), but it can be controlled to relatively low levels. Three major steps can control sampling risk in the sampling process:

1. *Determining an appropriate sample size.* As a higher percentage of items in the population is examined, sampling risk decreases.
2. *Ensuring that all items have an equal opportunity to be selected.* If all items have an equal opportunity to be selected, the likelihood of sampling risk decreases.
3. *Evaluating sample results to control sampling risk.* The results from a sample are "adjusted" to consider the likelihood that the sample being evaluated does not appropriately represent the population. We discuss this "adjustment" later.

EXHIBIT E.1

The Effect of Various Sample Averages on Conclusions

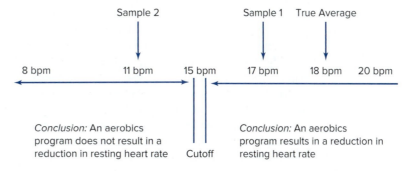

[5] Recall that the engagement team stipulated that the reduction must equal or exceed 15 beats per minute for it to reliably conclude that an aerobic program was effective in reducing resting heart rates. Therefore, even though the average reduction was 11 beats per minute, this difference is not large enough to provide the engagement team with a reliable conclusion.

AUDITING INSIGHT   Polling Problems

The results of the 2015 United Kingdom general election were surprising, not because of the outcome but because of the comfortable margin of victory for David Cameron and the Conservative Party. (A very close election was predicted.) Initially, the outcome was attributed to a late "swing" of votes to the Conservative Party; however, an inquiry commissioned by the British Polling Council and Market Research Society revealed that the difference was related to sampling. Their findings indicated that the sample of voters was heavily weighted to younger voters (who are more likely to be affiliated with the Labour Party) rather than older voters (who are more likely to be affiliated with the Conservative Party).

Source: "Poor Sampling Blamed for Pollsters' Failure to Predict U.K. Election," *The Wall Street Journal*, January 20, 2016, p. A9.

In evaluating the results of the 2016 United States Presidential election, two sampling issues may have contributed to the failure to predict Donald Trump's surprise victory. First, working-class white voters (who were generally supportive of Trump) were reluctant to respond to phone calls from pollsters, which understated Trump's level of support among the electorate. Second, Trump's heavy courtship of this group may have motivated them to vote in much higher rates than in previous elections, resulting in a higher level of support on Election Day than predicted.

Source: "Epic Fail," *The Economist*, November 12, 2016, pp. 29–30.

Nonsampling risk represents the probability that an incorrect conclusion will be reached as a result of reasons unrelated to the nature of the sample. Even if the auditors examine all items, they are still subject to nonsampling risk. Nonsampling risk typically occurs because of errors in judgment or execution. For example, if the engagement team incorrectly measures the resting heart rate of a member, the sample average will be incorrect and can result in an inappropriate conclusion. Note that this error is not caused by a nonrepresentative sample but by an *evaluator error*. In an auditing context, *nonsampling risk* arises when auditors use an inappropriate procedure or misinterpret evidence they have obtained.

Statistical Sampling versus Nonstatistical Sampling

The preceding section on the possible exposure to sampling risk notes a significant limitation with the use of sampling. This risk cannot be eliminated, but certain sampling plans allow the risk to be measured and controlled at acceptable levels. These plans are referred to as *statistical sampling plans*.

Statistical sampling plans apply the laws of probability to selecting sample items for examination and evaluating sample results. Specifically, statistical sampling methods enable the audit team to make quantitative statements about the results and to measure the sufficiency of evidence gathered (i.e., determine a sufficient sample size) and evaluate the results in such a way to control sampling risk. **Nonstatistical sampling** plans do not meet either of these criteria. Thus, these two types of plans differ in terms of how sample size is determined and how the results are evaluated.

Although the phrase *nonstatistical sampling* sounds less professional and less favorable, nonstatistical sampling methods can be appropriate in some circumstances. In certain cases, it is not necessary (or desirable) to use the laws of probability to select sample items.

Generally accepted auditing standards do *not* require the use of statistical sampling procedures. The use of nonstatistical sampling methods is often justifiable when the costs of using statistical sampling methods exceed the benefits of doing so. However, nonstatistical sampling should not be used solely as a means to reduce sample sizes.

The terms *statistical and nonstatistical sampling* and *sampling and nonsampling risk* are sometimes used interchangeably. However, it is important to note that they are indeed quite different. To understand this, sampling risk exists in both a statistical and nonstatistical sample because either type of sampling plan can result in the selection of a sample that does not appropriately represent the population. However, statistical sampling plans allow sampling risk to be measured and controlled to acceptable levels. Similarly, nonsampling risk can exist in either type of sampling approach because an individual could make a mistake in evaluating sample results in either a statistical or nonstatistical sampling application.

THE BASIC STEPS INVOLVED WITH SAMPLING

LO E-2
Understand the basic steps and procedures used in implementing a sampling plan.

In general, sampling can be viewed as including the following major steps:

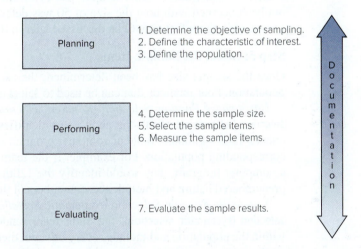

As an example of the process illustrated, consider our example of determining whether an aerobics program results in a reduction in the resting heart rate of participants. In this module, we provide an example of this process that does not involve calculations to illustrate how the sampling process works. Modules F and G provide a more comprehensive example of this process and how it is employed in various stages of the audit team's examination.

Planning

Steps 1–3: Determine the Objective, Define the Characteristic of Interest, and Define the Population

The *objective of the sampling application* is directly related to the question of interest. In this example, the objective is to determine whether an aerobics program results in a reduced resting heart rate; because the engagement team's conclusion with respect to this question is evidenced by whether the reduction is 15 bpm or greater, the reduction in resting heart rate is the *characteristic of interest*. Clearly defining the characteristic of interest in a sampling application is critical because it is the measure that will be obtained from the sample items and eventually evaluated against some criterion (related to the objective of the sampling application).

Defining the population can sound straightforward, but it must be defined carefully to be able to meet the objective of the sampling application. In our example, the population is defined as all members of Healthy Bodies clubs. If the population is defined more broadly (all residents of the city in which Healthy Bodies is located) or narrowly (all members of Healthy Bodies who are currently enrolled in an aerobics program), the results will not appropriately represent the population of interest.

Performing

Step 4: Determine Sample Size

Although many factors are considered in determining the appropriate sample size, the acceptable level of sampling risk is one important factor. Recall that an advantage of *statistical* sampling plans is that they determine a sample size that measures and controls exposure to sampling risk. An individual who wishes to reduce sampling risk to lower levels needs to select more items for examination as shown.

Assume that, based on an acceptable level of sampling risk of 10 percent, the engagement team determines that a sample size of 50 members is needed. At this point, do not be concerned with how the size of 50 was determined. Other factors also influence sample size; these factors will be discussed later in this module.

Step 5: Select the Sample Items

Once the sample size has been determined, the sample needs to be selected from the population. Four methods that can be used to select a sample are discussed next.

Unrestricted Random Selection (Random Selection) When using **unrestricted random selection (random selection)**, the audit team identifies a series of random numbers from either a random number table or computer program and selects the numbered item in the corresponding population. For example, if the team identified 120, 268, and 341 from a computer program, they would identify the 120th, 268th, and 341st members from a prenumbered listing and include these members in their test.

Systematic Random Selection (Systematic Selection) When using **systematic random selection (systematic selection)**, the audit team randomly selects a starting point from within the population and includes every *nth* item thereafter, where *n* is determined based on the number of items in the population and the necessary sample size. In this case, *n* is referred to as the **sampling interval** and represents the frequency with which items are selected within the population. The sampling interval is calculated by dividing the number of items in the population by the necessary sample size.

For example, assume the audit team identified a random starting point of 15 and a necessary sample size of 50. If the membership of Healthy Bodies clubs is 3,000, the sampling interval would be 60 (3,000 members ÷ 50 items = 60). In choosing the first three sample items, the audit team would select the 15th (starting point), 75th (15 + 60), and 135th (75 + 60) members from a prenumbered listing and include these members in their test.

One limitation of systematic selection is that the population must be randomly ordered. Because systematic selection essentially bypasses a number of items, a nonrandomly ordered population can result in bypassing a number of items having similar characteristics. For example, if the population of members were arranged alphabetically, bypassing a number of members whose last name begins with B (or any other letter) would not appear to influence the representativeness of the sample. However, if the population were arranged by member activity, then systematic selection could result in bypassing large groups of very active or very inactive members. This is obviously an unlikely scenario, but it should be considered.

Haphazard Selection When using **haphazard selection**, items are selected in an unstructured manner but without intentional bias. Although this can be done in any number of ways, two ways are to identify items (members) as they arrived at the club or flip through membership rosters selecting items until a total of 50 were selected. Contrary to the connotation of the word *haphazard,* items chosen by haphazard selection are not taken in a careless manner, and the results are expected to be representative of the population.

One significant limitation of haphazard selection is that, unlike either random selection or systematic selection, the sampling method cannot be described in sufficient detail to permit another individual to replicate it.

Block Selection   The use of **block selection** involves selecting a series of contiguous (or adjacent) items from the population. One example of block selection is the selection of the first 10 members from five pages of the membership roster for a total of 50 sample items. In this case, the population unit is really a list of members. Block selection is less desirable because it is difficult to efficiently obtain a representative sample; ordinarily, a relatively large number of blocks need to be selected to be representative.

Which Selection Method Should Be Used?   The use of statistical or nonstatistical sampling procedures has a significant impact on the method of sample selection. Random or systematic selection is used with statistical sampling because these methods (1) provide a reasonable likelihood of obtaining a representative sample, (2) allow the probability of obtaining sample items to be determined, and (3) allow the sample selection process to be replicated. As a result, these methods allow sampling risk to be measured and controlled to acceptable levels. In contrast, haphazard and block selection do not meet these criteria; they could result in a random sample, but quantitatively evaluating the randomness of the sample selected using them is difficult.

In practice, computer audit software has greatly increased the efficiency and effectiveness of selecting sample items, particularly when using systematic random selection or unrestricted random selection. Software applications use client data files and parameters designated by the audit team to select the appropriate sample items.

Step 6: Measure the Sample Items

Once the sample size has been determined and the sample has been selected, the next step is to *measure the sample items.* In our example, measuring the sample items consists of measuring the resting heart rate of each member prior to and following the aerobics program. It is at this point that nonsampling risk can occur. Examples of nonsampling risk include incorrectly transcribing a measurement or making some other mathematical error during the measurement process. After selecting the 50 members and averaging the reductions in resting heart rate, assume that an average reduction in the resting heart rate of 17.5 bpm is calculated.[6]

✅ REVIEW CHECKPOINTS

E.7   What are the seven major steps involved with sampling?

E.8   What is the importance of carefully defining the population of interest?

E.9   How does sampling risk affect sample size?

E.10   Briefly identify and explain the four methods used to select sample items.

E.11   What methods of sample selection are appropriate to use with a statistical sampling plan? Why?

Step 7: Evaluate the Sample Results

Based on the sample average reduction in resting heart rate of 17.5 bpm, can the engagement team conclude that an aerobics program results in a reduction in the average resting heart rate of participants? This average exceeds the 15 bpm criterion, but it is possible that the engagement team did not select a representative sample. (In addition, the engagement team could have made a computational error and introduced nonsampling risk, but we assume that no such errors were made.)

To evaluate the sample results, the sample average must be "adjusted" to control for the acceptable level of exposure to sampling risk (in this example, 10 percent). This is

[6] Of course, factors such as the time of day, recent physical exertion of the members, and any recent health issues experienced by members must be considered.

done by forming a range of estimates that have a certain probability of including the true (but unknown) population value. Assume that we can conclude with 90 percent probability that the true population average reduction in resting heart rate is between 15.5 bpm and 19.5 bpm (the sample estimate of 17.5 bpm plus and minus a 2.0 bpm adjustment factor). This example introduces the following concepts:

- The **precision** (or **allowance for sampling risk**) is the numeric distance from the estimated population value in which the true (but unknown) population value may lie with a given probability. In this case, the precision is 2.0 bpm.
- The **reliability** (or **confidence level**) is the likelihood of achieving a given level of precision. In the example, the reliability is 90 percent, which is equal to 100 percent minus the acceptable sampling risk of 10 percent.
- The **precision interval** is a range around the sample estimate that has a certain likelihood (equal to reliability) of including the true population value. In this example, the precision interval is 15.5 bpm to 19.5 bpm.

AUDITING INSIGHT How Many Jobs?

In the 2012 U.S. presidential election, the economy and job creation were significant issues in the minds of voters. How confident can voters be that the number of jobs actually created matches estimates given by the Bureau of Labor Statistics (BLS)?

When measuring the number of nonfarm jobs created, the BLS considers a pool of more than 130 million jobs, which translates into large margins of error. So, if the BLS estimates that 100,000 jobs were created in a given month, this measure really means that the BLS is 90 percent sure that the number of jobs created was between 9,000 and 191,000. In this example, the precision is 91,000, reliability is 90 percent, and the precision interval is 9,000 to 191,000.

Source: "Don't Let a Jobs Report Elect a President," www.businessweek.com/articles/2012-11-01/bloomberg-view-dont-let-a-jobs-report-elect-a-president," November 1, 2012.

Note that, for any given level of reliability, a unique level of precision exists (in this case, 2.0 bpm). If the engagement team desires a higher level of confidence regarding the closeness of a sample estimate to the true population value (say, 95 percent), the precision interval is wider (say, the sample estimate, ± 3.0 bpm). That is, the wider the range, the more confident one can be that a number falls within a range. Stated another way, each level of precision is associated with a given level of confidence.

What is the overall conclusion? Because the likelihood is 90 percent that the true population's average reduction in resting heart rate is 15.5 bpm to 19.5 bpm, the engagement team can reliably conclude that the average reduction is more than 15 bpm. Therefore, it appears that an aerobics program will provide participants with a reduction in their average resting heart rates. What is the chance that this conclusion is incorrect? It is less than 10 percent, which is less than the acceptable level of sampling risk. See Exhibit E.2 for the relationship between this precision interval and the 15 bpm criterion.

On the other hand, would the engagement team's conclusion change if, for the same confidence level, the precision were determined to be 3.0 bpm? In this case, the precision interval would be 14.5 bpm to 20.5 bpm (sample average of 17.5 bpm ± 3.0 bpm). As in Exhibit E.2, the results are a bit less certain because the lower level of the precision interval is below the criterion reduction of 15 bpm. In this case, statistical theory could be used to determine the precise probability that the true population's average was below 15 bpm and compare that to the acceptable level of sampling risk of 10 percent. However, the evidence in this latter case is clearly less convincing than that for a precision of 2.0 bpm.

In discussing the concept of precision, it is important to note that the terminology can be a bit misleading. Although the precision of 3.0 bpm is higher than that of 2.0 bpm, the latter is often referred to as being a *more precise* estimate because the precision interval is more closely centered on the sample estimate. In some instances, a more precise estimate is referred to as being characterized by *a higher level of precision*.

Summary: Healthy Bodies Example

At this point, the engagement team has performed the following sampling procedures:

1. *Define the objective of sampling.* In this case, the sampling objective is to determine whether an aerobics program results in a reduction in the resting heart rate of participants.

2. *Define the characteristic of interest.* The characteristic of interest is the reduction in resting heart rate of participants in an aerobics program (specifically, whether this reduction is at least 15 bpm).

3. *Define the population.* The population is defined as all members of Healthy Bodies clubs.

4. *Determine the sample size.* Based on the acceptable exposure to sampling risk of 10 percent, a sample size of 50 has been determined.

5. *Select the sample items.* Items may be selected using one of four selection methods (unrestricted random selection, systematic random selection, haphazard selection, or block selection).

6. *Measure the sample items.* Based on the resting heart rates prior to and following the aerobics program, the reduction in resting heart rate is 17.5 bpm.

7. *Evaluate the sample results.* The engagement team concludes that the true population's average reduction in resting heart rate is between 15.5 bpm and 19.5 bpm; as a result, they conclude that the average reduction is greater than 15 bpm.

Documenting the Sampling Procedure

For each of the seven major steps in the sampling process, important judgments and conclusions must be properly documented. Proper documentation for audit samples could be a focal point of supervisory or quality reviews. Some important information that would be documented in the Healthy Bodies example follows:

- *The objective of the sampling application, characteristic of interest, and definition of the population* (steps 1–3).
- *The factors affecting sample size (along with the method or rationale for the selected level of those factors) and determination of sample size;* in this case, the engagement team would document the acceptable level of sampling risk of 10 percent, the rationale for this level of sampling risk, and the determination of the sample size of 50 items (step 4).
- *The method of selecting the sample and description of items selected for examination.* If systematic selection is used, the engagement team would document the random starting point, the sampling interval of 20 items, and the list of the items selected (step 5).
- *The method of measuring sample items and summary of measurements.* In this case, the engagement team would document the resting heart rates of participants prior to

EXHIBIT E.2
Precision Intervals for Two Hypothetical Sample Results

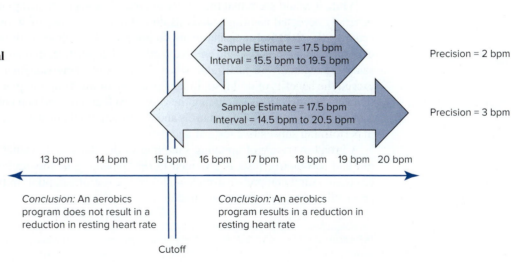

Sample Estimate = 17.5 bpm
Interval = 15.5 bpm to 19.5 bpm
Precision = 2 bpm

Sample Estimate = 17.5 bpm
Interval = 14.5 bpm to 20.5 bpm
Precision = 3 bpm

13 bpm   14 bpm   15 bpm   16 bpm   17 bpm   18 bpm   19 bpm   20 bpm

Conclusion: An aerobics program does not result in a reduction in resting heart rate

Conclusion: An aerobics program results in a reduction in resting heart rate

Cutoff

and following the aerobics program. In addition, the engagement team would document that the overall reduction in resting heart rates is 17.5 bpm (step 6).

- *The evaluation of sample results and overall conclusion with respect to the sample.* In this case, the engagement team would document the precision, reliability, and overall conclusions with respect to the sample (step 7).

The documentation prepared by the audit team should be sufficient for an experienced auditor to replicate the sampling procedure.

☑ REVIEW CHECKPOINTS

E.12 Define the terms *precision* (allowance for sampling risk), *reliability* (confidence), and *precision interval.*

E.13 Describe the basic procedure used to evaluate sample results.

USE OF SAMPLING IN THE AUDIT

LO E-3

Identify the two situations in which sampling is used in an audit.

Thus far in the text, we have discussed two main types of audit procedures performed by the audit team:

1. Tests of controls (which are used to determine the extent to which the entity's controls are functioning as intended).
2. Substantive tests (which are used to determine the accuracy of transactions or components of an entity's account balances.)

In performing these procedures, the audit team could evaluate each occurrence of a control or each transaction or component of an account balance. However, doing so would be cost prohibitive (and make it unlikely that the audit could be completed on a timely basis). As a result, audit teams will usually select a subset of controls, transactions, or components and base their conclusions on this subset (or sample) of items. The AICPA Audit Guide defines **audit sampling** as the "application of an audit procedure to less than 100 percent of the items within an account balance or class of transactions for the purpose of evaluating some characteristic of the balance or class."[7] As with the Healthy Bodies example discussed earlier in this module, the ability to draw a conclusion about a population by examining only a subset of items within that population is one of the primary benefits of sampling. That is, sampling provides an *efficiency* benefit to auditors. However, as noted throughout this module, sampling also exposes the auditors to *sampling risk,* creating a potential loss of *effectiveness.*

While it would seem that the ability to control exposure to sampling risk is important, generally accepted auditing standards do *not* require the use of statistical sampling procedures. **Nonstatistical sampling** plans do not provide auditors with the ability to control exposure to sampling risk and are frequently used in practice. In many cases, nonstatistical sampling methods are justifiable when the costs of using statistical sampling methods exceed the benefits of doing so. In fact, a survey of the sampling practices of six international accounting firms (including the Big Four) found that 50 percent used nonstatistical sampling methods in testing controls and 33 percent used nonstatistical sampling methods in performing substantive tests of details.[8]

A broad overview of applying sampling to the study and evaluation of internal control and substantive tests is provided in the remainder of this section; a more detailed discussion (and comprehensive example) of the use of sampling in these applications is provided in this and subsequent modules.

---

[7] AICPA Audit Guide *Auditing Sampling,* May 1, 2008, p. 133.
[8] B.E. Christensen, R.J. Elder, and S.M. Glover, "Behind the Numbers: Insights into Large Audit Firm Sampling Policies," *Accounting Horizons,* March 2015, pp. 61–81.

Study and Evaluation of Internal Control

With respect to the study and evaluation of the client's internal control, the audit team's objective is to determine whether they can rely upon important control policies and procedures to prevent or detect financial statement misstatements. The use of sampling in this context is referred to as **attributes sampling**.

The audit team uses attributes sampling in evaluating the effectiveness of the client's internal controls and assessing **control risk** (the likelihood that the client's internal control policies and procedures fail to prevent or detect a material misstatement). The general procedure used by the audit team to assess control risk is summarized here:

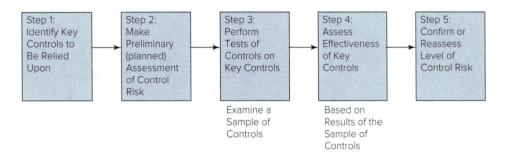

Attributes sampling is used in the third (perform tests of controls on key controls) and fourth (assess effectiveness of key controls) steps illustrated. Based on the results of these tests of controls, auditors evaluate their preliminary assessment of control risk and, ultimately, determine the *nature, timing,* and *extent* of further audit procedures.

Sampling Risks Associated with Attributes Sampling

When evaluating the effectiveness of the client's controls, auditors typically think in terms of the *maximum rate of deviation* that could exist before they would reduce reliance on that control (**tolerable rate of deviation [TRD]**). To illustrate, assume that the audit team decides that a control should function at least 96 percent of the time to be considered effective. (We illustrate how this percentage is determined in Module F.) Stated another way, the audit team is willing to accept that the control does not properly function 4 percent of the time (100 percent – 96 percent). This 4 percent represents the tolerable rate of deviation.

Next, the audit team will examine a sample of controls and calculate a **sample rate of deviation**, which provides one representation of the true population rate of deviation. Although auditors never know the true population rate of deviation with any certainty, they can use sampling tables to "adjust" the *sample rate of deviation* to one that has a certain probability of equaling or exceeding the true rate of deviation. Simply stated, this adjusted rate (the **upper limit rate of deviation [ULRD]**) provides a conservative estimate of the rate of deviation that allows the audit team to control exposure to sampling risk.

Once a tolerable rate of deviation has been established and upper limit rate of deviation has been computed, auditors compare the rates. The decision made by the audit team is as follows:

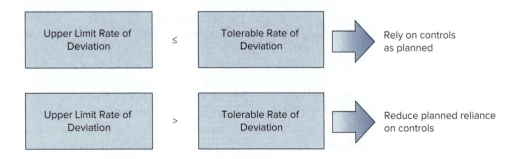

Because sampling is being used to evaluate the operating effectiveness of controls, the audit team is exposed to sampling risk. Consider the following matrix. The two columns represent the two possible outcomes if the entire population were examined; the two rows represent the two possible decisions that auditors could make based on their sample of controls (ARD = actual rate of deviation, TRD = tolerable rate of deviation, ULRD = upper limit rate of deviation). Auditors calculate upper limit rate of deviation by adjusting the rate of deviation in their sample for sampling error to determine the highest possible rate of deviation for a given confidence level.

		Decision Based on True State of the Population	
		ARD ≤ TRD (rely on internal control as planned)	ARD > TRD (reduce planned reliance on internal control)
Decision Based on Examining Sample	ULRD ≤ TRD (rely on internal control as planned)	A: Correct decision	B: Risk of overreliance (risk of assessing control risk too low)
	ULRD > TRD (reduce planned reliance on internal control)	C: Risk of underreliance (risk of assessing control risk too high)	D: Correct decision

Cells A and D do not expose the audit team to sampling risk because the decision to rely on the client's controls as planned (cell A) or to reduce the planned reliance on the client's controls (cell D) is consistent with the decision the audit team would have made had the entire population been examined.

Examine the outcome of cell C. In this instance, the auditors' sample of controls indicates that the rate of deviation exceeds the tolerable rate of deviation; as a result, they would choose to reduce the reliance on internal control and assess control risk at higher levels. However, unknown to the auditors, the rate of deviation in the population is actually lower than the tolerable rate of deviation. This situation is referred to as the **risk of underreliance** (or the **risk of assessing control risk too high**). In this instance, the auditors' sample results in the decision to reduce their reliance on internal control (i.e., *underrely on internal control*), which results in higher assessments of control risk.

In contrast, cell B represents a situation in which the auditors choose to maintain their reliance on internal control because the upper limit rate of deviation is less than or equal to the tolerable rate of deviation. However, in the population, the actual rate of deviation exceeds the tolerable rate of deviation. As a result, the auditors inappropriately rely on internal control and maintain the assessment of control risk at lower levels. This is referred to as the **risk of overreliance** (or the **risk of assessing control risk too low**). In this instance, the sample results in the auditors' decision to rely on internal control as planned (i.e., *overrely on internal control*), which results in lower assessments of control risk.

Which of these risks is of more concern to the auditor? If control risk is assessed at unnecessarily high levels (the risk of underreliance), the resulting detection risk is lower than is necessary to reduce audit risk to acceptable levels. As a result, the nature, timing, and extent of the further audit procedures is more effective than necessary. Ultimately, the overall level of audit risk that the auditors achieve is lower than necessary. Thus, assessing control risk too high causes an *efficiency loss* for the audit team because more extensive substantive procedures are performed than necessary to reduce overall audit risk to acceptable levels.

If control risk is assessed too low, the resulting detection risk is higher than appropriate in the circumstances. When this occurs, the auditors' substantive procedures do not reduce the overall audit risk to an acceptable level. This happens because the auditors believe that internal control is more effective in preventing or detecting misstatements than is the case. The ultimate result of failing to reduce audit risk to an acceptable level is issuing an unmodified opinion on financial statements that are materially misstated, resulting in a reputation loss or litigation by shareholders and other third parties relying on the auditors' work. Therefore, assessing control risk too low exposes the auditors to an *effectiveness loss.*

Given a choice of the two sampling risks, the risk of overreliance clearly is of more concern to auditors than the risk of underreliance. As a result, auditors explicitly control their exposure to the risk of overreliance to acceptable levels when (1) determining the necessary sample size and (2) evaluating sample results.

⍾ REVIEW CHECKPOINTS

E.14 Define *attributes sampling.* When is it used in the audit examination?

E.15 What is the *tolerable rate of deviation*? How does the audit team use it when deciding whether to rely on internal control?

E.16 What are the two sampling risks associated with attributes sampling? What types of losses are associated with each of these risks?

E.17 Why is the audit team more concerned with the risk of overreliance than with the risk of underreliance?

Substantive Procedures

When used in substantive procedures, the audit team's objective is to determine whether an account balance or class of transactions is recorded and presented according to generally accepted accounting principles. **Variables sampling** is used to examine a population when auditors want to estimate the amount (or value) of some characteristic of that population. Auditors use variables sampling when performing substantive procedures to evaluate the fairness of an account balance or class of transactions.

Sampling Risks Associated with Variables Sampling

As in the evaluation of internal control, auditors do not expect account balance or classes of transactions to have zero misstatements but are concerned when these misstatements reach a level that would influence the decisions of those relying on financial statements (referred to as *materiality*). When performing substantive procedures, auditors first determine the level of misstatement they are willing to accept without concluding that the account balance is materially misstated (**tolerable misstatement**). Next, based on a sample of transactions or components, the audit team will calculate a **sample estimate of misstatement**; similar to attributes sampling, this sample estimate of misstatement is then "adjusted" to a level that has a specified probability of equaling or exceeding the true level of misstatement (the **upper limit on misstatements [ULM]**). The ULM adds precision to the sample estimate of misstatement, allowing the audit team to control its exposure to sampling risk to desired levels.

The decision process then proceeds as follows:

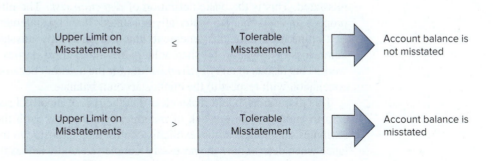

Auditors may be exposed to sampling risk if the sample of components or transactions of the account balance is not representative of the population in terms of the extent to which they are misstated. Consider the following matrix. The two columns represent the two possible outcomes if the entire population were examined; the two rows represent the two possible decisions auditors could make based on the sample of transactions or components of the account balance (AM = actual misstatement, TM = tolerable misstatement, ULM = upper limit on misstatements).

		Decision Based on True State of the Population	
		AM ≤ TM (conclude account is fairly stated)	AM > TM (conclude account is misstated)
Decision Based on Examining Sample	ULM ≤ TM (conclude account is fairly stated)	A: Correct decision	B: Risk of incorrect acceptance
	ULM > TM (conclude account is misstated)	C: Risk of incorrect rejection	D: Correct decision

Cells A and D do not represent sampling risk because the decision to conclude either that the account balance is fairly stated (cell A) or that the account balance is misstated (cell D) is consistent with the decision auditors would have made had the entire population been examined.

Examine the outcome of cell C. In this instance, the sample of transactions and components indicates that the misstatement might exceed the tolerable misstatement. As a result, auditors would conclude that the account is misstated. However, the amount of misstatement in the population is actually less than the tolerable misstatement, suggesting that the account balance is fairly stated. This is referred to as the **risk of incorrect rejection** because auditors' initial judgment is to *incorrectly reject* the account balance as fairly stated.

In contrast, cell B represents a situation in which auditors conclude that the account balance is fairly stated (because the upper limit on misstatements is less than or equal to the tolerable misstatement); however, in the population, the actual misstatement exceeds the tolerable misstatement. As a result, auditors inappropriately conclude that the account balance is fairly stated. This is referred to as the **risk of incorrect acceptance** because the auditors' judgment is to *incorrectly accept* the account balance.

Which of these risks is of more concern to auditors? If the auditors commit the risk of incorrect rejection and initially conclude that the account balance is misstated, the client typically requests that the auditors expand the sample size or gather additional evidence before making an adjustment to the financial statements. As this occurs and as the sample becomes more representative of the population, the auditors ultimately reach the correct conclusion. What is the cost to them? They were required to perform additional substantive procedures beyond those performed to control detection risk to acceptable levels. Thus, the incorrect rejection causes an *efficiency loss* for the auditors.

If the auditors commit the risk of incorrect acceptance and conclude that the account is not misstated, they most likely do not perform additional procedures or examine additional items related to that account balance or class of transactions. As a result, the auditors conclude that the account balance is fairly stated when, in fact, it is materially misstated. This is the basic definition of *detection risk*. The ultimate result of failing to propose an adjustment to materially misstated financial statements is issuing an unmodified opinion on financial statements that are materially misstated, resulting in a reputation loss or litigation by shareholders and other third parties relying on the auditors' work. This results in an *effectiveness loss* for the auditors because they made an incorrect conclusion with respect to the client's account balance.

This discussion should make clear that the risk of incorrect acceptance is of more concern to auditors than the risk of incorrect rejection. As with the risk of overreliance in attributes sampling, auditors explicitly control their exposure to the risk of incorrect acceptance when determining the necessary sample size and when evaluating sample results.

Summary: Sampling Risks for Audit Sampling

Exhibit E.3 summarizes the sampling risks associated with attributes and variables sampling. Note that both types of sampling have risks that expose auditors to effectiveness and efficiency losses. Although any form of sampling risk is not desirable, auditors are particularly concerned with sampling risks that expose them to effectiveness losses.

EXHIBIT E.3   Sampling Risks When Using Sampling in the Audit Examination

Type of Sampling	Risk	Type of Loss
Attributes	Risk of overreliance (assessing control risk too low)	Effectiveness (auditors could face litigation if misstatements are not detected)
	Risk of underreliance (assessing control risk too high)	Efficiency (auditors perform unnecessary procedures)
Variables	Risk of incorrect acceptance	Effectiveness (auditors could face litigation if misstatements are not detected)
	Risk of incorrect rejection	Efficiency (auditors perform unnecessary procedures)

✅ REVIEW CHECKPOINTS

E.18 Define *variables sampling*. When is it used in the audit examination?

E.19 What is *tolerable misstatement*? How do auditors use it when deciding whether account balances are fairly recorded?

E.20 What are the two sampling risks associated with variables sampling? What types of losses are associated with these risks?

E.21 Why are auditors more concerned with the risk of incorrect acceptance than the risk of incorrect rejection?

AN OVERVIEW OF AUDIT SAMPLING

LO E-4
Understand how the basic steps and procedures used in a sampling plan apply to an audit.

This subsection provides a brief overview of how this seven-step procedure is applied to sampling in an audit setting. Modules F and G apply this procedure using a comprehensive example for attributes and variables sampling, respectively.

Planning (Steps 1–3)

In the planning stages, auditors determine the objective of the sampling application and define the characteristic of interest and the population.

The populations are as follows:

- *Attributes sampling.* All possible applications of controls by client personnel.
- *Variables sampling.* All components or transactions comprising the account balance or class of transactions.

Auditors often perform **dual-purpose tests** by examining documents for both attributes and monetary misstatements. For example, an invoice might be examined for the attribute of a credit authorization signature (control test) and the monetary misstatement of an incorrect price (substantive test).

Performing

Determine the Sample Size (Step 4)

In either type of sampling application, four key factors affect the auditors' determination of sample size: (1) the population size, (2) the expected population deviation rate (or expected misstatement), (3) the tolerable rate of deviation (or tolerable misstatement), and (4) the auditors' acceptable exposure to sampling risk. In addition, for certain types of variables sampling applications, the population variability affects the sample size. The effect of these factors on sample size is summarized in Exhibit E.4. At this point, you should attempt to *conceptually* understand how these factors affect sample size and not become overly concerned with how the auditors assess them. The method of assessing these factors is discussed in more detail in Modules F and G.

As the size of the population increases, a larger sample is typically necessary to support conclusions based on that population. This relationship is fairly logical; a sample of 50 items drawn from a population of 100 items is more likely to be representative than the same sample of 50 drawn from a population of 100,000 items. Therefore, we can state that population size has a *direct relationship* with sample size. That is, as the population size increases, the sample size increases (and vice versa).[9]

As the expected population deviation rate or expected misstatement increases, the sample needs to be larger. Again, this relationship seems logical because higher rates of deviation (or higher levels of dollar misstatement) represent potential problems to the auditors, signaling the need for a larger sample size. As a result, like population size, expected population deviation rate or expected misstatements have a *direct relationship* with sample size.

As the tolerable rate of deviation (or tolerable misstatement) decreases, the sample needs to be increased. This larger sample size results from the fact that auditors are requiring the client's (1) controls to operate extremely effectively (small tolerable rate of deviation) or (2) account balance to be very accurately stated (small tolerable misstatement), and auditors need to examine a larger proportion of the population to ensure that they detect smaller rates of deviation or misstatements. In this case, the tolerable rate of deviation or tolerable misstatement has an *inverse relationship* with sample size. That is, as the tolerable rate of deviation (or tolerable misstatement) decreases, sample size increases (and vice versa).

Sampling risk represents the likelihood that the auditors' decision based on the sample differs from the decision that would be made based on the population. Recall that sampling risk results from a nonrepresentative sample. To increase the representativeness of the sample and reduce sampling risk, the audit team should increase the size of the sample (e.g., a sample of 100 percent would provide a zero sampling risk). Therefore, like the tolerable rate of deviation (or tolerable misstatement), sampling risk has an *inverse relationship* with sample size.

The variability of a population reflects differences between the value of individual items within the population and the mean of those items. Population variability is often measured as the **standard deviation** (or **standard error of the mean**). Clearly, as the components of a population differ more (i.e., have a higher level of variability), the audit team needs to examine a larger number of items to obtain a representative sample. As a result, population variability has a *direct relationship* with sample size.

EXHIBIT E.4
Factors Affecting Sample Size

Factor	Effect on Sample Size
Population size	*Direct* (as population size increases, sample size increases)
Expected population deviation rate (expected misstatement)	*Direct* (as expected population deviation rate or expected misstatement increases, sample size increases)
Tolerable rate of deviation (tolerable misstatement)	*Inverse* (as tolerable rate of deviation or tolerable misstatement decreases, sample size increases)
Sampling risk	*Inverse* (as acceptable sampling risk decreases, sample size increases)
Population variability	*Direct* (as variability increases, sample size increases)

[9] However, once a population size reaches a certain level, additional increases in population size do not have significant effects on sample size. This relationship is illustrated more completely in Module F.

Exhibit E.4 summarizes how the factors just discussed are related to sample size. The method of determining these factors, as well as calculations of sample size using these factors, is presented in subsequent modules.

Select Sample Items (Step 5)

Once the sample size has been determined, the auditors select the sample. The items selected are either potential applications of important controls (attributes sampling) or components or transactions of an account balance or class of transactions (variables sampling).

As noted previously, both *unrestricted random selection* and *systematic random selection* are appropriate to use with statistical sampling because all items in the population have an equal probability of selection, and these methods allow another individual to replicate the sample selection process. In contrast, *block selection* and *haphazard selection* do not meet these criteria and are not used with statistical sampling.

Measure Sample Items (Step 6)

After the sample items have been selected, auditors perform the appropriate audit procedures and measure each item. For attributes sampling, auditors perform tests of controls to evaluate whether client personnel have performed the control policy of interest. For variables sampling, auditors perform substantive procedures to determine the correct amount (audited value) of each component or transaction selected for examination.

Evaluate Sample Results (Step 7)

The final step in either attributes or variables sampling is to evaluate the sample results, which involves the following four-step procedure:

1. Identify either the rate of deviation (attributes sampling) or the difference between audited values and recorded balances (variables sampling) from the sample items.
2. Adjust the information in step 1 to control the auditors' exposure to sampling risk. This adjustment is referred to as the *allowance for sampling risk.*
3. Compare the adjusted estimate in step 2 to either the tolerable rate of deviation (attributes sampling) or the tolerable misstatement (variables sampling).
4. Based on the comparison in step 3, make the decision with regard to the effectiveness of the client's internal control (attributes sampling) or fairness of the account balance (variables sampling).

Documenting the Sampling Procedure

As they perform the procedures in each of these steps, auditors should document important judgments, assumptions, and conclusions because this documentation will provide evidence with respect to the operating effectiveness of the client's internal control and the fairness of the client's account balances. Documentation should be sufficient to enable another audit team to replicate the tests and for a reviewer to evaluate the results.

Example of Audit Sampling

Assume the audit team is evaluating an internal control that requires all purchases to be supported by an authorized purchase order. This is an attributes sampling application because it involves evaluating the presence or absence of a characteristic of interest in a population. The following is a very brief step-by-step illustration of how sampling would be applied in this context. (More detailed examples of attributes sampling and variables sampling are shown in Modules F and G, respectively.)

Step 1: The objective is to determine whether purchases are supported by an authorized purchase order.

Step 2: The characteristic of interest is the existence of an authorized purchase order.

Step 3: The population of interest is all receiving reports or other documentation related to a purchase.

Step 4: Based on a *population size* of 20,000 purchases, *expected population deviation rate* of 1 percent, *tolerable rate of deviation* of 4 percent, and *risk of overreliance* of 5 percent, a sample size of 156 is determined. (It is not important at this point that you know how this sample size was determined; this will be illustrated in greater detail in Module F.)

Step 5: A sample of 156 receiving reports (representing *bona fide* purchases) was selected using systematic random selection techniques.

Step 6: Based on tests of controls, the audit team identified one deviation (situations in which a receiving report was not supported by an authorized purchase order).

Step 7: Based on the one deviation in the sample of 156 receiving reports, the audit team determines an "adjusted" deviation rate of 3.2 percent. (It is not important at this point that you know how this adjusted rate was determined; this will be illustrated in greater detail in Module F.) Because the adjusted deviation rate is less than the tolerable rate of deviation of 4 percent, the audit team would conclude that the control is functioning effectively.

✓ REVIEW CHECKPOINTS

E.22 What are the objectives of attributes and variables sampling?

E.23 What factors affect the sample size used in an attributes sampling application? How do these factors affect sample size?

E.24 What factors affect the sample size used in a variables sampling application? How do these factors affect sample size?

Summary

This module introduces the sampling process and discusses how sampling is used in an audit. One of the major disadvantages of sampling is that the decision made based on the sample could differ from the decision that would have been made after examining the entire population. This disadvantage (referred to as *sampling risk*) can be overcome to some extent through the use of statistical sampling methods. Statistical sampling methods control the individual's exposure to sampling risk by selecting a sufficient sample size and evaluating sample results in such a way to control sampling risk.

Two major approaches to sampling used in an audit examination are *attributes sampling* (in the study and evaluation of internal control) and *variables sampling* (in the auditors' substantive procedures). This module discussed the risks associated with these sampling approaches and the various factors that influence the sample size. Attributes sampling and variables sampling are discussed in more detail in Modules F and G, respectively.

Key Terms

allowance for sampling risk (precision): The numeric distance from the estimated population value in which the true (but unknown) population value may lie with a given probability; used to adjust the sample estimate to control exposure to sampling risk.

attributes sampling: A form of sampling used to determine the extent to which some characteristic (attribute) exists within a population of interest; used by the audit team during tests of controls.

audit sampling: The application of an audit procedure to less than 100 percent of the items within an account balance or class of transactions for the purpose of evaluating some characteristic of the balance or class.

block selection: A method of choosing sample items in which a series of contiguous (or adjacent) items is chosen from the population.

confidence level (reliability): The likelihood that the true population value lies within the precision interval.

control risk: The likelihood that the client's internal control policies and procedures fail to prevent or detect a material misstatement.

detection risk: The likelihood that the auditors' substantive procedures will fail to detect a material misstatement that exists within an account balance or class of transactions.

dual-purpose test: An audit procedure used as both a test of controls and a substantive test.

haphazard selection: The method of choosing sample items in an unstructured manner but without intentional bias.

nonrepresentative sample: A sample that differs substantially from the population on one or more key characteristics of interest from which it is drawn.

nonsampling risk: The likelihood that an incorrect conclusion will be reached because of reasons unrelated to sampling.

nonstatistical sampling: A plan that does not apply the laws of probability to select representative items for examination and evaluate the results; does not allow an individual to control exposure to sampling risk.

population: The entire group of items about which a conclusion is desired in a sampling application.

precision: See *allowance for sampling risk.*

precision interval: The range around the sample estimate that has a likelihood equal to reliability of including the true population value.

random selection: See *unrestricted random selection.*

reliability: See *confidence level.*

risk of assessing control risk too high: See *risk of underreliance.*

risk of assessing control risk too low: See *risk of overreliance.*

risk of incorrect acceptance: The likelihood that the audit team will conclude that the client's account balance is fairly stated when it is materially misstated.

risk of incorrect rejection: The likelihood that the audit team will conclude that the client's account balance is materially misstated when it is fairly stated.

risk of overreliance (risk of assessing control risk too low): The likelihood that the audit team will conclude that the client's controls are functioning effectively when they are not functioning effectively.

risk of underreliance (risk of assessing control risk too high): The likelihood that the audit team will conclude that the client's controls are not functioning effectively when they are functioning effectively.

sample: A subset of items drawn from a population of interest.

sample estimate of misstatement: The difference between the recorded account balance and the audited account balance.

sample rate of deviation: The extent of variations found in the audit team's sample; determined by dividing the number of deviations by the sample size.

sampling: The process of making a statement about a population of interest based on examining only a subset (or sample) of that population.

sampling interval: An interval determined by dividing the recorded amount of the population (account balance) by the sample size.

sampling risk: The likelihood that the decision made based on the sample will differ from the decision that would have been made if the entire population had been examined.

standard deviation (standard error of the mean): A measure of the variability of the population.

standard error of the mean: See *standard deviation.*

statistical sampling: A plan that applies the laws of probability to select items for examination and evaluates the results; allows an individual to control the exposure to sampling risk.

systematic random selection (systematic selection): The method of selecting sample items in which a starting point is determined and a fixed number of items are bypassed between selections.

systematic selection: See *systematic random selection.*

tolerable misstatement: The maximum amount by which the account balance or class of transactions can be misstated without the audit team concluding that the account balance or class of transactions is materially misstated.

tolerable rate of deviation: The maximum rate of deviation permissible by the audit team without modifying the planned assessed level of control risk.

unrestricted random selection (random selection): A method of selecting items in which all items in the population are assigned a number and chosen based on random numbers.

upper limit on misstatements (ULM): A measure that adjusts the sample estimate of misstatement for the audit team's acceptable level of sampling risk.

upper limit rate of deviation (ULRD): A measure that adjusts the sample rate of deviation for the audit team's acceptable level of sampling risk.

variables sampling: A form of sampling used to examine a population to estimate the amount or value of some characteristic of that population; used by auditors during their substantive procedures.

Multiple-Choice Questions for Practice and Review

All applicable Exercises and Problems are available with *Connect*.

LO E-4

E.25 In an audit sampling application, an auditor
   a. Performs procedures on all items in a balance and makes a conclusion about the entire balance.
   b. Performs procedures on less than 100 percent of the items in a balance and formulates a conclusion about the entire balance.
   c. Performs procedures on less than 100 percent of the items in a class of transactions to become familiar with the client's accounting system.
   d. Performs analytical procedures on the client's unaudited financial statements when planning the audit.

LO E-1

E.26 Auditors consider statistical sampling to be characterized by the following:
   a. Representative sample selection and nonmathematical evaluation of the results.
   b. Carefully biased sample selection and mathematical evaluation of the results.
   c. Representative sample selection and mathematical evaluation of the results.
   d. Carefully biased sample selection and nonmathematical evaluation of the results.

LO E-1

E.27 In which of the following scenarios would the use of sampling be most appropriate?
   a. The population consists of a relatively small number of items.
   b. The need for precise information about the population is not important.
   c. The decision to be made is relatively critical.
   d. The costs associated with an incorrect decision are extremely high.

LO E-1

E.28 The risk that the decision made based on the sample will differ from the decision made based on the entire population is referred to as
   a. Audit risk.
   b. Examination risk.
   c. Sampling risk.
   d. Nonsampling risk.

LO E-1

E.29 Which of the following is *not* a method that auditors use to control their exposure to sampling risk during the examination?
   a. Determining an appropriate sample size.
   b. Performing the appropriate audit procedure.
   c. Ensuring that all items have an equal opportunity to be selected.
   d. Evaluating sample results using a mathematical basis.

LO E-1

E.30 Which of the following is an advantage of nonstatistical sampling?
   a. It measures the audit team's exposure to sampling risk.
   b. It is required by generally accepted auditing standards.
   c. It ensures that samples are randomly selected.
   d. It is typically less complex than statistical sampling.

LO E-1

E.31 Selecting a sample using a series of random numbers to identify sample items is referred to as
  a. Block selection.
  b. Haphazard selection.
  c. Systematic random selection.
  d. Unrestricted random selection.

LO E-2

E.32 If systematic selection is used with a starting point of 10, a population size of 100, and a necessary sample size of 20, the first three items selected for examination would be
  a. 10, 110, 210.
  b. 110, 210, 310.
  c. 10, 15, 20.
  d. 15, 20, 25.

LO E-1

E.33 A limitation of systematic random selection is that this method
  a. Has a relatively low likelihood of yielding a representative sample.
  b. Results in a larger sample size than other selection methods.
  c. Can result in bypassing a number of items having similar characteristics.
  d. Cannot be used with statistical sampling plans.

LO E-1

E.34 Which of the following is appropriately used for statistical sampling applications?

	Unrestricted Random Selection	Block Selection
a.	Yes	Yes
b.	Yes	No
c.	No	Yes
d.	No	No

LO E-1

E.35 Which of the following pairs of selection methods could appropriately be used in statistical sampling applications?
  a. Unrestricted random selection, block selection.
  b. Block selection, haphazard selection.
  c. Systematic random selection, haphazard selection.
  d. Unrestricted random selection, systematic random selection.

LO E-1

E.36 The distance from the sample estimate that has a certain likelihood (equal to reliability) of including the true population value is known as the
  a. Confidence.
  b. Mean.
  c. Precision.
  d. Precision interval.

LO E-1

E.37 The likelihood that an identified precision interval contains the true (but unknown) population value is the
  a. Confidence.
  b. Mean.
  c. Precision.
  d. Sampling risk.

LO E-1

E.38 Which of the following statements is *not* true if the precision interval for a sampling risk of 10 percent ranges from 60 to 70?
  a. A 10 percent probability exists that the true population value is less than 60 or more than 70.
  b. A 90 percent probability exists that the true population value is less than 60 or more than 70.
  c. The reliability is 90 percent.
  d. The precision is 5.

LO E-2

E.39 In audit sampling applications, sampling risk is
   a. A characteristic of statistical sampling applications but not of nonstatistical applications.
   b. The probability that the audit team will fail to recognize erroneous accounting in the client's documentation.
   c. The probability that accounting misstatements will arise in transactions and enter the accounting system.
   d. The probability that an audit team's conclusion based on a sample might be different from the conclusion based on an audit of the entire population.

LO E-3

E.40 The risks of incorrect acceptance in variables sampling and of overreliance in attributes sampling both relate to
   a. Effectiveness of an audit.
   b. Efficiency of an audit.
   c. Control risk assessment decisions.
   d. Evidence about assertions in financial statements.

LO E-3

E.41 The type of sampling most frequently used by auditors during their study of internal control is referred to as
   a. Attributes sampling.
   b. Control sampling.
   c. Monetary unit sampling.
   d. Variables sampling.

LO E-3

E.42 Which of the following components of the audit risk model is most closely associated with attributes sampling?
   a. Audit risk.
   b. Control risk.
   c. Detection risk.
   d. Inherent risk.

LO E-3

E.43 The audit team will choose to reduce the reliance on controls if the _____ is greater than the _____
   a. Tolerable rate of deviation; upper limit rate of deviation.
   b. Upper limit rate of deviation; tolerable rate of deviation.
   c. Expected population deviation rate; tolerable rate of deviation.
   d. Tolerable rate of deviation; expected population deviation rate.

LO E-1

E.44 An advantage of statistical sampling over nonstatistical sampling methods is that statistical methods
   a. Afford more assurance than a nonstatistical sample of equal size.
   b. Provide an objective basis for quantitatively evaluating sampling risk.
   c. Can more easily convert the sample into a dual-purpose test useful for substantive procedures.
   d. Eliminate the need to use judgment in determining appropriate sample sizes.

(AICPA adapted)

LO E-3

E.45 When using sampling in the study of internal control, the audit team would compare the upper limit rate of deviation to the
   a. Expected population deviation rate.
   b. Sample rate of deviation.
   c. Statistical rate of deviation.
   d. Tolerable rate of deviation.

LO E-1

E.46 Which of the following would *not* result in exposure to nonsampling risk?
   a. Measuring the characteristic of interest in an inappropriate manner.
   b. Selecting items that are not representative of the population of interest.
   c. Making an unintentional mistake in measuring the characteristic of interest.
   d. All of the above would result in exposure to nonsampling risk.

LO E-1

E.47 Which of the following statements is *not* true with respect to nonstatistical sampling?

    a. It cannot be used in an audit conducted in accordance with generally accepted auditing standards.

    b. It considers a number of factors in determining the appropriate sample size.

    c. When using it, an individual makes some estimate of the characteristic of interest.

    d. It requires the use of judgment on the part of the individual performing the sampling application.

LO E-2

E.48 In a sampling application to determine the average weight of students enrolled in a fitness class, if the sample estimate is 120 pounds, the precision is 10 pounds, and the reliability is 90 percent, which of the following statements is true?

    a. There is 10 percent likelihood that the average weight of a student in the class is more than 130 pounds.

    b. There is 10 percent likelihood that the average weight of a student in the class is less than 110 pounds.

    c. There is 90 percent likelihood that the average weight of a student in the class is less than 110 pounds or more than 130 pounds.

    d. There is a 90 percent likelihood that the average weight of a student in the class is between 110 and 130 pounds.

LO E-2

E.49 Which of the following steps would normally be performed last in a sampling application?

    a. Examine sample items and determine the sample estimate.

    b. Determine the level of reliability for the sampling application.

    c. Identify the objective of the sampling application.

    d. Determine the appropriate sample size.

LO E-3

E.50 The risk of incorrect rejection and the risk of underreliance relate to the

    a. Effectiveness of the audit.

    b. Efficiency of the audit.

    c. Preliminary estimates of performance materiality.

    d. Tolerable misstatement.

(AICPA adapted)

Exercises and Problems

connect   All applicable Exercises and Problems are available with *Connect.*

LO E-1

E.51 **Sampling Risk.** You and a friend are deciding whether to pack heavy clothing for a trip to the northeastern United States. You have decided that you would need heavy clothing only if the temperature is expected to fall below 50 degrees during your trip. You have studied the past 50 years' seasonal temperatures in the northeast. You are considering the use of sampling to calculate an expected average temperature; you will base your decision to pack heavy clothing on the results of your sample.

Required:

    a. What is *sampling risk*? What two types of sampling risks are present in this context?

    b. Describe the "costs" associated with the sampling risks in part (a).

    c. How would your sampling plan differ if you used statistical sampling versus nonstatistical sampling?

    d. What are the advantages and disadvantages of using statistical sampling methods in an attempt to answer your question?

LO E-1

E.52 **Sampling and Nonsampling Risk.** This module provided a detailed example of the use of sampling to determine whether individuals could reduce their resting heart rates through an aerobic exercise program.

Required:

Indicate whether each of the following situations reflects sampling risk (S), nonsampling risk (NS), both sampling risk and nonsampling risk (B), or neither sampling risk nor nonsampling risk (N).

a. The scale on the instrument used to measure heart rates is malfunctioning.

b. At one location, you selected only members who participated in a more rigorous aerobics program.

c. At one location, your assistant inadvertently recorded measures immediately after the conclusion of an aerobics activity rather than after a five-minute rest period, as done in other locations.

d. Attendance is not monitored at all of the exercise sessions.

e. Your assistant makes an error in recording a number of measures.

f. Your sample is comprised of a disproportionate number of club members over the age of 65.

LO E-1

E.53 **Sampling and Nonsampling Risk.** Read the following five independent sampling applications.

Required:

Indicate whether each situation is characteristic of sampling risk (S) or nonsampling risk (N). Provide a brief explanation for your answer.

a. You are estimating the average net income of passengers on a particular airline flight. You randomly select three rows of seats (a total of 18 passengers) and calculate the average income of those passengers.

b. When estimating the average time for swimmers in a 25-meter freestyle race, you inadvertently include the times of swimmers from other events (butterfly, breaststroke, and backstroke) in your sample.

c. When estimating the average time necessary to finish an examination, the class of students you randomly selected was an honors section of the course.

d. When estimating the percentage of sixth-grade students who plan to attend college, your sample includes a disproportionate number of students attending intermediate schools located in small college towns (many of the parents are affiliated with the local university).

e. When estimating the total amount of money held in savings accounts by people of various nationalities, you make some inadvertent mistakes in converting various currencies into U.S. dollars.

LO E-1

E.54 **Basic Sampling.** You are attempting to determine whether you are taller or shorter than the average of students currently enrolled in your university. You have just learned about sampling and have decided to sample students to determine the average height at your university.

Required:

a. Define *sampling*.

b. What are the advantages and disadvantages of using sampling to answer this question as opposed to examining the entire population?

c. In which situations would you be more likely to use sampling (applied to this particular example) as opposed to examining the entire population?

LO E-1, E-2

E.55 **Basic Sampling.** You are evaluating the feasibility of opening a new 10-screen movie theater in a town that has only one existing theater. To be viable, the proposed theater would need an average attendance of at least 15,000 patrons per month. The theater would show movies every day; each of the 10 screens would have a capacity of 120 patrons. An average month has the following characteristics with respect to potential patrons:

• Weekdays: 21 days with a total of 20 shows per day (2 show times × 10 screens)
• Weekends: 9 days with a total of 40 shows per day (4 show times × 10 screens)
• Because the current theater maintains no records, you must physically visit the theater and count patrons.

Required:

a. What are some possible methods you can use to estimate the number of patrons on the evenings you visit?

b. What are some precautions that you should consider to ensure a representative sample?

c. What are two possible types of sampling risk that are present in this context? Which of these risks is of more concern to you?

    d. Assume that your sampling procedure was employed to provide you 95 percent confidence. How would you react to the following independent outcomes? (Each sample estimate and precision represents an estimate of the number of patrons per day?)

       1. Sample estimate of 600 patrons, precision of 30 patrons.

       2. Sample estimate of 680 patrons, precision of 150 patrons.

       3. Sample estimate of 490 patrons, precision of 35 patrons.

LO E-1

E.56 **Basic Sampling.** You are employed by Northeast Airlines and have been asked to determine the rate of on-time arrivals for competing airlines at a proposed hub location. Northeast is known for its outstanding customer service and constantly ranks in the top three among all airlines in on-time arrivals with an average rate of 82 percent of all flights.

Because it would be a new entrant in this particular airport, Northeast does not believe it can compete unless its on-time arrival rate can surpass that of the airlines currently serving this hub. Because each of the four major competitors has hundreds of flights arriving at the hub on a daily basis, you are considering the use of sampling to estimate an on-time arrival rate.

Required:

    a. Define *sampling*. What are the primary advantages and primary disadvantages of using sampling in this application?

    b. Briefly describe how you would identify the population of flights from which you intend to sample.

    c. Define *sampling risk* and *nonsampling risk*. Provide an example of how each could be present in this situation.

    d. List some characteristics of various flights that could give you increased exposure to sampling risk in this application.

    e. Once you have estimated an on-time arrival rate for its competitors, what information can you provide to Northeast Airlines to assist it in its decision process?

LO E-2

E.57 **Sample Evaluation.** In the most recent local election between two candidates, you heard your local news anchor indicate that your preferred candidate had 48 percent of the vote with a margin for error (precision) of $\pm$ 6 percent. The news anchor also indicated a reliability of 99 percent for these results.

Required:

    a. Define the terms *sample estimate, precision,* and *reliability.*

    b. Based on the information given, what is the possible range of support that your preferred candidate could have when all votes are counted?

    c. Provide a brief summary (one sentence) describing what you can determine from the anchor's report.

    d. How do you feel about your candidate's chances of winning the election?

    e. How would you feel about your candidate's chances of winning if the anchor's report was identical except that the margin for error was only $\pm$ 1 percent?

LO E-2

E.58 **Sample Evaluation.** For each of the following independent cases, identify the missing value(s).

	1	2	3
Precision	20	(C)	10
Sample estimate	56	80	(E)
Reliability	95%	(D)	98%
Precision interval	(A)	75 to 85	111 to 131
Sampling risk	(B)	10%	(F)

LO E-2

E.59 **Sample Evaluation.** The National Football League (NFL) is interested in determining whether the average age of its fan base is less than 35 years of age to identify this demographic for potential advertisers. Following are the results for three different stadiums for fans attending an NFL game on a given weekend. In all cases, assume a sampling risk of 5 percent.

	Sample 1	Sample 2	Sample 3
Precision	5	3	8
Sample estimate	26	34	40

Required:

a. Construct a precision interval for each of these samples.

b. Given the sampling risk of 5 percent, provide a single-sentence summary of the results to the NFL for each sample.

c. What is your basic conclusion regarding each sample?

d. If the NFL increased its acceptable level of sampling risk, how would that affect the precision interval and your conclusions? If it decreased the acceptable level of sampling risk, how would that affect the precision interval and your conclusions? Why?

LO E-2

E.60 Sample Evaluation. Gloria Bush has performed a sampling plan to estimate the number of children per household in her neighborhood. In doing so, she established a 10 percent acceptable level of sampling risk and found a sample estimate of 2.5 children per household. Based on the acceptable level of sampling risk, she calculated a precision of 0.7 children per household.

Required:

a. Define the terms *precision* and *reliability*. How are these terms related?

b. What is the precision interval in this example? What statement can Bush make based on her sample evidence?

c. Assume that she desires a lower sampling risk (5 percent). How will this affect the precision interval?

d. If she is interested in knowing whether the number of children per household exceeds 1.5 children, how would you advise her based on the following outcomes? In all cases, assume that the sample estimate is 2.5 children per household.

1. Reliability = 90 percent; precision = 0.7 children per household.
2. Reliability = 95 percent; precision = 1.4 children per household.
3. Reliability = 99 percent; precision = 1.8 children per household.

e. What causes the differences in the relationships noted in part (d)?

LO E-2

E.61 Sample Evaluation. Your political consulting group, Electem Inc., is assisting a local political candidate, Alice Evans, to determine the likelihood of her election to office during the upcoming campaign. She would like to have an extremely high level of confidence (95 percent) that she would receive more than a majority of the ballots cast.

After conducting an extensive survey, you have determined that 53 percent of voters would prefer Evans with a precision of 5 percent and a corresponding reliability of 95 percent. In determining this information, your notes of the sampling process revealed the following information:

1. The district that she would represent is composed of eight neighborhoods. You randomly chose four of these neighborhoods and, within each, had workers poll voters (using a door-to-door technique) from the first 25 households that responded.

2. Your workers canvassed the neighborhoods during the day from 12 P.M. to 3 P.M.

3. Your workers asked voters to respond to the following question: "Do you support Alice Evans during the upcoming election?"

4. In one neighborhood (a community with restricted access to nonresidents), your workers could not obtain a sample of 25 voters using a door-to-door polling technique. As a result, they used a telephone survey to obtain the 25 responses for this neighborhood.

5. Some of your workers observed that, at homes indicating they would support Evans for office, campaign signs for her chief rival were present. The workers were surprised that these same households indicated they would support Evans.

6. George Clinton, one of your workers, indicated that he misunderstood the survey instructions, which indicated that a voter could indicate "yes," "no," or "undecided." George

thought that he was required to obtain a "yes" or "no" answer; when voters indicated they were undecided, he pressed them to make a decision (which they ultimately did).

7. Billy Bush, another worker, did not verify the names of the individuals to whom he was speaking.

Required:

a. Based on the sample results, without considering any of the information included in items (1) through (7), what would you advise Evans about her electability?

b. How would your advice to her change if she established the following levels of reliability? (Assume that the sample estimate of 53 percent is unchanged?)
   1. Reliability = 99 percent, precision = 8 percent.
   2. Reliability = 90 percent, precision = 2 percent.

c. Summarize why your advice to Evans would change based on the reliability and precision noted in part (b).

d. For each of the issues included in your sampling notes, indicate how that issue could affect the advice you provide to Evans and her ability to rely on the sample evidence.

LO E-2

E.62 **Sample Evaluation.** Marts Inc., a local fund-raising organization, is considering the feasibility of a fund-raising campaign to assist a youth organization in building a new recreation center in College Bryan, Texas. Marts has been asked to determine whether this campaign would be successful in raising $1.5 million, the amount needed to construct and equip the center.

Because unsuccessful fund-raising efforts have a negative impact on Marts' ability to obtain future clients and engagements, it has established a reliability of 99 percent; that is, Marts wants to have a very high level of confidence that the $1.5 million can be successfully raised in the local community. Because a total of 50,000 citizens live in the College Bryan area, the average gift necessary to ensure a successful campaign is $30 per person ($1,500,000 ÷ 50,000). Based on the sampling risk associated with 99 percent reliability, Marts determined a sample size of 200 and surveyed each of these individuals with respect to their willingness to donate to the fund-raising campaign. The average level of support indicated by these 200 persons was $35 per person.

Required:

a. Based on Marts's sample, calculate the sample estimate for the total amount that could be raised under this fund-raising effort.

b. Based only on the sample estimate, how would you advise Marts as to the potential success of its fund-raising campaign?

c. What is the primary limitation to Marts in making its decision based only on the sample estimate?

d. What is sampling risk? What types of factors could influence Marts's exposure to sampling risk in this particular situation?

e. Using the sample estimate calculated in part (a), determine the precision interval if the calculated precision were
   1. $100,000.
   2. $200,000.
   3. $300,000.

f. How would you advise Marts regarding the potential success of the fund-raising campaign based on the precision intervals calculated in part (e)?

g. Assume that Marts believes that 99 percent reliability is too stringent and is considering lowering the reliability to 95 percent. How will this change affect the precision interval and the likelihood that Marts will conclude that the fund-raising campaign will ultimately be successful?

LO E-1, E-2

E.63 **Basic Sampling: Comprehensive.** Reagan Russell is considering opening a multipurpose hardware and lawn store in Anytown, USA. Based on his knowledge of the industry, he believes that if the average household income is more than $35,000, the store will ultimately be successful. He was planning to attempt a census of the income levels in Anytown but has heard about sampling and is now considering using sampling to obtain the necessary information to make his decision.

Required:

a. What would you tell Russell about the advantages and disadvantages of sampling?

b. Russell is interested in knowing the advantages and disadvantages of statistical sampling. What would you tell him?

c. Russell has heard about sampling and nonsampling risk and is concerned about them.

1. Define *sampling risk* and *nonsampling risk*.

2. How can Russell control his exposure to sampling and nonsampling risk?

3. What are some possible examples of sampling and nonsampling risk in this situation?

d. Assume that Russell decided to use unrestricted random selection to obtain a sample of households for examination. If he determined a sample size of 100 households, describe how he could select the sample from the city's property tax rolls.

e. Instead of unrestricted random selection, Russell asked you whether he could just pick four or five streets and examine all of the households on those streets. What would you tell him?

f. Assume that Russell has set a sampling risk of 10 percent and found a sample estimate of $39,000 with a precision of $3,000. How would you explain the results to Russell? What advice would you give him?

g. Repeat part (f) assuming that Russell found a sample estimate of $42,000 and a precision of $10,000.

LO E-2

E.64 Sample Selection. Arianna Casey is trying to select a sample of registered voters in Hoops County to see how they intend to vote on funding a stadium for the local professional basketball team. She has determined that a sample of 1,000 voters will be necessary to provide an acceptable minimum level of sampling risk (15 percent). The state has more than 3 million registered voters who are listed (sorted by zip code) in an electronic data file maintained in the state commissioner's office. The commissioner has agreed to allow Casey to have access to this data file for her project.

Required:

a. What is sampling risk? What steps can Casey take to control her exposure to sampling risk?

b. How would she define the population in this case?

c. What are some potential methods of selecting the sample (as specifically applied to this application)?

d. What precautions should Casey take to ensure that she selects a representative sample?

LO E-2

E.65 Sample Selection Methods. You are employed by FishWrap Ltd., a local newspaper distribution company, and are attempting to determine the average level of customer satisfaction with the newspaper's delivery service. All customers are included in a comprehensive database that includes the following information: customer name, delivery address, telephone number, type of service (weekly only, weekend only, weekly/weekend), length of service (how long they have subscribed to the newspaper), and name of carrier.

Because the local area has 10,500 subscribers, FishWrap has decided to sample its customers instead of surveying the entire population. Based on a number of factors (including precision and reliability), FishWrap has determined that a sample of 150 customers is necessary.

Required:

a. In this application, what are some of the major characteristics of subscribers that should be considered to ensure that a representative sample is selected?

b. Identify and briefly define four major methods used to select a sample.

c. How could you select a sample from the population using each of these methods?

d. The information in each list is arranged in descending order based on length of service. Indicate how each of the following factors could impact your ability to use the four methods of selecting a sample from a population:

1. The database is a typed list of information.

2. The database is an electronic list of information and cannot be sorted on any characteristic.

3. The database is an electronic list of information and can be sorted on any characteristic.

e. How does each of the following factors impact your ability to evaluate whether you have selected a representative sample from the population?

1. The delivery address does not include zip code or another reasonable way of identifying physical location within the subscription area.

2. The length of service is classified as follows: less than six months, six months to one year, more than one year.

3. If customers have relocated within the subscription area, their length of service has been reset to zero even when they continued their subscriptions.

LO E-1

E.66 **Sampling and Nonsampling Risk.** Arthur Castle is interested in identifying the average number of family members living in each household in his neighborhood. He has heard about sampling and thinks that it could help him identify this information. In considering the application of sampling to this particular situation, he considers the following characteristics of his neighborhood:

a. Many of his neighbors are dual-income career couples and are away from home in the mornings and afternoons.

b. His neighborhood has two distinct types of homes. The value of the homes in the more established section is in the $300,000 and above price range; most of the individuals have resided in this section for quite some time. The value of homes in the newer section is in the $150,000 to $200,000 range, most of which have been built and occupied within the last two years.

c. A small park has been built in the neighborhood. Because of safety considerations, many families with small children have chosen to live near the park.

d. A wooded area backs up to one section of his neighborhood. Because of the privacy offered by the wooded area, as well as the relative lack of traffic, older residents have chosen to live in this part of the neighborhood.

e. Several families have frequent visitors to their homes, particularly on the weekends.

Required:
For each of these characteristics, indicate whether it has the potential to affect sampling risk, nonsampling risk, both sampling risk and nonsampling risk, or neither sampling risk nor nonsampling risk.

LO E-1

E.67 **Sampling and Nonsampling Risk.** You are conducting a research study to determine the effect of a two-week workout and diet regimen on the weight loss experienced by individuals between the ages of 30 and 35 years. Health Busters, a local fitness club, has allowed you access to some of its members for their voluntary participation. Your research study will use the following methodology:

1. Solicit participation from health club members.

2. Ask members who agree to participate to weigh themselves and self-report their weight to you at a specific time.

3. Provide members a scheduled set of workouts and dietary restrictions for the upcoming two weeks.

4. Via telephone survey, obtain the members' weights following the two-week period.

5. Based on the initial weight measurement and final weight measurement, calculate the net weight gain or loss.

Required:
a. How would each of the following characteristics of the methodology affect sampling risk and nonsampling risk?

1. You solicited member participation during the early morning hours when most of the members working out were doing so before going to work that day.

2. Males constituted 85 percent of your sample.

3. The health club is located near downtown where most residents are either single or married without children.

4. Because of traffic, expensive parking, and reasonable proximity of their homes to their offices, most of the patrons walk to their offices (or, in inclement weather, take taxicabs or public transportation).

5. Because of privacy concerns, you agreed to allow participants to self-report their initial and final weight measurements.

6. Because of time constraints, you were unable to monitor participants' workouts or diets during the two-week period.

b. Suggest some improvements to the methodology described to reduce potential exposure to sampling risk and nonsampling risk.

LO E-2

E.68 Sample Selection Methods. You are interested in selecting a sample of 100 students on your campus to participate in a survey of the effects of coffee on students' ability to comprehend material from a faculty member's lecture. You have decided to limit your selection to business majors and have obtained a comprehensive list (ranked in descending order based on grade point average) of all business majors. This list is 22 pages long and contains the names of 2,200 business majors.

Required:

a. When selecting your sample, what precautions should you take to ensure a representative sample?

b. Briefly describe how you might select the sample using each of the following methods: (1) unrestricted random selection, (2) systematic random selection, (3) haphazard selection, and (4) block selection.

c. What are some of the advantages and disadvantages of using the selection methods described in part (b)?

LO E-4

E.69 Factors Affecting Sample Size. Indicate how each of the following factors influences the sample size in an attributes and variables sampling application by using I (inverse relationship), D (direct relationship), or U (unrelated).

	Attributes Sampling	Variables Sampling
Population size		
Expected population deviation rate (expected misstatement)		
Tolerable rate of deviation (tolerable misstatement)		
Sampling risk		
Population variability		

LO E-2

E.70 General Sampling. Alex Fishkin is trying to decide on a new location for an ice cream and candy shop. He has decided that if the average number of children per household within a one-mile radius of a proposed shop exceeds 1.3, it would be financially successful and would provide him an annual net income of $50,000 (the minimum acceptable amount). If not, he would stand to lose his initial investment of $150,000.

Required:

a. What factors would influence Fishkin's decision to use sampling to answer this question?

b. What are some of the advantages and disadvantages of using sampling to answer this question?

c. Define *sampling risk*. Describe two different outcomes that may reflect Fishkin's exposure to sampling risk. Which of these outcomes would be of more concern to him?

d. If the initial investment was $10,000 instead of $150,000, how do you think Fishkin would evaluate the potential outcomes of the two sampling risks noted in part (c)?

e. Define *nonsampling risk*. Describe some potential nonsampling risks that Fishkin could encounter in this application.

LO E-3

E.71 Audit Sampling: Types of Audit Samples. You have been assigned to the audit of Phillip's Inc., a chain of convenience stores. As part of the audit planning, you decide to perform the following tests:

1. Perform a walkthrough of purchase transactions by selecting one purchase and following it through all processing steps from the initial purchase order to recording in the general ledger.

2. Select a sample of purchase vouchers and ensure they are supported by receiving documents.

3. Select a sample of payroll checks and agree the time to the time cards and ensure they have supervisor approval. Using the sample, project the total payroll expense for the year.

4. Select a sample of items from the inventory on hand and estimate the total inventory on hand at the balance sheet date.

5. Vouch all long-term debt issued during the year to the loan agreement and the cash received.

6. Select a sample of long-term debt agreements and ensure they have been approved in the board of directors' minutes.

7. Evaluate the control environment by inquiring of personnel as to the existence of a code of conduct.

Required:

a. Define the terms *attributes sampling, variables sampling,* and *dual-purpose testing.*

b. Indicate whether each of the items (1) through (7) suggests an attributes sample, a variables sample, a dual-purpose test, or is not an example of sampling.

LO E-4

E.72 **Various Sampling Concepts.** You overheard the following comments during a conversation between Roger Nadal and Rafael Federer about a specific sampling application.

Required:

Refer to appropriate professional standards and comment on the validity of each of these statements.

a. "Using nonstatistical sampling is so much easier than using statistical sampling. Statistical sampling requires far too many judgments. Under nonstatistical sampling, I can just pick items, evaluate them, and make my decision."

b. "I wish nonstatistical sampling were allowable in generally accepted auditing standards audits. In some cases, the additional time required by statistical sampling just isn't worth the benefits."

c. "Once we control the sampling risk, we're home free. Assuming we select a representative sample, there's nothing else that we need to worry about."

d. "Be careful if you try to set sampling risk at too low a level. You will need to select more items, which will increase the amount of audit time."

e. "Those transactions with Wimbledon are always so difficult to audit. Let's exclude them from our sampling frame. We can pick other items and have a sufficiently large sample to meet generally accepted auditing standards."

f. "I'm about to perform a walkthrough on Flushing's processing of sales transactions to understand their nature. What level of sampling risk should I consider in planning my sample of transactions?"

LO E-4

E.73 **General Sampling.** The accounting firm of Mason & Jarr performed the work described in each of the following separate cases. The two partners are worried about properly applying auditing standards regarding sampling. They have asked your advice.

Required:

Write a report addressed to Mason & Jarr stating whether they did or did not observe the essential elements of auditing standards in each case. When applicable, refer to the appropriate professional standards regarding audit sampling.

a. Mason selected three purchase orders for the purchase of raw materials from LIZ Corporation's files. He started at the beginning in the accounting process and traced each one through the accounting system. He saw the receiving reports, purchasing agent's approvals, receiving clerks' approvals, vendors' invoices (now stamped PAID), entry in the cash disbursement records, and canceled checks. This work gave him a first-hand familiarity with the cash disbursement system, and he felt confident about understanding related questions in the internal control questionnaire completed later.

b. Jarr observed the physical inventory at SER Corporation. She had a list of the different inventory descriptions with the quantities taken from the perpetual inventory records. She selected the 200 items with the largest quantities and counted them after the client's shop foreperson had completed his count. She decided not to verify the count accuracy of the other 800 items. The shop foreperson miscounted in 16 cases. Jarr concluded the rate of miscount was 8 percent and that as many as 80 of the 1,000 items might be counted incorrectly. As a result, she asked him to recount everything.

c. CSR Corporation issued seven separate commercial paper notes near the fiscal year-end to finance seasonal operations. Jarr confirmed the obligations under each series with the independent trustee for the holders, studied all seven indenture agreements, and traced the proceeds of each issue to the cash receipts records.

d. At the completion of the EH&R Corporation audit, Mason obtained written representations as required by generally accepted auditing standards from the president, the chief financial officer, and the controller. He did not ask the chief accountant at headquarters or the plant controllers in the three divisions for written representations.

e. Jarr audited the Repairs and Maintenance account of Kerr Corporation by vouching all entries of more than $5,000 (totaling $278,000) to supporting documents. She compared the sum of all remaining entries ($75,000, a material amount) in relation to the prior-year total of $56,000 and decided the amounts were reasonable, so she did not perform additional procedures with respect to these entries.

LO E-4

E.74 **Basic Attributes Sampling.** Fournette, CPA, is studying and evaluating Tiger Inc.'s internal controls over cash disbursements. In planning the engagement, Fournette has identified the requirement that vendor invoices are authenticated (through a formal approval process) prior to being submitted for payment as a key control. Because of the large number of purchase transactions, Fournette has decided to use attributes sampling during his evaluation of this control. In so doing, he has established a risk of overreliance of 5 percent and a tolerable rate of deviation of 3 percent.

Required:

a. What is the appropriate population from which Fournette should select his sample?

b. After selecting and evaluating his sample, Fournette determined an upper limit rate of deviation of 6 percent.

1. Provide a brief explanation about the meaning of the term *upper limit rate of deviation*.
2. What would Fournette conclude with respect to Tiger's internal control?
3. What sampling risk(s) is Fournette exposed to in this situation?

c. Repeat part (b), assuming that Fournette determined an upper limit rate of deviation of 2 percent.

d. If Fournette were willing to accept a risk of overreliance of 10 percent, how would that affect the likelihood of relying on Tiger's internal controls?

LO E-4

E.75 **Basic Variables Sampling.** Henry, CPA, is performing substantive tests of Crimson Company's accounts receivable (which have a recorded balance of $200 million) and decided to confirm customer account balances. Because of the large number of customer balances, Henry has decided to use variables sampling and has established a risk of incorrect acceptance of 5 percent and a tolerable misstatement of $10 million.

Required:

a. What is the appropriate population from which Henry should select his sample?

b. After selecting and evaluating his sample, Henry has determined an upper limit on misstatements of $17 million.

1. Provide a brief explanation about the meaning of the term *upper limit on misstatements*.
2. What would Henry conclude with respect to Crimson Company's accounts receivable?
3. What sampling risk(s) is Henry exposed to in this situation?

c. Repeat part (b), assuming that Henry determined an upper limit on misstatements of $6 million.

d. If Henry were willing to accept a risk of incorrect acceptance of 10 percent, how would that affect the likelihood of accepting Crimson Company's accounts receivable balance as fairly stated?

Attributes Sampling

There are five kinds of lies: lies, damned lies, statistics, politicians quoting statistics, and novelists quoting politicians on statistics.

Stephen K. Tagg, marketing faculty member, University of Strathclyde

Professional Standards References

Topic	AU-C/ISA Section	PCAOB Reference
Consideration of Internal Control in an Integrated Audit	265	2201
Identifying and Assessing the Risks of Material Misstatement	315	2110
Auditors' Responses to Risks of Material Misstatement	330	2301
Audit Sampling	530	2315

LEARNING OBJECTIVES

Module F provides a comprehensive example of the use of attributes sampling in the audit team's study of internal control.

Your objectives are to be able to:

LO F-1 Identify the objectives of attributes sampling, define *deviation conditions*, and define the population for an attributes sampling application.

LO F-2 Understand how various factors influence the size of an attributes sample and how to determine the sample size for an attributes sampling application.

LO F-3 Identify various methods of selecting an attributes sample.

LO F-4 Evaluate the results of an attributes sampling application by determining the *upper limit rate of deviation.*

LO F-5 Understand how to use *sequential sampling, discovery sampling,* and *nonstatistical sampling* in attributes testing.

INTRODUCTION

Role of Attributes Sampling in the Audit

The need for audit teams to control their exposure to *audit risk* (the risk that a material misstatement occurs, is not prevented or detected by the client's internal control, and is not detected by the audit team's substantive procedures) has been discussed throughout the text. The following provides a general overview of how audit teams control this risk:

1. Establish the desired level of audit risk.
2. Based on the susceptibility of the account balance or class of transactions to material misstatement, assess *inherent risk*.
3. Based on the effectiveness of the client's internal controls in preventing or detecting misstatements, assess *control risk*.
4. Determine *detection risk*, which includes *analytical procedures risk* and *test of details risk* (which reflects the nature, timing, and extent of the audit team's substantive tests).

In evaluating the effectiveness of the client's internal controls (step 3), the audit team conducts tests of the operating effectiveness of important control activities. These tests of controls (and the assessment of control risk) are directly related to the audit team's need to select an appropriate sample of control activities to ensure that they are functioning as intended.

Auditors apply sampling for tests of controls on almost every engagement. As you read in Chapter 5, the Sarbanes–Oxley Act requires auditors of public companies to test the effectiveness of internal controls. Moreover, auditors of all entities should test the operating effectiveness of controls where control risk is less than 100 percent and the audit team is relying on them to reduce substantive procedures. This module focuses on the use of attributes sampling in conducting tests of controls to assess control risk, control the audit team's overall exposure to audit risk, and meet the objectives of the audit.

The importance of attributes sampling is evidenced by the following deficiencies noted by PCAOB inspection teams when reviewing tests of controls by large auditing firms:[1]

- The Firm failed to sufficiently test an important control over the loan grading process that it selected, as the sample size the Firm used in its testing was too small to obtain the necessary level of assurance that the control was operating effectively to prevent or detect material misstatements.

- For these compensating controls [over revenue and accounts receivable transactions], the sample used by the Firm to test the compensating controls was inadequate because the Firm underestimated the number of times the control operated when computing the necessary sample size.

These deficiencies illustrate the potential issues involved with properly identifying the population and determining sample size, two important steps in the attributes sampling process.

---

[1] *PCAOB Report on 2014 Inspection of KPMG* (September 24, 2014); *PCAOB Report on 2013 Inspection of Ernst & Young* (June 28, 2013).

PLANNING

LO F-1

Identify the objectives of attributes sampling, define *deviation conditions,* and define the population for an attributes sampling application.

Attributes sampling is used to determine the extent to which some attribute (or characteristic) exists within a population of interest. In tests of controls, that attribute is whether a specific control was properly applied by client personnel and is appropriately functioning to prevent or detect material financial statement misstatements.

The following seven-step procedure serves as the basis for our illustration of attributes sampling.

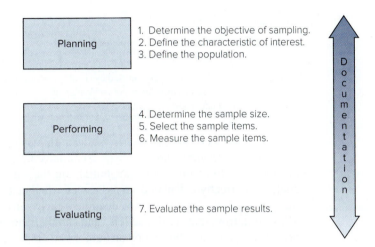

To illustrate the application of the process, we focus on the audit team's study and evaluation of important controls for the revenue cycle of AirCon Company, a manufacturer of high-technology products.

Step 1: Determine the Objective of Sampling

The first step in the attributes sampling process is to identify the objective of attributes sampling, which is related to examining key controls corresponding to the management assertions of interest to the audit team. For the examination of AirCon's revenue cycle, the two major assertions of interest are *occurrence* (does the recorded sale represent an actual sale made to a customer?) and *accuracy* (has the sale been recorded at the proper dollar amount?). Once the relevant assertions have been determined, the audit team then specifies one or more controls that, if functioning, allow the client to meet the recording objectives related to these assertions. The following is a summary of the assertions and one relevant control that will be tested.[2]

Assertion	Control
Occurrence	Sales invoices are supported by a valid shipping document[3]
Accuracy	Sales invoices are initialed by client personnel as evidence of verification of mathematical accuracy

Step 2: Define the Characteristic of Interest

Once the specific controls have been identified, the audit team must next define the characteristic of interest; in an attributes sampling context, this is a deviation condition. The word **deviation** (commonly referred to as **exception**) refers to instances in which the client or its personnel do *not* follow prescribed controls; in other words, deviations are instances in which

---

[2]In practice, a greater number of controls would pertain to the occurrence and accuracy assertions. We limit the number of controls examined by the audit team to focus on the application of attributes sampling.

[3] Of course, the possibility exists that the shipping document was fraudulently prepared in an effort to increase sales. However, this possibility is beyond the scope of our discussion of attributes sampling.

controls *are not functioning as intended.* Defining the deviation conditions at the outset is important because deviation conditions provide the audit team evidence regarding the *operating effectiveness* of the client's internal control.

AirCon's control activities indicate that authorized client personnel should write their initials in a preprinted "verified by" space on the invoice after mathematically verifying the accuracy of each sales invoice. For the control activity that a sales invoice must be supported by a valid shipping document, a deviation would be a situation in which a shipping document does not exist to support a sales invoice. The deviation conditions defined by the audit team are as follows:

Assertion	Control	Example of Deviation
Occurrence	Sales invoices are supported by a valid shipping document	Instance in which sales invoice is not accompanied by a valid shipping document
Accuracy	Sales invoices are initialed by client personnel as evidence of verification of mathematical accuracy	Lack of authorized employee initials on sales invoice or mathematically incorrect invoice

A deviation does not necessarily indicate that an error in processing a transaction has occurred. For example, an employee could have mathematically verified a sales invoice but forgotten to record his or her initials on the sales invoice. In addition, the invoice could be correctly calculated regardless of whether the invoice was verified. However, the failure of client employees to document their performance of key controls represents a deviation from that control activity and should be investigated. Further, the documentation may be initialed, but not by an authorized employee.

Step 3: Define the Population

The *population* is the set of all items about which a conclusion is desired. In attributes sampling, the population represents all potential occurrences of the control activity of interest. Population definition is important because audit conclusions can be made only about the population from which the sample was selected. For example, consider the following relationships between the sales invoice and shipping document in the revenue cycle:

Have all sales been recorded?

(Completeness)

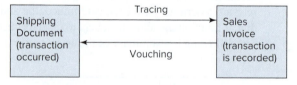

Are all recorded sales valid?

(Occurrence)

Notice that, by defining the population as sales invoices, the audit team is examining only transactions that have been recorded. As a result, this population cannot be used to provide evidence for the *completeness* assertion. However, this population is appropriate if the audit team is interested in verifying that all recorded sales invoices represent valid transactions (as evidenced by the presence of shipping documents), which corresponds to the *occurrence* assertion. As a result, the population should be defined as all sales invoices prepared by AirCon during the period under audit.

When defining the population, the audit team also needs to determine the **physical representation of the population.** The physical representation is the frame of reference that the audit team uses in selecting the sample, also referred to as the *source* of the sample.

That is, the audit team will select the sample from the physical representation. Some possible physical representations for selecting a sample of sales invoices include these:

- A journal list of recorded sales invoices.
- Copies of sales invoices contained in a file.
- A computerized list of sales invoices.

The primary concerns about the physical representation are that it is complete and corresponds with the actual population. If tests of controls are performed at an interim date, the audit team should extend tests from the interim date to the date of the financial statements and ensure that the final population includes all transactions (and possible applications of controls) for the period under audit. This can be done by footing a sales journal and agreeing the total of sales to the general ledger.

AirCon Company has a computerized list of all sales invoices prepared during the year. It can be sorted by date, customer, or dollar amount. The audit team will use this listing to select the sample.

The first three steps in the sampling process for AirCon Company are summarized next.

Summary: Steps 1–3 in the Sampling Process for Aircon Company

Step 1 The audit team's objective in sampling is to evaluate the operating effectiveness of controls related to the occurrence and accuracy assertions.

Step 2 The audit team defined deviation conditions as (a) lack of employee initials on sales invoices or mathematical error on a sales invoice (accuracy) and (b) a sales invoice that is not accompanied by a shipping document (occurrence).

Step 3 The audit team defined the population as a computerized list of all sales invoices prepared during the year and verified the completeness and accuracy of the listing.

✔ REVIEW CHECKPOINTS

F.1 Define *attributes sampling*. In what stage of the audit would it be used?

F.2 How do the management assertions relate to the objectives of attributes sampling?

F.3 Define *deviation condition*. Why are deviation conditions so important in an attributes sampling application?

F.4 Why is appropriately defining the population of interest so important in an attributes sampling application?

PERFORMING

LO F-2
Understand how various factors influence the size of an attributes sample and how to determine the sample size for an attributes sampling application.

At this point, the audit team has completed the planning stage of its sampling process and is ready to begin performing the sampling application. The next three steps are determining the sample size, selecting the sample, and measuring sample items, as shown here. We begin by discussing how audit teams determine the appropriate sample size.

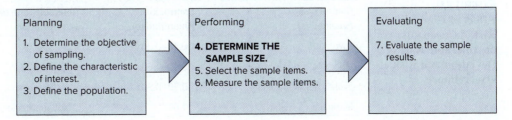

Planning	Performing	Evaluating
1. Determine the objective of sampling. 2. Define the characteristic of interest. 3. Define the population.	**4. DETERMINE THE SAMPLE SIZE.** 5. Select the sample items. 6. Measure the sample items.	7. Evaluate the sample results.

Step 4: Determine the Sample Size

The *sample size* represents the number of items that the audit team examines within a population of interest. Four main factors influence the sample size in an attributes sampling application:

- Tolerable rate of deviation.
- Sampling risk (risk of overreliance, or risk of assessing control risk too low).
- Expected population deviation rate.
- Population size.

Tolerable Rate of Deviation

Because of human involvement and error, audit teams cannot expect controls to be functioning 100 percent of the time. In evaluating whether controls are functioning effectively, the question does remain about the extent to which deviations are permissible while still allowing the audit team to appropriately rely on the control.

The **tolerable rate of deviation** is the maximum rate of deviations permissible by the audit team without modifying the planned assessed level of control risk. In determining the tolerable rate of deviation, the audit team should consider (1) the planned assessed level of control risk and (2) the degree of assurance desired by the audit evidence in the sample. Generally, if a control is judged to be more important and would result in a more significant reduction in substantive testing, the tolerable rate of deviation should be established at lower levels.

Exhibit F.1 illustrates how the tolerable rate of deviation can be related to control risk assessments. Although control risk is rarely assessed numerically in practice, note that lower levels of control risk are associated with lower tolerable rates of deviation (and vice versa). Using Exhibit F.1, if the audit team established a low acceptable control risk (between 0.10 and 0.30), the corresponding tolerable rate of deviation would range from 3 to 7 percent.

Assume that AirCon Company's control risk was assessed at a low level (0.30) for the occurrence assertion and a moderate level (0.50) for the accuracy assertion. Using the matrix in Exhibit F.1, the audit team translated these assessments into tolerable rate of deviation of 6 percent and 10 percent for the controls related to the occurrence and accuracy assertions, respectively.

Sampling Risk

Sampling risk is the likelihood that the decision made based on the sample differs from the decision that would have been made had the entire population been examined. There are two types of sampling risks for attributes sampling applications: the **risk of underreliance** and the **risk of overreliance** (sometimes referred to as the *risk of assessing control risk too high* and the *risk of assessing control risk too low,* respectively). Exhibit F.2 summarizes some of the key characteristics of these risks.

As shown in Exhibit F.2, the risk of overreliance occurs when the audit team's sample evidence suggests that the control is functioning effectively (the adjusted sample rate of deviation is less than or equal to the tolerable rate of deviation) when the true (but unknown) state of the population is that the control is *not* functioning effectively

EXHIBIT F.1
Effect of Control Risk Assessments on Tolerable Rate of Deviation and Risk of Overreliance

Control Risk (Qualitative)	Control Risk (Quantitative)	Tolerable Rate of Deviation	Risk of Overreliance
Low	0.10–0.30	3%–7%	5%
Moderate	0.40–0.60	6%–12%	5%–10%
Slightly below maximum	0.70–0.90	11%–20%	10%
Maximum	1.00	Not applicable	Not applicable

EXHIBIT F.2 **Sampling Risks Associated with Attributes Sampling**

Sampling Risk	Sample Results	Unknown State of the Population	Loss
Risk of underreliance (risk of assessing control risk too high)	Adjusted sample rate of deviation > Tolerable rate of deviation *Conclusion:* Control is not functioning effectively	Population rate of deviation ≤ Tolerable rate of deviation *Conclusion:* Control is functioning effectively	Efficiency loss because additional substantive procedures will be performed
Risk of overreliance (risk of assessing control risk too low)	Adjusted sample rate of deviation ≤ Tolerable rate of deviation *Conclusion:* Control is functioning effectively	Population rate of deviation > Tolerable rate of deviation *Conclusion:* Control is not functioning effectively	Effectiveness loss because an insufficient level of substantive procedures will be performed

(population rate of deviation is higher than the tolerable rate of deviation). Because the risk of overreliance results in the audit team's failure to reduce audit risk to acceptable levels (an effectiveness loss), controlling exposure to this risk is of primary importance. Although the risk of underreliance is also a form of sampling risk, this risk will actually result in the audit team achieving a lower level of audit risk than planned. Therefore, in an attributes sampling plan, the audit team will typically control only the exposure to the risk of *overreliance* in determining the appropriate sample size.

How does the audit team assess the acceptable level of the risk of overreliance? This risk depends on the planned level of control risk (which reflects the degree of reliance that the audit team wishes to place on the client's internal control). As the planned level of control risk is lower, it becomes quite important for the audit team to reduce the exposure to the risk of overreliance.

Refer to Exhibit F.1 and recall that the audit team has decided to assess control risk at low levels (0.30) for the occurrence assertion and moderate levels (0.50) for the accuracy assertion. Based on the relationships in Exhibit F.1, these assessments of control risk are translated into 5 percent and 10 percent risks of overreliance for the controls related to the occurrence and accuracy assertions, respectively.[4]

Expected Population Deviation Rate

Audit teams usually know or suspect that some level of deviation occurs in the client's internal control activities; this rate is referred to as the **expected population deviation rate**. The concept of reasonable assurance suggests that the client's internal control activities will not function perfectly (i.e., a zero rate of deviation). Thus, some level of deviations is typically observed and is incorporated into the determination of sample size.

How is the expected population deviation rate determined? If the client represents a recurring engagement, the audit team has some knowledge of rate of deviations from prior engagements. These rates might need to be adjusted if changes in the client's controls have occurred since the prior audit, but previous-year rates serve as a reasonable starting point. For example, if the observed rate of deviation from prior audits was 4 percent but the audit team is aware of improvement in controls, the current-year rate of deviation could be estimated at a lower level (say, 3 percent). If, on the other hand, the engagement is a first-year engagement, the audit team might use a small sample (referred to as a *pilot sample*) to estimate the rate of deviations.

Based on their previous experience in examining the operating effectiveness of these controls for AirCon Company, the audit team assessed the expected population deviation rate at 2 percent and 3.5 percent for the controls related to the occurrence and accuracy assertions, respectively.

---

[4]Exhibit F.1 reflects the common practice of selecting one of two levels of the risk of overreliance (5 percent and 10 percent).

Population Size

Common sense probably tells you that samples should be larger for larger populations (a *direct relationship*). Strictly speaking, your common sense is accurate; clearly, the sample size for a population of 10 items would be smaller than for a population of 1,000 items. However, once a population reaches a certain size, any increase has a minimal effect on sample size. As a result, unless the population size is very small (which is not common for most attributes sampling applications), the audit team does not consider population size in determining sample size to a great extent.

To illustrate, the AICPA Audit Guide *Auditing Sampling* provides the following sample sizes for different populations for the same level of the risk of overreliance, expected population deviation rate, and tolerable rate of deviation:

Population Size	Sample Size
100	33
200	35
500	37
1,000	37
1,500	38
2,000	38

The preceding illustrates that, once the population exceeds 500 items, the effect of population size on sample size is relatively limited. Because AirCon processes more than 20,000 sales invoices per year, the population is of sufficient size not to influence the audit team's sample size. What about extremely small sample sizes? Often, controls such as bank reconciliations are only performed monthly or at some other interval; as such, this type of control has a population size of only 12 items in a given year. Exhibit F.3 suggests the sample sizes in such circumstances.

Summary of Sample Size Factors

Exhibit F.4 summarizes the general relationships between the factors discussed in this section and sample size.

A recent survey of the sampling practices of six international accounting firms (including the Big Four) revealed the following levels of parameters used in practice (these parameters provided a range of sample sizes for the six firms from 22 items to 59 items:)[5]

- Risk of overreliance: Between 5 percent and 10 percent.
- Expected population deviation rate: Generally 0 percent.
- Tolerable rate of deviation: Between 5 percent and 10 percent.

EXHIBIT F.3
Sample Sizes for Small Audit Populations

Control Frequency and Population Size	Sample Size
Quarterly (4)	2
Monthly (12)	2–4
Semimonthly (24)	3–8
Weekly (52)	5–9

Source: AICPA Audit Guide *Audit Sampling.*

[5]B. E. Christensen, R.J. Elder, and S.M. Glover, "Behind the Numbers: Insights into Large Audit Firm Sampling Policies," *Accounting Horizons,* March 2015, pp. 61–81.

EXHIBIT F.4   Factors Affecting Sample Size

Factor	Determination Based On	Relationship with Sample Size	Level for AirCon
Tolerable rate of deviation	Level of control risk	Inverse	6% (occurrence) 10% (accuracy)
Sampling risk (risk of overreliance)	Level of control risk	Inverse	5% (occurrence) 10% (accuracy)
Expected population deviation rate	Prior audits (for recurring engagements) or a pilot sample of controls (for first-year engagements)	Direct	2% (occurrence) 3.5% (accuracy)
Population size	Number of applications of control to transactions	Direct	Greater than 20,000 invoices

Using AICPA Sampling Tables

How does the audit team use the preceding factors in determining sample size? The AICPA has developed sampling tables that specifically incorporate the (1) risk of over-reliance, (2) expected population deviation rate, and (3) tolerable rate of deviation. These tables also identify the number of deviations the audit team can find and still accept the control as operating effectively (number of expected deviations), which can give the audit team an idea of whether the sample size is realistic. In practice, computer programs are frequently used to determine sample size; these programs follow the logic of the statistical formulas that are used to construct the AICPA sampling tables. The AICPA tables are used as follows:

1. Based on the risk of overreliance, select the appropriate sample size table in Appendix F.A. Tables for a 5 percent and 10 percent risk of overreliance are reproduced as Exhibits FA.1 and FA.2, respectively.
2. Identify the row of the table corresponding to the expected population deviation rate for the control being examined.
3. Identify the column of the table representing the assessed tolerable rate of deviation for the control being examined.
4. Determine the sample size by identifying the junction of the row from step 2 and the column from step 3.

Referring to the sample size table in Exhibit FA.1 (5 percent risk of overreliance) and reading the sample size at the intersection of the 2 percent expected population deviation rate row and the 6 percent tolerable rate of deviation column reveals a sample size for the control related to the occurrence assertion of 127 items.

This can be seen using the following excerpt from Exhibit FA.1.

Expected Population Deviation Rate	Tolerable Rate of Deviation		
	5%	6%	7%
1.00%	93	78	66
2.00%	181	127	88
3.00%	361	195	129

Using the sample size table in Exhibit FA.2 (10 percent risk of overreliance) and reading the sample size at the intersection of the 3.5 percent expected population deviation

EXHIBIT F.5
Sample Audit
Documentation for
AirCon Company
Sample Selection

Control Examined	Control Risk	ROO (%)	TRD (%)	EPDR (%)	n(A)
Occurrence: Sales invoices are prepared only for items shipped to customers	Low (0.30)	5.0%	6.0%	2.0%	127
Accuracy: Extensions and footings on sales invoices are mathematically verified	Moderate (0.50)	10.0	10.0	3.5	52

ROO = Risk of overreliance
TRD = Tolerable rate of deviation
EPDR = Expected population rate of deviation
n = sample size
NOTE A: Items were selected using a random starting point of 667. The entire sample is shown on workpaper TC-1-A (not illustrated in text).

rate row and the 10 percent tolerable rate of deviation column reveals a sample size for the test of controls related to the accuracy assertion of 52 items.[6]

In reviewing Exhibit FA.1, you can see how the various factors affect sample size, as follows.

- Reading across the 2 percent expected population deviation rate row, you see that if the tolerable rate of deviation for the control related to the occurrence assertion was reduced from 6 percent to 5 percent, the necessary sample size would increase from 127 items to 181 items, reflecting an *inverse relationship* with sample size.
- Reading down the 6 percent tolerable rate of deviation column, you see that if the expected population deviation rate were reduced from 2 percent to 1 percent, the sample size for the control related to the occurrence assertion would decrease from 127 items to 78 items, reflecting a *direct relationship* with sample size.[7]
- Comparing the cell entries in Exhibits FA.1 and FA.2, increasing the risk of overreliance from 5 percent to 10 percent results in a reduction in sample size from 127 to 88 (using a expected population deviation rate of 2 percent and a tolerable rate of deviation of 6 percent), reflecting an *inverse relationship* with sample size.

Exhibit F.5 is an example of partial audit documentation prepared for tests of controls for AirCon Company. It summarizes the controls examined, assessed level of control risk, various factors considered in determining the sample size, and the sample size itself.

Summary: Step 4 in the Sampling Process for AirCon Company

Step 4 Based on the acceptable risk of overreliance, expected population deviation rate, and tolerable rate of deviation, the audit team determined sample sizes of 127 (for the control related to the occurrence assertion) and 52 (for the control related to the accuracy assertion).

---

[6]The AirCon example illustrates different risks of overreliance, tolerable rates of deviations, and expected population deviation rates for the two controls examined for AirCon Company. We do so primarily to show how these factors affect sample size. In practice, the cost of identifying and selecting sample items in attributes sampling is often far higher than the cost of measuring and evaluating these items. As a result, when selecting a single document to evaluate more than one control, the audit team may use the largest of the sample sizes and examine all controls related to the document selected.

[7]Note that the sample size does not necessarily change with each incremental change in the expected deviation rate. For example, using a 6 percent tolerable rate of deviation and a 5 percent acceptable risk of overreliance, the sample size is 78 for expected deviation rates ranging from 0.25 percent to 1.25 percent. However, the sample size increases to 103 when the expected deviation rate increases to 1.50 percent.

In practice, audit teams utilize software in performing sampling plans. Throughout this module, we illustrate the use of IDEA Data Analysis Software in various stages of the attributes sampling process.

To determine sample size using IDEA, access the **Analysis> Sample>Attribute** function and enter the population size of 20,000 transactions,[8] tolerable rate of deviation of 6 percent, expected population deviation rate of 2 percent, and confidence level of 95 percent (corresponding to a risk of overreliance of 5 percent).

After selecting "Compute," IDEA will provide the appropriate sample size of 127 items for the control related to the occurrence assertion. (Inputting parameters of 20000, 10 percent, 3.5 percent, and 90 percent for the control related to the accuracy assertion would result in a sample size of 52 items).

More detailed information and sample input and output screens can be found in Connect.

✅ REVIEW CHECKPOINTS

F.5 Define the terms (a) *sampling risk,* (b) *tolerable rate of deviation,* and (c) *expected population deviation rate.* How does the audit team assess or determine these factors?

F.6 What two types of sampling risks could an audit team encounter when performing attributes sampling?

F.7 In attributes sampling, why is the risk of overreliance more important than the risk of underreliance?

F.8 What is the relationship between sample size and (a) sampling risk, (b) tolerable rate of deviation, and (c) expected population deviation rate?

F.9 Describe the general procedure used by the audit team to determine sample size using AICPA sampling tables.

LO F-3
Identify various methods of selecting an attributes sample.

Step 5: Select the Sample Items

After determining the appropriate sample size, the audit team then selects sample items from the population.

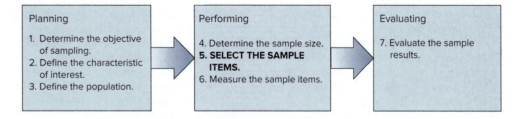

Planning	Performing	Evaluating
1. Determine the objective of sampling. 2. Define the characteristic of interest. 3. Define the population.	4. Determine the sample size. **5. SELECT THE SAMPLE ITEMS.** 6. Measure the sample items.	7. Evaluate the sample results.

The audit team's basic goal in selecting a sample is to increase the likelihood that it is representative of the population, thereby reducing sampling risk. For example, if the audit team is examining a sample of sales invoices, this sample should include sales invoices that

- Have been prepared throughout the year.
- Represent both large and small dollar amounts.
- Have been prepared by different individuals involved in the invoice preparation process.
- Represent different customers or geographic areas.

---

[8]While AirCon processed more than 20,000 sales transactions, once a population reaches a certain size, that factor has a minimal effect on sample size.

For example, considering the first item, if sales invoices for only the month of November are examined, differences in the persons, processes, or other factors involved in the preparation or processing of sales invoices in the month of November can result in a nonrepresentative sample.

The audit team then selects the sample from the population. Two common methods used are unrestricted random selection and systematic random selection.

- When using **unrestricted random selection** (also known as **random selection**), the audit team identifies a series of random numbers equal to the desired sample size and selects the numbered item in the corresponding population (for example, selecting the 120th, 268th, 341st, etc. sales invoices comprising AirCon's population of sales invoices).

- When using **systematic random selection** (commonly referred to as **systematic selection**), the audit team identifies a random starting point in the population and then bypasses (or "skips") a fixed number of items (referred to as the **sampling interval**) and selects the corresponding items until the appropriate number of items has been selected. The sampling interval is determined by dividing the number of items in the population by the desired sample size.

Two other methods of selecting samples are **block selection** (which involves the selection of a series of contiguous or adjacent items) and **haphazard selection** (which selects items in an unstructured manner without intentional bias). A recent survey of the sampling practices of six international accounting firms (including the Big Four) concluded that unrestricted random selection and systematic random selection are generally preferred, with haphazard selection being the least preferred method.[9]

Summary: Step 5 in the Sampling Process for AirCon Company

Step 5 The audit team determined the completeness and accuracy of the population and selected 127 invoices. The first 52 were examined for both the controls related to the accuracy and occurrence assertions and the final 75 were examined for the control related to the occurrence assertion (recall that the sample sizes for the controls related to the accuracy and occurrence assertions were 52 and 127, respectively.)

USING IDEA IN THE AUDIT — Selecting the Sample

For populations maintained in electronic format, IDEA can be used to select sample items as follows.

For unrestricted random selection, using the **Analysis>Sample> Random** function, the audit team enters the number of records to select (sample size); the random start, starting record number, and ending record number will all be populated by IDEA. When "OK" is selected, the sample is automatically drawn from the population.

For systematic random selection, the **Analysis>Sample>Other> Systematic** function will provide two tabs: "Number of Records" and "Selection Interval," either of which can be used to select the sample. Depending upon the tab chosen, the audit team will enter the sample size ("Number of records") or sampling interval ("Selection Interval") as well as the random starting point in the sample ("Starting record number to select"). IDEA will then select a sample from the population using the random starting point and the sampling interval.

More detailed information and sample input and output screens can be found in Connect.

Step 6: Measure the Sample Items

Once the audit team has determined the sample size (step 4) and selected the sample items (step 5), they are ready to measure the sample items. When measuring the sample items in an attributes sampling application, the audit team determines whether the control has

[9]B.E. Christensen, R.J. Elder, and S.M. Glover, "Behind the Numbers: Insights into Large Audit Firm Sampling Policies," *Accounting Horizons,* March 2015, pp. 61–81.

been appropriately performed. It is important that the audit team not reperform the control activity but rather examine some form of evidence that client personnel performed it. If there is no evidence of the control being performed, the item will be classified as a deviation. The audit team examines evidence on the operating effectiveness of important controls by performing *tests of controls.*

This stage of the sampling process is illustrated here.

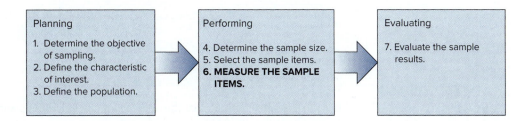

Although measuring sample items is typically straightforward, one issue that could arise relates to missing items. For example, when evaluating a control related to a sales invoice that cannot be located, the audit team would classify this particular item as a deviation. The fact that the document is missing could indeed reflect the fact that a control was not applied in the intended manner and the related document has been intentionally destroyed or removed from the physical representation of the population.

Measuring sample items is the step in the sampling process when nonsampling risk can occur. *Nonsampling risk* is the risk that the audit team's sample provides an incorrect conclusion for reasons other than the representativeness of the sample. For example, the audit team could make an unintentional error in evaluating evidence (such as classifying a deviation as a nondeviation or *vice versa*) or may fail to recognize that initials on a document are not those of an appropriate individual.

As noted earlier, the audit team's tests of controls were to verify the existence of valid shipping documents to support sales invoices (control related to the occurrence assertion) and verify the initials of client employees indicating mathematical verification of sales invoices (control related to the accuracy assertion).

Summary: Step 6 in the Sampling Process for AirCon Company

Step 6 The audit team's tests of controls identified two deviations for the control related to the occurrence assertion and four deviations for the control related to the accuracy assertion.

☑ REVIEW CHECKPOINTS

F.10 What are some important considerations for the audit team when selecting sample items?

F.11 What are *tests of controls*? What is the audit team's goal in performing them in an attributes sampling application?

F.12 When performing tests of controls, how would the audit team classify a situation when encountering a missing item?

STEP 7: EVALUATE THE SAMPLE RESULTS

LO F-4

Evaluate the results of an attributes sampling application by determining the upper limit rate of deviation.

Calculating the Upper Limit Rate of Deviation

At this point, the audit team is now ready to evaluate the sample results, the final step in the sampling process.

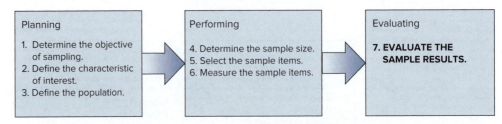

After measuring sample items, the audit team can calculate a **sample rate of deviation**, which represents the rate of deviations from key controls noted by the audit team members in their sample. The sample rate of deviation is calculated by dividing the number of deviations noted in the sample by the sample size. Thus, the sample rate of deviation for the controls related to the occurrence and accuracy assertions were 1.6 percent (2 deviations ÷ 127 invoices) and 7.7 percent (4 deviations ÷ 52 invoices), respectively. Because the tolerable rate of deviation for these controls are 6 percent and 10 percent, respectively, the audit team's initial conclusion might be to rely on the controls as planned because the sample rate of deviation is less than the tolerable rate of deviation.

What is the fallacy with this approach? The audit team's sample might not represent the population, and the sample rate of deviation may significantly understate the true population rate of deviation. Although audit teams never know the true population rate of deviation with any certainty, they can use sampling tables to "adjust" the sample rate of deviation to one that has a certain probability of equaling or exceeding the true rate of deviation. Simply stated, this adjusted rate (the **upper limit rate of deviation,** or **ULRD**) provides a conservative estimate of the population rate of deviation that allows the audit team to control exposure to sampling risk to acceptable levels.

The ULRD provides the following information:

- There is a (1 − *Risk of overreliance*) probability that the true population rate of deviation is less than or equal to the ULRD.
- There is a (*risk of overreliance*) probability that the true population rate of deviation exceeds the ULRD.

Exhibits F.B.1 and F.B.2 in Appendix F.B allow the ULRD to be determined for an acceptable risk of overreliance of 5 percent and 10 percent, as follows:

1. Based on the acceptable risk of overreliance, select the appropriate evaluation table.
2. Identify the row representing the appropriate sample size.
3. Identify the column corresponding to the number of deviations found by the audit team.
4. The ULRD is the value found at the intersection of the row in step 2 and the column in step 3.

To illustrate the use of sample evaluation tables, consider the findings for the control activity related to the occurrence assertion for AirCon Company. Recall that the audit team examined a sample of 127 sales invoices for the potential functioning of this control, found two deviations, and calculated a sample rate of deviation of 1.6 percent. Using Exhibit F.B.1 (for a risk of overreliance of 5 percent), the audit team would locate the row corresponding to a sample size of 127 items and the column for two deviations. Note that Exhibit F.B.1 contains a row for sample sizes of 125 and 150 but not 127. When choosing between two samples to use in this table, it is more conservative to use the smaller number. In this instance, the audit team can do one of the following:

1. Select an additional 23 items for examination for a sample size of 150 (the next highest sample size in the sample evaluation table).

2. Evaluate the results of the sample using a smaller sample size of 125. This provides a conservative (higher) measure of the ULRD because the same number of deviations will be attributed to a smaller number of sample items.

3. Interpolate the values in Exhibit FB.1 and estimate a ULRD for a sample of 127 items.

Because the original sample of 127 is very close to the sample size row of 125, assume that the audit team evaluates the two deviations using a sample size of 125. Reading the value in the table at the intersection of this row and column reveals a ULRD of 5.0 percent, as shown in the following excerpt from Exhibit FB.1.

	Actual Number of Deviations Found		
Sample Size	0	1	2
100	3.0	4.7	6.2
125	2.4	3.8	5.0
150	2.0	3.2	4.2

The ULRD is composed of the following components:

- A sample rate of deviation of 1.6 percent (2 deviations ÷ 127 items = 1.6%).[10]
- An **allowance for sampling risk** of 3.4 percent (ULRD of 5.0% − Sample rate of deviation of 1.6% = 3.4%). The allowance for sampling risk represents the "adjustment" of the sample rate of deviation for the acceptable risk of overreliance.

Now let us consider the results for the control related to the accuracy assertion. Using a risk of overreliance of 10 percent (Exhibit FB.2), note that a row for a sample of 52 items is not shown. Again, because this sample size is close to the row for a sample size of 50 and using 50 is more conservative than using 55 (the next available row in Exhibit FB.2), the four deviations would be evaluated using a sample size of 50. Reading the ULRD at the intersection of the row for a sample size of 50 and the column for 4 deviations yields a ULRD of 15.4 percent. This ULRD is comprised of a sample rate of deviation of 7.7 percent[11] and an allowance for sampling risk of 7.7 percent (15.4% − 7.7% = 7.7%). In this case, the ULRD of 15.4 percent exceeds the tolerable rate of deviation of 10 percent.

✅ REVIEW CHECKPOINTS

F.13 What is the sample rate of deviation? How does the audit team calculate it?

F.14 What is the ULRD? What information does the ULRD provide to the audit team?

F.15 What factors influence the determination of the ULRD?

F.16 Describe the general process used to determine the ULRD using AICPA sampling tables.

F.17 What options are available to the audit team for determining the ULRD if the audit team's sample size is not included in the AICPA sampling tables?

F.18 If the audit team examines a sample of 100 items, finds six deviations, and calculates a ULRD of 10.3 percent, what is the allowance for sampling risk?

---

[10]The fact that the audit team uses a sample size of 125 items to determine the ULRD does not affect the calculation of the sample rate of deviation using the original sample size (127 items).

[11]The fact that the audit team uses a sample size of 50 items to determine the ULRD does not affect the calculation of the sample rate of deviation using the original sample size of 52 items (4 deviations ÷ 52 items = 7.7% sample rate of deviation).

Making the Evaluation Decision

The audit team's decision rule after calculating the ULRD can be summarized as follows:

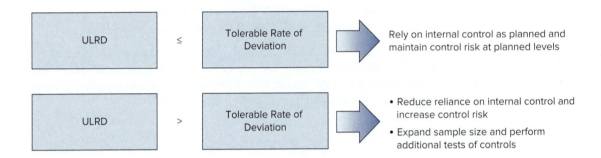

How would the audit team proceed from this point? Because the ULRD for the control related to the occurrence assertion (5.0 percent) is less than the tolerable rate of deviation (6.0 percent), it appears that the control for the occurrence assertion is functioning effectively. As a result, the audit team could decide to rely on internal control as planned and maintain the planned level of control risk as well as the planned level of detection risk.

For the control related to the accuracy assertion, since the ULRD (15.4 percent) exceeds the tolerable rate of deviation (10.0 percent), the audit team has one of two options. The first option is to reduce the planned degree of reliance on internal control, increase the planned level of control risk, and reduce the planned level of detection risk by performing more effective substantive procedures. Referring to Exhibit F.1, assume that a tolerable rate of deviation of 16 percent corresponds to a control risk assessment of 0.80 (slightly below maximum). Thus, without gathering any further evidence, the audit team could increase the assessment of control risk from 0.50 (moderate) to 0.80 (slightly below maximum) and correspondingly decrease the necessary level of detection risk. This decrease in the necessary level of detection risk would require the audit team to perform more effective substantive procedures.

Alternatively, the audit team could attempt to reduce the ULRD to a level below the tolerable rate of deviation of 10 percent by examining an expanded sample of controls. The following excerpted rows from Exhibit FB.2 show the ULRDs corresponding to situations in which four deviations are identified (reflecting the deviations identified by the audit team). As shown, if a total of 80 items is examined and no additional deviations are noted, the ULRD is 9.8 percent. Therefore, one option available to the audit team is to examine an additional 28 items (80 items − original sample of 52 items). Because additional deviations are likely to be identified, examining additional items is generally not an effective solution unless the ULRD is very close to the tolerable rate of deviation.[12]

Sample Size	Deviations = 4
40	19.0%
50	15.4
60	12.9
70	11.1
80	9.8

ULRD calculated based on original sample

Potential ULRD if additional items examined with no deviations

[12]The AICPA Audit Guide *Audit Sampling* recommends as a rule of thumb that if the audit team decides to test more items, then the team members increase the sample by at least the number of items in the original sample.

Which option would the audit team select? This decision depends on the relative costs of increasing the tests of controls versus the costs associated with performing more extensive substantive procedures. If the cost of examining additional items is relatively low and the likelihood of observing no additional deviations is high, the audit team would likely decide to extend the sample of controls. However, if the cost of selecting and evaluating additional items is relatively high and the audit team is likely to encounter additional deviations, it could be more cost effective to perform more effective substantive procedures. Either approach will maintain audit risk at an acceptable level.

One final issue in calculating the ULRD is the effect of the acceptable risk of overreliance on the ULRD. Conceptually, it would seem logical that lower levels of this risk would provide a more conservative (i.e., higher) ULRD. By examining Exhibit FB.2, you should note that the ULRD for a sample size of 200 items, five deviations, and a 10 percent risk of overreliance is 4.6 percent. Compare this to the ULRD of 5.2 percent for a risk of overreliance of 5 percent (Exhibit FB.1). Essentially, a higher acceptable risk of overreliance would increase the likelihood that the audit team can conclude to rely on internal control as planned.

Qualitative Evaluation of Deviations

The focus thus far has been on quantitative factors: sample sizes, numbers of deviations, tolerable rate of deviation, and ULRD. Regardless of the results of the attributes sampling application, the audit team should conduct a *qualitative evaluation* of deviations to determine their nature and cause. In some cases, deviations can truly represent an isolated incident on a specific transaction; in others, they can represent something far more serious.

A qualitative evaluation of deviations attempts to answer questions such as these with regard to observed deviations:

- Do deviations represent a pervasive error made consistently on all transactions or an isolated mistake made on a specific transaction?
- Are deviations intentional or unintentional in nature?
- Do deviations represent a misunderstanding of instructions or careless attention to duties?
- Do deviations have implications with regard to the effectiveness of other controls (for example, information technology general controls or other Committee of Sponsoring Organizations of the Treadway Commission, or COSO, components)?

If any deviations appear to be pervasively occurring throughout the sample, to represent intentional actions on the part of client employees, to represent careless attention, or to have implications with respect to other controls, they have additional implications for the audit and should be discussed with the client and its audit committee. In addition, for public entities, these deviations may reflect significant deficiencies or material weaknesses that must be disclosed in the audit team's report on internal control over financial reporting.

Summary: Step 7 in the Sampling Process for AirCon Company

Step 7 The audit team determined a ULRD of 5.0 percent and 15.4 percent for the controls related to the occurrence and accuracy assertions, respectively. Based on a comparison of the ULRD to the tolerable rate of deviation, the audit team would

- Conclude that the control related to the occurrence assertion is functioning effectively and rely on internal control as planned.

- Conclude that the control related to the accuracy assertion is not functioning effectively and either (1) reduce reliance on internal control or (2) expand the sample to examine a larger number of items.

AUDITING INSIGHT — PCAOB Findings for Attributes Sampling

This module began with an example of a deficiency related to attributes sampling disclosed in a PCAOB inspection report. The following excerpts from 2013–2015 PCAOB inspection reports of audits conducted by the Big Four firms (Deloitte, EY, KPMG, and PwC) illustrate issues identified in the attributes sampling applications conducted by these firms.

- For an automated control that the Firm tested . . . the Firm's procedures were limited to testing a sample of one transaction for each of three locations, even though the control addressed different types of transactions that involved varying processing mechanisms.

- The Firm's selection of a sample of contracts for testing the issuer's analysis was not designed in a manner that would reasonably be expected to produce a sample that was representative of the population of service contracts sold separately...

- The Firm . . . failed to evaluate whether the controls [over review of journal entries] operated at a level of precision that would prevent or detect misstatements. Further, the Firm failed to select its sample for testing these controls from the complete population of journal entries.

- [For two compensating controls selected for testing], the sample used by the Firm to test the compensating controls was inadequate because the Firm underestimated the number of times the control operated when computing the necessary sample size.

Source: PCAOB website, www.pcaobus.org/Inspections/Reports/Pages/default.aspx.

Summary

This module discusses attributes sampling, which the audit team uses to evaluate the operating effectiveness of internal control activities. When performing attributes sampling, the audit team's primary objective is to assess the extent to which the client's internal control activities are functioning effectively. As with any sampling application, the audit team is exposed to sampling risk (the risk that the decision made based on the sample differs from the decision that would have been made if the entire population had been examined). The audit team controls this sampling risk (referred to as the *risk of overreliance* or the *risk of assessing control risk too low*) in determining the appropriate sample size and evaluating the sample results.

After the sample is selected, the audit team performs tests of controls to determine whether the control is functioning as intended. A sample rate of deviation is determined by dividing the number of deviations by the sample size; this rate is adjusted to control for the acceptable exposure to the risk of overreliance to determine the upper limit rate of deviation (ULRD). The ULRD is a measure that has a (1 − *Risk of overreliance*) probability of equaling or exceeding the true rate of deviation in the population.

Once calculated, the ULRD is compared to the tolerable rate of deviation. If the ULRD is less than the tolerable rate of deviation, the audit team can rely on internal control as planned and accept the planned level of control risk. If the ULRD is higher than the tolerable rate of deviation, the audit team can either increase the assessed level of control risk (which will increase the necessary level of substantive procedures) or expand the sample to attempt to provide a ULRD that is lower than the tolerable rate of deviation. Decisions regarding the assessed level of control risk should consider the costs of performing additional tests of controls versus the cost savings from reduced substantive procedures.

Key Terms

allowance for sampling risk (or precision): The difference between the upper limit rate of deviation and the sample rate of deviation; "adjusts" the sample rate of deviation to allow the audit team to control the exposure to the risk of overreliance.

attributes sampling: A form of sampling used to determine the extent to which some characteristic (attribute) exists within a population of interest; used by the audit team during tests of controls.

block selection: A method of choosing sample items in which a series of contiguous (or adjacent) items is chosen from the population.

deviation: A condition that refers to instances in which client personnel do not follow prescribed controls and controls are not functioning as intended.

discovery sampling: A form of attributes sampling that audit teams use when deviations from controls are very critical but are expected to occur at a relatively low rate.

expected population deviation rate: The rate of variations anticipated by the audit team in the client's internal control activities; based on prior experience or a pilot sample.

haphazard selection: The method of choosing sample items in an unstructured manner but without intentional bias.

physical representation of the population: An audit team's frame of reference for selecting a sample.

random selection: See *unrestricted random selection.*

risk of overreliance (risk of assessing control risk too low): The likelihood that the audit team's sample will provide evidence that the client's controls are functioning effectively when examining the entire population would indicate they are not functioning effectively.

risk of underreliance (risk of assessing control risk too high): The likelihood that the audit team's sample will provide evidence that the client's controls are not functioning effectively when examining the entire population would indicate that they are functioning effectively.

sample rate of deviation: The extent of variations found in the audit team's sample; determined by dividing the number of deviations by the sample size.

sampling interval: An interval determined by dividing the recorded amount of the population (account balance) by the sample size.

sequential sampling: A plan in which an initial sample is selected and the audit team (1) draws a final conclusion regarding the effectiveness of the control or (2) selects additional items before drawing a final conclusion regarding the effectiveness of the control; also referred to as *stop-or-go sampling.*

systematic random selection (systematic selection): The method of choosing sample items in which a starting point is selected and a fixed number of items are bypassed between selections

systematic selection: See *systematic random selection.*

tolerable rate of deviation: The maximum rate of variation permissible by the audit team without modifying the planned assessed level of control risk.

unrestricted random selection (random selection): A method of choosing items in which all items in the population are assigned a number and selected based on random numbers picked from a random number table or generated from a computer program.

upper limit rate of deviation (ULRD): A measure that adjusts the sample rate of deviation for the audit team's acceptable level of sampling risk; the rate of deviation that has a (1–*Risk of overreliance*) probability of equaling or exceeding the true population rate of deviation.

Multiple-Choice Questions for Practice and Review

 All applicable Exercises and Problems are available with *Connect.*

LO F-1

F.27 Which of the following major stages of the audit is most closely related to attributes sampling?

a. Determining preliminary levels of materiality.

b. Performing tests of controls.

c. Performing substantive procedures.

d. Searching for the possible occurrence of subsequent events.

LO F-1

F.28 Which of the following steps in attributes sampling is most closely related to identifying key controls corresponding to the relevant management assertions?

a. Determine the objective of sampling.

b. Define the deviation condition.

c. Define the population.

d. Determine the sample size.

LO F-2

F.29 Which of the following factors has a *direct* relationship with sample size in an attributes sampling application?

	Tolerable Rate of Deviation	Expected Population Deviation Rate
a.	Yes	Yes
b.	No	Yes
c.	Yes	No
d.	No	No

LO F-2

F.30 Which of the following sampling risks does the audit team control in an attributes sampling application (ROO = risk of overreliance, ROU = risk of underreliance)?

	ROO	ROU
a.	Yes	Yes
b.	No	Yes
c.	Yes	No
d.	No	No

LO F-2

F.31 Why is the audit team more concerned with controlling the exposure to the risk of overreliance than with the risk of underreliance?

a. Only the risk of overreliance results in an incorrect audit decision.

b. The risk of underreliance is not related to the audit team's study and evaluation of internal control.

c. The risk of overreliance can ultimately result in the audit team's failing to reduce audit risk to acceptable levels.

d. The risk of underreliance can be controlled by performing tests of controls during the interim period.

LO F-2

F.32 Which of the following would *not* result in the audit team's selecting a larger sample of controls for examination?

a. A reduction in the risk of overreliance from 10 percent to 5 percent.

b. An increase in the tolerable rate of deviation from 3 percent to 6 percent.

c. An increase in the expected population deviation rate from 2 percent to 4 percent.

d. All of the above would result in a larger sample of controls.

LO F-2

F.33 Baily Cox, an audit manager, judged that the test of controls of the company's 50,000 purchase transactions should be based on a tolerable rate of deviation of 6 percent, a risk of overreliance of 5 percent, and an expected population deviation rate of 3 percent. Using AICPA sample size tables, Cox determined that the appropriate sample size in this situation would be

a. 49.

b. 78.

c. 132.

d. 195.

LO F-2

F.34 Francona Madden, an audit manager, considered the control risk assessments listed in the left column of the following table in evaluating A. Cardinal's internal control over sales transactions. The sample sizes for the substantive procedures of the customer accounts receivable are shown to the right of each control risk. What risk of overreliance (ROO) could be assigned for tests of controls at each control risk level?

Control Risk	Accounts Receivable Sample	ROO
0.20	400	?
0.50	390	?
0.80	350	?
0.90	190	10%

a. From top to bottom: 5 percent, 10 percent, 1 percent.

b. From top to bottom: 10 percent, 1 percent, 5 percent.

c. From top to bottom: 1 percent, 10 percent, 5 percent.

d. From top to bottom: 1 percent, 5 percent, 10 percent.

LO F-4   F.35   Assume that Dylan Lee found two deviations in a sample of 90 transactions. Using AICPA sample evaluation tables, Lee determined that the ULRD at a 5 percent risk of overreliance is

a. 2.0 percent.

b. 2.2 percent.

c. 5.9 percent.

d. 6.9 percent.

LO F-4   F.36   The interpretation of the ULRD in an attributes sampling application is

a. The estimated rate of deviation in the population with probability equal to the risk of overreliance that the population deviation rate is higher.

b. The estimated rate of deviation in the population with probability equal to the risk of overreliance that the actual rate of deviation is lower.

c. The estimated rate of deviation in the population with certainty that the actual rate of deviation is lower.

d. The estimated rate of deviation in the population with certainty that the actual rate of deviation is higher.

LO F-4   F.37   If an audit team examined 100 transactions and found one deviation from an important control activity, the audit conclusion could be that control risk can be assessed at the associated control risk level when

a. The tolerable rate of deviation is 2 percent.

b. The tolerable rate of deviation is 3 percent.

c. The tolerable rate of deviation is 4 percent.

d. More information about decision criteria is available.

LO F-4   F.38   If an audit team calculated a ULRD of 5 percent when the tolerable rate of deviation was 4 percent, both at the same risk of overreliance, control risk should be

a. Assessed at the level associated with the 4 percent tolerable rate of deviation.

b. Increased and substantive procedures should be adjusted accordingly.

c. Assessed at the maximum level (100 percent) because the company's performance failed the test.

d. Decreased and substantive procedures should be adjusted accordingly.

LO F-1   F.39   In which of the following circumstances would the audit team most likely use attributes sampling?

a. Selecting customer accounts receivable for confirmation.

b. Selecting inventory items for verification of physical quantities.

c. Selecting purchase orders for indication of proper authorization.

d. Selecting additions to property, plant, and equipment during the year.

LO F-4   F.40   Using AICPA sample evaluation tables, determine the conclusion from a statistical sample of internal controls when a sample of 125 documents indicates five deviations if the tolerable rate of deviation is 5 percent, the expected population deviation rate is 2 percent, and the allowance for sampling risk is 3 percent.

a. Accept the evidence as support for assessing a low control risk because the tolerable rate of deviation less the allowance for sampling risk is less than the expected population deviation rate.

b. Use the evidence to assess a higher control risk than planned because the sample rate of deviation plus the allowance for sampling risk exceeds the tolerable rate of deviation.

c. Use the evidence to assess a higher control risk than planned because the tolerable rate of deviation plus the allowance for sampling risk exceeds the expected population deviation rate.

d. Accept the evidence as support for assessing a low control risk because the sample rate of deviation plus the allowance for sampling risk exceeds the tolerable rate of deviation.

LO F-4

F.41 An audit team designed a sample that would provide a 10 percent risk of overreliance that not more than 7 percent of sales invoices lacked credit approval. From previous audits, the audit team expected that 3 percent of the sample invoices lacked proper approval. From the sample of 90 invoices, 7 were found to lack credit approval. Using AICPA sample evaluation tables, the audit team determined that the ULRD was

a. 3.3 percent.

b. 4.5 percent.

c. 7.8 percent.

d. 12.8 percent.

LO F-4

F.42 Based on the information in the preceding question, the audit team determined that the allowance for sampling risk was

a. 2.2 percent.

b. 5.0 percent.

c. 7.8 percent.

d. 10.0 percent.

LO F-4

F.43 If the _____ exceeds the _____, the audit team would decide to rely on internal control as planned and maintain control risk at planned levels.

a. ULRD; tolerable rate of deviation.

b. tolerable rate of deviation; ULRD.

c. expected population deviation rate; tolerable rate of deviation.

d. tolerable rate of deviation; expected population deviation rate.

LO F-4

F.44 If the sample evidence does *not* support the planned level of control risk, the audit team could

a. Increase the assessed level of control risk.

b. Perform additional substantive procedures, reducing the necessary level of detection risk.

c. Expand the sample to achieve an observed ULRD less than the tolerable rate of deviation.

d. All of the above are acceptable.

LO F-4

F.45 Which of the following best describes the method of determining the ULRD?

a. Expected population deviation rate + Allowance for sampling risk.

b. Risk of underreliance + Allowance for sampling risk.

c. Sample rate of deviation + Allowance for sampling risk.

d. Tolerable rate of deviation + Allowance for sampling risk.

LO F-2

F.46 Which of the following factors used to determine sample size is normally based on the extent to which the audit team expects to rely on the internal control being examined?

a. Allowance for sampling risk.

b. Expected population deviation rate.

c. Sample rate of deviation.

d. Tolerable rate of deviation.

LO F-5

F.47 A type of sampling application in which a relatively small initial sample is examined and decisions regarding expanding that sample are based on the results of this initial sample is known as

a. Attributes sampling.

b. Discovery sampling.

c. Sequential sampling.

d. Statistical sampling.

LO F-5

F.48 Jerry Tim is examining an important internal control in the audit of Langly Company. In past audits, deviations from this control have been observed at a minimal rate (less than 0.1 percent); however, because the account balance affected by this control is highly susceptible to fraud, it is important that Tim obtain a high level of assurance that deviations occur at no higher than a predetermined (low) rate. Which of the following sampling methods would Tim most likely use to evaluate this control?

a. Attributes sampling.

b. Discovery sampling.

c. Sequential sampling.

d. Statistical sampling.

LO F-5   F.49 In which step of a sampling plan is nonstatistical sampling different from statistical sampling?

a. Define the characteristic of interest.

b. Define the population.

c. Measure the sample items.

d. Evaluate the sample results.

LO F-5   F.50 The primary benefit of using nonstatistical sampling is that

a. It generally results in a smaller sample size.

b. It removes the need to consider allowance for sampling risk.

c. It is simpler to use.

d. All of the above are true.

Exercises and Problems

connect All applicable Exercises and Problems are available with *Connect*.

LO F-1   F.51 **Test of Controls Objectives and Deviations.**

Required:

Review each of the following controls. Identify (1) the objective of the audit team's test of controls and (2) one example of a deviation from the control.

a. The credit department supervisor reviews each customer's order and approves credit by making a notation on the order.

b. The billing department must receive written notice from the shipping department of actual shipment to a customer before a sale is recorded. The sales record date is supposed to be the shipment date.

c. Billing clerks carefully identify the correct catalog list prices for goods shipped and calculate and verify the amounts billed on invoices for the quantities of goods shipped.

d. Billing clerks review invoices for intercompany sales and mark each one with the code 9 so they will be posted to intercompany sales accounts.

LO F-2, F-4   F.52 **General Attributes Sampling.** Frazier Holyfield, a new staff accountant, is evaluating important controls over the revenue cycle and, more specifically, assessing the operating effectiveness of the control that all shipments made to customers by Top Rank Inc. have been properly invoiced.

Required:

Comment on the following actions that Holyfield performed. You should evaluate each action independently of any other actions.

a. Holyfield decided to inspect documentary evidence that all shipments made by Top Rank have been invoiced by matching shipping documents with invoices. Accordingly, she has identified the population from which she intends to sample as all sales invoices. Top Rank has a computerized list of invoiced sales that she can use to select the appropriate sample.

b. Because Holyfield plans to place a high degree of reliance on this particular control, she assesses the risk of overreliance at 5 percent. In previous years, a 10 percent level was used, but consultation with the engagement manager (Mike Evander) and partner (Donna Arum) indicate that a higher degree of reliance is planned in the current audit.

c. Holyfield assessed the expected population deviation rate at 1 percent. Although the rate of deviation from prior audits has approximated 2 percent, Top Rank has made several improvements in its processing of sales invoices; as a result, she believes that a lower expected population deviation rate is appropriate.

d. Based on the risk of overreliance (5 percent), the expected population deviation rate (1 percent), and the tolerable rate of deviation (4 percent), Holyfield uses sampling tables to calculate a sample size of 156. She then increases the sample size to 175 because the population of sales invoices is extremely large. (More than 30,000 sales invoices are processed per year.)

a. You need to select a sample of recorded cash disbursements. The client used two bank accounts for general disbursements. Account 1 was used during January–August and issued checks numbered 3633–6632. Account 2 was used during May–December and issued checks numbered 0001–6000.

b. You need to select a sample of purchase orders. The client issued prenumbered purchase orders in the sequence 9000–13999. You realize that if you select five-digit random numbers from a table and look for numbers in this sequence, 95 percent of the random numbers you scan will be discards because a table has 100,000 different five-digit random numbers. (The computer is down today!) How can you alter this sequence to reduce the number of instances in which the numbers in the table do not correspond to numbers in the population?

c. You need to select a sample of 100 perpetual inventory records so you can count the quantities while the stock clerks take the physical inventory. The perpetual records have been printed in a control list showing location, item description, and quantity. You have a copy of the list. It is 75 pages long, with 50 lines to a page (40 lines on the last page).

LO F-3

F.58 **Sample Selection.** Robert Janice, CPA, is verifying a sample of controls related to the approval of vouchers for payment. His client, Fave Company, uses a prenumbered voucher system in which a voucher is prepared and approved for all receiving reports and the corresponding vendor's invoice. Based on the prior audit, Janice has verified that the first receiving report number for the year is 12794 and the final receiving report prepared this year is 38121.

Required:

Indicate how Janice could use (1) unrestricted random selection and (2) systematic random selection to select the sample for sample sizes of 50, 100, and 500.

LO F-3

F.59 **Sample Selection.** Hunter McNeal is studying and evaluating Branyon's internal controls related to the mathematical verification of sales invoices. In this verification, Branyon's control activities require that employees perform the following procedures:

- Verify that sales invoices are prepared only for items actually shipped to customers. This activity is evidenced by requiring employees to place a checkmark next to quantities on the sales invoices.
- Verify that prices charged to customers are from approved price lists. This activity is evidenced by requiring employees to place a checkmark next to prices on the sales invoice.
- Verify that extensions and footings on invoices are mathematically accurate. This activity is evidenced by requiring employees to initial the bottom of the invoice in a section marked "Mathematically verified by."

To verify the operating effectiveness of these activities, McNeal established an expected population deviation rate of 3 percent, a tolerable rate of deviation of 6 percent, and a risk of overreliance of 10 percent. Using these parameters, McNeal determined a necessary sample size of 132 invoices, is now ready to select invoices for examination, and is considering the use of systematic selection.

Required:

a. McNeal wants to ensure the selection of a representative sample of sales invoices. What are some of the characteristics that should be considered to ensure that the sample is representative of the population of sales invoices?

b. What issues does the use of systematic selection introduce with respect to McNeal's ability to select a representative sample of sales invoices from the population?

c. Identify any issues associated with the use of systematic selection in the following independent circumstances.

1. Branyon does not maintain invoices in a computerized format but maintains hard copy by date. McNeal has full access to the files containing the invoices.

2. Branyon does not maintain invoices in a computerized format but maintains hard copy according to customer classification ("A" represents high-volume customers; "B," middle-volume customers; and "C," low-volume customers). McNeal has full access to the files containing the invoices.

3. Branyon does not maintain invoices in a computerized format but maintains hard copy by date. Because they are maintained off-site, McNeal does not have full access to the files; however, Branyon has offered to pull invoices selected by McNeal and make them available for the tests of controls.

4. Branyon maintains invoices in a computerized format arranged alphabetically by customer name. This file can be sorted by date, amount of sale, customer number, customer classification, and zip code. McNeal has full access to the computerized files.

LO F-2

F.60 **Sample Size Determination.** Jule Phillips is examining the internal control of Cowboy Company and has identified the mathematical verification of sales invoices as an important control and decided to test this control. Based on a discussion with Cowboy's management, Phillips determined that Cowboy Company's employees were required to indicate their compliance with this control by writing their initials in an appropriate place on the invoice copy.

Assume that Phillips established an acceptable risk of overreliance of 5 percent, an expected population deviation rate of 3 percent, and a tolerable rate of deviation of 9 percent.

Required:

a. Using AICPA sample size tables, determine the appropriate sample size.

b. Indicate how Phillips would assess the three parameters that are used to determine sample size (risk of overreliance, expected population deviation rate, and tolerable rate of deviation).

c. Use the original parameters but now assume that Phillips is willing to increase the acceptable risk of overreliance to 10 percent. Using AICPA sample size tables, determine the new sample size to examine.

d. Provide an explanation for the change in sample size noted in part (c).

LO F-2

F.61 **Sample Size Determination.** Review each of the following independent sets of conditions.

Required:

Use AICPA sample size tables to identify the appropriate sample size for use in a statistical sampling application (ROO = risk of overreliance, EPDR = expected population deviation rate, TRD = tolerable rate of deviation). What is your conclusion regarding the relationship of each of these factors to sample size based on comparing the sample sizes across different combinations of these factors?

a. ROO = 5%, EPDR = 0%, TRD = 7%.

b. ROO = 5%, EPDR = 3%, TRD = 7%.

c. ROO = 5%, EPDR = 3%, TRD = 6%.

d. ROO = 10%, EPDR = 0%, TRD = 7%.

LO F-2

F.62 **Sample Size Determination.** Review each of the following independent sets of conditions.

Required:

Use AICPA sample size tables to identify the appropriate sample size for use in a statistical sampling application (ROO = risk of overreliance, EPDR = expected population deviation rate, TRD = tolerable rate of deviation). What is your conclusion regarding the relationship of each of these factors to sample size based on comparing the sample sizes across different combinations of these factors?

a. ROO = 5%, EPDR = 1%, TRD = 4%.

b. ROO = 5%, EPDR = 1.5%, TRD = 4%.

c. ROO = 5%, EPDR = 1.5%, TRD = 6%.

d. ROO = 10%, EPDR = 1.5%, TRD = 4%.

LO F-2

F.63 **Sample Size Determination.** For each of the following independent cases, use AICPA sample size tables to identify the missing value(s).

	Control			
	1	2	3	4
Risk of overreliance	5.0%	5.0%	10.0%	(d)
Expected population deviation rate	1.25%	2.5%	(c)	1.25%
Tolerable rate of deviation	7.0%	(b)	6.0%	6.0%
Sample size	(a)	68	153	78

F.64 **Sample Size Determination.** Grady Cambridge, CPA, is performing attributes sampling to determine whether all purchases on account are properly approved by the client. Because the client typically makes more than 2,000 purchases on account per year, Cambridge has decided to use sampling instead of examining the entire population of purchases. Based on past experience with this client, Cambridge anticipates a rate of deviation of 1 percent.

Required:

a. What factors should Cambridge consider in determining the necessary sample size? How would the level of these factors be determined?

b. Once the appropriate factors have been determined, describe the process that Cambridge would use in determining the necessary sample size.

c. Assume that Cambridge established a risk of overreliance of 10 percent and a tolerable rate of deviation of 6 percent. Using AICPA sample size tables, determine the appropriate sample size to use in evaluating the controls over approval of purchases on account.

d. How would the following changes impact (a) the factors used to determine sample size and (b) the sample size examined by Cambridge? (Do *not* determine an exact sample size but indicate whether the sample size would be larger, smaller, or unchanged. Treat each of these changes in factors independently in providing your answers.)

  1. Because of increased sales and new lines of business, the number of purchases made by the client on account increased markedly from more than 2,000 to nearly 5,000 during the current year.

  2. The client remediated some control deficiencies related to the purchasing function noted in Cambridge's prior audits. One of these control deficiencies related specifically to the approval of purchases made by the client.

  3. The client has had turnover in the purchasing function during the most recent year. This turnover resulted in a higher-than-normal number of deviations during the first few months of the new employees' tenure. The deviation rate since then has decreased to historical levels.

  4. Cambridge has decided that it would be cost beneficial to seek a reduction in control risk from moderate to low.

  5. Cambridge has decided that it is no longer efficient to test controls at current levels and accordingly increased control risk from moderate levels to high levels.

  6. Because some of its previous suppliers are no longer in business or no longer competitive with respect to price, the client has added a number of new vendors to its approved vendor listing.

e. What are the trade-offs Cambridge must make between increasing the reliance on internal control and maintaining the current level of reliance on internal control?

f. What factors should Cambridge consider in deciding whether to increase the reliance on internal control?

F.65 **Sample Results Evaluation.** Jamie Plane is testing the effectiveness of an important control for Blackheart Inc. Plane is placing a high level of reliance on this control and has assessed a relatively low risk of overreliance (5 percent) and tolerable rate of deviation (6 percent). Based on the acceptable risk of overreliance, expected population deviation rate, and tolerable rate of deviation, Plane determined a sample size of 60 items. The tests of controls revealed three deviations.

Required:

a. Calculate the sample rate of deviation.

b. Using AICPA sample evaluation tables, calculate the ULRD and allowance for sampling risk.

c. Why does the ULRD differ from the sample rate of deviation?

d. What would Plane's conclusion be with respect to the operating effectiveness of the control? What options are available at this time?

e. Ignoring the effects on sample size, how would Plane's decision to accept a higher risk of overreliance (10 percent) affect the conclusions made with respect to the operating effectiveness of the control?

LO F-4

F.66   Sample Results Evaluation.

Required:

Review each of the following independent sets of conditions. For each condition, calculate the (1) sample rate of deviation, (2) ULRD and (3) allowance for sampling risk (n = sample size, d = deviations, ROO = risk of overreliance). What is your conclusion regarding the relationship of each of these factors to the ULRD based on comparing the ULRD across different combinations of these factors?

a. $n = 60$, d = 4, ROO = 5%.

b. $n = 60$, d = 6, ROO = 5%.

c. $n = 60$, d = 6, ROO = 10%.

LO F-4

F.67   Sample Results Evaluation.

Required:

Review each of the following independent sets of conditions. For each condition, calculate the (1) sample rate of deviation, (2) ULRD, and (3) allowance for sampling risk (n = sample size, d = deviations, ROO = risk of overreliance). What is your conclusion regarding the relationship of each of these factors to the ULRD based on comparing the ULRD across different combinations of these factors?

a. $n = 100$, d = 8, ROO = 5%.

b. $n = 100$, d = 4, ROO = 5%.

c. $n = 100$, d = 8, ROO = 10%.

LO F-4

F.68   Sample Results Evaluation.

Required:

	Control			
	1	**2**	**3**	**4**
Sample size	30	(d)	200	50
Number of deviations	2	4	(g)	2
Sample rate of deviation	(a)	(e)	2.5%	(i)
Risk of overreliance	5.0%	5.0%	10.0%	(j)
ULRD	(b)	12.6%	(h)	(k)
Allowance for sampling risk	(c)	(f)	2.1%	8.1%

For each of the following independent cases, use AICPA sample size and sample evaluation tables to identify the missing value(s).

LO F-4

F.69   Sample Results Evaluation. Assume that you are working on the audit of a small company and are examining purchase invoices for the presence of a "received" stamp. The omission of the stamp is thus a deviation. The population is composed of approximately 4,000 invoices processed by the company during the current year.

You decide that a rate of deviation in the population as high as 5 percent would not require any extended audit procedures. However, if the population rate of deviation is more than 5 percent, you would want to assess a higher control risk and conduct more extensive substantive tests.

In each case, write the letter of the sample (A or B) that, in your judgment, provides the best evidence that the rate of deviation in the population is 5 percent or lower (using a risk of overreliance of 5 percent). Assume that each sample is selected at random. Refer to AICPA sample evaluation tables if necessary.

	Case 1		Case 2		Case 3		Case 4		Case 5	
Sample	**A**	**B**	**A**	**B**	**A**	**B**	**A**	**B**	**A**	**B**
Number of invoices examined	75	200	150	25	200	100	100	125	200	150
Number of deviations	1	4	2	0	6	2	1	3	8	4
Sample rate of deviation	1.3	2.0	1.3	0.0	3.0	2.0	1.0	2.4	4.0	2.7

LO F-4

F.70   **Sample Results Evaluation.** Kendall Jackson, CPA, is examining the operating effectiveness of the internal control of Town Mo, a large conglomerate in the music industry. As part of the evaluation, Jackson determined a necessary sample size of 93 items (based on a tolerable rate of deviation of 5 percent, an expected population deviation rate of 0.5 percent, and a risk of overreliance of 5 percent). After properly selecting the 93 items, Jackson found no deviations from the prescribed control activities.

Required:

a. Based on Jackson's sample, determine the sample rate of deviation and ULRD. (Because the AICPA sample evaluation tables do not contain a row for a sample size of 93, round down and use a sample size of 90.)

b. Explain the difference between the ULRD and the sample rate of deviation observed in part (a). How does this difference relate to the use of statistical sampling?

c. What would Jackson conclude with respect to the operating effectiveness of Town Mo's internal control?

d. If Jackson found three deviations in the sample, calculate the sample rate of deviation and use AICPA sample evaluation tables to determine the ULRD. What would Jackson conclude with respect to the operating effectiveness of Town Mo's internal control in this case?

e. Using AICPA sample evaluation tables, determine the maximum number of deviations that Jackson could identify without reducing the reliance on Town Mo's internal control.

f. Repeat part (e) using a 10 percent risk of overreliance. What is the explanation for any differences between this number of deviations and that in part (e)?

LO F-1–F-4

F.71   **Evaluating a Sampling Application.** Tom Barton, an assistant accountant with a local CPA firm, recently graduated from Other University. He studied statistical sampling for auditing in college and wants to impress his employers with his knowledge of modern auditing methods.

Barton decided to select a random sample of payroll checks for the test of controls using a tolerable rate of deviation of 5 percent and an acceptable risk of overreliance of 5 percent. The senior accountant told Barton that 2 percent of the checks audited last year had one or more errors in the calculation of net pay. He decided to audit 100 random checks. Because supervisory personnel had paychecks with higher amounts than production workers, he selected 60 of the supervisor checks and 40 checks of the others. He was very careful to see that the selections of 60 from the April payroll register and 40 from the August payroll register were random.

The audit of this sample yielded two deviations, exactly the 2 percent rate experienced last year. The first was the deduction of federal income taxes based on two exemptions for a supervisory employee whose W-4 form showed four exemptions. The other was payment to a production employee at a rate for a job classification one grade lower than it should have been. The worker had been promoted the week before, and Barton found that in the next payroll he was paid at the correct (higher) rate.

When he evaluated this evidence, Barton decided that these two findings were really not control deviations at all. The withholding of too much tax did not affect the expense accounts, and the proper rate was paid the production worker as soon as the clerk caught up with the change orders. Barton decided that having found zero deviations in a sample of 100, the ULRD at 5 percent risk of overreliance was 3 percent, which easily satisfied his predetermined criterion.

The senior accountant was impressed. Last year he had audited 15 checks from each month, and Barton's work represented a significant time savings. The reviewing partner on the audit also was impressed because she had never thought that statistical sampling could be so efficient, and that was the reason she had never studied the method.

Required:

Identify and explain the mistakes made by Barton.

LO F-2

F.72   **Comprehensive Attributes Sampling.** Audra Dodge, CPA, is performing an attributes sampling plan for her audit of Truck Company. In her audit of cash disbursements, she has identified preparing a voucher and marking it as "paid" prior to preparing and mailing a check to the vendor as an important control. Dodge defined any voucher that was not marked as "paid" as being a deviation.

In performing her sampling application, she established the following parameters:

Risk of overreliance	5%
Expected population deviation rate	1.5%
Tolerable rate of deviation	4%

Required:

a. Identify what factors Dodge considered in establishing the risk of overreliance, expected population deviation rate, and tolerable rate of deviation.

b. Assume that Dodge wished to place additional reliance on this control. How would that affect the three parameters in part (a)?

c. Based on the original parameters, use AICPA sample size tables to determine the appropriate sample size.

d. If Dodge selected the sample size in part (c) and found four deviations, what is the sample rate of deviation?

e. Using AICPA sample evaluation tables, determine the ULRD. (*Note:* If the sample size cannot be directly located on the sample evaluation table, round down to the next highest sample size.)

f. What would Dodge's conclusion be with respect to the functioning of this control?

LO F-1, F-3, F-5   F.73 **Nonstatistical Attributes Sampling.** Aubrey Marblehead is conducting tests of controls on the control that quantities on Rock's receiving reports are appropriately verified. In so doing, Marblehead has inquired of Rock's receiving personnel, who said that they place a mark near the quantities verified and sign the receiving report upon delivery. Marblehead has decided to use nonstatistical sampling for this engagement. Based on the importance of this control and the rate of deviation that has been observed in prior audits, Marblehead has established the following parameters.

Risk of overreliance	5%
Expected population deviation rate	2.75%
Tolerable rate of deviation	7%

Based on the parameters established, Marblehead decides to use a sample of 100 receiving reports.

Required:

a. How would Marblehead define a deviation condition?

b. How would Marblehead appropriately define the population? What steps should be taken to ensure that it is complete?

c. If Rock has a computerized list of all receiving reports, what are some options available to Marblehead in selecting specific items for examination? What precautions should be taken before undertaking the selection of items?

d. For each of the following deviations, determine the sample rate of deviation and indicate Marblehead's decision with respect to the functioning of the control.

   1. 2 deviations.

   2. 4 deviations.

   3. 10 deviations.

LO F-1, F-3, F-5   F.74 **Nonstatistical Attributes Sampling.** Monroe Curtis is auditing the revenue cycle of Kentucky Distilleries and has elected to perform a nonstatistical test of controls. Kentucky Distilleries sells Old Horse Bourbon to wholesale distributors around the country. Because the sale of bourbon is strictly controlled, Curtis does not expect deviations to be present in the system and has assessed control risk as low and selected a sample size of 50 sales. Curtis has defined a deviation as a recorded sale not being supported by a shipping document with a federal tax stamp.

Deciding to use nonstatistical sampling this year to reduce audit hours, Alewine selected 100 invoices from the December invoice files, reasoning that tests closer to year-end are more effective, by selecting every 10th invoice until 100 invoices had been identified. Two invoices differed in amount from the shipping document, and one invoice could not be located. Alewine decided to accept the controls as effective again this year, reasoning the sample rate of deviation was only 2 percent, which is much less than the tolerable rate of deviation used last year.

Required:

As the manager of the Doxey Electronics audit, you have been reviewing the audit documentation. Prepare a list of reviewer comments to discuss with Alewine.

LO F-5

F.78 **Discovery and Sequential Attributes Sampling.** Sydney Siebenthaler, the audit manager for Jennifer's Running Shirts Inc., has just returned from a continuing education class on audit sampling and now wants to use discovery sampling or sequential sampling on the Jennifer's audit because the class instructor said that the sample sizes would be significantly smaller. "Talk about a no-brainer!" Siebenthaler exulted.

Jennifer's has good controls, and the audit team has performed tests of controls over the payroll procedures in previous years to reduce substantive tests of payroll accounts to only analytical procedures. In the previous year, the audit team used the following parameters: risk of overreliance, 10 percent; expected population deviation rate, 2 percent; and tolerable rate of deviation, 10 percent, which resulted in a sample size of 38. The auditors increased (rounded) the sample size to 40 items, and one deviation was found. The resulting ULRD rate was 9.4 percent, and the control was accepted as operating effectively.

Required:

a. Define *discovery sampling*.

b. Do you agree that discovery sampling should be used on the audit of Jennifer's?

c. How would discovery sampling be used?

d. Define *sequential sampling*.

e. Do you agree that sequential sampling should be used on the audit of Jennifer's?

f. How would sequential sampling be used?

USING IDEA IN ATTRIBUTES SAMPLING

Exercises F.79, F.80, and F.81 require the use of IDEA in an attributes sampling context. Elm Manufacturing Company (ELM) is a small manufacturer of backpacks located in Rochelle, Illinois. You are testing controls related to the authorization of sales made to customers on account and are interested in ensuring that goods are only shipped to customers following a formal credit approval. You have access to ELM's electronic records in Connect. The appropriate file for these exercises is the Sales 2017–4th Q data set. Detailed information about ELM, instructions for accessing data sets, a data directory for data sets, and a detailed attributes sampling example (with IDEA screenshots) can be found in Connect.

NOTE: The Sales 2017–4th Q data set contains a total of 410 transactions; because you are only examining the credit approval for goods that have been shipped, you would only examine orders through No. 17383 (a total of 388 shipments).

LO F-2,F-3,F-4

F.79 **Attributes Sampling with IDEA: Determining Sample Size, Selecting Sample Items, and Evaluating Sample Results.** Your audit team has established the following parameters for the examination of ELM's control over the authorization of sales:

Population size	388 shipments
Risk of overreliance	10%
Expected population deviation rate	1%
Tolerable rate of deviation	6%

Required:

Using IDEA, perform the following related to ELM's control over credit approvals.

a. Determine the appropriate sample size. Based on the sample size and preceding parameters, how many deviations could be observed without the audit team reducing their reliance on the authorization control?

b. Using systematic random selection, a random start of 23, as well as the sample size in part (a), select sample items from the population. What are the first five transactions that will be selected for examination?

c. After performing your tests of controls, you have identified three deviations in your sample. What is the ULRD? What conclusion would you draw with respect to the functioning of ELM's controls over the authorization of sales?

LO F-2

F.80 **Attributes Sampling with IDEA: Determining Sample Size.** Your audit team has established the following parameters for the examination of ELM's control over the authorization of sales:

Population size	388 shipments
Risk of overreliance	10%
Expected population deviation rate	1%
Tolerable rate of deviation	6%

Required:

a. Use IDEA to determine the necessary sample size, given the preceding parameters.

Parts (b), (c), and (d) are independent scenarios that affect sample size.

b. Assume the audit team has decided to increase its reliance on this control and reduce control risk related to the authorization of sales on account. Accordingly, it has decided to reduce the risk of overreliance to 5 percent. What is the necessary sample size, holding all other factors constant?

c. Assume that in the past year the audit team noted a greater extent of deviations in the population and decided that an expected population deviation rate of 2 percent would be more appropriate. What is the necessary sample size, holding all other factors constant?

d. Assume that the audit team has decided to reduce its reliance on this control and is willing to increase the tolerable rate of deviation from 6 percent to 8 percent. What is the necessary sample size, holding all other factors constant?

e. How do the results in parts (b), (c), and (d) reflect the relationship between various parameters and sample size?

LO F-4

F.81 **Attributes Sampling with IDEA: Evaluating Sample Results.** Based on a population size of 388 shipments, a 10 percent desired risk of overreliance, an expected population deviation rate of 1 percent, and a tolerable rate of deviation of 6 percent, the audit team selected a sample of 58 items.

In performing tests of controls, your audit team identified three shipments that were not supported by an approved sales order and concluded that these represent deviations from the control activity.

Required:

a. Use IDEA to determine the ULRD. What would the audit team's conclusion be with respect to the functioning of ELM's control over the authorization of sales transactions?

Part (b) is a set of independent scenarios that affect the evaluation of sample results.

b. For each of the following numbers of deviations, use IDEA to determine the ULRD and provide the audit team's conclusion with respect to the functioning of ELM's control over the authorization of sales transactions.

1. 0 deviations.

2. 1 deviations.

3. 2 deviations.

c. How do the results in part (b) reflect the relationship between the number of deviations and the ULRD?

Appendix F.A

AICPA Sample Size Tables

EXHIBIT FA.1 Sample Size Table for 5 Percent Risk of Overreliance (Number of Expected Deviations)

Expected Population Deviation Rate	Tolerable Rate of Deviation										
	2%	3%	4%	5%	6%	7%	8%	9%	10%	15%	20%
0.00%	149 (0)	99 (0)	74 (0)	59 (0)	49 (0)	42 (0)	36 (0)	32 (0)	29 (0)	19 (0)	14 (0)
0.25	236 (1)	157 (1)	117 (1)	93 (1)	78 (1)	66 (1)	58 (1)	51 (1)	46 (1)	30 (1)	22 (1)
0.50	313 (2)	157 (1)	117 (1)	93 (1)	78 (1)	66 (1)	58 (1)	51 (1)	46 (1)	30 (1)	22 (1)
0.75	386 (3)	208 (2)	117 (1)	93 (1)	78 (1)	66 (1)	58 (1)	51 (1)	46 (1)	30 (1)	22 (1)
1.00	590 (6)	257 (3)	156 (2)	93 (1)	78 (1)	66 (1)	58 (1)	51 (1)	46 (1)	30 (1)	22 (1)
1.25	1,030 (13)	303 (4)	156 (2)	124 (2)	78 (1)	66 (1)	58 (1)	51 (1)	46 (1)	30 (1)	22 (1)
1.50		392 (6)	192 (3)	124 (2)	103 (2)	66 (1)	58 (1)	51 (1)	46 (1)	30 (1)	22 (1)
1.75		562 (10)	227 (4)	153 (3)	103 (2)	88 (2)	77 (2)	51 (1)	46 (1)	30 (1)	22 (1)
2.00		846 (17)	294 (6)	181 (4)	127 (3)	88 (2)	77 (2)	68 (2)	46 (1)	30 (1)	22 (1)
2.25		1,466 (33)	390 (9)	208 (5)	127 (3)	88 (2)	77 (2)	68 (2)	61 (2)	30 (1)	22 (1)
2.50			513 (13)	234 (6)	150 (4)	109 (3)	77 (2)	68 (2)	61 (2)	30 (1)	22 (1)
2.75			722 (20)	286 (8)	173 (5)	109 (3)	95 (3)	68 (2)	61 (2)	30 (1)	22 (1)
3.00			1,098 (33)	361 (11)	195 (6)	129 (4)	95 (3)	84 (3)	61 (2)	30 (1)	22 (1)
3.25			1,936 (63)	458 (15)	238 (8)	148 (5)	112 (4)	84 (3)	61 (2)	30 (1)	22 (1)
3.50				624 (22)	280 (10)	167 (6)	112 (4)	84 (3)	76 (3)	40 (2)	22 (1)
3.75				877 (33)	341 (13)	185 (7)	129 (5)	100 (4)	76 (3)	40 (2)	22 (1)
4.00				1,348 (54)	421 (17)	221 (9)	146 (6)	100 (4)	89 (4)	40 (2)	22 (1)
5.00					1,580 (79)	478 (24)	240 (12)	158 (8)	116 (6)	40 (2)	30 (2)
6.00						1,832 (110)	532 (32)	266 (16)	179 (11)	50 (3)	30 (2)
7.00								585 (41)	298 (21)	68 (5)	37 (3)
8.00									649 (52)	85 (7)	37 (3)
9.00										110 (10)	44 (4)
10.00										150 (15)	50 (5)
12.50										576 (72)	88 (11)
15.00											193 (29)
17.50											720 (126)

Note: This table assumes a large population. Sample sizes of more than 2,000 not shown.
Source: AICPA Audit Guide *Audit Sampling.*

EXHIBIT FA.2   Sample Size Table for 10 Percent Risk of Overreliance (Number of Expected Deviations)

Expected Population Deviation Rate	Tolerable Rate of Deviation										
	2%	3%	4%	5%	6%	7%	8%	9%	10%	15%	20%
0.00%	114 (0)	76 (0)	57 (0)	45 (0)	38 (0)	32 (0)	28 (0)	25 (0)	22 (0)	15 (0)	11 (0)
0.25	194 (1)	129 (1)	96 (1)	77 (1)	64 (1)	55 (1)	48 (1)	42 (1)	38 (1)	25 (1)	18 (1)
0.50	194 (1)	129 (1)	96 (1)	77 (1)	64 (1)	55 (1)	48 (1)	42 (1)	38 (1)	25 (1)	18 (1)
0.75	265 (2)	129 (1)	96 (1)	77 (1)	64 (1)	55 (1)	48 (1)	42 (1)	38 (1)	25 (1)	18 (1)
1.00	398 (4)	176 (2)	96 (1)	77 (1)	64 (1)	55 (1)	48 (1)	42 (1)	38 (1)	25 (1)	18 (1)
1.25	708 (9)	221 (3)	132 (2)	77 (1)	64 (1)	55 (1)	48 (1)	42 (1)	38 (1)	25 (1)	18 (1)
1.50	1,463 (22)	265 (4)	132 (2)	105 (2)	64 (1)	55 (1)	48 (1)	42 (1)	38 (1)	25 (1)	18 (1)
1.75		390 (7)	166 (3)	105 (2)	88 (2)	55 (1)	48 (1)	42 (1)	38 (1)	25 (1)	18 (1)
2.00		590 (12)	198 (4)	132 (3)	88 (2)	75 (2)	48 (1)	42 (1)	38 (1)	25 (1)	18 (1)
2.25		974 (22)	262 (6)	132 (3)	88 (2)	75 (2)	65 (2)	42 (1)	38 (1)	25 (1)	18 (1)
2.50			353 (9)	158 (4)	110 (3)	75 (2)	65 (2)	58 (2)	38 (1)	25 (1)	18 (1)
2.75			471 (13)	209 (6)	132 (4)	94 (3)	65 (2)	58 (2)	52 (2)	25 (1)	18 (1)
3.00			730 (22)	258 (8)	132 (4)	94 (3)	65 (2)	58 (2)	52 (2)	25 (1)	18 (1)
3.25			1,258 (41)	306 (10)	153 (5)	113 (4)	82 (3)	58 (2)	52 (2)	25 (1)	18 (1)
3.50				400 (14)	194 (7)	113 (4)	82 (3)	73 (3)	52 (2)	25 (1)	18 (1)
3.75				583 (22)	235 (9)	131 (5)	98 (4)	73 (3)	52 (2)	25 (1)	18 (1)
4.00				873 (35)	274 (11)	149 (6)	98 (4)	73 (3)	65 (3)	25 (1)	18 (1)
5.00					1,019 (51)	318 (16)	160 (8)	115 (6)	78 (4)	34 (2)	18 (1)
6.00						1,150 (69)	349 (21)	182 (11)	116 (7)	43 (3)	25 (2)
7.00							1,300 (91)	385 (27)	199 (14)	52 (4)	25 (2)
8.00								1,437 (115)	424 (34)	60 (5)	25 (2)
9.00									1,577 (142)	77 (7)	32 (3)
10.00										100 (10)	38 (4)
12.50										368 (46)	63 (8)
15.00											126 (19)
17.50											457 (80)

Note: This table assumes a large population. Sample sizes of more than 2,000 not shown.
Source: AICPA Audit Guide *Audit Sampling*.

Appendix F.B

AICPA Sample Evaluation Tables

EXHIBIT FB.1 Sample Evaluation Table for 5 Percent Risk of Overreliance

Sample Size	Actual Number of Deviations Found										
	0	1	2	3	4	5	6	7	8	9	10
20	14.0	21.7	28.3	34.4	40.2	45.6	50.8	55.9	60.7	65.4	69.9
25	11.3	17.7	23.2	28.2	33.0	37.6	42.0	46.3	50.4	54.4	58.4
30	9.6	14.9	19.6	23.9	28.0	31.9	35.8	39.4	43.0	46.6	50.0
35	8.3	12.9	17.0	20.7	24.3	27.8	31.1	34.4	37.5	40.6	43.7
40	7.3	11.4	15.0	18.3	21.5	24.6	27.5	30.4	33.3	36.0	38.8
45	6.5	10.2	13.4	16.4	19.2	22.0	24.7	27.3	29.8	32.4	34.8
50	5.9	9.2	12.1	14.8	17.4	19.9	22.4	24.7	27.1	29.4	31.6
55	5.4	8.4	11.1	13.5	15.9	18.2	20.5	22.6	24.8	26.9	28.9
60	4.9	7.7	10.2	12.5	14.7	16.8	18.8	20.8	22.8	24.8	26.7
65	4.6	7.1	9.4	11.5	13.6	15.5	17.5	19.3	21.2	23.0	24.7
70	4.2	6.6	8.8	10.8	12.7	14.5	16.3	18.0	19.7	21.4	23.1
75	4.0	6.2	8.2	10.1	11.8	13.6	15.2	16.9	18.5	20.1	21.6
80	3.7	5.8	7.7	9.5	11.1	12.7	14.3	15.9	17.4	18.9	20.3
90	3.3	5.2	6.9	8.4	9.9	11.4	12.8	14.2	15.5	16.9	18.2
100	3.0	4.7	6.2	7.6	9.0	10.3	11.5	12.8	14.0	15.2	16.4
125	2.4	3.8	5.0	6.1	7.2	8.3	9.3	10.3	11.3	12.3	13.2
150	2.0	3.2	4.2	5.1	6.0	6.9	7.8	8.6	9.5	10.3	11.1
200	1.5	2.4	3.2	3.9	4.6	5.2	5.8	6.5	7.2	7.8	8.4
300	1.0	1.6	2.1	2.6	3.1	3.5	4.0	4.4	4.8	5.2	5.6
400	0.8	1.2	1.6	2.0	2.3	2.7	3.0	3.3	3.6	3.9	4.3
500	0.6	1.0	1.3	1.6	1.9	2.1	2.4	2.7	2.9	3.2	3.4

Note: This table presents ULRDs as percentages and assumes a large population.
Source: AICPA Audit Guide *Audit Sampling.*

EXHIBIT FB.2 Sample Evaluation Table for 10 Percent Risk of Overreliance

Sample Size	Actual Number of Deviations Found										
	0	1	2	3	4	5	6	7	8	9	10
20	10.9	18.1	24.5	30.5	36.1	41.5	46.8	51.9	56.8	61.6	66.2
25	8.8	14.7	20.0	24.9	29.5	34.0	38.4	42.6	46.8	50.8	54.8
30	7.4	12.4	16.8	21.0	24.9	28.8	32.5	36.2	39.7	43.2	46.7
35	6.4	10.7	14.5	18.2	21.6	24.9	28.2	31.4	34.5	37.6	40.6
40	5.6	9.4	12.8	16.0	19.0	22.0	24.9	27.7	30.5	33.2	35.9
45	5.0	8.4	11.4	14.3	17.0	19.7	22.3	24.8	27.3	29.8	32.2
50	4.6	7.6	10.3	12.9	15.4	17.8	20.2	22.5	24.7	27.0	29.2
55	4.2	6.9	9.4	11.8	14.1	16.3	18.4	20.5	22.6	24.6	26.7
60	3.8	6.4	8.7	10.8	12.9	15.0	16.9	18.9	20.8	22.7	24.6
65	3.5	5.9	8.0	10.0	12.0	13.9	15.7	17.5	19.3	21.0	22.8
70	3.3	5.5	7.5	9.3	11.1	12.9	14.6	16.3	18.0	19.6	21.2
75	3.1	5.1	7.0	8.7	10.4	12.1	13.7	15.2	16.8	18.3	19.8
80	2.9	4.8	6.6	8.2	9.8	11.3	12.8	14.3	15.8	17.2	18.7
90	2.6	4.3	5.9	7.3	8.7	10.1	11.5	12.8	14.1	15.4	16.7
100	2.3	3.9	5.3	6.6	7.9	9.1	10.3	11.5	12.7	13.9	15.0
125	1.9	3.1	4.3	5.3	6.3	7.3	8.3	9.3	10.2	11.2	12.1
150	1.6	2.6	3.6	4.4	5.3	6.1	7.0	7.8	8.6	9.4	10.1
200	1.2	2.0	2.7	3.4	4.0	4.6	5.3	5.9	6.5	7.1	7.6
300	0.8	1.3	1.8	2.3	2.7	3.1	3.5	3.9	4.3	4.7	5.1
400	0.6	1.0	1.4	1.7	2.0	2.4	2.7	3.0	3.3	3.6	3.9
500	0.5	0.8	1.1	1.4	1.6	1.9	2.1	2.4	2.6	2.9	3.1

Note: This table presents ULRDs as percentages and assumes a large population.
Source: AICPA Audit Guide *Audit Sampling.*

MODULE G

Variables Sampling

> *Facts are stubborn, but statistics are more pliable.*
>
> Mark Twain, (pseudonym of Samuel L. Clemens), famous American writer 1835–1910

Professional Standards References

Topic	AU-C/ISA Section	AS Section
Identifying and Assessing the Risks of Material Misstatement	315	2110
Materiality	320	2105
Evaluation of Misstatements	450	2810
Audit Evidence	500	1105
Audit Sampling	530	2315

LEARNING OBJECTIVES

Module G provides a comprehensive example of the use of variables sampling in the audit team's substantive procedures.

Your objectives are to be able to:

LO G-1 Define *variables sampling* and understand when it is used in the audit.

LO G-2 Understand the basic process underlying *monetary unit sampling* (MUS) and when to use MUS.

LO G-3 Identify the factors affecting the size of an MUS sample and calculate the sample size for an MUS application.

LO G-4 Evaluate the results for an MUS sample by calculating the projected misstatement, incremental allowance for sampling risk, and basic allowance for sampling risk.

LO G-5 Understand the basic process underlying *classical variables sampling* and the use of classical variables sampling in an audit (Appendix G.B).

LO G-6 Understand the use of nonstatistical approaches to variables sampling (Appendix G.C).

combined attributes-variables (CAV) sampling, cumulative monetary amount (CMA) sampling, and *dollar-unit sampling (DUS).*

The unique feature of MUS is its definition of the population as the number of dollars (euros, yuan, yen, etc.) in an account balance or class of transactions. (Viewed another way, individual dollars within an account balance or class of transactions are identified as sampling units.) Thus, if a client's accounts receivable are recorded at $300,000, the population is defined as 300,000 one-dollar units. Under MUS, the audit team randomly selects individual dollars from the population for examination. When a dollar is selected in this fashion, the entire "logical unit" (transaction or component of the account balance) is selected for examination. This feature typically makes MUS samples efficient because a small number of transactions or components can be selected for examination yet account for a relatively large dollar amount.

The following are advantages associated with the use of MUS:

- MUS typically results in relatively smaller sample sizes (in terms of the number of transactions or components selected for examination) compared to classical variables sampling.
- MUS samples typically include transactions or components reflecting relatively large dollar amounts.
- MUS is more effective in identifying misstatements in accounts when overstatement is the primary concern (such as revenues and assets).
- MUS is generally simpler to use than classical variables sampling, which often requires complex calculations.

In contrast, the following are disadvantages associated with the use of MUS:

- MUS provides a more conservative (higher) estimate of misstatement in the account balance or class of transactions compared to classical variables sampling. As a result, MUS is more likely to signal the need for an adjustment in the account balance or class of transactions, which will likely entail performance of additional procedures by the audit team.
- MUS is not effective in identifying misstatements in accounts when understatement is the primary concern (such as liabilities and expenses).
- The expansion of an MUS sample is difficult when preliminary results indicate that the account balance or class of transactions is materially misstated.
- MUS requires special considerations for logical units having a zero or negative balance. In some cases, logical units having these characteristics indicate employee fraud.

In summary, MUS is best used when the audit team expects to find few or no misstatements and when overstatement (existence assertion) is of greatest concern. In contrast, when a relatively large number of misstatements is expected or when understatement (completeness assertion) is of greatest concern, MUS is less effective.

In today's audit environment, computerized audit techniques are used to conduct MUS. Consider the following illustration of the audit team's examination of sales transactions using the *Sample-Detailed Sales* database in IDEA. This database contains 900 sales transactions totaling $12,563,283 (rounded); of these, four transactions have a zero balance, and one has a negative balance ($52.71, or rounded to $53.) Because zero and negative items require special consideration in MUS, the audit team will exclude these transactions from the population to be sampled, resulting in a population of 895 transactions with a recorded balance of $12,563,336. (For the remainder of this illustration, all amounts will be rounded to the nearest dollar.)

The audit team is examining the *existence* and *valuation and allocation* assertions and selects sales transactions for confirmation. This example illustrates how the audit team calculates sample size, selects sample items, and evaluates sample results through manual calculations. When the client maintains its records in computerized format (it would be difficult to imagine many instances where this would not be the case), computer software is used to perform these tasks.

Steps 1–3: Planning

Recall that, in the planning stages of MUS, the audit team (1) determines the objective, (2) defines the characteristic of interest, and (3) defines the population. The objective of any variables sampling application is to provide evidence regarding the fairness of the relevant assertions for the account being examined. These assertions determine the type of substantive procedures selected by the auditor for an account balance or class of transactions, which ultimately determines the nature of items selected for examination. To verify the *existence* and *valuation and allocation* assertions, the audit team confirms accounts receivable and selects a sample of "items" for confirmation.

Once the objective of sampling has been determined, the audit team defines the characteristic of interest. In a variables sampling application, the audit team is interested in determining the proper amount at which the items *should be* recorded; this amount is often referred to as the **audited value**, which is simply the dollar amount at which the item would be recorded assuming that no mistakes in judgment or mistakes in the application of generally accepted accounting principles were made. In an MUS application, the characteristic of interest is the difference between the recorded balance and the audited value, or the amount of *misstatement*.

The final step in the planning stage of MUS is to define the population of interest. As noted earlier, one of the most important distinctions of MUS is that the population is defined as all of the *individual dollars* (or euros, yuan, yen, etc.) within the account balance or class of transactions. Recall that the population of sales transactions is 895 transactions recorded at $12,563,336. As a result, MUS defines the population as 12,563,336 individual dollars of accounts receivable. Once defined, it is important that the audit team ensure the completeness and accuracy of the population prior to beginning the sampling process.

AUDITING INSIGHT	Are These Transactions Too Small?

One reason that **Ernst & Young** may have failed to detect a massive fraud at **HealthSouth** (a large provider of diagnostic imaging, outpatient surgery, and rehabilitation services) is its definition of the population from which its team selected transactions. HealthSouth executives knew that Ernst & Young would not examine items of less than $5,000; as a result, instead of preparing large dollar entries to reclassify expenses as assets, they prepared thousands of individual journal entries having amounts of less than $5,000.

Source: "Behind the Wave of Corporate Fraud: A Change in How Auditors Work," *The Wall Street Journal*, March 25, 2004, pp. A1, A14.

✅ REVIEW CHECKPOINTS

G.3 Define *monetary unit sampling (MUS)*. What is the unique feature of MUS?

G.4 What are the advantages and disadvantages of using MUS? Under what conditions is it best used?

G.5 How are the substantive procedures performed by the audit team related to the objective of MUS?

G.6 What is the typical characteristic of interest in an MUS application?

Step 4: Determine the Sample Size

LO G-3
Identify the factors affecting the size of an MUS sample and calculate the sample size for an MUS application.

The *sample size* represents the number of items that the audit team examines. In variables sampling, these items are transactions or components underlying the account balance or class of transactions being audited. Four main factors influence the sample size in an MUS application:

- Sampling risk (risk of incorrect acceptance).
- Tolerable misstatement.
- Expected misstatement.
- Population size.

As with all statistical sampling applications, the audit team must now adjust the detected misstatements to control for exposure to the risk of incorrect acceptance. This process requires the audit team to calculate a conservative estimate of the total misstatement composed of three separate components: projected misstatement, incremental allowance for sampling risk, and basic allowance for sampling risk.

Projected Misstatement

The **projected misstatement** assumes that the entire sampling interval contains the same percentage of misstatement as the item examined by the auditor. From Exhibit G.4 the audit team detected three misstatements. Exhibit G.5 illustrates how these misstatements are projected to the sampling interval from which they were drawn. (The columns for Invoice, Difference, and Tainting Percentage were drawn from Exhibit G.4.)

EXHIBIT G.5
Calculation of Projected Misstatement for Sales Transactions

Invoice	Difference	Tainting Percentage		Sampling Interval		Projected Misstatement
1000413	$ 4,650	10%	×	$147,804	=	$ 14,780
1000762	3,291	20	×	147,804	=	29,561
1000091	85,797	2	×	N/A	=	85,797
	$93,738				=	$130,138

Although the calculations in Exhibit G.5 are straightforward, note that the misstatement related to invoice 1000091 is not projected to the sampling interval in the same manner as the other two misstatements. Why? Recall from Exhibit G.4 that this transaction has a recorded balance of $4,289,855 and an audited value of $4,204,058. *Because the recorded balance is higher than the sampling interval, there is no need to project the misstatement to the sampling interval.* As a result, the projected misstatement for this particular transaction would equal the actual misstatement detected by the audit team.

Incremental Allowance for Sampling Risk

The calculation of the projected misstatement in Exhibit G.5 assumes that the remainder of the sampling interval is misstated to the same extent (based on the tainting percentage) as the item examined by the auditor. Of course, the remainder of the interval could be misstated to a higher, lower, or same extent as the item examined. To control exposure to sampling risk, the audit team calculates an adjustment to the projected misstatement that uses the confidence factors shown in Appendix G.A. (An excerpt of this table is shown here.)

Number of Overstatement Misstatements	Risk of Incorrect Acceptance = 5%	Risk of Incorrect Acceptance = 10%
0	3.00	2.31
1	4.75	3.89
2	6.30	5.33
3	7.76	6.69
4	9.16	8.00

This adjustment is referred to as the **incremental allowance for sampling risk** and is calculated as follows:

1. For all projected misstatements whose recorded balance is less than the sampling interval, rank the projected misstatements in descending order based on the dollar amount.
2. For each misstatement in step 1, determine the incremental confidence factor associated with the discovery of the misstatement. The confidence factor associated with zero overstatement errors and a 10 percent risk of incorrect acceptance from the above excerpt is 2.31; for one overstatement error, the factor is 3.89. As a result, the *incremental confidence factor* for the discovery of the first overstatement error is 1.58 (3.89 − 2.31).

EXHIBIT G.6
Calculation of Incremental Allowance for Sampling Risk for Sales Transactions

Invoice	Projected Misstatement		Incremental Confidence Factor		Incremental Allowance for Sampling Risk
1000762	$29,561	×	(3.89 − 2.31) − 1.00	=	$17,145
1000430	14,780	×	(5.33 − 3.89) − 1.00	=	6,503
					$23,648

The incremental confidence factor for the second overstatement error is 1.44 (5.33 − 3.89). These factors are highlighted in the above excerpt.

3. For each misstatement in step 1, multiply the projected misstatement by the incremental confidence factor (determined in step 2) minus 1.00 (subtracting 1.00 accounts for the fact that the misstatement has already been projected over the sampling interval when determining the projected misstatement).[4] For projected misstatements when the recorded balance is higher than or equal to the sampling interval, no incremental allowance for sampling risk needs to be determined because the projected misstatement exceeds the sampling interval.

The calculation of the incremental allowance for sampling risk is shown in Exhibit G.6. The incremental allowance for sampling risk attempts to control for the possibility that the misstatements detected in items examined by the audit team were not representative of the misstatements in the remainder of the sampling interval that was not examined by the auditor.

Basic Allowance for Sampling Risk

Both the projected misstatement and the incremental allowance for sampling risk apply to sampling intervals in which the audit team's substantive procedures revealed a misstatement. However, what about those sampling intervals in which no misstatement was discovered? For example, assume that the audit team evaluated an invoice recorded at $42,821 and found no misstatement. Is it reasonable to conclude that the entire sampling interval of $147,804 represented by that invoice contained no misstatements? To account for this possibility, the audit team calculates a **basic allowance for sampling risk** to provide a statistical measure of the misstatement that could be included in sampling intervals in which the audit team did not detect a misstatement.

Although the philosophy behind the calculation of the basic allowance for sampling risk is somewhat technical, the calculation is relatively straightforward. To calculate the basic allowance for sampling risk, multiply the sampling interval by the confidence factor for the risk of incorrect acceptance. The confidence factor corresponding to zero overstatement errors is selected because these sampling intervals did not contain an overstatement error. The basic allowance for sampling risk is calculated as follows:

$$\text{Basic allowance for sampling risk} = \text{Sampling interval} \times \text{Confidence factor}$$
$$= \$147,804 \times 2.31$$
$$= \$341,427$$

Note that the basic allowance for sampling risk would be calculated in all instances, even when the audit team detected no misstatements.

Upper Limit on Misstatements

The **upper limit on misstatements (ULM)** is the sum of the three components discussed in this subsection: the projected misstatement, the incremental allowance for sampling risk, and the basic allowance for sampling risk. The upper limit on misstatements is the amount that has a (1 − *Risk of incorrect acceptance*) probability of equaling or exceeding the true amount of misstatement in the population. Stated another way, there is a

[4]Alternatively, the audit team could multiply the projected misstatement by the incremental confidence factor and subtract the projected misstatement from this same amount. This calculation yields the same result as that illustrated in Exhibit G.6.

Both MUS and classical variables sampling are statistical sampling methods that explicitly control the audit team's exposure to sampling risk in determining sample size, selecting sample items, and evaluating sample results. However, it is important to note that generally accepted auditing standards do not require the use of statistical sampling methods; in many cases, it is easier and more efficient to use **nonstatistical sampling methods**. Further discussion of nonstatistical sampling, as well as an example of using nonstatistical sampling, is shown in Appendix G.C.

AUDITING INSIGHT   Audit Sampling in Practice

A recent survey of the sampling practices of six international accounting firms (including the Big Four) revealed the following with respect to variables sampling techniques.

1. While both MUS and classical variables sampling approaches were used, MUS approaches were used more frequently.
2. Four of the six firms emphasized the use of statistical sampling methods but permitted the use of nonstatistical methods. Three

of these four firms indicated that a larger sample size would be required if a nonstatistical technique was used (essentially imposing a "penalty" for the use of nonstatistical methods).

Source: B.E. Christensen, R.J. Elder, and S.M. Glover, "Behind the Numbers: Insights into Large Audit Firm Sampling Practices," *Accounting Horizons,* March 2015, pp. 61–81.

VARIABLES SAMPLING: DOCUMENTING

The audit team is required to document various information related to the sampling procedure. The information that would be documented depends upon the type of sampling application (MUS, classical variables sampling, or nonstatistical sampling) but generally includes the following:

- Information on the objective of sampling and assertions evaluated; definition of the characteristic of interest; and definition of the population and the sampling unit, including how the audit team verified the completeness and accuracy of the population being sampled (steps 1–3).[5]

AUDITING INSIGHT   "Big Data" and the Future of Audit Sampling

New technologies and the use of "Big Data" have the potential to significantly affect the traditional audit engagement. Previously, audit teams were limited to gathering traditional forms of evidence as to the fairness of financial statement account balances (or individual classes of transactions) by performing substantive tests of details on only a sample of items that comprise the entire population. In effect, under current auditing standards and practice, a significant portion of many audit populations are not subjected to any form of testing or assurance.

The potential now exists to use new technologies and both qualitative and quantitative data to provide some level of assurance on an entire audit population. For example, assume that a client's accounts receivable is comprised of more than 150,000 customer accounts and that the audit team has identified a number of factors that can be used to identify components or transactions that have an extremely low likelihood of being misstated. Based on initial screens of all 150,000 accounts, the audit team concludes that all but 100 of these accounts have an extremely low likelihood of being misstated; the audit team

then decides to perform substantive tests of detail (e.g., traditional positive confirmation procedures with customers) on each of these 100 accounts.

The audit team's testing could be viewed through one of two perspectives. From a traditional perspective, the audit team has performed substantive tests and obtained assurance on 100 of the 150,000 customer accounts. Alternatively, the use of qualitative and quantitative factors as an initial screen could be viewed as having provided some assurance (albeit a lower level than confirmation) on 149,900 components, with the audit team using confirmations to provide higher levels of assurance on the remaining 100 components. In this latter case, it could be argued that the audit team did not sample, but has examined the entire population.

As the existence and availability of new technologies and the use of Big Data increase, auditing standards setting bodies will face situations such as that described above. These considerations will obviously impact the role and nature of sampling in the audit.

[5]Steps refer to the seven-step procedure discussed at the beginning of this module.

- The sampling technique used and definition of a misstatement.
- The method and parameters used to determine sample size, as well as the rationale for these assessments (step 4).
- The sample size determined based on the parameters (step 4).
- Information on the selection of sample items and a list of items selected and examined by the audit team (step 5).
- A description of the substantive procedures performed on each item selected; a list of misstatements (step 6); and the determination of the upper limit on misstatements (MUS), precision interval (classical variables sampling), or estimated audited balance (nonstatistical sampling) (step 7).
- The audit team's conclusion with respect to the fairness of the recorded balance, including qualitative factors considered, and the effect of this conclusion on the financial statement opinion.

☑ REVIEW CHECKPOINTS

G.21 Define *classical variables sampling* and *nonstatistical sampling.* Are these methods viable options to monetary unit sampling?

G.22 What information related to variables sampling applications does the audit team typically document?

Summary

This module discusses variables sampling, which the audit team uses in performing substantive procedures. When performing variables sampling, the audit team has the primary objective of determining whether an account balance or class of transactions is fairly stated. As with any sampling application, the audit team is exposed to sampling risk (the risk that the decision made based on the sample differs from the decision that would have been made if the entire population were examined). Using statistical sampling allows the audit team to control this sampling risk (referred to as the *risk of incorrect acceptance*) in determining the appropriate sample size and evaluating the sample results. Two primary statistical types of variables sampling plans are monetary unit sampling (MUS) and classical variables sampling (of these, MUS is more commonly used in practice).

When using MUS, the audit team calculates an upper limit on misstatements, which has a (1 − *Risk of incorrect acceptance*) probability of equaling or exceeding the true amount of misstatement in the population. If the upper limit on misstatements is less than or equal to the tolerable misstatement, the audit team would conclude that the account balance is fairly stated; in contrast, if the upper limit on misstatements exceeds the tolerable misstatement, the audit team would either propose an adjustment to the account balance or class of transactions or expand the sample. MUS is unique in defining the sampling unit as an individual dollar in an account balance or class of transactions. As a result, MUS tends to select larger dollar components for examination.

Classical variables sampling uses normal distribution theory and the central limit theorem to provide a range of either the recorded balance of the account balance or class of transactions or the misstatement in the account balance or class of transactions.

Nonstatistical sampling is acceptable under generally accepted auditing standards. Instead of using statistical theory to determine sample size and allowance for sampling risk, auditors rely on their professional judgment in making these decisions.

LO G-2

G.28 The unique feature of monetary unit sampling is that
    a. Sampling units are not chosen at random.
    b. A dollar unit selected in a sample is not replaced before the sample selection is completed.
    c. Auditors need not worry about the risk of incorrect acceptance decision.
    d. The population is defined as the number of monetary units in an account balance or class of transactions.

LO G-3

G.29 When determining sample size under monetary unit sampling, an audit team does *not* need to make a judgment or estimate of
    a. Audit risk.
    b. Tolerable misstatement.
    c. Expected misstatement.
    d. Standard deviation.

LO G-2

G.30 Which of the following statements is *correct* about monetary unit sampling?
    a. The risk of incorrect acceptance must be specified.
    b. Smaller logical units have a higher probability of selection in the sample than larger units.
    c. Each logical unit in the population has an equally likely chance of being selected in the sample.
    d. The projected misstatement cannot be calculated when one or more misstatements are discovered.

LO G-2

G.31 One of the primary advantages of monetary unit sampling is the fact that
    a. It is an effective method of sampling for evidence of understatement in asset accounts.
    b. The sample selection automatically achieves high-dollar selection and stratification.
    c. The sample selection provides for including a representative number of small-value components.
    d. Expanding the sample for additional evidence is relatively simple.

LO G-3

G.32 Which of the following would *not* cause the audit team to select a larger sample of items under a monetary unit sampling application?
    a. A reduction in the risk of incorrect acceptance from 10 percent to 5 percent.
    b. An increase in the tolerable misstatement from $30,000 to $60,000.
    c. An increase in the expected misstatement from $20,000 to $40,000.
    d. All of these would result in selecting a larger sample.

LO G-4

G.33 Assume that an account with a recorded balance of $5,000 has an audited value of $3,000. By using monetary unit sampling, if the sampling interval is $1,500, the projected misstatement would be
    a. $600.
    b. $900.
    c. $2,000.
    d. $3,000.

LO G-4

G.34 If the _____ is less than the _____, the audit team would conclude that the account balance is fairly stated.
    a. Projected misstatement; tolerable misstatement.
    b. Tolerable misstatement; projected misstatement.
    c. Upper limit on misstatements; tolerable misstatement.
    d. Tolerable misstatement; upper limit on misstatements.

LO G-4

G.35 If the upper limit on misstatements is calculated at $17,800 and the tolerable misstatement is $15,000, what is the minimum amount of adjustment necessary for the audit team to issue an unmodified opinion on the client's financial statements?
    a. $0.
    b. $2,800.
    c. $4,800.
    d. $14,800.

LO G-5

G.36 (Appendix G.B) Alice Rathermel audited LoHo Company's inventory using sampling. She examined 120 items from an inventory compilation list and discovered net overstatement of $480. The audited items had a book (recorded) value of $48,000. There were 1,200 inventory items listed, and the total recorded inventory amount was $490,000. What is the projected misstatement using mean-per-unit estimation?

a. $480.

b. $576,000.

c. $10,000.

d. $480,000.

LO G-5   G.37 (Appendix G.B) To determine the sample size for a classical variables sampling application, an audit team should consider the tolerable misstatement, risk of incorrect acceptance, risk of incorrect rejection, population size, population variability, and

a. Expected misstatement in the account.

b. Overall materiality for the financial statements taken as a whole.

c. Risk of assessing control risk too low.

d. Risk of assessing control risk too high.

LO G-4   G.38 Which of the following components is *not* used in determining the upper limit on misstatements?

a. Basic allowance for sampling risk.

b. Incremental allowance for sampling risk.

c. Projected misstatement.

d. Tolerable misstatement.

LO G-4   G.39 The projected misstatement is determined by multiplying the sampling interval by the

a. Risk of incorrect acceptance.

b. Incremental confidence factor.

c. Confidence factor.

d. Tainting percentage.

LO G-4   G.40 Which of the following steps involved with determining the upper limit on misstatements is ordinarily performed *earliest*?

a. Multiply the sampling interval by the tainting percentage.

b. Determine the audited value of the item and compare it to the recorded balance.

c. Calculate the basic allowance for sampling risk.

d. Calculate the incremental allowance for sampling risk.

LO G-3   G.41 A component of an account balance has a recorded balance of $10,000 and an audited value of $8,000. By using monetary unit sampling, if the sampling interval is $20,000, the projected misstatement would be

a. $2,000.

b. $4,000.

c. $5,000.

d. $10,000.

LO G-4   G.42 Which of the following statements is *not* true with respect to the calculation of the upper limit on misstatements?

a. The tainting percentage is determined based on the difference between the recorded balance and the audited value.

b. A separate incremental allowance for sampling risk is calculated for each misstatement discovered by the auditor.

c. If no misstatements are detected, the basic allowance for sampling risk equals zero.

d. The projected misstatement is determined by multiplying the sampling interval by the tainting percentage.

LO G-5   G.43 (Appendix G.B) Which of the following courses of action would an audit team most likely follow in planning a sample of cash disbursements if the audit team is aware of several unusually large cash disbursements?

a. Increase the sample size to reduce the effect of the unusually large disbursements.

b. Continue to draw new samples until all unusually large disbursements appear in the sample.

c. Set the tolerable deviation rate at a lower level than originally planned.

d. Stratify the cash disbursements population so that the unusually large disbursements are selected.

(AICPA adapted)

LO G-3

G.50 Sample Size and Sampling Interval Determination: Monetary Unit Sampling. Blythe Drake is conducting an audit of Newman and is using MUS to select a sample of customer accounts receivable for confirmation. Newman's accounts receivable are recorded at $10,000,000 and comprise 2,000 customer accounts. Drake has established the following parameters for the investigation:

- Risk of incorrect acceptance = 5%.
- Tolerable misstatement = $250,000.
- Expected misstatement = $50,000.

Required:

a. Determine the sample size and sampling interval that Drake used in the audit of Newman's accounts receivable.

b. Based on the calculations in part (a), briefly describe how Drake would select customer accounts from the population of accounts receivable balances for confirmation.

c. Holding all other factors constant, determine the sample size and sampling interval assuming each of the following independent changes in Drake's sampling parameters:

1. Because of improvements in Newman's internal control policies related to accounts receivable processing from previous years, Drake believes that a risk of incorrect acceptance of 10 percent is now acceptable in the current engagement.

2. Because of the closeness of certain ratios to key debt covenants (particularly the current and quick ratios, which are highly influenced by accounts receivable), Drake believes that the tolerable misstatement should be decreased from $250,000 to $125,000.

3. Because of unusual circumstances in the previous year, some misstatements occurred in sales transaction processing that resulted in misstatements in accounts receivable. These misstatements are not anticipated to occur during the upcoming year. As a result, Drake believes that expected misstatement can be decreased from $50,000 to $25,000.

d. How do the changes noted in part (c) illustrate the relationship between sample size and various factors?

e. Describe the relationship between the sample size and sampling interval. Provide a brief explanation as to the nature of this relationship.

LO G-3

G.51 Sample Size Relationships: Monetary Unit Sampling. For each of the following cases, provide the missing information.

Recorded balance	$1,500,000	$190,000	(C)
Sample size	115	(B)	124
Sampling interval	(A)	$4,222	$18,000

LO G-3

G.52 Sample Size Relationships: Monetary Unit Sampling. Noel Frehley is examining the accounts receivable of Kiss Company and is considering the use of MUS. Kiss's accounts receivable are recorded at $400,000. Based on the necessary level of risk, Frehley has established a risk of incorrect acceptance of 5 percent. In addition, based on previous audits, Frehley estimates misstatements of $10,000. Finally, based on the overall level of performance materiality, Frehley has established tolerable misstatement at $20,000.

Required:

a. Determine the necessary sample size for Frehley's examination of Kiss Company's accounts receivable.

b. Assume that Frehley was interested in trying to reduce the necessary sample size. What are some options available in this regard?

c. Based on a discussion with the senior manager, Frehley knows that increasing the level of the risk of incorrect acceptance will reduce sample size. For the same level of expected misstatement, tolerable misstatement, and population size, determine the sample size for a risk of incorrect acceptance of 10 percent.

LO G-4   G.53 **Projected Misstatement Calculation: Monetary Unit Sampling.** For each of the following independent misstatements, identify the missing value:

	1	2	3	4
Recorded balance	$15,000	$30,000	(e)	$12,000
Audited value	$12,000	(c)	$6,000	(g)
Tainting percentage	(a)	5%	25%	(h)
Sampling interval	$50,000	(d)	$25,000	$48,000
Projected misstatement	(b)	$5,000	(f)	$24,000

LO G-4   G.54 **Upper Limit on Misstatements Calculation: Monetary Unit Sampling.** Jordan Thomas is using MUS to examine a client's accounts receivable balance. Using a sample size of 100 items and a sampling interval of $12,300, Thomas identified the following misstatements:

Item	Recorded Balance	Audited Value
1	$15,000	$12,500
2	10,000	4,000
3	3,000	2,000

Required:

a. Calculate the upper limit on misstatements assuming a risk of incorrect acceptance of (1) 5 percent and (2) 10 percent.

b. Based on your calculations in part (a), comment on the relationship between the risk of incorrect acceptance and the upper limit on misstatements.

LO G-4   G.55 **Upper Limit on Misstatements Calculation: Monetary Unit Sampling.** Carson Allister is performing an MUS application in the audit of Bird Company's accounts receivable. Based on the acceptable level of the risk of incorrect acceptance of 5 percent and a tolerable misstatement of $120,000, Allister has calculated a sample size of 75 items and a sampling interval of $25,000. After examining the sample items, the following misstatements were identified:

Item	Recorded Balance	Audited Value
1	$35,000	$28,000
2	10,000	8,000
3	6,000	3,000

Required:

a. Calculate the upper limit on misstatements for Bird Company's accounts receivable.

b. Provide a brief description of the meaning of the upper limit on misstatements calculated in part (a).

c. What would Allister's conclusion be with respect to the fairness of Bird's accounts receivable balance?

LO G-4   G.56 **Upper Limit on Misstatements Calculation: Monetary Unit Sampling.** The auditors mailed positive confirmations on 60 customers' accounts receivable balances. The company's accounts receivable balance comprised 2,356 customer accounts with a total recorded balance of $19,600,000, and the sampling interval was $280,000. The auditors received four positive confirmation returns reporting exceptions. Upon follow-up, they found the following:

- *Account 2333.* Recorded balance $8,345. The account was overstated by $1,669 because the client made an arithmetic mistake recording a credit memo. The company issued only 86 credit memos during the year. The auditors examined all of them for the same arithmetic mistake and found no similar misstatements.
- *Account 363.* Recorded balance $7,460. The account was overstated by $1,865 because the company sold merchandise to a customer with payment due in six months plus 15 percent interest. The billing clerk made a mistake and recorded the sales price and the unearned interest as the sale and receivable amount. Inquiries revealed that the company always sold on "payment due immediately" terms but had made an exception for this customer.

d. Based on the four overstatements identified by Mayo, calculate the upper limit on misstatements. Based on this upper limit on misstatements, what general statement can be made with respect to the extent of misstatement in the account balance?

e. What is your initial decision with respect to the fairness of Foley's accounts receivable balance?

f. Review each of the parameters established by Mayo (expected misstatement, tolerable misstatement, and risk of incorrect acceptance). Do any differences in the current engagement raise questions with respect to the level of these parameters?

g. What are the potential effect(s) of the changes in parameters noted in part (f) on the sampling application?

LO G-3, G-4   G.60 **Comprehensive Problem: Monetary Unit Sampling.** Clint Walker was examining the accounts receivable of Country Music Inc. Its accounts receivable were recorded at $1,500,000. Based on past audits, Walker established tolerable misstatement at 10 percent of the recorded account balance and anticipated a very small level of misstatement in Country Music's accounts receivable ($50,000). In his previous assessments of audit risk, risk of material misstatement, and analytical procedures risk, Walker had established a necessary risk of incorrect acceptance of 10 percent.

Required:

a. Calculate the sampling interval and sample size that Walker would use in the audit of Country Music.

b. Reperform the calculations in part (a) if Walker had established a risk of incorrect acceptance of (1) 5 percent and (2) 20 percent. Based on your calculations, describe the relationship between the necessary level of the risk of incorrect acceptance and the sample size and sampling interval.

c. [*Note: Part (c) is unrelated to parts (a) and (b).*] If Walker had detected the following four overstatements, determine the projected misstatement.

Recorded Balance	Audited Value	Sampling Interval
$ 3,500	$ 1,750	$ 8,000
1,000	200	8,000
12,000	10,000	8,000
5,000	4,000	8,000

d. Based on the results in part (c) and using a 10 percent risk of incorrect acceptance, calculate the upper limit on misstatements.

e. Reperform the calculation in part (d) using a risk of incorrect acceptance of (1) 5 percent and (2) 20 percent. Based on your calculation, describe the relationship between the necessary level of the risk of incorrect acceptance and the upper limit on misstatements.

f. Using a risk of incorrect acceptance of (1) 5 percent, (2) 10 percent, and (3) 20 percent, determine what Walker's conclusion would be with respect to Country Music's accounts receivable. How do different levels of the risk of incorrect acceptance influence the likelihood of concluding that the account balance is fairly stated?

LO G-3, G-4   G.61 **Comprehensive Problem: Monetary Unit Sampling.** Dylan Mays is auditing the accounts receivable of Channel Company. Channel's accounts receivable were recorded at $2,000,000 and comprised more than 1,500 customer accounts. However, Channel's ten largest customers' balances comprised a high percentage of the recorded accounts receivable (over $500,000, or 25 percent). As a result, Mays is considering the use of MUS.

Based on prior audits and other judgments, Mays has established the following parameters:

Risk of incorrect acceptance	5%
Tolerable misstatement	$120,000
Expected misstatement	$ 24,000

Required:

a. Briefly identify what factors Mays should consider in determining sample size and how these factors would be assessed.

b. Calculate the necessary sample size and sampling interval used by Mays in the audit of Channel Company.

c. Given the information in part (b), describe how Mays would select the sample from Channel's computerized accounts receivable ledger.

d. [*Note: Part (d) is unrelated to parts (b) and (c).*] If Mays detected the following three misstatements, determine the projected misstatement.

Recorded Balance	Audited Value	Sampling Interval
$ 45,000	$ 40,000	$ 13,000
8,000	6,000	13,000
12,000	9,000	13,000

e. Based on the results in part (d) and a 5 percent risk of incorrect acceptance, calculate the upper limit on misstatements.

f. Based on the calculation in part (e), determine what Mays's conclusion would be with respect to Channel Company's accounts receivable.

LO G-2

G.62 Mistakes in a Monetary Unit Sampling Application. Kelsey Mead, CPA, was engaged to audit Jiffy Company's financial statements for the year ended August 31.

For the current year, Mead decided to use MUS to select accounts receivable for confirmation because MUS uses each account in the population as a separate sampling unit. Mead expected to discover many overstatements but presumed that the MUS sample size still would be smaller than the corresponding sample size for classical variables sampling.

Mead reasoned that the MUS sample would automatically result in a stratified sample because each account would have an equal chance of being selected for confirmation. Additionally, the selection of negative (credit) balances would be facilitated without special considerations.

Mead computed the sample size using the risk of incorrect acceptance, the total recorded book amount of the receivables, and the number of misstated accounts allowed. Mead divided the total recorded book amount of the receivables by the sample size to determine the sampling interval and then calculated the standard deviation of the dollar amounts of the accounts selected for evaluation of the receivables.

Mead's calculated sample size was 60 and the sampling interval was determined to be $10,000. However, only 58 different accounts were selected because two accounts were so large that the sampling interval caused each of them to be selected twice. Mead proceeded to send confirmation requests to 55 of the 58 customers. Each of the three accounts originally selected for the sample had insignificant recorded balances under $20. Mead ignored these three small accounts and substituted the three largest accounts that had not been selected by the random selection procedure. Each of these accounts had balances in excess of $7,000, so Mead sent confirmation requests to these customers.

The confirmation process revealed two differences. One account with an audited value of $3,000 had been recorded at $4,000. Mead projected this to be a $1,000 misstatement. Another account with an audited value of $2,000 had been recorded at $1,900. Mead did not count the $100 difference because the purpose of the procedure was to detect overstatements.

In evaluating the sample results, Mead decided that the accounts receivable balance was not overstated because the projected misstatement ($1,000) was less than the allowance for sampling risk.

Required:

Describe each incorrect assumption, statement, and inappropriate application of sampling in Mead's procedures.

(AICPA adapted)

LO G-2, G-3

G.63 Sampling Application Evaluation: Variables Sampling. The law firm of Spade & Associates hired Dylan Sayers to review the audit of the 2017 financial statements that Hammer & Wimsey, CPAs, had completed for Golden Sound and Records Company. Specifically, the attorneys engaged Sayers to determine whether the audit of Golden Sound's inventory of sound equipment and CDs conformed to generally accepted auditing standards. After Golden Sound declared bankruptcy three months ago (eight months after the 2017 audited financial statements were issued), stockholders sued Golden Sound, alleging distribution of misleading financial statements, and Hammer & Wimsey hired Spade & Associates to prepare a defense in the event that Hammer & Wimsey were included later in the lawsuit. The first time Golden Sound had been audited was 2017.

Golden Sound's business had grown rapidly. The company had 40 stores in 2015, opened 36 more in 2016, and added 23 more (for a total of 99) during 2017. The following accounting information shows the growth of the inventory:

	June 30		
	2015	**2016**	**2017**
Sound equipment	$5,800,000	$10,000,000	$12,200,000
CDs	2,200,000	6,800,000	9,000,000
Total inventory	$8,000,000	$16,800,000	$21,200,000
Number of stores	40	76	99

Sayers reviewed the Hammer & Wimsey audit documentation and prepared this summary:

In April 2017, Bobby Earl (Hammer & Wimsey audit manager on the Golden Sound engagement) met with Golden Sound's managers and discussed the procedures for taking the physical inventory as of June 30. Mikki LaTouche (Golden Sound's chief financial officer) suggested that the auditors' inventory observation be conducted at the stores located in large cities where Golden Sound had started business. According to LaTouche, "These stores are well stocked with a representative selection of all types of equipment and musical releases available across all the stores. The store managers are well acquainted with the inventory and can conduct an accurate counting with experienced store employees. The newer stores carry less stock, and the managers are relatively new to their jobs. You'll get a more accurate inventory-taking observation in the more established stores."

Earl agreed and noted in the audit documentation that the prospect of sending audit teams to distant stores in the Midwestern and Southeastern states (where Golden Sound had established new stores in the past year or so) would be very costly in terms of auditors' time and travel expenses. Together, LaTouche and Earl selected eight of the stores in the Western Region. Earl supervised experienced audit teams as they observed the inventory counts at these eight stores. The auditors observed that the Golden Sound store managers gave good instructions to the inventory takers and that the count records were in good order. Test counts showed only minor mistakes, which the managers promptly and conscientiously corrected.

Everyone was interested in making accurate counts because Golden Sound had no reliable perpetual inventory records, and the financial statement amounts for inventory were determined by this physical inventory. In fact, Earl wrote in the internal control communication to the board of directors and in the management letter addressed to the CFO the observation that Golden Sound needed to establish reliable inventory records for physical control and profit enhancement. The auditors determined the following inventory amounts in the eight stores. Using the total inventory of $1,712,700 in these stores, Earl divided by eight to find the average per store, then multiplied by 99, and projected the total inventory in the amount of $21,194,663. Because this amount was only $5,337 less than the recorded balance of inventory in the general ledger, Earl and the reviewing partner did not perform further work and incorporated the recorded inventory amount of $21,200,000 in the 2017 financial statements along with a standard unmodified auditor's report.

Required:

Complete Sayers's engagement by evaluating the Hammer & Wimsey conduct of the inventory portion of the Golden Sound 2017 audit. Organize your answer using the fundamental principles of "Responsibilities" and "Performance" in Chapter 2.

LO G-4

G.64 **Monetary Unit Sampling.** Georgie Costanza, CPA, is auditing the accounts receivable of Vandalay Industries and is considering the use of MUS techniques. Costanza has a number of questions regarding the use of MUS and has asked you to provide answers to them.

Required:

a. Under generally accepted auditing standards, can Costanza use nonstatistical sampling in the examination of Vandalay accounts receivable?

b. What are the advantages to using statistical sampling in the audit?

c. What are the risks associated with sampling, and to what type of losses do they expose Costanza?

d. How does Costanza establish the appropriate level of the risk of incorrect acceptance?

e. Is Costanza permitted to specify that certain items be examined, or do all items need to be randomly selected?

f. How can Costanza increase the likelihood that the items in the sample are representative of the population?

g. Other than the dollar amount of the misstatements, are any other factors important for Costanza to consider with respect to the misstatements?

USING IDEA IN MONETARY UNIT SAMPLING

Exercises G.65 through G.68 require the use of IDEA in a monetary unit sampling context.

Elm Manufacturing Company (ELM) is a small manufacturer of back packs located in Rochelle, Illinois. Your audit team is conducting substantive tests of sales made to customers on account and will select a sample of transactions and confirm them with customers. You have access to ELM's electronic records in Connect. The appropriate file for these exercises is the Sales 2017–4th Q data set. Detailed information about ELM, instructions for accessing data sets, a data directory for data sets, and a detailed monetary unit sampling example (with IDEA screenshots) can also be found in Connect.

NOTE: The Sales 2017–4th Q data set contains a total of 410 transactions; of these, invoices have been prepared for the first 362 transactions (through Order No. 17357). You should use the INVAMT (which represents the amount of the sale prior to any discount) as the monetary unit from which to sample.

In selecting and evaluating the samples, select the following options:

- For extraction type, select "Fixed interval selection."
- For high values handling, select "High values in database."
- For evaluation, select "Multiple samples."

LO G-3

G.65 Monetary Unit Sampling with IDEA: Determining Sample Size. Assume that your audit team has established the following parameters for the examination of ELM's sales transactions:

Risk of incorrect acceptance	10%
Tolerable misstatement	$311,711 (or 8% of the recorded balance of the transactions)
Expected misstatement	$77,928 (or 2% of the recorded balance of the transactions)

Required:

a. Use IDEA to determine the necessary sample size, given the above parameters.

Parts (b), (c), and (d) are independent scenarios that affect the sample size in this example.

b. Assume that your audit team has decided to increase their reliance on internal control and permit a corresponding increase in the risk of incorrect acceptance from 10 percent to 15 percent, which maintains overall audit risk at the same level. What is the necessary sample size, holding all other factors constant?

c. Assume that your audit team has decided to reduce the level of tolerable misstatement from $311,711 to $233,783 (or 6 percent of the recorded balance of the transactions). What is the necessary sample size, holding all other factors constant?

d. Assume that based on additional controls implemented by ELM, your audit team has decided to reduce the expected misstatement from $77,928 to $19,482 (0.5 percent of the recorded balance of the transactions.) What is the necessary sample size, holding all other factors constant?

e. How do the results in parts (b), (c), and (d) reflect the relationship between various parameters and sample size?

G.66 **Monetary Unit Sampling with IDEA: Determining Sample Size and Selecting Sample Items.** Assume that your audit team has established the following parameters for the examination of ELM's sales transactions:

Risk of incorrect acceptance	10%
Tolerable misstatement	$389,638 (or 10% of the recorded balance of the transactions
Expected misstatement	$58,446 (or 1.5% of the recorded balance of the transactions)

Required:

a. Use IDEA to determine the necessary sample size, given the above parameters.

b. What is the sampling interval? Show how the sampling interval can be arithmetically determined from the sample size and the population size.

c. Assuming a random start of 5,678, use IDEA to extract sample items from the population. List the transactions associated with the sample items selected by your audit team for examination. (Be sure to use "fixed interval extraction" and "high values in database" as options.)

d. Describe how IDEA extracts sample items from the population of sales transactions.

e. Based on the items selected from the population, does it appear that monetary unit sampling selects larger dollar items for examination? Provide the basis for your answer.

f. Why does the number of transactions extracted in part (c) differ from the sample size? Is this a concern?

G.67 **Monetary Unit Sampling with IDEA: Evaluating Sample Results.**

Assume that your audit team has established the following parameters for the examination of ELM's sales transactions:

Risk of incorrect acceptance	10%
Tolerable misstatement	$292,229 (or 7.5% of the recorded balance of the transactions
Expected misstatement	$38,964 (or 1% of the recorded balance of the transactions)

Based on these parameters and a random start of 9,876, your audit team determined a sample size of 38 items and a corresponding sampling interval of $102,536.42.

The IDEA files for items selected by your audit team are included as Monetary Sample G.67 and High Values G.67 in Connect.

Students should begin a new project for each part of this exercise and copy the IDEA files into the folder related to that project, as IDEA automatically overwrites the file being used with the audited value.

Required:

a. After receiving replies to confirmations, you noted the following discrepancies:

Order No.	Recorded Balance	Audited Value
17025	$89,039.21	$88,126.24
17302	$16,617.54	$15,500.00
17020	$144,515.21	$140,967.20

Use IDEA to calculate the upper limit on misstatements. What would your conclusion be with respect to the recorded balance of ELM's sales transactions?

b. [*Note: Part (b) is independent of part (a)*] After receiving replies to confirmations, you noted the following discrepancies:

Order No.	Recorded Balance	Audited Value
17050	$23,239.34	$20,000.00
17215	$79,231.54	$71,308.39
17260	$7,001.52	$5,000.00
17190	$151,469.58	$145,000.00

Use IDEA to calculate the upper limit on misstatements. What would your conclusion be with respect to the recorded balance of ELM's sales transactions?

LO G-3, G-4

G.68 **Monetary Unit Sampling with IDEA: Comprehensive Problem.** Assume that your audit team has received the electronic file of sales transactions from ELM and is preparing to use monetary unit sampling in evaluating the fairness of ELM's sales transactions.

Required:

a. How many transactions are included in ELM's sales transaction file? Using the "Field Statistics" function, what is the recorded balance of the population of sales transactions (INVAMT)?

b. By double-clicking on the INVAMT column of the file, sort the population by dollar amount. Based on the composition of this population, which specific item(s) might your audit team wish to consider separately as it designs its MUS application?

c. Determine the sample size and sampling interval for each of the following combinations of parameters. Based on comparisons among these scenarios, describe the impact of each of these parameters on sample size:

	Confidence (Risk of Incorrect Acceptance)	Tolerable Misstatement	Expected Misstatement
1.	90% (10%)	$350,000	$100,000
2.	90% (10%)	$450,000	$100,000
3.	90% (10%)	$350,000	$50,000
4.	85% (15%)	$350,000	$100,000

d. Using the parameters in Scenario (c)(1) and a random start of $22,053, select a sample from the population of sales transactions. How many transactions were selected (including high value items)?

e. Express your sample in terms of the percentage of the number of transactions and percentage of total dollar value of transactions from the population. Does this appear to give you adequate coverage of the population? (You can use the "Field Statistics" function or export the transactions selected to an Excel file to simplify your calculations.)

For part (f), the IDEA files for items that were selected by the audit team are included as Monetary Sample G.68 and High Values G.68 in Connect. Students may wish to make copies of the data files for this part of the exercise, as IDEA automatically overwrites the file being used with the audited value entered.

f. Assume that the audit team's procedures identified the following misstatements:

Order No.	Recorded Balance	Audited Value
17005	$62,812.33	$60,000.00
17183	$4,676.54	$4,529.92
17326	$14,725.48	$12,000.00
17190	$151,469.58	$148,992.56

Use IDEA to calculate the upper limit on misstatements. What would your conclusion be with respect to the recorded balance of ELM's sales transactions?

N (the number of transactions) can be readily determined from the client's records; in this case, accounts receivable include 900 transactions.[8] The factors for R(IR) and R(IA) correspond to a risk of incorrect rejection of 15 percent and risk of incorrect acceptance of 10 percent and are drawn from Exhibit GB.1. Based on previous audits, the audit team estimated that the standard deviation was $3,173. Tolerable misstatement determined based on the total of the transactions and overall financial statement materiality was established at $628,167. Finally, the audit team judgmentally established the expected misstatement of $188,450 based on previous audits. We use the sample size of 312 in the remainder of this example to illustrate classical variables sampling.

Earlier, we noted that stratified sampling can be useful in reducing sample sizes if a great deal of variability exists in the population. By using the preceding formula, if the audit team decided to examine the two individually significant sales transactions and reduce the variability of the remainder of the population from $3,173 to $2,202, the sample size for the nonsignificant items would be 150 transactions.[9] Including the two individually significant items, the total sample would be 152. This provides an example of how using stratification can result in a more efficient sample for the auditor.

✅ REVIEW CHECKPOINTS

GB.4 What is *stratification*? What are the benefits to the audit team of stratifying the sample?

GB.5 What is the *standard deviation*? How does it affect the necessary sample size?

GB.6 Identify differences between the determination of sample size under classical variables sampling and MUS.

Step 5: Select the Sample Items

One of the basic tenets of statistical sampling methods is that each sampling unit has an equal probability of selection. The sample of sales transactions could be selected in either of the following ways:

1. Identify 312 random numbers and select the corresponding transactions for confirmation (unrestricted random selection).
2. Randomly select a starting point (or a number of starting points) in the population and select every *n*th transaction thereafter for confirmation (systematic random selection).

One very important difference between sample selection under classical variables sampling and MUS is the definition of the sampling unit. Classical variables sampling defines the sampling unit as a logical unit (in this case, a sales transaction). As a result, the audit team will select 312 of the 900 sales transactions for examination. In contrast, MUS defines the sampling unit as an individual dollar of a sales transaction and selects individual dollars for examination. Unlike MUS, classical variables sampling does not ensure that the highest dollar transactions are selected for examination. Under classical variables sampling, a $1 transaction has the same probability of being selected as a $1 million transaction! This characteristic is why the use of stratification to automatically select high dollar items is so important under classical variables sampling, as *individually significant items* can be identified and selected.

---

[8]In this example, we did not stratify the sample by excluding the two large transactions to focus on the methodology and calculations associated with mean-per-unit estimation. In an actual audit context, these two transactions would undoubtedly be examined and not subject to selection.

[9]The sample size formula would be modified by replacing the 900 sales transactions with 898 and the $3,173 sample standard deviation with $2,202.

Step 6: Measure the Sample Items

Once the sample size has been determined and the sample has been selected, the audit team measures the sample items. In the audit of sales transactions, measuring sample items requires the audit team to determine the audited value of the transaction. This will be done using standard accounts receivable confirmation procedures as well as additional procedures necessary to follow up on any discrepancies revealed by the confirmation procedures.

Assume that the audit team's examination of the 312 customer sales transactions revealed a total audited value of $4,259,736. Therefore, the mean audited value per unit is $13,653 ($4,259,736 ÷ 312). Also assume that the audit team calculated a $2,425 standard deviation of audited values.

Step 7: Evaluate the Sample Results

Evaluating the sample results requires the audit team to determine an overall estimate of the audited value (based on the mean audited value per unit) and construct an interval of sample estimates that controls the exposure to the risk of incorrect acceptance (10 percent) and risk of incorrect rejection (15 percent) to desired levels. This interval is referred to as the *precision interval,* and once it has been constructed, the audit team's decision rule is as follows:

- Accept the account balance as being fairly stated if the difference between the recorded balance and the farthest precision estimate is smaller than or equal to the tolerable misstatement.
- Reject the account balance as being fairly stated if the difference between the recorded balance and the farthest precision estimate is larger than the tolerable misstatement.

The first step in the construction of the precision interval is to determine the overall estimate of the audited value. If the mean audited value of the sample of sales transactions is $13,653, the audit team's best estimate of the audited value of the entire account is determined by multiplying $13,653 by the number of transactions in the population (900), or $12,287,700 ($13,653 × 900 = $12,287,700).

Next, the audit team determines the appropriate level of precision. *Precision* is the numeric distance from the estimated population value in which the true (but unknown) population value may lie with a given probability. The determination of precision allows the audit team to construct a precision interval that controls exposure to sampling risk to acceptable levels.

Recall from the calculation of sample size that the population size is 900 transactions, the confidence factor for the risk of incorrect acceptance is 1.28, and the sample size is 312. Also, after measuring the sample items, recall that the standard deviation of audited values is $2,425. The precision is calculated as $158,156:

$$\text{Precision} = N \times R(IA) \times (SD \div \sqrt{n})$$

$$= 900 \times 1.28 \times (\$2,425 \div \sqrt{312})$$

$$= \$158,156$$

n	=	Sample size
N	=	Population size (number of sales transactions)
R(IA)	=	Confidence factor for the risk of incorrect acceptance
SD	=	Standard deviation (for items selected for examination)

Once the precision has been calculated, the precision interval can be determined by adding and subtracting it from the sample estimate. The relationship between the sample estimate, precision, and the recorded balance is shown as

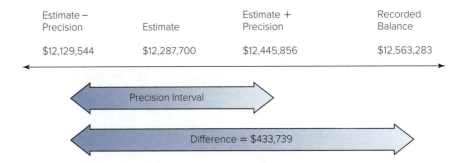

| Estimate −
Precision | Estimate | Estimate +
Precision | Recorded
Balance |
|---|---|---|---|
| $12,129,544 | $12,287,700 | $12,445,856 | $12,563,283 |

Precision Interval

Difference = $433,739

The significance of the precision interval is that it has a (1 − *Risk of incorrect acceptance*) probability of including the true balance; conversely, the true balance has a (*risk of incorrect acceptance*) probability of falling outside the precision interval. The difference between the recorded balance and the farthest end of the precision interval ($12,563,283 − $12,129,544 = $433,739) is compared to the tolerable misstatement ($628,167). In this case, the population can be accepted as being fairly stated and the audit team has limited its exposure to the risk of incorrect acceptance to 10 percent.

MUS versus Classical Variables Sampling

When considering the use of MUS and classical variables sampling, recall that MUS defines the sampling unit as an individual dollar within an account balance or class of transactions. As a result, this method tends to identify large-dollar items for examination, which is the primary benefit associated with the use of MUS. Compared to classical variables sampling, MUS is most appropriate when:

1. Overstatements are of greater concern to the audit team (such as the audit of assets and revenues) because MUS automatically selects items with larger recorded balances for examination.
2. It is difficult or impractical to estimate the standard deviation. (While not illustrated in the text, classical variables sampling methods require an estimate of the standard deviation in determining sample size and evaluating sample results.)
3. Zero or few misstatements are anticipated.
4. The population is relatively heterogeneous with respect to the dollar amount of components and a number of relatively large-dollar items exist (i.e., a high level of variability exists).

With respect to this final matter, when using classical variables sampling, the audit team may choose to subdivide the population into more homogenous groups based on size. (This process is known as *stratification* and has been discussed previously.) In particular, any large items (including individually significant items) may be selected for examination, and the audit team would then sample from the remainder of the population. In addition to ensuring that large items are examined, stratification reduces the variability of the remaining population and reduces the necessary sample size.

✓ REVIEW CHECKPOINTS

GB.7   How does sample selection under classical variables sampling differ from sample selection under MUS?

GB.8   Define *precision* and the *precision interval*. What factors are used to determine the level of precision?

GB.9   What is the audit team's decision rule when comparing the recorded balance to the precision interval?

GB.10   When selecting a variables sampling approach, when should the audit team use MUS and when should it use classical variables sampling?

Appendix G.C

LO G-6
Understand the use of
nonstatistical approaches to
variables sampling.

NONSTATISTICAL SAMPLING

The primary advantage of statistical sampling methods is that they explicitly measure and control the audit team's exposure to sampling risk in determining the sample size and evaluating sample results. However, it is important to note that generally accepted auditing standards do not require the use of statistical sampling methods; in many cases, it is easier and more efficient to use **nonstatistical sampling methods**.

The primary differences in statistical and nonstatistical sampling methods are as follows:

1. *Determining sample size.* While the AICPA Audit Guide *Audit Sampling* suggests using the MUS table to determine sample size, the audit team members can use their professional judgment in determining the appropriate sample size.
2. *Selecting sample items.* Nonstatistical sampling permits the audit team to use nonprobabilistic selection techniques, such as **haphazard selection** (e.g., picking vouchers from a drawer) and **block selection** (e.g., selecting all cash disbursements for a particular month). These methods allow the audit team to use their professional judgment when selecting the sample.
3. *Evaluating sample results.* After estimating the account balance or amount of misstatement and considering the tolerable misstatement, the audit team can judgmentally draw a conclusion about the fairness of the account balance or class of transactions without controlling for exposure to sampling risk. For example, if the recorded balance is $12,563,283, the audit team's estimated account balance is $12,200,000, and tolerable misstatement is $628,167, the team may conclude that the account if fairly stated without further analyses or formal calculation of a range of account balances.

Comprehensive Example: Nonstatistical Sampling

To illustrate the use of nonstatistical sampling, consider the IDEA example introduced in the module. Recall that the population consisted of 900 sales transactions totaling $12,563,283. (This included the five transactions with zero or negative amounts.) Also recall the following parameters that were established by the audit team:

- Risk of incorrect acceptance = 10%
- Expected misstatement = $188,450
- Tolerable misstatement = $628,167

In determining sample size under nonstatistical sampling, *Audit Sampling* notes that the audit team may use tables similar to those for MUS (see Exhibit GA.1). Alternatively, a nonstatistical sample size can be calculated through the use of the following formula:

$$\text{Sample size} = \frac{\text{Recorded balance of population}}{\text{Tolerable misstatement}} \times \text{Confidence factor}$$

The confidence factor incorporates the level of confidence desired through the substantive tests, as expressed in the risk of incorrect acceptance. For a 10 percent risk of incorrect acceptance, the appropriate confidence factor would be 2.3, as shown below (drawn from Table C.2 in *Audit Sampling*):

	Risk of Incorrect Acceptance					
	5%	10%	15%	20%	25%	30%
Factor	3.0	2.3	1.9	1.6	1.4	1.2

The appropriate sample size would be 46 transactions, as shown here:

$$\frac{\$12,563,283}{\$628,167} \times 2.3 = 46 \text{ transactions}$$

Recall that this population includes two transactions that exceed the tolerable misstatement and total $8,179,960 (65 percent of the recorded balance of the population). Because nonstatistical sampling does not require the audit team members to use random selection techniques, they would undoubtedly select these two transactions for examination and select 44 transactions from the remainder of the population. Unlike statistical sampling, the audit team can use either *block selection* (select transactions occurring on specific dates) or *haphazard selection* (select items without any conscious bias from the listing of transactions).

While the selection process is not illustrated, assume that the 46 transactions had a total recorded balance of $8,455,139, as follows:

Large items	2	$8,179,960
Other items	44	275,179
Total	46	$8,455,139

After selecting the sample items, the audit team performs the appropriate substantive procedures to determine the audited value of the transaction. In this case, assume that the audited value for these transactions was $8,252,216. Using ratio estimation, the audit team would estimate the account balance as follows:

$$\frac{\text{Audited value of sample}}{\text{Recorded balance of sample}} \times \text{Recorded balance of population}$$

$$\frac{\$8,252,216}{\$8,455,139} \times \$12,563,283 = \$12,261,765$$

Comparing the audited value of the population to the recorded balance of the population reveals an estimated misstatement of $301,518 ($12,563,283 − $12,261,765). Because this is significantly lower than the tolerable misstatement ($628,167), the audit team would likely conclude that the account balance is fairly stated.

✅ REVIEW CHECKPOINTS

GC.1 How does nonstatistical sampling differ from statistical sampling?

GC.2 What factors are considered in determining the sample size in a nonstatistical sampling application?

MODULE H

Auditing and Information Technology

A common mistake that people make when trying to design something completely foolproof is to underestimate the ingenuity of complete fools.

Douglas Adams, author of The Hitchhiker's Guide to the Galaxy

To err is human, but to really foul things up you need a computer.

Attributed to Paul R. Ehrlich, American biologist, author, and technology commentator

Professional Standards References

Topic	AU-C/ISA Section	AS Section
Consideration of Internal Control in an Integrated Audit		2201
Identifying and Assessing the Risks of Material Misstatement	315	2110
Auditors' Responses to Risks of Material Misstatement	330	2301
Reporting on Controls at a Service Organization	AT-C 320	2601

LEARNING OBJECTIVES

Given its extensive use by clients, audit teams must consider clients' information technology (IT) during all stages of the audit engagement. A textbook cannot describe fully all of the complexities of automated processing of business transactions, so this module assumes that you have had a course in accounting information systems. Chapter 3 provides a brief introduction to the effect of automated processing on audit planning; the focus of this module is on the audit team's examination of the client's accounting information system and its related computer controls. The module is subdivided into three parts. The first part reviews the basic elements of an accounting information system system and the related controls. The second part describes the procedures that audit

teams perform to test the operating effectiveness of the client's IT controls. The module concludes with a discussion of computer fraud and the controls that can be used to prevent it.

Your objectives are to be able to:

LO H-1 Identify how the use of an automated transaction processing system affects the audit examination.

LO H-2 Provide examples of general controls and understand how these controls relate to transaction processing in an accounting information system.

LO H-3 Provide examples of automated application controls and understand how these controls relate to transaction processing in an accounting information system.

is conducted in accordance with entity policies, and supports the entity's financial reporting requirements; (2) appropriate users participate in the software acquisition or program development process; (3) programs and software are tested and validated prior to being placed into operation; and (4) all software and programs have appropriate documentation.

An important program development control is the entity's use of the **systems development life cycle (SDLC)** process to plan, develop, and implement new accounting information systems (or databases). The SDLC begins with the identification of system requirements (basically, what does the entity need the system to do?); see Exhibit H.2. The feasibility analysis stage examines whether the entity should purchase the system "off the shelf" (i.e., from a commercial vendor), develop the system internally, or modify an off-the-shelf system for internal use. The answer depends on the entity's resources and expertise. Once a decision has been made that a new system is feasible, system specifications are developed. Programmers next write programs to accomplish those specifications and then design procedures. On conversion from the old system to the new one, training employees to use the new system is critical. Upon successful implementation, the system must continue to be monitored to ensure that problems do not arise. As they do occur (e.g., due to capacity constraints), the cycle begins anew: Is there a better system to meet the entity's needs?

Effective SDLC controls ensure that the entity:

- Follows established policies and procedures for acquiring or developing software or programs.
- Involves users in the design of programs, selection of prepackaged software and programs, and testing of programs.
- Tests and validates new programs and develops proper implementation and "back out" plans (plans to cancel the results of processing in the event of an error or program failure) prior to placing the programs into operation.
- Periodically reviews policies and procedures for acquiring and developing software or programs for continued appropriateness and modifying these policies and procedures as necessary.

In addition to the use of the SDLC, it is important that appropriate documentation exist for each of the entity's programs. *Documentation* describes the system and its controls and is the means of communicating the essential elements of the accounting information system to both current and potential users. In evaluating controls over documentation, audit teams review the documentation to (1) gain an understanding of the system and determine whether the documentation is adequate to support the proper use

EXHIBIT H.2

Systems Development Life Cycle

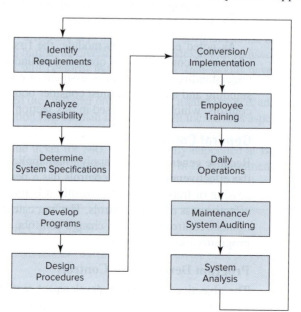

of the programs and (2) determine whether client personnel follow standards. Of utmost importance is whether the client has established systems development and documentation standards. Unless written standards exist, determining whether the program development controls and the documentation are adequate is difficult.

The accompanying Auditing Insight illustrates common problems that have been observed related to the implementation of new systems and programs.

AUDITING INSIGHT   The Problems with New Systems

The following common control issues have been identified related to the implementation of new accounting information systems. To the extent that these issues result in inaccurate processing of transactions or the inability to identify errors in processing, they will impact the integrity of the data generated by the systems and, ultimately, the fairness of the entity's financial statements.

- Imposing unrealistic deadlines, resulting in inadequate testing of the system.
- Failing to use controls that are packaged with the new systems.

- Failing to review reports generated by new systems.
- Providing inadequate training to employees on the use of new systems.
- Failing to ensure that system access capabilities reflect appropriate separation of duties.
- Allowing excessive customization of new systems, which compromises the integrity of these systems.

Source: "IT-Control Weakness Wanes," *CFO.com*, September 16, 2010.

Program Change Controls

The objectives of **program change controls** parallel those related to program development in the preceding subsection. These controls are implemented by the entity to provide reasonable assurance that requests for modifications to existing programs (1) are properly authorized, conducted in accordance with entity policies, and support the entity's financial reporting requirements; (2) involve appropriate users in the program modification process; (3) are tested and validated prior to being placed into operation; and (4) have been appropriately documented. Like program development controls, the use of an SDLC (and the analogous controls related to the use of an SDLC) is an important consideration when modifying existing programs. It is also important that the entity prepare appropriate documentation with respect to the program modifications. The accompanying Auditing Insight describes two recent examples in which the failure to properly implement system updates resulted in negative consequences for the companies involved.

AUDITING INSIGHT   Be Careful of System Upgrades

HERSHEY'S HARROWING HALLOWEEN

Like all organizations, immediately before the turn of this century, **Hershey Foods** faced a potential "Y2K" problem involving program coding that used only two-year digits instead of four (e.g., 99 for 1999), therefore causing problems for date-related procedures. To address the problem and update its old systems, Hershey undertook an ambitious system upgrade. In September 1999, facing implementation delays due to software integration complexities and a December 31, 1999, implementation deadline, Hershey decided to switch from its old system to its new system with a flip of a switch (the cold-turkey approach) rather than the originally planned module-by-module approach. Unfortunately, the implementation didn't take. Customer Halloween candy orders fell through the cracks. Candy inventory was "lost," remaining

unaccounted for in warehouses. The consequence was an estimated $150 million in lost sales.

OVERSTOCK AND UNDERREPORT

Implementation of a system upgrade by Overstock.com (an Internet retailer that primarily sells surplus and returned merchandise) resulted in the failure to properly reduce its revenue for customer returns. In his letter to shareholders, CEO Patrick Byrne indicated that "when we upgraded our system, we didn't hook up some of the accounting wiring; however, we thought we had manual fixes in place. We've since found that these manual fixes missed a few of the unhooked wires." The result? Overstock restated its financial statements for the period 2003–2007, reducing revenues by $12.9 million and increasing net losses by $10.3 million.

Source: "Botched ERP Hookup Spurs Restatement," *CFO.com*, October 24, 2008.

a negative inventory quantity). These conditions and others that are considered important should generate error reports for supervisor review.

- *Error correction and resubmission procedures.* Although previously mentioned as an input control, controls related to the identification of errors or unusual conditions encountered in processing transactions on a timely basis and correction and resubmission for processing should also be implemented by entities as transactions are processed.

Output Controls

Output controls represent the final check on the accuracy of the results of automated transaction processing. Output controls are concerned with detecting errors rather than preventing errors (as was the focus with input and processing controls). These controls also should be designed to provide reasonable assurance that only authorized persons receive output (or other types of reports generated by the accounting information system) or have access to files produced by the system. Typical output controls are the following:

- *Review of output for reasonableness.* An individual knowledgeable about the nature of the transactions and processing should perform an overall review of the output for reasonableness. This allows systematic errors that might otherwise go undetected in more detailed testing to be identified (e.g., an employee being paid 10 times his or her normal salary).
- *Control total reports.* Control totals produced as output should be compared and/or reconciled to input and run-to-run control totals produced during transaction processing. An independent data control group should be responsible for reviewing output control totals and investigating differences.
- *Master file changes.* During automated transaction processing, permanent information stored in master files is often updated or modified; these files should be viewed as outputs of the automated processing. Any changes should be properly authorized by the entity and reported in detail to the user department from which the request for change originated because an error can be pervasive. For example, as noted in the Auditing Insight "Always Lower Prices," incorrectly changing prices can cause the sale of products and services to be billed at incorrect levels.
- *Output distribution.* Systems' output (whether electronic or hard copy) should be distributed only to persons authorized to receive the output. A distribution list should be maintained and used to deliver report copies. The number of copies produced should be restricted to the number needed to prevent unauthorized use.

AUDITING INSIGHT   Always Lower Prices

- Customers at **Meijer Inc.** (a retailer of groceries and general merchandise in the midwestern United States) received an unexpected windfall when all items the chain sold were mistakenly discounted by 50 percent in the company's master price file; the discount was supposed to have applied only to Oriental rugs.

- In October 2009, British Airways PLC mistakenly offered tickets from the United States to India for $40 (it had intended to *increase* its ticket prices by $40) and had to cancel 1,200 reservations for

2,200 passengers. In a similar type of mistake contained in a computerized file, United Airlines inadvertently dropped a zero from its ticket prices and offered round-trip business class flights from Los Angeles and San Francisco to New Zealand for $1,062 (rather than $10,620). Unlike British Airways, United honored all tickets sold.

Sources: "Meijer Glitch Led to Discount," *Chicago Tribune,* May 24, 2007; "When Airline Fares Are Too Good to Be True," *The Wall Street Journal,* March 25, 2010, p. D1, D3.

EXHIBIT H.4   Automated Application Controls

	Input of Individual Transactions and Data Is Accurate (Accuracy)	All Transactions Are Entered (Completeness)	Transactions Are Entered Only Once (Occurrence)	Processing of Transactions Is Accurate (Accuracy)	Other
Data entry and formatting				X	Ensures that input is approved and authorized
Check digits	X				
Record counts		X	X	X	
Batch totals	X	X	X	X	
Hash totals	X	X	X	X	
Valid character tests	X				
Valid sign tests	X				
Missing data tests	X				
Sequence tests		X			
Limit and reasonableness tests	X			X	
Error correction and resubmission	X			X	
Periodically testing and evaluating processing accuracy of programs				X	
File and operator controls				X	Ensures that appropriate files are used in applications
Run-to-run totals				X	
Control total reports				X	
Review of output for reasonableness				X	
Master file changes				X	Ensures that changes to master file data are authorized
Output distribution					Ensures output is distributed only to authorized users

Exhibit H.4 is a summary of the automated application controls discussed in the preceding section. Note that some of these controls (record counts, batch totals, hash totals, and limit and reasonableness tests) may be used as both input controls and processing controls. Also note that the columns of Exhibit H.4 correspond to the following management assertions. (Notice that some of these controls affect multiple assertions:)

- Accuracy: Input of individual transactions and data is accurate.
- Completeness: All transactions are entered.
- Occurrence: Transactions are entered only once.
- Accuracy: Processing of transactions is accurate.

Summary

The differences between general controls and application controls are complex, often highly technical, and difficult to easily understand. To better differentiate these two types of controls, think of an iPhone or another type of smartphone. A number of general controls "surround" the smartphone environment, such as requiring a password (system access control) to unlock the phone. For operating system program changes, you must download any upgrades from an approved "App Store" distribution channel. With respect to program development, all apps must be approved by Apple before releasing them to iPhone users. Another general control protecting your iPhone is the iCloud that backs up all of your critical data to an off-site location should your iPhone be lost or stolen.

There are also often controls within each app ("application controls"), such as password requirements to access many apps (such as Facebook). Error messages appear if you input the wrong password or enter otherwise incorrect data. Other app controls include requesting user permission when accessing Google Maps from dining apps (such as Urbanspoon or OpenTable). Hopefully, this smartphone analogy makes the differences between general and application controls clearer and easier to understand.

☑ REVIEW CHECKPOINTS

H.9   What is the objective of input controls?

H.10 How can data entry and formatting controls minimize the likelihood of input errors?

H.11 Briefly describe record counts, batch totals, and hash totals. What types of errors in input would each of these controls likely identify?

H.12 How do input controls affect management's assertions with respect to the financial statements?

H.13 What is the objective of processing controls? List and briefly describe different processing controls.

H.14 What is the objective of output controls? List and briefly describe different output controls.

ASSESSING CONTROL RISK IN AN IT ENVIRONMENT

LO H-4

Describe how the audit team assesses control risk in an IT environment.

Recall from our earlier discussion the three major phases in the audit team's evaluation of internal control. The first phase is *obtaining an understanding of internal control;* during this phase, the audit team identifies the various controls (manual controls, general controls, and automated application controls) that the client has implemented. At this point, the audit team is aware of the types of controls that have been implemented but has not considered how these controls influence the risk of material misstatement or the operating effectiveness of these controls.

When audit teams have obtained an understanding of internal control, they then *form an assessment of control risk* (the second phase in the audit team's evaluation of internal control), which involves the following major steps:

1. Identify the types of misstatements that can occur in significant accounting applications.
2. Identify the points in the flow of transactions where specific types of misstatements could occur.
3. Identify specific control procedures (such as the automated application controls described in the preceding section) designed to prevent or detect these misstatements.
4. Evaluate the design of control procedures to determine whether the design suggests a low control risk and whether tests of controls might be cost effective.

These four steps parallel those in a manual processing environment. In addition to the type of controls that the audit team considers (general controls and automated application controls), one important difference in assessing control risk in an IT environment is identifying the points in the flow of transactions where misstatements could occur (step 2) because many additional steps and sources of potential misstatement are introduced. These sources can be classified as in Exhibit H.5.

EXHIBIT H.5   Points of Potential Misstatement in an IT Environment

Potential Source of Misstatement	Control(s)
1. Preparing and converting data to machine-readable form	Various input controls
2. Accessing files and programs during computer processing	Computer operations controls related to file identification (external labels and header and trailer labels)
3. Transferring data between computer programs and applications	Processing controls (run-to-run totals, control totals)
4. Updating master file information following processing	Output controls (related to master file changes)
5. Processing transactions by computer programs	Processing controls and output controls
6. Correcting and resubmitting errors at input or during processing	Error correction and resubmission procedures

Once the audit team has identified the points where a misstatement could occur, it focuses on specific control procedures implemented by the client to prevent or detect such misstatements. For example, one possible misstatement could involve preparing invoices (and billing customers) using incorrect prices because an inappropriate inventory price file is used in processing transactions. In this case, one control procedure might be as follows:

Source of Misstatement		Control Procedure
Use of inappropriate inventory price file to prepare invoices	→	The billing program should identify the most current version of the inventory price file

At this point, the audit team has

1. Obtained an understanding of internal control, including the general controls and automated application controls implemented by the client for the automated processing of transactions (phase 1).
2. Formed a preliminary assessment of control risk based on considering the general controls and automated application controls implemented by the client for the computerized processing of transactions (phase 2).

The next step in the audit team's evaluation of internal control is to test the operating effectiveness of these controls (phase 3). Because automated controls operate similarly for similar transactions, it is only necessary to test each control once to determine effectiveness. The following illustrates three important controls that would mitigate the risk of material misstatement for the accuracy assertion for sales transactions along with how the audit team would test these controls in a manual processing environment and the implications for testing these controls in an IT environment:

Control	Manual Test of Controls	Implication for Testing in an IT Environment
Credit sales are approved by the credit department	Examine invoice for evidence of credit approval	If authorized customer file is updated and accurate, audit team can examine input controls to ensure that only authorized customer numbers are accepted for processing
Quantities shipped to customers are compared to quantities invoiced	Compare quantities shipped from shipping documents to quantities on sales invoices or examine evidence of client comparison of quantities	If sales invoice processing program uses input from computerized shipping document transaction file, audit teams can ensure that quantities are appropriately accepted from shipping document transaction file
Mathematical accuracy of invoices is checked by client personnel	Recalculate mathematical accuracy of invoices or examine evidence of client verification of mathematical accuracy	If calculations are made by the sales invoice processing program, audit teams can verify the (1) operating effectiveness of limits and reasonableness tests and (2) accuracy of the invoice processing program

LO H-5

H.35 When processing controls within the accounting information system may not leave visible evidence that could be inspected by audit teams, the teams should
  a. Make corroborative inquiries.
  b. Observe the separation of duties of personnel.
  c. Review transactions submitted for processing and compare them to related output.
  d. Review the run manual.

LO H-5

H.36 Which of the following statements most likely represents a control consideration for an entity that performs its accounting using mobile computing devices?
  a. It is usually difficult to detect arithmetic errors.
  b. Unauthorized persons find it easy to access the computer and alter the data files.
  c. Transactions are coded for account classifications before they are processed on the computer.
  d. Random errors in report printing are rare in packaged software systems.

LO H-5

H.37 A customer intended to order 100 units of product Z96014 but incorrectly ordered product Z96015, which is not an actual product. Which of the following controls most likely would detect this error?
  a. Check digit verification.
  b. Record count.
  c. Hash total.
  d. Redundant data check.

LO H-6

H.38 Which of the following automated application controls would offer reasonable assurance that inventory data were completely and accurately entered?
  a. Sequence checking.
  b. Batch totals.
  c. Limit tests.
  d. Check digits.

LO H-2

H.39 Which of the following persons is responsible for controlling access to systems documentation and access to program and data files?
  a. Programmers.
  b. Data conversion operators.
  c. Librarians.
  d. Computer operators.

Exercises and Problems

 All applicable Exercises and Problems are available with *Connect.*

LO H-5

H.40 **Auditing Automated Controls.** You are auditing payroll for Alexander Inc., which uses computerized processing for its payroll transactions; the various steps in Alexander's system follow:
  - As employees provide services, they enter the number of hours worked on time sheets that their supervisor approves at the conclusion of the pay period. Time sheets have an identifying field that indicates whether the employee is an hourly (H) or a salaried (S) employee.
  - The following data are entered into the input file: (1) employee number, (2) number of hours worked, and (3) employee status (hourly versus salaried).
  - For hourly employees, the number of hours worked is multiplied by the wage rate (obtained from the employee master file) to calculate gross pay. For salaried employees, the employee's salary rate is obtained from the employee master file.
  - When gross pay has been determined, deductions are automatically calculated using information from the employee master file and standard deduction tables (for federal tax withholdings, FICA withholdings, and Medicare withholdings).
  - Net pay is calculated by subtracting deductions from gross pay.

Required:

a. What are the primary sources of error that can occur in the accounting information system just described?

b. How would you examine Alexander's payroll? What key controls would you evaluate?

LO H-2, H-5

H.41 **Tests of Controls: General Controls.** The audit team of Packer Company identified the following general controls in obtaining its overall understanding of Packer's internal control over the automated processing of transactions:

1. Packer has routine maintenance on its computer equipment and related technology scheduled and performed every six months.

2. Packer has formal, written systems development and documentation standards for the implementation of new programs.

3. Prior to implementing modifications to its existing programs, Packer tests and validates the program changes to ensure accurate processing.

4. Packer has appropriately separated the responsibilities of systems analysts, programmers, and computer operators.

5. Packer's computer files are protected from loss through frequent backups and storage at an off-site location.

6. Access to computer files and programs is protected through the use of passwords.

7. On a monthly basis, Packer reviews any revisions in the access rights of its employees to ensure consistency between their new job responsibilities and files and programs they may access.

Required:

Consider the four methods of testing the operating effectiveness of controls (inquiry, observation, document examination, and reperformance). For each of the preceding controls, provide an example of how Packer's audit team might choose to test the operating effectiveness of the control using the four methods of test of controls (e.g., how would the audit team use inquiry, observation, document examination, and reperformance to test control #1, routine maintenance on computer equipment and related technology?). [*Note:* Not all types of tests of controls are appropriate for testing all of the controls.]

LO H-3, H-5

H.42 **Tests of Controls: Input Controls.** Knight Company is a medium-size manufacturing entity that uses an automated transaction system to process its customer orders. Orders are collected and processed on a daily basis in batches. In its processing of customer orders, Knight requires input of the following information into a daily customer order file (# represents a numeric field; A represents an alphabetic field):

- Customer number (###).
- Item number (AA###).
- Quantities (##).

After this information has been entered, the computer program accesses the valid customer master file to ensure that the sale is to an authorized customer and does not exceed that customer's credit limit. The program then accesses the inventory master file, verifies that the appropriate quantities are on hand, and identifies the most current price. The program then prepares an invoice by multiplying the quantities the customer ordered by the appropriate price and generates a total amount for the sale.

To prevent and detect errors during the input process, Knight has established the following controls:

1. Data entry personnel must enter a valid password to access the data entry program.

2. A check digit is appended to the customer number as a seventh digit.

3. The following control totals are manually determined prior to input and then compared to a total generated by the computer program: (a) number of records entered, (b) sum of customer numbers, and (c) sum of quantities.

4. The program rejects a customer number or inventory quantity containing an alphabetic character and any entry for item numbers having an inappropriate character in the given field. Data entry personnel are prompted to reenter the information upon rejection of the original entry.

5. Any quantities ordered in excess of 9,999 are highly unusual and require special authorization by Knight's management. Any such entries are rejected and written to a rejected order file for follow-up and authorization.

6. If data entry is attempted for a customer whose number is not in the customer master file (either a new customer or an erroneous entry for an existing customer), the transaction is rejected and written to a rejected order file. Depending on the reason for the invalid customer number, a credit check is conducted (if an order from a new customer) or the entry is corrected (if an erroneous entry of the customer number).

Required:

Consider the four methods of testing the operating effectiveness of controls (inquiry, observation, document examination, and reperformance). For each of the preceding controls, provide an example of how Knight's audit team might choose to test the operating effectiveness of the control using the four methods of test of controls (e.g., how would the audit team use inquiry, observation, document examination, and reperformance to test control #1, use of valid passwords?). [*Note:* Not all types of tests of controls are appropriate for testing all of the controls.]

LO H-3, H-5   H.43 **Tests of Controls: Processing and Output Controls.** Mark Company's audit team is evaluating the controls that Mark has implemented over the automated processing of payroll transactions. During the understanding and assessment stages of the audit, the following processing and output controls have been identified as being important in this processing:

1. To detect unauthorized access to payroll programs and processing, a system log is generated and reviewed on a weekly basis. This log identifies the programs that have been accessed during the past week, the individual(s) who have accessed those programs, and the time(s) during which the programs have been accessed. This log is reviewed, and any unexpected or unauthorized access is investigated immediately.
2. Control totals are determined prior to the input of data and compared to computer-generated totals following transaction processing.
3. Any gross pay calculations in excess of $25,000 per month are identified and written to a rejected transaction file for separate investigation because Mark's highest paid employee whose salary is processed through the system earns $300,000 per year.
4. The system generates a report of any errors or unusual situations identified during transaction processing. This report is reviewed and any items are resolved in a timely manner, and the resolution is documented by notations made on the report.
5. Any changes to employee master file information since the last payroll period are evaluated to ensure that they have been properly authorized by the appropriate personnel.
6. The output is reviewed for reasonableness prior to distribution to users.

Required:

Consider the four methods of testing the operating effectiveness of controls (inquiry, observation, document examination, and reperformance). For each of the preceding controls, provide an example of how Mark's audit team might choose to test the operating effectiveness of the control using the four methods of test of controls (e.g., how would the audit team use inquiry, observation, document examination, and reperformance to test control #1, the generation and review of the system log?). [*Note:* Not all types of tests of controls will be appropriate for testing all of the controls.]

LO H-3   H.44 **Computer Internal Control Questionnaire Evaluation.** Assume that, when conducting procedures to obtain an understanding of Denton Seed Company's internal controls, you checked "No" to the following internal control questionnaire items:

- Does access to online files require specific passwords to be entered to identify and validate the terminal user?
- Does the user establish control totals prior to submitting data for processing? (Order entry application subsystem.)
- Are input control totals reconciled to output control totals? (Order entry application subsystem.)

Required:

Describe the errors and frauds that could occur because of the weaknesses indicated by the lack of IT controls.

LO H-2   H.45 **Separation of Duties and General Control Procedures.** You are engaged to examine the financial statements of Horizon Incorporated, which has its own computer installation. During the preliminary understanding phase of your study of Horizon's internal control, you found that Horizon lacked proper separation of the programming and operating functions.

As a result, you intensified the evaluation of the internal control surrounding the computer and concluded that the existing compensating general controls provided reasonable assurance that the objectives of internal control were being met.

Required:

a. In a properly functioning IT environment, how is the separation of the programming and operating functions achieved?

b. What are the compensating general controls that you most likely found?

(AICPA adapted)

LO H-2, H-3, H-7

H.46   Computer Frauds and Missing Control Procedures. The following are brief stories of actual employee thefts and embezzlements perpetrated in an IT environment.

Required:

What type of control procedure that might have prevented or detected the fraud was missing or inoperative?

a. An accounts payable terminal operator at a subsidiary entity fabricated false invoices from a fictitious vendor and entered them in the parent entity's central accounts payable/cash disbursement system. Five checks totaling $155,000 were issued to the "vendor."

b. A bank provided custodial and record-keeping services for several mutual funds. A proof-and-control department employee substituted his own name and account number for those of the actual purchasers of some shares. He used the accounting information system to conceal and shift balances from his name and account to names and accounts of the actual investors when he needed to avoid detection because of missing amounts in the investors' accounts.

c. The university's accounting information system was illegally hacked. Vandals changed many students' first name to Susan, student telephone numbers were changed to the number of the university president, grade point averages were modified, and some academic files were completely deleted.

d. A computer operator at a state-run horse race betting agency set the computer clock back three minutes. After the race was completed, he quickly telephoned bets to his girlfriend, an input clerk at the agency, gave her the winning horse and the bet amount, and won every time!

H.47   General Controls. Indicate the benefits of each of the following examples of general controls.

a. Echo checks are designed and built into the computer by the manufacturer.

b. The company schedules regular maintenance on its computer hardware.

c. The company involves users in its design of programs and selection of prepackaged software and programs.

d. New programs are tested and validated prior to being implemented.

e. Documentation is required prior to modifying existing programs using "emergency" change orders.

f. The duties of system analysts, programmers, and computer operators are appropriately separated.

g. Appropriate backup and data retention policies are implemented.

h. The access rights granted to employees are periodically reviewed and evaluated, giving consideration to known changes resulting from promotions and transfers within the company.

LO H-2

H.48   General Controls. For each of the following examples of general controls, classify the control based on appropriate category (program development controls, program change controls, computer operations controls, and access to programs and data controls). In addition, for each, provide the objective of the control and one example of how audit teams might test the operating effectiveness of the control.

a. The entity requires the use of passwords and requires these passwords to be modified every three months.

b. Proper documentation exists for "emergency" change requests for programs.

c. Important files, programs, and documentation are backed up and stored in a safe, offsite location.

d. The entity involves users in the design of programs and selection of prepackaged software.

e. The entity resolves failures for transactions processed in a real-time environment on a timely basis.

    f. All program development activities are consistent with the entity's needs and objectives.

    g. All modifications to existing programs are properly documented.

    h. The functions of systems analyst, computer programmer, and computer operator are performed by different individuals.

    i. The entity monitors which individuals access various programs and cross-checks this use against an authorized user listing.

LO H-3

H.49 **Automated Application Controls: Input Controls.** In its automated processing system over payroll transactions, Brady Company enters the following data from its employees' attendance records (# corresponds to a numeric field; A corresponds to an alphabetic field):

- Employee number (##-#-##, the employees' Social Security number).
- Entity division (AA#, an alphanumeric field containing two letters corresponding to the location of the employee and two numbers corresponding to that employees' supervisor).
- Hours worked (##.#, a weekly total of hours worked in 0.25-hour increments).

After data entry, these data are processed against the information maintained in that employee's master file record. The records are accessed based on employee number. If the employee is an hourly employee, the number of hours worked is multiplied by the pay rate; if a salaried employee, the hours worked are checked against a range of acceptable hours. After the gross pay is determined, information in the master file record is used to calculate income tax, FICA, and other withholdings from that employee's pay.

Required:

Provide an example of how Brady Company might incorporate each of the following input controls to verify the accuracy of input of employee attendance record information.

    a. Data entry and formatting controls.

    b. Check digit.

    c. Record counts.

    d. Batch totals.

    e. Hash totals.

    f. Valid character tests.

    g. Valid sign tests.

    h. Limit or reasonableness tests.

    i. Error correction and resubmission procedures.

LO H-2, H-3

H.50 **Identify Computer Control Weaknesses.** Ajax Inc., an audit client, recently installed a new accounting information system to process its shipping, billing, and accounts receivable records more efficiently. During interim work, an assistant completed the review of the accounting information system and the internal controls. The assistant determined the following information concerning the new accounting information system and the processing and control of shipping notices and customer invoices.

Each major computerized function (i.e., shipping, billing, accounts receivable) is permanently assigned to a specific computer operator who is responsible for making program changes, running the program, and reconciling the computer log. Responsibility for custody and control over the various databases and system documentation is randomly rotated among the computer operators on a monthly basis to prevent any one person from access to the database and documentation. Each computer programmer and computer operator has access to the computer room via a magnetic card and a digital code that is different for each card. The systems analyst and the supervisor of computer operators do not have access to the computer room.

The computer system documentation consists of the following items: program lists, error lists, logs, and database dictionaries. To increase efficiency, control totals (both batch totals and hash totals) and processing controls are not used in the system.

LO H-2

Ajax ships its products directly from two warehouses that forward shipping notices to general accounting. There, the billing clerk enters the price of the item and accounts for the numerical sequence of the shipping notices. The billing clerk also prepares daily summaries of the units shipped and the sales amounts. Shipping notices and summaries that are forwarded to the computer department for processing the computer output consist of the following:

- A three-copy invoice that is forwarded to the billing clerk.
- A daily sales register showing the aggregate totals of units shipped and sales amounts that the computer operator compares to the summaries.

The billing clerk mails two copies of each invoice to the customer and retains the third copy in an open invoice file that serves as a detail accounts receivable record.

Required:

a. Prepare a list of weaknesses in internal control (manual and computerized) and describe one or more ways to address each.

b. Suggest how Ajax's automated processing over shipping and billing could be improved through the use of remote terminals to enter shipping notices. Describe appropriate IT controls for such an online data entry system.

LO H-2, H-3

H.51 **Identify Control Weaknesses and Recommendations.** Georgia Beemster, CPA, is examining the financial statements of the Louisville Sales Corporation, which recently installed a computerized processing system. The following comments have been extracted from Beemster's notes on computer operations and the processing and control of shipping notices and customer invoices:

- To minimize inconvenience, Louisville made the conversion to the new accounting information system without changing its existing system. The vendor supervised the conversion and trained all computer department employees in systems design, operations, and programming.
- Each computer run is assigned to a specific employee who is responsible for making program changes, running the program, and answering questions. This procedure has the advantage of eliminating the need for records of computer operations because each employee is responsible for her or his own computer runs.
- At least one computer department employee remains in the computer room during office hours and only computer department employees have keys to the computer room.
- The vendor provided Louisville with systems documentation consisting of a set of record formats and program lists. This documentation and the files are maintained in the computer department.
- Louisville considered the desirability of IT controls but decided to retain the manual controls from its existing system.
- Louisville's products are shipped directly from public warehouses, which forward shipping notices to general accounting. There, a billing clerk enters the price of the items and accounts for the numerical sequence of shipping notices from each warehouse. The billing clerk also prepares daily summaries of the units shipped and the unit prices.
- Shipping notices and daily summaries are forwarded to the computer department for input and processing. Extension calculations are made on the computer. Output consists of invoices (in six copies) and a daily sales register. The daily sales register shows the aggregate totals of units shipped and unit prices, which the computer operator compares to the daily summaries.
- All copies of the invoice are returned to the billing clerk. The clerk mails three copies to the customer, forwards one copy to the warehouse, maintains one copy in a numerical file, and retains one copy in an open invoice file that serves as a detailed accounts receivable record.

Required:

Describe the weaknesses in the internal control over information and data flows and the procedures for processing shipping notices and customer invoices. Recommend some improvements in these control policies and procedures. Organize your answer sheet with two columns, one headed Weaknesses and the other headed Recommended Improvements.

(AICPA adapted)

LO H-3

H.52 **Automated Application Controls.** The following provides a brief description of the computerized payroll system used by Merriman in its biweekly processing of payroll for its employees.

1. Employees automatically record their attendance (hours worked) as they log in at the beginning and end of the workday.

2. At the end of each payroll period (every two weeks), employees print and authorize their attendance records, submitting them to their supervisor. The computer prenumbers these attendance records and generates them in chronological order based on when the employee submits his or her final attendance for that payroll period.

3. Supervisors review the attendance records submitted by their employees and authorize these records, which the supervisors then forward to data entry conversion operators.

4. Data conversion operators input the attendance record number, employee number, and hours worked from the attendance records that have been approved by the employee supervisors into a file to be used for computerized processing.

5. Once the entire batch of records has been accepted for processing, the computer program accesses the payroll master file data. Gross salary is then calculated as follows:
   - Gross salary for hourly wage employees is determined by multiplying the number of hours worked from the transaction file by the wage rate contained in that employee's master file record.
   - Gross salary for salaried employees is determined directly from the employee's master file record.
6. After the calculation of gross salary, information from the employee's payroll master file data as well as federal income tax and FICA withholding tables is used to calculate deductions from that employee's pay.
7. A payroll register is generated, distributed, and reviewed for reasonableness and obvious processing errors.
8. Following the review of the payroll register, funds are transferred into the account designated by the employee (for those employees who have authorized electronic transfer of funds) or paychecks are prepared and held for employees (for employees who have not authorized electronic transfer of funds).

Required:

For each of the preceding steps in Merriman's payroll processing, identify appropriate controls that the company has either implemented or should implement to ensure the authorized and accurate processing of payroll transactions.

LO H-3

H.53 **Flowchart Control Points.** Each number of the flowchart in Exhibit H.53.1 identifies a control point in the computerized payroll processing system. List the control points and, for each point, describe the type of internal control procedure that should be implemented.

EXHIBIT H.53.1
Flowchart Control Points

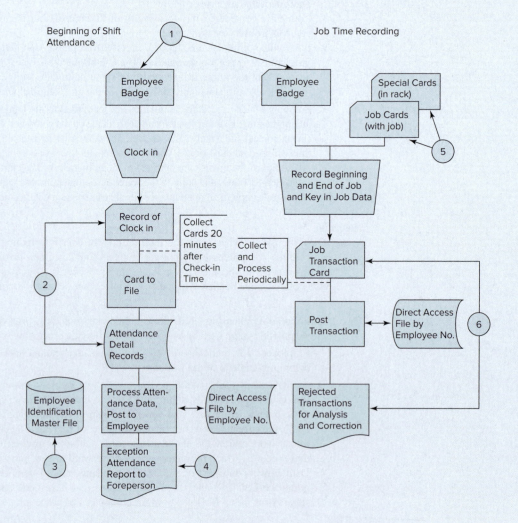

LO H-6

H.54 **Internal Control Considerations in End-User Computing Environments.** Because of the use of personal computers by many businesses, audit teams must know about the potential internal control weaknesses inherent in such an environment. This knowledge is crucial if audit teams are to make a proper assessment of the related control risk and to plan an effective and efficient audit approach.

Required:

In the following case study, assume that you are participating in the audit of Chicago Appliance Company and that the background information was obtained during the planning phase of the engagement. You have been asked to (a) consider the potential internal control weaknesses that exist in this end-user application and (b) assess how those internal control weaknesses could alter the audit plan for the current year.

Background Information

Chicago Appliance is a wholesale distributor of electric appliances. Its sales in each of the last two years have been approximately $40 million. All accounting applications are handled at Chicago's corporate office.

Automated processing operations have historically centered on an onsite mainframe computer. The computer applications include accounts payable and cash disbursements, payroll, inventory, and general ledger. Accounts receivable and fixed asset records have been prepared manually in the past. Internal controls in all areas have been considered strong in the last few years.

During the past year, financial management decided to automate the processing of sales, accounts receivable, and fixed asset transactions and accounting. Management also concluded that purchasing personal computers (PCs) and related available software was more cost effective than increasing the mainframe computer capacity and hiring a second computer operator. The controller and accounting clerks have been encouraged to find additional uses for the PCs and to "experiment" with them when they are not too busy.

The accounts receivable clerk is enthusiastic about the PCs, but the fixed-asset clerk seems somewhat apprehensive about them because he has limited prior experience with computers. The accounts receivable clerk explained that the controller had purchased a "very easy-to-use" accounts receivable software application program for the PC, which enables her to input the daily information regarding billings and receipts quickly and easily. The controller has added some personally developed programs to the software to give it better report-writing features.

During a recent demonstration, the accounts receivable clerk explained that the program required her to input only the customer's name and invoice amount in the case of billings or the customer's name and check amount in the case of receipts. The computer then automatically updates the respective customer's account balance. At the end of every month, the clerk prints and reconciles the accounts receivable trial balance to the general ledger balance and the controller reviews the reconciliation.

The fixed asset program also was purchased from an outside vendor. The controller indicated that the software package had just recently been put on the market and that it was programmed to compute tax depreciation based on recent changes in the federal tax laws. The controller also stated that, because of the fixed asset clerk's reluctance to use the computer, information from the manual fixed asset records had been input. The controller indicated, however, that the fixed asset clerk would be responsible for the future processing related to the fixed asset files and for generating the month-end and year-end reports used to prepare the related accounting entries.

All the various accounts receivable and fixed asset files are adequately labeled as to the type of program or data file. They are arranged in an organized manner near the PC.

(Adapted from a case contributed by PwC to *The Auditor's Report.*)

LO H-3, H-5

H.55 **Test Data Transactions in a Payroll Processing Program.** Use the computer-based electronic audit documentation on the textbook website to perform a test of the computerized payroll processing program.

The electronic audit documentation contains a simple program that accepts payroll transaction input and calculates an individual's weekly gross and net pay. When you come to the proper place in the program, you will see places to input these data:

- Employee identification (Social Security number).
- Regular pay rate (round dollars, no cents).
- Regular time (hours, 40 or fewer).

- Overtime (hours over 40).
- Gross earnings to date (gross pay prior to this payroll entry).

According to the client's description of the IT controls in the system:

1. The program checks for valid employee identification.
2. The regular pay rate is tested for reasonableness.
3. The system will accept no more than 40 regular-time hours.
4. There is a limit on the number of overtime hours that will be paid (32 hours). Overtime hours are paid only if the employee works 40 regular-time hours.
5. Overtime is paid at the rate of 150 percent of the regular pay rate.
6. Social Security and Medicare taxes and federal income tax withholdings are calculated automatically according to applicable laws and regulations.

Applicable Laws and Regulations (assume the following for this case)

- The minimum wage is $7.25 per regular hour.
- Social Security tax is 6.2 percent on the first $118,500 of gross pay, and Medicare tax is 1.45 percent of all pay.
- Federal income tax withholding is assumed to be 23 percent of gross pay.

Required:

The payroll calculation program contains control deficiencies. Your job is to identify and describe them. Follow the instructions in the electronic audit documentation. Devise and enter test transactions of your own making. Write a memo to the audit partner identifying and describing the control failures in the payroll calculation program.

Cases

Andersen: An Obstruction of Justice?

PROBLEM

Students may be familiar with **Arthur Andersen,** the CPA firm that failed to detect fraudulent financial activities in the audits of several companies including **Sunbeam, Waste Management, Enron,** and **WorldCom.** Many articles and papers have been written about the quality of these audits and how increasing the firm's revenues from both audit and nonaudit services may have supplanted audit quality as the main objective of Andersen as a firm. However, we should not lose sight of the facts that led to Andersen's demise and the findings that have occurred since Andersen ostensibly closed its doors as an audit and accounting firm.

In effect, Andersen had already received the maximum penalty even before its trial began. Once Anderson had been indicted, most of its clients had decided that an audit by a firm under indictment would be of little value even if allowed by the Securities and Exchange Commission (SEC). During the shareholder proxy season in early 2002, company after company announced it would no longer retain Andersen as its auditor. Whether the firm was able to defend itself or not, the days of Andersen as a viable audit firm had come to an end.

ANDERSEN GOES TO TRIAL

In May 2002, Arthur Andersen LLP was tried for obstruction of justice in connection with the destruction of documents during a time period prior to a formal SEC investigation of Enron, one of Andersen's largest clients. The main witness for the prosecution was David Duncan, a former Andersen partner in charge of the Enron audit, who had already pleaded guilty to obstruction of justice. The guilt or innocence of Andersen hinged on the question of corporate direction. If Duncan had acted illegally on his own in an effort to save himself from consequences resulting from an SEC investigation of Enron, then Andersen as a firm would not likely be found guilty of obstructing justice. However, if Duncan had acted illegally on the direction of Andersen's management within the scope of his position in an attempt to save Andersen from the consequences of Enron, the firm as a whole would be held liable. Therefore, the issues to be determined were (1) whether illegal acts had been committed and (2) if they had been committed on behalf of Duncan or on behalf of Andersen.

The Prosecution's Case

The chief prosecutor for the government was Samuel Buell. The main points in Buell's case follow:

- Top partners in Arthur Andersen's Chicago office had permitted Enron to use aggressive accounting practices that were very questionable given the nature of Enron's business.
- In late September through early October 2001, Andersen's legal department had begun creating a strategy designed to protect Andersen from regulators and litigants.
- A major part of the strategy was to invoke Andersen's document retention policy, which, according to prosecutors, was an obscure policy that its employees seldom read or followed on its audits. In addition, the policy had been revised in 2000 by an Andersen partner who had been disciplined by the SEC for his involvement in the Waste Management audits. According

to Buell, management had known that invoking the policy would lead to the destruction of "tons of papers and tens of thousands of computer files" that would be of interest to investigators.[1]

- The prosecution presented notes from an October 9 conversation between Nancy Temple, Andersen's legal counsel, and attorneys in Andersen's legal department. This conversation indicated that Temple had believed an SEC investigation was imminent and that such an investigation could have devastating consequences for Andersen. Andersen was still operating under a court order signed in 2000 (due to a settlement of the Waste Management lawsuits) that could trigger a suspension of its license to audit publicly traded companies if it was found to have engaged in additional securities law violations.

- Duncan had admitted to destroying documents to keep them out of the investigation and that his actions were taken under direction and with the consent of Andersen management in Chicago.

- Finally, C. E. Andrews, an Andersen partner, in his testimony before Congress in January 2002, had said that Duncan had given every appearance of destroying documents in anticipation of requests for documents from federal investigators.[2]

Andersen's Defense

Andersen's attorneys, led by Rusty Hardin, defended Andersen against all charges brought by the government.

- The government's case had fallen short of proving Andersen's guilt or even proving that a crime had occurred.

- Duncan had shredded documents prior to any formal investigation (Andersen was not subpoenaed until November 8, 2001), and the elimination of unnecessary documents was a normal audit procedure.

- It was clearly sound business practice to consult with the corporate attorneys with regard to potential litigation and the firm's rights and obligations with regard to that investigation. In fact, Duncan, at Temple's request, had saved many documents that could have proved detrimental to Andersen.

- Hardin argued that Duncan was innocent and that the government had overstated its case against him in order to pressure him to cooperate with its investigation in exchange for a reduced sentence.

- While the prosecution focused on the part of the document retention policy that instructed auditors on the documents that could be destroyed, parts of the retention policy indicated which documentation was required to be retained in the audit files.

THE CASE GOES TO THE JURY

Although the prosecution and defense presentations were very contentious, possibly the most contentious part of the case focused on the instructions that Judge Melinda Harmon gave to the jury. The instructions hinged on the wording of the statute that makes it a crime to

> *knowingly* use intimidation or physical force, threaten, or *corruptly persuade* another
> person . . . with intent to . . . cause that person to withhold documents from or alter documents
> for use in an official proceeding [emphasis added].[3]

Although both sides believed that the jury needed instructions that clarified the meaning of the statute in question, two issues were paramount in the argument concerning the instructions:

1. The phrase *knowingly . . . corruptly persuade* had been discussed at length. The government had contended that the word *knowingly* was not meant as a modifier of the term *corruptly persuade*. The jury had been instructed that

> Even if the petitioner honestly and sincerely believed that the conduct was lawful, you may
> find the petitioner guilty.[4]

[1] Alexi Barrionuevo and Jonathan Weil, "High Noon: Andersen's Criminal Case Goes to the Jury," *The Wall Street Journal*, June 6, 2002, pp. C1, C20.
[2] Ibid.
[3] 18 U.S.C. § 1512 (b)(2)(a) and (b).
[4] William Rehnquist, "Flawed Instruction Led to Andersen Verdict," *Chicago Daily Law Bulletin*, June 1, 2005.

2. The government had contended that the word *corruptly* needed to be defined for the jury. Prior rulings in the 5th District Court (the same court district that was trying the Andersen case) had stated that *corruptly* was

   knowingly and *dishonestly,* with specific intent to *subvert or undermine* the integrity of the proceedings [emphasis added].

   The government had insisted on excluding the word *dishonestly* and adding the word *impede* to the phrase "subvert and undermine." The instruction provided to the jury had not included the word *dishonestly* and included the phrase "subvert, undermine, or impede" government fact finding.[5]

Having heard the testimony and been given these instructions, the jury convicted Andersen of obstruction of justice after deliberating for 10 days.

ROUND TWO

On May 31, 2005, in a unanimous decision, the U.S. Supreme Court overturned the Andersen conviction on the basis of flawed instructions to the jury. In writing the opinion, Chief Justice William Rehnquist cited the following arguments:

- Merely providing a person with information regarding a course of action cannot be construed as persuading *another person . . . with intent to . . . cause* that person to withhold documents.
- It is not necessarily corrupt in *persuading another person . . . with intent to . . . cause* that person to withhold documents. It may be proper for an attorney to persuade a client to withhold documents under attorney–client privilege from an investigation. In this circumstance, such persuasion would not be corrupt. Therefore, the withholding of documents from an investigation cannot by itself be presumed to be a *corrupt* action.
- Document retention polices are created to keep documents from being obtained by certain individuals and organizations, including the government. These policies are common in business, and it is not wrongful for a manager to instruct employees to abide by such a policy.
- The term *knowingly* does modify the term *corrupt* both linguistically and per the intent of the statute. The jury instructions did not convey the requisite consciousness of wrongdoing that should be required for conviction.
- Substituting the term *impede* in place of *dishonestly* in the jury instructions removed the requirement that the action be with knowledge and forethought of wrongdoing. The term *impede* has a much broader concept. Anyone who innocently persuades another to withhold information might be considered to impede an investigation. Clearly, the term *corruptly* was included in the statute to exclude such innocent behavior from being consisted unlawful.
- A *knowingly corrupt persuader* cannot be someone who persuades others to shred documents under a document retention policy that was not enacted with regard to any particular proceeding in which those documents might be material. A series of events is not sufficient to indicate an intent to obstruct an investigation.

CONCLUSION

The headlines following the Supreme Court decision were telling:

"A Posthumous Victory," *USA Today,* June 1, 2005.
"Arthur Andersen's Hollow Victory," *The Economist,* June 4, 2005.
"Too Late for Andersen," *Legal Times,* June 6, 2005.
"A Bittersweet Court Victory for Andersen," *Legal Times,* June 6, 2005.

Although Arthur Andersen's verdict had been overturned because of faulty jury instructions, it was far from a vindication that what Andersen had done was correct. In addition, such a decision came much too late to provide anything but a moral victory to Andersen's former employees.

   The government has chosen not to retry Andersen. First, there was little to gain in terms of either financial or other penalties. Andersen had already received the "death penalty" (and was no longer a viable entity), whether guilty or innocent. Second, if Andersen was to be retried and found not guilty, the Department of Justice and the SEC would have suffered severe blows to their reputation and received a multitude of criticism from the business community. On the other hand, a retrial might have been what the government needed to fend off criticism of being overzealous and overreaching in its prosecution of Andersen. However, because the government did not retry the case, it appears that the risks outweigh the rewards. Third, the government received everything that it wanted with regard to Enron, WorldCom, and Andersen with the passage of the Sarbanes–Oxley Act. Most notably, as a result of the Andersen case, a stricter document retention policy with more severe penalties for not following that policy was enacted.

It is interesting to note that many legal experts believe that the Department of Justice and the SEC took a vastly different attitude toward the 2005 tax-shelter problems of **KPMG** because of the lessons learned from the Andersen prosecution. Clearly, in the Andersen case, there had been no winners, and the elimination of another international CPA firm caused significant harm to innocent employees and created substantial chaos in the business community.

Finally, in March 2007, a federal judge gave final approval to a $72.5 million settlement between Andersen and investors who sued the accounting firm over its role in Enron's collapse.[6] This finally put to rest the case of Andersen and Enron, but the repercussions may live on indefinitely.

DISCUSSION QUESTIONS

1. Look up the term *corrupt* in the dictionary. What is its definition? Was *corrupt* appropriately applied to the actions of Arthur Andersen?

2. The issues that overturned the Andersen verdict were based on faulty jury instructions, not on whether Andersen was, in fact, guilty or innocent. Based on the information in this case and other information you know, do you believe Andersen violated the law?

3. Do you believe that the Supreme Court's opinion overturning the lower court's decision was appropriate?

4. Should the SEC and the Department of Justice have tried Andersen as a firm, or should they have targeted specific individuals who had engaged in acts the two bodies believed to be unlawful?

5. Although Andersen's conviction was overturned, do you believe that its employees acted in an ethical manner?

6. Comment on the actions of David Duncan and Nancy Temple. Which of these parties do you believe was more responsible for the Andersen saga?

7. The class-action lawsuit against Andersen also named the **Canadian Imperial Bank of Commerce, JPMorgan Chase, Citigroup, Merrill Lynch,** and **Credit Suisse Group** as codefendants with Andersen. Why would the plaintiffs name so many entities in their lawsuit? Merrill Lynch and Credit Suisse asked a U.S. appeals court to rule that the complaint should not have been certified as a class action suit. Why would these entities make such a claim?

[6] Jeff Feely, "Settlement Approved for Enron Investors," *Washington Post*, March 10, 2007.

PTL Club–The Harbinger of Things to Come?

The PTL scandal is a picture-perfect, suitable-for-framing example of how auditors with a modicum of skepticism and alertness could have been heroes instead of goats. PTL was an accident waiting to happen even before Tammy got the notion that heading to the mall was the perfect cure for her blues. Auditors who were concerned with doing more than the absolute bare minimum required by GAAS and GAAP could have exposed this fraud much earlier, saving innocent and gullible viewers tens of millions of dollars.

Robert A. Prentice, "Anatomy of a Fraud: Inside the Finances of the PTL Ministries," American Business Law Journal, *November 1, 1993*

In January 1974, Jim and Tammy Faye Bakker launched the **PTL Club,** which for more than a decade was one of the most successful television ministries. At its peak, the PTL Club broadcast from nearly 200 television stations to a national audience estimated at 12 million viewers. PTL stood for both "Praise the Lord" and "People That Love." The Bakkers combined a traditional talk show format with religious entertainment, emotional personal testimonies, and frequent campaigns for financial support. The Bakkers established a Christian theme park, **Heritage USA,** which attracted fundamentalist Christians for prayer and fun. They had the country's third most popular amusement park with biblically themed rides and attractions and a large shopping mall selling Christian tapes, records, books, and religious action figures. At its height in 1986, more than 5 million people visited Heritage USA annually, and the PTL Club was raising $10 million a month.

The Bakker's ministry was so popular that, in the final days of the 1980 presidential campaign, Jimmy Carter summoned Jim Bakker to pray with him aboard Air Force One. Ronald Reagan invited Jim and Tammy to his first inaugural, and three years later, Reagan told the National Association of Religious Broadcasters' convention that "The PTL TV network is carrying out a master plan for people that love."[1]

While millions of people tuned into the PTL Club for its entertainment and religious inspiration, it had many detractors. Many concluded that "PTL" stood for "Pass the Loot," a reference to the Bakkers' frequent, passionate fund-raising appeals and to Jim and Tammy's lavish lifestyle. The Bakkers' perceived excesses (remember to think in 1980s dollars) included

- A vacation retreat in the Great Smoky Mountains.
- A $449,000 Palm Springs home with a spectacular view of the Santa Rosa Mountains from the heated pool and hot tub.
- Vacations in $350-a-night hotel suites in Hawaii.
- A 1981 Christmas bash for PTL executives at Cafe Eugene in Charlotte that included $9,000 worth of truffles flown in from Brussels.
- An oceanfront condominium near Palm Beach, which PTL bought for the Bakkers and spent more than $200,000 to furnish. (The Bakker's had recently made a vow to be "good stewards of God's money.")
- A $340,000 five-level lakeside home with another $73,000 in renovations and, of course, a 43-foot houseboat tied to the dock.
- A heated and air-conditioned doghouse for Tammy's dogs.
- Tammy's minks and Gucci handbags.
- A new Mercedes, a 1953 Rolls-Royce, a Corvette, and several Cadillac limousines.
- A basement health spa and indoor pool in their home in Heritage USA. In his dressing room, Bakker installed gold-plated bathroom fixtures and an $11,000 sauna and Jacuzzi.

The crown jewel in the Bakkers' opulent lifestyle was the 4,000-square-foot suite at the PTL ministry's Heritage USA theme park and retreat. The "presidential suite" in the Heritage Grand Hotel was designed for use by the Bakkers, although they often preferred their nearby lakeside home. The suite included gold-plated swan bathroom fixtures, antique beds, and mirrored walls in the bedroom. The suite also included Tammy's 10-by-60-foot closet. Other celebrities also used

[1] Art Harris, "The Good Life at PTL: A Litany of Excess," *The Washington Post,* May 22, 1987, p. A1.

the presidential suite, but they had to be cleared through Bakker's office. One prosecutor noted the hypocritical conduct in the suite. "People sent their money in for an attractive place where there was no smoking, no alcohol—no alcohol except for Mr. Bakker in the Presidential Suite,"[2] referring to Bakker's secret taste for wine and vodka screwdrivers that former staffers detailed in interviews with *The Washington Post*.

Bakker's frequent explanation for his expenditures was that "God wants his people to go first class." At the same time, this lifestyle inspired Ray Stevens's country song, "Would Jesus Wear a Rolex on His Television Show?"

TROUBLE IN PARADISE

The world of PTL and Heritage USA began to collapse in 1987. Jim Bakker had a tryst with church secretary, Jessica Hahn. The PTL Club paid her $256,000 to drop her $12 million lawsuit (later to be characterized as a bribe or "hush money" in court). The Internal Revenue Service questioned $1.3 million of PTL expenditures for the Bakkers, threatening the PTL's tax-exempt status (which eventually was revoked, causing the organization to pay back taxes and penalties). The Pentecostal Assemblies of God, which had ordained Bakker, defrocked him.

A confidential payroll account was kept without the board's knowledge. When Laventhol & Horwath (L&H) became PTL's auditor in May 1985, William Spears, a senior L&H partner, "kept the books" for this secret account. After writing checks for each other, friends, or themselves, the Bakkers or other top executives would call Spears with the information so the check register would be accurate and additional funds could be transferred if the account balance dwindled. Prosecutors categorized this fund as "unrecorded payroll"; creditors who lost millions and defrauded donors called it a "slush fund."

The funds for all these activities were primarily generated from partnership interests sold in four different resort hotels built or planned at Heritage USA. These resort properties were to be financed solely by selling "lifetime partnerships" to persons "donating" $1,000. Similar to a time-share, the donors received four days and three nights for their immediate family in one of the resort hotels, annually, for the rest of their lives. To induce donors to provide money, Bakker supposedly limited the number of partnerships in each project and often exaggerated the number of lifetime partnerships that had been sold. Although the money from selling partnership interests was to be used only for construction of the buildings, more than $100 million was diverted from just two of the projects to fund PTL day-to-day operations.

Eventually, many more than the limited number of lifetime memberships were sold, making it physically impossible for every member to exercise their hotel rights. Bakker sold more than 66,000 partnerships in his Heritage Grand Hotel, although he promised followers only 25,000 would be sold, and 74,000 partnerships in the never-finished Towers Hotel, even though he had said only 30,000 would be sold. The followers contributed $158 million between 1984 and 1987 for the partnerships. In addition, a lifetime partnership could be worth over a million dollars if a family of five came to PTL each year and used all facilities and other perks associated with their membership. In the criminal case against Bakker, the government characterized the financing of building operations through lifetime partnerships as a giant Ponzi scheme.

WHERE WAS THE OVERSIGHT?

Following PTL's bankruptcy, evidence surfaced indicating that the PTL's board of directors had functioned improperly. When Jim Bakker needed money, he simply told other key PTL officials to tell a board member to introduce a resolution recommending a bonus. The board met 23 times between July 5, 1983, and February 16, 1987, when it approved bonuses ranging from $10,000 to $390,000 for Jim Bakker 13 times. In 21 of those meetings, the board also approved bonuses of $2,000 to $170,000 for Tammy Bakker. From June 1986 to March 1987, Jim and Tammy Bakker received more than $1 million and $335,000 in bonuses, respectively. These bonuses were over and above salary and expenses the Bakkers used to maintain their lavish lifestyles. From 1984 to 1987, they received more than $4.8 million in salary, bonuses, and other payments. Each of two other PTL executives, David Taggart and Richard Dortch, received bonuses of almost half a million dollars. Despite receiving this exorbitant amount of money, Jim Bakker announced on TV that he was too poor to buy his $1,000 lifetime membership this month but would put it on his credit card (as viewers were urged to do) and pay for it the following month.

[2] Art Harris, "Jim Bakker, Driven by Money or Miracles?" *The Washington Post*, August 29, 1989, p. C1.

WHAT DID THE AUDITORS KNOW?

The mid-1980s had six very large international accountings firms (called the "Big Six") including Deloitte, Haskins & Sells (now a part of **Deloitte**), PTL's auditor until May 1985. **Laventhol & Horwath (L&H)** was then the seventh largest accounting firm. Jim Bakker used both of these highly regarded firms to reassure his viewers of the PTL Club's financial integrity. He often appeared on television to present audited financial statements as indicators of his personal honesty and the PTL Club's financial integrity. After all, PTL paid large fees to nationally reputable accounting firms to inspect its books. Would someone hiding financial misconduct do that? For example, on April 18, 1986, in the midst of allegations against Jim Bakker, he told his television audience

> We don't mind letting you know that we print audits of this ministry. We have done it for, what, ten years now, and we go through an audit almost a hundred percent of the time. An outside auditing firm, one of the big audit firms of America, is in here at all times auditing this ministry at our own expense, thousands of dollars, tens of thousands of dollars, to be responsible. And we are going to go forward, but it's time God's people say enough is enough.[3]

However, as Jim Bakker repeatedly used the auditors' good reputation to assure his audiences of the PTL Club's honesty and integrity, the accounting firms should have known that Jim Bakker was misleading PTL members.

Deloitte admitted that it had known of the advertised limit on the sale of memberships but argued that no oversales occurred until shortly after May 31, 1984, the end of the fiscal year for which it had prepared its last PTL financial statements. However, it took considerable criticism for not knowing or reporting on the oversale occurring shortly after May 31, 1984, because its report was dual dated August 31, 1984, and October 24, 1984. (While auditing standards specify the auditors' responsibilities for subsequent events when the report is dual dated, the judicial system and the court of public opinion may not always see these responsibilities similarly.) Conversely, L&H admitted that it had known that more than 25,000 Grand Hotel lifetime partnerships had been sold but denied that it had any knowledge that a limit was placed on the number of partnerships even though this limit was widely publicized.

Both Deloitte and L&H wrote checks from the PTL secret account to the Bakkers and other key employees (but did not sign them to avoid an obvious conflict of interest with their audit roles). Both firms prepared the Bakkers' tax returns. Tax law prohibits tax-exempt organizations from providing excessive private enumeration. Both accounting firms claimed to have been unaware that the IRS was seriously considering revoking PTL's tax-exempt status due to the compensation being paid to the Bakkers. Furthermore, after one outside law firm resigned because of concerns over excessive compensation, PTL's new law firm argued that the compensation was not excessive because the auditors reviewed the amounts paid.

Many red flags should have been evident to both audit firms. Although legal issues were raised regarding the lifetime partner concept, neither audit firm had indicated that this concept presented audit issues. Deloitte had addressed its concerns about the excessive compensation; the dramatically increasing personal expenses of senior executives; and the selling of merchandise at astronomical markups (PTL purchased statues of David and Goliath for $10 and represented them on television as being worth $1,000). But these issues did not lead to a modified audit report opinion or other disclosures.

Financial documentation was often designed to hide items from the auditors. For example, bonuses were not recorded in the minutes of the board of directors meetings but in "addendums" to the minutes that were added at a later date. A year's worth of records regarding travel and other expenses were "lost" and were never provided to L&H. Auditors could not find documentation for other expenditures, including $27 million of $80 million spent on construction projects. In a 23-page memo, Deloitte spent 22 pages listing inadequacies in PTL's internal controls. Both accounting firms knew that PTL had an unreasonably high number of separate bank accounts and a tremendous problem with bounced checks. A draft of Deloitte's 1984 audit report expressed a concern over "whether PTL would be able to continue as 'a going concern' based on current assets of only $8.6 million against $28.5 million in current liabilities." A going-concern issue was not included, however, in the issued audit report.

[3] Robert A. Prentice, "Anatomy of a Fraud: Inside the Finances of the PTL Ministries," *American Business Law Journal*, November 1, 1993.

AFTER THE FALL

Jim Bakker relinquished his ministry after admitting to the extramarital tryst, and he and his wife, Tammy Faye, exiled themselves to Palm Springs, California. In March 1987, to help avoid bankruptcy and restore its reputation, the PTL Club's new boards appointed the Rev. Jerry Falwell, then a well-respected and well-known television minister, to take over the organization. He was to defend the PTL Club against legal threats from creditors, disgruntled contributors, and the IRS.

The IRS Examination Report contended that tax-exempt rules had been violated because of excessive payments to Bakker, his family, and other PTL officers. Revenue examiners asserted that Bakker's compensation of $968,000 in a three-year period was "unreasonable" and that his total compensation should not have exceeded $331,000. PTL Club lawyers argued that Bakker's compensation was reasonable "because he is the guiding light of the ministry and is the key to PTL's success in fund raising."[4]

The PTL Club hired Arthur Andersen to extensively audit PTL activities in an effort to gain a true picture of its financial position. Besides those problems already outlined, the new auditors found the following:

- $92 million in funds that could not be accounted for (later reduced to $12 million as PTL executives found documents).
- $71 million debt.
- Missing records documenting $27 million in construction expenditures. (Building contractors insisted that they submitted the records to PTL as they performed the work.)
- Operating losses of $27 million sustained by the organization in the nine months preceding Bakker's resignation.

Based on the new information, PTL officials were convinced that Bakker knew that the ministry's financial situation was out of control long before the scandal over the sexual encounter forced him to step down.

LAVENTHOL & HORWATH

Founded in 1915 in New York, Horwath & Horwath merged in 1967 with Laventhol Krekstein Griffith & Co. of Philadelphia. L&H experienced massive growth exemplified by a nearly quadrupling of revenues during the 1980s, fueled through acquisitions by developing expertise in unique areas of practice and by accepting risky clients. From 1984 to 1990, L&H acquired 64 small practices increasing its revenues to $345 million. At its peak, the firm had more than 50 offices and 460 partners. Merging so many practices and commensurate different cultures created a patchwork of ethics and values and a sense that increasing the revenue stream was the firm's paramount objective. The drive for growth led the firm to accept clients without appropriately screening them and to accept clients known to be risky.

L&H often sought expertise that pushed the envelope. One of its most notable and lucrative revenue streams was finding tax write-offs for investors in hotels. This practice waned when the IRS reformed the tax code. L&H also developed a specialty in services to the commercial real estate industry, an industry which, in the late 1980s, was mired in an economic recession that resulted in empty buildings and falling prices. One client was pushing a bogus tax shelter involving genetically engineered cows, resulting in L&H's being the first accounting firm to lose a jury trial under federal racketeering law. L&H often found itself in court fighting allegations of sloppy audit work. Following the filing of lawsuits associated with their PTL work, the firm had 115 legal actions against it, seeking a total of $362 million.

L&H tried to survive despite the legal and fiscal pressures. Before its collapse, employees had accepted a 10 percent pay cut, and the payments to retired partners were significantly cut. Still, the firm found itself so short of cash that appeals from employees to borrow money occurred daily. Finally, the firm gathered its partners in Houston for a special meeting to address the critical situation. The vote was unanimous to dissolve Laventhol, resulting in what was then the largest collapse of an accounting firm. On November 21, 1990, Laventhol & Horwath declared bankruptcy, and 3,273 employees were out of work.

---

[4] Gary Klott, "PTL's Ledgers: Missing Records and Rising Debt," *The New York Times*, June 6, 1987, sect. 1, p. 8.

GOING TO COURT

In a 28-page indictment, Jim Bakker was charged with 24 counts of fraud and conspiracy. The jury convicted Bakker, who was sentenced to 45 years in prison. (The sentence was reduced on appeal, and Bakker was in prison only from 1989 to 1994.) In a civil case brought by disgruntled lifetime partners, Bakker was found liable for common law fraud and almost $130 million in damages (although no money was ever collected). The same jury exonerated Deloitte & Touche (successor to Deloitte, Haskins & Sells) from fraud because the intention (scienter) to aid in the fraud had not been proved.

Richard Dortch, PTL's former second in command, and Bakker aides David and James Taggart were also charged. Dortch, who was to have stood trial with Bakker, agreed to plead guilty to four counts of conspiracy and fraud and was sentenced to eight years (later reduced to two years) in prison and a $200,000 fine. His light sentence was in part due to his agreement to testify against Bakker. Taggart, former PTL executive vice president, received the maximum sentence of 18 years and 5 months on a conviction for income tax evasion. His brother, James Taggart, PTL's decorator, was sentenced to 17 years and 9 months.

L&H declared bankruptcy to shield itself from lawsuits, debt repayment (much of which was incurred to finance its acquisitions), and other liabilities. Once L&H declared bankruptcy, all lawsuits, including the PTL lawsuits, were suspended, and in 1992, the bankruptcy court combined the PTL claims and other lawsuits into the bankruptcy proceedings. PTL creditors and members joined a long list of creditors in bankruptcy court with total claims of nearly $2 billion. A federal bankruptcy court approved a plan to collect $47 million from 629 partners and other professional-level firm members, although L&H was not "conceding any allegations in the complaint."[5] The assessments, which were to be paid over 10 years, averaged between $75,000 and $400,000 per employee. Although PTL creditors received only a few cents on the dollar, members received nothing.

CONCLUSION

The AICPA has stated that the accounting profession must learn from past cases to prevent the reoccurrences of similar detrimental activities. Although the PTL engagement by itself did not destroy L&H, it contributed greatly at a time when the firm was already awash in debt and legal proceedings. PTL became the proverbial "straw that broke the camel's back." Furthermore, the PTL engagement is viewed as emblematic of the types of clients and quality of audit work that characterized Laventhol in the mid-1980s.

The L&H case changed the face of the accounting profession. Historically, the accounting profession had demanded that accountants practice as partnerships on the theory that professionals should stand by their work and not be shielded from the costs of their mistakes. It also made financial sense to adopt that structure because profits in a partnership are divided and taxed to the individual. Corporations, on the other hand, are taxed twice—once as a company and then as individuals on their corporate dividends. After Laventhol, the accounting profession moved to organizing under limited liability partnerships (LLPs) and companies (LLCs). These structures provide legal protection to the partners and top executives in the firm.

ADDITIONAL INFORMATION

Hour-long show highlighting the opening of Heritage USA: *PTL Club: Jim and Tammy on Location from Heritage Island,* www.youtube.com/watch?v=XdkiehVHDVU

PTL CLUB 1987—Jim & Tammy's Goodbye, www.youtube.com/watch?v=we18_hqy5O8

Short interview with Barbara Walters: *The Fall of Televangelist Conman Jim Bakker,* www.youtube.com/watch?v=V1nw7A54OvI

Long interview and fraud outline with Barbara Walters. Excellent overview of the scam and Jim Bakker: *American Scandals—Season 1, Episode 7,* "Jim Bakker: Fall from Grace," www.youtube.com/watch?v=ixWerYnIPJE

---

[5] "Laventhol Bankruptcy Plan," *The New York Times,* August 25, 1992.

DISCUSSION QUESTIONS

1. Although audit reports should provide assurance to investors and creditors that financial information presented is free of material misstatements and in accordance with GAAP, should audit reports be used to solicit investments, credit, or sales in a manner similar to Jim Bakker's? How can a CPA firm prevent such behavior?

2. During the trial, Mary K. Cline, senior auditor for Deloitte, Haskins and Sells stated:

   "Well, we made a lot of judgments during the audit, and we were auditing the balance sheet as of May 31, and there was no reason in my judgment to look at this number after May 31."[6]

   a. Should the oversale of lifetime partnerships be classified as a subsequent event?

   b. Should Deloitte have evaluated the sales occurring after the balance sheet date of May 31, 1984?

   c. Should L&H have been aware of the sales limits on lifetime memberships? If so, what should they have done about it?

3. Why do you think audit firms are willing to accept high-risk clients?

4. What analytical and audit procedures could have led Deloitte and L&H to have more easily detected and reported PTL Club's financial problems?

5. Why would a staff auditor want to be "part of the client's team" and consent to questionable practices rather than being an "independent watchdog" and contest such practices?

6. How could the auditors have known and understood the PTL business better in order to audit more efficiently and effectively?

7. Is it the auditors' responsibility to verify that the client meets tax-exempt status?

8. Did the preparation of checks violate the auditors' Code of Ethics?

ADDITIONAL SOURCES

Carol F. Venable, "Anatomy of a Fraud: Inside the Finances of the PTL Ministries," *American -Business Law Journal,* November 1, 1993.

Gary L. Tidwell, *Anatomy of a Fraud: Inside the Finances of the PTL Ministries* (New York: John Wiley, 1993).

Alison Leigh Cowan, "Bankruptcy Filing by Laventhol," *The New York Times,* November 22, 1990, p. 1.

J. Weber and M. Galen, "Behind the Fall of Laventhol," *BusinessWeek,* December 24, 1990, pp. 54–55.

William E. Schmidt, "For Jim and Tammy Bakker, Excess Wiped Out a Rapid Climb to Success," *The New York Times,* May 16, 1987, p. 8.

"Former Leader of PTL Ministry Is Found Liable for $130 Million," *The New York Times,* December 15, 1990, p. 12.

Art Harris and Michael Isikoff, "The Good Life at PTL: A Litany of Excess," *The Washington Post,* May 22, 1987, p. A1.

Art Harris, "Jim Bakker, Driven by Money or Miracles?" *The Washington Post,* August 29, 1989, p. C1.

Richard N. Ostling and Joseph J. Kane, "Jim Bakker's Crumbling World," *Time,* December 19, 1988, p. 72.

"Laventhol Bankruptcy Plan," *The New York Times,* August 25, 1992, p. D2.

Gregory Richards, "The Other Big Accounting Firm Meltdown—Laventhol & Horwath's Final Days: a 'Sad Tragedy to Watch,'" *Philadelphia Business Journal,* August 2, 2002.

Michael Isikoff, "PTL Contributors Sue Ministry's Accounting Firm," *The Washington Post,* November 19, 1987, p. C10.

Gary Klott, "PTL's Ledgers: Missing Records and Rising Debt," *The New York Times,* June 6, 1987, p. 8.

M. Galen and J. Weber, "Too Big, Too Fast," *BusinessWeek,* December 3, 1990, pp. 35–36.

[6] *Anatomy of a Fraud: Inside the Finances of the PTL Ministries, 1993* (New York: John Wiley), p. 215.

GM: Running on Empty?

Founded in 1908, **General Motors Corp.** (GM) is truly an iconic American corporation. From 1931 through 2008, GM was the world's largest automobile manufacturer, and in 1955, it became the first company in any industry to report more than $1 billion in revenues. GM's market share peaked at 51 percent in 1962. GM's domination in the market was such that many recommended the company be subject to scrutiny under antitrust laws. In 1971, former President Lyndon Johnson made the statement "now what's good for General Motors really is good for America."[1]

GM's net income reached an all-time high of $6.7 billion in 1997, and the automaker continued to generate positive net income through 2004. In 2005, things began to change. GM reported a net loss of more than $10 billion and continued to post losses through 2008, with a loss of almost $31 billion in that year. (GM's cash flow from operations in 2008 was a negative $12 billion.) A summary of various measures of GM's financial condition for the six-year period from 2003 through 2008 is presented in GM Exhibit 1.[2]

GM EXHIBIT 1

Summary of Financial Information: General Motors Corp. (amounts in millions)

	2003	2004	2005	2006	2007	2008
Total assets	$448,507	$479,603	$476,078	$186,192	$148,883	$91,047
Stockholders' equity	25,268	27,726	14,597	(5,441)	(37,094)	(86,154)
Revenues	182,543	193,571	192,605	207,349	181,112	148,979
Operating income	2,862	12,081	(16,931)	(7,668)	(4,390)	(21,284)
Net income	3,822	2,805	(10,567)	(1,978)	(38,732)	(30,860)
Cash flow from operations	7,600	13,061	(16,856)	(11,759)	7,731	(12,065)

Source: General Motors Corp. 2003–2008 10-K reports.

Because of concerns with the ultimate impact of GM's financial struggles on the world economy, GM received $13.4 billion in government loans in December 2008. President Barack Obama's administration pledged interim financing to allow GM to develop a restructuring plan, requested then-CEO Rick Wagoner to resign, and announced a plan to replace at least 6 of the 12 members of GM's board of directors. All of these events occurred in a market in which the economic conditions sharply decreased demand for automobile purchases. Not surprisingly, GM's stock reached a low (at that time) of $0.75 per share on May 29, 2009 (for comparison, GM's stock traded between $27 per share and $94 per share from 1983 to 2004). GM's high, low, and closing stock prices for the period 2003–2008 are summarized in GM Exhibit 2.

In its March 4, 2009, report on GM's financial statements, GM's auditors (**Deloitte & Touche**) concluded that GM's financial statements were fairly presented in conformity with GAAP.

GM EXHIBIT 2

Annual High, Low, and Closing Stock Prices: General Motors Corp.

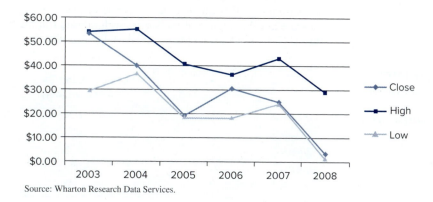

Source: Wharton Research Data Services.

[1] "The Black on GM's Board," *Time*, September 6, 1976.
[2] Data for 2003 through 2005 include General Motors Acceptance Corporation (GMAC), which served as the financial services arm of General Motors Corp. GM sold a controlling interest in GMAC in November 2006; as a result, data for 2006 through 2008 do not include results related to GMAC.

However, Deloitte expanded its report to include the following paragraph to recognize uncertainties regarding GM's ability to continue as a going concern:

> The accompanying consolidated financial statements for the year ended December 31, 2008, have been prepared assuming that the Corporation [GM] will continue as a going concern. As discussed in Note 2 to the consolidated financial statements, the Corporation's recurring losses from operations, stockholders' deficit, and inability to generate sufficient cash flow to meet its obligations and sustain its operations raise substantial doubt about its ability to continue as a going concern. Management's plans concerning these matters are also discussed in Note 2 to the consolidated financial statements. The consolidated financial statements do not include any adjustments that might result from the outcome of this uncertainty.

GM'S REORGANIZATION

In April 2009, GM's Chief Executive Officer Frederick "Fritz" Henderson (who succeeded Rick Wagoner) created a restructuring plan to save GM. Under this plan, the debt owed to unsecured bondholders, the United Auto Workers, and the U.S. government (which totaled $74.4 billion across the three groups) would be reduced by $44.6 billion in exchange for a 99 percent interest in the emerging company. In addition, the terms of this plan called for the closure of 42 percent of GM's dealers.[3]

On June 1, 2009, the once unthinkable happened: GM filed for Chapter 11 bankruptcy. Under the terms of the bankruptcy plan, two entities were created: an "old GM" (subsequently named **Motors Liquidation Company**), a public company that owns four brands in the process of being phased out (Hummer, Saab, Pontiac, and Saturn), and a "new GM," a private company that is majority owned by the U.S. government (a 60 percent stake), with the Canadian government (11.7 percent), United Auto Workers (17.5 percent), and GM's unsecured bondholders (10 percent) owning large minority stakes. The new GM (known as **General Motors Co.**) received the Buick, Cadillac, Chevrolet, and GMC brands. General Motors Co. emerged from bankruptcy and began its operations on July 10, 2009, just 40 days after the filing. A brief profile of GM (the combined entity prebankruptcy) and General Motors Co. (the new GM that emerged postbankruptcy) is shown in GM Exhibit 3.[4]

A BOOST FOR THE AUTO INDUSTRY

On July 1, 2009, the U.S. government announced the Car Allowance Rebate Program (popularly known as the "Cash for Clunkers" program) to provide incentives for the automobile industry. Initially, $1 billion was appropriated for this program, but overwhelming demand from consumers resulted in an additional $2 billion allocation when the original funds were exhausted. More than 690,000 transactions were rebated under this program, 17.6 percent of which were for General Motors Co. automobiles.[5] Despite this program, GM's 2009 retail sales were down 17 percent from 2008.

EPILOGUE

In November 2010, GM returned to public company status with an initial public offering that raised $23.1 billion, one of the largest such offerings in the history of the United States at that time;[6] GM's stock price closed at $34.19 that day. Deloitte & Touche's opinion on GM's 2010

GM EXHIBIT 3
Profile of General Motors Corp. and General Motors Co.

	General Motors Corp. (prebankruptcy)	General Motors Co. (postbankruptcy)
Debt (billions)	$176	$48
Employees	91,000	68,500
Brands	8	4
Dealers	5,900	3,600
Manufacturing plants	47	34

[3] "Plan Seeks a Smaller, Focused—and Profitable—GM," *The Wall Street Journal,* April 28, 2009, p. A8B.
[4] "GM Set to Exit Bankruptcy," *The Wall Street Journal,* July 10, 2009, p. A1.
[5] "Cash for Clunkers Wraps Up with Nearly 700,000 Car Sales and Increased Fuel Efficiency, U.S. Transportation Secretary Declares Program 'Wildly Successful,'" *U.S. Department of Transportation Press Release 2009-08-26.*
[6] "Total for GM Offering Rises to $23.1 Billion," *The Wall Street Journal,* November 27, 2010, p. B4.

financial statements (issued on March 1, 2011) concluded that GM's financial statements were presented in conformity with GAAP and made no reference to the going-concern uncertainties that GM had previously faced. GM has returned to profitability with reported net income (before non-controlling interests and preferred dividends) of $6.2 billion, $9.2 billion, and $6.2 billion in 2010, 2011, and 2012, respectively; however, as of mid-2013, its stock price had risen only slightly above its public offering price, to $34.96 per share. On June 5, 2013 (less than four years after its bankruptcy), GM rejoined the S&P 500, replacing **Heinz** following its acquisition by **Berkshire Hathaway.**

In 2014, GM was forced to recall over 29 million automobiles, a number that exceeded their combined sales for 2005 through 2014.[7] Most notable among the defects prompting these recalls were faulty ignition switches that prevented airbags from deploying in the event of a crash. (GM was aware of this potential fault prior to announcing the recall.)

In September 2015, GM entered into a deferred prosecution agreement with the U.S. Department of Justice, paying $900 million.[8] However, GM still has significant potential liability related to the defective ignition switches.[9] Through January 2016, a total of 121 putative class action suits are pending against GM related to these recalls, alleging diminution in value of the vehicles, punitive damages, and injunctive and other relief. In addition, a total of 244 personal injury cases are pending against GM alleging injury or death as a result of the defects. To date, GM has taken total charges of $2.0 billion against net income in 2014 and 2015 and has recognized a liability of $66 million for future payments as of December 31, 2015.

In spite of these matters, GM has remained highly profitable, reporting net income of $3.9 billion in 2014 and $9.7 billion in 2015. And, it has received unmodified opinions from its auditors (Deloitte & Touche), with no mention of this potential liability in their reports.

DISCUSSION QUESTIONS

1. Reviewing GM's financial information in GM Exhibit 1 and its stock price in GM Exhibit 2, when do you first see signs of GM's impending financial distress?
2. In referencing professional standards, what factors should auditors consider in evaluating potential going-concern uncertainties?
3. Considering your response to questions 1 and 2, do you believe that the going-concern uncertainty was warranted? Do you believe that Deloitte & Touche should have issued a going-concern opinion prior to 2008?
4. What economic factors existing in the United States during 2008 might have accelerated Deloitte & Touche's decision to issue an audit opinion modified to disclose going-concern uncertainties?
5. Do you believe that the events immediately following GM's bankruptcy alleviated the concerns that led to the issuance of the going-concern uncertainty? What issues would auditors need to consider in evaluating the ability of General Motors Co. (the new GM) to continue as a going concern?
6. Many companies believe that a going-concern opinion is a *self-fulfilling prophecy* (i.e., when a company receives a going-concern opinion, customers will not purchase products with warranties, suppliers will not provide short-term credit, and investors and creditors will not invest or loan). Would GM's going-concern opinion influence your decisions regarding either purchasing a car from GM or investing in GM's stock? Is a going-concern a self-fulfilling prophecy?

[7] "GM to Recall 8.45 Million More Vehicles in North America," *The Wall Street Journal Online*, June 30, 2014.
[8] "U.S. Charges GM with Wire Fraud, Concealing Facts on Ignition Switch," *The Wall Street Journal Online* September 18, 2015.
[9] All information in the remainder of this paragraph was drawn from General Motors Corp. 2015 *Form 10-K*.

Unhealthy Accounting at HealthSouth

PROBLEM

In 1996, key executives of **HealthSouth,** one of the nation's largest providers of health care services, began a massive fraud that eventually amounted to $2.7 billion.[1] HealthSouth is a textbook case of unbridled greed combined with a lack of corporate governance, which illustrates the difficult situation that auditors face when clients perpetrate a massive, collusive fraud.

HealthSouth was founded in 1984 by Richard Scrushy and coworkers at **Lifemark,** a Houston-based company that owned and managed hospitals.[2] They took HealthSouth public in 1986, and by 1996, the company's market value had grown to $12 billion.[3] According to the government's complaint, Scrushy, the chief executive officer, insisted that the company meet or exceed earnings expectations established by Wall Street analysts. Senior officers would present actual accounting earnings to Scrushy, and if they did not meet the forecasts, he reportedly told them to "fix it." Unbeknownst to Scrushy (according to his testimony at trial), a team of senior accounting personnel, known as "the family," held "family meetings" to determine ways to increase accounting earnings. They would look for "holes" in the balance sheet to be filled. The fictitious accounting entries they used to plug those holes were referred to as "dirt." Methods included overestimating insurance reimbursements, overstating fixed assets, improperly capitalizing expenses, and over-booking reserve accounts.[4]

The "family" members started by manipulating contractual allowances by consolidating entry adjustments after the end of each quarter. The allowances accounted for the differences between what HealthSouth charged patients and the amounts the company could collect from the patients' health insurers. By lowering the allowances improperly, HealthSouth improved its net revenue and bottom-line earnings. To offset the contractual allowances, the company increased inventory, intangible assets, fixed assets, and even cash. The fictitious fixed asset line item at each facility was listed as "AP summary."[5] The company's CFO, William Owens, a former **Ernst & Young** (EY) senior manager and one of five CFOs who eventually pleaded guilty to the fraud, also used the acquisition of **Horizon/CMS** to book $400 million worth of goodwill as part of the cover-up. He pulled the trick off with the help of two HealthSouth colleagues and a finance executive from Horizon.[6]

On paper, HealthSouth maintained impeccable corporate policies. The company established a confidential whistleblower hotline in 1997; developed a nonretaliation policy, which gave the compliance director direct access to the board; and established a centralized finance function. This centralized function seemed to be a particular advantage because other health care companies were falling apart as a result of problems in field offices. Reviewing these policies, it is not difficult to see why a massive fraud did not seem likely.[7]

Despite outward appearances, actual corporate governance was quite different. Many decisions were made at the executive level, which limited checks and balances along the way. The audit committee met only once a year. The accounting systems in the field did not interface with the corporate enterprise-resource-planning software, making it necessary for results to be consolidated at the corporate level, where it was easier to "cook" the numbers.[8]

Scrushy, a former gas station attendant, fit the profile of the domineering CEO who set the wrong tone at the top. He reportedly managed by fear and intimidation. Scrushy installed security cameras throughout headquarters to watch employees. He allowed rank-and-file employees into his executive suite only when he wanted to berate them.[9] According to the government's complaint, accounting personnel advised Scrushy in 1997 to abandon the fraud, but he refused, saying,

---

[1] "Keeping Secrets: How Five CFOs Cooked the Books at HealthSouth," *CFO.com*, June 1, 2005.
[2] www.richardmscrushy.com/biography.aspx.
[3] "HealthSouth Faked Profits, SEC Charges—A $1.4 Billion Overstatement Cited as CEO Is Accused of Ordering 'Massive Accounting Fraud,'" *The Wall Street Journal*, March 20, 2003, p. C1.
[4] *Securities and Exchange Commission v. HealthSouth Corp. and Richard M. Scrushy,* Civ. Action No. CV-03-J-0615-S (N.D. Ala. filed March 19, 2003), Complaint for Injunctive and Other Relief.
[5] Ibid.
[6] "Keeping Secrets."
[7] Ibid.
[8] "Questioning the Books: Audit Committee Met Only Once during 2001," *The Wall Street Journal*, March 21, 2003, p. A2.
[9] "Keeping Secrets."

"Not until I sell my stock."[10] The five CFOs realized the error of their ways, but most felt helpless to blow the whistle or even leave the company. One, Michael Martin, testified he tried to quit, but Scrushy reportedly said, "Martin, you can't quit. You'll be the fall guy."[11] Later, when Treasurer Leif Murphy decided to leave the company because of the fraud, Martin punched him twice at his going-away party and wrote on his farewell card, "Eat [expletive] and die."[12]

AUDIT APPROACH

HealthSouth was the largest client of the Birmingham office of EY. The 2001 audit fee was $1.2 million, and the firm billed an additional $2.5 million for other services. Many of Health-South's senior accounting staff had been EY employees.[13]

In hindsight, there had been red flags for the auditors to pursue. For example, from 1999 to 2001, net income rose nearly 500 percent while revenue grew only 5 percent.[14] The audit team also took no action when members learned that internal auditors were denied access to the corporate books. Finally, the team did not sufficiently investigate employee complaints.

The auditors were not oblivious to HealthSouth's risky profile. Jim Lamphron, a partner on the audit, said they focused on two risk factors: (1) "Company officials harboring a strong interest in seeing a rising stock price" and (2) "Management ranks dominated [by] those at the top. . . . Specifically, we were focusing on Richard Scrushy."[15] Despite EY's awareness of important fraud risks, the "family" was adept at the cover-up, making it difficult to detect certain aspects of the fraud. The SEC said that HealthSouth employees knew that EY questioned additions to fixed assets at any particular facility only if the additions exceeded a certain dollar threshold ($5,000), so the company avoided exceeding that dollar amount by spreading the adjustments below this materiality limit to various accounts and locations. When the auditors did question an accounting entry, HealthSouth officials created false documents to cover their tracks. When EY auditors asked for fixed assets ledgers for various facilities, accounting personnel would regenerate the ledgers, replacing the AP Summary line with the name of a specific fixed asset that did not exist at the facility.[16]

DISCOVERY

The fraud scheme was noticed by company whistle-blowers, whose concerns seemed to be disregarded. One anonymous e-mail was sent to the auditors saying the company "fleeced shareholders" and listed four suspicious accounting practices. EY's review determined that the issues raised by the author of the e-mail "did not affect the presentation of HealthSouth's financial statements." Another e-mail, from former employee Michael Vines and forwarded to audit partner Jim Lamphron, was passed to CFO William Owens and George Strong, the audit committee chairman. Owens provided fake invoices for the questioned entries and dismissed the seriousness of this e-mail, indicating that Vines was just a disgruntled former employee.[17] (Vines had made frequent comments about the company's accounting on the employee electronic chat room and was regarded as something of a pest.)[18]

In October 1999, Diana Henze, assistant vice president of finance, noticed that earnings would jump with each iteration of quarter-end consolidations. She confronted Owens, who was controller at the time, and accused him of fraud. When she went to Kelly Cullison, the company's corporate compliance officer, she was told that the compliance officer "did not have access to the supporting documents" to determine whether or not the journal entries were legitimate. Henze brought the matter to her supervisor, cofounder Tony Tanner, who told her the entries were the result of

[10] *SEC v. HealthSouth Corp.*, Civ. Action No. CV-03-J-0615-S, Complaint for Injunctive and Other Relief.

[11] "Keeping Secrets."

[12] "Former HealthSouth Executive Describes Deception and Abuse," *The Washington Post*, February 18, 2005, p. E04.

[13] "Did Ernst Miss Key Fraud Risks at HealthSouth?" *The Wall Street Journal*, April 10, 2003, p. C1.

[14] "Missing the Red Flags," *BusinessWeek*, April 14, 2003, p. 72.

[15] "Scrushy Watch: The End Is Near: With Only a Handful of Witnesses Left, the Defense Needs a Lucky Break," www.birminghamweekly.com, December 1, 2005.

[16] *SEC v. HealthSouth Corp.*

[17] "Missed Signal: Accountant Tried in Vain to Expose HealthSouth Fraud—Ex-Employee Took His Case to Auditors, Then Web—But Convinced No One—What about the Others?" *The Wall Street Journal*, May 20, 2003, p. A1.

[18] "The Economy: Ernst & Young Got a Warning on HealthSouth," *The Wall Street Journal*, April 24, 2003, p. A2.

reversing out a number of reserves and that the matter was closed.[19] Henze said that she was subsequently passed over for a promotion that would have given her more involvement with the books. When she asked why a less-qualified person got the job, Owens told her, "You have made it clear you won't do what we asked."[20]

William Owens finally went to the authorities when his wife threatened to divorce him because she thought (correctly) that he would end up in jail.[21] Owens agreed to wear a wire when meeting with Scrushy. Scrushy is on tape as saying, "You got accountants signing off on all this." In an impromptu meeting at a lake, Scrushy is recorded as telling Owens, "Just remember, I got eight kids. I got a bunch of babies at home. They need their daddy." Scrushy also told Owens, "If you want to go public with all this, get ready to get fired, and everyone goes down with you," according to the transcript of the recording that Owens made.[22] Once Owens came forth, the investigation quickly uncovered the massive fraud as other employees quickly cut deals with prosecutors.

Scrushy was a local hero in Birmingham with supporters in all corners. A lavish donor to local colleges, libraries, and medical centers, he was also a regular preacher at area churches. He even aired his own TV talk show each day before he appeared in court and hosted his own website (www.richardmscrushy.com).[23] His defense attorneys sought to depict him as a detached leader and visionary rather than a micromanager with unchallenged influence. In the end, he was acquitted of all charges in what many see as a blow to enforcement of the Sarbanes–Oxley Act. (Scrushy had certified statements on the 10-K dated August 14, 2002, under the Sarbanes–Oxley Act.)[24] Jurors said key witnesses were not credible, and the prosecution failed to present substantial evidence linking the fraud to Scrushy: "The smoking gun wasn't pointing toward Mr. Scrushy."[25]

Scrushy subsequently settled claims from the SEC by paying $81,000,000.[26] However, in October 2006, he was convicted of improperly paying $500,000 to a campaign of former Alabama Governor Don Siegelman in exchange for a seat on a hospital regulatory board. He was sentenced in June 2007 to nearly seven years in prison.[27] In July 2009, a jury awarded $2.88 billion in a civil suit brought by HealthSouth shareholders. It is believed to be the largest penalty ever levied against one executive. This case was brought before a lone judge, not a jury.[28] In April 2011, the Alabama Supreme Court denied Scrushy's appeal of the verdict.[29] Scrushy was released from prison in 2012 and now is on the speaker circuit.

DISCUSSION QUESTIONS

1. What are several red flags that E&Y either was or should have been aware of in the audit of HealthSouth?

2. What procedures can auditors perform to detect fraudulent entries made during the consolidation process?

3. How can auditors determine a company's true "tone at the top"?

4. What is the appropriate response by auditors to information from "disgruntled" employees?

5. HealthSouth concealed the fraud by keeping the fraudulent transactions below $5,000. What recommendation would you have given to E&Y to improve its sampling practices?

[19] "Executives on Trial: Witness Says HealthSouth Tried to Appease Street," *The Wall Street Journal*, February 23, 2005, p. C4.

[20] "Witness Lost Promotion after Asking Questions," *USA Today*, February 22, 2005, www.usatoday.com/money/industries/health/2005-02-22-scrushy-usat_x.htm.

[21] "Keeping Secrets."

[22] Ibid.

[23] Ibid.

[24] *SEC v. HealthSouth Corp.*

[25] "Clean Sweep: HealthSouth's Scrushy Is Acquitted; Outcome Shows Challenges for Sarbanes-Oxley Act; SEC Suit Still Ahead; No Job Offer from Company," *The Wall Street Journal*, June 29, 2005, p. 1.

[26] "Scrushy Case Comes to Muted Settlement," *The Wall Street Journal*, April 24, 2007, p. A3.

[27] "Business and Finance," *The Wall Street Journal*, June 29, 2007, p. A1.

[28] Valerie Bauerlein and Mike Esterl, "Judge Orders Scrushy to Pay $2.88 Billion in Civil Suit," *The Wall Street Journal*, June 19, 2009, p. B1.

[29] "Scrushy's Appeal Request Denied by Alabama High Court," *Modern Healthcare* 41, no. 16 (April 18, 2011), p. 4–4.

KPMG: How Many Firms?

BACKGROUND

How many major accounting firms are needed to provide companies sufficient choice? Because of their scale, expertise, and international presence, the world's largest corporations have traditionally relied on the largest accounting firms to conduct their audits. As late as 1988, the "Big Eight" firms (**Arthur Andersen & Co., Arthur Young & Company, Coopers & Lybrand, Deloitte Haskins & Sells, Ernst & Whinney, KPMG, Price Waterhouse & Co.,** and **Touche Ross & Co.**) dominated the market for audit services. In 1989, mergers between Ernst & Whinney and Arthur Young (to form Ernst & Young) and Deloitte Haskins & Sells and Touche Ross (to form Deloitte & Touche, now Deloitte) reduced choices to six providers. The merger of Price Waterhouse and Coopers & Lybrand in 1998 as **PricewaterhouseCoopers** (PwC) limited them to five.

Although a company's options with respect to the choice of an independent auditor were reduced by almost 50 percent, not until the Justice Department's dissolution of Arthur Andersen in 2002 were concerns raised about the lack of choices in the market for audit services and its impact on the competitiveness of the industry. (Arthur Andersen's verdict was overturned by the Supreme Court in 2005, but its partners and personnel had pursued other employment opportunities.)

The gulf between the Big Four and the remaining accounting firms can be best illustrated by comparing KPMG (the smallest of the Big Four, in terms of revenues) with **RSM** (formerly **McGladrey**) the fifth-largest accounting firm. In 2015, KPMG's U.S. revenues from audit and assurance services totaled $6.9 billion, compared to $1.6 billion at McGladrey.[1] Viewed from a consumer's standpoint, in 2015, Big Four firms audited all but one of the *Fortune* 100 companies (**Energy Transfer**) and all but four of the *Fortune* 500 companies (Energy Transfer, **Henry Schein, Inc., Icahn Enterprises,** and **NGL Energy Partners**).

In addition to a smaller set of large accounting firms, public companies are constrained by provisions of the Sarbanes–Oxley Act. In an effort to enhance auditor independence, Sarbanes–Oxley prohibits auditors from providing various types of nonaudit services to their audit clients. This prohibition was in response to the large shift of accounting firm revenues from primarily audit revenues to revenues for other services.[2] For example, in 1975, the percentage of total revenues from the Big Eight firms derived from audit services ranged from 62 percent (Touche Ross & Co.) to 76 percent (Price Waterhouse & Co.); in 2000, this same percentage ranged from 31 percent (Deloitte & Touche) to 45 percent (KPMG).[3]

As a result of Sarbanes–Oxley, public companies have engaged other Big Four firms for nonaudit services. As just one example, at one time, the Big Four firms provided **Wabtec Corp.** auditing (Ernst & Young), internal control testing (Deloitte & Touche), acquisitions advising (KPMG), and tax services (PricewaterhouseCoopers). If Wabtec decided to change auditors yet retain a Big Four firm, it would need to consider the effect of these services on the independence of its new auditor. A survey by J.D. Power & Associates of the 400 companies with more than $1 billion in revenue revealed that 55 percent of these companies are using more than one Big Four firm to provide various types of services (including audit services).[4]

The bottom line is that two independent developments (a smaller number of international accounting firms and Sarbanes–Oxley's limitations on the nonaudit services that can be provided by a company's auditors) have significantly impacted companies' choices of auditors. This dilemma can be best reflected by the experiences of two large organizations.

First, in 2005, **Intel Corp.** considered proposals for its audit engagement from all four firms. It retained Ernst & Young, which has audited Intel's financial statements for more than 30 years. This decision was largely driven by the nonaudit service provided to Intel by the other Big Four

---

[1] *Inside Public Accounting (IPA) Special Report: The 2015 IPA 100 Firms.*

[2] One particularly striking example of this shift was Arthur Andersen's revenues derived from providing services to Enron. In the last year of the firm's audit of Enron, Andersen's audit revenues were $25 million, while revenues from other services provided to Enron were $27 million. These other services included business process and risk management consulting, tax compliance and consulting, due diligence procedures related to acquisitions or other activities, work performed in connection with registration statements, and various statutory or other audits (information drawn from Enron's March 27, 2001, proxy statement filed with the Securities and Exchange Commission).

[3] Stephen A. Zeff, "How the U.S. Accounting Profession Got Where It Is Today: Part II," *Accounting Horizons,* December 2003, p. 270.

[4] "Firms' Auditor Choices Dwindle," *The Wall Street Journal,* June 21, 2005, p. C1.

firms. Cary Klafter, Intel's corporate secretary, noted that "because there are only a limited number of large multinational audit firms that do the kind of work that we need, if we were to switch audit firms, all sorts of dominos would fall."[5]

Second, when **Fannie Mae** dismissed KPMG as its auditor in the wake of an accounting scandal, its choices for a successor were slim: Deloitte & Touche had been advising the federal government in its probe of Fannie Mae, Ernst & Young had been providing consulting services to Fannie Mae's audit committee responding to the probes related to the scandal, and PricewaterhouseCoopers audited **Freddie Mac,** a major competitor.[6]

Could something happen to limit companies' choices even further?

THE PROBLEM

From 1996 through 2002, KPMG received $124 million in tax consulting fees from promoting tax shelters that allowed individuals and corporations to improperly avoid more than $1.4 billion in federal taxes.[7] E-mail messages obtained and released by the Internal Revenue Service indicated that KPMG officials were aware that the tax shelters were questionable.

As one example, a shelter referred to as *bond-linked issue premium structures (BLIPS)* created $5 billion in tax losses for investors. Under this shelter, clients would purchase foreign currency from offshore banks with funds borrowed from those same banks only to sell the currency back to the same bank a few months later. These investments were presented to the Internal Revenue Service as seven-year investments.[8] Other shelters in question carried similar names such as *FLIP, OPIS,* and *SOS.*

THE OUTCOME

On August 26, 2005, KPMG admitted to criminal tax fraud and agreed to a payment of $456 million in penalties (an average of $300,000 per KPMG partner); the government agreed to deferred adjudication and, in January 2007, dismissed all criminal charges against the firm. Subsequently, Judge Lewis Kaplan of the U.S. District Court for the Southern District of New York dismissed indictments against 13 of 16 former KPMG partners and, on December 18, 2008, two of the remaining three partners were convicted on multiple counts of tax evasion. (The remaining partner was acquitted.)[9]

In the midst of this activity, federal prosecutors indicted four current and former partners of Ernst & Young on similar charges. The shelters designed and sold by these partners brought Ernst & Young $120 million in fees. Those familiar with the matter do not expect that the firm itself will face criminal charges in this matter[10]; however, on May 8, 2009, four current and former E&Y executives were convicted.

THE ISSUE

KPMG has avoided the fate of Arthur Andersen: dissolution. However, the KPMG case has raised numerous questions about the future of the accounting profession if the small number of international accounting firms should become even smaller. For example, the Securities and Exchange Commission discussed various actions to assist companies in changing auditors if KPMG was indicted, including allowing companies to seek waivers to the stricter independence rules on a case-by-case basis and allowing KPMG to continue to perform audits if it were indicted. An unidentified SEC official indicated that "we have scenarios in place for any eventuality that could come out of this."[11] In addition, prior to the settlement, Deloitte & Touche, Ernst & Young, and PricewaterhouseCoopers reportedly requested that their partners not solicit current KPMG clients.[12]

[5] Ibid.
[6] "Fannie Mae's Dismissal of KPMG Shows Dwindling Choices among Big Four," *The Wall Street Journal,* December 23, 2004, p. C1.
[7] "Grand July Investigating KPMG Tax Shelters," *CFO.com,* February 23, 2004.
[8] "Inside the KPMG Mess," *BusinessWeek,* September 12, 2005, pp. 46–47.
[9] "Former KPMG Executives Convicted of Tax Evasion," *The Wall Street Journal,* December 18, 2008, p. C4.
[10] "Tax-Shelter Indictments Leave a Cloud over Ernst," *The Wall Street Journal,* May 31, 2007, p. C1.
[11] "SEC Weighs a 'Big Three' World," *The Wall Street Journal,* June 22, 2005, p. C1.
[12] "No Poaching from KPMG, Say Audit Firms," *CFO.com,* August 24, 2005.

DISCUSSION QUESTIONS

1. Do professional standards allow a company's auditors also to provide tax services and retain their independence?

2. How have provisions of the Sarbanes–Oxley Act limited a public company's choice of auditors?

3. What are some of the advantages and disadvantages of permitting auditors to provide nonaudit services (such as tax services) to clients?

4. What is the impact of a smaller number of major international accounting firms on public companies?

Something Went Sour at Parmalat[1]

PROBLEM

There was much confusion when Italian dairy food giant **Parmalat** defaulted on a $187 million bond payment in mid-November 2002. Default on a bond payment seemed difficult to believe considering that a Parmalat subsidiary in the Cayman Islands had a $4.9 *billion* cash balance in a **Bank of America** account. The problem was that the cash account did not exist.

Subsequent investigation revealed that, over a 15-year period, Parmalat's management had falsified accounts and created assets to hide losses of $10 billion from Parmalat's Latin American operations. Other allegations charged that Parmalat's management had lied about repurchasing $3.6 billion in bonds, which they had never done. By hiding losses and increasing assets on its balance sheet, Parmalat was able to continue to borrow enough money from investors and creditors to conceal and perpetuate the massive fraud.

AUDIT APPROACH

From 1990 to 1999, the Italian branch of Grant Thornton audited Parmalat. Under Italian law, however, Parmalat was forced to change auditors periodically and chose the Italian branch of **Deloitte Touche Tohmatsu** (Deloitte & Touche SpA) to be the company's new auditor in 2000. Grant Thornton, however, continued to audit Parmalat's offshore subsidiaries located in the Cayman Islands.

The new auditors first inquired about the Cayman Islands account in December 2002 and received a letter on Bank of America letterhead in March 2003, confirming the existence of the account. The letter, however, was a forgery, created in Parmalat's headquarters. Nevertheless, the $4.9 billion was listed on the subsidiary's balance sheet as of December 31, 2002, and was consolidated into Parmalat's balance sheets dated December 31, 2002, and June 30, 2003.

The auditors missed several red flags. First, the size of the account, on its own, should have been a red flag. It is very unusual for a large company to have so much cash in a single bank account. In addition, between January 2000 and September 2003, Parmalat raised more than $5 billion in debt offerings. With so much cash available in the Cayman Islands, why was Parmalat continuing to borrow money?

Second, the communication received from the Bank of America was in the form of a fax (see Parmalat Exhibit 1), which raises two issues. First, a fax transmission is not subject to the same level of control as returning an original confirmation. Essentially, a fax can be sent from almost anywhere, and the originating phone number can be falsified by simply changing the phone number in the transmitting fax machine. A mailed confirmation, however, passes through the federal mail system and is postmarked with the originating zip code. Also, this particular fax was smudged, raising more suspicions. Forgers routinely "age" their "originals" by repeatedly photocopying them to obscure any telltale photocopying lines. Given these circumstances, the auditors should have followed up directly with the bank.

Third, when such large balances represent a significant portion of a company's balance sheet (in this case, 38 percent of Parmalat's assets were in the subsidiary's bank account), auditors should take additional care to obtain further corroboration. All told, the combination of a large bank account and a questionable form of confirmation should have provided Deloitte & Touche SpA with sufficient warning to dig deeper.

DISCOVERY

Parmalat management also told Deloitte & Touche SpA that the company had a $617 million investment in an open-ended mutual fund that it could access at any time. The company, however, was unsuccessful in its attempts to retrieve the funds. Because no evidence was available to support management's claims, Deloitte & Touche SpA included a qualification in its audit review report highlighting the lack of evidence and alerted regulators of suspicions of a larger fraud.

Initial investigation revealed that massive amounts (estimates as high as $19 billion) of assets were missing or nonexistent. Parmalat and its subsidiaries filed for bankruptcy protection in Italy on December 27, 2003.

---

[1] G. Edmondson and L. Cohn, "How Parmalat Went Sour," *BusinessWeek Online*, January 12, 2004.

PARMALAT EXHIBIT 1

DEC 17 2003 16:01 FR BANK OF AMERICA   2019743539 TO 918467334872   P 01
17 DIC 2003 11:58   GRFN THORNTON SPA   NR.201   P.3

BankofAmerica

New York Branch

Grant Thornton Spa   March 6, 2003
Largo Augusto, 7
20122 MILANO, ITALY

                        Re: Bonlat Financing Corporation
                        BANY Account No.:   6550-2-52252
                        BANY Securities Deposits No.:   6550-2-85419

Dear Sir/Madam

We have received your request for audit purposes dated December 20,2002. We confine our response to certain information concerning account balances and securities deposits from our records at this office.

1. As of the close of business on December 31,2002, our records indicate the following deposit balance(s):

Account Type	Account Name	Account Number	Account Balance
Demand Deposit	Bonlat Financing Corporation	6550-2-52252	USD $336,812,328.64 CR
AutoInvest Account	Bonlat Financing Corporation	N/A	N/A

2. As of the close of business on December 31,2002, our records indicate the following Securities Deposit balance(s):

Account Type	Account Name	Account Number	Account Balance
Securities Deposit	Bonlat Financing Corporation	6550-2-85419	EUR €2,811,000,000.00
Securities Deposit	Bonlat Financing Corporation	6550-2-85419	USD $949,000,000.00

3. As of the close of business on December 31,2002, our records indicate the following Letter of Credit balance.

Trade Finance	Customer Name	Reference Number	Outstanding
	N/A	N/A	N/A

This information is for your CONFIDENTIAL use and is furnished in reply to your inquiry. No responsibility is assumed by Bank of America or its officers to the accuracy or completeness of this information. No representation is made as to any other relationship the subject may have with other Bank of America offices.

Sincerely,

Agnes Belgrave

Bank of America
100 West 33rd Street, New York, NY 10001

During the ongoing investigation, a Parmalat employee who had disobeyed orders to destroy company documents turned over a number of incriminating computer disks to investigators. With evidence mounting, Parmalat's founder and CEO Calisto Tanzi admitted to prosecutors that he was aware of the fraud. He also admitted to misappropriating Parmalat assets (more than $1 billion, prosecutors believe) to cover losses in other family-owned companies. It is unlikely that investigators will ever know for certain what happened to the missing funds (whether they were used to cover operating losses, pay creditors, or illegally enrich management). Twenty other Parmalat executives, including members of Tanzi's family, and the company's former CFO, former board members, and even lawyers, were indicted on charges including fraud, embezzlement, false accounting, and misleading investors. On June 28, 2005, a judge accepted plea bargains from 11 of those charged and sentenced them to prison ranging from 10 months to 2.5 years. In his January 2008 trial, Calisto Tanzi was found guilty of securities laws violations and was sentenced to 10 years in prison for his role in the fraud. More than two years later, in December 2010, Tanzi was also found guilty of fraudulent bankruptcy and criminal association and sentenced to an additional 18 years in jail. After he unsuccessfully appealed that verdict in 2011, the court added another nine years to his sentence. He should be about 105 years old when he is finally released.

DISCUSSION QUESTIONS

1. What steps does an auditor ordinarily take when confirming cash balances held on deposits with financial institutions?
2. What additional steps should the auditors have taken when they received the smudged fax copy printed on Bank of America letterhead?
3. What *red flags* did the auditors miss in the Parmalat case? Please be specific.
4. What steps should Deloitte & Touche SpA have taken with respect to Grant Thornton's audit of the Cayman Island subsidiaries?

GE: How Much Are Auditors Paid?

The financial report accompanying this letter is historic in that it is our first one covered by Section 404 of The Sarbanes–Oxley Act of 2002 (SOX). . . . But what does it mean to you? Is it a "check-the-box" bureaucracy based on an overreaction to the market scandals of yesterday? None of us likes more regulation, but I actually think SOX 404 is helpful. It takes the process control discipline we use in our factories and applies it to our financial statements. Implementing SOX 404 cost GE $33 million in 2004. But we think it is a good investment.

Jeffrey R. Immelt, Chairman of the Board and Chief Executive Officer, General Electric, in his Letter to Shareholders from the 2004 annual report

BACKGROUND

Since its required implementation in 2004, section 404 of Sarbanes–Oxley has generated a great deal of controversy. Its requirement that auditors assess the operating effectiveness of their clients' internal controls over financial reporting and express opinions on the effectiveness of their clients' internal controls over financial reporting and on management's assessment of its internal control over financial reporting (this latter responsibility has since been rescinded) has imposed significant costs on accelerated filers.[1]

The costs of Sarbanes–Oxley have been cited as having significant impact on the U.S. capital markets. For example, a higher dollar amount of initial public offerings (IPOs) has been made on overseas exchanges since the implementation of section 404. Many companies cite the high costs of Sarbanes–Oxley compliance as a factor in their choice of stock market listing; in 2002 (prior to Sarbanes–Oxley), 9 of the top 20 IPOs were on U.S. stock exchanges compared with only 3 of the top 20 IPOs in 2006. In addition, during 2006, total IPO values on both the London/AIM and Hong Kong stock exchanges exceeded values on the New York Stock Exchange.[2]

Among other reasons, the high costs of compliance with section 404 resulted in the issuance of *Auditing Standard No. 5 (AS 5)*, which superseded *Auditing Standard No. 2.* (AS 5 has subsequently been recodified as AS 3101.) Major changes under AS 5 include (1) eliminating the requirement for auditors to evaluate and opine on management's assessment of internal control over financial reporting, (2) encouraging auditors to adopt a "top-down, risk-based" approach, resulting in more efficient audits, and (3) expanding the potential use of others' work in the assessment of internal control over financial reporting. Then-SEC Chairman Christopher Cox noted that, as a result of the passage of AS 5, "the unduly high costs of implementing section 404 of the [Sarbanes–Oxley] act will come down" because companies "will be able to focus on the greatest risk of material misstatements in the financials."[3] Some estimate that this reduction could be as much as 10 percent.[4]

In addition to the provisions of section 404 related to internal control over financial reporting, Sarbanes–Oxley reduced auditors' ability to provide nonaudit services to their clients. Section 201 prohibits two major types of services that had become significant revenue sources for accounting firms: (1) financial information systems design and implementation and (2) internal audit outsourcing. Not coincidentally, these were two areas in which **Arthur Andersen** provided extensive services to **Enron** prior to its failure. Furthermore, section 202 requires that the entity's audit committee approve all nonaudit services (with the exception of those less than 5 percent of the total revenues paid to the accounting firm).

---

[1] *Accelerated filers* are those public entities filing financial statements with the SEC that have market capitalizations of more than $75 million. Initially, public entities with market capitalizations of less than $75 million were to be subject to the provisions of section 404 in 2005 (one year following the effective date for accelerated filers). In 2010, the Dodd-Frank Wall Street Reform and Consumer Protection Act permanently exempted smaller entities from these requirements.

[2] "Business Wins Its Battle to Ease a Costly Sarbanes-Oxley Rule," *The Wall Street Journal,* November 10, 2006, p. A1.

[3] "Painful Memories: SEC Grilled on 404 Costs," *CFO.com,* June 12, 2007.

[4] "AS5 Could Trim Audit Bills by 10%," *CFO.com,* May 4, 2007.

HOW DID SARBANES–OXLEY AFFECT ACCOUNTING FIRM REVENUES?

The preceding suggests that Sarbanes–Oxley could have a significant (yet indeterminable) effect on accounting firm revenues. On one hand, the internal control requirements of section 404 would presumably increase total revenues; however, the prohibition against providing financial information systems design and implementation and internal audit outsourcing services would likely reduce revenues. In addition, the requirement that the entity's audit committee approve all nonaudit services would presumably heighten these individuals' awareness of potential conflicts related to these services and reduce the likelihood that such services will be approved (or reduce the dollar level at which they are approved).

GE Exhibit 1 summarizes fees paid by General Electric to its auditors (**KPMG, LLP**) for various years both preceding and following the issuance of Sarbanes–Oxley; GE Exhibit 2 provides similar information for the average of *Fortune* 100 companies during these same years.[5] GE has among the highest fees in the *Fortune* 100, with only **Bank of America** ($100.9 million), **American International Group** (**AIG**) ($100.2 million), and **Citigroup** ($99 million) having higher total fees and only Bank of America ($82.2 million) having higher audit fees in 2014.

"Audit fees" are identified based on SEC rules and include fees paid for the (1) audit of the annual financial statements, (2) review of quarterly financial statements, (3) audit of the effectiveness of internal control over financial reporting, (4) attestation of management's report on the effectiveness of internal control over financial reporting, and (5) other services provided in connection with statutory and regulatory filings and engagements. "Audit-related" fees include other fees that can be reasonably related to the preceding services as well as fees paid for due diligence and audit services on mergers and acquisitions and fees paid for audit services on employee benefit plans.

SEC-REQUIRED FEE DISCLOSURES

One additional phenomenon that may influence the fees reported by General Electric and the *Fortune* 100 companies in Exhibits GE 1 and GE 2 is the disclosure requirements implemented by the SEC. In November 2000, the SEC adopted requirements that registrants disclose the various types of fees paid to its financial statement auditors; under this initial guidance, audit fees included fees paid for the annual financial statement audit and those paid for the reviews of quarterly financial

GE EXHIBIT 1
Fees Paid by General Electric to KPMG (in millions)

	2000	2004	2010	2014
Audit fees	$23.9	$78.2	$89.8	$78.2
Audit-related fees	15.5	15.5	9.7	10.7
Tax fees	13.8	8.9	9.3	2.2
Financial information systems fees	50.4	0.0	0.0	0.0
Other fees	0.0	0.0	0.0	0.0
Total fees	$103.6	$102.6	$108.8	$91.1

Source: Various General Electric proxy statements.

GE EXHIBIT 2
Average Fees Paid by *Fortune* 100 Companies to Auditors (in millions)

	2000	2004	2010	2014
Audit fees	$7.1	$16.3	$21.7	$22.3
Audit-related fees	0.9	2.8	3.5	4.5
Tax fees	1.1	4.0	2.8	2.5
Financial information systems fees	3.9	0.0	0.0	0.0
Other fees	16.2	0.5	0.3	0.8
Total fees	$29.2	$23.6	$28.3	$30.1

Source: Data extracted from Wharton Research Data Services.

[5] The fees shown in Exhibits GE 1 and GE 2 reflect only those amounts paid to the entity's financial statement auditors. It is likely that other accounting firms that are not involved with the financial statement audit also provide services to these entities. However, these latter data are not publicly available.

statements. Beginning in 2003, the SEC expanded the definition of *audit fees* to include services that "generally only the independent accountant can reasonably provide, such as comfort letters, statutory audits, attest services, consents and assistance with and review of documents filed with the [SEC]."[6] Some argued that broadening the definition of audit fees would be misleading in terms of user perceptions of auditors' independence. Barbara Roper, director of investor protection for the Consumer Federation of America, noted that "it's absolutely industry's water that's being carried here. It makes it look like their audit fees are bigger, their nonaudit fees are smaller, and it masks the conflict of interest."[7] Clearly, any comparison of fee breakdowns prior to and following Sarbanes–Oxley must consider the SEC's revised definition of audit fees.

DISCUSSION QUESTIONS

1. From a conceptual standpoint, how do the requirements of Sarbanes–Oxley related to nonaudit services affect perceptions of the auditors' independence?

2. Assume that your firm was auditing General Electric in 2000 and was recommending an adjustment to its financial statements that reduced net income. Based on the fees paid to your firm in 2000, what incentive(s) might your firm consider in insisting upon this adjustment? How would your firm's incentive(s) differ after 2004?

3. Compare General Electric's fees prior to (2000) and following (2004, 2010, and 2014) the implementation of Sarbanes–Oxley. Based on the trends in these fees and various components of these fees, comment on the effect of Sarbanes–Oxley on General Electric's fees.

4. Repeat question 3 for the *Fortune* 100 companies. Are the trends for these companies similar to those for General Electric?

5. For General Electric and the *Fortune* 100 companies, can you identify the increased costs of section 404 compliance cited in the press?

6. Comparing the fees in 2004 versus those in 2010 and 2014 for General Electric and *Fortune* 100 companies, does it appear that *AS 5* has reduced costs of section 404 compliance?

[6] Securities and Exchange Commission, "Strengthening the Commission's Requirements Regarding Auditor Independence," *Release No. 33-8183*, March 26, 2003.
[7] "Redefined by the SEC, 'Audit Fees' Get Murky," *The Wall Street Journal*, January 22, 2003, p. C1.

Satyam Computer Services Ltd.—India's Enron

Imagine that you are on the board of directors of **Satyam Computer Services** and you receive a letter from the chairman of the board that starts, "With deep regret and tremendous burden that I am carrying on my conscience"[1] and goes on to say that the company's balance sheet includes: 1) cash of more than $1 billion; 2), $77 million (m) of accrued interest that is nonexistent; 3), $253m of understated liability arranged by the chairman; 4), overstated receivables of $101m; and 5) overstated income statement profits for each of the last several years. Next, imagine that you were the audit partner for Satyam! This is exactly what happened in January 2009 to both the board of directors and its auditor **Price Waterhouse India** (PWI).

HISTORY OF SATYAM

Satyam, which means "truth" in Sanskrit, was founded by B. Ramalinga Raju in 1987 and grew to be a leading outsourcing firm used by major international companies. India's fourth-largest software and services firm, it reported revenue of $555m (actual revenue of $434m) and had 53,000 employees in 2008 (or did it? Stay tuned).

Chairman of the board Raju's confession seemed to spring from the board of directors' denial of the purchase of Maytas (Satyam spelled backward), a Raju family-controlled company owning thousands of acres of property. Apparently, Raju planned to use Maytas assets to offset the fictitious assets at Satyam.

The press had noted the company's related-party dealings. Raju's family members were on the Satyam board and friends were in senior management. Even though it was a large company, no financial experts were on the audit committee.

INDIAN ACCOUNTING ENVIRONMENT

Indian accounting standards are broadly similar to international standards, and the Indian accounting profession is largely self-regulated. Traditionally, general standards of corporate ethics and accounting have been suspect in India. Many companies had been created during License Raj, a period of government intervention in which businesses had to work with politicians and pay bribes. In India "promoters,"[2] who include business families and other corporate insiders, held almost half of the shares on the National Stock Exchange. However, because of its listing on the NYSE, Satyam was subject to the Sarbanes–Oxley Act, which should have induced stricter governance.

Although the Big Four accounting firms have been eagerly touting the growth potential in India, development there has been hampered by heavy national restrictions on the size and number of audit clients a partner can serve. The relationship between PwC and PWI underlines what many see as the patchwork nature of the big accounting firms. Each is a collection of national partnerships under a global umbrella organization. The profession has tried to standardize practices and ethics across the firms, but senior partners privately admit that quality can still be patchy. Some say the Big Four firms in India rely on trainee chartered accountants, and sometimes accountants simply copy the previous years' audits and the internal auditors' work because they have limited time to complete the current audit.

THE FRAUD

This fraud, which is India's biggest corporate fraud, apparently started in April 2002 when IT companies' American depository receipts (ADRs)[3] were popular among foreign investors. At that time,

---

[1] Joe Nocera, "In India, Crisis Pairs with Fraud," *The New York Times*, January 9, 2009, www.nytimes.com/2009/01/10/business/10nocera.html?ref=ramalingaraju (accessed September 14, 2011).
[2] Persons who are in overall control of the company and who are instrumental in formulating a plan to offer securities to the public. A promoter group includes the promoter, an immediate relative, and if the promoter is a company, any subsidiary or other company in which the parent company holds more than 10 percent of equity. http://iepf.gov.in/IEPF/Other_Aspects.html.
[3] Shares of overseas-based companies are traded as ADRs on U.S. stock markets in U.S. dollars

Raju decided to maintain two subaccounts under a single company bank account. He and his cronies controlled the main bank account, and the statements of the subsidiary account were under the control of the company's finance and account reconciliation (FAR) team. The accounting team would receive two bank statements for the same account: a genuine set of statements from the bank and a second set of fictitious statements provided by Raju and his team. The FAR team had to accept the fictitious bank statements (and related interest accruals). Allegedly, even the auditors relied on the documents supplied by Raju instead of obtaining third-party verification. The CFO, Srinivas Vadlamani, who was arrested, said he had not been directly involved but knew there had been something suspicious for more than five years. He had been specifically asked not to look at deposits. Vadlamani said the plan was carried out by creating a paper trail of fabricated invoices, forged balance sheets, and counterfeit bank statements in a scheme involving about 10 junior staff accountants.

Initial investigations have revealed that an in-house Satyam team developed software to generate altered invoices that included the genuine name of a client and of the client's project manager but with an overstated invoice amount. For example, a Satyam client, XYZ, pays 100 rupees to Satyam's bank account as fees. The original bank statement showed 100 rupees deposited by XYZ, but the statement provided by Raju overstated this figure. Year after year, altered invoices in the name of genuine clients and employees were created and went unnoticed by auditors.

The unrecorded liability of $253m was the amount that private companies owned by Raju lent to Satyam. To keep analysts and investors at bay, the loan amount was not shown in the books. Had it been shown, it would have raised eyebrows. After all, why would a company incur this liability when it had so much cash on its books?

In addition, the public prosecutor noted that the CFO (Vadlamani) had admitted during interrogation that Satyam had just 40,000 employees versus the 53,000 officially claimed, and the fictitious wages were siphoned off. The prosecutor claims Raju used a fictitious name to divert $4m a month from the company's account for his personal wealth. India's Serious Fraud Investigation Office has found that $100m raised through the issuance of ADRs did not end up in the company's bank accounts and has still not been found.

Although the company's bank balance was fictitious, the employees had to be paid real salaries. To meet these expenses, Raju and his family started pledging their stake in the company. The shares were pledged by a holding company, SRSR Holdings, which in turn had approximately 300 subsidiaries. India's Central Bureau of Investigation (CBI) has found that some of the documents of the companies created by Raju contained land records and names of land mafia agents,[4] indicating that the case may be more than just an accounting fraud.

THE AUDITORS

Even though PWI had been Satyam's auditor since 2000, it resigned. Indian police have arrested two partners of PWI on charges of criminal conspiracy and cheating. PwC says, "The audits were conducted by PWI in accordance with applicable auditing standards."[5] Vadlamani, the former CFO, said the auditors had not been complicit in cooking the books and had been given forged documents. The auditors had relied on documents provided by management such as account balance statements and letters of confirmation of account balances.

More specifically, Dennis Nally, then global leader of PwC, said to *Business Today:*

> If our job was described as to provide a 100 per cent assurance that there have been no material mistakes and no frauds have been committed, that would require audit firms to significantly increase the amount of work we do today and have much more forensic and different types of auditing. As we all know, when there is a desire at the top of an organization to commit a massive fraud, individuals in the organization that have participated in the fraud can do a lot of different things to keep it away from individuals, including auditor firms, the Board of Directors and the analyst community.[6]

[4] These agents formed a network of mafia-style operators that obtained illegal permits and illegally developed low-priced subsidized land and apartments and sold them to the public for high prices.
[5] Jackie Range and Scott Patterson, "Price Waterhouse Defends Its Audit Procedures," *The Wall Street Journal,* January 9, 2009, p. B5.
[6] Puja Mehra, "Our Job Is Not to Certify That There's No Fraud," *Business Today,* July 26, 2009.

FOLLOW-UP

Indian authorities arrested Raju and his brother Rama on complaints of cheating, forgery, breach of trust, and other charges. Police called in cyberforensic experts who can retrieve erased data from computers. In all, 10 people have been arrested.

PWI suspended its chief relationship partner and engagement leader on the Satyam audit, set up an advisory board, conducted a review of work and processes, and appointed a new head of quality assurance and risk management. While screening through the minutes of some of the board meetings, investigators found that the total audit fees paid to PWI for its domestic and international accounts was around $1.4m, almost double the figure mentioned in the balance sheet.

The information concerning the probe initiated by the Crime Investigation Department (CID), the Serious Fraud Investigation Office (SFIO), and Institute of Chartered Accountants of India (ICAI) was handed to the CBI. After some initial work, the CBI confirmed to *Business Today* that Raju seems to have come clean in his confession letter except for his statement about not having benefited in financial terms as a result of inflated results. "We are yet to establish if there was any diversion of funds from Satyam to any of Raju's entities. This will take some time to investigate," added the CBI official.[7] Decoding the biometric laptops used by Raju and his team, screening the internal financial software of the company and minutes of the board meetings for the final six years, scanning papers of the approximately 300 companies created by Raju and his family, and scrutinizing the land records under these companies was expected to keep the CBI busy for months.

In fact, during an interrogation session, Raju is believed to have said that he never did anything wrong because everyone else in the industry does it.

On April 5, 2011, the PCAOB and the SEC announced a joint penalty of $7.5m against the five firms composing PW India, a member of PwC. At the time, it was the largest such penalty ever assessed against a registered foreign accounting firm. The firms were also given other sanctions, including a six-month ban on accepting new SEC clients and the imposition of quality controls. In addition, the Institute of Chartered Accountants of India (ICAI) has barred two Indian auditors, Pulavarthi Siva Prasad and Chintapatla Ravindernath, from "the register of members permanently" for their role in the crisis.[8]

In the release of its findings, the PCAOB said the auditors had relied on management to send confirmation requests to Satyam's bank and to return responses to the auditors even though the audit programs "explicitly acknowledged that the engagement team should maintain control of the process of sending confirmation requests and receiving confirmation responses relating to the confirmation of cash."[9] Moreover, a network firm partner reviewing the documentation "advised that the engagement team 'can only take credit for [cash] confirmations we send [to] and receive directly [from the banks].'"[10] The partner "noted that the Company had a significant balance of fixed deposits and advised the engagement team to 'document that confirmations have been received [from the banks] for such amounts.'" There had been similar shortcomings in the confirmation of accounts receivable, even though the firm had noted numerous internal control deficiencies. "These confirmation deficiencies contributed directly to the auditors' failure to uncover the Satyam fraud," said James R. Doty, PCAOB Chairman.[11]

DISCUSSION QUESTIONS

1. Do you agree with Dennis Nally's comments?
2. How do you think Raju could have used Maytas assets to cover up the fraud?
3. Why are related-party frauds more difficult to detect than frauds with no related parties?
4. Should U.S. public accounting firms try to audit internationally in cultures they may not understand? If so, how can they maintain quality audits?

[7] Rachna M. Koppikar and Puja Mehra, "Satyam: Unraveling the Fraud," *Business Today*, July 2009.
[8] Keith Nuthall, "Auditors Barred for Life over Satyam Scandal," *Accountancy Age*, December 8, 2011.
[9] PCAOB, "PCAOB Announces Settled Disciplinary Order Against PricewaterhouseCoopers International Firms in India for Audit Violations Related to Satyam," April 5, 2011.
[10] Ibid.
[11] Ibid.

5. Can an international firm have one set of absolute ethics standards that must be followed at all times, or do ethics standards need to be flexible enough to account for variations in cultures?
6. How can auditors ensure they are receiving authentic documentation, not forgeries?
7. In your opinion, should PWI be subject to civil litigation?

ADDITIONAL SOURCES

Anand Adhikari, "The Problem Within: When the Bulk of the Auditing Work Involves Junior Auditors, Trouble Can't Be Too Far Behind," *Business Today,* February 22, 2009.

Geeta Anand and Romit Guha, "Corporate News: Satyam Bank Documents at Issue—Fraud Probe Sheds Light on How Outsourcing Company Inflated Its Balance Sheet," *The Wall Street Journal,* January 20, 2009, p. B3.

Eric Bellman and John Satish Kumar, "Founder Arrested, Board Out at Satyam," *The Wall Street Journal,* January 10, 2009, p. B1.

Eric Bellman and Jackie Range, "Corporate News: Satyam Probe Scrutinizes CFO, Audit Committee," *The Wall Street Journal,* January 14, 2009, p. B3.

"Corporate News: Satyam Backs Removal of Auditors," *The Wall Street Journal,* February 23, 2009, p. B3.

Jennifer Hughes, "Accountants Go into Shock at 'India's Enron,'" *Financial Times,* January 9, 2009, p. 16.

Nandini Lakshman, "Nine Charged in Hyderabad in Satyam Fraud," *BusinessWeek,* April 7, 2009.

Joe Leahy, "Details of Alleged Satyam Fraud Emerge," www.ft.com, January 22, 2009.

Kenan Machado and Romit Guha, "Satyam Founder Raju Is Granted Bail," *The Wall Street Journal,* August 19, 2010, p. B8.

Nandini Lakshman, and Manjeet Kripalani, "Is the Worst Over for Satyam?" *BusinessWeek,* February 4, 2009.

"Offshore Inmates: The Satyam Scandal," *The Economist,* January 17, 2009, p. 64.

PCAOB, Release No. 105-2011-002, April 5, 2011.

"PricewaterhouseCoopers Speaks to Puja Mehra on Improving Audit Practices," *Business Today,* July 2009.

Jackie Range and Joann S. Lublin, "The Satyam Scandal: Spotlight on India's Corporate Governance," *The Wall Street Journal,* January 8, 2009, p. A9.

Jackie Range, "Corporate News: Additional $100 Million Said to Be Missing from Satyam," *The Wall Street Journal,* May 1, 2009, p. B2.

Jackie Range and R. Jai Krishna, "Corporate News: More Staff Arrested at Satyam—Former Finance Chief at Indian Software Firm Defends Outside Auditors," *The Wall Street Journal,* April 7, 2009, p. B2.

Jackie Range, "Corporate News: Accountants for Satyam Arrested by Indian Police," *The Wall Street Journal,* January 26, 2009, p. B3.

Ahmed Rumman, "Satyam Auditor Seeks to Repair Image," *The Wall Street Journal,* March 6, 2009, p. B5.

Joshi Sonal, "India after Busting Land Mafia Organized Crime Involving Former Government Officials and Apartment Developers," www.indiadaily.com/editorial/3897.asp, August 1, 2005.

Salil Tripathi, "India Faces an 'Enron Moment,'" *The Wall Street Journal,* January 9, 2009, p. A11.

Craig Whitcher, Tyler Caskill, Andrew Reece, and Jake Denoncourt, "Satyam Case," Working Paper, George Mason University, 2009.

Auditor Changes at Daily Journal Corporation

Charlie Munger is vice chairman of **Berkshire Hathaway Inc.** and is informally known as Warren Buffett's "right arm." Munger also serves as chairman of **Daily Journal Corporation,** which publishes 10 newspapers and offers specialized information services and technology-based products. While often mentioned in the media because of his association with Buffett and long tenure and leadership at Berkshire Hathaway, Munger was recently in the news for another reason: his penchant to change auditors at Daily Journal.

REPORTING DELAYS

On December 16, 2013, Daily Journal informed the Securities and Exchange Commission (SEC) that it would not meet the filing deadline for its 2013 *Form 10-K*. (Daily Journal has a September 30 fiscal year-end.) The reason stated in its *Form 12b-25* filing was that Daily Journal's auditor (**EY**) had not completed its audit of the financial statements or internal control over financial reporting. Subsequently, Daily Journal informed the SEC that it would also miss the filing deadline for its December 31, 2013 and March 31, 2014 *Forms 10-Q*.[1] Once again, the reason stipulated in the filings was additional time required by EY to complete its audit and assessment of internal control over financial reporting. (While EY had audited Daily Journal's financial statements since 2000, 2013 was the first year EY reported on Daily Journal's internal control over financial reporting.)

DISMISSAL OF EY

On June 24, 2014, Daily Journal filed its 2013 *Form 10-K* (almost seven months after the filing deadline), in which EY issued an unqualified opinion on the financial statements but an adverse opinion on Daily Journal's internal control over financial reporting. Two days later, Daily Journal reported that its audit committee approved the dismissal of EY, effective June 24, 2014. An excerpt from Daily Journal's *Form 8-K* filing is shown here:[2]

> The Audit Committee of the Board of Directors of Daily Journal Corporation (the "Company") approved the dismissal of Ernst & Young LLP ("EY") as the Company's independent registered public accounting firm, effective June 24, 2014 . . .

> The reports of EY on the Company's financial statements for the past two fiscal years contained no adverse opinion or disclaimer of opinion and were not qualified or modified as to uncertainty, audit scope or accounting principles.

> During the Company's two most recent fiscal years and the subsequent interim period, there have been no disagreements with EY on any matter of accounting principles or practices, financial statement disclosure, or auditing scope or procedure, which disagreement(s) if not resolved to the satisfaction of EY would have caused EY to make reference to the subject matter of such disagreement(s) in its report on the Company's financial statements.

> During the Company's two most recent fiscal years and the subsequent interim period, there have been no reportable events of the kinds described in Item 304(a)(1)(v) of Regulation S-K under the Securities Exchange Act of 1934, *except that EY expressed an adverse opinion in its report on the Company's internal control over financial reporting as of September 30, 2013 (emphasis added)* . . . The Audit Committee of the Company's Board of Directors has discussed this matter with EY and has authorized EY to respond fully to the inquiries of the Company's successor independent registered public accounting firm.

> The Company requested and has received a letter from EY addressed to the Securities and Exchange Commission stating whether or not EY agrees with the statements in this Item 4.01. A copy of the letter, dated June 26, 2014, is filed as Exhibit 16.1 to this Form 8-K.

---

[1] These *Form 12b-25* filings were dated February 10, 2014 and May 12, 2014 for Daily Journal's first and second quarter 2014 *Forms 10-Q*, respectively.
[2] *Daily Journal Form 8-K* (filed with the SEC June 26, 2014).

APPOINTMENT OF BDO USA, LLP

On July 3, 2014, Daily Journal announced the appointment of **BDO USA, LLP** as auditor to replace EY. Shortly following BDO's appointment, Daily Journal filed its *Forms 10-Q* for the first (filed on August 13, 2014), second (filed on August 15, 2014), and third (filed on August 18, 2014) quarters of 2014, bringing Daily Journal current with respect to its SEC filings.

SEC COMMENT LETTER

Almost on cue, the Division of Finance at the SEC sent a letter of comment to Gerald Salzman (CEO of Daily Journal) that raised concerns with the 2013 *Form 10-K*. This letter (dated September 25, 2014) referenced Daily Journal's disclosure of intangible assets from an acquisition, the effectiveness of Daily Journal's internal controls, and discrepancies between preliminary financial filings on *Form 8-K* and subsequent filings on *Form 10-Q*. With respect to the intangible assets, Salzman's response to the SEC noted the following:

> At the time of the New Dawn acquisition, the Company discussed the purchase price allocation with EY. Accordingly, the Company was surprised when EY first raised the [accounting] issue after the original filing deadline. As further discussed below, the Company does not believe that the adjustments were necessary under GAAP, but EY required them as a condition to the delivery of its audit report. The Company did not view this as a disagreement with EY, but rather a matter of the parties making different judgment calls about the requirements in these specific circumstances regarding a matter the Company believed was not material to investors. Accepting EY's position was a practical decision on the part of the Company, and not the result of deficiencies in the Company's close process or in the areas where the adjustments were made.[3]

In the midst of these distractions, Daily Journal notified the SEC that it would not meet the filing deadline for its 2014 *Form 10-K* (which was ultimately filed 28 days after the December 31, 2014 deadline). BDO issued an unqualified opinion on Daily Journal's financial statements and an adverse opinion on its internal control, citing in part issues noted in the SEC's letter of comment in this latter opinion:

> The Company does not have sufficient technical expertise in assessing and applying accounting standards to non-routine transactions, reviewing the quarterly and annual tax analysis and provision, and assessing the adequacy of disclosures in the quarterly and annual consolidated financial statements. The Company amended its *Form 10-Q* for the third quarter of fiscal 2014 to restate amounts to correct a misstatement in the accounting for income taxes in connection with one of its acquisitions. This resulted in material audit adjustments the Company recorded to primarily offset the previously recorded income tax benefit as well as additional disclosures in the consolidated financial statements.[4]

ANOTHER AUDITOR CHANGE

BDO's opinion on Daily Journal's 2015 financial statements and internal control over financial reporting was issued on December 14, 2015 (ahead of the December 31, 2015 deadline). As in the previous two years, Daily Journal received an unqualified opinion on its financial statements and an adverse opinion on internal control over financial reporting; in this latter report, BDO cited a material audit adjustment that was required in the fourth quarter of fiscal 2015.

In February 2016, Daily Journal announced the dismissal of BDO and the appointment of **Squar Milner LLP,** a regional accounting firm with offices in California that provides audit or tax services to 30 public companies.[5] Ironically, less than one week earlier, Daily Journal shareholders ratified the appointment of BDO as its auditor with a positive vote of 95 percent of all shares voted.[6]

[3] Letter from Gerald Salzman to Securities and Exchange Commission, January 26, 2015.
[4] *Daily Journal 2014 Form 10-K* (filed with the SEC on January 28, 2015).
[5] http://squarmilner.com/services/audit-and-other-attest-services/public-companies/.
[6] *Daily Journal Form 8-K* (filed with the SEC on February 11, 2016).

CONCLUSION

Over a three-year period, Daily Journal engaged the following auditors:[7]

Period	Auditor	No. Offices	Revenue	*Inside Public Accounting* Revenue Rank
2000–2014	EY	80	$9.9 billion	3
2014–2016	BDO	63	$1.1 billion	7
2016–current	Squar Milner	5	$47.4 million	71

Academic research[8] examining auditor changes has concluded that clients receiving adverse internal control opinions are more likely to dismiss their incumbent auditors and choose a higher-quality replacement (represented by the size and level of firm, with Big Four being highest quality); this decision may reflect a desire of clients to improve their financial reporting quality. A more recent study[9] found that clients engage in "opinion-shopping" by dismissing auditors prior to potentially receiving an adverse opinion on internal control and often do so later in the fiscal year, in response to anticipating a negative report on their internal control.

DISCUSSION QUESTIONS

1. From the SEC website or other sources, locate Daily Journal's 2013 *Form 10-K* and review EY's report on Daily Journal's internal control over financial reporting. What were some of the weaknesses noted in this report?

2. Review the excerpt (presented in the case) of Daily Journal's *Form 8-K* (filed with the SEC June 26, 2014) related to the dismissal of EY. What type of disclosures are provided in this excerpt? What are some reasons that Daily Journal would provide these disclosures?

3. Review the excerpt (presented in the case) from Gerald Salzman's response to the SEC. Do you believe this response is consistent with the *Form 8-K* filing related to the dismissal of EY? What implications might this response have with respect to Daily Journal's internal control over financial reporting?

4. From the SEC website or other sources, locate Daily Journal's *Form 8-K* (filed July 3, 2014) related to the appointment of BDO. What type of disclosures are provided in this filing? What are some reasons that Daily Journal would provide these disclosures? (*Note:* Daily Journal filed two different *Form 8-Ks* on July 3, 2014.)

5. Referring to the professional standards (AU-C 210), what is BDO's responsibility with respect to communicating with EY?

6. From the SEC website or other sources, locate Daily Journal's *Form 8-K* (filed February 17, 2016) that announced the dismissal of BDO and engagement of Squar Milner. Compare the disclosures in this filing to those in questions (2) and (4) related to the dismissal of EY and engagement of BDO.

7. Why might adverse opinions on internal control over financial reporting prompt Daily Journal to change auditors? Are Daily Journal's auditor change activities consistent with the results of the academic studies summarized in this case? Why or why not?

---

[7] All data based on *Inside Public Accounting Special Report: The 2015 IPA 100 Firms.*
[8] M.E. Ettredge, J. Heintz, C. Li, and S. Scholz, "Auditor Realignments Accompanying Implementation of SOX 404 ICFR Reporting Requirements," *Accounting Horizons,* March 2011, pp. 17–39.
[9] N.J. Newton, J.S. Persellin, D. Wang, and M.S. Wilkins, "Internal Control Opinion Shopping and Audit Market Competition," *The Accounting Review,* March 2016, pp. 603–623.

London Has Fallen

Scott London seemed to have it all. One of three sons of a Los Angeles certified public accountant, he followed his father into the accounting business. He graduated in 1984 from California State University–Northridge and soon landed a job at a firm that later became part of **KPMG.** From an outsider's perspective, London appeared to have an ideal personal life. He and his wife Michele had two children and lived in an expensive home at the end of a cul-de-sac in a Los Angeles suburb known as the gateway to the Santa Monica Mountains. Professionally, as the KPMG partner in charge of the firm's Pacific Southwest Audit practice, he had more than 50 partners and 500 employees reporting to him. After 29 years with the firm, he seemed to be set financially, making close to $900,000 per year in salary.

With all this going for him, London shocked his colleagues and friends when he pled guilty to passing confidential client information to his golf buddy Bryan Shaw who had then traded on the information to make more than $1.5 million in illegal gains. Although the information was initially passed "innocently" in casual conversation on the golf course, London began accepting gifts of cash and jewelry in exchange for the tips. Shaw was caught when his trading account began showing up linked to trades made just before releases of corporate information to the public, a tell-tale sign of insider trading. When confronted, he agreed to cooperate with authorities, including agreeing to wear a wire to gain evidence against London. The sting operation that nabbed London was the result of a joint investigation by the FBI, SEC, and Department of Justice.

When first notified of the allegations, KPMG acted immediately and decisively, firing London, who the firm said "violated the firm's rigorous policies and protections, betrayed the trust of clients as well as colleagues, and acted with deliberate disregard for KPMG's long-standing culture of professionalism and integrity." Due to independence concerns, the firm resigned as auditor of **Skechers** and **Herbalife,** companies whose audits London oversaw. KPMG also announced that it would reassess its quality control standards, which include employee training, monitoring key employees' personal investments, and a whistle-blowing hot line.

In return for the confidential information, London received more than $50,000 in cash and gifts, including a $12,000 Rolex watch; however, the amount of these "gifts" was seemingly immaterial given London's almost seven-figure annual salary. In addition to losing his job and being sued by his former employer, London ended up serving 14 months in prison and paying $100,000 in fines. He has openly confessed to his misconduct and has expressed his remorse: "I cannot begin to apologize for my incredibly stupid actions. There is no excuse for my wrongful conduct." However, even in hindsight, London has trouble explaining his behavior: "I felt guilt about it regularly—I can't explain it to be honest with you. . . . I look back at when this started and I can't explain it . . . . I guess [the] best way to describe it is that humans make mistakes."[1]

We may never know the true motives behind his actions, but we do know that London made a conscious decision to betray his employer, his clients, and his profession, violating a number of rules from the AICPA Code of Professional Conduct in the process.

DISCUSSION QUESTIONS

1. What code violations have occurred in this case?
2. What is the range of penalties that the PCAOB could have levied against London? By the California State Board of Accountancy?
3. What do you think is the appropriate penalty?
4. What penalties were assessed?

[1] "Insider Trader Is Identified," *The Wall Street Journal,* April 11, 2013, p. C1.

Investment Management in Boston; yet, ultimately the SEC was unable to uncover Madoff's Ponzi scheme. In May 2000, Markopolos submitted evidence to the SEC that questioned the legitimacy of the returns on Madoff's hedge fund. In his submission, Markopolos wrote that Madoff's reported performance, which when charted rose roughly at a 45-degree angle, did not exist in finance.[7]

Markopolos e-mailed a second submission to the SEC on March 1, 2001, in which he presented additional analysis on Madoff's returns. Markopolos wrote that Madoff reportedly earned more than 15.5 percent a year for more than seven years, with an extremely low standard deviation of 4.3 percent. This was in contrast to the S&P 500, which earned more than 19.5 percent but with an annual standard deviation of 12.9 percent. In addition, Madoff's fund had only three down months in contrast to the market being down 26 months during the same period. "For example, in 1993 when the S&P returned 1.33%, Bernie returned 14.55%; in 1999 the S&P returned 21.04%, and there was Bernie at 16.69%. . . . His returns were always good, but rarely spectacular. So it wasn't his returns that bothered me so much—his returns each month were possible—it was that he *always* returned a profit. There was no mathematical model that could explain the consistency."[8] "This program earned 80% of the market's return with only one third of the risk. Think about it! Is this really possible, or is it too good to be true?" wrote Markopolos.[9]

In October 2005, Markopolos made his third submission, titled "The World's Largest Hedge Fund Is a Fraud," to the SEC. Markopolos's submission included 30 red flags that indicated that it was "highly likely" that Madoff was operating a Ponzi scheme. Each red flag fell into one of three categories: (1) Madoff's obsessive secrecy; (2) the impossibility of Madoff's returns, particularly the consistency of those returns; and (3) the unrealistic volume of options Madoff was supposedly trading.[10] Despite all of the warnings, the SEC failed to uncover the Madoff Ponzi scheme on its own.

MADOFF'S AUDITOR

From 1991 through 2008, **Bernard L. Madoff Investment and Securities'** (BLMIS) financial statements were audited by the accounting firm **Friehling & Horowitz.** In March 2009, David Friehling, who was a CPA licensed by the state of New York, was arrested and charged with securities fraud, aiding Madoff with investment advisor fraud, and filing false audit reports with the SEC. The charges brought against Friehling include that he failed to do the following[11]:

- Conduct independent verification of BLMIS revenues, assets, liabilities related to BLMIS client accounts, and the purchase and custody of securities by BLMIS.
- Test internal controls over areas such as the payment of invoices for corporate expenses or the purchase of securities by BLMIS on behalf of its clients.
- Examine a bank account through which BLMIS client funds flowed.

The SEC also filed a civil case against Friehling and his firm Friehling & Horowitz. The AICPA and the New York State Society of CPAs have expelled Friehling from membership. Under the AICPA's peer review program, auditors are monitored through mandatory peer review every three years. Friehling's work was not peer-reviewed because, since 1993, he had informed the AICPA that he did not perform audits, and therefore, would not need a peer review.[12] At the time, New York was one of only six states that did not require accounting firms to be peer-reviewed. However, beginning January 1, 2012, New York firms with three or more accounting professionals must be peer-reviewed once every three years.[13]

On November 3, 2009, Madoff's auditor David Friehling changed his plea from not guilty to guilty for the crimes involving the filing of falsely certified audits and financial statements with the SEC. Although Friehling was initially supposed to be sentenced in 2010, the sentencing was repeatedly postponed due to his cooperation with the government. In May 2015, citing his cooperation with the government, a federal judge sentenced Friehling to one year of home detention and one year of supervised release. Friehling lost his CPA license in July 2010.

[7] Harry Markopolos, *No One Would Listen* (Hoboken NJ: John Wiley & Sons, 2010).
[8] Ibid.
[9] Ibid.
[10] Ibid.
[11] United States Attorney, Southern District of New York, "Accountant for Bernard L. Madoff, Investment Securities, LLC Charged with Fraud Stemming from Accounting Violations," March 18, 2009.
[12] AccountingWeb, "Madoff's Accountant: When Is an Auditor Not an Auditor?" http://www.accountingweb.com/item/107303, March 30, 2009.
[13] Alyssa Abkowitz, "Madoff's Auditor . . . Doesn't Audit?," *Fortune*, December 19, 2008, available at http://money.cnn.com/2008/12/17/news/companies/madoff.auditor.fortune.

DISCUSSION QUESTIONS

1. Refer to the fundamental principles governing an audit (see Chapter 2). Under the responsibilities principle, auditors are required to exercise due care and maintain professional skepticism throughout the audit. Based on the case information, do you believe that the auditors from Friehling & Horowitz exercised due care and maintained professional skepticism throughout the audit? Why or why not?

2. After the Madoff case, the SEC instituted a number of reforms to its operations. Please visit the SEC's website (www.sec.gov) and search for Post-Madoff reforms. Next, please identify the two reforms that you believe will have the best chance of catching a criminal like Madoff. Make sure to provide justification for your choices.

3. Consider section 24 of the Securities Act of 1933 and section 32 of the Securities Exchange Act of 1934 (see Module C). Based on the case information, do you believe that Madoff's auditor, Friehling, should be facing criminal charges? Why or why not?

When the Music Stops: Crazy Eddie's

BACKGROUND

In the 1980s, Crazy Eddie was a fast-growing electronics retailer business specializing in stereos, televisions, VCRs, and computer gaming systems. Founded by Eddie Antar, Crazy Eddie was well known for its outlandish commercials (see www.youtube.com/watch?v=fO9XC3tAbkQ). Most of the key business positions were filled by members of the Antar family, including CFO Sam Antar, Eddie's cousin, and a CPA.

While the stores were successful, to avoid paying taxes, the family skimmed large amounts of cash from the business. According to Sam Antar, cash received from each day's business was brought to a family member's house, where a decision was made regarding how much cash to skim before the day's receipts were deposited in the bank. As much as $50,000 was skimmed from a day's sales on any given day. In 1979, which was the height of the skimming operation, approximately $3 million was taken out of the business. In fact, so much money was being skimmed that the Antars had difficulty finding places to keep it. (Remember, you cannot put large amounts of cash into the bank without the bank notifying the IRS.) Eventually, the Antars sent couriers to Israel with large amounts of cash to be deposited in Israeli banks. (Israel has favorable bank secrecy laws.)

Unsatisfied with the cash already being taken, Eddie and the Antar family decided that the type of money they desired could only be obtained by taking Crazy Eddie public. Because the family would retain large amounts of stock, a favorable IPO and subsequent increases in the company stock would net them tens of millions of dollars. In order to make Crazy Eddie appear more profitable, the family decided to reduce the skimming operation. With less money going into the Antars' pockets and more money being recorded as sales, the company's profits appeared to be increasing each year at an extraordinary rate. Further, the family transferred millions of dollars from the bank in Israel to a bank in Panama and included drafts drawn on the bank in Panama as store sales. This process was known as the "Panama Pump." Consecutively numbered drafts for $25,000, $50,000, $75,000, and even $100,000 were included in the sales figures for various stores on various days. This process was repeated several times. In 1985, $1.5 million received via the Panama Pump and another $500,000 in previous skimmed cash (stored in safe deposit boxes in local banks) were included in store sales to make Crazy Eddie appear to meet Wall Street's lofty expectations for a growing business. This process increased Crazy Eddie same-store-sales ratio, an important Wall Street measurement for retail companies' success. By the time of the IPO, Crazy Eddie looked like a gem that needed to be owned by savvy investors. In 1987, its first year as a public company, Crazy Eddie had 43 stores with reported sales of $350 million. Crazy Eddie was the new darling of Wall Street, with an IPO price of $8 per share that rose to more than $80 per share at its peak. Between 1988 and 1989, Antar family members sold more than $90 million worth of stock.

In 1984, Eddie Antar divorced his wife, and the Crazy Eddie family organization began to fracture. Many family members remained loyal to Eddie—who always relied on a charismatic personality to charm employees, customers, and vendors—while other members of the family decided to side with Eddie's ex-wife. Family turmoil persisted and escalated from 1984 through 1987. Profit increases began to slow as the Panama Pump slowed and the dollars necessary to maintain its expected phenomenal sales growth increased. A private equity firm, believing that the slowing growth was a result of Eddie's family problems and not a business problem, purchased Crazy Eddie in a hostile takeover. The new owners dismissed family members who occupied key business positions and immediately implemented a complete inventory count. In a very short time, the new owners found they had acquired a failing business with inflated assets. In June 1989, Crazy Eddie filed for Chapter 11 bankruptcy.

Eddie Antar is alleged to have made $75 million during the short public life of Crazy Eddie. Facing multiple charges in connection with the fraud, Eddie fled the country and lived using assumed names and the millions he had stashed in foreign bank accounts in several countries. In 1992, he was caught in Israel and, after a lengthy extradition fight, was brought back to the United States where, in 1997, he was convicted on 17 counts of fraud and sentenced to eight years in prison. His cousin, Sam Antar, was a major witness against him.

THE HIDE AND SEEK OF THE AUDIT

The audited financial statements for Crazy Eddie included not only fictitious sales, but inflated inventory, inaccurate accounts payable, deferred billing from vendors, side deals with vendors for inventory (included in inventory counts but not paid for) and fictitious vendor discounts used to offset accounts payable). Yet, from before its IPO all the way until the takeover in 1987, Crazy Eddie received unqualified opinions from its auditor each year. Inventory was a key issue in the Crazy Eddie fraud, yet the auditor's work shows no special attention to the inventory account balance—even when analytical procedures indicated significant red flags. Inventory more than quadrupled between 1984 and 1987, while inventory turnover slowed and the average age of inventory increased. Further, an increase in inventory logically requires more purchases, which should result in a corresponding increase in accounts payable, yet accounts payable actually decreased during this period. When observing the physical inventory, the auditor noted that the inventory in the warehouse was stacked and placed in rows. However, the auditors did not ask for inventory to be moved so that items in back of the rows could be verified. In addition, when the auditor noted changes to the inventory counts, they inquired of management but failed to follow up on the issue or include any concerns in the audit documentation.

Keeping the fraud from the auditors took hard work and a lot of nerve! In one instance, Crazy Eddie employees opened the auditors' records and altered the inventory counts on the auditors' sheets. (Remember these were pen-and-paper workpapers back in the 1980s.) Keys to the "Audit Trunk" (the bag with all the audit workpapers, plans, and information) were left accessible to the client.[1] Transfers of inventory were made to intentionally double-count inventory and make an accurate inventory count as difficult as possible for the auditors. Deals were made with vendors to provide merchandise before the year-end but to delay the billing until after year-end. This inventory on hand helped Crazy Eddie's close some of the inventory discrepancies between the physical inventory and the recorded inventory.

Because auditors assigned to inventory were often young men (in the 1980s, many more males entered the accounting and auditing profession than females), Sam always assigned very attractive young women to assist the auditors in the inventory count. Sam indicated that many of these auditors tended to focus attention on the attractive assistants, thereby placing less focus on the inventory. Further, female employees were encouraged to flirt with young male auditors and even to discuss audit issues over lunch or dinner. Sam even took senior audit team members to bars and clubs that were frequented by attractive young women.

While the Panama Pump was working, many stores had $25,000 or $50,000 drafts included in the day's sales. This resulted in sale spikes on those days for those stores. Had the auditors investigated these drafts in detail, they may have seen a $50,000 item, which was highly unusual especially in the 1980s. Further, these large cash items had no corresponding customer receipt to indicate what might have been purchased for $50,000. The consecutive numbers on these drafts at different stores, and the fact these were drafts and not checks,[2] should have been a glaring red flag for the auditors. But no such investigation was ever made by the auditors.

It is alleged that Main Hurdman had underbid the initial audit (1985) and, in an attempt to have a profitable engagement, did not perform adequate procedure. Further, the following year (1986), Main Hurdman merged with Peat Marwick, and new auditors were part of the engagement team. In 1997, following the takeover, Peat Marwick was terminated and Touche Ross was hired. It is certainly possible that the lack of consistency resulting from changing auditors helped Crazy Eddie hide its misconduct.

CONCLUSION

Sam Antar is very forthcoming regarding the fraud and his efforts to fool the auditor. In fact, Sam has a website (http://whitecollarfraud.com/) and travels the country speaking to professional groups and university students. A portion of an interview Sam did for the Association of Certified Fraud Examiners can be viewed at www.youtube.com/watch?v=5f6ZpC2bmbs.

Eddie and Sam Antar went their separate ways, and Eddie was eventually released from prison. CNBC arranged for Sam and Eddie to meet after years of never seeing or speaking to each other. A summary of the Crazy Eddie's case and the Sam and Eddie reunion can be seen at www.youtube.com/watch?v=Y_7ntzgTvhs.

---

[1] In the days of pen-and-paper audits, the last person to leave at night would lock up the workpapers. However, that person might have been the first person in the next day. Sometimes, the key was placed in a paperclip box or in a planter in the audit area so that the workpapers could be accessed by whoever was in early the next day.

[2] A draft looks similar to a check and can be deposited in the bank in a similar matter, but it is different. Individuals and most business write checks, not drafts. An auditor should know the difference and should understand why a draft would be used in any situation instead of a check.

McGraw Hill Education connect®

With Connect for Louwers/Blay/Sinason/Strawser/Thibodeau *Auditing and Assurance Services*, 7e, you receive the most proven study tools as well as an adaptive eBook.

What kind of study tools?

- **SmartBook®** Proven to help you improve grades and study more efficiently, SmartBook contains the same content as the print book, but actively tailors that content to the needs of the individual. Smart-Book's adaptive technology provides precise, personalized instruction on what you should do next, guiding you to master and remember key concepts, targeting gaps in knowledge and offering customized feedback, and driving you toward comprehension and retention of the subject matter.

- **End-of-Chapter Material** helps you apply the concepts in accounting and, in more comprehensive material, analyze the information to form business decisions. Assignable material includes exercises, problems and test bank material. Based on your instructor's settings, you can receive instant feedback on your work either while working on an assignment or after the assignment is submitted for a grade.

- **Interactive Applications** like "drag and drop" and "comprehension case" activities help you apply important concepts you learned in each chapter. These engaging materials are auto-graded, so you receive feedback on your work immediately.

 **New!** This product includes sample CPA Exam preparation questions from Roger CPA Review. For more information about the CPA Exam and products to prepare for successful completion of the exam, visit www.rogercpareview.com.

Connect gives you a complete digital solution that allows you to access your course materials from any computer, anytime.

Try out Connect using our *COURTESY ACCESS* feature!
How? Just ask your instructor for the section's Connect course URL. At the course home page, click the "Register Now" button, type in your email address, and click "Courtesy Access."

It's that simple to begin using Connect today!

McGraw Hill Education